Annotated Canada Pension Plan and Old Age Security Act
14th Edition

The Honourable Gordon Killeen, Q.C.

Andrew James

 LexisNexis

Annotated Canada Pension Plan and Old Age Security Act, 14th Edition, 2015

Library and Archives Canada Cataloguing in Publication

Killeen, Gordon; James, Andrew
    Annotated Canada Pension Plan and Old Age Security
Act/Gordon Killeen, Andrew James.

[1st ed.] 2001-
ISBN 978-1-55496-797-1 (14th edition)

    1. Canada Pension Plan.   2. Old age pensions — Law and legislation —
Canada.

KE3432.A31K55   344.7102'30263   C00-906067-3
KF3649.K55

Published by LexisNexis Canada, a member of the LexisNexis Group
LexisNexis Canada Inc.
123 Commerce Valley Dr. E., Suite 700
Markham, Ontario
L3T 7W8

Customer Service
Telephone: (905) 479-2665 ● Fax: (905) 479-2826
Toll-Free Phone: 1-800-668-6481 ● Toll-Free Fax: 1-800-461-3275
Email: customerservice@lexisnexis.ca
Web Site: www.lexisnexis.ca

Printed and bound in the United States of America.

Preface and Acknowledgments

There have been a number of legal developments since the 2014 edition of the *Annotated Canada Pension Plan and Old Age Security Act* was published. All have been reflected in this new 2015 edition.

With respect to CPP disability claims, a major change has been introduced by the amendment to the Canada Pension Plan Regulations clarifying the meaning of "substantially gainful employment". The new formula for determining a threshold for "substantially gainful occupation" sets it as essentially 12 times the maximum monthly retirement benefit. This objective standard should make the decision making on this issue much less opaque.

The overhanging decisions of the Review Tribunal and the Pension Appeals Board, which ceased hearing new appeals on March 31, 2013, have been issued, and those bodies are now defunct. The General Division and Appeal Division of the newly established Social Security Tribunal have begun handing down decisions that by and large have respected the approach to disability and other issues established by the former tribunals. These decisions have been incorporated into the 2015 edition.

Of course, the annotations in the 2015 edition also reflect the significant Federal Court of Appeal and Federal Court decisions over the last year into the annotations under the appropriate legislative provisions. Recent Federal Court of Appeal decisions have enunciated and/or clarified the law on a host of important issues; including the impact of the Ministry policy regarding benevolent employers (*Atkinson*), admissibility of new evidence on judicial review (*Gaudet*), standard of review (*Kaminski, Atkinson*), issue estoppel (*Kaminski*), and the availability of garnishment of benefits (*Simon*).

Once again, the 14th edition of this book was the result of a team effort. The authors thank Amichai Wise, Counsel with the federal Department of Justice, for assistance in identifying the significant cases. We are also grateful to Michel Mathieu, General Counsel for the Social Security Tribunal, for keeping us up to date in changes to administrative policies.

We again thank Iver Chong for his immaculate editing of the manuscript. Of course, any mistakes in the published material were introduced by the authors, who also take sole responsibility for the opinions expressed herein.

Gordon Killeen
Andrew James

November 2014

iii

Table of Contents

List of Abbreviations

The following list of abbreviations used in this book is provided for your reference.

CCH Sources

    CEB & PG — Canadian Employment Benefits and Pensions Guide

    TB — Transfer Binder

Government

    PAB — Pension Appeals Board

    RT — Review Tribunal

    SST — Social Security Tribunal

Ministers

    AG — Attorney General

    MCI — Minister of Citizenship and Immigration

    MEI — Minister of Employment and Immigration

    MHRD — Minister of Human Resources Development

    MMI — Minister of Manpower and Immigration

    MNHW — Minister of National Health and Welfare

    MNR — Minister of National Revenue

CPP Terms

    MQP — Minimum Qualifying Period

    ROE — Record of Earnings

    UPE — Unadjusted Pensionable Earnings

    YBE — Year's Basic Exemption

    YMPE — Year's Maximum Pensionable Earnings

The Canada Pension Plan Disability Pension — Procedure and Entitlement

Table of Contents

The Canada Pension Plan Disability Pension — Procedure and Entitlement

(see detailed table of contents on previous page)

Overview

The *Canada Pension Plan*, R.S.C. 1985, c. C-8, as amended ("CPP") provides seven types of benefits: (i) a survivor's pension; (ii) a death benefit; (iii) an orphan's benefit; (iv) a retirement pension; (v) a disability pension; and (vi) a disabled contributor's child's benefit; and (vii) starting in 2012, a post-retirement benefit.

The most contentious issue under the CPP is that of individual entitlement to a disability pension. Traditionally, more than 95% of the appeals from Ministerial reconsideration relate to disability claims — i.e., the Minister of Human Resources and Skills Development ("MHRD") has taken the position that the claimant is not "disabled" within the meaning of s. 42(2)(*a*) of the CPP, and therefore does not qualify to receive a disability pension.

In the 50 years since the CPP came into existence, the overseeing tribunal has had thousands of opportunities to apply the statutory meaning in the circumstances of the case before it. A large body of law, reflected in the Disability Case Table that follows this chapter, has developed. The following discussion analyzes the meaning of the CPP disability provisions generally and specific issues that have arisen in the case law. It also reviews the procedure by which disability applications are resolved.

I. Introduction

A. Overview of the CPP

The CPP was enacted on April 3, 1965, as S.C. 1964-1965, c. 51, coming into force on May 5, 1965 and effective as of January 1, 1966. After a 10-year transitional period, the program became fully effective in 1976. The federal government did not have authority to enact such a program under the *British North America Act, 1867*. A 1964 constitutional amendment, with provincial permission, was to needed to permit the federal government to offer a broad, national program that included survivor's and disability benefits.

One of the crucial aspects about the CPP is that it is not a general social welfare program. It is a self-financing program, and benefits are only available to contributors and their families. Contributors are those persons who have made mandatory monthly contributions by virtue of their employment in Canada. In this respect, the CPP may be seen as a mandatory insurance scheme, similar to the Employment Insurance ("EI") program. However, participation of self-employed individuals in the CPP is compulsory, which is not the case under EI.

Entitlement to CPP benefits, therefore, does not depend on means testing. When the CPP was introduced in the House of Commons as Bill C-136 in 1964, Judy LaMarsh, the Minister of National Health and Welfare, said:

> This plan, the Canada Pension Plan, is one which provides help as of right rather than on a need or a means test, for those who suffer the loss of a loved breadwinner or those who find themselves disabled and unable to carry on work. I think hon. members will agree this is a giant step forward in Canada's social security program. (House of Commons Debates, November 9, 1964, p. 9899.)

A second key point is that the CPP is not intended to provide the sole source of income for recipients. The CPP retirement pension, for example, is intended only to supplement the old age pension under the *Old Age Security Act*, private retirement pension plans and RRSPs and RRIFs. The August 1964 White Paper (the third and last in a series on this controversial proposal) stated in this regard:

> The plan is comprehensive in the sense of covering as many people as is practicable. It is *not* intended to provide all the retirement income or survivors' income which many Canadians wish to have. This is a matter of individual choice and, in the Government's view, should properly be left to personal savings and to private pension plans ...

> The purpose of the *Canada Pension Plan* is to make reasonable minimum levels of income available at normal retirement ages, and to people who become disabled, and to the dependents of people who die. There will be scope for the continuation and extension of private pension plans to provide benefits over these minimum levels. (p. 7, Emphasis in original.)

A third point is that the CPP is not easy to change. As observed by the Pension Appeals Board in *Tan v. MSD* (December 8, 2006), CP 20525, 22316, 22452, 22453, 23253 (PAB),

> While the *Plan* is administered by the federal government, major amendments require the approval of Parliament and at least two-thirds of the provinces with at least two-thirds of the population of Canada. Major changes cannot come into force any earlier than the first day of the third year following the year in which a notice of intention to introduce a measure containing a provision to that effect is laid before Parliament. By convention, this provision can only be waived with the unanimous consent of the provinces. Substantial amendments that alter or effect, directly or indirectly, immediately or in the future, the general level of benefits, the classes of benefits and the contribution rates or the formula for calculating the contributions and benefits payable also require provincial consent. [para. 15]

B. Financial Statistics

According to the 2006-2007 Annual Report of the CPP, contributors paid $32.4 billion into the CPP during that fiscal year, while $26.1 billion was paid out in benefits.

Not surprisingly, the retirement pension represents the lion's share of CPP benefits paid out each year. The 2006-2007 Annual Report says $23.3 billion was paid out in this form in the fiscal year, or approximately 72% of the total. Survivor's and children's benefits represented 14% of the total benefit dollars, while death benefits were at 1%. CPP administration costs were 2.2% of the total expenditures, supporting the government's claim that the CPP is more efficient than most large pension plans or RRSPs.

About 304,000 people with disabilities and approximately 90,000 children of disabled contributors received benefits from the CPP disability plan in 2006-2007. Disability benefits paid amounted to approximately $4.2 billion. This amount represents 13% of the total CPP benefit dollars paid out, less than the 17.3% in 1994 and the 14% in 2003. It should also be noted that nearly one-third of disability benefits paid each month are payable to contributors between the ages of 61 and 65, who would otherwise be eligible for early retirement pension if they were not receiving disability pensions. Therefore, total disability pension payments to persons who are not eligible for early retirement pensions represent approximately 10% of all CPP benefits paid from year to year.

C. Contributions

Contributions to the CPP are compulsory and are based on employee earnings that exceed a minimum level known as the Year's Basic Exemption ("YBE"), up to a ceiling known as the Year's Maximum Pensionable Earnings ("YMPE"). Since 1996, the YBE has been $3,500, although for purposes of calculating the Minimum Qualifying Period ("MQP") on disability-related claims, the YBE continues to increase. The YMPE is linked to the average Canadian wage and is adjusted annually. For 2014, the YMPE is $52,500, and the YBE is $5,200 for disability related claims. Contributions cannot be made (i) before age 18 or after age 70, (ii) after 65, where the contributor is in receipt of a CPP retirement pension or elects not to include income (effective January 1, 2012), or (iii) while an individual is receiving a CPP disability benefit. The specific rules for calculating contributions are set out in sections 11.1 to 20 of the CPP in Part III of this book.

It is well known that the balancing of CPP contributions and payouts over the long term is complicated by the aging population and dropping birthrates over the last three decades. A 49% increase in the number of CPP recipients is projected between 1999 and 2015, which is why combined employer/employee contribution rates rose from 3.6% in 1986 to 9.9% in 2003 and subsequent years.

II. CPP Disability Pension

A. Background

This plan, the Canada Pension Plan, is one which provides help as of right rather than on a need or a means test, for those who suffer the loss of a loved breadwinner or those who find themselves disabled and unable to carry on work ...

These disability benefits under the Canada Pension Plan will provide help in family crises when it is most needed ...

For those who become disabled there is at least the comfort of knowing that a pension will be payable, on a temporary or on a permanent basis as needed. (Minister LaMarsh, House of Commons Debates, November 9, 1964, p. 9899.)

The CPP disability pension, like other CPP benefits, is designed to supplement the disabled contributor's income. It was not necessarily intended to be the contributor's sole source of support, although it very often is. In addition to, or apart from the CPP disability pension, several options are open to persons who become disabled, some of which include:

- workers' compensation — if the injury or disease was employment-related;
- private disability insurance — available through employers. Note that coverage is expensive and hard to get for self-employed workers;
- early retirement (if 60 or over);

5

- student loans, scholarships and grants, and retraining programs;

- provincial/municipal welfare agencies;

- encroachment on capital; and

- assistance from family, friends and charities.

Note that if a disability pension recipient starts earning income from a business or employment, the disability may be deemed to have ceased under s. 70 of the CPP. Section 80.1 of the CPP authorizes the federal government to enter into agreements with other federal or provincial government bodies (or bodies which administer a non-legislated "federal or provincial activity") to apportion payments to a beneficiary. Undoubtedly, some disabled persons apply for and receive employment insurance benefits while still eligible, although they are required to state that they ready and willing to work. Now that EI benefits can no longer be claimed where the cessation of employment was voluntary, this option is not available to disabled persons who quit their jobs.

B. Requirements

There are five requirements for obtaining a disability pension. The applicant must:

1. be between the ages of 18 and 64 inclusive;

2. not be in receipt of a retirement pension;

3. fall within the minimum contributory requirement time frame (s. 44(2));

4. be determined to be disabled as defined in the CPP within such time frame (s. 42(2)(*a*) and Regulation s. 68); and

5. continue to be disabled up until the final determination of the disability claim.

A person's "contributory period" for purposes of the disability benefit or disabled contributor's child's benefit begins on the later of January 1, 1966 or the date he or she turns 18, and ends in the month he or she became disabled, or was deemed to become disabled. This period does not include months excluded by reason of the person's disability, or months in which the person was in receipt of family allowance benefits in a year in which the person's unadjusted pensionable earnings were less than the YBE (the "child care drop-out" provision).

The minimum contributory, or qualifying, period ("MQP") in practice refers to the last month in which the applicant qualified to receive a CPP benefit by virtue of CPP contributions made. Under s. 44(2), the MQP is determined as follows:

1. If the applicant has only four calendar years in his or her contributory period, he or she must have contributed in all those years.

2. If the applicant has more than four years in his or her contributory period, then contributions must have been made in four of the last six years.

3. If the applicant had previously been in receipt of a CPP disability pension, the above "four out of six" rule may waived, but only if the applicant has contributed each year after benefits were cancelled, including the year of cancellation.

6

If first-time applicants meet all the conditions of eligibility except that their contributions were made too long ago to meet the MQP, they may still qualify if:

1. They meet the rules in effect at the time they became disabled (see chart in the synopsis under CPP s. 44), and

2. They have been continuously disabled from that time to the date of the application.

Finally, where an applicant can not meet the MQP requirements only because of a division of unadjusted pensionable earnings was made between the applicant and their former spouse or common-law partner, the MQP is determined as if the division had not been made.

C. Definition of "Disabled"

1. The CPP and Regulations

"Disability" is defined by s. 42(2)(*a*) of the CPP as follows:

> **Sec. 42.** (2) For the purposes of this Act,
>
> (a) a person shall be considered to be disabled only if he is determined in prescribed manner to have a severe and prolonged mental or physical disability, and for the purposes of this paragraph,
>
>> (i) a disability is severe only if by reason thereof the person in respect of whom the determination is made is incapable regularly of pursuing any substantially gainful occupation, and
>>
>> (ii) a disability is prolonged only if it is determined in prescribed manner that the disability is likely to be long continued and of indefinite duration or is likely to result in death;

The "prescribed manner" referred to in s. 42(2)(*a*) for determining whether the disability is prolonged appears to be set out in ss. 68–70 of the CPP Regulations under the heading "Determination of disability". Notably, s. 68(1) reads as follows:

> **Sec. 68.** (1) Where an applicant claims that he or some other person is disabled within the meaning of the Act, he shall supply the Minister with the following information in respect of the person whose disability is to be determined:
>
> (a) a report of any physical or mental impairment including
>
>> (i) the nature, extent and prognosis of the impairment,
>>
>> (ii) the findings upon which the diagnosis and prognosis were made,
>>
>> (iii) any limitation resulting from the impairment, and
>>
>> (iv) any other pertinent information, including recommendations for further diagnostic work or treatment, that may be relevant;
>
> (b) a statement of that person's occupation and earnings for the period commencing on the date upon which the applicant alleges that the disability commenced; and
>
> (c) a statement of that person's education, employment experience and activities of daily life.

It wasn't until 2014 that the phrase "substantially gainful occupation" was clarified. In May 2014, s. 68.1 of the CPP Regulations was added to provide a formula for determining a threshold.

Sec. 68.1. (1) For the purpose of subparagraph 42(2)(*a*)(i) of the Act, "substantially gainful", in respect of an occupation, describes an occupation that provides a salary or wages equal to or greater than the maximum annual amount a person could receive as a disability pension. The amount is determined by the formula

$$(A \times B) + C$$

where

A   is .25 × the **Maximum Pensionable Earnings Average;**

B   is .75; and

C   **is the flat rate benefit, calculated as provided in subsection 56(2) of the Act, × 12.**

(2) If the amount calculated under subsection (1) contains a fraction of a cent, the amount is to be rounded to the nearest whole cent or, if the amount is equidistant from two whole cents, to the higher of them.

This is essentially 12 times the maximum monthly CPP retirement benefit, and therefore subject to change quarterly.

The definition in s. 42(2) is a somewhat circular. A person is *disabled* if he or she has a severe and prolonged mental or physical *disability*. Not "impairment". Not "disease" or "illness" or "handicap". While s. 68(1)(*a*) of the Regulations does refer to "impairment" in the context of what information the applicant is obligated to provide to the Minister, it does not explicitly state that an "impairment" is necessary to make a finding of disability.

So what exactly does s. 42(2)(*a*) mean? Before that question can be answered, we must establish the process by which all such provisions are to be interpreted and applied by courts and tribunals. What is legally relevant, and what should not be considered?

2. Statutory Interpretation Generally

Legislative provisions such as s. 42(2)(*a*) are not to be viewed in a vacuum. In *Rizzo & Rizzo Shoes Ltd. (Re)*, [1998] 1 S.C.R. 27, the Supreme Court of Canada found that it was not sufficient to restrict analysis of a provision to the plain meaning of the statutory words. This is particularly true with respect to "benefits-conferring" legislation, which is to be interpreted in a broad and generous manner in favour of the claimant. Attention must be directed to the scheme and object of the Act, the intention of the legislature, as well as the context of the words in issue (see *Rizzo*, para. 23). In inferring legislation intent, recourse may be made to Parliamentary debates and to legislative history.

The *Rizzo* approach to statutory interpretation was applied to s. 42(2)(*a*) of the CPP by the Federal Court of Appeal in *Villani v. Canada (A.G.)*, [2001] FCA 248.

The remainder of this part will examine the plain meaning, objects, scheme, legislative history, and overall context of s. 42(2)(*a*).

3. Plain Meaning Approach

Section 42(2)(*a*) is a complex, three-level definition section. The first level is the word "disabled", which the section purports to define. This is done by the phrase "severe and prolonged mental and physical disability", the second level of the definition. Finally, the words "severe" and "prolonged" are themselves defined.

The *Oxford English Dictionary* (1933) provides the following definitions:

"disability":

1. Want of ability (to discharge any office or function); inability, incapacity, impotence.

"disabled":

Rendered incapable of action or use, esp. by physical injury; incapacitated: see the verb.

"disable":

1. *trans.* To render unable or incapable; to deprive of ability, physical or mental, to incapacitate

(b) *spec.* To render (a man, animal, ship, etc.) incapable of action or use by physical injury or bodily infirmity; to cripple

(c) To injure, impair, or render less able *in* some capacity; to deprive of the use *of* (some faculty, power, or possession)

These definitions make it clear that the concept of disability has no intrinsic meaning apart from what the individual is prevented from doing. To have a mental or physical disability does not connote a condition that can be diagnosed in and of itself. The PAB decisions emphasize that "disability" in the context of s. 42(2)(*a*) is solely with respect to the applicant's capacity for employment, and is not referable to a medical condition *per se.* It is a red herring to focus on whether a given physical or mental condition (such as blindness) renders a person "disabled" in the abstract.

The Disability Case Table in the next chapter contains a survey of the various conditions relied on by applicants in support of their request for disability benefits. Some conditions are harder to establish than others, but the question is always the effect that the specified condition has on the ability of the applicant to work.

The second level under s. 42(2)(*a*) is that the disability be "severe" and "prolonged". These words are not definitive on their own. They are simply a way station on the road to the final destination — the determination as to whether the applicant has been rendered incapable (by his or her mental or physical condition) of engaging in "any substantially gainful occupation" for a "long-continued" and "indefinite" period of time.

According to the shorter *Oxford English Dictionary*, "substantial" means "having substance; not imaginary, unreal or apparent only; true, solid, real". This definition was employed in *Boles v. MEI* (June 30, 1994), CP 2794, CEB & PG ¶8553 (PAB), and its application is explored in the cases set out in the Disability Case Table. Note that in May 2014, s. 68.1 of the CPP Regulations was added to provide a formula for determining a threshold for "substantially gainful occupation". Essentially, the threshold amount of income is 12 times the maximum monthly CPP retirement benefit.

The terms "long-continued" and "indefinite" duration seem fairly vague or subjective. Is it sufficient that the disability not be transitory — i.e., that it not is expected to disappear in a few months? The *Oxford English Dictionary* (1933) definitions are as follows:

"indefinite"

Undefined, unlimited, the opposite of DEFINITE

I. *generally*

1. Without distinct limitation of being or character; having no clearly defined or determinate character; indeterminate, vague, undefined.

2. Of undetermined extent, amount, or number; unlimited.

"long"

6. Of a period of time, or a process, state, or action, viewed as extending over a period of time: Having a great extent in duration.

9. With implication of excessive duration.

11. That has continued or will continue in action, operation, or obligation for a long period.

Not surprisingly, these descriptions often do little to clarify the imprecise language. Was this lack of precision intentional? It would appear to be so when s. 42 is compared to the language of earlier public pension legislation.

In the hearings of the Special Joint Committee of the Senate and House of Commons, which reviewed the original CPP draft legislation in 1964, Dr. Willard, the witness on behalf of the Ministry of Department of Health and Welfare, said:

> Hon. Mr. Croll: How does [the definition] vary from the definition in the disability act at the present time?
>
> Dr. Willard: Mr. Chairman, the disabled persons' legislation that we have at the present time as the definition of permanent and total disability, which would be a more severe definition than the one set out here. You will notice in this Bill that the severity is related to a person being capable of regularly pursuing any substantially gainful occupation. It, therefore, brings in an additional concept of employability. Subparagraph (ii) relates to a disability that is prolonged, which means that it is not a temporary sickness cash benefit, or a benefit that is payable for an illness for a short period of time.
>
> Mr. Monteith: In this phrase "severe and prolonged mental or physical disability", would a terminal illness be covered?
>
> Dr. Willard: Yes, that would be covered; for instance, a terminal cancer case would be covered. (at p. 247)

In summary, and consistent with the approach set out in the Supreme Court of Canada's decision in *Rizzo*, s. 42(2)(*a*) is a provision that cannot be interpreted outside of its context. We must therefore examine the object and scheme of the CPP and its legislative history.

4. Objectives of the CPP

The CPP lacks a preamble, but there is no shortage of extrinsic sources as to its purpose and rationale. According to the 1964 White Paper:

> The *Canada Pension Plan* is designed to extend social insurance protection to people in retirement, to widows, orphans and the disabled. It will be a basic part of Canada's social security system. (p. 5.)
>
> The purpose of the *Canada Pension Plan* is to make reasonable minimum levels of income available at normal retirement ages, and to people who become disabled, and to the dependents of people who die. There will be scope for the continuation and extension of private plans to provide benefits over these minimum levels. (p. 7.)
>
> The *Canada Pension Plan* will be entirely self-financing. That is, the contributions will cover the cost of benefits, including the cost of administration. (p. 10.)
>
> The *Canada Pension Plan* is a social security program which is realistically geared to the growth of the economy. Within a moderate transition period, people of average incomes will be assured a reasonable retirement

pension, together with related social insurance protection for widows and children and people who become disabled. If our economy continues to grow in the way that it has been, with incomes rising both in money terms and in real value, people who make contributions now can be assured of pensions which will be appropriate to real income levels at the time they retire.

Related in this way to economic circumstances, the plan provides a level of pension which is appropriate to a society that values the security and dignity of those whose working life is past or who suffer the major misfortune of death or disablement of the family breadwinner.

Protection beyond that level will be a matter of individual choice. (p. 23.)

When the CPP was introduced in Parliament, Minister LaMarsh referred to the proposed legislation as a:

... comprehensive social insurance measure ... which provides help as of right rather than on a need or a means test, for those who suffer the loss of a loved breadwinner or those who find themselves disabled and unable to carry on work. I think hon. members will agree this is a giant step forward in Canada's social security program. (26th Parl., 2nd Session, November 9, 1964, *Hansard* at 9899.)

The Minister described supplementary benefits under the proposed CPP, such as the disability pension in the following manner:

In a sense, therefore, supplementary benefit pensions are more generous, especially for those in lower income brackets, than the new retirement pensions. This approach is justified because of the special need of widows, orphans and disabled contributors, and is certainly warranted on both humanitarian and economic grounds. (*Ibid.* at 9923.)

In *Villani v. Canada (A.G.)*, [2001] FCA 248, the Federal Court of Appeal considered the above extracts from the Parliamentary Debates to be relevant in interpreting s. 42(2).

Notably, there was no explicit statement in the White Paper regarding the importance of keeping contribution rates low. Minister LaMarsh referred to the contribution rate in the following terms:

The new program now envisaged being a richer one, there is a somewhat higher rate of contribution required. This higher rate of contribution will make it possible not only to finance the more generous retirement benefit, and the new survivors' and disability benefits, but will also result in higher investment reserves. (*Ibid.* at 9900.)

While contribution costs were a source of concern in the 1960s (see Torjman), the increases in employer and employee contribution rates beginning in 1987 and especially since 1997 have heightened awareness of the issue. The effect of high payroll taxes on the willingness of employers to hire or retain employees has been much debated. With the recent shift towards self-employment after corporate downsizing on the 1990s, the increasing combined contribution rates (levelling out at 9.9% of the maximum contributory earnings by 2003) result in a significant reduction of disposable income.

With increasing demographic pressure being exerted on CPP benefit payouts for the next generation, it is fair to say that minimizing contribution costs has become one of the objectives of the legislation. Chapter 5 of a joint federal–provincial–territorial government consultation paper ("An Information Paper for Consultations on the Canada Pension Plan", February 1996) is entitled "Options for Reducing CPP Costs".

5. Scheme of the CPP

The "scheme" of the Act, as that term is used by the Supreme Court of Canada in the *Rizzo* decision, appears to refer to the tools used by the legislation to achieve its intended goals.

> Finally, with regard to the scheme of the legislation, since the ESA is a mechanism for providing minimum benefits and standards to protect the interests of employees, *it can be characterized as benefits-conferring legislation. As such, according to several decisions of this Court, it ought to be interpreted in a broad and generous manner. Any doubt arising from difficulties of language should be resolved in favour of the claimant.* (para. 36.) (Emphasis added.)

Can the CPP be similarly characterized as "benefits-conferring legislation"? The Federal Court of Appeal in *Villani* replied to this question in the affirmative, stating:

> It is evident to me that the [CPP] is benefits-conferring legislation analogous to the *Unemployment Insurance Act, 1971*. The *Plan* provides for the payment of disability benefits to claimants who have been contributors under the scheme. (para. 28.)

This position is clearly correct. While it has often been observed that the CPP is not "welfare" legislation, the conferring of benefits on contributors and former contributors who meet the statutory criteria is undeniably central to its scheme. If employment standards legislation is "benefits-conferring", *a fortiori* the CPP must also qualify.

Therefore, the CPP ought to be interpreted in a broad and generous manner, with any doubts arising from difficulties of language to be resolved in favour of the applicant. In relation to s. 42(2)(*a*)(i), the Federal of Appeal in *Villani* stated the following:

> Accordingly, subparagraph 42(2)(*a*)(i) of the *Plan* should be given a generous construction. Of course, no interpretive approach can read out express limitations in a statute. The definition of a severe disability in the *Plan* is clearly a qualified one which must be contained by the actual language used in subparagraph 42(2)(*a*)(i). However, the meaning of the words used in that provision must be interpreted in a large and liberal manner, and any ambiguity flowing from the those words should be resolved in favour of a claimant for disability benefits. (para. 29.)

6. Legislative History

(a) Canadian Statutory Programs

The first disability pension in Canada was introduced under the auspices of the *Disabled Pensions Act* (S.C. 1953-54, c. 55). This was a provincially administered program with costs being shared by the federal and provincial governments. Allowances were paid to "totally and permanently disabled" persons aged 18 to 65. Subsections 2(2) and (3) of the Regulations read as follows:

> (2) For the purpose of the Act and these regulation, a person shall be deemed to be totally and permanently disabled only when
>
> (a) the person is suffering from a major physiological, anatomical or psychological impairment, verified by objective medical findings;
>
> (b) the impairment is likely to continue without substantial improvement during the lifetime of the person and is one to which the concept of cure cannot be applied; and
>
> (c) as a result of such impairment, the person is severely limited in activities pertaining to self-care and normal living, such as being

(i) bedridden or chairfast,

(ii) unable to leave home without being accompanied by another person,

(iii) normally in need of care and supervision for one or more of such self-care activities as dressing, body hygiene or eating,

(iv) unable to perform such routine activities as climbing a short stairway or walking a limited distance on a level surface, or

(v) certified by a qualified physician to be under medical instructions to forbear from activities of the kind mentioned in subparagraph (iv).

(3) Notwithstanding subsection (2), a person shall be deemed not to be totally and permanently disabled where, in respect of that person, a favourable rehabilitation prognosis is obtained, or approved therapeutic measures are recommended, by the provincial authority, the requisite rehabilitation services or therapeutic measures are available.

It can be seen that this provision shares very little with the CPP provision. In the first place, it adopts a much more restrictive approach such that the applicant must be practically helpless. Secondly, its degree of specificity stands in stark contrast to the generality of s. 42(2). Three elements that have no counterpart in s. 42(2) or s. 68 of the Regulations are as follows:

• The applicant must suffer from a major physiological, anatomical or psychological impairment.

• The express requirement of objective medical findings to support the applicant's claim.

• The impairment must be likely to continue without substantial improvement during the lifetime of the person and is one to which the concept of cure cannot be applied.

It is to be noted that many PAB decisions have taken the view that "objective medical findings" in support of the applicant's claim are virtually mandatory, despite the absence of such a requirement in the legislation. However, one could easily presume that Parliament made an intentional decision not to impose such a requirement on applicants. The necessity of "objective" evidence under the current scheme is discussed further below.

The 1964 White Paper states as follows (at p. 15):

A contributor will be regarded as disabled if an examination reveals a medically determinable impairment in which physical or mental disability is so severe and prolonged that he is unable to secure regular, substantially gainful employment. This does not mean he has to be completely helpless to qualify; it means he must be found unable to support himself by reason of his disability.

Clearly the White Paper was trying to establish a break with the then existing restrictive "totally and permanently disabled" approach, and to large extent the above paragraph is reflected in s. 42(2). However, the requirement that there be a "medically determinable impairment" did not make it into the CPP. Generally, the process of arriving at a consensus regarding the definition of disability was marked by heated debate and numerous false starts. Its possible inclusion raised serious questions about disincentives to work, criteria and cost. As a result of these concerns, a decision was made to employ a restricted definition of disability at the outset in order to determine how the program would evolved over time (see Torjman.)

(b) Comparison with U.S. Position

The current s. 42(2) definition was based largely on the definition used at the time by the U.S. *Social Security Act*. In the hearings of the Special Joint Committee of the Senate and House of Common that reviewed the original CPP draft legislation in 1964, the following exchange took place:

> Mr. Basford: Why do we have to have different tests?

> Dr. Willard [on behalf of the Ministry]: Mr. Chairman, the reason for a more stringent test in the case of disability arises from the problems that have surrounded the provision and administration of disability benefits. We have tried to develop the disability benefit along the lines of the one in the United States, but in some instances it is actually more generous. For instance, they have a six-month waiting period in the United States; we have a three-month waiting period in this Bill. (at p. 250)

It is therefore instructive to compare the s. 42(2) definition with its U.S. counterpart. The Social Security program was introduced in 1935 during the Great Depression as a major component of President Roosevelt's "New Deal". Originally, Social Security did not provide for a general disability benefit, although the blind were eligible for cash benefits. This distinction in the Social Security program between the blind and disabled persons generally has continued down to the present day.

In 1956, a general disability pension was introduced for persons between 50 and 65. "Disability" was defined by s. 223(*c*)(2) as follows:

> (2) The term disability means inability to engage in any substantial gainful activity by reason of any medically determinable physical or mental impairment which can be expected to result in death or to be of long-continued and indefinite duration. An individual shall not be considered to be under a disability unless he furnishes such proof of the existence thereof as may be required. (*Social Security Amendments of 1956*, Public Law 880, c. 836, s. 103.)

The first sentence is clearly the source for the CPP definition as it was enacted in 1965 and as it still reads today. There are several differences in the wording, which may or may not be meaningful (see discussion below), but the essence of the definition is identical. It is interesting to note that the U.S. definition did not fully reflect how it was intended to be applied by the Social Security Agency ("SSA"). As noted by Diller:

> The SSA's plans for consideration of age, education, and work experience were disclosed to Congress during the debate over passage. The Associate Chairman of the Advisory Council stated that "our definition requires that [the claimant] be disabled not only for the occupation which he has been pursuing but any occupation which he might be reasonably expected, by reason of education, experience, general background, age, and so forth, to pursue." Implicit in this statement is the point that a claimant would not be denied benefits when vocational factors made it "unreasonable" to expect him or her to pursue a particular type of work that he or she has the physical capacity to perform.

U.S. appellate-level decisions have articulated the following principles, which interpret and apply the 1956 definition:

- Unemployment compensation cannot be ordered under the guise of disability insurance. To establish a disability, a claimant must do more than show that he is unable to do his former work; he must be unable to perform any substantial, gainful work, including work of a physically or emotionally lighter type. The word "any" includes former work and work of a different nature: *Hicks v. Flemming*, 5 Cir. 1962, 302 F.2d 470 (C.A.)

- When a claimant's former employment is the only type of work he is capable of performing, then "former work" means "any work" and the requirements of the Act are met. But impairment to carry on one's *former work* is not enough in itself to satisfy the statutory definition of "any substantial gainful activity." The Secretary's showing of the claimant's ability to perform light work of a various nature is all the answer he is required to make to the claimant. "What jobs are there" means, within the context of the Act, what kinds of work can the claimant perform, not what jobs are there available for him in where he is located: *Celebrezze v. O'Brient*, 323 F.2d 989 (5th Cir. 1963); see also *Kerner v. Flemming*, 2 Cir. 1962, 283 F.2d 916; *Graham v. Ribicoff*, 9 Cir. 1962, 295 F.2d 391; *Rinaldi v. Ribicoff*, 2 Cir. 1963, 305 F.2d 548.

- Even though severe physical limitations have been established, it is still necessary in applying the legal standard to relate such limitation to the claimant's work history and educational background: *Underwood v. Ribicoff*, 4 Cir. 1962, 298 F.2d 850, 852.

- "Any substantial gainful work" must have reference to a claimant's education, training, experience, and physical and mental capacities, in addition to the effect of the impairment on former work activities: *Aaron v. Flemming*, M.D.Ala. 1958, 168 F. Supp. 291, 295. (C.A.) (Note: In *Celebrezze v. O'Brient*, 323 F.2d 989 (5th Cir. 1963) the court noted that "This test has become standard.")

While the Canadian definition has remained static since it was introduced, the U.S. definition continued to evolve throughout the 1960s. The minimum age of 50 requirement was eliminated in 1960. In 1965, the requirement that the disability be "long-continued or indefinite" was discontinued in favour of the current one-year period. The report of the U.S. Senate Committee on Finance remarked that:

> The effect of the provision the committee is recommending is to provide disability benefits for a totally disabled worker even though his condition may be expected to improve after a year. As experience under the disability program has demonstrated, in the great majority of cases in which total disability continues for at least a year the disability is essentially permanent.

In 1967, the definition was made substantially more detailed, with the eligibility requirements tightened in response to greater than expected demands on the system. It was made clear that it was not sufficient that the claimant was rendered unable to do his or her former job, and that "objective medical evidence" was required. The Senate and House committee reports both stated that:

> Statements of the applicant or conclusions of others with respect to the nature and extent of impairment or disability do not establish the existence of disability ... unless they are supported by clinical or laboratory findings or other medically acceptable evidence confirming such statements or conclusions.

The current definition reads as follows:

TITLE II — FEDERAL OLD-AGE, SURVIVORS, AND DISABILITY INSURANCE BENEFITS

§223.(a)(1) Every individual who —

(A) is insured for disability insurance benefits (as determined under subsection (c)(1)),

(B) has not attained retirement age (as defined in section 216(l)),

(C) has filed application for disability insurance benefits, and

(D) is under a disability (as defined in subsection (d))

15

shall be entitled to a disability insurance benefit ...

(*d*)(1) The term "disability" means —

(A) inability to engage in any substantial gainful activity by reason of any medically determinable physical or mental impairment which can be expected to result in death or which has lasted or can be expected to last for a continuous period of not less than 12 months; or

(B) in the case of an individual who has attained the age of 55 and is blind (within the meaning of "blindness" as defined in section 216(i)(1)), inability by reason of such blindness to engage in substantial gainful activity requiring skills or abilities comparable to those of any gainful activity in which he has previously engaged with some regularity and over a substantial period of time.

(2) For purposes of paragraph (1)(*a*) —

(A) An individual shall be determined to be under a disability only if his physical or mental impairment or impairments are of such severity that he is not only unable to do his previous work but cannot, considering his age, education, and work experience, engage in any other kind of substantial gainful work which exists in the national economy, regardless of whether such work exists in the immediate area in which he lives, or whether a specific job vacancy exists for him, or whether he would be hired if he applied for work. For purposes of the preceding sentence (with respect to any individual), "work which exists in the national economy" means work which exists in significant numbers either in the region where such individual lives or in several regions of the country.

(B) In determining whether an individual's physical or mental impairment or impairments are of a sufficient medical severity that such impairment or impairments could be the basis of eligibility under this section, the Commissioner of Social Security shall consider the combined effect of all of the individual's impairments without regard to whether any such impairment, if considered separately, would be of such severity. If the Commissioner of Social Security does find a medically severe combination of impairments, the combined impact of the impairments shall be considered throughout the disability determination process.

(C) An individual shall not be considered to be disabled for purposes of this title if alcoholism or drug addiction would (but for this subparagraph) be a contributing factor material to the Commissioner's determination that the individual is disabled.

(3) For purposes of this subsection, a "physical or mental impairment" is an impairment that results from anatomical, physiological, or psychological abnormalities which are demonstrable by medically acceptable clinical and laboratory diagnostic techniques.

(4)(*a*) The Commissioner of Social Security shall by regulations prescribe the criteria for determining when services performed or earnings derived from services demonstrate an individual's ability to engage in substantial gainful activity. No individual who is blind shall be regarded as having demonstrated an ability to engage in substantial gainful activity on the basis of earnings that do not exceed an amount equal to the exempt amount which would be applicable under section 203(*f*)(8), to individuals described in subparagraph (D) thereof, if section 102 of the *Senior Citizens' Right to Work Act* of 1996 had not been enacted. Notwithstanding the provisions of paragraph (2), an individual whose services or earnings meet such criteria shall, except for purposes of section 222(c), be found not to be disabled. In determining whether an individual is able to engage in substantial gainful activity by reason of his earnings, where his disability is sufficiently severe to result in a functional limitation requiring assistance in order for him to work, there shall be excluded from such earnings an amount equal to the cost (to such individual) of any attendant care services, medical devices, equipment, prostheses, and similar items and services (not including routine drugs or routine medical services unless such drugs or services are necessary for the control of the disabling condition) which are necessary (as determined by the Commissioner of Social Security in regulations) for that purpose, whether or not such assistance is also needed to enable him to carry out his normal daily functions; except that the amount to be excluded shall be subject to such reasonable limits as the Commissioner of Social Security may prescribe.

(b) In determining under subparagraph (A) when services performed or earnings derived from services demonstrate an individual's ability to engage in substantial gainful activity, the Commissioner of Social Security shall apply the criteria described in subparagraph (A) with respect to services performed by any individual without regard to the legality of such services.

(5)(a) An individual shall not be considered to be under a disability unless he furnishes such medical and other evidence of the existence thereof as the Commissioner of Social Security may require. An individual's statement as to pain or other symptoms shall not alone be conclusive evidence of disability as defined in this section; there must be medical signs and findings, established by medically acceptable clinical or laboratory diagnostic techniques, which show the existence of a medical impairment that results from anatomical, physiological, or psychological abnormalities which could reasonably be expected to produce the pain or other symptoms alleged and which, when considered with all evidence required to be furnished under this paragraph (including statements of the individual or his physician as to the intensity and persistence of such pain or other symptoms which may reasonably be accepted as consistent with the medical signs and .findings), would lead to a conclusion that the individual is under a disability. Objective medical evidence of pain or other symptoms established by medically acceptable clinical or laboratory techniques (for example, deteriorating nerve or muscle tissue) must be considered in reaching a conclusion as to whether the individual is under a disability. Any non-Federal hospital, clinic, laboratory, or other provider of medical services, or physician not in the employ of the Federal Government, which supplies medical evidence required and requested by the Commissioner of Social Security under this paragraph shall be entitled to payment from the Commissioner of Social Security for the reasonable cost of providing such evidence.

(b) In making any determination with respect to whether an individual is under a disability or continues to be under a disability, the Commissioner of Social Security shall consider all evidence available in such individual's case record, and shall develop a complete medical history of at least the preceding twelve months for any case in which a determination is made that the individual is not under a disability. In making any determination the Commissioner of Social Security shall make every reasonable effort to obtain from the individual's treating physician (or other treating health care provider) all medical evidence, including diagnostic tests, necessary in order to properly make such determination, prior to evaluating medical evidence obtained from any other source on a consultative basis.

(6)(*a*) Notwithstanding any other provision of this title, any physical or mental impairment which arises in connection with the commission by an individual (after the date of the enactment of this paragraph) of an offense which constitutes a felony under applicable law and for which such individual is subsequently convicted, or which is aggravated in connection with such an offense (but only to the extent so aggravated), shall not be considered in determining whether an individual is under a disability.

(*b*) Notwithstanding any other provision of this title, any physical or mental impairment which arises in connection with an individual's confinement in a jail, prison, or other penal institution or correctional facility pursuant to such individual's conviction of an offense (committed after the date of the enactment of this paragraph) constituting a felony under applicable law, or which is aggravated in connection with such a confinement (but only to the extent so aggravated), shall not be considered in determining whether such individual is under a disability for purposes of benefits payable for any month during which such individual is so confined.

One administrative aspect of the U.S. model that Canada did not follow was the SSA's Listing of Impairments. This listing outlined impairments for which coverage would automatically be granted assuming that the claimant established through objective medical evidence that he or she suffered from the listed condition. As such, it was intended as a convenient screening devise, and not to exclude those whose conditions were not listed. The operation of the U.S. approach is set out in the Code of Federal Regulations 20 C.F.R. 416.920 (1994), which outlines the five-step sequential analysis used by the SSA in determining whether a claimant is disabled. Essentially, the analysis is as follows:

1. Is the claimant engaging in a substantially gainful activity at the present time? If so, then he or she is not disabled.

2. Does the claimant have a severe impairment or combination of impairments that significantly limits the ability to perform basic work? If not, then the claimant is not disabled.

3. If the impairment does limit the ability to do basic work, does the impairment meet or is it equivalent to an impairment described on the Listing of Impairments? If yes, then the claimant is disabled.

4. If the impairment does not meet any of the listed impairments, does the impairment prevent doing past relevant work? If the claimant can perform past relevant work, she is not disabled. [Note that the SSA's restrictive view that "past relevant" need not be work that currently exists in the national economy is a reasonable construction of the legislation — see *Barnhart v. Thomas* (November 12, 2003) Doc. 02-763 (U.S.S.C.)]

5. If the impairment prevents the claimant from performing other significant gainful activity, the burden shifts to the Secretary to prove that jobs exist in the national economy that the claimant could perform, taking into account his or her age, education and work experience.

The basic tests in the Canadian and U.S. definitions are still similar, although the present U.S. provision is more detailed. Substantively, some of the key differences between the U.S and Canadian definitions are as follows:

• The U.S. definition requires (and has always required) that the disability arise out of a "medically determinable physical or mental impairment". The CPP statute does not specify this, but does provide that the determination of disability be made in the "prescribed manner." Section 68(1)(*a*) of the Regulations requires an applicant to supply a report of "any physical or mental impairment" to the Minister. This clearly does not make such an impairment a mandatory requirement for receiving a disability pension.

- For non-terminal conditions, the U.S. provision no longer requires that the disability must be "long-continued" or of "indefinite duration." Instead, the impairment must have lasted or be expected to last for a continuous period of at least 12 months. Under the CPP, the disability must be "prolonged or of indefinite duration." Note that the U.S. change was prompted by the observation that a disability of over one year's duration was usually going to fulfill the criteria in any event. The U.S. amendment was therefore not considered to be a substantive change, but merely to simplify the problems of proof.

- The U.S. provision now expressly permits the court to consider the applicant's age, education, and work experience in determining his or her inability to work. This essentially codifies the case law under the original 1956 definition. The CPP is silent on this point, although s. 68(1)(c) of the Regulations requires the applicant to furnish such information to the Minister.

- On the other hand, the U.S. provision deems irrelevant the issue of whether the applicant "would be hired if he applied for work". Again this is not addressed in the CPP, but according to the *Leduc* line of cases it is appropriate to ask whether a "real-world" employer would even consider hiring the applicant.

Of course, the U.S. definition should not be considered in isolation from the overall program. Perhaps surprisingly, the U.S Social Security contribution rate is considerably higher than Canada's. Since 1989, the U.S. rate has been 6.2% for both employers and employees, and 12.4% on self-employed income. It is called a "tax" and collected as part of the *Internal Revenue Code of 1986* (ss. 1401, 3101 and 3111). This tax is in addition to other taxes, and therefore contributions are not deductible or subject to a tax credit as they are in Canada.

From 1995 to 1999, roughly half of the workers who applied for disability benefits in the U.S. were successful. However, in previous years, the success rate had been as low as 29.1% (in 1981). (Source: www.ssa.gov/OACT/STATS/table6c7.html) In Canada, the first instance refusal rate has increased from 56% in 1995 to 70% in 1999.

It should be noted that there are two other components of the U.S. scheme for disabled. The first is the Supplemental Security Income (SSI) program for needy, blind or disabled individuals who are not contributors. The definition of "disabled" for SSI purposes is the same as that for disabled workers. The second is the *Americans With Disabilities Act* (ADA), which permits "qualified disabled individuals" to bring civil suit against employers who discriminate. A line of cases has arisen in the U.S. that argue that a previous application for Social Security disability benefits prevents a disabled person from suing an employer for not hiring (or terminating) that individual on the basis of his or her disability. (See M.C. Sims, "Estop It! Judicial Estoppel and it use in Americans with Disabilities Act Litigation" (1997), 34 Hous. L. Rev. 843, A.C. Luby "Estopping Enforcement of the Americans with Disabilities Act" 13 J. L. & Politics 415; J.M. Leon "Two Hats, One Head: Reconciling Disability Benefits and the Americans with Disabilities Act of 1990", [1997] U. Ill. L. Rev. 1139; M.C. Weston, "The Road Best Travelled: Removing Judicial Roadblocks that Prevent Workers from Obtaining both Disability Benefits and ADA Civil rights Protection" 26 Hofstra L. Rev. 377; M. Diller, "Dissonant Disability Policies: The Tensions Between the Americans with Disabilities Act and Federal Disability Benefit Programs" 76 Tex. L. Rev. 1003.)

Outside of federal and provincial human rights legislation, the only direct Canadian equivalent of the ADA is the *Ontarians With Disabilities Act, 2001*, S.O. 2001, c. 32. Apparently, the estoppel argument has not yet been raised in Canada.

III. Specific Issues

The following discussion applies the legislative analysis set out above to the following issues:

A. Objective Evidence: Is It an Absolute Requirement?

The phrase "objective medical evidence" does not appear in the CPP or regulations, but it is a common touchstone in PAB decisions. The phrase has never been definitely defined in Canada, but can conceivably refer to any one of three scenarios:

1. results of medical tests that unambiguously support a specific medical diagnosis;

2. clinical findings of an independent specialist in that area of medicine based on patient interviews, where such findings are not inconsistent with the results of medical tests; or

3. findings of any physician, even the patient's own family doctor, where such findings are not inconsistent with the results of medical tests.

In the U.S., by contrast, the phrase "objective medical evidence" has been specifically defined (see regulations §404.1528 and §404.1529 under the *Social Security Act*) to exclude symptoms reported by the claimant and to refer exclusively to the following two concepts:

> *Signs* ... anatomical, physiological, or psychological abnormalities which can be observed, apart from [the applicant's] statements (symptoms). Signs must be shown by medically acceptable clinical diagnostic techniques. Psychiatric signs are medically demonstrable phenomena that indicate specific psychological abnormalities, e.g., abnormalities of behavior, mood, thought, memory, orientation, development, or perception. They must also be shown by observable facts that can be medically described and evaluated.

> *Laboratory findings* ... anatomical, physiological, or psychological phenomena which can be shown by the use of medically acceptable laboratory diagnostic techniques. Some of these diagnostic techniques include chemical tests, electrophysiological studies (electrocardiogram, electroencephalogram, etc.), roentgenological studies (X-rays), and psychological tests.

The PAB often finds objective clinical findings of a specialist to be the most persuasive evidence of the applicant's entitlement to a disability pension. Some panels go even further, stating that objective evidence is an absolute requirement either generally (see *Cameron v. MHRD* (August 15, 1996), CP 4448; *Evagelou v. MEI* (March 5, 1996), CP 992, CEB & PG 8602) or with respect to specific conditions (*Smith v. MHRD* (September 16, 1996), CP 4364 — alcoholism; *Walsh v. MHRD* (October 4, 2000), CP 08755 — chronic pain syndrome).

However, other panels of the PAB have been reluctant to fetter their discretion to award in favour of a highly credible applicant. Many cases echo the principle that while objective medical evidence is helpful and greatly assists the PAB in its determination of disability, the CPP does not make a finding of disability conditional on "objective evidence" (see *MHRD v. Chase* (November 5, 1998), CP 6540).

The PAB has also held that s. 68 of the CPP Regulations, which provides that an applicant must furnish the Minister with a "report" of any physical or mental impairment, has the effect of requiring that the determination must be made on the basis of cogent medical evidence pertaining to the nature and extent and prognosis of the impairment, based on actual clinical findings, as opposed to only subjective testimony (see *Cameron* above; *Holliday v. MHRD* (October 23, 1996), CP 3959, CEB & PG 8661). Less rigidly, *Vukcevic v. MHRD* (November 22, 2000), CP 10947, suggests that an applicant will be determined eligible in the absence of such reports only on rare occasions.

The courts have not stepped in to resolve the issue. However, in *Villani v. Canada (A.G.)*, [2001] FCA 248, after substantially loosening the test for qualifying for a disability, the Federal Court of Appeal stated:

> This restatement of the approach to the definition of disability does not mean that everyone with a health problem who has some difficulty finding and keeping a job is entitled to a disability pension. Claimants still must be able to demonstrate that they suffer from a "serious and prolonged disability" that renders them "incapable regularly of pursuing any substantially gainful occupation". *Medical evidence will still be needed as will evidence of employment efforts and possibilities.* Cross-examination will, of course, be available to test the veracity and credibility of the evidence of claimants and others. (para. 50.) (Emphasis added.)

The italicized portion was relied on by the PAB in *Vega v. MHRD* (February 13, 2002), CP 13999 in support of the proposition that it is still "generally necessary" to have objective medical evidence. But if this is what the Federal Court of Appeal meant, it is easy to imagine how they could have been much clearer on that point.

It should also be pointed out that the Federal Court of Appeal in *Vogt v. MHRD*, [2002] FCA 52 implicitly endorsed the objective medical evidence standard applied by the PAB decision in dismissing the claimant's application for judicial review, stating the following:

> In our view the Board's reasons were sufficiently comprehensive to demonstrate the reasoning on which its conclusions were based. The Pension Appeals Board reviewed the substantive evidence and concluded that *there was no reliable objective evidence* to support a finding that the applicant suffered from a disability such as to prevent him from regularly pursuing a substantially gainful occupation.
>
> We are not able to find that this was a patently unreasonable conclusion. (paras. 4-5.) (Emphasis added.)

But it does not appear from the court's brief decision in *Vogt* that the need for "reliable objective evidence" had been challenged by the applicant.

There is certainly no support in the legislation for an absolute requirement of objective medical evidence on a disability application. It is impossible to conclude that Parliament intended that there be a rigid rule against determinations of entitlement based on subjective evidence, in light of the following:

- Section 42(2)(*a*) does not impose a requirement of any medically-determinable condition, in stark contrast to the regulations under the legislation that preceded it (1953-54 *Disabled Pensions Act*) and the U.S. *Social Security Act* definition on which the current provision was clearly based. Instead, the focus is exclusively on whether the applicant is capable of working or not. Without a medically determinable condition being required, it is difficult to justify imputing an requirement of medical findings.

- The regulations under the legislation that preceded it also required that such medical determinations be "verified by objective medical findings". There is no such requirement under s. 42(2)(*a*).

- While s. 42(2)(*a*) required that the disability is to be determined "in a prescribed manner", the Regulations merely require that the applicant to furnish information including a "report of any medical or mental impairment" (s. 68(1)(*a*)). Who the author of the report should be or what qualifications they must have are not specified. Nor does the provision state that the contents of such report will be determinative.

21

- The applicant is also required (by s. 68(1)(*b*) and (*c*) of the Regulation) to furnish other non-medical evidence, such as occupation, earnings, education, employment experience and daily activities. It has not been suggested that entitlement is *conditional* on such evidence being favourable to the claim, so why should success be conditional on the evidence required by s. 68(1)(*a*)?

An application for disability benefits is not comparable to a serious personal injury claim in terms of the potential dollar amounts involved. Clearly, there should be restrictions on the amount of expert medical evidence that a party is required to furnish in order to secure an entitlement to an average of $676.91 (up to a maximum benefit $935.12) per month in 2001. Given the four-stage application and appeal process, with new or updated reports being required for every one, pursuing a disability claim could eventually get very expensive for an applicant.

At the same time, the PAB, in carrying out its mandate, may appropriately have regard for the purposes of the CPP, one of which is to provide an affordable program of social insurance to Canadians. While keeping CPP premiums a low as possible should not be a primary consideration, the PAB can hardly ignore the "floodgates" argument as it applies to the more subjective of the chronic illnesses such as chronic fatigue syndrome and fibromyalgia. The constitutional difficulty of enacting changes to the CPP justifies an incremental approach to any relaxation of requirements.

One of the leading PAB decisions on subjective evidence is *Macri v. MEI* (January 9, 1995), CP 3079, CEB & PG 8669. In *Macri*, the PAB defined the situation where subjective complaints were out of proportion to findings of organic impairments as "functional overlay situations". An entitlement to a pension had to be based on a proper psychiatric diagnosis of a mental illness or emotional disorder severe enough to be disabling in its own right.

The *Macri* approach is more restrictive than the approach used in the U.S. even though, as noted above, a medically determinable physical or mental disability is expressly required to be shown on a disability claim under the *Social Security Act*. The U.S. case law has set out specific parameters for taking subjective evidence into account. Allowing for the differences in the legislation and regulatory context, these parameters are worth considering by Canada adjudicators.

The leading American decision on point is *Polaski v. Heckler*, 739 F.2d 1320 (8th Cir. 1984). In this case, the 8th Circuit Court of Appeal adopted the following statement as the correct approach to dealing with subjective complaints on disability claims:

> Symptoms such as pain, shortness of breath, weakness, or nervousness are the individual's own perceptions of the effects of a physical or mental impairment(s). Because of their subjective characteristics and the absence of any reliable techniques for measurement, symptoms (especially pain) are difficult to prove, disprove, or quantify.

*   *   *

> While the claimant has the burden of proving that the disability results from a medically determinable physical or mental impairment, direct medical evidence of the cause and effect relationship between the impairment and the degree of claimant's subjective complaints need not be produced. The adjudicator may not disregard a claimant's subjective complaints solely because the objective medical evidence does not fully support them.

> The absence of an objective medical basis which supports the degree of severity of subjective complaints alleged is just one factor to be considered in evaluating the credibility of the testimony and complaints. The adjudicator must give full consideration to all of the evidence presented

relating to subjective complaints, including the claimant's prior work record, and observations by third parties and treating and examining physicians relating to such matters as:

1. the claimant's daily activities;

2. the duration, frequency and intensity of the pain;

3. precipitating and aggravating factors;

4. dosage, effectiveness and side effects of medication;

5. functional restrictions.

The adjudicator is not free to accept or reject the claimant's subjective complaints solely on the basis of personal observations. Subjective complaints may be discounted if there are inconsistencies in the evidence as a whole.

In *Ghant v. Bowen*, 930 F.2d 633 (8th Cir.1991), it was held that the adjudicator must expressly explain the reason for discrediting the subjective complaints.

Under this approach, subjective complaints can be corroborated by a wide range of more "objective" evidence, not just medical reports. This is still a hurdle for applicants, but not an unduly high one, and could easily be applied in the Canadian legislative context.

B. The Test for Severity

1. Personal Factors

The Federal Court of Appeal in *Villani* resolved a long-standing dispute regarding the relevance of personal factors in determining whether a disability was "severe" within the meaning of s. 42(2)(a)(i). At the PAB level, the weight of recent authority was in favour of a restrictive approach under which personal factors such as age, education and employment background were not relevant. The minority approach was embodied by the *Leduc v. MNHW* (January 29, 1988), CEB & PG 8546, where the following was stated:

> ... the Appellant does not live in an abstract and theoretical world. He lives in a real world, people [*sic*] by real employers who are required to face up to the realities of commercial enterprise. The question is whether it is realistic to postulate that, given all of the Appellant's well documented difficulties, any employer would even remotely consider engaging the Appellant. (pp. 6021-6022.)

The Court of Appeal in *Villani* came down firmly in favour of this "real world" test, stating:

> [s. 42(2)(a)(i)] indicates ... that Parliament viewed as severe any disability which renders an applicant incapable of pursuing with consistent frequency any truly remunerative occupation. In my view, it follows from this that the hypothetical occupations which a decision-maker must consider cannot be divorced from the particular circumstances of the applicant, such as age, education level, language proficiency and past work and life experience. (para. 38.)

* * *

The proper test for severity is the one that treats each word in the definition as contributing something to the statutory requirement. Those words, read together, suggest that the severity test involves an aspect of employability. (para. 44.)

2. External Socio-Economic Conditions

An important issue not unequivocally determined by *Villani* is whether socio-economic conditions, such as the availability of work in the local community or in the national economy, is a relevant consideration in determining whether the disability is severe. The traditional approach to the relevance of personal circumstances and economic factors was set out in the PAB decision in *Villani:*

> It is very important to note that the words "regularly pursuing *any* substantially gainful occupation ..." means just that: *any* occupation. It is not, as some insurance policies say, "... any occupation for which the applicant is reasonably suited ..." It is *any* occupation, even though the applicant may lack education, special skills, or basic language.

> A second factor is availability of work. This is not a matter that is or can be considered by this Board. So the state of the local job market is irrelevant: It is legally assumed that work is available to do. (Emphasis in original.)

After quoting the above two paragraphs (at par. 43), the Court of Appeal in *Villani* went on to state that the PAB had imposed a far too restrictive test of severity, but did not specifically accept or reject the second paragraph. Judicial review was granted, and the case was referred the case back to the PAB for a rehearing before a different panel.

While the "availability of work" issue was not addressed, the court, in embracing the real-world concept of "employability", did say:

> Unfortunately for decision-makers under the *Plan*, employability is not a concept that easily lends itself to abstraction. Employability occurs in the context of *commercial realities and the particular circumstances of an applicant.* (Emphasis added.) (para. 45.)

After discussing circumstances in the sense of what alternative occupations may realistically be considered, the Court concludes its analysis by stating the following:

> This restatement of the approach to the definition of disability does not mean that everyone with a health problem who has some difficulty finding and keeping a job is entitled to a disability pension. Claimants still must be able to demonstrate that they suffer from a "serious and prolonged disability" that renders them "incapable regularly of pursuing any substantially gainful occupation". Medical evidence will still be needed as will evidence of employment efforts *and possibilities.* Cross-examination will, of course, be available to test the veracity and credibility of the evidence of claimants and others. (para. 50.) (Emphasis added.)

It also should be noted that the court, in the course of its review of early PAB decisions issued before the "real world" test was first articulated by *Leduc*, noted the following:

> Similarly, in *Minister of National Health and Welfare v. Raymond G. Russell, CCH Employment Benefits and Pension Guide Reports, Transfer Binder 1968–1985* at ¶8684, pp. 66279-6280 (June 26, 1974), the Board restated its jurisprudence *to that time* in the following words:

> > The Board has always interpreted the language of the statute to mean exactly what it says, and in many cases has had to say that the fact that suitable work has not been available to an applicant is irrelevant to the question of whether or not he qualifies. However, various circumstances have been held to bear upon this question, such as age, education and aptitude. (para. 35.) (Emphasis added.)

Nowhere does the court directly refer to the availability of work as a factor. The only list of relevant factors expressly set out by the court is in the following extract:

Each word in the subparagraph must be given meaning and when read in that way the subparagraph indicates, in my opinion, that Parliament viewed as severe any disability which renders an applicant incapable of pursuing with consistent frequency any truly remunerative occupation. In my view, it follows from this that the hypothetical occupation which a decision maker must consider cannot be divorced from the particular circumstances of the applicant, such as *age, education level, language proficiency and past work and life experience.* (para. 38.) (Emphasis added.)

The underlined factors above pertain only to personal characteristics of the claimant. On the other hand, the court expressly endorses the PAB decision in *Barlow v. MHRD* (November 22, 1999), CP 07017, and in paragraph 37 quotes the PAB as saying:

... it is difficult, if not impossible, to find that [the appellant] was at age 57 in a position to qualify for any usual or customary employment, *which actually exists,* is not illusory, and is of real importance. (Emphasis added.)

To impose a requirement that the hypothetical job "actually exist" would seem to make the availability of work a relevant consideration.

It is hard to know how to interpret the Court of Appeal's omitting to comment on the PAB's views regarding the irrelevance of the availability of work. Of course, any comment the court did make would have been *obiter.*

Perhaps the Court of Appeal thought that economic conditions were so obviously a component of the "real world" approach endorsed by the court that the issue required no further elucidation. Certainly, some of the *dicta* with respect to the meaning of employability could be considered to support the view that "commercial realities" (in addition to personal characteristics) and "employment possibilities" (in addition to employment efforts) are factors to be considered. The court was emphasizing a non-restrictive approach to interpreting the meaning of "severe" under s. 42(2)(a)(i); it is possible that it overshot the mark.

Six months later, a different panel of the Federal Court of Appeal did confront this issue head-on. In *MHRD v. Rice*, [2002] FCA 47, the Federal Court of Appeal refused judicial review of an PAB decision in favour of the claimant. The PAB had found that the claimant's disability was severe, having regard to his physical limitations and his lack of reading and writing ability, but also went on to state in *obiter:*

We therefore hold that Mr. Rice's disability is severe, and keeping in mind that Weymouth is a small community, the primary industry being fishing, and the Minister acknowledging he cannot return to his former employment, the possibility of obtaining regular gainful employment is remote, if not impossible. (page 8.)

The Minister sought judicial review. The Federal Court of Appeal confirmed the PAB's finding of severity, stating that it was made on the basis of appropriate principles and was not patently unreasonable. But the court also went on to add, in *obiter,* that:

... we would take this opportunity to make the point that indeed, as the Minister has argued, socio-economic factors such as labour market conditions are irrelevant in a determination of whether an individual is disabled pursuant to subsection 42(2) of the *Canada Pension Plan,* R.S.C. 1985, c. C-8. (para. 8.)

The Court of Appeal in *Rice* also found that the panel in *Villani* did not contradict this principle, stating that:

Isaac J.A.'s reference to "the hypothetical occupation" makes it clear that what is relevant is any substantially gainful occupation having regard to the individual's personal circumstances, but not whether real jobs are available in the labour market. (para. 10.)

While the generous interpretation afforded to subparagraph 42(2)(*a*)(i) and the necessity to take into account the "real world" context is a more liberal approach than may have been previously taken by some Boards, there is no suggestion in *Villani* that socio-economic considerations such as labour market conditions are relevant in a disability assessment. Indeed, Isaac J.A. quotes, *with apparent approval* the Board's decision in the *Minister of National Health and Welfare v. Raymond G. Russell* ... (para. 11.) (Emphasis added.)

It should be pointed out that the court in *Villani* quoted the *Russell* paragraph only to show how s. 42(2)(*a*) had been interpreted in its early years, before the "real world" test had been enunciated in the *Leduc* decision. The *Villani* court was clearly not endorsing *Russell* as being representative of the current test, contrary to the assertion in *Rice* above. The court in *Rice* then goes on to put an additional gloss on the loose phraseology used in *Villani* with the following comment:

While Isaac J.A. refers to the necessity of "evidence of employment efforts and possibilities" (para. 50), we read these words as referring to the capacity of an individual to be employed in any substantially gainful occupation, and not to whether, in the context of the labour market, it is possible to get a job. (para. 12.)

It seems unlikely that the *Villani* court was using the phrase "and possibilities" in the manner suggested by the *Rice* court. The full sentence in paragraph 50 reads as follows: "Medical evidence will still be needed as will evidence of employment efforts and possibilities". This appears refer not to the claimant's capacity to work — i.e., the basic issue to be decided in the severity test — but to various types of ancillary evidence all of which are ultimately relevant to a finding of incapacity. If the *Villani* court had really meant "possibilities" in the sense of what types of work the claimant could possibly (physically) do, then it would at least have said "evidence of employment possibilities and efforts" instead, to more accurately reflect the relative importance of the two factors.

Finally, the *Rice* court provides a policy argument to justify the exclusion of work availability as a relevant factor in making a determination of disability:

When the words of subparagraph 42(2)(*a*)(i) are considered, it is apparent that they refer to the capability of the individual to regularly pursue any substantially gainful occupation. They do not refer to labour market conditions. There is other legislation such as the *Employment Insurance Act* which is directed at helping individuals to cope with the fluctuations in the labour market. The disability provisions of the *Canada Pension Plan* have a different purpose. That purpose is to provide individuals who have been disabled in accordance with the words of that Act with a disability pension because they are incapable of regularly pursuing any substantially gainful employment. The disability provisions are not a supplementary employment insurance scheme. (para. 13.)

It is true that as a matter of statutory interpretation, the CPP should be interpreted to avoid overlap with the objects and provisions of the *Employment Insurance Act*. But it should be remembered that we are dealing with claimants who have established that they have a physical or mental impairment. The question is, which legislative regime is better suited to deal with the employment difficulties that inevitably arise as a result of such impairment? In dealing with two pieces of benefits-conferring legislation, it must also be a principle of statutory interpretation that claimants should not be allowed to fall between the cracks.

But whether or not this aspect of the *Rice* decision was *obiter dicta*, the Federal Court of Appeal has since strongly reaffirmed the irrelevance of local labour market conditions in determining the severity of a disability — see *Canada (Minister of Human Resources Development) v. Angheloni*, 2003 FCA 140 and *Canada (Minister of Human Resources Development) v. Harmer*, 2002 FCA 321.

This leaves open the question as to what the law should be. Is the availability of work a necessary ingredient of the "real world" test espoused in *Villani*? Or are all such concerns addressed by the entirely separate employment insurance regime in place federally?

It is interesting to examine the U.S. law in this regard. As noted above, the original U.S. *Social Security Act* definition of disability was quite vague on this point, and this vagueness was carried over to the very similar CPP definition in 1965. In *Celebrezze v. O'Brient*, 323 F.2d 989 (5th Cir. 1963), a leading court case under the original provision, the Court of Appeal held that only the kind of work the claimant could perform was relevant, not what jobs were available for him *where he was located*. Subsequent amendments to the SSA clarified this principle, and § 223(d)(2)(A) now reads:

> An individual shall be determined to be under a disability only if his physical or mental impairment or impairments are of such severity that he is not only unable to do his previous work but cannot, considering his age, education, and work experience, engage in any other kind of substantial gainful work which exists in the national economy, regardless of whether such work exists in the immediate area in which he lives, or whether a specific job vacancy exists for him, or whether he would be hired if he applied for work. For purposes of the preceding sentence (with respect to any individual), "work which exists in the national economy" means work which exists in significant numbers either in the region where such individual lives or in several regions of the country.

So disability pension claimants in the U.S. are not entitled to remain passive in the face of a depressed local economy. They are expected to move elsewhere in the region, or to other regions of the country, to obtain work that they can capably perform.

It also should be pointed out that the Canadian employment insurance regime certainly acknowledges differences between regions. It has never been the law that the unemployed lose eligibility for benefits unless they move to another region to look for work in their field. But unlike disability pension benefits, employment insurance benefits are of a temporary nature and in the long run, EI claimants do have an incentive to relocate to a more suitable region.

To return to the issue as to whether the availability of work is an inherent part of the "real world" test, it would seem to make sense to differentiate local and national conditions as is explicitly done in the U.S. legislation. It would almost certainly contradict the spirit of the "real world" test to disqualify a claimant who can only perform work that is not currently available in Canada. In the context of light office duties, such work may possibly be said to be unavailable when the Canadian economy as a whole is severely depressed, as it was in the early 1980s and 1990s.

The more common question is whether a claimant who has lived all his or her life in say, Thunder Bay, should be expected to move to Toronto to find a job calling for light office duties. What happens if a proven physical or mental impairment interferes with the ability of the claimant to move? What if the physical or mental impairment can be more readily borne in the claimant's locality because of the assistance of family and friends? Are claimants expected to give up their support system in the hopes of finding a job elsewhere?

It would seem that the "real world" test endorsed by the Federal Court in *Villani* is intended to provide maximum flexibility to decision-making bodies to allow them to take into account the availability of work in the local region in light of factors referred to in the previous paragraph. Since the contrary position taken by the court in *Rice* is clearly *obiter dicta*, nothing prevents decision makers from adopting this approach.

C. Res Judicata

1. What is Res Judicata?

Res judicata is a form of estoppel — i.e., a legal bar preventing a party from making an allegation or denial in certain circumstances. The overall goal is judicial finality, given that it is in no one's interest to argue the same points repeatedly.

The doctrine of *res judicata* embraces both cause of action estoppel and issue estoppel. Cause of action estoppel forbids a party from claiming to assert a new and distinct cause of action by manipulation of the factual elements, if what remains is essentially the same claim (*Town of Grandview v. Doering*, [1976] 2 S.C.R. 621).

Issue estoppel is more relevant in the context of a CPP claim. It prohibits the re-litigation of an issue that a court or tribunal has decided in a previous proceeding, with the underlying rationale of balancing the public interest in the finality of litigation with the public interest in ensuring that justice is done on the facts of a particular case (*Danyluk v. Ainsworth Technologies Inc.*, [2001] SCC 44). The three requirements of issue estoppel are:

1. That the same question has been decided. Issue estoppel covers fundamental issues of fact or law determined in the original proceeding that were essential to the decision — such as whether the claimant was disabled within the meaning of CPP s. 42(2)(*a*).

2. That the judicial decision which is said to create the estoppel was final. This embraces two requirements: the decision must be judicial and it must be final. A decision may be "final" even if it is appealable. The decision of an administrative tribunal may be "judicial" for this purpose even though the tribunal's procedures do not conform to the procedures in a civil trial as long as they meet fairness requirements and the tribunal is carrying out a judicial function. In determining whether the earlier decision is a "judicial" decision, three elements must be taken into account: (a) is the administrative authority issuing the original decision capable of receiving and exercising adjudicative authority, (b) as a matter of law, is the particular decision one that was required to be made in a judicial manner, and (c) as a mixed question of law and fact, was the decision made in a judicial manner. Both Review Tribunal and PAB hearings and decisions generally meet both the "judicial" and "finality" requirements, although a failure to act judicially may be found to exist in a particular hearing. It has been held that any hearing which is designed to be an independent, fair, impartial and binding adjudicative process satisfies the spirit of the requirement even if it is not technically "judicial" in the sense of a formal court hearing (*Rasanen v. Rosemount Instruments Ltd.* (1994), 17 O.R. (3d) 267 (C.A.)).

3. That the parties to the judicial decision were the same persons as the parties to the proceedings in which the estoppel is raised. Whether a person is a party for the purpose of issue estoppel depends on its degree of participation in the first hearing.

Even where these three requirements are not met, the court retains a discretion to refuse to apply issue estoppel when to do so would cause unfairness or work an injustice. Courts have refused to apply issue estoppel where "special circumstances" are found to exist, such as a change in the law since the original decision or the availability of further relevant material (see generally *Danyluk (supra)*, *Angle v. M.N.R.*, [1975] 2 S.C.R. 248 and *Minott v. O'Shanter Development Co.* (1999), 42 O.R. (3d) 321 (C.A.).)

2. Jurisdiction of the Social Security Tribunal To Reopen a Case

(a) Finality Generally

Neither decisions of the Minister nor of the Social Security Tribunal ("SST") are immune from reconsideration. Section 68 of the *Department of Human Resources and Social Development Act* ("DHRSDA") only refers to decisions of the SST as being "final" subject to judicial review under *Federal Courts Act.* There is no express requirement in section 81 of the CPP that Ministerial decisions or reconsiderations be judicial or final.

As a result, the Minister is not precluded from considering multiple applications or requests for reconsideration by a single claimant, for as long as the claimant continues to apply within his or her minimum qualifying period ("MQP"). But for tribunals such as the SST, the general rule was stated in *Chandler v. Alberta Association of Architects*, [1989] 2 S.C.R. 848 as follows:

> ... once such a tribunal has reached a final decision in respect to the matter that is before it in accordance with its enabling statute, that decision cannot be revisited because the tribunal has changed its mind, made an error within jurisdiction or because there has been a change of circumstances. It can only do so if authorized by statute or if there has been a slip or error ...

In *Chandler*, the Supreme Court of Canada did go on to observe that a tribunal that makes a determination which is a nullity is permitted to reconsider the matter afresh and render a valid decision.

(b) New Facts

The existence of new facts can trigger a reopening of the case by the tribunal. Subsection 84(2) of the CPP formerly read:

> (2) The Minister, a Review Tribunal or the Pension Appeals Board may, notwithstanding subsection (1), on new facts, rescind or amend a decision under this Act given by him, the Tribunal or the Board, as the case may be.

It was also pointed out by the Federal Court of Appeal in *MHRD v. Skoric*, [2000] 3 F.C. 265 (C.A.), that subsection 84(2) of the former CPP expressly permitted the Pension Appeals Board to reconsider its decisions "on new facts". With the advent of the Social Security Tribunal in 2013, paragraph 66(1)(*b*) of the DHRSDA now reads:

> (1) The Tribunal may rescind or amend a decision given by it in respect of any particular application if
>
>   ...
>
> (*b*) in any other case, a new material fact is presented that could not have been discovered at the time of the hearing with the exercise of reasonable diligence.

New facts sufficient to trigger a re-examination of the original decision are required by paragraph 66(1)(*b*) to be (i) material and (ii) not discoverable at the time of the original hearing with the exercise of reasonable diligence. This traditional common law test for admitting new evidence on appeal does not contradict this test, but is more specific:

1. The evidence could not have been obtained for the original hearing by due diligence.

2. The evidence must be relevant in the sense that it bears upon a decisive or potentially decisive issue at the hearing.

3. The evidence must be credible in the sense that it is reasonably capable of belief.

4. The evidence must be such that, if believed, it could reasonably be expected to have affected the result when taken with the other evidence adduced at the original hearing.

See *R. v. Stolar*, [1988] 1 S.C.R. 480. Other formulations of the test and additional procedural issues are addressed later in this book in the annotations under DHRSDA s. 66.

Note that paragraph 66(1)(*b*) of the DHRSDA essentially codifies the law as stated by the Federal Court of Appeal in *MHRD v. MacDonald*, [2002] FCA 48, where the Court stated the following:

> We agree with the Minister that the doctrine of *res judicata* applies to decisions of the Minister, Review Tribunal and Pension Appeals Board under the Canada Pension Plan subject to statutory provisions to the contrary, including subsection 84(2) of the Act providing for reconsideration based on new facts. The new facts must not have been previously discoverable with reasonable diligence, and must be material. (para. 2.)

The Court went on to refuse the Minister's application of judicial review, finding that in the circumstances the PAB was entitled to consider medical reports written subsequent to the initial Review Tribunal decision. While the above quote is *obiter*, the statement is worth examining because of the importance of the issue of *res judicata* in the context of disability appeals. First, it should be observed that there is no statutory or common law support for the proposition that the Minister is bound by the doctrine of *res judicata*.

IV. Disability Claims Procedures

A. The Social Security Tribunal

The Social Security Tribunal (the "SST") replaces the Review Tribunal and the Pension Appeals Board ("PAB") for CPP and OAS appeals after March 31, 2013. It will also hear appeals under the *Employment Insurance Act*. The lower level is called the General Division, and the appeal level is called the Appeal Division. **Appeals filed with the Office of the Commissioner of the Review Tribunals and the PAB which have not been heard by April 1, 2013 have been transferred to the SST.**

In addition to a chairperson and three vice-chairs for its Income Security, Employment Insurance and Appeal Divisions, the SST comprises 74 full-time members and up to 11 part-time members. The term for full-time members is five years, and the part-timer members are appointed for two years. Appointees may be reappointed for additional terms. The appointees are deemed by section 49 of the *Department of Human Resources and Skills Development Act* to be employed in the public service.

B. The Appeal Route

The process for determining CPP applications has four stages:

1. **Application to the Minister.** There is no time limit for making an application for CPP disability benefits (CPP s. 60), but retroactive benefits can only be paid for up to 15 months prior to the making of the application (CPP s. 42(2)(*b*)), less the three-month "waiting period" (CPP s. 69).

The applicant is required by section 68 of the CPP Regulations to provide the Minister with "a report of any physical or mental impairment", a statement of the applicant's occupation and earnings following the onset of the alleged disability, and a statement of the applicant's "education, employment experience, and activities of daily life". The Minister is also entitled to seek a statement of the applicant's occupation and earnings for any period, and to require the applicant (at the Minister's expense) to submit to examinations and supply reports as are deemed necessary by the Minister for determining whether the applicant is in fact disabled.

Applications for a disability benefit are now assessed by independent nurse adjudicators who determine whether the contributory and definition requirements are met. The adjudicators follow established Ministerial guidelines in making this determination. Applicants must submit all necessary information, such as proof of citizenship, and must arrange for a physician to complete the necessary forms (see *Torjman*). Although from 1989 to 1995 Ministerial guidelines permitted the adjudicator to consider socio-economic factors in making the determination (reflecting the PAB's decision in *Leduc*), after 1995 such factors could no longer be considered. It should be noted that recently the guidelines have been eased again to permit Ministry staff to consider the age, work history, and education of the applicant. As a result, an increasing percentage of applications for disability benefits are being denied, rising from 56% in 1995 to 67–70% over the 1997–1999 period. Still, over 90% of applications for disability benefits are resolved at this stage. In 2001, a letter from the Deputy Minister indicated that Ministry staff were permitted to consider the age, work history, and education of the applicant, but not socio-economic factors such as the availability of employment.

2. **Reconsideration of refusal by Minister.** If the Minister initially refuses to approve the application, the second stage is for the applicant to request the Minister to make a reconsideration of the determination within **90 days** of receiving the written notification (CPP s. 81, CPP Reg. s. 74.2). The request must be in writing and set out the grounds for the request and include a statement of the relevant facts (CPP Reg. s. 74.1). The Minister has discretion to extend the 90-day period (CPP Reg. s. 81(1)), but this discretion is rarely exercised. The success rate of requests for reconsiderations is approximately 28%.

3. **Appeal to SST General Division.** Appeals to the General Division of the SST from the reconsideration by the Minister must be brought within 90 days. Extensions are permitted, but in no case may an appeal be brought more than one year after the decision is communicated to the claimant. The General Division must summarily dismiss an appeal if it is satisfied that it has no reasonable chance of success. See sections 52–54 of the *Department of Human Resources and Skills Development Act* and annotations thereunder later in this book.

4. **Appeal to the SST.** Appeals to the Appeal Division of the SST from the decision of the General Division must be brought within 90 days. An appeal to the Appeal Division may only be brought if leave to appeal is granted, except for an appeal from a summary dismissal by the General Division. Leave is refused if the appellant has no reasonable chance of success. Extensions are permitted, but in no case may an appeal be brought more than one year after the General Division decision was communicated to the claimant. The only permitted grounds of appeal to the Appeal Division are that

(a) the General Division failed to observe a principle of natural justice or otherwise acted beyond or refused to exercise its jurisdiction;

(b) the General Division erred in law in making its decision, whether or not the error appears on the face of the record; or

(c) the General Division based its decision on an erroneous finding of fact that it made in a perverse or capricious manner or without regard for the material before it.

See sections 55–59 of the *Department of Human Resources and Skills Development Act* and annotations thereunder later in this book.

V. Bill C-51 Amendments to the Act

The federal government, with the required assent of the provincial governments, introduced important changes to the CPP via the *Economic Recovery Act*, S.C. 2009, c. 31 (Bill C-51). Highlights of the changes are as follows:

1. Changes to the Actuarial Factor for Early and Late Retirement

The adjustments for early and late receipt of the CPP retirement pension will be changed to further increase the pension for those who start receiving it after age 65, and further reduce it for those who start receiving it before age 65. These changes will be phased in gradually between 2011 and 2016.

Retirement pension taken after age 65

Before the changes, CPP retirement pensions increased by 0.5% for each month after age 65 (up to age 70) that contributors delayed receiving them. For example, if contributors started receiving their CPP pensions at the age of 70, their pension amounts were 30% more than if taken at age 65. From 2011 to 2013, the government will gradually increase this percentage from 0.5% per month (6% per year) to 0.7% per month (8.4% per year). This means that by 2013, if contributors start receiving their CPP pension at the age of 70, their pension amounts will be 42% more than if taken at age 65.

The following table outlines the increase in the monthly actuarial factor for each year.

Year	% (monthly increase)
2011	0.57
2012	0.64
2013	0.70

Retirement pension taken before age 65

Before the changes, CPP retirement pensions were reduced by 0.5% for each month before age 65 that contributors began receiving them. For example, if contributors started receiving their CPP pensions at the age of 60, their pension amounts were 30% less than if taken at age 65. From 2012 to 2016, the amount by which a contributor's early pension will be reduced will increase from 0.5% per month (6% per year) to 0.6% per month (7.2% per year). This means that by 2016, if contributors start receiving their CPP pensions at the age of 60, their pension amounts will be 36% less than if taken at age 65.

The following table outlines the increase in the monthly actuarial factor for each year.

Year	% (monthly reduction)
2012	0.52
2013	0.54
2014	0.56
2015	0.58
2016	0.60

2. Changes to the General Drop-Out Provision

Virtually all contributors are entitled to the general drop-out provision, which allows them to exclude a portion of their zero or low earnings from the calculation of their retirement benefit. Under the Bill C-51 changes, the pension formula will eventually exclude up to eight years of low earnings under the general drop-out provision.

Starting in 2012, the number of years of low or zero earnings that are automatically dropped from the calculation of CPP pensions will increase. Before the changes, 15% of the contributor's career period with the lowest earnings was automatically dropped. Under this provision, if contributors took their CPP retirement pension at 65, up to seven years of their lowest earnings were automatically dropped from the calculation of their average earnings.

Starting in 2012, the percentage of low earnings will increase to 16%, which may allow up to 7.5 years of a contributor's lowest earnings to be dropped from the calculation. In 2014, the percentage will increase to 17%, which may allow up to eight years of a contributor's lowest earnings to be dropped.

3. Elimination of the Work Cessation Test (s. 67)

Starting in 2012, contributors can begin receiving their CPP retirement pensions without any work interruption.

4. Introduction of the Post-Retirement Benefit

Starting in 2012, if contributors are receiving CPP retirement pensions and they choose to work, they could continue to make CPP contributions that will increase their payments through the Post-Retirement Benefit (PRB). The newly created PRB will be comprised of contributions made while contributors are receiving their CPP retirement pensions. If they are under age 65, contributions will be mandatory for them and their employers. If they are age 65 to 70, contributions will be voluntary (their employers will have to contribute if they do). People between the ages of 60 and 70 who make these contributions may begin to receive the PRB the following year.

- Self-employed beneficiaries will pay both employee and employer portions.

- Working CPP retirement pension recipients who wish to opt out of contributing to the Plan after age 65 will be required to inform the Canada Revenue Agency.

- Contributions made while beneficiaries are receiving their CPP retirement pensions will build up only the PRB. These contributions will not create eligibility or increase the amount of other CPP benefits, nor be subject to a credit split or retirement pension sharing.

- Each year of work will provide an additional PBR that will begin the following year and will be paid for life.

- The PRB will be added to an individual's CPP retirement pension, even if the maximum pension amount is already being received.

Selected sources

S. Torjman, "The CPP Disability Benefit", Caledon Institute for Social Policy (Ottawa: 2001) (prepared for the Office of the Commissioner or the Review Tribunal)

M. Diller, "Entitlement and Exclusion: The Role of Disability in the Social Welfare System" (1996), 44 UCLA L. Rev. 361

C. Meysenburg, "Doctor, Is She Disabled? The Eighth Circuit's Struggle With The Treating Physician's Testimony In Social Security Cases: Casenote on *Morse v. Shalala*" (1995), 28 Creighton L. Rev. 855

"Historical Development of the Canada Pension Plan: 1966-1991 — Twenty-Five Years of Service to Canadians", Income Security Branch, Policy and Legislation, Health and Welfare Canada (Ottawa: 1992)

G. Killeen, "The Pension Appeals Board: Some Comments on Practice and Procedure", Disability Insurance Law Programme (Ottawa: 2001)

Disability Case Table

Table of Contents

Disability Case Table

By far the most litigated aspect of the *Canada Pension Plan* is the determination of disability under s. 42(2)(*a*). Each year, the Pension Appeals Board issues thousands of decisions that confirm or deny disability benefits to claimants. These decisions are largely fact-specific, but over the years, trends have emerged as to how the Pension Appeals Board deals with various types of claims.

The following table summarizes the facts and legal principles articulated in leading Pension Appeals Board, Federal Court and Supreme Court of Canada decisions in CPP disability claim cases, and highlights continuing points of disagreement.

Please refer to the introductory chapter of this book for an analysis of the contentious issue as to which evidence is or is not relevant in a disability claim, and how claims proceed before the Pension Appeals Board. The authors address procedural issues in the annotations under specific sections of the CPP, especially sections 81 and 82. The starting date for disability benefits is discussed under CPP s. 42 §6. Cases making general observations regarding the disability regime are found under CPP s. 44 §1(a). The minimum qualifying period is discussed under CPP s. 44 §1(b), and the effect of the Canadian Charter of Rights and Freedoms under CPP s. 44 §1(c). Termination of benefits is dealt with in CPP s. 70 and the cases thereunder.

Part I. Overview of Scheme

Digest	Citation
The clear purpose of CPP disability benefits is to supplement the incomes of disabled Canadians who have difficulty meeting day-to-day expenses because of their inability to work, that is, their status as disabled.	*Sarvanis v. Canada*, 2002 SCC 28
The CPP is a compulsory social insurance scheme enacted to provide contributors and their families with reasonable minimum levels of income in the event that those contributors retire, die or become disabled.	*Del Zotto v. Canada*, [1999] 1 S.C.R. 3
The CPP was designed to provide social insurance for Canadians who experience a loss of earnings owing to retirement, disability, or the death of a wage-earning spouse or parent. It is not a social welfare scheme. It is a contributory plan in which Parliament has defined the benefits and the terms of entitlement, including the level and duration of an applicant's financial contribution.	*Granovsky v. Canada*, [2000] 1 S.C.R. 703

Obiter: CPP disability benefits can arguably be seen to compensate for the loss of earning capacity but they cannot reasonably be construed as intending to indemnify a disabled person for loss of income.	*Cugliari v. White* (1998), 38 O.R. (3d) 641 (C.A.)
The purpose of the CPP disability provisions is to provide individuals who have been disabled with a disability pension, in accordance with the words of the legislation, because they are incapable of regularly pursuing any substantially gainful employment. The disability provisions are not a supplementary insurance scheme.	*MHRD. v. Rice,* 2002 FCA 47
Many applicants for disability benefits are suffering pain and discomfort at the time of the hearing and the judicial review by the Federal Court of Appeal. Many are unsuccessful. This is no reflection on them or their condition. It is a reflection only of the difficult standard applicants must meet in order to demonstrate their disability is "severe and prolonged" within the meaning of CPP s. 42(2).	*Gaudet v. Canada (Attorney General),* 2013 FCA 254
Disability benefits are meant to address a very serious condition, one that prevents the earning of meaningful income to sustain oneself. Parliament could not have intended the final disposition of disability benefits in these circumstances to take eight years.	*D'Errico v. Canada (Attorney General),* 2014 FCA 95
The CPP's definition of "disabled" is highly restrictive; the focus is on those physical and mental limitations that affect a claimant's capacity to work. Thus, individuals who experience significant and prolonged health challenges may nonetheless not qualify for a disability pension if they are found to be capable regularly of pursuing a substantially gainful occupation.	*Atkinson v. Canada (Attorney General),* 2014 FCA 187
While the term "disability" has different meanings under different insurance and pension plans, under the CPP, the measure is employability. To support a claim, disability must normally be demonstrated on more than the claimant's evidence that he or she suffers pain or discomfort that prevents employment. Once evidence of employability is established, evidence that the claimant made efforts to obtain and maintain employment but failed by reason of a serious health condition is usually also required.	*Canada (Attorney General) v. Fink,* 2006 FCA 354

A disability pension is paid to a claimant who is a qualified contributor under the CPP in relation to his or her disability, without reference to the cause of that disability. It is not paid in respect of the "injury, damage or loss" claimed in this action, i.e., for pain and suffering, loss of enjoyment of life, or out-of-pocket expenses arising from the claimant's injuries. The pension is terminable, if the claimant's condition of disability ends, if the claimant becomes 65 years of age or qualifies for another federal or provincial pension, or if he or she dies. It is paid on the basis of a statutory formula without regard to whether the claimant has suffered any pecuniary loss, or any injury. While it may be possible to trace the claimant's disability to injuries suffered as a result of an accident, such injury is not the basis of or the reason for disability pension entitlement under the CPP.	*Sarvanis v. Canada*, (1998), 156 F.T.R. 265 (T.D.), reversed (2000), 184 D.L.R. (4th) 124 (C.A.), reversed 2002 SCC 28
The policy of the disability benefits provisions of the CPP reflect a socio-economic policy, not a medical policy. The test is whether a person is so disabled he or she can no longer be gainfully employed, not whether a grant of benefits will contribute to recovery. That the receipt of a disability pension may encourage inactivity and impede the applicant's recovery is not relevant.	*Benoit v. MHRD* (September 12, 1997), CP 5406
The CPP is not a substitute for other social programs, but has its own strict criteria.	*Mazzocca v. MNHW* (May 10, 1990), CP 1925
The focus of workers' compensation claims is causation, while the focus of CPP disability claims is capacity.	*Michaud v. MHRD* (July 1997), CP 4510
Although the CPP has been held not to be social welfare legislation, the principles of interpretation for such legislation — i.e., that it be liberally construed to advance its benevolent purpose, with reasonable doubts and ambiguities being resolved in the claimant's favour to ensure that the legislative benefits reach the person for whom they were designed — are still worthy of consideration in this context.	*MHRD v. Sartey* (November 21, 1997), CP 4883 CEB & PG ¶8705
The CPP disability pension is not sickness insurance, nor unemployment insurance. It is insurance against disastrous damage to the human body, available within certain time limits after the last date of contribution.	*MHRD v. Getchell* (March 10, 1999), CP 05999 CEB & PG ¶8764

Disability Case Table

Part II. "Severe and Prolonged"

(A) Definition of "Severe"

Section 42(2)(*a*)(i): a disability is severe only if by reason thereof the person in respect of whom the determination is made is incapable regularly of pursuing any substantially gainful occupation.

1. General Principles

The two requirements of paragraph 42(2)(*a*) of the CPP are cumulative, so that if an applicant does not meet one or the other condition, his application for a disability pension under the CPP fails. It was therefore not an error for the PAB to have concentrated primarily on the "severe" part of the test and not made any finding regarding the "prolonged" part of the test. The measure of whether a disability is "severe" is not whether the applicant suffers from severe impairments, but whether his disability "prevents him from earning a living". In other words, it is an applicant's capacity to work and not the diagnosis of his disease that determines the severity of the disability under the CPP. A corollary to this principle is that the determination of the severity of the disability is not premised upon an applicant's inability to perform his regular job, but rather on his inability to perform any work, i.e. "any substantially gainful occupation".	*Klabouch v. Canada (Social Development)*, 2008 FCA 33
See also:	*Granovsky v. Canada (Minister of Employment and Immigration)*, [2001] 1 S.C.R. 703
Employability is not to be assessed in the abstract, but rather in light of "all of the circumstances". The circumstances fall into two categories: 1. The claimant's background (age, education level, language proficiency, and past work and life experience), and 2. The claimant's medical condition.	*Bungay v. Canada (Attorney General)*, 2011 FCA 47
To come within the definition of "severe" disability, a claimant must not only show that he or she has a serious health problem but where there is evidence of work capacity, must also show that efforts at obtaining and maintaining employment have been unsuccessful by reason of that health condition	*Inclima v. Canada (Attorney General)*, 2003 FCA 117
The suffering of the claimant is not an element on which the test of "disability" rests. The claimant must suffer from disabilities which, in a "real world" sense, render him or her incapable regularly of pursuing any substantially gainful occupation.	*Canada (Minister of Human Resources Development) v. Angheloni*, 2003 FCA 140
Each word in s. 42(2)(*a*)(i) must be given meaning, and when so read, it must indicate that Parliament views as "severe" any disability that renders an applicant incapable of pursuing with consistent frequency any truly remunerative occupation. The test is not whether the applicant is incapable at all times of pursuing any conceivable occupation.	*Villani v. Canada (Attorney General)*, 2001 FCA 248

The severity of a disability refers to the capacity of the claimant to work. A finding of severity is not based on medical diagnosis alone, nor is it based solely on the subjective evidence of the claimant as to the degree of pain suffered when attempting to perform the claimant's usual or customary occupation. Such evidence must always be considered, of course, but it is relevant only to determine whether the claimant is able to perform any substantially gainful employment.	*Gorgiev v. Canada (Minister of Human Resources Development),* 2005 FCA 55
Section 42(2)(*a*)(i) calls for a "whole person" assessment of the claimant consistent with the "real world" approach taken by the Federal Court of Appeal in *Villani.* In that case, the court emphasized that, in every case, the decision-maker must not read out such important words as "regularly," "substantially" and "gainful" in the statutory language and should approach each case cognizant that the severity test is implicated in the concept of "employability".	*Villani v. MHRD* (February 12, 2002), CP 19801
The key question in these cases is not the nature or name of the medical condition, but its functional effect on the claimant's ability to work.	*Ferreira v. AGC* 2013 FCA 81
The definition of "severe" addresses the capacity of an applicant to work in a meaningful and competitive work environment. An employer should not have to put up with occasional absences from work and make accommodations by creating a flexible work environment to enable the individual to have a job that he or she would not otherwise be able to perform in a normal competitive work environment.	*L.F. v. MHRSD* (September 20, 2010), CP 26809 (PAB)
The term "severe" is expressed in terms of capacity to work. A finding of severity is not based on a medical diagnosis alone, or on a disease description. Nor is it based upon the applicant's ability to perform his or her usual occupation, rather than any substantially gainful employment. Capacity to perform regular part-time work, modified activities or sedentary occupations has been held to preclude a finding of severity.	*Kotsopoulos v. MHRD* (May 27, 2004), CP 21310
It is not the diagnosis of a condition or disease that automatically precludes one from working. It is the effect of the disease or condition on the person that must be considered.	*Petrozza v. MSD* (October 27, 2004), CP 12106 (PAB)
Entitlement is not based on a diagnosis of a condition but on capability of work. Many people who have cancer of various types are still capable of work; and they work until the illness becomes disabling for CPP purposes. Even though the condition may mean risks in the future, the Board must look at capacity for work in the relevant period.	*Demers v. MHRD* (June 11, 1999), CP 06825 CEB & PG ¶8723
There is no definition more regularly misunderstood than that of "severity". The determination of severity involves an assessment of the capacity for regularly pursuing any substantially gainful occupation remaining in the applicant's physical and/or mental framework. Nothing else is relevant.	*MHRD v. Getchell* (March 10, 1999), CP 05999 CEB & PG ¶8764
There is no provision in the CPP for partial disability.	*Wilson v. MEI* (May 31, 1996), CP 4109

41

"Severe" is expressed in terms of capacity for work, not on a medical diagnosis. Both "severe" and "prolonged" conditions must be present at the same time.	*Macri v. MEI* (January 9, 1996), CP 3079 CEB & PG ¶8669
The words "incapable regularly of pursuing any substantially gainful occupation" must be read in their ordinary grammatical sense to mean that: (a) the applicant lacks the capacity, whether for physical or mental reasons; (b) to engage in, on a reasonably consistent and regular basis; (c) any form of occupation; (d) which provides gainful remuneration; (e) of a substantial nature, i.e., not trivial, token, or minimal, but, on the other hand, not necessarily totally adequate.	*Herd v. MHRD* (August 15, 1996), CP 4048
It is the severity of the physical or mental condition preventing an applicant from engaging regularly in substantially gainful employment, not the lack of occupational skills.	*MEI v. Hallowes* (September 15, 1994), CP 2484 CEB & PG ¶8573
For the disability to be "severe", not only must it preclude the applicant from returning to his former employment (or employment of like nature), but also from rejoining the workforce in any substantially gainful occupation, of whatever nature. The applicable test is whether the physical capacity exists to perform or undertake some form of such employment, regardless of whether or not such employment is readily available, whether or not the applicant is actually trained to do such work, or whether or not the applicant possesses the linguistic or communicative skills which the job might require.	*Bains v. MHRD* (January 24, 1997), CP 04153
The applicant must be totally disabled, with no residual capacity to work.	*Crossett v. MEI* (May 8, 1996), CP 3377
The test is whether a person is unable to do any kind of job.	*Mapplebeck v. MHRD* (May 19, 2000), CP 08904
Severe The claimant's statement that he may be able to work part-time for two hours per day, provided his limitations could be respected, can be attributed more to honesty than common sense. The claimant could not realistically pursue any substantially gainful employment on a regular basis.	*MHRD v. Ethier* (July 24, 1998), CP 6086

Not severe	
Effective treatment for the claimant was readily available.	*Bell v. MHRD* (December 13, 2000), CP 12664
A family physician did not refer the applicant to psychiatrist for psychotherapy, and the inference drawn was that condition was not severe.	*Hamzagic v. MHRD* (November 29, 1999), CP 08831
The degree of pain reported by the applicant greatly exceeding the objective clinical findings.	*Braun v. MHRD* (October 5, 1999), CP 09172

2. "Person in Respect of Whom the Determination is Made"

The "person in respect of whom the determination is made" is the applicant. It may be unrealistic to suggest that the applicant could be retrained to perform light work in light of his age, work history and limited education.	*Whynot v. MHRD* (September 21, 2000), CP 13536

3. "Incapable"

The test is "capacity for", not "likelihood of", employment.	*MEI v. Campoverde* (December 12, 1994), CP 3272 CEB & PG ¶8556
See also:	*Laurin v. MEI* (August 11, 1994), CP 4368
The issue is the capacity of the applicant to perform some type of alternative employment, not whether that employment, whatever it may be, is available to the applicant.	*Montilla v. MHRD* (November 28, 2000), CP 06657
The profitability of the claimant's business venture is not necessarily an indictor of his capacity to do work. His claim that his business went bankrupt because he was unable to devote enough time to it to make it successful could not override the medical evidence that the claimant was capable of working.	*Kiriakidis v. Canada (Attorney General)*, 2011, FCA 316
Although the claimant may regard himself or herself as a store manager for a period of time after the MQP, all of the circumstances must be reviewed, including the claimant's limited role in the business, irregular attendance, salary, medical condition, education, and employment experience.	*R.P. v. MHRSD* (July 22, 2011) CP 26124 (PAB)
In finding the claimant disabled, the PAB was entitled to not give weight to the claimant's admissions, made at or around the time of her minimum qualifying period, that she was willing and able to engage in gainful employment.	*Canada (Attorney General) v. Davison*, 2011 FCA 78
Voluntary retirement does not equate to disability.	*Larouche v. MHRD* June 2003, CP 20275

4. "Regularly"

Predictability is the essence of regularity within the CPP definition of "disability".	*Atkinson v. Canada (Attorney General),* 2014 FCA 187
"Regularly" does not refer to the employment requirements but to the claimant's incapacity.	*Miller v. MSD,* (October 7, 2005), CP 23304 (PAB)
It is the incapacity, not the employment, which must be "regular", and the employment can be any substantially gainful occupation.	*Canada (Minister of Human Resources Development) v. Scott,* 2003 FCA 34
"Regularly" means that the applicant must be capable of coming to work as often as is necessary. Predictability is the essence. Credible evidence may establish that a degree of predictable interruption to a work schedule has rendered an individual unemployable.	*Chandler v. MHRD* (November 25, 1996), CP 4040
Despite brief periods of work capacity, the unpredictability of the Appellant's chronic fatigue and pain and his need to have frequent rests rendered him incapable regularly of maintaining any substantially gainful occupation in the real world.	*B.B. v. MHRSD* (October 14, 2008), CP 25356 (PAB)
Predictability of reporting for work is the essence of "regularly" reporting for an occupation. An applicant who could not commit himself to a work schedule from one day to the next, because of varying levels of pain, was disabled.	*Gallant v. MHRD* (June 25, 1998), CP 06612
An individual who is prevented from attending work regularly due to intermittent and unpredictable flare-ups of a chronic disease may be considered disabled.	*MSD v. Schuurmans* (January 15, 2007), CP 23478 (PAB)
The claimant was disabled where his chronic pain left with him the ability to work a maximum of two or three hours in a day in a sedentary position, and would prevent him from attending at a workplace at all on many days.	*Kean v. MSD* (July 23, 2004), CP 21315
Although the paraplegic claimant was "disabled" for CPP purposes while working sporadically an average of two days per week, he ceased to be disabled after the physician indicated that he could three days per week at his desk job.	*Swalwell v. MHRD* (October 25, 2001), CP 11228

5. "Any"

The word "any" is important. Where the applicant cannot pursue his previous occupation, but has the capacity for sedentary work, he or she is obliged to pursue such avenues, even though the CPP does not provide for retraining.	*Mosher v. MHRD* (May 1998), CP 5053 CEB & PG ¶8713
Definition of severe does not set any remunerative standard beyond what might be considered appropriate compensation for work performed — even if sedentary.	*MNHW v. Hanuik* (February 11, 1994), CP 2734
"Any" substantially gainful occupation means any kind of remunerative employment within the capabilities of the applicant. The applicant must show an honest effort to attain requisite skills for work within the range of his or her abilities.	*Croskery v. MHRD* (June 1, 1999), CP 11166 CEB & PG ¶8779
The test is not whether the applicant can do his or her former job or a job which would pay a comparable wage. He or she must be physically unable to do any job that is substantially gainful, even if the pay is significantly lower than in the previous job.	*Brunet v. MEI* (March 6, 1996), CP 3476

The occupation is not necessarily a job commensurate with the applicant's previous occupation.	*Donaldson v. MHRD* (May 1998), CP 4910 CEB & PG ¶8712

6. "Substantially Gainful Occupation"

Editor's note: In May 2014, s. 68.1 of the CPP Regulations (reproduced later in this book) was added. It provides a formula for determining a threshold for "substantially gainful occupation", which is essentially 12 times the maximum monthly retirement benefit. As it is tied to the retirement benefit, it can change quarterly with the adjustment in the benefit rate.

It may not be an error of law to describe the test as being whether the claimant can no longer work at a job which will provide "an appropriate livelihood", but it is generally unwise to formulate the legal test in words other than those contained.	*Canada (Minister of Human Resources Development) v. Quesnelle,* 2003 FCA 92
Where a letter written after the MQP by the family physician stated that the claimant was incapable of a full day's work, it was reasonable to draw the inference that she was capable of part-time employment and that her medical condition was thus not "severe" within the meaning of the CPP.	*Ferreira v. AGC* 2013 FCA 81
Employment is not automatically considered "gainful" once a person earns the maximum retirement benefit. The determination for "substantially gainful" cannot be decided by a one-size-fits-all figure. It requires a judgmental assessment, which could involve considering local income levels and cost of living, as well as other factors specific to the circumstances of the individual.	*MSD v. Nicholson* (April 17, 2007), CP 24143 (PAB)
While "substantially gainful" is not defined by the CPP, the term includes occupations where the remuneration for the services rendered is not merely nominal, token, or illusory compensation, but compensation that reflects the appropriate award for the nature of the work perfomed.	*G.T. v. Minister of Human Resources and Skills Development,* 2013 SSTAD 5
Part-time work is substantially gainful work.	*Landry v. MSD* (October 17, 2007), CP 24673 (PAB)
The term "substantially gainful" in s. 42(2)(a)(i) imposes a less stringent condition than would be the case if a claimant was required to be incapable of performing a "gainful" occupation. Whether a monetary reward is indicative of a "substantially gainful occupation" must be determined by an objective assessment of the remuneration and benefits received by the employee for his or her best services at the time of the application. For the purposes of the section, "substantial" means something "having substance; not imaginary, unreal or apparent only; true, solid, real". "Substantially gainful occupation" would therefore include occupations where the remuneration for the services rendered was not merely nominal, token or illusory compensation, but rather compensation which reflects an appropriate reward for the nature of the work performed.	*Boles v. MEI* (June 30, 1994), CP 2794 CEB & PG ¶8553

45

The test is not whether the occupation/business renders the applicant better off financially but rather whether the business is substantially gainful.	*Ellis v. MEI* (March 15, 1994), CP 2830
Substantially gainful may be determined relative to the claimant's income in previous years	*P.S. v. MHRSD* (January 28, 2011), CP 26937 (PAB)
A "substantially gainful occupation" will not necessarily be a job commensurate with the applicant's former occupation.	*Donaldson v. MHRD* (May 27, 1998), CP 04910 CEB & PG ¶8712
It is patently ridiculous to consider part-time employment well short of a regular workweek to constitute the capacity to regularly pursue gainful employment. The average workweek in Canada is between 37 and 40 hours. Therefore, working 14–16 hours per week at $8.40 per hour is not gainful employment. See also:	*Carvery v. MHRD* (April 28, 2003), CP 18772 (PAB) *M.D. v. MHRSD* (October 10, 2012), CP26650 (PAB)
While the applicant's attitude that he expected "nine hours work for eight hours work" of others and of himself was exemplary, it was not the standard under the CPP.	*Taylor v. MHRD* (July 4, 1997), CP 4436
The meaning and application of the phrase "substantially gainful occupation" may differ from case to case, reflecting the varied facts and circumstances of each.	*Lummiss v. MHRD* (May 3, 1999), CP 8229
It is not the function of the PAB to answer the question: What type of work can the applicant do? Nor is it is incumbent on the Minister to define or describe specifically what types of employment lie within the capabilities of the applicant or whether such employment is actually or imediately available. See also:	*Montilla v. MHRD* (November 28, 2000), CP 06657 *Kostoglou v. MHRD* (September 3, 1998), CP 5623 *St. Onge v. MHRD* (November 29, 2000), CP 11409
A person cannot be both a recipient of CPP disability benefits and a CPP contributor at the same time.	*Childerhose v. MHRD* (October 5, 1998), CP 04290
The phrase "semi-sedentary work", insofar as it purports to represent a finding as to the applicant's capacity, is incapable of conveying clear meaning for the purposes of assessing disability under the CPP.	*Wirachowsky v. Canada* (December 20, 2000), Doc. A-72-97 (Fed. C.A.)
Monies received by the applicant from his previous employer did not amount to proof of him being capable regularly of pursuing any substantially gainful occupation. Each case stands on its own facts.	*Alexander v. MHRD* (March 2000), CP 9448
The fact that there are earnings after the MQP, in itself, will not preclude a finding of disability. This is just one piece of evidence that must be weighed. Significant remuneration should never be an absolute bar to the receipt of disability benefits.	*MHRD v. Porter* (December 1998), CP 5616

Disabled	
The only work the claimant was able to pursue recently — part-time yoga instruction at $75 a week — was neither regular nor substantially gainful. Some other work she tried to do intermittently in the year leading up to her minimum qualifying period paid her $50-$160 per week for between 2-8 hours of work per week. When the claimant tried to work, her condition worsened from its already poor state.	*D'Errico v. Canada (Attorney General),* 2014 FCA 95
The claimant's earnings over a period of 10 years were less than what a person in Ontario would earn working half-time at minimum wage. In addition, it was unskilled work, although the claimant had skills as an engineer, in construction and renovation, as well as in running a business.	*G.T. v. Minister of Human Resources and Skills Development,* 2013 SSTAD 5
The claimant had been in a profession where the income is higher than the average population's income; his earnings of $19,538 for a year as a part-time massage therapist were not "substantial" when compared to his earnings in other years.	*P.S. v. MHRSD* (January 28, 2011), CP 26937 (PAB)
Employment as rehabilitation assistant working 12 hours per week (three 4-hour shifts) at $20.83 an hour.	*A.K. v. MHRSD* (September 2, 2009), CP 25905 (PAB)
Post-MQP earnings of $7,000 doing work which was casual, part-time, a few hours per day, when the individual could handle it, and for a benevolent employer.	*MSD v. Kuipers* (July 12, 2007), CP 24448 (PAB)
Former liquor store clerk now only able to earn $140, less deductions, for 20 hours work per week.	*Boyle v. MSD* (November 9, 2004), CP 25905 (PAB)
The applicant, whose eyesight was failing, owned 800-acre farm, which he ran in partnership with his wife. The applicant, continuing to live on the farm, played a part in its direction and earned income from it.	*Spencer v. MHRD* (December 8, 1999), CP 09277
The applicant continued part-time employment as courier truck driver for Canada Post.	*Heathcote v. MEI* (September 15, 1995), CP 3704
The applicant was no longer able to "manage" the farm.	*MNHW v. Perchak* (January 18, 1989), CP 1442 CEB & PG ¶8565
Not disabled	
While physical work was done by others, claimant worked 4 hours a day, served customers, made sales, oversaw employees, and looked after the administrative duties of the business.	*R.G. v. Minister of Human Resources and Skills Development* (February 26, 2014) CP 28699 (SSTGD)

Disability Case Table

47

Not disabled (cont'd)	
Claimant made $5,703 in 2009, but only started to work in August 2009 after her surgery. Earnings in 2010 were $14,000 from part-time work at $18 an hour, 3 days per week over 36 weeks annually, the fact that the employer was a benevolent employer was not a consideration.	*L.B. v. MHRSD*, (January 9, 2012) CP 27616 (PAB)
In every year after her accident, claimant filed income tax returns showing self-employment income earned for babysitting two grandchildren at her home.	*Gill v. Canada (Attorney General)*, 2011 FCA 195
Claimant owned and operated a fishing and hunting lodge for four years, reporting nil net income despite gross earnings of around $80,000 a year. The failure to generate a profitable venture does not substantiate a severe and prolonged incapacity to regularly pursue substantially gainful work	*T.C. v. MHRSD* (June 1, 2011) CP 26949 (PAB)
Earnings of $14,561 and $16,028 are considered substantially gainful even though earned through part-time work.	*Landry v. MSD* (October 17, 2007), CP 24673 (PAB)
Claimant worked regularly about 20 hours/wk for $15.40/hr.	*MSD v. Olsen* (October 26, 2006), CP 23908 (PAB)
Claimant earned gross farming income of $151,666, although net income was $3,430 after depreciation. Claimant worked regularly and performed useful functions on the farm and was able to live from such proceeds.	*Beres v. MSD* (September 28, 2007), CP 25136 (PAB)
Annual compensation in the range of $40,000 to $70,000 earned from sales by claimant and associates under her in a multi-level marketing company.	*MSD v. Hornsby* (September 26, 2007), CP 24266 (PAB)
Earnings of $10,875 and $38,857 over 2 years and then 20 hours a week at an hourly rate of $20 were found to be substantially gainful occupation.	*Miller v. MSD* (October 7, 2005), CP 23304 (PAB)
Claimant capable of running lawn-mowing business over last few years, which had produced substantial income during 8–12 week summer season; claimant capable of maintaining contract for longer periods, if necessary.	*Fehr v. Canada (Attorney General)* (January 23, 2004), 2005 FCA 299
Former welder and heavy duty mechanic who could now only eke out a subsistence living on his unprofitable farm with the help of neighbours and family members.	*Sudnik v. MHRD* (January 23, 2004), CP 19633
Joint owner of a farm, who continued to direct its operation.	*Nykipilo v. MHRD* (June 2003), CP 18831
The applicant received over $30,000 from family corporation for paying bills, filing receipts and doing errands as part of an income splitting device.	*Hrabec v. MHRD* (May 17, 2001), CP 12185
The claimant's former job was still available but at a reduced income.	*Bertram v. MHRD* (August 17, 2001), CP 12549
The applicant was in fact gainfully employed, although overpaid and working in the family business.	*Guindon v. MEI* (June 27, 1996), CP 3770
The applicant exercised degree of control of business and was actively engaged in all aspects.	*Campbell v. MHRD* (May 8, 1997), CP 4542 CEB & PG ¶8681

Not disabled (cont'd)	
The applicant's ROE showed self-employed earnings of $7,000 from 1990–1995 (except for 1991 where earnings were $15,000). Limit of $7,000 set by accountant for tax purposes, therefore inference drawn that the applicant could have earned more (i.e., had greater capacity).	*Larcher v. MHRD* (November 20, 1998), CP 05785
The applicant had earnings of $2,000 per month for 7 months annually, plus overtime.	*Childerhose v. MHRD* (October 5, 1998), CP 04290
Professional income was reduced due to poor economic times, rather than the applicant's condition.	*MacDonald v. MEI* (March 28, 1996), CP 3364 CEB & PG ¶8613
The applicant was employed seasonally from 1984–89, earning between $8,000 to $13,000 annually. In off-season, collected EI, declaring himself ready, willing and able to work.	*Macohonic v. MEI* (October 31, 1995), CP 3320
The applicant owned a barbershop, where he worked as a barber, employed others and handled the administrative work of the business by himself. This administrative role was a major factor in finding that he was not disabled.	*Palma v. MEI* (May 31, 1996), CP 4228 CEB & PG ¶8623
Earnings were noted on ROE for period during which the applicant seeking disability benefits; employment not merely for trial period.	*Welton v. MHRD* (November 6, 1998), CP 06142
The applicant has been working part-time in nursery and as homemaker.	*Kainth v. MHRD* (January 23, 1997), CP 4623
The applicant has been working two days a week, Mondays and Fridays, 7 hours/day; cannot work back-to-back days due to fatigue.	*Mayo v. MHRD* (June 10, 1998), CP 5688
The applicant has been working 15 hours per week.	*Orr v. MEI* (February 22, 1995), CP 2730
The applicant claimed to be severely disabled by rheumatoid arthritis, while being paid at the going rate of $10.30 per hour for part-time switchboard services, mostly on weekends, totalling $16,699.37 for the year.	*Boles v. MEI* (June 30, 1994), CP 2794 CEB & PG ¶8553

(B) Definition of "Prolonged"

Section 42(2)(*a*)(ii): a disability is prolonged only if it is determined in a prescribed manner that the disability is likely to be long continued and of indefinite duration or is likely to result in death.

1. General Principles

If medical prognosis at the time of treatment cannot project, not necessarily a cure, but a recovery to the degree that the individual in question would, within a foreseeable and reasonable time, having regard to the nature of the injuries and the resultant disability, recover sufficiently to enable him or her to pursue or engage in some form of substantially gainful employment, the disability may be held to be "prolonged". The issue is whether the applicant's future return to the work force in whatever capacity within a reasonable time is medically uncertain.	*MNHW v. Lauzon* (October 2, 1991), CP 2126 CEB & PG ¶9202
It is not only the existence of the condition that must be prolonged but its severity must be prolonged to meet the definition of disability under the CPP.	*Cutting v. MHRD* (October 7, 1998), CP 05743
It is the expectation of being able to return to work, not the time required for recovery, that should be the focus of the inquiry.	*MHRD v. Scott* (July 1998), CP 5741 CEB & PG ¶8716
Even though a condition may appear to be "severe" (and may even be conceded as such) it will not meet the requirement if it is not also "prolonged".	*Smazynski v. MHRD* (January 5, 2001), CP 09468
The CPP does not provide short-term or partial benefits to persons who are incapable of work but are reasonably expected to return to work.	*McKee v. MHRD* (June 19, 2003), CP 17139
Not prolonged There were three consecutive years of disability but no objective evidence as to disability was present beyond that period. The applicant had coronary bypass surgery. Evidence was clear that he was expected to recover within a specified time frame. The applicant had good recovery from back surgery. Evidence showed that the applicant was likely to recover from her depression.	*Smazynski v. MHRD* (January 5, 2001), CP 09468 *MNHW v. Ward* (January 23, 1989), CP 1645 CEB & PG ¶8570 *Anderson v. MHRD* (March 20, 1998), CP 4692 *Hall v. MEI* (March 26, 1996), CP 3233

2. Closed Period

The use of the word "indefinite" in subparagraph 42(2)(a)(ii) of the Plan makes clear that Parliament did not intend that disability pensions would be available in cases of temporary disability. The fact that a House of Commons Standing Committee recommended changes to this rule is not of great weight, unless of course, their suggestions are enacted. Similarly, a Physician's Guide distributed by the government department is of little value in offsetting the statutory language and the jurisprudence of this Court.	*Litke v. MHRSDC,* 2008 FCA 366
A disability cannot be "prolonged" unless it is determined to be of "indefinite duration". The restrictive language of s. 42 indicates that the purpose of the CPP is to provide a pension to those who are disabled from working on a long-term basis, not to tide claimants over a temporary period where a medical condition prevents them from working. The PAB's "closed period" decisions should be confined to situations where the medical opinion prior to the prescribed treatment does not clearly indicate the likelihood of the claimant's recovery and his or her subsequent ability to work.	*Canada (Minister of Human Resources Development) v. Henderson,* 2005 FCA 309
The Federal Court of Appeal in *Henderson* determined that s. 42 is aimed at assisting people with "long-term" disability and not to "tide over" those with short-term problems.	*Begley v. MSD,* (June 19, 2007), CP 24213 (PAB)
"Long continued" and "indefinite duration" must be read together and given a combined meaning. While a disability period of one and one-half years may be long continued, medical advice that the individual would be able to return to work within a reasonably precise time period did not indicate an indefinite duration.	*MSD v. Sparkes* (September 11, 2007), CP 24561 (PAB)
PAB decisions have consistently discouraged the awarding of disability pensions for closed or limited periods of time. The reason for this being that the purpose of the *Canada Pension Plan* is not to provide a source of compensation for temporarily disabled persons no matter how long their recovery period may be. While the PAB has on a few rare and infrequent occasions awarded disability pensions that begin and end within a closed period, these have occurred when at the time of application or earlier, it was expected or anticipated that the applicant would be disabled for a prolonged period of time but for some unforeseen or unexplained reason, the applicant recovered and returned to the workplace more quickly than anticipated.	*Kinney v. MSD* (February 24, 2005), CP 21314
"Closed period" decisions should be confined to situations where the medical opinion prior to the prescribed treatment does not clearly indicate the likelihood of the claimant's recovery and his subsequent ability to work. A closed period was not available where the claimant drywaller had been injured in a car accident, followed the prescribed treatment and returned to work gradually at his former job, with substantial employment earnings.	*MSD v. Sgotto* (May 26, 2006), CP 23601 (PAB)
The purpose of the CPP is not to provide a source of compensation for temporarily disabled persons no matter how long their recovery period may be. Closed period benefits were not available where the claimant teacher's gastrointestinal problems and depression prevented him from working for eight years, but he was now able to do manual labour.	*Saulnier v. MSD* (June 21, 2006), CP 24113 (PAB)

"Closed period awards" of disability pensions under the CPP usually arise when, after a period of disability and unemployment, the applicant subsequently becomes employed. Where the prognosis at the time of application is not positive, the PAB has awarded a closed period pension.	*Tibbo v. MSD* (August 23, 2004), CP 21704
There might be circumstances where an applicant is expected to be disabled for a prolonged period and recover more quickly than anticipated, thus being entitled to a disability pension for a closed period of time.	*Pankiw v. MHRD* (August 30, 2000), CP 08243
Applications for disability benefits for closed periods are generally to be discouraged, as they were not intended by the CPP. If the alleged disability has ceased on the date of hearing, the applicant will rarely succeed.	*Hornung v. MHRD* (June 16, 1998), CP 5795 CEB & PG ¶8718
It is not the purpose of the CPP to provide a form of compensation during a period of recovery, no matter how long.	*Boudreau v. MEI* (September 19, 1994), CP 3129
The issue is whether the applicant met the criteria for a severe and prolonged disability at the point she says she could no longer work, and if so, did her disability remain as such until she returned to full-time employment.	*MHRD v. Upshaw* (January 6, 2000), CP 07832 CEB & PG ¶8879
To claim a closed period, one must show that at the time or prior to the application, the prognosis was such as to indicate a prolonged condition.	*Stinson v. MHRD* (July 24, 1996), CP 3440
A closed period is not to be equated with convalescence or loss of temporary revenue.	*Couture v. MHRD* (September 29, 2000), CP 06735
Claim denied During alleged seven-year period of incapacity, claimant did janitorial work for his parents such as taking out garbage, shovelling snow and household chores. Claimant owned his own car which he drove locally, had his own bank account which he accessed, picked up his own prescriptions, made and kept his own medical appointments and played cards occasionally.	*Kayrouz v. HRSD* (April 28, 2008), CP 25444 (PAB)
Claimant returned to work after fourth severe depressive episode.	*MSD v. Sparkes* (September 11, 2007), CP 24561 (PAB)
Long distance operator suffering tendonitis in both wrists making it impossible to work at that job; claimant's diligent efforts towards rehabilitation finally succeeding after four years and she returned to work; despite prolonged recovery period, claimant and her physicians consistently expected recovery to point where she would be able to return to workforce; doctors consistently stated that claimant should be offered re-training for some form of employment.	*Davies v. MSD* (January 27, 2005), CP 07610
Claimant suffering from acute situational stress after medical negligence during the claimant's hysterectomy resulted in a sponge being left inside the claimant.	*Tibbo v. MSD* (August 23, 2004), CP 21704

Claim denied (cont'd) In the 14 months from the time of the injury until the applicant actually returned to work on a full-time basis, it was always expected that he would, in the not too distant future, be able to return to work, albeit not work of a heavy nature.	*Pankiw v. MHRD* (August 30, 2000), CP 08243
See also:	*Swalwell v. MHRD* (October 25, 2001), CP 11228
Applicant injured non-dominant hand and missed 20 months work; while injury more serious than first thought and hand still not fully healed, localized injury did not prevent applicant from finding alternate employment.	*Boudreau v. MEI* (September 19, 1994), CP 3129
There was a 10-month period after hip surgery and return to intermittent work.	*Brewer v. MHRD* (October 22, 1996), CP 3487
The claimant attended school during part of the closed period.	*Lauzon v. MNHW* (October 2, 1991), CP 2126 CEB & PG ¶9202
Claim allowed There was 5^1/$_2$-year period of fibromyalgia before retraining and the claimant returned to full-time work.	*MHRD v. Upshaw* (January 6, 2000), CP 07832 CEB & PG ¶8879
There was a 10-year period of a mild ankylosis spondylitis on applicant's spine, precipitated by lifting injury.	*Heathcote v. MEI* (September 15, 1995), CP 3704
There was 34 months conceded by the Minister with respect to reflex sympathetic dystrophy that was subsequently resolved.	*Brown v. MHRD* (July 22, 1997), CP 3873
There was a period of two years after the claimant became a paraplegic and before the person was able to work 3 days per week.	*Swalwell v. MHRD* (October 25, 2001), CP 11228

3. Disabled at Time of Application or MQP

The disability must be one that is actively in existence at the time of application.	*MNHW v. Shepard* (November 1, 1991), CP 2286
By virtue of s. 44(1)(*b*) and s. 60, benefits are payable to someone who is disabled, and the application must be filed and approved before benefits are payable. The claim was denied where the applicant had applied in the same month as he underwent back surgery, prior to which it was unknown whether the condition would improve but following which the prognosis was good. Whether the applicant would have qualified for benefits had the physician provided a medical report prior to the surgery was not relevant.	*Bryson v. MEI* (September 14, 1994), CP 2999
A subsequent event may be considered in determining whether a prognosis was incorrect. The fact that a diagnosis was not made until after the applicant's MQP was not fatal to the claim if the condition is causally connected to the MQP time frame.	*Orozco v. MHRD* (July 2, 1997), CP 5390
Although the applicant had claimed in her application that she became disabled after her MQP, the PAB found on all the facts that she was actually disabled prior to her MQP. The applicant should not be disqualified from receiving benefits because of her claimed date of disability.	*S.S. v. MHRSD* (March 24, 2011), CP 26627 (PAB)

Disability Case Table

53

4. "Prescribed Manner" — See Part VI. Evidentiary Issues and s. 68 of Regulations

Part III. Medical Issues

(A) Generally

Determining the claimant's medical condition is a broad inquiry, requiring that the condition be assessed in its totality. All of the possible impairments of the claimant that affect employability are to be considered, not just the biggest impairment or the main impairment. The approach of assessing the claimant's condition in its totality is consistent with s. 68(1) of the CPP Regulations, which requires claimants to submit highly particular information concerning "any physical or mental disability", not just what the claimant might believe is the dominant impairment.	*Bungay v. Canada (Attorney General)*, 2011 FCA 47
Where multiple medical problems are cited, the applicant's physical condition must be considered as a whole.	*Taylor v. MHRD* (July 4, 1997), CP 4436
A personality disorder is not a physical or mental disability within the meaning of the CPP.	*Babister v. MHRD* (January 16, 2001), CP 05707

(B) Specific Ailments

1. Alcohol-Related Disability

Although alcoholism might be considered a voluntary self-induced condition, it may, by its very nature, affect different people in different ways. It may or may not be a curable condition, and it may result in a condition that is more mental than physical, insofar as future employment capacity is concerned. Each case must be considered as a unique case, dependent upon its own specific facts and circumstances. While corroborating evidence may be particularly useful, it may not always be necessary. Oral evidence adduced by the applicant, either personally or on his behalf, may well be equally important and possibly overriding. Both objective and subjective evidence must be reviewed, considered and analyzed, with equal deliberation given to each category in determining its relative probative effect.	*Smallwood v. MHRD* (July 20, 1999), CP 09274 CEB & PG ¶8800
If it could be said that the applicant was disabled by reason of the fact that he was an alcoholic, then his incapacity to pursue substantially gainful occupation was not because of disability but by reason of his refusal to give up alcohol.	*Sandu v. MHRD* (January 18, 2000), CP 12150
There must be objective medical evidence to support a claim of disability due to alcoholism. Alcoholism is a malady that can be remedied but that requires intent, motivation and therapy.	*Smith v. MHRD* (September 16, 1996), CP 4364
Claim refused The place of alcohol in applicant's lifestyle was problem, not partial or total disability; the applicant had a choice; he could if he wished to reduce or eliminate the use of alcohol.	*Schmidt v. MNHW* (September 16, 1993), CP 2464

Claim refused (cont'd) One-month attendance at detox centre did not demonstrate sufficient motivation to recover.	*Smith v. MHRD* (September 16, 1996), CP 4364
Claim allowed A 59-year-old former factory labourer and video store co-operator (with wife) suffered from alcohol-induced brain damage and depression.	*Walsh v. MHRD* (September 25, 2001), CP 16544
The applicant became addicted to alcohol while in armed forces; he underwent various forms of treatment after discharge while unsuccessfully attempting to engage in several forms of employment; no objective medical evidence was presented as to mental or physical condition as of critical date, but there was convincing and credible personal testimony.	*Smallwood v. MHRD* (July 20, 1999), CP 09274 CEB & PG ¶8800

2. Amputations and Loss of Use of Limb

It was common knowledge, arising out of human observation and experience, that someone who has lost use of dominant limb can re-condition the other limb to perform virtually all physical functions.	*Vaughn v. MNHW* (May 1992), CP 1997
See also:	*B.G. v. MHRSD*, (June 10, 2008), CP 25254 (PAB)
The loss of the full use of one hand by a person who is otherwise able bodied does not prevent that person from seeking and obtaining employment in the real world.	*Bines v. MHRD* (November 15, 2001), CP 14261
It was not unreasonable to think that jobs exist which an otherwise reasonably fit middle-aged man, even lacking full use of dominant arm, would have physical capacity to perform.	*Brunet v. MEI* (March 6, 1996), CP 3476
The applicant's amputation below the knee did not constitute a disability.	*Sutton v. MHRD* (April 21, 1998), CP 5339
A defective knee joint is not sufficient to exclude a person from all employment. Workers with a bad arm or leg and, in some cases, a limb that is of no use at all, find modified work.	*Watson v. MHRD* (September 29, 1999), CP 08040
See also:	*G.L. v. MHRSD*, (May 19, 2011) CP 26973 (PAB)
The applicant was disabled by virtue of his various conditions, which included Carpal Tunnel Syndrome and Repetitive Stress Injury. The applicant had difficulty shaving and couldn't tie his necktie, button his collar, wash his hair, work with children, write cheques, or carry cups.	*Giakoumatos v. MHRD* (September 26, 2000), CP 08884

Disability Case Table

55

3. Cancer

Claim refused Breast cancer was diagnosed and treated, and in remission for 5 years, although a medical report indicated that fear of recurrence had affected applicant psychologically.	*Giustini v. MHRD* (August 23, 1999), CP 8067 CEB & PG ¶8807

4. Chemical and Environmental Sensitivities

The impact of the environment on health is not fully understood, and is a developing area in medicine. The onus of establishing, on a preponderance of evidence, the case for a claimant is therefore not easy. In the absence of supportive objective evidence, there is great difficulty in simply weighing the applicant's credibility. Where the applicant's complaints are real to him, it may be helpful for psychiatric evidence to be available to support a disability claim on such a psychiatric basis.	*Smith v. MHRD* (August 13, 1998), CP 5924
Whether environmental illnesses are worthy of compensation is a contentious issue in the medical profession. Where the applicant is not a malingerer, reasonable doubts and ambiguities may be resolved in his favour.	*MHRD v. Sartey* (November 21, 1997), CP 4883 CEB & PG ¶8705
Claim refused On a claim based on multiple chemical sensitivity, the applicant's refusal to attend the Board hearing out of fear of exposure to environmental allergens made it impossible for opposing counsel to cross-examine the applicant, and the applicant failed to establish her disability.	*Lawson v. MHRD* (April 29, 2002), CP 15396
Although choosing to wear special face mask to protect her from contaminants, the applicant still had capacity to work at jobs where she was not dealing directly with public; further psychiatric evidence may have been helpful.	*MHRD v. LeBlanc* (September 25, 1997), CP 4900 CEB & PG ¶8699

Claim refused (cont'd)	
Despite the applicant's multiple chemical sensitivities, she had been able to work in a controlled environment for 16 years with no problems; instead of looking for similar work, applicant chose to pursue master's degree and worked as student assistant as well as being single mother for 3 children.	*Jewett v. MHRD* (November 10, 2000), CP 10572
The applicant's lack of energy, subsidiary pains and sleep requirements were not established to be beyond improvement or domination; applicant's medical report contained scanty and unexplained assertions.	*Sass-Gauthier v. MHRD* (June 13, 1997), CP 05211
Medical evidence did not support complaints of reaction to wide spectrum of irritants, although it did objectively supported a reaction to low levels of contaminants in the industrial setting of the applicant's previous job.	*Smith v. MHRD* (August 13, 1998), CP 5924
Claim allowed	
Claimant looking for work, but required controlled employment environment and employers refusing to hire persons with chemical sensitivities.	*MSD v. Ridley* (August 23, 2007), CP 25040 (PAB)
The area of medicine dealing with multiple chemical sensitivity problems is evolving, and new discoveries may be made in the future that may help to improve the claimant's condition. It was prudent to have the claimant tested every five years to ascertain if there has been any improvement.	*MSD v. McGinley* (October 18, 2006), CP 23202 (PAB).
A 53-year-old cleaner developed vocal chord dysfunction as a result of repeated exposure by cleaning agents. A protective mask was unlikely to prevent her exposure to cleaning fumes, odours, and perfumes.	*Cramm v. MHRD* (July 19, 2001), CP 16230
The claimant had worked for a synthetic textile manufacturer in a small, poorly ventilated work space, using various solvents continuously; the provincial workers' compensation regime did not recognize chemical sensitivities.	*MHRD v. Harris* (August 14, 1997), CP 5150 CEB & PG ¶8702

5. Chronic Fatigue Syndrome (CFS)

Process of elimination is used to arrive at a diagnosis of CFS. Organic sources of problem should first be eliminated, and then a psychiatrist should be consulted to examine psychiatric problems.	*Fullarton v. MHRD* (October 21, 1996), CP 3712 CEB & PG ¶8659
CFS and Irritable Bowel Syndrome (IBS) are amenable to psychotherapy and cognitive behaviour therapy.	*Jelley v. MHRD* (May 5, 1999), CP 06704
Because of the very nature of the symptoms of CFS, those who suffer from it are thereby unable to function adequately so as to be capable regularly of pursuing any substantial gainful occupation.	*Nitska v. MHRD* (October 25, 2000), CP 10867

Disability Case Table

Claim denied	
Anti-depression treatment and psychological intervention would likely improve the applicant's self-perception and symptoms.	*Jelley v. MHRD* (May 5, 1999), CP 06704
All alternative explanations had not yet been examined, e.g., there was no referral to specialists to assess cognitive problems.	*Fullarton v. MHRD* (October 21, 1996), CP 3712 CEB & PG ¶8659
Doctor is a researcher, not a treating physician, who constricted file in manner that would only demonstrate disability (he decided what was relevant to put in file). Therefore, little weight was placed on his evidence.	*Mueller v. MHRD* (October 20, 2000), CP 13317
Claim allowed	
There was no reason to disbelieve the applicant's evidence, although there were no reliable objective medical findings to establish CFS.	*Nitska v. MHRD* (October 25, 2000), CP 10867

6. Chronic Pain Syndrome (CPS) and Fibromyalgia

There is no authoritative definition of chronic pain. It is, however, generally considered to be pain that persists beyond the normal healing time for the underlying injury or is disproportionate to such injury, and whose existence is not supported by objective findings at the site of the injury under current medical techniques. Despite this lack of objective findings, there is no doubt that chronic pain patients are suffering and in distress, and that the disability they experience is real.	*Nova Scotia (Workers' Compensation Board) v. Martin,* [2003] 2 S.C.R. 504
The importance of the *Martin* judgment is that the Supreme Court of Canada has recognized chronic pain as a compensable disability.	*Hunter v. MSD* (February 6, 2007), CP 23431 (PAB)
Although the evidence proved that the applicant had chronic pain, it still must be established that the pain prevented him from regularly pursuing any substantially gainful occupation.	*Klabouch v. Canada (Social Development),* 2008 FCA 33
Identifying a medical condition as sarcoidosis or fibromyalgia in and of itself does not bring the applicant closer to a disability pension in the absence of persuasive evidence that the applicant was disabled within the meaning of the CPP as of the MQP date.	*Gaudet v. Canada (Attorney General),* 2010 FCA 59
A lack of "serious pathology" is beside the point. The very nature of fibromyalgia is such that it does not appear on diagnostic tests. Still the label of fibromyalgia is not sufficient to satisfy a severe finding; the tribunal must look at the effect on the individual.	*P.R. v. Minister of Human Resources and Skills Development,* 2014 SSTGDIS 1
It is incumbent on a claimant to show conscious effort to seek relief from the number of pain management and pain control medical facilities that are often effective in providing sufficient relief to allow engaging in gainful work appropriate to the claimant's disabilities.	*M.C. v. M.S.D.* (July 8, 2011), CP 26647 (PAB)
Chronic pain cannot be proven by objective evidence and there is no medical test that can measure pain or take a picture of pain, and the main evidence that must be relied on is subjective evidence or the claimant's verbal description of his pain. The statutory criteria for a disability claim do not require proof to the level of objective medical evidence.	*G.B. v. MHRSD* (May 27, 2010), CP 26475 (PAB)
Chronic pain or fibromyalgia are not of themselves so debilitating that such diagnoses preclude any work. Indeed as has also been found, the vast majority of such sufferers are able to continue working, managing their pain through medication, passive treatment, active regular exercise and in some cases pain counselling.	*Butler v. MSD* (April 27, 2007) CP 21630 (PAB)

See also:	*Romanin v. MSD* (November 18, 2004), CP 21597 *Thawer v. MHRD* (December 3, 2003), CP 18204
It is not sufficient for CPS to be found to exist. The pain must be such as to prevent the sufferer from regularly pursuing a substantially gainful occupation. This difficult judgment call, generally made without the assistance of objective clinical signs, will be one of credibility on a case by case basis as to the severity of the pain complained of. The applicant must show that treatment was sought and efforts were made to cope with the pain. Although it is not essential in all cases, it will be desirable, and helpful for the applicant, that evidence of a psychiatric, psychological or physiatric nature be adduced from medical practitioners who have experience and general expertise in this difficult area of medicine. See also:	*MNHW v. Densmore* (June 2, 1993), CP 2389 CEB & PG ¶8508 *N.S. v. Minister of Human Resources and Skills Development*, 2014 SSTGDIS 2
The proof of fibromyalgia or CPS is somewhat more demanding than other facts. Special care and caution must be exercised in dealing with such complaints. There are three important considerations in determining whether the applicant is disabled owing to fibromyalgia or CPS or neither: 1. the quality of the applicant's evidence and its acceptance; 2. expert medical evidence adduced regarding fibromyalgia and CPS; and 3. any support for the applicant's claim to be found in the Minister's medical evidence.	*MHRD v. Warrick* (August 13, 1996), CP 4568 CEB & PG ¶8642
Chronic pain syndrome creates difficulty in determining its exact onset. It is a progressive disability. It cannot be said that it first occurred only when some medical practitioner actually put a name upon it. All of the evidence must be looked at to make its decision of the date of onset. That date can be prior to the date of the minimum qualifying period even if no medical practitioner so-named it until afterwards.	*Curnew v. MHRD* (June 25, 2001), CP 12886
To say that there is no corroborating medical evidence directly on the point of inability to work is tantamount to questioning whether the disease that come to be known as "fibromyalgia" in fact exists. Physicians in making the diagnosis must choose whether or not to believe what the applicant tells them.	*Hildebrandt v. MHRD* (August 14, 2000), CP 7641
The remedy for the collection of symptoms known under the heading of fibromyalgia is self-discipline involving pain and constant effort on the part of the patient, who must struggle in an atmosphere which often involves many aspects of an often unsatisfactory life. As by its nature there may be a lack of objective evidence, a tribunal faced with assessing disability must look for evidence that can confirm a believable story.	*Lajeunesse v. MHRD* (May 11, 2001), CP 13684
A diagnosis of fibromyalgia does not of itself equate to total disability or satisfy the issue of severity. Indeed the majority of sufferers can and do carry on with their jobs, the pain notwithstanding.	*McGillivray v. MHRD* (January 3, 2002), CP 14102

Disability Case Table

59

The family physician's supportive role with respect to the applicant's disability failed to challenge the applicant's notions about his problems and limitations. Instead, the applicant should be referred to an appropriate rehabilitation specialist to be integrated into an activating program of exercise in association with supportive counselling.	*Agostino v. MHRD* (May 7, 1997), CP 4171 CEB & PG ¶8671
The actual physical or mental capacity of the applicant must be examined and ascertained. The subjective pain experienced by the applicant, and its classification as fibromyalgia or CPS, does not throw any light on the cause of the pain or the applicant's capacity.	*Galloway v. MHRD* (March 19, 1998), CP 5043
Psychiatric evidence may be helpful, and efforts to cope with pain and treatment were imperative.	*Reichel v. MEI* (January 27, 1992), CP 2283
Neither fibromyalgia nor CPS are a significant basis, if a basis at all, for a finding of disability.	*Card v. MHRD* (July 30, 1996), CP 4279 CEB & PG ¶8649
It is incumbent on the applicant to show that she had made a conscientious effort to seek relief from the number of pain management and pain control medical facilities that are often effective in providing sufficient relief to patients to allow them to engage in gainful work appropriate to their disabilities.	*Croskery v. MHRD* (June 1, 1999), CP 11166 CEB & PG ¶8779
Medical approaches and statistics	
Diagnosis of fibromyalgia does not, just by the label itself, automatically preclude all employment. The medical evidence suggested that perhaps as many as 95% of patients with fibromyalgia are capable of some sedentary work.	*Hughes v. MHRD* (September 17, 1999), CP 06718
The American Psychiatric Association's definition of a pain disorder can usefully be applied in determining whether the applicant is disabled by CPS, with the presence or absence of:	*Van Horne v. MHRD* (August 29, 2000), CP 08903
1. pain in one or more anatomical sites and of sufficient severity to warrant clinical attention;	
2. clinically significant distress or impairment of functioning;	
3. existence of psychological factors important in the onset, severity, exacerbation and maintenance of pain; and	
4. feigned symptoms.	

Medical approaches and statistics (cont'd)	
A special 1994 report on the fibromyalgia syndrome, prepared under the auspices of the Physical Medicine Research Foundation, found in *The Journal of Rheumatology 1996*, states as follows: "Prognosis. The majority of patients with FM have chronic symptoms of varying severity that wax and wane. Most are capable of work, often with job modifications. Changing a job to suit the patient's abilities help maintain employability. Only a minority of patients are unable to work." [page 536]	*MHRD v. Bruneau* (April 24, 1997), CP 3865
Claim refused	
The applicant had allowed herself to become seriously deconditioned by ignoring or lacking the motivation to follow the treatment suggested by medical specialists who deal with fibromyalgia patients.	*Kerr v. MHRD* (January 3, 2002), CP 16349
The Board also noted the applicant's lack of motivation to perform work at lower pay than his prior employment.	*Reichel v. MEI* (January 27, 1992), CP 2283
Symptoms were prolonged but not severe enough to prevent applicant from doing light work; applicant received UI payments for part of period of claimed disability.	*MHRD v. Bruneau* (April 24, 1997), CP 3865
The applicant was at risk of developing CPS, which did not meet the definition of severe.	*Johnston v. MNHW* (September 6, 1993), CP 8563
Claim allowed	
Disc herniation causing severe pain; claimant could only work a maximum of two or three hours in a day in a sedentary position, and on many days could not attend at workplace at all.	*Kean v. MSD* (July 23, 2004), CP 21315
It was not possible to divide the applicant's day-to-day symptoms of fibromyalgia into categories of "good days" and "bad days". Even on her good days, the disabling symptoms were always present to some degree, and she was unable to maintain any schedule.	*MHRD v. Upshaw* (January 6, 2000), CP 07832 CEB & PG ¶8879
The applicant was not required to undergo a cognitive therapy and pain management program for CPS, as suggested by a psychologist. It was not offered in the applicant's community and did not offer a predictable expectation of relief from the applicant's symptoms.	*Benoit v. MHRD* (September 12, 1997), CP 5406

Claim allowed (cont'd)	
CPS followed reaction to antibiotics after serious cancer surgery; the applicant was not a malingerer, no physicians doubted her sincerity and two psychiatrists agreed on diagnosis of CPS.	*MNHW v. Densmore* (June 2, 1993), CP 2389 CEB & PG ¶8508
There was no denial that applicant suffers pain; no certainty regarding timing of return to work despite incremental improvements; balance was marginally in the applicant's favour.	*MHRD v. Warrick* (August 13, 1996), CP 4568 CEB & PG ¶8642
The applicant, a former firefighter, was a very credible witness and received a WCB pension.	*Van Horne v. MHRD* (August 29, 2000), CP 08903

7. Circulatory and Related Problems

Disabled	
Deep venous thrombosis caused pulmonary embolism. It was a recurring problem. The applicant also had a speech impediment and was precluded even from sedentary employment.	*Coltman v. MHRD* (October 22, 1996), CP 4318

Not disabled	
The applicant had vascular problems that resulted in pain. No psychiatric evidence and no evidence was presented to prove that the applicant attended pain clinic to help cope with pain.	*Parsons v. MHRD* (June 2, 1997), CP 4482

7.1 Hearing Loss

Being hearing-impaired is a serious limitation with an isolating effect on the individual and reduces the level of oral communication which can readily be undertaken, and in the employment context, such communication is generally quite important. Technical aids can help, but they have their limitations. Nonetheless, it does not necessarily render an applicant incapable regularly of pursuing all forms of substantially gainful employment. The workplace has room for the hearing-impaired and technological aids exist to help overcome the impairment. There are jobs in which the requirement for on-going oral communication is minimal or less important, in which a person with even a moderate bilateral neurosensory hearing loss could function satisfactorily. However, it is not incumbent upon the Minister to produce evidence in each case to show just where and in what job the claimant can expect to be engaged.	*Buckley v. MHRD* (November 29, 2001), CP 15265

8. Heart Conditions

Not disabled	
While applicant suffered from long-standing history of asthma which could progress to Chronic Obstruction Pulmonary Disease ("COPD") if not properly treated, medical evidence supporting serious condition of COPD was very "skimpy".	*Hutchinson v. Canada (Minister of Social Development)*, 2006 FCA 231
The applicant's fear of having an imminent heart attack does not equate with a severe disabled condition.	*Chamberlain v. MHRD* (September 14, 1999), CP 07918
The applicant had suffered a heart attack in 1994. Her lifestyle was now somewhat more restricted than before the heart attack. Her current chest pains were not related to her heart condition, and the fact that nitroglycerine pills were apparently giving her some relief could be attributable to the placebo effect.	*MHRD v. Mackinnon* (June 11, 1999), CP 06919
Disabled	
A 53-year-old applicant suffered a heart attack after quitting work due to heart problems. "Stress", resulting from frequent, sometimes lengthy, arrhythmias and rapid palpitations lasting up to an hour, was a factor.	*Osachoff v. MHRD* (July 7, 1997), CP 5635 CEB & PG ¶8684

9. Irritable Bowel Syndrome (IBS) and Incontinence

Disabled	
The applicant had suffered many humiliating experiences in public due to IBS, which was her main problem. It was difficult to imagine a more frustrating and embarrassing medical condition. When combined with other ailments, the applicant's medical condition was severe and prolonged.	*Burn (F.) v. MHRD* (April 11, 1997), CP 3498
While the applicant's frequency and/or urgency of urination would likely not be sufficient to entitle her to a pension, other related difficulties had a direct impact on her capacity for employment. These included recurrent, continuing and prolonged urinary tract infections, sometimes requiring self-catherization.	*Mainville v. MHRD* (June 27, 1997), CP 4873

10. Knee Pain

Not disabled	
The applicant's pain (arthritic left knee) was not constant and the knee joint had not been destroyed. He could therefore do sedentary work, now and after joint-replacement surgery.	*Charron v. MHRD* (June 25, 1997), CP 4939
A painful arthritic left knee did not constitute a severe disability.	*Suban v. MEI* (June 28, 1996), CP 3461
A defective knee joint hardly seems sufficient to exclude a person from all employment. Workers with a bad arm or leg, and in some cases a limb that is of no use at all, find modified work.	*Watson v. MHRD* (September 29, 1999), CP 08040
The applicant's main problem was being overweight. If that could be corrected, there were procedures available to remedy problems with the right knee.	*MacLeod v. MHRD* (August 16, 1996), CP 4016

11. Multiple Sclerosis (MS)

Disabled	
The 64-year-old claimant with Grade 12 education worked as a secretary all her life. She was diagnosed with MS and emotional problems, although she refused to see a psychiatrist.	*Presland v. MHRD* (June 17, 2002), CP 16815
The applicant was able to establish that she had been disabled by MS for four years prior to being officially diagnosed with the condition.	*Hilton v. MHRD* (August 28, 2000), CP 10982
Not disabled	
Post-MQP diagnosis of MS and report that this would have caused walking difficulties going back 10 years did not warrant reversing original denial of claim; report not giving opinion on claimant's condition or ability to work as of MQP; there was nothing that solidly connected a diagnosis of MS to a loss of ability to work.	*J.K. v. MHRSD* *(May 20, 2009),* CP 25953 (PAB)

12. Myofascial Pain Syndrome

Not disabled	
After whiplash resulting from a series of three motor vehicle accidents, the applicant was able to engage in light work, although she would experience episodes of aggravation that could be readily treated with a two- to three-week course of physical therapy. If the episodes did happen often and required taking two or three weeks off work for each episode, then the applicant would not be capable of regularly pursuing gainful employment.	*Vanneste v. MHRD* (November 8, 1996), CP 4397

13. Non-Specific Low Back Pain

Low back pain is a symptom and not a diagnosis. In the absence of objective medical findings or psychological explanation, the following principles apply: 1. Non-specific low back pain should be re-defined as a problem of activity intolerance, not a "medical" condition. 2. Non-specific low back pain should be considered as temporary, not a permanent disability. 3. Complaints of pain are not adequate to define a medically based problem. 4. Psychological factors identified as critical to the worker's activity intolerance (inability to work) might be diagnosed as a psychological, not a pain, disability.	*D.M. v. MHRD* (February 19, 1997), CP 3858 (PAB) CEB & PG ¶8664
Consistent with the four principles set out in *Mehlenbacher* (above), low back pain is a symptom and not a diagnosis. Non-specific low back pain should be redefined as a problem of activity intolerance, not a medical problem. There are many employed people who continue to work with muscular and mechanical back problems that limit their work capacity.	*O'Neill v. HRSD* (October 4, 2007), CP 24738 (PAB)
Non-specific low back pain is a problem of activity intolerance that should be considered temporary since the degree of activity is increased with proper back care and management.	*Pereira v. MHRD* (March 18, 1998), CP 5180
Many employed people continue to work with muscular and mechanical back problems that limit their work capacity.	*Watson v. MHRD* (September 29, 1999), CP 08040

14. Obesity

Not disabled There were procedures available to remedy the right-knee problems, but they were only available once the applicant (5'8", 237 lbs.) lost weight.	*MacLeod v. MHRD* (August 16, 1996), CP 4016
Disabled The 47-year-old female applicant (5'2", 300 lbs.) had other debilitating medical problems, some of which were caused by the obesity, others not. Morbid obesity alone would not qualify the applicant for a disability pension unless she was so obese that she could not function at all. A drastic or even significant weight loss was unlikely to occur at this point.	*Scala v. MHRD* (March 31, 1997), CP 4712 CEB & PG ¶8672

Disabled (cont'd)	
The 53-year-old female claimant was 5'3" tall and 318 lbs., and came from a family of grossly overweight individuals. The debilitating effects of her back injury, arthritis in knees, asthma and severe depression, were exacerbated by her weight, which she had tried to reduce without success.	*Adamson v. MHRD* (August, 1, 2002), CP 13422

15. Psoriasis

Disabled	
Psoriasis has varied in coverage of the applicant's body between 50% to 90% over the years. It is incurable, and the applicant could not be faulted for refusing to take prescribed drugs out of fear of the potential side-effects. It was difficult to imagine a more debilitating, embarrassing and frustrating affliction.	*McKenzie v. MHRD* (March 4, 1997), CP 4196

16. Respiratory Problems

Not disabled	
The applicant's asthma and persistent cough prevented her from continuing to work in her previous janitorial capacity, but did not prevent her from obtaining other employment despite her age (54 years) and lack of English.	*Megalos v. MHRD* (February 17, 1997), CP 4685

17. Sleep Disorder

Not disabled	
While there was no question that the applicant suffered from sleep disorder, i.e., persistent insomnia, there was no evidence that the disorder was severe and prolonged. No report from the sleep clinic physician who examined the applicant was produced.	*MacIntyre v. MEI* (March 28, 1996), CP 3279

18. Vision Impairment

Disabled	
The applicant, whose eyesight was failing, owned 800-acre farm, which he ran in partnership with his wife. The applicant, continuing to live on the farm, played a part in its direction and earned income from it.	*Spencer v. MHRD* (December 8, 1999), CP 09277
The 62-year-old claimant, a former bookkeeper and ice cream depot manager, had a detached retina in one eye and distorted vision in both eyes, exacerbated by irregular back spasm flare-ups.	*Barton v. MHRD* (October 11, 2002), CP 16824
The 50-year-old claimant with double vision, who had last been employed in janitorial work, had reasonably refused an operation on her right, or good eye, which if successful would have reduced the vision in her right eye to the reduced vision in her left eye, and made it easier for her to read.	*Lorna v. MHRD* (October 2, 2002), CP 18517
The 50-year-old claimant with Grade 12 education had a detached retina in right eye and severe headaches. She complained of a decrease in visual acuity in both eyes, although there was no medical explanation for this claim.	*Hack v. MHRD* (March 25, 2003), CP 13779
Not disabled	
The 54-year-old claimant with Grade 12 education could not drive, or read without a magnifying glass after becoming blind in his right eye following a cataract operation and developing a cataract in his left eye. While the PAB appreciated the claimant's refusal to have an operation for the left eye, the operation was of a minor nature and would lead to a significant improvement to his lifestyle and ability to work. The loss of vision in the right eye was not due to the first operation.	*Boutros v. MHRD* (October 29, 2002), CP 19520
The 62-year-old claimant, who had been a meteorological technician with a Grade 12 education, suffered a detached retina in his right eye. Surgery left him with 6/90 in that eye, and he also suffered from a hearing impairment.	*Maybroda v. MHRD* (2001), CP 12528
The 64-year-old claimant with Grade 6 education and 15 years experience as auto mechanic was no longer physically able to stand on his feet all day, but had not asked his employer for any other kind of work.	*Simson v. MHRD* (May 10, 2002), CP 16426

19. Whiplash/Soft-Tissue Injury

It is generally accepted that "whiplash" or soft-tissue accident injuries produce little objective evidence. Medical practitioners are therefore dependent on the subjective evidence of the patient.	*Simon v. MSD* (December 10, 2007), CP 24556 (PAB)

Disability Case Table

67

(C) Miscellaneous Physical Ailments

Not disabled	
While cystic fibrosis is prolonged, the applicant's condition was not severe and had not deteriorated in the three years since diagnosis, due to advances made in treating the disease.	*MHRD v. Getchell* (March 10, 1999), CP 05999 CEB & PG ¶8764
An essential tremor was treatable, and the family physician was not available to be examined on her affidavit.	*Bell v. MHRD* (December 13, 2000), CP 12664
A latex allergy was developed by a nurse.	*MacMillan v. MHRD* (November 6, 2000), CP 12183
The nature of somotoform disorder is that it does not have an objective medical foundation of the kind that would allow for a determination with a fair measure of confidence, that the applicant is disabled for CPP purposes. In the absence of any or of insufficient objective medical evidence, the oral evidence must be convincing and preferably bolstered by psychiatric evidence or evidence of a psychological nature, tending to show that the disability is severe.	*Sicoli v. MHRD* (July 22, 1999), CP 09472 CEB & PG ¶8801
Tennis elbow (chronic lateral epicondylitus) was developed by farm labourer.	*Sandhu v. MHRD* (October 7, 1999), CP 09161 CEB & PG ¶8832

(D) Mental Disability

Where mental stability is a significant issue, proper psychiatric evidence is required in order to establish entitlement under CPP.	*Duffield v. MHRD* (April 21, 1997), CP 3870
One who suffers from a psychological problem, which is within his or her ability to overcome, cannot be considered disabled under the CPP.	*Giampa v. MEI* (November 30, 1994), CP 3255 CPP 8557
A psychiatric report is required to support an allegation of depression.	*Lacy v. MHRD* (December 10, 1999), CP 05872
A family physician is capable of diagnosing depression where it exists. The failure of the family physician to make such a diagnosis may be taken as evidence that the claimant was not suffering from depression at that time.	*MSD v. Kumar* (March 14, 2005), CP 21326 (PAB)
Scope of s. 42(2)(a)(ii) is not restricted solely to mental disability or to physical disability, but includes a disability resulting from a cumulative combination of both mental and physical aspects.	*MNHW v. McDonald* (October 1988), CP 1527 CEB & PG ¶8564

68

"Mental disability" as it is used in s. 42(2)(*a*) is not limited to severe psychiatric illness or endogenous depression, but may encompass a condition or disorder that makes it impossible for the applicant to work without extended leaves of absence.	*MEI v. McFadden* (May 6, 1996), CP 3474 CEB & PG ¶8634
Disabled	
51 years old at the time of the hearing, and not working since 1995 motor vehicle accident in which her 11-year-old son was killed. She was diagnosed with major depression, and was unable to work or function normally ever since. She followed a sort of obsessive-compulsive lifestyle that no normal person would choose.	*Raisi v. MHRD* (February 12, 2004), CP21607
The 64-year-old claimant with Grade 12 education worked as a secretary all her life. She was diagnosed with MS and emotional problems, although she refused to see a psychiatrist.	*Presland v. MHRD* (June 17, 2002), CP 16815
The applicant clinically identified an untreatable phobia of medical treatment for his physical disability, which would otherwise render the applicant employable.	*MNHW v. McDonald* (October 7, 1988), CP 4643 CP 1527, CEB & PG ¶8564
The applicant had borderline intelligence, functioned personally, socially and interpersonally at a very dysfunctional level; she couldn't care for herself and had poor memory and cognitive problems.	*Tremblay v. MHRD* (January 23, 1997), CP 4682
The applicant was no longer able to cope with the job he hated after 23 years and chose to "drop out" of society to live a secluded lifestyle.	*MEI v. McFadden* (May 6, 1996), CP 3474 CEB & PG ¶8634
Dissent: There was no medical diagnosis of any mental or physical disorder that would preclude all employment. A personality disorder is a neurotic as opposed to psychotic diagnosis, and depression is reactive, not endogenous.	
The applicant's post-traumatic stress disorder went undiagnosed for over 30 years.	*Burris v. MHRD* (June 4, 1999), CP 04839 CEB & PG ¶8781
Not disabled	
It is possible to divide intellectual function into certain compartments, however, there must come a time when the sheer number of those activities along with their varied nature will inevitably lead to the inference that lack of capacity or competency to form an intention can no longer be legitimately argued. The medical evidence and the claimant's activities must both be considered in the determination of incapacity.	*Danielson v. MHRSD* (June 11, 2008), CP 25782 (PAB)
Two specialists diagnosed depression, but claimant refused their advice to take anti-depressants. He tried to take one once, but ceased taking it before the six-week trial ended because he thought the drug made him feel "weird." The claimant never sought an alternative drug because he did not like the idea of taking such medications.	*Roberts v. MHRD* (November 6, 2003), CP 20598

69

Not disabled (cont'd)	
The applicant's physical symptoms were compounded by depression over several traumatic years spent being tortured by and "on the run" from the authorities in Argentina before coming to Canada in 1988, However, the applicant was educated but had not learned English.	*de Montana v. MHRD* (February 15, 2002), CP 16285
The applicant suffered anxiety and depression but had not been prescribed medication.	*Michaud v. MEI* (September 27, 1995), CP 3631
Learning difficulties, or learning problems, do not translate into a mental disability. The applicant presented no medical or psychiatric evidence in this regard.	*Mapplebeck v. MHRD* (May 19, 2000), CP 08904
Low-grade depression precipitated by death of applicant's son and mother resulted in no motivation to return to workforce or rehabilitation course. The applicant had simply "given up".	*Cardadeiro v. MHRD* (November 17, 1998), CP 05757
The anxiety syndrome experienced by applicant out of proportion to clinical findings.	*Morden v. MHRD* (September 4, 1998), CP 05858 CEB & PG ¶8728

Part IV. Factors Associated with Medical Condition

(A) Adopting a Disabled Lifestyle

Claimants must show that reasonable and earnest efforts were made to find and maintain employment which can accommodate their limitations. Where the claimant made only two brief efforts at home-based work, did not look for other employment, and did not attempt retraining, her claim was undermined because it raised a suspicion that she has simply chosen to adopt a disabled lifestyle in the belief she is unemployable.	*F.E. v. MHRSD* (June 17, 2011), CP 26480 (PAB)
The applicant adopted a disabled life-style, while medical evidence indicated that not all employment was foreclosed.	*Caseley v. MEI* (April 21, 1994), CP 2904
The applicant adopted a disabled life-style, despite objective medical evidence. The applicant had not pursued recommended counselling, was involved in pending litigation over the motor vehicle accident he had been injured in, and was making more per month on social assistance than at his former employment.	*Hamou v. MHRD* (May 24, 1996), CP 3475
The applicant patterned her lifestyle according to belief that she was disabled. Mere belief, not buttressed by objective medical evidence, must be seriously questioned when considering an application under the CPP.	*Mazzocca v. MHRD* (May 10, 1990), CP 1925
There was no evidence that the obese applicant ever sought work again, on any level, after back pain induced him to stop work when he was 28 years old.	*Lombardo v. MHRD* (July 23, 2001), CP 12731

(B) Capacity to Work and to Retrain

To establish severe disability, appellants must not only show a serious health problem, but where there is evidence of work capacity, must also show effort at obtaining and maintaining employment has been unsuccessful by reason of the health condition.	*Inclima v. Attorney General (Canada)*, 2003 FCA 117
Where the true cause of the claimant's inability to return to work was his failure to make greater effort between the time of his accident and his MQP, there is no need to make an in-depth "real-world" analysis of the constraints on the claimant's capacity to return to the work force by his educational level, language proficiency and past work or life experience.	*Doucette v. MHRD*, 2004 FCA 292
An essential element of qualifying for a disability pension is evidence of serious efforts by the applicant to help himself or herself. This requirement extends to both the obligation to aggressively seek treatment and to the burden which accrues to all applicants of establishing that reasonable and realistic efforts were made to find and maintain employment while taking into account the *Villani* personal characteristics and his employability.	*A.P. v. MHRSD*, (December 15, 2009) CP 26308 (PAB)
Attendance in a retraining school program is not tantamount to evidence of work capacity, particularly where the claimant was doing so only to cooperate with the workers' compensation board and ensure the continuation of such benefits. While a claimant's ability to undertake retraining might be a factor, depending upon context, in assessing severity, in the post-*Villani* era it can no longer be elevated to the level of a rule or principle which would justify the denial of a claim, *per se*.	*Romanin v. MSD* (November 18, 2004), CP 21597
The stringent test in 42(2)(*a*), coupled with the civil burden of proof carried by an applicant, means that an applicant is expected to call some credible evidence directed to his or her efforts to retrain and participate in rehabilitation and vocational training programs — especially in those cases where the issue is really whether the given applicant has the capacity to carry out gainful alternative employment.	*Dorion v. MHRD* (December 21, 2000), CP 10672
Looking for work and attempting to work should not disqualify the applicant.	*Clement v. MHRD* (July 31, 1998), CP 5319
The fact that there is no provision in the CPP for retraining unless the applicant has already been found to be disabled (Reg. s. 69(2)) is not an impediment to a finding that the disability is not severe because the applicant can be retrained.	*Mosher v. MHRD* (May 28, 1998), CP 5053
The usual suggestion that appellants retrain or seek other employment, although attempted to some extent, was perceived to be unnecessary since the claimant understood that a job was always open with his previous employer if he could handle it.	*Boyle v. MHRD* (June 10, 2003), CP 18508

Not disabled	
Claimant worked as cashier at a supermarket 6 years after her MQP, but was dismissed after a short time because of performance. Claimant also made soap and candles for sale, and ran artisans' craft store for three years. Post-MQP medical reports mentioned her residual capacity for work.	*Simpson v. Canada (Attorney General)*, 2012 FCA 82
Applicant had no desire to have employment or retraining of any nature, and had made insufficient effort to mitigate. There were no moderate or severe limitations on his ability to maintain employment by reason of his asthmatic condition.	*S.D. v. MHRSD*, (April 15, 2010), CP 26280 (PAB)
Claimant, a former machinist, was attending classes in a business course for 25–27 hours each week, plus 15 hours each week studying. Claimant was maintaining an 80% average in program.	*Stratton v. MSD*, (November 2, 2006), CP 24370 (PAB)
Medical evidence indicated that the claimant had the capacity for jobs such as a gas station attendant, dispatcher or telemarketer, despite his misgivings regarding job satisfaction and salary expectations.	*Doucette v. MHRD*, 2004 FCA 292
No satisfactory evidence that the appellant could have worked at lighter work, therefore no requirement for the applicant to show that she made reasonable efforts at retraining to do less strenuous work, and to make efforts to secure less strenuous work.	*Adatia v. MHRD* (June 2003), CP 20124
The applicant's return to work to earn $5,000 in a year, while not a bar to a disability finding, is evidence that supports the Minister's position, particularly where the work was performed in a commercial setting and therefore more than merely doing household chores in her own residence at her own pace.	*Fitzgerald v. MHRD* (October 3, 2001), CP 14116
Sources for help in furthering the applicant's basic educational skills such as reading, writing and retraining for other work were available within five or six miles from the applicant's home.	*Hibbitts v. MHRD* (July 19, 2001), CP 13049
The applicant was employed, working full time at an hourly rate of $12.00, although she would prefer not to be. Her husband, however, was unemployed.	*Kalra v. MHRD* (October 23, 2001), CP 14989
The applicant had an obligation, indeed a duty, to attempt to rehabilitate himself and an obligation to seek alternative employment in earnest.	*Brunette v. MHRD* (October 24, 2000), CP 11722
The applicant declined to accept modified work which had been offered by the employer.	*Bowerman v. MHRD* (November 14, 2000), CP 09667
The applicant's stated intentions to seek work after rehabilitation and training with WCB indicated a capacity for work.	*Major v. MHRD* (July 10, 1998), CP 06460
Disabled	
Applicant consulted with two rehabilitation facilities, which were not able to identify any employment for which he was capable.	*MHRSD v. A.B.R.* (April 2, 2009), CP 26100 (PAB)
The applicant's valiant attempts to return to work for six months were not a sufficient basis for determining that disability had ceased.	*Hawkins v. MHRD* (September 12, 1997), CP 4276 CEB & PG ¶8695
An attempt to participate in employment training, as required by welfare authorities, during a few months one year, was not evidence of capacity to engage in employment. It merely confirmed the opposite.	*Hilton v. MHRD* (August 22, 2000), CP 10982

(C) Capacity to Attend School

Disabled	
The applicant's participation in several courses, in an effort to qualify himself for whatever kind of work would be suited to his condition, is indicative of good faith.	*Marriott v. MHRD* (January 31, 2000), CP 08452 CEB & PG ¶8892
The applicant had no transferable marketable skills and retraining was unlikely due to age, education and episodes of pain.	*Appleton v. MHRD* (November 21, 1997), CP 4619 CEB & PG ¶8709
The applicant was 56 years old and had spent his entire working life doing heavy labour. As with most men who have spent almost 40 years in various positions doing manual labour, it is difficult to imagine work of a less demanding nature or any feasible retraining options.	*Whynot v. MHRD* (September 21, 2000), CP 13536
The applicant, who had MS and successfully attended technical school after the disability, was alleged to have commenced until the illness forced her to drop out. While attending classes during the day, the applicant had to rest repeatedly.	*Fraser v. MHRD* (September 20, 2000), CP 11086
It is not the purpose of the CPP to provide financial assistance to those undertaking or terminating a course of study. Full-time attendance at an educational institution amounts to a persuasive indication of a capacity to work. However, other factors must be considered, such as the degree of incapacity, the study load, and the difficulty in attendance and participation in the program.	*Elwood v. MEI* (June 23, 1994), CP 2781 CEB & PG ¶8541
The applicant's attendance at school, or retraining, is often a useful reference to determine capacity.	*Bell v. MEI* (June 27, 1996), CP 3882 CEB & PG ¶8644
It is not reasonable for an applicant to fail to take advantage of the retraining opportunities offered by federal government programs, and such refusal must be treated as a negative factor.	*Eddy v. MHRD* (July 20, 1998), CP 5253
The ability to pursue a reasonably demanding course of study can be equated to the capability of pursuing a substantially gainful employment.	*MNHW v. Dupuis* (July 1985), CCH 8502
The physical demands on the applicant of full-time university attendance was equal to some form of modified or sedentary work.	*Buchanan v. MNHW* (August 11, 1993), CP 2643
There is no principle of law equating the applicant's school experience with a position in the workforce of modified or light duty. Each case turns on its own facts.	*Fraser v. MHRD* (September 20, 2000), CP 11086

Disability Case Table

73

Not disabled The claimant suffered from constant pain, yet successfully completed a Certificate of Architectural Technology from a community college, maintaining an 80% average and spending 15–20 hours a week in class and about the same amount of time at home studying and completing his class work.	*R.B. v. MHRSD* (June 14, 2012), CP 28005 (PAB)
The applicant pursued a master's degree and worked as student assistant as well as being a single mom caring for 3 children.	*Jewett v. MHRD* (November 10, 2000), CP 10572
The applicant obtained a 2-year graduate diploma from technical school while being single parent.	*MEI v. Hallowes* (September 15, 1994), CP 2484 CEB & PG ¶8573
The applicant's participation in a course of studies — 15 months community college, upgrading from Grades 8 to 12 and $5^{1}/_{2}$-month security course out of province — was equivalent in physical demands to engaging in modified or sedentary employment.	*MHRD v. Fillis* (May 8, 1997), CP 4446
Ne peut être invalide au sens de la loi celui qui est en mesure de suivre des cours. De formation sur une base quotidienne.	*Cloutier c. MHRD* (July 23, 1998), CP 4014
The fact that the applicant did not attempt to improve his English-language skills and thereby improve his chances at obtaining light, sedentary work reflected negatively on the claim.	*Ferreira v. MHRD* (November 27, 2000), CP 08160
The applicant had a severely disabled left arm, which made him unemployable in his former occupations, but was currently attending school full-time to upgrade his education to Grade 12.	*Hann v. MEI* (November 3, 1995), CP 03381
The applicant had completed a one-year upgrading program and three years of university.	*Jolicoeur v. MEI* (July 15, 1994), CP 2931

(D) Capacity to Perform Household Chores

The physical capacity to perform household chores that can generally be done at one's own convenience is not to be equated to capacity to perform light duties in the commercial marketplace.	*Morley v. MEI* (November 1995), CP 3296 CEB & PG ¶8592
The capacity to perform household tasks does not equate to capacity to perform substantially gainful employment.	*Wong v. MEI* (January 26, 1996), CP 03777 CEB & PG ¶8599
Not disabled The applicant could function despite her CPS to perform certain household chores, e.g., preparing meals, dusting, sweeping, driving a car.	*Stephens v. MEI* (March 8, 1996), CP 3782
Applicant's ability to care for her parents throughout period prior to appeal indicated she was capable of regularly pursuing substantially gainful employment.	*Canada (Attorney General) v. Causey* 2007 FC 422

(E) Recreation, Holidays and Volunteer Work

An individual who devoted a substantial portion of each week to training, practicing and playing professional wheelchair rugby was not disabled.	*MSD v. Hickling* (May 10, 2007), CP 24344 (PAB)
The CPP does not require applicants for a disability pension to remain housebound as a condition of eligibility. They are entitled to take holidays.	*Walton v. MHRD* (April 28, 2003), CP 20706
The fact that the applicant has volunteered for religious and charitable tasks requiring limited time and skill should not be held against him as evidence of his ability to take employment in the marketplace. The amount of effort and time expended in such work is entirely dependent on the applicant's physical and mental condition from time to time.	*Marriott v. MHRD* (January 31, 2000), CP 08452 CEB & PG ¶8892

(F) Functional Overlay

Part of a complaint may be real and part may be "functional overlay", or symptom exaggeration. A lack of organic symptoms is not necessarily determinative in deciding whether the applicant is a malingerer. Functional overlay is a delicate problem and pain can be subjective.	*Crossett v. MEI* (May 8, 1996), CP 3377 CEB & PG ¶8618
In functional overlay situations, where subjective complaints are out of proportion to findings of organic impairments, an entitlement to a pension must be based on a proper psychiatric diagnosis of a mental illness or emotional disorder severe enough to be disabling in its own right.	*Macri v. MEI* (January 9, 1995), CP 3079 CEB & PG ¶8669
The principle in *Macri* governs except in very limited situations.	*MHRD v. Wade* (January 20, 1998), CP 5294 CEB & PG ¶8708
The absence of evidence from the many specialists who examined a claimant alleging chronic pain to suggest that the claimant is malingering or exaggerating the pain, or of a psychogenic overlay or hysterical reaction which might explain the complaints of pain in the absence of objective evidence of injury, lends considerable weight and credence to the claimant's medical history.	*Gobeil v. MHRD* (July 9, 2001), CP 09864
Medical witnesses were entitled to take into account surveillance videotape of the applicant performing tasks which were beyond what he claimed he could do, although the videotape had not been seen by the Board.	*Petros v. MHRD* (August 20, 2001), CP 13059
Functional overlay, and its consequences, take precedence over medical opinion only in rarest of circumstances, e.g., where the applicant is obviously credible.	*Heritt v. MEI* (October 29, 1991), CP 2228

Functional overlay, diseases of psychogenic origin, and hysterical reactions do not in themselves constitute a disability under the CPP, unless they are established, by proper psychiatric evaluation, to be so severe as to prevent any employment and to be of indefinite duration.	*MNHW v. Menard* (January 18, 1980), CP 00402 CEB & PG ¶8805
The fact that the medical reports expressly refer to functional overlay and question the applicant's motivation to work, lessens the weight to be given the applicant's evidence a good deal.	*Lazzara v. MEI* (May 10, 1996), CP 3494
39-year-old claimant reported severe back pain after a workplace accident. Expert medical reports indicated functional overlay, and the claimant was receiving $1400/month from Ontario disability. She refused to attend the recommended "Function Restoration Program" because of child-care concerns. Claimant had computer skills, and was too young and too intelligent to be written off as permanently disabled at this time.	*Klasen v. MSD* (May 17, 2004), CP 20518

(G) Refusal to Follow Recommended Treatment

The "real world" context also means that the PAB must consider whether the claimant's refusal to undergo physiotherapy treatment is unreasonable and what impact that refusal might have on the claimant's disability status should the refusal be considered unreasonable.	*Lalonde v. Canada (Minister of Human Resources Development)*, 2002 FCA 211
Claimants have a personal responsibility to cooperate in their health care. See also:	*Kambo v. MHRD*, 2005 FCA 353 *N.J. v. MSD* (October 22, 2007), CP 25044 (PAB)
It is incumbent on an applicant to show a conscious effort to seek relief from the number of pain management and pain control medical facilities that are often effective in providing sufficient relief to allow engaging in gainful work appropriate to the applicant's disabilities.	*M.C. v. MHRSD* (July 8, 2011), CP 26647 (PAB)
Claimants for a disability pension must show that they responded to recommendations of health care advisors and made reasonable efforts to do the things necessary to likely improve their condition. However, they will not automatically be disqualified if they are not successful in those endeavours. Miracles cannot be expected and superhuman efforts should not be insisted on. If a claimant has taken reasonable steps to comply with recommendations but has been unable, despite those efforts, to attain the hoped-for results, it cannot simply be concluded that the individual in question did not show sufficient self-discipline and should be refused the disability pensions sought.	*Adamson v. MHRD* (August, 1, 2002), CP 13422
An applicant for a disability pension is obligated to make all reasonable efforts to undertake and submit to programs and treatments recommended by treating and consulting physicians. Such programs quite often offer the only hope of ever regaining the capacity to engage in gainful occupation. Only after reasonable attempts and efforts fail can it be determined that the disability is "severe". The applicant's failure to make an earnest effort to undertake recommended types of special activities amounts to an unreasonable refusal to accept treatment. See also:	*Ramirez v. MHRD* (January 27, 1999), CP 05222 CEB & PG ¶8769 (PAB) *MHRD v. Mulek* (September 13, 1996), CP 4719

To be entitled to a disability pension, an applicant is obligated to abide by and submit to treatment recommendations and, if this is not done, the applicant must establish the reasonableness of his/her non-compliance. Compliance must be viewed in the context of applicant's circumstances. Persons afflicted with fibromyalgia and experiencing the constant diffuse pain, lack of proper sleep, loss of energy, feelings of despair and associated depression cannot be expected to engage in treatment programs with the same enthusiasm, regularity and positive attitudes as persons recovering from fracture or a trauma injury. Another factor is the lack of publicly funded secondary health care facilities including pharmacotherapy.	*Bulger v. MHRD* (May 18, 2000), CP 9164
The refusal of certain suggested treatments may in certain circumstances be justified, but a broad rejection to a reasonable use of medication may weigh disapprovingly in the determination of one's qualification to a disability pension.	*L.L. v. MHRSD* (December 10, 2009), CP 26013 (PAB)
The applicant was not required to undergo a cognitive therapy and pain management program for CPS suggested by a psychologist. It was not offered in the applicant's community and did not offer a predictable expectation of relief from the applicant's symptoms.	*Benoit v. MHRD* (September 12, 1997), CP 5406
The applicant has an obligation to take counselling where it has been recommended by physicians, and if it is not successful, to provide an appropriate explanation.	*Hamou v. MHRD* (May 24, 1996), CP 3475
The applicant must establish that his or her incapability of engaging in any gainful occupation must have, as its cause, a physical condition or a psychological condition which the applicant is unable to overcome by reasonable conduct on his or her part.	*Giampa v. MEI* (November 30, 1994), CP 3255 CPP 8557
The applicant's clinically identified and untreatable phobia of medical treatment constitutes a mental illness in its own right, rendering him disabled even though treatment for his physical disability might render the applicant employable.	*MNHW v. McDonald* (October 7, 1988), CP 4643 CP 1527 CEB & PG ¶8564
The term "prolonged disability" contains an element of reasonable self-discipline or personal responsibility. Following medical advice to exercise, diet, take medication, avoid alcohol or tobacco, or follow other conservative and reasonable treatments, is expected of a person if such will ameliorate a potentially disabling condition. There may, of course, be circumstances in which such remedial action may not reasonably be expected of a person. But a person who continues to suffer from a condition that is reasonably avoidable or can reasonably be ameliorated, by taking available measures, cannot be said to be suffering from a disability that is of prolonged or indefinite duration.	*Smith v. MHRD* (May 29, 1998), CP 5068
The decision to undergo or refuse surgery lies with the person involved. If that decision is based on reasonable grounds, it should not adversely affect the claim to a disability pension. If the decision to refuse surgery is not a reasonable one, then such refusal should be considered as a negative factor in determining entitlement to a CPP disability pension.	*Forrester v. MHRD* (December 2, 2003), CP 20899
Disabled	
While the claimant did undergo physiotherapy following his workplace accident, he received only five sessions. Although he would have benefited from further physiotherapy, the claimant didn't have the resources to pay for it, the WSIB having rejected his application for coverage.	*G.D. v. Minister of Human Resources and Skills Development*, 2014 SSTGDIS 3
Applicant could not be faulted for not attending a pain clinic as recommended by one of his doctors, because his primary care physician chose not to make such a referral.	*MHRSD v. A.B.R.* (April 2, 2009), CP 26100 (PAB)

Disability Case Table

77

Disabled (cont'd)	
Applicant's reluctance to follow physicians' advice to do more exercises was not unreasonable in light of her past experiences, having hurt herself doing physiotherapy a few years ago and getting swollen feet from walking. Her tobacco addiction prevented her from giving up the smoking habit.	*Heisler v. MHRD* (September 12, 2001), CP 13450
Not disabled	
Claimant with back pain chose not to accept recommendations that he seek help to manage pain and further treatment including injections and possible surgery, although surgery would have a good chance of success.	*MHRSD v. R.K.* (January 7, 2013), CP 27791 (PAB)
A 39-year-old mother of young children with an MBA had previously worked in senior management and product development, but had made no attempts to work. She had various ailments leading to pain, but the expert witness noted all are treatable.	*M.C. v. MHRSD* (July 8, 2011), CP 26647 (PAB)
Claimant failed to follow the recommendations on how to treat fibromyalgia.	*D.C. v. MHRSD* (December 21, 2011), CP 27993 (PAB)
Claimant was 63-year-old man with grade seven education, with a 30-year history of being a truck driver, suffered a knee injury, but continued to drive the trucks for a year post-injury. Claimant missed a surgery date for a knee replacement as he was in the hospital with pneumonia, but made no subsequent attempts to seek information about a different surgery date. Although knee problems were limiting at MQP, they worsened afterwards. It was claimant's responsibility to follow the reasonable and available medical advice of his doctors and he failed to provide cogent reasons for not doing so.	*R.M. v. MHRSD* (November 16, 2010), CP 25286 (PAB)
Applicant suffering from stress, anxiety, and depression had a general aversion to use of medications or drug treatments, and had refused some treatments for cancer earlier. Taking the recommended medication did allow her to return to work.	*L.L. v. MHRSD* (December 10, 2009), CP 26013 (PAB)
Claimant worked 11 months after MQP and made two attempts to work; claimant could work in seated position; claimant failing to do any exercises as recommended, to stop smoking or make any effort at lighter employment after she stopped working.	*J.E.B. v. MHRSD,* (March 6, 2009), CP 24563 (PAB)
Claimant refused to travel 80 km to undertake aqua fitness or a fibromyalgia program to improve her chronic pain, although she regularly travelled this distance to get to her doctors.	*Bicho v. HRSD* (March 10, 2008), CP 24949 (PAB)
Obese claimant voluntarily quit part-time job to return to country of origin to arrange her daughters' marriages. Claimant did not comply with doctor's recommendations for treatment, medication and counseling, did not attempt to return to work or obtain medical treatment while in country of origin, and did not report any new or worsening symptoms. There were no tests to suggest a material deterioration in her condition from when she was working.	*N.J. v. MSD* (October 22, 2007), CP 25044 (PAB)
Claimant giving inconsistent reasons for refusing knee surgery to doctors and to PAB.	*Forrester v. MHRD* (December 2, 2003), CP 20899
Two specialists diagnosed depression, but claimant refused their advice to take anti-depressants. He tried to take one once, but ceased taking it before the six-week trial ended because he thought the drug made him feel "weird". The claimant never sought an alternative drug because he did not like the idea of taking such medications.	*Roberts v. MHRD* (November 6, 2003), CP 20598
The 44-year-old claimant did not follow structured conditioning program recommended by occupational therapist. The fact that the program would having been at claimant's expense was not accepted as an excuse.	*Ryan v. MHRD* (July 26, 2002), CP 19040

Not disabled (cont'd)	
The claimant admitted that she has never tried or considered any form of work after she was only 40 years old, nor has she undertaken a March of Dimes or other functional evaluation, notwithstanding a family physician's recommendation in two reports that such an evaluation would be helpful in determining a future course of gainful employment for her.	*Culp v. MHRD* (October 25, 2002), CP15328
The applicant's physical symptoms were aggravated by his obesity.	*McKerrow v. MHRD* (August 31, 2001), CP 15306
The 317-pound applicant's back problems would have been mitigated greatly if he had committed to a weight loss and exercise program 12 years previously.	*Lombardo v. MHRD* (July 23, 2001), CP 12731
The applicant with pacemaker was not reducing her weight, which may not have any bearing on her shoulder and arm problem, and was making no effort to seek lighter duty employment or follow any exercise regime.	*Saran v. MHRD* (October 12, 2001), CP 13048
The applicant's back ailment had the prospect of improvement with treatment, but she had not followed through with the physiotherapy made available to her. Nor was the applicant referred to other resources that could have assisted her such as a pain management clinic or vocational rehabilitation assessment, or to a physician or rheumatologist who may have helped.	*German v. MHRD* (August 1, 2001), CP 11005
The applicant's failure to take medications to ease the pain is not reasonable and must be treated as a negative factor.	*Eddy v. MHRD* (July 20, 1998), CP 5253
The applicant did not comply with the advice of a specialist to lose weight and exercise.	*Smaha v. MHRD* (January 22, 1997), CP 4643
The applicant was obese and a smoker, although suffering from chronic obstructive pulmonary disease.	*Smith v. MHRD* (May 29, 1998), CP 5068
The applicant's failure to attend four appointments to determine whether surgery is an option amounted to an unreasonable refusal to accept what could be a remedy for his disabilities.	*Wilganowski v. MHRD* (August 28, 2000), CP 10857
The applicant declined to do any of the following recommended actions: (1) trigger-point injections; (2) attempt to lose weight, quit smoking and exercise; (3) attend a pain clinic program; and (4) cease to abuse alcohol.	*Picard v. MHRD* (June 10, 1998), CP 5939

(H) Workers' Compensation Scheme

The fact that a provincial workers' compensation board determined that the specific injury was not compensable was irrelevant, since the CPP does not make it a condition that the disability be work-related.	*Halvorsen v. Canada (Minister of Human Resources Development)*, 2004 FCA 377

(I) Refusal To Look for Alternative Work

The issue as to whether the claimant attempted to find alternative work or lacked motivation to do so was clearly a relevant consideration in determining whether his disability was "severe".	*Klabouch v. Canada (Social Development)*, 2008 FCA 33
Applicant should not be penalized for attempting to do the only kind of work that he knew in light of his continued hope that his condition would improve.	*C.D. v. MHRSD* (July 22, 2011), CP 27430 (PAB)

Claimants seeking CPP disability benefits are expected to show meaningful effort to find other employment to suit their skills and limitations and follow recommended treatment programs. Failing that, they are obliged to provide reasonable explanations or be disentitled.	*M.C. v. MHRSD* (October 10, 2010), CP 26420 (PAB)
Claim denied Claimant MBA was 39, mother of young children, and previously worked in senior management and product development. She suffered migraines and pelvic pain. She had various ailments leading to pain, but all were treatable. No evidence of claimant's attempts to find work.	*M.C. v. M.S.D.* (July 8, 2011), CP 26647 (PAB)
Claimant voluntarily stopped working two years before MQP because "she could not handle the workload", with no mention of her subsequent medical complaints of memory loss and heart problems; claimant made no attempt to obtain other employment.	*Canada (Attorney General) v. Ryall,* 2008 FCA 164
64-year-old former bus driver suffering from visual impairment. Claimant admitted he could get a job doing something that does not require driving, however he is receiving disability benefits from his insurer; and if he got another job he would lose those benefits, which he could not afford to do at his age. The Board noted that his decision not to look for work was understandable; it is clear that he is not incapable of regularly pursuing any substantially gainful occupation.	*G.H. V. MHRSD* (January 28, 2009), CP 25623 (PAB)
Claim allowed Minister unsuccessfully argued that if applicant had attempted to retrain in lighter sedentary work before the MQP instead of continuing hard labour, he might not be so severely limited by his back pain.	*C.D. v. MHRSD* (July 22, 2011), CP 27430 (PAB)

Part V. Factors Extrinsic to the Applicant's Health

(A) General Principles

The hypothetical occupations that must be considered cannot be divorced from the particular circumstances of the applicant, such as age, education level, language proficiency and past work and life experience. The mandatory requirement under s. 68 of the CPP Regulations that applicants supply the Minister with information related to their education level, employment background and daily activities means that such "real world" details are indeed relevant to a severity determination made in accordance with the statutory definition in s. 42(2)(a)(i). "Employability" is not a concept that easily lends itself to abstraction, and occurs in the context of commercial realities and the particular circumstances of an applicant. The statutory test for severity requires an air of reality in assessing whether an applicant is incapable regularly of pursuing any substantially gainful occupation. This does not mean that everyone with a health problem who has some difficulty finding and keeping a job is entitled to a disability pension. Claimants still must be able to demonstrate that they suffer from a "serious and prolonged disability" that renders them "incapable regularly of pursuing any substantially gainful occupation". Medical evidence will still be needed as will evidence of employment efforts and possibilities. Cross-examination will be available to test the veracity and credibility of the evidence of claimants and others.	*Villani v. Canada (Attorney General),* 2001 FCA 248

The reference to "the hypothetical occupation" in *Villani* makes it clear that what is relevant is any substantially gainful occupation having regard to the individual's personal circumstances, but not whether real jobs are available in the labour market. "Evidence of employment efforts and possibilities" refers to the capacity of an individual to be employed in any substantially gainful occupation, and not to whether, in the context of the labour market, it is possible to get a job.	*MHRD v. Rice,* 2002 FCA 47
While the case of *Villani* may have changed the landscape to some extent, the onus is still on the applicant to prove his or her claim.	*Keddy v. MHRD* (September 11, 2001), CP 15005
The "real world" approach should also consider that many applicants for disability pension are not disabled as defined in the CPP but consider that they are entitled, however trifling their complaint, to a disability pension under the Plan, because "as they have paid into the Plan they are entitled to a payment out."	*Maritsa v. MHRD* (December 11, 2001), CP 13197
Where the true cause of the claimant's inability to return to work was his failure to make greater effort between the time of his accident and his MQP, there is no need to make an in-depth "real-world" analysis of the constraints on the claimant's capacity to return to the work force by his educational level, language proficiency and past work or life experience.	*Doucette v. MHRD,* 2004 FCA 292
Failure of the PAB to cite the *Villani* decision or conduct its analysis in accordance with the *Villani* principles is an error of law. That the claimant's mobility problems were aggravated by fatigue and she would have to alternate sitting and standing; making her performance of a sedentary office or related job problematic was the "real world" context required to be considered by *Villani.*	*Garrett v. Canada (Minister of Human Resources Development),* 2005 FCA 84
One must not assume that every applicant who is theoretically capable of doing sedentary work is capable of substantially gainful employment. One must look at the whole person in his or her situation to effectively apply the real world test. It was a reasonable inference to draw that a person who had shown a good work ethic, performing heavy labour over a 30-year period, would not sit idly at home if he could possibly work.	*Ronald v. MSD,* (June 8, 2005), CP 21909 (PAB)
Not disabled A 49-year-old female health care aide with Grade 12 education was suffering from back pain.	*Miller v. MHRD* (September 28, 2001), CP 13707
A 55-year-old garbage truck striker with Grade 5 education was suffering from arthritis and back and knee problems.	*Kelly v. MHRD* (November 12, 2001), CP 17219
A 50-year-old female factory worker with disc herniation that had resolved was deconditioned and longer able to do heavy lifting.	*Lainas v. MHRD* (February 5, 2002), CP 13644
A 42-year-old shipper/handler with Grade 8 education was suffering dizziness and blackouts from heart problems, ultimately requiring pacemaker. Applicant was no longer able to drive or work around machinery, but was not taking steps to retrain.	*Keddy v. MHRD* (September 11, 2001), CP 15005
A 50-year-old hotel housekeeper with elementary school education was suffering pain in right forearm.	*Maritsa v. MHRD* (December 11, 2001), CP 13197
A 47-year-old computer word processor was suffering constant pain in neck and upper spine areas after motor-vehicle accident.	*Griffiths v. MHRD* (November 1, 2001), CP 16610

Disability Case Table

81

Disabled	
A 60-year-old construction worker with Grade 8 education was suffering from arthritis and chronic pain.	*Zoldy v. MHRD* (November 27, 2001), CP 15071
A 60-year-old immigrant machine adjuster had multiple muscle, spinal disc, vision and hearing problems as a result of many injuries. The applicant was making strong efforts to retrain.	*Villani v. MHRD* (February 12, 2002), CP 19801
A 51-year-old female ambulance attendant with Grade 12 education was suffering various muscle pains and depression.	*Vacon v. MHRD* (March 11, 2002), CP 17596
A 43-year-old female manual labourer with lower back pain was unable to return to previous job involving heavy lifting, and unable to sit for long periods of time; while there may well be certain tasks or occupations which the applicant could perform for short periods of time, it was unrealistic to expect that any employer would hire her knowing that attendance would be irregular, that she would be in pain and taking much medication, and would require bed rest for indeterminate periods.	*Heisler v. MHRD* (September 12, 2001), CP 13450
A 50-year-old immigrant logger with limited English skills was suffering from arthritis and slipped disc.	*Hedar v. MHRD* (October 3, 2001), CP 15326

(B) "Real World" Employability — The *Leduc* Approach

Note: the *Leduc* approach was adopted by the Federal Court of Appeal in *Villani*.

An applicant may be determined to be disabled for CPP purposes, while in an abstract and theoretical sense, there may exist the possibility that he or she could perform some unspecified form of substantially gainful employment despite the handicaps under which he or she suffers. The applicant lives in the real world, peopled by real employers who are required to deal with the realities of commercial enterprise. The question is whether it is realistic to postulate that, given the applicant's well-documented difficulties, any employer would even remotely consider engaging the applicant.	*Leduc v. MNHW* (June 29, 1988), CP 1376 CEB & PG ¶8546
It is necessary to consider the total person and the combined disabilities, mental and physical, for cumulative effect. Where the applicant is a "slow learner" with a "learning deficit" or a "learning disability", thereby making retraining a very remote possibility or indicating that retraining would not be useful at all, he or she is at a considerable occupational disadvantage.	*Bennett v. MNHW* (October 22, 1993), CP 2549 CEB & PG ¶8690
Even where the applicant admits that she might at very limited times be capable of modest and limited sedentary work, the question remains as to who would hire her.	*Osachoff v. MHRD* (July 7, 1997), CP 5635 CEB & PG ¶8684
Some of those special and restricted circumstances present in *Leduc* and the decisions following *Leduc* are as follows: (1) a total disability depending on combined conditions both medical and non-medical and somewhat complicated in nature;	*Crossett v. MEI* (May 8, 1996), CP 3377 CEB & PG ¶8618

(2) a limitation on the possibility of control of those combined conditions — the difficulty of that control; (3) a formal restriction on driving an automobile as opposed to voluntary relinquishment; (4) there being some "unspecified" form of substantial gainful employment, as opposed to a number of specified gainful employments; (5) an unqualified acceptance of symptoms by certain medical witnesses and Board members; (6) a conflict of opinion between medical specialists and the family doctor, with the family doctor being considered in a better position to assess the applicant; (7) the consideration of slow learning and learning disability; and (8) the disability applicant being well motivated.	
The "person in respect of whom the determination is made" under s. 42(2)(*a*)(i) is the applicant. It may be unrealistic to suggest that the applicant could be retrained to perform light work in light of his age, work history and limited education.	*Whynot v. MHRD* (September 21, 2000), CP 13536
While a claimant may have legitimate potential as an artist, in the "real world" individuals must find the means to sustain themselves in a practical way if they do not have the financial means to "follow their dreams". One does not always have the luxury of pursuing their employment of choice.	*Kaminski v. MSD*, 2008 FCA 225
Before the Board can consider the "real world" context of *Villani*, it must be satisfied that the Appellant suffered from a serious and prolonged disability at MQP.	*Eng v. MSD* (October 22, 2007), CP 24980 (PAB)

(C) Learning Deficits

Disabled	
Limited intellectual ability and physical limitations made employment, at an unskilled level, impossible.	*Austin v. MEI* (May 17, 1995), CP 3311
The applicant's functional illiteracy made him unfit for retraining for non-physical work compatible with his physical limitations.	*Daly v. MEI* (August 11, 1994), CP 2919 CEB & PG ¶8564
The applicant's low IQ, failure to complete Grade 8 and psychological make-up rendered him untrainable for light work.	*King v. MEI* (April 5, 1995), CP 2941
Not disabled	
Although the applicant was functionally illiterate, retraining does not have to be directed to academic skills. The applicant could still develop manual skills.	*Noiles v. MEI* (October 27, 1995), CP 3417

(D) Socio-Economic Factors and Availability of Jobs

Socio-economic factors, such as labour market conditions in the community where the applicant resides, are irrelevant in determining whether the applicant is disabled. What is relevant is any substantially gainful occupation having regard to the individual's personal circumstances, but not whether real jobs are available in the labour market. Other legislation such as the *Employment Insurance Act* is directed at helping individuals to cope with the fluctuations in the labour market. The disability provisions are not a supplementary employment insurance scheme.	*MHRD v. Rice,* 2002 FCA 47
Section 42(2)(*a*)(i) refers to the capability of the individual to regularly pursue any substantially gainful occupation and not to labour market conditions. The PAB is bound by the *Rice* decision in this respect.	*Canada (Minister of Human Resources Development) v. Angheloni,* 2003 FCA 140
Obiter: The words of s. 42 (2)(*a*)(i) refer to the capability of the individual to regularly pursue any substantially gainful occupation. They do not refer to labour market conditions. There is other legislation such as the *Employment Insurance Act* which is directed at helping individuals to cope with the fluctuations in the labour market. By contrast, the purpose of the *Canada Pension Plan* is to provide individuals who have been disabled in accordance with the words of that Act with a disability pension because they are incapable of regularly pursuing any substantially gainful employment. The disability provisions are not a supplementary employment insurance scheme. There is no suggestion in *Villani* that socio-economic considerations such as labour market conditions are relevant in a disability assessment.	*Canada (Minister of Human Resources Development) v. Harmer,* 2002 FCA 321
While it is the capacity to work that predominates and not the availability of work in the job market, displacement of a contributor to another locality other than his residence may be too demanding and impractical in the context of the "real world".	*Deschamps v. MHRD* (November 18, 2002), CP 1703
While evidence of employment opportunities and job search efforts may be helpful in determining the claimant's degree of functional impairment, the statutory inquiry flowing from s. 42(2) is focused primarily upon the functional capacity of an individual and not upon the particular job market.	*Buckley v. MHRD* (November 29, 2001), CP 15265
The "real world" may be one of substantial unemployment, even for persons whose work capacity is unrestricted. While cognizance may be taken of the current economic realities, the proper application of the CPP does not involve an evaluation of the likelihood of an individual finding a particular type of employment in a particular location, but requires an assessment of the capability of the individual to regularly pursue any substantially gainful occupation.	*Wolfe v. MEI* (May 16, 1994), CP 3028
Not disabled Claimant suffering from lower back pain was 58 years old with a grade 11 education and lived in a small community in Newfoundland. Light and sedentary work was likely possible, and one thing keeping claimant from working was difficulty of getting a job in such a small town.	*L.R. v. MHRSD* (April 8, 2013), CP 28783 (PAB)
Fish plant worker with grade 8 education in small town having neck and back pain. Claimant returning to work before second injury occurring.	*Cox v. MHRD* (September 25, 2002), CP 18941
Claimant with two masters degrees and working as teacher and superintendent having bowel irregularities exacerbated by two accidents, chronic back pain, a bilateral carpal tunnel syndrome; claimant burned bridges by suing local school board, but unwilling to move to other municipality.	*Deschamps v. MHRD* (November 18, 2002), CP 17036

The applicant's difficulties were caused by the market's failure to provide the kind of jobs that he had the capacity and the training to fill, not by his lack of capacity to engage in a substantially gainful occupation.	*Lanthier v. MHRD* (October 24, 2000), CP 08141
Lack of job opportunities is not a factor.	*Sisson v. MHRD* (January 8, 2001), CP 11238
Discrimination against epileptics in the workplace is not covered by the CPP.	*Stubb v. MHRD* (November 16, 1998), CP 4734
Applicant was living in a small rural community.	*Wolfe v. MEI* (May 16, 1994), CP 3028

Disabled	
It would be unrealistic to expect a 44-year-old with Grade 7 education, who had always lived in the same small community with his family, to leave the area and relocate to a larger centre where he might find some sedentary employment that would accommodate his physical limitations.	*Smith v. MSD* (September 26, 2007), CP 24972 (PAB)

(E) Benevolent or Flexible Employer

The Government of Canada's website sets out a "Canada Pension Plan Adjudication Framework" in order to assist CPP decision makers interpreting and applying CPP s. 42(2). This document explains that individuals who are working for a "benevolent employer" could still be considered severely disabled under subparagraph 42(2)(a)(i), even if they work regular hours and receive income that is considered "substantially gainful." A "benevolent employer" is someone who will vary the conditions of the job and modify their expectations of the employee, in keeping with her or his limitations. The demands of the job may vary, the main difference being that the performance, output, or product expected from the client are considerably less than the usual performance output or product expected from other employees. This reduced ability to perform at a competitive level is accepted by the benevolent employer and the client is incapable regularly of pursuing any work in a competitive workforce. Work for a benevolent employer is not considered to be an "occupation" for the purposes of eligibility or continuing eligibility for a CPP disability benefit. There is no requirement under the CPP that the Minister prove that an employer is not benevolent in order to cease benefits. Rather, the burden lies on the Minister to prove on a balance of probabilities that the claimant has ceased to be disabled and thus that the requirements of s. 42(2)(a) were no longer met. Whether an individual's employer is benevolent is but one factor to be considered in determining whether or not an individual is incapable regularly of pursuing any substantially gainful occupation.	*Atkinson v. Canada (Attorney General),* 2014 FCA 187
It is not reasonable to expect the applicant to find a supportive employer with a flexible work schedule or productivity requirement in today's competitive marketplace.	*MHRD v. Bennett* (July 10, 1997), CP 4757 CEB & PG ¶8690

It is difficult, at best, to decide a disability case when the circumstances are such that the capacity to work is predicated upon a flexible work environment and an understanding employer. The Board has tended, in all appropriate cases, to not impose upon an applicant for benefits the burden of earnestly seeking employers possessed of these qualities to an exceptional degree.	*Chaisson v. MHRD* (July 14, 1998), CP 4821
Example situations Despite serious physical handicaps, the claimant attended work at least 70% of the time and there was no evidence of any complaints or disciplinary action because of missed time. While the claimant received some help from her coworkers and husband, she was able to perform the essential tasks of her job without assistance. Her work was productive and there is no evidence to suggest that her employer was dissatisfied with her work performance or experienced hardship from the accommodations made. Her employer was not benevolent as she did have the ability to perform at a competitive level and there was no evidence that the work expected from her was considerably less than the work expected from other employees.	*K. A. v. Minister of Human Resources and Skills Development,* 2013 SSTAD 6, affirmed *Atkinson v. Canada (Attorney General),* 2014 FCA 187
With respect to a 63-year-old man with grade 12 education and limitations in reading, writing and communicating who did a variety of physical and low paying jobs through his work life, it was unrealistic to expect the claimant to perform any jobs suggested by a Job Focus Assessment done for WCB or any form of substantially gainful sedentary employment. He would require a benevolent employer who would be prepared to put up with his occasional absences due to his health problems. CPP s. 42(2)(a) is concerned with the capacity of an applicant to work in a meaningful and competitive work environment. It cannot be said to be so if an employer may have to make accommodations by creating a flexible work environment to enable him to have a job that he would not otherwise be able to perform in a normal competitive work environment and to put up with occasional absences from work.	*L.F. v. MHRSD* (October 5, 2010), CP 26809 (PAB)
Claimant was disabled where he had been looking for work, but required controlled employment environment and employers refused to hire persons with chemical sensitivities.	*MSD v. Ridley* (August 23, 2007), CP 25040 (PAB)
Claimant's employer accommodated her disabilities and allowed her to work from 7-20 hours per week as a nurse's aid for $15/hr. Claimant was not disabled for CPP purposes.	*MSD v. Olsen* (October 26, 2006), CP 23908 (PAB)

Part VI. Evidentiary Issues

(A) Credibility of Claimant

Determining whether CPS is disabling is a difficult process, and comes down to the genuineness of what are strictly subjective symptoms. A judgment call as to credibility must be made on a case-by-case basis.	*Densmore v. MNHW* (June 2, 1993), CP 2389
It is important for the applicant to attend and testify at the hearing so that a proper assessment of his or her claim can be made. This is particularly true of CPS claims, even where none of the treating physicians expressed doubt as to the genuineness of the complaints. Failure to testify in person, unless adequately explained, will weigh heavily in the balance against genuineness of the claim.	*Di Caro v. MHRD* (April 24, 1997), CP 4068
An adverse inference could be drawn where claimant was present at the hearing, but did not testify. The PAB was justified in drawing inference that his evidence would have been unfavourable to his case.	*Gay v. MSD* (May 30, 2006), CP 22774 (PAB)
An adverse inference could be drawn where neither the applicant's spouse nor child testified to fill gaps in the evidence regarding the applicant's earnings following the onset of the disability.	*Dinas v. MHRD* (April 25, 1997), CP 4024
To meet the onus on them to prove disability, applicants usually choose to testify before the Board instead of relying exclusively on the medical reports. Oral testimony may usefully address issues such as the applicant's daily routine, the extent to which he or she can drive, what alternative employment has been sought, whether the applicant has been employed since the accident or whether the applicant is now gainfully employed.	*Montilla v. MHRD* (November 28, 2000), CP 06657
In a case where credibility looms large, it would be exceptional if, in spite of the lack of objective findings and testing, the applicant were able to satisfy the onus on the basis of documentary evidence alone. A court is not prevented from assessing credibility by the fact that the applicant requires an interpreter to testify, although it is not the ideal situation.	*Duhra v. MHRD* (January 21, 1998), CP 5021
It is not the function of the Board to "rubber stamp" medical opinions, and they must be weighed against oral testimony.	*Morley v. MEI* (November 1995), CP 3296 CEB & PG ¶8592
The oral testimony of the applicant can be, and very often is, material to the resolution of the matter. If deemed credible, it is entitled to due weight and serious consideration.	*Pettit v. MHRD* (April 1998), CP 4855 CEB & PG ¶8711
The fact that the applicant was receiving regular Employment Insurance benefits was telling against her credibility.	*B.R. v. MHRSD* (December 12, 2011), CP 27675 (PAB)
The PAB was impressed that the applicant alleging chronic back pain stood through most of the hearing, and did not turn head without turning entire body.	*D.D. v. MHRSD* (February 16, 2011), CP 27150 (PAB)

Where it appeared that the claimant had knowingly withheld important information or evaded answering truthfully questions asked of her by the various medical and professional persons who attended on her, considerable doubt was cast on the reliability of the assessments.	*Taylor v. MHRD* (October 2, 2001), CP 11966
The Board drew an adverse inference against the claimant when a medical witness had observed the claimant walking to the hearing with a normal gait and noted that the claimant had not appeared to be in physical discomfort while giving evidence.	*Sidhu v. MHRD* (December 7, 2001), CP 12198
There was an inconsistency in the answers given in the application questionnaire describing problems and limitations that did not reflect the near helpless condition the applicant described in her daily life at the Board hearing.	*Jagnandan v. MHRD* (November 1, 2001), CP 13436
The Board could not adopt the Review Tribunal's finding that the applicant was a very credible witness where, without explanation, the applicant had not appeared or testified before the Board although represented by counsel. The Board can only base its decision on the evidence presented to it and not on the evidence presented before the Review Tribunal.	*MHRD v. Taylor* (November 6, 1996), CP 3918

(B) Minister's Witnesses

Ministry doctors are requested to complete and submit a summary of their proposed evidence at the hearing.	Letter from Chairman of Board to Legal Services (November 12, 1997)
It is the practice of the Ministry to give the applicant notice that it will be calling a medical doctor as an expert witness to clarify the reports. This should be done at the time the Ministry files its appeal or reply. While the Rules are silent on last minute filing, as a matter of fairness the medical summary should state the doctor's area of expertise and should be filed and sent to the other party at least 10 days prior to the hearing. Where this is not done, the Board may exclude the evidence of the Ministry doctor.	*MHRD v. Pestawka* (January 4, 2002), CP 09228

The purpose of s. 68(2) of the CPP Regulations is to enable the Minister to require a pension applicant to submit to a special examination and to supply such reports as the Minister deems necessary for the purpose of determining the disability of that person. This is not a barrier to the adducing by the Minister of expert evidence from a medical witness who has not personally examined the applicant. Section 16(1) of *The Pension Appeals Board Rules of Procedure (Benefits)*, which expressly authorizes the panel to "summon before it by subpoena any person and require him to give evidence on oath and to produce such documents as it deems requisite", provides the PAB with ample authority to require the testimony of the Ministry's doctor at the hearing. Where the applicant had been previously informed that the purpose of the Ministry's doctor was to assist the panel in the interpretation of the medical record, this did not require that the doctor confine his or her testimony to that of interpreting the reports of the applicant's medical advisors or that he or she would not suggest for the PAB's consideration possible alternative employment for the applicant in the labour market.	*Spears v. Canada* (Attorney General), 2004 FCA 193
The proposed evidence of the Minister's expert witness will be admitted where it satisfied the four preconditions set out by the Supreme Court of Canada in *R. v. Mohan* of relevance, necessity, absence of an exclusionary rule, and qualification. The determination of whether the benefits of admissibility outweigh its cost can be done after the medical expert testifies at the appeal hearing. This could be done in a *voir dire* or after presentation of the evidence.	*E.G. v. Minister of Human Resources and Skills Development* (April 7, 2014) CP 29099 (SSTGD)
Knowledge of the evidence of an expert witness to be called by the Minister in advance is of obvious benefit to the applicant's counsel in preparing the case for presentation. Particularly where the applicant's counsel has made a specific written request for some sort of account of the evidence to be produced orally by an expert, it is not unreasonable to expect a responsive reply to be forthcoming prior to the hearing.	*Grandy v. MEI* (June 13, 1996), CP 3827
An adjournment may be granted to permit the applicant to review a summary of the Ministry doctor's proposed opinion evidence.	*Leone v. MHRD* (June 9, 1997), CP 5080
A Ministry doctor can testify in a province where he or she is not licensed to practice.	*Nitska v. MHRD* (October 25, 2000), CP 10867
The Minister's witness should be permitted to respond to new issues raised by a physician called by the claimant, and to answer the contradictions between the physician's testimony and his report. The usual practice before the Board is that experts are frequently, if not routinely, allowed to give testimonial evidence that goes beyond their reports.	*Canada (MHRD) v. Cantwell*, 2006 FCA 75

Disability Case Table

(C) Medical Reports for Claimant

Little weight is to be given to the psychiatric reports that display the appearance of a lack of objectivity and risk impinging the expert's credibility. By crossing the line from treating psychiatrist to advocate for his patient he does not really assist his patient, in fact he has the potential to hurt his patient's claim.	*R.D.G. v. Minister of Human Resources and Skills Development* (December 17, 2013) CP29131 (SSTGD)
While use of statutory wording in a medical report provides greater certainty, it is not essential if compliance with the statutory requirements has clearly been shown.	*Chehade v. MHRD* (November 14, 2000), CP 14165
Expert medical opinion pointing to a residual capacity to work is to be accorded great respect, particularly if the contrary medical opinion has little in the way of clinical finding or objective basis to support it.	*MHRD v. Warrick* (August 13, 1996), CP 4568 CEB & PG ¶8642
A family physician of long standing probably knows the patient best and an astute family physician, having a broad understanding of the patient's history and overall condition, will usually be able to say whether that person's complaints are feigned or exaggerated.	*Hunter v. MSD* (February 6, 2007), CP 23431 (PAB)
Questions remained where the applicant's family physician filed an affidavit but did not appear to be examined on it.	*Bell v. MHRD* (December 13, 2000), CP 12664
Little weight should be given to reports of general practitioners where: (a) the reports are plainly intended to influence outcome of appeal; (b) the authors of the reports are not called to testify and therefore be subject to examination; and (c) the reports do not substantively link the applicant's medical condition to the claimed disability.	*Correia v. MHRD* (November 27, 2000), CP 14447
Even if sworn, documents containing information about an applicant's recent condition and giving some background to a medical report in the record are not normally admissible on an application for judicial review.	*Gaudet v. Canada (Attorney General)*, 2013 FCA 254

Where a letter written after the MQP by the family physician stated that the claimant was incapable of a full day's work, it was reasonable to draw the inference that she was capable of part-time employment and that her medical condition was thus not "severe" within the meaning of the CPP.	*Ferreira v. AGC,* 2013 FCA 81
Where the family doctor's report and clinical notes contained some evidence to support his opinion and he was in the best position to make an overall assessment of the applicant's physical capacity, the family doctor was not an advocate for his patient.	*MHRSD v. A.B.R.* (April 2, 2009), CP 26100 (PAB)
The treating physician's evidence should be given little weight where he failed to relate the incapacity of the applicant to the MQP time frame.	*Pavicic v. MHRD* (August 31, 2000), CP 11123
The Board can only respond to the medical and other evidence put before it. Applicants should provide helpful chronological medical evidence going as far back in time as possible. This will enable the Board to have a complete and accurate medical picture.	*Dorion v. MHRD* (December 21, 2000), CP 10672
Where medical reports (in this case from the family doctor) are missing, clinical and physical findings will be given less weight.	*Pereira v. MHRD* (April 11, 1997), CP 425
An occupational therapist, while not a physician, is highly qualified to express an opinion in his or her area of expertise.	*Ryan v. MHRD* (July 26, 2002), CP 19040

(C.1) Conflicting Medical Reports

It is often the case that the medical evidence is not entirely *ad idem* and not entirely clear one way or the other. Failure to specifically refer to a letter written by the claimant's physician did not constitute a reviewable error, where the PAB in its reasons had alluded to the claimant's argument regarding the subject matter of the letter.	*Klabouch v. Canada (Social Development),* 2008 FCA 33
The PAB must be vigilant in assessing the documentary evidence of a family doctor, especially one who did not testify at the hearing, where there are *indicia* that his required and expected neutrality has been lost. (per concurring judgment of Létourneau J.A.)	*MHRD v. Angheloni,* 2003 FCA 140

Disability Case Table

91

The family physician in attempting to assist a patient who is seeking a disability pension may go beyond the role of a medical advisor and become an advocate for the claim and, in so doing, diminish the credibility of the evidence. The family doctor's statement that the claimant would "never be able to be gainfully employed again, because of his significant arthritic problems" was not accepted where it was not supported by pre-MQP clinical evidence.	*Williams v. MHRD* (January 29, 2004), CP 18713
Where the preponderance of the evidence contained in 30 medical reports was that disability was not "severe" so as to prevent claimant from working, this very considerable body of apparently credible evidence could not be rejected without explanation.	*Canada (Minister of Human Resources Development) v. Quesnelle,* 2003 FCA 92
Where the applicant's family physician of 20 years also serves as advocate on his behalf in the proceedings, the family physician's evidence is cast in a certain light, which may result in a reduction of its weight.	*Bent v. MHRD* (October 13, 2000), CP 11659
There is no rule that the Board will favour a specialist opinion over the opinion of a family physician. Whether to accept opinion of family doctors and specialist doctors is a matter of weighing all the evidence. The opinions of specialist and family physicians are to be considered in concert with diagnosis and prognosis of the family physician determining the nature and cause of the disability and to be verified or otherwise by reference to specialist. Differences are a matter of relative probity.	*Brown v. MEI* (March 8, 1996), CP 3778 CEB & PG ¶8605
Some family physicians are notorious for the loyal support of their patient's subjective claims, often taking on the mantle of advocacy to the detriment of their objectivity.	*Calamusa v. MHRD* (November 22, 1999), CP 07709
A determination of disability must be grounded on objective medical findings. The unsupported opinion of even a highly qualified specialist will not be accepted, particularly where it runs counter to the opinions of the two other equally eminent medical specialists. This position is supported by the provisions of s. 68(1)(*a*) of the Regulations.	*Cameron v. MHRD* (August 15, 1996), CP 4448
Opinions of specialists that do not rule out the applicant's return to the work-force are usually preferred to those of the family doctor which preclude return.	*Cantwell v. MHRD* (October 4, 2000), CP 10073
The family physician's assertion that the applicant was completely disabled, not only contradicted the opinion of specialist doctors who had examined the applicant thoroughly, but did not provide the positive reinforcement to the applicant that she required to be functional. A specialist concluded that the applicant needed to be convinced that her diagnosis was not disabling and that it was not going to cause her to be crippled.	*Dempsey v. MHRD* (May 8, 1997), CP 4078

A family physician is not a "specialist".	*Mejia v. MHRD* (August 30, 1996), CP 05587
A general practitioner refers patients to the specialists because the latter have the experience and knowledge of a particular disease not possessed by the general practitioner. Where there is a conflict of opinion, the opinions of the specialists are preferred save for exceptional circumstances. See also:	*Nicoletti v. MHRD* (May 7, 1999), CP 05587 CEB & PG ¶8770 *Talsma v. MHRD* (April, 1999), CP 07366
Preference may be given to the opinion of the applicant's family physician over that of the many specialists who only saw the applicant for between 20 and 50 minutes.	*Barlow v. MNHW* (November 22, 1991), CP 07017
The considered opinion of recognized medical and rehabilitation experts was preferred to the opinion of the applicant's family physician.	*Doyle v. MHRD* (May 6, 1997), CP 4864

(C.2) Medical Reports Prepared by Other Parties

The SST could review reports prepared by medical professionals retained through the claimant's WCB process whose stated opinions were supported by objective medical evidence. There was no reason to disregard these reports based on a bald allegation of bias.	*J.T. v. Minister of Human Resources and Skills Development,* 2013 SSTAD 9

(D) Requirement for / Definition of "Objective Medical Evidence"

1. Generally

A claimant must provide some objective medical evidence of his or her disability.	*Warren v. Canada(A.G.),* 2008 FCA 377
It is unclear what is meant by "objective" medical evidence. It might refer to X-ray, lab tests, or other clinical evidence. Or "objective" medical evidence might be opposed to the subjective evidence given by the claimant. His or her suffering, however, is not an element on which the test of "disability" rests. The PAB must be satisfied that the claimant suffers from disabilities which, in a "real world" sense, render him or her incapable of regularly pursuing any substantially gainful occupation.	*MHRD v. Angheloni,* 2003 FCA 140

Medical evidence will still be needed as will evidence of employment efforts and possibilities.	*Villani v. Canada (Attorney General),* 2001 FCA 248
The above statement in *Villani* confirms that it is still generally necessary to have objective medical evidence.	*Vega v. MHRD* (February 13, 2002), CP 13999
There have been cases in which evidence tendered by the applicant and his or her supporting witnesses was not only highly credible, but also equally highly persuasive, which called upon the Board to exercise its judicial capacity and function, thereby refusing to abdicate its decision-making role to the medical profession.	*Martin v. MHRD* (August 10, 2001), CP 14001
While objective medical evidence is helpful and greatly assists the Board in its determination of disability, the CPP does not make a finding of disability conditional on "objective evidence". The applicant usually gives oral testimony at a Board hearing. The subjective experiences of the applicant in regard to the pathology, with resulting consequences on his or her ability to engage in regularly substantially gainful occupation, are important considerations.	*MHRD v. Chase* (November 5, 1998), CP 6540
To make a determination that a disability is severe and prolonged, it must first be found that there is a clear and definite cause and effect relationship between the symptoms complained of and the disability, based on clinically objective medical findings. See also:	*Evangelou v. MEI* (March 5, 1996), CP 992 CEB & PG ¶8602 *MacKinnon v. MHRD* (June 9, 1999), CP 06919
The CPP does not restrict entitlement to a disability pension to those who furnish objective medical evidence of their conditions.	*Hounsell v. MHRD* (September 18, 2000), CP 10061
Notwithstanding a lack of objective evidence presented by the applicant, the totality of the evidence must be considered and undue emphasis should not be placed on its absence.	*Osachoff v. MHRD* (July 7, 1997), CP 5635 CEB & PG ¶8684
It is exceptional to accept subjective evidence that conflicts with objective evidence.	*Pearson v. MNHW* (August 10, 1993), CP 2614
All of the evidence must be considered in making a determination as to disability. Objective medical evidence supporting a finding of disability is not an absolute requirement.	*Reilly v. MHRD* (May 7, 1999), CP 08741

2. Particular Diseases

The condition of fibromyalgia is difficult to prove by objective findings.	*Arthurs v. Canada (Minister of Social Development),* 2006 FC 1107
Chronic pain cannot be proven by objective evidence and there is no medical test that can measure pain or take a picture of pain, and the main evidence that must be relied on is subjective evidence or the claimant's verbal description of his pain. The statutory criteria for a disability claim do not require proof to the level of objective medical evidence.	*G.B. v. MHRSD* (May 27, 2010, CP 26475 (PAB)
It is generally accepted that "whiplash" or soft-tissue accident injuries produce little objective evidence. Medical practitioners are therefore dependent on the subjective evidence of the patient.	*Simon v. MSD* (December 10, 2007), CP 24556 (PAB)
In the absence of objective evidence of a cause for chronic pain, the Board is inclined to regard the claimant's medical history with skepticism. However, the absence of evidence from the many specialists who examined the claimant to suggest that the claimant is malingering or exaggerating the pain, or of a psychogenic overlay or hysterical reaction which might explain the complaints of pain in the absence of objective evidence of injury, lends considerable weight and credence to the claimant's medical history.	*Gobeil v. MHRD* (July 9, 2001), CP 09864
Resolution of chronic pain cases depends upon the view ultimately taken of the reality of what are strictly subjective symptoms. The judgment call made generally without the assistance of objective clinical signs will be one of credibility on a case-by-case basis as to the severity of the pain complained of. It is incumbent upon the person who applied for benefits to show that treatment was sought and efforts were made to cope with the pain. As a result, it will be desirable although by no means essential in all cases, that evidence of a psychiatric or psychological or physiatric nature be adduced from the medical practitioners who have experience and general expertise in this difficult area of medicine.	*MNHW v. Densmore* (June 2, 1993), CP 2389 CEB & PG (TB) 8508
Ordinarily the Board will not be satisfied with subjective evidence alone to prove the existence of CPS. There is the additional difficulty of having to rely almost totally on subjective evidence to determine that the pain is so severe that it prevents the applicant from regularly pursuing any substantially gainful occupation.	*Walsh v. MHRD* (October 4, 2000), CP 08755
While corroborating evidence may be particularly useful in determining whether the applicant's alcoholism is disabling, it may not always be necessary. Oral evidence adduced by the applicant, either personally or on his behalf, may well be equally important and possibly overriding. Both objective and subjective evidence must be reviewed, considered and analyzed, with equal deliberation given to each category in determining its relative probative effect.	*Smallwood v. MHRD* (July 20, 1999), CP 09274 CEB & PG ¶8800

3. Effect of s. 68 of CPP Regulations

Section 68(1)(*a*) of the CPP Regulations supports the adoption of medical reports which include medical findings. The opinion of a specialist without supporting medical findings will not be accepted.	*Cameron v. MHRD* (August 16, 1996), CP 4448
Section 68 requires medical reports and medical findings. Oral testimony is not a sufficient basis for grounding a determination of disability.	*Dean v. MHRD.* (October 23, 1996), CP 3686
Section 68 requires evidence on the "nature, extent and prognosis of the impairment and the findings upon which the diagnosis and prognosis were made". The determination must be made on the basis of cogent medical evidence pertaining to the nature, extent and prognosis of the impairment, based on actual clinical finding, as opposed to only subjective testimony.	*Holliday v. MHRD* (October 23, 1996), CP 3959 CEB & PG ¶8661
In view of s. 68, it is only on rare occasions that an applicant will be determined eligible in the absence of such reports.	*Vukcevic v. MHRD* (November 22, 2000), CP 10947
It cannot be the case that before reviewing an application, there is an onus on the Ministry to obtain whatever evidence is available from the family doctor or any specialist listed in an application or prior application, whether or not it is filed by the claimant, to explain the CPP to the claimant, and to tell the claimant what information is missing from his or her file, including whether the claimant should file additional evidence. If there was such an onus, then the fact that the CPP Regulations put the burden of proof on the claimant would have no meaning.	*Jones v. Canada (Attorney General),* 2010 FC 740
The Minister has clear legislative authority under s. 68(1)(*a*) and (2) of the Regulations to require a claimant to provide medical information and submit to a medical examination "from time to time". The fact that information and consents were given previously at the initial stage of the claim does not mean that as the claim moves through the successive stages of review, more current information cannot be sought by the Minister. Consents given originally may be time limited on their face and have expired. Information furnished in earlier stages is necessarily dated, and newer and current developments in the physical and mental health of a claimant for disability benefits may well shed light on whether the claimant was, at the relevant time when she met the MQP, suffering from a "severe and prolonged" disability.	*Zhang v. Canada (Attorney General),* 2012 FC 808

(E) Other Public and Private Disability Plans

The criteria and issues for entitlement under Ontario workers compensation legislation are different from those under s. 42(2)(*a*) of the CPP. A workers compensation award for pain did not assist the claimant in a subsequent claim for CPP disability benefits, particularly where it could be inferred from documentation in the claimant's workers compensation file that she never wished to make a good-faith effort to obtain employment.	*R.T. v. MHRSD,* (April 2, 2009), CP 24572 (PAB)
A statement by a private insurer that the claimant should work as a taxi dispatcher was not determinative where there was no evidence that the claimant had any training as a dispatcher or operator or that she was familiar with the area in which she would have to work or with the marketing strategies of the taxi company and its policies. There was no indication that the taxi company would have hired her and trained her.	*Leduc v. MSD* (August 21, 2007), CP 23800 (PAB)
The fact that the claimant had been approved for a disability pension under the U.S. Social Security system was not in itself proof of qualification under the CPP. Under the U.S. system, once a claimant has demonstrated that she lacks the residual functional capacity to perform the requirements of any past relevant work, the burden shifts to the Social Security Administration to show that there are other jobs that the claimant can perform. There is no such shifting burden under the CPP.	*Butler v. MSD* (April 27, 2007), CP 21630 (PAB)
The fact that the claimant is qualified for and is receiving disability benefits under a private insurance plan is not relevant. The provisions of other public and private plans for disability pensions or other similar periodic payments vary from those of the CPP. The legislation rules that determine eligibility for a disability pension under the CPP are strict and inflexible. The threshold for a disability pension under the Plan is a high and stringent one, perhaps one of the highest, if not the highest, in any such legislation in North America.	*Heller-Pereira v. MHRD* (May 26, 2004), CP 18522
Reasonable inferences regarding the apparently dramatic deterioration of the applicant's condition prior to the hearing since his last examination may be drawn from the fact that the applicant was receiving maximum compensation under private plan for his disability and the CPP appeal was launched at the insurer's initiative. The insurer would reduce the private benefit payable to the applicant by the amount of the CPP disability pension payable.	*MNHW v. Brown* (April 21, 1989), CP 1501
Other public and private insurance disability plans/pensions besides the CPP do exist and their requirements vary. Although the CPP rules are strict and inflexible and the threshold is a high and stringent one, it is not an insurmountable threshold.	*R.S. v. Minister of Human Resources and Skills Development* (December 17, 2013) CP 29025 (SSTGD)

Disability Case Table

97

(F) Employment Insurance (EI)

Where claimant received regular EI benefits in three years post-MQP, this was a factor in concluding that claimant was not disabled, in addition to the lack of medical records prior to the expiry of the MQP and the fact that she worked post-MQP.	*M.R. v. MHRSD* (September 17, 2010), CP 26904 (PAB)
Term of claimant's retirement package was that she was considered "laid off" and was to apply for EI benefits to continue until her full retirement date. This required her to assert regularly that she was "capable of and available for work" by virtue of section 18 of the *Employment Insurance Act*. Claimant understood this and was able to return to her former job if it had become available.	*D.W. v. MHRSD* (April 15, 2011), CP 26887 (PAB)
Unemployment insurance (now EI) benefits payments received during the period in which the applicant claimed to be disabled can be considered, although they are not conclusive as to whether the degree of disability required by CPP has been met. However, they can also raise serious questions of credibility on the part of the applicant.	*MHRD v. Bruneau* (April 24, 1997), CP 3865
A disability pension should not be denied based on false claims to EI that the applicant was able to work. It is but one factor that is assessed for credibility.	*MHRD v. LeBlanc* (September 27, 1996), CP 4093
The fact that the applicant was receiving regular Employment Insurance benefits was telling against her credibility.	*B.R. v. MHRSD* (December 12, 2011), CP 27675 (PAB)
Unemployment insurance benefits are an indication that the applicant was "ready, able and willing to work" at the relevant time. See also:	*Gall v. MEI* (June 18, 1996), CP 3567 *G.L. v. MHRSD* (May 19, 2011), CP 26973 (PAB)
It was permissible for the applicant to have collected employment insurance benefits while agreeing to undergo EI-sponsored retraining after the onset of the alleged disability. She had disclosed her back injury to EI, and her disability made her unable to complete the training course. (Note: The Board stated that the applicant did not have to certify that she was ready, willing and able to work during the training period, which is incorrect.)	*Maranda v. MHRD* (October 12, 2000), CP 11202
The applicant receiving regular EI benefits in three years post-MQP was a factor in finding she was not disabled in addition to the lack of medical records prior to the expiry of the MQP and the fact that she worked post-MQP.	*M.R. v. MHRSD* (September 17, 2010), CP 26904 (PAB)

The Review Tribunal and Board expressly placed no weight on the applicant's statement to EI that he was "ready, able and willing to work", but found no disability on other grounds.	*Taylor v. MHRD* (July 4, 1997), CP 4436
By accepting regular EI benefits and submitting the required bi-weekly declarations of capability for work, the applicant was not, until the end of EI benefits, incapable regularly of pursuing substantially gainful occupation. To say that it is common practice for UI applicants to make knowingly false declarations cannot be used as justification for doing so in any particular case.	*Williamson v. MNHW* (January 26, 1978), CEB & PG ¶8747

(G) Post-MQP Diagnosis

Reports indicating a sharp deterioration in the claimant's condition after the MQP did not constitute new facts; existing condition just became more acute.	*Gilroy v. Canada (Attorney General)*, 2010 FCA 302
Where MQP ended six years prior to hearing date, PAB should not put too much emphasis on improvement in claimant's condition before hearing, and not give sufficient weight to medical reports contemporaneous with MQP expiry which indicated permanent disability.	*Cochran v. Canada (Attorney General)*, 2003 FCA 343
Evidence referred to in a report was relevant where it was based on a consultation by the claimant during the MQP, although the report itself was issued after the MQP.	*Toris v. Canada (Attorney General)*, 2003 FCA 231
The MQP date must have some meaning. The claim should be denied where many of the medical problems arose after MQP, caused at least in part by injuries from a motor vehicle accident six months after MQP, and there was evidence of work capacity and a complete lack of efforts to find work at MQP.	*Khalida, Alvi v. HRSD* (December 12, 2007), CP 25289 (PAB)
Contributor diagnosed with bipolar disorder approximately five years after MQP, but evidence indicated that contributor had been suffering from effects of the disorder prior to MQP.	*MHRSD v. J.R.* (February 6, 2009), CP 25889 (PAB)
Post-MQP diagnosis of MS and report that this would have caused walking difficulties going back 10 years did not warrant reversing original denial of claim; report not giving opinion on claimant's condition or ability to work as of MQP; there was nothing that solidly connected a diagnosis of MS to a loss of ability to work.	*J.K. v. MHRSD* (May 20, 2009), CP 25953 (PAB)
Although symptoms of fibromyalgia had appeared during the MQP, a definitive post-MQP diagnosis of fibromyalgia did not qualify the claimant for a disability pension where she was still gainfully employed even after the expiry of her MQP.	*Dillen v. MSD*, (June 6, 2006), CP 22581 (PAB)

Disability Case Table

99

Having risk factors for a stroke prior to MQP (diabetes and high blood pressure) which resulted in having a post-MQP stroke did not mean the claimant was disabled at MQP.	*Hilkemich v. MSD,* (December 12, 2005), CP 22395 (PAB)
Judicial review was denied where the fresh evidence presented by the claimant was new medical reports which only related to post-MQP condition.	*Ellis v. Canada (Minister of Social Development),* 2006 FCA 250
The mere fact that someone continues to work after the MQP expires should not automatically preclude entitlement to a disability pension. The person must be commended, not discouraged, for making an effort to remain financially self-supporting.	*Stanziano v. MHRD* (November 26, 2002), CP 17926
A letter from a family physician describing claimant's condition resulting from motor vehicle accident many years before when claimant was not his patient at time and he had no clinical records relating to such injuries was not accepted.	*Andrews v. MHRD* (June 20, 2002), CP 17788
While a new diagnosis voiced $3^1/_2$ years after MQP constituted fresh evidence, the diagnosis did not suggest that the claimant had disease at the relevant time.	*MacRae v. MHRD* (October 2, 2002), CP 19741
Letters of physicians written three years after MQP, indicating that the claimant's fibromyalgia had markedly restricted her from performing most activities for the last five years and diagnosing new conditions, did not meet the materiality test for new evidence.	*Spiece v. MHRD* (April 7, 2003), CP 19047
Even if it could be determined that the applicant had a disease 14 years before it was diagnosed (in this case, Parkinson's), the test is whether the applicant had been disabled by the disease at that earlier time. The fact that the applicant's business was not successful, was not sufficient indication of disability under the CPP.	*Braam v. MHRD* (June 9, 1998), CP 5413
If events subsequent to the onset of disability, such as the applicant's return to work, can be considered for the purpose of confirming a prognosis that a disability was not prolonged, subsequent events may also be examined to determine if an initially favourable prognosis was incorrect. Although the applicant at the time of her emergency surgery was expected to regain her health, that had not happened.	*MEI v. Gaspich* (April 13, 1994), CP 2592 CEB & PG ¶8539

(H) Subsequent Earnings

The fact of earnings after the MQP is only one piece of evidence to be weighed with all the other evidence respecting disability, and does not necessarily preclude a determination of disability.	*St. Gelais v. MEI* (September 13, 1994), CEB & PG ¶8558
Applicant returned to employment and reported earnings of some $10,000 and $38,000 following expiry of MQP, despite diagnosis of fibromyalgia and chronic fatigue.	*Miller v. Canada (Attorney General),* 2007 FCA 237

(I) Window Period

In a window situation, what must be decided is whether there is evidence that the applicant became, after the Review Tribunal hearing and before the MQP, incapable regularly of pursuing any substantially gainful occupation.	*H.D. v. MHRSD* (December 7, 2011), CP 23992 (PAB)
A window period should begin at the date of the Review Tribunal hearing, not the date the reasons are delivered. The period of a window should not depend upon the speed with which a Review Tribunal delivers its decision. The reasons for the decision relate to the evidence presented at the hearing, and not to a claimant's condition at the date the decision is issued.	*Candelaresi v. MSD* (February 21, 2005), CP 21406 (PAB)
Date of hearing was appropriate starting date for five months window; however no new disability arose during the window period and there was no evidence that the claimant became disabled during that period.	*M.M. v. MHRSD* (April 2, 2009), CP 20545 (PAB)

Disability Case Table

Canada Pension Plan

Table of Contents

Canada Pension Plan

R.S.C. 1985, c. C-8, as amended by R.S.C. 1985, c. 6 (1st Supp.), in force January 1, 1985; R.S.C. 1985, c. 41 (1st Supp.), s. 12, in force June 28, 1985; R.S.C. 1985, c. 5 (2nd Supp.), ss. 1 and 2 in force February 13, 1986, except s. 1(1), proclaimed in force January 1, 1987; R.S.C. 1985, c. 13 (2nd Supp.), proclaimed in force December 11, 1986; R.S.C. 1985, c. 27 (2nd Supp.), proclaimed in force July 23, 1986; R.S.C. 1985, c. 30 (2nd Supp.), ss. 1 to 60 and 62, except ss. 45 and 46, proclaimed in force January 1, 1987, ss. 45 and 46 proclaimed in force December 31, 1991; R.S.C. 1985, c. 18 (3rd Supp.), proclaimed in force July 2, 1987; R.S.C. 1985, c. 38 (3rd Supp.), in force December 17, 1987; R.S.C. 1985, c. 1 (4th Supp.), in force February 4, 1988; R.S.C. 1985, c. 46 (4th Supp.), in force September 13, 1988; R.S.C. 1985, c. 51 (4th Supp.), ss. 9, 25 and 30 in force January 1, 1991; S.C. 1990, c. 8, in force February 1, 1992; 1991, c. 14, in force March 15, 1991; 1991, c. 44, ss. 1 to 14, 16 to 19, 23 to 26 and 28 in force January 27, 1992, s. 15 in force June 1, 1993, ss. 20 to 22 and 27 in force January 1, 1992, ss. 34 and 35 in force December 13, 1991; 1991, c. 49, ss. 203 to 215 in force December 17, 1991; 1992, c. 1, ss. 23 to 25 in force February 28, 1992; 1992, c. 2, s. 1 in force June 26, 1992, s. 2 in force February 28, 1992; 1992, c. 27, s. 90 in force February 28, 1992; 1992, c. 48, s. 28(1) in force January 1, 1993; 1993, c. 24, in force June 10, 1993; 1993, c. 27, in force June 10, 1993; 1994, c. 13, s. 8(1)(a), in force May 12, 1994; 1994, c. 21, ss. 123 and 124, in force June 15, 1994; 1995, c. 33, in force July 13, 1995, except ss. 16, 25, 35(1) and (3), 36(1), 39 and 42 in force January 1, 1997; 1996, c. 11, in force July 12, 1996, except ss. 49(2) and 101(a); 1996, c. 16. ss. 60, 61, in force July 12, 1996; 1996, c. 23, ss. 187(a), 189(c), in force June 30, 1996; 1997, c. 40, ss. 58 to 99, assented to and in force, with exceptions, December 18, 1997[1]; 1998, c. 19, ss. 251 to 256 in force June 18, 1998; 1999, c. 17, ss. 111 and 112, assented to April 29, 1999 and in force November 1, 1999; 2000, c. 12, ss. 42 to 65, assented to June 29, 2000 and in force, with exception, July 31, 2000[2]; 2000, c. 14, ss. 45 and 46, assented to June 29, 2000[3]; 2000, c. 30, s. 155, in force October 20, 2000; 2001, c. 4, s. 67, in force June 1, 2001; 2001, c. 17, s. 254(1) in force June 14, 2001; 2002, c. 7, s. 111, assented to March 27, 2002 and in force April 1, 2003; 2002, c. 8, s. 121 and 182(1)(f), assented to March 27, 2002 and in force July 2, 2003; 2003, c. 5, assented to April 3, 2003[4]; 2003, c. 22, ss. 129-130, in force April 1, 2005; 2004, c. 22, ss. 15-24, in force January 31, 2005, except subsection 18(1), which is deemed to have come into force on March 18, 2003; 2004, c. 25, ss. 111-113, in force December 15, 2004; 2005, c. 35,

---

[1] Sections 58, 59, 61, 69 to 71, 76, 74, 77(1), 81, 83, 92 to 94 and 96 to 98 came into force on January 1, 1998. Sections 89 to 91 came into force on April 1, 1998.

[2] Note: section 65 amends only the French version of the Act.

[3] Section 46 of Bill C-32, *An Act to implement certain provisions of the budget tabled in Parliament on February 28, 2000*, came into force with part of the Act on June 29, 2000. Section 45 came into force on January 31, 2001, pursuant to SI/2001-19. Note: Subsection 46(1) specifically states that subsection 114(2) of the *Canada Pension Plan* does not apply in respect of the amendments to that Act contained in this Act.

[4] The following sections of Chapter 5 came into force April 1, 2004: ss. 1–3, 4(2), 5(1), (2), (4), (6), (8), (9) and (11), 6, 7, and 9(2); all remaining sections, except section 8 (ss. 4(1) and (3), 5(3), (5), (7) and (10), 9(1) and (3), 10, and 11) come into force three years after April 1, 2004, the date section 19 came into force. Section 8 came into force April 1, 2008, four years after April 1, 2004, the date section 19 came into force. The following are transitional provisions, in force April 1, 2004:

(continued on next page)

ss. 45-48, 50-52, 66 and 67 in force October 5, 2005; 2005, c. 38, s. 138, effective December 12, 2005; 2005, c. 47, s. 137, in force September 18, 2009; 2007, c. 11, assented to May 3, 2007, and most sections in force with exceptions[5]; 2008, c. 28; 2009, c. 31[5.1]; 2010, c. 12, s. 1668-1669, in force March 16, 2012; 2010, c. 25, s. 70, in force December 15, 2010; 2011, c. 24, s. 172-175, deemed in force January 1, 2006; 2012, c. 19, s. 226, 230(2), and (3), 233, 234, 251, and 253 to 262, in force June 29, 2012; s. 225, 227 to 229, 230(1), 231, and 232 in force April 1, 2013; s. 292 to 295, 305, 306, 694(a)(i) to (ix), 695(1)(a)(i), and (ii) in force March 1, 2013; 2012, c. 31, s. 193, 194, and 197 to 203 in force on December 15, 2012; 2013, c. 33, s. 155 in force June 26, 2013; 2013, c. 40, s. 236(1)(*b*), 237(1)(*b*), and 238(1)(*b*) in force December 12, 2013.

An Act to establish a comprehensive program of old age pensions and supplementary benefits in Canada payable to and in respect of contributors.

Short Title

1. *Short title* **— This Act may be cited as the** *Canada Pension Plan.*

(continued from previous page)

Sec. 19. Transfer of securities to the Board — (1) On the first day of each month after the coming into force of this section, $1/36$ of the right, title or interest of the Minister of Finance in each security that was purchased by the Minister under section 110 of the *Canada Pension Plan*, and that is held by that Minister on the first day of the first month following the coming into force of this section, is transferred to the Canada Pension Plan Investment Board established under section 3 of the *Canada Pension Plan Investment Board Act* ("the Board").

(2) *Transfer of replacement securities* — If a security referred to in subsection (1) is replaced within the 36-month period beginning on the first day of the first month following the coming into force of this section,

    (*a*) the Board is deemed to have acquired a right, title or interest in the replacement security in the same proportion as the right, title or interest it had acquired in the security being replaced; and

    (*b*) on the first day of each month after the day on which the replacement security is purchased, for each month then remaining in the 36-month period, an equal portion of the right, title or interest of the Minister of Finance in the replacement security is transferred to the Board, so that the replacement security is fully transferred to the Board on the same day as the security that it replaced would have been fully transferred.

(3) *Rights extinguished* — If a security referred to in subsection (1) is redeemed during the 36-month period referred to in subsection (2) and is not replaced, any right, title or interest of the Board in the security is extinguished.

[5](1) Subsection 114(2) of the *Canada Pension Plan* does not apply in respect of the amendments to that Act contained in sections 2, and 12 to 14 of this Act. (2) Sections 2, and 12 to 14 of this Act came into force March 3, 2008. (3) Subsection 4(2), sections 6 and 7, subsection 28(2) and sections 32 and 33 of this Act come into force on a day or days to be fixed by order of the Governor in Council (S.C. 2007, c. 11, s. 39).

[5.1]Subsection 114(2) of the *Canada Pension Plan* does not apply in respect of the amendments to that Act contained in S.C. 2009, c. 31, ss. 25 to 42 (S.C. 2009, c. 31, s. 43(1).) Sections 30 and 31, subsection 32(2) and sections 33, 34, 41 and 42 in force September 1, 2010; sections 25 to 29, 32(1) and 35 to 40 in force January 1, 2012.

———————— **Notes** ————————

Case Law

§1. Purpose of CPP

Granovsky v. Canada (MEI), [2000] 1 S.C.R. 703

The CPP was designed to provide social insurance for Canadians who experience a loss of earnings owing to retirement, disability, or the death of a wage-earning spouse or parent. It is not a social welfare scheme. It is a contributory plan in which Parliament has defined both the benefits and the terms of entitlement, including the level and duration of an applicant's financial contribution.

Del Zotto v. Canada, [1999] 1 S.C.R. 3

The CPP is a compulsory social insurance scheme enacted in 1965 in order to provide contributors and their families with reasonable minimum levels of income upon the retirement, disability or death of contributors.

Miceli-Riggins v. Canada (Attorney General), 2013 FCA 158

Social benefits legislation, like the CPP, is aimed at ameliorating the conditions of particular groups. However, social reality is complex: groups intersect and within groups individuals have different needs and circumstances, some pressing, some not so pressing depending on situations of nearly infinite variety. Accordingly, courts should not demand that legislation must always correspond perfectly with social reality in order to comply with s. 15(1) of the Charter. Distinctions arising under social benefits legislation will not lightly be found to be discriminatory. The CPP is not a general social welfare regime intended to bestow benefits upon all. It is not supposed to meet everyone's needs. Instead, it is a contributory plan that provides partial earnings replacement in certain technically defined circumstances. It is designed to be supplemented by private pension plans, private savings, or both. It cannot even be said that the CPP is intended to bestow benefits upon demographic groups of one sort or another. Instead, it is best regarded as a contributory-based compulsory insurance and pension scheme designed to provide some assistance — far from complete assistance — to those who satisfy the technical qualification criteria. Like an insurance scheme, benefits are payable on the basis of highly technical qualification criteria. Based on personal circumstances, some can make contributions, others not. Benefits are paid from direct contributions of employees, employers, and monies earned from the investment of contributory funds not required to pay current benefits. As a general matter, the quantum of benefits under the Plan is related to earnings. Like most insurance schemes, over time some contributors get significant benefits and can say they got their money's worth in terms of benefits received. Others, due to their personal circumstances, can contribute for years and get little in return. Far from providing universal welfare benefits, writ large, the CPP provides six specific benefits: retirement pension, disability pension, death benefits, survivor's pension, disabled contributor's child benefits, and benefits for the child of a deceased contributor. What's more, the CPP was never intended to meet all the needs of persons receiving those benefits, but rather was designed to provide only partial benefits.

Canada v. Bear, 2003 FCA 40

The CPP was deliberately designed as a universal, mandatory, pension scheme to which, with few exceptions, anyone 18 years of age or over would have to contribute if they had taxable income. There was no provision for individuals to opt-in. Those with taxable income who were excluded were defined by categories, such as employees of foreign or provincial governments. In the latter case, while it was thought inappropriate and probably unconstitutional to impose pension contributions on provincial governments (their property being immune from taxation by section 125 of the *Constitution Act, 1867*) provision was made for provincial governments to agree to inclusion of their employees and this was in fact what happened. The underlying principle was that coverage would be universal or determined by such categories without regard to personal choice. This was no doubt important actuarially to the success of the scheme as it was, and remains, self-sustaining, wholly dependent on contributions and investment revenue. It cannot be supplemented by money from general revenues found in the Consolidated Revenue Fund.

Canada Pension Plan

Layden v. HRSD, 2008 FC 619

The scheme of the CPP is intended to allow for inexpensive and informal access to timely pension benefits adjudication.

MHRD v. Kirby (November 27, 2001), CP 17189 (PAB)

The CPP is primarily intended as a source of income payable to qualified contributors during their lifetime. Its purpose is to assure a reasonable level of income to those in retirement, their immediate survivors, and to those who become disabled. The CPP is not a vehicle for the accumulation of assets or the enhancement of estates.

Mazzotta v. Canada (Attorney General), 2007 FCA 297

The CPP contains adjudicative and review mechanisms and a process designed to provide an easy, flexible and affordable access to these mechanisms.

Taylor v. MSD (August 18, 2006), CP 22241 (PAB)

The CPP is a legislated compulsory income replacement social insurance program to provide Canadians with a reasonable level of income upon retirement, disability, and death of a wage earner. Benefits under the CPP would hopefully be supplemented by *OAS (Old Age Security)* pension, private and public pensions, and investments and savings. The CPP cannot provide help to all and it was never intended to meet all of the needs of all Canadians.

Tan v. MSD (December 8, 2006), CP 20525, 22316, 22452, 22453, 23253 (PAB)

The CPP was not intended to provide all the retirement or survivors' income individuals might wish to have. It is a basic support vehicle that is meant to be supplemented by other means of individual choice such as savings and private pension plans. It is not a social welfare scheme.

§2. Constitutionality

Kroeker v. MNR (1969), 69 D.T.C. 380 (T.A.B.)

It was entirely within the jurisdiction of the federal Parliament to enact the CPP, particularly in light of the constitutional amendment adding s. 94A, which gave it the right to make laws in relation to old age pensions and supplementary benefits without affecting the operation of any present or future law of a provincial legislature in relation to any such matter. The CPP does not violate the Canadian Bill of Rights. While failure to apply for a Social Insurance Number does not relieve an individual from liability to make contributions called for by the CPP, the CPP lays down a system of appeals for employers or employees affected by its provisions.

Harris v. MHRSD, 2009 FCA 22

Eligibility for benefits under the CPP, and other social benefit programs, inevitably involves the somewhat arbitrary drawing of lines in complex schemes involving the balancing of competing interests. Hence, courts have been reluctant to conclude that Parliament has drawn those lines at constitutionally impermissible points. In order to ensure that Parliament has sufficient room to manoeuvre, courts should not define at too high a level of generality the legislative purpose underlying a particular benefit. The CPP is a self-funded, contributory, and compulsory social insurance program, in which the period of insured coverage is related to the date when a contributor ceases to pay premiums. A program aimed at all parents who leave employment to care for a child with a disability, for a maximum of another 12 years, would constitute such an extension of the period of coverage that the program would be qualitatively different from the one enacted.

§3. Interpretation

Villani v. Canada (Attorney General), [2001] FCA 248

The CPP is benefits-conferring legislation. It must be interpreted in a large and liberal manner, and any ambiguity in the language of provisions conferring benefits should be resolved in favour of the claimant for such benefits.

MHRD v. Woodcock (October, 2000), CP 14202 (PAB)

It is a well established principle of statutory interpretation that statutes should be interpreted in a manner which avoids absurd results.

Interpretation

2. *Definitions* — **(1) In this Act,**

"applicant" **means, in Part II,**

    (*a*) **a person or an estate that has applied for a benefit,**

    (*b*) **a person who has applied for a division of unadjusted pensionable earnings under section 55 or paragraph 55.1(1)(*b*) or (*c*), or**

    (*c*) **a person in respect of whom a division of unadjusted pensionable earnings has been approved under paragraph 55.1(1)(*a*); (R.S.C. 1985, c. 30 (2nd Supp.), s. 1(2).)**

"average monthly pensionable earnings" **of a person means an amount calculated in accordance with section 47 or 48;**

"balance-due day" **of a person for a year means**

    (*a*) **where the person died after October in the year and before May in the immediately following year, the day that is 6 months after the day of death, and**

    (*b*) **[6]in any other case, April 30 in the immediately following year; (S.C. 1991, c. 49, s. 203(2).)**

"basic exemption" **of a person for a year means an amount calculated in accordance with section 19;**

"beneficiary" **means a person, estate or other body to whom a benefit has become payable; (R.S.C. 1985, c. 30 (2nd Supp.), s. 1(2).)**

"benefit" **means a benefit payable under this Act and includes a pension;**

"business" **includes a profession, calling, trade, manufacture or undertaking of any kind whatever, and includes an adventure or concern in the nature of trade but does not include an office or employment;**

"common-law partner", **in relation to a contributor, means a person who is cohabiting with the contributor in a conjugal relationship at the relevant time, having so cohabited with the contributor for a continuous period of at least one year. For greater certainty, in the case of a contributor's death, the "relevant time" means the time of the contributor's death. (S.C. 2000, c. 12, s. 42(2).)**

"Consumer Price Index" **means the Consumer Price Index for Canada, as published by Statistics Canada under the authority of the *Statistics Act*;**

"contribution" **means a contribution under this Act;**

"contribution rate", **in respect of an employee, an employer and a self-employed person for a year, means the contribution rate for that employee, employer and self-employed person for the year determined in accordance with or pursuant to this Act; (R.S.C. 1985, c. 30 (2nd Supp.), s. 1(3).)**

---

[6] Pursuant to 1991, c. 49, s. 203(3), this definition is applicable after 1989.

"contributor" **means a person who has made an employee's contribution or a contribution in respect of the person's self-employed earnings, and includes a person the amount of whose earnings on which a contribution has been made for a year under this Act calculated as provided in subparagraph 53(1)(b)(i) exceeds zero and a person to whom unadjusted pensionable earnings have been attributed under section 55, 55.1 or 55.2; (R.S.C. 1985, c. 30 (2nd Supp.), s. 1(2); 2012, c. 31, s. 193.)**

"contributory period" **of a contributor has, subject to paragraph 44(2)(b) and subsection 56(5), the meaning assigned by section 49; (R.S.C. 1985, c. 30 (2nd Supp.), s. 1(2).)**

"contributory salary and wages" **of a person for a year means an amount calculated in accordance with section 12;**

"contributory self-employed earnings" **of a person for a year means an amount calculated in accordance with section 13;**

"deduct" **includes withhold;**

"disabled" **has the meaning assigned by section 42;**

"employee" **includes an officer;**

"employer" **means a person liable to pay salary, wages or other remuneration in relation to employment, and, in relation to an officer, includes the person from whom the officer receives their remuneration; (2011, c. 24, s. 172.)**

"employment" **means the state of being employed under an express or implied contract of service or apprenticeship, and includes the tenure of an office; (2011, c. 24, s. 172.)**

"excepted employment" **means employment specified in subsection 6(2);**

"maximum contributory earnings" **of a person for a year has the meaning assigned by section 16;**

"maximum pensionable earnings" **of a person for a year has the meaning assigned by section 17;**

"office" **and** "officer" **means the position of an individual entitling him to a fixed or ascertainable stipend or remuneration and includes a judicial office, the office of a minister of the Crown, the office of a lieutenant governor, the office of a member of the Senate or House of Commons, a member of a legislative assembly or a member of a legislative or executive council and any other office the incumbent of which is elected by popular vote or is elected or appointed in a representative capacity, and also includes the position of a corporation director, and** "officer" **means a person holding such an office;**

"pension" **means a pension payable under this Act;**

"Pension Appeals Board" **(Repealed by S.C. 2012, c. 19, s. 225, in force March 1, 2013.)**

"Pension Index" **has the meaning assigned by section 43;**

"pensionable employment" **means employment specified in subsection 6(1);**

"prescribed" **means**

(a) **in the case of a form or the information to be given on a form, authorized by the Minister having the control and direction of the administration of the Part of this Act to which the context extends; and** (*b*) in any other case, prescribed by regulation or determined in accordance with rules prescribed by regulation; (S.C. 1991, c. 49, s. 203(1).)

"Record of Earnings" **means the Record of Earnings established under section 95;**

"representative" **means, in respect of any person, a guardian, curator, committee, executor, liquidator of a succession, administrator or other legal representative of that person; (S.C. 2004, c. 25, s. 111.)**

"Review Committee" **(Repealed by R.S.C. 1985, c. 30, s. 1(1).)**

"Review Tribunal" **(Repealed by S.C. 2012, c. 19, s. 225, in force April 1, 2013.); (R.S.C. 1985, c. 30 (2nd Supp.), s. 1(3); 1995, c. 33, s. 25.)**

"salary and wages on which a contribution has been made" **for a year means an amount calculated in accordance with section 15;**

"self-employed earnings" **of a person for a year means an amount calculated in accordance with section 14;**

"Social Insurance Number" **means a Social Insurance Number assigned to an individual under the authority of any Act of Parliament, and "Social Insurance Number Card" means a Social Insurance Number Card issued to an individual under that authority;**

"spouse" **(Repealed by 2000, c. 12, s. 42(1)); (R.S.C. 1985, c. 30 (2nd Supp.), s. 1(3); 2000, c. 12, s. 42(1).)**[7]

"total pensionable earnings" **of a contributor means an amount calculated in accordance with section 50;**

"total pensionable earnings of a contributor attributable to contributions made under this Act" **means an amount calculated in accordance with section 78;**

"unadjusted pensionable earnings" **of a contributor for a year means an amount calculated in accordance with section 53;**

"year" **means a calendar year;**

"Year's Basic Exemption" **has the meaning assigned by section 20;**

"Year's Maximum Pensionable Earnings" **has the meaning assigned by section 18. (R.S.C. 1985, c. 30 (2nd Supp.), s. 1; 1991, c. 49, s. 203; 1995, c. 33, s. 25; 1996, c. 11, s. 95.)**

(2) *When specified age deemed to be reached* — **For the purposes of any provision of this Act in which reference is made to the reaching by a person of a specified age — other than a reference in paragraph 13(1)(*c*) or (*e*) or (1.2)(*c*), 17(*c*), 19(*c*) or (*d*) or**

---

[7] Prior to the repeal of the definition of "spouse" by 2000, c. 12, s. 42(1), effective July 31, 2000, the definition was as follows:

spouse — "spouse", in relation to a contributor, means,

   (a) except in or in relation to section 55,

      (i) if there is no person described in subparagraph (ii), a person who is married to the contributor at the relevant time, or

      (ii) a person of the opposite sex who is cohabiting with the contributor in a conjugal relationship at the relevant time, having so cohabited with the contributor for a continuous period of at least one year; and

   (b) in or in relation to section 55, a person who is married to the contributor at the relevant time;

and, in the case of a contributor's death, the "relevant time", for greater certainty, means the time of the contributor's death; (R.S.C. 1985, c. 30 (2nd Supp.), s. 1(3).)

44(3)(*a*), section 70 or paragraph 72(1)(*c*) — the person is deemed to have reached the specified age at the beginning of the month following the month in which the person actually reached that age, and in computing (S.C. 1991, c. 44, s. 1; 2009, c. 31, s. 25.)

    (*a*) any period of months ending with the time when he reached a specified age, the month in which he actually reached that age shall be included; and

    (*b*) any period of months commencing with the time when he reached a specified age, the month in which he actually reached that age shall not be included.

(R.S.C. 1985, c. 30 (2nd Supp.), s. 1; S.C. 1991, c. 44, s. 1; 1991, c. 49, s. 203; 1995, c. 33, s. 25; 2004, c. 25, s. 111; 2009, c. 31, s. 25; 2011, c. 24, s. 172; 2012, c. 19, s. 225; 2012, c. 31, s. 193.)

—————— **Notes** ——————

Synopsis

This section defines the meaning of various words and phrases used in the CPP. Subsection (2) essentially provides that for the purposes of determining the timing of the contribution requirement and benefit entitlement, a person reaches 65 at the end of the month in which he or she actually turns 65.

Recent Amendments

The term "common-law partner" is new, coming into force on July 31, 2000, and replacing the former term "spouse". The new term essentially broadens entitlement to survivor's benefits to include partners in same-sex relationships who would otherwise have qualified for benefits prior to the amendment if they had been opposite sex partners. Recent Supreme Court of Canada case law on the issue had made it obvious that to continue to exclude same-sex partners from CPP survivor benefits would not have withstood a court challenge under the *Canadian Charter of Rights and Freedoms*. However, entitlement has also been narrowed in that cohabitation for the year prior to death is now the sole basis for receipt survivor's benefits, with no special status for estranged spouses of the deceased contributor. Note that the possible ambiguity in the former definition of spouse as to whether the one-year cohabitation in a conjugal relationship must immediately precede the contributor's death has been carried over to the definition of "common-law partner".

Case Law

Contents

§1. Benefit

Mintzer v. The Queen (1998), 97-1485-IT-I (TCC)

A CPP benefit that was never actually received by the claimant, having been set off against taxes allegedly owing by the claimant in previous years, must, for income tax purposes, still be included in the claimant's income for the year.

§2. Common-Law Partner

Hodge v. MHRD, 2004 SCC 65

Section 2(1) defines the requisite common law relationship in terms of cohabitation. "Cohabitation" in this context is not synonymous with co-residence. Two people can cohabit even though they do not live under the same roof and, conversely, they may not be cohabiting in the relevant sense even if they are living under the same roof. Periods of physical separation do not end a common law relationship if there is a mutual intention to continue. Subject to whatever provision may be made in a statute, a common law relationship ends "when either party regards it as being at an end and, by his or her conduct, has demonstrated in a convincing manner that this particular state of mind is a settled one". In the context of entitlement to a survivor's pension, the definition of "spouse" [now "common law partner"] in s. 2(1) does not infringe s. 15(1) of the *Canadian Charter of Rights and Freedoms* by requiring that the partners have cohabitated for the year previous to the contributor's death. The proper comparator group for former common law partners who never married is former married spouses, and they are treated the same by the legislation.

Obiter: Until the issue of same-sex marriage is resolved, different considerations may possibly apply to gay and lesbian relationships in respect of a survivor's pension because, at least in the past, the institution of a legal marriage has not been available to them.

E.S. v. MHRSD (July 24, 2012), CP 25586 (PAB)

While cohabitation under the same roof is not determinative to decide if there was a common-law relationship in order to qualify for a survivor's pension, living under the same roof is still a significant factor to be taken into account in assessing the overall relationship. Other important factors to consider include various documents such as the income tax report, pension document, and OAS application where they declared themselves as "single" and "separated".

Brandon v. MHRD (November 30, 2001), CP 14937 (PAB)

The weight to be accorded the various elements or factors to be considered in determining whether a couple is in a conjugal relationship will vary widely and will be almost infinitive. Monogamy is not a requirement, and the existence of infidelity by one of the partners will not in itself be fatal to a finding of conjugal relationship.

Betts v. Shannon (2001), CCH CEB & PGR No. 8661, pp. 6775-6782

Cohabitation in a conjugal relationship will usually involve many of the following elements or questions, although not necessarily all of them:

1. Financial interdependence — e.g., shared bank accounts, credit cards with the same number, the acquisition and ownership of property;

2. A sexual relationship. Did the parties have sexual relations? If not, why not?

3. A common residence. Did the parties live under the same roof? Did they eat their meals together? What were their sleeping arrangements?

4. Expenses for each other on special occasions. Did the parties buy gifts for each other on special occasions?

5. A sharing of responsibilities in the running of the household. Who prepared the meals? Who washed the clothes? Who did the shopping? Who looked after the maintenance of the home?

6. A shared use of assets such as cars, boats, etc.

7. A shared responsibility in the raising of the children;

8. Shared vacations;

9. The expectation each day that there will be continued mutual dependency;

10. Each party named as beneficiary in the will of the other;

11. Each party named as beneficiary in the insurance policy of the other;

12. Where each of them kept their clothing;

13. In cases of illness, who cared for the one who was ill? Which one visited the ill one if in hospital?

14. Who had knowledge of the medical needs of the other?

15. Communications between the parties;

16. Public recognition of the parties;

17. The attitude and conduct of the community and the parties' families towards the parties, and, in the particular circumstances, the common-law relationship between the deceased and the respondent;

18. What marital status was declared by the parties on various applications, on other forms, completed by them?

19. Who took care of the deceased's funeral arrangements? Was there a funeral notice, and, if so, how were the parties described therein? Who was billed for the funeral costs? Who paid for the funeral? Who attended the funeral? Where did they sit?

Squance v. MNHW (1993), CCH CEB & PGR, No. 8523, pp. 5994-5997 (PAB)

The cessation of the sexual part of the marriage relationship does not necessarily terminate cohabitation.

Molodowich v. Penttinen (1980), 17 R.F.L. (2d) 376 (Ont. Dist Ct.). See also *M. v. H.* (1996), 25 R.F.L. (4th) 116 (Ont. C.A.), affd. (1999), 171 D.L.R. (4th) 577 (S.C.C.).

The following factors are relevant to determining whether unmarried parties are cohabiting:

1. Shelter

   ● Did the parties live under the same roof?

   ● What were the sleeping arrangements?

   ● Did anyone else occupy or share the available accommodation?

2. Sexual and Personal Behaviour

   ● Did the parties have sexual relations? If not, why not?

   ● Did they maintain an attitude of fidelity to each other?

   ● What were their feelings toward each other?

   ● Did they communicate on a personal level?

   ● Did they eat their meals together?

   ● What, if anything, did they do to assist each other with problems or during illness?

   ● Did they buy gifts for each other on special occasions?

3. Services

What was the conduct and habit of the parties in relation to:

   ● preparation of meals;

   ● washing and mending clothes;

   ● shopping;

- household maintenance; and

- any other domestic services?

4. Social

- Did they participate together or separately in neighbourhood and community activities?

- What was the relationship and conduct of each of them toward members of their respective families and how did such families behave toward the parties?

5. Societal

- What was the attitude and conduct of the community toward each of them and as a couple?

6. Economic Support

- What were the financial arrangements between the parties regarding the provision of or contribution toward the necessities of life such as food, clothing, shelter, and recreation?

- What were the arrangements concerning the acquisition and ownership of property?

- Was there any special financial arrangement between them which both agreed would be determinant of their overall relationship?

7. Children

- What was the attitude and conduct of the parties concerning their children?

McLaughlin v. Canada (Attorney General), 2012 FC 556

A decision-maker should not evaluate the *quality* of the relationship between two individuals to determine whether or not the relationship should fall within the definition of a "common-law partnership". Whether the common-law spouse had committed breaches of trust or engaged in other wrongful conduct to the detriment of the deceased was irrelevant to the person's status as a common-law spouse.

A.L. v. D.P. and MHRSD (November 16, 2011), CP 27238 (PAB)

It is not possible to establish one definition of what constitutes a conjugal relationship. Rather, keeping in mind the endlessly variable nature of marriage in our society, the circumstances of each case must be assessed to determine whether, in that specific case, the parties had a marriage-like relationship. Although it is not possible to set out factors which are determinative of the existence of a common-law relationship, it is possible to set out the following factors which do not prevent the existence of a finding of common-law relationship:

1. Involuntary separation neither terminates a conjugal relationship nor even suspends the counting of time. The mere fact that parties are not physically cohabiting does not mean that a conjugal relationship has come to an end. On the contrary, where parties are in a conjugal relationship, they can be separated for a period of time without in any way affecting the quality of that relationship. For example, one of the parties could, as a member of the military, be deployed outside of Canada for a six-month rotation; for that couple, the conjugal relationship is maintained, so long as the parties intend the relationship to continue. Obviously, when one of the parties in a conjugal relationship is in hospital, the hospital stay alone does not necessarily affect the quality of the relationship. The key to the correct characterization of the relationship is not physical cohabitation, but the intention of the parties.

2. A single residence is not necessary for a conjugal relationship.

3. Sex — In order to conclude that a relationship is "conjugal", it is not necessary to find that the putative partners had sex, or had monogamous sex.

115

Conjugal relationships are, by their nature, less formal than marriages: they do not have a clear start date as is achieved by a wedding ceremony and, more importantly for the purposes here, they have no clear termination date as is achieved by a divorce judgment. A conjugal relationship begins when the parties intend it to, and terminates when one of the parties to the relationship intends the termination. The key to deciding when a common-law relationship ends is the intention of a least one of the parties.

MHRSD v. S.S. (October 6, 2011), CP 27386 (PAB)

There can be intervals of separation, for one reason or another, without disturbing the legal status of a conjugal relationship. Separation due to an abusive relationship did not interrupt cohabitation where there was a mutual intention to continue the relationship.

MSD v. Pratt (April 11, 2006), CP 22323 (PAB)

While married couples may have almost infinite variations on a theme in their conjugal or cohabitation arrangements, they must have a core starting point, failing which the relationship dissolves to a vanishing point. The core of the relationship is that the parties have by their acts and conduct shown a mutual intention to live together in a marriage-like relationship of some permanence. If this core is absent, there can be no common-law partnership. In testing this core element, the checklist of questions posed in *Molodowich* will be of substantial help.

MSD v. Lenz (November 1, 2005), CP 23437 (PAB)

Cohabitation involves a common residence as a general rule, but each case turns on its facts. Where each party continued to reside at his or her respective residence for 18 years prior to the contributor's death, they were still common-law partners under the CPP as the relationship contained many essential elements of cohabitation in a conjugal relationship.

R.P. v. MHRSD (May 31, 2010), CP 26623 (PAB)

Cohabitation can exist where the couple was not living in the same residence due to the deceased contributor's addiction problems.

Mills v. MSD (July 27, 2005), CP 18867 (PAB)

The parties' separation for three months did not end the common-law relationship as there was a mutual intention to continue. There was no "intent" by both parties to end relationship nor, did it appear that entering a facility for medical treatment would end cohabitation.

Rogers v. MSD (December 16, 2004), CP 20699 and CP 21436 (PAB)

A common-law relationship ends when either party regards it as being at an end and, by his or her conduct, has demonstrated in a convincing manner that this particular state of mind is a settled one. While the physical separation of parties following "a fight" might, in some cases, appear to amount to an ending of a cohabitation the test should be realistic and flexible enough to recognize that a brief "cooling off" does not bring the relationship to an end. Such conduct does not convincingly demonstrate a settled state of mind that the relationship is at an end.

MSD v. Briggs (May 2, 2005), CP 22224 (PAB)

Incidents of cohabitation include varied evidence such as joint bank accounts, keys to one another's house, survivor looking after the funeral arrangements, mutual beneficiaries of life insurance, clothes at each other's home, joint financial affairs, and joint operation of the home(s).

J.H. v. MHRSD (January 5, 2012), CP 27594 (PAB)

An affair is not necessarily a common-law relationship. Where the claimant was clearly in a common-law relationship with the contributor at the time of the contributor's death, and had been carrying on an affair with the married contributor over a number of years, it must be determined at what point the common-law relationship began. While public recognition is an important factor in determining whether a common-law relationship existed, it was plausible that the contributor would want to keep his common-law relationship secret until his financial situation was resolved by divorce.

116

MHRSD v. S.S. (October 6, 2011), CP 27386 (PAB)

Although infidelity is improper conduct, it does not mean that the conjugal relationship ceases to exist. Nor did the fact that the claimant had left the house several times with their child in the course of their 15-year relationship to go to an abused women's shelter and swore an affidavit in a claim for a child support claim which contained the statement that "There is no reasonable prospect of reconciliation" derogate from the fact of a common-law relationship.

Cahoon v. Allred (September 9, 1997), CP 5556 (PAB)

Parties to a relationship who maintained their separate residences were not cohabiting, regardless of the number of times or nights they spent together. Where they did not share the use of the furnishings, had no common bank account and neither took responsibility for the other's basic living expenses, there was no common enterprise one expects when two people are cohabiting in a conjugal relationship.

Obiter. It would be wrong to place the words cohabitation in a conjugal relationship in a straightjacket, preventing their flexible application to novel and evolving situations in a changing society. But while it cannot be said in all cases that for people to cohabit, they must leave their respective residences and embark upon cohabitation in a common residence, the PAB cannot rewrite the CPP.

MHRD v. Haynes (June 28, 2001), CP 15179 (PAB)

While as a general rule, cohabitation involves a common residence, each case must be dealt with on its own specific facts. Cohabitation was found to exist although the parties maintained separate apartments a few doors apart on the same floor of their apartment building because they needed the space. The other attributes of a conjugal relationship, such as spending nights together, preparing and eating meals together, sharing household and other expenses according to ability to pay and spending their time and holidays together, and holding themselves out as a couple to society at large, were present.

Clendening v. MHRD (February 4, 2002), CP 14849 (PAB)

There can be no comprehensive definition of conjugal cohabitation beyond saying that it is a manifestation of the intention of the parties as evidenced by their social and economic interaction one with the other. Cohabitation may be found where the parties maintain separate residences, but each has the key to other's apartment and there was mutual sharing of each residence on a more or less equal basis.

Downey v. Emberley (July 12, 1995), CP 3330, CEB & PG 8580 (PAB)

Cohabitation in a conjugal relationship does not necessarily exclude residing under separate roofs, particularly if that is a temporary necessity for occupational reasons.

MNHW v. Decoux, Elaine (October 4, 1991), CP 2046, CEB & PG (TB) ¶9203 (PAB). See also *Beaudoin v. Canada (MNHW)*, [1993] 3 FC 518 (C.A.); *Siou v. MHRD* (April 16, 2002), CP 14667 (PAB).

Since s. 2 does not specifically state that the continuous period of one year must immediately precede the contributor's death, it should not be given that interpretation. (Note: Decided under former definition of "spouse".)

Crowe v. MNHW (1989), CP01808 (PAB)

"Cohabitating ... in a conjugal relationship" can be defined as the setting up of a matrimonial home together, and would involve a bilateral intention on the part of both spouses to do so living together as man and wife.

Ancher v. MHRD (1997) CP03808 (PAB)

It is doubtful any exhaustive definition of the phrase "cohabitating ... in a conjugal relationship" can be given, nor is it desirable that one is available when account is taken of the vastly differing circumstances from one case to the next.

Dilka v. Canada (Attorney General), 2009 FCA 90

The claimant and deceased were held not to have been cohabitating at the time of death where they had previously lived together for four years, but had maintained separate residences for nearly 20 years. Although there had been considerable interaction between the two since 1987, they had not held themselves out as being married or in a common-law relationship, and had described themselves to tax and social welfare authorities as "single", and not as being in a common-law relationship.

M.P. v. MHRSD (July 9, 2009), CP 26318 (PAB)

The deceased contributor's drinking and abuse made it impossible for the claimant for a survivor's pension to continue living with him. Although the claimant had regarded the deceased contributor as her common-law spouse until his death, s. 2(1) and case law requires that the parties actually cohabit and that the cohabitation be continuous for a period of at least one year immediately preceding the contributor's death for the common-law spouse to qualify for a survivor's pension.

Schwartz v. MHRD (October 29, 2002), CP 18791 (PAB)

The parties were cohabiting in a conjugal relationship although they were using both of their respective houses and vehicles where they represented themselves as such to their small social circle, and they traveled together and slept in the same bed. The parties had not set up a single common home or merged their financial affairs because the deceased was still in the throes of divorcing his wife.

§3. Contributions

Kroeker v. MNR (1969), 69 D.T.C. 380 (T.A.B.)

Payments made by contributors are defined as contributions under s. 2, and are not in the nature of a "tax".

§4. Employment Status

(a) The English Definition

Stevenson Jordan and Harrison, Ltd. v. MacDonald and Evans (1951), T.L.R. 101 (C.A.). See also *Wiebe Door Services Ltd.* (1986), 87 D.T.C. 5025 (Fed. C.A.)

Under a contract of service, a person is employed as part of the business and his or her work is done as an integral part of the business. Under a contract for services, the work, although done for the business, is only accessory to it, not integrated into it.

Market Investigations, Ltd. v. MSS, [1968] 3 All E.R. 732. See also *Moose Jaw Kinsmen Flying Fins Inc. v. MNR,* (1988), 88 D.T.C. 6099 (Fed. C.A.)

The fundamental test to be applied is this: "Is the person who has engaged himself to perform these services performing them as a person in business on his own account?" If the answer to that question is "yes", then the contract is a contract for services. If the answer is "no", then the contract is a contract of service. No exhaustive list has been compiled and perhaps no exhaustive list can be compiled of considerations which are relevant in determining that question, nor can strict rules be laid down as to the relative weight which the various considerations should carry in particular cases. The most that can be said is that control will no doubt always have to be considered, although it can no longer be regarded as the sole determining factor. Factors which may be of importance, are matters such as whether the man performing the services provides his own equipment, whether he hires his own helpers, the degree of financial risk be taken, the degree of responsibility for investment and management he has, and whether and how far he has an opportunity of profiting from sound management in the performance of his task. The application of the general test may be easier in a case where the person who engages himself to perform the services does so in the course of an already established business of his own. However, this factor is not decisive, and a person who engages himself to perform services for another may well be an independent contractor even though he has not entered into the contract in the course of an existing business carried on by him.

(b) Leading Canadian Cases

671122 Ontario Ltd. v. Sagaz Industries Canada Inc., [2001] S.C.J. No. 61, 2001 SCC 59

The Market Investigations approach is approved. The central question is whether the person who has been engaged to perform the services is performing them as a person in business on his own account. In making this determination, the level of control the employer has over the worker's activities will always be a factor. However, other factors to consider include whether the worker provides his or her own equipment, whether the worker hires his or her own helpers, the degree of financial risk taken by the worker, the degree of responsibility for investment and management held by the worker, and the worker's opportunity for profit in the performance of his or her tasks. The above factors constitute a non-exhaustive list, and there is no set formula as to their application. The relative weight of each will depend on the particular facts and circumstances of the case. [Note: This was a tort case dealing with the vicarious liability of the employer.]

Precision Gutters Ltd v. Canada (Minister of National Revenue), [2002] FCA 207

After the Supreme Court of Canada's decision in Sagaz, the central question to be decided is whether the person who has been engaged to perform the services is performing them as a person in business on his own account or is performing them in the capacity of an employee. In order to make this determination the four criteria set out in Wiebe Door are factors to be considered. While the "integration test" is not to be completely rejected, it could be difficult to apply. The ability to negotiate the terms of a contract entails a chance of profit and risk of loss in the same way that allowing an individual the right to accept or decline to take a job entails a chance of profit and risk of loss. The court must approach the analysis from the perspective of the alleged employees, and not of the employers.

Wolf v. Canada, [2002] FCA 96

Great weight may be given to how the parties viewed their relationship.

Per Décary J.A.: In an era of globalization, when a worker decides to keep his or her freedom to come in and out of a contract almost at will, when the hiring person wants to have no liability towards a worker other than the price of work and when the terms of the contract and its performance reflect those intentions, the contract should generally be characterized as a contract for services. Specific factors include lack of job security, disregard for employee-type benefits, freedom of choice and mobility concerns.

Royal Winnipeg Ballet v. Canada (Minister of National Revenue), 2006 FCA 87

Wolf does not stand for the proposition that the parties' contractual description of their legal relationship is to be treated as a kind of tie-breaker. If it is established that the terms of the contract, considered in the appropriate factual context, do not reflect the legal relationship that the parties profess to have intended, then their stated intention will be disregarded.

Wiebe Door Services Ltd. (1986), 87 D.T.C. 5025 (Fed. C.A.)

The case law has established a series of tests to determine whether a contract is one of service or for the provision of services. While not exhaustive, the following are four tests most commonly referred to:

1. The degree or absence of control exercised by the alleged employer.

2. Ownership of tools.

3. Chance of profit and risks of loss.

4. Integration of the alleged employee's work into the alleged employer's business.

The test is not fourfold, as it is often described as being, but rather a four-in-one test with emphasis always retained on the combined force of the whole scheme of operations, even while the usefulness of the four subordinate criteria is acknowledged. It is a general, over-arching test, which involves examining the whole of the various elements that constitute the relationship between the parties. In using the test to determine the character of the relationship the four

119

tests should be combined and integrated in order to seek out the meaning of the whole transaction.

The organization test, espoused in *Stevenson Jordan and Harrison, Ltd.* (previously mentioned), produces entirely acceptable results when properly applied. That is, when the question of organization or integration is approached from the persona of the "employee" and not from that of the "employer," because it is always too easy from the superior perspective of the larger enterprise to assume that every contributing cause is so arranged purely for the convenience of the larger entity. It is with respect to the business of the employee in asking the question: "Whose business is it?"

The fact of mutual dependency between the "employer" and the contractor is not determinative of the issue. If the businesses of both parties are so structured as to operate through each other, they could not survive independently without being restructured. While that is a consequence of their surface arrangement, it is not necessarily expressive of their intrinsic relationship.

1392644 Ontario Inc. (Connor Homes) v. Canada (National Revenue), 2013 FCA 85

The ultimate question to determine if a given individual is working as an employee or as an independant contractor is deceivingly simple. It is whether or not the individual is performing the services as his own business on his own account. Since the trend in the workforce for the past few years has been toward increased outsourcing and short-term contracts, this question has taken on added importance, and has led to much litigation in the Tax Court of Canada. The test, though simple in theory, is often very difficult to apply with any degree of certainty, in part due to the specific nature of the question and the variability of the ever-changing workplace. Alongside the test as set out in *Wiebe Door* and *Sagaz*, in the past few years another jurisprudential trend has emerged that affords substantial weight to the stated intention of the parties. *Royal Winnipeg Ballet* stands for the proposition that what must first be considered is whether there is a mutual understanding or common intention between the parties regarding their relationship. Where such a common intention is found, be it as independent contractor or employee, the test set out in *Wiebe Door* is then to be applied by considering the relevant factors in light of that mutual intent for the purpose of determining if, on balance, the relevant facts support and are consistent with the common intent. The approach set out in *Royal Winnipeg Ballet* simply emphasizes the well-known principle that persons are entitled to organize their affairs and relationships as they best deem fit. The relationship of parties who enter into a contract is generally governed by that contract. Thus the parties may set out in a contract their respective duties and responsibilities, the financial terms of the services provided, and a large variety of other matters governing their relationship. However, the legal effect that results from that relationship, i.e., the legal effect of the contract, as creating an employer-employee or an independent contractor relationship, is not a matter that the parties can simply stipulate in the contract. In other words, it is insufficient to simply state in a contract that the services are provided as an independent contractor to make it so.

Because the employee-employer relationship has important and far-reaching legal and practical ramifications extending to tort law (vicarious liability), to social programs (eligibility and financial contributions thereto), to labour relations (union status), and to taxation (GST registration and status under the *Income Tax Act*), etc., the determination of whether a particular relationship is one of employee or of independent contractor cannot simply be left to be decided at the sole subjective discretion of the parties. Consequently, the legal status of independent contractor or of employee is not determined solely on the basis of the parties declaration as to their intent. That determination must also be grounded in a verifiable objective reality. Consequently, *Wolf* and *Royal Winnipeg Ballet* set out a two-step process of inquiry that is used to assist in addressing the central question, as established in *Sagaz* and *Wiebe Door*, which is to determine whether or not the individual is performing the services as his own business on his own account. Under the first step, the subjective intent of each party to the relationship must be ascertained. This can be determined either by the written contractual relationship the parties have entered into or by the actual behaviour of each party, such as invoices for services rendered, registration for GST purposes, and income tax filings as an independent contractor.

The second step is to ascertain whether an objective reality sustains the subjective intent of the parties. It is also necessary to consider the *Wiebe Door* factors to determine whether the facts are consistent with the parties' expressed intention. In other words, the subjective intent of the parties cannot trump the reality of the relationship as ascertained through objective facts. In this second step, the parties intent as well as the terms of the contract may also be taken into account since they colour the relationship. The relevant factors must be considered in light of the parties' intent. However, that being stated, the second step is an analysis of the pertinent facts for the purpose of determining whether the test set out in *Wiebe Door* and *Sagaz* has been in fact met, i.e., whether the legal effect of the relationship the parties have established is one of independent contractor or of employer-employee.

The central question at issue remains whether the person who has been engaged to perform the services is, in actual fact, performing them as a person in business on his own account. In making this determination, no particular factor is dominant and there is no set formula. The factors to consider will thus vary with the circumstances. Nevertheless, the specific factors discussed in *Wiebe Door* and *Sagaz* will usually be relevant, such as the level of control over the worker's activities, whether the worker provides his own equipment, hires his helpers, manages and assumes financial risks, and has an opportunity of profit in the performance of his tasks.

Pluri Vox Media Corp. v. Canada, 2012 FCA 295

An unusual situation is where an individual enters into more than one contract with his or her own company and provides services in different capacities. The simple fact that an individual is a director or an officer of a company does not, in and of itself, exclude the possibility that other services may be provided by that individual as an independent contractor. When that occurs, it will be necessary, for the purposes of the *Income Tax Act* and the CPP to apportion the amounts paid between the services performed in one capacity and the other. In assessing the control factor where the individual concerned is providing services to his or her own corporation, the corporation is a separate person and the corporate veil is not to be pierced, except in limited situations. The issue to be considered is the corporation's legal power to control the employee, not whether the employee feels subject to that control. Where the principal of the corporation company was supervising an independent contractor who was providing services to the corporation, but with whom the principal had no contractual relationship, the principal must have been providing such supervisory services as an employee of the corporation.

Montreal v. Montreal Locomotive Works Ltd., [1947] 1 D.L.R. 161 (P.C.)

In many cases, the question can only be settled by examining the whole of the various elements which constitute the relationship between the parties. This way, it is possible, in some cases, to decide the issue by raising as the crucial question whose business is it, or in other words by asking whether the party is carrying on the business, in the sense of carrying it on for himself or on his own behalf and not merely for a superior.

Charbonneau v. Canada (MNR), [1996] F.C.J. No. 1337 (Fed. C.A.). See also *Attaches Premier Ltée (Les) v. Ranger* (1997), FC A-905-96 (Fed. C.A.)

The tests laid down are not the ingredients of a magic formula. They are guidelines which are generally useful to consider, but not to the point of jeopardizing the ultimate objective of the exercise, which is to determine the overall relationship between the parties. Once it has been determined that there is a genuine contract, the issue is always whether there is a relationship of subordination between the parties such that there is a contract of employment or, whether there is such a degree of autonomy that there is a contract of enterprise or for services. The parts must give way to the whole. Monitoring the result of the work done is not to be confused with the concept of controlling the worker.

Moose Jaw Kinsmen Flying Fins Inc. v. MNR, 88 D.T.C. 6099 (Fed. C.A.)

The tests are useful subordinates in weighing all of the facts relating to the operations of the employer. This is now the preferable and proper approach because, in a given case, one or more of the tests can have little or no applicability. To formulate a decision in such a case, the overall evidence must be considered, taking into account those of the tests which may be applicable and giving to all the evidence the weight which the circumstances may dictate.

Canada Pension Plan

Toronto Transit Commission v. Canada (National Revenue), 2010 FCA 33

Subsection 2(1) defines "employment" as an activity: the performance of services under a contract of service. It does not include long-term disability payments to an employee under an employer-funded program.

Nametco Holdings Ltd. v. Canada (Minister of National Revenue), 2002 FCA 474

The Board of Referees is without jurisdiction to determine the issue of whether or not the worker was an independent contractor, and therefore the Minister was not estopped from asserting before the Tax Court a position contrary to that adopted by the Board of Referees and not appealed. Nor could the matter be *res judicata* by virtue of the decision of the Board of Referees, and it was not an abuse of process for the Minister to argue a different position before the Tax Court.

Southland Livestock Feeders Ltd. v. M.N.R., 2011 TCC 209

The fact that a worker is not registered for GST does not mean he or she is an employee where the worker's gross income was less than the threshold amount that would have triggered an obligation to register.

(c) Effect of Agreement

TBT Personnel Services Inc. v. Canada, 2011 FCA 256

Where a personnel agency hired 96 truck drivers, 43 who had signed a written agreement with the agency, and 53 who had not, it was appropriate for a court to treat the two groups of drivers separately. The written agreements contained clauses acknowledging that the driver was an independent contractor, suggesting a common intention that the driver would be engaged as a person carrying on his own business. However, such clauses were not binding, and in view of the circumstances all 96 drivers were held to be employees.

Wiebe Door Services Ltd. (1986), 87 D.T.C. 5025 (Fed. C.A.)

An agreement that contractors would be running their own businesses and would therefore be responsible for their own taxes and any contributions for workers' compensation, unemployment insurance and CPP is not of itself determinative of the relationship between the parties. A court must carefully examine the facts in order to come to its own conclusion.

Royal Winnipeg Ballet v. Canada (Minister of National Revenue), 2006 FCA 87

It is wrong in principle to set aside, as worthy of no weight, the uncontradicted evidence of the parties as to their common understanding of their legal relationship, even if that evidence cannot be conclusive. It was still a factor, even in the absence of a written agreement that purported to characterize the legal relationship between the parties, where there was no dispute between the parties as to what they believe that relationship to be.

National Capital Outaouais Ski Team v. Canada (National Revenue), 2008 FCA 132

The minister's assessment of the overall legal relationship of the parties to a contract is based on assumptions of fact that the minister makes. The assumed facts are presumed to be true unless they are rebutted. There is no presumption with respect to the intention of the parties to the contract. The fact that a corporation may perceive itself to be a not-for-profit organization and not a business *per se*, and merely a framework which gives individuals an opportunity to excel, does not derogate from its status as a corporation which can legally be an employer within the meaning of the *Employment Insurance Act* and the CPP.

IT/Net Consultants Inc. v. MNR (2000), Docs. 98-757-UI; 98-110-CPP (T.C.C.)

The fact that an arrangement is structured in such a way as to best benefit the parties from an EI and CPP contribution point of view is not the end of the matter. The parties are free to structure their arrangement as best suits their purposes.

(d) Standard of Review

Candor Enterprises Ltd. v. MNR (2000), FC A-636-98 (Fed. C.A.). See also *MNR v. Jencan Ltd.* (1997), 215 N.R. 352 (Fed. C.A.)

The Minister's determination that employment is not pursuant to a contract of service is a quasi-judicial decision that is subject, on appeal, to independent review by the Tax Court. In this review, the Court is required to consider the factual assumptions stated in the Minister's pleadings against all the evidence before it.

Wiebe Door Services Ltd. (1986), 87 D.T.C. 5025 (Fed. C.A.)

The Federal Court Appeal cannot, on an application under s. 28 of the *Federal Court Act*, engage in an examination of the evidence as such, unless a particular result is so inevitable on the facts that any other conclusion would be perverse. Where the Court is left with an inconclusive result after excising the lower court's erroneous application of the legal principle to the facts, it is appropriate to set aside the lower court decision and refer the matter back to the Tax Court Judge for a determination consistent with the proper principle.

(e) Recent Example Cases — Employees

- Dive tender and deckhand for commercial fishing business: *D.W. Thomas Holdings Inc. v. Canada*, 2009 FCA 371

- Corporation giving athletes an opportunity to strive towards national team status in their sport: *National Capital Outaouais Ski Team v. Canada (National Revenue)*, 2008 FCA 132

- Office worker for real estate agent paid $10/hr: *1351678 Ontario Limited v. M.N.R.*, 2011 TCC 252

- Person giving home care to invalid paid hourly wage for set weekly hours and schedule: *Garneau v. M.N.R.*, 2004 TCC 456. See also *North Shore Association for the Mentally Handicapped v. MNR*, 2003 TCC 657

- Nurses working for association which locates temporary placements; hours set by clients; nurses paid amount billed by agency to client, less 11% administration fee; association being employment agency: *Central Registry of Graduate Nurses v. M.N.R.*, 2003 TCC 822

- Inexperienced drywall installer for drywall business paid on a weekly basis, did not supply own tools and did not have vehicle; worker hired after answering employer's ad: *Da Ponte v. MNR*, 2003 TCC 523

- Worker providing child-care services for family each weekday from 7:30 am to 5:30 p.m.: *Mohr v. MNR* (1997), Docs. 97-481-UI; 97-90-CPP (T.C.C.)

- Travel agents formerly working in office now working out of respective homes for same employer and paid on commission basis in relation to individual sales: *Polimark Ltd. v. MNR* (2000), Doc. 98-41-CPP (T.C.C.)

- Secretary on short-term disability leave doing part-time work at employer's; worker being paid by employer and employer reimbursed by disability plan: *Desender v. MNR* (1999), Docs. 1999-978-EI; 1999-988-CPP; 1999-978-EI; 1999-988-CPP (T.C.C.)

- Seasonal deliveries by pool of drivers using employer's trucks; employer paying associated expenses such as fuel, repairs, and tolls; drivers receiving hourly rate on basis of long trip should take and having to keep log book of trips supplied by employer: *942259 Ontario Inc. v. MNR* (1999), 97-990-UI; 97-106-CPP (T.C.C.)

- Managers of chain of convenience stores having no ownership interest in stores and working 60-hour weeks; remuneration based purely on profit, with monthly draw permitted; managers having little autonomy as to operation of stores: *Avondales Stores Limited v. MNR* (1997), TCC 96-2165-UI

Canada Pension Plan

- Placement agency matching child and youth rehabilitative workers with insurance companies on per job basis; worker having written agreement with agency and invoicing broker at hourly rate; worker required to provide set amount of time per week with child, although schedule was flexible; worker obliged to meet objectives set by client and insurance company: *Bartimaeus Inc. v. MNR* (1999), 98-307(UI) (T.C.C.). See also *Sheridan v. Canada (MNR)*, [1985] F.C.J. No. 230 (C.A.)

- Auto repair shop engaging services of mechanic for hourly rate and providing tools; mechanic working irregular hours, but working exclusively for shop on virtually a daily basis: *Chanor Truck Repairs Ltd. v. MNR* (1999), 98-739-UI; 98-109-CPP (T.C.C.)

- Manufacturer hiring sales representative initially as employee, but unilaterally purporting to change worker's status to independent contractor after two years; worker still covered by various company plans such as life insurance, dental insurance and health insurance at company expense; worker working at company, at home and on road, but required to be working for company during regular business hours: *Chantler Packaging Inc. v. MNR* (1999), Doc. 98-50 (UI) (T.C.C.)

- Company providing oilfield services including maintenance for well sites and plants; worker responsible for the maintenance and supervision of particular gas plant: worker paid daily rate plus overtime by company, although providing own equipment: *Dyck v. MNR* (1999), Docs. 1999-1521-EI; 1999-1522-CPP; 1999-1523-EI; 1999-1524-CPP (T.C.C.)

- Beauty technicians working in salon paying no rent, using employer's equipment and paid fixed percentage of individual billings; working hours prescribed by employer: *493900 Ontario Ltd. o/a Forma Cosmetics v. MNR* (August 15, 1990), CEB & PG (TB) ¶8609 (PAB)

- Legal researcher engaged by sole practitioner lawyer who paid her law society fees and professional insurance; researcher working on lawyer's files at his office or at courthouse library: *Cram v. MNHW* (January 7, 1992), CEB & PG (TB) ¶9213 (PAB)

- Secretary not required to work specific hours, not supervised on day-to-day basis and free to work for other parties; "independent contractor's agreement" signed by secretary not determinative as she economically required to sign: *Motani v. MNR* (March 29, 1993), CEB & PG (TB) ¶8507 (PAB)

- Pizza delivery drivers controlled by the company; most of equipment necessary for pizza business being owned by company: *872538 Ontario Inc. v. MNR* (Court file no. 92-644(UI)) (T.C.C.)

(f) Recent Example Cases — Independent Contractors

- Fibre optic welders having equity stake in business; nature of highly specialized job required flexible hours, and it was imperative to avoid restrictions on employee working hours imposed by provincial legislation; workers received no salary but only profit from project: *1663255 Ontario Inc. v. M.N.R.*, 2011 TCC 19 (January 24, 2011)

- Workers engaged to construct fences for fence design and construction company; no commitment given to workers as to work hours and they were only offered work when it was available; workers not obligated to accept jobs and it was expected that they may have other sources of income: *Booker v. M.N.R.*, 2011 TCC 44 (January 26, 2011)

- High school student working for roofing company over summers; all other company workers were independent contractors, and worker was to be treated the same: *Norman v. M.N.R.*, 2011 TCC 217 (April 19, 2011)

- Paralegal retained by parking lot to issue and enforce parking tickets; worker having expertise not amenable to supervision; no set hours: *Pichugin v. M.N.R.*, 2011 TCC 16

- Feedlot worker paid in cash: Minister only interested because worker reported income as "other employment income": *Southland Livestock Feeders Ltd. v. M.N.R.*, 2011 TCC 209

- Driving instructor who provided own car and paid all expenses, had no set schedule: *Bansal v. M.N.R.*, 2010 TCC 340

- Drywall installer working for contractor provided his own tools: *McKenna v. M.N.R.*, 2010 TCC 601 (November 25, 2010)

- Thirteen car sales agents working for dealership on pure commission basis; although dealer had to approve of all sales, bulk of business came from agent's own prior clients: *126873 Ontario Limited o/a Autopark Superstore v. M.N.R.*, 2007 TCC 442

- Dancers with a ballet company; company performs four ballets per September to May season, planned two to three years in advance; dancers recruited from company's ballet school and from open auditions; remuneration set for most dancers by Canadian Ballet Agreement, although principals may negotiate slightly better rate; common intention of parties that dancers were independent contractors; company's extensive control of dancers not inconsistent with independent contractor status, given the same control is exercised over guest dancers: *Royal Winnipeg Ballet v. Canada (Minister of National Revenue)*, 2006 FCA 87

- Worker was engaged to perform loss control surveys and property risk evaluations; worker set own schedule, and invoiced business once per month: *Insurers' Advisory Organization Inc. v. MNR*, 2003 TCC 443

- Sales force paid straight commission by sales distributor and operating independently, but with no ability to complete a deal except through the distributor: *Scott v. M.N.R,* 2003 TCC 120

- Professional nurse flying to hospital in remote location to work two weeks at a time; paid fixed daily amount, including travel days: *Uranium City Hospital v. M.N.R.*, 2003 TCC 439

- Account manager/broker working for equipment leasing brokerage company on pure commission basis; company supplied office, but individual supplying own equipment and cell phone: *Topolovich v. M.N.R.*, 2003 TCC 651

- Wood cutters using own tools and paid by the cord by lumber company; payor did not know when workers worked: *Jaillet v. Canada (Minister of National Revenue),* 2002 FCA 394, affirming (November 1, 2000) Doc. 2000-2476-EI (T.C.C.)

- Fishers working on boats owned by fish processing company supplying some of their own minor equipment and must have licence; decisions as to how and where fishing to take place influenced by Department of Fisheries, company and fishers themselves; fishers not paid salaries but rather share in proceeds of each catch with company after deductions for expenses: *Canada (Minister of National Revenue) v. Comeau's Sea Foods Ltd.,* 2002 FCA 516

- Individuals hired to install building gutters manufactured by company; each installer using own judgment to decide when to work or not; 20-30% of contracts with installers negotiated; no guarantee of ongoing work for installers: *Precision Gutters Ltd v. Canada (Minister of National Revenue)*, [2002] FCA 207

- Mechanical engineer resident in the U.S. with no fixed base in Canada signing renewable one-year contract dependent entirely on available workload; contract expressly stating that individual is an independent contractor, although paying individual for all hours worked with increased rate for overtime and employer exercising control over hours worked and tools used: *Wolf v. Canada*, [2002] FCA 96

- Worker hired by not-for-profit group to develop projects, worker required to periodically report on status; worker paid $200/day not to exceed $600/week; worker charging GST: *Women in Film & Television Toronto Inc. v. MNR* (1998), Docs. TCC 97-1402 (UI) (T.C.C.)

- Dental hygienists for dental practice: *Tsimerman v. MNR* (1998), Doc. 97-851 (UI) (T.T.C.). See also *Bradford v. MNR* (1988), 88 D.T.C 1661 (T.C.C.)

125

- Workers delivered advertising flyers door-to-door or verified such deliveries as part of sub-operation of cartage company; high turnover rate and minimal training; workers had own vehicle, although bags and postal keys supplied on payment of deposit by worker; remuneration on piece-work basis: *W.A. Pacific Rim Company Inc. v. MNR* (1997), Docs. 94-2355-UI; 94-74-CPP (T.C.C.)

- Worker hired by management and technology consulting company to work full time on temporary contract for third party; worker located on third-party's premises and invoicing daily rate with overtime subject to approval; worker not paid for days missed: *IT/Net Consultants Inc. v. MNR* (2000), Docs. 98-757-UI; 98-110-CPP (T.C.C.)

- Management consultant providing services to company for 10 hours per week for flat rate through business operated with wife; consultant working from own premises and also serving competitors of company: *H.J. Jones-Sons Limited v. MNR* (1999), Docs. 98-433-UI; 98-71-CPP (T.C.C.)

- Delivery service hired drivers with their own vehicles to perform delivery orders obtained by service; drivers received 65% commission on deliveries and paid all expenses for vehicles; drivers assuming risk of damage to packages; driver wearing uniform of service and displaying sign on vehicle: *Flash Courier Services Inc. v. MNR* (2000), Docs. 1999-2239-EI; 1999-2240-CPP (T.C.C.)

- Cosmetic company using contract demonstrators at store locations on seasonal basis at hourly rate; non-exclusive arrangement and worker could refuse to work on a particular day or at a particular location; worker paid own CPP contribution: *Drummond v. MNR* (1998), Doc. 96-862-UI (T.C.C.)

- Unsupervised workers for roofing contractor could work on own time, refuse work from contractor and work for others; workers owning own tools; written contract naming workers as subcontractors: *Rainbow Holdings Corp. v. MNR* (February 9, 1994), CEB & PG (TB) ¶8554 (PAB)

- Not-for-profit agency using roster of service providers to provide in-home support for disabled children; once family agrees to process, agency and provider enter into support contract naming times and rate; agency providing basic training to providers, and compensating them for expenses, but exercising little control: *Family Services Perth-Huron v. MNR* (2000), Doc. 98-106-CPP (T.C.C.)

- Computer trainer working out of Learning Centre's facilities for 10 years, but not exclusively; price negotiated for each job; trainer using Centre's manual, but otherwise having complete autonomy over program: *Bastasic v. MNR* (1999), Doc. 98-251-UI (T.C.C.)

(g) Recent Example Case — Employers

International Minerals & Chemical (Canada) Global Limited v. M.N.R. (2001-05-08), TCC 2000-2851-EI (T.C.C.)

While a limited partnership is a business entity, it is not a person within the definition of "employer" in the CPP nor is it a person at common-law. However, the general partner of a limited partnership can be an employer through the partnership.

(h) Constitutional Issues

Kreutz v. Canada (Attorney General), 2002 FCA 94

Even if contractual freedom were to be protected by section 7 of the *Canadian Charter of Rights and Freedoms*, the *Wiebe* principle is not unconstitutional. It does not prevent an employer from entering into an agreement to hire an independent contractor, but involves a question of what evidence is sufficient to prove for statutory purposes what kind of contract has in fact been made. It merely means that evidence of a specific agreement is not necessarily determinative where there is other evidence, as there was here, of a kind of legal relationship different from what the parties purported to create. In the final analysis, the question must be determined by applying a legal test to all the facts and not merely by taking the parties' word for it.

(i) Holding an Office

Canada (National Revenue) v. Conseil central des syndicats nationaux du Saguenay/Lac St-Jean, 2009 FCA 375

The relevant legal tests underlying the existence of an office are twofold: first, the individuals involved must hold an "office, the incumbent of which is elected by popular vote or is elected or appointed in a representative capacity" and, second, the position in question must entitle the individual to a fixed or ascertainable stipend or remuneration. Where once elected, union officials undertook to assume the powers and duties associated with their union positions for which they were entitled to their usual remuneration, the officials could not be said to be volunteering where the union paid them amounts for lost salary, child care expenses and travel expenses with respect to the performance of union duties while taking time off their regular work. The fact that the union officials were not expressly entitled to such remuneration under any contractual relationship or any central council constitution or by-laws was immaterial. The only issue was whether the union officials were paid for their activities as union officers during their union leave.

Canada (Minister of National Revenue) v. Ontario, 2011 FCA 314

Those who hold a position and are given a *per diem* payment are given a "fixed or ascertainable stipend or remuneration" within the meaning of the CPP s. 2(1) and the ITA s. 248(1). The phrase "fixed or ascertainable" does not require an advance determination of the total remuneration for a particular year. An advance annual determination normally will be sufficient to meet the test, but that does not mean that it is necessary. By the combined operation of section 6 of the CPP, the definition of "office" in section 2 of the CPP, and section 24 of the *Canada Pension Plan Regulations,* C.R.C. c. 385, a member of the Ontario Judicial Appointments Committee is engaged in pensionable employment if that position carries the entitlement to a "fixed or ascertainable stipend or remuneration".

Canada (Minister of National Revenue) v. Real Estate Council of Alberta, 2012 FCA 121. See also *Vachon Estate v. Canada,* 2009 FCA 375

The phrase "the position ... [must be one] entitling" the individual to "stipend or remuneration," means nothing more than a position for pay. That the office-holder would not be paid in a year if there were no tasks to perform in that year takes nothing away from the fact that his or her position was a position for pay.

Payette v. M.N.R., 2002 CarswellNat. 4668 (Fed. Ct.)

It cannot be said that a person does not occupy a position because that person's main professional activity is exercised elsewhere than with the Commission. That said, it is not enough to occupy a position: the position must entitle the person to a "fixed or ascertainable stipend or remuneration", according to the definition set out in CPP s. 2(1). The words "stipend" and "remuneration" mean gross income, not income net of expenses. The descriptor "ascertainable" must refer to something that can be ascertained a priori; otherwise it would have no meaning since everything can be ascertained a posteriori. Thus if the "stipend" or "remuneration" is not fixed, it must still be ascertainable in advance with at least some degree of accuracy by using some formula or by referring to certain set factors. Merely indicating the hourly rate is insufficient to establish that the position itself makes a member eligible for a "fixed or ascertainable stipend or remuneration", where it is not known how many times each member is called upon to sit on the review committee or how many days or hours are spent on this activity in a given year.

Doblej v. Canada (Canadian Employment Insurance Commission), 2004 FCA 19

An Indian band councillor who achieved her position via election by popular vote came within the definition of "officer" under CPP s. 2(1).

§5. Review Tribunals

Canada (MHRD) v. Fleming, 2004 FCA 288

There is no such thing in the CPP as a review tribunal constituted under s. 84(2). By virtue of s. 2, a review tribunal is established under section 82. It is more proper, therefore to refer to review tribunals constituted for the purpose of dealing with appeals pertaining to s. 81 proceedings and to review tribunals constituted for the purpose of dealing with s. 84(2) applications.

Application and Operation of Act

3. *Definitions* — **(1) In this Act,**

province providing a comprehensive pension plan — **"province providing a comprehensive pension plan" means a province prescribed by a regulation made on the recommendation of the Minister of Employment and Social Development for the purposes of this Act as a province (2005, c. 35, s. 67(a)(i); 2012, c. 19, s. 694(a)(i); 2013, c. 40, s. 238(1)(b)(i).)**

    (a) the government of which has, on or before May 3, 1965, signified the intention of that province to provide for the establishment and operation in that province, in lieu of the operation therein of this Act, of a plan of old age pensions and supplementary benefits providing for the making of contributions thereunder commencing with the year 1966 and providing for the payment of benefits thereunder comparable to those provided by this Act; or

    (b) the government of which has, at any time after May 3, 1965, given notice in writing to the Minister of Employment and Social Development of the intention of that province to provide (1996, c. 11, s. 95(b); 2013, c. 40, s. 238(1)(b)(i).)

        (i) for the establishment and operation in that province, in lieu of the operation therein of this Act, of a plan of old age pensions and supplementary benefits providing for the making of contributions thereunder commencing with the third year following the year in which the notice was given and providing for the payment of benefits thereunder comparable to those then provided by this Act or by any provincial pension plan other than that plan, and

        (ii) for the assumption under that plan of all obligations and liabilities accrued or accruing to the first day of that third year with respect to the payment of benefits under this Act attributable to contributions made under this Act in respect of employment in that province or in respect of self-employed earnings of persons resident in that province;

"provincial pension plan" means a plan of old age pensions and supplementary benefits for the establishment and operation of which provision has been made as described in paragraph (a) or (b) of the definition "province providing a comprehensive pension plan" under a law of a province providing a comprehensive pension plan.

(S.C. 1996, c. 11, s. 95.)

    (2) *Prescription of province after notice given* — **Notwithstanding anything in subsection (1), where, not later than twelve months before the first day of the third year following the year in which notice in writing as described in paragraph (b) of the definition "province providing a comprehensive pension plan"in subsection (1) was given to the Minister of Employment and Social Development by the government of a province, the legislature of the province has provided by law for the establishment and operation in that province of a plan of old age pensions and supplementary benefits as described in that paragraph and for the assumption under that plan of all obligations and liabilities accrued or accruing as described in that paragraph, the Governor in Council shall, by regulation made on the recommendation of the Minister of Employment and Social Development for the purposes of this Act, prescribe that province as a**

province described in that paragraph. (S.C. 1996, c. 11, s. 95(*b*); 2005, c. 35, s. 67(*a*)(ii); 2012, c. 19, s. 694(1)(*a*)(ii); 2013, c. 40, s. 238(1)(*b*)(i).)

(3) *Effective date of prescription* — Any regulation made pursuant to subsection (2) becomes effective on the first day of the third year following the year in which the notice referred to in that subsection was given to the Minister of Employment and Social Development. (S.C. 1996, c. 11, s. 95(*b*); 2005, c. 35, s. 67(*a*)(ii); 2012, c. 19, s. 694(1)(*a*)(ii); 2013, c. 40, s. 238(1)(*b*)(i).)

(S.C. 1996, c. 11, s. 95; 2005, c. 35, s. 67; 2012, c. 19, s. 694; 2013, c. 40, s. 238.)

─────────── Notes ───────────

Synopsis

This section and s. 4 authorize the federal Minister to enter into agreements with provinces which have enacted a "comprehensive pension plan" whereby employees in that province are not subject to the CPP. Quebec is the only province to date that has brought in a comprehensive pension plan, the QPP.

Related Regulations

● Prescribed Province Pension Regulations, C.R.C. 1978, c. 391

───────────────

4. *Application in respect of province providing comprehensive pension plan* — **(1)** Notwithstanding anything in this Act, except as provided in subsection (2),

    (*a*) the provisions of this Act with respect to the making of contributions by employees and employers in respect of pensionable employment and the provisions of Part III with respect to employees in pensionable employment do not apply in relation to employment in a province providing a comprehensive pension plan; and

    (*b*) the provisions of this Act with respect to the making of contributions by persons for any year in respect of self-employed earnings do not apply in relation to persons who on the last day of that year were resident in a province providing a comprehensive pension plan.

(2) *Exception* — Subject to subsection (3), all of the provisions of this Act apply to

    (*a*) employment by Her Majesty in right of Canada or by an agent of Her Majesty in right of Canada in a province providing a comprehensive pension plan; and

    (*b*) any employment in a province providing a comprehensive pension plan if and to the extent that the establishment and operation of the plan referred to in paragraph (*a*) or (*b*) of the definition "province providing a comprehensive pension plan" in subsection 3(1), as the case may be, in relation to persons employed in that employment is outside the legislative authority of the legislature of that province,

as though that employment were employment in a province other than a province providing a comprehensive pension plan.

(3) *Agreement with government of province providing comprehensive pension plan* — The Minister of Employment and Social Development, with the approval of the Governor in Council, may on behalf of the Government of Canada enter into an agreement with the government of a province providing a comprehensive pension plan

Canada Pension Plan

whereby, in accordance with such terms and conditions as may be set out in the agreement, any persons employed in employment described in subsection (2), and any employers of any persons employed in such employment, with respect to any persons so employed, shall be subject to the provisions of the provincial pension plan of that province in all respects as though the establishment and operation of that plan in relation to any persons so employed were within the legislative authority of the legislature of that province, and with respect to any period while the agreement continues in force, the agreement has the force of law according to the provisions thereof. (1996, c. 11, s. 95(*b*); 2005, c. 35, s. 67(*a*)(iii); 2012, c. 19, s. 694(*a*)(iii); 2013, c. 40, s. 238(1)(*b*)(ii).)

(4) *Province in which person deemed employed* — For the purposes of this Act, a person shall be deemed to be employed in the province in which the establishment of his employer to which he reports for work is situated, and where the employee is not required to report for work at any establishment of his employer, he shall be deemed to be employed in the province in which the establishment of his employer from which his remuneration is paid is situated.

(5) *Reference to last day of year* — A reference in paragraph (1)(*b*) to the last day of a year shall, in the case of a person who resided in Canada at any time in that year but ceased to reside in Canada before the last day thereof, be deemed to be a reference to the last day in that year on which he resided in Canada.

(S.C. 1996, c. 11, s. 95; 2005, c. 35, s. 67; 2012, c. 19, s. 694; 2013, c. 40, s. 238.)

——————————— **Notes** ———————————

Synopsis

See Synopsis for s. 3.

———————————————————

Electronic Alternatives[8]

4.1. *Minister's power* — The Minister of National Revenue may use electronic means to create, communicate, make available, collect, receive, store or otherwise deal with documents or information under this Act.

(S.C. 2007, c. 11, s. 1; 2012, c. 19, s. 226.)

Part I

Contributions

5. *Definition of "Minister"* — (1) In this Part, "Minister" means the Minister of National Revenue. (S.C. 1998, c. 19, s. 251(1).)

———————————————————————————————

[8] The heading before section 4.1 was added by 2007, c. 11, s. 1.

(2) *Delegation* — [9]The Minister may authorize an officer or a class of officers to exercise powers or perform duties of the Minister under this Part. (S.C. 1998, c. 19, s. 251(1).)

(S.C. 1998, c. 19, s. 251.)

——————— Notes ———————

Synopsis

This section provides that the Minister responsible for overseeing contributions to the CPP is the Minister of National Revenue, i.e., the same Minister who administers the *Income Tax Act*.

Division A: Contributions Payable

Pensionable Employment

6. *Pensionable employment* — **(1)** Pensionable employment is

(a) employment in Canada that is not excepted employment;

(b) employment in Canada under Her Majesty in right of Canada that is not excepted employment; or

(c) employment included in pensionable employment by a regulation made under section 7.

(2) *Excepted employment* — Excepted employment is

(a) employment in agriculture or an agricultural enterprise, horticulture, fishing, hunting, trapping, forestry, logging or lumbering by an employer who either pays the employee less than two hundred and fifty dollars in cash remuneration in a year or employs the employee, on terms providing for payment of cash remuneration, for a period of less than twenty-five working days in a year;

(b) employment of a casual nature otherwise than for the purpose of the employer's trade or business;

(c) employment as a teacher on exchange from a country other than Canada;

(d) employment of a person by the person's spouse or common-law partner, unless the remuneration paid to the person may be deducted under the *Income Tax Act* in computing the income of the spouse or common-law partner; (S.C. 2000, c. 12, s. 43.)

(e) employment of a member of a religious order who has taken a vow of perpetual poverty and whose remuneration is paid either directly or by the member to the order;

(f) employment for which no cash remuneration is paid where the person employed is the child of, or is maintained by, the employer;

(g) employment as a member of the Canadian Forces or the Royal Canadian Mounted Police, except as provided by any other Act of Parliament;

---

[9] Pursuant to S.C. 1998, c. 19, s. 251(2): "Any power or duty of the Minister of National Revenue delegated to an officer or a class of officers by a regulation made under subsection 40(2) of the Act before the day on which this Act is assented to continues to be delegated to that officer or that class of officers until an authorization by the Minister made under subsection 5(2) of the Act, as enacted by subsection 251(1) of 1998, c. 19, changes the delegation of that power or duty."

(*h*) employment in Canada by an employer who employs persons in Canada but under the terms of a reciprocal agreement between the Government of Canada and the government of another country is exempt from liability to make the contribution imposed on an employer by this Act;

(*i*) employment by Her Majesty in right of a province or by an agent of Her Majesty in right of a province;

(*j*) employment in Canada by the government of a country other than Canada or by an international organization; (R.S.C. 1985, c. 30 (2nd Supp.), s. 2.)

(*j.1*) employment of an Indian as defined in the *Indian Act*, in respect of which the earnings are not included in computing income for purposes of the *Income Tax Act*; or (R.S.C. 1985, c. 30 (2nd Supp.), s. 2.)

(*k*) employment excepted from pensionable employment by a regulation made under section 7.

(R.S.C. 1985, c. 30 (2nd Supp.), s. 2; 2000, c. 12, s. 43.)

———————— Notes ————————

Synopsis

This section sets out the types of employment that are, and are not, subject to CPP contributions. "Pensionable employment" is defined very broadly to include all employment in Canada that does not fit under one of the specific exceptions in ss. 6(2).

Recent Amendments

Section 6(2)(*c*) was amended in 2000 to refer to "common-law partners" instead of "spouse".

Related Provisions

● Section 7 — Regulations respecting employment to be included in or excepted from pensionable employment

Case Law

Bear v. Canada (Attorney General), [2001] FCT 1192

The pre-1988 prohibition against reserve Indians contributing to the CPP because were not subject to taxation and therefore did not have pensionable income was contrary to the equality guarantee in the Canadian Bill of Rights, and was therefore of no effect. Reserve Indians were entitled to make retroactive CPP contributions with respect to pensionable income earned before 1988.

———————————————

7. *Regulations respecting employment to be included in pensionable employment* — **(1) The Governor in Council may make regulations for including in pensionable employment**

(*a*) any employment outside Canada or partly outside Canada, being employment that would be pensionable employment if it were in Canada;

(*b*) the entire employment under one employer of a person who is engaged by the employer partly in pensionable employment and partly in other employment;

(*c*) any employment if it appears to the Governor in Council that the nature of the work performed is similar to the work performed by persons employed in pensionable employment;

(*d*) the performance of services for remuneration if it appears to the Governor in Council that the terms or conditions on which the services are performed and the remuneration is paid are analogous to a contract of service, whether or not they constitute a contract of service;

(*e*) pursuant to an agreement with the government of a province, employment in Canada by Her Majesty in right of the province or by an agent of Her Majesty in right of the province;

(*f*) pursuant to an agreement with the employing government or organization, employment in Canada by the government of a country other than Canada or by an international organization; and

(*g*) any excepted employment other than employment described in paragraph 6(2)(*g*) or (*i*).

(**2**) *Regulations respecting employment to be excepted from pensionable employment* — The Governor in Council may make regulations for excepting from pensionable employment

(*a*) any employment if it appears to the Governor in Council by reason of the laws of any country other than Canada that a duplication of contributions or benefits will result;

(*b*) any employment of a person by an employer resident outside Canada unless arrangements satisfactory to the Minister have been made for the payment of the contributions required by this Act to be made in respect of that employment;

(*c*) the entire employment under one employer of a person who is engaged by the employer partly in pensionable employment and partly in other employment;

(*d*) any employment if it appears to the Governor in Council that the nature of the work performed by persons employed in that employment is similar to the nature of the work performed by persons employed in employment that is not pensionable employment;

(*e*) any employment if it appears to the Governor in Council that the services are performed and the remuneration is paid in a manner analogous to the earning of income from the carrying on of a business; and

(*f*) any employment in which persons are ordinarily employed to an inconsiderable extent.

(**3**) *Extent of authority to make regulations* — A regulation made under subsection (1) or (2) may be conditional or unconditional, qualified or unqualified, and may be general or restricted to a specific area, a person or a group or class of persons, and the authority conferred by subsection (1) to make regulations to include in pensionable employment any employment described in that subsection includes authority to make such other regulations to provide for the manner in which the provisions of this Act shall apply with respect thereto, and to adapt the provisions of this Act with respect thereto, as appear to the Governor in Council to be necessary to give effect to the regulations made under that subsection.

(**4**) *Limitation* — No regulation under this section shall require the payment of an employer's contribution by the government of a country other than Canada or by an international organization unless the regulation is made pursuant to an agreement referred to in paragraph (1)(*f*).

————————— Notes —————————

Synopsis

This section confers very broad authority on the federal government to make regulations adding to the types of employment to be included in pensionable employment, as well as to the types of employment that may be excepted from pensionable employment. Other countries and international organizations cannot be required to remit the employer's CPP contribution by regulation in the absence of an agreement. The CPP Regulations and Schedules noted below provide specific inclusions and exceptions.

Related CPP Regulations

- Section 16 — Employment outside Canada
- Section 17 — Employment in international transportation
- Section 18 — Ships
- Section 19 — Aircraft
- Section 20 — Freight and passenger trains
- Section 21 — Motor vehicles
- Section 22 — Employment in Canada by employer resident outside Canada
- Section 23 — Directors resident outside Canada
- Section 24 — Employment by province or agent of province (see also Schedules III and IV)
- Section 25 — Employment by international organization (see also Schedules V and VI)
- Section 26 — Employment by country other than Canada (See also Schedules VII and VIII)
- Section 27 — Employment by member of religious order who has taken vow of poverty
- Section 28 — Employment to inconsiderable extent
- Sections 29–34.1 — Pensionable employment

Case Law

Silverside Computer Systems Inc. v. MNR (1997), FC A-105-97 (Fed. C.A.)

Section 24 of the CPP Regulations is consistent with the rule-making authority conferred by s. 7(1)(*d*), and indicates that the Minister has implicitly concluded that the activities of a person who is placed by an agency to perform services for and under the direction and control of an agency's client, as well as the nature of the work done, are "similar" or "analogous" to services performed under a contract of service.

Dataco Utility Services Ltd. v. M.N.R., (2001-06-07) T.C.C. 2000-4444-EI, 2000-4445-CPP (T.C.C.)

The intention of CPP Regulation 34 and Regulation 6(g) under the *Employment Insurance Act* is to bring into the basket of the two social schemes those workers, whether they are employees under a contract of service or independent contractors under contracts for services, who simply contract with entity A for a fee (or other recompense), to be found or placed in work (employment) with or under the direction and control of a third entity B. In determining whether entity A is a "placement or employment agency" within the meaning of the regulations, the first question to be asked is whether the worker is performing services for entity A as part of the business of the latter, albeit part of that business may be a contract for entity A to provide a service for entity B, or whether entity A is simply acquiring personnel as its very business with no contract to undertake anything further than to pass the worker on to entity B to undertake whatever the business of entity B might be. The simple question to ask is whether entity A is under any obligation to provide a service to entity B other than simply provide personnel. Is it obligated to perform in some other way than simply to make people available? If the answer is yes, it clearly has business of its own as does any general contractor on a building site and the worker is not covered by the regulations under either statute. If however, the answer is no, that is, it is not obligated to carry out any service other than to provide personnel, then clearly the worker in such a situation is covered by the Regulations under both statutes.

Canada (Minister of National Revenue) v. Mastech Quantum Inc., [2002] FCA 131

Section 34(1) of the CPP Regulations presumes that either the agency or the client will pay the remuneration and thus be deemed to be the employer of the individual. Where the client does not pay the individual, the fact that a payroll service used by the agency pays the individual does change the fact that the agency is responsible for his or her remuneration.

Supreme Tractor Services Ltd. v. M.N.R., 2001 CanLII 748 (T.C.C.)

In determining whether an entity is a placement agency for the purposes of s. 34(2) of the CPP Regulations, the first question to be asked is whether the worker is performing services for entity A as part of the business of the latter, albeit part of that business may be a contract for entity A to provide a service for entity B, or whether entity A is simply acquiring personnel as its very business with no contract to undertake anything further than to pass the worker on to entity B to undertake whatever the business of entity B might be. The simple question to ask is whether entity A is under any obligation to provide a service to entity B other than simply provide personnel. Is it obligated to perform in some other way than simply to make people available? If the answer is yes, it clearly has business of its own as does any general contractor on a building site and the worker is not covered by the Regulations under either statute. If however, the answer is no, that is, it is not obligated to carry out any service other than to provide personnel, then clearly the worker in such a situation is covered by the Regulations under both statutes. The question is not so much about who is the ultimate recipient of the work or services provided as this will cover every single possible subcontract situation, but rather who is under obligation to provide the service. If the entity alleged to be the placement agency is under an obligation to provide a service over and above the provision of personnel, it is not placing people, but rather performing that service and is not covered by the Regulations.

OLTCPI Inc. v. Canada (National Revenue), 2010 FCA 74

Where the company supplied dieticians to a client, with the client paying the dietician directly, the company was acting as a placement agency for the purpose of s. 34(2) of the CPP Regulations. The dieticians were directed to answer to the client's specific needs and provide the particular services which they were called upon to provide by the client's staff. It was therefore open for a court to hold that the company's situation was not analogous to that of a contractor providing personnel in the performance of a distinct service, and that the dietician was not an independent contractor, but an employee of the client.

Contributions by Employees and Employers in respect of Pensionable Employment

8. *Amount of employee's contribution* — **(1) Every employee who is employed by an employer in pensionable employment shall, by deduction as provided in this Act from the remuneration in respect of the pensionable employment paid to the employee by the employer, make an employee's contribution for the year in which the remuneration is paid to the employee of an amount equal to the product obtained when the contribution rate for employees for the year is multiplied by the lesser of (2011, c. 24, s. 173.)**

> **(a) the employee's contributory salary and wages for the year paid by the employer, minus such amount as or on account of the basic exemption for the year as is prescribed; and**

> **(b) the employee's maximum contributory earnings for the year, minus such amount, if any, as is determined in prescribed manner to be the employee's salary and wages paid by the employer on which a contribution has been made for the year by the employee under a provincial pension plan.**

(1.1) *Contributions for 1997* — Notwithstanding subsection (1), for 1997 the contribution required by that subsection, in this subsection referred to as the "basic contribution", shall be calculated as though the contribution rate for employees were 2.925% and every employee who is required to make a contribution under that subsection shall make an additional contribution of an amount equal to 1/39 of the basic contribution. (S.C. 1997, c. 40, s. 58.)

(1.2) *Interest on unpaid additional contributions* — Where the amount paid by an employee on or before the employee's balance-due day for a year on account of the additional contribution required to be made under subsection (1.1) is less than the amount of the additional contribution required to be made, interest at a prescribed rate per annum is payable by the employee on the difference between those amounts from the balance-due day for the year to the day of payment. (S.C. 1997, c. 40, s. 58.)

(1.3) *Application of certain provisions* — Subsection 30(1) and sections 32, 36 and 37 apply in respect of the additional contribution required to be made under subsection (1.1) as though it were a contribution required to be made under this Act in respect of self-employed earnings. (S.C. 1997, c. 40, s. 58.)

(2) *Excess amount* — An excess amount has been paid when the aggregate of all amounts deducted as required from the remuneration of an employee for a year, whether by one or more employers, on account of the employee's contribution for the year under this Act or under a provincial pension plan exceeds the sum obtained by adding the following amounts:

(a) the product obtained when the contribution rate for employees for the year under this Act is multiplied by the lesser of

  (i) the employee's contributory salary and wages for the year in respect of pensionable employment to which the provisions of this Act relating to the making of contributions apply, plus the employee's contributory self-employed earnings for the year in the case of an individual who is described in section 10 and to whom the provisions of this Act relating to the making of contributions apply, minus the prorated portion of the employee's basic exemption for the year calculated under subsection (4), and

  (ii) the prorated portion of the employee's maximum contributory earnings for the year calculated under subsection (5); and

(b) the product obtained when the contribution rate for employees for the year under a provincial pension plan is multiplied by the lesser of

  (i) the employee's contributory salary and wages for the year in respect of pensionable employment to which the provisions of a provincial pension plan apply, minus the prorated portion of the employee's basic exemption for the year calculated under subsection (6), and

  (ii) the prorated portion of the employee's maximum contributory earnings for the year calculated under subsection (7).

(2013, c. 33, s. 155.)

(3) *Overpayment* — The overpayment made by the employee on account of an employee's contribution for the year under this Act is the product obtained when the excess amount determined under subsection (2) is multiplied by the ratio that

(a) the employee's contributory salary and wages for the year in respect of pensionable employment to which the provisions of this Act relating to the making of contributions apply, subject to the maximum pensionable earnings in respect of each pensionable employment,

bears to

(b) the aggregate of the employee's contributory salary and wages for the year in respect of pensionable employment to which the provisions of this Act relating to the making of contributions apply or to which the provisions of a provincial pension plan apply, subject to the maximum pensionable earnings in respect of each pensionable employment.

(2013, c. 33, s. 155.)

(4) *Prorated portion of employee's basic exemption* — For the purposes of subparagraph (2)(a)(i), the prorated portion of the employee's basic exemption for the year is the product obtained when the employee's basic exemption is multiplied by the ratio that

(a) the employee's contributory salary and wages for the year in respect of pensionable employment to which the provisions of this Act relating to the making of contributions apply, subject to the maximum pensionable earnings in respect of each pensionable employment,

bears to

(b) the aggregate of the employee's contributory salary and wages for the year in respect of pensionable employment to which the provisions of this Act relating to the making of contributions apply or to which the provisions of a provincial pension plan apply, subject to the maximum pensionable earnings in respect of each pensionable employment.

(2013, c. 33, s. 155.)

(5) *Prorated portion of employee's maximum contributory earnings* — For the purposes of subparagraph (2)(a)(ii), the prorated portion of the employee's maximum contributory earnings for the year is the product obtained when the employee's maximum contributory earnings is multiplied by the ratio that

(a) the employee's contributory salary and wages for the year in respect of pensionable employment to which the provisions of this Act relating to the making of contributions apply, subject to the maximum pensionable earnings in respect of each pensionable employment,

bears to

(b) the aggregate of the employee's contributory salary and wages for the year in respect of pensionable employment to which the provisions of this Act relating to the making of contributions apply or to which the provisions of a provincial pension plan apply, subject to the maximum pensionable earnings in respect of each pensionable employment.

(2013, c. 33, s. 155.)

(6) *Prorated portion of employee's basic exemption* — For the purposes of subparagraph (2)(b)(i), the prorated portion of the employee's basic exemption for the year is the difference between the employee's basic exemption, determined without taking into account paragraphs 19(b) and (c), and the prorated portion calculated under subsection (4). (2013, c. 33, s. 155.)

(7) *Prorated portion of employee's maximum contributory earnings* — For the purposes of subparagraph (2)(b)(ii), the prorated portion of the employee's maximum contributory earnings for the year is the difference between the employee's maximum contributory earnings, determined without taking into account paragraphs 17(b) and

Canada Pension Plan

(c) and 19(b) and (c), and the prorated portion calculated under subsection (5). (2013, c. 33, s. 155.)

(R.S.C. 1985, c. 30 (2nd Supp.), s. 3; 1997, c. 40, s. 58; 2011, c. 24, s. 173; 2013, c. 33, s. 155.)

—————— **Notes** ——————

Synopsis

This section sets out the formula for determining the amount of CPP contributions from each employee.

Employee's contribution for year

=

Contribution rate for employees for year (4.95% in 2003 and subsequent years)

×

LESSER OF

Employee's contributory salary and wages - basic exemption

AND

Employee's maximum contributory earnings for year - Employee's salary and wages paid by employer on which contribution had been made for the year by employee under the provincial pension plan

In 1997, employees were required to make an addition contribution equal to 1/39 of the basic contribution as determined above (ss. (1.1)–(1.3)).

Where an employee works for one or more employers, makes contributions under either the CPP or QPP, and the total of all contributions exceeds 4.95% of the contributory salary or wages up to the maximum ceiling, plus the employee's contributory self-employed earnings, if any, minus the basic exemption, the excess is deemed to be an overpayment and the employee may apply for a refund. Overpayments are calculated as follows:

Overpayment by employee on account of employee's contribution for year

=

Contribution rate for employees for year (4.95% in 2003 and subsequent years)

×

LESSER OF

Employee's contributory salary and wages + employee's contributory self-employment earnings for year - basic exemption

AND

Employee's maximum contributory earnings for year

Related Provisions

- Section 10 — Amount of contribution in respect of self-employment earnings
- Section 11.1 — Contribution rate
- Section 12 — Amount of contributory salary and wages of employees
- Section 16 — "Maximum contributory earnings" defined
- Section 38 — Refund of overpayment where application made within 4 years
- Section 39 — Refund of overpayment in accordance with agreement

- Schedule

Related CPP Regulations

- Section 5 — Basic exemption

- Section 6 — Contribution to provincial pension plan

- Sections 8–8.1 — Payment of contributions to Receiver General

- Section 15 — Amount of salary and wages on which contribution made for the year

- Sections 35–36 — Interest rate on overpayments

Case Law

Agpro Services Inc. v. MNR (1999), 96-136-CPP (T.C.C.)

There is no automatic refund issued on behalf of an employer and an application has to be made for it. However, the CPP provides for the process of an application for overpayment by an employer. Where an overpayment is made and an application for a refund is made then this may be granted in an appropriate case, but the employer must provide evidence that it was entitled to a refund. Even if the employer shows that its calculations are accurate, the employer would still not be entitled to a refund unless the Court was satisfied that the Minister had acted beyond its authority in pro-rating the basic exemption allowed to the persons named in the PD24(E)s submitted to the Minister.

Davitt v. MNR, 2012 FCA 27

The Tax Court of Canada lacks jurisdiction to hear a constitutional challenge brought under the CPP s. 28 to the premium rates imposed by the CPP.

---

9. *Amount of employer's contribution* — **(1) Every employer shall, in respect of each employee employed by the employer in pensionable employment, make an employer's contribution for the year in which remuneration in respect of the pensionable employment is paid to the employee of an amount equal to the product obtained when the contribution rate for employers for the year is multiplied by the lesser of (2011, c. 24, s. 174.)**

  (a) **the contributory salary and wages of the employee for the year paid by the employer, minus such amount as or on account of the employee's basic exemption for the year as is prescribed, and**

  (b) **the maximum contributory earnings of the employee for the year, minus such amount, if any, as is determined in prescribed manner to be the salary and wages of the employee on which a contribution has been made for the year by the employer with respect to the employee under a provincial pension plan.**

(2) *Succession of employers* — **If, in a year after 2003, one employer immediately succeeds another as the employer of an employee as a result of the formation or dissolution of a corporation or the acquisition — with the agreement of the former employer or by operation of law — of all or part of a business of the former employer, the successor employer may, for the application of subsections (1) and 8(1) and section 21, take into account the amounts paid, deducted, remitted or contributed under this Act by the former employer in respect of the year in relation to the employment of the employee as if they had been paid, deducted, remitted or contributed by the successor employer. If the employer takes those amounts into account with respect to the employer's contributions, the employer shall also take them into account with respect to the employee's contributions. (S.C. 2004, c. 22, s. 15.)**

Canada Pension Plan

(3) *Self-employment succeeded by employment* — **For the application of subsections (1) and 8(1) and section 21, if a person, in a year after 2003, is self-employed, ceases to be self-employed and becomes an employee of a corporation controlled by the person, the corporation may**

> (*a*) **take into account the amount of contributory self-employed earnings of the person in the year as contributory salary and wages paid by the corporation to the employee in that year; and**

> (*b*) **take into account one half of the contributions by the person in respect of self-employed earnings in the year as an amount deducted, remitted or contributed in relation to employee's contributions for that year, and one half of that amount as an amount remitted or contributed in relation to employer's contributions for that year.**

(S.C. 2004, c. 22, s. 15.)

> **(R.S.C. 1985, c. 30 (2nd Supp.), s. 3; 2004, c. 22, s. 15; 2011, c. 24, s. 174.)**

——————— **Notes** ———————

Synopsis

This section sets out the formula for determining the amount of CPP contributions from an employer for each employee:

Employer's contribution for employee for year

=

Contribution rate for employer for year (4.95% in 2003 and subsequent years)

×

LESSER OF

Contributory salary and wages of employee for year paid by employer - employee's basic exemption

AND

Maximum contributory earnings of employee for year - Employee's salary and wages paid by employer on which contribution had been made for the year by employee under provincial pension plan

Related Provisions

> • Section 11.1 — Contribution rate
> • Section 12 — Amount of contributory salary and wages of employees
> • Section 15 — Amount of salary and wages on which contribution made for the year
> • Section 16 — "Maximum contributory earnings" defined Schedule

Related CPP Regulations

> • Section 7 — Employer's contribution

Case Law

Toronto Transit Commission v. Canada (National Revenue), 2010 FCA 33

Subsection 9(1) provides that "remuneration" paid by an employer to an employee must be *for* the pensionable employment in order to require an employer's contribution. Long-term disability payments to employees under an employer-funded program are not for the pensionable performance of services, but instead are an indemnity for the wages lost by employees who could not work.

140

Gary Jackson Professional Corporation v. Canada (National Revenue), 2013 FCA 142

The Canada Revenue Agency takes the position that the payment of amounts by an employer to the trustees under a valid employees' profit sharing plan (and the allocation of such payments to employees) will not result in contributions being payable under the CPP. An employees' profit sharing plan is defined in s. 144(1) of the *Income Tax Act.* Under the ITA, the payments made by the employer to the trustees under the arrangement are deductible (ITA ss. 144(5) and 20(1)(*w*)) and the amounts allocated to the employees are included in their income as income from an office or employment (ITA ss. 144(3) and 6(1)(*d*)) in the year that the amounts are allocated. Since the amounts are included in the income of the employees when the amounts are allocated to them, when the amounts are subsequently paid to those employees no amount is then included in their income (ITA s. 144(6)). The definition of "employees' profit sharing plan" now makes it clear that the employer is required to make payments computed by reference to profits. If the employer election under the ITA s. 144(10) is made, and the arrangement specifically provides that the payments will be made from profits, the condition that the arrangement must provide that payments computed by reference to profits are required will be satisfied. If the election has not been made, there must be a set formula which, when applied, will produce an amount that has been computed by reference to profits and the employer must be obligated to pay that amount to the trustees under the arrangement. A valid profit sharing plan requires that the formula is worked out by reference to the employer's profits whereby a total amount of profits to be distributed to his employees or shared by the employer with them is determined and must be paid to a trustee when there is such a profit. There must be a binding obligation by the employer to make payments in accordance with a formula which refers to profits and which must be paid in the event of profits. Arbitrary payments made by the employer to the employee from profits which bore no relationship to the agreed upon formula did not qualify, and were to be assessed for CPP.

Agpro Services Inc. v. MNR (1999), 96-136-CPP (T.C.C.)

The Minister is entitled to pro-rate the basic exemption with respect to each employee based upon the percentage of time the employee worked in the year.

Davitt v. MNR, 2012 FCA 27

The Tax Court of Canada lacks jurisdiction to hear a constitutional challenge brought under the CPP s. 28 to the premium rates imposed by the CPP.

Contributions by Persons in respect of Self-Employed Earnings

10. *Amount of contribution in respect of self-employed earnings* — **(1) Every individual who is resident in Canada for the purposes of the *Income Tax Act* during a year and who has contributory self-employed earnings for the year shall make a contribution for the year of an amount equal to the product obtained when the contribution rate for self-employed persons for the year is multiplied by the lesser of**

    (*a*) the individual's contributory self-employed earnings for the year, minus the amount by which the individual's basic exemption for the year exceeds the aggregate of

        (i) all amounts deducted as prescribed on account of the individual's basic exemption for the year whether by one or more employers pursuant to section 8, and

        (ii) all amounts deducted as prescribed by or under a provincial pension plan on account of any like exemption for the year whether by one or more employers pursuant to that plan, and

    (*b*) the individual's maximum contributory earnings for the year, minus the individual's salary and wages, if any, on which a contribution has been made for the year and such amount, if any, as is determined in prescribed manner to be

141

the individual's salary and wages on which a contribution has been made for the year by the individual under a provincial pension plan.

(2) *Employment succeeded by self-employment* — **For the purpose of subsection (1), if a person, in a year after 2003, is an employee of a corporation controlled by the person, ceases to be employed by that corporation and becomes self-employed, the person may**

> (a) **take into account the amount of contributory salary and wages paid by the corporation to the employee in the year as contributory self-employed earnings of the person in the year; and**
>
> (b) **take into account the amounts deducted, remitted or contributed by the corporation in relation to the employee's contributions and the employer's contributions in respect of the person for the year as contributions by the person in respect of self-employment earnings in that year.**

(S.C. 2004, c. 22, s. 16.)

(R.S.C. 1985, c. 30 (2nd Supp.), s. 3; 2004, c. 22, s. 16.)

——————————— **Notes** ———————————

Synopsis

This section sets out the following formula for determining the contribution with respect to self-employment income earned by a Canadian resident individuals in the year. Note that the test for "residence" is the same as under the *Income Tax Act*.

Contribution for year on self-employed earnings

=

Contribution rate for self-employed persons for year (9.9% in 2003 and subsequent years)

×

LESSER OF

Individual's contributory self-employed earnings for year - [individual's basic exemption - (amounts deducted from contribution on account of basic exemption as applied to contribution on employment salary and wages under s. 8 + amounts deducted from contribution on account of similar exemption under provincial pension plan)]

AND

Individual's maximum contributory earnings of employee for year - individual's salary and wages on which contribution had been made for the year under CPP and/or provincial pension plan

Related Provisions

> ● Section 11 — Election by members of designated religious sect not to contribute in respect of self-employed earnings
>
> ● Section 13 — Contributory self-employed earnings
>
> ● Section 15 — Amount of salary and wages on which contribution made for the year
>
> ● Section 16 — "Maximum contributory earnings" defined
>
> ● Section 30 — Return with respect to self-employed earnings to be filed

Davitt v. MNR, 2012 FCA 27

The Tax Court of Canada lacks jurisdiction to hear a constitutional challenge brought under
the CPP s. 28 to the premium rates imposed by the CPP.

---

11. *Election not to contribute in respect of self-employed earnings* — **(1) Subject to
subsections (2) and (5), section 10 does not apply with respect to any year in respect of
any individual who, being a member of a religious sect or a division of a religious sect
certified by the Minister pursuant to subsection (6), elects not to make a contribution
with respect to that year.**

(2) *Idem* — **An election referred to in subsection (1) shall**

(*a*) **be made in such manner and form as may be prescribed;**

(*b*) **commence to have effect, if approved by the Minister, on and from January 1
of the year in which the election is filed with the Minister; and**

(*c*) **cease to have effect on January 1 of the year next following the day on which
a revocation of the election made in prescribed manner is received by the
Minister.**

(3) *Minister to be satisfied* — **The Minister shall approve an election referred to
in subsection (1) where he is satisfied that**

(*a*) **the person making the election**

(i) **is a member of a religious sect or a division of a religious sect that has been
certified pursuant to subsection (6), and**

(ii) **has been certified as such a member by a spokesman for that sect or
division; and**

(*b*) **the spokesman**

(i) **has been authorized by the sect or division to certify persons as being
members of the sect or division, and**

(ii) **has certified that the sect or division maintains tenets, teachings and
practices of kinds referred to in subparagraphs (6)(*a*)(i) and (ii).**

(4) *Return of contribution* — **Any contribution made by a contributor with respect
to a year for which he elects under this section not to make a contribution shall, on
application, be returned to him.**

(5) *Only one election permitted* — **Where an individual who has elected not to
make a contribution with respect to any year revokes the election, he may not make an
election under this section with respect to any subsequent year.**

(6) *Certification of religious sect or division* — **The Minister shall certify a religious sect or a division of a religious sect for the purposes of this section where**

(*a*) **he is satisfied that the religious sect**

(i) **is a religious organization that has established tenets and teachings that
oppose the acceptance of benefits from any private or public insurance that
provides for payments in the event of death, disability, old age or retirement,**

(ii) **does, as a practice, make provisions for the support of dependent members
that are reasonable in view of their general level of living, and**

(iii) **was in existence in Canada on January 1, 1966 and has been maintaining the tenets, teachings and practices referred to in subparagraphs (i) and (ii) since that date; and**

(*b*) **the religious sect or division thereof has applied to him in prescribed form for certification.**

———————— Notes ————————

Synopsis

This section authorizes the Minister to permit members of designated religious sects not to contribute in respect of self-employed earnings.

———————

Division B: Calculation of Contributions

Contribution Rate

11.1. *Contribution rate — 1966 to 1986 —* **(1) The contribution rate for the years 1966 to 1986 is:**

(*a*) **for employees, 1.8% of contributory wages and salaries;**

(*b*) **for employers, 1.8% of contributory wages and salaries; and**

(*c*) **for self-employed persons, 3.6% of contributory self-employed earnings.**

(2) *Contribution rates after 1986 —* **The contribution rate for employees, employers and self-employed persons for 1987 and subsequent years is as set out in the schedule, as amended from time to time (S.C. 1997, c. 40, s. 59.)**

(R.S.C. 1985, c. 30 (2nd Supp.), s. 4; 1997, c. 40, s. 59.)

———————— Notes ————————

Synopsis

This section establishes the contribution rate for employees, employers and self-employed persons. The contribution rate for years after 1986 is found in the Schedule to the CPP, after s. 118.

Related Provisions

- Schedule

———————

Contributory Salary and Wages

12. *Amount of contributory salary and wages —* **(1) The amount of the contributory salary and wages of a person for a year is the person's income for the year from pensionable employment, computed in accordance with the *Income Tax Act* (read without reference to subsection 7(8) of that Act), plus any deductions for the year made in computing that income otherwise than under paragraph 8(1)(*c*) of that Act, but does not include any such income received by the person (S.C. 2001, c. 17, s. 254(1); 2004, c. 22, s. 17.)**

(*a*) **before he reaches eighteen years of age;**

(*b*) during any month that is excluded from that person's contributory period under this Act or under a provincial pension plan by reason of disability; (R.S.C. 1985, c. 30 (2nd Supp.), 5(1).)

(*c*) after they reach sixty-five years of age if

(i) a retirement pension is payable to them under this Act or under a provincial pension plan, and

(ii) subject to subsection (1.1), they make an election to exclude the income; or

(S.C. 2009, c. 31, s. 26(1).)

(*d*) after they reach seventy years of age. (S.C. 2009, c. 31, s. 26(1).)

(1.1) *Election* — An election referred to in subparagraph (1)(*c*)(ii)

(*a*) shall be made or revoked in the prescribed form and manner;

(*b*) shall commence to have effect on the first day of the month following the month in which it is made;

(*c*) shall cease to have effect on the first day of the month following the month in which it is revoked;

(*d*) may be made only once in a year;

(*e*) may not be revoked in the year in which it is made;

(*f*) may not be made in a year in which an election is revoked; and

(*g*) is deemed to be an election in respect of the person's income from all pensionable employment and in respect of their self-employed earnings.

(S.C. 2009, c. 31, s. 26(2).)

(1.2) *Consequence of not revoking election in prescribed form and manner* — If a person does not revoke — in respect of an employer — an election in the prescribed form and manner, the contributory salary and wages referred to in paragraphs 8(1)(*a*) and 9(1)(*a*) do not, for the purposes of those paragraphs, include income from that employment. However, they may — in respect of that income — make an election under subsection 13(3) and pay the contribution required under section 10 within one year after their balance-due day. (S.C. 2009, c. 31, s. 26(2).)

(2) *Idem* — In the case of a person who is a contributor under the *Public Service Superannuation Act* there shall be included in computing the amount of that person's contributory salary and wages for a year the amount of his salary, as defined in that Act, that is not otherwise included in computing income for the purposes of the *Income Tax Act*.

(2.1) *Idem* — In the case of an Indian, as defined in the *Indian Act*, to the extent provided by regulations pursuant to subsection 7(1) and subject to any conditions prescribed by those regulations, there shall be included in computing the amount of that person's contributory salary and wages for a year the amount of his income from employment that would otherwise be excepted pursuant to paragraph 6(2)(*j*.1). (R.S.C. 1985, c. 30 (2nd Supp.), s. 5(2).)

(3) *Remuneration paid in respect of employment in province* — A reference in this Act to the contributory salary and wages of a person for a year shall, in relation to any remuneration paid to him in respect of pensionable employment in a province providing a comprehensive pension plan, be construed as a reference to his income for the

145

year from that employment as that income is required to be computed under the provincial pension plan of that province.

(R.S.C. 1985, c. 30 (2nd Supp.), s. 5; 2001, c. 17, s. 254; 2004, c. 22, s. 17; 2009, c. 31, s. 26.)

————————— Notes —————————

Synopsis

This section defines the total annual contributory salary and wages of employees for the purpose of calculating employee and employer contributions under ss. 8 and 9 respectively. The employee's income as calculated under the *Income Tax Act* is used as the basis for calculating income, although allowable *Income Tax Act* deductions (except for the residence of clergy) must be added back in.

Note, however, that four types of income are exempt from inclusion under this section — income received before the employee turned 18, income received in month that was not part of the employee's contributory period owing to the employee's disability during that month, income received after the employee turns 70, and income received after the employee turns 65 and is in receipt of a CPP or private pension, where the employee elects to exclude income from pensionable employment or self-employed earnings. This election may be made annually, cannot be made if a revocation of election has already been made for that year, and cannot be revoked the year it is made.

Case Law

Canada v. Bear, 2003 FCA 40

While there is no specific exclusion of Indians in the CPP, the effect of s. 12 is to base CPP contributions on income defined by and calculated under the *Income Tax Act*. Under s. 81 of the *Income Tax Act* and s. 87 of the *Indian Act*, contributions to the CPP could not be based on, nor required from, Indian income exempt from taxation. Income earned by an Indian on a reserve is exempt from taxation by virtue of s. 87 of the *Indian Act*. This exemption is not discriminatory for the purposes of s. 15 of the *Canadian Charter of Rights and Freedoms*, and does not constitute a denial of equality before the law within the meaning of s. 1(*b*) of the *Canadian Bill of Rights*. The exemption is therefore constitutionally valid.

————————————

Contributory Self-Employed Earnings

13. *Amount of contributory self-employed earnings* — **(1) The amount of the contributory self-employed earnings of a person for a year is the amount of the self-employed earnings except that,**

(*a*) **for a year in which the person reaches eighteen or seventy years of age, in which their contributory period ends under this Act or under a provincial pension plan by reason of disability or in which a disability pension ceases to be payable to them under this Act or under a provincial pension plan, the amount of the contributory self-employed earnings is equal to that proportion of the amount of the self-employed earnings that the number of months in the year**

(i) **after**

(A) **they reach eighteen years of age, or**

(B) **the disability pension ceases to be payable, or**

(ii) **before**

(A) **they reach seventy years of age, or**

(B) **the month following the month in which their contributory period ends under this Act or under a provincial pension plan by reason of disability,** is of 12;

　(b) despite paragraph (a), for a year in which a retirement pension is payable to them under this Act or under a provincial pension plan and for which they make an election to exclude self-employed earnings, the amount of the contributory self-employed earnings is equal to that proportion of the amount of the self-employed earnings that the number of months in the year before the election is deemed to be made — minus the number of months that are excluded from the contributory period under this Act or under a provincial pension plan by reason of disability — is of 12;

　(c) despite paragraph (a), for a year in which a retirement pension is payable to them under this Act or under a provincial pension plan and for which they revoke an election to exclude self-employed earnings, the amount of the contributory self-employed earnings is equal to that proportion of the amount of self-employed earnings that the number of months in the year after the election is deemed to be revoked — minus the number of months after they reach seventy years of age — is of 12;

　(d) despite paragraph (a), for a year in which an election referred to in subparagraph 12(1)(c)(ii) is made, the amount of the contributory self-employed earnings is equal to that proportion of the amount of the self-employed earnings that the number of months in the year before the election is made — minus the number of months that are excluded from the contributory period under this Act or under a provincial pension plan by reason of disability — is of 12; and

　(e) despite paragraph (a), for a year in which an election referred to in subparagraph 12(1)(c)(ii) is revoked, the amount of the contributory self-employed earnings is equal to that proportion of the amount of the self-employed earnings that the number of months in the year after the election is revoked — minus the number of months after they reach seventy years of age — is of 12.

(R.S.C. 1985, c. 30 (2nd Supp.), s. 6; 2009, c. 31, s. 27(1).)

　(1.1) *Election* — An election referred to in paragraph (1)(b) or (c)

　(a) shall be made or revoked in the prescribed form and manner;

　(b) may be made only once for a year;

　(c) may not be revoked for the year for which it is deemed to be made;

　(d) may not be made for a year for which an election is revoked;

　(e) is deemed to be made or revoked on the first day of the month referred to in the election or revocation, as the case may be; and

　(f) may not be made for a year for which the person has income from pensionable employment.

(S.C. 2009, c. 31, s. 27(1).)

　(1.2) *Condition* — For the purposes of paragraph (1.1)(e), the month may not be

　(a) before the one in which the person reaches sixty-five years of age;

　(b) before the one in which the retirement pension becomes payable; or

　(c) after the one in which they reach seventy years of age.

(S.C. 2009, c. 31, s. 27(1).)

　(2) *Excluded earnings* — Subject to subsection (1), the contributory self-employed earnings of a person do not include earnings for

　(a) any period described in paragraph 12(1)(a), (b), (c) or (d); or

　(b) any year that

(i) follows a year for which the person makes an election to exclude self-employed earnings, and

(ii) is not a year for which they revoke the election.

(S.C. 2009, c. 31, s. 27(1).)

(**3**) *Election to include certain earnings* — Despite subsection (1), the amount of the contributory self-employed earnings of a person for a year for the purposes of section 10 shall, if the person or their representative makes an election in the prescribed manner within one year from June 15 in the following year — or, in the case of an employee to whom the Minister refunds an amount under section 38, from the day on which the Minister refunds the amount — include any amount by which (S.C. 1997, c. 40, s. 60; 2009, c. 31, s. 27(2).)

(*a*) the lesser of

(i) his contributory salary and wages for the year, and

(ii) his maximum pensionable earnings for the year,

exceeds

(*b*) the aggregate of

(i) his salary and wages on which a contribution has been made for the year and such amount, if any, as is determined in prescribed manner to be his salary and wages on which a contribution has been made for the year by him under a provincial pension plan, and

(ii) the lesser of

(A) the aggregate of all amounts deducted as prescribed on account of his basic exemption for the year by one or more employers pursuant to section 8 and all amounts deducted as prescribed by or under a provincial pension plan on account of any like exemption for the year by one or more employers pursuant to such a plan, and

(B) his basic exemption for the year.

(**4**) *Self-employed earnings where resident in province* — A reference in this Act to the contributory self-employed earnings of a person for a year shall, in relation to any self-employed earnings of a person who was resident on the last day of the year in a province providing a comprehensive pension plan, be construed as a reference to his self-employed earnings for the year as such earnings are required to be computed under the provincial pension plan of that province.

(R.S.C. 1985, c. 30 (2nd Supp.), s. 6; 1997, c. 40, s. 60; 2009, c. 31, s. 27.)

——————— Notes ———————

Synopsis

This section defines the total annual contributory self-employed earnings for the purpose of calculating the contribution in respect of self-employed earnings under s. 10. Four types of income are exempt from inclusion — income received before the employee turned 18, income received in month that was not part of the employee's contributory period owing to the employee's disability during that month, income received after the employee turns 70, and income received after the employee turns 65 and is in receipt of a CPP or private pension, where the employee elects to exclude income from pensionable employment or self-employed earnings. Where such income is received for part of a given year, the contribution is prorated on a month-by-month basis for that part of the year before or after such income is received.

Where there has been an over-deduction of the basic exemption, s. 13(3) allows the individual to elect to make up any deficiency. This may occur where an individual had more than one employer and was allowed too much for his or her basic exemption during the year, thereby denying the individual an opportunity to contribute on his or her full earnings for the year. This election may be made within one year from June 15 in the year following the year in issue.

Related Provisions

- Section 14 — Amount of self-employed earnings for a year
- Section 30 — Return required to be filed in respect of self-employed earnings
- Section 31 — Estimate of amount of contribution required to be made
- Section 33 — Payment of contribution
- Section 34 — Interest on unpaid contributions
- Section 35 — Failure to file return
- Section 36 — Assessments, objections, interest, penalties and refunds
- Section 37 — Priority in which payment to be applied
- Section 38(4), (4.1) — Refund of excess contribution

---

14. *Amount of self-employed earnings for a year* — **The amount of the self-employed earnings of a person for a year is the aggregate of**

(a) an amount equal to

    (i) his income for the year from all businesses, other than a business more than fifty per cent of the gross revenue of which consisted of rent from land or buildings, carried on by him,

    minus

    (ii) all losses sustained by him in the year in carrying on those businesses,

    as such income and losses are computed under the *Income Tax Act*, except any such income or losses from the performance of services described in paragraph 7(1)(d) that has been included in pensionable employment by a regulation made under subsection 7(1) or by a regulation made under a provincial pension plan, (R.S.C. 1988, c. 30 (2nd Supp.), s. 7.)

(b) his income for the year from employment described in paragraph 7(2)(e) that has been excepted from pensionable employment by a regulation made under subsection 7(2) or by a regulation made under a provincial pension plan, as that income is computed under the *Income Tax Act*, and (R.S.C. 1985, c. 30 (2nd Supp.), s. 7.)

(c) in the case of an Indian, as defined in the *Indian Act*, to the extent provided by regulations and subject to any conditions prescribed by those regulations, his income for the year from self-employment on a reserve, as defined in the *Indian Act*, that is not otherwise included in computing income for the purposes of the *Income Tax Act*. (R.S.C. 1985, c. 30 (2nd Supp.), s. 7.)

(R.S.C. 1985, c. 30 (2nd Supp.), s. 7.)

--------------- **Notes** ---------------

Synopsis

This section sets out the formula for calculating an individual's annual self-employed earnings for the purpose of s. 13. Essentially, the amount of business income and losses is determined by application of the federal *Income Tax Act*. Income from businesses that derive more than half their gross revenue for the rental of real property is entirely excluded. While business deductions permitted by the *Income Tax Act* in getting to net income will be allowed, further deductions — e.g., personal exemptions, charitable donations, gifts to the Crown, optional standard deduction and businesses losses from other years — used to arrive at an individual's "taxable income" for *Income Tax Act* purposes are not permitted. The income from different businesses must be computed separately, and a loss from one business cannot be used to reduce the income from a different business. Taxable capital gains (and losses) are not included. Under *Income Tax Act* s. 67, expenses are deductible only to the extent that they are reasonable.

Related Provisions

- Section 2 — "Business" defined

- Section 14.1 — Communal organizations

- Section 30 — Return required to be filed in respect of self-employed earnings

---

14.1. *Idem* — [10]**For the purposes of paragraph 14(a), where a member of a family in a congregation is specified in an election under subsection 143(2) of the *Income Tax Act* for a year, such part of the total of all amounts allocated to the family under that subsection for the year as may reasonably be regarded as having been derived from a business carried on by the congregation shall be deemed to be the member's income (as computed under that Act) from such a business carried on by the member.**

(S.C. 1991, c. 49, s. 204.)

─────────── **Notes** ───────────

Synopsis

This section addresses the situation where income is earned by a family that is part of a communal organization whose members do not own the property as individuals. Under the *Income Tax Act*, the property is deemed to be owned in trust, and under s. 143(2), the trustees may elect to have the income from the property deemed to have been payable to the individual members of the congregation in a taxation year.

Salary and Wages on which Contribution Made

15. *Amount of salary and wages on which contribution made for a year* — **(1)** **The amount of the salary and wages of a person on which a contribution has been made for a year is an amount equal to**

    (*a*) **the aggregate of all amounts deducted as required from the remuneration of that person on account of the employee's contribution for the year under this Act, minus the amount of any refund made to him under section 38 in respect of any amounts so deducted on account thereof, or such part of the amount of any refund in respect thereof made to him as described in section 39 as might have been made to him under subsection 38(1) if no agreement had been entered into under subsection 39(1), and**

    (*b*) **where an employer has failed to deduct an amount as required from the remuneration of that person on account of the employee's contribution for the year under this Act and that person has notified the Minister of the employer's failure so to deduct that amount on or before April 30 in the following year, an**

---

[10] Pursuant to 1991, c. 49, s. 204(2), section 14.1 applies to 1982 and subsequent years.

amount equal to the amount that should have been so deducted by the employer on account thereof,

divided by the contribution rate for employees for the year. (R.S.C. 1985, c. 30 (2nd Supp.), s. 8(1).)

(2) *Effect of payment by employer of amount not deducted as required* — **For the purposes of subsection 8(2) and this section, where an amount that an employer has failed to deduct as required from the remuneration of an employee on account of the employee's contribution for a year under this Act is paid by the employer on account of the employee's contribution for that year under this Act, the amount so paid shall be deemed to have been deducted by the employer on account of that contribution.**

(3) *Special rule applicable in prescribed circumstances* — **Where an employer has filed a return pursuant to this Part showing an amount as the salary and wages on which a contribution has been made by an employee for a year under this Act, the amount so shown, multiplied by the contribution rate for employees for the year, may, in prescribed circumstances, be substituted for the amount shown therein as the aggregate of the amounts deducted by that employer on account of the employee's contribution for the year under this Act, in calculating the amount to be determined under subsection (1). (R.S.C. 1985, c. 30 (2nd Supp.), s. 8(2).)**

(R.S.C. 1985, c. 30 (2nd Supp.), s. 8.)

—————————— Notes ——————————

Synopsis

This section determines the amount of an employee's salary and wages on which contribution has been made for the year for the purposes of ss. 8-10. This amount is equal to:

(Total of the employee's actual contributions - any refund of contributions + any contributions the employer did not deduct) / employee's contribution rate

Where an employer has paid an amount on account of the employee's contribution, but has not deducted that amount from the employee's remuneration, the amount contributed is deemed to have been deducted for the purpose of determining the salary and wages on which a contribution has been made.

—————————————————————

Maximum Contributory Earnings

16. *Amount of maximum contributory earnings for a year* — **The amount of the maximum contributory earnings of a person for a year is the amount of his maximum pensionable earnings for the year, minus the amount of his basic exemption for the year.**

—————————— Notes ——————————

Synopsis

For 2014, the maximum contributory earnings was $52,500 - $3,500, or $49,000.

Related Provisions

- Section 17 — Amount of Maximum Pensionable Earnings

- Section 19 — Amount of basic exemption

Related CPP Regulations

- Section 5(5) — Computation of employee's contribution

Maximum Pensionable Earnings

17. *Amount of maximum pensionable earnings* — **The amount of the maximum pensionable earnings of a person for a year is the amount of the Year's Maximum Pensionable Earnings except that,**

(a) **for a year in which the person reaches eighteen or seventy years of age or die, in which their contributory period ends under this Act or under a provincial pension plan by reason of disability or in which a disability pension ceases to be payable to them under this Act or under a provincial pension plan, the amount of the maximum pensionable earnings is equal to that proportion of the amount of the Year's Maximum Pensionable Earnings that the number of months in the year**

  (i) **after**

   (A) **they reach eighteen years of age, or**

   (B) **the disability pension ceases to be payable, or**

  (ii) **before**

   (A) **they reach seventy years of age,**

   (B) **they die, or**

   (C) **the month following the month in which their contributory period ends under this Act or under a provincial pension plan by reason of disability,**

including, if they die, the month in which they die, is of 12;

(b) **despite paragraph (a), for a year in which an election referred to in subparagraph 12(1)(c)(ii) is made or one referred to in paragraph 13(1)(b) is deemed to be made, the maximum pensionable earnings is equal to that proportion of the amount of the Year's Maximum Pensionable Earnings that the number of months in the year before the election is made or deemed to be made, as the case may be — minus the number of months that are excluded from the contributory period under this Act or under a provincial pension plan by reason of disability — is of 12; and**

(c) **despite paragraph (a), for a year in which an election referred to in subparagraph 12(1)(c)(ii) is revoked or one referred to in paragraph 13(1)(c) is deemed to be revoked, the maximum pensionable earnings is equal to that proportion of the amount of the Year's Maximum Pensionable Earnings that the number of months in the year after the election is revoked or deemed to be revoked, as the case may be — minus the number of months after they reach seventy years of age or die, whichever is earlier — is of 12.**

(R.S.C. 1985, c. 30 (2nd Supp.), s. 9; 2009, c. 31, s. 28.)

——————— **Notes** ———————

Synopsis

This section establishes that a person's maximum pensionable earnings for the year, used to determine the amount of maximum contributory earnings for the year, is the Year's Maximum Pensionable Earnings (YMPE) as calculated in s. 18, except where during the year:

  1. the person has turned 18 or 70, or has died;

2. the person has become entitled to receive a retirement pension under the CPP or QPP;

3. the person has become disabled such that the contributory period ends under the CPP or QPP;

4. a disability pension under the CPP or QPP ceases to be payable.

This calculation is also subject to whether an employee, being 65 or older, has elected to exempt his or her pensionable employment or self-employed earnings in a year, or has revoked an earlier election.

In these years, the person's maximum pensionable earnings are determined by dividing the YMPE by 12 and multiplying it by the number of the months in the year from the month after the person reaches 18, a disability pension ceases to be payable, the contributory period ends by reason of disability, before the person turns 70, a retirement pension becomes payable or the person dies. Where a person dies, the month of death in included in the contributory period.

Related Provisions

- Section 2(2) — When specified age deemed to be reached
- Section 18 — Amount of Year's Maximum Pensionable Earnings ("YMPE")

Year's Maximum Pensionable Earnings

18. *Amount of Year's Maximum Pensionable Earnings* — **(1) The amount of a Year's Maximum Pensionable Earnings is**

(*a*) **for 1987, $25,900;**

(*b*) **subject to subsection (2), for 1988, an amount calculated by multiplying the Year's Maximum Pensionable Earnings for 1987 by the ratio that**

(i) **the average for the twelve month period ending on June 30, 1987 of the Wage Measure for each month in that period**

bears to

(ii) **the average for the twelve month period ending on June 30, 1986 of the Wage Measure for each month in that period; and**

(*c*) **subject to subsection (2), for 1989 and each subsequent year, an amount calculated by multiplying the Year's Maximum Pensionable Earnings for the preceding year, calculated without reference to subsections (2) and (3), by the ratio that**

(i) **the average for the twelve month period ending on June 30 of the preceding year of the Wage Measure for each month in that period**

bears to

(ii) **the average for the twelve month period ending on June 30 of the year immediately preceding the preceding year of the Wage Measure for each month in that period.**

(S.C. 1991, c. 44, s. 2.)

(2) *Rounding off* — **Where the amount calculated in accordance with paragraph (1)(*b*) or (*c*) for any year is not a multiple of one hundred dollars, the Year's Maximum Pensionable Earnings for that year is the amount that is the next multiple of one hundred dollars below that amount. (S.C. 1991, c. 44, s. 2.)**

(3) *Minimum amount of Year's Maximum Pensionable Earnings* — **Where the amount calculated in accordance with paragraph (1)(*b*) or (*c*) in respect of any year is**

less than the Year's Maximum Pensionable Earnings for the preceding year, it shall be increased to the amount of the Year's Maximum Pensionable Earnings for the preceding year. (S.C. 1991, c. 44, s. 2.)

(4) *Idem* — (Repealed by 1991, c. 44, s. 2.)

(5) *Wage Measure* — The Wage Measure for a month is the average weekly wages and salaries of

    (*a*) the Industrial Aggregate in Canada for the month as published by Statistics Canada under the authority of the *Statistics Act*; or

    (*b*) in the event that the Industrial Aggregate ceases to be published, such other measure as is prescribed by regulation for the month as published by Statistics Canada under the authority of the *Statistics Act*.

(6) *Idem* — For the purpose of calculating the amount of a Year's Maximum Pensionable Earnings, where Statistics Canada has published any revisions of the Industrial Aggregate or the other measure referred to in paragraph (5)(*b*) for any month, the revision of the Industrial Aggregate or the other measure referred to in paragraph (5)(*b*) that has been published most recently prior to the calculation in respect of that month shall be used in calculating the amount of the Year's Maximum Pensionable Earnings.

(7) *Adjustment of Industrial Aggregate* — Where, at any time after the coming into force of this section, a new time or content basis is adopted by Statistics Canada in determining the Industrial Aggregate or the other measure referred to in paragraph (5)(*b*) for a month and the adoption of that new basis would cause a difference between

    (*a*) the average for the twelve month period ending on June 30 of any year of the Industrial Aggregate or the other measure referred to in paragraph (5)(*b*) for each month in that period calculated pursuant to this section on the former time or content basis, as the case may be; and

    (*b*) the average for the twelve month period of the Industrial Aggregate or the other measure referred to in paragraph (5)(*b*) for each month in that period calculated pursuant to this section on the new time or content basis, as the case may be,

of more than one per cent of the average for that twelve month period of the Industrial Aggregate or the other measure referred to in paragraph (5)(*b*) for each month in that period calculated pursuant to this section on the former time or content basis, the average of that twelve month period calculated on the new time or content basis shall be adjusted by the Minister, on the advice of the Chief Statistician of Canada, to reflect the former time or content basis, and any other averages that are calculated in determining the Year's Maximum Pensionable Earnings for the year following that twelve month period shall be adjusted accordingly.

(8) *Limitation on adjustment* — Subsection (7) shall cease to apply when the Industrial Aggregate or the other measure referred to in paragraph (5)(*b*) for a month has been calculated on the new time or content basis referred to in that subsection for a period of twenty-four consecutive months ending on June 30 of a year.

(R.S.C. 1985, c. 30 (2nd Supp.), s. 10; S.C. 1991, c. 44, s. 2.)

─────────── **Notes** ───────────

Synopsis

The Year's Maximum Pensionable Earnings ("YMPE") is calculated by multiplying the YMPE for the preceding year, calculated without rounding-off, by the following ratio:

the average for the 12-month period ending on June 30 of the preceding year of the average wages and salaries (the "Wage Measure") for each month in that period: the average for the 12-month period ending on June 30 of the year immediately prior to the preceding year of the Wage Measure for each month in the period

This amount is then rounded down to a $100 multiple. For 2002, the YMPE was $39,100. For 2003, the YMPE was $39,900. For 2004, the YMPE was $40,500. For 2005, the YMPE was $41,100. For 2006, the YMPE was $42,100. For 2007, the YMPE was $43,700. For 2008, the YMPE was $44,900. For 2009, the YMPE was $46,300. For 2010, the YMPE was $47,200. For 2011, the YMPE was $48,300. For 2012, the YMPE was $50,100. For 2013, the YMPE was $51,100. For 2014, the YMPE is $52,500.

───────────────

Basic Exemption

19. *Amount of basic exemption* — **The amount of the basic exemption of a person for a year is the amount of the Year's Basic Exemption except that,**

    (*a*) **for a year in which the person reaches eighteen or seventy years of age or die, in which their contributory period ends under this Act or under a provincial pension plan by reason of disability or in which a disability pension ceases to be payable to them under this Act or under a provincial pension plan, the amount of the basic exemption is equal to that proportion of the amount of the Year's Basic Exemption that the number of months in the year**

    (i) **after**

      (A) **they reach eighteen years of age, or**

      (B) **the disability pension ceases to be payable, or**

    (ii) **before**

      (A) **they reach seventy years of age,**

      (B) **they die, or**

      (C) **the month following the month in which their contributory period ends under this Act or under a provincial pension plan by reason of disability,**

    including, if they die, the month in which they die, is of 12;

    (*b*) **despite paragraph (*a*), for a year in which an election referred to in subparagraph 12(1)(*c*)(ii) is made or one referred to in paragraph 13(1)(*b*) is deemed to be made, the amount of the basic exemption is equal to that proportion of the amount of the Year's Basic Exemption that the number of months in the year before the election is made or deemed to be made, as the case may be — minus the number of months that are excluded from the contributory period under this Act or under a provincial pension plan by reason of disability — is of 12;**

    (*c*) **despite paragraph (*a*), for a year in which an election referred to in subparagraph 12(1)(*c*)(ii) is revoked or one referred to in paragraph 13(1)(*c*) is deemed to be revoked, the amount of the basic exemption is equal to that proportion of the amount of the Year's Basic Exemption that the number of months in the year after the election is revoked or deemed to be revoked, as the case may be**

155

— minus the number of months after they reach seventy years of age or die, whichever is earlier — is of 12;

(*d*) despite paragraphs (*a*) to (*c*), for a year in which a retirement pension becomes payable to them under this Act or under a provincial pension plan, the amount of the basic exemption is equal to that proportion of the amount of the Year's Basic Exemption that the number of months in the year before the retirement pension becomes payable — minus the number of months that are excluded from the contributory period under this Act or under a provincial pension plan by reason of disability — is of 12 unless the aggregate of the contributory salary and wages and the contributory self-employed earnings exceeds the amount, adjusted by that proportion, of the Year's Maximum Pensionable Earnings, in which case, the amount of the basic exemption is increased by the lesser of

(i) the product obtained by multiplying

(A) the Year's Basic Exemption

by

(B) one-twelfth of the amount by which the number of months in the year for which a retirement pension is payable exceeds the greater of

(I) the number of months for which an election referred to in subparagraph 12(1)(*c*)(ii) or paragraph 13(1)(*b*) has effect, and

(II) the number of months after they reach seventy years of age or die, whichever is earlier, and

(ii) the amount by which the aggregate of the contributory salary and wages and the contributory self-employed earnings exceeds the product obtained by multiplying

(A) the Year's Maximum Pensionable Earnings

by

(B) one-twelfth of the amount by which the number of months in the year before the retirement pension becomes payable exceeds the number of months that are excluded from the contributory period under this Act or under a provincial pension plan by reason of disability.

(S.C. 2009, c. 31, s. 29.)

——————— Notes ———————

Synopsis

This section establishes that a person's basic exemption for the year, used to determine the amount of maximum contributory earnings for the year, is the Year's Basic Exemption ("YBE") as set out in s. 20 (i.e., $3,500), except where during the year:

1. the person has turned 18 or 70, or has died,

2. the person has become entitled to receive a retirement pension under the CPP or QPP,

3. the person has become disabled such that the contributory period ends under the CPP or QPP,

4. a disability pension under the CPP or QPP ceases to be payable.

In these years, the person's basic exemption is determined by dividing the YBE by 12 and multiplying it by the number of the months in the year from the month after the person reaches 18, a disability pension ceases to be payable, the contributory period ends by reason of disability, before the person turns 70, a retirement pension becomes payable or the person dies. Where a person dies, the month of death is included in the contributory period.

Case Law

Miceli-Riggins v. Canada (Attorney General), 2013 FCA 158

The proration provision in the CPP s. 19 is an ameliorative provision designed to mitigate possible harsh results. Section 19 is designed to ensure that a contributor is not disadvantaged when the contributor cannot make sufficient contributions in a year. Under proration, the contributor's required contribution level for the year is reduced in proportion to the number of months the contributor was able to work. Proration is available when a contributor reaches 70 years of age, dies, becomes disabled, or the CPP retirement pension is payable. It is also available when a person turns 18 years of age or ceases to receive a disability pension under the CPP or provincial counterparts. It is not available when a person gives birth to a child, or becomes or ceases to be eligible for the CRDO.

MHRD v. Snowdon (December 3, 2007), CP 25013 (PAB)

Section 19 allows proration for the year the contributory period ends because of disability under the Plan. In the year that the contributory period ends, the prorated amount is established by dividing the YBE by 12 and multiplying by the number of months before and including the month the claimant became disabled.

Pleasant-Joseph v. MSD (November 13, 2007), CP 24934 (PAB), judicial review denied 2009 FCA 173

Proration cannot apply to two years, even where the claimant's contributions were only short by $138.00 in the previous year. The PAB could not apply equitable principles to its decision to assist the claimant.

MSD v. Gorman (August 1, 2006), CP 22414 (PAB)

Section 19 provides that proration may be allowed for the year the contributory period ends because of the disability under the CPP. To be eligible for disability benefits the claimant would have to be found to be disabled within the meaning of the CPP during the extended period.

Related Provisions

- Section 20 — Amount of Year's Basic Exemption

Year's Basic Exemption

20. *Amount of Year's Basic Exemption* — **(1) Subject to subsection (2), the amount of a Year's Basic Exemption is the highest multiple of $100 that is less than or equal to 10% of the Year's Maximum Pensionable Earnings for the year. (S.C. 1997, c. 40, s. 61.)**

(2) *Limitation* — **For each year after 1997 the amount of a Year's Basic Exemption is $3,500. (S.C. 1997, c. 40, s. 61.)**

(S.C. 1997, c. 40, s. 61.)

—————— **Notes** ——————

Synopsis

As of January 1, 1998, the Year's Basic Exemption (YBE) has been generally frozen at $3,500. However, s. 20(2) does not apply for disability-related claims purposes (see s. 44(2)(a)). In 2014, the YBE to be used in calculating the minimum qualifying period on disability and disabled contributor's child's benefit claims is $5,200.

Division C: Collection of Contributions

Employees and Employers

21. *Amount to be deducted and remitted by employer* — [11](1) Every employer paying remuneration to an employee employed by the employer at any time in pensionable employment shall deduct from that remuneration as or on account of the employee's contribution for the year in which the remuneration in respect of the pensionable employment is paid to the employee any amount that is determined in accordance with prescribed rules and shall remit that amount, together with any amount that is prescribed with respect to the contribution required to be made by the employer under this Act, to the Receiver General at any time that is prescribed and, if at that prescribed time the employer is a prescribed person, the remittance shall be made to the account of the Receiver General at a financial institution (within the meaning that would be assigned by the definition "financial institution" in subsection 190(1) of the *Income Tax Act* if that definition were read without reference to its paragraphs (*d*) and (*e*). (S.C. 2011, c. 24, s. 175.)

(1.1) *Exception — remittance to financial institution* — For the purpose of subsection (1), a prescribed person referred to in that subsection is deemed to have remitted an amount to the account of the Receiver General at a financial institution referred to in that subsection if the prescribed person has remitted the amount to the Receiver General at least one day before the day on which the amount is due. (S.C. 2008, c. 28, s. 38(1).)

(2) *Liability for failure to deduct and remit* — Subject to subsection (3), every employer who fails to deduct and remit an amount from the remuneration of an employee as and when required under subsection (1) is liable to pay to Her Majesty the whole amount that should have been deducted and remitted from the time it should have been deducted.

(3) *Subsequent decision — limit on liability* — An employer is not liable for any amount that the employer fails to deduct as required by this Act from the remuneration of an employee, or for any interest or penalties for that failure, if

(a) the employer is informed in writing in a ruling under section 26.1 that the employer is not required to make the deduction;

(b) the ruling is not based on information provided by the employer to the Minister that was incorrect in a material particular; and

(c) it is subsequently decided under subsection 27.2(3) or section 28 that the deduction should have been made. (S.C. 1997, c. 40, s. 62.)

(3.1) *Subsequent decision — other consequences* — Once the decision under subsection 27.2(3) or section 28 is communicated to the employer, the employer is liable without interest or penalties under this Act to pay the contribution required to be paid by the employer with respect to the employee. On payment by the employer of any amount as or on account of that contribution, the employee is deemed to have notified the Minister as required by paragraph 15(1)(*b*) of the employer's failure to deduct the amount of that contribution from the remuneration of the employee. (S.C. 1997, c. 40, s. 62.)

(4) *Deduction from subsequent payment of remuneration* — An employer who fails to deduct an amount that is required by subsection (1) to be deducted from a payment

---

[11] Pursuant to 1993, c. 24, s. 143(3), subsection 21(1) applies after 1992.

of remuneration to an employee may deduct an amount equal to the amount from any subsequent payment of remuneration made to the employee within 12 months after the making of the payment from which the amount was required to be deducted, but no employer may deduct from a payment of remuneration made to an employee, in addition to the amount required by subsection (1) to be deducted therefrom, any amount with respect to more than one such amount that the employer previously failed to deduct. (R.S.C. 1985, c. 6 (1st Supp.), s. 1(2).)

(5) *Amount deducted deemed received by employee* — Where an amount has been deducted under subsection (1), it shall be deemed for all purposes to have been received at that time by the employee to whom the remuneration was payable.

(6) *Interest on amounts not remitted* — Where an employer has failed to remit to the Receiver General an amount that the employer was required to remit at the time when he was required to do so, the employer shall pay to the Receiver General interest on that amount at the prescribed rate computed from the day on which the employer was so required to remit the amount to the day of remittance of the amount to the Receiver General. (R.S.C. 1985, c. 46 (4th Supp.), s. 1.)

(7) *Penalty for failure to remit* — Every employer who in a calendar year fails to remit to the Receiver General an amount that the employer is required to remit at the time when he is required to do so is liable to a penalty of

(a) subject to paragraph (b), if

(i) the Receiver General receives that amount on or before the day it was due, but that amount is not paid in the manner required, three per cent of that amount,

(ii) the Receiver General receives that amount

(A) no more than three days after it was due, three per cent of that amount,

(B) more than three days and no more than five days after it was due, five per cent of that amount, or

(C) more than five days and no more than seven days after it was due, seven per cent of that amount, or

(iii) that amount is not paid or remitted on or before the seventh day after it was due, ten per cent of that amount; or

(S.C. 2008, c. 28, s. 38(2).)

(b) [12]where, at the time of the failure a penalty under this subsection was payable by the employer in respect of an amount that the employer was required to remit during the year and the failure was made knowingly or under circumstances amounting to gross negligence, twenty per cent of the amount. (S.C. 1991, c. 49, s. 205; 1993, c. 24, s. 143(3).)

(R.S.C. 1985, c. 46 (4th Supp.), s. 1.)

(R.S.C. 1985, c. 6 (1st Supp.), s. 1; R.S.C. 1985, c. 46 (4th Supp.), s. 1; 1991, c. 49, s. 205; 1993, c. 24, s. 143; 1997, c. 40, s. 62; 2008, c. 28, s. 38; 2011, c. 24, s. 175.)

---

[12] Pursuant to 1993, c. 24, s. 143(4), this section applies after 1992, except in respect to amounts required to be submitted before 1993.

——————— **Notes** ———————

Synopsis

This section states that an employer must withhold an amount from every remuneration payment to each employee. The withheld amount (see CPP Regulation, s. 5) is to be held by the employer on account of the employee's CPP contribution. Such amount must be remitted on a regular basis (see CPP Regulation, s. 8) to the Receiver General, or, where the employer is "prescribed person" (see CPP Regulation s. 8.2) the account of the Receiver General at a financial institution along with the employer's contribution with respect to each employee. In the *Income Tax Act*, the definition for "financial institution" in s. 190(1) *(a)–(c)* reads as follows:

"financial institution" means a corporation that

(a) is a bank,

(b) is authorized under the laws of Canada or a province to carry on the business of offering its services as a trustee to the public, [or]

(c) is authorized under the laws of Canada or a province to accept deposits from the public and carries on the business of lending money on the security of real estate or investing in mortgages on real estate[.]

Even if the employer failed to withhold the amounts from its employees, it is liable to remit the total amount of the employee and employer contributions unless the employer was relying on an erroneous Minister's written ruling that it did not have to withhold the amounts. The employer has 12 months to deduct the employee contribution from subsequent remuneration payments to the employee from the time of the missed deduction.

The employer must pay interest at the prescribed rate on amounts it fails to remit, and is also liable to a penalty of 10% of the amount, or 20% if the employer knowingly failed to remit or was grossly negligent.

Related Provisions

- Section 21.1 — Liability of directors

- Section 26 — No liability against person deducting

- Section 26.1(4) — Presumption that deduction or non-deduction in accordance with Act

- Section 41(1) — Offence or punishment

Related CPP Regulations

- Sections 4–5 — Computation of employee's contribution

- Sections 8–8.1 — Payment of contribution

- Section 8.2 — Prescribed persons

- Section 10–11 — Filing of employer's returns

- Section 12 — Filing by legal representatives

- Section 13 — Distribution of employee's portion of return

- Section 14 — Penalties

- Sections 35–36 — Prescribed interest rates

Case Law

Soper v. The Queen (1997), 97 D.T.C. 5407 (Fed. C.A.)

In reality, employers do not actually set aside funds relating to source deductions every time an employee is issued a paycheque. The withholding of source deductions is a notional concept that does not materialize until the obligation to remit actually arises.

Kroeker v. MNR (1969), 69 D.T.C. 380 (T.A.B.)

CPP payments withheld at source only enter into the computation of the taxpayer's net taxable income as deductions from gross income and do not form part of the taxes levied. CPP contributions withheld at source become simply another premium deducted by the employer, and for income tax purposes are treated in the same way as employee's contributions to Blue Cross, provincial hospital plans, employer's pension funds, union dues and other such payments.

Aboriginal Federated Alliance Inc. v. The Queen, 2004 TCC 336

Amounts that have been withheld by the employer must be remitted. The employer cannot avoid its obligation to remit by arguing that it should not have withheld.

Allan A. Greber Professional Corporation v. M.N.R., 2007 TCC 78

Funds paid by an employer into a *bona fide* employee profit sharing plan allocated to the principals of the employer and paid out to them by the trustees of the plan were not remuneration "paid" by an employer to "an employee", and accordingly there was no obligation on the Appellant to deduct or remit CPP contributions with respect thereto.

DNS Signs Ltd. v. M.N.R., 2006 TCC 407

In the normal course of events, allocations to beneficiaries of *bona fide* employees profit sharing plans are not subject to source deductions. This exemption from source deductions stems from the fact that allocations to beneficiaries from employees profit sharing plans are of trust income computed with reference to an employer's profit from the employer's business, and are not employees' contributory salaries and wages within the meaning of the CPP. The same considerations do not apply if the EPSP is not *bona fide.* The purpose of section 144 of the *Income Tax Act* is to provide certainty regarding the income tax consequences of contributions to employees profit sharing plans; of incentive allocations to employees out of such plans; of income earned on trust assets; and of distributions thereof. The section is not intended to be used as a means of circumventing the CPP and avoiding the contributions required by it. The CPP is remedial legislation designed to provide social insurance for Canadians. It should therefore be given fair, large and liberal construction, and its objectives should not be frustrated by improper use of section 144 of the ITA.

21.1. *Liability* — **(1) If an employer who fails to deduct or remit an amount as and when required under subsection 21(1) is a corporation, the persons who were the directors of the corporation at the time when the failure occurred are jointly and severally or solidarily liable, together with the corporation, to pay to Her Majesty that amount and any interest or penalties relating to it. (S.C. 2004, c. 25, s. 112.)**

(2) *Application of Income Tax Act provisions* — **Subsection 227.1(2) to (7) of the *Income Tax Act* apply, with such modification as the circumstances require, in respect of a director of a corporation referred to in subsection (1).**

(3) *Assessment provisions applicable to directors* — **The provisions of this Act respecting the assessment of an employer for an amount payable by the employer under this Act and respecting the rights and obligations of an employer so assessed apply in respect of a director of a corporation in respect of an amount payable by the director under subsection (1) in the same manner and to the same extent as if the director were the employer referred to in those provisions.**

(R.S.C. 1985, c. 6 (1st Supp.), s. 2; 2004, c. 25, s. 112.)

———————— **Notes** ————————

Synopsis

Where a corporation fails to deduct or remit CPP employer or employee contributions, this section renders the directors of liable for such amounts, along with interest and penalties thereon. Liability is joint and several (with the corporation), which means that the Minister can recover the entire amount or a portion thereof from any one or more of the directors. In the *Income Tax Act*, s. 227.1(2)–(7) reads as follows:

(2) *Limitations on liability* — A director is not liable under subsection 227.1(1), unless

(a) a certificate for the amount of the corporation's liability referred to in that subsection has been registered in the Federal Court under section 223 and execution for that amount has been returned unsatisfied in whole or in part;

(b) the corporation has commenced liquidation or dissolution proceedings or has been dissolved and a claim for the amount of the corporation's liability referred to in that subsection has been proved within six months after the earlier of the date of commencement of the proceedings and the date of dissolution; or

(c) the corporation has made an assignment or a receiving order has been made against it under the *Bankruptcy and Insolvency Act* and a claim for the amount of the corporation's liability referred to in that subsection has been proved within six months after the date of the assignment or receiving order.

(3) *Idem* — A director is not liable for a failure under subsection 227.1(1) where the director exercised the degree of care, diligence and skill to prevent the failure that a reasonably prudent person would have exercised in comparable circumstances.

(4) *Limitation period* — No action or proceedings to recover any amount payable by a director of a corporation under subsection 227.1(1) shall be commenced more than two years after the director last ceased to be a director of that corporation.

(5) *Amount recoverable* — Where execution referred to in paragraph 227.1(2)(a) has issued, the amount recoverable from a director is the amount remaining unsatisfied after execution.

(6) *Preference* — Where a director pays an amount in respect of a corporation's liability referred to in subsection 227.1(1) that is proved in liquidation, dissolution or bankruptcy proceedings, the director is entitled to any preference that Her Majesty in right of Canada would have been entitled to had that amount not been so paid and, where a certificate that relates to that amount has been registered, the director is entitled to an assignment of the certificate to the extent of the director's payment, which assignment the Minister is hereby empowered to make.

(7) *Contribution* — A director who has satisfied a claim under this section is entitled to contribution from the other directors who were liable for the claim.

Related Bulletins and Circulars

● IC 89-2R: Directors' Liability — Section 227.1 of the *Income Tax Act* and s. 323 of the *Excise Tax Act*

Case Law

§1. Purpose and Scope of *Income Tax Act* s. 227.1

Smith v. R., [2001] 2 C.T.C. 192 (Fed. C.A.)

The directors' liability provisions of the *Income Tax Act* and the *Excise Tax Act* were enacted to strengthen the Crown's ability to enforce the statutory obligation imposed on certain taxpayers to remit taxes payable by other parties, such as tax withheld at source from wages paid to employees, and net GST collected from customers. Normally, the Crown's remedies against a corporation that fails to remit these third party taxes would be limited to the corporation's assets. That is a necessary incident of separate corporate personality. However, it was perceived that a corporation, particularly a corporation in financial difficulty, might prefer to default on its obligation to remit taxes, in order to satisfy creditors whose claims were more immediately pressing. It was apparently thought necessary to enact legislation that would deter corporations from making such a choice. Consequently, the ITA s. 227.1(1) and ETA s. 323(1) were enacted to impose liability, subject to certain conditions, on the directors of a corporation that had failed to remit tax collected from others. This is based on the presumption that a decision by a corporation to default on its remittance obligations would originate with the directors.

Canada v. Buckingham, 2011 FCA 142

Parliament did not require that directors be subject to an absolute liability for the remittances of their corporations. Consequently, Parliament has accepted that a corporation may, in certain circumstances, fail to effect remittances without its directors incurring liability. What is required is that the directors establish that they were specifically concerned with the tax remittances and that they exercised their duty of care, diligence, and skill with a view to preventing a failure by the corporation to remit the concerned amounts. The amounts withheld from employee remuneration for income tax, CPP, and Employment Insurance purposes are deemed to have been paid by the employee for all purposes associated with these statutes, including for the purposes of assessing the liability of directors for the failure of their corporation to remit the amounts so withheld. The same standard of care, diligence, and skill defence is to apply to each.

Clements v. The Queen, 2003 TCC 289

The analysis in *Smith* (above) applies to the director's liability provisions in the CPP.

Canada v. Corsano, [1999] 3 FC 173 (C.A.)

The rationale for *Income Tax Act* s. 227.1(1) is the ultimate accountability of the directors of a company for the deduction and remittance of employees' taxes. Such accountability cannot depend on whether the company is a profit or not-for-profit company, whether the directors are paid or not or whether they are nominal but active or merely passive directors.

Soper v. The Queen (1997), 97 D.T.C. 5407 (Fed. C.A.)

Non-remittance of taxes withheld on behalf of a third party commonly occurred during the 1981–82 recession. Faced with a choice between remitting such amounts to the Crown or drawing such amounts to pay key creditors whose goods or services were necessary to the continued operation of the business, corporate directors often followed the latter course. Such patent abuse and mismanagement on the part of directors constituted the "mischief" at which *Income Tax Act* s. 227.1 was directed.

Liddle v. R., 2011 FCA 159

The fact that another director was heavily involved in the company was not a defence. The express words of the provisions of s. 21.1(1) of the CPP make the director "jointly and severally, or solidarily, liable" for the full amounts that the company had failed to remit to the Minister.

Zen v. Canada (National Revenue), 2010 FCA 180

Section 227.1(1) imposes on directors a continuing liability for interest on their corporation's unpaid tax debt and the amount of their liability in respect of that debt as assessed. The Minister can take collection measures with respect to the interest without a further assessment.

§2. Director

Kalef v. R., [1996] 2 C.T.C. 1 (Fed. C.A.)

The *Income Tax Act* does not define "director" either for the purposes of the *Income Tax Act* as a whole or for the purposes of section 227.1. It is therefore appropriate to look to the corporation's incorporating legislation for guidance as to who is a "director" for the purposes of section 227.1. Where the director in question did not fulfil any of the requirements under the *Business Corporations Act* (Ont.), which would indicate that he had ceased to be a director of the company, he remained a director notwithstanding the appointment of a trustee in bankruptcy for the company.

Canada v. Corsano, [1999] 3 FC 173 (C.A.)

Occupying the position of director brings a person within the definition a director under *Income Tax Act* s. 227.1, regardless of how the position may be designated. The word "director" does not only connote a person qualified to act as such under the governing legislation. Persons who are not statutorily qualified to be directors of the company who nonetheless act as directors in conformity with the will of the shareholders should not be allowed to assert their lack of qualification to escape the liability cast upon directors under s. 227.1.

Per Letourneau J.A.: In interpreting the word "director" in subsection 227.1(1), the court can look to the common-law definition of director as well as the governing company legislation.

§3. Standard of Care

Canada v. Buckingham, 2011 FCA 142

The reference to a "reasonably prudent person" in s. 227.1(3) of the *Income Tax Act* is a clear indication that the test is objective rather than subjective. This objective standard has set aside the common law principle that a director's management of a corporation is to be judged according to his own personal skills, knowledge, abilities, and capacities. It is the factual aspects of the circumstances surrounding the actions of the director that are important, not the subjective motivations of the directors. The emergence of stricter standards puts pressure on corporations to improve the quality of board decisions through the establishment of good corporate governance rules. Stricter standards also discourage the appointment of inactive directors chosen for show or who fail to discharge their duties as director by leaving decisions to the active directors. Consequently, a person who is appointed as a director must carry out the duties of that function on an active basis and will not be allowed to defend a claim for malfeasance in the discharge of his or her duties by relying on his or her own inaction. An objective standard does not however entail that the particular circumstances of a director are to be ignored. These circumstances must be taken into account, but must be considered against an objective "reasonably prudent person" standard. The focus of the inquiry under s. 227.1(3) will however be different than that under s. 122(1)(*b*) of the CBCA, since the former requires that the director's duty of care, diligence, and skill be exercised to prevent failures to remit. In order to rely on these defences, a director must thus establish that he turned his attention to the required remittances and that he exercised his duty of care, diligence, and skill with a view to preventing a failure by the corporation to remit the concerned amounts.

Soper v. The Queen (1997), 97 D.T.C. 5407 (Fed. C.A.)

The traditional common-law principles with respect to the appropriate standard of care of a company director are as follows:

1. Directors of a company are not to be equated with trustees. Directors are agents of the company and, as such, stand in a fiduciary relationship to their principal, the company.

2. A director need not exhibit, in the performance of his or her duties, a greater degree of skill and care than may reasonably be expected from a person of his or her knowledge and experience. The standard of care is therefore partly objective (the standard of the reasonable person), and partly subjective in that the reasonable person is judged on the basis that he or she has the knowledge and experience of the particular individual. It is a hybrid "objective subjective standard".

3. A director is not obliged to give continuous attention to the affairs of the company, nor is he or she even bound to attend all meetings of the board. However, when, in the circumstances, it is reasonably possible to attend such meetings, a director ought to do so.

4. In the absence of grounds for suspicion, it is not improper for a director to rely on company officials to perform honestly duties that have been properly delegated to them. It is the exigencies of business and the company's articles of association that,

together, will determine whether it is appropriate to delegate a duty. The larger the business, the greater the need to delegate will be.

The common-law standard of care, while altered slightly, has not been significantly upgraded by statute. The standard of care laid down in *Income Tax Act* s. 227.1(3) is inherently flexible. Rather than treating directors as a homogeneous group of professionals whose conduct is governed by a single, unchanging standard, the provision embraces a subjective element which takes into account the personal knowledge and background of the director, as well as his or her corporate circumstances in the form of, *inter alia*, the company's organization, resources, customs and conduct. Therefore, more is expected of individuals with superior qualifications (e.g., experienced business persons).

The standard of care set out in s. 227.1(3) is, therefore, not purely objective. Nor is it purely subjective. It is not enough for a director to say he or she did his or her best, for that is an invocation of the purely subjective standard. Equally clear, is that honesty is not enough. However, the standard is not a professional one. Nor is it the negligence law standard that governs these cases. Rather, the *Income Tax Act* contains both objective elements embodied in the reasonable person language and subjective elements inherent in individual considerations like "skill" and the idea of "comparable circumstances". Accordingly, the standard can be properly described as "objective subjective".

Whether a company is in serious financial difficulty, such as to suggest a problem with remittances, cannot be determined simply by the fact that the monthly balance sheet bears a negative figure. Many firms operate on a line of credit to deal with fiscal fluctuations. In each case, it will be for the Tax Court Judge to determine whether the director ought to have known that there was a problem or potential problem with remittances based on the financial information or documentation available to him or her. Whether the standard of care has been met is predominantly a question of fact to be resolved in light of the personal knowledge and experience of the director at issue.

Canada v. Corsano, [1999] 3 FC 173 (C.A.)

All directors of all companies are liable for their failure if they do not meet the single standard of care provided for in *Income Tax Act* s. 227.1(3) to exercise the degree of care, diligence and skill to prevent the failure that a reasonably prudent person would have exercised in comparable circumstances. It is the application of the standard that is flexible because of the varying and different skills, factors and circumstances that are to be weighed in measuring whether a director in a given situation has lived up to the standard of care established by the *Income Tax Act*.

Comparelli v. Canada 2010 FCA 13

The conduct of the director of a start-up company which never really got off the ground and has repeatedly defaulted on its obligations to remit will be judged more harshly than the director of a company which has a history of success.

§4. Inside/Outside Directors

Soper v. The Queen (1997), 97 D.T.C. 5407 (Fed. C.A.)

While liability is not dependent simply upon whether a person is classified as an inside director, as opposed to an outside director, inside directors will face a significant hurdle when arguing that the subjective element of the standard of care should predominate over its objective aspect. Precautionary measures may be regarded as persuasive evidence of due diligence on the part of a director, but such steps are not necessary conditions precedent to the establishment of that defence. This is particularly true with respect to the establishment of a separate trust account for source deductions to be remitted to the Receiver General. An outside director cannot be required to go to the lengths outlined in paragraph 7 of IC 89-2 or to establish and monitor a trust account from which both employee wages and remittances owing to the Crown would be paid. Although a director cannot adopt an entirely passive approach, it is permissible to rely on the day-to-day corporate managers to be responsible for the payment of debt obligations, such as those owing to the Crown, unless there is reason for suspicion. A positive duty to act arises where a director obtains information, or becomes aware of facts, which might

165

lead one to conclude that there is, or could reasonably be, a potential problem with remittances. It is incumbent upon an outside director to take positive steps if he or she knew, or ought to have known, that the corporation could be experiencing a remittance problem.

Bianco v. MNR (1991), 2 B.L.R. (2d) 255 (T.C.C.). See also *Edmondson (S.G.) v. MNR*, [1988] 2 C.T.C. 2185 (T.C.C.); *Shindle (B.) v. Canada*, [1995] 2 C.T.C. 227 (F.C.T.D.); *Snow v. MNR* (1991), 38 C.C.E.L. 70 (T.C.C.).

Liability will not be imposed on an inside director in cases where he or she is an innocent party who has been misled or deceived by co-directors.

§4.1. Corporation in difficulty

Canada v. Buckingham, 2011 FCA 142

The liability of the directors under s. 227.1(1) is not conditional on the existence of sufficient cash in the corporation to pay the remittances of employee source deductions. The time frame in which to assess the director's conduct does not begin when the corporation runs out of cash. Instead, it begins when it becomes apparent to the director, acting reasonably and with due care, diligence, and skill, that the corporation is entering a period of financial difficulties. A director of a corporation cannot justify a defence under the terms of s. 227.1(3) where he condones the continued operation of the corporation by diverting employee source deductions to other purposes. The entire scheme of s. 227.1, read as a whole, is precisely designed to avoid such situations.

§5. Preventive Steps

Smith v. R., [2001] 2 C.T.C. 192 (Fed. C.A.). See also *Clements v. The Queen*, 2003 TCC 289

What may reasonably be expected of a director for the purposes of subsection 227.1(1) of the *Income Tax Act* and subsection 323(1) of the *Excise Tax Act* depends upon the facts of the case, and has both an objective and a subjective aspect. The subjective aspect of the standard of care applicable to a particular director will depend on the director's personal attributes, including knowledge and experience. Generally, a person who is experienced in business and financial matters is likely to be held to a higher standard than a person with no business acumen or experience whose presence on the board of directors reflects nothing more, for example, than a family connection. However, the due diligence defence probably will not assist a director who is oblivious to the statutory obligations of directors, or who ignores a problem that was apparent to the director or should have been apparent to a reasonably prudent person in comparable circumstances. In assessing the objective reasonableness of the conduct of a director, the factors to be taken into account may include the size, nature and complexity of the business carried on by the corporation, and its customs and practices. The larger and more complex the business, the more reasonable it may be for directors to allocate responsibilities among themselves, or to leave certain matters to corporate staff and outside advisers, and to rely on them. The inherent flexibility of the due diligence defence may result in a situation where a higher standard of care is imposed on some directors of a corporation than on others. For example, it may be appropriate to impose a higher standard on an "inside director" (for example, a director with a practice of hands-on management) than an "outside director" (such as a director who has only superficial knowledge of and involvement in the affairs of the corporation). That is particularly so if it is established that the outside director reasonably relied on assurances from the inside directors that the corporation's tax remittance obligations were being met. In certain circumstances, the fact that a corporation is in financial difficulty, and thus may be subject to a greater risk of default in tax remittances than other corporations, may be a factor that raises the standard of care. For example, a director who is aware of the corporation's financial difficulty and who deliberately decides to finance the corporation's operations with unremitted source deductions may be unable to rely on the due diligence defence. In every case, however, it is important to bear in mind that the standard is reasonableness, not perfection.

Canada v. McKinnon, [2001] 2 FC 203 (C.A), 2000 D.T.C. 6593 (*sub nom. Worrell v. Canada*), [2001] 1 C.T.C. 79

The relevant question is whether the directors exercised due diligence to prevent the company's failure to remit. This is not necessarily the same as asking whether it was reasonable from a business point of view for the directors to continue to operate the business. In order to avail themselves of the defence provided by *Income Tax Act* s. 227.1(3), directors must normally have taken positive steps which, if successful, could have prevented the company's failure to remit from occurring. The question then is whether the directors' actions to prevent the failure meets the standard of the care, diligence and skill that would have been exercised by a reasonably prudent person in comparable circumstances. It will normally not be sufficient for the directors to have simply carried on the business, knowing that a failure to remit was likely but hoping that the company's fortunes would revive with an upturn in the economy or in their market position. In such circumstances, directors will generally be held to have assumed the risk that the company will subsequently be able to make its remittances. If directors decide to continue the business in the expectation that the company will turn around and will be able to make good its remittance defaults after they have occurred, and the company nonetheless fails without paying its tax debts, it is no defence for the directors to say that the risk that they took would have been taken by a reasonable person. The s. 227.1(3) defence only applies if it can be demonstrated that the directors exercised the care, diligence and skill that a reasonably prudent business person in comparable circumstances would have exercised to prevent a future default.

Canada v. Buckingham, 2011 FCA 142

A director's duty is to prevent the failure to remit, not to condone it in the hope that matters can be rectified subsequently. Contrary to the suppliers of a corporation who may limit their financial exposure by requiring cash-in-advance payments, the Crown is an involuntary creditor. The level of the Crown's exposure to the corporation can thus increase if the corporation continues its operations by paying the net salaries of the employees without affecting employee source deductions remittances, or if the corporation decides to collect GST/HST from customers without reporting and remitting these amounts in a timely fashion. In circumstances where a corporation is facing financial difficulties, it may be tempting to divert these Crown remittances in order to pay other creditors and thus ensure the continuation of the operations of the corporation. It is precisely such a situation which s. 227.1 seeks to avoid. The defence under s. 227.1(3) should not be used to encourage such failures by allowing a due diligence defence for directors who finance the activities of their corporation with Crown monies on the expectation that the failures to remit could eventually be cured. The Federal Court of Appeal's decision in *Worrell* (see *McKinnon,* above) did not modify the focus of the defence of care, diligence, and skill, which is to prevent the failure to remit, not to cure failures to do so.

Ruffo v. MNR (2000), Doc. A-429-97 (Fed. C.A.)

The director's duty is to anticipate and prevent the failure to pay the sums owing and not to commit such failure or perpetuate it in the hope that at the end of the day the firm would again become profitable or there would be enough money, even if it were wound up, to pay all the creditors.

Soper v. The Queen (1997), 97 D.T.C. 5407 (Fed. C.A.)

The purpose of s. 227.1(3) is to prevent failure to make remittances and not to cure default after the fact. Although, as a practical matter, the provision should have the latter effect as well.

Canada v. Corsano, [1999] 3 FC 173 (C.A.)

A director's duty is to prevent default, not to condone it in the hope that matters can be rectified subsequently.

Machula v. The Queen, 2003 TCC 563

Physical intervention and evidence of active corrective measures and follow-up by the director are called for where Revenue Canada takes garnishee action or employees' pay cheques are NSF.

Canales v. The Queen (1997), 97 D.T.C. 49 (T.C.C.)

It is a well-established principle that the director must demonstrate that a reasonable attempt was made to prevent the failure to deduct and remit, and not just an attempt to remedy the situation after the failure.

Canada Pension Plan

§6. Effect of Bankruptcy, Receivership and Loss of Control

Robitaille v. The Queen, 90 D.T.C. 6059 (T.C.C.)

Where effective control of a corporation has been taken over by a bank without a request by the directors, and where decisions as to issuing cheques are exclusively made by the bank, again without consultation with the board of directors, the corporation's actions regarding remittances, payments or, withholdings will be essentially those of the bank. Consequently, since the ITA s. 227.1(1) contemplates that a corporation is acting freely through its board of directors, in these circumstances there would be no liability on the directors.

Champeval v. M.N.R., 90 D.T.C. 1291 (T.C.C.)

If directors do not have free choice in the corporate decisions due to factors completely beyond their control, they cannot be bound by the ITA s. 227.1(1).

Liddle v. R., 2009 TCC 451, affirmed 2011 FCA 159

Where the managing director ignored a letter from an investor ostensibly relieving him of his duties as director for repeated violations of a forbearance agreement, the director did not cease to be responsible for CPP and other remittances.

Canada (Attorney General) v. McKinnon (2000), Doc. A-421-98 (Fed. C.A.)

It is inappropriate to import into s. 227.1(1) a requirement that it is only engaged if the directors have *de facto* control over the financial operation of the company, particularly the payment of its bills.

§7. Procedure

Amyot v. Canada, 2006 FCA 55

The Minister's failure to file notices of assessment with the proof of claim submitted to the trustee in bankruptcy did not render the proof of claim insufficient to meet the requirements of s. 227.1(2)(*c*) of the ITA.

---

22. *Minister may assess amount payable* — **(1) The Minister may assess an employer for an amount payable by him under this Act, or may re-assess the employer or make additional assessments as the circumstances require, and the expression "assessment" when used in this Act with reference to any action so taken by the Minister under this section includes any such re-assessment or additional assessment.**

(2) *Notice of assessment and liability of employer* — **After assessing an employer for an amount payable by him under this Act, the Minister shall send the employer a notice of assessment, and on that notice being sent to the employer, the assessment shall be deemed to be valid and binding, subject to being varied or vacated on appeal under this Act, and the employer is liable to pay to Her Majesty the amount thereof forthwith.**

(3) *Limitation on assessments* — **Notwithstanding subsection (1) or (2), no assessment, re-assessment or additional assessment of an amount payable by an employer under this Act may be made by the Minister under this section after four years have elapsed from the earliest of the days on or before which any contribution in relation to which that amount is payable should have been paid, unless the employer has made any misrepresentation or committed any fraud in filing any return or in supplying any information pursuant to this Part in relation thereto.**

——————— **Notes** ———————

Synopsis

This section authorizes the Minister to assess an employer for CPP contributions. The assessment must be conducted within four years of the allegedly unpaid contribution, in the absence of fraud or misrepresentation on the part of the employer.

Related Provisions

- Section 27.1 — Appeal of assessments
- Section 27.2 — Notification of appeal
- Section 27.3 — Minister's authority not restricted

Case Law

742190 Ontario Inc. (Van Del Manor Nursing Homes) v. Canada (Customs and Revenue Agency), 2010 FCA 162

The CPP, the *Income Tax Act* and the *Employment Insurance Act* share four elements in common: (1) the assessment of the liability to pay, (2) the notification of the assessment, (3) the right to a Ministerial review of the assessment, and (4) the right to a judicial appeal of the assessment. The word "assessment" generally refers to the determination by the Minister of the amount of a person's liability, and includes the act of making the determination and the product of the determination. The assessment may be based on a return or report filed by the person or information obtained by the Minister from another source. The review may be cursory (such as an administrative processing of the person's return or report) or it may involve an audit or a more extensive investigation. Typically, the statute will also provide that the notice of assessment is determinative of the amount of the liability of the assessed person subject only to changes that may be made by a reassessment, including a reassessment after a Ministerial review or judicial appeal. The statute stipulates the period within which that right must be exercised, and may provide that the limitation period may be extended. The statute may also state one or more presumptions that may be made if it becomes necessary to prove the date of the commencement of the limitation period. The Tax Court has no jurisdiction to consider an appeal of an assessment unless the person assessed has validly exercised the right to request a Ministerial review or, in the case of an income tax assessment, to object.

Kroeker v. MNR (1969), 69 D.T.C. 380 (T.A.B.)

Obiter: It is apparently government policy that the simplest way of accomplishing the form of assessment under what is now s. 22, is to include the amount payable under the CPP in the employer's income tax assessment for the year.

———————————————————

23. *Recovery of contributions, etc., as debt due to Her Majesty* — **(1) All contributions, interest, penalties and other amounts payable by a person under this Act are debts due to Her Majesty and recoverable as such in the Federal Court or any other court of competent jurisdiction or in any other manner provided for by this Act. (S.C. 1997, c. 40, s. 63.)**

(2) [13]*Application of Income Tax Act provisions* — **Section 160, subsections 161(11) and 220(3.1), (4) and (5), sections 221.1, and 223 to 224.3, subsections 227(9.1) and (10), sections 229, 236 and 244 (except subsections 244(1) and**

——————————————————————————————————————

[13] Pursuant to 1991, c. 49, s. 206(2). Subsection 23(2) is applicable to 1985 and subsequent years, except that

(a) before 1987, subsection 23(2) of the said Act, as enacted by subsection (1), shall be read without reference to subsection 248(11) of the *Income Tax Act;*

(continued on next page)

Canada Pension Plan

(4)) and subsections 248(7) and (11) of the *Income Tax Act* apply, with such modifications as the circumstances require, in relation to all contributions, interest, penalties and other amounts payable by a person under this Act, and for the purposes of this subsection,

    (a) the reference in subsection 224(1.2) of that Act to "subsection 227(10.1) or a similar provision" shall be read as a reference to "section 22 of the *Canada Pension Plan*"; and

    (b) subsection 224(1.2) of the *Income Tax Act* shall apply to employer's contributions, employee's contributions, and related interest, penalties or other amounts, subject to subsections 69(1) and 69.1(1) of the *Bankruptcy and Insolvency Act* and section 11.09 of the *Companies' Creditors Arrangement Act*. (S.C. 2005, c. 47, s. 137; 2007, c. 36, s. 108.)

(R.S.C. 1985, c. 5 (2nd Supp.), s. 1(1); R.S.C. 1985, c. 38 (3rd Supp.), s. 1(1); 1991, c. 49, s. 206; 2000, c. 30, s. 155(1).)

    (3) *Where amount deducted not remitted* — [14]Where an employer has deducted an amount from the remunerations of an employee as or on account of any contribution required to be made by the employee but has not remitted the amount to the Receiver General, the employer is deemed, notwithstanding any security interest (as defined in subsection 224(1.3) of the *Income Tax Act*) in the amount so deducted, to hold the amount separate and apart from the property of the employer and from property held by any secured creditor (as defined in subsection 224(1.3) of the *Income Tax Act*) of that employer that but for the security interest would be property of the employer, in trust for Her Majesty and for payment to Her Majesty in the manner and at the time provided under this Act. (S.C. 1998, c. 19, s. 252(1).)

    (4) *Extension of trust* — [15]Notwithstanding the *Bankruptcy and Insolvency Act* (except sections 81.1 and 81.2 of that Act), any other enactment of Canada, any enactment of a province or any other law, where at any time an amount deemed by subsection (3) to be held by an employer in trust for Her Majesty is not paid to Her Majesty in the manner and at the time provided under this Act, property of the employer and property held by any secured creditor (as defined in subsection 224(1.3) of the *Income Tax Act*) of that employer that but for a security interest (as defined in

---

(continued from previous page)

    (b) the references in subsection 23(2) of the *Canada Pension Plan*, as enacted by subsection (1), to subsections 227(9.1) and 248(7) of the *Income Tax Act* are applicable to remittances in respect of amounts paid after 1987;

    (c) the reference in subsection 23(2) of the *Canada Pension Plan*, as enacted by subsection (1), to subsection 227(10) of the *Income Tax Act* is applicable to amounts payable after December 17, 1987;

    (d) the reference in subsection 23(2) of the *Canada Pension Plan*, as enacted by subsection (1), to section 160 of the *Income Tax Act* is applicable after July 13, 1990; and

    (e) the reference in subsection 23(2) of the *Canada Pension Plan*, as enacted by subsection (1), to section 221.1 of the *Income Tax Act* is applicable with respect to amendments and enactments assented to or promulgated after 1989, and shall be deemed to have come into force on January 1, 1990.

    (f) the reference in Chapter 30, subsection 155(2) states as follows: Subsection (1) is deemed to have come into force on November 30, 1992 except that, before September 30, 1997, paragraph 23(2)(b) of the *Canada Pension Plan*, as enacted by subsection (1), shall be read without reference to "and section 11.4 of the *Companies' Creditors Arrangement Act*".

[14] Subsection (3) as added by 1998, c. 19, s. 252(1) is in force as of June 15, 1994.

[15] Subsection (4) as added by 1998, c. 19, s. 252(1) is in force as of June 15, 1994.

subsection 224(1.3) of the *Income Tax Act)* would be property of the employer, equal in value to the amount so deemed to be held in trust is deemed

(*a*) to be held, from the time the amount was deducted by the employer, separate and apart from the property of the employer, in trust for Her Majesty whether or not the property is subject to such a security interest, and

(*b*) to form no part of the estate or property of the employer from the time the amount was so deducted, whether or not the property has in fact been kept separate and apart from the estate or property of the employer and whether or not the property is subject to such a security interest

and is property beneficially owned by Her Majesty notwithstanding any security interest in such property or in the proceeds thereof, and the proceeds of such property shall be paid to the Receiver General in priority to all such security interests. (S.C. 1998, c. 19, s. 252(1).)

(4.1) *Meaning of "security interest"* — [16]For the purposes of subsections (3) and (4), a security interest does not include a prescribed security interest. (S.C. 1998, c. 19, s. 252(1).)

(5) *Certificate before distribution* — Every person, other than a trustee in bankruptcy, who is an assignee, liquidator, receiver, receiver-manager, administrator, executor, liquidator of a succession or any other like person, in this section referred to as the "responsible representative", administering, winding-up, controlling or otherwise dealing with a property, business or estate of another person, before distributing to one or more persons any property over which he or she has control in his or her capacity as the responsible representative, shall obtain a certificate from the Minister certifying that all amounts (S.C. 2004, c. 25, s. 113.)

(*a*) for which any employer is liable under this Act up to and including the date of distribution, and

(*b*) for the payment of which the responsible representative is or can reasonably be expected to become liable in his capacity as the responsible representative

have been paid or that security for the payment thereof has been accepted by the Minister. (R.S.C. 1985, c. 5 (2nd Supp.), s. 1(2).)

(5.1) *Personal liability* — Where a responsible representative distributes to one or more persons property over which he has control in his capacity as the responsible representative, without obtaining a certificate under subsection (5) in respect of the amounts referred to in that subsection, the responsible representative is personally liable for the payment of those amounts to the extent of the value of the property distributed and the Minister may assess the responsible representative therefor in the same manner and with the same effect as an assessment made under section 22. (R.S.C. 1985, c. 5 (2nd Supp.), s. 1(2).)

(6) *Trustee in bankruptcy* — Where an employer has become a bankrupt, the trustee in bankruptcy shall be deemed to be the agent of the bankrupt for all purposes of this Act.

(7) *Priority* — (Repealed by R.S.C. 1993, c. 24, s. 154(1).)

(8) *Amount secured* — (Repealed by R.S.C. 1993, c. 24, s. 154(1).)

(9) *Property charged* — (Repealed by R.S.C. 1993, c. 24, s. 154(1).)

(10) *Third party demand* — (Repealed by R.S.C. 1993, c. 24, s. 154(1).)

---

[16] Subsection (4.1) as added by 1998, c. 19, s. 252(1) is in force as of June 15, 1994.

(11) *Provisions of Income Tax Act applicable* — **(Repealed by R.S.C. 1993, c. 24, s. 154(1).)**

(12) *Definitions* — **(Repealed by R.S.C. 1993, c. 24, s. 154(1).)**

(13) *Substituted property* — **(Repealed by R.S.C. 1993, c. 24, s. 154(1).)**

(R.S.C. 1985, c. 5 (2nd Supp.), s. 1; R.S.C. 1985, c. 38, (3rd Supp.), s. 1; 1991, c. 49, s. 206; 1992, c. 27, s. 90; 1993, c. 24, s. 154; 1994, c. 21, s. 123; 1997, c. 40, s. 63; 1998, c. 19, s. 252; 2004, c. 25, s. 113; 2005, c. 47, s. 137; 2007, c. 36, s. 108.)

————————— **Notes** —————————

Synopsis

This section sets out the enforcement mechanism for recovering unpaid contributions from an employer or self-employed person. Unpaid CPP contributions take priority to all other claims against the employer, except registered mortgages (see CPP Regulation, 8.3).

Related Provisions

● Section 41(1) — Offence or punishment

Related CPP Regulations

● Section 8.3 — Security interests

————————————————————

24. *Books and records* — **(1)** Every employer paying remuneration to an employee employed by him in pensionable employment shall keep records and books of account at his place of business or residence in Canada, or at such other place as may be designated by the Minister, in such form and containing such information as will enable any contributions payable under this Act or any contributions or other amounts that should have been deducted or paid to be determined, and where any such employer has failed to keep adequate records and books of account, the Minister may require him to keep such records and books of account as he may specify, and the employer shall thereafter keep records and books of account as so required.

(2) *Keeping of records and books of account* — Every employer required by this section to keep records and books of account shall retain those records and books of account and every account and voucher necessary to verify the information contained therein until the expiration of six years from the end of the year in respect of which those records and books of account are kept or until written permission for their prior disposal is given by the Minister.

(2.1) *Electronic records* — Every employer required by this section to keep records who does so electronically shall retain them in an electronically readable format for the retention period referred to in subsection (2). **(S.C. 1998, c. 19, s. 253.)**

(2.2) *Exemption* — The Minister may, on such terms and conditions as are acceptable to the Minister, exempt an employer or a class of employers from the requirement in subsection (2.1). **(S.C. 1998, c. 19, s. 253.)**

(3) *Retention for ruling or appeal* — If the employer or an employee of the employer is subject to a ruling under section 26.1 or has made an appeal to the Minister under section 27 or 27.1, the employer shall retain every record, book of account, account and voucher necessary for dealing with the ruling or the appeal until the ruling is made or the appeal is disposed of and any further appeal is disposed of or the time for filing a further appeal has expired. (S.C. 1997, c. 40, s. 64.)

(S.C. 1991, c. 49, s. 207; 1997, c. 40, s. 64; 1998, c. 19, s. 253.)

—————————— Notes ——————————

Synopsis

This section requires employers to keep accounting books and records for at least six years, or longer, if a proceeding to which they pertain is underway or is the subject of an appeal.

Related Provisions

- Section 25 — Inspections
- Section 41(2) — Offence or punishment

———————————————————

25. *Interpretation* — **(1) In this section,**

"authorized person" **means a person authorized by the Minister for the purposes of this section;**

"documents" **includes money, securities and any of the following, whether computerized or not: books, records, letters, telegrams, vouchers, invoices, accounts and statements (financial or otherwise); (S.C. 1991, c. 49, s. 208.)**

"dwelling-house" **means the whole or any part of a building or structure that is kept or occupied as a permanent or temporary residence and includes**

    (*a*) **a building within the curtilage of a dwelling-house that is connected to it by a doorway or by a covered and enclosed passageway, and**

    (*b*) **a unit that is designed to be mobile and to be used as a permanent or temporary residence and that is being used as such a residence;**

"judge" **means a judge of a superior court having jurisdiction in the province where the matter arises or a judge of the Federal Court.**

(2) *Inspections* — **An authorized person may, at any reasonable time, for any purpose relating to the administration or enforcement of this Act, inspect, audit or examine any document that relates or may relate to the information that is or should be contained in the records or books of account or to the amount of any contribution payable under this Act and, for those purposes, the authorized person may**

    (*a*) **subject to subsection (3), enter any premises or place where any records or books of account are or should be kept; and**

    (*b*) **require the owner, occupant or person in charge of the premises or place to give to the authorized person all reasonable assistance and to answer all proper questions relating to the administration or enforcement of this Act and, for that purpose, require the owner, occupant or person in charge of the premises or place to attend at such premises or place with the authorized person.**

(3) *Warrant required to enter dwelling-house* — **Where a premises or place referred to in subsection (2) is a dwelling-house, an authorized person may not enter that dwelling-house without the consent of the occupant except under the authority of a warrant issued under subsection (4).**

(4) *Warrant or order* — Where, on *ex parte* application by the Minister, a judge is satisfied by information on oath

(*a*) that there are reasonable grounds to believe that a dwelling-house is a premises or place referred to in subsection (2),

(*b*) that entry into the dwelling-house is necessary for any purpose relating to the administration or enforcement of this Act, and

(*c*) that entry into the dwelling-house has been refused or that there are reasonable grounds for believing that entry thereto will be refused

the judge shall issue a warrant authorizing an authorized person to enter that dwelling-house subject to such conditions as may be specified in the warrant but, where the judge is not satisfied that entry into that dwelling-house is necessary for any purpose relating to the administration or enforcement of this Act, the judge shall

(*d*) order the occupant of the dwelling house to provide an authorized person with reasonable access to any document that is or should be kept therein, and

(*e*) make such other order as is appropriate in the circumstances to carry out the purposes of this Act

to the extent that access has been or may be expected to be refused and that the document is or may be expected to be kept in the dwelling-house.

(5) *Requirement to provide documents or information* — Notwithstanding any other provision of this Act, the Minister may, subject to subsection (6), for any purpose related to the administration or enforcement of this Act, by notice served personally or by registered or certified mail, require that any person provide, within such reasonable time as is stipulated in the notice,

(*a*) any information or additional information, including a return of income or a supplementary return; or

(*b*) any document.

(6) *Unnamed persons* — The Minister shall not impose on any person, in this section referred to as a "third party", a requirement under subsection (5) to provide information or any document relating to one or more unnamed persons unless the Minister first obtains the authorization of a judge under subsection (7).

(7) *Judicial authorization* — On *ex parte* application by the Minister, a judge may, subject to such conditions as the judge considers appropriate, authorize the Minister to impose on a third party a requirement under subsection (5) relating to an unnamed person or more than one unnamed person, in this section referred to as the "group", where the judge is satisfied by information on oath that

(*a*) the person or group is ascertainable; and (S.C. 1998, c. 19, s. 254(1).)

(*b*) the requirement is made to verify compliance by the person or persons in the group with any duty or obligation under this Act;

(*c*) (Repealed by 1998, c. 19, s. 254(1).)

(*d*) (Repealed by 1998, c. 19, s. 254(1).)

(8) *Service authorization* — Where an authorization is granted under subsection (7), the authorization shall be served together with the notice referred to in subsection (5).

(9) *Review of authorization* — Where an authorization is granted under subsection (7), a third party on whom a notice is served under subsection (5) may, within 15 days after the service of the notice, apply to the judge who granted the authorization or, where the judge is unable to act, to another judge of the same court for a review of the authorization.

(10) *Powers on review* — **On hearing an application under subsection (9), a judge may cancel the authorization previously granted if the judge is not then satisfied that the conditions in paragraphs (7)(*a*) and (*b*) have been met and the judge may confirm or vary the authorization if satisfied that those conditions have been met. (S.C. 1998, c. 19, s. 254(2).)**

(11) *Additional remedy* — **Where a person is found guilty of an offence under subsection 41(2) for failing to comply with a requirement under subsection (5), the court may make such order as it deems proper in order to enforce compliance with the requirement.**

(12) *Copies as evidence* — [17]**Where any document is inspected, audited, examined or provided under this section, the person by whom it is inspected, audited or examined or to whom it is provided or any officer of the Canada Revenue Agency may make, or cause to be made, one or more copies thereof and, in the case of an electronic document, make or cause to be made a print-out of an electronic document, and any document purporting to be certified by the Minister or an authorized person to be a copy of the document, made pursuant to this subsection is evidence of the nature and content of the original document and has the same probative force as the original document would have if it were proven in the ordinary way. (S.C. 1998, c. 19, s. 254(3); 1999, c. 17, s. 111(*a*); 2005, c. 38, s. 138(*c*)(i).)**

(13) *Compliance* — **No person shall hinder, molest or interfere with any person doing anything that he is authorized to do by or pursuant to this section or prevent or attempt to prevent any person from doing any such thing and, notwithstanding any other Act or law, every person shall, unless he is unable to do so, do everything he is required to do by or pursuant to this section.**

(R.S.C. 1985, c. 5 (2nd Supp.), s. 2; 1991, c. 49, s. 208; 1994, c. 13, s. 8(1)(*a*); 1998, c. 19, s. 254; 1999, c. 17, s. 111(*a*); 2005, c. 38, s. 138.)

——————————— Notes ———————————

Synopsis

This section authorizes the inspection, audit or examination of the accounting books and records by the Minister's agents. Warrants may be obtained to enter dwelling houses without the owner's consent.

Related Provisions

- Section 41(2) — Offence or punishment

26. *No action against person deducting* — **(1) No action lies against any person for deducting any sum of money in compliance or intended compliance with this Act.**

(2) *Receipt of Minister sufficient discharge* — **The receipt of the Minister for an amount deducted by any person as required by or under this Act is a good and sufficient discharge of the liability of any debtor to his creditor with respect thereto to the extent of the amount referred to in the receipt.**

---

[17] Pursuant to S.C. 1998, c. 19, s. 254(4), subsection (12) applies to copies and print-outs made after June 18, 1998.

——————— **Notes** ———————

Synopsis

This section exempts employers from liability for withholding sums for the intended purpose of complying with their statutory duty under the CPP.

———————————————

Rulings and Appeals

26.1. *Request for rulings* — **(1) The Minister of Employment and Social Development, an employer, an employee or a person claiming to be an employer or an employee may request an officer of the Canada Revenue Agency authorized by the Minister of National Revenue to make a ruling on any of the following questions: (2005, c. 35, s. 67(a)(iv); 2005, c. 38, s. 138(c)(ii); 2012, c. 19, s. 694(a)(iv); 2013, c. 40, s. 238(1)(b)(iii).)**

   (*a*) **whether an employment is pensionable;**

   (*b*) **how long an employment lasts, including the dates on which it begins and ends;**

   (*c*) **what is the amount of any earnings from pensionable employment;**

   (*d*) **whether a contribution is payable;**

   (*e*) **what is the amount of a contribution that is payable; and**

   (*f*) **who is the employer of a person in pensionable employment.**

(S.C. 1997, c. 40, s. 65; 1999, c. 17, s. 111(*b*); 2005, c. 35, s. 67(*a*)(iv).)

   (2) *Time limit* — **The Minister of Employment and Social Development may request a ruling at any time, but a request by any other person must be made before June 30 of the year after the year in respect of which the question relates.** (1997, c. 40, s. 65; 2005, c. 35, s. 67(*a*)(iv); 2012, c. 19, s. 694(*a*)(iv); 2013, c. 40, s. 238(1)(*b*)(iii).)

   (3) *Ruling* — **The authorized officer shall make the ruling within a reasonable time after receiving the request.** (S.C. 1997, c. 40, s. 65.)

   (4) *Presumption* — **Unless a ruling has been requested with respect to a person in pensionable employment,**

   (*a*) **an amount deducted from the remuneration of the person or paid by an employer as a contribution for the person is deemed to have been deducted or paid in accordance with this Act; or**

   (*b*) **an amount that has not been so deducted or paid is deemed not to have been required to be deducted or paid in accordance with this Act.**

(S.C. 1997, c. 40, s. 65.)

(S.C. 1997, c. 40, s. 65; 1999, c. 17, s. 111; 2005, c. 35, s. 67; 2005, c. 38, s. 138; 2012, c. 19, s. 694; 2013, c. 40, s. 238.)

——————— **Notes** ———————

Synopsis

This section provides that an authorized officer of the Department of National Revenue may make a ruling on specified aspects relevant to determining the required contribution. Such a request may be made by the Minister of Human Resources Development at any time, or by an employer or employee or a person claiming to be an employer or employee before June 30 of the year following the transaction in question. In the absence of a ruling, the status quo is presumed to be in accordance with the CPP.

Related Provisions

- Section 27 — Appeal of rulings

- Section 27.2 — Notification of appeal, and where appeal to be sent

- Section 27.3 — Minister's authority not restricted

- Section 29 — Decision final

Case Law

Davitt v. Canada (National Revenue) 2009 FCA 362

Under s. 26.1(1), an employer, an employee, or a person claiming to be an employer or employee, or the Minister of Human Resources and Skills Development, may request an officer of the Canada Revenue Agency authorized by the Minister of National Revenue to make a ruling of the questions in s. 26.1(1)(*a*) to (*f*). Section 26.1(1)(*e*) refers to a challenge to the correctness of the arithmetic result of the calculation of the contribution payable. Its scope is not broad enough to encompass a challenge to the validity of the statutory provisions by which a taxpayer was obliged to pay CPP contributions, either expressly or by necessary implication.

---

27. *Appeal of rulings* — **An appeal to the Minister from a ruling may be made by the Minister of Employment and Social Development at any time, and by any other person concerned within 90 days after the person is notified of the ruling.**

(**S.C. 1997, c. 40, s. 65; 2005, c. 35, s. 67(***a***)(v); 2012, c. 19, s. 694(1)(***a***)(v); 2013, c. 40, s. 238(1)(***b***)(iv).)**

—————— **Notes** ——————

Synopsis

This section permits the Minister of Human Resources Development to appeal a ruling under s. 26 to the Minister of National Revenue at any time. However, employers and employees only have 90 days after being notified of the ruling in which to appeal.

Related Provisions

- Section 27.2 — Notification of appeal, and where appeal to be sent

- Section 27.3 — Minister's authority not restricted

- Section 28 — Appeal to Tax Court of Canada

- Section 29 — Authority of Minister or Tax Court of Canada to decide questions — Decision final

- Section 38(2) — Refund after decision on appeal

Case Law

Agpro Services Inc. v. MNR (1997), 96-136-CPP (T.C.C.)

There is a three-step process for appealing assessment set out in ss. 27 and 28:

1. the appeal to the Minister referred to in s. 27(2),

2. the decision of the Minister on the appeal to the latter for the reconsideration of his assessment contemplated by s. 27(5), and

3. the appeal to the Tax Court of Canada under s. 28(1).

27.1. *Appeal of assessments* **— An employer who has been assessed under section 22 may appeal to the Minister for a reconsideration of the assessment, either as to whether an amount should be assessed as payable or as to the amount assessed, within 90 days after being notified of the assessment.**

(S.C. 1997, c. 40, s. 65.)

——————— **Notes** ———————

Synopsis

This section permits an employer to apply for a reconsideration of an assessment within 90 days of being notified of the assessment.

Case Law

741290 Ontario Inc. (Van Del Manor Nursing Home) v. Canada (Revenue Agency), 2009 FC 985

The provision respecting timelines of assessment appeals under the CPP is now triggered by *notice* to the employer. This provision applies for new appeals even if the assessments relate to periods where the predecessor provision — which referred to the date of mailing — applied.

Related Provisions

- Section 27.3 — Minister's authority not restricted
- Section 28 — Appeal to Tax Court of Canada
- Section 29 — Authority of Minister or Tax Court of Canada to decide questions — Decision final
- Section 38(2) — Refund after decision on appeal

27.2. *Notification of appeal* **— (1) Where an appeal is made to the Minister under section 27 or 27.1, the Minister shall**

    (a) **notify any person who may be affected by the appeal that the Minister intends to decide the appeal, including the Minister of Employment and Social Development in the case of an appeal of a ruling; and (2005, c. 35, s. 67(a)(vi); 2012, c. 19, s. 694(a)(vi); 2013, c. 40, s. 238(1)(b)(v).)**

    (b) **give the person an opportunity to provide information and to make representations to protect the person's interests, as the circumstances require. (S.C. 1997, c. 40, s. 65.)**

(2) *Where appeal to be sent* **— An appeal shall be addressed to the Assistant Director of Appeals in a Tax Services Office of the Canada Revenue Agency and delivered or mailed to that office. (S.C. 1997, c. 40, s. 65; 1999, c. 17, s. 111(c); 2005, c. 38, s. 138(c)(iii).)**

(3) *Decision* **— The Minister shall decide the appeal within a reasonable time after receiving it and shall notify the affected persons of the decision in any manner that the Minister considers adequate. (S.C. 1997, c. 40, s. 65.)**

(S.C. 1997, c. 40, s. 65; 1999, c. 17, s. 111; 2005, c. 35, s. 67; 2005, c. 38, s. 138; 2012, c. 19, s. 694; 2013, c. 40, s. 238.)

————————— **Notes** —————————

Synopsis

This section requires the Minister to notify other interested persons, including the Minister of Human Resources Development, of an appeal of a ruling or assessment, and to give such persons an opportunity to make representations or provide evidence.

Related Provisions

- Section 27.3 — Minister's authority not restricted

Case Law

742190 Ontario Inc. (Van Del Manor Nursing Homes) v. Canada (Customs and Revenue Agency), 2010 FCA 162

The Minister has a public duty to review an assessment on a timely basis when requested to do so. The Minister has no discretion to decline to review the assessment. The Minister has no adequate alternative remedy. In this context, the remedy of a waiver is not adequate because it is granted only at the discretion of the Minister. The Minister cannot rely on the doctrine of *laches* to preclude a Ministerial review that is made on a timely basis. Nor does the fact that the employer had previously requested waivers of interest and penalties necessarily mean that the employer has conceded that they were correctly assessed, where there is no evidence that the Minister had notified the employer that the making of a waiver request would be construed as a concession.

27.3. *Minister's authority not restricted* — **Nothing in sections 26.1 to 27.2 restricts the authority of the Minister to make a decision under this Part on the Minister's own initiative or to make an assessment after the date mentioned in subsection 26.1(2).**

(S.C. 1997, c. 40, s. 65.)

————————— **Notes** —————————

Synopsis

The section clarifies that the Minister's discretion to make any decision regarding CPP contributions or an assessment at any time is not limited by ss. 26.1–27.2.

Case Law

Care Nursing Agency Ltd. v. MNR, 2008 FCA 334. See also *Drosdovech v. MNR,2009 FCA 55*

Section 27.3 of the CPP permits the Minister to make assessments against the employer in the absence of rulings under s. 26.1(1). The consequences of such an interpretation are neither unreasonable nor absurd.

---

28. *Appeal of Tax Court of Canada* — [18]**(1) A person affected by a decision on an appeal to the Minister under section 27 or 27.1, or the person's representative, may, within 90 days after the decision is communicated to the person, or within any longer time that the Tax Court of Canada on application made to it within 90 days after the expiration of those 90 days allows, appeal from the decision to that Court in accordance with the *Tax Court of Canada Act* and the applicable rules of court made thereunder. (S.C. 1998, c. 19, s. 255(1).)**

---

[18] Pursuant to 1998, c. 19, s. 255(3), subsection (1) applies to appeals instituted after the fourth month after the month in which this Act is assented to.

Canada Pension Plan

(1.1) *Communication of decision* — **The determination of the time at which a decision on an appeal to the Minister under section 27 or 27.1 is communicated to a person shall be made in accordance with the rule, if any, made under paragraph 20(1.1)(*h*.1) of the *Tax Court of Canada Act*. (S.C. 1997, c. 40, s. 65.)**

(1.2) *Extension of time to appeal* — **Section 167, except paragraph 167(5)(*a*), of the *Income Tax Act* applies, with such modifications as the circumstances require, in respect of applications made under subsection (1). (S.C. 1998, c. 19, s. 255(2).)**

(2) *Decision of court* — **On an appeal under this section, the Tax Court of Canada may vacate, confirm or vary a decision on an appeal under section 27 or an assessment that is the subject of an appeal under section 27.1 or, in the case of an appeal under section 27.1, may refer the matter back to the Minister for reconsideration and reassessment, and shall without delay**

  (*a*) **notify the parties to the appeal in writing of its decision; and**

  (*b*) **give reasons for its decision, but, except where the Court deems it advisable in a particular case to give reasons in writing, the reasons given by it need not be in writing. (S.C. 1997, c. 40, s. 65.)**

(S.C. 1997, c. 40, s. 65; 1998, c. 19, s. 255.)

———————— **Notes** ————————

Synopsis

This section authorizes appeals to the Tax Court of Canada by any person affected by the Minister's decision on an appeal of an assessment or ruling within 90 days of the decision being communicated to the person. The Court is authorized to vacate, confirm or vary the assessment or ruling, and may refer the assessment back to the Minister for reconsideration and reassessment. The court must also immediately give written notification to the parties of its decision, and must give reasons although they need not be in writing.

The 90-day period for bringing an appeal can be extended by the Court. Section 167 of the *Income Tax Act* reads as follows:

  167. *Extension of time to appeal* — (1) Where an appeal to the Tax Court of Canada has not been instituted by a taxpayer under section 169 within the time limited by that section for doing so, the taxpayer may make an application to the Court for an order extending the time within which the appeal may be instituted and the Court may make an order extending the time for appealing and may impose such terms as it deems just.

  (2) *Contents of application* — An application made under subsection 167(1) shall set out the reasons why the appeal was not instituted within the time limited by section 169 for doing so.

  (3) *How application made* — An application under subsection 167(1) shall be made by filing in the Registry of the Tax Court of Canada, or by sending by registered mail addressed to an office of the Registry, 3 copies of the application accompanied by 3 copies of the notice of appeal.

  (4) *Copy to Deputy Attorney General* — The Tax Court of Canada shall send a copy of each application made under this section to the office of the Deputy Attorney General of Canada.

  (5) *When order to be made* — No order shall be made under this section unless

  (*a*) the application is made within one year after the expiration of the time limited by section 169 for appealing; and

  (*b*) the taxpayer demonstrates that

(i) within the time otherwise limited by section 169 for appealing the tax-payer

    (A) was unable to act or to instruct another to act in the taxpayer's name, or

    (B) had a *bona fide* intention to appeal,

(ii) given the reasons set out in the application and the circumstances of the case, it would be just and equitable to grant the application,

(iii) the application was made as soon as circumstances permitted, and

(iv) there are reasonable grounds for the appeal.

Related Provisions

- Section 29 — Authority of Minister or Tax Court of Canada to decide questions — Decision final — Witness fees

- Section 38(2) — Refund after decision on appeal

Case Law

Davitt v. MNR, 2012 FCA 27

Section 12 of the *Tax Court of Canada Act* allows for CPP appeals only to the extent that they are permitted by the EI Act and the CPP. While an appeal of the Minister's decision may be taken to the Tax Court by virtue of CPP s. 28, an appeal to the Minister under s. 27 is from a ruling under paragraphs 26.1(1)(*a*)-(*f*), which do not relate to the contribution rate. The Tax Court of Canada therefore lacks jurisdiction to hear a constitutional challenge to the premium rates imposed by the CPP.

Agpro Services Inc. v. MNR (1997), 96-136-CPP (T.C.C.)

The jurisdiction of the Tax Court, being a statutory body, is limited under Part I to matters referred to in s. 28. The Tax Court does not have jurisdiction to decide claims relating to a refund of contributions, and the central issue in an appeal from an assessment under Part I must be the validity of the assessment. However, the reference to a refund of CPP contributions in an appeal to the Tax Court from an assessment, under CPP Part I, does not affect the validity of an appeal in view of the close link between such assessment and an overpayment of contributions. Section 18.15(4) of the *Tax Court of Canada Act,* which provides that appeals shall be dealt by this Court "as informally and expeditiously as the circumstances and consider-ations of fairness permit", applies as well to appeals under Part I by virtue of s. 18.29(1)(*a*) of the *Tax Court of Canada Act.* The Tax Court of Canada Rules of Procedure respecting the CPP do not require a description of the relief sought in a notice of appeal.

Agpro Services Inc. v. MNR (1999), 96-136-CPP (T.C.C.)

There is no restriction on the employer's right of appeal of the Minister's determination under s. 27, and the Tax Court may hear the appeal without having to decide if it is an appeal from an assessment.

R. v. Bauman (1998), 97-2315-IT-I (T.C.C.)

Section 28 does not provide contributors who are not employers or employees with a right of appeal to the Tax Court of Canada. The *Canada Pension Plan* does not grant the Tax Court jurisdiction for their appeals, and the Tax Court has no inherent jurisdiction to hear them. Self-employed persons who seek an exemption from having to contribute must apply for judicial review of the Minister's refusal in a superior court with jurisdiction respecting the CPP.

Grunwald v. Canada, 2005 FCA 421

While s. 165(1) of the ITA provides that a notice of objection is to be served on the Minister on or before the day that is 90 days after the day of mailing of the notice of assessment, personal service of the notice of assessment on the taxpayer also starts the time for serving the notice of objection.

Canada Pension Plan

29. *Authority to decide questions* — **(1) The authority of the Minister or the Tax Court of Canada to decide an appeal under section 27, 27.1 or 28 includes the authority to decide any question of fact or law necessary to be decided in the course of the appeal and to decide whether a person is or may be affected by the decision of the appeal. (S.C. 1997, c. 40, s. 65.)**

(2) *Decisions and rulings final* — **Except as otherwise provided in this Act, the decision of the Minister or the Tax Court of Canada of an appeal under section 27, 27.1 or 28 and a ruling of an authorized officer under section 26.1 is final and binding for all purposes of this Act. (S.C. 1997, c. 40, s. 65.)**

(3) *Allowance for attending appeal* — **If, on an appeal to the Tax Court of Canada from a decision of the Minister, a person affected by the decision is requested by the Court to attend before it on the consideration of the appeal and so attends, the person shall be paid such travel and other allowances, including compensation for loss of remunerative time, as are approved by the Treasury Board. (S.C. 1997, c. 40, s. 65.)**

(S.C. 1997, c. 40, s. 65.)

——————— Notes ———————

Synopsis

This section authorizes the Minister or the Tax Court of Canada to decide any necessary question of fact or law on an appeal. The section also precludes any further or additional right of appeal from a ruling assessment or decision of the Tax Court of Canada. Witness fees for attending hearings in the Tax Court of Canada are provided for.

Division D: Collection of Contributions in Respect of Self-Employed Earnings

30. *Return to be filed* — [19]**(1) Where a person is required to make a contribution for a year in respect of self-employed earnings, a return of the person's self-employed earnings for the year shall, without notice or demand for it, be filed with the Minister in the prescribed form and manner and containing the prescribed information, by that person (or, if the person is unable for any reason to file the return, by their representative) on or before the day on or before which the person's return of income under Part I of the *Income Tax Act* is required by that Part to be filed or would be required by that Part to be filed if tax under that Part were payable for the year. (S.C. 1997, c. 40, s. 66(1).)**

(2) *Demand for return* — **Whether or not he is liable to make a contribution for a year in respect of his self-employed earnings and whether or not a return has been filed under subsection (1), every person shall, on demand from the Minister, served personally or by registered letter, file with the Minister in prescribed form and containing prescribed information, within such reasonable time as may be stipulated in the demand, a return of his self-employed earnings for the year designated therein.**

(3) *Return by trustee, etc.* — **Every trustee in bankruptcy, assignee, liquidator, curator, receiver, trustee or committee and every agent or other person administering, managing, winding-up, controlling or otherwise dealing with the property, business, estate or income of a person who has not filed a return of his self-employed earnings**

---

[19] Pursuant to 1997, c. 40, s. 66(3), subsection 30(1) applies to 1996 and subsequent years.

for a year as required by this section shall file with the Minister a return in prescribed form of that person's self-employed earnings for the year.

(4) *Identification of province of residence* — The prescribed information to be contained in any return of the self-employed earnings of a person for a year required by this section to be filed with the Minister shall identify the province in which that person was resident on the last day of that year.

(5) *Where no return filed within four years* — [20]The amount of any contribution required by this Act to be made by a person for a year in respect of their self-employed earnings for the year is deemed to be zero where

(a) the return of those earnings required by this section to be filed with the Minister is not filed with the Minister before the day that is four years after the day on or before which the return is required by subsection (1) to be filed; and

(b) the Minister does not assess the contribution before the end of those four years. (S.C. 1997, c. 40, s. 66(2).)

(S.C. 1991, c. 49, s. 209; 1997, c. 40, s. 66.)

——————— **Notes** ———————

Synopsis

This section provides that a return must be filed by an individual who is required by s. 10 to make a contribution in respect of his or her self-employed earnings. The deadline for filing the return is the same as for the individual's income tax return. Even if an individual is not required to make a contribution for the year, the Minister may demand that a return setting out the individual's self-employed earnings be filed. If no return is filed within the four years from April 30 in the following year and the Minister has not in the interval assessed the contribution, no contribution is required to be paid and the individual would receive no corresponding benefit in respect of that year.

Case Law

Torrance v. Canada (National Revenue), 2008 FC 1083

Subsection 30(5)(a) and (b) overrides any discretion that the Court might have to apply an income tax refund from the previous year to a CPP contribution payable in a subsequent year, to ensure that the contribution is made for that subsequent year.

Related Provisions

- Section 31 — Estimate of contribution to be made in the return
- Section 35 — Failure to file return
- Section 41(3) — Offence or punishment

31. *Estimate to be made* — **Every person required by section 30 to file a return of his self-employed earnings shall in the return estimate the amount of the contribution to be made by him in respect thereof.**

32. *Examination of return and notice of assessment* — **The Minister shall, with all due dispatch, examine each return of self-employed earnings and assess the contribution for the year in respect thereof and the interest and penalties, if any, payable, and, after the examination, shall send a notice of assessment to the person by whom the return was filed.**

[20] Pursuant to 1997, c. 40, s. 66(3), subsection 30(5) applies to 1996 and subsequent years.

33. *Payment of contribution* — [21](1) Where

(a) the amount of the contribution required to be made by a person for a year in respect of his self-employed earnings is forty dollars or less, or

(b) a person who is required by this Act to make a contribution for a year in respect of his self-employed earnings is not required by section 155 or 156 of the *Income Tax Act* to pay instalments for that year in respect of his income tax,

the person shall, on or before the person's balance-due day for the year, pay to the Receiver General the whole amount of the contribution. (S.C. 1991, c. 49, s. 210(1).)

(2) *Farmers and fishermen* — [22]Every person to whom section 155 of the *Income Tax Act* applies, other than a person to whom subsection (1) applies, shall pay to the Receiver General on or before December 31 in each year, two-thirds of

(a) the contribution required to be made by the person for the year in respect of the person's self-employed earnings, as estimated by the person, or

(b) the contribution required in respect of the person's self-employed earnings for the preceding year,

and, on or before the person's balance-due day for the year, the remainder of the contributions as estimated under section 31, except that paragraph (a) and (b) shall not require the payment of any amount in respect of the person that would otherwise become due after the death of the person. (S.C. 1991, c. 49, s. 210(2); 1993, c. 24, s. 145(1).)

(3) *Other persons* — [23]Every person, other than a person to whom subsection (1) or (2) applies, shall pay to the Receiver General in respect of each year

(a) on or before March 15, June 15, September 15 and December 15 in the year, an amount equal to one-quarter of

(i) the contribution required to be made by the person for the year in respect of the person's self-employed earnings, as estimated by the person, or

(ii) the contribution required in respect of the person's self-employed earnings for the preceding year, or

(b) on or before

(i) March 15 and June 15 in the year, an amount equal to one quarter of the contribution required in respect of the person's self-employed earnings for the second preceding year, and

(ii) September 15 and December 15 in the year, an amount equal to one-half of the amount, if any, by which

(A) the contribution, required in respect of the person's self-employed earnings for the preceding year

exceeds

(B) one half of the contribution required in respect of the person's self-employed earnings for the second preceding year,

and, on or before the person's balance-due day for the year, the remainder of the contributions as estimated under section 31, except that paragraph (a) and (b) shall not require the payment of any amount in respect of the person that would otherwise

---

[21] Pursuant to 1991, c. 49, s. 210(3), the change to 33(1) is applicable to 1990 and subsequent years.

[22] Pursuant to 1993, c. 24, s. 145(2), subsection 33(2) applies to 1992 and subsequent years.

[23] Pursuant to 1993, c. 24, s. 145(2), subsection 33(3) applies to 1992 and subsequent years.

become due after the death of the person. (S.C. 1991, c. 49, s. 210(3); 1993, c. 24, s. 145(1).)

(S.C. 1991, c. 49, s. 210; 1993, c. 24, s. 145.)

—————————— Notes ——————————

Synopsis

This section states the general rule that self-employed individuals must pay CPP contributions in quarterly installments on or before March 15, June 15, September 15 and December 15 of each year. The individual has three choices as to how to calculate the amount to be paid each quarter, based on (i) the previous year's CPP contribution, (ii) the estimated contribution for the current year, or (iii) a blend of the contributions made for the preceding year and the second preceding year. Any unpaid balance should be paid on or before April 30 of the following year.

Installment payments on self-employed earnings are not required where the annual contribution amount is $40 or less, or where the individual is exempt from making installment payments under the *Income Tax Act*. Farmers and fishermen must pay two-thirds of the contribution required in respect of estimated self-employed earnings by December 31 of the year, and the balance by April 30 of the following year.

Related Provisions

- Section 34 — Interest on unpaid contributions and installments

—————————————————

34. *Interest on unpaid contributions* — [24](1) **Where the amount paid by a person on or before the person's balance-due day for a year on account of contributions required to be made by the person for the year in respect of the person's self-employed earnings is less than the amount of the contribution so required to be made, interest at a prescribed rate per annum is payable by the person on the difference between those amounts from the balance-due day for the year to the day of payment. (S.C. 1991, c. 49, s. 211(1).)**

(2) *Interest on instalments* — **In addition to any interest payable under subsection (1), where a person, being required by section 33 to pay a part or instalment of a contribution, has failed to pay all or any part thereof as required, he shall, on payment of the amount he failed so to pay, pay interest thereon at a prescribed rate per annum from the day on or before which he was required to make the payment to the day of payment or the beginning of the period in respect of which he is liable to pay interest thereon under subsection (1), whichever is the earlier.**

(3) *Limitation for farmers and fishermen* — [25]**For the purposes of subsection (2), where a person is required by subsection 33(2) to pay a part or instalment of a contribution in respect of the person's self-employed earnings, the person shall be deemed to have been liable to pay on or before the day referred to in subsection 33(2) a part or instalment computed by reference to**

    (*a*) **the contribution required to be made by the person for the year in respect of the person's self-employed earnings, minus forty dollars,**

    (*b*) **the contribution required in respect of the person's self-employed earnings for the preceding year, or**

—————————————————

[24] Pursuant to 1991, c. 49, s. 211(2), subsection 34(1) is applicable to 1990 and subsequent years.

[25] Pursuant to 1993, c. 24, s. 146(2), and 1994, c. 21, s. 124(2), subsections 34(3) and (4) are applicable to 1992 and subsequent years.

Canada Pension Plan

(*c*) the amount stated to be the amount of the instalment payable by the person for the year in the notice, if any, sent to the person by the Minister,

whichever method gives rise to the least amount required to be paid by the person on or before that day. (S.C. 1993, c. 24, s. 146(1).)

(4) *Limitation for other persons* — [26]For the purposes of subsection (2), where a person is required by subsection 33(3) to pay a part or instalment of a contribution in respect of the person's self-employed earnings, the person shall be deemed to have been liable to pay on or before each day referred to in subsection 33(3) a part or instalment computed by reference to

(*a*) the contribution required to be made by the person for the year in respect of the person's self-employed earnings, minus forty dollars,

(*b*) the contribution required in respect of the person's self-employed earnings for the preceding year,

(*c*) the amounts determined under paragraph 33(3)(*b*) in respect of the person for the year, or

(*d*) the amounts stated to be the amounts of instalment payable by the person for the year in the notices, if any, sent to the person by the Minister,

whichever method gives rise to the least total amount of those parts or instalments required to be paid by the person by that day. (S.C. 1993, c. 24, s. 146(1); 1994, c. 21, s. 124(1).)

(S.C. 1991, c. 49, s. 211; 1993, c. 24, s. 146; 1994, c. 21, s. 124(1).)

——————————— Notes ———————————

Synopsis

Where a person pays less than the required contributions by April 30 of the following year, this section imposes interest at the prescribed rate on the unpaid balance. Interest may also be charged on unpaid installments based on the required contribution for the year less $40.

Related CPP Regulations

- Sections 35–36 — Prescribed interest rates

———————————————————

35. *Failure to file return* — [27](1) Every person who fails to file a return of that person's self-employed earnings for a year as and when required by section 30 is liable to a penalty of five per cent of such part of the amount of the contribution required to be made by that person for the year in respect thereof as remained unpaid at the expiration of the time the return was required to be filed, except that, where that person is liable to a penalty under subsection 162(1) or (2) of the *Income Tax Act* in respect of the year, the Minister may reduce the penalty to which that person is liable under this section or may remit the penalty in whole or in part. (S.C. 1991, c. 49, s. 212(1).)

———————————————————

[26] Pursuant to 1993, c. 24, s. 146(2), and 1994, c. 21, s. 124(2), subsections 34(3) and (4) are applicable to 1992 and subsequent years.

[27] Pursuant to 1992, s. 212(2), subsection 35(1) is applicable with respect to penalties exigible after September 12, 1988.

(2) *Idem* — **Every person who fails to file a return as required by subsection 30(3) is liable to a penalty of five dollars for each day of default, but not exceeding in all fifty dollars.**

(S.C. 1991, c. 49, s. 212.)

—————————— Notes ——————————

Synopsis

This section establishes a penalty of 5% of the unpaid amount for failure to file a return of self-employed earnings. If the person is also liable to penalty under *Income Tax Act* s. 162(1), the Minister may reduce the penalty under this section. Every trustee in bankruptcy, liquidator and similar type of person required to file a return of self-employed earnings on behalf of a bankrupt is liable to a penalty of $5 for each day of default.

—————————————————

36. *Application of Income Tax Act provisions* — **Subject to this Part and except as otherwise provided by regulation, the provisions of Divisions I and J of Part I of the** *Income Tax Act* **with respect to assessments, payment of tax, objections to assessments, appeals, interest, penalties and excess refunds, and the provisions of Part XV (except section 221) and subsections 248(7) and (11) of that Act apply, with such modifications as the circumstances require, in relation to any amount paid or payable as or on account of the contribution for a year in respect of self-employed earnings as though that amount were an amount paid or payable as or on account of tax under that Act. (R.S.C. 1985, c. 38 (3rd Supp.), s. 2(1); 1991, c. 49, s. 213.)**

(R.S.C. 1985, c. 38 (3rd Supp.), s. 2(1); 1991, c. 49, s. 213.)

—————————— Notes ——————————

Synopsis

This section makes applicable provisions of the *Income Tax Act* dealing with assessments, payment of tax and appeal, appeals to the Tax Court of Canada and Federal Court, and administration and enforcement.

Case Law

R. v. Bauman (1998), 97-2315-IT-I (T.C.C.)

Self-employed persons who seek an exemption from having to contribute must apply for judicial review of the Minister's refusal in a superior court with jurisdiction respecting the CPP.

Kroeker v. MNR (1969), 69 D.T.C. 380 (T.A.B.)

An assessment made by the MNR comes before the court with a presumption of validity. If it is challenged, the onus is on the contributor to demonstrate error in the assessment to the point of destroying the basis upon which it rests. A bare factual statement by the contributor is not sufficient.

—————————————————

37. *Priority in which payment to be applied* — **Where any payment is made by a person to the Minister on account of taxes specified in section 228 of the** *Income Tax Act* **and of a contribution under this Act in respect of self employed earnings, notwithstanding any direction made by the person making the payment with respect to its application, the part of the payment that would be applied under that section in payment of tax under the** *Income Tax Act* **shall be applied in payment of the contribution under this Act and shall be deemed to be a payment on account thereof, and to the**

Canada Pension Plan

extent of the amount so applied shall not discharge liability for tax under the *Income Tax Act*, and any amount then remaining shall be applied in payment of tax under the *Income Tax Act* and shall discharge the liability of the person making the payment for that tax to the extent of that amount.

––––––––––––– Notes –––––––––––––

Synopsis

Where individuals are in arrears on payment of CPP contributions and federal income tax, this section deems that any payments made are applied first to the CPP contribution.

Division E: General

Refunds of Overpayments

38. *Refund of overpayment* — **(1)** If an overpayment has been made by an employee on account of the employee's contribution under this Act for a year, the Minister must, if application in writing is made to the Minister by the employee not later than four years — or, in the case of an employee who, in respect of a disability pension, is notified after September 1, 2010 of a decision under subsection 60(7) or 81(2), a decision under subsection 82(11) or 83(11) as those subsections read immediately before their repeal or a decision under section 54 or 59 of the *Department of Employment and Social Development Act*, 10 years — after the end of the year, refund to the employee the amount of the overpayment. (S.C. 2009, c. 31, s. 30(1); 2012, c. 19, s. 227(1); 2013, c. 40, s. 236(1)(*b*)(i).)

(2) *Refund after decision on appeal* — Where an amount on account of a contribution is deducted from the remuneration of an employee or is paid by an employer with respect to an employee, and it is decided by a decision on an appeal made under section 27, 27.1 or 28 that the amount exceeds the amount required by this Act to be deducted or paid, the Minister shall refund the excess if the employee or employer applies for it in writing to the Minister not later than 30 days after the decision is communicated to the employee or employer, as the case may be. (S.C. 1997, c. 40, s. 67(1).)

(3) *Refund of excess — employee* — Despite anything in this Part, if an employee applies to the Minister and satisfies the Minister that, for any year, the amount deducted from the employee's remuneration exceeds the contribution for the year required of the employee under subsection 8(1), the Minister may refund the amount of the excess. The application must be made within four years — or, in the case of an employee who, in respect of a disability pension, is notified after September 1, 2010 of a decision under subsection 60(7) or 81(2), a decision under subsection 82(11) or 83(11) as those subsections read immediately before their repeal or a decision under section 54 or 59 of the *Department of Employment and Social Development Act*, 10 years — after the end of the year. (S.C. 2004, c. 22, s. 18(1); 2009, c. 31, s. 30(2); 2012, c. 19, s. 227(2); 2013, c. 40, s. 236(1)(*b*)(i).)

(3.1) *Refund of amount remitted in excess of required amount — employer* — Subject to subsection (3.2) but despite any other provision of this Part, if an employer applies to the Minister and satisfies the Minister that, for any year, the amount remitted by the employer as employer's contributions with respect to an employee exceeds the contribution for the year required of the employer under section 9 with respect to the employee, the Minister may refund the amount of the excess. The application must be made within four years after the end of the year. (S.C. 2004, c. 22, s. 18(1).)

(3.2) *No refund of employers' contributions* — No refund may be made of any contribution required to be made as an employer's contribution under section 9. (S.C. 2004, c. 22, s. 18(1).)

(4) *Refund of excess contribution in respect of self-employed earnings* — Where a person has paid, on account of the contribution required to be made by him for a year in respect of his self-employed earnings, an amount in excess of the contribution, the Minister

  (*a*) may refund that part of the amount so paid in excess of the contribution on sending the notice of assessment of the contribution, without any application having been made for the refund; and (S.C. 2010, c. 25, s. 70.)

  (*b*) must make such a refund after sending the notice of assessment, if application is made in writing by the contributor not later than four years — or, in the case of a contributor who, in respect of a disability pension, is notified after September 1, 2010 of a decision under subsection 60(7) or 81(2), a decision under subsection 82(11) or 83(11) as those subsections read immediately before their repeal or a decision under section 54 or 59 of the *Department of Employment and Social Development Act*, 10 years — after the end of the year. (S.C. 2009, c. 31, s. 30(3); 2010, c. 25, s. 70; 2012, c. 19, s. 227(3); 2013, c. 40, s. 236(1)(*b*)(i).)

(4.1) *Refund after correction of record of earnings* — Where an amount on account of a contribution is paid by a person in respect of self-employed earnings or is deducted from the remuneration of an employee and the Minister determines, taking into consideration an amendment made under section 97 to the Record of Earnings, that the amount paid or deducted is in excess of the amount required by this Act to be paid or deducted, the Minister may refund the excess. (S.C. 1997, c. 40, s. 67(2).)

(5) *Recovery of amount refunded or credited on liability* — Where an application under this section has been made to the Minister for a refund of any amount deducted on account of an employee's contribution for a year and, whether on the basis of incorrect or incomplete information contained in the application or otherwise, the Minister has refunded an amount to the employee or applied an amount to a liability of the employee to Her Majesty in right of Canada, in excess of the amount that should have been refunded or applied, the amount of the excess may be recovered at any time from the employee as a debt due to Her Majesty. (S.C. 1991, c. 49, s. 214.)

(6) *Application of refund to other debts* — Instead of making a refund that might otherwise be made under this section, the Minister may, where the person to whom the refund is payable is liable or about to become liable to make any payment to Her Majesty in right of Canada, apply the amount of the refund to that liability and notify the person of his action. (S.C. 1991, c. 49, s. 214.)

(7) *Interest on overpayments* — If an amount in respect of an overpayment is refunded or applied under this Act to any other liability, interest shall be paid or applied on the amount at a prescribed rate per annum under the circumstances and for the period or periods determined as prescribed, except that

  (*a*) no interest shall be paid or applied if the amount of the interest is less than one dollar; and (*b*) **no interest shall be paid or applied on an amount that is refundable under subsection (4.1). (S.C. 1997, c. 40, s. 67(3).)**

(S.C. 1991, c. 49, s. 214; 1997, c. 40, s. 67; 2004, c. 22, s. 18; 2009, c. 31, s. 30; 2010, c. 25, s. 70; 2012, c. 19, s. 227; 2013, c. 40, s. 236.)

———————— Notes ————————

Synopsis

This section imposes a four-year time limit on applications for refunds of overpayments by employees and self-employed individuals in respect of their CPP contribution. Where the entitlement to a refund arises by way of a decision is on appeal, the employer or employee has 30 days after being informed of the decision to apply to the Minister for the refund. The Minister has discretion to refund the excess amount where the employer or employee satisfies the Minister that an overpayment has been made, or where an correction to the Record of Earnings has been made. The Minister has the right to recover for overpayment of a refund as well as the right to apply any excess amount to debts owing by the contributor to the Crown — e.g., income tax in arrears. Interest at the prescribed rate is payable by the Minister on overpayments, except where the amount owing is less than $1.00 or where the refund resulted from an amendment to the Record of Earnings.

Related CPP Regulations

● Sections 35–36 — Prescribed interest rates and refunds of overpayment

Case Law

Agpro Services v. Canada (Minister of National Revenue), [2002] FCA 253

Where the employer and the employee's have overpaid CPP contributions and the employees have received their refund, the Minister did not have authority to limit the employer's entitlement to a refund by pro-rating the basic exemption in the computation of an employer's contribution. The only pro-ration that could take place under the CPP is the one provided for in s. 5(5) of the Regulations, and the pro-ration thereby authorized applied equally to the computation of an employer's and an employee's contribution.

————————

39. *Refund of overpayment in accordance with agreement* — **(1) Notwithstanding anything in this Act, where an overpayment has been made by an employee on account of the employee's contribution for a year under this Act, the Minister may, in accordance with any agreement that may be entered into by him with the approval of the Governor in Council with the appropriate authority of a province having the administration of the provincial pension plan referred to in subsection 8(2), if application in writing is made to the Minister by the employee not later than four years after the end of the year, refund to the employee the whole amount of the excess referred to in that subsection, in which case the whole of that amount shall be deemed to be an overpayment made by the employee on account of his contribution for that year under this Act.**

(2) *Saving* — **Where in accordance with any agreement entered into under subsection (1) the appropriate authority of a province has refunded to an employee the whole amount of the excess referred to in subsection 8(2) with respect to that employee, the whole of that amount shall be deemed to be an overpayment made by the employee on account of his contribution for that year under the provincial pension plan referred to in that subsection.**

(3) *Provision for making of financial adjustments* — **Any agreement entered into under subsection (1) may provide therein for the making of any financial adjustments required to be made by reason of any payments made to employees in accordance with**

that agreement and for the crediting or charging of the amount of those adjustments to the Canada Pension Plan Account.

———————— **Notes** ————————

Synopsis

This section provides the mechanism for obtaining a refund in the situation addressed in s. 8(2), where the employee makes an overpayment of his or her contribution under the CPP or QPP. The employee has four years to apply to the Minister for a refund, which may be granted in accordance with the agreement between the federal government and Quebec.

———————————————

Regulations

40. *Regulations* — **(1) The Governor in Council may make regulations**

(*a*) prescribing or providing anything that, by this Part, is to be prescribed or is to be provided by regulations;

(*b*) requiring any class of persons to file information returns respecting any class of information required in connection with contributions under this Act, including information respecting contributions of employees of any such persons identified by the province in which the employees were employed;

(*c*) requiring a person who is, by a regulation made under paragraph (*b*), required to file an information return to supply a copy of the return or a prescribed portion thereof to the person or persons in respect of whose contributions the return or portion thereof relates;

(*d*) prescribing a penalty not exceeding ten dollars a day for each day of default and not exceeding in all two hundred and fifty dollars to which a person who fails to comply with a regulation made under paragraph (*b*) or (*c*) shall be liable;

(*e*) defining the expressions "agriculture", "agricultural enterprise", "employment of a casual nature", "forestry", "horticulture", "fishing", "hunting", "international organization", "logging", "lumbering", "trapping"or "working days" for the purposes of this Act;

(*f*) respecting the manner in which any provision of this Act that applies or extends to an employer of an employee shall apply or extend to any person by whom the remuneration of an employee for services performed in pensionable employment is paid either wholly or in part, and to the employer of any such employee;

(*f.1*) providing for the right of a person to whom a provision of this Act applies or extends by virtue of a regulation made under paragraph (*f*) to recover from the employer any amounts that the person becomes liable to pay by virtue of that regulation; (S.C. 2004, c. 22, s. 19.)

(*g*) specifying the circumstances in which and the conditions on which a person shall be deemed to be or have been, or not to be or have been, a member of the Canadian Forces or the Royal Canadian Mounted Police for the purposes of paragraph 6(2)(*g*);

(*h*) authorizing the Minister on behalf of the Government of Canada to enter into any agreement for giving effect to the provisions of paragraph 6(2)(*h*) or paragraph 7(1)(*e*) or (*f*);

(*i*) regulating the procedure to be followed in the determination by the Minister of questions under this Part;

Canada Pension Plan

191

(*j*) respecting the terms and conditions governing the making of refunds in accordance with any agreement under subsection 39(1) that may be entered into by the Minister on behalf of the Government of Canada; and

(*k*) generally for carrying out the purposes and provisions of this Part.

(2) *Regulations of Minister* — (Repealed by 1998, c. 19, s. 256.)

(3) *Effective date of regulations* — A regulation made under paragraph (1)(*a*) prescribing rules referred to in subsection 21(1) shall have effect from the day it is published in the *Canada Gazette* or from such earlier day as may be specified in the regulation. (S.C. 1991, c. 49, s. 215.)

(4) *Effective date of certain agreements* — Any agreement for giving effect to the provisions of paragraph 6(2)(*h*) or 7(1)(*f*) that is entered into by the Minister pursuant to regulations made under paragraph (1)(*h*) has effect with reference to a period before it was entered into if the agreement provides for that effect.

(S.C. 1991, c. 49, s. 215; 1998, c. 19, s. 256; 2004, c. 22, s. 19.)

Offences

41. *Offence and punishment* — (1) Every employer who fails to comply with subsection 21(1) or 23(3) is guilty of an offence and, in addition to any penalty otherwise provided, is liable on summary conviction to

(*a*) a fine not exceeding five thousand dollars; or

(*b*) both the fine described in paragraph (*a*) and imprisonment for a term not exceeding six months.

(2) *Idem* — Every person who fails to comply with or contravenes section 24 or 25 is guilty of an offence punishable on summary conviction.

(3) *Idem* — Every person who fails to comply with or contravenes section 30 or a regulation made under paragraph 40(1)(*b*) or (*c*) is guilty of an offence and, in addition to any penalty otherwise provided, is liable on summary conviction to a fine of not less than twenty-five dollars a day for each day of default, but not exceeding in all one thousand dollars.

(4) *Idem* — Every person who

(*a*) makes, or participates in, assents to or acquiesces in the making of, false or deceptive statements in a return, certificate, statement or answer filed or made as required by or under this Part or a regulation,

(*b*) to evade payment of a contribution imposed by this Act, destroys, alters, mutilates, secretes or otherwise disposes of the records or books of account of an employer,

(*c*) makes, or assents to or acquiesces in the making of, false or deceptive entries, or omits, or assents to or acquiesces in the omission, to enter a material particular, in records or books of account of an employer,

(*d*) wilfully, in any manner, evades or attempts to evade, compliance with this Act, or payment of contributions imposed by this Act, or

(*e*) conspires with any person to commit an offence described in any of paragraphs (*a*) to (*d*),

is guilty of an offence and, in addition to any penalty otherwise provided, is liable on summary conviction to

(*f*) a fine of not less than twenty-five dollars and not more than five thousand dollars plus, in an appropriate case, an amount not exceeding double the amount of the contribution that should have been shown to be payable or that was sought to be evaded, or

(g) both the fine described in paragraph (f) and imprisonment for a term not exceeding six months.

(5) *Saving provision* — Where a person has been convicted under this section of failing to comply with subsection 21(1) or a regulation made under paragraph 40(1)(b) or (c), he is not liable to pay any penalty imposed under section 21 or under any regulation made under section 40 for the same failure unless he was assessed for that penalty or that penalty was demanded from him before the information or complaint giving rise to the conviction was laid or made.

(6) *Information or complaint* — An information or complaint under this section may be laid or made by any officer of the Canada Revenue Agency, a member of the Royal Canadian Mounted Police or any person thereunto authorized by the Minister and, where an information or complaint purports to have been laid or made under this section, it shall be deemed to have been laid or made by a person thereunto authorized by the Minister and shall not be called in question for lack of authority of the informant or complainant except by the Minister or a person acting for him or Her Majesty. (S.C. 1999, c. 17, s. 111(d); 2005, c. 38, s. 138(c)(iv).)

(S.C. 1999, c. 17, s. 111; 2005, c. 38, s. 138.)

——————— **Notes** ———————

Synopsis

This section sets out the offences and punishment for violation of specific provisions of Part I of the CPP, including failure to deduct and remit contributions, failure to keep proper books and records or permit audit or inspection of records, failure to submit returns, false statements and entries, and evasion of payment of contributions. Note that s. 90(2) provides for a 5-year limitation on the bringing of prosecutions under the CPP from the time the Minister becomes aware of the subject matter of the proceedings.

———————

Part II
Pensions and Supplementary Benefits
Interpretation

42. *Definitions* — (1) In this Part,

"basic number of contributory months" in the case of any contributor, means one hundred and twenty minus the number of months that were excluded from the contributor's contributory period under this Act or under a provincial pension plan by reason of disability; (R.S.C. 1985, c. 30 (2nd Supp.), s. 12(1).)

"child" of a contributor means a child of the contributor, whether born before or after the contributor's death, and includes

(a) an individual adopted legally or in fact by the contributor while the individual was under twenty-one years of age, and

(b) an individual of whom, either legally or in fact, the contributor had, or immediately before the individual reached twenty-one years of age did have, the custody and control, but does not include a child of the contributor who is adopted legally or in fact by someone other than the contributor or the contributor's spouse or common-law partner prior to the death or disability of the contributor, unless the contributor was maintaining the child, as defined by regulation; (R.S.C. 1985, c. 30 (2nd Supp.), s. 12(1); 2000, c. 12, s. 44(2).)

"dependent child"[28] of a contributor means a child of the contributor who
  (a) is less than eighteen years of age,
  (b) is eighteen or more years of age but less than twenty-five years of age and is in full-time attendance at a school or university as defined by regulation, or
  (c) is a child other than a child described in paragraph (b), is eighteen or more years of age and is disabled, having been disabled without interruption since the time he reached eighteen years of age or the contributor died, whichever occurred later;

(R.S.C. 1985, c. 30 (2nd Supp.), s. 12(1).)

"disabled contributor's child" or any form of that expression of like import means a dependent child of a contributor who is disabled, but does not include a dependent child described in paragraph (c) of the definition "dependent child" in this section; (R.S.C. 1985, c. 30 (2nd Supp.), s. 12(1).)

"family allowance recipient" means a person who received or is in receipt of an allowance or a family allowance pursuant to the *Family Allowances Act*, chapter F-1 of the Revised Statutes of Canada, 1970, as it read immediately before being repealed or the *Family Allowances Act* for that period prior to a child reaching seven years of age, and such other persons as may be prescribed by regulation;

"Maximum Pensionable Earnings Average" in respect of a contributor for a year, means the average of the Year's Maximum Pensionable Earnings for that year and
  (a) where the year is before 1998 or the date of birth of the contributor is before January 1, 1933, the two previous years, or
  (b) in any other case,
    (i) where the year is 1998, the three previous years, and
    (ii) where the year is after 1998, the four previous years;

(S.C. 1997, c. 40, s. 68.)

---

[28] The amendment to that portion of the definition "dependent child" preceding paragraph (a) thereof made by R.S.C. 1985, c. 30 (2nd Supp.), s. 12(1) applies in respect of all benefits payable after the coming into force of this section. (R.S.C. 1985, c. 30 (2nd Supp.), s. 12(3).)

Where, before the coming into force of R.S.C. 1985, c. 30 (2nd Supp.), s. 12, a children's benefit to an applicant was terminated or an applicant was denied a children's benefit on the ground that the applicant was not a "dependent child" due to marital status, application may be made for that benefit and, if the application is approved, payment shall be effective starting with the month in which this section comes into force or the eleventh month before the month in which the application was received, whichever is the later. (R.S.C. 1985, c. 30 (2nd Supp.), s. 12(4).)

With regard to the amendments made by R.S.C. 1985, c. 30 (2nd Supp.), s. 12(1) to paragraph (b) of the definition "dependent child" and to the definition "disabled contributor's child", application may be made for benefits that had been terminated or denied, in accordance with those definitions, before the coming into force of this section, but no such benefit is payable in respect of such an application for any month before January, 1987. (R.S.C. 1985, c. 30 (2nd Supp.), s. 12(5).)

Minister — "Minister" means the Minister of Employment and Social Development; (1996, c. 11, s. 95(*b*); 2005, c. 35, s. 67(*a*)(vii); 2012, c. 19, s. 694(*a*)(vii); 2013, c. 40, s. 238(1)(*b*)(vi).)

"orphan" of a contributor means a dependent child of a contributor who has died but does not include a dependent child described in paragraph (*c*) of the definition "dependent child";

"substantially gainful", in respect of an occupation, has the meaning that may be prescribed; (2012, c. 31, s. 194.)

"surviving spouse with dependent children" **(Repealed by 2000, c. 12, s. 44(1).);**

"survivor" in relation to a deceased contributor, means

    (*a*) if there is no person described in paragraph (*b*), a person who was married to the contributor at the time of the contributor's death, or

    (*b*) a person who was the common-law partner of the contributor at the time of the contributor's death;

(S.C. 2000, C. 12, s. 44(3).)

"survivor with dependent children" means a survivor of a contributor who wholly or substantially maintains one or more dependent children of the contributor; (S.C. 2000, c. 12, s. 44(3).)

"wholly or substantially" has such meaning as may be prescribed.

    (2) *When person deemed disabled* — **For the purposes of this Act,**

    (*a*) a person shall be considered to be disabled only if he is determined in prescribed manner to have a severe and prolonged mental or physical disability, and for the purposes of this paragraph,

        (i) a disability is severe only if by reason thereof the person in respect of whom the determination is made is incapable regularly of pursuing any substantially gainful occupation, and

        (ii) a disability is prolonged only if it is determined in prescribed manner that the disability is likely to be long continued and of indefinite duration or is likely to result in death; and

    (*b*) a person is deemed to have become or to have ceased to be disabled at the time that is determined in the prescribed manner to be the time when the person became or ceased to be, as the case may be, disabled, but in no case shall a person — including a contributor referred to in subparagraph 44(1)(*b*)(ii) — be deemed to have become disabled earlier than fifteen months before the time of the making of any application in respect of which the determination is made. (S.C. 1992, c. 1, s. 23; 2009, c. 31, s. 31.)

(R.S.C. 1985, c. 30 (2nd Supp.), s. 12(2).)

    (R.S.C. 1985, c. 30 (2nd Supp.), s. 12; 1992, c. 1, s. 23; 1996, c. 11, s. 95(*b*); 1997, c. 40, s. 68; 2005, c. 35, s. 67; 2009, c. 31, s. 31; 2012, c. 19, s. 694; 2012, c. 31, s. 194; 2013, c. 40, s. 238.)

——————— **Notes** ———————

Synopsis

    This section explains the meaning of words and phrases used in Part II of the CPP.

By far the most contentious provision of the entire CPP is s. 42(2), which sets out the test for when a claimant is disabled. To be considered disabled, a person must be determined to have a severe and prolonged mental or physical disability. "Severe" means that the disability renders the person incapable of regularly pursuing any substantially gainful occupation. "Prolonged" means that the disability is either likely to be long continued and of indefinite duration, or likely to result in death. Sections 68–70 of the CPP Regulations provide more details as to the procedure by which a person is determined to be disabled. The issue of whether or not a claimant is disabled is extensively discussed in the Introduction at the beginning of this book.

Another key issue is: who qualifies to receive a survivor's pension following the death of a married contributor who is living with a "common-law partner" at the time of his or her death: the legal spouse or the common-law partner? The definition of "survivor" in s. 42(1) must be read in conjunction with that of "common-law partner" in s. 2. The case law has made it clear that the test for being considered a common-law partner under s. 2(1) is that he or she must be someone with whom the deceased contributor (i) cohabited for at least one continuous year in a conjugal relationship recently or at some point in the past, and (ii) cohabited in a conjugal relationship at the time of his or her death.

The definition of "family allowance recipient" is required for the "child-rearing drop-out" provisions of s. 44(2)(b)(iv). By virtue of s. 77(c), (d) of the CPP Regulations, an "eligible individual" and "qualified dependent" for the purpose of ss. 122.6 and 122.62 of the federal *Income Tax Act* are part of the definition. The *Income Tax Act* definitions read as follows:

122.6 *Definitions.* —

"*eligible individual*" in respect of a qualified dependant at any time means a person who at that time

> (a) resides with the qualified dependant,

> (b) is the parent of the qualified dependant who primarily fulfills the responsibility for the care and upbringing of the qualified dependant,

> (c) is resident in Canada or, where the person is the cohabiting spouse of a person who is deemed under subsection 250(1) to be resident in Canada throughout the taxation year that includes that time, was resident in Canada in any preceding taxation year,

> (d) is not described in paragraph 149(1)(a) or 149(1)(b), and

> (e) is, or whose cohabiting spouse is, a Canadian citizen or a person who

>> (i) is a permanent resident (within the meaning assigned by the *Immigration Act*),

>> (ii) is a visitor in Canada or the holder of a permit in Canada (within the meanings assigned by the *Immigration Act*) who was resident in Canada throughout the 18 month period preceding that time, or

>> (iii) was determined before that time under the *Immigration Act*, or regulations made under that Act, to be a Convention refugee, and for the purpose of this definition,

> (f) where the qualified dependant resides with the dependant's female parent, the parent who primarily fulfills the responsibility for the care and upbringing of the qualified dependant is presumed to be the female parent,

> (g) the presumption referred to in paragraph 122.6 eligible individual (f) does not apply in prescribed circumstances, and

> (h) prescribed factors shall be considered in determining what constitutes care and upbringing;

"*qualified dependant*" at any time means a person who at that time

> (a) has not attained the age of 18 years,

> (b) is not a person in respect of whom an amount was deducted under paragraph (a) of the description of B in subsection 118(1) in computing the tax

payable under this Part by the person's spouse for the base taxation year in relation to the month that includes that time, and

(c) is not a person in respect of whom a special allowance under the *Children's Special Allowances Act* is payable for the month that includes that time;

* * *

122.62 *Eligible individual.* — (1) For the purposes of this subdivision, a person may be considered to be an eligible individual in respect of a particular qualified dependant at the beginning of a month only if the person has, no later than 11 months after the end of the month, filed with the Minister a notice in prescribed form containing prescribed information.

(2) *Extension for notices* — The Minister may at any time extend the time for filing a notice under subsection 122.62(1).

(3) *Exception* — Where at the beginning of 1993 a person is an eligible individual in respect of a qualified dependant, subsection 122.62(1) does not apply to the person in respect of the qualified dependant if the qualified dependant was an eligible child (within the meaning assigned by subsection 122.2(2) because of subparagraph (a)(i) of the definition "eligible child" in that subsection) of the individual for the 1992 taxation year.

(4) *Person ceasing to be an eligible individual* — Where during a particular month a person ceases to be an eligible individual in respect of a particular qualified dependant (otherwise than because of the qualified dependant attaining the age of 18 years), the person shall notify the Minister of that fact before the end of the first month following the particular month.

(5) *Death of cohabiting spouse* — Where

(a) before the end of a particular month the cohabiting spouse or common-law partner of an eligible individual in respect of a qualified dependant dies, and

(b) the individual so elects, before the end of the eleventh month after the particular month, in a form that is acceptable to the Minister, for the purpose of determining the amount deemed under subsection 122.61(1) to be an overpayment arising in any month after the particular month on account of the individual's liability under this Part for the base taxation year in relation to the particular month, subject to any subsequent election under subsection 122.62(6) or 122.62(7), the individual's adjusted income for the year is deemed to be equal to the individual's income for the year.

(c) (Repealed by S.C. 1998, c. 21, s. 95.)

(d) (Repealed by S.C. 1998, c. 21, s. 95.)

(6) *Separation from cohabiting spouse* — Where

(a) before the end of a particular month an eligible individual in respect of a qualified dependant begins to live separate and apart from the individual's cohabiting spouse, because of a breakdown of their marriage, for a period of at least 90 days that includes a day in the particular month, and

(b) the individual so elects, before the end of the eleventh month after the particular month, in a form that is acceptable to the Minister, for the purpose of determining the amount deemed under subsection 122.61(1) to be an overpayment arising in any month after the particular month on account of the individual's liability under this Part for the base taxation year in relation to the particular month, subject to any subsequent election under subsection 122.62(5) or 122.62(7), the individual's adjusted income for the year is deemed to be equal to the individual's income for the year.

(c) (Repealed by S.C. 1998, c. 21, s. 95.)

(d) (Repealed by S.C. 1998, c. 21, s. 95.)

197

(7) *Person becoming a cohabiting spouse* — Where

(a) at any particular time before the end of a particular month a taxpayer has become the cohabiting spouse of an eligible individual, and

(b) the taxpayer and the eligible individual jointly so elect in prescribed form filed with the Minister before the end of the eleventh month after the particular month,

for the purpose of determining the amount deemed by subsection 122.61(1) to be an overpayment arising in any month after the particular month on account of the eligible individual's liability under this Part for the year, the taxpayer is deemed to have been the eligible individual's cohabiting spouse throughout the period that began immediately before the end of the base taxation year in relation to the particular month and ended at the particular time.

Income Tax Regulations 6300, 6301, and 6302 read as follows:

6300. *Interpretation* In this Part, "qualified dependant" has the meaning assigned by section 122.6 of the Act. (SOR/93-13, s. 1.)

6301. *Non-Application* **(1)** For the purposes of paragraph (g) of the definition "eligible individual" in section 122.6 of the Act, the presumption referred to in paragraph (f) of that definition does not apply in the circumstances where

(a) the female parent of the qualified dependant declares in writing to the Minister that the male parent, with whom she resides, is the parent of the qualified dependant who primarily fulfills the responsibility for the care and upbringing of each of the qualified dependants who reside with both parents;

(b) the female parent is a qualified dependant of an eligible individual and each of them files a notice with the Minister under subsection 122.62(1) of the Act in respect of the same qualified dependant;

(c) there is more than one female parent of the qualified dependant who resides with the qualified dependant and each female parent files a notice with the Minister under subsection 122.62(1) of the Act in respect of the qualified dependant; or

(d) more than one notice is filed with the Minister under subsection 122.62(1) of the Act in respect of the same qualified dependant who resides with each of the persons filing the notices if such persons live at different locations.

(2) For greater certainty, a person who files a notice referred to in paragraph (1)(b), (c) or (d) includes a person who is not required under subsection 122.62(3) of the Act to file such a notice. (SOR/93-13, s. 1; SOR/99-17, s. 9.)

6302. *Factors* For the purposes of paragraph (h) of the definition "eligible individual" in section 122.6 of the Act, the following factors are to be considered in determining what constitutes care and upbringing of a qualified dependant:

(a) the supervision of the daily activities and needs of the qualified dependant;

(b) the maintenance of a secure environment in which the qualified dependant resides;

(c) the arrangement of, and transportation to, medical care at regular intervals and as required for the qualified dependant;

(d) the arrangement of, participation in, and transportation to, educational, recreational, athletic or similar activities in respect of the qualified dependant;

(e) the attendance to the needs of the qualified dependant when the qualified dependant is ill or otherwise in need of the attendance of another person;

(f) the attendance to the hygienic needs of the qualified dependant on a regular basis;

(g) the provision, generally, of guidance and companionship to the qualified dependant; and (*h*) the existence of a court order in respect of the qualified dependant that is valid in the jurisdiction in which the qualified dependant resides. (SOR/93-13, s. 1.)

Recent Amendments — Substantially Gainful Employment

In May 2014, s. 68.1 of the CPP Regulations (reproduced later in this book) was added. It provides a formula for determining a threshold for "substantially gainful occupation" which is essentially 12 times the maximum retirement benefit. As it is tied to the retirement benefit, it can change quarterly with the adjustment in the benefit rate.

Related CPP Regulations

- Sections 47–50 — Determination of age
- Section 65 — Whole or substantial maintenance of dependent children
- Section 65.1 — Maintenance of child
- Section 66 — Full-time attendance at a school or university
- Section 67 — Declaration of enrolment or attendance at a school or university
- Sections 68–70 — Determination of disability
- Section 77 — Definition of "family allowance recipient"

Case Law

§1. Child

(a) General

Bajwa v. MHRD (April 4, 2002), CP 14184 (PAB)

The statutory requirement is related to both care and control of the child. Both are required. One alone falls short. Care and control of religious matters, schooling, professional education and the like, standing alone, may fall short. Influence and concern in these areas standing alone are not sufficient.

J.D. v. MHRSD (August 14, 2012), CP 26564 (PAB)

It does not matter that a non-parent contributor or recipient has assumed the primary caregiving role for their granddaughter. Although the grandparent recipient of CPP disability benefits resided with the mother and the child, the grandparent was not entitled to the disabled contributor's child's benefits because the mother of the child had the custody and control of the child. The grandparent never applied for the legal custody or adoption of their grandchild.

Limer v. MNHW (June 29, 1988), CP 1222, CEB & PG (TB) ¶8545 (PAB)

The common-law presumption as to the husband's paternity of a child conceived during a marriage applies even after separation of the parties. This principle is rebuttable only on proof by cogent evidence to the contrary.

(b) Example Case — Custody and Control or Adoption in Fact

- Deceased contributor having had excellent rapport with spouse's one-year-old child during eight-month cohabitation and marriage; contributor's poor physical condition (lung cancer) militating against adoption in fact: *MNHW v. Glitnak* (May 23, 1990), CP 1807, CEB & PG (TB) ¶8605 (PAB)

§2. Dependent Child

(a) Attendance at School or University

MHRD v. Attewell (January 14, 1999), CP 06345, CEB & PG (TB) ¶8762 (PAB)

The "full-time attendance" aspect of s. 67(*a*) of the CPP Regulations is a procedural rather than a substantive requirement, and therefore non-compliance does not nullify the application.

Canada Pension Plan

199

MHRD v. Ruelland (March 21, 1997), CP 04084, CEB & PG (TB) ¶8677 (PAB)

The CPP and Regulations are not very specific or clear as to the meaning of "full-time attendance at a school or university", and the definitions are to be given their most liberal interpretation.

MSD v. Allemano, (February 24, 2006), CP 23393 (PAB)

It was clear under s. 66(2) of the CPP Regulations that where the child was unable to attend school at the beginning of a school year due to illness, there was no entitlement to DCCB benefits unless he or she returned to school during that school year.

MEI v. Coates (April 29, 1994), CP 3022, CEB & PG (TB) ¶8529 (PAB)

For a scholastic vacation to exist, there must be full-time attendance at a recognized school or university. The applicant's intention in March to attend university in September could not qualify where the applicant was not then in a recognized program.

(b) Example Cases — Full-Time Attendance

- "Up With People" qualifies as an educational institution providing training or instruction of an educational, professional, vocational or technical nature: *MHRD v. Monk* (June 12, 1998), CP 06223 (PAB)

- Taking upgrading night courses at Adult Training Centre four nights per week, three hours per night; applicant dropping one of two courses in April, but awarded attendance until September to allow for vacation: *MHRD v. Ruelland* (March 21, 1997), CP 04084, CEB & PG ¶8677 (PAB)

- Internship at teaching hospital required as part of formal training to obtain diploma as dietitian; applicant receiving monthly stipend: *MNHR v. Gouthro* (September 13, 1993), CP 2668, CEB & PG (TB) ¶8526 (PAB)

- Attending VAST Centre which enabled students who had dropped out of regular school system to continue studies; program involving 8 hours of in-class time per week: *MHRD v. Attewell* (January 14, 1999), CP 06345, CEB & PG (TB) ¶8762 (PAB)

(c) Example Cases — Not in Full-Time Attendance

- Child took compassionate leave from TQ3 army training upon death of contributor father, before slipping into a long period of depression, drug use and drinking; child finally applying for orphan's benefit payment at age 36, 13 years after father's death; sisters received benefit during statutory period: *Sloan v. MHRD,* (October 4, 2002), CP 16188 (PAB)

- Participation in Canada World Youth Program: *MEI v. Coates* (April 29, 1994), CP 3022, CEB & PG (TB) ¶8529 (PAB)

- Employment as apprentice electrician with electrical firm; instruction provided by firm being incidental to its main commercial profit-making enterprise: *MNHW v. Hyrnuik* (June 11, 1985), CEB & PG (TB) ¶8961 (PAB)

§3. Survivor

(a) Generally

Carter v. Canada (Minister of Social Development), 2006 FCA 172

The "or" at the end of para. (*a*) in the definition of "survivor" in s. 42(1) is clearly disjunctive, not conjunctive. Only one person can qualify as a "survivor".

Farrell v. Canada (Attorney General), 2010 FC 34

There can only be one recipient of CPP survivor benefits. The potential benefits of a married but separated spouse can be usurped by a person who was a common-law partner of the deceased at the time of his death. Section 2(1) of the CPP defines "common-law partner" partner in relation to a contributor as "a person who is cohabiting with the contributor in a conjugal relationship at the relevant time, having so cohabited with the contributor for a continuous period of at least one year". The question is not whether the person living with the deceased at the time of death is a good person or whether she behaved in an appropriate manner. Nor is the question whether the legally married spouse was more deserving of the deceased's CPP survivor benefits than the common-law spouse. The sole question is whether the deceased and the person living with him at the time of death were in a common-law relationship for at least one year prior to his death.

Betts v. Shannon (October 22, 2001), CP 11654 (PAB)

Where there are two alleged survivors at time of the contributor's death, the onus is on common-law partner to prove on balance of probabilities that was cohabiting with deceased in a conjugal relationship at time of contributor's death, having so cohabited with him for a continuous period of at least one year.

Park v. Ribson (December 13, 1996), CP 3700, CEB & PG ¶8656 (PAB)

The one-year continuous cohabitation in a conjugal relationship does not have to be in the year immediately preceding the contributor's death. It is sufficient if the one-year cohabitation is followed later by a further period of cohabitation in a conjugal relationship of whatever duration ending with the contributor's death. To repudiate earlier relationship would require a clear and precisely indicated intention on the part of deceased contributor that it was irrevocably terminated.

D.H. v. MHRSD, (June 12, 2013), CP 28303 (PAB)

A common law relationship ends when either party regards it as being at an end and, by conduct, has demonstrated in a convincing manner that this particular state of mind is a settled one. A couple not living under the same roof is not decisive in determining whether they are still in a common law relationship. The deceased rented a room at work and may have told a daughter and the intervener that the relationship with the claimant common law spouse was over. However, the deceased gave no indication to others that that was the case.

Hunsigner v. MHRD, (December 16, 2002), CP 18406 (PAB)

There must have been a conjugal relationship for a claimant to be entitled to receive survivor's benefits. The fact that the claimant had lived with and taken care of her father and her contributor sister, who was not well, until their respective deaths did not mean that she qualified as a "survivor" under the CPP.

Siou v. Rundle (April 18, 2002), CP 14667 (PAB)

Where the common-law partner and the deceased contributor separated for a period before the contributor's death, they were held to have resumed cohabitation although they continued to hold leases on separate premises. The common-law partner's lengthy apartment lease did not prevent her from moving in with the contributor and caring for him until he entered the hospital.

Craig v. MHRD; Morrow v. MHRD (January 13, 2000), CP 13521, CEB & PG 13354 (PAB)

Despite the amendments to the definition of common-law partners in 2000, the version of the legislation in effect at the time of the contributor's death should govern the appeal of the matter from the Review Tribunal. Where the contributor resided with two women alternately at the same time without their knowledge, neither woman qualified for the survivor benefit. Neither relationship was uninterrupted for a continuous period of at least one year throughout period of cohabitation. CPP provides for only one spouse to be granted a survivor's pension.

Charuk v. Sullivan (October 4, 1996), CP 4366, CEB & PG ¶8646 (PAB)

While "cohabitation" is not defined in the CPP, it implies the bilateral intention of both parties to set up a matrimonial home together; living together as man and wife with some measure of mutual intercourse. The conjugal relationship aspect implies something in the nature of an ongoing arrangement — i.e., one that is continuing on a regular basis. It must be by way of a bilateral, or mutually agreed upon, intention, to be of such an ongoing nature. Finally, it seems implicit that the arrangement in question be of a monogamous nature, also by mutual and bilateral intention. The intention of the deceased, if it exists at all, must necessarily be clearly deduced from whatever actual evidence is brought before the PAB. Where two parties seek survivor's benefits, it may well be that due to the particular circumstances of the situation neither putative "spouse" may meet those somewhat rigid requirements.

MSD v. Whiteway (August 15, 2006), CP 24313 (PAB)

Multiple false statutory declarations by the claimant that she and the deceased contributor were living separate and apart could be ignored in finding that they in fact were common law spouses, even where the explanation given for making the false declarations was less than satisfactory.

Sawatzky v. MSD (October 16, 2006), CP 22318 (PAB)

A seven-year relationship without cohabitation was explainable given that both parties had children and wanted to avoid problems associated with merging the families.

MSD v. Riddell (July 27, 2006), CP 22465 (PAB)

Section 12(1) of the *Divorce Act* states that a divorce takes effect on the 31st day after the day on which the judgment granting the divorce is rendered. The *Divorce Act* has built into it a 30-day appeal period. When that period expires, the divorce is final, that is, at the end of the 30th day. The contributor's death on the 31st day after the divorce was granted meant that the former spouse was not a "survivor" for CPP purposes.

Trevena v. MHRD (October 30, 1998), CP 05060, CEB & PG (TB) ¶8725 (PAB)

For a common-law spouse to move furniture and all her clothes out of the contributor's residence and give a change of address notice was indicative of a termination of the relationship, and not a mere temporary cooling-off period. There was no pattern in the relationship of temporary separations always followed by reconciliation.

Mansell v. MHRD (March 1, 2000), CP 04765 (PAB)

It is desirable that there be consistency in the definitions of "spouse" among the CPP, the *Divorce Act*, provincial statutes related to family law, and pensions under federal control, such as those for military and civil servants.

MSD v. Briggs (May 2, 2005), CP 22224 (PAB). See also *Rogers v. MSD* (December 16, 2004), CP 20699 and CP 21436 (PAB).

The fact that the parties had originally lived together at one point, raised four children together and continued their exclusive relationship with occasional sleepovers over 28 years up until the contributor's death was not sufficient to qualify as cohabitation in a conjugal relationship at the time of the contributor's death. The parties maintained separate bank accounts, there was no evidence to mutual access to both residences or of vacations or trips together, death benefits were paid to the deceased's daughter from a previous marriage, and the application for survivor's benefits stated that the parties were living apart at the time of the contributor's death.

Keiller-Pearce v. MHRD (December 5, 1997), CP 04078, CEB & PG (TB) ¶8707 (PAB)

Where the parties had gone through a form of marriage while the deceased contributor was still married to his previous spouse, the purported second marriage was void *ab initio* and could not by itself form the basis of a claim for survivor status.

Reinberger, Estate of v. Holmes (April 29, 1994), CP 2914, CEB & PG (TB) ¶8532 (PAB)

The estate of the legal wife of the deceased contributor does not having standing to appeal a decision of the Review Tribunal that the common-law partner applicant was entitled to survivor's benefits instead of the legal wife, where the Minister had provided written confirmation that the estate would not be required to return any benefits already paid to the legal wife. The estate therefore lacked any economic interest in the appeal.

(b) Canadian Charter of Rights and Freedoms

Hughes v. HRSD (October 9, 2007), CP 24000 (PAB)

The definition of "survivor" in s. 42(1) does not violate s. 15(1) of the Charter by discriminating against separated widows and widowers on the basis of sex, age and marital status. No appropriate comparable group which receives a survivor's pension on the basis of a listed or analogous ground in s. 15(1) of the Charter that is denied to the Appellant on the same ground. In federal benefits such as CPP, competing claims will have to be balanced. On occasion, improving the lot of one group of persons necessarily involves transferring some disadvantage from a previously privileged group to a more disadvantaged one. This does not constitute discrimination within the meaning of s. 15(1) of the Charter.

Trevena v. MHRD (October 30, 1998), CP 05060, CEB & PG (TB) ¶8725 (PAB)

The requirement that a common-law spouse (now partner) must be cohabiting with the contributor at the time of death does not violate the equality rights guarantee under s. 15 of the *Canadian Charter of Rights and Freedoms*. The nature of a common-law relationship is that it lacks formality and it is therefore more difficult to define when such a relationship ceases. The requirement of cohabitation on death is not an unreasonable method of establishing one's status to defeat the claim of the legal spouse.

§4. Survivor with Dependent Children

Bennett v. MEI (July 10, 1995), CP 2708, CEB & PG (TB) ¶8579 (PAB)

Benefits were not payable where the child was in the contributor's custody at the time of the contributor's death and the former spouse had not been wholly or substantially maintaining the child at that time.

§5. Disability

(Disability determination cases under s. 42(2)(a) are organized in the Disability Case Table, starting at p. 35.)

§6. Starting Date for Disability Benefits

Galay v. MSD (June 3, 2004), CP 21768 (PAB)

The words "before the time of the making of any application" in s. 42(2)(b) refer to the time that the application was received by the Minister.

Sarazin v. MHRD (June 27, 1997), CP 5300, CEB & PG (TB) ¶8682 (PAB)

Section 42(2)(b) limits the retroactive time to 15 months, before the later of (i) the time when a successful application for disability benefits was made, or (ii) when the amendments came into force in June 1992. It is irrelevant whether the claimant had actually become disabled prior to that time, or had made a previous claim for benefits which was denied because it was too late under the legislation in force prior to the June 1992 amendments to s. 44(1)(b).

MSD v. Zicarelli (December 7, 2004), CP 21971 (PAB)

The use of the word "deemed" in s. 42(2)(b) does not create an ambiguity between that section and s. 69. The reference in s. 69 to the "month in which the applicant became disabled" is the month when he was deemed to be disabled in s. 42(2)(b).

Baines v. Canada (HRSD), 2011 FCA 158, leave to appeal to SCC refused, 2012 CanLII 22038 (SCC).

Where the claimant's initial application was refused seven years before, the fact that a subsequent application was allowed for the same injury did not permit the tribunal to backdate the award beyond the 15-month statutory maximum to the date of the initial application. The Review Tribunal did not have jurisdiction to reopen the original file, and the PAB could only consider issues within the Review Tribunal's jurisdiction (CPP s. 83(11)).

Dillon v. Canada (Attorney General), 2007 FC 900

Where a previous application for disability benefits had been dismissed many years before, and that decision was not appealed from, the granting of benefits for the same condition on a subsequent application could not be made retroactive to the date of the first application. The earlier decision was *res judicata.*

King v. Canada, 2007 FC 272

There is no automatic right to interest on disability pension payments which have been delayed and for which the disabled person is entitled to a retroactive pension payment. Moreover, the PAB in granting the plaintiff a disability pension under the Plan has no authority to award interest. However, it may be possible for the plaintiff to obtain a favourable decision from the Minister under s. 66(4). The following is the proper course of proceeding:

1. the plaintiff asks that the Minister consider remedial action under s. 66(4) not to award interest on the retroactive pension payment; and

2. if the Minister denies the request for interest, the plaintiff can commence an application for judicial review of that decision in the Federal Court under s. 18.1 of the *Federal Courts Act.*

A.T. v. MHRSD (May 15, 2013), CP 28176 (PAB)

Where the claimant was already in receipt of early retirement CPP benefits at the time of the application for a disability benefit, under s. 42(2)(*b*) he or she cannot be deemed disabled more than 15 months prior to the application. As the retirement pension had already been in pay for three years at the time of the application, the claim for a disability pension failed.

Pettipas v. MSD (March 30, 2007), CP 24333 (PAB)

Nothing in the CPP limits the application of the maximum retroactivity provision in s. 42(2)(*b*) to disability claims and to exclude it from the determination of claims for death and survivor's benefits.

MSD v. Somani (August 8, 2005), CP 23329 (PAB)

For the purpose of determining when an application for disability benefits was made, the submission of a doctor's medical report is not a substitute for the filing of a formal application for disability benefits. A medical report does not meet the requirements of an application for benefits in "prescribed manner" as stipulated in s. 60(6) nor does it provide the important personal information required by ss. 43, 52 and 68 of the Regulations.

Whitter v. MSD (May 15, 2006), CP 23649 (PAB)

The PAB does not have statutory jurisdiction to use an earlier, unsuccessful application for disability benefits by a claimant in fixing the onset dates for benefits granted to the same claimant under a subsequent application.

Law v. MSD (October 18, 2006), CP 24157 (PAB)

Where a medical report established that the claimant was disabled as of a certain date, and there was no evidence of any change in the year previous to that date, then disability benefits should commence as of one year before the date of the medical report.

Meseyton v. MSD (June 4, 2004), CP 21108 (PAB)

The fact that the claimant had previously made an unsuccessful application for benefits, but failed to appeal the Minister's refusal, did not entitle the claimant to an extension of the 15-month period of retroactivity on his subsequent successful application.

Batho v. MHRD (January 23, 1997), CP 4735 (PAB)

The U.S.–Canada treaty only came into effect in 1984, and there is no provision for retroactivity.

Cavalieri v. MHRD (October 25, 1996), CP 3925 (PAB)

The fact that the claimant waited three years before applying for a disability pension was not grounds for denying the 15 months, retroactive payments under this section. The claimant was young and was making a sincere attempt get back into the workforce before applying for benefits.

MHRD v. Andryjowich (August 15, 1996), CP 3593, CEB & PG (TB) ¶8639 (PAB)

Section 42(2)(*b*) qualifies and restricts the ambit of "the time of the making of any application" where there might be two or more successive applications brought before the adjudicating body, and dealt with or otherwise disposed of on successive occasions. The deemed 15 months relates not to "any application" regardless of its place in the sequence which might have been made, but specifically to "any application in respect of which the determination is made" — i.e., the application then currently being adjudicated.

MNHW v. Carroll (February 11, 1994), CP 2952, CEB & PG (TB) ¶8534 (PAB)

Following an unsuccessful application for a disability pension, the fact that fresh medical evidence becomes available to justify an award does not give the Review Tribunal or PAB jurisdiction to backdate the award to the time the original application was made, beyond the 15-month maximum period in s. 42(2)(*b*).

Bueno v. MHRD (April 23, 1997), CP 03253, CEB & PG (TB) ¶8674 (PAB)

The triggering date for entitlement to a disability pension is the date of the application. Section 69, which provides that payment of disability pension commences on the fourth month after the month in which the applicant became disabled, does not override the mandatory 15-month deemed disability onset. Although the claimant actually became disabled years prior to the time of making the application, the four-month period commences from the earliest time in which the claimant is deemed to be disabled by virtue of s. 42(2)(*b*) — i.e., 15 months prior to the application.

Proulx v. Minister of Human Resources Development (June 15, 2000), CP 07859 (PAB)

The only exception to the 15-month maximum retroactivity is if the claimant was mentally incapacitated and unable to form the intention to make an application prior to the actual date of the application.

MNHW v. Kartisch (February 25, 1991), CP 1552, CEB & PG (TB) ¶8625 (PAB). See also *MSD v. Zicarelli* (December 7, 2004), CP 21971 (PAB).

The 15-month limitation in what is now s. 42(2)(*b*) allows disability to be consistently and accurately established on a retroactive basis for a reasonable period. It helps to ensure an equitable balance between persons who have disabilities with a readily verifiable onset and persons with chronic progressive conditions where the onset is not so readily ascertainable. It prescribes a period of time which is neither unreasonable nor intrinsically unfair within which a contributor or someone acting on his or her behalf may make an application for benefits. The provision does not involve a restriction of a person's physical liberty and security, nor does it violate the right to life, liberty and the security of the person under s. 7 of the Charter. What is now s. 42(2)(*b*) is purely in the realm of public policy to which s. 7 has no application in that the principles of fundamental justice are not brought into play.

Pension Index

43. *Pension Index for subsequent years* — **(1) Subject to subsection (2), the Pension Index for each year shall be calculated, in prescribed manner, as the average for the twelve month period ending October 31 in the preceding year of the Consumer Price Index for each month in that twelve month period.**

(2) *Exception* — **For any year for which the calculation required by subsection (1) yields a Pension Index that is less than the Pension Index for the preceding year, the Pension Index shall be taken to be the Pension Index for the preceding year.**

(3) *Where basis of Consumer Price Index is changed* — **Where at any time the Consumer Price Index is adjusted to reflect a new time basis or a new content basis with a resulting percentage adjustment being made in the figures for that Index, a corresponding percentage adjustment shall, at the time of the next calculation of the Pension Index, be made in all values then existing of the Pension Index. (S.C. 1991, c. 44, s. 3.)**

(S.C. 1991, c. 44, s. 3.)

——————— Notes ———————

Synopsis

The Pension Index is used as the basis for calculating increases in the amount of CPP benefits payable from year to year. This section states that the Pension Index is tied to the Consumer Price Index (CPI), except that if the CPI drops from a previous year the Pension Index remains the same.

Related Provisions

- Section 45(2) — Annual benefits adjustments

Related CPP Regulations

- Section 75 — Pension index

—————————————————

Division A: Benefits Payable

44. *Benefits payable* — [29]**(1) Subject to this Part,**

(a) a retirement pension shall be paid to a contributor who has reached sixty years of age; (R.S.C. 1985, c. 30 (2nd Supp.), s. 13(1).)

(b) a disability pension shall be paid to a contributor who has not reached sixty-five years of age, to whom no retirement pension is payable, who is disabled and who

(i) has made contributions for not less than the minimum qualifying period,

(ii) is a contributor to whom a disability pension would have been payable at the time the contributor is deemed to have become disabled if an application for a disability pension had been received before the contributor's application for a disability pension was actually received, or (S.C. 1997, c. 40, s. 69(1).)

(iii) is a contributor to whom a disability pension would have been payable at the time the contributor is deemed to have become disabled if a division of unadjusted pensionable earnings that was made under section 55 or 55.1 had not been made (S.C. 1997, c. 40, s. 69(1).)

(iv) (Repealed by 1997, c. 40, s. 69(1).)

(R.S.C. 1985, c. 30 (2nd Supp.), s. 13(1).

---

[29] Pursuant to 1997, c. 40, s. 69(5), subparagraphs 44(1)(*b*)(i)–(iii) and (1)(*e*)(ii)–(iii) apply only in respect of contributors who are deemed disabled for purpose of the Act after December 31, 1997.

(c) a death benefit shall be paid to the estate of a deceased contributor who has made contributions for not less than the minimum qualifying period;

(d) subject to subsection (1.1), a survivor's pension shall be paid to the survivor of a deceased contributor who has made contributions for not less than the minimum qualifying period, if the survivor (R.S.C. 1985, c. 30 (2nd Supp.), s. 13(2); 2000, c. 12, s. 45(1).)

   (i) has reached sixty-five years of age, or

   (ii) in the case of a survivor who has not reached sixty-five years of age, (S.C. 2000, c. 12, s. 64.)

      (A) had at the time of the death of the contributor reached thirty-five years of age,

      (B) was at the time of the death of the contributor a surviving spouse with dependent children, or

      (C) is disabled;

(e) a disabled contributor's child's benefit shall be paid to each child of a disabled contributor who

   (i) has made contributions for not less than the minimum qualifying period,

   (ii) is a contributor to whom a disability pension would have been payable at the time the contributor is deemed to have become disabled if an application for a disability pension had been received before the contributor's application for a disability pension was actually received, or (S.C. 1997, c. 40, s. 69(2).)

   (iii) is a contributor to whom a disability pension would have been payable at the time the contributor is deemed to have become disabled if a division of unadjusted pensionable earnings that was made under section 55 or 55.1, had not been made; (S.C. 1997, c. 40, s. 69(2).)

   (iv) (Repealed by S.C. 1997, c. 40, s. 69(2).)

(f) an orphan's benefit shall be paid to each orphan of a deceased contributor who has made contributions for not less than the minimum qualifying period; and

(g) a post-retirement benefit shall be paid to a beneficiary of a retirement pension under this Act or under a provincial pension plan. (S.C. 2009, c. 31, s. 32(1).)

(1.1) *Limitation* — In the case of a common-law partner who was not, immediately before the coming into force of this subsection, a person described in subparagraph (a)(ii) of the definition "spouse" in subsection 2(1) as that definition read at that time, no survivor's pension shall be paid under paragraph (1)(d) unless the common-law partner became a survivor on or after January 1, 1998. (S.C. 2000, c. 12, s. 45(2).)

(2) [30]*Calculation of minimum qualifying period in case of disability pension and disabled contributor's child's benefit* — For the purposes of paragraphs (1)(b) and (e),

(a) a contributor shall be considered to have made contributions for not less than the minimum qualifying period only if the contributor has made contributions on earnings that are not less than the basic exemption of that contributor, calculated without regard to subsection 20(2),

---

[30] Pursuant to 1997, c. 40, s. 69(5), paragraph 44(2)(a) and subparagraph 44(2)(b)(iv) apply only in respect of contributors who are deemed disabled for purpose of the Act after December 31, 1997.

On proclamation the portion of s. 44(2)(a) before subparagraph (i), will be replaced by S.C. 2012, c. 31, s. 195(1), and will read as follows:

(a) a contributor shall be considered to have made contributions for not less than the minimum qualifying period only if the contributor has made contributions during the contributor's contributory period on earnings that are not less than the contributor's basic exemption, calculated without regard to subsection 20(2),

(i) for at least four of the last six calendar years included either wholly or partly in the contributor's contributory period or, where there are fewer than six calendar years included either wholly or partly in the contributor's contributory period, for at least four years,

(i.1) for at least 25 calendar years included either wholly or partly in the contributor's contributory period, of which at least three are in the last six calendar years included either wholly or partly in the contributor's contributory period, or (S.C. 2007, c. 11, s. 2[30.1].)

(ii) for each year after the month of cessation of the contributor's previous disability benefit; and

(S.C. 1997, c. 40, s. 69(3).)

(b) the contributory period of a contributor shall be the period

(i) commencing January 1, 1966 or when he reaches eighteen years of age, whichever is the later, and

(ii) ending with the month in which he is determined to have become disabled for the purpose of paragraph (1)(b),

but excluding

(iii) any month that was excluded from the contributor's contributory period under this Act or under a provincial pension plan by reason of disability, and

(iv) in relation to any benefits payable under this Act for any month after December, 1977, any month for which the contributor was a family allowance recipient in a year for which the contributor's unadjusted pensionable earnings are less than the basic exemption of the contributor for the year, calculated without regard to subsection 20(2). (S.C. 1997, c. 40, s. 69(4).)

(2.1) *Proration — late applications for disability pensions —* **For the purposes of determining the minimum qualifying period of a contributor referred to in subparagraph (1)(b)(ii), the basic exemption for the year in which they would have been considered to have become disabled, and in which the unadjusted pensionable earnings are less than the relevant Year's Basic Exemption for that year, is an amount equal to that proportion of the amount of that Year's Basic Exemption that the number of months that would not have been excluded from the contributory period by reason of disability is of 12. (S.C. 2009, c. 31, s. 32(2).)**

On proclamation s. 44(2.2) will be added by S.C. 2012, c. 31, s. 195(2), and will read as follows:

[30.1] Subparagraph 44(2)(a)(i.1) of the *Canada Pension Plan*, as enacted by section 2, applies in respect of an application for a disability pension made in or after the month in which that section comes into force. However, in the case of a contributor referred to in subparagraph 44(1)(b)(ii) of the *Canada Pension Plan*, subparagraph 44(2)(a)(i.1) of that Act, as enacted by section 2, applies only if the contributor is deemed to have become disabled no earlier than 15 months before the month in which that section comes into force.

(2.2) *Family allowance — late applications for disability pensions* — **A contributor referred to in subparagraph (1)(b)(ii) is deemed to have made contributions for not less than the minimum qualifying period for the purposes of subparagraph (1)(b)(i) if**

    (a) they became disabled in a month in which they were a family allowance recipient;

    (b) in the year in which they became disabled

        (i) the child in respect of which they were a family allowance recipient reached seven years of age, and

        (ii) their unadjusted pensionable earnings were less than their basic exemption, calculated without regard to subsection 20(2); and

    (c) in the absence of this subsection, a disability pension would not be payable to them, but had they become disabled in the year immediately before the year in which they became disabled, a disability pension would have been payable to them under subparagraph (1)(b)(ii).

(3) *Calculation in case of other supplementary benefits* — **For the purposes of paragraphs (1)(c), (d) and (f), a contributor shall be considered to have made contributions for not less than the minimum qualifying period only if the contributor has made contributions**

On proclamation s. 44(3), the portion before paragraph (a), will be replaced by S.C. 2012, c. 31, s. 195(3), and will read as follows:

(3) *Calculation for other supplementary benefits* — **For the purposes of paragraphs (1)(c), (d) and (f), a contributor shall be considered to have made contributions for not less than the minimum qualifying period only if the contributor has made contributions during the contributor's contributory period**

    (a) for at least one-third of the total number of years included either wholly or partly within his contributory period, excluding from the calculation of that contributory period any month in a year after the year in which he reaches sixty-five years of age and for which his unadjusted pensionable earnings were equal to or less than his basic exemption for that year, but in no case for less than three years; or (S.C. 1991, c. 44, s. 4.)

    (b) for at least ten years.

(R.S.C. 1985, c. 30 (2nd Supp.), s. 13; 1991, c. 44, s. 4; 1997, c. 40, s. 69; 2000, c. 12, ss. 45, 64; 2007, c. 11, s. 2; 2009, c. 31, s. 32.)

—————————— Notes ——————————

Synopsis

This section sets out the seven types of pensions and benefits provided for in the CPP. These are: (i) a retirement pension for contributors 60 years old and older, (ii) a disability pension, (iii) a death benefit to the estate of a deceased contributor, (iv) a survivor's pension to the spouse or common-law partner of a deceased contributor, (v) a benefit to the child or children of a disabled contributor, (vi) a benefit to the orphan of a deceased contributor, and (vii) a post-retirement benefit.

Of course, not everybody automatically qualifies to receive benefits. A retirement pension can only be claimed by a "contributor". As defined in s. 2(1), a contributor is a person who has made a CPP contribution in respect of employment or self-employment earnings, or a person who has obtained a division of his or her spouse's unadjusted pensionable earnings.

To qualify for receiving a disability pension, the claimant must be:

    1. Less than 65 years old,

2. Not receiving a retirement pension,

3. Disabled (defined in s. 42(1)), and

4. A contributor who (i) either made net CPP contributions above the Year's Basic Exemption for at least 4 of the last 6 years included in whole or in part in the contributor's "contributory period" (see below), or 3 of the last 6 years where 25 years of contributions were made by the contributor, or, where the contributor had previously received CPP disability benefits, for each year after the month that such benefits had ceased, (ii) could have received a disability pension on the date he or she was deemed disabled if an application for a disability pension had been received before the application was actually received, or (iii) could have received a disability pension on the date he or she was deemed disabled if a division of unadjusted pensionable earnings had not been made.

A person's "contributory period", for purposes of the disability benefit or disabled contributor's child's benefit, begins on the later of January 1, 1966 or the date he or she turns 18, and ends in the month he or she became disabled, or was deemed to become disabled. This period does not include months excluded by reason of the person's disability, or months in which the person was in receipt of family allowance benefits in a year in which the person's unadjusted pensionable earnings were less than the Year's Basic Exemption — i.e., the "child-rearing dropout" provisions (s. 44(2)(iv)).

If less than 6 calendar years are included in whole or in part of the person's contributory period, contributions must have been made for at least 4 years or, where the contributor had previously received CPP disability benefits, for each year after the month that such benefits had ceased.

Note that the Year's Basic Exemption on a claim for disability or disabled contributor's child's benefit is calculated without reference to s. 20(2) (s. 44(2)(a)), and therefore unlike the general YBE has not been frozen at $3,500 since 1998. The YBE over the past has been as follows:

Year	Basic Exemption	
	Generally	Disability
2014	3,500	5,200
2013	3,500	5,100
2012	3,500	5,000
2011	3,500	4,800
2010	3,500	4,700
2009	3,500	4,600
2008	3,500	4,400
2007	3,500	4,300
2006	3,500	4,200
2005	3,500	4,100
2004	3,500	4,000
2003	3,500	3,900
2002	3,500	3,800
2001	3,500	3,800
2000	3,500	3,700
1999	3,500	3,700
1998	3,500	3,600
1997	3,500	3,500
1996	3,500	3,500
1995	3,400	3,400
1994	3,400	3,400
1993	3,300	3,300
1992	3,200	3,200
1991	3,000	3,000

To qualify for payment to the beneficiary of a death benefit, a survivor's pension or an orphan's benefit, the contributor must have made contributions for at least: (i) 3 calendar years included either wholly or partly within a contributory period of 9 years or less; (ii) 1/3 of the total number of calendar years included either wholly or partly within a contributory period of between 9 and 30 years; or (iii) 10 years where the person's contributory period is longer than 30 years.

Legislative History

The Minimum Qualifying Period ("MQP") for CPP disability benefits has been altered several times over the years. This chart sets out the MQP for specific periods.

Calendar year in which disability benefit would begin	Minimum number of calendar years with valid contributions
1966–1969	no pension available
1970–1975	5 years
1976–1980	5 of the last 10 years
1981–1983	5 of the last 10 years*
1984–1986	5 of the last 10 years**
1987–1997	5 of the last 10 years or 2 of the last 3 years, or 2 years when there are only 2 years in the contributory period
1998–current	4 of the last 6 years, or 3 of the last 6 years if at least 25 years of contributions made, or each year since cessation of disability benefits previously payable

Notes:

* plus one additional year of contributions if the contributory period is more than 15 years

** plus two additional years of contributions if the contributory period is more than 15 years

Section 44(2) of the *Canada Pension Plan*, 1984–1985, reads as follows:

(2) Calculation of minimum qualifying period in case of disability pension and disabled contributor's child's benefit — For the purposes of paragraphs (1)(b) and (f),

(a) a contributor shall be considered to have made contributions for not less than the minimum qualifying period only if he has made contributions

(i) for at least 5 calendar years and at least 3 of the total number of calendar years included either wholly or partly within his contributory period, and where the number of calendar years included either wholly or partly within his contributory period exceeds 10, for at least 5 of the last 10 calendar years so included, or

(ii) for at least 10 calendar years and at least 5 of the last 10 calendar years included either wholly or partly within his contributory period; and

(a) the contributory period of a contributor shall be the period

(i) commencing January 1, 1966 or when he reaches 18 years of age, whichever is the later, and

(ii) ending with the third month following the month in which he is determined to have become disabled

but does not include any month for which a disability pension was payable to him under this Act or under a provincial pension plan and on or after January 1, 1978, that period does not include any month for which he was a family allowance recipient in a year for which his unadjusted pensionable earnings were equal to or less than this basic exemption for the year.

(1974-75-76, c. 4, s. 25(3); 1976-77, c. 36, s. 3)

Section 44(2) of the *Canada Pension Plan*, 1996, reads as follows:

> **(2) Calculation of minimum qualifying period in case of disability pension and disabled contributor's child's benefit** — [31]For the purposes of paragraphs (1)(*b*) and (*e*),
>
>> (*a*) a contributor shall be considered to have made contributions for not less than the minimum qualifying period only if he has made contributions
>>
>>> (i) for at least five of the last ten calendar years included either wholly or partly within his contributory period, or
>>>
>>> (ii) where there are fewer than ten calendar years included either wholly or partly within his contributory period, for at least five of those years; and
>>
>> (*b*) the contributory period of a contributor shall be the period
>>
>>> (i) commencing January 1, 1966 or when he reaches eighteen years of age, whichever is the later, and
>>>
>>> (ii) ending with the month in which he is determined to have become disabled fit, the purpose of paragraph (1)(*b*),
>>
>> but excluding
>>
>>> (iii) any month that was excluded from the contributors contributory period under this Act or under a provincial pension plan by reason of disability, and
>>>
>>> (iv) in relation to any benefits payable under this Act for any month after December, 1977, any month for which he was a family allowance recipient in a year for which his unadjusted pensionable earnings were equal to or less than his basic exemption for the year.

(R.S.C. 1985, c. 30 (2nd Supp.), s. 13(4).)

Recent Amendments

The 2000 amendment makes same-sex partners of deceased contributors entitled to survivor's benefits retroactive to contributors' deaths occurring on or after January 1, 1998. The 2007 amendment (in force March 3, 2008) provides the contributory requirement for disability benefits for contributors with at least 25 years of contributions to the CPP is reduced to only 3 of the last 6 years. For other disability pension claimants, the contribution requirement remains 4 of the last 6 years.

Related Provisions

- Section 19 — Proration of amount of basic exemption
- Section 45 — Basic amount of benefits
- Section 46 — Amount of retirement pension
- Section 56 — Amount of disability pension
- Section 57 — Amount of death benefit
- Section 58 — Amount of survivor's pension
- Section 59 — Amount of disabled contributor's child benefit and orphan's benefit
- Section 60 — Application for benefit
- Section 61 — Approval of interim benefit
- Section 69 — Commencement of disability pension
- Section 70 — When disability pension ceases to be payable
- Section 74(1) — Who may apply for disabled contributor's child benefit and orphan's benefit
- Section 77 — Amount of benefit payable
- Section 108(3) — Amounts to be charged to CPP Account

---

[31] Pursuant to R.S.C. 1985, c. 30 (2nd Supp.), c. 13(5), the amendments to section 44(2) caused by R.S.C. 1985, c. 30 (2nd Supp.), s. 13(4) apply only in respect of contributors who are determined to be disabled for the purpose of paragraph 44(1)(*b*) of the Act on or after January 1, 1987.

Related CPP Regulations

- Sections 47–50 — Determination of age

Case Law

Contents

§1. Disability Claims [See also Disability Case Table]

(a) Generally

Lila v. MSD (November 20, 2007), CP 24412 (PAB), see also *B.S. v. MHRSD* February 21, 2008), CP 25049 (PAB)

The CPP does not allow the payment of any pension, retirement or disability to anyone who continues to make contributions.

MEI v. Spielberger (January 26, 1995), CP 3026, CEB & PG ¶8576 (PAB)

What is now s. 44(1)(*b*)(ii) provides a remedy to a contributor who has no retirement pension and is disabled and would have been entitled to a disability pension, but failed to apply at a time when he or she had sufficient contributions. In effect, it backdates the application to a time when the contributor was deemed disabled and had sufficient contributions. It does not assist those who did not become disabled within the six months that they received a retirement pension. (See s. 66.1(1.1).)

MHRD v. Andryjowich (August 15, 1996), CP 3593, CEB & PG (TB) ¶8639 (PAB)

The enactment of what is now s. 44(1)(*b*)(ii) (formerly s. 44(1)(*b*)(iv)) in conjunction with s. 42(2)(*b*) did not have the effect of retroactively reinstating any previous application which may have been dealt with adversely through the adjudicative process. What is now s. 44(1)(*b*)(ii) means that a disability pension shall be paid to a contributor (i) who is disabled, (ii) to whom a disability pension would have been payable, (iii) when he or she would have been deemed to have become disabled, (iv) if he or she had applied, or (v) at a time earlier than the time in which he or she actually did apply.

Lazzara v. MEI (May 10, 1996), CP 3494 (PAB)

Under what is now s. 44(1)(*b*)(ii), the claimant had to establish that he or she was continuously disabled for the entire period between the latest date at which the claimant could satisfy the minimum contribution requirements of the Act and the commencement of the 15-month period prior to the receipt of the claimant's application for a disability pension.

MNHW v. Carroll (February 11, 1994), CP 2952, CEB & PG (TB) ¶8534 (PAB)

What is now s. 44(1)(*b*)(ii) is not relevant where following an unsuccessful application for a disability pension, fresh medical evidence became available to justify an award. There is no jurisdiction to backdate the award to the time the original application was made, beyond the 15-month maximum period in s. 42(2)(*b*).

Canada Pension Plan

213

Sarvanis v. Canada (1998), FC T-2075-92

A disability pension is paid to a claimant who is a qualified contributor under the CPP in relation to his or her disability, without reference to the cause of that disability. It is not paid in respect of the "injury, damage or loss" claimed in this action, i.e., for pain and suffering, loss of enjoyment of life, or out-of-pocket expenses arising from the claimant's injuries. The pension is terminable, if the claimant's condition of disability ends, if the claimant becomes 65 years of age or qualifies for another federal or provincial pension, or if he or she dies. It is paid on the basis of a statutory formula without regard to whether the claimant has suffered any pecuniary loss, or any injury. While it may be possible to trace the claimant's disability to injuries suffered as a result of an accident, such injury is not the basis of or the reason for disability pension entitlement under the CPP.

Prevost v. MSD (June 7, 2005), CP 13312 (PAB)

Section 44 deals with the qualifications for entitlement for a disabled contributor's child's benefit award, but does not deal with the timetable for payment thereof.

(b) Minimum Qualifying Period

MHRD v. Woodcock, [2002] FCA 296

The former s. 44(1)(*b*)(iv) [now s. 44(1)(*b*)(ii)] is intended to relieve applicants for a disability pension from the prejudice they would otherwise suffer because of a late application, and therefore requires the Minister to determine whether an applicant would have qualified for a disability pension if the application had been submitted earlier than it was. A s. 55.1 attribution may be given retrospective effect where the former s. 44(1)(*b*)(iv) [now s. 44(1)(b)(*ii*)] applies because of a late disability pension application, but only if the facts of the case make it reasonable to presume that the application for the disability pension and the s. 55.1 application would have been submitted at or about the same time, and there is no reason to conclude that the s. 55.1 application would not have been accepted if it had been made at that time.

Walters v. MEI, [1996] FCJ No. 176 (C.A.)

Where a claimant becomes disabled part-way through a year, that year must be counted as being the first year "partly" within the claimant's contributory period for the purpose of s. 44(2)(*a*)(i). The claimant does not have the option to start counting the years from the year immediately prior to the year he or she became disabled, although such year was the first calendar year entirely within the claimant's contributory period. The clear meaning of the CPP requires the inclusion of all years "wholly or partly" within the contributory period.

Pleasant-Joseph v. Canada (Attorney General), 2009 FCA 173

It was not an error for the PAB to conclude that the claimant had not made valid contributions for at least four of the last six years of her contributory period, where the claimant had been short by $138.00 for one of the years in question. The PAB did not have the power to remedy the shortfall so as to qualify the claimant for a disability pension. Both the Federal Court and the PAB are bound to apply the provisions of the CPP and cannot disregard those provisions so as to remedy what might be considered or perceived as an unfair and/or unjust result.

Wiley v. MHRD (November 3, 1998), CP 5686 (PAB)

Proration of the year's basic exemption under s. 19 can only be contemplated if the claimant can be declared disabled in the month in question.

MHRD v. Stevens (November 3, 1998), CP 06087 (PAB)

Eligible pensionable employment is confined to earnings between the ages of 18 and 69 that are greater than the year's basic exemption.

Stratichuk v. MHRD (July 16, 1996), CP 4115 (PAB)

A contribution made in a year, which contribution had been fully refunded, was not effective to render such year a contributory year.

MHRD v. Macfayden (March 11, 2002), CP 15656 (PAB)

The language of s. 42(2)(*b*) is clear that a person cannot be deemed disabled earlier than fifteen months before the time of the making of any application in respect of which the determination is made. Where the claimant had unsuccessfully applied for a disability pension in 1982 with respect to his alleged disability commencing in 1979 but failing to meet the contributory qualifications in place at the time, could not under his re-application in 1992 (backdated to 15 months to 1991) be considered to be disabled in 1979 for the purposes of meeting the current contribution requirements under the CPP. As such, his contributory period was the 25-year period between 1966 and 1991, meaning that he would have to have made contributions for at least one-third — i.e., nine — of those years.

(c) Canadian Charter of Rights and Freedoms

Canada (Attorney General) v. Hislop, 2007 SCC 10

Section 44(1.1) is of no force and effect. Such a limitation on the rights of same sex partners to obtain benefits was contrary to s. 15 of the *Canadian Charter of Rights and Freedoms,* and could not be justified under s. 1 of the Charter.

Lezau v. Canada (MSD), 2008 FCA 99

The CPP contributory rules apply to all Canadians, immigrants and non-immigrants. While the CPP created a differential treatment between contributors who have made sufficient contributions and those who have not, this is an attribute of any social benefit legislation that requires a person to qualify for benefits by meeting certain criteria. Calculations of contributory periods for the CPP do not violate the s. 15 Charter rights of immigrants who come from countries where no international agreement is in place.

Xinos v. MEI (March 19, 1997), Doc. A-212-96 (Fed. C.A.)

The disability pension contributory requirements were not contrary to s. 15 of the Charter. Equal benefit and protection of the law does not require every beneficiary under a CPP income replacement scheme to be entitled to identical benefits or conditions of eligibility. The proper criteria for social program benefits as set by Parliament should not be second-guessed quickly by courts and tribunals.

Sudnik v. MHRD (January 23, 2004), CP 19633 (PAB)

Entitlement to a disability pension was a property right, not falling within the right to life, liberty and security of the person, and as such was not protected by the s. 7 of the *Canadian Charter of Rights and Freedoms* requirement of fundamental justice before such could be taken away.

MNHW v. Poland (March 29, 1993), CP 2343, CEB & PG (TB) ¶8500 (PAB)

The CPP does not discriminate against a person whose disability prevents them from qualifying as contributors so as to be in violation of s. 15 of the Charter. In fact, the CPP establishes a special benefit, not available to the non-disabled, but available to all members of the disabled group who meet the minimum condition established by the legislation.

MNHW v. Johnston (October 4, 1991), CP 2048, CEB & PG (TB) ¶9214 (PAB). See also *MNHW v. Sinclair* (March 29, 1993), CP 2373, CEB & PG (TB) ¶8501 (PAB).

The fundamental difference between the retirement pension and the disability pension requires that different criteria apply in either case, and these are clearly defined within the legislation. The CPP is omnibus legislation, and the differences between its separate programs are not discriminatory. Under s. 15 of the Charter, difference is not to be equated with discrimination.

MNHW v. Kartisch (February 25, 1991), CP 1552, CEB & PG (TB) ¶8625 (PAB). See also *MNHW v. Sinclair* (March 29, 1993), CP 2373, CEB & PG (TB) ¶8501 (PAB).

The minimum contributory period requirements of the CPP do not violate the right to life, liberty and the security of the person under s. 7 of the Charter. Economic rights are not encompassed by s. 7.

Moses-Brown v. MNHW (November 23, 1990), CP 1630, CEB & PG (TB) ¶8651 (PAB)

Neither the Charter nor the CPP could be given retrospective effect so as to allow a claimant to use the legislative MQP requirement 1987 to validate her contributions for 1977–1980 which were not sufficient to qualify the claimant at the time. The claimant never acquired any right under the CPP and, therefore, could not contend that a right conferred by the CPP or the Charter was infringed.

(d) Non-Deductibility from Tort Awards

Canadian Pacific Ltd. v. Gill, [1973] S.C.R. 654

The main goal of tort law is to compensate injured plaintiffs for the full extent of their losses but not to overcompensate them. This prohibition on overcompensation, known as the rule against double recovery, has allowed for limited exceptions. The exception applicable to this appeal is the private insurance exception, also known as a collateral benefits rule. Under this exception, payments received under an insurance policy are not deducted from an injured plaintiff's tort award even though the effect of this exception may be to "overcompensate" the plaintiff. This private insurance exception includes CPP payments because they are much of the same nature as contracts of insurance.

Ratych v. Bloomer, [1990] 1 S.C.R. 940

Indemnity payments — that is — payments intended to compensate an injured plaintiff for a pecuniary loss are deductible from a tort award. However, CPP disability benefits are non-indemnity payments, being paid to the recipient on account of her disability and do not depend on her having incurred an income loss. They are therefore not deductible from such a tort award.

Sarvanis v. Canada, 2002 SCC 28

A disability benefit awarded under the *Canada Pension Plan* does not constitute a pension or compensation "in respect of death, injury, damage or loss" for the purposes of s. 9 of the *Crown Liability and Proceedings Act*. CPP disability payments are not to be considered indemnity payments, and are not to be deducted from tort damages compensating injuries that factually caused or contributed to the relevant disability. This rule is premised on the contractual or contributory nature of the CPP. Only contributors are eligible, at the outset, to receive benefits, provided that they then meet the requisite further conditions.

Demers v. Monty, 2012 ONCA 384

Section 267.8(1)2 of the *Insurance Act* (Ontario) does not override the non-deductibility of CPP disability benefits from a tort award at common law. If the legislature intended to change the non-deductibility of certain benefits, such as CPP disability benefits, it did not make that intention clear. The addition of the term "loss of earning capacity" in the Bill 59 regime does not clearly and unambiguously change the non-deductibility of CPP benefits at common law, because the jurisprudence has not treated the phrase in a consistent way. CPP disability benefits are not paid to a claimant "in respect of the incident" and therefore are not captured by s. 267.8(1)2.

§2. Survivor's Pension

(a) Purpose

Law v. MEI, [1999] 1 S.C.R. 497

The purpose and function of survivor's pension provisions of the CPP is not to remedy the immediate financial need experienced by widows and widowers, but rather to enable older widows and widowers to meet their basic needs during the longer term. Parliament's intent in enacting a survivor's pension scheme with benefits allocated according to age appears to have been to allocate funds to those persons whose ability to overcome need was weakest. The concern was to enhance personal dignity and freedom by ensuring a basic level of long-term financial security to persons whose personal situation makes them unable to achieve this goal, that is so important to life and dignity.

Canada (Minister of Human Resources Development) v. Tait, 2006 FCA 380

Whether the common-law spouse files an application for benefits or files and withdraws it later is totally irrelevant to a determination of who is the spouse in s. 2(1) and the surviving spouse for the purposes of s. 44(1)(d). If the Minister has established on the balance of probabilities that a common-law spouse exists, as defined in s. 2(1), then s. 2(1) states that the person is the spouse for the purpose of survivor's benefits regardless of whether there is a married spouse in existence: the common-law spouse takes or is entitled to take and the married spouse loses out, subject to the *de novo* appeal rights vested in an applicant to have these issues ventilated before the Review Tribunal and the Board. Spouses and others may give up voluntarily certain rights they enjoy under statutory regimes of a variety of kinds. What they cannot do is trench upon the legislature's role to set clear-cut statutory criteria for a pension or entitlement. Parties may be able to contract out of a statute but what they cannot do is contract themselves into a statute's benefits, absent authority to do so within the four corners of the statute. The CPP does not specify that the Minister, or anyone else for that matter, cannot provide evidence, where the alleged common-law partner fails to apply, or does not provide relevant evidence. The designation of common law requires evidence and is a question of mixed fact and law. In light of CPP s. 65(1), survivor benefits cannot be assigned or designated.

McLaughlin v. Canada (Attorney General), 2012 FC 556

The CPP provisions create a presumption that the individual who is married to the contributor at the time of his or her death is entitled to the survivor pension. This presumption, however, is displaced where the contributor no longer cohabits with the person to whom he or she is married and, instead, enters into a conjugal relationship with a common-law partner. Where such relationship exists for at least a year prior to the contributor's death, the statute provides that survivor benefits are entirely payable to the common-law partner, regardless of how long the contributor might have been married.

MHRD v. Martin (July 17, 2000), CP 03884 (PAB)

The decision to include a surviving spouse's benefit in the CPP, and the eligibility requirements, were based on the assumption that the majority of married women did not participate in the labour force, especially when they were raising children, and that most families were supported by male wage earners. Thus, it was considered fair to have a portion of the contributor's retirement pension paid to these widows who were suddenly faced with the responsibility of maintaining a family and who had little or no experience in the labour force. The eligibility requirements for the survivor's pension, under the CPP, reflects Parliament's intent that the greatest possible benefit be provided to survivors who are least likely to be in a position to become self-supporting following the death of the contributor. The survivor's pension is also designed to protect the integrity of the CPP and keep the contribution rate within the reach of average wage earners.

Mansell v. MHRD (March 1, 2000), CP 04765 (PAB)

The survivor benefit was intended to provide some financial assistance as a matter of right on the death of a contributor towards the loss of earnings that he or she had contributed to household expenses prior to death. The low monthly amount makes any splitting of that pension impractical. While the purposes and intent of the statutory change, allowing common-law partners to claim a survivor's pension, was a move towards equality of treatment of married and common-law spouses, the definition, in fact, continues to contain an element of discrimination in favour of the legal spouse. The legal spouse has been given a continuing residual right to become entitled again if a subsequent common-law union should end, without any requirement to re-enter a conjugal relationship.

B.P. v. MHRSD (June 18, 2010), CP 25325 (PAB)

An application for death benefits under the CPP cannot be deemed to include an application for a survivor's pension. There is no duty on the Minister to search through the file of the Department to determine that a person is eligible for a pension and inform her of her eligibility. Policies and directives of the Department are not enforceable.

S.K. v. MHRSD (July 26, 2010), CP 25866 (PAB)

Where the file contained a few discrepancies with respect to the date of separation between the intervenor common-law spouse and the deceased contributor and the intervenor was not present at the hearing to clarify them, the intervener had not met the onus that was upon her.

(b) Canadian Charter of Rights and Freedoms

Law v. MEI, [1999] 1 S.C.R. 497

The survivor's pension provisions of the CPP (ss. 44(1)(d) and 58) are not discriminatory and do not violate the equality rights guaranteed by s. 15(1) of the Charter. While both the delay in the receipt of benefits and the reduced entitlement to benefits constitute a denial of equal benefit of the law, and clearly draw distinctions on the basis of the enumerated ground of age, there is no violation of human dignity.

Hodge v. MHRD, 2004 SCC 65

The definition of "spouse" [now "common law partner"] in s. 2(1) does not infringe s. 15(1) of the *Canadian Charter of Rights and Freedoms* by requiring that the partners have cohabitated for the year previous to the contributor's death. The proper comparator group for former common law partners who never married is former married spouses, and they are treated the same by the legislation. Therefore, to be entitled to a survivor's pension, an common law partner who was not married to the contributor at the time of the contributor's death must have been cohabitating with the contributor for a continuous period of at least one year prior to the contributor's death.

Obiter: Until the issue of same-sex marriage is resolved, different considerations may possibly apply to gay and lesbian relationships in respect of a survivor's pension because, at least in the past, the institution of a legal marriage has not been available to them.

Sutherland v. Canada, [1997] F.C.J. No. 3, (Fed. C.A.)

The date a pensioner turned 60 or retired must be considered an "event", and not an ongoing condition. Where this critical event occurred before s. 15 came into force, the Charter could not apply. [See also *Yates v. MSD* (February 21, 2008), CP 22807 (PAB), where the Board ruled that the same analysis applied regarding s. 7 of the Charter.]

Yates v. MSD (February 21, 2008), CP 22807 (PAB)

A virtually universal contributory social insurance program such as the CPP is not constitutionally required to establish special rules to accommodate senior citizens of foreign lands, such as the United Kingdom, which have refused to negotiate a reciprocal agreement with Canada that could have led to increased credits towards a Canadian CPP pension.

Mansell v. Minister of Human Resources Development (March 1, 2000), CP 04765 (PAB)

The survivor's pension provisions of the CPP do not violate s. 15 of the Charter by discriminating against abandoned legal spouses. Such a group has not historically been discriminated against, and unequal treatment alone does not establish a breach of s. 15.

(c) Worthiness

Canada (Procureur Général) v. St-Hilaire, [2001] FCA 63

To determine whether a recipient is worthy to receive a pension under federal legislation, the court may look to the Civil Code or the common-law. The claimant's conviction for manslaughter in relation to the spouse committed under the influence of drugs can render the claimant unworthy to receive a pension. (Note: The pension being claimed was the monthly allowance under s. 13(3) of the *Public Service Superannuation Act*. The court extensively reviewed the common-law authorities in this area.)

§3. Minimum Qualifying Period — Non-Disability Situations

Canada (MHRD) v. Skoric, [2000] 3 FC 265 (C.A.)

A contribution made after the expiry of the contributory period counts towards meeting the minimum qualifying period. The words "within his contributory period", in s. 44(3)(*a*), serve only to define the number of years for which contributions must be made, and not to prescribe when they must be made. There is no requirement that only contributions made within the contributory period count towards the ten-year period referred to in s. 44(3)(*b*). To deprive a person of the benefit of a contribution that he or she has in fact made, simply because it was made outside the contributory period, would be unfair and inconsistent with a statutory scheme in which eligibility is based on the contributions made. The CPP does not permit a part of a year of a minimum qualifying period to be "rounded down" to the nearest whole number if that would result in a period that was less than the statutorily required one third of the contributory period.

Pastorius v. MSD (May 12, 2005), CP 22401 (PAB)

Under CPP s. 44(1)(*c*) and (*d*), payments of death benefits are conditional upon the deceased contributor having made contributions for not less than the minimum qualifying period. Section 44(3) requires that the minimum qualifying period be at least one third of the total number of years included either totally or partly within the contributory period, but not less than three years; or for at least 10 years. Under s. 52(3)(*a*), a contributor is deemed to have made a contribution for any year for which her unadjusted pensionable earnings exceed her basic exemption for the year. Further, she is deemed to have made no contribution for any year for which her unadjusted pensionable earnings did not exceed her basic exemption for the year. Section 44(2)(*b*)(iv) of the CPP and s. 77 of the Regulations, commonly referred to as the CRDO provisions, exclude from the contributory period those years where earnings were below the "years' unadjusted pensionable earnings".

MNHW v. Zimmer (July 19, 1991), CP 2109, CEB & PG (TB) ¶8632 (PAB) See also *Lipske v. MHRD* (July 6, 2001), CP 14662 (PAB).

Section 44(3) is to be interpreted to mean the following:

1. The length of the contributory period must be determined in terms of years.

2. Any part of a year falling within the contributory period constitutes a full year.

3. Contributions must have been made for not less than one-third of the total number of years that constitute the contributory period.

4. The qualifying period shall, in any event, be not less than three years.

Vousden v. MHRD (July 16, 2003), CP 19687 (PAB)

When considering eligibility for survivor pension under s. 44(3)(*a*) — i.e., a third of total number of years — the words "wholly or partly" are plain and unambiguous. It does not permit a calculation which considers the number of years to be inclusive or exclusive, or a calculation based on months rather than years.

MHRD v. Brown (August 20 2003), CP 20353 (PAB)

Where one-third of the contributory period resulted in a fractional number, it could not be rounded down to the lesser whole number in order to match the number of years that the claimant made contributions. Therefore, if the contributory period was 17 years, the claimant must have contributed for at least 6 years. The Federal Court of Appeal's decision in *Villani* that any ambiguities in CPP were to be interpreted in favour of the claimant did not alter the reasoning in *Zimmer*.

MHRSD v. W.W. (September 10, 2009), CP 19623 (PAB)

Regardless of when a contributor *becomes* disabled, the contributory period cannot end earlier than 15 months before the date of the disability application. Although the contributor was found disabled in 1988 (her MQP), her contributory period for seeking entitlement to the death benefit and the survivor's pension ended when the applicant was deemed to be disabled — i.e., 15 months prior to her disability benefit application.

§4. Child Rearing Drop-Out (CRDO) Provision (s. 44(2)(*b*)(iv))

- See also CPP Regulations, s. 77

Runchey v. Canada (A.G.), 2013 FCA 16

In certain situations, the CPP allows contributors to "drop out" low-earning periods so that reduced earnings are removed from the calculation of benefits. These are governed by "drop out provisions" in the CPP. Most contributors are entitled to a "general low-earnings drop out" (s. 48(4)). This provision allows contributors to drop out a certain percentage of years when their contributions are low for any reason. In addition to this general drop out, the CPP also contains drop out provisions for specific cases. The CRP, sometimes also described as the Child Rearing Drop Out ("CRDO"), is one such provision. Under it, parents can remove from their calculation of benefits under the Plan time spent caring for young children. In this way, the CRP ensures that parents who leave or reduce their workforce participation to raise pre-school age children are not penalized in determining future pension benefits. The CRP provision does not automatically exclude "child rearing" years from the qualifying parent's benefit calculations. Periods are only dropped if doing so will result in higher pension benefits (s. 48(2)(*a*)). The CRP does not necessarily apply to the parent that had primary caregiving responsibility for the child or children. Because of the definition of "family allowance recipient," eligibility for the CRP is generally limited to parents that, before 1992, qualified for a family allowance or, after 1992, the Canada Child Tax Benefit. While family allowances and Canada Child Tax Benefit will generally have gone to the parent with primary caregiving responsibility, this is not always the case. Rather, both programs presumptively apply to the female parent, except when the male parent has sole custody of the child or in other limited circumstances. Therefore, the CRP program favours women as a whole. Under the Division of Unadjusted Pensionable Earnings ("DUPE") provisions, certain pension credits may be divided between ex-spouses in certain circumstances (s. 55.1).

Miceli-Riggins v. Canada (Attorney General), 2013 FCA 158

People might not be able to work and make contributions under the CPP for good reason. For example, parents may need to stay at home to care for a child. This scenario continues to disproportionately occur with women rather than men. Leaving the workforce to care for a child could have consequences for benefits under the CPP. The failure to make contributions under the CPP in a given year may reduce the benefits payable in the future. It may also affect the operation of rules such as the "four in six" rule. To eliminate these potentially unfair effects, the CPP allows certain periods to be excluded from the contributory period. These are known as the "dropout provisions" in the CPP. There are three types of dropout provisions: the general dropout provisions, the disability dropout provisions, and the child rearing dropout ("CRDO") provisions. The CRDO is designed to ensure that a person who stays home to raise a child under the age of seven is not penalized during that time for having low or no earnings. It protects eligibility for benefits and preserves the level of benefits eventually paid out under the CPP. This feature of the design of the CPP plays a vital role in advancing the financial security of women who have their work interrupted by child rearing. The CRDO provisions related to the workplace attachment test for disability benefits are available to all eligible contributors, irrespective of gender, who stay home to care for children under the age of seven and have pensionable earnings in a particular year below the minimum amount of contribution required for that year (s. 44(2)(b)(iv)). Specifically, the CRDO provisions allow any month to be excluded from the contributory period where: (1) the contributor is a "family allowance recipient" as defined in the CPP Regulations; and (2) the contributor has earnings for the year below the minimum amount of contribution required for that year. In light of the ameliorative nature of the CRDO provisions and the proration provision in the CPP s. 19, the CRDO provisions do not discriminate against women who give birth to children early in the calendar year, before they have had a chance to earn $3,500 for that year. To the extent that they are aimed at ameliorating or remedying the condition of women, an enumerated group under s. 15(1) of the Charter, they may be said to be a "law, program or activity" within the meaning of s. 15(2) of the Charter.

Harris v. MHRSD, 2009 FCA 22

The CRDO provisions are designed to extend the period of CPP coverage for a relatively short and well-defined period of time. They do this by directing the benefit to parents who stay at home with pre-school age children; that is, who temporarily leave employment for a maximum of seven years. In enacting the CRDO, Parliament has chosen to relax the "recency requirement" in favour of parents who temporarily leave employment to look after *young* children. The extent of the relaxation is defined by reference to the *age* at which children in Canada can attend public school. The age of seven in the CRDO provisions is not merely a proxy for a child's being in full-time school. Rather, it was chosen by Parliament to define when a child is no longer young enough to require a parent to stay at home, without prejudicing *her* ability to satisfy the "recency requirement" for eligibility for CPP. That the rationale of the selection of the age was that children are then old enough for full-time school, and their parents can thus more easily return to work, does not mean that the program should be divorced from the age of the children. The failure to allow parents of older disabled children the ability to stay at home to take care of their children does not violate the rights of such parents under s. 15 of the Charter. Whether the CRDO provisions should extend to parents who are at home looking after children with disabilities beyond the age of seven is a matter of social and economic policy and priorities to be decided in the political realm, not of constitutionally guaranteed human rights to be determined by the courts.

Graceffa v. HRSD (October 15, 2007), CP 16882 (PAB)

Subparagraph 44(2)(b)(iv) is known as the Child Rearing Drop-out (CRDO) provision. The CRDO helps parents maintain their level of pensionable earnings during child rearing years. The purpose of the provision is to ensure that a CPP contributor will not be penalized where he or she has made low or zero earnings and contributions to the CPP. It allows for those periods to be excluded from the contributory period when calculating the CPP benefits where a contributor is in receipt of family allowance and does not have earnings equal to or less than their basic exemption for the year they seek to exclude. They may exclude up to seven years per child from their contributory period. Subsection 42(1) of the CPP and paragraph 77(1)(a) of the CPP Regulations are clear. The primary caregiver of the child or children is to be the recipient of the CRDO relief from CPP contributions. There can only be one person first in importance to provide care to a child or children in a family unit. Two cohabiting parents in a family unit cannot be considered to be family allowance recipients for the same period of time. Further, the CRDO cannot belong to a child as the child is not a family allowance recipient or a contributor to the CPP. There is no provision for the division of the CRDO on a per-child basis.

HRSD v. Harris (November 27, 2007), CP 24279 (PAB)

The CRDO provisions in s. 44(2)(b)(iv) and s. 77(1)(a) of the CPP Regulations do not infringe subsection 15(1) of the Charter on the enumerated grounds of age, disability and gender. The purpose of the CRDO provision is to recognize the needs of young children for parental input and to prevent the penalization of parents of young children, in terms of CPP entitlement, who accept the role of primary caregiver for a stated number of years.

Owsiany v. MEI (March 14, 1996), CP 2987 (PAB). See also *Ley v. MHRD* (October 28, 2002), CP 17771 (PAB).

The use of the words "calendar year" in s. 44(2)(a)(i) means that the period in which a contributor is considered to have made contributions is to be determined by way of calendar years, that is January 1 to December 31 of any given year. The MQP is to be resolved by the measure of calendar years and not by yearly periods which may be any accumulation of 12-month periods. The length of the MQP can therefore not be expanded by the number of months the contributor was qualified for the child benefit drop-out under s. 44(2)(b)(iv).

Ley v. MHRD (October 28, 2002), CP 17771 (PAB)

Any 12-month period related to the child-rearing drop-out ("CRDO") provision will not suffice unless it falls within a calendar year, nor will individual months within a calendar year be excluded where a child under seven years of age has resided in the contributor's home.

Di Falco v. MSD (February 26, 2007), CP 23374 (PAB)

According to s. 44(2)(b)(iv), only months for which the contributor was *in receipt* of family allowances can be dropped from the contributory period in calculating the effect of the CRDO. Payments under the *Family Allowances Act* cannot be made until a child is born. Accordingly, a claimant cannot be in receipt of family allowances while she is still pregnant, and the MQP can occur during that time.

Abbott v. MSD (January 10, 2006), CP 21427 (PAB)

Section 44(2)(a)(i) speaks of "ten calendar years included wholly or partly in his contributory period" and s. 44(2)(b)(iv) only excludes the months of family allowance benefits. Where the claimant received family allowance benefits for three months in a calendar year, but did not make any contributions for the remainder of that year, the year could not be included in the CRDO. The approach taken by the board in *Owsiany* and *Ley* was followed.

§5. Proof of Age

Atri v. Canada (Attorney General), 2007 FCA 178

Where the applicant is seeking to establish that his age is as set out in documents issued by his native country rather than his Canadian immigration documents, he is entitled as a matter of fairness to be told by the PAB why it did not accept his national documents as proof of his age, especially where the applicant alleged that his Identification Booklet is a birth certificate. The PAB failed to discharge its statutory duty to provide adequate reasons for its decision where it did not refer specifically to the national documents, nor explain why it preferred the immigration documents as proof of the applicant's age. Birth certificates are one of the categories of documents on which the Minister must determine the age and identity of a claimant by virtue of s. 47(1), (3) of the CPP Regulations.

Division B: Calculation of Benefits

Basic Amount and Annual Adjustment

45. *Basic amount of benefit* — **(1) A reference in this Part to the basic amount of any benefit shall be construed as a reference to the amount thereof calculated as provided in this Part without regard to subsection (2). (R.S.C. 1985, c. 30 (2nd Supp.), s. 14.)**

(2) *Annual adjustments* — **Where any benefit has become payable commencing with a month in any year, the basic monthly amount of the benefit shall be adjusted annually, in prescribed manner, so that the amount payable for a month in any following year is an amount equal to the product obtained by multiplying**

(a) the amount that would have been payable for that month if no adjustment had been made under this section with respect to that following year,

by

(*b*) the ratio that the Pension Index for that following year bears to the Pension Index for the year preceding that following year.

(R.S.C. 1985, c. 30 (2nd Supp.), s. 14.)

————————— Notes —————————

Synopsis

This section defines the "basic amount" of a benefit to mean the amount calculated before the annual adjustment according to the Pension Index.

Related Provisions

- Section 43 — Pension Index
- Section 77 — Amount of benefit payable

Related CPP Regulations

- Section 62 — Annual adjustment of benefits

Case Law

Wagler v. MSD (November 14, 2005), CP 22744 (PAB)

The claim for "fair rate of interest" on retroactive benefit payments is not possible because the CPP does not provide for the payment interest on such payments. To award interest on retroactive benefit payments without express statutory authority would be an error in law.

————————————————

Retirement Pension

46. *Amount of retirement pension* — **(1)** Subject to this section, a retirement pension payable to a contributor is a basic monthly amount equal to twenty-five per cent of his average monthly pensionable earnings.

(2) *Special case* — Subject to this section, the basic monthly amount of retirement pension payable to a former disability pension recipient in respect of whom a division of unadjusted pensionable earnings is approved either before or after the commencement of the retirement pension, where the division reduces the retirement pension otherwise payable, shall be calculated by dividing

(*a*) the aggregate of

   (i) the basic monthly amount of the retirement pension calculated in subsection (1) that would be payable to the contributor had his unadjusted pensionable earnings not been subject to the division, multiplied by the number of months that have been excluded from the contributor's contributory period by reason of disability, and

   (ii) the basic monthly amount of the retirement pension calculated in subsection (1) that would be payable following the division, multiplied by the number of months in contributor's contributory period calculated in accordance with section 49

by

(*b*) the aggregate of

   (i) the number of months that have been excluded from the contributor's contributory period by reason of disability, and

   (ii) the number of months in the contributor's contributory period calculated in accordance with section 49.

(3) *Upward or downward adjustment factor — up to 2010* — Subject to subsections (4) to (6), a retirement pension that becomes payable after December 31, 1986 and before January 1, 2011 commencing with a month other than the month in which the contributor reaches 65 years of age is a basic monthly amount equal to the basic monthly amount calculated in accordance with subsection (1) or (2), as the case may be, adjusted by a factor fixed by the Minister, on the advice of the Chief Actuary of the Office of the Superintendent of Financial Institutions, to reflect the time interval between the month in which the retirement pension commences and the month in which the contributor reached, or would reach, 65 years of age, but the time interval is deemed never to exceed five years. (R.S.C. 1985, c. 18 (3rd Supp.), s. 29; 2009, c. 31, s. 33.)

(3.1) *Upward or downward adjustment factor — after 2010 —* Subject to subsections (4) to (6), a retirement pension that becomes payable after December 31, 2010 commencing with a month other than the month in which the contributor reaches 65 years of age is a basic monthly amount equal to the basic monthly amount calculated in accordance with subsection (1) or (2), as the case may be, adjusted by a factor fixed under subsection (7). (S.C. 2009, c. 31, s. 33.)

(4) *Exception if division of unadjusted pensionable earnings increases retirement pension —* Subject to subsection (5), if, as a result of a division of unadjusted pensionable earnings under section 55 or 55.1, a retirement pension that was payable increases, the adjustment factor applicable after the increase to the basic monthly amount of the retirement pension calculated in accordance with subsection (1) or (2), as the case may be, instead of the adjustment factor referred to in subsection (3) or (3.1), as the case may be, shall be determined by the formula

$$\frac{[(F1 \times P1) + (F2 \times E)]}{P2}$$

where

F1 is an amount equal to the adjustment factor referred to in subsection (3) or (3.1), as the case may be, at the time the retirement pension first became payable;

P1 is the basic monthly amount of the retirement pension calculated in subsection (1) or (2), as the case may be, before the division;

F2 is the lesser of
   (a) an amount equal to what the adjustment factor referred to in subsection (3) or (3.1), as the case may be, would have been if the retirement pension had commenced in the month in which the increase commences to be payable, and
   (b) 1;

E is equal to the excess of P2 over P1; and

P2 is the basic monthly amount of the retirement pension immediately following the division.

(S.C. 2009, c. 31, s. 33.)

(5) *Exception if survivor's pension reduced —* Unless otherwise provided by an agreement under section 80, if a person receives a retirement pension under this Act and a survivor's pension under this Act and the survivor's pension is at any time reduced from its full amount under subsection 58(2), any downward adjustment factor resulting from the application of subsection (3), (3.1) or (4) at that time shall not be applied to the whole of the basic monthly amount of the retirement pension calculated in subsection (1) or (2), as the case may be, but only to the amount remaining when that basic monthly amount is reduced by the product obtained by multiplying
   (a) the amount by which the survivor's pension has been reduced
by
   (b) the ratio that the Pension Index for the year in which the retirement pension first commenced to be payable bears to the Pension Index for the year in which the survivor's pension is reduced.

(S.C. 2009, c. 31, s. 33.)

(6) *Exception if division after age 65 precedes commencement of retirement pension* — **If, after a person has reached 65 years of age but before the person commences to receive a retirement pension, a division of unadjusted pensionable earnings takes place under section 55 or 55.1 in respect of that person, the upward adjustment factor referred to in subsection (3) or (3.1), as the case may be, to be applied to any increase in the retirement pension that is attributable to the division shall be based on the time interval between the taking place of the division and the commencement of the retirement pension, and shall not take into account the time interval between the month in which the person reaches 65 years of age and the month in which the division takes place. (S.C. 1991, c. 44, s. 5(2); 2009, c. 31, s. 33.)**

(7) *Regulations* — **For the purposes of subsection (3.1), the Governor in Council may make regulations fixing one or more adjustment factors or the methods of calculating them — including factors or methods that may apply on specified dates — to reflect the time interval between the month in which the retirement pension commences and the month in which the contributor reached, or would reach, 65 years of age, but the time interval is deemed never to exceed five years. (S.C. 2009, c. 31, s. 33.)**

(8) *Condition* — **The Governor in Council may only make regulations under subsection (7) or repeal them on the recommendation of the Minister of Finance and only if the lieutenant governor in council of each of at least two thirds of the included provinces, as defined in subsection 114(1), having in total not less than two thirds of the population of all of the included provinces, has signified the consent of that province to the making or repeal of the regulations. (S.C. 2009, c. 31, s. 33.)**

(9) *Amendment* — **Regulations made under subsection (7) may only be amended in accordance with subsection 113.1(14). (S.C. 2009, c. 31, s. 33.)**

(R.S.C. 1985, c. 30 (2nd Supp.), s. 15; c. 18 (3rd Supp.), s. 29; 1991, c. 44, s. 5; 2009, c. 31, s. 33.)

——————— **Notes** ———————

Synopsis

This section establishes as a general rule that a person's monthly retirement pension is equal to 25% of the person's average monthly pensionable earnings, adjusted to reflect the average of the final five-year maximum pensionable earnings. Between the ages of 60 and 65, the pension is reduced by $1/2$% for each month (6% annually) preceding the 65th birthday. This amount, together with the yearly indexation, will be paid for the rest of the retiree's life. A contributor who elects to apply for retirement pension after age 65 will see the amount of amount of the amount of the retirement pension increased by $1/2$% for each month (6% annually) following his or her 65th birthday up to a maximum increase of 30%. The maximum monthly retirement pension payable in 2014 is $1038.33.

Additional calculation rules are used if a division of unadjusted pension credits has taken place following a marital breakdown, where (i) the contributor had formerly received a disability pension and was the subject of a division resulting in a reduction of the retirement pension otherwise payable (s. 46(2)), (ii) where the division increases the contributor's retirement pension s. 46(4), or (iii) the division takes place after the person reaches the age of 65 but before he or she starts to receive a retirement pension (s. 46(6)).

Related Provisions

- Section 47 — Amount of average monthly pensionable earnings where pension commencing before January, 1976

- Section 48 — Average monthly pensionable earnings where pension commencing after December, 1975

- Section 60 — Application for benefit

- Section 77 — Amount of benefit payable

Related CPP Regulations

- Section 56 — Payment of certain benefits at intervals greater than monthly

---

47. *Amount of average monthly pensionable earnings* — **Where a retirement pension becomes payable to a contributor commencing with any month before January, 1976, his average monthly pensionable earnings are an amount calculated by dividing his total pensionable earnings by the basic number of contributory months.**

———————— **Notes** ————————

Synopsis

This section sets out the following formula for determining the average monthly pensionable earnings of a contributor whose retirement pension becomes payable before January 1976:

Average monthly pensionable earnings = Total pensionable earnings / Basic number of contributory months

The average monthly pensionable earnings of a contributor is used to determine the amount of retirement pension payable (see s. 46).

Related Provisions

- Section 48 — Average monthly pensionable earnings where pension commencing after December, 1975

- Section 49 — Contributory period

- Section 50 — Calculation of total pensionable earnings

- Section 77 — Amount payable under CPP where receiving from other plan

---

48. *Average monthly pensionable earnings in case of pension commencing after December, 1975* — **(1) Subject to subsections (2), (3) and (4), where a retirement pension becomes payable to a contributor commencing with any month after December, 1975, his average monthly pensionable earnings are an amount calculated by dividing his total pensionable earnings by the total number of months in his contributory period or by the basic number of contributory months, whichever is the greater.**

(2) *Deductions in calculating average monthly pensionable earnings of certain months during child raising years* — **In calculating the average monthly pensionable earnings of a contributor in accordance with subsection (1) for the purpose of calculating or recalculating benefits payable for a month commencing on or after January 1, 1978, there may be deducted**

- **(a) from the total number of months in a contributor's contributory period, those months during which he was a family allowance recipient and during which his pensionable earnings were less than his average monthly pensionable earnings calculated without regard to subsections (3) and (4), but no such deduction shall reduce the number of months in his contributory period to less than the basic number of contributory months, except**

  - **(i) for the purpose of calculating a disability benefit in respect of a contributor who is deemed to have become disabled for the purposes of this Act after December 31, 1997, in which case the words "the basic number of contributory months" shall be read as "48 months", (S.C. 1997, c. 40, s. 70.)**

  - **(i.1) for the purpose of calculating a disability benefit in respect of a contributor who is deemed to have become disabled for the purposes of this Act in 1997, in which case the words "the basic number of contributory months" shall be read as "24 months", and (S.C. 1997, c. 40, s. 70.)**

Canada Pension Plan

225

(ii) for the purpose of calculating a death benefit and a survivor's pension, in which case the words "the basic number of contributory months" shall be read as "thirty-six months"; and

(R.S.C. 1985, c. 30 (2nd Supp.), s. 16(1); 1997, c. 40, s. 70.)

(b) from his total pensionable earnings, the aggregate of his pensionable earnings attributable to the months deducted pursuant to paragraph (a).

(3) *Deductions allowed where contributory period ends after age 65* — Where a contributor's contributory period ends after the month preceding the month in which he reaches sixty-five years of age and the total number of months in his contributory period remaining after the deduction under paragraph 2(a) exceeds the basic number of contributory months, in calculating his average monthly pensionable earnings in accordance with subsection (1) there shall be deducted **(R.S.C. 1985, c. 30 (2nd Supp.), s. 16(2).)**

(a) from the total number of months remaining in his contributory period, the number of months therein after he reached sixty-five years of age or by which the total exceeds the basic number of contributory months, whichever is the lesser; and

(b) from his total pensionable earnings remaining after the deduction under paragraph (2)(b), the aggregate of his pensionable earnings for a number of months equal to the number of months deducted under paragraph (a), for which months that aggregate is less than the aggregate of his pensionable earnings for any other like number of months in his contributory period other than for months for which a deduction has already been made under subsection (2).

On proclamation s. 48(3)(b) will be replaced by S.C. 2012, c. 31, s. 196(1), and will read as follows:

(b) from the contributor's total pensionable earnings remaining after the deduction under paragraph (2)(b), the aggregate of the contributor's pensionable earnings for a number of months equal to the number of months deducted under paragraph (a), for which months that aggregate is less than — or, if not less than, then equal to — the aggregate of the contributor's pensionable earnings for any other like number of months in the contributor's contributory period other than for months for which a deduction has already been made under subsection (2).

(4) *Deductions allowed where number of months remaining exceeds 120* — Where the number of months remaining after making any deduction under subsection (2) or (3) from the total number of months in the contributory period of a contributor exceeds one hundred and twenty, in calculating his average monthly pensionable earnings in accordance with subsection (1) there shall be deducted

(a) from the number of months remaining, a number of months equal to the lesser of

(i) subject to subsection (5), if the retirement pension or other benefit becomes payable commencing with a month before January 2012, fifteen per cent of the number remaining — and sixteen per cent commencing with a month after December 2011 and before January 2014 and seventeen per cent commencing with a month after December 2013 — and, if that per cent includes a fraction of a month, the fraction shall be taken to be a complete month, and

(ii) the number of months by which the number remaining exceeds one hundred and twenty; and

(S.C. 2009, c. 31, s. 34(1).)

(b) from his total pensionable earnings remaining after making any deduction under subsection (2) or (3), the aggregate of his pensionable earnings for a number of months equal to the number of months deducted under para-

Y

graph (*a*), for which months that aggregate is less than his aggregate pensionable earnings for any like number of months in his contributory period other than for months for which a deduction has already been made under subsection (2) or (3).

On proclamation s. 48(4)(*b*) will be replaced by S.C. 2012, c. 31, s. 196(2), and will read as follows:

(*b*) **from the contributor's total pensionable earnings remaining after making any deduction under subsection (2) or (3), the aggregate of the contributor's pensionable earnings for a number of months equal to the number of months deducted under paragraph (*a*), for which months that aggregate is less than — or, if not less than, then equal to — the contributor's aggregate pensionable earnings for any like number of months in the contributor's contributory period other than for months for which a deduction has already been made under subsection (2) or (3).**

(5) *Exception — same percentage* — **The percentage used in a calculation of the amount of average monthly pensionable earnings under subsection (4) is to be used in the calculation of other benefits based on that amount. (S.C. 2009, c. 31, s. 34(2).)**

(R.S.C. 1985, c. 30 (2nd Supp.), s. 16; 1997, c. 40, s. 70; 2009, c. 31, s. 34.)

———————— Notes ————————

Synopsis

This section sets out the following formula for determining the average monthly pensionable earnings of a contributor whose retirement pension becomes payable after December 1975:

Average monthly pensionable earnings = Total pensionable earnings / Greater of total number months in contributory period or basic number of contributory months

The average monthly pensionable earnings of a contributor is used to determine the amount of retirement pension payable (see s. 46).

Related Provisions

● Section 50 — Total pensionable earnings

Case Law

Runchey v. Canada (A.G.), 2013 FCA 16

The CRP provision does not automatically exclude "child rearing" years from the qualifying parent's benefit calculations. Periods are only dropped if doing so will result in higher pension benefits (s. 48(2)(*a*)). Section 48(2)(*a*) specifies that contributors only qualify for the CRP in months that they (i) are a "family allowance recipient", and (ii) have pensionable earnings that are "less than his [or her] average monthly pensionable earnings." A parent is considered a "family allowance recipient" if he or she received a payment under the old *Family Allowances Act* or qualified for the Canada Child Tax Benefit. The definition also includes the spouse or partner of someone who received a payment under the old *Family Allowances Act,* but only if the recipient of the family allowance waives his or her entitlement to the CRP. The second requirement — earnings below average monthly pensionable earnings — ensures that the CRP does not drop out months that would otherwise increase the contributor's pension benefits.

The most recent version of the *Family Allowances Act* (R.S.C. 1985, c. F-1) was repealed as of January 1, 1993. After this date, parents were not eligible for family allowances. Accordingly, family allowances are not relevant to defining "family allowance recipient" after 1993. As a result, the family allowance cannot be a basis for determining CRP eligibility after 1992. Section 42 solves this problem by including in the definition of "family allowance recipient" "such other persons as may be prescribed by regulation." Subsection 77(1) of the CPP Regulations expands the definition of "family allowance recipient." In so doing, it adds new categories of contributors that are eligible for the CRP. Paragraph 77(1)(*a*) extends the definition to the spouses and common-law partners of those who received a family allowance under the *Family Allowances Act.* It does so on two conditions: the spouse or common-law partner must have remained at home as the primary caregiver of a child under the age of seven and the "period has not already been or cannot be excluded or deducted from the [recipient of an allowance's] contributory period under Part II of the Act." Section 42 of the CPP and s. 77(1) of the CPP Regulations establish three circumstances when a contributor is a "family allowance recipient":

1. before 1992, he or she received a family allowance under the old *Family Allowances Act*; or

2. he or she remained at home as the primary caregiver of the child, he or she is the present or former spouse or common-law partner of a person who received a family allowance, and the person who received a family allowance does not qualify or waives his or her right to the CRP; and

3. after 1992, he or she did or could qualify for the Canada Child Tax Benefit.

The CRP therefore does not necessarily apply to the parent that had primary caregiving responsibility for the child or children. Because of the definition of "family allowance recipient," eligibility for the CRP is generally limited to parents who, before 1992, qualified for a family allowance or, after 1992, the Canada Child Tax Benefit. While family allowances and the Canada Child Tax Benefit will generally have gone to the parent with primary caregiving responsibility, this is not always the case. Rather, both programs presumptively apply to the female parent, except when the male parent has sole custody of the child or in other limited circumstances. Therefore, the CRP program favours women as a whole.

Like the Family Allowance, the female parent is automatically eligible for the Canada Child Tax Benefit in most circumstances. However, unlike the Family Allowance, the male parent is usually eligible if he is the primary caregiver, even if both parents live with the child. According to s. 122.6 of the *Income Tax Act*, the parent that is the "eligible individual" of the "qualified dependant" receives the Canada Child Tax Benefit. The eligible individual is the parent who "primarily fulfils the responsibility for the care and upbringing of the qualified dependant" (ITA s. 122.6(a)). Section 122.6(f) presumes that the female parent is the primary caregiver when she is living with the child. Therefore, when both parents reside with the child, the female parent benefits from a presumption that she is the eligible individual and collects the Canada Child Tax Benefit. However, this presumption is rebuttable. Subsection 122.6(h) of the definition authorizes factors for determining which parent is the primary caregiver. These factors are set out in the *Income Tax Regulations*, C.R.C., c. 945, s. 6302. Furthermore, the presumption can be excluded by regulations made under s. 122.6(g) of the definition. For example, the presumption does not apply when the woman advises the Minister in writing that the man is the primary caregiver, nor, when competing claims are made, there are two female parents or the parents reside in different locations (*Income Tax Regulations* s. 6301(a), (c), and (d)). In these circumstances, the male parent may claim the Canada Child Tax Benefit without documentation. The requirement that the female parent sign a declaration before the male can benefit is an administrative obstacle to the male parent that female parents do not encounter. And it might be quite an onerous obstacle where the marriage has broken down and the parents are not cooperating with each other. Therefore, the *Income Tax Act* does not preclude male parents from claiming the Canada Child Tax Benefit. However, because of the presumption in subsection 122.6(f), male parents can face an additional administrative burden to qualify when both the parents live with the child. Thus, it is easier for women to qualify for the Canada Child Tax Benefit as compared to men, and thus gain access to the CRDO. Meanwhile, the DUPE provisions of the CPP are aimed at transferring pension credits from the high-income-earning spouse to the low-earning spouse upon divorce or separation. In many families, the low-earning spouse is the woman. However, the overlap affects only some men in certain circumstances and is a consequence of an intricate scheme and not a singling out of men for different treatment. Consequently, the distinction did not perpetuate prejudice or stereotyping that would demonstrate discrimination against men, and did not violate the equality rights guarantee under section 15 the Charter.

L.L. v. Minister of Human Resources and Skills Development and A.C., 2013 SSTAD 12

The CRP provision does not automatically exclude "child rearing" years from the qualifying parent's benefit calculations. Periods are only dropped if doing so will result in higher pension benefits. The plain meaning of s. 77(1)(a) of the CPP Regulations is that the other spouse (the non-family allowance recipient) cannot qualify for the same period as the family allowance recipient. As such, the other parent can only qualify for the CRP when the person who received the family allowance does not.

Taylor v. MSD (August 18, 2006), CP 22241 (PAB)

The general 15% dropout provision under s. 48(4) takes into account many of life's events and interrupted earnings, including time out from earning income to look after family members, and others.

---

49. *Contributory period* — **The contributory period of a contributor is the period commencing January 1, 1966 or when he reaches eighteen years of age, whichever is the later, and ending**

  (*a*) **where a benefit other than a disability pension commences before the end of 1986, when he reaches sixty-five years of age, or if he makes a contribution for earnings after he reaches sixty-five years of age, with the month for which he last made such a contribution, and in any case not later than the month in which he dies, or**

  (*b*) **where a benefit other than a disability pension commences after the end of 1986, with the earliest of**

  (i) **the month preceding the month in which he reaches seventy years of age,**

  (ii) **the month in which he dies, or**

  (iii) **the month preceding the month in which the retirement pension commences,**

but excluding

  (*c*) **any month that was excluded from the contributor's contributory period under this Act or under a provincial pension plan by reason of disability, and**

  (*d*) **in relation to any benefits payable under this Act for any month after December, 1977, any month for which he was a family allowance recipient in a year for which his unadjusted pensionable earnings were equal to or less than his basic exemption for the year.**

(R.S.C. 1985, c. 30 (2nd Supp.), s. 17.)

——————— **Notes** ———————

Synopsis

This section defines the "contributory period" of a contributor — i.e., the amount of time he or she was making net CPP contributions from employment or self-employment income — for the purposes of calculating the retirement pension, death benefit, survivors' pension or orphan's benefit. Note that a person's "contributory period" for purposes of the disability benefit or disabled contributor's child's benefit is defined in s. 44(2)(*b*).

The contributory period begins on the later of January 1, 1966 or the date a person turns 18. The contributory period ends:

  1. Either (i) when he or she turns 65, or (ii) the month where he or she last made a contribution after turning 65, or (iii) at the latest, the month when he or she dies, if the contributor starts receiving a benefit (except for a disability pension) before 1987, or

  2. The earliest of (i) the month before the contributor turns 70, (ii) the month in which he or she dies, or (iii) the month before the month he or she starts receiving the retirement pension, if the contributor starts receiving a benefit (except for a disability pension) after 1986.

The contributory period excludes months where the person was receiving a CPP or QPP disability pension, or months in which the person was in receipt of family allowance benefits in a year in which the person's unadjusted pensionable earnings were less than the basic exemption (now $3,500 for non-disability claims).

Case Law

Canada (Attorney General) v. Storto (1994), 174 N.R. 221 (Fed. C.A.). See also *Armstrong-Lane v. MHRD* (February 5, 2001), CP 10538 (PAB)

Where the deceased contributor was never determined to be disabled, s. 49(c) had no application.

Van De Wetering v. Canada (Attorney General), 2003 FCT 588

Where the claimant raises the issue of his or her disability and its impact on the calculation of the contributory period, the Ministry and tribunals must determine whether the claimant was in fact disabled so as to affect such calculation, whether or not the claimant complied with every technical detail of the procedure to ensure that such a determination was made.

Townley v. MHRD (January 26, 1997), CP 3202, CEB & PG (TB) ¶8663 (PAB)

Section 49(c) can only operate when there has been a specific finding or determination of disability under the CPP. The years following a determination that the claimant had qualified for a military disability pension and during which he made no CPP contributions could not be excluded from the contributory period.

MNHW v. Hunter (August 15, 1990), CP 1762, CEB & PG (TB) ¶8608 (PAB)

The effect of the "child rearing drop-out" provisions, under s. 49(d), is to permit certain periods of time to be excluded from the calculation of average monthly pensionable earnings. The purpose is clearly to ensure that those parents who choose to limit their income to care for young children are not penalized. However, to be eligible, the applicant must be receiving family allowance for the child or be the spouse of a family allowance recipient who remained home to care for the child, and the child must be under 7 years old. A claimant who quit work to care for her grandchildren after her daughter's death did not come within the provision where neither she nor her spouse was receiving family allowance payments.

Taylor v. MSD (August 18, 2006), CP 22241 (PAB)

The s. 49(d) CRDO provision drops out months during which parents care for their children under the age of seven, from their contributory period and from the calculation of their pension. Sections 48(1), 48(2) and 49(d) do not violate or contravene s. 15(1) of the *Canadian Charter of Rights and Freedoms* respecting the care the contributor provided to her adult stepson and her mother, and if there is a violation or contravention of s. 15(1) of the Charter, then such violation or contravention is justified under s. 1 of the Charter. The CRDO provisions do not marginalize, stigmatize or demean the sense of worth of women who give unpaid care to adults. The s. 49(d) CRDO provision enables those who remain at home to care for their child or children up to seven years old, not to be penalized during this period of care when they have zero or low income earnings. This also helps the children in their development and growth, as the early years of maturity are crucial to the health and overall development of young children. The s. 49(d) CRDO provision is of great benefit to children under the age of seven, and also to their parents, which combined together helps to build a healthy and stable society. While many persons do, on a short-term basis, care for an ill child or stepchild, or an ill parent or step-parent, or other person (e.g., an ill friend or other family member) over the age of seven, such caregivers do not, generally, on a regular basis, devote all or much of their time, effort, and resources towards nourishing or providing care for such care recipients, 24 hours a day, seven days a week, 365 days a year, as do all parents, in caring for, raising, nourishing, and providing for their children under the age of seven.

Zchoch v. MSD (April 21, 2006), CP 23937 (PAB)

Article 25 of the Canada-Austria social security agreement provides that periods of coverage completed under the legislation of one of the countries before the entry into force of the agreement must also be taken into consideration in determining entitlement to a benefit under this agreement. Therefore, the claimant's pre-1966 contributions in Austria could be taken into account, despite CPP s. 49. [Note: the PAB distinguished the *Henry* decision (below) dealing with the Finland agreement on the basis that there was no reference in that decision to an equivalent provision to Article 25 in the Finland agreement.]

Henry v. MHRD (April 27, 2001), CP 11844 (PAB)

The contributor's pre-1966 employment in Finland does not count toward the contributory period, which by virtue of s. 49 cannot commence before January 1, 1966. The

Canada–Finland agreement does not define "contributory period", so the CPP definition must govern.

---

50. *Total pensionable earnings* — **The total pensionable earnings of a contributor are the total for all months in his contributory period of his pensionable earnings for each month calculated as provided in section 51.**

————————— **Notes** —————————

Synopsis

This section calculates the total pensionable earnings in a contributory period to be used in computing the average monthly pensionable earnings under ss. 47 and 48.

Related Provisions

● Section 49 — Contributory period defined

---

51. *Calculation of pensionable earnings for a month* — **(1) The pensionable earnings of a contributor for a month (in this subsection referred to as the "particular month") are the amount determined by the formula**

$$A \times B$$

where

A   is the earnings for which the contributor is deemed by section 52 to have made a contribution for the particular month; and

B   is
  (*a*) where the contributor was born after December 31, 1932 and the contributor's retirement pension did not commence before January 1, 1998 and, after the contributor's 60th birthday, a month was excluded from the contributor's contributory period by reason of disability, the product determined by the formula

$$(C/D) \times (E/F)$$

where

C   is the contributor's Maximum Pensionable Earnings Average for the year in which a benefit first became payable to the contributor under this Act or a provincial pension plan that caused a month after the contributor's 60th birthday to be excluded from the contributor's contributory period by reason of disability,

D   is the Year's Maximum Pensionable Earnings for the year that includes the particular month,

E   is the Pension Index for the year in which a benefit becomes payable to the contributor under this Act or a provincial pension plan, and

F   is the Pension Index for the year referred to in the description of C, and
  (*b*) in any other case, the ratio

$$G/D$$

where

G   is the Maximum Pensionable Earnings Average in respect of the contributor for the year in which a benefit becomes payable to the contributor under this Act or under a provincial pension plan, and

D   is as described in paragraph (*a*).

Canada Pension Plan

231

(2) *Exception* — **For the purposes of subsection (1), where the year referred to in the description of C is 1987 or earlier, the Maximum Pensionable Earnings Average for the year shall be calculated as if the Year's Maximum Pensionable Earnings for a particular year before 1986 were calculated as the greatest multiple of $100 that is equal to or less than an amount calculated by multiplying the Year's Maximum Pensionable Earnings for 1986, which are $25,800, by the ratio**

$$A/B$$

where

A   **is the average for the twelve month period ending on June 30 of the year preceding that particular year of the average weekly wages and salaries of the Industrial Composite in Canada as published by Statistics Canada for each month in that period, and**

B   **is the average for the twelve month period ending on June 30, 1985 of the average weekly wages and salaries of the Industrial Composite in Canada as published by Statistics Canada for each month in that period.**

(3) *Pension Index before 1974* — **For the purpose of subsection (1), where the beginning of a period that is excluded from the contributor's contributory period by reason of disability is in a year before 1974, in calculating the Pension Index for the year in which that period begins, paragraph 43.1(2)(a) of the *Canada Pension Plan*, R.S.C. 1970, c. C-5, as amended by section 24 of chapter 4 of the Statutes of Canada, 1974-75-76, shall be read without reference to the words "or 1.02 times the Pension Index for the preceding year, whichever is the lesser".**

(S.C. 1997, c. 40, s. 71.)

———————— Notes ————————

Synopsis

This section sets out the formula for calculating a contributor's pensionable earnings for a month during a given contributory period. In making the calculation, the general rule is that the earnings on which the contributor has contributed for a particular month are multiplied by the ratio of the Maximum Pensionable Earnings Average ("MPEA") for the year in which pension is payable and the Year's Maximum Pensionable Earnings ("YMPE" — $52,000 in 2014) for the year in which the relevant contribution was deemed to have been made. An alternate formula is prescribed if the contributor received a disability pension after his or her 60th birthday.

This calculation allows the contributory earnings for each month to be adjusted to reflect changes in the value of the YMPE from the year in which the contribution was made to the year in which the benefit is paid, thereby maintaining the real value of contributions and neutralizing the effect of inflation.

Related Provisions

- Section 18 — Amount of Year's Maximum Pensionable Earnings
- Section 42(1) — Maximum pensionable earnings average defined
- Section 43 — Pension index

———————————

52. *Amount of earnings for which contribution deemed to have been made for a month* — **(1) For the purpose of calculating the pensionable earnings of a contributor for a month in any year for which the contributor has made a contribution, the contribution shall be deemed to have been made for all months in the year, and the earnings for which he shall be deemed to have made a contribution for each month in the year are an amount calculated by dividing his unadjusted pensionable earnings for the year by twelve, except that**

(*a*) for a year in which the contributor reaches eighteen years of age or in which a disability pension ceases to be payable to him under this Act or under a provincial pension plan, the contribution shall be deemed to have been made for earnings for the months in the year after he reached that age or after the pension ceased to be payable, as the case may be, and

(*b*) for a year in which the contributor reaches seventy years of age or dies, in which a retirement pension becomes payable to him under this Act or under a provincial pension plan or in which any month is excluded from his contributory period under this Act or under a provincial pension plan by reason of disability, the contribution shall be deemed to have been made for earnings for the months in the year before the contributor reached seventy years of age or died, before the retirement pension became payable or that were not so excluded, as the case may be; (R.S.C. 1985, c. 30 (2nd Supp.), s. 19.)

in which case the earnings for which he shall be deemed to have made a contribution for each such month shall be an amount calculated by dividing his unadjusted pensionable earnings for that year by the number of those months.

(2) *Where no contribution made* — For the purpose of calculating the pensionable earnings of a contributor for a month in any year for which the contributor made no contribution, the amount of the earnings for which a contribution shall be deemed to have been made for any month in the year shall be deemed to be zero.

(3) *When contribution deemed to have been made* — For the purposes of this Part,

(*a*) a contributor shall be deemed to have made a contribution for any year for which his unadjusted pensionable earnings exceed his basic exemption for the year, and shall be deemed to have made no contribution for any year for which his unadjusted pensionable earnings do not exceed his basic exemption for the year; and

(*b*) a contributor shall be deemed to have made a contribution for earnings for any month for which a contribution is deemed by subsection (1) to have been made by him.

(R.S.C. 1985, c. 30 (2nd Supp.), s. 19.)

──────── **Notes** ────────

Synopsis

In general; under this section, monthly earnings on which a person is deemed to have made a contribution are the unadjusted pensionable earnings for a year, as defined in s. 53, divided by 12. The exception is where the contributor could not have made contributions for the full 12 months of a given year, either because (i) he or she turned 18 during that year, or (ii) the contributor had been in receipt of a disability payment which ceased to be payable in that year. In such circumstances, the contribution to deemed to have been made for the months in the year following the event.

Where (i) the contributor either turns 70 or dies in a year, (ii) a retirement pension becomes payable in a year, or (iii) any month is excluded from a contributor's contributory period by reason of disability, the contribution is deemed to have been made for the months in the year before the event occurred. In the cases of (ii) and (iii), the earnings for which the contributor is deemed to have made a contribution for each month is the amount calculated by dividing unadjusted pensionable earnings for that year by the number of months for which the contributor is deemed to have made a contribution.

The earnings for which a contributor is deemed to have made a contribution for each month in a year in which the contributor did not make a CPP contribution is deemed to be zero (s. 52(2)). A contribution is deemed to have been made in year in which the unadjusted pensionable earnings exceed the basic exemption, but not where the unadjusted pensionable earnings fail to exceed to basic exemption. Monthly contributions are deemed to have been made in the same manner as contributions for that year are deemed to have been made (s. 52(3)).

Related Provisions

• Section 53 — Unadjusted pensionable earnings for a year

Case Law

Walters v. MEI, [1996] FCJ No. 176 (C.A.)

While s. 97 makes it indisputable that the amount shown in the Record is accurate, however small, whether such payment was sufficient to be a valid yearly contribution is determined by s. 52(3).

MNHW v. Poland (March 29, 1993), CP 2343, CEB & PG (TB) ¶8500 (PAB).

By virtue of s. 52(3)(*a*), if the annual earnings do not exceed the basic exemption, then there cannot have been a valid contribution for that year which might create an eligibility for pension rights. The fact that the claimant did not seek a refund of his invalid contribution triggered by minimal earnings could not be allowed to defeat the clear intention of s. 2(3)(*a*). This substantive section overrides the purely administrative s. 99 provision that the record is closed after 4 years. Therefore, *MNHW v. Sawyer* (September 5, 1989), CP 1581 (PAB) was wrongly decided.

---

53. *Unadjusted pensionable earnings for a year* — **(1) Subject to section 54, the unadjusted pensionable earnings of a contributor for a year are an amount equal to**

    (*a*) the aggregate of

        (i) his contributory salary and wages for the year, and

        (ii) his contributory self-employed earnings for the year in the case of an individual described in section 10,

    (*b*) the aggregate of

        (i) his earnings on which a contribution has been made for the year under this Act, calculated as the aggregate of

            (A) his salary and wages on which a contribution has been made for the year, and

            (B) the amount of any contribution required to be made by the contributor for the year in respect of the contributor's self-employed earnings divided by the contribution rate for self-employed persons for the year, (R.S.C. 1985, c. 30 (2nd Supp.), s. 20(1).)

        (ii) his earnings on which a contribution has been made for the year under a provincial pension plan, calculated as the aggregate of

            (A) such amount as is determined in prescribed manner to be his salary and wages on which a contribution has been made for the year by him under a provincial pension plan, and

            (B) the amount of any contribution required to be made by the contributor for the year under a provincial pension plan in respect of the contributor's self-employed earnings divided by the contribution rate for self-employed persons for the year, (R.S.C. 1985, c. 30 (2nd Supp.), s. 20(2).)

        (iii) his basic exemption for the year, or

    (*c*) his maximum pensionable earnings for the year,

whichever is the least, except that where the amount calculated as provided in paragraph (*a*) is equal to or less than the amount of his basic exemption for the year, his unadjusted pensionable earnings for that year shall be deemed to be zero.

    (2) *Year in which retirement pension commences* — **For the purposes of subsection (1), for the year in which a retirement pension becomes payable under this Act,**

    (*a*) the contributor's basic exemption is equal to that proportion of the amount of the Year's Basic Exemption that the number of months in the year that are not excluded from the contributory period — and are before the retirement pension becomes payable — is of 12; and

(b) the contributor's maximum pensionable earnings is equal to that proportion of the amount of the Year's Maximum Pensionable Earnings that the number of months in the year that are not excluded from the contributory period — and are before the retirement pension becomes payable — is of 12.

(S.C. 2009, c. 31, s. 35.)

(R.S.C. 1985, c. 30 (2nd Supp.), s. 20; 2009, c. 31, s. 35.)

——————————— **Notes** ———————————

Synopsis

The unadjusted pensionable earnings of a contributor for a year is the amount which is actually posted to the credit of the contributor in the government's Record of Earnings for all pension purposes. Essentially, this section provides the dollar amount of the earnings upon which a person has made contributions under the CPP, plus the basic exemption ($3,500). It is this amount which is subsequently adjusted in order to obtain the average pensionable earnings. Under s. 52, the unadjusted pensionable earnings of a contributor for a year is used to determine the amount of earnings for which a contribution is deemed to have been made for a month.

Related Provisions

- Section 54 — Unadjusted pensionable earnings for years of division

Related CPP Regulations

- Section 41 — Salary and wages on which a contribution has been made under a provincial pension plan

———————————————————————

54. *Unadjusted pensionable earnings for years of division* — **The amount of the unadjusted pensionable earnings of a contributor for a year determined under section 53 shall be adjusted for each year in which there is a division of unadjusted pensionable earnings under section 55 or 55.1 and under a provincial pension plan.**

(R.S.C. 1985, c. 30 (2nd Supp.), s. 21.)

——————————— **Notes** ———————————

Synopsis

This section provides for the adjustment of the amount of unadjusted pensionable earnings of a contributor in a year in which the pension credits have been divided between separating couples under ss. 55 and 55.1.

———————————————————————

Division of Unadjusted Pensionable Earnings for Divorces and Annulments before the Coming into Force of Section 55.1

55. *Application for division* — **(1) Subject to this section, subsections 55.2(2), (3) and (4) and section 55.3, an application for a division of the unadjusted pensionable earnings of former spouses may be made in writing to the Minister by or on behalf of either former spouse, by the estate or succession of either former spouse or by any person that may be prescribed, within 36 months or, if both former spouses agree in writing, at any time after the date of a judgment granting a divorce or of a judgment of nullity of the marriage, rendered on or after January 1, 1978 and before January 1, 1987.** (R.S.C. 1985, c. 30 (2nd Supp.), s. 22(1); 1991, c. 44, s. 6(1); 1995, c. 33, s. 26; 2000, c. 12, s. 46(1); 2012, c. 31, s. 197(1).)

(2) *Idem* — **For the purposes of this section,**

Canada Pension Plan

(*a*) notwithstanding paragraphs (*b*) and (*c*), the former spouses must have cohabited for at least thirty-six consecutive months during the marriage before an application made under subsection (1) may be approved by the Minister;

(*b*) the marriage is deemed to have been solemnized or nullified or a divorce is deemed to have been made final on the last day of the year preceding the registered date of the marriage or the judgment of nullity or the effective date of the judgment granting a divorce; and (R.S.C. 1985, c. 30 (2nd Supp.), s. 22(2); 2012, c. 31, s. 197(2).)

(*c*) the former spouses shall be deemed to have cohabited throughout the year in which the marriage was solemnized, and shall be deemed not to have cohabited at any time during the year of divorce or of annulment of the marriage.

(3) *Period of cohabitation* — In determining the period for which the unadjusted pensionable earnings of the former spouses shall be divided, only those months during which the former spouses cohabited during the marriage shall be considered and, for the purposes of this section, months during which former spouses cohabited shall be determined in the prescribed manner. (S.C. 1991, c. 44, s. 6(2).)

(4) *Division of unadjusted pensionable earnings* — On approval by the Minister of an application referred to in subsection (1), the unadjusted pensionable earnings for each former spouse for the period of cohabitation attributable to contributions made under this Act, determined in the same manner as the total pensionable earnings attributable to contributions made under this Act are determined in section 78, shall be added and then divided equally and the unadjusted pensionable earnings so divided shall be attributed to each former spouse.

(5) *On division unadjusted pensionable earnings under this Act* — Where there is a division under subsection (4) and under a provincial pension plan, for the purposes of benefit calculation and payment under this Act, the total unadjusted pensionable earnings of a contributor for a year of division shall be the aggregate of his unadjusted pensionable earnings attributed under subsection (4) and his unadjusted pensionable earnings attributed under a provincial pension plan.

(6) *No division* — No division of unadjusted pensionable earnings for a period of cohabitation shall be made

(*a*) where the total unadjusted pensionable earnings of the former spouses in a year does not exceed twice the Year's Basic Exemption; (S.C. 2000, c. 12, s. 46(3).)

(*b*) for the period before which one of the former spouses reached eighteen years of age or after which a former spouse reached seventy years of age; (R.S.C. 1985, c. 30 (2nd Supp.), s. 22(3); 2000, c. 12, s. 46(3).)

(*c*) for the period in which one of the former spouses was a beneficiary of a retirement pension under this Act or under a provincial pension plan; and (R.S.C. 1985, c. 30 (2nd Supp.), s. 22(3); 2000, c. 12, s. 46(3).)

(*d*) for any month that is excluded from the contributory period of one of the former spouses under this Act or a provincial pension plan by reason of disability. (R.S.C. 1985, c. 30 (2nd Supp.), s. 22(3); 2000, c. 12, s. 46(3).)

(7) *Benefits in pay* — Where an application referred to in subsection (1) has been approved and a benefit is payable under this Act to or in respect of either of the former spouses for any month commencing on or before the day of receipt of an application under subsection (1), the basic amount of the benefit shall be calculated and adjusted in accordance with section 45 but subject to the division of unadjusted pensionable earnings made under this section and the adjusted benefit shall be paid effective the month following the month the application referred to in subsection (1) is received. (S.C. 2000, c. 12, s. 46(3).)

(8) *Notification of division* — On approval by the Minister of an application for division of unadjusted pensionable earnings, an applicant and the former spouse or the

former spouse's estate shall be notified in a manner prescribed by regulation and, where the applicant or the former spouse or the former spouse's estate is dissatisfied with the division or the result thereof, the right of appeal as set out in this Part applies. (S.C. 2000, c. 12, s. 46(3).)

(9) *Regulations* — The Governor in Council may make regulations prescribing the time, manner and form of making applications for division of unadjusted pensionable earnings or withdrawal of applications for that division, the procedures to be followed in dealing with and approving those applications and the information and evidence to be furnished in connection therewith.

(R.S.C. 1985, c. 30 (2nd Supp.), s. 22; 1991, c. 44, s. 6; 1995, c. 33, s. 26; 2000, c. 12, s. 46; 2012, c. 31, s. 197.)

———————— **Notes** ————————

Synopsis

When a marriage or common-law relationship ends, the CPP credits that the parties accumulated during the time they lived together can be divided equally between them. For legal marriages ending between January 1, 1978 and December 31, 1986, this section sets out how the division of unadjusted pensionable earnings will be achieved where a decree absolute of divorce, a judgment granted divorce, or a judgment of nullity of marriage has been obtained.

Related Provisions

- Section 55.1 — CPP division after January 1, 1987
- Section 55.2(2), (3) — Effect of spousal agreement
- Section 55.3 — Incapacity of one of the parties
- Section 66(5) — Where person denied division because of written agreement
- Section 81 — Request for reconsideration by Minister

Related CPP Regulations

- Section 43 — Application for division of unadjusted pensionable earnings
- Section 44 — Application on behalf of incapable person
- Section 45(3)–(5) — Withdrawal of application
- Section 46 — Notification in writing
- Sections 52, 54 — Information and evidence required from applicant
- Section 78 — Cohabitation

Case Law

MEI v. Neil (September 20, 1995), CP 8590, CEB & PG (TB) ¶8590 (PAB)

Under s. 55, an application for division must be made by one of the former spouses within 36 months from the date of the divorce judgment. The legislation does not expressly prohibit the former spouses from opting out of its provisions.

Murray v. Canada (MNHW) (1998), A-697-93 (Fed. C.A.)

The provision expressly limits pension credit splitting to spouses divorced on or after January 1, 1978. While spouses who divorced prior to 1978 are not given the right to apply for pension-splitting, s. 15 of the Charter could not be applied retrospectively to "cure" this failure and the provision is therefore valid.

Obiter: The past injustice to women was recognized and rectified by what is now s. 55, but only in cases of divorces granted after the law came into effect. The proclamation into force of the amendment was held up for nearly 6 months after the date of its enactment, to allow for adjustments in negotiations involving divorce cases that were in progress, recognizing the difficulties that would be caused to those cases if the delay were not allowed. This delay also indicated conclusively that the characterization of the discrimination in this case has to be based on an event — a divorce obtained after January 1, 1978 — not on the ongoing status of a divorced person. It is, therefore, the date of the divorce, not the fact of the divorce, that is most significant. If it were otherwise, then all the divorce settlements completed prior to 1978 might have to be reopened.

Tippett v. Canada (Attorney General), 2012 FCA 301

Section 15 of the Charter came into force on April 17, 1985, and applies to the three-year limitation period under s. 15 in circumstances where the limitation period has expired after that date. It is irrelevant that the parties might have divorced before that date.

Von Der Kammer v. MNHW (July 19, 1991), CP 1916, CEB & PG (TB) ¶8629 (PAB). See also *Warner v. MEI* (November 1995), CP 2710 (PAB).

Despite the use of the word "may" in s. 55(1), the application for a division of unadjusted pensionable earnings must be made within 36 months of the date of the parties' decree absolute. The PAB has no jurisdiction to extend the time period.

Harrison-Wilson v. MSD (April 14, 2005), CP 22023 (PAB)

While s. 55 allows for an application by an estate within the 36-month time limit following divorce, it makes no reference to allowing an estate to agree to waive the time limit imposed by the legislation. A waiver signed by the administrator of the deceased contributor spouse's estate was inoperative where it was granted more than 36 months after the spouses were divorced and more than 36 months after the contributor spouse's death, notwithstanding the Minister advised the surviving spouse to obtain it.

D.T. v. MHRSD (November 26, 2007), CP 24399 (PAB)

The words in s. 43(1) of the Regulation "made in writing at any office of the Department" mean, in effect, "exists in the office" or "is in office".

Squance v. MNHW (November 19, 1993), CP 2550, CEB & PG (TB) ¶8523 (PAB)

CPP Regulation 78(2)(a) only applies to deem a couple to be cohabiting when spouses were living separately solely because occupation, unemployment or illness. It did not apply when one of the spouses made a decision to remain in a country after the other spouse returned to Canada. In that case, the question turned on the common-law definition of "cohabitation".

Canada (Attorney General) v. Leer, 2012 FC 932

The only real distinction between ss. 55 and 55.1 is their application to the dissolution of relationships in different periods. The result is the same regardless of whether s. 55.1 and the related provision of s. 55.2(8) was formally applied. The fact that a decision may have been erroneously based on s. 55 rather than s. 55.1 was not in itself grounds for granting leave to appeal, where the outcome would have been the same.

Division of Unadjusted Pensionable Earnings

55.1. *When mandatory division to take place* — **(1) Subject to this section and sections 55.2 and 55.3, a division of unadjusted pensionable earnings shall take place in the following circumstances:**

   (a) in the case of spouses, following a judgment granting a divorce or a judgment of nullity of the marriage, on the Minister's being informed of the judgment and receiving the prescribed information; (S.C. 1991, c. 44, s. 7(1); 2000, c. 12, s. 47; 2012, c. 31, s. 198.)

   (b) in the cases of spouses, following the approval by the Minister of an application made by or on behalf of either spouse, by the estate or succession of either spouse or by any person that may be prescribed, if (S.C. 1997, c. 40, s. 72(1); 2007, c. 11, s. 3(1).)

      (i) the spouses have been living separate and apart for a period of one year or more, and

      (ii) in the event of the death of one of the spouses after they have been living separate and apart for a period of one year or more, the application is made within three years after the death; and

   (c) in the case of common-law partners, following the approval by the Minister of an application made by or on behalf of either former common-law partner, by

the estate or succession of one of those former common-law partners or by any person that may be prescribed, if (S.C. 1997, c. 40, s. 72(2); 2000, c. 12, s. 47.)

(i) the former common-law partners have been living separate and apart for a period of one year or more, or one of the former common-law partners has died during that period, and

(ii) the application is made within four years after the day on which the former common-law partners commenced to live separate and apart or, if both former common-law partners agree in writing, at any time after the end of that four-year period.

(S.C. 2000, c. 12, s. 47; 2007, c. 11, s. 3(2).)

(2) *Calculation of period of separation* — For the purposes of this section,

(a) persons subject to a division of unadjusted pensionable earnings shall be deemed to have lived separate and apart for any period during which they lived apart and either of them had the intention to live separate and apart from the other; and

(b) a period during which persons subject to such a division have lived separate and apart shall not be considered to have been interrupted or terminated

(i) by reason only that either person has become incapable of forming or having an intention to continue to live separate and apart or of continuing to live separate and apart of the spouse's own volition, if it appears to the Minister that the separation would probably have continued if the person had not become so incapable, or

(ii) by reason only that the two persons have resumed cohabitation during a period of, or periods totalling, not more than ninety days with reconciliation as its primary purpose.

(S.C. 2000, c. 12, s. 47.)

(3) *Period of cohabitation* — For the purposes of this section, persons subject to a division of unadjusted pensionable earnings must have cohabited for a continuous period of at least one year in order for a division of unadjusted pensionable earnings to take place, and, for the purposes of this subsection, a continuous period of at least one year shall be determined in a manner prescribed by regulation. (S.C. 2000, c. 12, s. 47.)

(4) *Period for purposes of division* — In determining the period for which the unadjusted pensionable earnings of the persons subject to a division shall be divided, only those months during which the two persons cohabited shall be considered, and, for the purposes of this subsection, months during which the two persons cohabited shall be determined in the prescribed manner. (S.C. 1991, c. 44, s. 8(1); 2000, c. 12, s. 47.)

(5) *Minister's discretion* — Before a division of unadjusted pensionable earnings is made under this section, or within the prescribed period after such a division is made, the Minister may refuse to make the division or may cancel the division, as the case may be, if the Minister is satisfied that

(a) benefits are payable to or in respect of both persons subject to the division; and

(b) the amount of both benefits decreased at the time the division was made or would decrease at the time the division was proposed to be made.

(S.C. 1995, c. 33, s. 27; 2000, c. 12, s. 47.)

(R.S.C. 1985, c. 30 (2nd Supp.), s. 23; 1991, c. 44, ss. 7, 8; 1995, c. 33, s. 27; 1997, c. 40, s. 72; 2000, c. 12, s. 47; 2007, c. 11, s. 3; 2012, c. 31, s. 198.)

———————— **Notes** ————————

Synopsis

This section makes the division of unadjusted pensionable earnings mandatory with few exceptions. To divide the spouses' unadjusted pensionable earnings, the Minister must be informed of the decree or judgment in the case of married couples. Spouses may apply for the Minister's approval of a division, if the parties have been living separate and apart for at least one year, or one of the parties has died after they had been living separate and apart for at least one year and application is made within three years after death.

The Minister has discretion to refuse to make a division or to cancel a division only if satisfied that (i) both parties are entitled to benefits, and (ii) the amount of both benefits would decrease upon division or when the division was proposed to be made (s. 55.1(5)).

Recent Amendments

The 2000 amendments formally introduced the concept of "common-law partners", which includes same-sex partners, and eliminated the former extended definition of "spouse" (see Synopsis and Case Law under s. 2). "Spouse" as it is now used in s. 55(1)(*a*) and (*b*), once again, refers to one of the parties to a legal marriage.

Related Provisions

- Section 55.11 — Application of s. 55.1
- Section 55.2 — Separation agreements and court orders; notification of parties; effect of division; provincial pension plans; where no division
- Section 55.3 — Incapacity of one of the parties
- Section 56(6) — Calculation of disability pension where division occurring
- Section 66(5) — Where person denied division because of written agreement
- Section 81 — Request for reconsideration by Minister

Related CPP Regulations

- Section 43 — Application for division of unadjusted pensionable earnings
- Section 44 — Application on behalf of incapable person
- Section 45(3)–(5) — Withdrawal of application
- Section 46(3) — When Minister's discretion may be exercised
- Sections 52, 54 — Information and evidence required from applicant
- Section 54.2 — Effective date of division
- Section 78.1 — Cohabitation — Division of unadjusted pensionable earnings (post-1986)

Case Law

§1. The Post-1986 Regime Generally

MHRD v. Woodcock, [2002] FCA 296

Section 55.1 is intended to facilitate the division of "unadjusted pensionable earnings" (colloquially referred to as "pension credits") between former spouses following a divorce.

Runchey v. Canada (A.G.), 2013 FCA 16.

See also Upshall v. Canada (Attorney General), 2013 FCA 174

The overlap between the DUPE credit split and the CRDO under CPP ss. 48–49 creates a qualitatively subtle distinction based on gender. It is easier for women to qualify for the Canada Child Tax Benefit as compared to men, and thus gain access to the CRDO. Meanwhile, the DUPE provisions of the CPP are aimed at transferring pension credits from the high-income-earning spouse to the low-earning spouse upon divorce or separation. In many families, the low-earning spouse is the woman. However, the overlap affects only some men in certain circumstances and is a consequence of an intricate scheme and not a singling out of men for different treatment. Consequently, the distinction did not perpetuate prejudice or stereotyping that would demonstrate discrimination against men, and did not violate the equality rights guarantee under s. 15 the Charter.

MEI v. Neil (September 20, 1995), CP 8590, CEB & PG (TB) ¶8590 (PAB)

The pension division regime under ss. 55.1 and 55.2 is broader in its application than under s. 55 in that the splitting provisions have been extended to separated married spouses and common-law spouses provided certain conditions are satisfied. The division is now automatic under s. 55.1(1)(*a*) in the sense that applications no longer have to be made. All that is required for a division to take place is for the Minister to be informed of the divorce and to receive the prescribed information. There are only two exceptions to the compulsory regime under s. 55.1:

1. A spousal agreement has been entered into, indicating an intention by the former spouses that there be no division of their pension credits, and meeting the three enumerated conditions set out in s. 55.2(3) that make it binding on the Minister — i.e., it was entered into on or after June 4, 1986, the opting out or waiver provisions are expressly permitted by legislation enacted in the applicable province, and the provisions of the agreement have not been judicially invalidated.

2. The Minister has discretion to refuse a division, or to cancel one made within 60 days (see Regulation s. 46(3)) after the making of the division, where the Minister is satisfied that the division is to the detriment of both spouses.

The opting-out feature is, therefore, within provincial control, in deference to constitutional requirements. To date, only Quebec and Saskatchewan (and B.C.) have enacted the enabling legislation. Sections 55.1(4) and 55.2(3) provide narrow exceptions to compulsory pension credit splitting and cannot serve as vehicles to negate the clear intention of the CPP. Where exceptions apply, these must meet the strict statutory criteria laid down in the legislation.

Before a s. 55.1(1) division can take place, the Minister is required to make an inquiry and be satisfied that the proposed division is not caught by s. 55.1(5)(*b*). Such a finding is implicitly part of each decision to make a division, and is therefore subject to appeal under s. 81 notwithstanding the 60-day limitation on the Minister's determination.

MHRD v. Wiemer, [1998] FCJ No. 809, 228 N.R. 341, 42 R.F.L. (4th) 242 (Fed. C.A.)

Sections 55.1 and 55.2 establish a regime of mandatory division of unadjusted pensionable earnings in the circumstances described in that section which refer to spouses living separate and apart after the breakdown or nullity of their marriage or the breakdown of their common-law relationship. The intent clearly is to install a regime of compulsory credits splitting to protect spouses or former spouses in case of a failure of their marriage or common-law relationship. The only exceptions to the mandatory nature of the regime are to be found in subsections 55.1(5) and 55.2(3).

Conkin v. Canada (Attorney General), 2005 FCA 351

There is no time limit set for the information prescribed in s. 55(1)(*a*) to be sent. Paragraph 55.1(1)(*c*) *in fine* only applies to paragraph 55.1(1)(*c*), and does not set a condition which applies to paragraphs 55.1(1)(*a*), (*b*) and (*c*).

Upshall v. Canada (Attorney General), 2008 FC 813, judicial review granted 2009 FCA 284

No adjustments are to be made to the parties' pensionable earnings prior to a division of pension credits taking place. This would presumably include an adjustment to a spouse's pension entitlement based upon the Child Rearing Drop-out provisions of the CPP. The only other basis upon which the Minister could potentially take remedial action in relation to a division of pension credits is under CPP s. 66(4). This provision allows for relief in some, but not all, cases where an individual has been provided with erroneous advice by departmental officials.

Upshall v. Canada (Attorney General), 2009 FCA 284

The Review Tribunal under CPP ss. 81 and 82 may hear the appeal of a former spouse who is dissatisfied with any decision made under s. 55.1, where the essence of the former spouse's argument was that the Minister's interpretation of s. 55.1 was unfair, discriminatory and wrong in law. Only if the argument was that the benefit had been denied due to departmental error did the Tribunal lack jurisdiction to consider the appeal.

Canada Pension Plan

MSD v. Holmes (April 19, 2005), CP 23407 (PAB)

Where the parties separate for less than one year before attempting a reconciliation which lasts for more than 90 days, pension credits earned during the temporary separation are included in the splitting exercise.

R.H. v. MHRSD (May 5, 2008), CP 25329 (PAB)

Although the spouses lived in the same home for some months following the date of marital breakdown and continued to share meals and socialize occasionally with friends, they were legally separated. The husband's admitted homosexuality made reconciliation impossible from the perspective of the claimant wife.

D.T. v. MHRSD (November 26, 2007), CP 24399 (PAB)

The words in s. 43(1) of the Regulation "made in writing at any office of the Department" mean, in effect, "exists in the office" or "is in office".

Bernier v. Canada (Minister of Human Resources Development), 2005 FCA 4

The PAB had no jurisdiction to remedy the inequitable result of the aggregate amount of retirement pensions being reduced following credit splitting.

Allen v. MHRD (October 30, 2002), CP 18634 (PAB)

A decree *nisi* is not a judgment of nullity. A decree absolute is required to make a divorce final.

MHRD v. Balding, (March 31, 2003), CP 17439 (PAB)

The physical or medical condition of an applicant for a pension credit split is not a factor to be considered. It is not required to be disclosed by the applicant, nor is it considered by the Minister. A request for a division is a right, subject to some requirements, and effectuating it is mandatory. A request for division can even be made by an estate.

§2. Effect of Separation Agreement

MHRD v. Wiemer, [1998] FCJ No. 809, 228 N.R. 341, 42 R.F.L. (4th) 242 (Fed. C.A.). See also *Williston v. MHRD* (March 4, 1997), CEB & PG (TB) ¶8673 (PAB).

The "approval by the Minister" mentioned in paragraph 55.1(1)(c) does not give the Minister discretion to approve or disapprove of the division. Such approval merely relates to the conditions required by an individual to qualify as an applicant under the Act. The Minister may refuse to approve an application for division of the earnings if the applicant does not meet the conditions imposed by statute. However, once the Minister has approved the application because the applicant meets the conditions, a mandatory division is to take place unless the two exceptions to the regime are applicable. There is no residual discretion not to divide the unadjusted pensionable earnings, and consideration is not to be given to any separation agreement or the intention of the parties thereto outside the parameters of s. 55.2(3).

MHRSD v. D.M.B. v. E.C. (July 19, 2010), CP 26360 (PAB)

Agreements in writing by former common-law partners to waive the four-year time limit must occur after May 3, 2007 when s. 55.1(c) was amended to allow such agreement. The agreement must also contain a specific and express waiver of the four-year limitation.

Y.A.O. v. MHRSD v. D.O. (May 30, 2011), CP 26786 (PAB)

Where the parties had governed themselves by the terms of a 1998 separation agreement that cited they were living separate and apart since 1986, they could not avail themselves of s. 55.11 (which governs the application of s. 55.1) without showing they had resumed cohabitation after December 1986. Had their marriage been legally terminated by divorce or a judgment of nullity rendered on or after January 1, 1978 and before January 1, 1987, the claimant would have been eligible to apply under s. 55(1) where mandatory division takes place for married couples after one year of separation only if the commencement of the separation was on or after January 1, 1987.

MEI v. Taylor (May 10, 1994), CP 2840, CEB & PG (TB) ¶8542 (PAB)

Where the CPP is not expressly mentioned in the spousal agreement, the agreement is not binding on the Minister and cannot restrain the Minister from dividing pension credits under ss. 55 and 55.1, even though it was the intent of both parties to waive any claim to each other's pension credits through the agreement.

Dominie v. MSD (June 16, 2004), CP 21228 (PAB), application for judicial review dismissed 2005 FCA 242

The Minister's six-year delay in processing the former wife's application did not alter the mandatory nature of the provisions. The waiver of CPP rights in the separation agreement between the spouses was not effective in Newfoundland.

Gainor v. MHRD (November 26, 1996), CP 3933, CEB & PG (TB) ¶8653 (PAB)

The PAB has no jurisdiction to prevent the division of pension credits where the fact that the payor husband fell on hard economic times after the matrimonial breakdown and signing of the separation agreement.

MHRD v. Grail (November 6, 2001), CP 09559 (PAB). See also *Poirier v. MHRD* (August 7, 2001), CP 14597 (PAB)

The PAB did not have discretion to cancel the division of unadjusted pensionable earnings even where the parties had clearly attempted to settle their affairs in a settlement agreement and the applying spouse died six months after the pension was divided.

§3. Living Separate and Apart Before January 1, 1987

MHRD v. Jackman (July 17, 2001), CP 16276 (PAB). See also *Heschl v. MHRD* (August 29, 2001), CP 12028 (PAB)

Division of unadjusted pensionable earning credits is mandatory where a decree absolute of divorce occurring after 1986, even though separation took place prior to 1986, except in those provinces where the parties may waive the division. The Minister has no discretion not to divide once it is informed of the divorce.

Christensen v. MSD (May 4, 2004), CP 21785 (PAB)

A couple had separated prior to January 1, 1987, and had never obtained a final divorce order. After the husband died suddenly in 2001, the wife was not entitled to apply for a division of CPP credits under s. 55.1. The parties' 1986 separation agreement, under which they agreed that contributions made by them to the date of the agreement to the CPP should be distributed evenly between them, did not give the Minister discretion to make a division of unadjusted pensionable earnings otherwise than in accordance with the CPP.

Schlaepfer v. MHRD (April 9, 2003), CP 12615 (PAB)

Credibility is an issue when determining the date on which the parties ceased to cohabit. The parties may be found to have continued cohabitating despite living in different cities.

Blais v. Blais (January 25, 1996), CP 3860, 4003, CEB & PG (TB) ¶8601 (PAB)

Where the common-law partners began to live separate and apart considerably prior to January 1, 1987, albeit still living under the same roof, they did not come within s. 55.1 and neither could apply for a division of pension credits.

MHRD v. O'Halloran (September 24, 1996), CP 4407, CEB & PG (TB) ¶8657 (PAB)

Section 55.1 applies only to spouses, whether married or common-law, who separated after 1986. It did not have retrospective effect to allow legal spouses who had separated prior to 1987 to apply for a division of pension credits.

§4. Procedure

MHRD v. Wiemer, [1998] FCJ No. 809, 228 N.R. 341, 42 R.F.L. (4th) 242 (Fed. C.A.)

There is no requirement under the CPP that approval of an application for a division of unadjusted pensionable earnings be given by the Minister personally. Under s. 24(2) of the *Interpretation Act*, powers given to a Minister to do an act or a thing can be exercised by a person appointed to serve in the department over which the Minister presides in a capacity appropriate to the doing of the act. This merely recognizes in legislation an existing practice dictated by the diversity and complexities of modern public administrations. An official form issued by the Division of Unadjusted Pensionable Earnings ("Pension Credits") CPP and signed by a person in a section reserved to office use only under a heading called "Authorized Signature" is presumptively sufficient. The onus then shifts to the party challenging the approval to adduce evidence that the person who signed was not authorized to sign the approval and which could have, if not rebutted, at least sufficiently undermined the presumption of validity which attaches to the signature of an official document so as to displace the burden and put on governmental officials the obligation to establish the validity of the signature as well as the existence of a proper authority vested in the signatory. Mere unsubstantiated allegations or speculations are not sufficient to displace the presumed authority under s. 24(2) of the *Interpretation Act* and the presumption of validity of the signature.

MHRD v. Woodcock, [2002] FCA 296

Under section 55.1, the only right that arises automatically upon divorce is the right to apply for an attribution of pension credits, and the attribution itself depends upon an application being made. There is nothing in the CPP that would preclude the Minister from recognizing a retrospective s. 55.1 attribution where the former s. 44(1)(*b*)(iv)) [now s. 44(1)(*b*)(ii)] requires eligibility for a disability pension to be determined on the basis of a hypothetical application as of some earlier date. A s. 55.1 attribution may therefore be given retrospective effect where the former s. 44(1)(*b*)(iv) [now s. 44(1)(*b*)(ii)] applies because of a late disability pension application, but only if the facts of the case make it reasonable to presume that the application for the disability pension and the s. 55.1 application would have been submitted at or about the same time, and there is no reason to conclude that the s. 55.1 application would not have been accepted if it had been made at that time.

Naslovar v. MHRD (September 2007), CP 24392 (PAB)

Where a DUPE application is made following a post-1986 divorce, no withdrawal of the application is permitted, even if both parties wish to withdraw it.

Strezov v. Canada (Attorney General), 2007 FC 417

While the Minister does have the power to grant relief under s. 66(4) where someone has been given erroneous advice, the Minister can only do so where the effect of the erroneous advice is to deny the individual a benefit, including a division of pensionable earnings, to which the person would otherwise have been entitled. Relief was not available to cancel a split of pension credits where Ministry staff had allegedly told a claimant that her pension credits would not be split if the result was not favourable to her.

Canada (Attorney General) v. Leer, 2012 FC 932

The only real distinction between ss. 55 and 55.1 is their application to the dissolution of relationships in different periods. The result is the same regardless of whether s. 55.1 and the related provision of s. 55.2(8) was formally applied. The fact that a decision may have been erroneously based on s. 55 rather than s. 55.1 was not in itself grounds for granting leave to appeal, where the outcome would have been the same.

Cornwell v. MHRD (September 8, 2003), CP 19665 (PAB)

The spouse of the applicant for a division of credits was not entitled to apply for a cancellation of the division 8 years after the application, even where the applicant spouse had died three weeks after the effective date of the division and never received any increased benefit from the division. However, the estate of the applicant spouse did receive an increased death benefit as a result of the division.

Dominie v. MSD (June 16, 2004), CP 21228 (PAB), application for judicial review dismissed 2005 FCA 242

The former wife's estate, for which the former husband was the executor and sole beneficiary, was not entitled to withdraw the wife's application for a division of CPP credits made before she died. Section 45(3) of the Canada Pension Plan Regulations does not apply to divorced spouses as the legislative intent was that credit splitting be mandatory and automatic following a divorce. Since after divorce no application is required to activate a credit split, there can be no application to withdraw.

§5. Canadian Charter of Rights and Freedoms

Moore v. MSD (April 6, 2006), CP 21922 (PAB)

A claimant's differential treatment based upon his "province of residence" does not give rise to a Charter argument of discrimination. Differential treatment resulting from the proper exercise of constitutional powers cannot be the subject of a challenge under s. 15 of the Charter on the basis only that it creates distinctions based upon province of residence. Section 55.1 of the CPP does not amount to a distinction which is based upon a "personal characteristic" for the purpose of s. 15 of the Charter.

Conway v. MHRD (February 17, 1998), CP 04447, CEB & PG (TB) ¶8704 (PAB)

While the four-year limitation on applications by common-law spouses (now partners) under s. 55.1(1)(c) violates the equality rights of common-law partners vis-à-vis legal spouses, who are under no such limitation, the discrimination was demonstrably justified in a free and democratic society given the pressing and substantial objective of striking a balance between the rights of common-law spouses.

55.11. *Application of section 55.1* — **Section 55.1 applies**

(a) in respect of judgments granting a divorce and judgments of nullity of a marriage, rendered on or after January 1, 1987; (S.C. 2012, c. 31, s. 199.)

(b) in respect of spouses and former spouses who commence to live separate and apart on or after January 1, 1987 but before the coming into force of this section ("spouse" having in this paragraph the meaning that it had immediately before that coming into force); and

(c) in respect of spouses and former common-law partners who commence to live separate and apart after the coming into force of this section.

(R.S.C. 1985, c. 30 (2nd Supp.), s. 23; S.C. 2012, c. 31, s. 199.)

———————— **Notes** ————————

Synopsis

This section establishes that the following persons may seek a division under s. 55.1: (i) spouses and former spouses who obtain decrees absolute and judgments granting a divorce or judgments granting a nullity of a marriage after January 1, 1987, (ii) spouses and former spouses (including opposite sex common-law partners) who commence living separate and apart after January 1, 1987 and prior to July 31, 2000, and (iii) spouses and former spouses or former common-law partners who commence living separate and apart after July 31, 2000.

Case Law

R.H. v. MHRSD (March 15, 2010), CP 06689 (PAB)

The limitation in what is now s. 55.11(b) on eligibility for a division of unadjusted pensionable earnings (DUPE) to married couples separated on or after January 1, 1987 does not violate s. 15 equality guarantee under the Charter. The DUPE provisions did not create a distinction on the basis of a personal characteristic required in order to show an infringement of s. 15(1) of the Charter. Even if the DUPE provisions were found to be discriminatory, any Charter breach would be a justifiable limit on the appellant's rights under s. 1 of the Charter. In any case, the applicant was not entitled to have the Charter applied retrospectively to a separation that occurred in 1984, before s. 15 of the Charter came into force in April 1985.

Y.A.O. v. MHRSD v. D.O. (May 30, 2011), CP 26786 (PAB)

Where the parties had governed themselves by the terms of a 1998 separation agreement that cited they were living separate and apart since 1986, they could not avail themselves of s. 55.11 (which governs the application of s. 55.1) without showing they had resumed cohabitation after December 1986.

55.2. *Definition of "spousal agreement"* — **(1) (Repealed by 2000, c. 12, s. 48(1).)**

(2) *Spousal agreement or court order not binding on Minister* — **Except as provided in subsection (3) where, on or after June 4, 1986, a written agreement between persons subject to a division under section 55 or 55.1 was entered into, or a court order was made, the provisions of that agreement or court order are not binding on the Minister for the purposes of a division of unadjusted pensionable earnings under section 55 or 55.1. (S.C. 2000, c. 12, s. 48(2).)**

(3) *Spousal agreement binding on Minister* — **Where**

(a) a written agreement between persons subject to a division under section 55 or 55.1 entered into on or after June 4, 1986 contains a provision that expressly mentions this Act and indicates the intention of the persons that there be no division of unadjusted pensionable earnings under section 55 or 55.1,

(b) that provision of the agreement is expressly permitted under the provincial law that governs such agreement,

(c) the agreement was entered into

(i) in the case of a division under section 55 or paragraph 55.1(1)(b) or (c), before the day of the application for the division, or

(ii) in the case of a division under paragraph 55.1(1)(a), before the rendering of the judgment granting a divorce or the judgment of nullity of the marriage, as the case may be, and (S.C. 2012, c. 31, s. 200(1).)

(d) that provision of the agreement has not been invalidated by a court order,

that provision of the agreement is binding on the Minister and, consequently, shall not make a division under section 55 or 55.1. (S.C. 2000, c. 12, s. 48(2).)

(4) *Minister to notify parties* — The Minister shall, without delay after being informed of a judgment granting a divorce or a judgment of nullity of a marriage or after receiving an application under section 55 or paragraph 55.1(1)(b) or (c), notify each of the persons subject to the division, in the prescribed manner, of the periods of unadjusted pensionable earnings to be divided, and of any other information that the Minister considers necessary. (S.C. 2000, c. 12, s. 48(2); 2012, c. 31, s. 200(2).)

(5) *Division of unadjusted pensionable earnings* — Where there is a division under section 55.1, the unadjusted pensionable earnings for each person subject to the division for the period of cohabitation attributable to contributions made under this Act, determined in the same manner as the total pensionable earnings attributable to contributions made under this Act are determined in section 78, shall be added and then divided equally, and the unadjusted pensionable earnings so divided shall be attributed to each person. (S.C. 1991, c. 44, s. 8(1); 2000, c. 12, s. 48(2).)

(6) *Effect of division* — Where there is a division under section 55.1 and under a provincial pension plan, for the purposes of benefit calculation and payment under this Act, the total unadjusted pensionable earnings of a contributor for a year of division shall be the aggregate of his unadjusted pensionable earnings attributed under subsection (5) and his unadjusted pensionable earnings attributed under a provincial pension plan.

(7) *Provincial pension plans* — No division under section 55.1 shall be made for any month during which the persons subject to the division cohabited and for which either of them contributed to a provincial pension plan (and, for the purposes of this subsection, months during which the persons cohabited shall be determined in the prescribed manner), unless the unadjusted pensionable earnings attributed to the persons under the provincial pension plan are divided for that month in a manner substantially similar to that described in this section and section 55.1. (S.C. 1991, c. 44, s. 8(2); 2000, c. 12, s. 48(3).)

(8) *No division* — No division under section 55.1 for a period of cohabitation of the persons subject to the division shall be made

(a) for a year in which the total unadjusted pensionable earnings of the persons does not exceed twice the Year's Basic Exemption;

(b) for the period before which one of the persons reached eighteen years of age or after which one of the persons reached seventy years of age;

(c) for the period in which one of the persons was a beneficiary of a retirement pension under this Act or under a provincial pension plan; and

(d) for any month that is excluded from the contributory period of one of the persons under this Act or a provincial plan by reason of disability.

(S.C. 2000, c. 12, s. 48(3).)

(9) *Payment of benefit* — **Where there is a division under section 55.1 and a benefit is or becomes payable under this Act to or in respect of either of the persons subject to the division for a month not later than the month following the month in which the division takes place, the basic amount of the benefit shall be calculated and adjusted in accordance with section 46 and adjusted in accordance with subsection 45(2) but subject to the division, and the adjusted benefit shall be paid effective the month following the month in which the division takes place but in no case shall a benefit that was not payable in the absence of the division be paid in respect of the month in which the division takes place or any prior month. (S.C. 1991, c. 44, s. 8(3); 2000, c. 12, s. 48(3).)**

(10) *Notification of division* — **Where there is a division under section 55.1, both persons subject to the division, or their respective estates shall be notified in the prescribed manner. (S.C. 1991, c. 44, s. 8(3); 1995, c. 33, s. 28; 2000, c. 12, s. 48(3).)**

(11) *Regulations* — **The Governor in Council may make regulations prescribing**
  (a) the time, manner and form of making applications for a division of unadjusted pensionable earnings or withdrawal of applications for such division;
  (b) the procedures to be followed in dealing with and approving such applications and the information and evidence to be furnished in connection therewith; and
  (c) the effective dates of the approval or taking place of a division and of the attribution of pensionable earnings following a division. (S.C. 1991, c. 44, s. 8(4).)

(R.S.C. 1985, c. 30 (2nd Supp.), s. 23; 1991, c. 44, s. 8; 1995, c. 33, s. 28; 1997, c. 40, s. 73; 2000, c. 12, s. 48; 2012, c. 31, s. 200.)

————————— **Notes** —————————

Synopsis

This section deals with the extent to which the Division of Unadjusted Pensionable Earnings ("DUPE") is affected by provisions in separation agreements and court orders which purport to allocate property between the spouses following the breakdown of a conjugal relationship. Written agreements between persons signed before June 4, 1986, which are intended to settle all property matters between the parties, preclude such division. However, written agreements between person signed on or after June 4, 1986 cannot prevent division unless (i) the terms of the agreement expressly mentions the CPP and the parties' intention that no division be made, (ii) such a provision is expressly permitted under the provincial law governing the agreement, and (iii) the provision of the agreement has not been invalidated by a court order.

To date, the following provinces have enacted DUPE opt-out provisions as part of their respective matrimonial property regimes:

Quebec — The registered earnings under the QPP or "similar plans" of each spouse during the marriage form part of the family patrimony, by virtue of Article 415 in the *Civil Code*. Article 423 (in force July 1, 1989) states:

423. The spouses may not, by way of their marriage contract or otherwise, renounce their rights in the family patrimony.

One spouse may, however, from the death of the other spouse or from the judgment of divorce, separation from bed and board or nullity of marriage, renounce such rights, in whole or in part, by notarial act *en minute*; that spouse may also renounce them by a judicial declaration which is recorded, in the course of proceedings for divorce, separation from bed and board or nullity of marriage. (S.C. 1992, c. 57, s. 716(2).)

Renunciation shall be entered in the register of personal and movable real rights. Failing entry within a period of one year from the time when the right to partition arose, the renouncing spouse is deemed to have accepted.

(S.C. 1992, c. 57, s. 716(2).)

Canada Pension Plan

Saskatchewan — Section 38(5) of the *Matrimonial Property Act, 1997,* S.S. 1997, c. M-6.11, (in force January 1, 1987) states:

38. *Interspousal contracts. —*

* * *

(5) Without limiting the generality of subsection (4), an interspousal contract entered into on or after June 4, 1986 may provide that, notwithstanding the *Canada Pension Plan,* there may be no division between the parties of unadjusted pensionable earnings pursuant to that Act.

British Columbia — Section 62 of the *Family Relations Act,* R.S.B.C. c. 128 (in force July 1, 1995) states:

62. *Canada Pension Plan. —* A marriage agreement or other written agreement between spouses entered into on or after June 4, 1986 may provide that, despite the *Canada Pension Plan,* there be no division of unadjusted pensionable earnings under that Act.

Alberta — Effective 2005, s. 82.2 of the *Family Law Act,* S.A. 2003, c. F-4.5 permits spouses to waive credit splitting by agreement in writing. The provision states:

82.2. *Agreement re unadjusted pensionable earnings.*–A written agreement between spouses or common-law partners entered into on or after June 4, 1986 may provide that, notwithstanding the *Canada Pension Plan* (Canada), there be no division between the parties of unadjusted pensionable earnings pursuant to that Act.

It is uncertain whether the provincial legislation can retroactively approve a waiver contained in a separation agreement signed before such legislation came into effect. In *Dortman,* the PAB expressly refused to rule on this point. The calculation of the amount of the unadjusted pensionable earnings to be divided is made be taking the total pensionable earnings attributable to each person's CPP contributions that are subject to the division and dividing it equally (s. 55.2(5)).

No DUPE will be made for a period of cohabitation:

(a) where the total unadjusted pensionable earnings of the persons in a year does not exceed twice the basic exemption ($3,500 $\times$ 2 = $7,000 in 2001);

(b) for the period prior to one of the person turning 18;

(c) for the period after one of the spouses or former spouses turns 70;

(d) for the period when one of the persons was a beneficiary of a CPP or QPP retirement benefit; and

(e) for any month excluded from one of the person's CPP or QPP contributory period due to disability.

Where there is a DUPE, both persons subject to the division or their respective estates must be notified in writing (s. 55.2(10)).

Recent Amendments

Before the 2000 amendment that extended the scope of the CPP to include same-sex relationships, s. 55.2 referred to "spousal" agreements.

Related Provisions

● Section 66(5) — Where person denied division because of written agreement

● Section 81 — Request for reconsideration by Minister

Related CPP Regulations

● Section 46 — Notification in writing

Case Law

§1. Pre-June 4, 1986 Regime

MNHW v. Preece (August 26, 1983), CEB & PG (TB) ¶8914 (PAB)

The CPP provisions permitting spouses to apply to divide pension credits do not prevent the freedom of spouses to contract out of such rights. Having given complete releases from further claims in a settlement agreement, minutes of settlement or a consent judgment, spouses are precluded from subsequently applying for and receiving a division of pension benefits.

MHRD v. Brickman (August 27, 1997), CP 4410 (PAB)

The existence of negotiations regarding a division of the CPP credits prior to June 4, 1986 did not meet the standard for an enforceable oral or written separation agreement under Ontario law.

Sands v. Sands (January 31, 1989), CP 1511, CEB & PG (TB) ¶8559 (PAB)

Where the language in a separation agreement is unclear, its interpretation is not dependent on the use of any magic words. The issue is whether the cumulative effect of the relevant clauses taken in the context of the whole agreement leads to the conclusion that the parties intended to resolve all property and financial matters arising out of their marriage.

MNHW v. Fielden (July 28, 1988), CEB & PG (TB) ¶8548 (PAB)

The PAB was bound by the law as expressed in the CPP, and not by statements of policy contained in a brochure issued by the Minister of Health and Welfare as to the divisibility of pension credits. Where the clauses in minutes of settlement signed before the Preese decision in 1983 indicated a clear intention to resolve all matters arising out of the parties' marriage, including any rights under the CPP, division was not permitted.

Clemenshaw v. Clemenshaw (January 24, 2000), CP 09042 (PAB)

While s. 66 gives the Minister, *but not the Board*, discretion to take "remedial action" where pre-June 4, 1986 settlement agreements exist, it does not provide that the other spouse's pension credits will be divided. Section 66 therefore only allows the Minister in rare cases to give an applicant an *ex gratia* pension without depriving the other spouse of his or her full pension. Parliament did not intend to negate *Preece* and make pre-June 4, 1986 agreements subject to the same conditions as s. 55.2(2) and (3).

§2. Post-June 4, 1986 Regime

Moore v. MSD (April 6, 2006), CP 21922 (PAB)

The distinction in s. 55.2(3) based on "province of residence" is constitutional. "Province of residence" is not an analogous ground of discrimination under s. 15 of the Charter. "Province of residence" has no bearing on whether a DUPE can be cancelled. A claimant's province of residence at the time an agreement is signed is only one of the factors to be used to determine who can contract out of mandatory DUPE provisions. It is not the sole determining factor. Once a DUPE has been made, the CPP provides the Minister with discretion to cancel that division in very limited circumstances. The Minister's inability to cancel the DUPE years after it has been effected is not based upon an applicant's province of residence at any time.

MHRSD v. C.C. (October 22, 2010), CP 26589 (PAB)

Section 55.2(9) comes into play when a benefit becomes payable as a result of a division of unadjusted pensionable earnings. Where the claimant needed this division, particularly the unadjusted pensionable earnings attributed to her record of earnings, to achieve an MQP that entitled her to apply for a disability pension, disability pension payments would commence the month after the claimant applied for DUPE, regardless of when she applied for the disability pension itself. The statutory limit created by s. 55.2(9) prevents the ordinary retroactivity rules from applying and limits the disability award to the future period from and after the month of application for DUPE.

MHRD v. Steinke (November 7, 2000), CP 07078 (PAB)

By virtue of s. 55.2(9), a claimant whose entitlement to receive benefits was dependent on her successful application for DUPE while her previous claim for a disability pension was making its way through the appeal process, was not entitled to have the commencement of payments backdated to 15 months before the application for benefits. The benefits could only start in the month after the DUPE took place.

Asner v. Asner and MHRD (November 1996), CP 4574, CEB & PG (TB) ¶8654 (PAB)

Ontario has not enacted legislation permitting agreements not to apply for DUPE. Under Ontario law, separation agreements are void unless made in writing. Where there was no agreement between the spouses prior to June 4, 1986, except regarding the quantum of support, one spouse may apply for a DUPE despite the existence of a 1987 agreement that specifically forbid such an application.

Canada Pension Plan

249

MHRD v. Dortman (January 10, 2000), CP 08891 (PAB). See also *Unger v. MHRD* (August 21, 2001), CP 13857 (PAB); *Bort v. MHRD* (June 29, 2001), CP 15060 (PAB).

Only strict compliance with the legislation will trigger the binding effect of "the waiver" on the Minister. A provision in a separation agreement that does not expressly mention the CPP or indicate any intention one way or the other that there would be no DUPE could not constitute a waiver.

MNHW v. Blackwood (June 16, 1992), CP 2326, CEB & PG (TB) ¶9223 (PAB)

The purpose of s. 55.2 is to make spousal agreements ineffective to determine whether or not the Minister divides the pension, unless expressly permitted by provincial legislation. Although the *Matrimonial Property Act* in Alberta does purport to release the parties to a property settlement from future claims by the other party, the Act does not mention pensions and therefore does not give the necessary "express" permission to allow spousal waivers. The CPP must be mentioned explicitly to engage s. 55.2(3), as it is in the *Saskatchewan Act.*

Blackwood v. MNHW (1993), 3 R.F.L. (4th) 337, 169 N.R. 236 (C.A.)

Sections 55.2(3)(*a*) and (*b*) are not unconstitutional, being valid legislation in relation to old age pensions and supplementary benefits pursuant to section 94A of the *Constitution Act, 1867.*

§3. Notice to Parties

Greco v. MHRD (October 23, 2002), CP 18977 (PAB)

Notice to both parties required by s. 55.2(4) was fundamental. The PAB determined that the husband did not receive notice as required by the CPP. A letter in the Minister's file purporting to notify the pension-holding spouse did not constitute evidence that it had been mailed to the spouse or received by him.

Obiter. The method and means of service of notice should be set out in the legislation.

55.3. *Incapacity* — [32](1) **Where an application for a division of unadjusted pensionable earnings is made under subsection 55(1) or paragraph 55.1(1)(*b*) or (*c*) or the Minister receives the prescribed information referred to in paragraph 55.1(1)(*a*) and the Minister is satisfied, on the basis of evidence provided by or on behalf of a person subject to the division, that the person had been incapable of forming or expressing an intention to make an application or to provide the information to the Minister on the day on which the application was actually made or the information was actually received, the Minister may deem the application to have been made or the information to have been received in the first month in which a division could have taken place or in the month that the Minister considers the person's last relevant period of incapacity to have commenced, whichever is the later. (S.C. 2000, c. 12, s. 49.)**

(2) *Idem* — **Where an application for a division of unadjusted pensionable earnings is made under subsection 55(1) or paragraph 55.1(1)(*b*) or (*c*) or the Minister receives the prescribed information referred to in paragraph 55.1(1)(*a*) and the Minister is satisfied, on the basis of evidence provided by or on behalf of a person subject to the division, that**

(a) the person had been incapable of forming or expressing an intention to make an application or to provide the information to the Minister before the day on which the application was actually made or the information was actually received by the Minister,

(b) the person had ceased to be so incapable before that day, and

(c) the application was actually made or the information was actually received by the Minister

(i) within the period that begins on the day on which the person had ceased to be so incapable and that comprises the same number of days, not exceeding twelve months, as in the period of incapacity, or

---

[32] Pursuant to 1991, c. 44, s. 9(*b*), section 55.3 applies only to individuals who are incapacitated on or after January 1, 1991.

(ii) **where the period referred to in subparagraph (i) comprises fewer than thirty days, not more than one month after the month in which the person had ceased to be so incapable,**

the Minister may deem the application to have been made or the information to have been received in the first month in which a division could have taken place or in the month in which the Minister considers the person's last relevant period of incapacity to have commenced, whichever is the later. (S.C. 2000, c. 12, s. 49.)

(3) *Period of incapacity* — **For the purposes of subsections (1) and (2), a period of incapacity must be a continuous period except as otherwise prescribed.**

(4) *Application* — **This section applies only to individuals who were incapacitated on or after January 1, 1991.**

(S.C. 1991, c. 44, s. 9.)

—————— Notes ——————

Synopsis

Where one of the parties is not capable of forming or expressing an intention to apply for division of unadjusted pensionable earnings, this section provides authority for the Minister to deem an application for a division to have been brought in the first month where a division could have taken place.

Recent Amendments

The 2000 amendments deleted the reference to "spouse or former spouse" so that the section now refers to a "person" who may be subject to a division of unadjusted pensionable earnings under ss. 55 or 55.1, which in the case of s. 55.1 can now include a same-sex partner.

Related Provisions

● Section 81 — Request for reconsideration by Minister

Case Law

MHRD v. Balding, (March 31, 2003), CP 17439 (PAB)

Section 55.3 deals with incapacity for the purpose of deeming of an earlier date of application, and not for the purpose of deeming an application null and void. It did not give the Minister the authority to consider an application null and void on the basis of capacity or incapacity.

Doherty v. MEI (July 15, 1996), CP 4207, CEB & PG (TB) ¶8651 (PAB)

The Review Tribunal and the PAB have jurisdiction to review a s. 55.3 Ministerial decision, by virtue of ss. 82 and 83. The 36-month limitation must govern where W was clearly aware and was capable of forming the intention to apply for a division of credits during the period. W had suffered long-standing physical abuse during the marriage and did not apply until after death of former H, 10 years after divorce, although she had taken steps to apply during that period. The fact that W had been dissuaded from carrying out her intention to apply meant that she could not bring herself within the strict and narrow confines of the remedial provisions of s. 55.3.

Obiter: This is not to say that the fear of spousal retribution could never operate to create an incapacity in a spouse to form the requisite intention.

Hoar v. MSD (April 10, 2006), CP 13993 (PAB)

Section 55.3 is not a transitional rule, but was crafted to bridge the old rules that made no allowance for mental incapacity and new rules (s. 55.3) that did. The cut-off date is the time the legislation came into force. The provision was made effective to a date a year before the legislation came into force in order that the provision allowing a person up to one year within which to apply after regaining capacity, could operate immediately. The different treatment of those injured before or after January 1, 1991 did not violate s. 15 of the *Canadian Charter of Rights and Freedoms.*

Greco v. MHRD (October 23, 2002), CP 18977 (PAB)

Notice to both parties required by s. 55.2(4) was fundamental. The PAB determined that the husband did not receive notice as required by the CPP. A letter in the Minister's file purporting to notify the pension-holding spouse did not constitute evidence that it had been mailed to the spouse or received by him. *Obiter.* The method and means of service of notice should be set out in the legislation.

MHRSD v. T.O. (September 24, 2008), CP 25465 (PAB)

The claimant's depression, obsessive compulsive disorder and attention deficit disorder resulted in incapacity to complete forms and incapacity to form the intention to make an application for DUPE.

Disability Pension

56. *Amount of disability pension* — [33]**(1) A disability pension payable to a contributor is a basic monthly amount consisting of**

(a) **a flat rate benefit, calculated as provided in subsection (2); and**

(b) **seventy-five per cent of the amount of the contributor's retirement pension calculated as provided in this section.**

(2) *Calculation of flat rate benefit* — **The amount of the flat rate benefit mentioned in paragraph (1)(a) is**

(a) **in the case of a flat rate benefit commencing to be payable for a month in the year 1986, ninety-one dollars and six cents;**

(b) **in the case of a flat rate benefit payable for a month in the year 1987, an amount calculated by multiplying**

(i) **two hundred and thirty-three dollars and thirty-eight cents**

by

(ii) **the ratio that the Pension Index for 1987 bears to the Pension Index for 1986; and**

(c) **in the case of a flat rate benefit commencing to be payable for a month in the year 1988 or any subsequent year, an amount calculated by multiplying**

(i) **the amount of the flat rate benefit that would have been payable for a month in the year preceding that year**

by

(ii) **the ratio that the Pension Index for the year in which the benefit commences to be payable bears to the Pension Index for the year preceding that year.**

(3) *Calculation of contributor's retirement pension* — **The amount of the contributor's retirement pension to be used for the purpose of paragraph (1)(b) is an amount equal to twenty-five per cent of his average monthly pensionable earnings calculated as provided in subsections (4) and (5).**

(4) *Average monthly pensionable earnings* — **For the purposes of subsection (3), the average monthly pensionable earnings of a contributor who is deemed to have become disabled for the purposes of this Act after December 31, 1997 is, subject to subsections 48(2) and (4), the amount obtained by dividing**

(a) **the contributor's total pensionable earnings**

by

---

[33] Pursuant to R.S.C. 1985, c. 30 (2nd Supp.), s. 24(2), subsection 56(1):

(a) insofar as it amends the method of calculating a flat rate benefit, applies regardless of whether the contributor is determined to be disabled for the purpose of paragraph 44(1)(b) of the said Act before or after the end of December, 1986; and

(b) insofar as it amends the method of calculating a contributor's retirement pension, applies only in respect of contributors who are determined to be disabled for the purpose of paragraph 44(1)(b) of the said Act on or after January 1, 1987.

(*b*) the total number of months in the contributor's contributory period or 48, whichever is greater.

(S.C. 1997, c. 40, s. 74.)

(**4.1**) *Average monthly pensionable earnings* — For the purposes of subsection (3), the average monthly pensionable earnings of a contributor who is deemed to have become disabled for the purposes of this Act in 1997 is, subject to subsections 48(2) and (4), the amount obtained by dividing

(*a*) the contributor's total pensionable earnings

by

(*b*) the total number of months in the contributor's contributory period or 24, whichever is greater.

(S.C. 1997, c. 40, s. 74.)

(**5**) *Contributory period* — For the purposes of subsection (4), the contributory period of a contributor is the period

(*a*) commencing January 1, 1966 or when he reaches eighteen years of age, whichever is the later, and

(*b*) ending with the month in which he is determined to have become disabled for the purpose of paragraph 44(1)(*b*),

but excluding

(*c*) any month that was excluded from the contributor's contributory period under this Act or under a provincial pension plan by reason of disability, and

(*d*) in relation to any benefits payable under this Act for any month after December, 1977, any month for which he was a family allowance recipient in a year for which his unadjusted pensionable earnings were equal to or less than his basic exemption for the year.

(**6**) *Where division of unadjusted pensionable earnings occurs* — The amount of the contributor's retirement pension to be used for the purpose of paragraph (1)(*b*), in the case of a contributor in respect of whom a division of unadjusted pensionable earnings takes place either before or after the commencement of the disability pension, where the division reduces the disability pension otherwise payable, shall be calculated by dividing (S.C. 1991, c. 44, s. 10.)

(*a*) the aggregate of

(i) the amount of the contributor's retirement pension calculated in accordance with subsections (3) to (5) before the division, multiplied by the aggregate of

(A) the number of months that have been excluded from the contributor's contributory period under this Act or a provincial pension plan by reason of disability, and

(B) the number of months remaining until the month in which the contributor reaches sixty-five years of age,

and

(ii) the amount of the contributor's retirement pension calculated in accordance with subsections (3) to (5) following the division, multiplied by the number of months in the contributor's contributory period calculated in accordance with subsection (5)

by

(*b*) the aggregate of

(i) the number of months that have been excluded from the contributor's contributory period under this Act or under a provincial pension plan by reason of disability,

Canada Pension Plan

253

   (ii) **the number of months remaining until the month in which the contributor reaches sixty-five years of age, and**

   (iii) **the number of months in the contributor's contributory period calculated in accordance with subsection (5).**

(R.S.C. 1985, c. 30 (2nd Supp.), s. 24; 1991, c. 44, s. 10; 1997, c. 40, s. 74.)

———————— **Notes** ————————

Synopsis

   This section sets out the formula for determining the monthly disability pension for individual contributors. There are two components: (i) a flat-rate benefit, and (ii) an earnings-related component of 75% of a person's retirement pension entitlement, equal to 25% of the person's average monthly pensionable earnings. The flat-rate component is indexed to the year-to-year Pension Index increase (if any). For persons deemed to have become disabled after December 31, 1997, the retirement pension is calculated by dividing the person's total pensionable earnings by the greater of 48 or the total number of months in the contributory period. Combining these amounts, the 2014 maximum monthly CPP disability pension is $1,236.35. The contributory period begins with the later of the month in which the contributor turns 18 or January 1, 1966, and ends with the month in which he or she became disabled, but excludes months when the contributory was receiving disability pension, or family allowance payments in a year in which the contributor's earnings were less than the basic exemption for that year (s. 56(5)). Special rules address the situation where a division of the unadjusted pensionable earnings has taken place (s. 56(6)).

Related Provisions

   ● Section 42(2) — When person deemed disabled

   ● Section 44(1)(*b*) — Entitlement to disability pension

   ● Section 60 — Application for benefit

   ● Section 69 — Commencement of disability pension

   ● Section 70 — When disability pension ceases to be payable

   ● Section 77 — Amount payable under CPP where receiving from other plan

   ● Section 81 — Request for reconsideration by Minister

————————————————

Death Benefit

   57. *Amount of death benefit* **— (1) Subject to subsection (1.1), a death benefit payable to the estate of a contributor is a lump sum amount equal to (S.C. 1997, c. 40, s. 75(1).)**

   (*a*) **six times the amount of the contributor's retirement pension, calculated as provided in subsection (2), or**

   (*b*) **ten per cent of the Year's Maximum Pensionable Earnings for the year in which the contributor died,**

whichever is the lesser.

   (1.1) *Maximum in cases of death after December 31, 1997* **— Where the contributor's death occurs after December 31, 1997, the lump sum referred to in subsection (1) shall not exceed $2,500. (S.C. 1997, c. 40, s. 75(2).)**

   (2) *Calculation of contributor's retirement pension* **— The amount of the contributor's retirement pension to be used for the purposes of subsection (1) is**

   (*a*) **in the case of a contributor who died before January 1, 1987 and to whom a retirement pension was payable for the month in which he died, the amount of such pension for that month, but where that contributor's contributory period ended before January 1976, the amount is the amount of the retirement pension payable for the month in which he died multiplied by the ratio that the** basic number of contributory months bears to the number of months in the contributor's contributory period;

(*b*) in the case of a contributor who died before January 1, 1987 and to whom no retirement pension was payable for the month in which he died, an amount equal to twenty-five per cent of his average monthly pensionable earnings, calculated as provided in sections 46 to 53 except that, in making that calculation,

(i) subsection 46(3) to (6) and section 47 are not applicable,

(ii) subsection 48(1) shall be read as follows:

"Sec. 48. (1) Subject to subsections (2), (3) and (4), the average monthly pensionable earnings of a contributor are an amount calculated by dividing his total pensionable earnings by the total number of months in his contributory period, and"

(iii) section 51 shall be read as though for the reference therein to the year in which a benefit becomes payable to the contributor there were substituted a reference to the year in which the contributor died; and

(*c*) [34]in the case of a contributor who died on or after January 1, 1987,

(i) where a retirement pension was not payable for the month in which the contributor died, an amount equal to twenty-five per cent of his average monthly pensionable earnings, calculated as provided in subsection (3), or

(ii) where a retirement pension was payable for the month in which the contributor died, the product obtained by multiplying

(A) an amount equal to twenty-five per cent of his average monthly pensionable earnings, calculated as provided in subsection (3),

by

(B) the ratio that the Pension Index for the year that includes that month bears to the Pension Index for the year in which the retirement pension first became payable, calculated, where the year in which the retirement pension first became payable was prior to 1974, as if the Pension Index for that year had not been subject to the limitation referred to in paragraph 43.1(2)(*a*) of the *Canada Pension Plan*, chapter C-5 of the Revised Statutes of Canada, 1970, of 1.02 times the Pension Index for the preceding year. (S.C. 1991, c. 44, s. 11(1).)

(R.S.C. 1985, c. 30 (2nd Supp.), s. 25.)

(3) *Calculation of average monthly pensionable earnings* — Subject to subsections 48(2), (3) and (4), the average monthly pensionable earnings of a contributor is an amount calculated by dividing his total pensionable earnings by the total number of months in his contributory period or by thirty-six, whichever is greater, and

(*a*) in the case of a contributor to whom a retirement pension was payable for the month in which he died, section 51 applies; or

(*b*) in the case of a contributor to whom no retirement pension was payable for the month in which he died, section 51 applies but the reference therein to the year in which a benefit becomes payable to the contributor shall be read as a reference to the year in which the contributor died.

(R.S.C. 1985, c. 30 (2nd Supp.), s. 25; 1991, c. 44, s. 11; 1997, c. 40, s. 75.)

[34] Pursuant to 1991, c. 44, s. 11(2), subsection 57(2)(*c*)(ii)(B) applies in respect of the calculation of any benefits payable or becoming payable on or after January 27, 1992.

———————— **Notes** ————————

Synopsis

This section sets out the formula for calculating the death benefit to which the survivor or the estate of a deceased contributor is entitled. If the contributor dies on or after January 1, 1998, essentially the amount is a lump sum payment of six times the contributor's monthly retirement pension to a maximum of $2,500. For contributors who die on or after January 1, 1987, calculation of the retirement pension depends on whether they were receiving a CPP retirement pension at the time of death. If not, the amount of the retirement pension for purposes of determining the death benefit equals 25% of the contributor's average monthly pensionable earnings. If so, the amount equals the average monthly pensionable earnings indexed to reflect increases in the Pension Index since the retirement pension first became payable.

Related Provisions

- Section 43 — Pension Index
- Section 44(1)(*c*) — Entitlement to death benefit
- Section 44(3) — Minimum qualifying period
- Section 51 — Calculation of pensionable earnings for a month
- Section 60 — Application for benefit
- Section 71 — Death benefit payable to estate
- Section 77 — Amount payable under CPP where receiving from other plan
- Section 81 — Request for reconsideration by Minister

Related CPP Regulations

- Section 63 — Determination of marital or filial status or death
- Section 64 — Payment of death benefit to other than estates

———————————————

Survivor's Pension

58. *Amount of survivor's pension* — **(1) Subject to this section, a survivor's pension payable to the survivor of a contributor is a basic monthly amount as follows: (S.C. 2000, c. 12, s. 64.)**

(*a*) in the case of a survivor who has not reached sixty-five years of age and to whom no retirement pension is payable under this Act or a provincial pension plan, a basic monthly amount consisting of (S.C. 2000, c. 12, s. 64.)

(i) a flat rate benefit, calculated as provided in subsection (1.1), and

(R.S.C. 1985, c. 30 (2nd Supp.), s. 26(1).)

(ii) $37^1/_2$ per cent of the amount of the contributor's retirement pension, calculated as provided in subsection (3),

reduced, unless the survivor was at the time of the death of the contributor a survivor with dependent children or unless he is disabled, by $^1/_{120}$ for each month by which the age of the survivor at the time of the death of the contributor is less than forty-five years, and reduced, if at any time after the death of the contributor the survivor ceases to be (S.C. 2000, c. 12, s. 64.)

(iii) a survivor with dependent children and is not at that time disabled, or (S.C. 2000, c. 12, s. 64.)

(iv) disabled and is not at that time a survivor with dependent children, (S.C. 2000, c. 12, s. 64.)

by $^1/_{120}$ for each month by which the age of the survivor at that time is less than forty-five years; and (S.C. 2000, c. 12, s. 64.)

(*b*) in the case of a survivor who has reached sixty-five years of age and to whom no retirement pension is payable under this Act or a provincial pension plan, a basic monthly amount equal to sixty per cent of the amount of the contributor's retirement pension, calculated as provided in subsection (3). (R.S.C. 1985, c. 30 (2nd Supp.), s. 26(2); 2000, c. 12, s. 64.)

(**1.1**) *Amount of flat rate benefit* — The amount of the flat rate benefit referred to in subparagraph (1)(*a*)(i) is

(*a*) in the year 1986, ninety-one dollars and six cents; or

(*b*) in the year 1987 or any subsequent year, an amount calculated by multiplying

(i) the amount of the flat rate benefit that would have been payable for a month in the year preceding that year

by

(ii) the ratio that the Pension Index for the year in which the flat rate benefit commences to be payable bears to the Pension Index for the year preceding that year.

(R.S.C. 1985, c. 30 (2nd Supp.), s. 26(3).)

(**2**) *Calculation of survivor's pension where retirement pension payable* — Where a survivor's pension under this Act and a retirement pension under this Act or under a provincial pension plan are payable to the survivor of a contributor, the basic monthly amount of the survivor's pension payable to the survivor is (S.C. 2000, c. 12, s. 64.)

(*a*) in the case of a survivor who has not reached sixty-five years of age and whose retirement pension commences to be payable after December 31, 1997, the aggregate of (S.C. 2000, c. 12, s. 64.)

(i) a flat rate benefit, calculated as provided in subsection (1.1), and

(ii) the lesser of

(A) the amount determined by the formula

$$C - D$$

where

C   is 37.5% of the amount of the contributor's retirement pension calculated as provided in subsection (3), and

D   is the lesser of

(I) 40% of C, and

(II) 40% of the survivor's retirement pension, calculated without regard to subsections 46(3) to (6) but in accordance with subsection 45(2), and

(B) an amount that, when added to the survivor's retirement pension (calculated without regard to subsections 46(3) to (6) but in accordance with subsection 45(2)), is equal to the amount of a benefit of 25% of $1/12$ of the survivor's Maximum Pensionable Earnings Average for the later of the year in which the surviving spouse first became qualified to receive the survivor's pension and the year in which the survivor's retirement pension commenced to be payable, adjusted in accordance with subsection 45(2) as if the benefit had commenced to be payable in the later of the year in which the survivor first became qualified to receive the survivor's pension and the year in which the survivor's retirement pension commenced to be payable;

(S.C. 1997, c. 40, s. 76(1).)

(*b*) in the case of a survivor who has not reached sixty-five years of age and whose retirement pension commences to be payable before January 1, 1998, the aggregate of

(i) a flat rate benefit, calculated as provided in subsection (1.1), and

(ii) the lesser of

(A) 37.5% of the amount of the contributor's retirement pension, calculated as provided in subsection (3), and

(B) an amount that, when added to the survivor's retirement pension (calculated without regard to subsections 46(3) to (6) but in accordance with subsection 45(2)), is equal to the amount of a benefit of 25% of $^1/_{12}$ of the average of the Year's Maximum Pensionable Earnings for the later of the year in which the survivor first became qualified to receive the survivor's pension and the year in which the survivor's retirement pension commenced to be payable, and for each of the two preceding years, adjusted in accordance with subsection 45(2) as if the benefit had commenced to be payable in the later of the year in which the survivor first became qualified to receive the survivor's pension and the year in which the survivor's retirement pension commenced to be payable; or

(S.C. 1997, c. 40, s. 76(1).)

(c) in the case of a survivor who has reached sixty-five years of age and who was born after December 31, 1932 and whose retirement pension commences to be payable after December 31, 1997, the lesser of

(i) the amount determined by the formula

$$A - B$$

where

A   is 60% of the amount of the contributor's retirement pension calculated as provided in subsection (3), and

B   is the lesser of

(I) 40% of A, and

(II) 40% of the survivor's retirement pension, calculated without regard to subsections 46(3) to (6) but in accordance with subsection 45(2), and

(ii) an amount that, when added to the survivor's retirement pension (calculated without regard to subsections 46(3) to (6) but in accordance with subsection 45(2)), is equal to the amount of a benefit of 25% of $^1/_{12}$ of the survivor's Maximum Pensionable Earnings Average for the later of the year in which the survivor first became qualified to receive the survivor's pension and the year in which the survivor's retirement pension commenced to be payable, adjusted in accordance with subsection 45(2) as if the benefit had commenced to be payable in the later of the year in which the survivor first became qualified to receive the survivor's pension and the year in which the survivor's retirement pension commenced to be payable; or (S.C. 1997, c. 40, s. 76(1).)

(d) in any other case, the lesser of

(i) 60% of the amount of the contributor's retirement pension, calculated as provided in subsection (3), and

(ii) an amount that, when added to the survivor's retirement pension (calculated without regard to subsections 46(3) to (6) but in accordance with subsection 45(2)), is equal to the amount of a benefit of 25% of $^1/_{12}$ of the average of the Year's Maximum Pensionable Earnings for the later of the year in which the survivor first became qualified to receive the survivor's pension and the year in which the survivor's retirement pension commenced to be payable, and for each of the two preceding years, adjusted in accordance with subsection 45(2) as if the benefit had commenced to be payable in the later of the year in which the survivor first became qualified to receive the survivor's pension and the year in which the survivor's retirement pension commenced to be payable.

(S.C. 1997, c. 40, s. 76(1); 2000, c. 12, s. 64.)

(3) *Calculation of contributor's retirement pension* — [35]The amount of the contributor's retirement pension to be used for the purposes of subsections (1) and (2) is an amount calculated as provided in paragraph 57(2)(*a*), (*b*) or (*c*) multiplied, for the purpose of calculating the monthly amount of the survivor's pension for months commencing with the month in which (S.C. 2000, c. 12, s. 64.)

(*a*) a survivor's pension became payable to survivor by reason of a disability that began after the death of the contributor, (S.C. 2000, c. 12, s. 64.)

(*b*) the survivor reached sixty-five years of age, not having reached that age at the time of the death of the contributor, (S.C. 2000, c. 12, s. 64.)

(*c*) the survivor's pension under this Act or the survivor's retirement pension under this Act or a provincial pension plan commenced to be payable, whichever is the later, (S.C. 2000, c. 12, s. 64.)

(*d*) a survivor's pension became payable to the survivor under this Act in circumstances other than those described in paragraph (*a*), (*b*) or (*c*), or (S.C. 2000, c. 12, s. 64.)

(*e*) the survivor has had an adjustment to the survivor's retirement pension pursuant to subsection 55(7) or 55.2(9) following a division of unadjusted pensionable earnings, (S.C. 2000, c. 12, s. 64.)

by the ratio that the Pension Index for the year that includes that month bears to the Pension Index for the year in which the contributor died. (R.S.C. 1985, c. 30, ss. 26(5), (6); 1991, c. 44, s. 12(3).)

(4) *Pension Index limitation removed* — For the purpose of calculating the monthly amount of a survivor's pension under subsection (3) in a case where the survivor's pension commences with a month in a year after 1973 and is in respect of a contributor who died prior to 1974, the ratio referred to in that subsection shall be calculated as if the Pension Index for the year in which the contributor died had not been subject to the limitation referred to in paragraph 43.1(2)(*a*) of the *Canada Pension Plan*, chapter C-5 of the Revised Statutes of Canada, 1970, of 1.02 times the Pension Index for the preceding year. (S.C. 2000, c. 12, s. 50(1).)

(5) *Calculation of amount of retirement pension to survivor* — [36]For the purposes of subsection (2), the monthly amount of the retirement pension payable to the survivor of a contributor shall be calculated without regard to any provision of the provincial pension plan referred to in that subsection that reduces the pensions of contributors who have reached the age of sixty-five years or precludes the payment of pensions to those contributors by reason of their employment earnings. (S.C. 1991, c. 44, s. 12(4); 2000, c. 12, s. 64.)

(6) *Calculation of disability pension where survivor's pension payable* — Subject to subsection (6.1), where a survivor's pension under this Act and a disability pension under this Act are payable to the survivor of a contributor and either the date of death of the contributor or the date on which the survivor is deemed to have become disabled for the purposes of this Act is after December 31, 1997, the amount of the disability pension is an amount that, when added to the amount of the survivor's pension for a month in the year in which the survivor's pension or the disability pension commenced to be payable, whichever is the later, equals the aggregate of

(*a*) the greater of

(i) the flat rate benefit payable under subparagraph (1)(*a*)(i), and

(ii) the flat rate benefit payable under paragraph 56(1)(*a*), and

(*b*) the lesser of

(i) the aggregate of

---

[35] Pursuant to 1991, c. 44, s. 12(6), subsection 58(3) applies in respect of benefits that commence to be paid before or after January 27, 1992.

[36] Pursuant to 1991, c. 44, s. 12(6), subsection (5) applies in respect of benefits that commence to be paid before or after January 27, 1992.

(A) the greater of

    (I) the amount payable under subparagraph (1)(*a*)(ii), and

    (II) the amount payable under paragraph 56(1)(*b*), and

(B) 60% of the lesser of the amount described in subclause (A)(I) and the amount described in subclause (A)(II), and

(ii) 75% of the amount of a benefit of 25% of $^{1}/_{12}$ of the survivor's Maximum Pensionable Earnings Average for the later of the year in which the survivor first became qualified to receive the survivor's pension and the year in which the survivor's disability pension commenced to be payable, adjusted in accordance with subsection 45(2) as if the benefit had commenced to be payable in the later of the year in which the survivor first became qualified to receive the survivor's pension and the year in which the surviving spouse's disability pension commenced to be payable.

(S.C. 1997, c. 40, s. 76(2); 2000, c. 12, s. 64.)

(6.1) *Saving* — Where subsection (6) applies and the aggregate amount of the survivor's pension and the disability pension are less than the amount of the disability pension that would be payable if the survivor's pension were not payable, the amount of the disability pension is the amount that results when

(*a*) the amount of the survivor's pension

is subtracted from

(*b*) the amount of the disability pension that would be payable if the survivor's pension were not payable.

(S.C. 1997, c. 40, s. 76(2).)

(6.2) *Calculation of disability pension where survivor's pension payable* — Where a survivor's pension under this Act and a disability pension under this Act are payable to the survivor of a contributor and subsection (6) does not apply, the amount of the disability pension is an amount that, when added to the amount of the survivor's pension for a month in the year in which the survivor's pension or the disability pension commenced to be payable, whichever is the later, equals the aggregate of

(*a*) the greater of

    (i) the flat rate benefit payable under subparagraph (1)(*a*)(i), and

    (ii) the flat rate benefit payable under paragraph 56(1)(*a*), and

(*b*) the lesser of

    (i) the aggregate of the amounts payable under subparagraph (1)(*a*)(ii) and paragraph 56(1)(*b*), and

    (ii) the amount of a benefit of 25% of $^{1}/_{12}$ of the average of the Year's Maximum Pensionable Earnings for the later of the year in which the survivor first became qualified to receive the survivor's pension and the year in which the survivor's disability pension commenced to be payable, and for each of the two preceding years, adjusted in accordance with subsection 45(2) as if the benefit had commenced to be payable in the later of the year in which the survivor first became qualified to receive the survivor's pension and the year in which the survivor's disability pension commenced to be payable.

(S.C. 1997, c. 40, s. 76(2); 2000, c. 12, s. 64.)

(7) *Special case* — Notwithstanding subsection (6), the Minister may, in prescribed circumstances and on the written request of the applicant, if in the Minister's opinion it would be to the applicant's advantage, pay the applicant the full amount of the disability pension and calculate the amount of the applicant's survivor's pension in a manner similar to that set out in subsection (6) for the calculation of the disability pension, but in no case may the aggregate of the two pensions exceed what it would have been had subsection (6) applied.

(8) *Calculation of survivor's pension when disability pension payable under provincial pension plan* — Except where otherwise provided by an agreement under section 80, where a survivor's pension under this Act and a disability pension under a provincial pension plan are payable to the survivor of a contributor and either the date of death of the contributor or the date on which the survivor is deemed to have become disabled for the purposes of a provincial pension plan is after December 31, 1997, the amount of the survivor's pension is an amount that, when added to the amount of the disability pension for a month in the year in which the survivor's pension or the disability pension commenced to be payable, whichever is the later, equals the aggregate of (S.C. 2000, c. 12, s. 50(2).)

(*a*) the greater of
    (i) the flat rate benefit payable under subparagraph (1)(*a*)(i), and
    (ii) the flat rate benefit payable under the provincial pension plan in respect of disability, and

(*b*) the lesser of
    (i) the aggregate of
        (A) the greater of
            (I) the amount payable under subparagraph (1)(*a*)(ii), and
            (II) the portion of the contributor's retirement pension payable to the survivor under the provincial pension plan in respect of disability, and
        (B) 60% of the lesser of the amount described in subclause (A)(I) and the amount described in subclause (A)(II), and
    (ii) 75% of the amount of a benefit of 25% of $^1/_{12}$ of the survivor's Maximum Pensionable Earnings Average for the later of the year in which the survivor first became qualified to receive the survivor's pension and the year in which the survivor's disability pension commenced to be payable, adjusted in accordance with subsection 45(2) as if the benefit had commenced to be payable in the later of the year in which the survivor first became qualified to receive the survivor's pension and the year in which the survivor's disability pension commenced to be payable.

(S.C. 1997, c. 40, s. 76(3); 2000, c. 12, s. 64.)

(8.1) *Calculation of survivor's pension when disability pension payable under provincial pension plan* — Except where otherwise provided by an agreement under section 80, where a survivor's pension under this Act and a disability pension under a provincial pension plan are payable to the survivor of a contributor and subsection (8) does not apply, the amount of the survivor's pension is an amount that, when added to the amount of the disability pension for a month in the year in which the survivor's pension or the disability pension commenced to be payable, whichever is the later, equals the aggregate of (S.C. 2000, c. 12, s. 50(3).)

(*a*) the greater of
    (i) the flat rate benefit payable under subparagraph (1)(*a*)(i), and
    (ii) the flat rate benefit payable under the provincial pension plan in respect of disability, and

(*b*) the lesser of
    (i) the aggregate of
        (A) the amounts payable under subparagraph (1)(*a*)(ii), and
        (B) the portion of the contributor's retirement pension payable to the survivor under the provincial pension plan in respect of disability, and
    (ii) the amount of a benefit of 25% of $^1/_{12}$ of the average of the Year's Maximum Pensionable Earnings for the later of the year in which the survivor first became qualified to receive the survivor's pension and the year in which the survivor's disability pension commenced to be payable, and for each of the two preceding years, adjusted in accordance with subsection 45(2) as if

Canada Pension Plan

the benefit had commenced to be payable in the later of the year in which the survivor first became qualified to receive the survivor's pension and the year in which the survivor's disability pension commenced to be payable.

(S.C. 1997, c. 40, s. 76(3); 2000, c. 12, s. 64.)

(9) *Interpretation* — [37]**For the purposes of this section, a survivor first becomes qualified to receive a survivor's pension in the month following the month in which the survivor first met the criteria of subsection 44(1) in relation to that pension. (S.C. 1991, c. 44, s. 12(5); 2000, c. 12, s. 64.)**

(R.S.C. 1985, c. 30 (2nd Supp.), s. 26; 1991, c. 44, s. 12; 1997, c. 40, s. 76; 2000, c. 12, s. 50; 2000, c. 12, s. 64.)

––––––––––––– **Notes** –––––––––––––

Synopsis

This section sets out the very technical rules for determining the amount of a survivor's pension payable in different circumstances. While there is no substitute for close reading of the specific provisions, the following is an overview of the survivor's entitlement where he or she is:

Aged 65 and over (not receiving a retirement pension) (s. 58(1)(*b*)) — Basic monthly amount equal to 60% of the amount of the deceased contributor's retirement pension. In 2014, the maximum survivor's pension is $623.00 per month.

Aged 65 and over (born after December 31, 1932 and retirement pension commencing after December 31, 1997) (s. 58(2)(*c*)) — Combined pensions equal retirement pension of survivor plus lesser of (i) 60% of deceased contributor's retirement pension minus lesser of 40% of that amount and 40% of the survivor's retirement pension before actuarial adjustment, and (ii) ceiling of maximum retirement pension in year of entitlement to second occurring benefit.

Aged under 65 (retirement pension becoming payable after December 31, 1997) (s. 58(2)(*a*),(*b*)) — Combined pensions equal adjusted retirement pension, plus survivor flat-rate benefit, plus lesser of (i) $37^{1}/2$% of deceased contributor's retirement pension, minus lesser of 40% of that amount and 40% of survivor's retirement pension before actuarial adjustments, and (ii) ceiling of maximum survivor's retirement pension in year of entitlement to the second benefit plus survivor flat-rate.

Aged 45 to 64 (no retirement pension payable) (s. 58(1)(*a*)) — Flat rate, plus $37^{1}/2$% of the amount of the deceased contributor's retirement pension, to a combined maximum of $567.91 per month in 2014.

Aged 35 to 45 (s. 58(1)(*a*)) — Same as amount for survivors aged 45–64, but reduced by $^{1}/_{120}$th for each month by which survivor is less than 45 years at time of contributor's death, unless survivor disabled or having dependent children.

Also receiving disability pension (s. 58(6)) — Larger of flat-rate portions of survivor or disability benefits, plus lesser of (i) total of (A) greater of $37^{1}/2$% of contributor's retirement pension and earnings-related portion of disability pension, and (B) 60% of lesser of amounts described in (A), and (ii) 75% of maximum retirement pension ($1,038.33 in 2014). [Note: Combined total not to exceed one maximum disability benefit ($1,236.35 in 2014).]

Having dependent children — Survivor's pension plus orphan's pension on behalf of children ($230.72 in 2014).

The survivor is qualified to receive the benefit starting in the month after the deceased contributor dies (s. 58(9)).

Recent Amendments

The 2000 amendments deleted references to "surviving spouse" in favour of the term "survivor".

Related Provisions

- Section 42(1) — Definition of "survivor"

––

[37] Pursuant to 1991, c. 44, s. 12(6), subsection (9) applies in respect of benefits that commence to be paid before or after January 27, 1992.

- Section 44(1)(*d*) — Entitlement to survivor's pension
- section 44(3) — Minimum qualifying period
- Section 60 — Application for benefit
- Section 63 — Where spouse remarried before survivor's pension payable
- Section 63.1 — Application for commencement or reinstatement of survivor's pension
- Section 72 — When survivor's pension commences
- Section 73 — Duration of payment of survivor's pension
- Section 77 — Amount of benefit payable
- Section 81 — Request for reconsideration by Minister

Related CPP Regulations

- Section 54.4 — Special case for calculation of survivor's pension
- Section 56 — Payment of certain benefits at intervals greater than monthly

Case Law

Law v. MEI, [1999] 1 S.C.R. 497

The purpose and function of survivor's pension provisions of the CPP is not to remedy the *immediate* financial need experienced by widows and widowers, but rather to enable older widows and widowers to meet their basic needs *during the longer term*.

Parliament's intent in enacting a survivor's pension scheme with benefits allocated according to age appears to have been to allocate funds to those persons whose ability to overcome need was weakest. The concern was to enhance personal dignity and freedom by ensuring a basic level of long-term financial security to persons whose personal situation makes them unable to achieve this goal, so important to life and dignity.

Canada (Attorney General) v. Borai, 2008 FC 999

The PAB does not have jurisdiction to grant leave to appeal a decision of the Review Tribunal affirming the Minister's decision denying survivor benefits where the grounds upon which leave was sought was the failure of the RT to alter the date of disability of the claimant's deceased spouse. Neither the RT nor the PAB have jurisdiction over the issue of the disability date in respect of the claimant's spouse.

MHRD v. Faulkner (January 18, 2000), CP 09347 (PAB)

Section 58(2)(*b*)(ii) does not speak of when an event should have taken place, but rather when the event does take place. Its effect was as if the benefit had commenced to be payable in the later point in time when the surviving spouse is qualified to receive the survivor's pension, and the year in which the surviving spouse's disability pension commenced to be payable. Where the claimant had previously received survivor's benefits but at the time was not yet eligible to receive a retirement pension, and the survivor's benefits had been cancelled in 1980 owing to the claimant's remarriage, the claimant was entitled to receive combined survivors benefits and retirement pension at the 1987 rate as opposed to the 1980 rate.

Makeiv v. MNHW (February 9, 1994), CP 2579, CEB & PG (TB) ¶8537 (PAB)

The PAB does not have jurisdiction to prorate the survivor's pension between competing spouses on the bases of the number of years of their respective co-habitation with the deceased contributor. Such a change would have to be made by Parliament.

Disabled Contributor's Child's Benefit and Orphan's Benefit

59. *Amount of benefit* — **A disabled contributor's child's benefit payable to the child of a disabled contributor and an orphan's benefit payable to the orphan of a contributor is a basic monthly amount consisting of**

(a) in the year 1991, one hundred and thirteen dollars and fourteen cents; or

(*b*) in the year 1992, the aggregate of (i) one hundred and thirteen dollars and fourteen cents, multiplied by the ratio referred to in subparagraph (*c*)(ii), and (ii) thirty-five dollars; or

(*c*) in the year 1993 or any subsequent year, an amount calculated by multiplying

(i) the amount of the benefit that would have been payable for a month in the year preceding that year

by

(ii) the ratio that the Pension Index for the year in which the benefit commences to be payable bears to the Pension Index for the year preceding that year.

(R.S.C. 1985, c. 30 (2nd Supp.), s. 27; 1991, c. 44, s. 13.)

―――――――――― Notes ――――――――――

Synopsis

This section provides that the benefits payable to each child of a disabled contributor and to each orphan are indexed flat-rate benefits, not dependent on earnings. Year-to-year increases are proportional to changes in the Pension Index, the amount for 2014 being $230.72.

Related Provisions

- Section 43 — Pension Index
- Section 44(1)(*e*), (*f*) — Entitlement to benefit
- Section 44(3) — Minimum qualifying period
- Section 60 — Application for benefit
- Section 74 — Person by whom application may be made; commencement of payment; no benefit in respect of more than two contributors
- Section 75 — Payment of benefit
- Section 76 — When benefit ceases to be payable
- Section 81 — Request for reconsideration by Minister

―――――――――――――――――――

Post-retirement Benefit

59.1. *Amount of post-retirement benefit* — **(1) Subject to subsections (2) and (3), a post-retirement benefit payable to a contributor is a basic monthly amount determined by the formula**

$$[(A \times F/B) \times C \times D \times E] / 12$$

where

A is the amount determined under subsection 53(1) for the year prior to the year in which the post-retirement benefit commences to be payable;

B is the Year's Maximum Pensionable Earnings for the year prior to the year in which the post-retirement benefit commences to be payable;

C is 0.00625;

D is the Maximum Pensionable Earnings Average for the year in which the post-retirement benefit commences to be payable;

E is the adjustment factor referred to in subsection 46(3) or (3.1), as the case may be, based on the age of the contributor on January 1 of the year in which the post-retirement benefit commences to be payable; and

F is the amount determined by the formula

G / H

where

G   is the amount of the earnings referred to in subparagraph 53(1)(*b*)(i), and

H   is the aggregate of the earnings referred to in subparagraph 53(1)(*b*)(i) and those referred to in subparagraph 53(1)(*b*)(ii).

(S.C. 2009, c. 31, s. 36.)

(**2**) *Unadjusted pensionable earnings for the year in which the retirement pension becomes payable* — For the purpose of the calculation under subsection (1), if the unadjusted pensionable earnings are earned in the year in which the contributory period ends under subparagraph 49(*b*)(iii), the amount determined for A in subsection (1) is the greater of

   (*a*) zero, and

   (*b*) the amount that is calculated by subtracting the Year's Maximum Pensionable Earnings for that year — multiplied by the number of months in the year before the retirement pension becomes payable and divided by 12 — from the amount determined under subsection 53(1).

(S.C. 2009, c. 31, s. 36.)

(**3**) *Adjustment factor for contributors who are 70 years of age or older* — For the purpose of the calculation under subsection (1), if the contributor is seventy years of age or older, the amount determined for E in subsection (1) is the adjustment factor for a contributor who is seventy years of age. (S.C. 2009, c. 31, s. 36.)

(S.C. 2009, c. 31, s. 36.)

Division C: Payment of Benefits: General Provisions

60. *Application for benefit* — (**1**) No benefit is payable to any person under this Act unless an application therefor has been made by him or on his behalf and payment of the benefit has been approved under this Act.

(**1.1**) *Application for post-retirement benefit deemed to be made* — An application for a post-retirement benefit under subsection (1) is deemed to be made on January 1 of the year following the year of the unadjusted pensionable earnings referred to in section 76.1 if

   (*a*) the person is a beneficiary of a retirement pension on that day; and

   (*b*) the Minister has the information necessary to determine whether a post-retirement benefit is payable to them.

(S.C. 2009, c. 31, s. 36.)

(**2**) *Application for benefit by estate, etc.* — Notwithstanding anything in this Act, but subject to subsections (2.1) and (2.2), an application for a benefit, other than a death benefit, that would have been payable in respect of a month to a deceased person who, prior to the person's death, would have been entitled on approval of an application to payment of that benefit under this Act may be approved in respect of that month only if it is made within 12 months after the death of that person by the estate, the representative or heir of that person or by any person that may be prescribed by regulation. (S.C. 1997, c. 40, s. 77(1).)

(**2.1**) *Certain applications may not be approved* — An application referred to in subsection (2) in respect of a disability benefit may not be approved if the application is received after December 31, 1997. (S.C. 1997, c. 40, s. 77(1).)

(**2.2**) *Restriction — retirement pension* — An application referred to in subsection (2) in respect of a retirement pension may only be approved in respect of a month after the deceased contributor had reached age 70. (S.C. 1997, c. 40, s. 77(1).)

(3) *Exception* — Where a disabled contributor's child's benefit would, if the application had been approved, have been payable to a child of a disabled contributor on application made prior to the death of the child or an orphan's benefit would, if the application had been approved, have been payable to an orphan of a contributor on application made prior to the death of the orphan and the child or orphan dies after December 31, 1977, not having reached eighteen years of age, and no application has been made at the time of the death of the child or orphan, an application may be made within one year after the death by the person or agency having custody and control of the child or orphan at the time of the death or, where there is at that time no person or agency having custody and control, by such person or agency as the Minister may direct. (R.S.C. 1985, c. 1 (4th Supp.), s. 44, Sch. II, item 4.)

(4) *Benefits payable to estate or other persons* — Where an application is made pursuant to subsection (2) or (3), a benefit that would have been payable to a deceased person referred to in subsection (2) or a deceased child or orphan referred to in subsection (3) shall be paid to the estate or such person as may be prescribed by regulation.

(5) *Application deemed to have been received on date of death* — Any application made pursuant to subsection (2) or (3) is deemed to have been received

   (*a*) on the date of the death of a person who, prior to his death, would have been entitled, on approval of an application, to payment of a benefit under this Act; or

   (*b*) on the date of the death of a child or an orphan referred to in subsection (3) where the person having custody and control of the child or orphan did not make an application prior to the death of the child or orphan.

(6) *How application to be made* — An application for a benefit shall be made to the Minister in prescribed manner and at the prescribed location. (R.S.C. 1985, c. 30 (2nd Supp.), s. 28(2).)

(7) *Consideration of application and approval by Minister* — The Minister shall forthwith on receiving an application for a benefit consider it and may approve payment of the benefit and determine the amount thereof payable under this Act or may determine that no benefit is payable, and he shall thereupon in writing notify the applicant of his decision.

(8) *Incapacity* — Where an application for a benefit is made on behalf of a person and the Minister is satisfied, on the basis of evidence provided by or on behalf of that person, that the person had been incapable of forming or expressing an intention to make an application on the person's own behalf on the day on which the application was actually made, the Minister may deem the application to have been made in the month preceding the first month in which the relevant benefit could have commenced to be paid or in the month that the Minister considers the person's last relevant period of incapacity to have commenced, whichever is the later. (S.C. 1991, c. 44, s. 14.)

(9) *Idem* — Where an application for a benefit is made by or on behalf of a person and the Minister is satisfied, on the basis of evidence provided by or on behalf of that person, that

   (*a*) the person had been incapable of forming or expressing an intention to make an application before the day on which the application was actually made,

   (*b*) the person had ceased to be so incapable before that day, and

   (*c*) the application was made

      (i) within the period that begins on the day on which that person had ceased to be so incapable and that comprises the same number of days, not exceeding twelve months, as in the period of incapacity, or

(ii) where the period referred to in subparagraph (i) comprises fewer than thirty days, not more than one month after the month in which that person had ceased to be so incapable,

the Minister may deem the application to have been made in the month preceding the first month in which the relevant benefit could have commenced to be paid or in the month that the Minister considers the person's last relevant period of incapacity to have commenced, whichever is the later. (S.C. 1991, c. 44, s. 14.)

(10) *Period of incapacity* — For the purposes of subsections (8) and (9), a period of incapacity must be a continuous period except as otherwise prescribed. (S.C. 1991, c. 44, s. 14.)

(11) *Application* — Subsections (8) to (10) apply only to individuals who were incapacitated on or after January 1, 1991. (S.C. 1991, c. 44, s. 14.)

(12) *Making claim or providing information in person* — The Minister may require an applicant or other person or a group or class of persons to be at a suitable place at a suitable time in order to make an application for benefits in person or to provide additional information about an application. (S.C. 1997, c. 40, s. 77(2).)

(R.S.C. 1985, c. 1 (4th Supp.), s. 44, Sch. II, item 4; c. 30 (2nd Supp.), s. 28(2); 1991, c. 44, s. 14; 1997, c. 40, s. 77; 2009, c. 31, s. 36.)

———————— Notes ————————

Synopsis

This section provides that CPP benefits must be applied for by claimants and approved by the Minister before they are payable. The regulations (see below) set out the prescribed manner and form of the application. The Minister may require the claimant to appear in person to make the application or provide additional information (ss. (12)). Written notification of the Minister's decision must be given (ss. (7)). Special rules apply to applications on behalf of incapable persons (ss. (8)–(11)).

Where the contributor has died after becoming being entitled to apply for CPP benefits, other than disability benefits, the estate, the representative or heir of the deceased must apply within 12 months of the date of the contributor's death (ss. (2), (2.1)). The estate may only apply in respect of a retirement pension, which the deceased could have applied for, in respect of months after the deceased had reach age 70 (ss. (2.2)). The parent of a child or an agency having custody of a child may apply for the disabled contributor's child's benefit or orphan's benefit within 12 months of the death of the child (ss. 3)). All such applications are deemed to be received by the Minister on the date of death.

Related Provisions

- Section 61 — Approval of interim benefits
- Section 62 — Where payment approved after month of commencement
- Section 70(2) — Cessation of disability pension at age 65
- Section 70.1 — Request for Reinstatement
- Section 76(3) — Cessation of disabled contributor's child's benefit on death of contributor
- Section 81 — Request for reconsideration by Minister

Related CPP Regulations

- Section 37(2) — Person entitled to make application
- Section 37(3) — Person entitled to receive benefits
- Section 43 — Application for benefits
- Section 44 — Application on behalf of incapable person
- Section 45 — Withdrawal of application

- Section 52 — Information and evidence required to be furnished by applicant or beneficiary
- Section 53 — Information from family allowance recipients
- Section 55 — Payments to persons on behalf of beneficiaries
- Section 57 — Payment of benefits unpaid at death
- Section 59 — Withholding of benefits
- Section 61 — Application for retirement pension
- Section 63 — Determination of marital or filial status or death
- Sections 68–70 — Determination of disability
- Section 90 — Offence and punishment for misrepresentation
- Section 90.1 — Penalty for misrepresentation

Case Law

§1. General Principles

Lewis v. MSD (March 16, 2007), CP 23913 (PAB)

An application for OAS benefits cannot be treated as an application for CPP retirement pension under s. 60. The applicant under s. 60 and the CPP Regulations is required to furnish additional information. Nor was the Department receiving the OAS application under an obligation to advise the applicant of her entitlement to CPP benefits. The wording of s. 60(1) puts the obligation squarely on the applicant, and not the department.

MHRD v. Lavoie (June 27, 1997), CP 5412, CEB & PG (TB) ¶8685 (PAB)

Decisions of the Minister, or of the Minister's officials, are not subject to the rule of *res judicata*. Such decisions are administrative, not judicial, as they are made by parties to the case, however impartial. The rejection by the Minister of a disability claim therefore did not prevent the applicant from making a subsequent claim, even where the Minister's original rejection had not been appealed by the claimant.

MHRD v. Kirby (November 27, 2001), CP 17189 (PAB)

Sections 60(8) and 60(2) are mutually exclusive, and the incapacity provisions cannot be invoked following the death of a contributor.

R.C. v. MHRSD (September 22, 2010), CP 21938 (PAB)

Section 60(2) applies where an application for benefits is made by an estate. The CPP doesn't contemplate a situation where a claimant dies prior to a scheduled hearing. Where the claimant died intestate, a court order was needed to authorize his widow or anyone else to pursue the appeal on his behalf.

B.P. v. MHRSD (June 18, 2010), CP 25325 (PAB)

Section 60(1) provides that no benefit is payable unless an application for the benefit is presented to the Minister by a claimant. At the time the claimant applied for a death benefit, she did not apply for a survivor's pension. The PAB could not deem that the application for a death benefit also includes an application for a survivor's pension.

MHRSD v. Estate of O.C. (November 17, 2008), CP 25411 (PAB)

Section 60(8) applies only to applications made by or on behalf of a living person and not an estate. However, the incapacity provision could be invoked by the estate based on the contributor's appeal of the start date of the disability pension where the contributor had applied for and received a disability pension before he died. Subsection 60(8) refers to "an application for a benefit" and not to an application to consider the incapacity of a recipient. [Note: The PAB distinguished *Kirby* (above) on the facts.]

Meyer v. MHRD (October 16, 2001), CP 15781 (PAB)

Where the contributor's estate applied for a retirement pension within one year of the death of the contributor, the maximum period of retroactivity under s. 67(3) of the twelve months prior to when the application was made applied.

Taylor v. MHRD (January 4, 2001), CP 11112 (PAB)

The spouse of a deceased contributor does not have to have a death certificate or court order for the presumption of death before he or she can complete the application form for survivor's benefits.

MacIsaac v. MEI (November 15, 1994), CP 2938, CEB & PG (TB) ¶8570 (PAB)

While there is nothing in the CPP that precludes a person from making more than one application, each application, once finally determined, is subject to the rules of *res judicata* and cannot be revived by a subsequent application.

Mandel v. MNHW (October 20, 1993), CP 2715, CEB & PG ¶8516 (PAB)

Where the applicant proves that he or she did what was necessary to complete and submit the application, receipt by the Minister is proven for the purpose of the Act.

MNHW v. Kearney (June 16, 1993), CP 2631, CEB & PG (TB) ¶8512 (PAB)

Affidavit evidence on the claimant's behalf may be accepted to prove an application for benefits had been made.

MEI v. Sidhu (January 26, 1996), CP 3486, CEB & PG (TB) ¶8610 (PAB)

An application for disability benefits by a person receiving a CPP retirement pension does not implicitly contain a request to cancel the retirement pension.

§1.1. Garnishment

Simon v. Canada, 2014 FCA 47

The Ministry may express its view that CPP benefits payable to the plaintiff may be subject to garnishment in the future. A negligence claim brought by the plaintiff against the Crown and Ministry officials in their personal capacities regarding an alleged effect of such a possible future administrative decision where any possible damage had not yet materialized did not disclose a viable cause of action.

§2. Incapacity

Canada (Attorney General) v. Danielson, 2008 FCA 78

Section 60 is precise and focused in that it does not require consideration of the capacity to make, prepare, process or complete an application for disability benefits, but only the capacity of forming or expressing an intention to make an application. The activities of a claimant during the period between the claimed date of commencement of disability and the date of application may be relevant to cast light on his or her continuous incapacity to form or express the requisite intention and ought to be considered.

Baines v. Canada (HRSD), 2011 FCA 158, leave to appeal to SCC refused, 2012 CanLII 22038 (SCC).

Section 60(9) applies only to applications for benefits, not to appeals from the rejection of applications. Incapacity in this context has been held to mean an incapacity to form an intention to apply, not the claimant's undoubted physical difficulties resulting from the accident.

Statton v. Canada (Attorney General), 2006 FCA 370. See also *Robbins v. Canada (Attorney General)* 2010 FCA 85.

Section 60(8) is not relevant to applications for benefits arising from the legal incapacity of an applicant. Section 74 governs applications for disabled contributors' child benefits, and s. 60(8) is inapplicable. See also *MSD v. Gartner* (August 28, 2007), CP 24311 (PAB)

Robbins v. Canada (Attorney General) 2010 FCA 85

Section 60(1) requires that an application be made before benefits can be paid and that s. 74 prescribes the maximum retroactivity applicable to the children of disabled contributors.

Sedrak v. Canada (Social Development), 2008 FCA 86

The capacity to form the intention to apply for benefits is not different in kind from the capacity to form an intention with respect to other choices which present themselves to an applicant. The fact that a particular choice may not suggest itself to an applicant because of his worldview does not indicate a lack of capacity. Subsections 60(8) and (9) taken together allow

Canada Pension Plan

269

for persons who lack the capacity to apply for benefits to either have an application made on their behalf, or to make the application themselves when they reacquire the capacity to do so. Nothing in this scheme requires that the word "capacity" be given a meaning other than its ordinary meaning.

Canada (Attorney General) v. Kirkland, 2008 CAF 144

The Court of Appeal decision in *Danielson* stands for the principle that the activities of a claimant during an alleged period of incapacity may be relevant in casting light on his or her continuous incapacity to form or express the requisite intention, and ought to be considered. The decision in *Sedrak* holds that the capacity to form an intention to apply for benefits is not different in kind from the capacity to form an intention with respect to other choices which present themselves to the claimant.

Slater v. Canada (Attorney General), 2008 FCA 375

In determining whether or not a claimant had the mental capacity to form or express an intention within the meaning of subsections 60(8) and (9), it was necessary to look at both the medical evidence and the relevant activities of the individual concerned — between the claimed date of commencement of disability and the date of application — which cast light on the capacity of the person concerned during that period of so "forming and expressing" the intent.

See also *J.F. v. Minister of Human Resources and Skills Development* (January 28, 2014) CP 27316 (SSTGD)

Morrison v. MHRD (1997), CP 4182 (PAB), CEB & PG ¶8679. See also *Devcic v. MHRD* (August 30, 2001), CP 14065 (PAB).

The provisions of s. 60(8)–(11) are precise and narrow, rather than general or flexible. The issue of whether the applicant was capable of forming or expressing an intention to make an application is a narrow question, but difficult to answer. The answer may involve expert medical opinion related, in particular, to the period between the claimed date of commencement of the disability and the date of eventual application for disability benefits, and very important, the relevant activities of the individual concerned between the claimed date of commencement of disability and the date of application which cast light on the capacity of the person concerned during that period of so "forming and expressing" the intent. The activities of the individual concerned during that period will be particularly significant if the expert medical opinions are of a general, varied or equivocal nature and perhaps not fully or adequately supported by medical evidence, and failure to apply for a disability pension at an earlier date. Moreover, the question of what occurred to "trigger" the application when it was in fact and finally made, with the required capacity present, will be an interesting and significant one. What changed and why will be an important question. There is a significant difference between capacity to form or express an intent to make an application for disability benefits and the capacity to make, complete, "fill in", or "meet the requirements" of an application. The psychological unwillingness to "deal with" an application for a disability pension and choosing to "walk away" from the problems in the claimant's life at the relevant time do not equate with being "incapable of forming or expressing an intent to make an application."

Janes v. MSD (August 24, 2006), CP 23479 (PAB)

The test under s. 60(9) is not the ability to complete and send in an application. The section says "incapable of forming or expressing an intention to make an application". Those are two alternate exceptions to the general rule. While "expressing an intention" arguably calls for some physical act, "forming ... an intention" calls for mental activity only. The evidence of forming an intention can come from the admission of the applicant or can be inferred from the activities of the applicant.

Nenshi v. MSD (January 9, 2006), CP 22251 (PAB)

It is not whether a person is capable to deal with the consequences of an application, but rather whether the person was capable of forming an intention to apply or not. The capacity lacking which an applicant must establish is of forming or expressing an intention to make an application, not the preparation process and completion of the application. In the circumstances, the appeal was denied even though medical reports showed due mental illness made it difficult for her to make important decisions. The claimant always knew she was ill and received treatment for such illness. She may not have been able to deal with the physical act of completing the forms, but she could form and express an intent to apply.

HRSDC v. Y.C. (January 10, 2012), CP 26648 (PAB)

Incapacity provisions do not apply to the children's benefits. The incapacity referred to in s. 60(8) applies only to the person on whose behalf the application was made and not to the person making it.

Prevost v. MSD (June 7, 2005), CP 13312 (PAB). See also *MHRD v. Slayer* (December 4, 2002), CP 17196 (PAB), and *MSD v. Statton* (January 21, 2005), CP 22564 (PAB).

The provisions of s. 60(8)-(11) deal with an application on behalf of an incapacitated person, and do not relate to a minor with regard to his or her lack of legal capacity. Section 74(1) permits the application for a DCCB to be made by a custodian of the child.

Weisberg v. MSD (December 8, 2004), CP 21943 (PAB)

Where a claimant was aware that something was wrong with him, the fact that he was incapable of recognizing that it was a disabling condition does not render him incapable for the purposes of s. 60(9). The incapacity to form an intention must encompass an incapacity different from an incapacity to express an intention. The incapacity of forming an intention must refer to a cognitive deficiency that precedes the expression of that intention. In other words, one must be able to form an intention before communicating it. An incapacity of expressing an intention, on the other hand, can be either a cognitive or a physical incapacity or both. Unless an applicant has some cognitive recognition that he or she is disabled, although not necessarily the extent of that disability, there would be no reason to apply for a pension. A person suffering from psychosis would be a person at one end of the spectrum who is likely incapable of forming an intention to apply for a disability pension. Such persons would not only be incapable of realizing the nature and extent of their illness, they would be incapable of realizing that they were mentally ill and probably "incapable regularly of pursuing any substantially gainful occupation." On the other hand, persons who know that they are suffering from a physical illness but unable to appreciate the nature and extent of that illness would not necessarily be considered incapable of forming or expressing an intention to apply for a disability pension.

Obiter. Subsection 60(9) deals with an applicant who has suffered incapacity and has since recovered. A simple example is where the applicant has been in a coma caused by a blow to the head and subsequently recovers. Such person is entitled to apply for a pension retroactive to the date of the incapacity provided that the application is made within the same number of days as the period of the incapacity and within twelve months after recovering capacity. For example, if a person has been rendered incapacitated for 350 days, he must apply within 350 day of regaining capacity. If he is incapacitated for 400 days, he must still apply within twelve months. If he is rendered incapacitated for less than 30 days, then he has up to 30 days to apply. Incapacity must have been continuous throughout the entire period. The purpose is to ensure that persons who are rendered incapacitated and seek to obtain retroactive disability payments make timely applications, otherwise their right to a retroactive payment will be lost.

Tatsiopoulos v. MSD (December 17, 2004), CP 21976 (PAB)

"Incapable", as used in s. 60, refers to a mental state that renders a person unable to intend to make an application, not the lack of knowledge. It is inapplicable where the claimant has the capacity to form or express an intention to file an application for disability benefits.

Gallant v. MHRD (October 2, 2001), CP 14706 (PAB)

Section 60 should not be narrowly interpreted. The requirement of being incapable of forming or expressing an intention to make an application for a disability benefit implies knowledge and being able to understand the nature of such an application.

Pedersen v. MHRD (May 1, 2001), CP 11660 (PAB)

The onus of establishing incapacity is on the claimant. The PAB cannot assume that a debilitating illness such as schizophrenia prevented the applicant from forming an intention to apply earlier.

Goodacre v. MHRD (June 21 2000), CP 7661 (PAB)

Section 60(8), (9) apply to the person on whose behalf the application is made or to a person who ceased to be incapable, but not to the person making the application on behalf of someone else. The provisions refer to medical incapacity, and do not import the common-law notions of legal incapacity. The fact that an orphan had been legally incapacitated by virtue of her status as an infant did not permit the PAB to backdate benefits to the date of the contributor's death.

271

Slater v. MHRD (January 3, 2003), CP 17196 (PAB)

The words "that person" as they appear in the fourth line of s. 60(8) refer to the person on whose behalf the application is made, not to the person making the application.

§3. Example Cases — Claimant Capable of Forming Intention to Apply

(a) Claimant Capable of Forming Intention to Apply

- Claimant diagnosed with schizophrenia over 20 years before application; main reason applicant did not apply earlier was due to lack of knowledge of entitlement to disability pension: *McDonald v. Canada (Attorney General)*, 2013 FCA 37

- Husband in shock and suffering major depression after contributor's death, and failing to apply for survivor's benefits until six years later; husband continuing to work during that time: *Lavery v. MSD* (April 21, 2007), CP 23950 (PAB)

- Applicant being frequently depressed, suffering from extreme grief over the loss of son, and diagnosed with schizophrenia and psychotic disorder; applicant showing lucidity by consenting to numerous tests and forms of treatment over an 18 year period after leaving employment: *Devcic v. MHRD* (August 30, 2001), CP 14065 (PAB)

- Despite applicant's schizophrenia, her lack of knowledge of entitlement rather than lack of capacity to form an intent resulted in delay of application: *Pedersen v. MHRD* (May 1, 2001), CP 11660 (PAB)

- Applicant for survivor's benefits not aware of husband's demise until more than 4 years after his death; applicant not lacking capacity to form intention to make application: *MHRD v. Robertson* (December 6, 1999), CP 08044 (PAB)

- Claimant delaying application for four years although condition not improving during that period; attending physician not suggesting that claimant's anxiety state or associated psychosomatic symptoms rendered him incapable: *MEI v. Hudon* (July 14, 1994), CP 2727, CEB & PG (TB) ¶8552 (PAB)

- Claimant suffering bouts of depression and anxiety, but not sufficiently intense or continuous: *Kumar v. MEI* (May 9, 1996), CP 3516 (PAB)

- Claimant teaching class part-time prior to making application, and making and keeping medical appointments: *Morrison v. MHRD* (1997), CP 4182 (PAB)

- Claimant suffering from agoraphobia, but indicating that had she known of availability of disability benefit at time of onset of illness, she would have applied: *Proulx v. MHRD* (June 15, 2000), CP 07859 (PAB)

(b) Claimant Not Capable of Forming Intention to Apply

- Applicant for survivor's benefits and orphan's benefits alleging that deceased husband had inflicted emotional abuse on her; applicant separated three years prior to husband's death and applying three years after his death; applicant participated in various activities during that period and discussed forms, understood their nature and decided not to complete them: *MHRSD v. J.C.* (April 13, 2010), CP 26612 (PAB)

- Claimant's orphan son was penalized by applicant's failure to file applications earlier, where applicant found not to be incapacitated: *H.H. v. MHRSD* (May 21, 2010), CP 25537 (PAB)

- Contributor's refusal to accept diagnosis of schizophrenia preventing earlier application for disabled contributor's child's benefit: *Gallant v. MHRD* (October 2, 2001), CP 14706 (PAB)

- Clear medical diagnosis of paranoid schizophrenia going back three years prior to application: *Raithby v. MHRD* (April 23, 1997), CP 4361, CEB & PG (TB) ¶8680 (PAB)

§4. Canadian Charter of Rights and Freedoms

Canada (Attorney General) v. Hislop, 2007 SCC 10

With respect to s. 60(2), the estates of those survivors who were same sex partners of the contributor and who died more than 12 months before the coming into force of the 2000 amendments do not have standing to claim a s. 15(1) Charter right on behalf of the deceased survivor. The use of the term "individual" in s. 15(1) of the Charter was intentional and indicates that s. 15(1) applies to natural persons only.

Kernerman v. HRSD (November 30, 2007), CP 20561 (PAB)

The claimant's estate lacked standing to commence a Charter challenge where no argument had taken place before any tribunal with respect to the issue of discrimination under s. 15(1) at the time that the claimant died.

---

61. *Approval of interim benefit* — **(1) Where application is made for a benefit and payment of the benefit would be approved except that the amount of the benefit cannot be finally calculated at the time the approval would otherwise be given, the Minister may approve payment of an interim benefit in such amount as he may fix and payment of the interim benefit may be made in a like manner as if the benefit had been approved.**

(2) *Adjustment to be made when benefit subsequently approved* — **Where an interim benefit has been paid under subsection (1) and payment of a benefit is subsequently approved,**

   (a) **if the amount of the interim benefit was less than the amount of the benefit subsequently approved, the beneficiary shall be paid the additional amount that he would have been paid if the benefit had been approved at the time the interim benefit was approved; and**

   (b) **if the amount of the interim benefit exceeded the amount of the benefit subsequently approved, the amount paid in excess thereof shall be deducted from subsequent payments of the benefit or otherwise recovered in such manner as the Minister may direct.**

—————— **Notes** ——————

Synopsis

This section authorizes the Minister to approve payment of an interim benefit to recipients who qualify for a benefit, the amount of which cannot yet be calculated. Once the amount can be confirmed, subsequent payments will be adjusted to reflect over- or under-payments during the interim period.

---

62. *Where payment approved after month of commencement* — **(1) Payment of a benefit for each month shall be made at such time during the month as the Minister directs, except that, where payment of a benefit is approved after the end of the month for which the first payment of the benefit is payable under this Part, monthly payments of the benefit shall be made for months commencing with the month following the month in which payment of the benefit is approved and payments of the benefit months preceding that month for which the benefit is payable under this Part shall be paid in one sum during that month. (R.S.C. 1985, c. 30 (2nd Supp.), s. 29.)**

(2) *When benefit deemed to have become payable* — **For the purposes of this Act, where a benefit is payable under this Part commencing with any month, the benefit shall be deemed to have become payable at the beginning of that month.**

(R.S.C. 1985, c. 30 (2nd Supp.), s. 29.)

—————— **Notes** ——————

Synopsis

This section provides that while monthly payments are deemed to become payable at the beginning of the month, they are to be paid at a time in the month directed by the Minister. Payments with respect to the period prior to the approval of the application for benefits may be paid as a single lump sum in the month when payments actually start.

Related Provisions

   • Section 69 — Commencement of disability pension

- Section 72 — Commencement of survivor's pension

Related CPP Regulations

- Section 76 — Deduction for excess payments and remittance to provincial or municipal authority

Case Law

Bueno v. MHRD (April 23, 1997), CP 03253, CEB & PG (TB) ¶8674 (PAB)

Section 62 is only an explanatory section dealing with the commencement of other benefits, and does not override s. 42(2)(*b*) and s. 69 with respect to the commencement date of a disability pension.

---

63. *Where spouse remarried before survivor's pension payable* — **(1) Where a person whose spouse has died remarries at a time when no survivor's pension is payable to him, no survivor's pension is payable to that person during the period of his remarriage and if following the death of his spouse of that or any subsequent remarriage a survivor's pension would be payable to him if he applied for such a pension, his deceased spouse for the purposes of this Act shall be deemed to be his spouse named in the application.**

(2) *Discontinuance of survivor's pension* — **Where a person to whom a survivor's pension is being paid remarries, the survivor's pension shall be discontinued commencing with the month following the month in which that person was married.**

(3) *Application for survivor's pension* — **Where the spouse of a person whose survivor's pension has been discontinued under subsection (2) dies, that person may on application therefore be paid a survivor's pension equal to the survivor's pension that was discontinued under subsection (2) or the survivor's pension that would have been payable by reason of the death of the spouse if no survivor's pension had been previously payable to that person, whichever is the greater.**

(4) *Payment of pension to former spouse* — **Where the marriage of a person whose survivor's pension has been discontinued under subsection (2) is terminated otherwise than by the death of his spouse, the survivor's pension previously payable to that person shall thereupon become payable to him.**

(5) *Calculation of basic amount of survivor's pension* — **Where a survivor's pension payable to a person has been discontinued under subsection (2) and subsequently a survivor's pension equal to the pension so discontinued becomes payable to that person or the pension so discontinued again becomes payable to him, the basic monthly amount of the pension thereupon payable to that person shall be calculated as though the pension discontinued under subsection (2) had not been discontinued.**

(6) *Only one survivor's pension payable* — **Where, but for this subsection, more than one survivor's pension would be payable concurrently to a person under this Act, or a survivor's pension would be payable concurrently to a person under this Act and under a provincial pension plan, only one survivor's pension shall be payable to that person, the amount of which shall be the greatest or greater of the survivor's pensions that would, but for this subsection, be payable to that person.**

(7) *Death within 1 year of marriage* — **Where a contributor dies within one year after his marriage, no survivor's pension is payable to his survivor if the Minister is not satisfied that the contributor was at the time of his marriage in such a condition of health as to justify him in having an expectation of surviving for at least one year thereafter. (S.C. 2000, c. 12, s. 64.)**

(7.1) *When subsection (7) does not apply* — **Subsection (7) does not apply if the aggregate of the following periods is one year or more:**

　　(*a*) the period during which the contributor and the survivor had cohabited during the marriage; and

(b) the period during which the contributor and the survivor had cohabited in a conjugal relationship immediately before the marriage.

(S.C. 2000, c. 12, s. 51.)

(8) *Application of subsection (3)* — Subsection (3) applies only to a person who has made an application pursuant to that subsection that is pending on the coming into force of section 63.1. (R.S.C. 1985, c. 30 (2nd Supp.), s. 30.)

(9) *Application of subsection (4)* — Subsection (4) applies only to a person whose marriage is terminated as described in that subsection before the coming into force of section 63.1. (R.S.C. 1985, c. 30 (2nd Supp.), s. 30.)

(10) *Subsection does not apply* — Subsection (5) does not apply in a respect of a survivor's pension that becomes payable pursuant to section 63.1. (R.S.C. 1985, c. 30 (2nd Supp.), s. 30.)

(R.S.C. 1985, c. 30 (2nd Supp.), s. 30; 2000, c. 12, s. 64.)

——————————— Notes ———————————

Synopsis

This section provides for the discontinuance of the survivor's pension to a survivor who remarries before January 1, 1987. Survivors of marriages to more than one deceased contributor are only entitled to the survivor's pension of the greatest amount (ss. (6)). When a contributor dies within one year after marrying, no survivor's pension is payable unless (i) his or her health condition was such as to justify an expectation of surviving for at least one year after the marriage, or (ii) the parties had cohabited for a total of at least one year immediately before the marriage and thereafter (ss. (7), (7.1)).

Recent Amendments

The 2000 amendments reflect the new terminology, abolishing the use of the term "surviving spouse" in favour of the term "survivor".

Related Provisions

● Section 63.1 — No discontinuance for remarriages on or after January 1, 1987; reinstatement of survivor's pension

———————————————————

63.1. *Subsections do not apply* — **(1)** Subsections 63(1) and (2) do not apply to a person who remarries after the coming into force of this section.

(2) *Application for commencement or reinstatement of survivor's pension* — Where, before the coming into force of subsection (1),

(a) a survivor's pension that, but for the operation of subsection 63(1), would have become payable to a person did not become payable to the person, or

(b) the payment of a survivor's pension to a person was discontinued under subsection 63(2),

and the person is not being paid a survivor's pension at the time that this section comes into force, an application in writing to the Minister for the commencement or reinstatement, as the case may be, of the survivor's pension may be made by the person or on behalf of the person by such other person as may be prescribed.

(3) *Commencement of survivor's pension* — On approval by the Minister of an application referred to in subsection (2), a survivor's pension is payable to the applicant for each month commencing with the later of

(a) the month in which this section comes into force, and

(b) the eleventh month preceding the month in which the application is received by the Minister.

(4) *Basic monthly amount of survivor's pension* — **Where a survivor's pension becomes payable under this section to a person, the basic monthly amount of the pension shall be calculated in accordance with section 58 as though**

    (a) in the case of a person referred to in paragraph (2)(a), the survivor's pension that would have become payable to the person but for the operation of subsection 63(1) became payable at the time that it would have become payable but for that subsection; and

    (b) in the case of a person referred to in paragraph (2)(b), payment of the survivor's pension to the person had not been discontinued under subsection 63(2).

(R.S.C. 1985, c. 30 (2nd Supp.), s. 31.)

————————— **Notes** —————————

Synopsis

This section provides that a survivor is not disentitled to survivor's pension if he or she remarries on or after January 1, 1987. If he or she remarried before that date, the survivor may apply for reinstatement of the survivor's pension for the period commencing January 1, 1987.

————————————————————

64. *Surviving spouse of contributor* — [38]**(Repealed by R.S.C. 1985, c. 30, (2nd Supp.), s. 32(1).)**

65. *Benefit not to be assigned, etc.* — **(1) A benefit shall not be assigned, charged, attached, anticipated or given as security, and any transaction purporting to assign, charge, attach, anticipate or give as security a benefit is void.**

(1.1) *Benefit not subject to seizure or execution* — **A benefit is exempt from seizure and execution, either at law or in equity. (S.C. 1995, c. 33, s. 29.)**

(2) *Exception* — **Notwithstanding subsections (1) and (1.1), where any provincial authority or municipal authority in a province pays a person any advance or assistance or welfare payment for a month or any portion of a month that would not be paid if a benefit under this Act had been paid for that period and subsequently a benefit becomes payable or payment of a benefit may be made under this Act to that person for that period, the Minister may, in accordance with any terms and conditions that**

---

[38] Pursuant to R.S.C. 1985, c. 30 (2nd Supp.), s. 32(2): Notwithstanding the repeal of s. 64, section 64 continues to apply where a contributor dies before January 1, 1987 and, in that case, the definition "spouse", as enacted by subsection 1(3) of R.S.C. 1985, c. 30 (2nd Supp.), does not apply to section 64. Section 64 originally read as follows:

"**Sec. 64. Surviving spouse of contributor** — (1) Subject to subsections (2) and (3), for purposes of this Part, the surviving spouse of a deceased contributor is the person who was by law married to the deceased contributor at the time of his death.

(2) *Person deemed to be surviving spouse of contributor* — For the purposes of this Part, where a person

    (a) established to the satisfaction of the Minister that he had, for a period of not less than three years immediately before the death of a contributor with whom he had been residing and whom by law he was prohibited form marrying by reason of a previous marriage either of the contributor or of himself to another person, been publicly represented by the contributor as the spouse of the contributor, or

    (b) establishes to the satisfaction of the Minister that he had, for not less than one year immediately before the death of a contributor with whom he had been residing, been publicly represented by the contributor as the spouse of the contributor, and that at the time of the death of the contributor neither he nor the contributor was married to any other person

that person shall, if the Minister so directs, be deemed to be the surviving spouse of the deceased contributor, in lieu of the surviving spouse, if any, described in subsection (1), and to have become married to the contributor at such time as he commenced being so represented as the spouse of the contributor.

(3) *Idem* — For the purposes of this Part, a person to whom subsection (2) would apply, but for his marriage to a contributor after such time as he commenced being so represented as the spouse of the contributor, shall, if the Minister so directs, be deemed to have become married to the contributor at the time when, in fact, he commenced being so represented."

may be prescribed, deduct from that benefit and pay to the provincial authority or municipal authority, as the case may be, an amount not exceeding the amount of the advance or assistance or welfare payment paid. (S.C. 1997, c. 40, s. 78.)

(3) *Exception* — Notwithstanding subsections (1) and (1.1), where an administrator of a disability income program who is approved by the Minister makes a payment under that program to a person for a month or any portion of a month that would not have been made if a benefit under paragraph 44(1)(*b*) had been paid to that person for that period and subsequently a benefit becomes payable or payment of a benefit may be made under this Act to that person for that period, the Minister may, in accordance with any terms and conditions that may be prescribed, deduct from that benefit and pay to the administrator an amount not exceeding the amount of the payment made under that program. (S.C. 1997, c. 40, s. 78.)

(S.C. 1991, c. 44, s. 15; 1995, c. 33, s. 29; 1997, c. 40, s. 78.)

——————————— Notes ———————————

Synopsis

This section prevents recipients of CPP pensions from transferring the right to receive the benefit to a third party. This means that a recipient cannot sell such right in return for a lump sum, or use it as collateral to obtain a loan. Nor can CPP payments be garnished by private creditors. However, the Minister may deduct amounts from the CPP benefit otherwise payable where public welfare agencies, or approved disability income programs, have made payments which would not have been made if they had been aware that the payee was also a recipient of CPP benefits. (See also the *Mintzer* case below.)

Related Provisions

● Section 65.1 — Assignment of retirement pension to spouse or common-law partner

Related CPP Regulations

● Section 76.1 — Deduction from a benefit and payment to an administrator for a disability income program

Case Law

Bouchard v. Canada (Attorney General) 2009 FCA 321

The Crown is not bound by the seizure exemption provisions set out in CPP s. 65, and can claim such monies by virtue of s. 224.1 of the *Income Tax Act*. Under s. 17 of the *Interpretation Act*, no enactment is binding on the Crown or affects the Crown or its rights or prerogatives in any manner, unless otherwise indicated. The provisions of the CPP and OASA appear to be aimed at ensuring that benefits payable under them be for the beneficiary's own use by preventing that person from alienating or encumbering them. Although CPP s. 65 applies to third parties, there is no indication of any intention to bind the Crown.

Mintzer v. Canada, [1996] 2 FC 146 (C.A.)

Section 65 does not prevent the Crown from exercising its right of set-off under section 224.1 of the *Income Tax Act* against CPP retirement benefits received by a person who owes income tax. The word "attached" in s. 65(1) signifies something that is given to or to be exercised by a third party rather than by the Crown. The subsection appears to be aimed at ensuring that benefits payable under the statute are for the beneficiary's own use by preventing that person from alienating or encumbering them. The exception contained in s. 65.1(1), allowing an assignment in favour of a spouse, supports this contention. But for this subsection, the prohibitions in s. 65(1) would clearly prevent such an assignment.

Canada (Minister of Human Resources Development) v. Tait, 2006 FCA 380

By virtue of s. 65(1), survivor benefits cannot be assigned or designated.

Kenny v. Canada (Attorney General), 2004 FC 460, affirmed 2005 FCA 370

Section 65 is designed to prohibit double-dipping. The Minister's decision to pay monies to Social Services involves two determinations. The first is to confirm that the applicable conditions set out in CPP s. 65(2) and s. 76 of the CPP Regulations have been met. The second is to determine whether the discretion conferred by s. 65(2) of the CPP and s. 76(2) of the CPP

Canada Pension Plan

Regulations will be exercised to authorize payment to a province. There is no appeal or review provision in either case. The first determination is administrative in nature and requires no particular expertise. The Court is as well-positioned as the Minister to determine whether the prescribed requirements have been met. This determination calls for little deference and the applicable standard of review is correctness. The second determination is vested exclusively with the Minister and lies within the Minister's discretion. The Minister has considerable expertise in the administration of the CPP and in federal–provincial relations and arrangements — matters of which the courts have little knowledge. The determination involves policy considerations associated with the rights of the individual and the rights of governments. The discretionary decision invites a high degree of deference and the applicable standard of review is patent unreasonableness. A "Consent to Deduction and Payment" form was not invalid although the claimant had not yet applied for his CPP disability benefits at the time he signed the form. Reference to an "arrangement" between the federal Minister and the provincial social services Minister with respect to deduction and payment does *not* meet the evidentiary requirement for a written agreement between the two levels of government set out in s. 76(4) of the CPP Regulations.

65.1. *Assignment of retirement pension to spouse or common-law partner* — **(1) Notwithstanding subsection 65(1) but subject to this section, the Minister may approve the assignment of a portion of a contributor's retirement pension to the contributor's spouse or common-law partner, on application in prescribed manner and form by the contributor or the spouse or common-law partner, if the circumstances described in either subsection (6) or (7) exist. (S.C. 2000, c. 12, s. 52(1).)**

(2) *Definition of "spousal agreement"* — **(Repealed by 2000, c. 12, s. 52(1).)**

(3) *Agreement or court order not binding on Minister* — **Except as provided in subsection (4), where, on or after June 4, 1986, a written agreement between persons subject to an assignment under this section was entered into, or a court order was made, the provisions of that agreement or court order are not binding on the Minister for the purposes of an assignment under this section. (S.C. 2000, c. 12, s. 52(2).)**

(4) *Agreement binding on Minister* — **Where**

(a) **a written agreement between persons subject to an assignment under this section entered into on or after June 4, 1986 contains a provision that expressly mentions this Act and indicates the intention of the persons that there be no assignment under this section,**

(b) **that provision of the agreement is expressly permitted under the provincial law that governs such agreements,**

(c) **the agreement was entered into before the day of the application for the assignment, and**

(d) **that provision of the agreement has not been invalidated by a court order,**

that provision of the agreement is binding on the Minister and, consequently, the Minister shall not approve an assignment under this section. (S.C. 2000, c. 12, s. 52(2).)

(5) *Minister to notify parties* — **The Minister shall, forthwith after receiving an application from one spouse or from one common-law partner for an assignment under this section, notify the other spouse or common-law partner, in prescribed manner, that such an application has been made, and of such other information as the Ministers deems necessary. (S.C. 2000, c. 12, s. 52(2).)**

(6) *Double assignment* — **Where**

(a) **a retirement pension is payable to both spouses or to both common-law partners under this Act, or**

(b) **a retirement pension is payable to one spouse or common-law partner under this Act and a retirement pension is payable to the other spouse or common-law partner under a provincial pension plan and an agreement under section 80 provides for an assignment in this circumstance,** the assignment shall be made in respect of both retirement pensions and, in the case described in paragraph (*b*), in accordance with the agreement. (S.C. 2000, c. 12, s. 52(2).)

(7) *Single assignment* — Where, in respect of spouses or common-law partners,

(*a*) one is a contributor under this Act and the other is not a contributor under either this Act or a provincial pension plan,

(*b*) a retirement pension is payable under this Act to the contributor, and

(*c*) the non-contributor has reached sixty years of age,

the assignment shall be made only in respect of the retirement pension of the contributor. (S.C. 2000, c. 12, s. 52(2).)

(8) *Definitions* — In subsection (9),

"joint contributory period" means the period commencing on January 1, 1966 or with the month in which the elder of the two spouses or of the two common-law partners reaches eighteen years of age, whichever is later, and ending

(*a*) where both spouses or common-law partners are contributors, with the month in which the later of their respective contributory periods ends, or

(*b*) where only one spouse or common-law partner is a contributor, with the later of

(i) the month in which the contributor's contributory period ends, and

(ii) the earlier of the month in which the non-contributor reaches seventy years of age and the month in which an application for an assignment of a retirement pension is approved,

but excluding, where subsection (6) applies, any month that is excluded from the contributory period of both spouses or common-law partners pursuant to paragraph 49(*c*) or (*d*);

(S.C. 2000, c. 12, s. 52(2).)

"period of cohabitation" has the prescribed meaning, but in all cases shall be deemed to end with the month in which the joint contributory period ends.

(9) *Portion of pension assignable* — The portion of a contributor's retirement pension to be assigned to the contributor's spouse or common-law partner under this section is an amount calculated by multiplying

(*a*) the amount of the contributor's retirement pension, calculated in accordance with sections 45 to 53,

by

(*b*) fifty per cent of the ratio that the number of months in the period of cohabitation bears to the number of months in the joint contributory period.

(S.C. 2000, c. 12, s. 52(2).)

(10) *When assignment commences* — An assignment under this section commences with the month following the month in which the application for the assignment is approved.

(11) *When assignment ceases* — An assignment under this section ceases with the earliest of

(*a*) with the month in which either spouse or either common-law partner dies; (S.C. 2000, c. 12, s. 52(3).)

(*b*) with the twelfth month following the month in which the spouses or the common-law partners commence to live separate and apart within the meaning of paragraphs 55.1(2)(*a*) and (*b*) (and in those paragraphs a reference to "persons subject to a division" shall be read as a reference to "spouses or common-law partners"), (S.C. 2000, c. 12, s. 52(3).)

Canada Pension Plan

279

(c) where subsection (7) applies, with the month in which the non-contributor spouse or the non-contributor common-law partner becomes a contributor; (S.C. 2000, c. 12, s. 52(3).)

(d) the month in which a decree absolute of divorce, a judgment granting a divorce under the *Divorce Act* or a judgment of nullity of a marriage is issued and (S.C. 2000, c. 12, s. 52(3).)

(e) the month following the month in which the Minister approves a request or requests in writing from both spouses or both common-law partners that the assignment be cancelled. (S.C. 1995, c. 33, s. 30(1); 2000, c. 12, s. 52(3).)

(S.C. 1991, c. 44, s. 16; 1995, c. 33, s. 30(1); 2000, c. 12, s. 52(3).)

(11.1) *Request for reinstatement* — Where paragraph (11)(e) applies, either spouse or either common-law partner may make a request in writing to the Minister to have the assignment reinstated. (S.C. 1995, c. 33, s. 30(2); 2000, c. 12, s. 52(3).)

(11.2) *When reinstatement effective* — An assignment shall be reinstated on the first day of the month following the month in which the Minister approves the request referred to in subsection (11.1). (S.C. 1995, c. 33, s. 30(2).)

(12) *Notification of assignment* — On approval by the Minister of an assignment under this section, both spouses or both common-law partners shall be notified in the prescribed manner. (S.C. 1995, c. 33, s. 30(2); 2000, c. 12, s. 52(4).)

(R.S.C. 1985, c. 30 (2nd Supp.), s. 33; 1991, c. 44, s. 16; 1995, c. 33, s. 30; 1997, c. 40, s. 79; 2000, c. 12, s. 52.)

————————— **Notes** —————————

Synopsis

This section authorizes the Minister to approve of assignments in valid written domestic agreements between spouses and common-law partners of the assignor's right to receive a retirement pension, but only where the province where the parties reside has enacted legislation which expressly permits such assignment.

Recent Amendments

The 2000 amendment substitutes the phrase "spouse and common-law partner" for the formerly used term "spouse".

Related Provisions

- Section 81 — Request for reconsideration by Minister
- Section 80 — Agreements with provinces

Related CPP Regulations

- Section 43 — Application form assignment of a portion of a retirement pension
- Section 44 — Application on behalf of incapable person
- Section 46.1 — Notification in writing
- Sections 52, 54.1 — Information and evidence required from applicant
- Section 78.2 — Meaning of "period of cohabitation"

Case Law

Mintzer v. Canada, [1996] 2 FC 146 (C.A.)

The words "seizure and execution" in subsection 65(1.1) are not intended to prevent a set-off under s. 224.1 of the *Income Tax Act* against retirement benefits payable, but were intended to be additions to the list of prohibitions already contained in subsection 65(1).

MEI v. Hastings (November 9, 1994), CP 2864, CEB & PG (TB) ¶8567 (PAB)

The federal government and the Quebec government have not entered agreement under s. 80 for the purpose of authorizing an assignment under s. 65.1(6)(b). Where the applicant's spouse was a contributor to the QPP, but not to the CPP, that spouse's failure to apply for the minimal benefits she would be entitled to under the QPP did not mean that the applicant was eligible to assign a portion of his CPP retirement pension to his spouse under s. 65.1(1). The QPP pension was "payable" to the spouse for the purposes of s. 65.1(6)(*b*), and therefore the parties' circumstances did not fall within s. 65.1(6).

---

66. *Return of benefit where recipient not entitled* — **(1) A person or estate that has received or obtained by cheque or otherwise a benefit payment to which the person or estate is not entitled, or a benefit payment in excess of the amount of the benefit payment to which the person or estate is entitled, shall forthwith return the cheque or the amount of the benefit payment, or the excess amount, as the case may be. (S.C. 1991, c. 44, s. 17(1).)**

(2) *Recovery of amount of payment* — **If a person has received or obtained a benefit payment to which the person is not entitled, or a benefit payment in excess of the amount of the benefit payment to which the person is entitled, the amount of the benefit payment or the excess amount, as the case may be, constitutes a debt due to Her Majesty and is recoverable at any time in the Federal Court or any other court of competent jurisdiction or in any other manner provided by this Act. (S.C. 1997, c. 40, s. 80; 2007, c. 11, s. 4(1).)**

(2.01) *Recovery of amount of interest* — **Interest payable under this Part constitutes a debt due to Her Majesty and is recoverable at any time in the Federal Court or any other court of competent jurisdiction or in any other manner provided by this Act. (S.C. 2007, c. 11, s. 4(1).)**

(2.02) *Recovery of amount of penalty* — **The amount of a penalty imposed on a person under section 90.1 constitutes a debt due to Her Majesty and is recoverable at any time in the Federal Court or any other court of competent jurisdiction or in any other manner provided by this Act. (S.C. 2007, c. 11, s. 4(2).)**

(2.1) *Set-off* — **Where any amount is or becomes payable to the person or the person's estate or succession under this Act or any other Act or program administered by the Minister, that indebtedness may, in the prescribed manner, be deducted and retained out of the amount payable. (S.C. 1997, c. 40, s. 80.)**

(2.2) *Certificates* — **All or part of the amount of that indebtedness that has not been recovered may be certified by the Minister**

    (*a*) **without delay, if in the Minister's opinion the person liable to pay the amount is attempting to avoid payment; and**

    (*b*) **in any other case, on the expiration of 30 days after the default. (S.C. 1997, c. 40, s. 80.)**

(2.3) *Judgment* — **On production to the Federal Court, the certificate shall be registered in the Court. When it is registered, it has the same force and effect, and all proceedings may be taken, as if the certificate were a judgment obtained in the Court for a debt of the amount specified in the certificate. (S.C. 1997, c. 40, s. 80.)**

(2.4) *Judgment* — **A certificate registered under subsection (2.3) may also be registered in the superior court of a province as if it were a document evidencing a judgment of that court. (S.C. 1997, c. 40, s. 80.)**

(2.5) *Costs* — **All reasonable costs and charges for the registration of the certificate are recoverable in the same way as if they had been certified and the certificate registered under this section. (S.C. 1997, c. 40, s. 80.)**

(2.6) *Charge on land* — **A document issued by the Federal Court or by a superior court of a province evidencing a certificate in respect of a debtor registered under subsection (2.3) or (2.4) may be recorded for the purpose of creating security, or a charge, lien or legal hypothec, on land in a province, or on an interest in land in a province, held or owned by the debtor, in the same manner as a document evidencing a**

Canada Pension Plan

judgment of the superior court of the province against a person for a debt owing by the person may be recorded in accordance with the law of the province to create security, or a charge, lien or legal hypothec, on land, or an interest in land, held or owned by the person. (S.C. 2001, c. 4, s. 67)

(2.7) *Garnishment* — If the Minister knows or suspects that a person is or is about to become indebted or liable to make a payment to a person liable to make a payment to Her Majesty under this Part, the Minister may, by a notice served personally or by confirmed delivery service, require the first person to pay the money otherwise payable to the second person in whole or in part to the Receiver General on account of the second person's liability. (S.C. 1997, c. 40, s. 80; 2007, c. 11, s. 4(4).)

(2.8) *Debt due to the Crown* — An amount not paid as required by a notice under subsection (2.7) is a debt due to Her Majesty. (S.C. 1997, c. 40, s. 80.)

(2.9) *Proof of personal service* — If provision is made by this Act or the regulations for personal service of a request for information or a notice or demand, an affidavit of the person effecting service stating that

(a) the person has charge of the appropriate records and has knowledge of the facts in the particular case,

(b) such a request, notice or demand was served personally on a named day on the person to whom it was directed, and

(c) the person identifies as an exhibit attached to the affidavit a true copy of the request, notice or demand,

is evidence of the personal service and of the request, notice or demand. (S.C. 1997, c. 40, s. 80.)

(3) *Remission of amount owing* — Notwithstanding paragraph 61(2)(b) and subsections (1) and (2) of this section, where a person has received or obtained a benefit payment to which he is not entitled, or a benefit payment in excess of the amount of the benefit payment to which he is entitled, and the Minister is satisfied that

(a) the amount or excess of the benefit payment cannot be collected within the reasonably foreseeable future,

(b) the administrative costs of collecting the amount or excess of the benefit payment are likely to equal or exceed the amount to be collected, (R.S.C. 1985, c. 30 (2nd Supp.), s. 34(1).)

(c) repayment of the amount or excess of the benefit payment would cause undue hardship to the debtor, or (R.S.C. 1985, c. 30 (2nd Supp.), s. 34(1).)

(d) the amount or excess of the benefit payment is the result of erroneous advice or administrative error on the part of the Minister or an official of the Department of Employment and Social Development acting in an official capacity in the administration of this Act, (R.S.C. 1985, c. 30 (2nd Supp.), s. 34(1); 1996, c. 11, s. 97(1)(b); 2005, c. 35, s. 66(a)(i); 2012, c. 19, s. 695(1)(a)(i); 2013, c. 40, s. 237(1)(b)(i).)

the Minister may, unless that person has been convicted of an offence under any provision of this Act or of the *Criminal Code* in connection with the obtaining of the benefit payment, remit all or any portion of the amount or excess of the benefit payment. (S.C. 1995, c. 33, s. 31(1).)

(4) *Where person denied benefit due to departmental error, etc.* — Where the Minister is satisfied that, as a result of erroneous advice or administrative error in the administration of this Act, any person has been denied (S.C. 1995, c. 33, s. 31(2).)

(a) a benefit, or portion thereof, to which that person would have been entitled under this Act,

(b) a division of unadjusted pensionable earnings under section 55 or 55.1, or

(c) an assignment of a retirement pension under section 65.1, the Minister shall take such remedial action as the Minister considers appropriate to place the person in the position that the person would be in under this Act had the erroneous advice not been given or the administrative error not been made. (R.S.C. 1985, c. 30 (2nd Supp.), s. 34(2); 1991, c. 14, s. 1; 1991, c. 44, s. 17(2); 1995, c. 33, s. 31.)

(5) *When person denied division* — Where the Minister is satisfied that a person has been denied a division of unadjusted pensionable earnings under section 55 or 55.1 as a result of the provisions of a written agreement entered into or a court order made before June 4, 1986, the Minister shall take such remedial action as the Minister considers appropriate to place the person in the position that the person would be in under this Act had the division been approved, including attributing to that person the earnings that would have been attributed had the division been approved, if (S.C. 2000, c. 12, s. 53.)

    (*a*) the agreement or order does not indicate that there be no division of unadjusted pensionable earnings under this Act; and (S.C. 2000, c. 12, s. 53.)

    (*b*) all other criteria specified by or under this Act respecting divisions are met. (S.C. 1991, c. 44, s. 17(2); 2000, c. 12, s. 53.)

(6) *Exclusion of Financial Administration Act* — Section 155.1 of the *Financial Administration Act* does not apply in relation to amounts owing to Her Majesty under this Part. (S.C. 2007, c. 11, s. 4(5).)

(R.S.C. 1985, c. 30 (2nd Supp.), s. 34; S.C. 1991, c. 14, s. 1; 1991, c. 44, s. 17; 1995, c. 33, s. 31; 1996, c. 11, s. 97; 1997, c. 40, s. 80; 2000, c. 12, s. 53; 2001, c. 4, s. 67; 2005, c. 35, s. 66; 2007, c. 11, s. 4; 2012, c. 19, s. 695; 2013, c. 40, s. 237.)

———————— Notes ————————

Synopsis

This section requires persons who receive a CPP benefit payment to which they are not entitled, to return the payment or amount of overpayment. The incorrect payment or overpayment amount is treated as a debt due to the Crown and is recoverable at any time. The Minister may set off the amount against other amounts owing to the person by the Ministry. The Minister is authorized to waive the debt if it is uncollectable, the costs of collecting it are prohibitive, repayment would cause undue hardship, or the payment or overpayment resulted from erroneous advice or administrative error by Ministry officials, unless the person has been convicted of an offence under the *Criminal Code* in connection with the payment or overpayment. Where an error has been made by Ministry officials, or where the Minister had failed to approve a division of pension credits on the basis of a written agreement or court order made before June 4, 1986, although the agreement or order did not expressly prohibit such a division, the Minister is required to do what is necessary to put the person in the same position he or she would be in if the error had not been made or the division be approved.

Recent Amendments

The 2000 amendment deleted references to the person's "spouse" in s. 66(5), consistent with the new terminology. The 2007 amendments specifically provide for the collection of interest and penalties on any overpayment.

Related CPP Regulations

    ● Section 42 — Recovery by deductions of amounts to which recipient not entitled

Case Law

§1. Generally

Canada (Attorney General) v. Jodhan, 2012 FCA 161

The method by which the federal government permits online access to potential claimants violates s. 15 of the Charter to the extent that it discriminates against visually impaired persons. The visually impaired have not been "reasonably accommodated" because they allegedly can obtain the same information available online by other channels, namely in person, by telephone and by mail. These other channels are difficult to access, less reliable, and not complete. Moreover, they fail to provide the visually impaired with independent access or the same dignity and convenience as the services online. For the blind and visually impaired, accessing information and services online gives them independence, self-reliance, control, ease of access, dignity, and self-esteem. A person is not handicapped if she does not need help. Making the government online information and services accessible provides the visually impaired with "substantive equality".

Canada (Attorney General) v. King, 2009 FCA 105

The term "erroneous advice", as it is used in s. 66(4), refers to advice given by the Department of Human Resources and Skills Development to a member of the public, and not to advice which, on occasion, may be given to the Minister in the course of deciding whether a pension should be awarded. The CPP is one of the largest social benefit schemes in the country. The statute and its regulations are complex, and many applicants are not represented by counsel. As such, department officials sometimes provide summary information over the phone or in person at local offices concerning eligibility for benefits, deadlines for filing, and so forth. Where an official gives a member of the public incorrect information, resulting in the denial of a benefit, the Minister may decide to provide a remedy. The plain and ordinary meaning of the word "advice" contemplates a communication of some sort. Decisions of medical adjudicators are not deemed to be advice always accepted by the Minister. A decision of the PAB overruling a decision of the Minister, in the absence of new evidence, does not constitute proof of erroneous advice. If it did, there would be no discretion for the Minister under s. 66(4), which provides that the Minister must satisfy herself that an error has been made. Where the Pension Appeal Board relied on new evidence in overruling the Minister to award a pension, the Minister's initial decision to deny the benefit could be said to have been based on erroneous advice for that reason alone.

§2. Erroneous advice (s. 66(4))

Robbins v. Canada (Attorney General), 2014 FC 689

Where a legislative officer is appointed to peruse the claimant's file and determine if there had been an administrative error under s. 66(4), this was a question of fact and of discretion and should be reviewed on the standard of reasonableness. The court should not intervene if the officer's decision is transparent, justifiable, intelligible, and within the range of acceptable outcomes. The court will set aside the officer's decision only if his reasons, read in the context of the record, fail to intelligibly explain why he reached his conclusions or how the facts and applicable law support the outcome. The fact that the Department made administrative errors in relation to the applicant's file in the past does not make it any more or less likely to make an administrative error in the future. Section 66(4) does not create an adversarial process. Ultimately, the CPP was enacted to benefit contributors. If errors in how the Act is administered are impeding that objective, then the Department has an interest in uncovering and correcting those errors. Thus, once a contributor has said that he or she was given erroneous advice or that an administrative error occurred, it may indeed be unfair or unreasonable for the Department not to collect evidence from its own files and about its own procedures. Indeed, that much is demanded by its policy guidelines. Therefore, while it may be technically true that the onus is on the applicant to prove an administrative error or erroneous advice, it is analytically unhelpful to the extent that it suggests that the Department can simply do nothing. It could be an error for an officer to dismiss claims that he believes solely because there is no corroborating evidence, especially where no corroborating evidence could reasonably be expected.

Bartlett v. Canada (Attorney General), 2012 FCA 230

The remedial powers of the Minister under s. 66 rest on a different statutory foundation from those which may result in a reconsideration or appeal under Division F of Part II of the CPP. The legislative intent behind s. 66(4) was to provide the Minister with special authorities beyond those available under a reconsideration or appeal so as to remedy denials of benefits resulting from erroneous advice or administrative errors in situations where such errors could not otherwise be adequately remedied under the other provisions of the CPP. A distinction exists in the CPP such that persons obtaining retroactivity redress through reconsiderations and appeals are not in the same position as those whose available retroactivity redress is under s. 66(4). Interest payments cannot be awarded as a remedy on reconsideration or appeal because there is no provision for them under the current legislative scheme. However, where a person has been denied a disability pension for decades as a result of a civil servant's administrative error, Parliament intended to empower the Minister under s. 66(4) to take all appropriate remedial measures required to correct that error, including providing both retroactive payments related to the entire period and related interest on those payments.

King v. Canada (Attorney General) 2010 FCA 122

An error of law on the part of the Minister in misrepresenting the definition of "disability" does not constitute either "erroneous advice" or "administrative error" within the scope of s. 66(4). For s. 66(4) to have any application, the alleged administrative error must have resulted in the denial of a benefit the appellant was entitled to. In an application for judicial review, pleadings must assert a factual foundation for the allegation the administrative error is what led the Minister to reach the wrong conclusion about the appellant's entitlement to remedial action. Reference to a failure by the Minister to disclose documents were irrelevant where there was no allegation that the non-disclosure led to the wrong conclusion.

Canada (Attorney General) v. Torrance, 2013 FCA 227

The question as to whether or not there was an administrative error is reviewable on a standard of reasonableness because it is a question of fact. The question as to whether the administrative error resulted in a deprivation of benefits that would otherwise have been payable is also a question of fact, reviewable on the standard of reasonableness. By this standard, the issue is whether the decision fell within the range of acceptable outcomes. While section 66(4) requires an examination of the officials' behaviour, not that of the claimant's, section 66(4) also requires that any administrative error have deprived a claimant of benefits to which he would otherwise have been entitled. It is therefore not inappropriate for officials to identify the reason the claimant was not entitled to benefits in order to show that any administrative error that may have occurred was not the cause of the claimant's ineligibility for benefits. The Minister's letter denying the claimant's initial claim for disability benefits on the ground of insufficient contributions was mailed to the wrong address and never received by the claimant. The claimant, who been rendered a quadriplegic by the accident that led to the claim, had delayed filing the income tax returns for the years in question for eight years, which returns would have proved that he had made sufficient contributions for those years. It was reasonable for the Minister to conclude that the failure of the letter to reach its destination was not the cause of the claimant's failure to file his income tax returns in a timely fashion.

Jones v. Canada (Attorney General), 2010 FC 740

The Federal Court of Appeal's 2010 decision in *King* (above) makes it clear that there must be a causal connection between the erroneous advice or administrative error and the denial of the benefit, the absence of which is fatal. Previous Ministerial decisions that the claimant was not disabled for the purposes of CPP s. 42 could only be challenged through the generous appeal process in the CPP and ultimately through judicial review, and not via s. 66(4). *Obiter:* The type of errors that entails the application of s. 66(4) include, for example, misplacing or losing an application, or seeking information about the wrong year. There is no legal obligation on the Minister to obtain further information from an applicant's doctor or specialist (also called "developing to" the doctor or specialist) before making a determination. While such may be current practice, the Minister's failure to do so in 1987 did not constitute an administrative error. It cannot be the case that before reviewing an application, there is an onus on the Ministry to obtain whatever evidence is available from the family doctor or any specialist listed in an application or prior application, whether or not it is filed by the claimant, to explain the CPP to the claimant, and to tell the claimant what information is missing from his or her file, including whether the claimant should file additional evidence. If there was such an onus, then the fact that the CPP Regulations put the burden of proof on the claimant would have no meaning, and an applicant would be better off providing no medical evidence at all, leaving it to the Department to do all the inquiries itself, so that if anything is missing, he or she can simply bypass the three-tier appeal process by going directly to s. 66(4) to obtain not only the benefits themselves but also the related interest which are not even otherwise payable under the CPP.

Kissoon v. Canada (Minister of Human Development Resources), 2004 FC 24, affirmed 2004 FCA 384

The decision of the Minister under s. 66(4) is discretionary. Although the Minister "shall" take remedial action that it considers appropriate, this duty arises only once the Minister is satisfied that erroneous advice has been given or that an administrative error has occurred. The requirement to take remedial action is conditional and, therefore, does not fetter the Minister's discretion to first satisfy herself that an error has been made. Given the discretionary nature of the Minister's decision, the standard of review is patent unreasonableness. This means that the Minister's decision should only be set aside if it is made arbitrarily or in bad faith, it cannot be supported on the evidence, or the Minister failed to consider the appropriate factors. A finding of erroneous advice or administrative error is one of fact, which also signals to a court that deference should be accorded to the Minister. Evidence should not be reweighed nor findings tampered with merely because this Court would have come to a different conclusion.

Leskiw v. Canada (Attorney General), 2003 FCT 582, affirmed 2004 FCA 177

Section 66(4) does not require that the claimant request that the Minister investigate a claim of erroneous advice. The Review Tribunal may refer an appeal to it based on an allegation of erroneous advice to the Income Security Programs Branch of the Ministry. The Branch then has jurisdiction to assess the claim and determine whether such advice was actually given, even though the claimant did not request such an assessment or mention "erroneous advice" or s. 66(4) in letters to the Ministry.

Scheuneman v. Canada (Human Resources Development), 2005 FCA 254

The existence of s. 66(4) should be taken to preclude a tort claim based on an administrative error that results in an incorrect termination of disability benefits. Where the error has been acknowledged and the benefit reinstated retroactive to when they had been terminated, the Court does not have the jurisdiction to compel the Minister to reconsider that remedy. The authority to award interest is included in the power conferred by s. 66(4).

Obiter: It remains open to the claimant to ask the Minister to reconsider the remedy on the basis that the reinstatement of benefits did not place him in the position he would have been in if the administrative error had not been made.

Raivitch v. Canada (Minister of Human Resources Development), 2006 FC 1279

There are no prescribed procedures for investigating s. 66(4) claims. The procedures are at the discretion of the Minister, which is in line with the discretionary nature of the decision itself. Where the decision-maker conducted numerous interviews with HRDC employees in an effort to ascertain whether an administrative error had indeed been committed with regard to the applicant, and considered all reasonable avenues for assessing a potential administrative error — documentary, archival, personal interviews with employees and correspondence, as well as the possible impact of the claimant's deficiencies in the English language on the situation, — this represented a reasonable and appropriate approach for determining the claim.

King v. Canada, 2007 FC 272

There is no automatic right to interest on disability pension payments which have been delayed and for which the disabled person is entitled to a retroactive pension payment. Moreover, the PAB in granting the plaintiff a disability pension under the Plan has no authority to award interest. However, it may be possible for the plaintiff to obtain a favourable decision from the Minister under s. 66(4). As indicated in *Scheuneman* (above), the proper course of proceeding is:

1. the plaintiff asks that the Minister consider remedial action under s. 66(4) not to award interest on the retroactive pension payment; and

2. if the Minister denies the request for interest, the plaintiff can commence an application for judicial review of that decision in the Federal Court under s. 18.1 of the *Federal Courts Act.*

Lee v. Canada (Attorney General), 2011 FC 689

There is no legal obligation on HRSDC to inform individuals of the availability of CPP benefits. There is no set procedure for the Ministry to investigate a claim of erroneous advice. There is no requirement to interview the applicants and other witnesses where the applicants had been given an opportunity to provide, and were specifically asked to provide, "all of the information, evidence and submissions" that they wished to provide.

Bessette v. Canada (Attorney General), 2011 FC 176

The Minister does not bear the onus of informing claimants of their entitlement to a benefit. Section 60(1) puts the onus on applicants to claim benefits. Even if the claimant had been erroneously informed by a Ministry official that the 11-month limit on retroactive benefits is generally waived with respect to the disabled contributor child benefit, the imposition of the limitation on retroactive benefits was not caused by any error. The cause of any loss of benefits was the failure to make a timely claim for them, not the conduct of the official to whom the claimant spoke. *Obiter:* It would be completely different if the claimant had been told that she did not have to make a claim for benefits when her children were born because benefits can be assessed retroactively whenever she applied for them. In that case, the claimant would have suffered a loss attributable to bad advice.

Bartlett v. Canada (Attorney General), 2007 FC 89

The Minister making a request to the Department of National Revenue regarding the claimant's contributions for the wrong year is an administrative error. [Note: This case was distinguished in *Jones v. Canada (Attorney General),* 2010 FC 740, where the Federal Court noted at para. 47 that in *Bartlett,* "it is clear that the decision-maker had undertaken some enquiry (thereby assuming the duty to do it correctly) and in the process of doing so mistakenly sought information about the wrong year. This case does not stand for the proposition that there is an administrative duty to seek evidence to establish an applicant's right to CPP benefits when he or his doctors failed to provide it".]

Canada (Attorney General) v. Dale, 2006 FC 1364

Neither the Review Tribunal nor the PAB has jurisdiction to entertain an appeal of a decision of the Minister under s. 66(4).

Mulveney v. Canada (Human Resources Development), 2007 FC 869

The determination of whether an overpayment arose as a result of erroneous advice or administrative error is a matter that falls within the expertise of the Minister and his delegate, and the delegate's expertise is superior to that of the court. The fact that the delegate had significant experience and expertise in handling requests for the exercise of discretion to remit overpayments and, as supervisor of the medical adjudication unit of HRDC, could be presumed to have superior knowledge as to what constitutes administrative error or erroneous advice, militated in favour of affording deference to the delegate's decision.

Strezov v. Canada (Attorney General), 2007 FC 417

While the Minister does have the power to grant relief under s. 66(4) where someone has been given erroneous advice, the Minister can only do so where the effect of the erroneous advice is to deny the individual a benefit, including a division of pensionable earnings, to which the person would otherwise have been entitled. Relief was not available to cancel a split of pension credits where Ministry staff had allegedly told a claimant that her pension credits would not be split if the result was not favourable to her.

Bartlett v. Canada (Attorney General), 2007 FC 89

The Minister's decision that there was no administrative error was patently unreasonable where department documents manifestly indicated that it had never actually attempted to verify the applicant's contributions for the years in question.

Barnes v. Canada (MHRD), 2004 FC 985

A finding by the Minister's delegate that the claimant "did not provide any evidence" to support the allegation of erroneous advice, was patently unreasonable where in fact the claimant had given uncontradicted testimony as to the erroneous advice, which the Review Tribunal, albeit in a gratuitous ruling, had no jurisdiction to make, had found credible. The Minister's delegate should have acknowledged this evidence and then gone on to assign its weight. On judicial review, the Minister's delegate was directed to specifically consider the findings of the Review Tribunal with respect to the claimant's and his mother's credibility.

Hussey-Roberts v. MHRD, (May 31, 2002), CP 19092

The PAB is without jurisdiction to hear a contributor's application for relief from administrative error or erroneous advice committed or given by any official person. Section 66(4) clearly provides that such remedial power is vested in the Minister.

Edwards v. MHRD, (May 17, 2002), CP 18011 (applying *Pincombe v. Canada (Attorney General),* (October 5, 1995) Doc. A-675-94 (Fed. C.A.)

The PAB does not have jurisdiction to deal with the sole issue of whether the Minister properly exercised his discretion with respect to repayment of benefits received while allegedly not entitled thereto. Instead, such a matter should be brought up by application before the Federal Court.

Larone v. MHRD (February 23, 2000), CP 09254 (PAB)

The PAB does not have jurisdiction to deal with the matter of recovery of any overpayment of disability benefits to a claimant. That matter is dealt with in s. 66, and under s. 66(2) any overpayment to Appellant is a debt due to Her Majesty and is recoverable at any time in the Federal Court or any other court of competent jurisdiction or in any manner provided by the CPP.

Clemenshaw v. Clemenshaw (January 24, 2000), CP 09042 (PAB)

While s. 66 gives the Minister, *but not the Board*, discretion to take "remedial action" where pre-June 4, 1986 settlement agreements exist, it does not provide that the other spouse's pension credits will be divided. Section 66 therefore only allows the Minister, in rare cases, to give an applicant an *ex gratia* pension without depriving the other spouse of his or her full pension.

Julian v. MHRD (September 10, 1999), CP 06550 (PAB)

Subsection 66(4) authorizes the Minister to take the appropriate remedial action with respect to any person *denied* a benefit as a result of erroneous advice or administrative error in the administration of the CPP. This applies exclusively to corrective measures taken by the Minister with regard to a contributor whose rights are infringed as a result of an error or erroneous advice by an administrative official. This recourse can therefore be taken only at the initiation of a contributor to correct an error that results in the denial of a benefit to which he would be entitled, or the division of unadjusted pensionable earnings under s. 55 or 55.1, or the assignment of a retirement pension under s. 65.1. Section 66(4) cannot be used by the Minister to end or cancel disability benefits payable that had been authorized by administrative error.

Funk v. MHRD (February 18, 1998), CP 5245 (PAB). See also *Margison v. MEI* (October 25, 1995), CP 3300 (PAB); *Townsend v. MEI* (November 25, 1995), CP 3267 (PAB).

Raising a false hope, e.g., where Ministry staff suggest that the claimant apply for a disability pension, does not equate to administrative error under s. 66(4). The provision gives the Minister a discretion, and once that discretion is exercised it is not reviewable by the PAB as there is no jurisdiction.

Graham v. MHRD (June 13, 1997), CP 5230, CEB & PG (TB) ¶8692 (PAB)

There is no authority in the legislation allowing the Review Tribunal or the PAB to forgive the repayment of disability benefits that have been paid in error to a claimant.

Pincombe v. Canada (Attorney General), [1995] F.C.J. No. 1320 (Fed. C.A.). See also *Canada (Minister of Human Resources Development) v. Tucker*, 2003 FCA 278, *MSD v. Goyetche* (June 30, 2004), CP 22050 (PAB).

The decision to remedy or not in CPP s. 66 is placed wholly within the Minister's department. Neither the Review Tribunal nor the PAB have jurisdiction to hear appeals from the Minister's decision or to interfere with the discretion exercised.

66.1. *Request to cancel benefit* — **(1) A beneficiary may, in prescribed manner and within the prescribed time interval after payment of a benefit has commenced, request cancellation of that benefit.**

(1.1) *Exception* — **Subsection (1) does not apply to the cancellation of a retirement pension in favour of a disability benefit where an applicant for a disability benefit under this Act or under a provincial pension plan is in receipt of a retirement pension and the applicant is deemed to have become disabled for the purposes of entitlement to the disability benefit in or after the month for which the retirement pension first became payable. (S.C. 1997, c. 40, s. 81.)**

(2) *Effect of cancellation* — **Where a request made under subsection (1) or under a substantially similar provision of a provincial pension plan is granted and the amount of the benefits paid is repaid within the prescribed time or, in the case of a provincial pension plan, the time provided thereunder, that benefit shall be deemed for all purposes of this Act not to have been payable during the period in question.**

(R.S.C. 1985, c. 30 (2nd Supp.), s. 35; 1997, c. 40, s. 81.)

————————— **Notes** —————————

Synopsis

This section permits a person receiving CPP benefits to request the Minister to cancel and repay them. The request must be in writing and made within six months of the commencement of receiving the retirement pension (Regulation s. 46.2).

Note that a person cannot be in receipt of retirement pension and a disability benefit under the CPP at the same time, by virtue of s. 44(1)(*b*) and s. 70(3). Where the recipient of a retirement pension is less than 65 years old and has been determined by the Minister to be disabled prior to or in the month that the retirement pension became payable, he or she may use s 66.1 to cancel the retirement pension in favour of the disability benefit. Subsection (1.1), which came into force January 1, 1998, clarifies that such a request can only be brought for this purpose where the claimant was deemed to be disabled prior to the month in which the retirement first became payable, and must be made within 60 days of receiving the notice of the determination (Regulation s. 46.2(2)).

Legislative History

Prior to December 18, 1997, before the coming into force of s. 66.1(1), the claimant could request a cancellation even if he or she was deemed to become disabled in or after the month that the retirement pension became payable.

Related Provisions

- Section 70(3) — Effect of receiving a retirement pension

Related CPP Regulations

- Section 46.2 — Cancellation of benefit within 6 months

Case Law

Funk v. MHRD (February 18, 1998), CP 5245 (PAB). See also *Margison v. MEI* (October 25, 1995), CP 3300 (PAB); *Townsend v. MEI* (November 25, 1995), CP 3267 (PAB).

The combined effect of ss. 70(3) and 66.1, and s. 46.2 of the Regulations, is that the last date an applicant who had been in receipt of a retirement pension since September 1992 could be found to be disabled is no more than six months after she was in receipt of a retirement pension, or March 1993. Where the application for disability benefit was received in December 1994, the earliest that the applicant could be deemed to be disabled is September 1993. In such a case, it was too late to obtain a withdrawal of the applicant's retirement pension in favour of a disability pension.

MSD v. Desjardins (October 5, 2006), CP 23966 (PAB)

Section 66.1(1.1) is clear and unequivocal. The CPP provisions allowing for the cancellation of retirement benefits in favour of disability benefits are not flexible. Neither the Review Tribunal nor the PAB is entitled to exercise an equitable jurisdiction in this regard. While s. 43(1) and (1.1) of the Regulations allow for an application for a disability pension that has been denied to be deemed an application for retirement benefits in prescribed circumstances, the reverse is not true.

Greathead v. MSD (March 14, 2006), CP 23044 (PAB)

A claimant cannot seek to cancel a CPP retirement pension which is already in pay in favour of a CPP disability pension if the date when he is disabled (or deemed disabled) for the purpose of entitlement to a disability pension, is during, or after, the month for which his retirement pension first became payable. By virtue of s. 42(2)(*b*) a person cannot be deemed to have become disabled more than 15 months earlier to their application for a disability pension, and therefore an application for a disability pension cannot succeed if made four years after the claimant began to receive a retirement pension.

MSD v. Galay (June 3, 2004), CP 21768 (PAB)

Where a claimant had already been in receipt of a CPP retirement pension more than 15 months prior to applying for disability benefits, he could not cancel the pension in favour of the disability benefits under s. 66.1.

MEI v. Sidhu (January 1996), CP 3486, CEB & PG (TB) ¶8610 (PAB)

An application for disability benefits by a person receiving a CPP retirement pension does not implicitly contain a request to cancel the retirement pension.

Boulard v. MSD (May 20, 2004), CP 22011 (PAB)

The claimant had been receiving a retirement pension since July 2000. Since the claimant's application for a disability pension was received in April 2002, the PAB ruled that he could not have been deemed disabled prior to January 2001, and the application to withdraw the retirement pension was dismissed.

Zoldy v. MHRD (November 27, 2001), CP 15071 (PAB)

In canceling his retirement pension and applying for a disability benefit, the applicant is entitled to rely on express instructions by the Ministry representative and should not be penalized for complying with their directive. The PAB may draw an adverse inference from the Minister's failure to call a knowledgeable witness in this regard.

Gudelj v. MHRD (May 17, 2001), CP 11806 (PAB). See also *MHRD v. Kerr* (June 11, 2001), CP 18095 (PAB).

The PAB did not have jurisdiction to reopen previous unsuccessful applications for disability benefits to allow the applicant to come within the allowed period for canceling retirement pension in favour of a disability benefits.

Hopkins v. MHRD (November 18, 1999), CP 07997 (PAB)

Obiter: Following the 1997 enactment of s. 66.1(1.1), it appears that applications for disability benefits to an applicant already in receipt of a CPP retirement pension are not longer permitted if the deemed date of disability is fixed on a date on or following the month for which the retirement pension became payable. The six-month window has been eliminated.

Division D: Payment of Benefits: Special Rules Applicable

Retirement Pension

67. *Commencement of retirement pension* **— (1) For a retirement pension that commences to be payable before January 1, 1987, subject to section 62, where an applicant, other than an estate, has reached sixty-five years of age and payment of the retirement pension is approved, the pension is payable for each month commencing with (R.S.C. 1985, c. 30 (2nd Supp.), s. 36(1).)**

(*a*) **the month in which the applicant reached sixty-five years of age,**

(*b*) **the latest of, the eleventh month preceding the month in which the application was received, the month following the month in which the contributor last worked and for which a contribution was made under this Act or a provincial pension plan and the month following the last month for which unadjusted pensionable earnings have been attributed under section 55, or (R.S.C. 1985, c. 1 (4th Supp.), s. 5.)**

(*c*) **the month for which the applicant applied for the pension to commence,** whichever is the latest.

(2) *Idem* **— For a retirement pension that commences to be payable on or after January 1, 1987 and where the applicant is not an estate, subject to section 62, where payment of the retirement pension is approved, the pension is payable for each month commencing with the latest of**

(*a*) **the month in which the applicant reached sixty years of age,**

(*b*) **the month following the month in which the applicant applied, if he was under seventy years of age when he applied,**

(*c*) **the month following the month in which the applicant wholly or substantially ceased to be engaged in paid employment or self-employment, if he is then under sixty-five years of age,**

(*d*) **the month in which the applicant reached sixty-five years of age, if he has not wholly or substantially ceased to be engaged in paid employment or self-employment,**

(*e*) **the twelfth month preceding the month following the month in which the applicant applied, if he was over seventy years of age when he applied,**

(*f*) **the month in which the applicant reached seventy years of age, if he applied after reaching that age,**

(g) the month of January 1987, if the applicant has reached sixty years of age but not sixty-five years of age before that month, and

(h) the month chosen by the applicant in his application.

(R.S.C. 1985, c. 30 (2nd Supp.), s. 36; R.S.C. 1985, c. 1 (4th Supp.), s. 5.)

(3) *Exception* — Where a person who has applied to receive a retirement pension attains the age of sixty-five years before the day on which the application is received, the pension is payable commencing with the latest of

(a) the twelfth month before the month after the month in which the applicant applied or the month of January 1995, whichever is later,

(b) the month in which the applicant reaches the age of sixty-five years, or

(c) the month chosen by the applicant in the application.

(S.C. 1995, c. 33, s. 32.)

(3.1) *Commencement of retirement pension — on or after January 1, 2012* — For a retirement pension that commences to be payable on or after January 1, 2012 and if the applicant is not an estate, subject to section 62, if payment of the retirement pension is approved, the pension is payable for each month commencing with the latest of

(a) the month in which the applicant reached sixty years of age,

(b) the month following the month in which the application was received if they were under sixty-five years of age when they applied,

(c) the eleventh month preceding the month in which the application was received if they have reached sixty-five years of age when they applied, but in no case earlier than the month in which they reached sixty-five years of age, and

(d) the month chosen by the applicant in their application.

(S.C. 2009, c. 31, s. 33.)

(4) *Deemed application where disability pension ceased* — Where a disability pension is no longer payable because a decision that the person was disabled has been reversed or because the person has ceased to be disabled, and on or before the day that is 90 days after the day on which the person is notified that the disability pension has ceased, or within any longer period that the Minister may either before or after the expiration of those 90 days allow, the person applies for a retirement pension, that application is deemed to have been received in the latest of

(a) the month in which the disability pension application was made,

(b) the last month for which the disability pension was payable, and

(c) the month before the month in which the contributor reached the age of 60 years. (S.C. 1997, c. 40, s. 82.)

(R.S.C. 1985, c. 30 (2nd Supp.), s. 36; R.S.C. 1985, c. 1 (4th) Supp.), s. 5; 1995, c. 33, s. 32; 1997, c. 40, s. 82; 2009, c. 31, s. 33.)

——————— **Notes** ———————

Synopsis

This section sets out the rules for when a contributor may start to receive his or her CPP retirement pension. The benefits are payable from the latest of:

Applicant between 60 and 64 years old

1. the month the applicant turns 60;

2. the month after the applicant wholly or substantially ceases employment;

3. the month after the application is received; and

4. the month chosen by the applicant in the application.

Applicant between 65 and 69 years old

1. the 12th month before the month after the application is received;
2. the month the applicant turns 65; and
3. the month chosen by the applicant in the application.

For applicants who have already turned 70, the pension can be paid retroactively to the month after the 70th birthday. However, retroactive payments can only be made for a maximum of 12 months, including the month in which the application is received.

Where the applicant is notified that his or her CPP disability pension is no longer payable, his or her application for a retirement pension made within 90 days (subject to extension) of the notification is deemed to be received in the latest of: (i) the month in which application for disability pension was made; (ii) the last month in which disability pension was payable; or (iii) the month before contributor turned 60.

Related Provisions

- Section 46 — Amount of retirement pension
- Section 60 — Application for benefit
- Section 68 — Duration of payment
- Section 68.1 — Cessation of employment

Related CPP Regulations

- Section 54.3 — Whole or substantial cessation of engagement in employment

Case Law

Mandel v. MNHW (October 20, 1993), CP 2715, CEB & PG (TB) ¶8516 (PAB)

Where the applicant proves that he or she did what was necessary to complete and submit the application, receipt by the Minister is proven for the purpose of the Act.

MNHW v. Kearney (June 16, 1993), CP 2631, CEB & PG (TB) ¶8512 (PAB)

Affidavit evidence on the claimant's behalf may be accepted to prove an application for benefits had been made.

Meyer v. Canada (Attorney General), 2003 FCA 107. See also *Thibault (Estate) v. Canada (Attorney General)*, 2005 FC 47.

Section 67(3) of the CPP applies to applications by estates, and therefore the limitation to 12 months' retroactivity of benefits also applies whether it is the living contributor, or his or her estate, that is applying. To read the legislation as conferring on survivors or beneficiaries of an estate access to greater benefits than living contributors would be patently absurd.

---

68. *Duration of payment* — **Subject to this Act, a retirement pension shall continue to be paid during the lifetime of the beneficiary, and shall cease with the payment for the month in which the beneficiary dies.**

68.1. *Proof of cessation of employment* — **(Repealed by S.C. 2009, c. 31, s. 39.)**

(R.S.C. 1985, c. 30 (2nd Supp.), s. 37; 2009, c. 31, s. 39.)

——————— **Notes** ———————

Related CPP Regulations

- Section 54.3 — Whole or substantial cessation of engagement in employment

Case Law

Armstrong-Lane v. MHRD (February 5, 2001), CP 10538 (PAB)

The Minister is not required to further investigate the applicant's intentions where the application indicates that the under-65 applicant wanted to receive a retirement pension in the earliest month eligible, but also that he or she had not ceased to be employed or self-employed. In such a situation, the Minister did not err by approving the application and granting the retirement pension in the month when the applicant turned 65.

Disability Pension

69. *Commencement of pension* — **Subject to section 62, where payment of a disability pension is approved, the pension is payable for each month commencing with the fourth month following the month in which the applicant became disabled, except that where the applicant was, at any time during the five-year period next before the month in which the applicant became disabled as a result of which the payment is approved, in receipt of a disability pension payable under this Act or under a provincial pension plan,**

    (a) the pension is payable for each month commencing with the month next following the month in which the applicant became disabled as a result of which the payment is approved; and

    (b) the reference to "fifteen months" in paragraph 42(2)(b) shall be read as a reference to "twelve months".

(R.S.C. 1985, c. 30 (2nd Supp.), s. 38.)

——————— **Notes** ———————

Synopsis

This section sets out the general rule that a disability pension is payable from the fourth month after the applicant became disabled. A CPP beneficiary who ceases to be disabled, then becomes disabled again within five years of the earlier disability, has to wait only until the month following the month in which he or she became disabled to receive a disability pension.

Related Provisions

• Section 42(2)(b) — When person deemed to become or cease to be disabled

Case Law

MSD v. Zicarelli (December 7, 2004), CP 21971 (PAB)

The reference in s. 69 to the "month in which the applicant became disabled" is the month when he was deemed to be disabled in s. 42(2)(b). Section 69(b) clearly varies s. 42(2)(b) by reducing the fifteen months maximum retroactive period set out in s. 42(2)(b) to twelve months for an applicant who had earlier, within five years, been receiving disability benefits under the CPP.

Bueno v. MHRD (April 23, 1997), CP 03253, CEB & PG (TB) ¶8674 (PAB)

Section 62 is only an explanatory section dealing with the commencement of other benefits, and does not override ss. 42(2)(b) and 69 with respect to the commencement date of a disability pension.

Johnson v. MHRD (February 17, 2004), CP 19002 (PAB)

Obiter: Without some limitation on retroactivity, it would be impossible to manage the CPP in an efficient way. One would never be able to know the amount of unrealized retroactive payments that might be accumulating and the result could well be chaotic. The CPP could not function for the benefit of the greater good without some limitation being placed on retroactivity.

Dillon v. Canada (Attorney General), 2007 FC 900

Where a previous application for disability benefits had been dismissed many years before, and that decision was not appealed from, the granting of benefits for the same condition on a subsequent application could not be made retroactive to the date of the first application. The earlier decision was *res judicata*.

Canada Pension Plan

70. *When pension ceases to be payable* — **(1) A disability pension ceases to be payable with the payment**

   (*a*) **for the month in which the beneficiary ceases to be disabled;**

   (*b*) **for the month immediately preceding the month in which the beneficiary commences to receive a retirement pension under this Act or under a provincial pension plan;**

   (*c*) **for the month in which the beneficiary reaches sixty-five years of age; or**

   (*d*) **for the month in which the beneficiary dies.**

(R.S.C. 1985, c. 30 (2nd Supp.), s. 39(1).)

   (2) *Application for retirement pension deemed to have been made* — **Where a disability pension ceases to be payable to a person by reason of his having reached sixty-five years of age, an application under section 60 shall be deemed to have been made by and received from that person, in the month in which he reached that age, for a retirement pension to commence with the month following that month.**

   (3) *Effect of receiving a retirement pension* — **A person who commences to receive a retirement pension under this Act or under a provincial pension plan is thereafter ineligible to apply or re-apply, at any time, for a disability pension under this Act, except as provided in section 66.1 or in a substantially similar provision of a provincial pension plan, as the case may be. (R.S.C. 1985, c. 30 (2nd Supp.), s. 39(2).)**

(R.S.C. 1985, c. 30 (2nd Supp.), s. 39.)

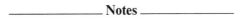

———————— **Notes** ————————

Synopsis

   In addition to setting out the rules for when a recipient is no longer entitled to receive a disability pension, this section deems an application for a retirement pension to have been made in the same month as a disability ceases because the recipient turned 65. This section also provides that the recipient of a retirement pension is forever disentitled from receiving a disability pension in the absence of a request to cancel the retirement pension under s. 66.1.

Related Provisions

   ● Section 42(2)(*b*) — When person deemed to become or cease to be disabled

Regulations

   ● Section 70.1 — Obligation to report return to work

Case Law

Kinney v. Canada (Attorney General), 2009 FCA 158

A request for reconsideration of a decision that the claimant had regained his capacity to work allowed the Minister to vary that decision to be effective as of an earlier time, but it did not allow the Minister to vary a prior decision confirming the claimant's eligibility as of that date.

Gervais v. Canada (MSD), 2010 FCA 53

The fact that the claimant had remained gainfully employed following the termination of disability benefits by the Minister was consistent with the conclusion that the Minister properly denied disability benefits for the entire period beginning with the termination, and so was a relevant consideration for the PAB.

E.D. v. Minister of Human Resources and Skills Development (May 27, 2014) CP29015 (SSTGD)

The claimant's claim of being unaware of the obligation to report her return to work was rejected where she had signed the application that states the obligation. The obligation is also provided for in s. 70.1 of the CPP Regulations. Further, the Minister does not have a duty to remind claimants of the obligation, although it does so through brochures.

C.S. v. MHRSD (February 2, 2012), CP 28021 (PAB)

Benefits are properly terminated where the recipient failed to provide additional information to the Minister. That they were later reinstated did not entitle the recipient to retroactive payments back to the date they were terminated. The Minister's admission that the claimant was disabled did not constituted new facts.

Scheuneman v. Canada (Human Resources Development), 2004 FC 1084

The Minister could not be held negligent for terminating the claimant's disability benefits, even where they were subsequently reinstated. Policy considerations preclude recognition of a duty of care on the Minister's part toward persons claiming benefits under the CPP. Nor did the claimant show that the Minister had violated his rights under s. 7 of the Charter by interfering with any fundamental life choices or causing him a sufficient level of psychological stress.

J.H. v. MHRSD, (October 17, 2012), CP 27289 (PAB)

The Minister's Adjudication Framework permits persons on disability benefits to earn up to 12 times the amount of the disability benefit annually without loss of benefits. Where the recipient was bipolar, and was capable of working and earning approximately $10,000 annually when working, it was not appropriate to cease benefits although the recipient had earnings of up to $13,000 in the year benefits were terminated. Such an amount was an anomaly.

R.P. v. MHRSD (October 4, 2010), CP 25589 PAB

Where the claimant was able to establish and operate a business that grossed between $100,000 and $200,000 annually — albeit minimal reported net income — while he was receiving CPP disability payments, it was irrelevant that the claimant had to change jobs or reduce his hours of work after the original accident. A doctor, lawyer, skilled worker, or farmer who suffered a physical impairment would have to change or adjust his career because he still had residual work capacity but could not work at the prior pace and hours. Each might have to be satisfied with much less income in less satisfactory circumstances but substantial gainful employment can be achieved at a scaled-down level.

T.C. v. MHRSD (June 1, 2011), CP 26949 (PAB)

While collecting a disability pension, the claimant owned and operated a fishing and hunting lodge for four years, reporting nil net income despite gross earnings of around $80,000 a year. The failure to generate a profitable venture did not substantiate a severe and prolonged incapacity to regularly pursue substantially gainful work. The claimant's active involvement in the operations of the business over four years was indicative that he had residual capacity to work as of the commencement of the business.

R.R. v. MHRSD (July 6, 2009), CP 26151 (PAB)

The Minister was entitled to cease payment of benefits where the recipient had returned to the workforce as a security guard, both full- and part-time, as well as a janitor, for a seven-month period for 32–40 hours a week. Over a three-year period, the recipient's reported earnings were $11,405, $9,728 and $15,769. It was irrelevant that the recipient had returned to work without the express authorization of his physician or because of his unfortunate financial circumstances, or that he considered himself unemployable as of the time of the hearing.

Milton v. MHRD (October 7, 2003), CP 18657 (PAB), application for judicial review dismissed 2004 FCA 235.

On the claimant's appeal of the Minister's decision to terminate benefits, the onus is on the Minister to show, on a balance of probabilities, that the claimant is no longer disabled at the time the benefits were terminated. It is a general rule of practice and procedure that a witness may only be cross-examined after he or she has been sworn. Where the Minister has presented its case and the claimant elects not to call evidence, the Minister is not entitled to call the claimant for cross-examination.

Obiter: in this case, the Minister did not apply to re-open its case, and then seek leave call and cross-examine the claimant. It remains an open question as to what the PAB might have done had such an application been made.

Lummiss v. MHRD (May 3, 1999), CP 8299 (PAB)

The purpose of a reassessment of a disability pension is to determine whether the pensioner's health or circumstances have improved to the extent that he or she is capable of regularly engaging in a substantially gainful occupation. To justify terminating a disability pension under s. 70(1) of the Regulations, the Minister is required to make a specific request to the pensioner to perform the work that had been selected for him or her. Where cessation of benefits has been ordered under s. 70, the burden of proving that the pensioner's disability has ceased lies with the Minister.

Canada Pension Plan

295

Doyle v. MHRD (July 26, 2001), CP 16627 (PAB), sent back to PAB for rehearing [2002] FCA 280

Where a recipient of CPP disability benefits contests a decision to terminate the pension, the onus is on the Minister to show, on a balance of probabilities, that the recipient is no longer disabled at the time the benefits were terminated. Upon reinstatement, it was open to the Minister to require that the recipient undergo such special examinations as the Minister may specify under s. 69 of the Regulations. If, at that time, the recipient failed without good cause to comply with any requirement of the Minister made under s. 69, he may be determined to have ceased to be disabled at such time as the Minister may specify except that such time shall not be earlier than the day of failure to comply.

M.D. v. MHRSD (July 13, 2010), CP 26312 (PAB)

The recipient's disability pension was rightfully ceased where she was working as a self-employed taxi driver despite her several physical disabilities. The fact that the business may not have been profitable was irrelevant to determining whether the recipient now had the capacity to work.

H.W. v. MHRSD (May 5, 2010), CP 26415 (PAB)

The recipient suffered severe depression requiring hospitalization, but had returned to work at various sales positions on commission by Spring 2004. He was not able to function as a full-time sales person until December 2004, and that was the date when his disability pension was properly terminated.

J.P. v. MHRSD (April 20, 2010), CP 26645 (PAB)

The PAB did not have equitable jurisdiction to grant compassionate consideration towards the recipient's request for an additional three-month trial work hardening/work strengthening program.

MHRSD v. J.M. (February 6, 2009), CP 24382 (PAB)

The claimant's disability pension was terminated after her mitral valve stenosis was successfully operated on, and she regained ability to work. She returned to modified work part-time as a teacher or in her husband's law office, over a prolonged period with regular attendance and no absences for medical reasons. Her earnings were substantially gainful ($8,682.00 to $10,922.00). The claimant had manifested the ability to work, while also carrying out all her household duties and tasks and other everyday needs of life, without ever requiring outside help.

MSD v. Drisdelle (March 1, 2006), CP 22236 (PAB)

The recipient's record of working every year for 6-12 weeks for $4,000 per week after a severe head injury merely constituted failed work attempts. The appellant remained a member of the union, and his co-workers covered for him as he was unable to work adequately.

70.1. *Reinstatement of disability pension* — [39]**(1) Subject to this section, a person who has ceased to receive a disability pension because they have returned to work is entitled to have that disability pension reinstated if, within two years after the month in which they ceased to receive the disability pension, they become incapable again of working. (S.C. 2004, c. 22, s. 20.)**

(2) *Request for reinstatement* — **A request by a person for reinstatement of a disability pension shall be made to the Minister in accordance with the regulations. Subsections 60(2), (4), (5) and (8) to (12) apply to the request, with any modifications that the circumstances require. (S.C. 2004, c. 22, s. 20.)**

(3) *Consideration and approval of request by Minister* — **The Minister shall approve a request made by a person under subsection (2) if the Minister is satisfied that**

---

[39] Note: Section 70.1 does not apply in respect of persons who, before the coming into force of section 20 of this Act, have ceased to receive a disability pension because they have returned to work (S.C. 2004, c. 22, s. 23.).

(*a*) the person has a severe and prolonged mental or physical disability that is the same as, or is related to, the disability that entitled the person to receive the disability pension that is the subject of the request;

(*b*) not more than two years have elapsed from the month in which the person ceased to receive the disability pension to the month when they became incapable again of working; and

(*c*) the person had not reached sixty-five years of age and was not receiving a retirement pension in the month in which they became incapable again of working.

(S.C. 2004, c. 22, s. 20.)

(**4**) *Reinstatement of disabled contributor's child benefit* — On reinstatement of a disability pension under subsection (3), the Minister shall approve the reinstatement of a disabled contributor's child benefit that had been payable to the child of the person whose disability pension is reinstated if the Minister is satisfied that the child meets the requirements under this Act for payment of a disabled contributor's child benefit. (S.C. 2004, c. 22, s. 20.)

(**5**) *Notification of decision — disability pension* — The Minister shall in writing inform a person who makes a request for reinstatement of a disability pension of the Minister's decision whether or not to approve the request. (S.C. 2004, c. 22, s. 20.)

(**6**) *Notification of decision — disabled contributor's child benefit* — The Minister shall in writing inform a person who has made a request for reinstatement of a disability pension, a child of that person or, in relation to that child, a person or agency referred to in section 75 of the Minister's decision whether or not to approve a disabled contributor's child benefit. (S.C. 2004, c. 22, s. 20.)

(**7**) *Application of provisions — disability pension* — The provisions of this Act that apply to a disability pension, except paragraphs 42(2)(*b*), 44(1)(*b*) and 44(2)(*a*) and section 69, apply to a disability pension that is reinstated under this section, with any modifications that the circumstances require. (S.C. 2004, c. 22, s. 20.)

(**8**) *Application of provisions — disabled contributor's child benefit* — The provisions of this Act that apply to a disabled contributor's child benefit, except paragraphs 44(1)(*e*) and 44(2)(*a*) and subsection 74(2), apply to a disabled contributor's child benefit that is reinstated under this section, with such modifications as the circumstances require. (S.C. 2004, c. 22, s. 20.)

(**9**) *Amount of disability pension and survivor's pension* — Despite subsection (7) and subject to any division of unadjusted pensionable earnings under sections 55 to 55.3, the basic monthly amount of a disability pension that is reinstated, and the monthly amount of any survivor's pension under this Act that is payable to the person whose disability pension is reinstated, shall not be less than the amount that was payable for the month immediately preceding the month in which the pension ceased to be payable, adjusted annually in accordance with subsection 45(2). (S.C. 2004, c. 22, s. 20.)

(**10**) *Commencement of payments* — A disability pension or a contributor's child benefit that is reinstated pursuant to a request under this section is payable commencing with the month following the month in which the person who made the request under this section became incapable again of working. (S.C. 2004, c. 22, s. 20.)

(S.C. 2004, c. 22, s. 20.)

————————— **Notes** —————————

Synopsis

This section, which came into force on January 31, 2005, allows persons whose CPP disability benefit was ceased because they returned to work to have their benefit reinstated if they are unable to continue working and the same or a related disability recurs within a maximum period of two years. Together with the timing provisions set out in the regulations, it is designed to ensure that eligible individuals will have their benefits quickly restarted if their attempt to return to work is not successful. Similarly, the consequential reinstatement of the disabled contributor's child benefit is provided for.

Related CPP Regulations

- Sections 71, 72 — Request for Reinstatement of Disability Pension

- Section 73 — Reinstatement of a Disabled Contributor's Child Benefit

Case Law

Perrotta v. MSD, March 17, 2004 (PAB)

Where the Minister is applying for a termination CPP disability benefits, the PAB's jurisdiction does not allow for any adjudication on the validity of the recipient's original claim for benefits. The PAB's jurisdiction is confined to the simple question as to whether the Minister has satisfied the onus on it to establish on a balance of probabilities that the recipient's disability had ceased. Proof that the recipient's health or circumstances had improved between the time that benefit payment commenced to the extent that he or she was capable of regularly engaging in a substantially gainful occupation would satisfy that onus.

—————————————

Death Benefit

71. *Payable to estate* **— (1) Where payment of a death benefit is approved, the Minister shall except as provided in subsections (2) and (3), pay the death benefit to the estate of the contributor.**

(2) *Exceptions* **— The Minister may direct payment of a death benefit in whole or in part to such person or body as is prescribed where**

   (a) he is satisfied, after making reasonable inquiries, that there is no estate;

   (b) the estate has not applied for the death benefit within the prescribed time interval following the contributor's death; or

   (c) the amount of the death benefit is less than the prescribed amount.

(3) *No double payment* **— Where a payment has been made pursuant to subsection (2), the Minister is not liable to make that payment to any subsequent applicant.**

(R.S.C. 1985, c. 30 (2nd Supp.), s. 40.)

————————— **Notes** —————————

Synopsis

This section authorizes the Minister to pay a death benefit to the estate on approval of an application, or to a prescribed person (see Regulation s. 64) unless there is no estate, the estate fails to apply within the 60 days following the death of the contributor, or the amount of the death benefit is less than 2/3 of 10% of the QMPE for the year of death.

Related CPP Regulations

- Section 64 — Payment of death benefit to other than estates

Case Law

Cormier v. Canada (Minister of Human Resources Development), 2002 FCA 514

The only statutory liability of the Minister to pay a death benefit is owed to the estate. If the estate fails to apply within 60 days of the death, the only effect of this failure is to trigger the discretion exercisable by the Minister under s. 71(2) to pay the benefit to statutorily prescribed persons, who do not include the estate of the contributor. The Minister's obligation to pay to the estate under s. 71(1) continues, even if representatives of the estate do not apply for death benefit within the 60 days. However, if the estate does not apply within 60 days and the Minister makes a discretionary payment under s. 71(2), s. 71(3) expressly provides that the Minister is no longer liable to pay the estate if it subsequently applies under s. 71(1).

MSD v. Gray (May 28, 2007), CP 24802 (PAB)

The spouse of the contributor is not, *ipso facto*, entitled to be paid the death benefit. Where the will appointing another person as the executor is subsequently found to have been revoked, giving the surviving spouse the right to be named administrator of the contributor's estate, which right she did not exercise, does not give the Minister the right to make a valid death benefit payment to her.

MSD v. Mankasingh (November 30, 2005), CP 23363 (PAB)

The divorced parents of the deceased child contributor individually arranged for two separate funeral services to be held, and each applied for death benefit. Both applications were returned due to incomplete documentation. When only the father resubmitted with proper documentation, the Minister was entitled to make direct payment to the father after the statutory 60-day waiting period from the date of the child's death had expired. At the time of payment, there was only one valid application on file, and the Minister could not have been aware that there had been two services after the child's death or that the mother even intended to pursue her claim.

Survivor's Pension

72. *Commencement of pension* — **(1) Subject to section (2) and section 62, where payment of a survivor's pension is approved, the pension is payable for each month commencing with the month following (S.C. 2000, c. 12, s. 54(2).)**

   (a) the month in which the contributor died, in the case of a survivor who at the time of the death of the contributor had reached thirty-five years of age or was a survivor with dependent children,

   (b) the month in which the survivor became a survivor who, not having reached sixty-five years of age, is disabled, in the case of a survivor other than a survivor described in paragraph (a), or

   (c) the month in which the survivor reached sixty-five years of age, in the case of a surviving spouse other than a survivor described in paragraph (a) or (b),

but in no case earlier than the twelfth month preceding the month following the month in which the application was received. (S.C. 2000, c. 12, s. 54; 2000, c. 12, s. 64.)

   (2) *Limitation* — In the case of a survivor who was the contributor's common-law partner and was not, immediately before the coming into force of this subsection, a person described in subparagraph (a)(ii) of the definition "spouse" in subsection 2(1) as that definition read at that time, no survivor's pension may be paid for any month before the month in which this subsection comes into force. (S.C. 2000, c. 12, s. 54(3).)

(S.C. 2000, c. 12, s. 54.)

Canada Pension Plan

―――――――――― **Notes** ――――――――――

Synopsis

This section sets out a flexible rule for when a survivor's pension begins to run, and permits going back up to 12 months prior to the date of the application.

Recent Amendments

The 2000 amendment replaces the former term "surviving spouse" with the term "survivor", which includes parties to a same-sex relationship, although no benefits are payable to same-sex couples for months to same-sex survivors before the amendment came into force on July 31, 2000.

Related Provisions

- Section 58 — Amount of survivor's pension

- Section 73 — Duration of payment

Related CPP Regulations

- Section 63 — Determination of marital or filial status or death

Case Law

Taylor v. MHRD (January 4, 2001), CP 11112 (PAB)

The spouse of a deceased contributor does not have to have a death certificate or court order for the presumption of death before he or she can complete the application form for survivor's benefits. The fact that the spouse of a person who went missing in 1989 had to wait 7 years before she could obtain an order for the declaration of his death under the *Insurance Act* was not grounds for ordering that benefits be paid from 1989, in the face of the 11-month restriction on retroactive payments under s. 72. Section 88 is clear and binding, and it is not relevant whether or not the Minister would have presumed the contributor's death if and when the application had been brought in 1989.

MHRD v. Leblanc (October 20, 2000), CP 13675 (PAB)

The PAB did not have discretionary power to extend the period of retroactivity beyond 11 months from date of application, even where a parent had chosen not to mention child from previous relationship when applying for benefits for children from another relationship and the other parent became aware of the child's entitlement years later. The Ministry's application form is clear in asking applicants to identify children in the care and control of others.

Canada (Attorney General) v. Hislop, 2007 SCC 10

Section 72(2) is of no force and effect. Such a limitation on the rights of same sex partners to obtain benefits was contrary to s. 15 of the Charter, and could not be justified under s. 1 of the Charter. Same-sex survivors are therefore entitled to up to 12 months of pension arrears for the period from August 1999 to July 2000, pursuant to s. 72(1). The claimants were not entitled to a constitutional exemption from the limitation on arrears in s. 72(1).

Johnson v. MHRD (February 17, 2004), CP 19002 (PAB)

Obiter. Even where a claimant living in an isolated aboriginal community had not been aware the survivor's pension, ss. 72(1) and 74 of the CPP could not be said to violate s. 15 of the *Canadian Charter of Rights and Freedoms*. It had not been established that the impugned provisions had a disproportionate impact on persons living in isolated aboriginal communities as compared with beneficiaries living in urban areas or as compared to non-aboriginal beneficiaries living in rural areas. Nor did the reduction of retroactive benefits due to the late application demean the applicant's essential human dignity such that s. 15(1) would be infringed.

―――――――――――――――――

73. *Duration of payment* — **(1) Subject to this Act, a survivor's pension shall continue to be paid during the lifetime of the beneficiary, and shall cease with the payment for the month in which the beneficiary dies. (S.C. 2000, c. 12, s. 55.)**

(2) *Special case* — **If**

(a) a contributor died on or after January 1, 1998 but before the coming into force of this subsection, and

(b) a survivor's pension was, immediately before that coming into force, payable to a survivor who had been married to the contributor at the time of the contributor's death,

the approval of payment of a survivor's pension, in respect of that contributor's death, to a survivor who was the contributor's common-law partner at the time of the contributor's death and was not a person described in subparagraph (a)(ii) of the definition of "spouse" in subsection 2(1) as that definition read at that time, does not affect the right of the survivor referred to in paragraph (b) to continue to receive the survivor's pension in accordance with subsection (1). (S.C. 2000, c. 12, s. 55.)

(S.C. 2000, c. 12, s. 55.)

——————— **Notes** ———————

Synopsis

This section provides that a survivor's pension continues to run for the life of the survivor, ceasing in the month of the survivor's death.

Recent Amendments

The section was amended in 2000 to deal with a transitional problem arising from the substitution of the former term "spouse", which included opposite sex common-law relationships, with "common-law partner". If a married contributor died between January 1, 1998 and July 31, 2000 while cohabiting in a same-sex relationship, the right of the same-sex partner to claim a survivor's pension does not impinge the right of the contributor's legal spouse to receive or continue to receive a survivor's pension.

Disabled Contributor's Child's Benefit and Orphan's Benefit

74. *Persons by whom application may be made* — **(1) An application for a disabled contributor's child's benefit or orphan's benefit may be made on behalf of a disabled contributor's child or orphan by the child or orphan or by any other person or agency to whom the benefit would, if the application were approved, be payable under this Part.**

(2) *Commencement of payment of benefit* — **Subject to section 62, where payment of a disabled contributor's child's benefit or orphan's benefit in respect of a contributor is approved, the benefit is payable for each month commencing with,**

(a) in the case of a disabled contributor's child's benefit, the later of

(i) the month commencing with which a disability pension is payable to the contributor under this Act or under a provincial pension plan, and

(ii) the month next following the month in which the child was born or otherwise became a child of the contributor, and

(b) in the case of an orphan's benefit, the later of

(i) the month following the month in which the contributor died, and

(ii) the month next following the month in which the child was born,

but in no case earlier than the twelfth month preceding the month following the month in which the application was received.

(3) *No benefit in respect of more than two contributors* — [40]Where a disabled contributor's child's benefit has become payable to a child under this Act or under a provincial pension plan in respect of any contributor thereunder or an orphan's benefit has become payable to an orphan under this Act or under a provincial pension plan in respect of any contributor thereunder, no disabled contributor's child's benefit or orphan's benefit is payable to that person under this Act in respect of any other such contributor except another parent of that person, and in no case shall such a benefit be paid to that person in respect of more than two contributors. **(R.S.C. 1985, c. 30 (2nd Supp.), s. 41(1).)**

(3.1) *Meaning of "parent"* — In subsection (3), "parent" has the reciprocal meaning to that of "child". **(R.S.C. 1985, c. 30 (2nd Supp.), s. 41(1).)**

(4) *Limitation on benefit payable* — **(Repealed by 1991, c. 44, s. 18.)**

(R.S.C. 1985, c. 30 (2nd Supp.), s. 41; 1991, c. 44, s. 18.)

——————— Notes ———————

Synopsis

This section provides a disabled contributor's child's benefit or an orphan's benefit may be made by the child or orphan, or on his or her behalf to a person or organization identified in s. 75. Where payment is approved, the benefit is payable monthly commencing with:

1. In the case of a disabled contributor's child, the later of the month in which a disability pension is payable, or the month next following the month in which the child was born or otherwise became a child of the contributor.

2. In the case of an orphan, the later of the month following the month in which the contributor dies or the month after the month the child was born.

However, a disabled contributor's child or orphan's benefit cannot in any case be paid for more than 12 months before the month in which the application was received.

Related Provisions

- Section 59 — Amount of benefit
- Section 70.1(4),(6),(8), (10) Reinstatement of disabled contributor's child benefit
- Section 75 — Payment of benefits
- Section 76 — When benefit ceases to be payable

Related CPP Regulations

- Section 63 — Determination of marital or filial status or death
- Section 73 — Reinstatement of disabled contributor's child benefit

Statton v. Canada (Attorney General), 2006 FCA 370

Section 74 exclusively governs applications for disabled contributors' child benefits, and CPP s. 60(8) is inapplicable.

———

[40] Pursuant to R.S.C. 1985, c. 30 (2nd Supp.), s. 41(2), subsection 74(3) applies whether the contributor died or became disabled before or after January 1, 1987, but no payment shall be made for any month before January, 1987.

Desrosiers v. MSD (January 4, 2006), CP 22965 (PAB)

The result of the Federal Court of Appeal's decision in *Statton* (above) is that the PAB has no discretionary power in the PAB to either amend the application of the parent to include the child, or to make an order effective retroactively to 11 months preceding the parent's application.

Obiter: This is a legislative gap which clearly allows a parent for whatever reason to prejudice a child's right to a benefit. Unfortunately while there is no question it is unfair and unjust the PAB cannot fill that legislative gap.

Bessette v. Canada (Attorney General), 2011 FC 176

By virtue of s. 74(2)(*a*)(ii), a DCCB is normally payable the month after the child's birth. However, s. 74(2) provides that in no case are benefits payable for a period earlier than 11 months before the application for benefits is received. The Minister does not bear the onus of informing claimants of their entitlement to the DCCB. Section 60(1) puts the onus on applicants to claim benefits. Even if the claimant had been erroneously informed by a Ministry official that the 11-month limit on retroactive benefits is generally waived with respect to the DCCB, the imposition of the limitation on retroactive benefits was not caused by any error. The cause of any loss of benefits was the failure to make a timely claim for them, not the conduct of the official to whom the claimant spoke. *Obiter:* It would be completely different if the claimant had been told that she did not have to make a claim for benefits when her children were born because benefits can be assessed retroactively whenever she applied for them. In that case, the claimant would have suffered a loss attributable to bad advice.

MHRSD v. H.H. (May 21, 2010), CP 25537 (PAB)

An extension of the statutory 11-month period of retroactivity was not available to the claimant's orphaned son where the claimant had not been incapacitated during the relevant time. The son was penalized by the claimant's failure to file applications earlier.

MSD v. Butler (August 11, 2006) CP 24230 (PAB)

An orphan who is receiving an orphan's benefit by reason of the deaths of both contributor parents is not entitled to receive DCCB payments upon his or her guardian becoming disabled. Parliament intended to limit the number of qualifying contributors to two, the second of which must be a parent. Only another parent may qualify as a contributor so as to entitle the child to an additional benefit, whether orphan's or DCCB.

Prevost v. MSD (June 7, 2005), CP 13312 (PAB)

While s. 74(1) permits the application for a disabled contributor's child's benefit ("DCCB") to be made by a child, it does not permit the application to be made by the custodian of the child when read in conjunction with s. 75. Section 74(1) by itself would permit a custodian of the child to apply. Section 74(2) provides for commencement of the DCCB in the same month that a disability payment is payable, but in no case earlier than the eleventh month preceding the month in which the application is received. The starting point for entitlement is that an appropriate application in writing for the DCCB must be made by an appropriate person or agency (s. 60(1)). The provisions of s. 60(8)-(11) deal with an application on behalf of an incapacitated person, and do not relate to a minor with regard to his or her lack of legal capacity.

Johnson v. MHRD (February 17, 2004), CP 19002 (PAB)

Section 74 did not unlawfully discriminate against orphaned minors. The CPP created no distinction among different classes of children, and they are all treated similarly under ss. 74 and 75.

Obiter: Even where a claimant living in an isolated aboriginal community had not been aware the survivor's pension, ss. 72(1) and 74 of the CPP could not be said to violate s. 15 of the *Canadian Charter of Rights and Freedoms.* It had not been established that the impugned provisions had a disproportionate impact on persons living in isolated aboriginal communities as compared with beneficiaries living in urban areas or as compared to non-aboriginal beneficiaries living in rural areas. Nor did the reduction of retroactive benefits due to the late

Canada Pension Plan

application demean the applicant's essential human dignity such that s. 15(1) would be infringed.

---

75. *Payment of benefit* — **Where a disabled contributor's child's benefit is payable to a child of a disabled contributor or an orphan's benefit is payable to an orphan of a contributor, payment thereof shall, if the child or orphan has not reached eighteen years of age, be made to the person or agency having custody and control of the child or orphan, or, where there is no person or agency having custody and control of the child or orphan, to such person or agency as the Minister may direct, and for the purposes of this Part,**

    (*a*) **the contributor, in relation to a disabled contributor's child, except where the child is living apart from the contributor, and**

    (*b*) **the survivor, if any, of the contributor, in relation to an orphan, except where the orphan is living apart from the survivor, (S.C. 2000, c. 12, s. 56.)**

shall be presumed, in the absence of any evidence to the contrary, to be the person having custody and control of the child or orphan.

(S.C. 2000, c. 12, s. 56.)

──────────── **Notes** ────────────

Synopsis

This section provides that payment of a CPP disabled contributor's child's benefit or an orphan's benefit is to be made to the person or agency having custody or control of the child or orphan, if the child or orphan is under 18. The disabled contributor is presumed to be the person having custody or control, unless the child is living apart from the contributor. With respect to an orphan, the survivor is presumed to be the person having custody and control unless the orphan is living apart. If the child or orphan is over 18 and capable of managing his or her own affairs, the benefit may be paid directly to the child or orphan.

Case Law

Ciavaglia v. MSD (May 25, 2007), CP 23489 (PAB). See also *MSD v. Willard Berendt* CP 24238 (PAB) and *MSD v. Berendt* CP 24179 (PAB).

Benefits could not be payable to more than one person having custody of the child. If Parliament had intended that there be multiple recipients, it would have inserted "person or persons" in the provision. The presumption in s. 70 is that the disabled contributor is the person having custody and control of the child except where the child is living apart from the contributor. The child benefits are not divisible between the various claimants as the Minister ought not to be obliged to divide or even attempt to divide those payments so as to reflect the periods in which the children reside away from their principle residence.

P.E. v. MHRSD (May 2008), CP 25371 (PAB)

Where custody of the children had been granted to the claimant by court order which was never varied, the mother continued to exercise custody and control during a five-month period when the children lived with the other parent by mutual consent.

MHRD v. Warren (December 12, 2001), CP 14995 (PAB)

Although the divorce judgment incorporated the agreement of the parties that there be joint custody, the PAB must also examine who in fact exercised control over the child, in other words, where the child resided and who took responsibility for the child's care and maintenance, schooling and participation in sports. The intention to have shared custody was insufficient where one of the parents was incapable of exercising his or her right.

Bajwa v. MHRD (April 4, 2002), CP 14184 (PAB)

The statutory requirement is related to both care and control of the child. Both are required. One alone falls short. Care and control of religious matters, schooling, professional education and the like, standing alone, may fall short. Influence and concern in these areas standing alone are not sufficient. The disabled contributor could not be said to have had "control" of the children of his second wife within the meaning of s. 75 where the children were attending college in Pakistan, although he was helping to support them.

J.D. v. MHRSD (August 14, 2012), CP 26564 (PAB)

Although the grandparent recipient of CPP disability benefits lives with the mother and the child, the grandparent was not entitled to the disabled contributor's child's benefits because the mother of the child had the custody and control of the child. The grandparent never applied for the legal custody or adoption of their grandchild. It does not matter that the grandparents assume the primary caregiving role for their granddaughter. The custody and control is the determining factor.

---

76. *When disabled contributor's child's benefit ceases to be payable* — **(1) A disabled contributor's child's benefit ceases to be payable with the payment for the month in which**

    (a) the child ceases to be a dependent child;

    (b) the child dies;

    (c) the contributor's disability benefit ceases to be payable; (S.C. 1991, c. 44, s. 19(1).)

    (d) the child is adopted legally or in fact by someone other than the disabled contributor or the disabled contributor's spouse or common-law partner, unless the disabled contributor is maintaining the child, as defined by regulation; or (S.C. 1991, c. 44, s. 19(1); 2000, c. 12, s. 57.)

    (e) the disabled contributor ceases to have custody and control of the child, where the child is a child as defined in subsection 42(1) by reason of the disabled contributor having had such custody and control. (S.C. 1991, c. 44, s. 19(1).)

    (2) *When orphan's benefit ceases to be payable* — **An orphan's benefit ceases to be payable with the payment for the month in which the child ceases to be a dependent child or dies.**

    (3) *Exception* — **Where, by reason of the death of a contributor, a disabled contributor's child's benefit ceases to be payable to a person who is 18 years of age or older at the time of that death, an application under section 60 for an orphan's benefit shall be deemed to have been made by that person in the month in which the contributor died. (S.C. 1991, c. 44, s. 19(2).)**

    (R.S.C. 1985, c. 30 (2nd Supp.), s. 42; 1991, c. 44, s. 19; 2000, c. 12, s. 57.)

—————————— Notes ——————————

Synopsis

This section sets out the test for when a disabled contributor's child's benefit or orphan's benefit are no longer payable. The section must be read in conjunction with the definition of "dependent child" in s. 42(1) and the regulations. Significantly, a child is dependent as long as he or she is enrolled in a school or university on a full-time basis.

Related Provisions

- Section 42(1) — "Dependent child" defined

Related CPP Regulations

- Section 65.1 — Maintenance of child

Post-retirement Benefit

76.1. *Commencement of benefit* — **Subject to section 62, a post-retirement benefit is payable to a beneficiary of a retirement pension for each month commencing with January 1 of the year following the year of a contributor's earnings if**

    (*a*) **a contribution has been made in respect of those earnings;**

    (*b*) **those earnings exceed the contributor's basic exemption; and**

    (*c*) **those earnings are for a period that**

        (i) **begins after 2011 and after the contributory period ends under subparagraph 49(*b*)(iii), and**

        (ii) **ends with the month preceding the month in which the contributor reaches seventy years of age.**

(S.C. 2009, c. 31, s. 40.)

76.2. *Duration of payment* — **Subject to this Act, a post-retirement benefit shall continue to be paid during the lifetime of the beneficiary and shall cease with the payment for the month in which the beneficiary dies.**

(S.C. 2009, c. 31, s. 40.)

Division E: Payment of Benefits: Amount Payable Under Canada Pension Plan

--- Notes ---

Synopsis

Sections 77-80.1 are required because some contributors will have contributed under both the CPP and QPP. The purpose of these sections is to determine the portion of the aggregate amount of pension that is payable under each of the CPP and QPP. Note that the share of the federal and Quebec plans in the unadjusted pensionable earnings for a year is the proportion of earnings on which a contribution has been made for the year under each plan bears to the total of such earnings.

---

77. *Amount of benefit payable under Act* — **Where, by virtue of any provision of this Act other than this section, a benefit is payable under this Act to or in respect of any contributor, notwithstanding anything in this Part except as provided in section 80, the amount of the benefit that is payable under this Act is an amount equal to that proportion of the amount of the benefit payable to or in respect of the contributor, calculated as provided in this Part without regard to this section, that**

    (*a*) **the total pensionable earnings of the contributor attributable to contributions made under this Act,**

are of

    (*b*) **the total pensionable earnings of the contributor.**

――――――――― **Notes** ―――――――――

Synopsis

This section allows the Minister to prorate the amount of benefits payable to a contributor who is also eligible for to receive similar benefits under a similar provincial plan (e.g., the QPP), depending on the relative total pensionable earnings under the CPP and the provincial plan. This section is subject to agreements made between the federal Minister and provinces with similar plans.

Related Provisions

- Section 78 — Total pensionable earnings attributable to contributions made under the Act

- Section 80 — Agreements with provinces

- Section 80.1 — Agreements with provinces respecting the apportionment of payments

――――――――――――――――――

78. *Total pensionable earnings attributable to contributions made under Act* — **The total pensionable earnings of a contributor attributable to contributions made under this Act are an amount equal to the amount that his total pensionable earnings would be if the unadjusted pensionable earnings of the contributor for a year were that proportion of his unadjusted pensionable earnings for the year that**

> (*a*) **the contributor's earnings on which a contribution has been made for the year under this Act, calculated as provided in subparagraph 53(1)(***b***)(i), (S.C. 2012, c. 31, s. 201(1).)**

are of

> (*b*) **the aggregate of the amount mentioned in paragraph (***a***) and the contributor's earnings on which a contribution has been made for the year under a provincial pension plan, calculated as provided in subparagraph 53(1)(***b***)(ii). (S.C. 2012, c. 31, s. 201(2).)**

(S.C. 2012, c. 31, s. 201.)

79. *Total pensionable earnings attributable to contributions made under Act as a result of division* — **For a year of a division as determined under section 55 or 55.1 and under a provincial pension plan, the total pensionable earnings of a contributor attributable to contributions made under this Act are an amount equal to the amount that his total pensionable earnings would be if the unadjusted pensionable earnings of the contributor for the year were that proportion of his unadjusted pensionable earnings for the year that**

> (*a*) **his unadjusted pensionable earnings attributed under subsection 55(4) or 55.2(5)**

are of

> (*b*) **his total unadjusted pensionable earnings for the year determined under subsection 55(5) or 55.2(6).**

(R.S.C. 1985, c. 30 (2nd Supp.), s. 43.)

80. *Agreements with provinces* — **(1)** **Notwithstanding section 77, the Minister, with the approval of the Governor in Council, may on behalf of the Government of Canada enter into an agreement with the appropriate authority of a province providing a comprehensive pension plan to provide for the administration and coordination of this Act and the provincial pension plan in respect of persons who are contributors**

Canada Pension Plan

under this Act or the provincial plan or both, including, without limiting the generality of the foregoing,

    (*a*) the determination and payment of any benefit, or portion thereof, payable under this Act or under the provincial pension plan;

    (*b*) the determination, processing and approval of divisions of unadjusted pensionable earnings under this Act and under the provincial pension plan;

    (*c*) the determination, processing and approval of applications for assignments, under this Act or under the provincial pension plan, of a retirement pension to the spouse or common-law partner of a contributor; (S.C. 2000, c. 12, s. 58.)

    (*d*) the exchange of such information obtained under this Act or under the provincial pension plan as is necessary to give effect to the agreement; and

    (*e*) the payment under this Act in accordance with the agreement of the whole amount of any benefit payable to or in respect of a contributor, calculated as provided in this Part without regard to section 77, in which case the whole amount of that benefit shall be deemed to be payable under this Act to or in respect of that contributor.

(R.S.C. 1985, c. 30 (2nd Supp.), s. 44.)

(2) *Saving* — **Where, in accordance with any agreement entered into under subsection (1), the whole amount of any benefit payable to or in respect of a contributor, calculated in a manner similar to that described in paragraph (1)(*e*), is payable under the provincial pension plan referred to in that subsection, the whole amount of that benefit shall be deemed to be payable under the provincial pension plan to or in respect of that contributor. (R.S.C. 1985, c. 30 (2nd Supp.), s. 44.)**

(3) *Provision for making of financial adjustments* — **Any agreement entered into under subsection (1) may provide therein for the making of any financial adjustments required to be made by reason of any payments made to or in respect of a contributor in accordance with that agreement, and for the crediting or charging of the amount of those adjustments to the Canada Pension Plan Account.**

(R.S.C. 1985, c. 30 (2nd Supp.), s. 44; 2000, c. 12, s. 58.)

———————— **Notes** ————————

Synopsis

This section authorizes the federal Minister to enter into an agreement with a province providing a similar plan to the CPP for the common administration of the plans by the province.

Related Provisions

    ● Section 89(1)(i), (j) — Regulations

    ● Section 107 — Reciprocal agreements with other countries

Related CPP Regulations

    ● Section 58(2) — Single payment of benefits

————————

80.1. *Agreements respecting the apportionment of payments* — **(1) The Minister may, with the approval of the Governor in Council, on behalf of the Government of Canada enter into an agreement with any person or body responsible for the administration of**

(*a*) any other Act of Parliament,

(*b*) an Act of the legislature of a province, or

(*c*) a federal or provincial activity established other than under an Act of Parliament or of the legislature of a province,

that provides for periodic payments to persons in respect of accidents, injuries, illnesses and occupational diseases for the purpose of limiting the total amount that is payable to a beneficiary as a disability benefit under this Act and as periodic payments under that other law or activity. (S.C. 1997, c. 40, s. 83.)

(2) *Apportionment of payments* — The agreement shall provide rules for determining how much, if any, of the total amount payable to a beneficiary shall be payable under this Act and how much, if any, shall be payable under that other law or activity. (S.C. 1997, c. 40, s. 83.)

(3) *Effect of agreement* — Notwithstanding anything in this Act, but subject to subsection (4), where an agreement entered into pursuant to subsection (1) applies in respect of a beneficiary, the only amounts that may be payable as disability benefits to the beneficiary under this Act are the amounts provided for by the agreement. (S.C. 1997, c. 40, s. 83.)

(4) *Limitation* — An agreement may not

(*a*) change a person's eligibility to receive a benefit as a disabled contributor's child or the amount of that benefit;

(*b*) change the determination of months that are excluded from a beneficiary's contributory period by reason of disability;

(*c*) result in a beneficiary receiving, in respect of any month, disability benefits under this Act and payments under the other law or activity that are less than the disability benefits that would be otherwise payable under this Act for the month if there were no such agreement; or

(*d*) result in a beneficiary receiving, in respect of any month, disability benefits under this Act that are greater than the disability benefits that would otherwise be payable under this Act if there were no agreement. (S.C. 1997, c. 40, s. 83.)

(S.C. 1997, c. 40, s. 83.)

——————— Notes ———————

Synopsis

This section authorizes the Minister to enter into agreements with the entities who administer any other federal or provincial Act or activity which provides periodic payments to persons due to accidents, injuries, illnesses and occupational diseases, for example, worker's compensation benefits. This is designed to eliminate "double-dipping" by injured employees, by limiting the total amount the beneficiary will receive as a CPP disability benefit.

Division F: Reconsiderations and Appeals

81. *Appeal to Minister* — (1) Where

(*a*) a spouse, former spouse, common-law partner, former common-law partner or estate is dissatisfied with any decision made under section 55, 55.1, 55.2 or 55.3,

(*b*) an applicant is dissatisfied with any decision made under section 60,

(c) A beneficiary is dissatisfied with any determination as to the amount of a benefit payable to the beneficiary or as to the beneficiary's eligibility to receive a benefit,

(d) a beneficiary or the beneficiary's spouse or common-law partner is dissatisfied with any decision made under section 65.1, or

(e) a person who made a request under section 70.1, a child of that person or, in relation to that child, a person or agency referred to in section 75 is dissatisfied with any decision made under section 70.1, (S.C. 2004, c. 22, s. 21.)

the dissatisfied party or, subject to the regulations, any person on behalf thereof may, within ninety days after the day on which the dissatisfied party was notified in the prescribed manner of the decision or determination, or within such longer period as the Minister may either before or after the expiration of those ninety days allow, make a request to the Minister in the prescribed form and manner for a reconsideration of that decision or determination. (S.C. 2000, c. 12, s. 59(1).)

(1.1) *Reconsideration where penalty assessed* — A person to whom a penalty has been assessed under section 90.1 or, subject to the regulations, any person on their behalf, who is dissatisfied with the decision to impose a penalty or with the amount of the penalty may, within 90 days after the day on which the person is notified in the prescribed manner of the decision or determination, or within any longer period that the Minister may, either before or after the expiration of those 90 days, allow, request, in the prescribed form and manner, that the Minister reconsider that decision or determination. (S.C. 1997, c. 40, s. 84.)

(2) *Reconsideration by Minister and decision* — The Minister shall reconsider without delay any decision or determination referred to in subsection (1) or (1.1) and may confirm or vary it, and may approve payment of a benefit, determine the amount of a benefit or determine that no benefit is payable, and shall notify in writing the party who made the request under subsection (1) or (1.1) of the Minister's decision and of the reasons for it. (S.C. 1997, c. 40, 84; 2000, c. 12, s. 59(1) and (2).)

(3) *Rescission or amendment of decision* — The Minister may, on new facts, rescind or amend a decision made by him or her under this Act. (S.C. 2012, c. 19, s. 228.)

(R.S.C. 1985, c. 30 (2nd Supp.), s. 45; 1991, c. 44, s. 20; 1995, c. 33, s. 34; 1997, c. 40, s. 84; 2000, c. 12, s. 59; 2004, c. 22, s. 21; 2012, c. 19, s. 228.)

—————— Notes ——————

Synopsis

This section imposes a time limit of 90 days on requesting a reconsideration of a Minister's decision with respect to a division of unadjusted pensionable earnings, an application for benefits, the amount of any benefit payable to a beneficiary or his or her entitlement to receive a benefit, the assignment of a retirement pension, or the or a request for reinstatement of a disability pension. The time starts to run after receipt of the written notification of the Minister's initial decision, and the 90-day limit may be extended by the Minister. The Minister's decision following a reconsideration must be in writing and be communicated to the requesting party, with reasons.

Bill C-38 Amendments

As of April 1, 2013, appeals under s. 82 from the Ministerial decision on reconsideration are to be taken to the General Division of the Social Security Tribunal. For appeals filed and heard prior to April 1, 2013, the Review Tribunal remains seized of the file and must make its decision no later than March 31, 2014 (or such date as is earlier prescribed under CPP s. 253(3)) — see CPP s. 255. Appeals filed under s. 82(1) but not heard before April 1, 2013 are deemed to have been filed with the General Division of the Social Security Tribunal on April 1, 2013 — see CPP s. 257. Note that the repealed provisions continue to apply to appeals of which a Review Tribunal remains seized, with any necessary adaptations — CPP s. 262.

The appeal procedure in the Social Security Tribunal is set out in Part 5 of the *Department of Human Resources and Skills Development Act*, reproduced in this book starting on page 587.

Related Provisions

- Section 82 — Appeal to Review Tribunal

Related CPP Regulations

- Section 74 — Reconsideration and appeal on behalf of incapable persons
- Section 74.1 — Request for reconsideration
- Section 74.2 — Notification of appealable decisions
- Section 74.4 — Notice of constitutional questions

Case Law

McMaster v. MSD (March 31, 2006), CP 23010 (PAB)

Neither the Review Tribunal nor the PAB have the authority to decide on the incapacity of a person to form or express an intention to make an application for disability benefits until the Minister makes a decision under s. 81.

Robsob-Belfrey v. MHRD (January 8, 2004), CP 15822 (PAB)

No appeal could be heard where the Minister had never, on the record, considered and given a decision in writing on the issue of capacity.

MHRD v. Lavoie (June 27, 1997), CP 5412, CEB & PG ¶8685 (PAB)

Decisions of the Minister, or of the Minister's officials, are not subject to the rule of *res judicata*. Such decisions are administrative and not judicial as they are made by parties to the case, however impartial. The rejection by the Minister of a disability claim therefore did not prevent the applicant from making a subsequent claim, even where the Minister's original rejection had not been appealed by the claimant.

MSD v. Kendall (June 7, 2004), CP 21960 (PAB)

Officials in the Ministry are entitled to act on behalf of the Minister in advising a claimant that his or her application for a reconsideration is refused for non-compliance with the 90-day leave period. Section 24(2) of the federal *Interpretation Act* expressly provides that the Minister may act through departmental staff.

MSD v. Forfar (June 23, 2005), CP 21246 (PAB)

Where the Review Tribunal had already dismissed the claimant's appeal, the Tribunal did not have jurisdiction to convert a s. 81 appeal of a subsequent application by the same claimant into a s. 84(2) application and make a determination that there are new facts to justify a different decision, even where the earlier decision was pre-*Villani*.

Panopoulos v. Canada (Attorney General) 2010 FC 877

An extention for reconsideration was refused where the applicant, despite having had assistance with other applications and appeals in the past, did not seek assistance with the Minister's letter until approximately 10 months later.

Wiemer v. Ganim (1996), Doc. T-1121-95 (Fed. T.D.)

Having rendered an initial decision to permit division of a pension, the Minister, including the Minister's delegate, is *functus officio*. The CPP has no provision which allows the Minister, once he has made an original decision in a case, to receive its reference back and to reconsider the decision, even if directed to do so by the PAB. This is clearly beyond the Minister's statutory powers.

MEI v. Neil (September 20, 1995), CP 8590, CEB & PG (TB) ¶8590 (PAB)

A finding by the Minister that a proposed division of pension credits is not caught by s. 55.1(5)(*b*) is implicitly part of each decision to make a division, and is therefore subject to appeal under s. 81, notwithstanding the 60-day limitation on the Minister's determination.

82. *Appeal to Social Security Tribunal* — **A party who is dissatisfied with a decision of the Minister made under section 81, including a decision in relation to further time to make a request, or, subject to the regulations, any person on their behalf, may appeal the decision to the Social Security Tribunal established under section 44 of the** *Department of Employment and Social Development Act.*

(R.S.C. 1985, c. 30 (2nd Supp.), s. 45; 1991, c. 44, s. 21; 1995, c. 33, s. 35; 1997, c. 40, s. 85; 2000, c. 12, s. 60; 2000, c. 12, s. 64; 2010, c. 12, s. 1668; 2012, c. 19, s. 229; 2013, c. 40, s. 236(1)(*b*)(ii).)

———————— **Notes** ————————

Synopsis

Note that appeal procedures in the Review Tribunal are governed by the Review Tribunal Rules of Procedure.

As of April 1, 2013, appeals under s. 82 from the Ministerial decision on reconsideration are to be taken to the General Division of the Social Security Tribunal. For appeals filed and heard prior to April 1, 2013, the Review Tribunal remains seized of the file and must make its decision no later than March 31, 2014 (or such date as is earlier prescribed under CPP s. 253(3)) — see CPP s. 255. Appeals filed under s. 82(1) but not heard before April 1, 2013 are deemed to have been filed with the General Division of the Social Security Tribunal on April 1, 2013 — see CPP s. 257. Note that the repealed provisions continue to apply to appeals of which a Review Tribunal remains seized, with any necessary adaptations — CPP s. 262.

The appeal procedure in the Social Security Tribunal is set out in Part 5 of the *Department of Human Resources and Skills Development Act*, reproduced in this book starting on page 587.

83. *Stay of benefits pending judicial review* — **If a decision is made by the Social Security Tribunal established under section 44 of the** *Department of Employment and Social Development Act* **in respect of a benefit, the Minister may stay payment of the benefit until the latest of (2013, c. 40, s. 236(1)(*b*)(iii).)**

(*a*) **the expiry of the period allowed for making an application for leave to appeal to the Appeal Division of that Tribunal,**

(*b*) **the expiry of the period allowed for making an application under the** *Federal Courts Act* **for judicial review of the decision, and**

(*c*) **if Her Majesty has made an application under the** *Federal Courts Act* **for judicial review of the decision, the month in which all proceedings in relation to the judicial review have been completed.**

(R.S.C. 1985, c. 41 (1st Supp.), s. 12; R.S.C. 1985, c. 27 (2nd Supp.), s. 7; R.S.C. 1985, c. 30 (2nd Supp.), s. 45; 1991, c. 44, s. 22; 1995, c. 33, s. 36; 1997, c. 40, s. 85.1; 2000, c. 12, s. 61; 2000, c. 12, s. 64; 2002, c. 8, s. 121; 2010, c. 12, s. 1669; 2012, c. 19, s. 229; 2013, c. 40, s. 236.)

———————— **Notes** ————————

Synopsis

This section provides for an automatic stay of benefits ordered by the General division of the SST during the period for launching an appeal or judicial review by the Minister.

---

84. *Authority to determine questions of law and fact* — **(Repealed by S.C. 2012, c. 19, s. 229, in force April 1, 2013.)**

(R.S.C. 1985, c. 30 (2nd Supp.), s. 45; 1990, c. 8, s. 46; 2002, c. 8, s. 182(1)(*f*); 2012, c. 19, s. 229, in force April 1, 2013; 2012, c. 31, s. 202.)

———————— **Notes** ————————

Synopsis

Until April 1, 2013, this section gives broad authority to the PAB and Review Tribunal to determine questions of law or fact with respect to disputes over CPP benefits, DUPE or assignments of retirement pension under s. 65.1. A decision of the PAB or Review Tribunal is final and binding, subject to the right to appeal the Review Tribunal decision to the PAB under s. 83, and the right to seek judicial review of a PAB decision, including a decision refusing leave to appeal to the PAB. Note that judicial review of a PAB decision refusing leave to appeal is made to the Federal Court under ss. 18 and 18.1 of the *Federal Court Acts*, whereas judicial review of substantive PAB decisions is made directly to the Federal Court of Appeal under s. 28 of that Act.

Federal Courts Act

18. — (1) *Extraordinary remedies, federal tribunals.* — Subject to section 28, the Federal Court has exclusive original jurisdiction

  (*a*) to issue an injunction, writ of *certiorari*, writ of prohibition, writ of *mandamus* or writ of *quo warranto*, or grant declaratory relief, against any federal board, commission or other tribunal; and

  (*b*) to hear and determine any application or other proceeding for relief in the nature of relief contemplated by paragraph (*a*), including any proceeding brought against the Attorney General of Canada, to obtain relief against a federal board, commission or other tribunal.

. . .

18.1. — (1) *Application for judicial review* — An application for judicial review may be made by the Attorney General of Canada or by anyone directly affected by the matter in respect of which relief is sought.

(2) *Time limitation* — An application for judicial review in respect of a decision or an order of a federal board, commission or other tribunal shall be made within 30 days after the time the decision or order was first communicated by the federal board, commission or other tribunal to the office of the Deputy Attorney General of Canada or to the party directly affected by it, or within any further time that a judge of the Federal Court may fix or allow before or after the end of those 30 days.

(3) *Powers of Federal Court* — On an application for judicial review, the Federal Court may

  (*a*) order a federal board, commission or other tribunal to do any act or thing it has unlawfully failed or refused to do or has unreasonably delayed in doing; or (*b*) declare invalid or unlawful, or quash, set aside or set aside and refer back for determination in accordance with such directions as it considers to be appropriate, prohibit or restrain, a decision, order, act or proceeding of a federal board, commission or other tribunal.

(4) *Grounds of review* — The Federal Court may grant relief under subsection (3) if it is satisfied that the federal board, commission or other tribunal

(*a*) acted without jurisdiction, acted beyond its jurisdiction or refused to exercise its jurisdiction;

(*b*) failed to observe a principle of natural justice, procedural fairness or other procedure that it was required by law to observe;

(*c*) erred in law in making a decision or an order, whether or not the error appears on the face of the record;

(*d*) based its decision or order on an erroneous finding of fact that it made in a perverse or capricious manner or without regard for the material before it;

(*e*) acted, or failed to act, by reason of fraud or perjured evidence; or

(*f*) acted in any other way that was contrary to law.

(5) *Defect in form or technical irregularity* — If the sole ground for relief established on an application for judicial review is a defect in form or a technical irregularity, the Federal Court may

(*a*) refuse the relief if it finds that no substantial wrong or miscarriage of justice has occurred; and

(*b*) in the case of a defect in form or a technical irregularity in a decision or an order, make an order validating the decision or order, to have effect from any time and on any terms that it considers appropriate.

* * *

28. — **(1)** *Judicial review* — The Court of Appeal has jurisdiction to hear and determine applications for judicial review made in respect of any of the following federal boards, commissions or other tribunals:

. . .

(*d*) the Pension Appeals Board established by the *Canada Pension Plan*.

. . .

(2) *Section applies* — Sections 18 to 18.5, except subsection 18.4(2), apply, with any modifications that the circumstances require, in respect of any matter within the jurisdiction of the Federal Court of Appeal under subsection (1) and, when they apply, a reference to the Federal Court shall be read as a reference to the Federal Court of Appeal.

(3) *Federal Court deprived of jurisdiction* — If the Federal Court of Appeal has jurisdiction to hear and determine a matter, the Federal Court has no jurisdiction to entertain any proceeding in respect of that matter.

Note that procedures in the Federal Court of Appeal with respect to CPP appeals are governed by the Tax Court of Canada Rules of Procedure respecting the *Canada Pension Plan*.

Bill C-38 Amendments

If no decision has been made before April 1, 2013, in respect of a request for rescission or amendment based on new facts made under s. 84(2), it is deemed to be an application made on April 1, 2013 under s. 66 of the *Department of Human Resources and Skills Development Act* and is deemed to relate to a decision made by the General Division of the Social Security Tribunal, in the case of a decision made by a Review Tribunal, or by the Appeal Division of the Social Security Tribunal, in the case of a decision made by the Pension Appeals Board.

85. *Appeals under provincial pension plan* — **(Repealed by S.C. 2012, c. 19, s. 229, in force April 1, 2013.)**

———————— **Notes** ————————

Synopsis

This section authorizes the PAB to hear appeals under provincial pension plans if the provincial legislation so provides. Section 196 of the QPP provides for appeals to the PAB.

86. *Attendance before Pension Appeals Board* — **(Repealed by S.C. 2012, c. 19, s. 229, in force April 1, 2013.)**

(R.S.C. 1985, c. 30 (2nd Supp.), s. 46; 1995, c. 33, s. 37; 2012, c. 19, s. 229.)

———————— **Notes** ————————

Synopsis

This section authorizes the payment of reasonable travel and living expenses to parties who are request to attend PAB hearings. A successful claimant represented by counsel in a PAB hearing is entitled to be compensated for his or her legal expenses.

Case Law

Canada (Attorney General) v. Burnham, 2008 FCA 380

The PAB does not have the legal authority to require the Minister to reimburse any person other than the claimant for expenses incurred or income lost as a result of attending a hearing of the PAB, or as a result of an adjournment.

86.1. *Stay of benefits pending judicial review* — **(Repealed by S.C. 2012, c. 19, s. 229, in force April 1, 2013.)**

(S.C. 1995, c. 33, s. 38; 2002, c. 8, s. 182(1)(f); 2012, c. 19, s. 229.)

———————— **Notes** ————————

Synopsis

This section authorizes the Minister to stay (i.e., refuse) payment of CPP benefits until the time for appealing or seeking judicial review of the Review Tribunal or PAB decision has expired, or until judicial review proceedings have been completed.

Division G: General

87. *Census information* — **Subject to such conditions as may be prescribed, for the purpose of ascertaining the age of any applicant or beneficiary, or of an appli-**

cant's or a beneficiary's spouse or common-law partner or former spouse or former common-law partner, the Minister is entitled to obtain from Statistics Canada, on request, any information respecting that person's age that is contained in the returns of any census taken more than thirty years before the date of the request.

(R.S.C. 1987, c. 330 (2nd Supp.), s. 47; 2000, c. 12, s. 62.)

_____ Notes _____

Synopsis

This section authorizes the Minister to obtain information relevant to determining the age of a person from the census records of Statistics Canada.

Related CPP Regulations

- Section 51 — Conditions on obtaining information from Statistics Canada

---

88. *Presumption as to death* — **(1)** Where a contributor or beneficiary or a contributor's or beneficiary's spouse or common-law partner or former spouse or former common-law partner has, either before or after the coming into force of this section, disappeared under circumstances that, in the opinion of the Minister, raise beyond a reasonable doubt a presumption that the person is dead, the Minister may determine the date for the purposes of this Act on which that person's death is presumed to have occurred, and thereupon that person shall be deemed for all purposes of this Act to have died on that date. (S.C. 2000, c. 12, s. 63.)

(2) *Change of date* — If, after having determined the date of a person's death pursuant to subsection (1), the Minister is satisfied from new information or evidence that the date of death is different from that determined, the Minister may determine a different date of death, in which case the person shall be deemed for all purposes of this Act to have died on that different date and the Minister shall forthwith cause to be paid any benefit that would have been payable if the determination of death had not been made.

(3) *Where person appears* — If, after having determined the date of a person's death pursuant to subsection (1), the Minister is satisfied from new information or evidence that the person is alive, the Minister shall forthwith cause to be paid any benefit that would have been payable in respect of the person had such determination not been made.

(4) *Benefits cease* — Where any benefit has been paid to any person as a result of the determination of another person's death pursuant to this section and the Minister is satisfied from new information or evidence that other person is alive, the benefit shall forthwith cease to be payable and any such benefit paid prior to the Minister's being satisfied that the person is alive shall be deemed to have been validly paid.

(5) *Death certificates issued by other authorities* — For the purposes of this section, the Minister is not bound by the issuance or revocation of a death certificate by any other authority.

(R.S.C. 1985, c. 330 (2nd Supp.), s. 48; 2000, c. 12, s. 63.)

─────────── **Notes** ───────────

Synopsis

This section authorizes the Minister to treat a person who has disappeared as being deceased as of a certain date. The most frequent use of this provision is qualify the spouse or partner of a disappeared contributor to receive a survivor's pension.

Case Law

Taylor v. MHRD (January 4, 2001), CP 11112 (PAB)

The spouse of a deceased contributor does not have to have a death certificate or court order for the presumption of death before he or she can complete the application form for survivor's benefits. The fact that the spouse of a person who went missing in 1989 had to wait 7 years before she could obtain an order for the declaration of his death under the *Insurance Act* was not grounds for ordering that benefits be paid from 1989, in the face of the 11-month restriction on retroactive payments under s. 72. Section 88 is clear and binding, and it is not relevant whether or not the Minister would have presumed the contributor's death if and when the application had been brought in 1989.

─────────────────

Regulations

89. *Regulations* — **(1) The Governor in Council may make regulations**

(*a*) **prescribing or defining anything that, by this Part, is to be prescribed or defined by regulations;**

(*b*) **prescribing the time, manner and form of making applications for benefits, the information and evidence to be furnished in connection therewith and the procedures to be followed in dealing with and approving applications;**

(*b.1*) **prescribing the time and manner for making requests for reinstatement of a disability pension under section 70.1, and the information and evidence to be furnished in connection with requests; (S.C. 2004, c. 22, s. 22.)**

(*b.2*) **prescribing the information and evidence to be furnished in connection with the reinstatement of disabled contributor's child benefits under section 70.1; (S.C. 2004, c. 22, s. 22.)**

(*c*) **setting out the circumstances in which the Minister may allow a longer period to make a request under subsection 81(1) or (1.1); (R.S.C. 1985, c. 330 (2nd Supp.), s. 49; S.C. 2012, c. 19, s. 230(1).)**

(*d*) **providing for the making of an application or appeal by and the payment of a benefit to any person or agency on behalf of any other person or beneficiary where it is established in such manner and by such evidence as may be prescribed that the other person or beneficiary is by reason of infirmity, illness, insanity or other causes incapable of managing his own affairs, and prescribing the manner in which any benefit authorized to be paid to any such person or agency on behalf of a beneficiary shall be administered and expended for the benefit of the beneficiary and accounted for;**

(*e*) **respecting the determination of disability subject to this Part and the conditions on which any amount as or on account of a benefit in respect of the disability of a person shall be paid or shall continue to be paid, including the initial and subsequent periodic or other assessments of that disability and the reasonable rehabilitation measures to be undergone by that person, and providing for the payment out of the Consolidated Revenue Fund of the cost of any such assessments of disability and rehabilitation measures and for the charging**

Canada Pension Plan

of the amount thereof to the Canada Pension Plan Account as a cost of administration of this Act;

(*f*) providing that the failure of a person to undergo any assessment of disability or reasonable rehabilitation measure as required by any regulation made under paragraph (*e*), without good cause as defined by regulation, shall be a ground on which that person may be determined to have ceased to be disabled;

(*g*) providing, in the case of any benefit that becomes payable to a person to whom no pension is then payable under the *Old Age Security Act*, the basic monthly amount of which benefit is less than such amount, not exceeding ten dollars, as may be prescribed, for the commutation of such benefit in such circumstances and in accordance with such methods and bases as may be prescribed and for the payment to that person in the place of that benefit of an amount equal to the commuted value thereof, or for the payment of that benefit at prescribed intervals less frequent than monthly;

(*h*) respecting the payment of any amount on account of a benefit under this Act that remains unpaid at any time after the death of the beneficiary;

(*i*) respecting the terms and conditions governing the payment of benefits in accordance with any agreement under subsection 80(1) that may be entered into by the Minister on behalf of the Government of Canada;

(*j*) providing, in any case or class of cases not covered by the provisions of an agreement under subsection 80(1), for the issue of cheques by the Government of Canada in the amount of any benefit payable under this Act to or in respect of a contributor and in the amount of any like benefit payable under a provincial pension plan to or in respect of the same contributor, or for the payment by other means by the Government of Canada of such amount, if arrangements satisfactory to the Governor in Council have been made with the government of that province for the issue of cheques, or for the payment by other means, by that government on a reciprocal basis and for the making of any financial adjustments by that government required to be made by reason thereof, and providing for the making of any financial adjustments by the Government of Canada required to be made by reason of those arrangements and for the crediting or charging of the amount thereof to the Canada Pension Plan Account; (S.C. 1991, c. 44, s. 23.)

(*k*) for the purpose of determining the first month for which the amount of a survivor's pension shall be reduced or increased as provided under this Act;

(*l*) providing for the conditions under which the payment of benefits may be withheld pending the furnishing of the Minister with information, evidence and documentation required under this Act and the regulations;

(*l.1*) (Repealed by S.C. 2012, c. 19, s. 230(2), in force June 29, 2012.)

(*l.2*) (Repealed by S.C. 2012, c. 19, s. 230(2), in force June 29, 2012.)

(*m*) generally for carrying out the purposes and provisions of this Part.

(2) *Regulations — payment of interest —* The Governor in Council may make regulations respecting the payment of interest on amounts owing to Her Majesty under this Part, including regulations prescribing

(*a*) the circumstances in which interest is payable;

(*b*) rates of interest or the manner of calculating rates of interest;

(*c*) terms and conditions for the imposition and payment of interest; and (*d*) terms and conditions under which the Minister may waive, reduce or remit the interest payable.

(S.C. 1995, c. 33, s. 39; 2007, c. 11, s. 5(2).)

(3) *Personal Information Protection and Electronic Documents Act* — (**Repealed by S.C. 2012, c. 19, s. 230(2), in force June 29, 2012.**)

(R.S.C. 1985, c. 330 (2nd Supp.), s. 49; 1991, c. 44, s. 23; 1995, c. 33, s. 39; 2004, c. 22, s. 22; 2007, c. 11, s. 5; 2012, c. 19, s. 230; 2012, c. 19, s. 230.)

———————— **Notes** ————————

Synopsis

This section authorizes the federal Governor in Council (the Cabinet) to make regulations under the Act.

Related CPP Regulations

- Canada Pension Plan Regulations
- Review Tribunal Rules of Procedure
- Pension Appeals Board Rules of Procedure (Benefits)
- Tax Court of Canada Rules of Procedure respecting the Canada Pension Plan

———————————

Offences

90. *Offence and punishment* — (**1**) **Every person who**

(*a*) **knowingly makes a false or misleading statement in any application or declaration or makes any application or declaration that by reason of any non-disclosure of facts is false or misleading, or obtains any benefit payment by false pretences,**

(*b*) **being the payee thereof, negotiates or attempts to negotiate any cheque for a benefit to which he is not entitled, or**

(*c*) **knowingly fails to return any cheque or the amount of any benefit payment or any excess amount as required by section 66, (S.C. 1991, c. 44, s. 24.)**

is guilty of an offence punishable on summary conviction.

(2) *Limitation period* — **Any proceedings under this Act in respect of an offence may be commenced at any time within, but not later than, five years after the Minister becomes aware of the subject-matter of the proceedings. (S.C. 1997, c. 40, s. 86.)**

(3) *Saving* — **No proceeding shall be commenced under this section or the *Criminal Code* for an act or omission if a penalty for that act or omission has been imposed under section 90.1. (S.C. 1997, c. 40, s. 86.)**

(S.C. 1991, c. 44, s. 24; 1997, c. 40, s. 86.)

———————— **Notes** ————————

Synopsis

This section makes it a summary conviction offence for a person to make a false or misleading statement, or cash or fail to return a CPP cheque to which he or she is not entitled. Note that summary conviction offences are subject to the *Criminal Code*. There is a 5-year "statute of limitations" on CPP offences, and criminal proceedings cannot be brought where the Minister has imposed a penalty on the person under s. 90.1.

Related Provisions

- Section 90.1 — Penalty for misrepresentation, etc.

Administrative Monetary Penalties[41]

90.1. *Penalty for misrepresentation, etc.* — **(1) The Minister may impose on a person a penalty for each of the following acts or omissions if the Minister becomes aware of facts that in the Minister's opinion establish that the person has**

- **(a) made a statement or declaration, in an application or otherwise, that the person knew was false or misleading;**
- **(b) made a statement or declaration, in an application or otherwise, that the person knew was false or misleading because of the non-disclosure of facts;**
- **(c) knowingly failed to declare to the Minister all or some of the person's earnings for a period for which the person received disability benefits;**
- **(d) received or obtained by cheque or otherwise a benefit payment to which the person knew that they were not entitled, or a benefit payment that the person knew was in excess of the amount of the benefit payment to which they were entitled, and did not return the cheque or the amount of the benefit payment, or the excess amount, as the case may be, without delay; or (S.C. 2007, c. 11, s. 7(2).)**
- **(e) participated in, assented to or acquiesced in an act or omission mentioned in any of paragraphs (a) to (d).**

(S.C. 1997, c. 40, s. 87.)

(1.1) *Purpose of penalty* — **The purpose of the penalty is to promote compliance with this Act and not to punish. (S.C. 2007, c. 11, s. 7(4).)**

(2) *Maximum penalty* — **The Minister may set the amount of the penalty for each act or omission at not more than $10,000. (S.C. 1997, c. 40, s. 87.)**

(3) *Limitation on imposition of penalties* — **A penalty shall not be imposed on a person under subsection (1) if**

- **(a) a prosecution for the act or omission has been initiated against the person; or**
- **(b) five years have passed since the day on which the Minister became aware of the act or omission.**

(S.C. 1997, c. 40, s. 87.)

(4) *Rescission, etc., of penalty* — **The Minister may rescind the imposition of a penalty under subsection (1), or reduce the penalty,**

- **(a) on the presentation of new facts;**
- **(b) on being satisfied that the penalty was imposed without knowledge of, or on the basis of a mistake as to, some material fact;**
- **(c) on being satisfied that the penalty cannot be collected within the reasonably foreseeable future; or**

---

[41] The heading before section 90.1 was added by S.C. 1997, c. 40, s. 87, and amended by 2007, c. 11, s. 6.

(*d*) on being satisfied that payment of the penalty would cause undue hardship to the debtor.

(S.C. 2007, c. 11, s. 7(5).)

(S.C. 1997, c. 40, s. 87; 2007, c. 11, s. 7.)

——————————— **Notes** ———————————

Synopsis

This section authorizes the Minister to impose a penalty of up to $10,000 on persons for making false or misleading statements to the Minister, or for cashing or failing to return a CPP cheque to which that person is not entitled. This penalty provision may not be used if criminal proceedings have already been brought against the person under s. 90, or where more than 5 years have passed since the Minister discovered the act or omission.

Related Provisions

- Section 81(1.1) — Request for reconsideration by Minister
- Section 90 — Offences and punishment

Administration and Enforcement[42]

90.2. *Interpretation* — **(1) The definitions in this subsection apply in this section.**

document — **"document" includes moneys, securities, books, records, letters, accounts, statements (financial or otherwise), correspondence, memoranda, film, microform, videotape, photographs, machine-readable records and other documentary material, regardless of form or characteristics, and any copy or printout of any of them.**

dwelling-house — **"dwelling-house" means the whole or a part of a building or structure that is kept or occupied as a permanent or temporary residence and includes**

(*a*) **a building within the yard of a dwelling-house that is connected to it by a doorway or by a covered and enclosed passageway; and**

(*b*) **a unit that is designed to be mobile and to be used as a permanent or temporary residence and that is being used as such a residence.**

judge — **"judge" means a judge of a superior court having jurisdiction in the province where the matter arises or a judge of the Federal Court.**

(S.C. 1997, c. 40, s. 87.)

(2) *Inspections* — **The Minister may, at any reasonable time, for any purpose relating to the administration or enforcement of this Act, examine any document that relates or may relate to the entitlement of a person to a benefit or the amount of a benefit and, for that purpose, the Minister may**

(*a*) **subject to subsection (3), enter any premises or place where the Minister believes that a document relating to the entitlement of a person to a benefit or the amount of a benefit is or should be kept; and**

(*b*) **require the owner, occupant or person in charge of the premises or place to give the Minister all reasonable assistance and to answer all proper questions relating to the administration or enforcement of this Act and, for that purpose,**

---

[42] The heading before section 90.2 was added by S.C. 2007, c. 11, s. 8.

require the owner, occupant or person in charge of the premises or place to attend at those premises or that place with the Minister.

(S.C. 1997, c. 40, s. 87.)

(3) *Warrant required to enter dwelling-house* — Where the premises or place referred to in subsection (2) is a dwelling-house, the Minister may not enter that dwelling-house without the consent of the occupant except under the authority of a warrant issued under subsection (4). (S.C. 1997, c. 40, s. 87.)

(4) *Warrant* — On *ex parte* application by the Minister, a judge may issue a warrant authorizing the Minister to enter a dwelling-house subject to the conditions that may be specified in the warrant, if the judge is satisfied by information on oath that

(a) there are reasonable grounds to believe that the dwelling-house is a premises or place referred to in subsection (2);

(b) entry into the dwelling-house is necessary for a purpose relating to the administration or enforcement of this Act; and

(c) entry into the dwelling-house has been refused or that there are reasonable grounds to believe that entry will be refused.

(S.C. 1997, c. 40, s. 87.)

(5) *Other access to document* — Where the judge is not satisfied that entry into that dwelling-house is necessary for a purpose relating to the administration or enforcement of this Act but is satisfied that access to a document that is or should be kept in the dwelling-house has been or may be expected to be refused, the judge may

(a) order the occupant of the dwelling-house to provide the Minister with reasonable access to the document; and

(b) make any other order that is appropriate in the circumstances to carry out the purposes of this Act.

(S.C. 1997, c. 40, s. 87.)

(6) *Requirement to provide documents or information* — Despite any other provision of this Act, the Minister may, subject to subsection (7), for any purpose relating to the administration or enforcement of this Act, by notice served personally or by confirmed delivery service, require that any person provide, within the reasonable time that is stipulated in the notice, any information or additional information or any document. (S.C. 1997, c. 40, s. 87.)

(7) *Unnamed persons* — The Minister shall not impose on a person, in this section referred to as a "third party", a requirement under subsection (6) to provide information or a document relating to one or more unnamed persons unless the Minister first obtains the authorization of a judge under subsection (8). (S.C. 1997, c. 40, s. 87.)

(8) *Judicial authorization* — On *ex parte* application by the Minister, a judge may, subject to the conditions that the judge considers appropriate, authorize the Minister to impose on a third party a requirement under subsection (6) relating to one or more unnamed persons, in this section referred to as the "group", where the judge is satisfied by information on oath that

(a) the person or group is ascertainable; and

(*b*) the requirement is made to verify compliance by the person or persons in the group with a duty or obligation under this Act.

(S.C. 1997, c. 40, s. 87.)

(9) *Service of authorization* — Where an authorization is granted under subsection (8), the authorization shall be served together with the notice referred to in subsection (6).

(S.C. 1997, c. 40, s. 87.)

(10) *Review of authorization* — Where an authorization is granted under subsection (8), a third party on whom a notice is served under subsection (6) may, not later than 15 days after the service of the notice, apply to the judge who granted the authorization or, if that judge is unable to act, to another judge of the same court for a review of the authorization. (S.C. 1997, c. 40, s. 87.)

(11) *Powers on review* — On hearing an application under subsection (10), a judge may cancel the authorization previously granted if the judge is not then satisfied that the conditions in paragraphs (8)(*a*) to (*d*) have been met, and the judge may confirm or vary the authorization if the judge is satisfied that those conditions have been met. (S.C. 1997, c. 40, s. 87.)

(12) *Copies as evidence* — Where a document is inspected, examined or provided in accordance with this section, the person by whom it is inspected or examined or to whom it is provided may make, or cause to be made, one or more certified copies of it and any such copy is evidence of the nature and content of the original document and has the same probative force as the original document would have if it were proven in the ordinary way. (S.C. 1997, c. 40, s. 87.)

(13) *Compliance* — No person shall interfere with any person doing anything that the person is authorized under this section to do or prevent or attempt to prevent any person from doing any such thing. (S.C. 1997, c. 40, s. 87.)

(S.C. 1997, c. 40, s. 87.)

——————————— Notes ———————————

Synopsis

This section authorizes the Minister to conduct an inspection of documents relating to the entitlement of persons to benefits, to obtain a search warrant where such documents are in a private residence, and to require individuals or groups of persons to product relevant documents. The Minister may make copies of documents obtained under this section.

Part III

Administration

Interpretation

91. *Definitions* — **The following definitions apply in this Part.**

"Investment Board" **means the Canada Pension Plan Investment Board established by section 3 of the Canada Pension Plan Investment Board Act.**

"Minister" means the Minister of Employment and Social Development. (2005, c. 35, s. 67(*a*)(viii); S.C. 2012, c. 19, s. 694(*a*)(viii); 2013, c. 40, s. 238(1)(*b*)(vii).)

(S.C. 1996, c. 11, s. 95; 2003, c. 5, s. 1; 2005, c. 35, s. 67; S.C. 2012, c. 19, s. 694; 2013, c. 40, s. 238.)

General

92. *Administration of Act* — **(1)** The Minister has the control and direction of the administration of this Act other than Part I.

(2) *Duties of Minister of National Revenue* — The Minister of National Revenue has the control and direction of the administration of Part I and shall from time to time each year report to the Minister

    (*a*) such information obtained under this Act with respect to the earnings and contributions of any contributor as is required by the Minister to permit the calculation of the amount of the unadjusted pensionable earnings to be shown to the account of the contributor in the Record of Earnings established under section 95, and to identify in the Record of Earnings the unadjusted pensionable earnings of contributors, according to information contained in returns made pursuant to Part I;

    (*b*) such information obtained with respect to the earnings of any person as is required by the Minister to permit the determination of the amount of any benefit that may be payable under this Act to or in respect of that person or of the amount of any benefit that may be payable to or in respect of that person by reason of which any financial adjustment may be required to be made pursuant to any agreement entered into under subsection 80(1); and

    (*c*) such statistical and other general information as is necessary for the administration of this Act including the conduct of actuarial and other studies relating to the operation of this Act.

93. *Duty of Minister of Public Works and Government Services* — The Minister of Public Works and Government Services shall furnish the Minister with such assistance in the administration of this Act as the Governor in Council may direct. (S.C. 1996, c. 16, s. 60(1)(b).)

(S.C. 1996, c. 16, s. 60.)

94. *Duty of Canada Employment Insurance Commission* — The Canada Employment Insurance Commission shall furnish the Minister and the Minister of National Revenue with such assistance in the administration of this Act as the Governor in Council may direct. (S.C. 1996, c. 11, s. 99.)

(S.C. 1996, c. 11, s. 99.)

Records and Information

95. *Record of Earnings* — The Minister shall cause to be established such records, to be known as the Record of Earnings, of information obtained under this Act with respect to the earnings and contributions of contributors, including information obtained pursuant to any agreement entered into under section 105 with respect to those earnings and contributions, as are necessary to permit

    (*a*) the determination of the amount of any benefit that may be payable under this Act to or in respect of any contributor;

(*b*) the calculation of the amount of any financial adjustment that may be required to be made pursuant to any agreement entered into under subsection 80(1); and

(*c*) the identification of the unadjusted pensionable earnings of contributors, according to information contained in returns made pursuant to Part I.

——————— Notes ———————

Related Provisions

- Section 97 — Entry in record of earnings presumed to be accurate

---

96. *Application for statement of earnings and request for reconsideration* — **(1) Subject to the provisions of any agreement entered into under section 105, every contributor may require the Minister, by application made in the prescribed manner, to furnish or make available to the contributor a statement of the unadjusted pensionable earnings shown to the contributor's account in the Record of Earnings, and if a contributor is not satisfied with the statement, they may request that it be reconsidered by the Minister. (S.C. 2007, c. 11, s. 9.)**

(2) *Application of sections 81 and 82* — **Sections 81 and 82 apply with any modifications that the circumstances require to any request made under subsection (1) as though it were an application for a benefit. (S.C. 2012, c. 19, s. 231.)**

(3) *Exception* — **(Repealed by S.C. 1995, c. 33, s. 40.)**

(S.C. 1995, c. 33, s. 40; 2007, c. 11, s. 9; 2012, c. 19, s. 231.)

——————— Notes ———————

Related CPP Regulations

- Section 39 — Application for statement of earnings

---

97. *Entry in record of earnings presumed to be accurate* — **(1) Notwithstanding section 96, except as provided in this section, any entry in the Record of Earnings relating to the earnings or a contribution of a contributor shall be conclusively presumed to be accurate and may not be called into question after four years have elapsed from the end of the year in which the entry was made. (S.C. 1995, c. 33, s. 41(1).)**

(2) *Rectification of Record in certain cases* — **If,**

(*a*) from information furnished by or obtained from the records of an employer or a former employer, or an employee or a former employee of an employer, or a person required to make a contribution in respect of his self-employed earnings, after the time specified in subsection (1), or

(*b*) for any other reason,

it appears to the Minister that the amount of the unadjusted pensionable earnings shown in the Record of Earnings to the account of an employee or former employee of that employer or to the account of that person is less than the amount that should be so shown in that Record, the Minister may cause the Record of Earnings to be rectified in order to show the amount of the unadjusted pensionable earnings of the contributor that should be so shown therein. (R.S.C. 1985, c. 30, (2nd Supp.), s. 50.)

(2.1) *Removal of entry* — **If, from information furnished pursuant to an agreement referred to in paragraph 105(1)(*a*), it appears to the Minister that an amount**

that is shown in the Record of Earnings to the account of a person as being a contribution under this Act relates instead to a contribution under the provincial pension plan of that province, the Minister may, at any time after that information is furnished, authorize the removal of that entry from the Record of Earnings. (S.C. 1995, c. 33, s. 41(2).)

(3) *Idem* — Where the amount of the unadjusted pensionable earnings of a contributor shown to his account in the Record of Earnings is increased pursuant to subsection (2) and it appears to the Minister that the earnings and contributions with respect to which that amount is so increased have been incorrectly shown in the Record to the account of another contributor, the Minister may cause the Record of Earnings to be rectified by reducing the amount of the unadjusted pensionable earnings shown in the Record to the account of that other contributor by such part of that amount as has been incorrectly so shown therein.

(4) *Notice of rectification to be given* — Whenever any reduction is made in the amount of the unadjusted pensionable earnings of a contributor shown to their account in the Record of Earnings, whether under subsection (3) or otherwise, and it appears from the Record of Earnings that before the making of the reduction the contributor had been informed under section 96 of the amount of the earnings shown to their account in the Record of Earnings, the Minister must notify the contributor in prescribed manner of his or her action and if the contributor is not satisfied with the amount of the reduction so made, they may request that such action be reconsidered by the Minister and sections 81 and 82 apply with any modifications that the circumstances require to that request as though it were an application for a benefit. (S.C. 2012, c. 19, s. 232.)

(R.S.C. 1985, c. 330 (2nd Supp.), s. 50; 1995, c. 33, s. 41; 2012, c. 19, s. 232.)

———————— **Notes** ————————

Related CPP Regulations

- Section 40 — Notification of contributor of reduction

Case Law

Walters v. MEI, [1996] FCJ No. 176 (C.A.)

While s. 97 makes it indisputable that the amount shown in the Record is accurate, whether such payment was sufficient to be a valid yearly contribution is determined by s. 52(3), a basic eligibility provision.

Pankewicz v. MHRD (August 27, 2001), CP 12908 (PAB)

Where on a claim for survivor's benefits the record showed the deceased had made only five years of contributions although seven were required, s. 97 requires that the record be conclusively presumed to be accurate and the claim denied.

———————————

98. *Application for assignment of Social Insurance Number* — (1) Every individual who applies for a division under section 55 or 55.1 shall, within thirty days of the date of application for such division, if he has not earlier been assigned a Social Insurance Number, file an application with the Minister, in such form and manner as may be prescribed, for the assignment to him of a Social Insurance Number. (R.S.C. 1985, c. 330 (2nd Supp.), s. 51.)

(2) *Idem* — Every individual who reaches eighteen years of age and is or becomes employed in pensionable employment on or after reaching that age shall, within thirty days after he reaches eighteen years of age or becomes employed in pensionable employment, as the case may be, if he has not earlier been assigned a Social Insur-

ance Number, file an application with the Minister, in such form and manner as may be prescribed, for the assignment to him of a Social Insurance Number.

(3) *Idem* — Every individual who is required by section 30 to file a return of his self-employed earnings for a year, other than an individual to whom subsection (1) or (2) applies, shall on or before the first day on or before which he is required by section 33 to pay any amount as or on account of the contribution required to be made by him for that year in respect of those earnings, if he has not earlier been assigned a Social Insurance Number, apply to the Minister, in such form and manner as may be prescribed, for the assignment to him of a Social Insurance Number.

(4) *Assignment of Number* — The Minister shall, on application by an individual to whom a Social Insurance Number has not earlier been assigned, cause a Social Insurance Number to be assigned to the individual and a Social Insurance Number Card may be issued to the individual. (2012, c. 19, s. 305.)

(5) *Employer to maintain record of Social Insurance Number* — Every employer who employs an employee in pensionable employment shall, in the case of an employee to whom subsection (2) applies, within 30 days after the day on which the employee reaches 18 years of age or becomes employed in pensionable employment, whichever is the later, require the employee to inform the employer of their Social Insurance Number, and the employer shall maintain a record of the Social Insurance Number of each employee. (2012, c. 19, s. 305.)

(6) *Employee to provide Social Insurance Number* — Every employee who is required under subsection (5) to inform the employer of their Social Insurance Number shall do so within 30 days after the day on which they are required to do so by the employer. (2012, c. 19, s. 305.)

(R.S.C. 1985, c. 330 (2nd Supp.), s. 51; 2012, c. 19, s. 305.)

——————— **Notes** ———————

Case Law

Kroeker v. MNR (1969), 69 D.T.C. 380 (T.A.B.)

Failure to apply for a Social Insurance Number does not relieve an individual from liability to make contributions called for by the CPP.

99. *Application to be signed by applicant* — **(1)** An application for a Social Insurance Number shall be signed by the applicant in his own hand but where the applicant is unable to sign his own name, he may attest the application by making his mark in the presence of two witnesses whose names and signatures shall be shown thereon.

(2) *Change of name* — When the name of an individual to whom a Social Insurance Number has been assigned changes, by reason of marriage or otherwise, the individual shall inform the Minister of their new name, unless they have already so informed another authority empowered to receive that information,

(a) if the individual is employed in pensionable employment, within 60 days after the day on which the change of name becomes effective; or

(b) if the individual is not employed in pensionable employment but later becomes so employed, or is required to make a contribution under this Act in respect of their self-employed earnings, within 60 days after the day on which the individual becomes so employed or after the first day on or before which they are required under section 33 to pay any amount as or on account of the contribution required to be made by them in respect of those earnings, as the case may be.

(S.C. 2012, c. 19, s. 306.)

(S.C. 2012, c. 19, s. 306.)

——————— Notes ———————

Case Law

MNHW v. Poland (March 29, 1993), CP 2343, CEB & PG (TB) ¶8500 (PAB).

Section 99 is an administrative provision and does not override the substantive provision of s. 52(3)(*a*). A claimant could not defeat the clear intention of s. 52(3)(*a*) merely by not seeking within four years a refund of an invalid contribution triggered by earnings less than the basic exemption. Therefore, *MNHW v. Sawyer* (September 5, 1989), CP 1581 (PAB) was wrongly decided.

100. *Agreement respecting assignment of Social Insurance Numbers* — **(1) The Minister may, on behalf of the Government of Canada, enter into an agreement with the government of a province providing a comprehensive pension plan under which the Minister may cause Social Insurance Numbers to be assigned to persons to whom Social Insurance Numbers have not earlier been assigned, on the basis of applications made by those persons to the appropriate authority in that province.**

(2) *Numbers deemed to have been assigned under Act* — **Any Social Insurance Numbers caused to be assigned by the Minister under any agreement entered into under subsection (1) shall be deemed for all purposes of this Act to have been assigned under this Act.**

101. *Regulations* — **(1) The Governor in Council may make regulations**

(*a*) **requiring employers to distribute to their employees applications and other material relating to applications for Social Insurance Numbers;**

(*b*) **prescribing districts for purposes of assigning Social Insurance Numbers, in which persons who reside therein may file their applications for Social Insurance Numbers and, having regard to the public convenience, the place or places within each district at which those persons may apply;**

(*c*) **prescribing the conditions on which and manner in which Social Insurance Number Cards that have been lost or destroyed may be replaced;**

(*d*) **authorizing the Minister and the Minister of National Revenue to cause a Social Insurance Number to be assigned and a Social Insurance Number Card to be issued to any individual who has not earlier been assigned a Social Insurance Number; (R.S.C. 1985, c. 330 (2nd Supp.), s. 52.)**

(*d.1*) **prescribing or defining anything that, by this Part, is to be prescribed or defined; (R.S.C. 1985, c. 330 (2nd Supp.), s. 52.)**

(*d.2*) **(Repealed by S.C. 2012, c. 19, s. 233(1), in force June 29, 2012.)**

(*d.3*) **(Repealed by S.C. 2012, c. 19, s. 233(1), in force June 29, 2012.)**

(*e*) **generally for carrying out the purposes and provisions of this Part.**

(2) *Personal Information Protection and Electronic Documents Act* — **(Repealed by S.C. 2012, c. 19, s. 233(2), in force June 29, 2012.)**

(R.S.C. 1985, c. 330 (2nd Supp.), s. 52; 1995, c. 33, s. 42; 2007, c. 11, s. 10; 2012, c. 19, s. 233.)

102. *Offence and punishment* — **(1)** Every person who, in his application for a Social Insurance Number, knowingly furnishes any false or misleading information is guilty of an offence punishable on summary conviction.

(2) *Idem* — Every person who has been assigned a Social Insurance Number and who knowingly makes application again to be assigned a Social Insurance Number, whether giving the same or different information in that application as in his previous application, and whether or not he is assigned a Social Insurance Number again, is guilty of an offence punishable on summary conviction.

(3) *Idem* — Every employer who fails to comply with subsection 98(5) or any regulation made under paragraph 101(1)(*a*) is guilty of an offence and is liable on summary conviction to a fine not exceeding one hundred dollars.

103. *Limitation period* — **(1)** A prosecution for an offence under this Act may be commenced at any time within, but not later than, five years after the time when the subject-matter of the prosecution arose.

(2) *Officers, etc., of corporations* — Where a corporation commits an offence under this Act, every officer, director or agent of the corporation who directed, authorized, assented to, acquiesced in or participated in the commission of the offence is a party to and guilty of the offence and is liable on conviction to the punishment provided for the offence whether or not the corporation has been prosecuted or convicted.

(3) *Information or complaint* — Subsection 41(6) applies with respect to an information or complaint under any of the provisions of this Act other than Part I, as though for the reference therein to the Canada Revenue Agency and the Minister thereof there were substituted a reference to the Department of Employment and Social Development and the Minister. (1996, c. 11, s. 97(1)(*b*); 1999, c. 17, s. 111(*e*); 2005, c. 35, s. 66(*a*)(ii); 2005, c. 38, s. 138; 2012, c. 19, s. 695(1)(*a*)(ii); 2013, c. 40, s. 237(1)(*b*)(ii).)

(S.C. 1996, c. 11, s. 97; 1999, s. 17, s. 111; 2005, c. 35 s. 66; 2005, c. 38, s. 138; 2012, c. 19, s. 695; 2013, c. 40, s. 237.)

Availability of Information[43]

104. *Definitions* — **(1)** The following definitions apply in this section and sections 104.1 and 105. (S.C. 2012, c. 19, s. 293(1).)

"administration" includes the development, operation, evaluation and enforcement of policies and programs.

"federal institution" means a department or any other body referred to in Schedule I, I.1, II or III to the *Financial Administration Act*. (S.C. 2003, c. 22, s. 129.)

"public officer" means an officer or employee of a federal institution, or a prescribed individual or a member of a prescribed class of individuals. (S.C. 1997, c. 40, s. 88.)

(2) *Interpretation* — The definition of a word or expression in subsection (1) does not affect its interpretation in any other provision of this Act. (S.C. 1997, c. 40, s. 88.)

(3) *Purpose* — (Repealed by S.C. 2012, c. 19, s. 293(2), in force March 1, 2013.) (S.C. 1997, c. 40, s. 88; 2005, c. 35, s. 45; 2012, c. 19, s. 293.)

(S.C. 1997, c. 40, s. 88; 2003, c. 22, s. 129; 2005, c. 35, s. 45; 2012, c. 19, s. 293.)

---

[43] The heading before section 104 was added by S.C. 1997, c. 40, s. 88 and replaced by 2012, c. 19, s. 292.

———————— **Notes** ————————

Related CPP Regulations

● Section 37 — Public officer: Prescribed individual

104.01. *Protection of information* — **(Repealed by S.C. 2012, c. 19, s. 294, in force March 1, 2013.)**

(S.C. 1997, c. 40, s. 88; 2005, c. 35, s. 46; 2007, c. 11, s. 11; 2012, c. 19, s. 294.)

———————— **Notes** ————————

Related CPP Regulations

● Section 60 — Access to privileged information on written request

---

104.02. *Availability of information within certain departments* — **(Repealed by S.C. 2012, c. 19, s. 294, in force March 1, 2013.)**

(S.C. 1997, c. 40, s. 88; 2005, c. 35, s. 47; 2012, c. 19, s. 294.)

104.03. *Availability of information within federal institutions* — **(Repealed by S.C. 2012, c. 19, s. 294.)**

(S.C. 1997, c. 40, s. 88; 1999, s. 17, s. 111(f); 2005, c. 35, s. 48; 2005, c. 35 s. 66; 2005, c. 38, s. 138; 2012, c. 19, s. 294.)

104.04. *Exception re war crimes* — **(Repealed by S.C. 2012, c. 19, s. 294, in force March 1, 2013.)**

(S.C. 1997, c. 40, s. 88; S.C. 2012, c. 19, s. 294.)

104.05. *Availability of information to provincial authorities* — **(Repealed by S.C. 2012, c. 19, s. 294, in force March 1, 2013.)**

(S.C. 1997, c. 40, s. 88; 2012, c. 19, s. 294.)

104.06. *Availability of information to certain persons or bodies* — **(Repealed by S.C. 2012, c. 19, s. 294, in force March 1, 2013.)**

(S.C. 1997, c. 40, s. 88; 2005, c. 35, s. 50; 2012, c. 19, s. 294.)

104.07. *Where Minister may permit information to be made available* — **(Repealed by S.C. 2012, c. 19, s. 294, in force March 1, 2013.)**

(S.C. 1997, c. 40, s. 88; 2012, c. 19, s. 294.)

104.08. *Evidence and production of documents* — **(Repealed by S.C. 2012, c. 19, s. 294, in force March 1, 2013.)**

(S.C. 1997, c. 40, s. 88; 2005, c. 35, s. 51; 2012, c. 19, s. 294.)

104.09. *Offence* — **(Repealed by S.C. 2012, c. 19, s. 294, in force March 1, 2013.)**

(S.C. 1997, c. 40, s. 88; 2005, c. 35, s. 51; 2012, c. 19, s. 294.)

104.1. *Availability of information within federal institutions* — **(1) Despite any other Act or law, any information obtained by a public officer of the Canada Revenue Agency, the Department of Finance, the Department of Public Works and Government Services or the Department of Citizenship and Immigration for the purpose of the administration of this Act may be made available to a public officer of the**

Department of Employment and Social Development, the Canada Revenue Agency, the Department of Finance, the Department of Public Works and Government Services, the Department of Citizenship and Immigration or the Office of the Superintendent of Financial Institutions for the purpose of the administration of this Act. (2012, c. 19, s. 294; 2013, c. 40, s. 237(1)(*b*)(iii).)

(2) *Secondary release of information* — Information obtained under this section shall not be made available to any other person or body unless the information is made available only for the same purpose and on any conditions that the Minister may specify. (S.C. 2012, c. 19, s. 294.)

(S.C. 1997, c. 40, s. 88; 2012, c. 19, s. 294; 2013, c. 40, s. 237.)

104.101. *Research or statistical purposes* — (Repealed by S.C. 2012, c. 19, s. 294, in force March 1, 2013.)

(S.C. 2005, c. 35, s. 52; 2012, c. 19, s. 294; 2013, c. 40, s. 237.)

104.102. *Use of information for research purposes* — (Repealed by S.C. 2012, c. 19, s. 294, in force March 1, 2013.)

(S.C. 1997, c. 40, s. 88; 2005, c. 35, s. 52; 2012, c. 19, s. 294.)

104.11. *Information obtained relative to Social Insurance Numbers* — (Repealed by S.C. 2012, c. 19, s. 294, in force March 1, 2013.)

(S.C. 1997, c. 40, s. 88; 2012, c. 19, s. 294.)

Agreements with Provinces[44]

105. *Agreement with province for exchange of records and furnishing of information* — The Minister may, on behalf of the Government of Canada, enter into an agreement with the government of a province providing a comprehensive pension plan

(*a*) under which any information obtained under this Act, including records of any amounts that are shown in the Record of Earnings to the accounts of individuals who have made contributions under this Act and under the provincial pension plan of that province and that relate to the contributions made by those individuals under this Act, may be made available under prescribed conditions to the appropriate authority of that province having the administration of the provincial pension plan, and under which any information obtained under the provincial pension plan may be made available on a reciprocal basis to the Minister; and

(*b*) under which the Minister or the appropriate authority of that province, in accordance with any terms and conditions that may be specified in the agreement, may make available to any individual who has made contributions under this Act and under the provincial pension plan a statement of any amounts shown in the Record of Earnings or the appropriate records established under the provincial pension plan, as the case may be, to the account of that individual, and may act on or give effect to any request made by that individual for reconsideration by the Minister or the appropriate authority, as the case may be, of any statement made available to the individual.

(S.C. 1997, c. 40, s. 88.)

(S.C. 1997, c. 40, s. 88.)

---

[44] The heading before section 105 was added S.C. 2012, c. 19, s. 294.

Oaths, Affidavits, Declarations and Affirmations[45]

106. *Commissioners for oaths* — **(1) A person who (S.C. 1995, c. 33, s. 44(1).)**

(a) is employed in the administration or enforcement of Part I or any regulations made thereunder and is authorized by the Minister of National Revenue for the purpose, or

(b) is employed in the administration or enforcement of this Part and Part II or any regulations made thereunder and is authorized by the Minister for the purpose,

may, in the course of their employment and subject to any other Act of Parliament or any Act of the legislature of a province, administer oaths and take and receive affidavits, declarations and solemn affirmations and every person so authorized has, with respect to any such oath, affidavit, declaration or solemn affirmation, all the powers of a commissioner for taking affidavits. (S.C. 1995, c. 33, s. 44(2).)

(2) *Acceptance of oaths, etc.* — **For the purposes of the administration of**

(a) Part I or any regulations made under that Part, any person described in paragraph (1)(a), or

(b) this Part or Part II or any regulations made under either of those Parts, any person described in paragraph (1)(b)

may accept any oath administered or affidavit, declaration or solemn affirmation given by any officer or employee of any department in, or other portion of, the federal public administration specified in Schedule I, IV or V to the *Financial Adminstration Act* or of any department of the government of a province who has all the powers of a commissioner for taking affidavits. (S.C. 1995, c. 33, s. 44(3); 2003, c. 22, s. 130.)

(S.C. 1995, c. 33, s. 44; 2003, c. 22, s. 130.)

Reciprocal Agreements with Other Countries

107. *Reciprocal arrangements re administration, etc.* — **(1) Where, under any law** of a country other than Canada, provision is made for the payment of old age or other benefits including survivors' or disability benefits, the Minister may, on behalf of the Government of Canada, on such terms and conditions as may be approved by the Governor in Council, enter into an agreement with the government of that country for the making of reciprocal arrangements relating to the administration or operation of that law and of this Act, including, without restricting the generality of the foregoing, arrangements relating to

(a) the exchange of such information obtained under that law or this Act as may be necessary to give effect to any such arrangements,

(b) the administration of benefits payable under this Act to persons resident in that country, the extension of benefits to and in respect of persons under that law or this Act and the increase or decrease in the amount of the benefits payable under that law or this Act to and in respect of persons employed in or resident in that country, and

(c) the administration of benefits payable under that law to persons resident in Canada, the extension of benefits to and in respect of persons under that law or this Act and the increase or decrease in the amount of the benefits payable under that law or this Act to and in respect of persons employed in or resident in Canada,

and, subject to subsection (4), any such agreement may extend to and include similar arrangements with respect to any provincial pension plan.

[45] The heading before section 106 was added S.C. 2012, c. 19, s. 295.

(2) *Minimum payment as a result of arrangement* — **(Repealed by R.S.C. 1985, c. 30 (2nd Supp.), s. 54.)**

(3) *Regulations for giving effect to agreements* — **For the purpose of giving effect to any agreement entered into under subsection (1), the Governor in Council may make such regulations respecting the manner in which this Act shall apply to any case or class of cases affected by the agreement, and for adapting this Act thereto, as appear to the Governor in Council to be necessary for that purpose, and any regulations so made may provide therein for the making of any financial adjustments required under the agreement and for the crediting or charging of the amount of any of those adjustments to the Canada Pension Plan Account.**

(4) *Agreements with respect to provincial pension plan* — **Where the government of a province providing a comprehensive pension plan requests the Government of Canada to enter into an agreement under this section with the government of a country under any law of which provision is made for the payment of old age or other benefits including survivors' or disability benefits, the Minister, with the approval of the Governor in Council, may enter into an agreement with the government of that country for the making of reciprocal arrangements relating to any of the matters referred to in subsection (1) with respect to the provincial pension plan of that province, if that plan makes provision for entering into such an agreement and for the carrying out of the provisions thereof, including the making of any financial adjustment required to be made for that purpose and the crediting or charging of the amount of any such adjustment to the appropriate account or accounts established under that plan.**

(R.S.C. 1985, c. 30 (2nd Supp.), s. 54.)

——————— **Notes** ———————

Case Law

Tan v. MSD (December 8, 2006), CP 20525, 22316, 22452, 22453, 23253 (PAB)

Section 107 authorizes the federal government to enter into agreements with other countries that have laws providing for the payment of old age or other benefits including survivor's and disability benefit. Such agreements allow individuals who have qualified under the CPP to move to signatory countries without the loss of benefits and for individuals who come to Canada having contributed to the plans of those countries to retain benefits. The purpose of the agreements is:

(a) to reduce or eliminate restrictions, based on citizenship, that may prevent Canadians from receiving pensions from other countries (equality of treatment);

(b) to reduce or eliminate restrictions on the payment of pensions abroad (export of benefits);

(c) to make it easier to become eligible for benefits by adding together periods of social security coverage under the programs of two or more countries (totalization); and

(d) to permit continuity of social security coverage when a person is working temporarily in another country and to prevent situations where a person would have to contribute to two countries' social security programs for the same work (continuity of coverage).

Four essential conditions must exist for Canada to enter into a social security agreement with another country. First, the other country must have a public pension system which can be co-ordinated with the CPP. The other country must have a system which is based on residence or contributions and benefits must be payable regularly on a weekly, monthly or other regular basis. Secondly, the other country must be prepared to grant reciprocity on such matters as the payment of benefits in a convertible currency, to persons residing in Canada. Thirdly, the financial basis of the other country's social security system must be reasonably sound, and fourthly, the other country's social security institution must be able to carry out its administrative obligations under an agreement.

Financial Provisions

107.1. *Donations* — **The Minister may acquire money, securities or other property by gift, bequest or otherwise and shall dispose of such securities or other property subject to the terms, if any, on which such money, securities or other property is given, bequeathed or otherwise made available to the Minister.**

(S.C. 1995, c. 33, s. 45.)

108. *Canada Pension Plan Account* — **(1) There is hereby established in the accounts of Canada an account to be known as the Canada Pension Plan Account.**

(2) *Amounts to be credited to Account* — **There shall be paid into the Consolidated Revenue Fund and credited to the Canada Pension Plan Account**

- (a) **all amounts received under this Act as or on account of contributions or otherwise;**
- (b) **all amounts required to be credited to the Canada Pension Plan Account pursuant to any agreement entered into under subsection 39(1) or 80(1) or pursuant to any regulation made under paragraph 89(1)(f) or subsection 107(3);**
- (c) **all interest on securities purchased by the Minister of Finance under section 110 and all interest credited to the Canada Pension Plan Account under that section;**
- (d) **any amount of money received under section 107.1 and any proceeds from the disposition of any securities or other property received under that section; (S.C. 1995, c. 33, s. 46(1); 1997, c. 40, s. 89(1).)**
- (e) **all amounts charged for the use of resources that are associated with the administration of this Act; (S.C. 1995, c. 33, s. 46(1).)**
- (f) **any interest or administrative charge collected in relation to money payable under this Act; and (S.C. 1997, c. 40, s. 89(1).)**
- (g) **all amounts received pursuant to section 56 of the *Canada Pension Plan Investment Board Act*. (S.C. 1997, c. 40, s. 89(1).)**

(2.1) *Costs of appeals related to Old Age Security Act* — **(Repealed by S.C. 2012, c. 19, s. 234(1), in force June 29, 2012.)**

(3) *Amounts to be charged to Account* — **There shall be paid out of the Consolidated Revenue Fund and charged to the Canada Pension Plan Account**

- (a) **all amounts payable under this Act as or on account of benefits or otherwise;**
- (b) **all amounts required to be charged to the Canada Pension Plan Account pursuant to any agreement entered into under subsection 39(1) or 80(1) or pursuant to any regulation made under paragraph 89(1)(f) or subsection 107(3);**
- (b.1) **all amounts credited to the Canada Pension Plan Account pursuant to paragraph (2)(e); (S.C. 1995, c. 33, s. 46(3); 1997, c. 40, s. 89(2).)**
- (c) **the costs of administration of this Act, under the authority of Parliament;**
- (d) **all amounts required to be charged to the Canada Pension Plan Account pursuant to section 57 of the *Canada Pension Plan Investment Board Act*; and (S.C. 1997, c. 40, s. 89(2).)**

(*e*) the costs of administering Part 5 of the *Department of Employment and Social Development Act* in respect of appeals respecting this Act. (2012, c. 19, s. 234(2); 2013, c. 40, s. 236(1)(*b*)(iv).)

(4) *Limitation* — **No payment shall be made out of the Consolidated Revenue Fund under this section in excess of the total of**

(*a*) **the amount of the balance to the credit of the Canada Pension Plan Account, and**

(*b*) **the fair market value of the assets of the Investment Board less its liabilities.**

(S.C. 2003, c. 5, s. 2.)

(S.C. 1995, c. 33, s. 46; 1997, c. 40, s. 89; 2003, c. 5, s. 2; 2012, c. 19, s. 234; 2013, c. 40, s. 236.)

———————————— Notes ————————————

Related CPP Regulations

● Section 58(2) — Single payment of benefits

Case Law

Mintzer v. Canada, [1996] 2 FC 146 (C.A.)

The role of the Crown with respect to monies credited to the CPP Account or to benefits not yet paid is that of an administrator in exercise of its governmental functions rather than of a trustee.

———————————————

108.1. *Management of Account* — **(1) Any amounts standing to the credit of the Canada Pension Plan Account that exceed the immediate obligations of that Account shall be transferred to the Investment Board, unless any agreement entered into under section 111.1 provides otherwise. The amounts shall be paid out of the Consolidated Revenue Fund and charged to the Canada Pension Plan Account. (S.C. 2003, c. 5, s. 3.)**

(2) *Payment by Investment Board* — **The Minister may, by notice, and in accordance with any agreement entered into under section 111.1, require the Investment Board to pay into the Consolidated Revenue Fund any amount necessary to offset amounts charged or required to be charged to the Canada Pension Plan Account under subsection 108(3) and any interest charged under subsection 110(2). (S.C. 2003, c. 5, s. 3.)**

(3) *Interest* — **The Minister of Finance shall credit interest to the Canada Pension Plan Account at market rates, as determined by that Minister, on any amount standing to the credit of that Account. The interest shall be paid out of the Consolidated Revenue Fund. (S.C. 2003, c. 5, s. 3.)**

(S.C. 2003, c. 5, s. 3.)

109. *Canada Pension Plan Investment Fund* — **(1) (Repealed by S.C. 2003, c. 5, s. 4(1).)**

(2) *Amounts to be charged and credited to Account* — **(Repealed by S.C. 2003, c. 5, s. 4(3).) (S.C. 2003, c. 5, s. 4(2) and (3).)**

(3) *Matured securities* — *amounts to be charged to Fund* — **(Repealed by S.C. 2003, c. 5, s. 4(3).) (S.C. 2003, c. 5, s. 4(2) and (3).)**

Canada Pension Plan

(4) *Redemption before maturity — amounts to be charged to Fund* — **(Repealed by S.C. 2003, c. 5, s. 4(3).) (S.C. 2003, c. 5, s. 4(2) and (3).)**

(S.C. 2003, c. 5, s. 4.)

110. *Definitions* — **(1) (Repealed by S.C. 2003, c. 5, s. 5(3).) (S.C. 1997, c. 40, s. 90(2); 2003, c. 5, s. 5(1), (2) and (3).)**

(2) *Interest shall be charged to Account* — **The Minister of Finance shall charge interest to the Canada Pension Plan Account at market rates, as determined by that Minister, on any amount paid out of the Consolidated Revenue Fund under subsection 108(3) that exceeds the balance to the credit of the Canada Pension Plan Account. Interest shall be charged for the period beginning on the day on which the amount is paid out of the Consolidated Revenue Fund under subsection 108(3) and ending on the day on which the Investment Board pays that amount into the Consolidated Revenue Fund under section 56 of the *Canada Pension Plan Investment Board Act*. (S.C. 2003, c. 5, s. 5(4).)**

(2.1) *Additional interest* — **(Repealed by S.C. 2003, c. 5, s. 5(5).) (R.S.C. 1985, c. 30 (2nd Supp.), s. 55(2); 2003, c. 5, s. 5(5).)**

(3) *Replacement security* — **(Repealed by S.C. 2003, c. 5, s. 5(7).) (S.C. 1997, c. 40, s. 90(4); 2003, c. 5, s. 5(6) and (7).)**

(4) *Principal amount* — **(Repealed by S.C. 2003, c. 5, s. 5(7).) (S.C. 1997, c. 40, s. 90(4); 2003, c. 5, s. 5(7).)**

(5) *Term to maturity* — **(Repealed by S.C. 2003, c. 5, s. 5(7).) (S.C. 1997, c. 40, s. 90(4); 2003, c. 5, s. 5(7).)**

(6) *Interest* — **(Repealed by S.C. 2003, c. 5, s. 5(7).) (S.C. 1997, c. 40, s. 90(4); 2003, c. 5, s. 5(7).)**

(6.1) *Features of replacement security* — **(Repealed by S.C. 2003, c. 5, s. 5(7).) (S.C. 1997, c. 40, s. 90(4); 2003, c. 5, s. 5(7).)**

(6.2) *Redemption* — **(Repealed by 2003, c. 5, s. 5(8).) (S.C. 1997, c. 40, s. 90(4); 2003, c. 5, s. 5(8).)**

(6.3) *Amount redeemable* — **(Repealed by 2003, c. 5, s. 5(8).) (S.C. 1997, c. 40, s. 90(4); 2003, c. 5, s. 5(8).)**

(6.4) *Redemption at request of province* — **(Repealed by 2003, c. 5, s. 5(10).) (S.C. 2000, c. 14, s. 45; 2003, c. 5, s. 5(9) and (10).)**

(6.5) (Repealed by 2003, c. 5, s. 5(10).) (S.C. 2000, c. 14, s. 45; 2003, c. 5, s. 5(10).)

(7) *Consolidation of securities* — **(Repealed by 2003, c. 5, s. 5(10).)**

(8) *Saving provision* — **(Repealed by 2003, c. 5, s. 5(11).)**

(R.S.C. 1985, c. 30 (2nd Supp.), s. 55; 1997, c. 40, s. 90; 2000, c. 14, s. 45; 2003, c. 5, s. 5.)

111. *Transfers — matured securities not replaced* — **(1) (Repealed by 2003, c. 5, s. 6.)**

(2) *Transfers — excess* — **(Repealed by 2003, c. 5, s. 6.)**

(S.C. 1997, c. 40, s. 91; 2003, c. 5, s. 6.)

111.1. *Administration agreement* — **(1) The Minister of Finance may, on terms and conditions satisfactory to the Minister, enter into an agreement with the Invest-ment Board with respect to the administration of any matter referred to in sections**

107.1 to 110, including the payment of amounts out of the Consolidated Revenue Fund to the Investment Board, and the payment of amounts by the Investment Board into the Consolidated Revenue Fund. (S.C. 2003, c. 5, s. 7.)

(2) *Administration agreement* — The Minister of Finance may enter into an agreement with the Investment Board with respect to the administration of any matter referred to in section 113. (S.C. 2003, c. 5, s. 7.)

(S.C. 1997, c. 40, s. 91; 2003, c. 5, s. 7.)

112. *Annual financial statements* — (1) The Minister shall, as soon as possible after the end of each fiscal year, prepare annual financial statements for the *Canada Pension Plan* in respect of that year setting out

(a) a statement of the amounts credited to or charged to the Canada Pension Plan Account during the year; (S.C. 2003, c. 5, s. 8.)

(b) a statement consolidating the accounts of the Canada Pension Plan Account and the Investment Board for the year; and (S.C. 2003, c. 5, s. 8.)

(c) any other accounts and information that the Minister considers appropriate to present fairly the financial transactions and the financial position of the *Canada Pension Plan* for the year.

(S.C. 1997, c. 40, s. 91.)

(2) *Reliance* — In preparing the annual financial statements, the Minister may rely on the annual financial statements prepared under subsection 39(4) of the *Canada Pension Plan Investment Board Act.*

(3) *Audit* — The annual financial statements of the *Canada Pension Plan* shall be audited annually by the Auditor General of Canada and a report of the audit shall be made to the Minister.

(4) *Duty to provide information* — The Investment Board and its auditor shall provide the Auditor General of Canada with any records, accounts, statements or other information that in the opinion of the Auditor General of Canada are necessary to audit the annual financial statements of the *Canada Pension Plan.*

(S.C. 1997, c. 40, s. 91; 2003, c. 5, s. 8.)

113. *Effect of regulation made under subsection 3(2)* — (1) Where any regulation has been made under subsection 3(2) prescribing a province as a province described in paragraph (b) of the definition "province providing a comprehensive pension plan" in subsection 3(1),

(a) all obligations and liabilities accrued or accruing as described in that paragraph, for the assumption of which under the provincial pension plan of that province provision has been made by any law of that province, shall, from and after the day on which the regulation became effective, cease to be obligations or liabilities accrued or accruing with respect to the payment of benefits under this Act attributable to contributions made under this Act in respect of employment in that province or in respect of self-employed earnings of persons resident in that province; and

(b) the Minister of Finance shall pay an amount calculated as provided in subsection (2) to the government of that province, by the transfer to that government in the first instance and to the extent necessary for that purpose, of securities of that province that are designated securities as defined in section 2 of the *Canada Pension Plan Investment Board Act*, and in the second instance and to the extent necessary for that purpose, of securities of Canada that are designated securities as defined in section 2 of that Act, and by the payment to that government of any balance then remaining in any manner that may be prescribed. (S.C. 2003, c. 5, s. 9(1).)

(1.1) *Transfer by Investment Board* — The Minister of Finance may, by notice, and in accordance with any agreement entered into under section 111.1, require the Investment Board to pay to that Minister any amount, and to transfer to that Minister any securities of the province or of Canada referred to in paragraph (1)(b), that are necessary for the purposes of subsection (1). (S.C. 2003, c. 5, s. 9(2) and (3).)

(1.2) *Rights in securities extinguished* — (Repealed by S.C. 2003, c. 5, s. 9(3).) (S.C. 2003, c. 5, s. 9(2) and (3).)

(2) *Amount to be paid to government of province* — For the purposes of subsection (1), the amount to be calculated as provided in this subsection in the case of any province shall be calculated by the Minister of Finance as the amount obtained by adding

(a) the total amount of all contributions credited to the Canada Pension Plan Account, to the day on which the regulation referred to in subsection (1) became effective, in respect of employment in that province or in respect of self-employed earnings of persons resident in that province, and

(b) the part of

(i) the net investment return of the Investment Board, and

(ii) all interest credited to or accrued to the credit of the Canada Pension Plan Account,

to the day on which the regulation referred to in subsection (1) became effective, that is derived from the contributions referred to in paragraph (a), (S.C. 1997, c. 40, s. 92.)

and subtracting from the total so obtained

(c) such part of all amounts paid as or on account of benefits under this Act as would not have been payable under this Act if that province had been a province described in paragraph (a) of the definition "province providing a comprehensive pension plan" in subsection 3(1), and

(d) such part of the costs of administration of this Act, to the day on which the regulation referred to in subsection (1) became effective, as is equal to the proportion of those costs that the total amount of the contributions referred to in paragraph (a) is of the total amount of all contributions credited to the Canada Pension Plan Account to that day.

(3) *Agreement respecting assumption of obligations and liabilities* — Where notice in writing has been given to the Minister by the government of a province as described in the definition "province providing a comprehensive pension plan" in subsection 3(1), the Minister, with the approval of the Governor in Council, may on behalf of the Government of Canada enter into an agreement with the government of that province,

(a) for the furnishing of that government under prescribed conditions with any information obtained under this Act, including records of any amounts that are shown in the Record of Earnings to the accounts of persons who have made contributions under this Act in respect of employment in that province or as persons resident in that province in respect of self-employed earnings; and

(b) generally for the making of all such arrangements as may be necessary to permit provision to be made for the assumption, under the provincial pension plan referred to in the notice, of all obligations and liabilities accrued or accruing as described in paragraph (b) of the definition "province providing a comprehensive pension plan" in subsection 3(1).

(S.C. 1997, c. 40, s. 92; 2003, c. 5, s. 9.)

Financial Review of the Canada Pension Plan[46]

113.1. *Review every three years* — **(1)** Once every three years after 1997, the Minister of Finance and ministers of the Crown from the included provinces shall review the financial state of the Canada Pension Plan and may make recommendations as to whether benefits or contribution rates or both should be changed. (S.C. 1997, c. 40, s. 94(1).)

(2) *Review of adjustment factors* — When the Chief Actuary of the Office of the Superintendent of Financial Institutions specifies adjustment factors in his or her report according to subsection 115(1.11), the Minister of Finance and ministers of the Crown from the included provinces shall, as part of their review, also review the adjustment factors fixed under subsection 46(7) and may make recommendations as to whether they should be changed. (S.C. 1997, c. 40, s. 94(2); 2009, c. 31, s. 41(1).)

(3) *Completion of review* — If possible, the review in each three year period must be completed in time to permit the Minister of Finance to make recommendations to the Governor in Council before the end of the second year of the three year period. (S.C. 1997, c. 40, s. 94(3).)

(4) *Factors to be considered* — In conducting any review required by this section and in making any recommendations, ministers shall consider

(a) the most recent report prepared by the Chief Actuary pursuant to section 115 and any changes between that report and earlier reports prepared by the Chief Actuary;

(b) any more recent estimates of the Chief Actuary in respect of

(i) the outstanding balance of the Canada Pension Plan Account,

(ii) the projected revenues into and payments out of the Canada Pension Plan Account,

(iii) the ratio of the projected assets of the Canada Pension Plan over the projected expenditures of the Canada Pension Plan, and (S.C. 1997, c. 40, s. 94(4).)

(iv) the changes, if any, to the amounts and ratio projected at the previous review under this section attributable to changing demographic and economic circumstances or to changes to the Canada Pension Plan affecting payments or contributions thereunder; (S.C. 1997, c. 40, s. 94(5).)

(c) the financing objective of having a contribution rate, without taking into account the changes referred to in paragraph (d) for which the contribution rate most recently calculated under subparagraph 115(1.1)(c)(ii) exceeds zero, that is no lower than the rate (S.C. 2007, c. 11, s. 12.)

(i) that, beginning with the year 2003, is the lowest constant rate that can be maintained over the foreseeable future, and

(ii) that results in the ratio of the projected assets of the Canada Pension Plan at the end of any given year over the projected annual expenditures of the Canada Pension Plan in the following year being generally constant; and (S.C. 1997, c. 40, s. 94(5).)

(d) that changes to the Act that increase benefits or add new benefits must be accompanied by a permanent increase in the contribution rates to cover the extra costs of the increased or new benefits and by a temporary increase in the contribution rates for a number of years that is consistent with common actuarial practice to fully pay any unfunded liability resulting from the increased or new benefits. (S.C. 1997, c. 40, s. 94(5).)

---

[46] The heading before section 113.1 was replaced by 1997, c. 40, s. 93.

(5) *Role of Minister when recommendations made* — On the completion of a review required by subsection (1), the Minister of Finance may recommend to the Governor in Council that the Governor in Council make regulations under subsection (6) to amend the schedule in accordance with that subsection to give effect to any recommendations made under subsection (1). Where the recommendations made under subsection (1) are that no changes be made to benefits or contribution rates, the Minister of Finance shall cause those recommendations to be published in the *Canada Gazette*. (S.C. 1997, c. 40, s. 94(6).)

(6) *Regulation to adjust rates* — Subject to subsections (7) and (8), the Governor in Council may, on the recommendation of the Minister of Finance made under subsection (5), by regulation amend the schedule to change the contribution rate for employees, employers and self-employed persons for any or all of the years following the review. (S.C. 1997, c. 40, s. 94(6).)

(7) *Limitation on adjustments* — The following shall apply with respect to any adjustment and setting of contribution rates pursuant to subsection (6):

  (a) the contribution rate for employees and employers for a year must be identical;

  (b) the contribution rate for self-employed persons for a year must be equal to the sum of the contribution rates for employees and employers for that year;

  (c) no contribution rate for employees and employers for a year may be increased by more than one-tenth of a percentage point above the contribution rate for the previous year; and

  (d) no contribution rate for self-employed persons for a year may be increased by more than two-tenths of a percentage point above the contribution rate for the previous year.

(8) *Coming into force of regulation* — Where a review takes place in a three year period as required by subsection (1) and the Governor in Council before October 1 of the third year of that period makes a regulation under subsection (6), the regulation shall, by order made by the Governor in Council, come into force, or is deemed to have come into force, on January 1 of the year after that period. (S.C. 1997, c. 40, s. 94(7).)

(8.1) *Provincial consent required* — An order made under subsection (8) may not be made unless the lieutenant governor in council of each of at least two-thirds of the included provinces, having in total not less than two thirds of the population of all of the included provinces, has, before the October 1 date referred to in that subsection, signified the consent of that province to the coming into force of the regulation. (S.C. 1997, c. 40, s. 94(7).)

(9) *Exemption from Statutory Instruments Act* — A regulation made pursuant to subsection (6) is exempt from the application of sections 3, 5 and 11 of the *Statutory Instruments Act*. (S.C. 1991, c. 44, s. 27.)

(10) *Publication in Canada Gazette* — Forthwith on the coming into force of any regulation made pursuant to subsection (6), the Minister of Finance shall cause a copy thereof to be published in the *Canada Gazette*.

(11) (Repealed by S.C. 2007, c. 11, s. 12(2).)

(11.01) (Repealed by S.C. 2007, c. 11, s. 12(2).)

(11.02) (Repealed by S. C. 2007, c. 11, s. 12(2).)

(11.03) (Repealed by S.C. 2007, c. 11, s. 12(2).)

(11.04) (Repealed by S.C. 2007, c. 11, s. 12(2).)

(11.05) *Insufficient rates* — Subject to subsections (11.12) and (11.13), if, at October 1 of the year before a three-year period for which a review is required by subsection (1), the contribution rate for self-employed persons for the years in that three-year period less the contribution rate most recently calculated under subparagraph 115(1.1)(*c*)(ii) is less than the contribution rate most recently calculated under subparagraph 115(1.1)(*c*)(i) for self-employed persons for those years, (S.C. 2007, c. 11, s. 12(3).)

    (*a*) the benefits payable in the three year period shall be determined as if the ratios referred to in paragraphs 45(2)(*b*) and 56(2)(*c*), subsection 58(1.1) and subparagraph 59(*c*)(ii) were each 1; and

    (*b*) the schedule is deemed to have been amended as of the next day after that October 1

      (i) to increase the contribution rate for employees and employers for each year after that October 1 to the rate determined under subsections (11.07) to (11.11) for that year, and

      (ii) to increase the contribution rate for self-employed persons for each year after that October 1 to twice the contribution rate determined under subsections (11.07) to (11.11) for employers for that year. (S.C. 1997, c. 40, s. 94(8).)

(11.06) *Interpretation* — In the calculations under subsections (11.07) to (11.11),

A is one half of the contribution rate most recently calculated under subparagraph 115(1.1)(*c*)(i) for self-employed persons for the years in the three-year period referred to in subsection (11.05);

B is the contribution rate for employees and employers at October 1 of the third year of the last three-year period for which contribution rates were set for employees and employers, by an Act of Parliament or by a regulation made under subsection (6), on the recommendation of ministers under subsection (1);

C is one half of the contribution rate most recently calculated under subparagraph 115(1.1)(*c*)(ii) for self-employed persons for the years in the three-year period referred to in subsection (11.05); and

D is the difference between B and C.

(S.C. 1997, c. 40, s. 94(8); 2007, c 11, s. 12(4).)

(11.07) *Determination of rate — 1st case* — If neither A nor D is greater than 4.95% and A is greater than D, the contribution rate for employees and employers for each year after the October 1 date referred to in subsection (11.05) is A plus C. (S.C. 1997, c. 40, s. 94(8); 2007, c. 11, s. 12(4).)

(11.08) *Determination of rate — 2nd case* — If A is greater than 4.95%, D is less than or equal to 4.95% and the percentage determined by the formula

$$^1/_2 (A - D)$$

is less than or equal to 0.1%, then the contribution rate for employees and employers for each year after the October 1 date referred to in subsection (11.05) is the rate determined by the formula

$$4.95\% + {}^1/_2 (A - 4.95\%) + C$$

(S.C. 1997, c. 40, s. 94(8); 2007, c. 11, s. 12(4).)

(11.09) *Determination of rate — 3rd case* — If A is greater than 4.95%, D is less than or equal to 4.95% and the percentage determined by the formula

$$^1\!/_2 \; (A - D)$$

is greater than 0.1%, then the contribution rate for employees and employers is

(*a*) for the first year after the October 1 date referred to in subsection (11.05), the rate determined by the formula

$$4.95\% + {}^1\!/_6 \; (A - 4.95\%) + C$$

(*b*) for the next year, the rate determined by the formula

$$4.95\% + {}^1\!/_3 \; (A - 4.95\%) + C$$

and

(*c*) for each subsequent year, the rate determined by the formula

$$4.95\% + {}^1\!/_2 \; (A - 4.95\%) + C$$

(S.C. 1997, c. 40, s. 94(8); 2007, c. 11, s. 12(4).)

(11.1) *Determination of rate — 4th case* — If subsections (11.07) to (11.09) do not apply and the percentage determined by the formula

$$^1\!/_2 \; (A - D)$$

is less than or equal to 0.1%, then the contribution rate for employees and employers for each year after the October 1 date referred to in subsection (11.05) is the rate determined by the formula

$$D + {}^1\!/_2 \; (A - D) + C$$

(S.C. 1997, c. 40, s. 94(8); 2007, c. 11, s. 12(4).)

(11.11) *Determination of rate — 5th case* — If subsections (11.07) to (11.1) do not apply, then the contribution rate for employees and employers is

(*a*) for the first year after the October 1 date referred to in subsection (11.05), the rate determined by the formula

$$D + {}^1\!/_6 \; (A - D) + C$$

(*b*) for the next year, the rate determined by the formula

$$D + {}^1\!/_3 \; (A - D) + C$$

and

(*c*) for each subsequent year, the rate determined by the formula

$$D + {}^1\!/_2 \; (A - D) + C$$

(S.C. 1997, c. 40, s. 94(8); 2007, c. 11, s. 12(4).)

(11.12) *Where paragraph (11.05)(a) does not apply* — **Paragraph (11.05)(a) does not apply if subsection (11.07) applies.** (S.C. 1997, c. 40, s. 94(8).)

(11.13) *Where subsection (11.05) does not apply* — **Subsection (11.05) does not apply where**

(*a*) a recommendation was made under subsection (1) in the three years before the three-year period referred to in subsection (11.05) that the contribution rates for one or more of the years in that three-year period be increased and the rates were increased before October 1 of the year before that three year period, by an Act of Parliament or by a regulation made under subsection (6), to give effect to that recommendation; or

(*b*) a recommendation was made under subsection (1) in the three years before the three-year period referred to in subsection (11.05) that the contribution rates for the years in that three-year period not be increased and the Minister of Finance before October 1 of the year before that three-year period has caused that recommendation to be published in the *Canada Gazette*. (S.C. 1997, c. 40, s. 94(8).)

(11.14) *Adjustment* — If a contribution rate determined under any of subsections (11.07) to (11.11) is not a multiple of 0.005%, the contribution rate is to be rounded to the nearest multiple of 0.005%. (S.C. 1997, c. 40, s. 94(8); 2007, s. 11, s. 12(5).)

(11.15) *Rates to be published* — The Minister of Finance shall publish in the *Canada Gazette* any amendment to the schedule deemed to have been made under this section. (S.C. 1997, c. 40, s. 94(8).)

(12) *Application of subsection 114(2)* — For greater certainty, subsection 114(2) does not apply to any amendments to the schedule made under subsection (6) or subsections (11.05) to (11.11). (S.C. 2007, s. 11, s. 12(6).)

(13) *Recommendation — adjustment factors* — On the completion of a review required by subsection (2), the Minister of Finance may recommend to the Governor in Council that the Governor in Council amend the regulations made under subsection 46(7) to give effect to any recommendations made under subsection (2). If the recommendations are that no changes be made to the adjustment factors, the Minister of Finance shall cause those recommendations to be published in the *Canada Gazette*. (S.C. 2009, c. 31, s. 41(3).)

(14) *Changes to adjustment factors — regulations* — The Governor in Council may, on the recommendation of the Minister of Finance made under subsection (13), amend the regulations to change one or more adjustment factors or the methods of calculating them. (S.C. 2009, c. 31, s. 41(3).)

(15) *Provincial consent* — The regulations may only be amended if the lieutenant governor in council of each of at least two thirds of the included provinces, having in total not less than two thirds of the population of all of the included provinces, has signified the consent of that province to the amendment. (S.C. 2009, c. 31, s. 41(3).)

(16) *Definition of "included province"* — In this section, included province has the same meaning as in subsection 114(1). (S.C. 2009, c. 31, s. 41(3).)

(R.S.C. 1985, c. 30 (2nd Supp.), s. 56; 1991, c. 44, s. 27; 1997, c. 40, s. 94; 2007, c. 11, s. 12; 2009, c. 31, s. 41.)

Amendments to Act

114. *Definition of "included province"* — **(1)** In this section, "included province" means a province other than Yukon or the Northwest Territories or Nunavut, except a province providing a comprehensive pension plan, unless at the time in respect of which the description is relevant, there is in force an agreement entered into under subsection 4(3) with the government of that province. (S.C. 2002, c. 7, s. 111.)

(2) *Effective date of major amendments* — Where any enactment of Parliament contains any provision that alters, or the effect of which is to alter, either directly or indirectly and either immediately or in the future, the general level of benefits provided by this Act or the contribution rate for employees, employers or self-employed persons for any year, it shall be deemed to be a term of that enactment, whether or not it is expressly stated in the enactment, that the provision shall come into force only on a day to be fixed by order of the Governor in Council, which day shall not in any case be earlier than the first day of the third year following the year in which any notice of intention to introduce a measure containing a provision to that effect was laid before Parliament. (S.C. 1997, c. 40, s. 95(1).)[47]

(3) *Notice* — A notice of intention described in subsection (2) shall be in such form as is sufficient to indicate the nature of the provision contained or proposed to be contained in the measure referred to in subsection (2) to the effect described in that subsection, and on any such notice being laid before Parliament the Minister shall forthwith cause a copy thereof to be sent to the lieutenant governor in council of each included province.

(4) *Coming into force of other amendments of substance* — Where any enactment of Parliament contains any provision that alters, or the effect of which is to alter, either directly or indirectly and either immediately or in the future,

(a) the general level of benefits provided by this Act,

(b) the classes of benefits provided by this Act,

(c) the contribution rate for employees, employers or self-employed persons for any year, (R.S.C. 1985, c. 30 (2nd Supp.), s. 57(2).)

(d) the formulae for calculating the contributions and benefits payable under this Act,

(e) the management or operation of the Canada Pension Plan Account, or (S.C. 2003, c. 5, s. 10.)

(f) the *Canada Pension Plan Investment Board Act,* (S.C. 1997, c. 40, s. 95(2).)

it shall be deemed to be a term of that enactment, whether or not it is expressly stated in the enactment, that the provision shall come into force only on a day to be fixed by order of the Governor in Council, which order may not be made and shall not in any case have any force or effect unless the lieutenant governor in council of each of at least two-thirds of the included provinces, having in the aggregate not less than two-thirds of the population of all of the included provinces, has signified the consent of that province to the enactment. (S.C. 1997, c. 40, s. 95(3).)

(4.1) *Exception* — Subsections (2) and (4) do not apply in respect of changes under any of subsections 113.1(11.05) to (11.11) to benefits or contribution rates. (S.C. 1997, c. 40, s. 95(4); 2007, c. 11, s. 13.)

(5) *Determination of population* — For the purposes of this section, the population of a province at any time in a year in respect of which the determination thereof is relevant means the population thereof on June 1 of that year, as estimated by the Chief Statistician of Canada.

(R.S.C. 1985, c. 30 (2nd Supp.), s. 57; 1997, c. 40, s. 95; 2002, c. 7, s. 111; 2003, c. 5, s. 10; 2007, c. 11, s. 13.)

Report of Chief Actuary

115. *Chief Actuary to report every three years* — (1) The Chief Actuary of the Office of the Superintendent of Financial Institutions shall, during the first year of each three year period for which a review is required by subsection 113.1(1), prepare a report setting out, as at a date not earlier than December 31 of the year before the three year period, the results of an actuarial examination of the operation of this Act

---

[47] Pursuant to 1997, c. 40, s. 99, subsection 114(2) does not apply in respect of the amendments to the *Canada Pension Plan* made by S.C. 1997, c. 40.

On proclamation of S.C. 2004, c. 22, s. 24(1) (January 31, 2007), subsection 114(2) does not apply in respect of the amendments to the *Canada Pension Plan* made by S.C. 2004, c. 22.

Pursuant to S.C. 2007, c. 11, s. 39, subsection 114(2) does not apply in respect of the amendments to the *Canada Pension Plan* made by S.C. 2007, c. 11, ss. 2, 12–14, and 36.

based on the state of the Canada Pension Plan Account and the investments of the Investment Board. (S.C. 1997, c. 40, s. 96(1).)

(1.1) *Contents of report* — The Chief Actuary shall, in the report,

(a) state the estimated revenues of the Canada Pension Plan Account and the estimated investment income of the Investment Board for each of the 30 years immediately following the date of the examination, and the estimated amount of all payments under subsection 108(3) in each of those 30 years;

(b) state, for each fifth year of a period of not less than 75 years from the date of the examination, an estimate of the percentage of total contributory salaries and wages and contributory self-employed earnings that would be required to provide for all payments under subsection 108(3) in that year if there were no balance in the Canada Pension Plan Account at the commencement of that year and the Investment Board had no investments;

(c) specify a contribution rate calculated, in respect of self-employed persons for each year of a period of not less than 75 years after the three-year period in which the report is prepared, by combining

(i) a contribution rate, calculated in the prescribed manner, without taking into account the changes referred to in paragraph 113.1(4)(d) for which the contribution rate most recently calculated under subparagraph (ii) exceeds zero, and

(ii) a contribution rate calculated in the prescribed manner in respect of the changes referred to in paragraph 113.1(4)(d);

(S.C. 2007, c. 11, s. 14.)

(c.1) specify the contribution rates referred to in subparagraphs (c)(i) and (ii); and (S.C. 2007, c. 11, s. 14.)

(d) set out the manner in which that contribution rate was calculated.

(S.C. 1997, c. 40, s. 96(1).)

(1.11) *Adjustment factors* — In the first report prepared after 2015 and in every third report that follows, the Chief Actuary shall specify, in reference to the adjustment factors fixed under subsection 46(7), the factors as calculated according to a methodology that he or she considers appropriate; the Chief Actuary may also, if he or she considers it necessary, specify the factors in any report prepared under subsection (1) after 2015. (S.C. 2009, c. 31, s. 42.)

(1.2) *Relationship between rates* — For the purpose of the calculation referred to in paragraph (1.1)(c),

(a) the contribution rate for employees and employers for a year must be identical; and

(b) the contribution rate for self-employed persons for a year must be equal to the sum of the contribution rates for employees and employers for that year. (S.C. 1997, c. 40, s. 96(1).)

(1.3) *Application of subsection 114(4)* — Subsection 114(4) applies, with such modifications as the circumstances require, to the making of the regulations prescribing the manner of the calculation referred to in paragraph (1.1)(c) and to the making of any regulation changing that manner of calculation. (S.C. 1997, c. 40, s. 96(1).)

(2) *Report when certain Bills introduced* — In addition to any report required under subsection (1) and in accordance with a request of the Minister of Finance, whenever any Bill is introduced in the House of Commons to amend this Act in a

manner that would in the opinion of the Chief Actuary materially affect any of the estimates contained in the most recent report made under that subsection, the Chief Actuary shall prepare a report as set out in subsection (3). (S.C. 2012, c. 31, s. 203.)

(3) *Report for section 113.1 review* — (Repealed by 1997, c. 40, s. 96(2).)

(4) *Single report allowed* — (Repealed by 1997, c. 40, s. 96(2).)

(5) *Rates in reports* — (Repealed by 1997, c. 40, s. 96(2).)

(6) *Contents of regulations* — (Repealed by 1997, c. 40, s. 96(2).)

(7) *Application of subsection 114(4)* — (Repealed by 1997, c. 40, s. 96(2).)

(8) *Report to be laid before House of Commons* — Forthwith on the completion of any report under this section, the Chief Actuary shall transmit the report to the Minister of Finance, who shall cause the report to be laid before the House of Commons forthwith on its receipt if Parliament is then sitting, or if Parliament is not then sitting, on any of the first five days next thereafter that Parliament is sitting, and if at the time any report under this section is received by the Minister of Finance Parliament is then dissolved, the Minister of Finance shall forthwith cause a copy of the report to be published in the *Canada Gazette.*

(R.S.C. 1985, c. 13 (2nd Supp.), s. 10; c. 30 (2nd Supp.), s. 58; c. 18 (3rd Supp.), s. 32; 1997, c. 40, s. 96; 2007, c. 11, s. 14; 2009, c. 31, s. 42; 2012, c. 31, s. 203.)

Annual Report to Parliament and the Provinces[48]

116. *Canada Pension Plan Advisory Board* — (Repealed by 1997, c. 40, s. 97(2).)

117. *Annual report to be made by Ministers* — **(1)** The Minister of Finance and the Minister of Employment and Social Development shall, as soon as possible after the end of each fiscal year, together prepare a report on the administration of this Act during that year, including (2005, c. 35, s. 67(a)(ix); 2012, c. 19, s. 694(a)(ix); 2013, c. 40, s. 238(1)(b)(viii).)

(a) the annual financial statements for that year prepared under section 112 and the report of the Auditor General of Canada on those statements;

(b) the number of contributors during that year and the number of persons to whom benefits were payable during that year; and

(c) any other information that the Ministers, and the appropriate provincial Ministers of the participating provinces, as defined in section 2 of the *Canada Pension Plan Investment Board Act*, consider appropriate. (S.C. 1997, c. 40, s. 97.)

(2) *Tabling in Parliament* — The Ministers shall cause the report to be laid before each House of Parliament on any of the first 15 days on which that House is sitting after the report is prepared. (S.C. 1997, c. 40, s. 97.)

(3) *Presentation to provinces* — As soon as possible after the report is prepared, the Ministers shall send the report to the appropriate provincial Minister of every province. (S.C. 1997, c. 40, s. 97.)

(4) *Definition of "appropriate provincial Minister"* — In this section, "appropriate provincial Minister", in respect of a province, means the province's minister of the

---

[48] The heading before sections 116 and 117 was replaced by 1997, c. 40, s. 97.

Crown who has primary responsibility for that province's finances. (S.C. 2003, c. 5, s. 11.)

(S.C. 1997, c. 40, s. 97; 2005, c. 35, s. 67; 2003, c. 5, s. 11; 2012, c. 19, s. 694; 2013, c. 40, s. 238.)

Government Employees

118. *Government contributions* — (1) There shall be charged to the Consolidated Revenue Fund and credited to the Canada Pension Plan Account an amount equal to

(*a*) the contributions required to be made by Her Majesty in right of Canada as employer's contributions under this Act, and

(*b*) the amount required by subsection 21(2) to be paid by Her Majesty in right of Canada as a result of the failure to deduct and remit, in accordance with this Act, the required amount as or on account of the employee's contributions,

in respect of persons in employment under Her Majesty in right of Canada that is not excepted employment under this Act.

(2) *Contributions under agreement* — There shall be charged to the Consolidated Revenue Fund and paid to the appropriate authority in a province with which an agreement has been entered into under subsection 4(3) an amount equal to

(*a*) the contributions required to be paid by Her Majesty in right of Canada under that agreement as employer's contributions, and

(*b*) the amount required to be paid by Her Majesty in right of Canada as a result of the failure to deduct and remit, in accordance with the agreement, the required amount as or on account of the employee's contributions,

in respect of persons employed by Her Majesty in right of Canada in employment designated in the agreement.

Canada Pension Plan

Schedule

(Subsection 11.1(2))

Year	For Employees	For Employers	For Self-Employed Persons
	Contribution Rates		
1987	1.9 %	1.9 %	3.8 %
1988	2.0	2.0	4.0
1989	2.1	2.1	4.2
1990	2.2	2.2	4.4
1991	2.3	2.3	4.6
1992	2.4	2.4	4.8
1993	2.5	2.5	5.0
1994	2.6	2.6	5.2
1995	2.7	2.7	5.4
1996	2.8	2.8	5.6
1997	3.0	3.0	6.0
1998	3.2	3.2	6.4
1999	3.5	3.5	7.0
2000	3.9	3.9	7.8
2001	4.3	4.3	8.6
2002	4.7	4.7	9.4
2003 and each subsequent year	4.95	4.95	9.9

(S.C. 1997, c. 40, s. 98, Schedule.)

TRANSITIONAL PROVISIONS

The following Transitional Provisions from S.C. 2010, c. 19 apply to the amendments made by S.C. 2012, c. 19, s. 225–234:

251. *Definitions* — **The following definitions apply in sections 252 to 270.**

"Pension Appeals Board" means the Pension Appeals Board established under section 83 of the *Canada Pension Plan*, as it read immediately before the coming into force of section 229.

"Review Tribunal" means a Review Tribunal established under section 82 of the *Canada Pension Plan*, as it read immediately before the coming into force of section 229.

"Social Security Tribunal" means the Social Security Tribunal established under section 44 of the *Department of Human Resources and Skills Development Act*.

252. *[Not reproduced].*

253. *Review Tribunal* — **(1) The members of a Review Tribunal referred to in subsection 255(1) continue to hold office until the earlier of the end of the term for which they were appointed and April 1, 2014.**

(2) *No compensation.* **Despite the provisions of any contract, agreement or order, no person appointed to hold office as a member of the Review Tribunal, other than the Commissioner of Review Tribunals and the Deputy Commissioner of Review Tribunals, has any right to claim or receive any compensation, damages, indemnity or other form of relief from Her Majesty in right of Canada or from any employee or agent of Her Majesty for ceasing to hold that office or for the abolition of that office by the operation of this Division.**

(3) *Earlier date* — **For the purposes of subsection (1), the Governor in Council may, by order, fix a day earlier than April 1, 2014.**

254. *Pension Appeals Board* — **(1) The members of the Pension Appeals Board continue to hold office until April 1, 2014.**

(2) *No compensation* — **Despite the provisions of any contract, agreement or order, no person appointed to hold office as a member of the Pension Appeals Board has any right to claim or receive any compensation, damages, indemnity or other form of relief from Her Majesty in right of Canada or from any employee or agent of Her Majesty for ceasing to hold that office or for the abolition of that office by the operation of this Division.**

(3) *Earlier date* — **For the purposes of subsection (1), the Governor in Council may, by order, fix a day earlier than April 1, 2014.**

255. *Appeals — Review Tribunal.* **(1) A Review Tribunal remains seized of any appeal filed and heard before April 1, 2013 under subsection 82(1) of the *Canada Pension Plan*, as it read immediately before the coming into force of section 229.**

(2) *Time limit* — **A Review Tribunal must make its decision no later than March 31, 2014 or, if an order is made under subsection 253(3), the day before the day fixed by that order.**

(3) *Failure to decide* — **The General Division of the Social Security Tribunal becomes seized of any appeal referred to in subsection (1) if no decision is made by the day referred to in subsection (2). The appeal is deemed to be an appeal filed with the**

General Division of the Social Security Tribunal on April 1, 2014 or, if an order is made under subsection 253(3), the day fixed by that order.

(4) *Appeals — Social Security Tribunal* **A person who is dissatisfied with a decision made under subsection (1) may appeal the decision to the Appeal Division of the Social Security Tribunal.**

256. *Appeals — Pension Appeals Board* — **An appeal from a decision of a Review Tribunal that could have been appealed to the Pension Appeals Board, but for the repeal of subsection 83(1) of the** *Canada Pension Plan* **by section 229, may be brought to the Appeal Division of the Social Security Tribunal.**

257. *Appeals — Social Security Tribunal* — **Any appeal filed before April 1, 2013 under subsection 82(1) of the** *Canada Pension Plan***, as it read immediately before the coming into force of section 229, is deemed to have been filed with the General Division of the Social Security Tribunal on April 1, 2013, if section 255 does not apply to it.**

258. *Appeals — Pension Appeals Board* — **(1) The Pension Appeals Board remains seized of any appeal filed and heard before April 1, 2013 under subsection 83(1) of the** *Canada Pension Plan***, as it read immediately before the coming into force of section 229.**

(2) *Time limit* **The Pension Appeals Board must make its decision no later than March 31, 2014.**

(3) *Failure to decide* **The Appeal Division of the Social Security Tribunal becomes seized of any appeal referred to in subsection (1) if no decision has been made by the day referred to in subsection (2). The Appeal Division of the Social Security Tribunal is deemed to have granted leave to appeal on April 1, 2014.**

259. *Appeals — Social Security Tribunal* — **The Appeal Division of the Social Security Tribunal is deemed to have granted leave to appeal on April 1, 2013 with respect to any application for leave to appeal filed before April 1, 2013 under subsection 83(1) of the** *Canada Pension Plan***, as it read immediately before the coming into force of section 229, if leave to appeal to the Pension Appeals Board has been granted but that Board has not yet heard that appeal.**

260. *Leave to appeal — Social Security Tribunal.* **Any application for leave to appeal filed before April 1, 2013 under subsection 83(1) of the** *Canada Pension Plan***, as it read immediately before the coming into force of section 229, is deemed to be an application for leave to appeal filed with the Appeal Division of the Social Security Tribunal on April 1, 2013, if no decision has been rendered with respect to leave to appeal.**

261. *Request for reconsideration* — **(1) If no decision has been made before April 1, 2013, in respect of a request made under subsection 84(2) of the** *Canada Pension Plan***, as it read immediately before the coming into force of section 229, it is deemed to be an application made on April 1, 2013 under section 66 of the** *Department of Human Resources and Skills Development Act* **and is deemed to relate to a decision made, as the case may be, by**

(a) the General Division of the Social Security Tribunal, in the case of a decision made by a Review Tribunal; or

(b) the Appeal Division of the Social Security Tribunal, in the case of a decision made by the Pension Appeals Board.

(2) *Deeming* An application made under section 66 of the *Department of Human Resources and Skills Development Act* after March 31, 2013 is deemed to relate to a decision made, as the case may be, by

(*a*) the General Division of the Social Security Tribunal, in the case of a decision made by a Review Tribunal; or

(*b*) the Appeal Division of the Social Security Tribunal, in the case of a decision made by the Pension Appeals Board.

262. *Continued application* — The provisions of the *Canada Pension Plan* and the *Old Age Security Act* repealed by this Act, and their related regulations, continue to apply to appeals of which a Review Tribunal or the Pension Appeals Board remains seized under this Act, with any necessary adaptations.

Canada Pension Plan Regulations

C.R.C. 1978, Vol. IV, c. 385, as amended by SOR/78-142, gazetted February 22, 1978 and effective February 10, 1978; SOR/78-591, gazetted August 9, 1978 and effective July 24, 1978; SOR/78-935, gazetted December 27, 1978 and effective January 1, 1979; SOR/79-141, gazetted February 28, 1979 and effective February 6, 1979; SOR/79-286, gazetted April 11, 1979 and effective March 23, 1979; SOR/79-402, gazetted May 23, 1979 and effective May 10, 1979; SOR/79-751, gazetted November 14, 1979 and effective October 22, 1979; SOR/79-957, gazetted December 26, 1979 and effective January 1, 1980; SOR/80-133, gazetted February 27, 1980 and effective January 1, 1980; SOR/80-320, gazetted May 14, 1980 and effective May 1, 1980; SOR/80-757, gazetted October 8, 1980 and effective September 19, 1980; SOR/80-813, gazetted November 12, 1980 and effective October 23, 1980; SOR/80-877, gazetted November 26, 1980 and effective November 13, 1980; SOR/80-930, gazetted December 24, 1980 and effective January 1, 1981; SOR/81-99, gazetted February 11, 1981 and effective January 29, 1981; SOR/81-197, gazetted March 11, 1981 and effective January 1, 1972; SOR/81-448, gazetted June 24, 1981 and effective January 1, 1980; SOR/81-733, gazetted October 14, 1981 and effective September 21, 1981; SOR/81-1029, gazetted December 23, 1981 and effective January 1, 1982; SOR/82-290, gazetted March 24, 1982 and effective March 5, 1982; SOR/82-321, gazetted March 24, 1982 and effective April 1, 1982; SOR/82-597, gazetted June 23, 1982 and effective July 1, 1982; SOR/82-784, gazetted September 8, 1982 and effective August 19, 1982; SOR/82-1096, gazetted December 22, 1982 and effective January 1, 1983; SOR/83-238, gazetted March 23, 1983 and effective April 1, 1983; SOR/83-270, gazetted April 13, 1983 and effective March 25, 1983; SOR/84-50, gazetted January 11, 1984 and effective December 22, 1983; SOR/84-115, gazetted February 8, 1984 and effective January 23, 1984; SOR/84-459, gazetted June 27, 1984 and effective June 14, 1984; SOR/85-39, gazetted January 9, 1985 and effective January 1, 1985; SOR/85-1087, gazetted December 11, 1985 and effective November 21, 1985; SOR/85-1164, gazetted December 25, 1985 and effective December 12, 1985; SOR/86-1133, gazetted December 24, 1986 and effective December 11, 1986; SOR/86-1134, gazetted December 24, 1986 and effective January 1, 1987; SOR/87-714, gazetted December 23, 1987 and effective December 10, 1987; SOR/87-719, gazetted December 23, 1987 and effective December 10, 1987; SOR/87-721, gazetted December 23, 1987 and effective December 10, 1987; SOR/88-239, gazetted April 27, 1988 and effective April 14, 1988; SOR/88-628, gazetted December 21, 1988 and effective December 7, 1988; SOR/88-631, gazetted December 21, 1988 and effective December 7, 1988; SOR/88-638, gazetted December 21, 1988 and effective December 7, 1988; SOR/88-639, gazetted December 21, 1988 and effective December 7, 1988; SOR/89-304, gazetted June 21, 1989 and effective June 8, 1989; SOR/89-345, gazetted July 19, 1989 and effective June 29, 1989; SOR/89-467, gazetted October 11, 1989 and effective September 21, 1989; SOR/89-580, gazetted December 20, 1989 and effective January 1,

1990; SOR/90-47, gazetted January 17, 1990 and effective December 27, 1989; SOR/90-687, gazetted October 10, 1990 and effective September 27, 1990; SOR/90-829, gazetted December 19, 1990 and effective November 29, 1990; SOR/90-832, gazetted December 19, 1990 and effective January 1, 1991; SOR/91-682, gazetted December 4, 1991 and effective November 21, 1991; SOR/92-17, gazetted January 1, 1992 and effective December 31, 1991; SOR/92-36, gazetted January 1, 1992 and effective January 1, 1992; SOR/92-736, gazetted December 30, 1992 and effective January 1, 1993; SOR/93-11, gazetted January 13, 1993 and effective January 1, 1993; SOR/93-94, gazetted March 10, 1993 and effective February 23, 1993; SOR/93-290, gazetted June 16, 1993 and effective June 1, 1993; SOR/93-398, gazetted August 11, 1993 and effective July 21, 1993; SOR/93-533, gazetted December 15, 1993 and effective December 2, 1993; SOR/94-173, gazetted February 23, 1994 and effective February 10, 1994, except sections 1, 2 and 4 which are effective January 1, 1994; SOR/95-156, gazetted April 5, 1995 and effective March 21, 1995; SOR/95-287, gazetted June 28, 1995 and effective June 13, 1995; SOR/96-161, gazetted April 3, 1996 and effective March 19, 1996; SOR/96-262, gazetted May 29, 1996 and effective January 1, 1996; SOR/96-522, gazetted December 5, 1996 and effective January 1, 1997; SOR/97-34, gazetted January 8, 1997 and effective December 19, 1996; SOR/97-384, gazetted August 8, 1997 and effective January 1, 1997; SOR/97-472, gazetted October 29, 1997 and effective October 9, 1997; SOR/98-258, gazetted May 13, 1998 and effective January 1, 1998; SOR/99-23, gazetted January 6, 1999 and effective January 1, 1999; SOR/99-60, gazetted February 3, 1999 and effective January 1, 1999, except section 3, effective January 21, 1999; SOR/99-192, gazetted May 12, 1999 and effective April 22, 1999; SOR/99-389, gazetted October 27, 1999 and effective October 6, 1999; SOR/2000-61, gazetted March 1, 2000 and effective January 1, 2000; SOR/2000-133, gazetted April 12, 2000 and effective March 30, 2000; SOR/2000-411, gazetted December 20, 2000 and effective November 30, 2000; SOR/2001-135, gazetted April 5, 2001 and effective January 1, 2001; SOR/2002-221, gazetted June 19, 2003 and effective June 6, 2003; SOR/2002-245, gazetted July 3, 2002 and effective January 1, 2002; SOR/2004-249, gazetted December 1, 2004 and effective November 16, 2004; SOR/2005-38, filed February 15, 2005 and effective January 31, 2005, the date sections 20-23 of 2004, c. 24 came into force; SOR/2007-55, s. 1, gazetted April 4, 2007 and effective March 22, 2007; SOR/2010-45, gazetted March 3, 2010 and effective February 23, 2010, except section 8, subsection 9(1) and section 10 which are effective April 1, 2010, and section 13 which is effective April 1, 2011; S.C. 2010, c. 12, s. 34(1), effective July 1, 2010; SOR/2010-300, effective January 1, 2011; SOR/2011-299, effective January 1, 2012; SOR/2013-20, effective March 1, 2013; SOR/2013-61, effective April 1, 2013; SOR/2013-83, effective April 30, 2013; SOR/2013-208, effective November 22, 2013; SOR/2013-233, effective December 6, 2013; SOR/2014-135, effective May 29, 2014; S.C. 2014, c. 20, s. 38, effective June 19, 2014.

Regulations Reporting the Administration of the Canada Pension Plan

Short Title

1. These Regulations may be cited as the *Canada Pension Plan Regulations*.

Interpretation

2. (1) In these Regulations,

"Act" means the *Canada Pension Plan*;

"Chairman" **(Repealed by SOR/2013-61, s. 1, in force April 1, 2013.)**

"Commissioner" **(Repealed by SOR/2013-61, s. 1, in force April 1, 2013.)**

"Minister" **means**

   (*a*) in Parts I, II, III and IV, the Minister of National Revenue, and

   (*b*) in Part V, the Minister as defined in subsection 42(1) of the Act; **(SOR/96-522, s. 1)**

"Vice-Chairman" **(Repealed by SOR/2013-61, s. 1, in force April 1, 2013.)**

   (2) For the purposes of the Act and these Regulations,

"agriculture" **means the operations of farming when carried on a farm for the benefit of an individual or other person who is a farmer and, without limiting the generality of the foregoing, includes the operation of**

   (*a*) the clearing of land for the purposes of farming,

   (*b*) the cultivation of the soil,

   (*c*) the conservation of the soil, including the construction, maintenance and operations of the drainage systems, ditches, canals, reservoirs or waterways exclusively for the purposes of farming,

   (*d*) the producing, harvesting, storing or grading of any natural product of farming,

   (*e*) the preparation of land for or the harvesting of wild berries,

   (*f*) the raising of bees and producing of honey,

   (*g*) the breeding or raising of horses, beasts of burden, cattle, sheep, goats, swine, fur bearing animals, birds of any kind or the production of eggs,

   (*h*) dairy farming and the processing of milk, butter or cheese on the farm where it is produced,

   (*i*) producing maple sap, maple syrup or maple sugar,

when carried on a farm for the benefit of an individual or other person who is a farmer, and includes

   (*j*) the offering for sale or selling, off the farm for the benefit of such farmer, of any of the products of the operations previously described in this definition where such offering for sale or selling is incidental to those operations, and

   (*k*) the exhibiting, advertising, assembling, freezing, storing, grading, processing, packing and transporting, off the farm for the benefit of such farmer, of the products described in paragraph (*j*) where the exhibiting, advertising, assembling, freezing, storing, grading, processing, packing or transporting is incidental to the offering for sale or selling described in that paragraph;

"agricultural enterprise" **means the business of agriculture carried on for the benefit of an individual or other person who is a farmer;**

"fishing" **means fishing for or catching any fish, including shell fish, crustaceans or molluscs, or any aquatic animal or plant by any method whatever;**

"forestry" **means the planting, breeding, propagation, producing, protection, measuring or harvesting of trees when carried on in a forest, on a woodlot or on a tree**

CPP REGULATIONS

farm, and includes all services incidental to any of those activities if such services are performed where the activities are carried on;

"horticulture" **means**

(a) the operations relating to the breeding, producing, raising or harvesting of

(i) vegetables, flowers, shrubs or ornamental grasses, and (SOR/2013-208, s. 1(2).)

(ii) seeds, seedlings, grafts and cuttings of vegetables, flowers, shrubs or ornamental grasses, and (SOR/2013-208, s. 1(2).)

(b) the operations relating to landscape gardening where the landscape gardening is incidental to the carrying on of

(i) any of the operations described in paragraph (a), or

(ii) agriculture,

and includes all services incidental to the carrying on of any of the operations described in paragraph (a) or (b) if such services are performed where the operations are carried on;

"hunting" **means** hunting for or catching or killing any wild animal by any method whatever, but does not include any operation involved in carrying on the business of rodent extermination;

"international organization" **means**

(a) any specialized agency of which Canada is a member that is brought into relationship with the United Nations in accordance with Article 63 of the Charter of the United Nations, and

(b) any international organization of which Canada is a member, the primary purpose of which is the maintenance of international peace or the economic or social well-being of a community of nations;

"logging" **means** the converting of trees into timber when carried on in a forest, on a woodlot or on a tree farm;

"lumbering" **means** the milling of timber into lumber or boards when carried on in a forest, on a woodlot or on a tree farm, and includes the preparation of timber for milling in such place;

"trapping" **means** the operations involved in using any trap, snare or other device for taking or destroying any wild animal, but does not include any operation involved in carrying on the business of rodent extermination.

(3) For the purposes of the definitions "logging" and "lumbering" in subsection (2), "timber" means logs of any size, lathwood, pulpwood, fuelwood, tiewood, veneerwood, posts, bolts, piles, pit props, spars, stakes, bark, chips or any crude wood before it has been milled or otherwise manufactured.

(SOR/92-17, s. 1; SOR/96-522, s. 1; SOR/2013-61, s. 1; SOR/2013-208, s. 1.)

Part I

Collection and Payment of Employees' and Employers' Contributions

Interpretation

3. The definitions in this section apply in this Part, (SOR/85-39, s. 1(1), (2); SOR/2002-245, s. 1(1).)

"employee's contribution" **means an amount determined in accordance with sections 5 and 6;**

"employer's contribution" **means an amount determined in accordance with section 7;**

"ordinary remuneration" **means the remuneration paid to an employee on a pay day in respect of employment in the relevant pay period and includes fees paid to a director of a corporation if no other remuneration is payable to the director by the corporation;**

"pay day" **means the day on which remuneration ordinarily is paid to an employee;**

"pay period" **means**
    (*a*) **the usual period for which an employee is paid on a pay day, or**
    (*b*) **where there is no usual period, the period for which the employee is actually paid on a pay day,**
and for the purposes of paragraphs (*a*) and (*b*) includes a period of an hour or a day; (SOR/85-39, s. 1(3).)

"remuneration" **has the same meaning as the expression "contributory salary and wages" as used in section 12 of the Act; (SOR/90-829, s. 1.)**

"year's maximum contribution" **means an amount calculated by multiplying the person's contribution rate for the year by the difference between the amount of the person's maximum pensionable earnings, and the amount of the person's basic exemption.**

(SOR/78-142, s. 1; SOR/78-935, s. 1; SOR/80-133, s. 1; SOR/81-99, s. 1; SOR/82-290, s. 1; SOR/83-270, s. 1; SOR/84-115, s. 1; SOR/85-39, s. 1; SOR/85-1164, s. 1; SOR/86-1134, s. 1; SOR/86-1164, s. 1; SOR/87-721, s. 1; SOR/88-639, s. 1; SOR/89-580, s. 1; SOR/90-829, s. 1; SOR/90-832, s. 1; SOR/92-36, s. 1; SOR/92-736, s. 1; SOR/94-173, s. 1; SOR/95-156, s. 1; SOR/96-262, s. 1; SOR/97-384, s. 1; SOR/98-258, s. 1; SOR/99-60, s. 1; SOR/2000-61, s. 1; SOR/2002-245, s. 1(2).)

(SOR/78-142, s. 1; SOR/78-935, s. 1; SOR/80-133, s. 1; SOR/81-99, s. 1; SOR/82-290, s. 1; SOR/83-270, s. 1; SOR/84-115, s. 1; SOR/85-39, s. 1; SOR/85-1164, s. 1; SOR/86-1134, s. 1; SOR/86-1164, s. 1; SOR/87-721, s. 1; SOR/88-639, s. 1; SOR/89-580, s. 1; SOR/90-829, s. 1; SOR/90-832, s. 1; SOR/92-36, s. 1; SOR/92-736, s. 1; SOR/94-173, s. 1; SOR/95-156, s. 1; SOR/96-262, s. 1; SOR/97-384, s. 1; SOR/98-258, s. 1; SOR/99-60, s. 1; SOR/2000-61, s. 1; SOR/2001-135, s. 1; SOR/2002-245, s. 1.)

Computation of Employee's Contribution

4. For the purposes of subsection 21(1) of the Act, the rules set out in section 5 are hereby prescribed for the purposes of determining an employee's contribution to be deducted by the employee's employer from any payment of remuneration in a year.

(SOR/85-39, s. 2; SOR/90-829, s. 2.)

CPP REGULATIONS

5. (1) For the purposes of this section, a "qualifying payment of remuneration" is that portion of a payment of remuneration that is ordinary remuneration from pensionable employment.

(2) Subject to subsections (6) to (8), the amount of an employee's contribution to be deducted by their employer from any qualifying payment of remuneration in a pay period in a year shall be determined using the following formula and rounding the result to the nearest multiple of $0.01 or, where that result is equidistant from two such multiples, to the higher thereof:

$(A - B) \times C$

where

A is the qualifying payment of remuneration for the pay period;

B is the employee's basic exemption in respect of the pay period; and

C is the contribution rate for employees for the year.

(SOR/86-1134, s. 2(1); SOR/2002-245, s. 2(1).)

(3) Subject to subsections (7) and (8), the amount of an employee's contribution in respect of that portion of a payment of remuneration from pensionable employment that is not a qualifying payment of remuneration is the product of that portion multiplied by the contribution rate for employees for the year, rounded in the manner set out in subsection (2). (SOR/86-1134, s. 2(2); SOR/2002-245, s. 2(1).)

(4) (Subsections 5(2) to (4) of the Regulations have been replaced by SOR/2002-245, s. 2(1).)

(5) For the purposes of subsection (2), the amount of an employee's basic exemption for each pay period in a year is (SOR/2002-245, s. 2(2).)

(a) in the case of an employee who is ordinarily paid
  (i) hourly, $1.75,
  (ii) daily, $14.58,
  (iii) weekly, $67.30,
  (iv) bi-weekly, $134.61,
  (v) quadri-weekly, $269.23,
  (vi) semi-monthly, $145.83,
  (vii) monthly, $291.66,
  (viii) quarterly, $875,
  (ix) semi-annually, $1,750, or
  (x) annually, $3,500;
(b) in the case of an employee who is ordinarily paid only in respect of a period of 10 months in the year and is paid
  (i) in 22 payments, $159.09
  (ii) semi-monthly, $175, or
  (iii) monthly, $350; and
(c) in any other case, the amount that is the greater of
  (i) the product obtained when $3,500 is multiplied by the fraction that the number of days in the period is of 365 days, and

(ii) $67.30.

(SOR/85-1164, s. 2; SOR/86-1134, s. 2; SOR/82-721; s. 2; SOR/88-639, s. 2; SOR/89-580, s. 2; SOR/90-832, s. 2; SOR/92-36, s. 1; SOR/92-736, s. 2; SOR/94-173, s. 2; SOR/96-262, s. 2.)

(6) Where there are 27 bi-weekly or 53 weekly pay periods ending in a year, there shall be added to the employee's contribution otherwise determined under subsection (2) for the pay period an amount equal to the amount determined when (SOR/2002-245, s. 2(3).)

    (a) the employee's basic exemption for the year is divided by 27 or 53, as the case may be, without taking into consideration amounts less than $0.01;

    (b) the amount determined under paragraph (a) is subtracted from the amount of the applicable basic exemption determined under subsection (5); and

    (c) the amount determined under paragraph (b) is multiplied by the contribution rate for employees for the year and the product obtained thereby is rounded to the nearest multiple of $0.01, or where that product is equidistant from two such multiples, to the higher thereof. (SOR/86-1134, s. 2(4).)

(7) Where a payment of remuneration in respect of an employee's pensionable employment for a pay period in a year exceeds the amount of the employee's basic exemption for the pay period, the amount of the employee's contribution in respect of that payment shall be at least $0.01.

(8) The aggregate of an employee's contributions for a year deducted by an employer in respect of pensionable employment with the employer shall not exceed the year's maximum contribution.

(SOR/78-142, s. 2; SOR/78-935, s. 2; SOR/80-133, s. 2; SOR/81-99, s. 2; SOR/82-290, s. 2; SOR/83-270, s. 2; SOR/84-115, s. 2; SOR/85-39, s. 2; SOR/85-1164, s. 2; SOR/86-1134, s. 2; SOR/82-721, s. 2; SOR/88-639, s. 2; SOR/89-580, s. 2; SOR/90-832, s. 2; SOR/92-36, s. 1; SOR/92-736, s. 2; SOR/96-262, s. 2; SOR/2002-245, s. 2.)

Provincial Pension Plan

6. (1) Where an employee has made a contribution for the year under a provincial pension plan in respect of salary and wages paid to him by an employer, the amount of the employee's contribution determined under section 5 in respect of a payment of remuneration to him in that year by that employer shall not exceed the amount remaining after subtracting from the year's maximum contribution the aggregate of that employee's contributions previously required to be deducted in that year by that employer under this Part or under a provincial pension plan.

(2) For the purposes of sections 10 and 13 of the Act, the salary and wages on which a contribution has been made for the year by an individual under a provincial pension plan is an amount equal to the aggregate of all contributions required to be made by the individual in that year under a provincial pension plan in respect of salary and wages, divided by the contribution rate for employees for the year. (SOR/86-1134, s. 3; SOR/90-829, s. 3.)

(SOR/86-1134, s. 3; SOR/90-829, s. 3.)

Employer's Contribution

7. The amount that an employer shall remit as the employer's contribution in respect of a payment of remuneration made by him to an employee employed by him in

pensionable employment is an amount equal to the employee's contribution required to be deducted under this Part in respect of that payment of remuneration.

Payment of Contributions

8. (1) Subject to subsections (1.1), (1.11), (1.12) and (2), the employee's contribution and the employer's contribution shall be remitted to the Receiver General on or before the 15th day of the month following the month in which the employer paid to the employee the remuneration in respect of which those contributions were required to be made. (SOR/97-472, s. 1(1).)

(1.1) Subject to subsection (1.11), where the average monthly withholding amount of an employer for the second calendar year preceding a particular calendar year is

> (a) equal to or greater than $25,000 and less than $100,000, the employer shall remit the employee's contribution and the employer's contribution to the Receiver General (S.C. 2014, c. 20, s. 38(1).)
>
>> (i) in respect of remuneration paid before the 16th day of a month in the particular calendar year, on or before the 25th day of the month, and
>>
>> (ii) in respect of remuneration paid after the 15th day of a month in the particular calendar year, on or before the 10th day of the following month; and
>
> (b) equal to or greater than $100,000, the employer shall remit the employee's contribution and the employer's contribution to the Receiver General on or before the third day, not including a Saturday or holiday, after the end of the following periods in which remuneration was paid, (S.C. 2014, c. 20, s. 38(2).)
>
>> (i) the period beginning on the first day of a month in the particular calendar year and ending on the 7th day of the month,
>>
>> (ii) the period beginning on the 8th day of a month in the particular calendar year and ending on the 14th day of the month,
>>
>> (iii) the period beginning on the 15th day of a month in the particular calendar year and ending on the 21st day of the month, and
>>
>> (iv) the period beginning on the 22nd day of a month in the particular calendar year and ending on the last day of the month.

(1.11) Where an employer referred to in paragraph (1.1)(a) or (b) would otherwise be required to remit the employee's contribution and employer's contribution in respect of a particular calendar year in accordance with that paragraph, the employer may elect to remit those contributions

> (a) in accordance with subsection (1), if the average monthly withholding amount of the employer for the calendar year preceding the particular calendar year is less than $25,000 and the employer has advised the Minister that the employer has so elected; or (S.C. 2014, c. 20, s. 38(3).)
>
> (b) if the average monthly withholding amount of the employer for the calendar year preceding the particular calendar year is equal to or greater than $25,000 and less than $100,000 and the employer has advised the Minister that the employer has so elected, (S.C. 2014, c. 20, s. 38(4).)
>
>> (i) in respect of remuneration paid before the 16th day of a month in the particular calendar year, on or before the 25th day of the month, and
>>
>> (ii) in respect of remuneration paid after the 15th day of a month in the particular calendar year, on or before the 10th day of the following month.

(1.12) If at any time

(*a*) the average monthly withholding amount in respect of an employer for either the first or the second calendar year before the particular calendar year that includes that time is less than $1,000,

(*b*) throughout the 12-month period before that time, the employer has remitted, on or before the day on or before which the amounts were required to be remitted, all amounts each of which was required to be

(i) deducted or withheld under subsection 153(1) of the *Income Tax Act,* or

(ii) remitted in Part IX of the *Excise Tax Act,* and

(*c*) throughout the 12-month period before that time, the employer has filed all returns each of which was required to be filed under the *Income Tax Act* or Part IX of the *Excise Tax Act* on or before the day on or before which those returns were required to be filed under those Acts,

contributions payable in a month that ends after that time and that is in the particular calendar year may be remitted by the employer to the Receiver General

(*d*) in respect of such contributions paid in January, February and March of the particular calendar year, on or before the 15th day of April of the particular year,

(*e*) in respect of such contributions paid in April, May and June of the particular calendar year, on or before the 15th day of July of the particular year,

(*f*) in respect of such contributions paid in July, August and September of the particular calendar year, on or before the 15th day of October of the particular year, and

(*g*) in respect of such contributions paid in October, November and December of the particular calendar year, on or before the 15th day of January of the year following the particular year. (SOR/97-472, s. 1(2).)

(SOR/87-714, s. 1; SOR/90-47, s. 1; SOR/93-94, s. 1; SOR/97-472, s. 1.)

(1.2) For the purpose of this section, the average monthly withholding amount of an employer for a calendar year is determined pursuant to subsections 108(1.2) and (1.3) of the Income Tax Regulations. (SOR/87-714, s. 1.)

(2) An employer carrying on a business or activity with respect to which he employs employees in pensionable employment shall, if he ceases to carry on that business or activity, with 7 days of so ceasing remit to the Receiver General any employee's contribution and any employer's contribution that he is required to remit with respect to those employees.

(3) Every payment by an employer of an employee's contribution or an employer's contribution shall be accompanied by a return in prescribed form.

(SOR/87-714, s. 1; SOR/90-47, s. 1; SOR/93-94, s. 1; SOR/97-472, s. 1; S.C. 2014, c. 20, s. 38--subsections 38(1) to (4) apply to amounts deducted or withheld after 2014.)

8.1. (1) Every person by whom the remuneration of an employee for services performed in pensionable employment is paid either wholly or in part is, for the purpose of calculating the employee's contributory salary and wages, maintaining records and filing returns, and paying, deducting and remitting the contributions payable thereon under the Act and these Regulations, deemed to be an employer of that employee in addition to the actual employer of that employee.

(1.1) The amount of any contributions paid by the person who is deemed to be the employer under subsection (1) is recoverable by that person from the actual employer. (SOR/98-258, s. 2(2).)

(2) Where a person who is deemed by subsection (1) to be an employer fails to pay, deduct or remit the contributions that an employer is required to pay, deduct and remit under the Act and these Regulations, the provisions of Part I of the Act shall apply to that person as if he were the actual employer. (SOR/79-402.)

(SOR/79-402; SOR/98-258, s. 2(2).)

Prescribed Persons

8.2. (1) The following are prescribed persons for the purposes of subsection 21(1) of the Act:

(a) an employer who is required, under subsection 21(1) of the Act and in accordance with paragraph 8(1.1)(b), to remit amounts deducted; and

(b) a person or partnership who, acting on behalf of one or more employers, remits the following amounts in a particular calendar year and whose average monthly remittance, in respect of those amounts, for the second calendar year preceding the particular calendar year, is equal to or greater than $50,000,

(i) amounts required to be remitted under subsection 21(1) of the Act,

(ii) amounts required to be remitted under subsection 153(1) of the *Income Tax Act* and a similar provision of a law of a province that imposes a tax on the income of individuals, where the province has entered into an agreement with the Minister of Finance for the collection of taxes payable to the province, in respect of payments described in the definition "remuneration" in subsection 100(1) of the Income Tax Regulations, and

(iii) amounts required to be remitted under subsection 53(1) of the *Unemployment Insurance Act*.

(2) For the purposes of paragraph 1(b), the average monthly remittance made by a person or partnership on behalf of all the employers for whom that person or partnership is acting, for the second calendar year preceding the particular calendar year, is the quotient obtained when the aggregate, for that preceding year, of all amounts referred to in subparagraphs (1)(b)(i) to (iii) remitted by the person or partnership on behalf of those employers is divided by the number of months, in that preceding year, for which the person or partnership remitted those amounts. (SOR/93-533, s. 1.)

Security Interests

8.3. (1) For the purpose of subsection 23(4.1) of the Act, "prescribed security interest", in relation to an amount deemed by subsection 23(3) of the Act to be held in trust by a person means that part of a mortgage securing the performance of an obligation of the person, that encumbers land or a building, where the mortgage is registered pursuant to the appropriate land registration system before the time the amount is deemed to be held in trust by the person.

(2) For the purpose of subsection (1), where, at any time after 1999, the person referred to in subsection (1) fails to pay an amount deemed by subsection 23(3) of the Act to be held in trust by the person, as required under the Act, the amount of the prescribed security interest referred to in subsection (1) is deemed not to exceed the amount by which the amount, at that time, of the obligation outstanding secured by the mortgage exceeds the total of (*a*) all amounts each of which is the value determined at the time of the failure, having regard to all the circumstances including the existence of any deemed trust for the benefit of Her Majesty pursuant to subsection 23(3) of the Act, of all the rights of the secured creditor securing the obligation, whether granted by the person or not, including guarantees or rights of set-off but not including the mortgage referred to in subsection (1), and

(*b*) all amounts applied after the time of the failure on account of the obligation,

so long as any amount deemed under any enactment administered by the Minister, other than the *Excise Tax Act*, to be held in trust by the person, remains unpaid.

(3) For greater certainty, a prescribed security interest includes the amount of insurance or expropriation proceeds relating to land or a building that is the subject of a registered mortgage interest, adjusted after 1999 in accordance with subsection (2), but does not include a lien, a priority or any other security interest created by statute, an assignment or hypothec of rents or of leases, or a mortgage interest in any equipment or fixtures that a mortgagee or any other person has the right absolutely or conditionally to remove or dispose of separately from the land or building. (SOR/99-389, s 1.)

(SOR/93-533; SOR/99-389.)

Part II

Information Returns

Interpretation

9. In this Part, all words and expressions have the same meaning as in Part I.

Filing of Employer's Returns

10. (1) Subject to subsection (2), every person who has made a payment of remuneration during a year to an employee employed by him in pensionable employment shall, without notice or demand therefor, file with the Minister an information return for that year in prescribed form on or before the last day of February of the year next following.

(2) A person carrying on a business or activity with respect to which he employs employees in pensionable employment shall, if he ceases to carry on that business or activity, within 30 days of so ceasing and without notice or demand therefor, file with the Minister, with respect to those employees, the information return required by subsection (1).

11. Every person who makes or has made a payment of remuneration at any time to an employee employed in pensionable employment shall on demand by registered letter from the Minister make an information return in prescribed form containing the information required therein and shall file the return with the Minister within such reasonable time as may be stipulated in the registered letter.

Legal Representatives and Others

12. (1) When a person who is required to make a return under this Part for a year dies before having made the return, the return shall be filed by his legal representatives within 90 days of his death and shall be in respect of that year or, if the return is required in respect of the year in which he dies, in respect of that part thereof prior to his death.

(2) Every trustee in bankruptcy, assignee, liquidator, curator, receiver, trustee or committee and every agent or other person administering, managing, winding-up, controlling or otherwise dealing with the property, business or estate of a person who has not filed a return for a year as required by this Part shall file such return on that person's behalf.

Distribution of Employee's Portion of Return

13. (1) Every person required by section 10 or 12 to file an information return for a year with the Minister shall supply, to each employee in respect of whose remuneration the return relates, two copies of the portion of the return relating to that employee.

(2) The copies referred to in subsection (1) shall, on or before the day the information return is required to be filed with the Minister, be sent to the employee by mail at his last known address or be delivered to him in person.

Penalties

14. (1) Every person who fails to file a return as and when required by this Part is liable to a penalty of $10 for each day of default, but not exceeding in all $250.

(2) Every person who fails to comply with section 13 is liable to a penalty of $10 for each day of default, but not exceeding in all $250.

Part III

Employment Included in or Excepted from Pensionable Employment by Regulation

Interpretation

15. (1) In this Part,

"employer operating in Canada" **includes**

(a) Her Majesty in right of Canada,

(b) Her Majesty in right of a province, if employment by Her Majesty in right of that province has been included in pensionable employment by regulation in accordance with paragraph 7(1)(e) of the Act,

(c) an agent of Her Majesty in right of a province, if employment by that agent has been included in pensionable employment by regulation in accordance with paragraph 7(1)(e) of the Act, and

(d) any employer who has an establishment in Canada and who

(i) is subject to income tax under Part I of the *Income Tax Act*, or

(ii) but for section 149 of the *Income Tax Act*, would be subject to income tax under Part I of that Act,

for any taxation year for which he has taxable income;

"employment in international transportation" **means employment that is primarily engaged in by a person in a pay period and that is performed partly within and partly outside Canada on**

(a) a ship,

(b) an aircraft used in the operation of a commercial air service by a person who is licensed to operate an international service under the *Canada Transportation Act*,

(c) a freight or passenger train, or

(d) a motor vehicle that is registered to operate in one or more provinces of Canada and in one or more states of the United States;

(SOR/2013-208, s. 2.)

"establishment in Canada", with respect to an employer, means any office, warehouse, factory, oil well, gas well, mine, workshop, farm, timber, land, pier, wharf, school, college, club, residence, hotel, motel, restaurant, tavern, bar or any other place or premises in Canada that is owned, leased or licensed by the employer and where the employer or one or more of his employees works or reports for work or from or at which one or more of his employees are paid;

"ship" means a vessel, boat or craft, used or designed to be used in navigation in, on, through or immediately above water. (SOR/2013-208, s. 2.)

(2) All other words and expressions in this Part have the same meaning as in Part I.

(SOR/2013-208, s. 2.)

Employment Outside Canada

16. (1) Pensionable employment includes employment outside Canada (except employment in international transportation) that would be pensionable employment if it were in Canada, if the employee employed therein

(a) ordinarily reports for work at an establishment in Canada of his employer;

(b) is resident in Canada and is paid at or from an establishment in Canada of his employer;

(c) is an employee, other than an employee engaged locally outside Canada,

(i) of Her Majesty in right of Canada, or

(ii) of Her Majesty in right of that province (if employment by Her Majesty in right of that province has been included in pensionable employment by regulation in accordance with paragraph 7(1)(e) of the Act),

who was resident in Canada immediately prior to becoming so employed outside Canada or who is in receipt of a representation allowance;

(d) performs services in a country other than Canada under an international development assistance program of the Government of Canada prescribed as such pursuant to paragraph 250(1)(d) of the *Income Tax Act* and was resident in Canada at any time in the three-month period preceding the day on which such services commenced;

(e) is the spouse or common-law partner of a person described in paragraph (c) or (d) or of a person described in paragraph 250(1)(b) of the *Income Tax Act* and SOR/2000-411, s. 1.)

(i) is living with that person,

(ii) is an employee of Her Majesty in right of Canada or of Her Majesty in right of a province (the government of which has entered into an agreement referred to in paragraph 7(1)(e) of the Act), and

(iii) was resident in Canada at any time before becoming so employed outside Canada;

(f) is an employee of Her Majesty in right of Canada who is engaged locally outside Canada and if the President of the Treasury Board signifies to the

365

Minister that he wishes the employment of such employee to be included in pensionable employment; or

(g) is an employee of Her Majesty in right of a province (the government of which has entered into an agreement referred to in paragraph 7(1)(e) of the Act), who is engaged locally outside Canada and if the government of the province signifies to the Minister that it wishes the employment of such employee to be included in pensionable employment.

(2) Pensionable employment includes employment in a country other than Canada (except employment described in subsection (1) or employment in international transportation) by an employer operating in Canada if

(a) the employment in that country would be pensionable employment if it were in Canada, and

(b) the employee

(i) was engaged by the employer at the time when the employee was in and was resident in Canada, or

(ii) was engaged by the employer not more than three months after the employee ceased to be employed outside Canada as a member of the Canadian Forces or in the circumstances described in paragraph 1(c), (d) or (e),

and the employer has undertaken in prescribed form to make payment of the employee's contributions and the employer's contributions in accordance with section 8 in respect of all such employees employed by him in such employment in that country.

(3) In this section, the expression "an employee engaged locally outside Canada" means an employee who is engaged outside Canada for the performance of services outside Canada.

(SOR/2000-411, s. 1.)

Employment in International Transportation

17. (1) Notwithstanding sections 18, 19, 20 and 21, employment in international transportation described in those sections is not pensionable employment unless it is employment that would be pensionable employment if it were wholly within Canada.

(2) Employment in international transportation, except employment therein that is included in pensionable employment by section 18, 19, 20, 21 or 22, is excepted from pensionable employment.

Ships

18. (1) In the case of an employer who is operating in Canada and who employs persons in international transportation on a ship that is operated under an agreement with the crew that is entered into in Canada, pensionable employment includes (SOR/2013-208, s. 3(1).)

(a) when that ship is engaged on a voyage other than an inland voyage, the employment on the ship of any person who has a place of domicile in Canada; and (SOR/2013-208, s. 3(2).)

(b) when that ship is engaged on an inland voyage, all persons employed on the ship. (SOR/2013-208, s. 3(2).)

(2) Where an employer operating in Canada employs persons in international transportation on a ship that is not operating under an agreement with the crew,

pensionable employment includes all employment on the ship if it is being operated mainly in and near Canada.

(3) For the purposes of this section, a person has a place of domicile in Canada if

(a) the person is a Canadian citizen; or (SOR/2013-208, s. 3(3).)

(b) the person is a permanent resident within the meaning of the *Immigration and Refugee Protection Act* and has a place in Canada to which they return from time to time as their place of permanent abode. (SOR/2013-208, s. 3(4).)

(4) The following definitions apply in this section:

"agreement with the crew" **means** articles of agreement entered into under the *Canada Shipping Act, 2001.*

"inland voyage" **means a voyage on**

(a) any river, lake or other navigable fresh waters within Canada, including the St. Lawrence River as far seaward as a straight line drawn from Cap-des-Rosiers to West Point, Anticosti Island and from Anticosti Island to the north shore of the St. Lawrence River along a meridian of longitude 63° degrees W.;

(b) any part of any lake or river forming part of the inland waters of Canada that lies within the United States;

(c) Lake Michigan; or

(d) any sheltered waters on the coasts of Canada that are described in Schedule 1 to the *Vessel Certificates Regulations.*

(SOR/2013-208, s. 3(5).)

(2001, c. 27, s. 273; SOR/2013-208, s. 3.)

Aircraft

19. Pensionable employment includes employment in international transportation on an aircraft used in the operation of a commercial air service by a person who is licensed to operate an international service and a domestic service under the *Canada Transportation Act.*

(SOR/2013-208, s. 4.)

Freight and Passenger Trains

20. (1) Pensionable employment includes, in the case of employment in international transportation on a freight or passenger train operated by a railway company whose principal place of business is in Canada, that part of the employment of a person that is determined by the employer (on a basis approved by the Minister) to be in respect of employment in Canada.

(2) Pensionable employment includes, in the case of employment in international transportation on a freight or passenger train operated by a railway company whose principal place of business is outside Canada, that part of the employment of a person that is determined by the employer (on a basis approved by the Minister) to be in respect of employment in Canada.

(3) In this section, "railway company" has the same meaning as in the *Canada Transportation Act.* (SOR/2013-208, s. 5.)

(SOR/2013-208, s. 5.)

CPP REGULATIONS

367

Motor Vehicles

21. Pensionable employment includes employment in international transportation on a motor vehicle that is registered to operate in one or more provinces of Canada and in one or more states of the United States, if (SOR/2013-208, s. 6.)

(a) the person so employed is resident in Canada; and

(b) the motor vehicle is operated for the purposes of an enterprise that is regarded, for the purpose of taxation under the *Income Tax Act*, as an enterprise of Canada.

(SOR/2013-208, s. 6.)

Employment in Canada by an Employer Resident Outside Canada

22. (1) The entire employment of a person by an employer who

(a) is not resident in Canada, and

(b) does not have an establishment in Canada,

is excepted from pensionable employment.

(2) Notwithstanding subsection (1) but subject to subsection (3), pensionable employment includes

(a) the employment in Canada of a person

(i) who is resident in Canada, and

(ii) who is employed by an employer who

(A) is not resident in Canada, and

(B) does not have an establishment in Canada, and

(b) in the case of a person

(i) who is resident in Canada, and

(ii) who is employed in international transportation on a motor vehicle that is registered to operate in one or more provinces of Canada and in one or more states of the United States and is operated for the purposes of an enterprise that is regarded, for the purpose of taxation under the *Income Tax Act*, as an enterprise of the United States, (SOR/2013-208, s. 7.)

that part of the employment of such person that is in Canada,

if the employer has made arrangements satisfactory to the Minister to make payments of the employee's contributions and the employer's contributions in respect of that employment in accordance with section 8 and to file information returns in respect of the employment as required by Part II.

(3) Where the employment described in paragraph (2)(a) or (b) is in a province providing a comprehensive pension plan, that employment is not included in pensionable employment unless the employer has made arrangements (in place of the arrangements satisfactory to the Minister described in subsection (2)) satisfactory to the authority having the administration of the provincial pension plan for the payment under that plan of contributions in respect of the employment.

(4) Paragraph 15(1)(b) of the Act does not apply in respect of the employment of a person in employment that is included in pensionable employment by subsection (2). (SOR/90-829, s. 4.)

(5) Where the employer of an employee referred to in subsection (2) does not have an establishment in Canada within the meaning of subsection 4(4) of the Act, the

employee shall be deemed to report for work at an establishment of the employer situated in the province

(a) where the employee ordinarily works or ordinarily does the most work in Canada; or

(b) in any case where a determination cannot be made under paragraph (a), where the employee resides in Canada.

(SOR/90-829, s. 4; SOR/2013-208, s. 7.)

Directors Resident Outside Canada

23. Notwithstanding any other provision of this Part, the employment of a person

(a) who is not ordinarily resident in Canada, and

(b) who is an employee within the meaning of the definition "employee" in subsection 2(1) of the Act by virtue only of his position as a corporation director,

is excepted from pensionable employment if his employment as such director is performed wholly or partly outside of Canada.

Employment by a Province or an Agent of a Province

24. (1) Employment by Her Majesty in right of a province set out in Schedule III and employment by an agent of Her Majesty in right of that province, except employment by an agent thereof who is specified in Schedule IV and any employment by Her Majesty in right of the province that is set out in that Schedule, is included in pensionable employment.

(2) Employment by Her Majesty in right of a province providing a comprehensive pension plan and employment by an agent of Her Majesty in right of that province is included in pensionable employment if such employment is pensionable employment under the provincial pension plan of that province.

(3) Where employment by Her Majesty in right of a province providing a comprehensive pension plan or by an agent of Her Majesty in right of that province is included in pensionable employment by virtue of subsection (2), the provisions of the Act with respect to the making of contributions by employees and employers in respect of pensionable employment and the provisions of Part III of the Act with respect to employees in pensionable employment do not apply in relation to any employment by Her Majesty in right of that province or by an agent of Her Majesty in right of that province, whether such employment is within or without the province.

Employment by an International Organization

25. Employment in Canada by an international organization set out in Schedule V, except employment by that international organization that is set out in Schedule VI, is included in pensionable employment.

Employment by a Country other than Canada

26. Employment in Canada by the government of a country other than Canada set out in Schedule VII, except employment by such government that is set out in Schedule VIII, is included in pensionable employment.

Employment of a Member of a Religious Order who has taken a Vow of Perpetual Poverty

27. Employment referred to in paragraph 6(2)(*e*) of the Act is included in pensionable employment if such employment

(*a*) is in a province providing a comprehensive pension plan; and

(*b*) is pensionable under the provincial pension plan of that province.

Employment to an Inconsiderable Extent

28. (1) Subject to subsections (3) to (5), employment in which persons are ordinarily employed to an inconsiderable extent is excepted from pensionable employment. (SOR/99-23, s. 1(1).)

(2) For the purposes of subsection (1), "employment in which persons are ordinarily employed to an inconsiderable extent" means

(*a*) employment in

(i) abating a disaster, or

(ii) a rescue operation,

if the person so employed is not in the regular employment of the employer who so employs him;

(*b*) employment, other than as an entertainer, at a circus, fair, parade, carnival, exposition, exhibition or other like activity, if the person so employed

(i) is not in the regular employment of the employer who so employs him, and

(ii) is so employed by the employer for less than 7 days in the year; or (SOR/99-23, s. 1(2).)

(*c*) [Repealed by SOR/99-23, s. 1(2).]

(*d*) employment of a person by the Government of Canada, the government of a province, a municipality or a school board in connection with a referendum or election to public office, if the person

(i) is not regularly employed by that employer, and

(ii) is employed by that employer in that employment for less than 35 hours in a year. (SOR/99-23, s. 1(3).)

(3) Where an employment that has been excluded from pensionable employment under paragraph 2(*b*) or (*d*) becomes a regular employment, the employment is pensionable employment beginning on the day or at the hour, as the case may be, that the employment became a regular employment. (SOR/99-23, s. 1(4).)

(4) Where a person has been employed by the same employer in one or more employments that have been excluded from pensionable employment under paragraph (2)(*b*) and the total period of those employments exceeds six days in the same year, the employments, taken together, constitute pensionable employment beginning on the first day of the total period. (SOR/99-23, s. 1(4).)

(5) Where a person has been employed by the same employer in one or more employments that have been excluded from pensionable employment under paragraph (2)(*d*) and the total period of those employments exceeds 34 hours in the same year, the employments, taken together, constitute pensionable employment beginning at the first hour of the total period. (SOR/99-23, s. 1(4).)

(SOR/99-23, s. 1.)

Pensionable Employment

29. Pensionable employment includes employment in Canada that is excepted from pensionable employment by virtue of

(*a*) section 28, or

(*b*) paragraph 6(2)(*a*), 6(2)(*b*) or 6(2)(*j*) of the Act

of an employee in a year who

(*c*) is resident in Canada in the year for the purposes of the *Income Tax Act*;

(*d*) is not, in respect of that employment, in pensionable employment by virtue of any other provision of the Act or these Regulations;

(*e*) elects in accordance with subsection 13(3), of the Act for the purposes of section 10 thereof; and (SOR/90-829, s. 5.)

(*f*) pays the contribution referred to in section 10 of the Act within one year from April 30 of the following year or within one year from the day on which an amount is refunded to the employee under section 38 of the Act. (SOR/2011-299, s. 1.)

(SOR/90-829, s. 5; SOR/2011-299, s. 1.)

29.1. (1) Subject to subsection (2), pensionable employment includes the employment of an Indian, as defined in the *Indian Act*, in Canada in a year, to the extent the employment is excepted from pensionable employment solely pursuant to paragraph 6(2)(*j*.1) of the Act if

(*a*) the Indian is resident in Canada for the purposes of the *Income Tax Act*; and

(*b*) the employer of the Indian elects, by completing the form authorized by the Minister for such purpose, that, from the date of filing the form with the Minister or such later date as the employer specifies in the form, the employment of each Indian employee of the employer whose employment is not excepted from pensionable employment by other than paragraph 6(2)(*j*.1) of the Act is pensionable employment.

(2) Where an employer does not make the election referred to in paragraph (1)(*b*), the employment of an Indian, as defined in the *Indian Act*, in a year in Canada, to the extent the employment is excepted from pensionable employment solely pursuant to paragraph 6(2)(*j*.1) of the Act, may be included in pensionable employment if

(*a*) the Indian is resident in Canada for the purposes of the *Income Tax Act*;

(*b*) the employment is not pensionable employment by virtue of any other provision of the Act or these Regulations;

(*c*) the Indian makes an election in accordance with subsection 13(3) of the Act; and (SOR/90-829, s. 6.)

(*d*) the Indian pays the contribution referred to in section 10 of the Act within one year after April 30 of the following year or within one year after the day on which an amount is refunded to the employee under section 38 of the Act. (SOR/2011-299, c. 2.)

(SOR/88-631, s. 1; SOR/90-829, s. 6; SOR/2011-299, c. 2.)

30. Pensionable employment includes employment in Canada, that is excepted from pensionable employment by virtue of subsection 22(1), of an employee in a year by an employer who

(*a*) is not resident in Canada, and

(*b*) does not have an establishment in Canada,

if the employee complies with the requirements of paragraphs 29(*c*) to (*f*) in respect of the year.

31. Pensionable employment includes employment in international transportation, that is excepted from pensionable employment by virtue of subsection 17(2), of an employee in a year if the employee complies with the requirements of paragraphs 29(*c*) to (*f*) in respect of the year and is not required in respect of that employment to contribute to a similar plan under the laws of a country other than Canada.

32. Pensionable employment includes employment outside Canada in a year that would be pensionable employment if it were in Canada in the year, of an employee if the employee complies with the requirements of paragraphs 29(*c*) to (*f*) in respect of the year and is not required in respect of that employment to contribute to a similar plan under the laws of the country in which he is employed.

33. For greater certainty, where the employment of an employee is, by virtue of the employee's compliance with the requirements of paragraphs 29(*c*) to (*f*) included in a pensionable employment under way of sections 29 to 32, the employer of that employee is not required to pay an employer's contribution in respect of the employment.

34. (1) Where any individual is placed by a placement or employment agency in employment with or for performance of services for a client of the agency and the terms or conditions on which the employment or services are performed and the remuneration thereof is paid constitute a contract of service or are analogous to a contract of service, the employment or performance of services is included in pensionable employment and the agency or the client, whichever pays the remuneration to the individual, shall, for the purposes of maintaining records and filing returns and paying, deducting and remitting contributions payable by and in respect of the individual under the Act and these Regulations, be deemed to be the employer of the individual.

(2) For the purposes of subsection (1), "placement or employment agency" includes any person or organization that is engaged in the business of placing individuals in employment or for performance of services or of securing employment for individuals for a fee, reward or other remuneration.

(SOR/78-142, s. 3.)

34.1. (1) Notwithstanding any other provision of this Part

(*a*) subject to subsection 6(2) of the Act, where by virtue of any of the circumstances described in an agreement entered into under subsection 107(1) of the Act the legislation of Canada applies to a person in any year, the employment of that person in those circumstances is included in pensionable employment for that year, if (SOR/96-522, s. 2(1).)

(i) his employer is an employer operating in Canada within the meaning given to that term by subsection 15(1),

(ii) his employer has, in respect of that employment, given an undertaking in prescribed form to pay the employee's contributions and the employer's contributions under section 8 and 9 respectively, of the Act for the year and to file information returns in accordance with Part II, or

(iii) in any case where his employer is not an employer operating in Canada and has not given the undertaking described in subparagraph (ii) or has not complied with the undertaking in the year, that person complies with the requirements of paragraphs 29(*c*) to (*f*) in respect of that year; and

(*b*) where by virtue of any of the circumstances described in an agreement entered into under subsection 107(1) of the Act the legislation of the other country that is party to the agreement applies to a person in any year, the employment of that person in those circumstances is excepted from pensionable employment for that year. (SOR/96-522, s. 2(2).)

(2) Paragraph 15(1)(*b*) of the Act does not apply in respect of the employment of a person in employment that is included in pensionable employment by virtue of subparagraph (1)(*a*)(ii). (SOR/90-829, s. 7.)

(3) For the purposes of this section, "legislation" has the meaning assigned to that term by the applicable agreement.

(SOR/80-877, s. 1; SOR/90-829, s. 7; SOR/96-522, s. 2.)

Part IV

Prescribed Interest Rates and Refunds of Overpayment

35. (1) Where

(*a*) an amount in respect of an overpayment of contributions is refunded to an employee or self-employed person or applied to a liability of the employee or self-employed person to Her Majesty in right of Canada, interest to be paid or applied under subsection 38(7) of the Act shall be calculated at the rate prescribed in paragraph 36(2)(*b*) and for the period that begins on the latest of

(i) May 1 of the year following the year for which the contributions were paid,

(ii) the day on which the application for the refund was received, and

(iii) the day when the overpayment arose,

and ends on the day on which the amount is so refunded or applied; and

(*b*) an amount in respect of an overpayment is refunded to an employer or applied to a liability of the employer to Her Majesty in right of Canada, interest to be paid or applied under subsection 38(7) of the Act shall be calculated at the rate prescribed in paragraph 36(2)(*b*) and for the period that begins on the later of

(i) the day on which the remittance that created the overpayment was received, and

(ii) the day on which the remittance that created the overpayment was due to be received,

and ends on the day on which the amount is so refunded or applied.

(SOR/79-141, s. 1; SOR/95-287, s. 1.)

36. (1) For the purposes of subsection (2), "quarter" means any of the following periods in a year:

(*a*) the period that begins on January 1 and ends on March 31;

(*b*) the period that begins on April 1 and ends on June 30;

(*c*) the period that begins on July 1 and ends on September 30; and

(*d*) the period that begins on October 1 and ends on December 31.

(2) For the purposes of

(a) every provision of the Act that requires interest at a prescribed rate to be paid to the Receiver General, the prescribed rate in effect during any particular quarter is the total of

    (i) the rate that is the simple arithmetic mean, expressed as a percentage per annum and rounded to the next higher whole percentage where the mean is not a whole percentage, of all amounts each of which is the weekly average equivalent yield, expressed as a percentage per annum, of Government of Canada Treasury Bills that mature approximately three months after their date of issue and that are sold at a weekly auction of Government of Canada Treasury Bills during the first month of the quarter preceding the particular quarter, and

    (ii) 4 per cent; and

(b) every provision of the Act that requires interest at a prescribed rate to be paid or applied on an amount payable by the Minister, the prescribed rate in effect during any particular quarter is the total of

    (i) the rate determined under subparagraph (a)(i) in respect of the particular quarter, and

    (ii) if the amount is payable to a corporation, zero per cent, and in any other case, 2 per cent. (S.C. 2010, c. 12, s. 34(1).)

(SOR/95-287, s. 1; SOR/97-557, s. 1; 2010, c. 12, s. 34.)

Part V

Pensions and Supplementary Benefits

Interpretation

37. (1) In this Part,

"Director" [Repealed by SOR/96-522, s. 3.]

"Child Tax Benefit" means the deemed overpayment determined in accordance with section 122.61 of the *Income Tax Act* in respect of a qualified dependant under seven years of age; (SOR/93-11, s. 1.)

"personal representative" means the executor, administrator, heir or other person having the ownership or control of property comprised in the estate of a deceased person or, where there is no estate, the survivor of the deceased person or, where there is no such survivor, the next of kin of the deceased person. (SOR/2000-411, s. 2.)

(2) For the purposes of subsection 60(2) of the Act, a person entitled to make an application includes a person or agency authorized to receive a benefit under section 57 of these Regulations. (SOR/90-829, s. 10.)

(3) For the purposes of subsection 60(4) of the Act, a person entitled to receive benefits includes a person or agency authorized to receive a benefit under section 57 of these Regulations. (SOR/90-829, s. 10.)

(4) For the purpose of the definition "public officer" in subsection 104(1) of the Act, a prescribed individual is a person employed in a federal institution or whose services are required by a federal institution, on a casual or temporary basis or under a student employment program. (SOR/99-192, s. 1.)

(SOR/86-1133, s. 1; SOR/89-345, s. 1; SOR/90-829, s. 10; SOR/92-17, s. 2; SOR/93-11, s. 1; SOR/96-522, s. 3; SOR/99-192, s. 1; SOR/2000-411, s. 2.)

38. [Repealed by SOR/96-522, s. 4.]

Application for Statement of Earnings

39. (1) An application under subsection 96(1) of the Act by a contributor to require the Minister to inform the contributor of the unadjusted pensionable earnings shown to the contributor's account in the Record of Earnings shall be made to the Minister in writing. The application may also be made to the Minister by way of the Internet on the electronic form prescribed for that purpose and made available on the Internet. (SOR/2004-249, s. 1.)

(2) An application made in writing shall include the contributor's name, address (including the postal code) and Social Insurance Number. (SOR/2004-249, s. 1; SOR/2010-45, s. 1.)

(3) An application made by way of the Internet shall include the contributor's name, Social Insurance Number and postal code. (SOR/2004-249, s. 1.)

(SOR/90-829, s. 12; SOR/96-522, s. 23; SOR/2004-249, s. 1.)

40. Where, pursuant to subsection 97(4) of the Act, a contributor is required to be notified of a reduction in the amount of the unadjusted pensionable earnings shown to the account of the contributor in the Record of Earnings, the contributor shall be notified of the reduction in writing addressed to the contributor at his latest known address.

(SOR/86-1133, s. 2; SOR/90-929, s. 12.)

Salary and Wages on which a Contribution has been made under a Provincial Pension Plan

41. For the purposes of clause 53(1)(b)(ii)(A) of the Act, the salary and wages on which a contribution has been made for the year by a contributor under a provincial pension plan is an amount equal to the aggregate of all contributions required to be made by the contributor in that year under the provincial pension plan in respect of salary and wages, multiplied by 100 and divided, (SOR/2013-83, s. 1.)

(a) in respect of the year 1992, by 2.4;

(b) in respect of the year 1993, by 2.5;

(c) in respect of the year 1994, by 2.6;

(d) in respect of the year 1995, by 2.7; and

(e) in respect of the year 1996, by 2.8.

(SOR/86-1133, s. 2; SOR/96-522, s. 5; SOR/2013-83, s. 1.)

Recovery by Deductions of Amounts to which Recipient not Entitled

42. For the purpose of subsection 66(2.1) of the Act, an amount of indebtedness that is owing may be deducted and retained out of the whole or any portion of a benefit that is payable to the person or the person's estate or succession, under this Act or any other Act or program administered by the Minister, that will recover the overpayment

CPP REGULATIONS

in a single payment or in instalments, in any amount that does not cause undue hardship to the person or the person's estate or succession.

(SOR/96-522, s. 6; SOR/99-192, s. 2.)

Application for Benefits, for Assignment of a Retirement Pension and for Division of Unadjusted Pensionable Earnings

43. (1) An application for a benefit, for a division of unadjusted pensionable earnings under section 55 or 55.1 of the Act or for an assignment of a portion of a retirement pension under section 65.1 of the Act shall be made in writing at any office of the Department of Human Resources Development or the Department of Human Resources and Skills Development. (SOR/79-751, s. 1; SOR/86-1133, s. 3; SOR/89-345, s. 2; SOR/96-522, s. 24; SOR/2004-249, s. 2.)

(1.1) Where an application for a disability pension has been denied, and the applicant has reached 60 years of age between the time of the application and the time of its denial or would have been entitled to a retirement pension if he had applied therefor at the time of application for the disability pension, that application shall, on request made by or on behalf of the applicant, be deemed to be an application for a retirement pension if the request is made

(*a*) in writing at the location of any office of the Department of Human Resources Development; and (SOR/90-829, s. 14(1); SOR/96-522, s. 24.)

(*b*) within 90 days following the month in which the applicant is notified of the denial or, where the denial is finally confirmed on appeal, within 90 days after the day on which the applicant is notified of the confirmation.

(SOR/86-1133, s. 3; SOR/93-290, s. 1.)

(2) Where by reason of section 80 of the Act and an agreement under that section with a province providing a comprehensive pension plan the whole amount of any benefit payable to an applicant is deemed to be payable under that plan or where the division of unadjusted pensionable earnings can be determined under that plan in accordance with the agreement, the Minister shall, as soon as possible after an application is received, forward the application, together with a statement of the date on which it was received, to the authority charged under that plan with the duty of receiving applications, calculating the division of unadjusted pensionable earnings and paying benefits. (SOR/90-829, s. 14(2); SOR/96-522, s. 23.)

(SOR/79-751, s. 1; SOR/86-1133, s. 3; SOR/89-345, s. 2; SOR/90-829, s. 14; SOR/93-290, s. 1; SOR/96-522, ss. 23, 24; SOR/2004-249, s. 2.)

43.1. (1) Despite subsection 43(1), an application for a retirement pension may also be made to the Minister by way of the Internet if

(*a*) the relevant information required under section 52 is sent to the Minister by way of the Internet on the electronic form prescribed for that purpose and made available on the Internet, unless the Minister requires that the information or evidence be provided to the Minister in writing; and

(*b*) the electronic confirmation sheet sent to the applicant by the Minister and bearing the date and time of receipt of the information by the Minister and a confirmation number assigned to the application by the Minister is signed by the applicant or their representative and delivered by hand, mail or courier to the Minister at an office of the Department of Human Resources Development or the Department of Human Resources and Skills Development.

(SOR/2004-249, s. 3.)

(2) When all the requirements of subsection (1) have been met, the application submitted electronically is considered to have been received on the date and at the time indicated on the electronic confirmation sheet. (SOR/2004-249, s. 3.)

(SOR/2004-249, s. 3.)

44. (1) Where the Minister is satisfied, by such medical certificates or other documentary evidence as is presented to the Minister or as the Minister may require, that a person, by reason of infirmity, illness, insanity or other cause, is incapable of managing the person's own affairs, an application for a benefit, for a division of unadjusted pensionable earnings under section 55 or 55.1 of the Act or for an assignment of a portion of a retirement pension under section 65.1 [66.1] of the Act may be made on that person's behalf by another person or by an agency if the Minister is satisfied that such other person or agency is authorized by or pursuant to a law of Canada or of a province to manage that person's affairs or, where it appears to the Minister that there is no other person or agency so authorized, by any other person or agency approved by the Minister. (SOR/80-757, s. 1; SOR/86-1133, s. 4; SOR/89-345, s. 3; SOR/96-522, s. 23.)

(2) Where either or both spouses, former spouses or former common-law partners are deceased, an application for a division of unadjusted pensionable earnings under section 55 or paragraph 55.1(1)(*b*) or (*c*) of the Act may be made by the personal representative or by or on behalf of a child of any of those deceased persons. (SOR/90-829, s. 15; SOR/2000-411, s. 3.)

(SOR/80-757, s. 1; SOR/86-1133, s. 4; SOR/89-345, s. 3; SOR/90-829, s. 15; SOR/96-522, s. 23; SOR/2000-411, s. 3.)

45. (1) Where no payment of a benefit has been made in respect of an application for a benefit made after May 28, 1975, the applicant may withdraw the application by sending to the Minister a written notice to that effect at any time before the commencement of payment of the benefit. (SOR/93-290, s. 2; SOR/96-522, s. 23.)

(2) Where an application for a benefit has been withdrawn pursuant to subsection (1), the application shall not thereafter be used for the purpose of determining the applicant's eligibility for a benefit.

(3) An applicant for a division of unadjusted pensionable earnings under section 55 or paragraph 55.1(1)(*b*) or (*c*) of the Act may withdraw the application by sending a notice in writing to the Director not later than 60 days after the date of receipt by the applicant of notification of the decision respecting the application. (SOR/86-1133, s. 5; SOR/89-345, s. 4.)

(4) Where an application for a division of unadjusted pensionable earnings under section 55 or paragraph 55.1(1)(*b*) or (*c*) of the Act is withdrawn pursuant to subsection (3), the application shall not thereafter be used for the purpose of determining whether the person in respect of whom the application was submitted is eligible for the division. (SOR/86-1133, s. 5; SOR/89-345, s. 4.)

(5) Where an application for a division of unadjusted pensionable earnings under section 55 or paragraph 55.1(1)(*b*) or (*c*) of the Act has been approved and subsequently withdrawn, notice in writing of the withdrawal shall be given by the Minister to the other spouse, former spouse or former common-law partner or to their respective estates, as the case may be. (SOR/86-1133, s. 5; SOR/89-345, s. 4; SOR/90-829, s. 16; SOR/200-41, s. 4; SOR/2002-221, s. 1.)

(SOR/86-1133, s. 5; SOR/89-345, s. 4; SOR/90-829, s. 16; SOR/93-290, s. 2; SOR/96-522, s. 23; SOR/2000-41, s. 4; SOR/2002-221, s. 1.)

CPP REGULATIONS

46. (1) A notification required by subsection 55.2(4) of the Act shall be effected by giving notice in writing. (SOR/90-829, s. 17(1).)

(2) A notification required by subsection 55(8) or 55.2(10) of the Act shall be effected by giving notice in writing containing such of the following information as is applicable: (SOR/90-829, s. 17(2).)

(a) the dates of marriage and dissolution of marriage of the persons subject to the division; (SOR/2000-411, s. 5(1).)

(b) the period of cohabitation for which the division of unadjusted pensionable earnings has been made;

(c) the amount of unadjusted pensionable earnings, prior to the division, of the persons subject to the division; (SOR/2000-411, s. 5(2).)

(d) the amount of unadjusted pensionable earnings of the persons subject to the division as a result of the division; (SOR/2000-411, s. 5(2).)

(e) the effect of the division on any benefit that is payable to or in respect of the persons subject to the division; (SOR/2000-411, s. 5(2).)

(f) a statement of the right to make a request for a reconsideration referred to in subsection 81(1) of the Act; and (SOR/90-829, s. 17(3); SOR/96-522, s. 7.)

(g) any other information that the Minister deems necessary. (SOR/96-522, s. 7.)

(3) A division referred to in subsection 55.1(5) of the Act may be cancelled pursuant to that subsection within the period of 60 days after the making of the division. (SOR/90-829, s. 17(4); SOR/2000-411, s. 5.)

(SOR/86-1133, s. 6; SOR/90-829, s. 17; SOR/96-522, s. 7; SOR/2000-411, s. 5.)

46.1. (1) A notification required by subsection 65.1(5) of the Act shall be effected by giving notice in writing.

(2) A notification required by subsection 65.1(12) of the Act shall be effected by giving notice in writing containing the following information:

(a) the month with which the assignment commences in accordance with subsection 65.1(10) of the Act;

(b) the portion of retirement pension assigned; and

(c) a statement of the right to make a request for a reconsideration referred to in subsection 81(1) of the Act. (SOR/96-522, s. 8)

(SOR/86-1133, s. 6; SOR/90-829, s. 18; SOR/96-522, s. 8.)

Cancellation of Benefit

46.2. (1) A beneficiary may submit to the Minister, within the interval between the date of commencement of payment of the benefit and the expiration of six months after that date, a request in writing that the benefit be cancelled. (SOR/96-522, s. 23.)

(2) Despite subsection (1), if there is a determination that an applicant for a disability pension under the Act or a comparable benefit under a provincial pension plan is deemed to have become disabled for the purpose of entitlement to the disability pension or benefit and is in receipt of a retirement pension, and the time when the applicant is deemed to be disabled is before the date on which the retirement pension became payable, the applicant may submit to the Minister, within the period beginning on the day of commencement of payment of the retirement pension and ending 60 days after the receipt by the applicant of the notice of the determination, a request in

writing that the retirement pension be cancelled. (SOR/96-522, s. 9(2); SOR/99-192, s. 3.)

(2.2) [Repealed by SOR/96-522, s. 9.]

(3) The Minister shall consider a request received pursuant to subsection (1) or (2) and, according to the applicable criteria, shall grant or refuse it. (SOR/93-290, s. 3(2); SOR/96-522, s. 9(3).)

(4) Where a request referred to in subsection 66.1(2) of the Act is granted under this section, the amount described in that subsection shall, for the purposes thereof, be repayable within the time beginning on the granting of the request and ending on the expiration of six months following the month in which the request is granted. (SOR/90-829, s. 19.)

(SOR/86-1133, s. 6; SOR/90-829, s. 19; SOR/93-290, s. 3; SOR/96-522, ss. 9, 23; SOR/99-192, s. 3.)

Evidence of Age and Identity[1]

47. (1) Subject to sections 49 and 50, the Minister shall determine the age and identity of a person for the purposes of the Act in accordance with whichever of subsections (2) to (4) is applicable. (SOR/86-1133, s. 7; SOR/2004-249, s. 4.)

(2) The Minister shall determine the age and identity of a person on the basis of any information provided to the Minister by the Canada Employment Insurance Commission under subsection 28.2(5) of the *Department of Human Resources and Skills Development Act.* (SOR/2004-249, s. 4; SOR/2013-20, s. 1.)

(3) The Minister shall determine the age and identity of a person on the basis of a birth certificate or a certified copy of one. (SOR/2004-249, s. 4.)

(4) If there is sufficient reason to believe that a birth certificate is not available, the Minister shall determine the age and identity of a person on the basis of any other evidence and information with respect to the age and identity of the person that is available from any source. (SOR/90-829, s. 20; SOR/2004-249, s. 4.)

(5) If the Minister is unable to determine the age and identity of a person under any of subsections (2) to (4), the Minister shall, if it is possible to do so, determine the age and identity of the person on the basis of information obtained from Statistics Canada in accordance with section 87 of the Act. (SOR/2004-249, s. 4.)

(SOR/86-1133, s. 7, SOR/90-829, s. 20; SOR/96-522, s. 23; SOR/2004-249, s. 4; SOR/2013-20, s. 1.)

48. [Revoked by SOR/86-1133, effective January 1, 1987.]

49. Where the age of a person has been determined under the *Old Age Security Act* or a provincial pension plan, that determination shall be accepted by the Minister for the purposes of the Act.

(SOR/96-522, s. 10.)

50. At any time after the age of a person has been determined pursuant to these Regulations, the Minister may, where facts not previously taken into account in determining the age of the person come to his attention, make a new determination of the age of the person.

(SOR/96-522, s. 23.)

---

[1] Heading amended by SOR/2004-249, s. 4.

CPP REGULATIONS

51. For the purposes of section 87 of the Act, the following are prescribed as the conditions subject to which any information specified in that section respecting the age of any applicant or beneficiary or the applicant's or beneficiary's spouse, former spouse, common-law partner or former common-law partner is obtainable from Statistics Canada on request and for the purpose specified in that section: (SOR/90-829, s. 21(1); SOR/2000-411, s. 6(1).)

    (*a*) the request to Statistics Canada for such information shall

        (i) be made in a form prescribed by the Chief Statistician,

        (ii) bear the signed consent of the applicant, beneficiary, spouse, former spouse, common-law partner or former common-law partner or of the person or agency that made the application on their behalf or, where there is no such person or agency, any other person or agency who would have been entitled to make the application on their behalf, and (SOR/2000-411, s. 6(2).)

        (iii) provide such information as may be necessary to enable a proper search to be made of the census records for the purpose of obtaining the information requested; and

    (*b*) information obtained pursuant to section 87 of the Act shall not be disclosed to any person except to an officer, clerk or employee of the Department of Human Resources Development or except as required by an agreement entered into under section 105 of the Act with the government of a province providing a comprehensive pension plan. (SOR/90-829, s. 21(2); SOR/96-522, s. 24.)

(SOR/86-1133, s. 9; SOR/90-829, s. 21; SOR/96-522, s. 24; SOR/2000-411, s. 6.)

Information and Evidence Required to be Furnished by an Applicant or Beneficiary

52. For the purposes of determining the eligibility of an applicant for a benefit, the amount that an applicant or beneficiary is entitled to receive as a benefit or the eligibility of a beneficiary to continue to receive a benefit, the applicant, the person applying on his behalf, or the beneficiary, as the case may be, shall, in the application or thereafter in writing when requested to do so by the Minister, set out or furnish the Minister with the following applicable information or evidence:

    (*a*) the name at birth and present name, sex, address and Social Insurance Number of

        (i) the applicant or beneficiary,

        (ii) the disabled or deceased contributor,

        (iii) the spouse or common-law partner of the disabled contributor or the survivor of the deceased contributor, SOR/86-1133, s. 10(1); SOR/2000-411, s. 7(17).)

        (iv) each dependent child of the disabled or deceased contributor, and (SOR/86-1133, s. 10(1).)

        (v) any former spouse or former common-law partner, where known to the applicant; (SOR/86-1133, s. 10(1); SOR/2000-411, s. 7(2).)

    (*b*) the date and place of birth of

        (i) the applicant or beneficiary,

        (ii) the disabled or deceased contributor,

        (iii) the survivor of the deceased contributor, and (SOR/2000-411, s. 18.)

        (iv) each dependent child of the disabled or deceased contributor;

(c) the date and place of death of the contributor;

(d) whether a dependent child of the contributor has died since

(i) the date on which the contributor claims to have become disabled, or

(ii) the death of the contributor;

(e) [Revoked by SOR/86-1133, s. 10(2).]

(f) whether the deceased contributor was married at the time of his death and, if so, to whom, and the date and place of the marriage;

(g) whether the deceased contributor was separated or divorced at the time of his death;

(h) whether there is a personal representative of the estate of the deceased contributor, and the name and address of any such personal representative;

(i) whether a dependent child of the disabled or deceased contributor

(i) is his child, (SOR/86-1133, s. 10(3).)

(ii) is his legally adopted child or was adopted in fact by him or is a legally adopted child of another person,

(iii) was legally or in fact in his custody and control,

(iv) is in the custody and control of the disabled contributor, the survivor of the contributor or another person or agency, (SOR/86-1133, s. 10(4); SOR/2000-411, s. 18.)

(v) is living apart from the disabled contributor or the survivor, or (SOR/86-1133, s. 10(4); SOR/2000-411, s. 18.)

(vi) is or was maintained by the disabled contributor; (SOR/86-1133, s. 10(4); SOR/2000-411, s. 18.)

(j) where a dependent child of the disabled or deceased contributor is 18 or more years of age, whether that child is and has been in full time attendance at a school or university; (SOR/86-1133, s. 10(5).)

(k) whether the applicant or beneficiary who is the survivor of a contributor maintains wholly or substantially one or more dependent children of the deceased contributor; (SOR/2000-411, s. 18.)

(k.1) (Repealed by SOR/2013-83, s. 2, in force April 30, 2013.)

(l) a statement evidencing the amount of the contributory salary and wages and of the contributory self-employed earnings of a disabled or deceased contributor for the year in which the contributor became disabled or died and for any preceding year;

(m) whether the applicant, beneficiary or deceased contributor is or was in receipt of or has applied for a benefit under the Act or under a provincial pension plan or a pension under the *Old Age Security Act*; and

(n) such additional documents, statements or records that are in the possession of the applicant or beneficiary or are obtainable by him that will assist the Minister in ascertaining the accuracy of the information and evidence referred to in paragraphs (a) to (m).

(SOR/86-1133, s. 10; SOR/96-522, s. 23; SOR/2000-411, ss. 5, 7 and 18; SOR/2013-83, s. 2.)

53. For the purposes of determining whether any months during which a contributor was a family allowance recipient should not be included in his contributory period, the applicant shall, in the application or thereafter in writing when requested to do so by the Minister, set out or furnish the Minister with such of the following additional information or evidence as is applicable:

CPP REGULATIONS

(*a*) the name and date of birth of all children in respect of whom the contributor received family allowance benefits or Child Tax Benefits; (SOR/93-11, s. 2.)

(*b*) the Social Insurance Number, if any, of each of those children; (SOR/93-11, s. 2.)

(*c*) the periods during which the contributor received family allowance benefits or Child Tax Benefits in respect of those children; (SOR/93-11, s. 2.)

(*d*) the province in which the contributor resided while in receipt of family allowance benefits or Child Tax Benefits in respect of those children; (SOR/93-11, s. 2.)

(*e*) the Social Insurance Number of the contributor to whom family allowance benefits or Child Tax Benefits were paid in respect of those children; (SOR/93-11, s. 2.)

(*f*) if known, the name and Social Insurance Number of any other person who received family allowance benefits or Child Tax Benefits in respect of those children; and (SOR/93-11, s. 2.)

(*g*) such additional documents, statements or records that are in the possession of the applicant or are obtainable by him that will assist the Minister in ascertaining the accuracy of the information and evidence referred to in paragraphs (*a*) to (*f*).

(SOR/93-11, s. 2; SOR/96-522, s. 23.)

54. (1) For the purposes of determining whether an application for a division of unadjusted pensionable earnings pursuant to section 55 or paragraph 55.1(1)(*b*) or (*c*) of the Act may be approved, the applicant shall, in the application or thereafter in writing when requested to do so by the Minister, set out or furnish the Minister with the information required under section 52 in the case of an application for a benefit, subject to such modifications as the circumstances may require, and with such of the following additional information or evidence as is applicable: (SOR/90-829, s. 22(1).)

(*a*) the name at birth and present name, the sex, address and Social Insurance Number of each spouse, former spouse or former common-law partner; (SOR/2000-411, s. 8(1).)

(*b*) the date and place of birth of each spouse, former spouse or former common-law partner; (SOR/2000-411, s. 8(1).)

(*c*) whether the spouse, former spouse or former common-law partner is or was in receipt of or has applied for a benefit under the Act or under a provincial pension plan; (SOR/2000-411, s. 8(1).)

(*d*) the date and place of marriage of the spouses or former spouses and their certificate of marriage;

(*e*) the date and place of the dissolution of the marriage of the former spouses;

(*f*) documentary evidence of any such dissolution of marriage, including the decree absolute of divorce, the judgment granting a divorce under the *Divorce Act, 1985* or the judgment of nullity; (SOR/90-829, s. 22(2).)

(*g*) the address of all residences where the spouses, former spouses or former common-law partners lived together; (SOR/2000-411, s. 8(3).)

(*h*) the dates of any periods when the spouses, former spouses or former common-law partners did not live together and whether the separations or any of them were for any reason set out in paragraph 78(2)(*a*) or subsection 78.1(3); (SOR/2000-411, s. 8(3).)

(*i*) the date that the spouses, former spouses or former common-law partners commenced to live separate and apart; (SOR/2000-411, s. 8(3).)

(*j*) the dates of all periods when the spouses, former spouses or former common-law partners lived together in a conjugal relationship; (SOR/2000-411, s. 8(3).)

(*k*) a copy of any written agreement between persons subject to a division that was entered into before June 4, 1986 or any written agreement between such persons that was entered into on or after that date and contains a provision that is binding on the Minister under subsection 55.2(3) of the Act; and (SOR/2000-411, s. 8(3).)

(*l*) such additional documents, statements or records that are in the possession of, or are obtainable by, the applicant as will assist the Minister in ascertaining the accuracy of the information and evidence referred to in paragraphs (*a*) to (*k*).

(2) The information relating to the marriage in question as provided in paragraph 55.1(1)(*a*) of the Act shall be such of the following information as is applicable: (SOR/90-829, s. 22(3).)

(*a*) the name at birth and present name, the sex, address and Social Insurance Number of each of the former spouses;

(*b*) the date and place of marriage of the former spouses and their certificate of marriage;

(*c*) the date and place of the dissolution of the marriage of the former spouses;

(*d*) a copy of the decree or judgment referred to in that paragraph;

(*e*) the addresses of all residences where the former spouses lived together;

(*f*) the dates of any periods when the former spouses did not live together and whether the separations or any of them were for any reason set out in paragraph 78(2)(*a*) or subsection 78.1(3); (SOR/2000-411, s. 8(6).)

(*g*) the date that the former spouses commenced to live separate and apart;

(*h*) the dates of all periods when the former spouses lived together in a conjugal relationship; and

(*i*) a copy of any written agreement between persons subject to a division that was entered into before June 4, 1986 or any written agreement between such persons that was entered into on or after that date and contains a provision that is binding on the Minister under subsection 55.2(3) of the Act. (SOR/2000-411, s. 8(8).)

(SOR/80-757, s. 3; SOR/86-1133, s. 11; SOR/90-829, s. 22; SOR/96-522, s. 23; SOR/2000-411, s. 8.)

54.1. For the purposes of determining whether an application for an assignment of a portion of a retirement pension under section 65.1 of the Act may be approved, the applicant shall, in the application or thereafter in writing when requested to do so by the Minister, set out or furnish the Minister with the information required under section 52, subject to such modifications as the circumstances may require, and with such of the following additional information or evidence as is applicable: (SOR/90-829, s. 23(1).)

(*a*) the name at birth and present name, the sex, address and Social Insurance Number of the applicant's spouse or common-law partner; (SOR/2000-411, s. 9(1).)

(*b*) the date and place of birth of the applicant's spouse or common-law partner; (SOR/2000-411, s. 9(1).)

CPP REGULATIONS

383

(c) whether the applicant's spouse or common-law partner is or was in receipt of or has applied for a benefit under the Act or under a provincial pension plan; (SOR/2000-411, s. 9(1).)

(d) the date and place of marriage of the spouses and their certificate of marriage;

(e) the month in which the spouses or common-law partners commenced to live together in a conjugal relationship; (SOR/2000-411, s. 9(3).)

(f) the dates of any periods when the spouses or common-law partners did not live together and whether the separations or any of them were for any reason set out in paragraph 78(2)(a) or subsection 78.1(3); (SOR/2000-411, s. 9(3).)

(g) documentary evidence of the dissolution of any previous marriage of the applicant, including the decree absolute of divorce, the judgment granting a divorce under the *Divorce Act*, or the judgment of nullity; and (SOR/90-829, s. 23(2).)

(h) such additional documents, statements or records that are in the possession of, or are obtainable by, the applicant as will assist the Minister in ascertaining the accuracy of the information and evidence referred to in paragraphs (a) to (g).

(SOR/86-1133, s. 11; SOR/90-829, s. 23; SOR/96-522, s. 23; SOR/2000-411, s. 9.)

Effective Dates of the Approval or Taking Place of a Division and of the Attribution of Pensionable Earnings Following a Division

54.2. (1) For the purposes of the Act,

(a) the effective date of the taking place of a division of unadjusted pensionable earnings is the last day of the month in which the information prescribed for the purposes of paragraph 55.1(1)(a) of the Act, and that is listed in subsection 54(2), is received by the Minister; or

(b) the effective date of the approval of a division of unadjusted pensionable earnings is the last day of the month in which the application referred to in paragraph 55.1(1)(b) or (c) is received.

(2) The effective date of the attribution of pensionable earnings following the division is the first day of the month following the month in which the effective date of the taking place or approval of the division falls.

(SOR/86-1133, s. 11; SOR/90-829, s. 24; SOR/93-290, s. 4.)

Whole or Substantial Cessation of Engagement in Employment (Heading repealed by SOR/2013-83, s. 3.)

54.3. (Repealed by SOR/2013-83, s. 3, in force April 30, 2013.)

(SOR/86-1133, s. 11; SOR/88-628, s. 1; SOR/90-829, s. 24; SOR/99-192, s. 4; SOR/2013-83, s. 3.)

Special Case for Calculation of Survivor's Pension

54.4. For the purposes of subsection 58(7) of the Act, where the applicant would be financially prejudiced on account of payment to the applicant of a survivor's pension as referred to in subsection 58(6) of the Act and would not be financially prejudiced on account of payment to the applicant of a disability pension pursuant to subsection 58(7) of the Act, the Minister's powers may be exercised in accordance with subsection 58(7) of the Act.

(SOR/86-1133, s. 11; SOR/90-829, s. 24.)

Payment of Benefits to Persons on Behalf of Beneficiaries

55. (1) Where the Minister is satisfied, on such information or evidence as is presented to him or as he may require, that a beneficiary, by reason of infirmity, illness, insanity or other cause, is incapable of managing his own affairs, the Minister may direct that the benefit be paid on behalf of such beneficiary to any person or agency that the Minister is satisfied is authorized by or pursuant to any law of Canada or of a province to manage that beneficiary's affairs or, where it appears to the Minister that there is no person or agency so authorized, to a person or agency approved by the Minister.

(2) Where the Minister directs, pursuant to subsection (1), that a benefit be paid on behalf of a beneficiary to a person or agency referred to in that subsection, no such benefit shall be paid to such person or agency until the person or agency, as the case may be, has undertaken in an agreement with the Minister

(a) to administer and expend the benefit on behalf of the beneficiary in accordance with the terms of the agreement; and

(b) to furnish any information or evidence and to do any thing that the Act or these Regulations require the beneficiary to furnish or do.

(3) Any person or agency to whom a benefit is paid pursuant to this section on behalf of a beneficiary shall account, in a form approved by the Minister and at such time or times as he directs, to the Minister for the benefit payments received and the disbursements made of the payments.

(SOR/96-522, s. 23.)

Payment of Certain Benefits at Intervals Greater than Monthly

56. Where any benefit the basic monthly amount of which is less than $2 becomes payable to a person to whom no pension is then payable under the *Old Age Security Act*, the Minister may direct that such benefit shall be paid in arrears at intervals, not greater than yearly, specified by the Minister.

(SOR/96-522, s. 23.)

Payment of Benefits Unpaid at Death

57. A benefit payment may be paid to the estate of a deceased beneficiary, or if there is no estate, to a person or agency designated by the Minister, where

(a) an amount is payable as a benefit to the deceased beneficiary; or

(b) a benefit payment made to the beneficiary or made on behalf of the beneficiary by cheque or otherwise is returned to the Minister after the beneficiary's death.

(SOR/96-522, s. 12.)

Single Payment of Benefits

58. (1) For the purposes of paragraph 89(1)(j) of the Act, where the Government of Canada paid a benefit in December 1974 to a person in respect of contributions made under the Act and under the *Quebec Pension Plan*, the Minister may direct that

385

a single monthly payment be made by cheque or otherwise for as long as the beneficiary remains entitled to the benefit. (SOR/96-522, s. 23.)

(2) Where a single monthly payment is made in respect of a beneficiary, that portion of the payment calculated as provided in the *Quebec Pension Plan* shall, in accordance with paragraph 108(3)(*b*) of the Act, be charged to the Canada Pension Plan Account and the amount remitted by the Government of the Province of Quebec in respect of the benefit payable to that beneficiary under the *Quebec Pension Plan* shall, in accordance with paragraph 108(2)(*b*) of the Act, be credited to the Canada Pension Plan Account.

(SOR/90-829, s. 25; SOR/93-290, s. 5; SOR/96-522, s. 23.)

Withholding of Benefits

59. (1) Where evidence is required under the Act or these Regulations to determine the eligibility or continuing eligibility of any beneficiary to receive any amount payable as a benefit and where the Minister has requested such evidence and the beneficiary has not complied with the request or the Minister is not satisfied with the evidence furnished by that beneficiary, the Minister may, on 30 days written notice, withhold payment of the benefit until such time as the beneficiary has furnished the evidence and the Minister is satisfied as to the eligibility of that beneficiary to receive benefits. (SOR/80-757, s. 4; SOR/96-522, s. 23.)

(2) Where payment of a benefit that has been withheld under subsection (1) is resumed, the benefit shall be paid for any portion of the period of withholding during which the beneficiary was entitled to receive benefits.

(SOR/80-757, s. 4; SOR/96-522, s. 23.)

Access to Privileged Information[2]

60. (Repealed by SOR/2013-20, s. 2, in force March 1, 2013.)

(SOR/80-813, s. 1; SOR/90-829, s. 26; SOR/93-290, s. 6; SOR/96-522, s. 14; SOR/99-192, s. 5; SOR/2013-20, s. 2.)

60.1. (Repealed by SOR/2013-20, s. 2, in force March 1, 2013.)

(SOR/2010-45, s. 3; SOR/2013-20, s. 2.)

Prescribed Federal Institutions and Federal Acts[3]

60.2. (Repealed by SOR/2013-20, s. 2, in force March 1, 2013.)

(SOR/2010-45, s. 3; SOR/2013-20, s. 2.)

Application for Retirement Pension

61. An applicant for a retirement pension shall, in addition to any other information or material that these Regulations require him to file or furnish, file with the Minister a statement of the amount of his contributory salary and wages and of his contributory self-employed earnings

(*a*) for the year in which the application is made; and

---

[2] Heading amended by SOR/2010-45, s. 2 and repealed by SOR/2013-20, s. 2, in force March 1, 2013.

[3] Heading added by SOR/2010-45, s. 3 and repealed by SOR/2013-20, s. 2, in force March 1, 2013.

(b) if the Minister so requires, for the year preceding the year in which the application is made.

(SOR/96-522, s. 23.)

Annual Adjustment of Benefits

62. (1) When the basic monthly amount of a benefit is adjusted annually pursuant to subsection 45(2) of the Act,

(a) the product obtained by multiplying the amount referred to in paragraph 45(2)(a) of the Act by the ratio referred to in paragraph 45(2)(b) thereof shall be adjusted to the nearest cent in accordance with subsection (2); and

(b) any quotient obtained from the ratio referred to in paragraph 45(2)(b) of the Act shall be expressed as a decimal fraction in accordance with subsection (3).

(SOR/86-1133, s. 12.)

(2) Where the product referred to in paragraph (1)(a) contains a fractional part of a dollar represented by three or more digits, and

(a) where the third digit is less than five, the third and subsequent digits shall be dropped; and

(b) where the third digit is five or greater than five, the second digit shall be increased by one and the third and subsequent digits shall be dropped.

(3) Where the quotient referred to in paragraph (1)(b) contains a fraction that is less than one, that fraction shall be expressed as a decimal fraction of four digits after the decimal point, and

(a) where the fourth digit after the decimal point is less than five, the third digit after the decimal point shall remain unchanged and the fourth digit shall be dropped; and

(b) where the fourth digit after the decimal point is five or greater than five, the third digit after the decimal point shall be increased by one and the fourth digit shall be dropped.

(SOR/86-1133, s. 11.)

Determination by the Minister

63. (1) Where a determination is made by the Minister as to whether a person is the spouse, common-law partner, child or parent of an applicant, a contributor or another person subject to a division or whether a person is deceased, the determination shall be made by the Minister on the basis of the information provided to the Minister pursuant to subsection (2) or (3), as the case may be, and any other information that the Minister may obtain. (SOR/2000-411, s. 10.)

(2) The applicant or beneficiary shall provide to the Minister any certificate of marriage, birth, baptism or death, as the case may be, that may enable the Minister to make a determination referred to in subsection (1). (SOR/2000-411, s. 10.)

(3) If a certificate referred to in subsection (2) is not available or is not adequate for the purpose of making the determination, the applicant or beneficiary shall provide to the Minister, at the Minister's request, any documentary or other information that is available with respect to the subject of the determination. (SOR/2000-411, s. 10.)

(SOR/86-1133, s. 12; SOR/96-522, s. 23; SOR/2000-411, s. 10.)

CPP REGULATIONS

Payment of Death Benefit to Other than Estates

64. (1) When paragraph 71(2)(*a*) of the Act applies or when the estate of a deceased contributor has not applied for the death benefit within the interval of 60 days after the contributor's death, or when the amount of the death benefit is less than two-thirds of 10% of the Year's Maximum Pensionable Earnings for the year in which the contributor died, in the case of a death that occurred before January 1, 1998, or less than $2,387, in the case of a death that occurred after December 31, 1997, a direction under subsection 71(2) of the Act may, subject to subsections (2) and (3), be given for payment of the death benefit (SOR/90-829, s. 27; SOR/96-522, s. 15; SOR/99-192, s. 6.)

    (*a*) to the individual or institution who has paid or is responsible for the payment of the deceased contributor's funeral expenses;

    (*b*) in the absence of an individual or institution described in paragraph (*a*), to the survivor of the deceased contributor; or

    (*c*) in the absence of an individual or institution referred to in paragraph (*a*) and a survivor referred to in paragraph (*b*), to the next of kin of the deceased contributor. (SOR/2000-411, ss. 11, 18.)

(2) No amount in excess of the actual funeral expenses shall be paid pursuant to paragraph (1)(*a*).

(3) Where, by virtue of subsection (2), an amount paid pursuant to paragraph (1)(*a*) is less than the amount of the death benefit, a direction pursuant to subsection (1), in so far as it relates to the remainder of the death benefit, may be given as if in the absence of an individual or institution described in that paragraph.

(SOR/86-1133, s. 14; SOR/90-829, s. 27; SOR/96-522, s. 15; SOR/99-192, s. 6; SOR/2000-411, ss. 11, 18.)

Whole or Substantial Maintenance

65. For the purposes of subsection 42(1) of the Act, "wholly or substantially" with reference to the maintenance of one or more dependent children of a deceased contributor, means that the survivor of that contributor provides more than 50 per cent of the maintenance provided for such children by all persons other than such children or any other dependent child of that contributor.

(SOR/90-829, s. 28; SOR/2000-411, s. 18.)

Maintenance of Child

65.1. For the purposes of subsection 42(1) and paragraph 76(1)(*d*) of the Act, "maintaining the child", (SOR/90-829, s. 29(1).)

    (*a*) with reference to the child of a deceased contributor, means making periodically, for the child, until the contributor's death, financial provision amounting to not less than the orphan's benefit payable under the Act; and

    (*b*) with reference to the child of a disabled contributor, means making periodically, for the child, financial provision amounting to not less than the disabled contributor's child's benefit payable under the Act.

(SOR/86-1133, s. 15; SOR/90-829, s. 29.)

Full-Time Attendance at a School or University

66. (1) For the purpose of paragraph (*b*) of the definition "dependent child" in subsection 42(1) of the Act, "full-time attendance at a school or university" means full-time attendance at a school, college, university or other educational institution that provides training or instruction of an educational, professional, vocational or technical nature and a dependent child shall be deemed to be or to have been in full-time attendance at a school or university during an absence by reason of a normal period of scholastic vacation. (SOR/90-829, s. 30.)

(2) Where a dependent child

(a) after having been in full-time attendance at a school or university at the beginning of an academic year, is absent from the institution, or

(b) is absent owing to his failure to resume full-time attendance at a school or university during an academic year

by reason of an illness, that child shall be considered to be or to have been in full-time attendance throughout that absence including the normal period of scholastic vacation if

(c) immediately after such absence the child resumes full-time attendance at a school or university at any time during that academic year, or

(d) where it is determined by the Minister that the child is unable to comply with paragraph (c), he resumes full-time attendance at a school or university in the next ensuing academic year.

(SOR/2000-133, s. 1.)

(3) Where a dependent child is absent after he has begun an academic year by reason of illness and it is determined by the Minister, on evidence satisfactory to him, that by reason of such illness it is not possible for the child to resume full-time attendance at a school or university during that academic year, the child shall be deemed to have been in full-time attendance at a school or university until the end of a normal period of scholastic vacation following that academic year. (SOR/96-522, s. 23.)

(4) Where a dependent child, after he has been in full-time attendance at a school or university at the beginning of an academic year, is absent from the institution by reason of illness and, during such absence or during a normal period of scholastic vacation, the child ceases to be a dependent child or a disabled contributor's child or dies, that child shall be considered to be in full-time attendance at a school or university until the end of the month in which he ceases to be a dependent child or a disabled contributor's child or dies.

(SOR/86-1133, s. 15; SOR/90-829, s. 30; SOR/96-522, s. 23; SOR/2000-133, s. 1.)

Declaration of Enrolment or Attendance at a School or University

67. An applicant or beneficiary shall, in support of his claim that a dependent child of 18 or more years of age

(a) is or has been enrolled in a course requiring full-time attendance at a school or university, file with the Minister a declaration signed by a responsible officer of the institution, certifying as to such enrolment; and

(b) is or has been for a period of time in full-time attendance at a school or university, file with the Minister a declaration of such attendance signed by the child.

(SOR/86-1133, s. 15; SOR/96-522, s. 23.)

CPP REGULATIONS

389

Determination of Disability

68. (1) Where an applicant claims that he or some other person is disabled within the meaning of the Act, he shall supply the Minister with the following information in respect of the person whose disability is to be determined:

(a)   a report of any physical or mental disability including (SOR/2010-45, s. 4(1).)

   (i)   the nature, extent and prognosis of the disability, (SOR/2010-45, s. 4(1).)

   (ii)   the findings upon which the diagnosis and prognosis were made,

   (iii)   any limitation resulting from the disability, and (SOR/2010-45, s. 4(2).)

   (iv)   any other pertinent information, including recommendations for further diagnostic work or treatment, that may be relevant;

(b)   a statement of that person's occupation and earnings for the period commencing on the date upon which the applicant alleges that the disability commenced; and

(c)   a statement of that person's education, employment experience and activities of daily life.

(2) In addition to the requirements of subsection (1), a person whose disability is to be or has been determined pursuant to the Act may be required from time to time by the Minister

(a)   to supply a statement of his occupation and earnings for any period; and

(b)   to undergo such special examinations and to supply such reports as the Minister deems necessary for the purpose of determining the disability of that person.

(3) The reasonable cost of any examination or report required under subsection (2) shall be

(a)   paid by way of reimbursement or advance, as the Minister deems fit;

(b)   paid out of the Consolidated Revenue Fund; and

(c)   charged to the Canada Pension Plan Account as a cost of administration of the Act.

(4) For the purposes of this section, "cost" includes travel and living expenses that the Minister deems necessary of the person whose disability is to be determined and of a person to accompany that person.

(SOR/96-522, s. 23; SOR/2010-45, s. 4.)

68.1. (1) For the purpose of subparagraph 42(2)(a)(i) of the Act, "substantially gainful", in respect of an occupation, describes an occupation that provides a salary or wages equal to or greater than the maximum annual amount a person could receive as a disability pension. The amount is determined by the formula

$$(A \times B) + C$$

where

A   is .25 $\times$ the Maximum Pensionable Earnings Average;

B   is .75; and

C   is the flat rate benefit, calculated as provided in subsection 56(2) of the Act, $\times$ 12.

(SOR/2014-135, s. 1.)

(2) If the amount calculated under subsection (1) contains a fraction of a cent, the amount is to be rounded to the nearest whole cent or, if the amount is equidistant from two whole cents, to the higher of them. (SOR/2014-135, s. 1.)

(SOR/2014-135, s. 1.)

69. (1) For the purpose of determining whether any amount shall be paid or shall continue to be paid as a benefit in respect of a person who has been determined to be disabled within the meaning of the Act, the Minister may require that person from time to time

(*a*) to undergo such special examinations,

(*b*) to supply such reports, and

(*c*) to supply such statements of his occupation and earnings for any period,

as the Minister may specify.

(2) Where the Minister is of the opinion that a person who has been determined to be disabled within the meaning of the Act may benefit vocationally from reasonable rehabilitation measures, he may, from time to time, require that person to undergo such reasonable rehabilitation measures as he may specify.

(3) The reasonable cost of any examination or report or rehabilitation measure required under this section shall be

(*a*) paid by way of reimbursement or advance, as the Minister deems fit;

(*b*) paid out of the Consolidated Revenue Fund; and

(*c*) charged to the Canada Pension Plan Account as a cost of administration of the Act.

(4) For the purposes of this section, "cost" includes travel and living expenses that the Minister deems necessary of the disabled person and of a person to accompany that person.

(SOR/96-522, s. 23.)

70. (1) Where a person who has been determined to be disabled within the meaning of the Act fails without good cause to comply with any requirement of the Minister made under section 69, he may be determined to have ceased to be disabled at such time as the Minister may specify except that such time shall not be earlier than the day of failure to comply. (SOR/96-522, s. 23.)

(2) For the purpose of subsection (1), "good cause" means a significant risk to a person's life or health.

(SOR/96-522, s. 23.)

Return to Work[4]

70.1. If a person who has been determined to be disabled within the meaning of the Act returns to work, the person shall so inform the Minister without delay.

(SOR/2005-38, s. 1.)

---

[4] Heading added by SOR/2005-38, s. 1.

CPP REGULATIONS

Request for Reinstatement of Disability Pension and Disabled Contributor's Child Benefit[5]

71. (1) A request for reinstatement of a disability pension under section 70.1 of the Act shall be made in writing at any office of the Department of Human Resources Development or the Department of Human Resources and Skills Development. (SOR/2005-38, s. 1.)

(2) The request shall be made within 12 months after the month in which the person became incapable again of working. (SOR/2005-38, s. 1.)

(SOR/89-345, s. 7; SOR/2005-38, s. 1.)

72. (1) The determination as to whether a person is entitled to have a disability pension reinstated shall be made by the Minister on the basis of the information and the evidence provided to the Minister under subsection (2). (SOR/2005-38, s. 1.)

(2) The applicant or the person making a request on the applicant's behalf shall furnish the Minister with the following information and evidence:

(a) the applicant's name, address and Social Insurance Number and, if applicable, the name and address of the person making the request on the applicant's behalf and that person's relationship to the applicant;

(b) the month in which the applicant ceased to receive the disability pension;

(c) the month in which the applicant became incapable again of working;

(d) the date that the applicant stopped working;

(e) the statement of a person qualified to practise medicine confirming that the applicant has a severe and prolonged mental or physical disability that is the same as, or is related to, the disability that entitled the applicant to receive the disability pension that is the subject of the request;

(f) the name of each dependent child of the applicant and whether the child is living with or apart from the applicant; and (SOR/2010-45, s. 6.)

(g) if the request includes a request to reinstate the disabled contributor's child benefit in respect of each of the applicant's children who are 18 years of age or more,

(i) the child's name, address and Social Insurance Number, and

(ii) evidence, established in accordance with section 67, that the child is in full-time attendance at a school or university.

(SOR/2005-38, s. 1; SOR/2010-45, s. 6.)

(SOR/89-345, s. 7; SOR/2005-38, s. 1; SOR/2010-45, s. 6.)

Reinstatement of a Disabled Contributor's Child Benefit[6]

73. (Repealed by SOR/2010-45, s. 7.)

(SOR/89-345, s. 7; SOR/2005-38, s. 1; SOR/2010-45, s. 7.)

Reconsideration and Appeal on Behalf of Certain Persons

74. If the Minister or the Social Security Tribunal established under section 44 of the *Department of Human Resources and Skills Development Act* is satisfied, on being presented with medical certificates or other written statements, that a person, by

---

[5] Heading added by SOR/2005-38, s. 1, and amended by SOR/2010-45, s. 5.

[6] Heading added by SOR/2005-38, s. 1, and repealed by SOR/2010-45, s. 7.

reason of infirmity, illness, insanity or other cause, is incapable of managing their affairs, a request for a reconsideration under subsection 81(1) or (1.1) of the Act or an appeal under section 82 of the Act or section 55 of the *Department of Human Resources and Skills Development Act* may be made on the person's behalf by another person or an agency if that other person or agency is authorized by or under a law of Canada or of a province to manage the person's affairs or, if it appears to the Minister or the Social Security Tribunal that there is no other person or agency so authorized, if that other person or agency is considered to be qualified to do so by the Minister or the Social Security Tribunal, as the case may be.

(SOR/90-829, s. 31; SOR/92-17, s. 3; SOR/96-522, s. 16; SOR/2010-45, s. 8; SOR/2013-61, 2.)

Request for Reconsideration

74.1. (1) A request for a reconsideration under subsection 81(1) or (1.1) of the Act shall be made in writing to the Minister and shall set out (SOR/2010-45, s. 9(1).)

    (a) the name, address and Social Insurance Number of the contributor;

    (b) if the person making the request for the reconsideration is not the contributor, that person's name and address and their relationship to the contributor; and (SOR/2010-45, s. 9(2).)

    (c) the grounds for the request for the reconsideration and a statement of the facts that form the basis of that request.

(SOR/2000-133, s. 2.)

(2) If it appears to the Minister that the person making the request for a reconsideration has failed to provide information in accordance with any of the requirements of paragraphs (1)(a) to (c) — or has failed to provide sufficient information to allow the Minister to determine if there are circumstances that allow for a longer period in which to make the request — the Minister may take any steps to obtain the information that is necessary to rectify the failure. (SOR/2013-61, s. 3.)

(3) For the purposes of subsections 81(1) and (1.1) of the Act and subject to subsection (4), the Minister may allow a longer period to make a request for reconsideration of a decision or determination if the Minister is satisfied that there is a reasonable explanation for requesting a longer period and the person has demonstrated a continuing intention to request a reconsideration. (SOR/2013-61, s. 3.)

(4) The Minister must also be satisfied that the request for reconsideration has a reasonable chance of success, and that no prejudice would be caused to the Minister or a party by allowing a longer period to make the request, if the request for reconsideration

    (a) is made after the 365-day period after the day on which the person is notified in writing of the decision or determination;

    (b) is made by a person who has applied again for the same benefit; or

    (c) is made by a person who has requested the Minister to rescind or amend a decision under subsection 81(3) of the Act.

(SOR/2013-61, s. 3.)

(SOR/92-17, s. 3; SOR/96-522, s. 16; SOR/2000-133, s. 2; SOR/2010-45, s. 9; SOR/2013-61, s. 3.)

CPP REGULATIONS

Notification of Appealable Decisions

74.2. A notification referred to in subsection 81(1) or (1.1) of the Act must in writing and sent by the Minister.

(SOR/92-17, s. 3; SOR/96-522, s. 16; SOR/2000-133, s. 3; SOR/2010-45, s. 10; SOR/2013-61, s. 4.)

Professionals Eligible for Review Tribunals Panel (Heading repealed by SOR/2013-61, s. 4.)

74.3. (Repealed by SOR/2013-61, s. 4.)

(SOR/92-17, s. 3; SOR/2013-61, s. 4.)

Constitutional Questions[7]

74.4. (Repealed by SOR/2010-45, s. 11.)

(SOR/92-17, s. 13; SOR/2010-45, s. 11.)

Pension Index

75. (1) For the purposes of subsection 43(2) of the Act, the Pension Index for each year shall be calculated as the quotient obtained by dividing the aggregate of the Consumer Price Index for each month in the 12-month period ending October 31 in the preceding year by 12, adjusted to one digit after the decimal point in accordance with subsection (2). (SOR/96-522, s. 17.)

(2) Where the quotient obtained pursuant to subsection (1) contains a fraction that is less than one, that fraction shall be expressed as a decimal fraction of two digits after the decimal point and

(a) the second digit after the decimal point shall be dropped if that digit is less than five; or

(b) the first digit after the decimal point shall be increased by one and the second digit dropped if the second digit is five or greater than five.

(SOR/90-829, s. 31; SOR/96-422, s. 17.)

76. (1) In this section,

"authority" means any provincial authority or municipal authority in a province that pays any advance or assistance or welfare payment to a person in the province; (SOR/96-522, s. 18(1).)

"excess payment" means the amount of any advance or assistance or welfare payment that was paid by an authority to a person for a month or any portion thereof and that would not have been paid if the benefit that was subsequently payable under the Act to that person in respect of that period had in fact been paid during that period.

(2) Subject to subsection (3) to (6), the Minister may, where an authority satisfies him that an excess payment has been paid to a person, authorize

(a) the deduction from the one sum amount payable to that person in accordance with subsection 62(1) of the Act in respect of the period for which the excess payment was paid, and (SOR/90-829, s. 32(1).)

---

[7] Heading amended by SOR/2010-45, s. 11.

(*b*) the payment to the provincial authority or municipal authority in the province in which the excess payment was paid, (SOR/96-522, s. 18(2).)
of an amount equal to the amount of the excess payment.

(3) An authority referred to in subsection (2) shall, before any deduction and payment from a benefit payable under the Act to any person is authorized under subsection (2), certify, in a form satisfactory to the Minister,

(*a*) the effective date of commencement and the effective date of termination, if applicable, of the advance or assistance or welfare payment;

(*b*) the amount that was paid to the person by the authority for the period during which the excess payment occurred or the amount that the authority applies to have reimbursed, whichever is the lesser; and

(*c*) the Social Insurance Number of the contributor as a result of whose participation under the Act the benefit is payable.

(4) No deduction and payment in respect of an excess payment shall be authorized pursuant to subsection (2) unless

(*a*) the Minister and the appropriate provincial official have concluded an agreement in writing authorizing the deduction and payment; (SOR/96-522, s. 18(3).)

(*b*) the certification required by subsection (3) has been received by the Minister;

(*c*) the irrevocable written consent of the person to the deduction and payment by the Minister has been received before the expiry of one year after the date of their signature; and (SOR/90-829, s. 32(2); SOR/96-522, s. 18(3); SOR/99-192, s. 7; SOR/2013-20, s. 3.)

(*d*) the amount of the excess payment is greater than $50.

(5) [Repealed by SOR/96-522, s. 18(3).]

(6) If, for any reason, no deduction has been made under sub-section (2) in respect of an excess payment or a deduction and payment have been made in respect of an excess payment in an amount less than the amount that might have been paid in respect thereof under subsection (2), the Minister shall not authorize the deduction and payment of any other amount in respect of that excess payment. (SOR/2002-221, s. 3.)

(SOR/90-829, s. 32; SOR/96-522, s. 18; SOR/99-192, s. 7; SOR/2002-221, s. 3; SOR/2013-20, s. 3.)

Deduction from a Benefit and Payment to an Administrator for a Disability Income Program

76.1. (1) For the purposes of subsection 65(3) of the Act, the Minister may deduct an amount as described in that subsection from a benefit payable to a person under paragraph 44(1)(*b*) of the Act and pay that amount to an administrator approved by the Minister where the following terms and conditions are met:

(*a*) the administrator submits to the Minister a record of the payment made under the disability income program, together with the person's irrevocable written consent to the deduction and payment; (SOR/99-192, s. 8.)

(*b*) the documents referred to in paragraph (*a*) are received by the Minister within one year after the date on which the consent is signed; and

(*c*) the amount exceeds $50.

CPP REGULATIONS

(2) For the purpose of subsection 65(3) of the Act, if, for any reason, no deduction has been made or a deduction and payment have been made by the Minister for an amount that is less than the amount that might have been paid under that subsection, the Minister shall not authorize any other deduction and payment. (SOR/99-192, s. 8; SOR/2002-221, s. 4.)

(SOR/93-290, s. 7; SOR/99-192, s. 8; SOR/2002-221, s. 4.)

Family Allowance Recipient

77. (1) For the purposes of the definition "family allowance recipient" in subsection 42(1) of the Act, "family allowance recipient" includes (SOR/86-1133, s. 16; SOR/89-345, s. 8; SOR/93-11, s. 3; SOR/96-522, s. 19.)

(a) the spouse, former spouse, common-law partner or former common-law partner of a person who is described in that definition as having received or being in receipt of an allowance or a family allowance in respect of a child for any period before the child reached the age of seven, if that spouse, former spouse, common-law partner or former common-law partner remained at home during that period as the child's primary caregiver and that period has not already been or cannot be excluded or deducted from the person's contributory period under Part II of the Act; (SOR/89-345, s. 8; SOR/96-522, s. 19; SOR/2010-45, s. 12(1).)

(b) a member of the Canadian Armed Forces who, before 1973, was posted to serve outside Canada, or the spouse or former spouse of such a member, who, but for the posting, would have received an allowance or family allowance for a child under seven years of age; (SOR/89-345, s. 8; SOR/96-522, s. 19; SOR/2010-45, s. 12(1).)

(c) the person who, under section 122.62 of the *Income Tax Act*, is considered to be an eligible individual for the purposes of subdivision a.1 of Division E of Part I of that Act (Child Tax Benefit) in respect of a qualified dependant under seven years of age; and (SOR/93-11, s. 3; SOR/96-522, s. 19.)

(d) the person who would have been considered to be an eligible individual for the purposes of subdivision a.1 of Division E of Part I of the *Income Tax Act* (Child Tax Benefit) had a notice been filed under subsection 122.62(1) of that Act, where no person was considered to be an eligible individual in respect of the same qualified dependant under seven years of age. (SOR/93-11, s. 3; SOR/96-522, s. 19.)

(2) (Repealed by SOR/2010-45, s. 12(2).) (SOR/2000-411, s. 12; SOR/2010-45, s. 12(2).)

(SOR/86-1133, s. 16; SOR/89-345, s. 8; SOR/93-11, s. 3; SOR/96-522, s. 19; SOR/2000-411, s. 12; SOR/2010-45, s. 12.)

Cohabitation

78. (1) For the purposes of section 55 of the Act, months during which the former spouses have cohabited include (SOR/90-829, s. 33(1).)

(a) all consecutive months during the marriage in which the former spouses have lived together as husband and wife without interruption for more than 90 days; and

(b) any period of the marriage preceding the minimum period of 36 consecutive months of cohabitation required by paragraph 55(2)(a) of the Act. (SOR/90-829, s. 33(2).)

(2) For the purpose of paragraph (1)(*a*), (SOR/2000-411, s. 13(2).)

(*a*) where the former spouses did not have the intention to live separate and apart but were separated by reason of the occupation, employment or illness of either spouse, the separation does not constitute interruption of cohabitation; and (SOR/86-1133, s. 17; SOR/2000-411, s. 13(7).)

(*b*) where, after having completed the minimum period of 36 consecutive months of cohabitation required by paragraph 55(2)(*a*) of the Act, the former spouses were separated for any reason for a period of more than 90 days and subsequently resumed cohabitation for a period of more than 90 days, the cohabitation of the former spouses shall be deemed not to have been interrupted. (SOR/90-829, s. 33(3).)

(3) For the purposes of section 55 of the Act, where the cohabitation of the spouses is interrupted for more than 90 days as referred to in paragraph (1)(*a*), the cohabitation shall be deemed to have ceased immediately before the year in which the interruption commenced. (SOR/90-829, s. 33(4).)

(SOR/86-1133, s. 17; s. 16; SOR/89-345, s. 8; SOR/90-829, s. 33; SOR/2000-411, s. 13; SOR/93-11, s. 3; SOR/96-522, s. 19.)

Cohabitation — Division of Unadjusted Pensionable Earnings

78.1. (1) In determining, for the purposes of subsections 55.1(4) and 55.2(7) of the Act, the months during which the spouses, former spouses or former common-law partners cohabited,

(*a*) those months shall, subject to paragraphs (b) and (c), be reckoned as beginning with the first month of the year in which the marriage of the persons subject to the division was solemnized or in which they commenced to cohabit in a conjugal relationship, whichever is applicable; (SOR/2000-411, s. 14.)

(*b*) the persons subject to the division shall be considered not to have cohabited at any time during the year in which they were divorced or their marriage annulled or in which they commenced to live separate and apart; and

(*c*) where, after having lived separate and apart for one year or more, the persons subject to the division resumed cohabitation for at least one year, the period of that separation shall be considered to have begun with the first month of the year in which they commenced to live separate and apart and to have ended with the last month of the year immediately preceding the year in which they resumed cohabitation.

(SOR/2000-411, s. 14.)

(2) In determining a continuous period of at least one year for the purposes of subsection 55.1(3) of the Act, such a period shall be considered to be constituted by any period of cohabitation by the persons subject to the division for twelve or more consecutive months, reckoned as beginning with the month in which the marriage was solemnized or in which they commenced to cohabit in a conjugal relationship and ending with the month immediately preceding the month in which they commenced to live separate and apart. (SOR/2000-411, s. 14.)

(3) For the purposes of this section, where the persons subject to the division did not have the intention to live separate and apart but were separated by reason of the occupation, employment or illness of either person, the separation does not constitute interruption of cohabitation. (SOR/2000-411, s. 14.)

(SOR/86-1133, s. 18; SOR/90-829, s. 34; SOR/93-290, s. 8; SOR/2000-411, s. 14.)

CPP REGULATIONS

Cohabitation — Assignment of a Retirement Pension

78.2. For the purposes of subsection 65.1(8) of the Act, "period of cohabitation" means the period comprising all months during which the contributor and spouse or common-law partner referred to in subsection 65.1(9) of the Act cohabited, and includes the month in which their marriage was solemnized or in which they commenced to cohabit in a conjugal relationship, whichever is applicable, but does not include any months that are not within their joint contributory period as defined in subsection 65.1(8) of the Act.

(SOR/86-1133, s. 18; SOR/90-829, s. 35; SOR/2000-411, s. 15.)

Pension Adjustments

78.3. For the purposes of subsection 46(3.1) of the Act, the adjustment factor for a retirement pension that becomes payable in a month before the month in which the contributor reaches 65 years of age shall be determined by the formula

$$1 - (A \times B)$$

where

A   is the number of months in the period beginning with the month in which the retirement pension becomes payable and ending with the month before the month in which the contributor reaches 65 years of age, or 60 months, whichever is less; and

B   is

  (a) 0.0050, if the month in which the retirement pension becomes payable is after December 31, 2010 and before January 1, 2012,

  (b) 0.0052, if the month in which the retirement pension becomes payable is after December 31, 2011 and before January 1, 2013,

  (c) 0.0054, if the month in which the retirement pension becomes payable is after December 31, 2012 and before January 1, 2014,

  (d) 0.0056, if the month in which the retirement pension becomes payable is after December 31, 2013 and before January 1, 2015,

  (e) 0.0058, if the month in which the retirement pension becomes payable is after December 31, 2014 and before January 1, 2016, and

  (f) 0.0060, if the month in which the retirement pension becomes payable is after December 31, 2015.

(SOR/2010-300, s. 1.)

78.4. For the purposes of subsection 46(3.1) of the Act, the adjustment factor for a retirement pension that becomes payable in a month after the month in which the contributor reaches 65 years of age shall be determined by the formula

$$1 + (A \times B)$$

where

A   is the number of months in the period beginning with the month after the contributor reaches 65 years of age and ending with the month in which the retirement pension becomes payable, or 60 months, whichever is less; and

B   is

(a) **0.0057**, if the month in which the retirement pension becomes payable is after December 31, 2010 and before January 1, 2012

(b) **0.0064**, if the month in which the retirement pension becomes payable is after December 31, 2011 and before January 1, 2013, and

(c) **0.0070**, if the month in which the retirement pension becomes payable is after December 31, 2012.

(SOR/2010-300, s. 1.)

Part VI
Miscellaneous

79. The Minister of National Revenue may, on behalf of the Government of Canada, enter into an agreement with

(*a*) the government of a country other than Canada,

(*b*) an international organization, or

(*c*) the government of a province,

for giving effect to the provisions of paragraph 6(2)(*h*) or 7(1)(*e*) or (*f*) of the Act.

80. [Repealed by SOR/99-192, s. 9, effective April 22, 1999.]

81. [Repealed by SOR/99-192, s. 9, effective April 22, 1999.]

82. The election referred to in paragraph 11(2)(*a*) of the Act shall be made by filing with the Minister the form prescribed therefor.

(SOR/90-829, s. 38.)

83. An individual, to whom section 10 of the Act is not applicable because an election made by the individual pursuant to section 11 of the Act has been approved by the Minister, may revoke the election by advising the Minister thereof in writing.

(SOR/90-829, s. 38.)

83.1. The election referred to in subsection 12(1.1) of the Act is made or revoked by providing the prescribed form to an employer of the person.

(SOR/2011-299, s. 3.)

83.2. The election referred to in subsection 13(1.1) of the Act is made or revoked by

(*a*) filing the prescribed form, together with the return of the person's self-employed earnings for the year, with the Minister within one year from June 15 in the year following the year for which the return is filed; or

(*b*) filing the prescribed form with the Minister within one year from June 15 in the year following the year for which the return of the person's self-employed earnings has been filed.

(SOR/2011-299, s. 3.)

84. (1) An individual to whom subsection 13(3) of the Act applies for a year may elect to have the individual's contributory salary and wages for the year included as self-employed earnings for the purposes of section 10 of the Act by filing with the Minister the form prescribed therefor. (SOR/90-829, s. 39.)

(2) The form referred to in subsection (1) shall be filed by an individual

CPP REGULATIONS

399

(*a*) with his income tax return, or

(*b*) if his income tax return has already been filed, with the Minister

within one year from April 30th of the year following the year for which he so elects.

(SOR/90-829, s. 39.)

84.1. For the purposes of paragraph 14(*c*) of the Act, in the case of an Indian, as defined in the *Indian Act,* the extent of the income of the Indian for the year from self-employment on a reserve, as defined in the *Indian Act,* is the amount described in paragraph 14(*a*) of the Act for that year.

(SOR/88-631, s. 2; SOR/90-829, s. 40.)

Year's Maximum Pensionable Earnings — Time and Manner of Calculation

85. (1) The Year's Maximum Pensionable Earnings for a year shall be calculated immediately following the date on which the first revision of the Industrial Aggregate in Canada for the month of June of the year preceding that year is published by Statistics Canada. (SOR/87-719, s. 1(1).)

(2) Where an average for a period is required pursuant to paragraph 18(1)(*b*) or (*c*) of the Act, it shall be calculated as the quotient obtained by dividing the aggregate of the Wage Measure for each month in the period by the number of months in the period, adjusted to two digits after the decimal point in accordance with subsection (4). (SOR/87-719, s. 1(1); SOR/90-829, s. 41(1); SOR/94-173, s. 3(1).)

(3) Where a ratio is calculated pursuant to paragraph 18(1)(*b*) or (*c*) of the Act and the ratio contains a fraction that is less than one, the fraction shall be expressed as a decimal fraction of four digits after the decimal point, and (SOR/87-719, s. 1(2); SOR/90-829, s. 41(2); SOR/94-173, s. 3(2).)

(*a*) the fourth digit after the decimal point shall be dropped if that digit is less than five; or

(*b*) the third digit after the decimal point shall be increased by one and the fourth digit dropped if the fourth digit is five or greater than five.

(4) Where the quotient obtained pursuant to subsection (2) or the product obtained pursuant to paragraph 18(1)(*b*) of the Act contains a fraction that is less than one, the fraction shall be expressed as a decimal fraction of three digits after the decimal point, and (SOR/90-829, s. 41(3); SOR/94-173, s. 3(3).)

(*a*) the third digit after the decimal point shall be dropped if that digit is less than five; or

(*b*) the second digit after the decimal point shall be increased by one and the third digit dropped if the third digit is five or greater.

(SOR/87-719, s. 1(3).)

(SOR/87-719, s. 1; SOR/90-829, s. 41; SOR/94-173, s. 3.)

Application of International Agreements

86. The agreements referred to in Schedule IX, which were entered into under subsection 107(1) of the Act for the making of reciprocal arrangements relating to the administration or operation of the Act, shall, in order to give full effect to the Act, be applied in Canada in a manner that extends to common-law partners the treatment afforded to spouses.

(SOR/2000-411, s. 16.)

Interest on Amounts Owing to Her Majesty

87. (1) The following definitions apply in this section.

"average bank rate" means the simple arithmetic mean of the bank rates that are established during the month before the month in respect of which interest is being calculated.

"bank rate" means the rate of interest established weekly by the Bank of Canada as the minimum rate at which the Bank of Canada makes short-term advances to members of the Canadian Payments Association.

"debt" means

    (a) a debt due under subsection 66(2) of the Act in respect of which a penalty has been imposed under section 90.1 of the Act; or

    (b) a debt due under subsection 66(2.02) of the Act.

"demand for payment" means a demand for payment in writing and includes a notification of a decision to impose a penalty under section 90.1 of the Act or of the amount of a penalty imposed under that section.

"due date" means, in respect of a debt,

    (a) where a payment schedule has been established, any day on which a scheduled payment is to be made; or

    (b) where no payment schedule has been established, the day that is 120 days after the day on which a demand for payment was issued.

(SOR/2010-45, s. 13.)

(2) Interest is payable on all debts that are recoverable on or after the day on which this section comes into force. (SOR/2010-45, s. 13.)

(3) The accrual of interest on a debt, at the rate set out in subsection (4), begins on the due date. (SOR/2010-45, s. 13.)

(4) Interest accrues on a debt at a rate that is calculated daily and compounded monthly at the average bank rate plus three per cent. (SOR/2010-45, s. 13.)

(5) Interest does not accrue on a debt during the period in which a reconsideration under subsection 81(2) of the Act, an appeal under subsection 82 of the Act or section 55 of the *Department of Human Resources and Skills Development Act*, or a judicial review under the *Federal Courts Act* is pending in respect of that debt. (SOR/2010-45, s. 13; SOR/2013-61, s. 5(1).)

(6) The accrual of interest on a debt or on a portion of the debt, as applicable, ceases on

    (a) the day before the day on which a scheduled payment in respect of the debt or a payment of the debt in full is received by Her Majesty;

    (b) the day on which the debt or the portion of the debt is remitted under subsection 66(3) of the Act;

    (c) the day on which the penalty that constitutes the debt is reduced or the decision imposing that penalty is rescinded under

        (i) subsection 90.1(4) of the Act, or

CPP REGULATIONS

401

  (ii) the latest of the following decisions in respect of a decision or determination of the Minister under section 90.1 of the Act:

   (A) a decision of the Minister under subsection 81(2) of the Act, and

   (B) a decision on an appeal under subsection 82 of the Act or section 55 of the *Department of Human Resources and Skills Development Act* or a judicial review under the *Federal Courts Act*; (SOR/2013-61, s. 5(1).)

 (*d*) the day on which the accrued interest is remitted under subsection (7); or

 (*e*) the day on which the debtor dies.

(SOR/2010-45, s. 13.)

 (7) The conditions under which the Minister may remit in whole or in part the interest payable under this section are that

 (*a*) the interest has ceased to accrue in accordance with paragraph (6)(*c*);

 (*b*) the interest cannot be collected within the reasonably foreseeable future;

 (*c*) the administrative costs of collecting the interest would exceed the amount of that interest; and

 (*d*) the payment of the interest would result in undue hardship to the debtor.

(SOR/2010-45, s. 13.)

(SOR/2010-45, s. 13; SOR/2013-61, s. 5.)

[Schedule I is repealed by SOR/2002-245, s. 3; Schedule II is not reproduced.]

Schedule III

(s. 24)

1. Province of Ontario.

2. Province of Alberta.

3. Province of Manitoba.

4. Province of Newfoundland.

5. Province of Nova Scotia.

6. Province of British Columbia.

7. Province of Saskatchewan.

8. Province of Prince Edward Island.

9. Province of New Brunswick.

Schedule IV

(s. 24)

1. Province of Ontario

(*a*) Employment as a judge appointed by the Government of Canada.

(*b*) Employment by appointment of Her Majesty in right of Ontario, or of an agent of Her Majesty in right of Ontario, as a member of an agency, board, commission, committee or other incorporated or unincorporated body, who is paid fees or other remuneration on a *per diem* basis, or a retainer or honorarium, and who is not in the full-time employment of Her Majesty in right of Ontario or of an agent of Her Majesty in right of Ontario.

(SOR/82-784, s. 1; SOR/2013-233, s. 1.)

2. Province of Alberta

(*a*) Employment as members of the Legislative Assembly of Alberta and who have not contributed to the General Revenue Fund such contributions as are required by the *Public Service Pension Act*, being chapter 299, Revised Statutes of Alberta, 1970, as amended.

(*b*) Employment as members of Commissions, Boards or Committees by appointment of Her Majesty in right of Alberta or of an agent of Her Majesty in right of the said Province and who are paid fees or other remuneration on a *per diem* basis and who are not regularly employed by Her Majesty in right of the Province of Alberta or by an agent of Her Majesty in right of the said Province.

(*c*) Employment to provide services for which the employee is paid a retainer, an honorarium, or on a fee basis.

3. Province of Manitoba

Employment as members of boards, commissions or committees by appointment of Her Majesty in right of Manitoba or of an agent of Her Majesty in right of that province, who are paid a retainer, an honorarium or on a fee basis. (SOR/2007-55, s. 1.)

4. Province of Newfoundland

(*a*) Employment as Chairman or a member of

   (i) the Labour Relations Board of Newfoundland;

   (ii) the Apprenticeship Board of Newfoundland;

   (iii) the Minimum Wage Board of Newfoundland;

   (iv) the Conciliation Boards of Newfoundland;

   (v) the Apprenticeship Advisory and Examining Committees of Newfoundland;

   (vi) the Industrial Inquiry Commissions of Newfoundland; or

   (vii) the Boiler Inspection Advisory Committees of Newfoundland.

(*b*) Employment as Chairman of the St. John's Metropolitan Area Board.

(*c*) Employment as a member of the Boiler Inspection Board of Examiners of Newfoundland.

(*d*) Employment as

   (i) a Government of Newfoundland charring contractor;

   (ii) a part-time medical practitioner or specialist who is paid a fixed annual retainer; or

   (iii) a local road employee.

5. Province of Nova Scotia

(*a*) Employment as a member of a Board, commission or agency of Her Majesty in right of Nova Scotia who is employed otherwise than full time as such member.

(*b*) Employment to provide services for which the employee is paid a retainer, an honorarium or on a fee basis.

(*c*) [Revoked by SOR/88-638, s. 1.]

6. [8]Province of British Columbia

Employment as members of agencies, boards, commissions or committees by appointment of Her Majesty in right of British Columbia or of an agent of Her Majesty in right of that province, who are paid fees or other remuneration on a per diem basis. (SOR/99-60, s. 3.)

7. Province of Saskatchewan

(*a*) [Revoked by SOR/89-304, s. 1.]

(*b*) Employment as Judges of the Surrogate Courts of Saskatchewan.

(*c*) Employment as members of Boards, Commissions or Committees by appointment of Her Majesty in right of Saskatchewan, who are paid fees or honorariums on a *per diem* basis.

(SOR/78-591, s. 1.)

8. Province of Prince Edward Island

(*a*) Substitute and remedial teachers employed on a casual basis.

(*b*) Highway road section foremen employed on a casual basis and labourers working under their supervision.

(*c*) Persons receiving training allowances during a period of education.

9. Province of New Brunswick

---

[8] SOR 99-60, s. 3, effective on the day of registration.

Employment as a member or an employee of any of the boards, commissions or committees hereinafter listed, except the employment as a member or an employee thereof whose duties require his full time attention and who receives for performing such duties a regular salary:

(a) Advisory Board to the Children's Hospital School, Lancaster.

(b) Advisory Board — Water Authority.

(c) Advisory Committee to the Alcohol Education and Rehabilitation Division.

(d) Barbering Advisory Committee.

(e) Board of Examiners for Stationary Engineers.

(f) Business Technology Board.

(g) Cancer Advisory Committee.

(h) Film Classification Board.

(i) Chemical Technology Board.

(j) Civil Service Commission.

(k) Civil Technology Board.

(l) Community Improvement Corporation.

(m) Conciliation Board.

(n) Electrical & Electronic Technology Board.

(o) Farm Adjustment Board.

(p) Federal — Provincial Manpower Committee.

(q) Fishermen's Loan Board of New Brunswick.

(r) Fitness and Amateur Sport Scholarship and Bursary Selection Committee.

(s) Hospital Services Advisory Board.

(t) Industrial Development Board.

(u) Labour Relations Board.

(v) Land Compensation Board.

(w) Loan and Scholarship Advisory Committee.

(x) Low Pressure Gas Board of Examiners.

(y) Mechanical Technology Board.

(z) Medical Review Board.

(aa) Minimum Wage Board.

(bb) Motor Carrier Board and Public Utilities Board.

(cc) Motor Vehicle Dealer Licensing Board.

(dd) Motor Vehicle Repair (Mechanical), Barbering, Powderman, Electrical, Plumbing, Heavy Equipment Repair Trade, Refrigeration and Air Conditioning Trade and the Oil Burner Installation and Service Trade Examining Committees.

(ee) Natural Products Control Board.

(ff) New Brunswick Dairy Products Commission.

(gg) New Brunswick Development Corporation.

(hh) New Brunswick Electric Power Commission.

(ii) New Brunswick Industrial Safety Council.

(jj) New Brunswick Liquor Control Commission.

(kk) New Brunswick Liquor Licensing Board.

(ll) New Brunswick Museum Board.

(*mm*) New Brunswick Parole Board.

(*nn*) New Brunswick Water Authority Board.

(*oo*) Old Age and Blind Assistance Board.

(*pp*) Plumbing Technical Advisory Council.

(*qq*) Provincial Apprenticeship Committee and its 10 Provincial Advisory Committees.

(*rr*) Provincial Equalization and Appeal Board.

(*ss*) Provincial Planning Commission.

(*tt*) Social Assistance Commissioners.

(*uu*) Study Committee on Mental Health.

(*vv*) Tradesmen's Qualification Board.

(*ww*) Vocational Education Board.

(*xx*) Workmen's Compensation Board.

(SOR/78-591, s. 1; SOR/82-784, s. 1; 88-638, ss. 1, 2; 89-304, s. 1; SOR/99-60, s. 3; SOR/2007-55, s. 1; SOR/2013-233, s. 1.)

Schedule V

(s. 25)

1. Northwest Atlantic Fisheries Organization. (SOR/81-448, s. 1.)

2. International Pacific Salmon Fisheries Commission.

3. International North Pacific Fisheries Commission.

4. Commonwealth of Learning. (SOR/90-687, s. 1.)

5. North Pacific Marine Science Organization.

6. North Pacific Anadromous Fish Commission. (SOR/96-161, s. 2.)

(SOR/81-448, s. 1; SOR/90-687, s. 1; SOR/96-161, s. 2.)

Schedule VI

(s. 25)

1. *Northwest Atlantic Fisheries Organization* (SOR/81-448, s. 2.)

(*a*) Employment of a person who is exempt from Canadian income tax by virtue of a Tax Convention to which Canada is a party.

(*b*) Employment of a person who is exempt from Canadian income tax by virtue of paragraph 149(1)(*a*) of the *Income Tax Act*.

(*c*) Employment of a person who is exempt from Canadian income tax by virtue of an order of the Governor in council.

(*d*) Employment of a person who is not

(i) a citizen within the meaning of section 3 of the *Citizenship Act*, or

(ii) a permanent resident as defined in subsection 2(1) of the *Immigration Act*.

(SOR/96-161, s. 3.)

2. *International Pacific Salmon Fisheries Commission*

(*a*) Employment of a person who is exempt from Canadian income tax by virtue of a Tax Convention to which Canada is a party.

(*b*) Employment of a person who is exempt from Canadian income tax by virtue of paragraph 149(1)(*a*) of the *Income Tax Act.*

3. *International North Pacific Fisheries Commission*

(*a*) Employment of a person who is exempt from Canadian income tax by virtue of a Tax Convention to which Canada is a party.

(*b*) Employment of a person who is exempt from Canadian income tax by virtue of paragraph 149(1)(*a*) of the *Income Tax Act.*

4. *Commonwealth of Learning*

(*a*) Employment of a person who is an official of the Commonwealth of Learning.

(*b*) Employment of a person who is exempt from Canadian income tax by virtue of paragraph 149(1)(*a*) of the *Income Tax Act.*

5. *North Pacific Marine Science Organization*

(*a*) Employment of a person who is exempt from Canadian income tax by virtue of a Tax Convention to which Canada is a party.

(*b*) Employment of a person who is exempt from Canadian income tax by virtue of paragraph 149(1)(*a*) of the *Income Tax Act.*

(*c*) Employment of a person who is exempt from Canadian income tax by virtue of an order of the Governor in Council.

(*d*) Employment of a person who is not

    (i) a citizen within the meaning of section 3 of the *Citizenship Act*, or

    (ii) a permanent resident as defined in sub section 2(1) of the *Immigration Act*.

(SOR/96-161, s. 4.)

6. *North Pacific Anadromous Fish Commission*

(*a*) Employment of a person who is exempt from Canadian income tax by virtue of a Tax Convention to which Canada is a party.

(*b*) Employment of a person who is exempt from Canadian income tax by virtue of paragraph 149(1)(*a*) of the *Income Tax Act.*

(*c*) Employment of a person who is exempt from Canadian income tax by virtue of an order of the Governor in Council.

(*d*) Employment of a person who is not

    (i) a citizen within the meaning of section 3 of the *Citizenship Act*, or

    (ii) a permanent resident as defined in subsection 2(1) of the *Immigration Act*.

(SOR/90-687, s. 2; SOR/96-161, s. 4.)

(SOR/81-448, s. 2; SOR/90-687, s. 2; SOR/96-161, s. 4.)

Schedule VII

(s. 26)

1. New Zealand.

2. United Kingdom of Great Britain and Northern Ireland.

3. Australia.

4. Finland.

5. France. (SOR/89-304, s. 2.)

CPP REGULATIONS

6. United States. (SOR/89-304, s. 2.) — Revoked by SOR/88-239, 1. 1.

7. Denmark [Revoked by SOR/88-239, s. 1.]

8. Japan.

9. India.

10. Belgium [Revoked by SOR/88-239, s. 1.]

11. Barbados [Revoked by SOR/88-239, s. 1.]

12. Sweden [Revoked by SOR/88-239, s. 1.]

13. South Africa.

14. Federal Republic of Germany.

15. Italy [Revoked by SOR/80-877, s. 2.]

16. Ireland.

17. Trinidad and Tobago.

18. Israel. (SOR/81-197, s. 1.)

19. Antigua and Barbuda. (SOR/90-687, s. 3.)

20. Malaysia. (SOR/90-687, s. 3.)

21. Senegal. (SOR/97-34, s. 1.)

(SOR/80-877, s. 2; SOR/81-197, s. 1; SOR/88-239, s. 1; SOR/89-304, s. 2; SOR/90-687, s. 3; SOR/97-34, s. 1.)

Schedule VIII

(s. 26)

1. *New Zealand*

Employment in Canada by the Government of New Zealand of a person who
(a) is a subject or citizen of New Zealand; or
(b) is exempt from Canadian income tax by virtue of the New Zealand–Canada Tax Convention.

2. *United Kingdom of Great Britain and Northern Ireland*

Employment in Canada by the Government of the United Kingdom of Great Britain and Northern Ireland of a person who
(a) is not a citizen of Canada; or
(b) is not permanently resident in Canada.

3. *Australia*

Employment in Canada by the Government of Australia of a person who
(a) is not a citizen of Canada; or
(b) is not permanently resident in Canada.

4. *Finland*

Employment in Canada by the Government of Finland of a person who
(a) is a subject or citizen of Finland; or
(b) is exempt from Canadian income tax by virtue of the Canada–Finland Tax Convention.

5. *France*

Employment in Canada by the Government of France of a person who
(a) contributes to a pension plan of the French Republic or on behalf of whom contributions are made to a pension plan by the French Republic; or
(b) is exempt from Canadian income tax.

(SOR/89-304, s. 3.)

6. *United States*

Employment in Canada by the Government of the United States of a person who
(a) is a citizen of the United States;
(b) participates in the Civil Service Retirement System of the United States or other pension plan financed by the Government of the United States, where that person has participated in that System or plan continuously since before October 1, 1983 and has elected not to participate in the *Canada Pension Plan*; or
(c) is not a locally engaged employee of the Government of the United States.

(SOR/89-304, s. 3.)

7. *Denmark* [Revoked by SOR/88-239, s. 2.]

8. *Japan*

Employment in Canada by the Government of Japan of a person who
(a) is a national of Japan and is neither a national of nor permanently resident in Canada; or
(b) is exempt from Canadian income tax by virtue of the *Canada–Japan Income Tax Convention Act, 1965.*

9. *India*

Employment in Canada by the Government of India of a person who is exempt from Canadian income tax by virtue of paragraph 149(1)(a) or (b) of the *Income Tax Act.*

10. *Belgium* [Revoked by SOR/88-239, s. 2.]

11. *Barbados* [Revoked by SOR/88-239, s. 2.]

12. *Sweden* [Revoked by SOR/88-239, s. 2.]

13. *South Africa*

Employment in Canada by the Government of the Republic of South Africa of a person who is exempt from Canadian income tax by virtue of paragraph 149(1)(a) or (b) of the *Income Tax Act.*

14. *Federal Republic of Germany*

CPP REGULATIONS

409

Employment in Canada by the Government of the Federal Republic of Germany at its official missions and posts of a person

(*a*) who is a German national, or

(*b*) who contributes to a pension plan of the Federal Republic of Germany by virtue of a bilateral or multilateral agreement or any supranational regulations.

15. *Republic of Italy* [Revoked by SOR/80-877, s. 3.]

16. *Ireland*

Employment in Canada by the Government of Ireland of a person who

(*a*) is a citizen of Ireland and is not permanently resident in Canada; or

(*b*) is exempt from Canadian income tax by virtue of paragraph 149(1)(*a*) or (*b*) of the *Income Tax Act*.

17. *Trinidad and Tobago*

Employment in Canada by the Government of Trinidad and Tobago of a person who

(*a*) is a subject or citizen of Trinidad and Tobago and is not permanently resident in Canada; or

(*b*) is by virtue of paragraph 149(1)(*a*) or (*b*) of the *Income Tax Act* exempt from Canadian income tax.

18. *Israel*

Employment in Canada by the Government of Israel of a person who

(*a*) is a citizen of Israel and is not permanently resident in Canada; or

(*b*) is exempt from income tax by virtue of paragraph 149(1)(*a*) or (*b*) of the *Income Tax Act*.

(SOR/81-197, s. 2.)

19. *Antigua and Barbuda*

Employment in Canada by the Government of Antigua and Barbuda of a person who is exempt from Canadian income tax by virtue of paragraph 149(1)(*a*) of the *Income Tax Act*. (SOR/90-687, s. 4.)

20. *Malaysia*

Employment in Canada by the Government of Malaysia of a person who

(*a*) is exempt from Canadian income tax by virtue of paragraph 149(1)(*a*) of the *Income Tax Act*; or

(*b*) participates in the Government of Malaysia's non-contributory gratuity scheme.

(SOR/90-687, s. 4.)

21. *Senegal*

Employment in Canada by the Government of Senegal of a person who

(*a*) is a citizen of Senegal and is not permanently resident in Canada; or (*b*) is exempt from Canadian income tax by virtue of paragraph 149(1)(*a*) or (*b*) of the *Income Tax Act.*

(SOR/97-34, s. 2.)

(SOR/80-877, s. 3; SOR/81-197, s. 2; SOR/85-1087, s. 1; SOR/88-239, s. 2; SOR/89-304, s. 3; SOR/90-687, s. 4; SOR/97-34, s. 2.)

Schedule IX

(Section 86)

Country	Agreement
Antigua and Barbuda	Agreement on Social Security between Canada and Antigua and Barbuda, signed at Ottawa on September 2, 1992
Australia	Reciprocal Agreement on Social Security between the Government of Canada and the Government of Australia, signed at Canberra on July 4, 1988
	Protocol amending the Reciprocal Agreement on Social Security between the Government of Canada and the Government of Australia, signed at Ottawa, on October 11, 1990
Austria (Republic of)	Agreement on Social Security between the Government of Canada and the Government of the Republic of Austria, signed at Vienna on February 24, 1987
	Supplementary Agreement to the Agreement on Social Security between Canada and the Republic of Austria, signed at Vienna on September 12, 1995
Barbados	Agreement on Social Security between the Government of Canada and the Government of Barbados, signed at Bridgetown on February 11, 1985
Belgium	Agreement on Social Security between the Government of Canada and the Government of Belgium, signed at Brussels on May 10, 1984
Chile (Republic of)	Agreement on Social Security between the Government of Canada and the Government of the Republic of Chile, signed on November 18, 1996
Croatia (Republic of)	Agreement on Social Security between the Government of Canada and the Government of the Republic of Croatia, signed on April 22, 1998
Cyprus (Republic of)	Agreement on Social Security between Canada and the Republic of Cyprus, signed at Ottawa on January 24, 1990
Denmark	Agreement on Social Security between the Government of Canada and the Government of Denmark, signed at Copenhagen on April 12, 1985
Dominica (Commonwealth of)	Agreement on Social Security between the Government of Canada and the Government of the Commonwealth of Dominica, signed at Roseau on January 14, 1988

SCHEDULE IX — *continued*

Country	Agreement
Finland (Republic of)	Agreement on Social Security between the Government of Canada and the Government of the Republic of Finland, signed at Ottawa on October 28, 1986
France	Agreement on Social Security between the Government of Canada and the Government of France, signed at Ottawa on February 9, 1979
Germany (Federal Republic of)	Agreement on Social Security between the Government of Canada and the Government of the Federal Republic of Germany, signed at Bonn on November 14, 1985
Greece (Hellenic Republic)	Agreement on Social Security between Canada and the Hellenic Republic, signed at Toronto on November 10, 1995
Grenada	Agreement on Social Security between the Government of Canada and the Government of Grenada, signed on January 8, 1998
Guernsey	Agreement on Social Security between Jersey, Guernsey and Canada, in force in Canada as of January 1, 1994
Iceland	Agreement on Social Security between the Government of Canada and the Government of Iceland, signed at Gimli on June 25, 1988
Ireland	Agreement on Social Security between Canada and Ireland, signed at Ottawa on November 29, 1990
Israel	Interim Agreement on Social Security between the Government of Canada and the Government of Israel, signed at Jerusalem on April 9, 2000
Italy (Italian Republic)	Agreement on Social Security between Canada and Italy, signed at Toronto on November 17, 1977 Agreement on Social Security between Canada and the Italian Republic, signed at Rome on May 22, 1995
Jamaica	Agreement between the Government of Canada and the Government of Jamaica with respect to Social Security, signed at Kingston, Jamaica on January 10, 1983
Jersey	Agreement on Social Security between Jersey, Guernsey and Canada, in force in Canada as of January 1, 1994

CPP REGULATIONS

413

SCHEDULE IX — *continued*

Country	Agreement
Korea (Republic of)	Agreement on Social Security between Canada and the Republic of Korea, signed at Seoul on January 10, 1997
Luxembourg	Agreement on Social Security between the Government of Canada and the Government of Luxembourg, signed at Ottawa on May 22, 1986
Malta (Republic of)	Agreement on Social Security between Canada and the Republic of Malta, signed at Toronto on April 4, 1991
Mexico (United Mexican States)	Agreement on Social Security between Canada and the United Mexican States, signed at Ottawa on April 25, 1995
Morocco (Kingdom of)	Convention on Social Security between the Government of Canada and the Government of the Kingdom of Morocco, signed on July 1, 1998
Netherlands (Kingdom of the)	Agreement on Social Security between the Government of Canada and the Government of the Kingdom of the Netherlands, signed at The Hague on February 26, 1987
New Zealand	Agreement on Social Security between Canada and New Zealand, signed on April 9, 1996
Norway (Kingdom of)	Agreement on Social Security between the Government of Canada and the Government of the Kingdom of Norway, signed at Oslo on November 12, 1985
Philippines (Republic of the)	Agreement on Social Security between Canada and the Republic of the Philippines, signed at Winnipeg on September 9, 1994 Supplementary Agreement to the Agreement on Social Security between the Government of Canada and the Government of the Republic of the Philippines, signed at Winnipeg on November 13, 1999
Portugal	Agreement between Canada and Portugal with respect to Social Security, signed at Toronto on December 15, 1980
Saint Lucia	Agreement on Social Security between the Government of Canada and the Government of Saint Lucia, signed at Castries on January 5, 1987
Saint-Vincent and the Grenadines	Agreement on Social Security between the Government of Canada and the Government of Saint-Vincent and the Grenadines, signed on January 6, 1998

SCHEDULE IX — continued

Country	Agreement
Slovenia (Republic of)	Agreement on Social Security between the Government of Canada and the Government of the Republic of Slovenia, signed on May 17, 1998
Spain	Protocol to the Convention on Social Security between Canada and Spain, signed at Ottawa on October 19, 1995
St. Kitts and Nevis (Federation of)	Agreement on Social Security between Canada and the Federation of St. Kitts and Nevis, signed at Ottawa on August 17, 1992
Sweden	Agreement on Social Security between the Government of Canada and the Government of Sweden, signed at Stockholm on April 10, 1985
Switzerland (Swiss Confederation)	Convention on Social Security between Canada and the Swiss Confederation, signed at Ottawa on February 24, 1994
Trinidad and Tobago (Republic of)	Agreement on Social Security between the Government of Canada and the Government of the Republic of Trinidad and Tobago, signed on April 9, 1997
Turkey (Republic of)	Agreement on Social Security between the Government of Canada and the Government of the Republic of Turkey, signed on June 19, 1998
United Kingdom of Great Britain and Northern Ireland	Memorandum of Understanding between the Government of Canada and the Government of the United Kingdom of Great Britain and Northern Ireland concerning Co-operation and Mutual Assistance in the Administration of Social Security Programmes, signed on January 16, 1997
United States of America	Agreement between the Government of Canada and the Government of the United States of America with respect to Social Security, signed at Ottawa on March 11, 1981
	Supplementary Agreement between the Government of Canada and the Government of the United States of America with respect to Social Security, signed at Ottawa on May 10, 1983
	Second Supplementary Agreement amending the Agreement between the Government of Canada and the Government of the United States of America with respect to Social Security, signed on May 28, 1996

SCHEDULE IX — continued

Country	Agreement
United States of America (*cont'd.*)	Administrative Understanding on Mutual Assistance, concluded pursuant to the Agreement between the Government of Canada and the Government of the United States of America with respect to Social Security and signed on December 4, 1996
Uruguay (Eastern Republic of)	Agreement on Social Security between the Government of Canada and the Government of the Eastern Republic of Uruguay, signed at Ottawa on June 2, 1999

(Repealed by SOR/96-522, s. 22; added by SOR/2000-411, s. 17.)

Canada Pension Plan — Prescribed Province Pension Regulations

C.R.C. 1978, c. 391.

Regulations Prescribing the Province of Quebec as a Province Providing a Comprehensive Pension Plan

Short Title

1. These Regulations may be cited as the *Prescribed Province Pension Regulations.*

General

2. The Province of Quebec is hereby prescribed, for the purposes of the *Canada Pension Plan*, as a province the government of which has, before the 30th day after April 3, 1965, signified the intention of such province to provide for the establishment and operation in that province, in lieu of the operation therein of the *Canada Pension Plan*, of a plan of old age pensions and supplementary benefits providing for the making of contributions thereunder, commencing with the year 1966 and providing for the payment of benefits thereunder comparable to those provided by the *Canada Pension Plan.*

Canada Pension Plan (Social Insurance Numbers) Regulations

C.R.C. 1978, c. 386 as amended by SOR/90-444, s. 1, gazetted August 15, 1990 and effective July 27, 1990; SOR/2000-133, gazetted April 12, 2000 and effective March 30, 2000; SOR/2013-84, effective April 30, 2013.

Regulations Respecting the Assigning of Social Insurance Numbers

Short Title

1. These Regulations may be cited as the *Canada Pension Plan (Social Insurance Numbers) Regulations.*

Interpretation

2. In these Regulations,

"Act" **means the** *Canada Pension Plan;*

"Card" **means a Social Insurance Number Card;**

"Commission" **means the Canada Employment Insurance Commission; (SOR/2000-133, s. 5.)**

"local office of the Commission" **means an office established by the Commission in any locality, and includes any office designated as such by the Commission and, in relation to an employer, the nearest local office servicing the area of their place of business and, in relation to any other person, the local office nearest to their residence; (SOR/2013-84, s. 7(a).)**

"Minister" **(Repealed by SOR/2013-84, s. 1, in force April 30, 2013.)**

(SOR/2000-133, s. 5; SOR/2013-84, ss. 1, 7.)

Manner of Making Application

3. (1) Every individual who is required by the Act to file an application with the Minister or to apply to the Minister for the assignment to him of a Social Insurance Number shall do so by delivering or mailing to a local office of the Commission, an application, in the form prescribed by the Minister for that purpose, containing

    (a) **their full name; (SOR/2013-84, s. 7(b).)**

    (b) **their name at birth if it differs from their name at the time of application; (SOR/2013-84, s. 7(b).)**

    (c) **their date of birth; (SOR/2013-84, s. 7(b).)**

    (d) **their place of birth; (SOR/2013-84, s. 7(b).)**

    (e) **their mother's surname at her birth; (SOR/2013-84, s. 7(b).)**

    (f) **the first given name of their father; and (SOR/2013-84, s. 7(b).)**

(g) any other information required in the form prescribed by the Minister.

(2) Every individual who changes their name, by reason of marriage or otherwise, and who is required by the Act to inform the Minister of their new name shall do so by delivering or mailing to a local office of the Commission a notification, in the form prescribed for that purpose, containing (SOR/2013-84, s. 2(1).)

    (a) the information required by subsection (1) in respect of an application for the assignment of a Social Insurance Number; (SOR/2013-84, s. 2(2).)

    (b) their Social Insurance Number; and (SOR/2013-84, s. 7(b).)

    (c) their full name before the change of name. (SOR/2013-84, s. 7(b).)

(3) Every individual whose Card has been lost or destroyed may apply to the Minister for a new Card by delivering or mailing to a local office of the Commission an application, in the form prescribed for that purpose, containing (SOR/2013-84, s. 2(3).)

    (a) the information required by subsection (1) in respect of an application for the assignment of a Social Insurance Number; and (SOR/2013-84, s. 2(4).)

    (b) their Social Insurance Number, or if it is unknown, a statement that they were previously assigned a Social Insurance Number. (SOR/2013-84, s. 2(4).)

(4) Every individual who expects to be an individual required by the Act to file an application with the Minister or to apply to the Minister for the assignment to them of a Social Insurance Number may, if they have not earlier been assigned a Social Insurance Number, make application, on the form and in the manner specified in subsection (1), for the assignment to them of a Social Insurance Number. (SOR/2013-84, s. 2(5).)

(SOR/2013-84, ss. 2, 7.)

Sources of Application Forms

4. Applications in the form prescribed by the Minister for the purposes of section 3 may be obtained from

    (a) any post office;

    (b) any local office of the Commission;

    (c) any office of the Department of National Revenue; and

    (d) any office of the Department of Human Resources and Skills Development. (SOR/2013-84, s. 3.)

(SOR/2000-133, s. 6; SOR/2013-84, s. 3.)

Duties of Employer

5. An employer who requires an employee to inform them of their Social Insurance Number shall provide the employee with the appropriate form to apply for a Social Insurance Number or Card if the employer ascertains that the employee

    (a) has not had a Social Insurance Number assigned to them;

    (b) has changed their name since their Social Insurance Number was assigned; or

    (c) has lost their Social Insurance Card or it has been destroyed.

(SOR/90-444, s. 1; SOR/2013-84, s. 4.)

6. (1) If an employee fails to inform their employer of their Social Insurance Number within the period set out in subsection 98(6) of the Act, the employer shall, within three days after the expiry of the period, report the circumstances of the failure to the local office of the Commission and provide it with the information necessary to identify the employee. (SOR/2013-84, s. 5.)

(2) If an employee who has been reported under subsection (1) subsequently informs the employer of their Social Insurance Number, the employer shall immediately notify the local office of the Commission. (SOR/2013-84, s. 5.)

(SOR/2013-84, s. 5.)

Authority of Minister

7. The Minister or the Minister of National Revenue may cause a Social Insurance Number to be assigned to an individual who has not been assigned a Social Insurance Number.

(SOR/2013-84, s. 6.)

8. The Minister or the Minister of National Revenue may cause a Card to be issued to an individual to whom a Social Insurance Number was caused to be assigned under section 7.

(SOR/2013-84, s. 6.)

CPP REGULATIONS

Calculation of Contribution Rates Regulations, 2007

SOR/2008-50.

Interpretation

1. The following definitions apply in these Regulations.

"Act" means the Canada Pension Plan.

"contributory earnings" means the contributory salary and wages and the contributory self-employed earnings referred to in sections 12 and 13, respectively, of the Act.

"increased or new benefits" means the increased or new benefits referred to in paragraph 113.1(4)(*d*) of the Act.

"payments" means the payments charged to the Canada Pension Plan Account under subsection 108(3) of the Act excluding any payments in respect of any increased or new benefits that resulted in a non-zero contribution rate under section 3.

"review period" means any three-year period for which the Chief Actuary prepares a report set out in subsection 115(1) of the Act.

Calculation of Contribution Rate

2. For the purposes of subparagraph 115(1.1)(*c*)(i) of the Act, the contribution rate is the one that is the smallest multiple of 0.001 percentage points and that results in a projected ratio of assets to expenditures for the 60th year after the review period that is not lower than the projected ratio of assets to expenditures for the 10th year after the review period which ratios are determined in accordance with the formula

$$(A + B - C) / D$$

where

A is the projected balance in the Canada Pension Plan Account on December 31 of that year;

B is the projected assets of the Investment Board on December 31 of that year;

C is the projected assets on December 31 of that year in respect of any increased or new benefits that resulted in a non-zero contribution rate calculated under section 3; and

D is the projected payments for the following year.

3. (1) For the purposes of subparagraph 115(1.1)(*c*)(ii) of the Act, the contribution rate with respect to any increased or new benefits is equal to the sum of the permanent increase in the contribution rate calculated in accordance with subsection

423

(2) and the temporary increase in the contribution rate calculated in accordance with subsection (3).

(2) The permanent increase in the contribution rate is calculated, in respect of contributory earnings for the year that, and the years after, the increased or new benefits come into effect, as the ratio of the present value of the projected extra costs related to the increased or new benefits in respect of those contributory earnings to the present value of those contributory earnings.

(3) The temporary increase in the contribution rate for a period not exceeding 15 years is calculated, in respect of contributory earnings for the years before the increased or new benefits come into effect, as the ratio of the present value of the projected extra costs related to the increased or new benefits in respect of those contributory earnings to the present value of contributory earnings for the same period as the temporary increase in the contribution rate.

(4) The present values referred to in this section shall be calculated as of the day on which the increased or new benefits come into effect.

(5) If the contribution rate calculated in accordance with subsection (1) is less than 0.02 percentage points, the contribution rate shall be deemed to equal zero.

Rounding of Amounts

4. If a contribution rate determined under section 2 and subsection 3(1) is not a multiple of 0.01 percentage points, it shall be rounded to the nearest multiple of 0.01 or, if the amount is equidistant from the two multiples, to the higher multiple.

Repeals

5. The Calculation of Contribution Rates Regulations are repealed.

6. The Calculation of Default Contribution Rates Regulations are repealed.

Coming into Force

7. These Regulations come into force on the day on which section 14 of *An Act to Amend the Canada Pension Plan and the Old Age Security Act*, chapter 11 of the Statutes of Canada, 2007, comes into force.

Delegation of Powers (Canada Pension Plan, Part I) Regulations

C.R.C. 1978, c. 387, as amended by SOR/78-731, gazetted September 27, 1978 and effective September 15, 1978; SOR/79-105, gazetted February 14, 1979 and effective January 26, 1979; SOR/80-828, gazetted November 12, 1980 and effective October 29, 1980; SOR/81-668, gazetted September 9, 1981 and effective August 24, 1981, SOR/82-446, gazetted May 12, 1982 and effective April 28, 1982; SOR/83-725, gazetted October 12, 1982 and effective September 26, 1983; SOR/84-410, gazetted June 13, 1984 and effective May 31, 1984; SOR/86-433, gazetted April 30, 1986 and effective April 11, 1986; SOR/87-700, gazetted December 23, 1987 and effective December 4, 1987; SOR/92-377, gazetted July 1, 1992 and effective June 11, 1992.

Regulations Providing for the Delegation of Powers Conferred by the Canada Pension Plan Upon the Minister of National Revenue

Short Title

1. These Regulations may be cited as the Delegation of Powers (Canada Pension Plan, Part I) Regulations.

Interpretation

2. In these Regulations,

"Act" means the *Canada Pension Plan*;

"Minister" means the Minister of National Revenue.

Delegation

3. The following persons may exercise all the powers and perform all the duties of the Minister under Part I of the Act:

    (*a*) the Deputy Minister of National Revenue for Taxation; and

    (*b*) an official holding a position of Assistant Deputy Minister of National Revenue for Taxation.

4. An officer holding the position of Director, Taxation, in a District Office of the Department of National Revenue, Taxation, may exercise the powers of the Minister under subsections 23(5) and (10), section 24 and subsections 25(4), (5) and (7), 30(2) and 35(1) of the Act.

5. The Director, Appeals and Referrals Division, the Director, Policy and Programs Division, the Chief, the Determination and Appeals Section, or an officer holding the position of Chief of Appeals in a District Office of the Department of National Revenue, Taxation, may exercise the powers and perform the duties of the Minister under sections 27 and 29 of the Act.

6. The Director General, Revenue Collection Programs Directorate of the Department of National Revenue, Taxation, may exercise the powers of the Minister under subsections 11(3) and (6), 23(10) and 25(5) of the Act.

7. The Director General, Assessment of Returns Directorate of the Department of National Revenue, Taxation, may exercise the powers of the Minister under subsections 25(5) and 30(2) of the Act.

8. An officer holding the position of Director in a Taxation Centre of the Department of National Revenue, Taxation, may exercise the powers of the Minister under subsections 23(5), 25(4), (5) and (7), 30(2) and 35(1) of the Act.

9. The Director, Source Deductions Division of the Department of National Revenue, Taxation, may exercise the powers and perform the duties of the Minister under subsections 11(3) and (6) of the Act.

10. The Chief, Coverage Policy and Legislation Section of the Department of National Revenue, Taxation, may perform the duties of the Minister under subsection 11(3) of the Act.

11. Where a power is conferred or a duty is imposed on the Minister by a provision of the *Income Tax Act* and that provision is made applicable, with such modifications as the circumstances may require, to the Act, by subsection 23(2) or (11) or section 36 thereof, as the case may be, the power or duty may, for the purposes of the Act, be exercised or performed by any officer to whom the power or duty is delegated by the Income Tax Regulations.

Rules of Procedure of the Pension Appeals Board for Appeals under Section 83 of the Canada Pension Plan

C.R.C. 1978, c. 390, as amended by SOR/90-811, gazetted December 5, 1990 and effective November 22, 1990; SOR/92-18, gazetted January 1, 1992 and effective December 31, 1991; SOR/96-524, gazetted December 5, 1996 and effective January 1, 1997; SOR/2000-133, gazetted April 12, 2000 and effective March 30, 2000; SOR/2010-45, gazetted March 17, 2010, effective February 23, 2010.

Short Title

1. These Rules may be cited as the Pension Appeals Board Rules of Procedure (Benefits).

Interpretation

2. In these Rules,

"Act" means the *Canada Pension Plan*;

"appellant" **means a person, or an agency referred to in section 74 of the *Canada Pension Plan Regulations*, who makes an application under subsection 83(1) of the Act for leave to appeal or for an extension of time within which to apply for leave to appeal;**

"Board" **means the Pension Appeals Board;**

"Chairman" **means the Chairman of the Board who is appointed under subsection 83(5) of the Act;**

"Commissioner" **means the Commissioner of Review Tribunals who is appointed under subsection 82(5) of the Act;**

"Director" **[Repealed by SOR/96-524, s. 1(1).];**

"interested party" **means [Repealed by SOR/96-524, s. 1(1).];**

"Minister" **means the Minister of Human Resources Development; (SOR/2000-133, s. 7.)**

"party" **means the appellant or the respondent who was a party to the proceedings before a Review Tribunal that rendered a decision appealed to the Board, and includes any person added as a party under subsection 83(10) of the Act; (SOR/96-524, s. 1(2).)**

"Registrar" **means the Registrar of the Board;**

"Vice-Chairman" means the Vice-Chairman of the Board who is appointed under subsection 83(5) of the Act.

(SOR/90-811, s. 2; SOR/92-18, s. 1; SOR/96-524, s. 1; SOR/2000-133, s. 7.)

Application

3. These Rules apply to appeals brought pursuant to section 83 of the Act.

(SOR/90-811, s. 3.)

Application for Leave to Appeal

4. An appeal from a decision of a Review Tribunal shall be commenced by serving on the Chairman or Vice-Chairman an application for leave to appeal, which shall be substantially in the form set out in Schedule I and shall contain

 (a) the date of the decision of the Review Tribunal, the name of the place at which the decision was rendered and the date on which the decision was communicated to the appellant; (SOR/92-18, s. 2.)

 (b) the full name and postal address of the appellant;

 (c) the name of an agent or representative, if any, on whom service of documents may be made, and his full postal address;

 (d) the grounds upon which the appellant relies to obtain leave to appeal; and

 (e) a statement of the allegations of fact, including any reference to the statutory provisions and constitutional provisions, reasons the appellant intends to submit and documentary evidence the appellant intends to rely on in support of the appeal. (SOR/96-524, s. 2.)

(SOR/92-18, s. 2; SOR/96-524, s. 2.)

Extension of Time

5. An application for an extension of time within which to apply for leave to appeal a decision of a Review Tribunal shall be served on the Chairman or Vice-Chairman and shall set out the information required by paragraphs 4(a) to (e) and the grounds on which the extension is sought.

(SOR/92-18, s. 3.)

Making of Applications

6. (1) An application under section 4 or 5 shall be made either by the appellant, on the appellant's own behalf, or in the name of the appellant by a representative, whose authority shall be indicated by the representative.

(2) An application served on the Chairman or Vice-Chairman pursuant to section 4 may be deemed by the Chairman or Vice-Chairman to be an application properly made for the purpose of section 5.

(SOR/92-18, s. 3.)

Disposition of Applications

7. An application under section 4 or 5 shall be disposed of *ex parte*, unless the Chairman or Vice-Chairman otherwise directs.

Information

8. (1) On receipt of an application for leave to appeal a decision of a Review Tribunal, the Registrar shall notify the Commissioner in writing that such an application has been filed.

(2) The Commissioner, after receiving a notification under subsection (1), shall provide to the Registrar, before the end of the third working day following the day on which the notification was received, the following:

(a) the names and addresses of the parties to the proceedings before the Review Tribunal;

(b) the decision of the Review Tribunal and the reasons therefor; and

(c) the documentary evidence that was filed with the Review Tribunal.

(SOR/92-18, s. 3.)

9. (1) The Chairman or Vice-Chairman may request the appellant or any party to produce documents or information required for the purpose of the granting or refusal of leave to appeal or an extension of time within which to apply for leave to appeal. (SOR/96-524, s. 8(a).)

(2) The appellant may produce any documents that the appellant considers useful in support of the application under section 4 or 5.

(SOR/92-18, s. 3; SOR/96-524, s. 8.)

Appeals

10. (1) Where leave to appeal is granted, the Registrar shall forthwith notify every party, in writing, of the granting of leave to appeal and send to every such party, other than the appellant, a copy of the notice of appeal together with a copy of any documents submitted in support of the appeal. (SOR/96-524, s. 8(b).)

(2) Where an interested party who receives a copy of a notice of appeal pursuant to subsection (1) wishes to be heard on the hearing of the appeal, that party shall, within thirty days after the day on which the copy of the notice of appeal was received, or such longer time as the Chairman or Vice-Chairman may allow, file with the Registrar a reply. (SOR/96-524, s. 8(b).)

(3) A reply referred to in subsection (2) shall contain

(a) a statement admitting or denying the allegations of fact in the notice of appeal; and

(b) a statement of any further allegations of fact and of the statutory provisions and reasons on which the party intends to rely. (SOR/96-524, s. 8(b).)

(4) On receipt of the reply of any party, the Registrar shall forward a copy of that reply to every other party to the appeal. (SOR/96-524, s. 3.)

(SOR/92-18, s. 3; SOR/96-524, ss. 3, 8.)

Notice of Motion

10.1. (1) Any matter that arises, in the course of an appeal or seeking leave to appeal, that can be considered in advance of the hearing of the appeal without the personal appearance of the parties and requires a decision or order of the board, may be brought before the Chairman or Vice-Chairman by notice of motion.

CPP REGULATIONS

(2) A notice of motion shall

(*a*) be in writing in any form;

(*b*) state the precise relief sought and the grounds to be argued, including a reference to any statutory provision or any rule contained in these Rules, and lists the documentary evidence to be used; and

(*c*) shall be accompanied by an affidavit verifying the facts that the applicant relies upon and all documentary evidence related thereto. Any other party may file an affidavit in reply.

(3) A notice of motion and all accompanying documents and representations of a party shall be filed with the Registrar and shall be served on every other party to the appeal not later that 10 days prior to the hearing of the appeal. A party opposing the motion shall file with the Registrar and shall serve on every other party to the appeal not later than five clear days prior to the hearing of the appeal any affidavit or written representations upon which the party intends to rely.

(4) A notice of motion may be disposed of by the Chairman or the Vice-Chairman without the requirement of an oral hearing, unless the Chairman or Vice-Chairman otherwise directs.

(5) A decision or order on a notice of motion shall be made and conveyed to the parties to the appeal not later than three days prior to the date set for the hearing of the appeal. Written reasons shall be issued on the request of any party to the appeal.

(6) Despite subsections (2) to (5), a notice of motion in connection with a matter that has not been served on a party prior to the commencement of the hearing of the appeal may be brought orally at the hearing and shall be disposed of in accordance with such procedures as the Board may direct.

(SOR/96-524, s. 4.)

10.2. (1) Where the constitutional validity, applicability or operability of any provision of the Act or any regulation made thereunder is to be put in issue before the Board in relation to a matter under appeal to the Board, the party raising the issue shall, within 60 days after the date that notice granting leave to appeal is received, file with the Registrar four copies of a brief containing a concise memorandum of the points to be argued and four copies of the authorities upon which the party intends to rely. The party shall also serve, at the same time, a copy of the brief and of the authorities on every other party to the appeal.

(2) The party shall, at least 10 days before the date set for the hearing of the appeal, also serve notice of the issue referred to in subsection (1) on the persons referred to in subsection 57(1) of the *Federal Courts Act* and provide a copy and proof of service of that notice to the Registrar. (SOR/2010-45, s. 14(1).)

(3) Within 30 days after the date of receipt of the brief referred to in subsection (1), the other parties shall file with the Registrar four copies of a brief containing a concise memorandum of the points to be argued and four copies of the authorities upon which they intend to rely. They shall also serve, at the same time, a copy of the brief and of the authorities on every other party to the appeal. (SOR/2010-45, s. 14(2).)

(4) Where the proof of service required by subsection (2) has not been provided in accordance with that subsection, the Board may, on the request of any party or on its own motion, adjourn the hearing. (SOR/2010-45, s. 14(2).)

(SOR/96-524, s. 4; SOR/2010-45, s. 14.)

11. (1) [Revoked by SOR/92-18, s. 3.]

(2) [Revoked by SOR/92-18, s. 3.]

Hearing of the Case

12. (1) After the time for filing a reply under subsection 10(2) has expired, the matter shall be deemed to be an action before the Board and, unless the Chairman or Vice-Chairman otherwise orders, ready for hearing. (SOR/92-18, s. 4.)

(2) The Board may, upon application by any party to an appeal, or of its own motion, appoint the time and place for the hearing of the appeal.

(3) The Registrar shall notify all parties to an appeal of the time and place appointed for the hearing of the appeal at least 20 days before the date so appointed.

(4) The Board may, upon application by any party to an appeal, or of its own motion, adjourn an appeal on such terms as in its opinion the circumstances of the case require.

(SOR/92-18, s. 4.)

13. (1) [Revoked by SOR/92-18, s. 5.]

(2) [Revoked by SOR/92-18, s. 5.]

Consolidation and Joinder

14. When there are two or more appeals, whether under the Act or under any provincial law referred to in section 85 of the Act, the Board may, on application by any party, or of its own motion, if it appears (SOR/96-524, s. 8(c).)

(*a*) that some common question of law or fact arises in both or all the appeals, or

(*b*) that for some other reason it is desirable in the interests of justice,

order such appeals to be consolidated on such terms as it deems fit, or may order the appeals to be heard at the same time, or consecutively, or may order any appeal to be stayed until the determination of any other appeal.

(SOR/90-811, s. 4; SOR/92-18, s. 6; SOR/96-524, s. 8(c).)

Discovery

15. (1) After the time limited for filing a reply has expired, any party to an appeal may apply to the Chairman, a member of the Board or the Registrar for an order

(*a*) directing any other party to the appeal to make discovery of such of the documents that are or have been in his possession relating to any matter in question therein;

(*b*) permitting him to examine for the purpose of discovery any party to the appeal; or

(*c*) directing or permitting both the discovery and examination described in paragraphs (*a*) and (*b*).

(2) The Chairman, a member of the Board or the Registrar may, on receipt of an application made pursuant to subsection (1), make such order as in his opinion the circumstances of the case require and, without restricting the generality of the foregoing, may in the order

CPP REGULATIONS

(*a*) specify the form of the affidavit to be used for the production of documents;

(*b*) designate the person to be examined, where the party is a corporation or unincorporated association;

(*c*) designate the person before whom the examination is to be conducted and the manner in which it is to be conducted; and

(*d*) provide for the use that may be made of the discovery at the hearing of the appeal.

——————————— Notes ———————————

Case Law

Andrews v. Canada (Attorney General), 2011 FCA 75

A claimant is not entitled to discovery for the purpose of finding someone in the Ministry who would say that he was disabled before the date of his deemed disability. No one would have the requisite statutory authority to conclude that he was disabled before the date determined by the Review Tribunal.

———————————————

Evidence

16. (1) The Board may by subpoena summon any person to appear before it and may require them to give evidence under oath and to produce any documents that it considers necessary. (SOR/2010-45, s. 15.)

(2) A subpoena in the form set out in Schedule II or III, as applicable, may be issued by the Registrar in blank and may be completed by a party to an appeal or their solicitor, and any number of names may be inserted in the subpoena. (SOR/2010-45, s. 15.)

(3) Witnesses shall be examined orally upon oath at the hearing of an appeal but, prior to the hearing or at any time during the hearing, any party to the appeal may apply to the Board for an order permitting that all facts or any particular fact or facts may be proven other than by oral evidence and the Board may make such order as in its opinion the circumstances of the case require. (SOR/2010-45, s. 15.)

(SOR/2010-45, s. 15.)

17. Any person swearing an affidavit to be used in an appeal may be requested to appear before a person appointed by the Chairman or a member of the Board for that purpose to be cross-examined thereon.

18. A hearing of an appeal shall be public unless the Board in special circumstances orders the case to be heard *in camera.*

18.1. At any time the Board, the Chairman or the Vice-Chairman, as the case might be, may, on their own initiative or at the request of any party, adjourn a hearing of an appeal on such terms, if any, as are just, including adjourning it until a decision has been rendered in another case before the Board or before any other court in Canada in which the issue is the same or substantially the same as the issue to be raised in the proceeding.

(SOR/96-524, s. 5.)

Withdrawals and Agreements

19. An application made or an appeal commenced under these Rules may at any time be withdrawn in whole or in part by the appellant on notification in writing to the Registrar, who shall forthwith inform the other parties of the withdrawal.

(SOR/92-18, s. 7.)

19.1. The Board may dispose of an appeal in accordance with any agreement made between the parties to the appeal, signed by them and filed with the Registrar.

(SOR/92-18, s. 7.)

Decisions

20. (1) The reasons for a decision of the Board on an appeal shall be in writing and shall be deposited with the Registrar who shall draw up and enter the decision and shall forthwith send by registered mail a copy of the decision and the reasons therefor to the parties to the appeal.

(2) The Registrar may arrange for the publication of the decisions of the Board, or a digest thereof, in such form and manner as the Board deems proper.

Service of Documents

21. (1) The service of any documents provided for in these Rules shall be effected by personal service or by letter addressed

(*a*) in the case of the Chairman, the Vice-Chairman, the Board or the Registrar, to the Registrar, Pension Appeals Board, Ottawa; (SOR/92-18, s. 8.)

(*b*) in the case of the Minister, to the address of the Minister's representative, as provided in the notice of appeal or in the reply to the notice of appeal, as the case may be; (SOR/96-524, s. 7(1).)

(*c*) in the case of the appellant or the respondent, other than the Minister, subject to subsection (2), to

(i) the address for service given in his application for leave to appeal or;

(ii) where no address for service is given in the application for leave to appeal, to the postal or other address given therein or in any written communication made by the appellant or respondent to the Board; and

(*d*) in the case of any other person, to the address given in the latest written communication made by that person to the Board or the Minister. (SOR/96-524, s. 7(2).)

(2) Any party to an appeal may in writing notify the Board and any other party of a change of address which address shall thereafter be that party's address for service.

(3) The date of service shall be deemed to be the date of mailing or when personal service is effected.

(4) Notwithstanding paragraphs (1)(*a*) to (*c*), the Registrar may in a particular case accept any other means of service that he considers appropriate.

(SOR/92-18, s. 8; SOR/96-524, s. 7.)

Non-Compliance with Rules

22. (1) Non-compliance with any of these Rules or with any rule of practice for the time being in force shall not render any proceedings void unless the Board so directs, but such proceedings may be set aside either wholly or in part as irregular and may be amended or otherwise dealt with in such manner and upon such terms as in the opinion of the Board the circumstances of the case require.

CPP REGULATIONS

(2) Where an application is made to set aside a proceeding for irregularity, the grounds therefor shall be stated clearly in the application.

23. [Revoked by SOR/92-18, s. 9.]

Quebec Appeals

24. Notwithstanding anything in these Rules, the procedure to be followed on any appeal to the Board under section 196 of the *Québec Pension Plan* shall be the *Rules of Procedure of the Review Commission* prescribed by Order in Council of the Lieutenant Governor in Council of the Province of Quebec, No. 1465-72 dated May 31, 1972, as amended from time to time.

Schedule I

(s. 4)

(Application for Leave to Appeal and Notice of Appeal)

IN THE MATTER of an appeal to the Pension Appeals Board pursuant to the *Canada Pension Plan* from the decision of a Review Tribunal rendered at _____ on the _____ day of _____ 20 _____.

_____
(Name of Appellant)

_____
(Name of Respondent)

APPLICATION FOR LEAVE TO APPEAL AND NOTICE OF APPEAL

To the Chairman/Vice-Chairman,
Pension Appeals Board,
Ottawa:

The above-mentioned decision was communicated to me on _____.

I am dissatisfied with the above-mentioned decision and hereby request leave to appeal and, if leave is granted, hereby appeal therefrom on the following grounds:

If leave is granted, the following is a statement of allegations of fact, the statutory provisions and the reasons which I intend to submit in support of my appeal to establish that the decision should be reversed or amended.

The name and full postal address of my agent or representative, if any, upon whom service of documents may be made are as follows:

DATED AT

on the _____ day of _____ 20 _____.

_____
(Signature of Appellant or Agent Representative)

_____
(Address for service of documents)

(SOR/92-18, s. 10; SOR/2010-45, s. 16.)

CPP REGULATIONS

Schedule II

(s. 16)

(Subpoena to testify)

THE PENSION APPEALS BOARD

To:

1. _____

2. _____

3. _____

4. _____

You are hereby required under the provisions of the *Pension Appeals Board Rules of Procedure (Benefits)* to appear personally before the

PENSION APPEALS BOARD

at ....
on the .... day of ....
.... o'clock in the .... noon, to testify
the truth according to your knowledge in an appeal pending in the Pension Appeals
Board, wherein .... is Appellant and ....
is Respondent, on the part of

Registrar,
PENSION APPEALS BOARD

(SOR/2010-45, s. 17.)

Schedule III

(s. 16)

(Subpoena to produce)

THE PENSION APPEALS BOARD

To:

1. _____

2. _____

3. _____

4. _____

You are hereby required under the provisions of the *Pension Appeals Board Rules of Procedure (Benefits)* to appear personally before the

PENSION APPEALS BOARD

at ....
on the .... day of ....
.... o'clock in the .... noon, to testify the truth according to your knowledge in an appeal pending in the Pension Appeals Board, wherein .... is Appellant and ....
is Respondent, on the part of ....
.... and to bring with you and there and then produce ....

Registrar,
PENSION APPEALS BOARD

(SOR/2010-45, s. 18.)

General Rules of the Tax Court of Canada Regulating the Practice and Procedure in the Court for Appeals under Section 28 of the Canada Pension Plan, Revised Statutes of Canada, 1985, Chapter C-8

SOR/90-689, gazetted October 24, 1990, effective January 1, 1991; as amended by; SOR/93-98, gazetted March 10, 1993 and effective February 23, 1993; SOR/95-116, gazetted March 8, 1995 and effective February 21, 1995; SOR/96-505, gazetted and effective November 12, 1996; SOR/99-213, gazetted May 26, 1999 and effective May 6, 1999; SOR/2004-98, gazetted May 19, 2004 and effective April 27, 2004; SOR/2007-145, gazetted June 27, 2007 and effective June 14, 2007; SOR/2008-305, gazetted December 10, 2008 and effective November 20, 2008.

Short Title

1. These rules may be cited as the *Tax Court of Canada Rules of Procedure respecting the Canada Pension Plan.*

Interpretation

2. In these rules,

"Act" means the *Canada Pension Plan*;

"appellant" means an employee or employer, or the representative of either of them, who appeals under section 28 of the Act;

"electronic filing" means the act of filing, by electronic means, through the Court's website (www.tcc-cci.gc.ca) or any other website referred to in a direction issued by the Court, any document listed on those sites; (SOR/2007-145, s. 1; SOR/2008-305, s. 1.)

"fax" means to transmit a facsimile of printed matter electronically or a document so transmitted;

"intervener" means a person affected by a determination by, or a decision on an appeal to, the Minister under section 27 of the Act and who has intervened in an appeal;

"Minister" means the Minister of National Revenue;

"Registrar" **means the person appointed as Registrar of the Court by the Chief Administrator of the Courts Administration Service in consultation with the Chief Justice; (SOR/2004-98, s. 1.)**

"Registry" **means the Registry established by the Chief Administrator of the Courts Administration Service at the principal office of the Court at 200 Kent Street, 2nd Floor, Ottawa, Ontario K1A 0M1 (telephone (613) 992-0901 or 1-800-927-5499; fax: (613) 957-9034; website: www.tcc-cci.gc.ca) or at any other local office of the Court specified in notices published by the Court. (SOR/2004-98, s. 1.)**

(SOR/93-98, s. 1; SOR/2004-98, s. 1; SOR/2007-145, s. 1.)

3. These rules shall be liberally construed to secure the just, least expensive and most expeditious determination of every appeal on its merits.

Application

4. These rules apply to appeals brought under section 28 of the Act.

Filing a Notice of Appeal[1]

5. (1) An appeal by an appellant from a ruling or a decision made by, or a decision on an appeal to, the Minister shall be instituted within the time period set out in subsection 28(1) of the Act, which is 90 days after the ruling or decision is communicated to the appellant, or within any longer time that the Court on application made to it within 90 days after the expiration of those 90 days allows.

(2) Where a ruling or decision referred to in subsection (1) is communicated by mail, the date of communication is the date it is mailed and, in the absence of evidence to the contrary, the date of mailing is that date specified on the ruling or decision.

(3) An appeal referred to in subsection (1) shall be made in writing and shall set out, in general terms, the reasons for the appeal and the relevant facts, but no special form of pleadings is required.

(4) An appeal referred to in subsection (1) shall be instituted by filing a notice of appeal, which may be in the form set out in Schedule 5, using one of the following methods:

   (a) depositing the notice with the Registry;

   (b) sending it by mail to the Registry; or

   (c) sending it by fax or by electronic filing to the Registry.

(SOR/2008-305, s. 3.)

(5) (Repealed by SOR/2008-305, s. 3.) (SOR/2007-145, s. 2; SOR/2008-305, s. 3.)

(6) *Filing Date* **— (Repealed by SOR/2008-305, s. 3.)**

(7) *Electronic Filing* **— (Repealed by SOR/2008-305, s. 3.)**

(8) *Form of Appeal* **— (Repealed by SOR/2008-305, s. 3.)**

(SOR/99-213, s. 1; SOR/2007-145, s. 2; SOR/2008-305, s. 3.)

---

[1] Heading amended by SOR/2008-305, s. 2, effective November 20, 2008.

Filing of Other Documents[2]

5.1. Except as otherwise provided in these rules and unless otherwise directed by the Court, a document other than a notice of appeal may be filed using one of the following methods:

(*a*) depositing it with the Registry;

(*b*) sending it by mail to the Registry; or

(*c*) sending it by fax or by electronic filing to the Registry

(SOR/2007-145, s. 3; SOR/2008-305, s. 4.)

Filing Date[3]

5.2. Except as otherwise provided in these rules and unless otherwise directed by the Court, the date of filing of a document is deemed to be

(*a*) in the case of a document filed with the Registry or sent by mail or by fax, the date shown by the date received stamp placed on the document by the Registry at the time it is received; or

(*b*) in the case of a document filed by electronic filing, the date shown on the acknowledgment of receipt issued by the Court.

(SOR/2008-305, s. 4.)

Electronic Filing[4]

5.3. (1) Except as otherwise provided in these rules and unless otherwise directed by the Court, when a document is filed by electronic filing, the copy of the document that is printed by the Registry and placed in the Court file is deemed to be the original version of the document. (SOR/2008-305, s. 4.)

(2) A party who files a document by electronic filing shall, if required by these rules or at the request of a party or the Court, provide a paper copy of the document and file it with the Registry. (SOR/2008-305, s. 4.)

(3) If the Registry has no record of the receipt of a document, it is deemed not to have been filed, unless the Court directs otherwise. (SOR/2008-305, s. 4.)

(SOR/2008-305, s. 4.)

Extension of Time

6. (1) An application for an order extending the time within which an appeal may be instituted may be in the form set out in Schedule 6. (SOR/2007-145, s. 4(2).)

(*a*) (Repealed by SOR/2007-145, s. 4(2).)

(*b*) (Repealed by SOR/2007-145, s. 4(2).)

(*c*) (Repealed by SOR/2007-145, s. 4(2).)

(2) An application under subsection (1) shall be made by filing with the Registrar, in the same manner as appeals are filed under section 5, three copies of the application accompanied by three copies of the notice of appeal. (SOR/2007-145, s. 4(2).)

(3) No application shall be granted under this section to an applicant unless

[2] Heading added by SOR/2007-145, s. 3; amended by SOR/2008-305, s. 3.

[3] Heading added by SOR/2008-305, s. 4.

[4] Heading added by SOR/2008-305, s. 4.

CPP REGULATIONS

(*a*) the application is made within 90 days after the expiration of 90 days after the day on which the Minister communicated his or her decision to the applicant; and

(*b*) the applicant demonstrates that

(i) within the initial 90-day period specified in paragraph (*a*), the applicant

(A) was unable to act or to instruct another to act in the applicant's name, or

(B) had a good faith intention to appeal,

(ii) given the reasons set out in the application and the circumstances of the case, it would be just and equitable to grant the application,

(iii) the application was made as soon as circumstances permitted it to be made, and

(iv) there are reasonable grounds for appealing the decision.

(SOR/2007-145, s. 4(2).)

(4) After having given the Minister an opportunity to make representations, the Court shall dispose of the application on the basis of the representations contained in it and any additional information, if any, that the Court may require. (SOR/2007-145, s. 4(2).)

(5) The Registrar, on being informed of the decision of the Court in respect of the application, shall inform the applicant and the Minister of the decision. (SOR/2007-145, s. 4(2).)

(6) The application pursuant to subsection (1) is deemed to have been filed on the date of its receipt by the Registry, even if the application is not accompanied by the notice of appeal referred to in subsection (2), provided that the notice of appeal is filed within 30 days after that date or within any reasonable time that the Court establishes. (SOR/2007-145, s. 4(2).)

(SOR/2007-145, s. 4.)

Preparation for Appeal

7. (1) The Registrar shall serve the Minister with a copy of the notice of appeal referred to in section 5 and notice of the Registry in which it was filed or to which it was mailed.

(2) The material referred to in subsection (1) may be served personally, and personal service on the Commissioner of Revenue is deemed to be personal service on the Minister, or by mail addressed to the Minister, and if served by mail, the date of service is the date it is mailed and, in the absence of evidence to the contrary, the date of mailing is that date appearing on the communication from the Registrar accompanying the material. (SOR/2004-98, s. 7(*a*); SOR/2007-145, s. 11(*a*).)

(SOR/2004-98, s. 7; SOR/2007-145, s. 11.)

8. (1) The Minister, on receipt of a copy of the notice of appeal referred to in section 7, shall

(*a*) serve a copy of the notice of appeal and notice of the Registry in which it was filed or to which it was mailed on every person to whom a notification was sent pursuant to subsection 27(5) of the Act in respect of the determination or decision that is the subject of the appeal, and

(*b*) serve notice at the Registry in which the notice of appeal was filed or to which it was mailed of the name and address of every person who was served with the material referred to in paragraph (*a*), and serve at that Registry a copy of

(i) the application to the Minister to determine a question made under paragraph 27(1)(*a*) of the Act, or

(ii) the assessment made by the Minister and a copy of the appeal in respect thereof made to the Minister under subsection 27(2) of the Act

and a copy of the notification given by the Minister under subsection 27(5) of the Act.

(2) The material referred to

(*a*) in paragraph (1)(*a*) may be served personally or by mail, and

(*b*) in paragraph (1)(*b*) may be served by filing it at the Registry or by mail

and if served by mail, the date of service is the date it is mailed and, in the absence of evidence to the contrary, the date of mailing is the date appearing on the communication from the Minister accompanying the material.

Intervention

9. (1) A person affected by a decision of the Minister may intervene as a party in an appeal by filing with the Registry a notice of intervention that may be in the form set out in Schedule 9. (SOR/2007-145, s. 5; SOR/2008-305, s. 5.)

(2) The notice of intervention shall be filed within 45 days after the day on which the notice of appeal was served on the intervener under section 8. (SOR/2008-305, s. 5.)

(3) An intervener may state in the notice of intervention that the intervener intends to rely on the reasons set out in the notice of appeal received by the intervener or the reasons set out in the notice of intervention of another intervener.

(4) The Registrar shall serve the Minister and the appellant with a copy of any notice of intervention received by the Registrar.

(5) The notice of intervention may be served personally, and personal service on the Commissioner of Revenue is deemed to be personal service on the Minister, or by mail addressed to the Minister, and if served by mail, the date of service is the date it is mailed and, in the absence of evidence to the contrary, the date of mailing is that date appearing on the communication from the Registrar accompanying the notice of intervention. (SOR/2004-98, s. 7(*b*); SOR/2007-145, s. 11(*b*).)

(SOR/2004-98, s. 7; SOR/2007-145, ss. 5 and 11; SOR/2008-305, s. 5.)

Consolidation of Appeals

10. (1) Where there are two or more appeals commenced in accordance with these rules, the Court may, upon application by the Minister or an appellant or by an intervener, direct that the appeals be

(*a*) consolidated on such terms as it may direct,

(*b*) heard at the same time,

(*c*) heard consecutively, or

(*d*) stayed until the determination of any other appeal,

if there is a common question of law or fact in both or all of the appeals, or it is desirable in the interests of justice.

(2) An application referred to in subsection (1) shall be filed in or mailed to the Registry in which the notices of appeal were filed or to which they were mailed and shall be served on the other parties to the appeals.

CPP REGULATIONS

Consolidation of Interventions

11. Where there are two or more notices of intervention served under these rules, the Court may direct that one notice of intervention be filed and served on behalf of all interveners if

 (*a*) there is a common question of law or fact in both or all notices of intervention, or

 (*b*) it is desirable in the interests of justice.

Reply

12. (1) The Minister shall reply in writing to every notice of appeal or notice of intervention filed in or mailed to a Registry under subsection 5(5) or 9(1).

 (2)

 (*a*) The Minister shall file the reply at the Registry and on the appellant or intervener, or both, as the case may be, within 60 days from the day on which the notice of appeal or notice of intervention was served on the Minister, or within such longer time as the Court upon application made to it within those 60 days may allow. (SOR/93-98, s. 2.)

 (*b*) The reply shall be filed in the Registry in which the notice of appeal or notice of intervention was filed or to which it was mailed, and it may be served on the appellant or intervener personally or by mail. (SOR/96-505, s. 1.)

 (*b.1*) A reply may be filed under paragraph (*b*) by mailing it to the appropriate Registry described in that paragraph. (SOR/96-505, s. 1.)

 (*c*) If the reply is served by mail, the date of service is the date it is mailed and, in the absence of evidence to the contrary, the date of mailing is that date appearing on the communication from the Minister accompanying the reply.

 (3) The reply referred to in subsection (1) shall

 (*a*) admit or deny the facts alleged in the notice of appeal or notice of intervention, and

 (*b*) contain a statement of any further allegations of fact on which the Minister intends to rely.

 (4) An application for an extension of time under paragraph (2)(*a*) shall be made by serving at the Registry an application setting out

 (*a*) the date on which the notice of appeal or notice of intervention was served on the Minister,

 (*b*) the additional time required, and

 (*c*) the reasons therefor.

 (5) The application to extend time may be served by filing it in the Registry in which the notice of appeal or notice of intervention was filed or to which it was mailed, or by sending a letter, telegram, telex or fax to that Registry.

 (6) If the application to extend time is served by telegram, telex or fax, the date of service is the date that the telegram, telex or fax is transmitted and, if the application is served by mail, the date of service is the date stamped on the envelope at the post office and, if there is more than one such date, the date of service shall be deemed to be the earliest date.

 (7) The Court shall dispose of the application on the basis of the representations contained in it and such additional information, if any, as the Court may require and after having given the appellant or intervener an opportunity to make representations.

(8) The Registrar, on being informed of the decision of the Court in respect of the application, shall inform the Minister and the appellant or intervener.

(SOR/93-98, s. 2; SOR/96-505, s. 1.)

Judgment by Consent

13. When all parties have consented in writing to a judgment disposing of an appeal in whole or in part and filed it with the Registry, the Court may
    (a) grant the judgment sought without a hearing;
    (b) direct a hearing; or
    (c) direct that written representations be filed.

(SOR/2008-305, s. 6.)

Disposition of Appeals

14. After the time for filing a reply under subsection 12(1) has expired, the matter shall, unless the Court otherwise directs, be deemed to be ready for hearing.

15. (1) Where a reply to a notice of appeal has not been served within the 60 days prescribed under paragraph 12(2)(a) or within such longer time as the Court may allow, the appellant may apply on motion to the Court for judgment in respect of the relief sought in the notice of appeal. (SOR/93-98, s. 3.)

(2) On the return of the application for judgment the Court may
    (a) (Repealed by SOR/2007-145, s. 6.)
    (b) direct that the appeal proceed to hearing on the basis that facts alleged in the notice of appeal are presumed to be true,
    (c) allow the appeal if the facts alleged in the notice of appeal entitle the appellant to the judgment sought, or
    (d) give such other direction as is just.

(3) The presumption in paragraph (2)(b) is a rebuttable presumption.

(SOR/93-98, s. 3; SOR/2007-145, s. 6.)

16. (1) An appeal may at any time be withdrawn in whole or in part by the appellant by serving notice in writing on the Registrar and thereupon the appeal is deemed to be dismissed in whole or in part.

(2) The Registrar shall forthwith serve any intervener or other person who may be directly affected by a notice of withdrawal served under subsection (1) with a copy of the notice of withdrawal.

17. After hearing an appeal, the Court may vacate, confirm or vary a decision on an appeal under section 27 of the Act or an assessment that is the subject of an appeal under section 27.1 of the Act or, in the case of an appeal under section 27.1 of the Act, may refer the matter back to the Minister for reconsideration and reassessment, and shall without delay
    (a) notify the parties to the appeal in writing of its decision; and
    (b) give reasons for its decision, but, except where the Court deems it advisable in a particular case to give reasons in writing, the reasons given by it need not be in writing.

(SOR/2004-98, s. 2.)

CPP REGULATIONS

445

Discovery

18. (1) After the time limited for replying under section 12 has expired, the Court may, on application by any party to an appeal, direct

(a) any other party to the appeal to make discovery on oath of the documents that are or have been in the possession of or under the control of that other party relating to any matter in question on the appeal,

(b) that the applicant is authorized to examine on oath, for the purposes of discovery, any other party to the appeal, or

(c) that there shall be both discovery of documents and examination for discovery.

(2) The Court may specify the form of affidavit to be used for the purpose of discovery of documents.

(3) The person to be examined for discovery shall be

(a) if the other party is an individual, that individual,

(b) if the other party is a corporation or any body or group of persons empowered by law to sue or to be sued, either in its own name or in the name of any officer thereof or any other person, any member or officer of such corporation, body or group,

(c) if the other party is the Minister, any departmental or other officer of the Crown nominated by the Deputy Attorney General of Canada, or

(d) a person who has been agreed upon by the examining party and the party to be examined with the consent of such person.

(4) The Court may designate the person before whom the examination for discovery is to be conducted and direct the manner in which it shall be conducted.

(5) All evidence given at an examination for discovery shall be recorded by a court reporter. (SOR/2008-305, s. 7.)

(6) Any party may, at the hearing of an appeal, use in evidence against another party any part of the examination for discovery of that other party, but, on the application of an adverse party, the Court may direct that any other part of the examination, that in the opinion of the Court, is so connected with the part to be used that the last-mentioned part ought not to be used without such other part, be put in evidence by the party seeking to use such examinations.

(SOR/2008-305, s. 7.)

Hearing of Appeals

19. The Court may, on application by the Minister or an appellant or by an intervener or of its own motion, fix the date, time and place for the hearing of an appeal.

20. When the Court has fixed the date for a hearing, the Registrar shall, no later than 30 days before that date, send by registered mail to all parties, or have served on all parties to the appeal, a notice of hearing.

21. The Court may, on application by the Minister or an appellant or by an intervener or of its own motion, adjourn an appeal on such terms as in its opinion the circumstances of the case require.

22. The Court, upon the application of a party to an appeal or of its own motion and after giving every party an opportunity to be heard, may, at any stage of the appeal, give directions for the further conduct of the appeal.

23. All parties to an appeal may appear in person or may be represented by counsel or an agent.

Subpoena

24. (1) A party who requires the attendance of a person as a witness at a hearing may serve the person with a subpoena requiring the person to attend the hearing at the time and place stated in the subpoena and the subpoena may also require the person to produce at the hearing the documents or other things in the person's possession, control or power relating to the matters in question in the appeal that are specified in the subpoena.

(2) On the request of a party or of counsel, the Registrar, or some other person authorized by the Chief Justice, shall sign, seal and issue a blank subpoena and the party or counsel may complete the subpoena and insert the names of any number of witnesses. (SOR/2004-98, s. 3.)

(3) A subpoena shall be served on a witness personally and, at the same time, witness fees and expenses in accordance with subsection (4) shall be paid or tendered to the witness.

(4) A witness, other than a witness who appears to give evidence as an expert, is entitled to be paid by the party who arranged for his or her attendance $75 per day, plus reasonable and proper transportation and living expenses. (SOR/2007-145, s. 7.)

(5) An amount is not payable under subsection (4) in respect of an appellant, a respondent or a person who has intervened under section 9 unless the appellant, respondent or person has been called upon to testify by another party to the appeal. (SOR/96-505, s. 2.)

(SOR/93-98, s. 4; SOR/96-505, s. 2; SOR/2004-98, s. 3; SOR/2007-145, s. 7.)

Evidence

25. (1) A party to an appeal may, prior to the hearing thereof or at any time during the hearing, apply to the Court for a direction permitting all facts or any particular fact or facts to be proved by other than oral evidence and the Court may give such direction as in its opinion the circumstances of the case require.

(2) All evidence given at the hearing of an appeal shall be recorded in a manner approved by the Registrar. (SOR/2008-305, s. 8.)

(3) Any person who swears an affidavit to be used in an appeal may be required to appear before a person appointed by the Court for that purpose to be cross-examined thereon.

(4) Where a party intends to call an expert witness at the hearing of an appeal, that party shall, as soon as practicable and not later than 20 days before the date of the hearing of the appeal, serve at the Registry and on every other party a copy of the report signed by that expert containing the expert's name, address and qualifications and a statement of the substance of that expert's proposed testimony.

(5) A copy of a report by an expert witness shall be served

(a) by filing it in the Registry in which the notice of appeal was filed or to which it was mailed or by sending the report by mail or fax to that Registry, and

CPP REGULATIONS

(*b*) on every other party to an appeal by personal service or by sending the report to that party by mail or fax

and, if a copy of the report is served by fax, the date of service is the date of the transmission of the fax, or if it is served by mail, the date of service is the date stamped on the envelope at the post office and, if there is more than one such date, the date of service shall be deemed to be the earliest date.

(6) A party who has failed to comply with subsection (4) is not permitted to call an expert witness without leave of the Court.

(7) Subsections (4) and (6) do not apply to evidence in rebuttal.

(8) The Court may, with the consent of all parties, receive in evidence at the hearing of the appeal a report served under subsection (4) without requiring the expert to attend and give oral evidence.

(9) Where it is impracticable or inconvenient for an expert witness to attend at the hearing of an appeal, the party intending to call the witness may, with leave of the Court or the consent of the parties, examine the witness under oath prior to the hearing of the appeal before a court reporter appointed by the Registrar for the purpose of having the evidence of that expert available for use at the hearing of the appeal.

(10) An expert witness who is examined under subsection (9) may be examined, cross-examined by a party adverse in interest, or re-examined in the same manner as a witness at the hearing of an appeal and, if any dispute arises during the course of the examination, any party to the appeal may make application to the Court to resolve the dispute.

(11) Where the evidence of an expert witness has been taken under subsections (9) and (10), that witness shall not be called to give evidence at the hearing of the appeal, except with leave of the Court or unless the Court requires the attendance of that witness at the hearing of the appeal.

(SOR/2008-305, s. 8.)

Service of Documents

26. (1) Unless otherwise provided in these rules, service of any document provided for in these rules shall be effected by personal service or by mail or by fax addressed

(*a*) in the case of the Court or the Registrar, to a Registry,

(*b*) in the case of the Minister, to the Commissioner of Revenue, Ottawa, Ontario K1A 0L8, (SOR/2004-98, s. 7(*c*); SOR/2007-145, s. 11(*c*).)

(*c*) in the case of the appellant or any intervener

   (i) to the address of the appellant or intervener for service as set out in the notice of appeal or notice of intervention, or

   (ii) where no address for service is set out in the notice of appeal or notice of intervention, to the postal or other address set out in the notice of appeal, notice of intervention or any written communication made by that person to the Court or Registrar, and

(*d*) in the case of any other person, to the address set out in the latest written communication made by that person to the Court or Registrar.

(2) Any party to an appeal who wishes to change address for service shall

(*a*) serve notice in writing of the change at the Registry to which the notice of appeal was sent, and

(*b*) serve a copy of the notice on all other parties,

which address shall thereafter be that party's address for service.

(3) Where service is effected by fax, the date of service is the date that the fax is transmitted and, if service is effected by mail, the date of service shall be deemed to be the date stamped on the envelope at the post office and, if there is more than one such date, the date of service shall be deemed to be the earliest date.

(SOR/2004-98, s. 7; SOR/2007-145, s. 11.)

Calculating Time

26.1. (1) For the purpose of calculating a time limit established under these rules, the period beginning on December 21 in any year and ending on January 7 of the next year shall be excluded.

(2) Where the time limited for the doing of a thing under these rules expires or falls on a holiday or a Saturday, the thing may be done on the day next following that is not a holiday or Saturday.

(SOR/93-98, s. 5.)

General

26.2. Subject to any order that the Court, in special circumstances, may make restricting access to a particular file by persons other than the parties to a matter before the Court, any person may, subject to appropriate supervision and when the facilities of the court permit without interfering with the ordinary work of the court,

(*a*) inspect any Court file relating to a matter before the Court; and

(*b*) on payment of $0.40 per page, obtain a photocopy of any court document on a Court file.

(SOR/95-116, s. 1.)

27. (1) Failure to comply with these rules shall not render any proceedings void unless the Court so directs, but such proceedings may be set aside either in whole or in part as irregular and may be amended or otherwise dealt with in such manner and upon such terms as, in the opinion of the Court, the circumstances of the case require.

(2) Where a person makes an application to set aside a proceeding for irregularity, the objections intended to be put forward shall be stated clearly in the application.

(3) The Court may, where and as necessary in the interests of justice, dispense with compliance with any rule at any time.

(4) Where matters are not provided for in these rules, the practice shall be determined by the Court, either on a motion for directions or after the event if no such motion has been made. (SOR/2004-98, s. 4(2).)

(SOR/2004-98, s. 4.)

Contempt of Court

28. (1) A person is guilty of contempt of court who

(*a*) at a hearing of the Court fails to maintain a respectful attitude, remain silent or refrain from showing approval or disapproval of the proceeding;

CPP REGULATIONS

(*b*) wilfully disobeys a process or order of the Court;

(*c*) acts in such a way as to interfere with the orderly administration of justice or to impair the authority or dignity of the Court;

(*d*) is an officer of the Court and fails to perform his or her duties;

(*e*) is a sheriff or bailiff and does not execute a writ forthwith or does not make a return thereof; or

(*f*) contrary to these rules and without lawful excuse,

    (i) refuses or neglects to obey a subpoena or to attend at the time and place appointed for his or her examination for discovery,

    (ii) refuses to be sworn or to affirm or to answer any question put to him or her,

    (iii) refuses or neglects to produce or permit to be inspected any document or other property, or

    (iv) refuses or neglects to answer interrogatories or to make discovery of documents.

(SOR/2004-98, s. 5.)

(2) Subject to subsection (6), before a person may be found in contempt of court, the person alleged to be in contempt shall be served with an order, made on the motion of a person who has an interest in the proceeding or at the Court's own initiative, requiring the person alleged to be in contempt

(*a*) to appear before a judge at a time and place stipulated in the order;

(*b*) to be prepared to hear proof of the act with which the person is charged, which shall be described in the order with sufficient particularity to enable the person to know the nature of the case against the person; and

(*c*) to be prepared to present any defence that the person may have.

(SOR/2004-98, s. 5.)

(3) A motion for an order under subsection (2) may be made *ex parte*. (SOR/2004-98, s. 5.)

(4) An order may be made under subsection (2) if the Court is satisfied that there is a *prima facie* case that contempt has been committed. (SOR/2004-98, s. 5.)

(5) An order under subsection (2) shall be personally served, together with any supporting documents, unless otherwise ordered by the Court. (SOR/2004-98, s. 5.)

(6) In a case of urgency, a person may be found in contempt of court for an act committed in the presence of a judge in the exercise of his or her functions and condemned at once, provided that the person has first been called on to justify his or her behaviour. (SOR/2004-98, s. 5.)

(7) A finding of contempt shall be based on proof beyond a reasonable doubt. (SOR/2004-98, s. 5.)

(8) A person alleged to be in contempt may not be compelled to testify. (SOR/2004-98, s. 5.)

(9) Where the Court considers it necessary, it may request the assistance of the Attorney General of Canada or any other person in relation to any proceedings for contempt. (SOR/2004-98, s. 5.)

(10) Where a person is found to be in contempt, a judge may order, in addition to any other order made in respect of the proceedings, any or all of the following:

(*a*) that the person be imprisoned for a period of less than two years;

(*b*) that the person pay a fine;

(*c*) that the person do or refrain from doing any act;

(*d*) that the person's property be sequestered; and

(*e*) that the person pay costs.

(SOR/2004-98, s. 5.)

(SOR/2004-98, s. 5.)

Costs in Vexatious Proceedings

29. Where a judge has made an order under section 19.1 of the *Tax Court of Canada Act*, costs may be awarded against the person in respect of whom the order has been made.

(SOR/2004-98, s. 5.)

CPP REGULATIONS

Schedule 5

(Section 5)

FORM OF NOTICE OF APPEAL

IN THE TAX COURT OF CANADA

In re the Canada Pension Plan

BETWEEN:

Appellant,

and

The Minister of National Revenue,

Respondent.

NOTICE OF APPEAL

Notice of appeal is hereby given by *(here insert name and full postal address of Appellant)* ....
.... from,

Applies to a ruling on request under para. 26.1(1)(d) or (e) C.P.P.

(i) the ruling regarding a contribution, made by the Respondent on a request made to the Respondent on the *(here insert the date the request for a ruling was made to the Respondent)* .... day of .... to rule on the question *(here describe question ruled on by Respondent)*
....
which the Respondent ruled *(here describe ruling made)* ....
....
and that ruling was communicated to the Appellant on the *(here insert the date of mailing of the ruling)* .... day of .....

Applies to a decision made under s. 27.3 C.P.P.

(ii) the decision on a question, regarding a contribution, made by the Respondent on the Respondent's own initiative, namely, whether *(here describe question determined by Respondent)* ....
....
which the Respondent decided by stating that *(here describe decision made)* ....
....
and that decison was communicated to

the Appellant on the *(here insert the date of mailing of the decision)* .... day of ....

Applies to a decision on appeal under s. 27.1 C.P.P.

(iii) the decision of the Respondent on an appeal to the Respondent for the reconsideration of an assessment made on the *(here insert the date of the appeal for reconsideration of the assessment)* .... day of .... whereby *(here describe assessment that was appealed for reconsideration)* ....
....
and the decision of the Respondent on the reconsideration was that *(here insert the decision made on the reconsideration of the assessment)* ....
....
which decision was communicated to the Appellant on the *(here insert the date of mailing of the decision)* .... day of ....

A. Statement of Facts

(Here set out in consecutively numbered paragraphs a statement of the allegations of fact.)

B. The Reasons which the Appellant Intends to Submit

(Here set out the reasons on which the Appellant intends to rely.)

C. Address for Service

(Here set out the address for service of documents.)*

(a) name and address of Appellant's counsel, if any; or

(b) name and address of Appellant's agent, if any.)

Dated at *(city, town or village)*, this ....
day of .... 20 ...

....
Signature of Appellant, Appellant's counsel or Appellant's agent

(SOR/99-213, s. 2; SOR/2007-145, s. 8.)

(*) If the Appellant is not represented by counsel or an agent, the address given at the commencement of the notice of appeal shall be the Appellant's address for service.

Schedule 6

(Section 6)

APPLICATION FOR EXTENSION OF TIME WITHIN WHICH AN APPEAL MAY BE INSTITUTED

TAX COURT OF CANADA

In re the Canada Pension Plan

BETWEEN:

(name)

Applicant,

and

HER MAJESTY THE QUEEN,

Respondent.

APPLICATION FOR EXTENSION OF TIME WITHIN WHICH AN APPEAL MAY BE INSTITUTED

I HEREBY apply for an order extending the time within which an appeal may be instituted (*identify the date the decision to the Minister was communicated to the applicant*).

(*Here set out the reasons why the appeal to the Court was not instituted before the expiration of 90 days after the day the decision was communicated and any other relevant reasons in support of the application.*)*

Date:

TO: The Registrar   *(Set out name,*
Tax Court of   *address for service*
Canada   *and telephone*
200 Kent Street   *number of applicant,*
Ottawa, Ontario   *applicant's counsel or*
K1A 0M1   *applicant's agent)*

or
Any other office
of the Registry.

(SOR/2007-145, s. 9.)

(*) NOTE that three copies of this application accompanied by three copies of a notice of appeal must be filed with the Registrar of the Tax Court of Canada in the same manner as appeals are filed under subsections 5(5) and (7).

Schedule 9

(Section 9)

FORM OF NOTICE OF INTERVENTION

IN THE TAX COURT OF CANADA

In re the Canada Pension Plan

BETWEEN:

Appellant

and

the Minister of National Revenue,

Respondent.

NOTICE OF INTERVENTION

Notice of intervention is hereby given by *(here insert name and full postal address of Intervener)* ....
....
....
..........on the appeal of *(here insert name of Appellant)* ....
made on the *(here insert the date of the notice of appeal)* ....
day of.........

A. Statement of Facts*

(Admit or deny the facts alleged in the notice of appeal and set out in consecutively numbered paragraphs a statement of such further facts upon which the Intervener intends to rely.)

B. The Reasons which the Intervener Intends to Submit**

(Here set out the reasons on which the Intervener intends to rely.)

C. Address for Service

(Here set out the address for service of documents.)**

(a) *name and address of Intervener's counsel, if any, or*

(a) *name and address of Intervener's agent, if any.)*

Dated at *(city, town or village)*, this.......day of..........20...

....
Signature of Intervener, Intervener's counsel or Intervener's agent

(SOR/2004-98, s. 6; SOR/2007-145, s. 10.)

---

* Attention is directed to subsection 9(3), which permits Interveners, instead of setting forth a statement of facts and reasons, to rely on the statements of facts and reasons pleaded in the notice of appeal or any other intervention.

** If the Intervener is not represented by a counsel or an agent, the address given at the commencement of the notice of intervention shall be the Intervener's address for service.

Old Age Security Act

Table of Contents

Old Age Security Act

R.S.C. 1985, c. O-9, as amended by R.S.C. 1985, c. 34 (1st Supp.), in force September 1, 1985, except s. 6, in force June 28, 1985; R.S.C. 1985, c. 1 (4th Supp.), s. 28, in force February 4, 1988; R.S.C. 1985, c. 51 (4th Supp.), s. 15, in force January 1, 1991; 1990, c. 39 in force October 23, 1990, except s. 57(1), deemed in force September 13, 1988; 1991, c. 44, ss. 32 and 33 in force January 1, 1992; 1992, c. 24, s. 17, in force July 1, 1992; 1992, c. 48, s. 29 in force January 1, 1993; 1995, c. 33, ss. 1–24, in force July 13, 1995, except s. 3(1), in force November 1, 1995, except s. 16 in force January 1, 1997; 1996, c. 11, in force July 12, 1996, except ss. 32, 49(2) and 101(a); 1996, c. 18, ss. 50–56, deemed in force April 1, 1996; 1996, c. 21, s. 74, in force June 20, 1996; 1996, c. 23, s. 187, in force June 30, 1996; 1997, c. 40, ss. 100–107, assented to December 18, 1997, subsections 102–105, 106 where it enacts subsection 44(3) and 107 where it enacts section 44.2 in force December 18, 1997, sections 100–101, 106 where it enacts subsection 44(4) and 107 where it enacts section 44.1 not yet in force; 1998, c. 19, s. 288, assented to and in force June 18, 1998; 1998, c. 21, ss. 105–119, assented to and in force June 18, 1998; 1999, c. 22, ss. 87–89, assented to and in force June 17, 1999; 2000, c. 12, ss. 192–209, assented to June 29, 2000 and effective July 31, 2000; 2001, c. 4, s. 111, in force June 1, 2001; 2001, c. 27, ss. 263–267, assented to November 1, 2001 and effective June 28, 2002; 2002, c. 8, s. 182(1)(z.5), assented to March 27, 2002 and in force July 2, 2003; 2003, c. 22, 178–179, assented to November 7, 2003 and in force April 1, 2005; 2005, c. 30, ss. 136–137, assented to and in force June 29, 2005; 2005, c. 35, ss. 55–58, 60–62, 66(e) and 67(e), assented to July 20, 2005 and in force October 5, 2005; 2005, c. 38, s. 138, in force December 12, 2005; 2005, c. 9, s. 7, in force November 25, 2005; 2006, c. 4, s. 180, in force July 1, 2006; 2007, c. 11, assented to May 3, 2007, and most sections in force with exceptions[1]; 2007, c. 35; 2008, c. 28, s. 156, in force July 1, 2008; 2009, c. 33, ss. 31–32, in force January 1, 2010; 2010, c. 22, ss. 1–11, in force December 15, 2010; 2011, c. 15, ss. 13–14, in force June 26, 2011; 2012, c. 19, ss. 237(2), 238, 239, 445, 447, 452, 461, 464, and 465 in force on assent — June 29, 2012; ss. 235, 236, and 237(1) in force April 1, 2013; ss. 296 to 299 in force March 1, 2013; ss. 446, 448, and 451 in force July 1, 2013; ss. 449, 450, and 453 in force March 1, 2013; 466 in force April 1, 2014; ss. 694(f)(i) and (ii) in force March 1, 2013; ss. 454 to 460, 462, 463 come into force on a day or days to be fixed by order of the Governor in Council and are not yet in force; 2013, c. 40, ss. 236(1), 237(1), and 238(1), in force December 12, 2013.

An Act to provide for old age security

Short Title

1. *Short title* — **This Act may be cited as the *Old Age Security Act*.**

---

[1]Subsection 114(2) of the Canada Pension Plan does not apply in respect of the amendments to that Act contained in section 36 of this Act. (2) Section 36 of this Act comes into force in accordance with subsections 114(4) of the Canada Pension Plan. (3) Subsection 7 of this Act come into force on a day or days to be fixed by order of the Governor in Council (S.C. 2007, c. 11, s. 39).

—————— **Notes** ——————

Case Law

Canada (Minister of Human Resources Development) v. Gerstel, 2006 FCA 93 (CanLII)

The object of the OAS Act is to provide assistance to the elderly, and low income Canadians, and as such, there is no reason why claimants should not compute their income in the manner which is most advantageous to them, so long as they comply with the rules of the *Income Tax Act,* as modified by the OAS Act.

Collins v. Canada, [2002] FCA 82

The OAS Act is intended to provide income support to elderly persons, which is a pressing and substantial public policy objective.

Canada (Minister of Human Resources Development) v. Stiel, 2006 FC 466

The OAS regime is altruistic in purpose. Unlike the CPP, OAS benefits are universal and non-contributory, based exclusively on residence in Canada. This type of legislation fulfills a broad-minded social goal. It should therefore be construed liberally, and persons should not be lightly disentitled to OAS benefits. However, it cannot be ignored that the OAS Act provides benefits, first and foremost, to residents of Canada. It has been described as the building block of the Canadian retirement income system.

B-67374 v. MHRD (January 15, 2003) (RT)

The *OAS Act* does not provide for the grant of a benefit on compassionate grounds, and requires all applications to be made in writing. A person otherwise entitled to a pension has no right to one unless he or she applies for it. The application for a pension is to be dealt with on the basis of the law as it stands when the pension is applied for, not when a person might first become eligible to apply. There is nothing in the Act that provides for the consideration of any special circumstances for the purpose of establishing qualification for a pension. Although the appellant is a low income earner, financial difficulties are not relevant to a determination of entitlement under the *OAS Act.*

———————————

Interpretation

2. *Definitions* — **In this Act,**

"allowance" **means the allowance authorized to be paid under Part III; (S.C. 2000, c. 12, s. 192(5).)**

"applicant" **means a person who has applied, or is deemed to have applied, for a benefit, or with respect to whom an application for a benefit has been waived; (S.C. 1995, c. 33, s. 1(1).)**

"application" **means an application for a benefit;**

"beneficiary" **means a person to whom payment of a benefit has been approved;**

"benefit" **means a pension, supplement or allowance; (S.C. 2000, c. 12, s. 209.)**

"cheque" **means any instrument issued in payment of a benefit;**

"common-law partner", **in relation to an individual, means a person who is cohabiting with the individual in a conjugal relationship at the relevant time, having so cohabited with the individual for a continuous period of at least one year. For greater certainty, in the case of an individual's death, the "relevant time" means the time of the individual's death; (S.C. 2000, c. 12, s. 192(4).)**

"Consumer Price Index", **with respect to any adjustment quarter, means the average for that adjustment quarter of the Consumer Price Index for Canada, as published by Statistics Canada under the authority of the *Statistics Act*, for each month in that adjustment quarter;**

"first adjustment quarter", **in relation to a payment quarter, means,**

    (*a*) **if the payment quarter commences on the first day of April in a payment period, the period of three months commencing on the first day of November immediately before that first day of April,**

    (*b*) **if the payment quarter commences on the first day of July in a payment period, the period of three months commencing on the first day of February immediately before that first day of July,**

    (*c*) **if the payment quarter commences on the first day of October in a payment period, the period of three months commencing on the first day of May immediately before that first day of October, and**

    (*d*) **if the payment quarter commences on the first day of January in a payment period, the period of three months commencing on the first day of August immediately before that first day of January; (S.C. 1998, c. 21, s. 119(2)(*a*).)**

"income[2]" **of a person for a calendar year means the person's income for the year, computed in accordance with the *Income Tax Act*, except that**

    (*a*) **there shall be deducted from the person's income from office or employment for the year**

        (i) **a single amount in respect of all offices and employments of that person equal to**

            (A) **for the purpose of determining benefits payable in respect of any month before July 2008, the lesser of $500 and one fifth of the person's income from office or employment for the year, or**

            (B) **for the purpose of determining benefits payable in respect of any month after June 2008, the lesser of $3,500 and the person's income from office or employment for the year,**

(S.C. 2008, c. 28, s. 156.)

        (ii) **the amount of the employee's premiums paid by the person during the year under the *Employment Insurance Act*, and**

        (iii) **the amount of employee's contributions made by the person during the year under the *Canada Pension Plan* or a provincial pension plan as defined in section 3 of that Act,**

    (*b*) **there shall be deducted from the person's self-employment earnings for the year**

        (i) **the amount of contributions made in respect of those self-employed earnings by the person during the year under the *Canada Pension Plan* or a provincial pension plan as defined in section 3 of that Act, and**

        (ii) **the amount of premium paid by the person during the year under Part VII.1 of the *Employment Insurance Act*,**

(S.C. 2009, c. 33, s. 31.)

---

[2] Pursuant to 1999, c. 22, subsections 87(3) and 87(4), this definition of "income", as enacted by 1999, c. 22, subsections 87(1) and 87(2), applies for the purposes of determining benefits payable under the *Old Age Security Act* for months after June 1999, with the exception of paragraph (*d*), which applies for the purpose of determining benefits payable under the *Old Age Security Act* for months after June 2000.

Old Age Security Act

(*c*) there shall be deducted from the person's income for the year, to the extent that those amounts have been included in computing that income,

   (i) the amount of any benefit under this Act and any similar payment under a law of a provincial legislature,

   (ii) the amount of any death benefit under the *Canada Pension Plan* or a provincial pension plan as defined in section 3 of that Act, and

   (iii) the amount of any social assistance payment made on the basis of a means, a needs or an income test by a registered charity as defined in subsection 248(1) of the *Income Tax Act* or under a program provided for by an Act of Parliament or a provincial legislature that is neither a program prescribed under the *Income Tax Act* nor a program under which the amounts referred to in subparagraph (i) are paid;

(S.C. 1999, c. 22, s. 87(1).)

(*d*) there shall be deducted from the person's income for the year three times the amount, if any, by which

   (i) the total of any amounts that may be deducted under section 121 of the *Income Tax Act* in computing the person's tax payable for the year

   exceeds

   (ii) the person's "tax for the year otherwise payable under this Part" (within the meaning assigned by subsection 126(7) of the *Income Tax Act* for the purposes of paragraph 126(1)(*b*) of that Act) for the year, and

(S.C. 1999, c. 22, s. 87(2).)

(*e*) there shall be deducted from the person's income for the year any amount included under paragraph 56(1)(*q*.1) or subsection 56(6) of the *Income Tax Act* and there shall be included in the person's income for the year any amount that may be deducted under paragraph 60(*y*) or (*z*) of that Act; (S.C. 2006, c. 4, s. 180; 2007, c. 35, s. 129[3].)

Minister — "Minister" means the Minister of Employment and Social Development; (1996, c. 11, s. 95(*k*); 2005, c. 35, s. 67(*e*)(i); 2012, c. 19, s. 694(*f*)(i); 2013, c. 40, s. 238(1)(*k*)(i).)

"payment period", in relation to a month, means

   (*a*) the fiscal year that includes the month, where the month is before April, 1998,

   (*b*) the period that begins on April 1, 1998 and ends on June 30, 1999, where that period includes the month, and

   (*c*) the period after June 30, 1999 that begins on July 1 of one year and ends on June 30 of the next year, where that period includes the month; (S.C. 1998, c. 21, s. 105(1).)

"payment quarter" means a period of three months commencing on the first day of April, July, October or January in a payment period; (S.C. 1998, c. 21, s. 119(2)(*a*).)

"pension" means a monthly pension authorized to be paid under Part I;

"pensioner" means a person whose application for a pension has been approved;

"prescribed" means prescribed by the regulations;

---

[3] Section 129 applies to the 2008 and subsequent taxation years (S.C. 2007, c. 35, s. 135.).

"release" in relation to a person who has been incarcerated, means release from custody on earned remission, at the expiry of a sentence, or on parole or statutory release that has not been terminated or revoked; (S.C. 2010, c. 22, s. 2.)

"Review Tribunal" (Repealed by S.C. 2012, c. 19, s. 235.) (S.C. 1995, c. 33, s. 1(2); 2012, c. 19, s. 235.)

"second adjustment quarter", in relation to a payment quarter, means,

(a) if the payment quarter commences on the first day of April in a payment period, the period of three months commencing on the first day of August immediately before that first day of April,

(b) if the payment quarter commences on the first day of July in a payment period, the period of three months commencing on the first day of November immediately before that first day of July,

(c) if the payment quarter commences on the first day of October in a payment period, the period of three months commencing on the first day of February immediately before that first day of October, and

(d) if the payment quarter commences on the first day of January in a payment period, the period of three months commencing on the first day of May immediately before that first day of January; (S.C. 1998, c. 21, s. 119(2)(a).)

"special qualifying factor" of a person for a month before April 1996 means one and for a month after March 1996 means

(a) one, where the person is not a specially qualified individual, and

(b) where the person is a specially qualified individual, the fraction of which

(i) the numerator is the aggregate period (expressed in the number of years and, where the number of years is not a whole number, rounded down to the next lower whole number) as of the last day of the immediately preceding month, during which the individual has resided in Canada after attaining eighteen years of age, and

(ii) the denominator is 10; (S.C. 1996, c. 18, s. 50.)

"specially qualified individual" means a person who has not resided in Canada after attaining eighteen years of age for an aggregate period of ten or more years other than such a person to whom a pension or allowance was payable (S.C. 2000, c. 12, s. 209.)

(a) for the month of March 1996 or an earlier month, or

(b) for the month of January 2001 or an earlier month, where, before March 7, 1996, the person was residing in Canada as a Canadian citizen or a permanent resident within the meaning of subsection 2(1) of the *Immigration and Refugee Protection Act*; (S.C. 2000, c. 12, s. 209; 2001, c. 27, s. 263.)

"spouse" [Repealed by 2000, c. 12, s. 192(1)];

"spouse's allowance" [Repealed by 2000, c. 12, s. 192(2)];

"supplement" means a monthly guaranteed income supplement authorized to be paid under Part II;

"survivor" means a person whose spouse or common-law partner has died and who has not thereafter become the spouse or common-law partner of another person; (S.C. 2000, c. 12, s. 192(4).)

"widow" **[Repealed by 2000, c. 12, s. 192(1)].**

(R.S.C. 1985, c. 34 (1st Supp.), s. 1; 1995, c. 33, s. 1; 1996, c. 11, s. 95; 1996 c. 18, s. 50; 1998, c. 21, ss. 105, 119(2)(a); 1999, c. 22, s. 87; 2000, c. 12, ss. 192 and 209; 2001, c. 27, s. 263; 2005, c. 35, s. 67; 2006, c. 4, s. 180; 2007, c. 35, s. 129; 2008, c. 28, s. 156; 2009, c. 33, s. 31; 2010, c. 22, s. 2; 2012, c. 19, ss. 235 and 694; 2013, c. 40, s. 238.)

―――――――― **Notes** ――――――――

Case Law

§1. Spouse (Note: Definition repealed in 2000.)

Canada (Minister of Human Resources Development) v. Leavitt, 2005 FC 664

At the same time that the definition of "spouse" was deleted, the term "common-law partner" was added. As currently worded, where the term spouse is used in the Act, it is followed by the term common-law spouse. It was not Parliament's intention to extend the commonly understood meaning of "spouse" to include emotional ties or other measures of the strength or nature of the relationship. Rather, the intent was simply to avoid a definition of "spouse" that no longer accords with today's understanding of that term.

M-36223 v. MHRD (February 24, 2000) (RT). See also *P-47857 v. MHRD* (November 30, 1999) (RT).

The former definition of "spouse" required public representation as "husband and wife". Although the parties acknowledged in a statutory declaration that they represented each other as "common-law spouse", the parties had not become each other's spouse as defined in Section 2.

§2. Survivor

T-32201 v. MHRD (June 22, 1999) (RT)

"Spouse" for this purpose should be given a broad, rather than narrow and technical interpretation. Public representation as husband and wife is not relevant, for the purposes of coming within the definition of "spouse", in situations of "long and permanent" relationships.

C-51751 v. MHRD (February 8, 2000) (RT)

The former definition of a "widow" as a person whose spouse has died necessarily excludes a former widow and recipient of a survivor's allowance who subsequently remarries. The survivor's argument that the second spouse had been hospitalized for mental illness, and that the subsequent marriage was therefore not a true marriage, was not accepted.

Canada (Attorney General) v. Landry, [1997] F.C.J. No. 224 (T.D.)

An ecclesiastical annulment of a second marriage was not relevant for purposes of, what is now, the survivor's allowance under the OAS, where the second marriage was also terminated by a civil divorce. The necessary implication of the decree absolute of divorce was that, for civil law purposes, the applicant had been married and had become "the spouse of another person", thereby excluding her from being considered a widow of the her first husband.

P-47086 v. MHRD (February 8, 2000) (RT)

Where the applicant had stated on her application for OAS benefits and a renewal for GIS benefits that she had formed a common-law relationship with a person following her husband's death, the applicant was not a "survivor" despite her testimony that she was mistaken in so stating and despite her neighbours' letters indicating that she lived in a room-mate relationship with the person. She represented the person as her spouse, they shared bank accounts, life insurance and jointly signed documents.

§3. Income

　　● See also cases regarding qualification for GIS under s. 13 (below)

MHRD v. Mahy, 2004 CFA 340

There is no concept of negative income under the *OAS Act.* The negative income of one member of a couple therefore cannot be used to reduce or offset the income of the other member. There is reason to believe that the notion of "income" under the *OAS Act* loses its usual conceptual meaning, especially in view of the interaction that s. 2 makes with the computation of income under the Income Tax Act. Section 2 "income" (*c*)(i) allows for a deduction from income the amount of any benefit received by a pensioner under the Act. It is a social measure designed to assist low-income pensioners. The purpose of that deduction is not to create or determine a loss, but simply to ensure that the benefits of pensioners under the *OAS Act* are not reduced by reason of receiving such income. The purpose of these deductions is also to determine the amount of the benefits payable and whether a pensioner is entitled to receive maximum benefits. Thus, a pensioner is entitled to a payment of maximum benefits when, pursuant to s. 2, he has no income or zero income. Where the pensioner has a spouse, maximum benefits are available to them if they jointly have no income or if their joint income is zero. Under the legislative scheme, even if they had a negative or minus income, it would not increase the amount of the maximum benefits payable to these pensioners. Conversely, any income left after the deductions authorized by s. 2 "income" (*c*)(i) will reduce the amount of benefits in a proportion established by the legislative scheme.

Bakht v. MHRD, [2002] FCA 252

The deduction from taxes payable provided by s. 118(3) of the *Income Tax Act* is not a deduction made in determining a taxpayer's income and has therefore no application for purposes of computing the applicant's income as defined under OAS Act s. 2. Foreign taxes paid on foreign pension income of the applicant were therefore not deductible from the pension income included for purposes of computing the applicant's GIS entitlement.

2.1. *Amount of full pension* — **(1) In this Act, a reference to the amount of a full monthly pension means the amount of a full monthly pension that has not been increased under subsection 7.1(1) or (2). (S.C. 2012, c. 19, s. 446.)**

(2) *Monthly pension* — **The terms "pensioner's monthly pension" in subsections 12(5) and 22(2) and "pension" in subsection 12(5.1) mean, respectively, a pensioner's monthly pension and a pension that have not been increased under subsection 7.1(1) or (2). (S.C. 2012, c. 19, s. 446.)**

(S.C. 2012, c. 19, s. 446.)

2.2. *References to "sixty years"* — **(1) In this Act, a reference to the age of "sixty years" or "60 years" is to be read for the applicable period set out in column 1 of the table to this subsection as a reference to the corresponding age in column 2.**

(S.C. 2012, c. 19, s. 447.)

Column 1 Period	Column 2 Age
From April 1, 2023 to June 30, 2023	60 years and one month
From July 1, 2023 to September 30, 2023	60 years and two months
From October 1, 2023 to December 31, 2023	60 years and three months
From January 1, 2024 to March 31, 2024	60 years and four months
From April 1, 2024 to June 30, 2024	60 years and five months
From July 1, 2024 to September 30, 2024	60 years and six months
From October 1, 2024 to December 31, 2024	60 years and seven months

Column 1 Period	Column 2 Age
From January 1, 2025 to March 31, 2025	60 years and eight months
From April 1, 2025 to June 30, 2025	60 years and nine months
From July 1, 2025 to September 30, 2025	60 years and 10 months
From October 1, 2025 to December 31, 2025	60 years and 11 months
From January 1, 2026 to March 31, 2026	61 years
From April 1, 2026 to June 30, 2026	61 years and one month
From July 1, 2026 to September 30, 2026	61 years and two months
From October 1, 2026 to December 31, 2026	61 years and three months
From January 1, 2027 to March 31, 2027	61 years and four months
From April 1, 2027 to June 30, 2027	61 years and five months
From July 1, 2027 to September 30, 2027	61 years and six months
From October 1, 2027 to December 31, 2027	61 years and seven months
From January 1, 2028 to March 31, 2028	61 years and eight months
From April 1, 2028 to June 30, 2028	61 years and nine months
From July 1, 2028 to September 30, 2028	61 years and 10 months
From October 1, 2028 to December 31, 2028	61 years and 11 months
After December 31, 2028	62 years

(2) *Reference to "sixty-five years"* — **In this Act, a reference to the age of "sixty-five years" or "65 years" is to be read for the applicable period set out in column 1 of the table to this subsection as a reference to the corresponding age in column 2. (2012, c. 19, s. 447.)**

Column 1 Period	Column 2 Age
From April 1, 2023 to June 30, 2023	65 years and one month
From July 1, 2023 to September 30, 2023	65 years and two months
From October 1, 2023 to December 31, 2023	65 years and three months
From January 1, 2024 to March 31, 2024	65 years and four months
From April 1, 2024 to June 30, 2024	65 years and five months
From July 1, 2024 to September 30, 2024	65 years and six months

Column 1 Period	Column 2 Age
From October 1, 2024 to December 31, 2024	65 years and seven months
From January 1, 2025 to March 31, 2025	65 years and eight months
From April 1, 2025 to June 30, 2025	65 years and nine months
From July 1, 2025 to September 30, 2025	65 years and 10 months
From October 1, 2025 to December 31, 2025	65 years and 11 months
From January 1, 2026 to March 31, 2026	66 years
From April 1, 2026 to June 30, 2026	66 years and one month
From July 1, 2026 to September 30, 2026	66 years and two months
From October 1, 2026 to December 31, 2026	66 years and three months
From January 1, 2027 to March 31, 2027	66 years and four months
From April 1, 2027 to June 30, 2027	66 years and five months
From July 1, 2027 to September 30, 2027	66 years and six months
From October 1, 2027 to December 31, 2027	66 years and seven months
From January 1, 2028 to March 31, 2028	66 years and eight months
From April 1, 2028 to June 30, 2028	66 years and nine months
From July 1, 2028 to September 30, 2028	66 years and 10 months
From October 1, 2028 to December 31, 2028	66 years and 11 months
After December 31, 2028	67 years

(3) *Reference to "seventy years"* — **In this Act, a reference to the age of "seventy years" or "70 years" is to be read for the applicable period set out in column 1 of the table to this subsection as a reference to the corresponding age in column 2. (2012, c. 19, s. 447.)**

Column 1 Period	Column 2 Age
From April 1, 2028 to June 30, 2028	70 years and one month
From July 1, 2028 to September 30, 2028	70 years and two months
From October 1, 2028 to December 31, 2028	70 years and three months
From January 1, 2029 to March 31, 2029	70 years and four months
From April 1, 2029 to June 30, 2029	70 years and five months
From July 1, 2029 to September 30, 2029	70 years and six months
From October 1, 2029 to December 31, 2029	70 years and seven months
From January 1, 2030 to March 31, 2030	70 years and eight months
From April 1, 2030 to June 30, 2030	70 years and nine months
From July 1, 2030 to September 30, 2030	70 years and 10 months
From October 1, 2030 to December 31, 2030	70 years and 11 months
From January 1, 2031 to March 31, 2031	71 years
From April 1, 2031 to June 30, 2031	71 years and one month

Old Age Security Act

Column 1 Period	Column 2 Age
From July 1, 2031 to September 30, 2031	71 years and two months
From October 1, 2031 to December 31, 2031	71 years and three months
From January 1, 2032 to March 31, 2032	71 years and four months
From April 1, 2032 to June 30, 2032	71 years and five months
From July 1, 2032 to September 30, 2032	71 years and six months
From October 1, 2032 to December 31, 2032	71 years and seven months
From January 1, 2033 to March 31, 2033	71 years and eight months
From April 1, 2033 to June 30, 2033	71 years and nine months
From July 1, 2033 to September 30, 2033	71 years and 10 months
From October 1, 2033 to December 31, 2033	71 years and 11 months
After December 31, 2033	72 years

(2012, c. 19, s. 447.)

Part I

Monthly Pension

Pension Payable

3. *Payment of full pension* — **(1) Subject to this Act and the regulations, a full monthly pension may be paid to**

(*a*) **every person who was a pensioner on July 1, 1977;**

(*b*) **every person who**

(i) **on July 1, 1977 was not a pensioner but had attained twenty-five years of age and resided in Canada or, if that person did not reside in Canada, had resided in Canada for any period after attaining eighteen years of age or possessed a valid immigration visa,**

(ii) **has attained sixty-five years of age, and**

(iii) **has resided in Canada for the ten years immediately preceding the day on which that person's application is approved or, if that person has not so resided, has, after attaining eighteen years of age, been present in Canada prior to those ten years for an aggregate period at least equal to three times the aggregate periods of absence from Canada during those ten years, and has resided in Canada for at least one year immediately preceding the day on which that person's application is approved; and**

(*c*) **every person who**

(i) **was not a pensioner on July 1, 1977,**

(ii) **has attained sixty-five years of age, and**

(iii) **has resided in Canada after attaining eighteen years of age and prior to the day on which that person's application is approved for an aggregate period of at least forty years.**

(2) *Payment of partial pension* — **Subject to this Act and the regulations, a partial monthly pension may be paid for any month in a payment quarter to every person who is not eligible for a full monthly pension under subsection (1) and**

(*a*) **has attained sixty-five years of age; and**

(*b*) **has resided in Canada after attaining eighteen years of age and prior to the day on which that person's application is approved for an aggregate period of at least ten years but less than forty years and, where that aggregate period is less than twenty years, was resident in Canada on the day preceding the day on which that person's application is approved.**

(3) *Amount of partial pension* — **Subject to subsection 7.1(3), the amount of a partial monthly pension, for any month, shall bear the same relation to the full monthly pension for that month as the aggregate period that the applicant has resided in Canada after attaining 18 years of age and before the day on which the application is approved, determined in accordance with subsection (4), bears to 40 years. (S.C. 2012, c. 19, s. 448.)**

(4) *Rounding of aggregate period* — **For the purpose of calculating the amount of a partial monthly pension under subsection (3), the aggregate period described in that subsection shall be rounded to the lower multiple of a year when it is not a multiple of a year.**

(5) *Additional residence irrelevant for partial pensioner* — **Once a person's application for a partial monthly pension has been approved, the amount of monthly pension payable to that person under this Part may not be increased on the basis of subsequent periods of residence in Canada.**

(S.C. 2012, c. 19, s. 448.)

——————————— **Notes** ———————————

Synopsis

This section provides for the payment of a full or partial monthly pension to persons 65 and older. Entitlement to, and the amount of, the pension depends on residence — how many years the applicant resided in Canada after turning 18. The minimum number of years of residence is 10. The number of years of Canadian residence (up to a maximum of 40) is divided by 40 to arrive at the fraction of the basic OAS pension amount that the applicant is entitled to receive. Therefore, 10 years of Canadian residence entitles an applicant to 10/40 (or one-quarter) of the full monthly pension. At least 40 years of Canadian residence entitles the applicant to the full monthly pension.

The most contested issue that arises in this context is whether the applicant has been resident in Canada in a given time period. Section 21 of the OAS Regulations must be examined in detail in making this determination. Section 21 permits people working overseas for certain purposes to maintain Canadian residence. Applicants are also permitted to be temporarily absent from Canada, for up to one year, without interrupting their residence. The decisions below discuss what happens when an applicant has spent more than a year outside of Canada. Essentially, it is a question of fact, to be determined case-by-case, whether the extended absence will interrupt residence.

Note that where an applicant has emigrated to Canada from another country with which Canada has signed a social security agreement, the years of contribution to that country's social insurance scheme may count towards the total number of years of residence in Canada for the purposes of the above calculation. (See s. 40 and cases thereunder.)

Related Regulations

- Sections 18, 19 — Proof of age

- Section 20 — Statement of particulars of residence required
- Section 21 — "Residence" defined

Case Law

§1. Generally

Flitcroft v. Canada (Attorney General), 2012 FC 782

The words "for any period" in s. 3(1)(*b*)(i) meant any period on or before July 1, 1977, and not any period prior to the 10 years immediately preceding the day the application was approved. Either the claimant had to have been residing in Canada on that day, or he or she had to have resided here at some period when he or she was between the ages of 18 and 25. The provision is not vague and there is no need to resort to the history of the statute or Hansard to interpret it.

K-67133 v. MHRD (July 15, 2002) (RT)

Ministry officials have a positive duty to inform CPP applicants of their eligibility for the OAS.

W-44040 v. MHRD (March 24, 1999) (RT)

Where the appellant already accepted a partial pension benefit, the Tribunal has no jurisdiction to re-open the issue.

Ata v. Canada, [1985] F.C.J. No. 800 (C.A.). See also *Canada v. Pattison,* [1990] F.C.J. No. 1142 (T.D.).

Under s. 3(2), it is clear that a person otherwise entitled to a pension has no right to one unless he applies for it. Once he has applied, he has a right to have the application dealt with according to the law. Right to the pension vests upon approval of the application. An application for a pension is to be dealt with on the basis of the law as it stands when the pension is applied for.

Canada (Attorney General) v. Pike, [1995] F.C.J. No. 15 (T.D.)

There is nothing in the Act or Regulations which provides for the consideration of any special circumstances for the purpose of establishing qualification for a full pension.

S-33497 v. MHRD (January 21, 1999) (RT)

Financial and family difficulties faced by the applicant were not relevant to a determination of entitlement under the Act.

§2. Proof of Age

Hussaini v. Canada (Attorney General), 2011 FC 26

A birth date is essentially a question of fact and accordingly reviewable on the standard of reasonableness. The duty of fairness does not require the Review Tribunal to seek evidence, in general or expert evidence, when an appeal proceeds before it. On a dispute over the claimant's age, the Review Tribunal did not breach the duty of fairness owed to the claimant by failing to demand that she produce a forensic report to authenticate the family records.

E-46357 v. MHRD (November 8, 1999) (RT)

In proving the applicant's age, documentation from the applicant's home country and credible testimonial evidence may be accepted over the age stated on the applicant's official Canadian documentation.

Example Cases — Applicant not Establishing Different Age

- Applicant's passport and other documentation indicating 1940 DOB; birth certificate issued in India indicating 1932 DOB, but no name on certificate; applicant taking no steps to amend documentation between arrival in Canada in 1974 and date of application; applicant's spouse stating on 1993 OAS application that wife's DOB was in 1940: *M-38624 v. MHRD* (March 24, 1999) (RT)

- While Chinese immigrants to Canada may have often changed their dates of birth in order to get the children admitted in the country, the official DOB must be upheld in the absence of any credible documentation confirming the alleged earlier date, given the mass of evidence indicating a later DOB: *S-31353 v. MHRD* (December 18, 1998) (RT)

§3. Residence

- See also cases under **s. 40 — Agreements regarding the effect of international social security treaties**

(a) Generally

Ata v. Canada, [1985] F.C.J. No. 800 (C.A.)

Permanent residence is a status to be obtained by compliance with particular provisions of Canadian immigration laws, not merely by personal intention and lawful presence, of whatever duration, in Canada.

Duncan v. Canada (Attorney General), 2013 FC 319

The common-law definition of "residence" is relevant to consideration of the term under both the OAS Act and the ITA and the material factors to be considered in determining residence may be the same under both statutes. There is no exhaustive definition of "residence" in the ITA. Despite the fact that an individual's liability for income tax is based on the concept of residency, the ITA leaves the meaning of residence to be defined in the common law, although it may deem an individual to be or not to be a resident in certain circumstances regardless of its conclusions regarding factual residence. The CRA has expressed the opinion that courts have held "residence" to be "a matter of the degree to which a person in mind and fact settles into or maintains or centralizes his ordinary mode of living with its accessories in social relations, interests, and conveniences at or in the place in question." In determining the residence status of an individual for the purposes of the Act, it is also necessary to consider the ITA s. 250(3), which provides that in the Act a reference to a person "resident" in Canada includes a person who is "ordinarily resident" in Canada. Courts have held that an individual is ordinarily resident in Canada for tax purposes if Canada is the place where the individual, in the settled routine of his or her life, regularly, normally, or customarily lives. In making a determination of residence status, all of the relevant facts in each case must be considered, including residential ties with Canada and length of time, object, intention, and continuity with respect to stays in Canada and abroad. The meaning of the term may vary not only in the contexts of different matters, but also in different aspects of the same matter. Decision makers must be wary of precedent, such that the context of the statute in question as well as a claimant's specific factual circumstances must always be kept in mind. While the claimant's intention is a legitimate factor to consider, it should not be relied on at the expense of all other factors. Although the OAS Act and the ITA serve different aims, the purpose of considering residency after age 18 in the OAS Act may link the availability of an OAS pension to the contributions a claimant has made to Canada in the years during which a person could most contribute to the economy.

Canada (Minister of Human Resources Development) v. Stiel, 2006 FC 466

The legislative scheme appears focused on the provision of benefits to persons living their retirements in Canada. It is only through the operation of specific, added provisions that non-residents obtain even a partial OAS pension.

Kiefer v. Canada (Attorney General), 2008 FC 786

The mental state of the claimant's spouse with respect to loyalty and ties to Canada were not material to a determination of the claimant's residency in Canada.

Singh v. Canada (Attorney General), 2013 FC 437

The term "missionary" is not defined in the OAS Act or OAS Regulations, but a common attribute of a missionary assignment is that one has been sent from their home country to another country to propagate a religion.

Old Age Security Act

L-74700 v. MHRD (July 28, 2003) (RT)

Even though the Ministry had given an incomplete and misleading explanation of the qualification requirements for a full OAS pension to the applicant, the Ministry was not required to grant a full pension where the applicant had not relied on such advice.

C-74893 v. MHRD (September 30, 2003) (RT)

Additional periods of Canadian residence after a partial pension is granted could not be used to increase the pension amount, although it was relevant to determining whether the pension could be exported.

G-63886 v. MHRD (November 7, 2001), (RT)

There is no exemption under the *OAS Act* for status Indians such that they did not need to prove residence for the purpose of receiving OAS benefits. One cannot be ordinarily resident in two countries at the same time.

R-35036 v. MHRD (October 14, 1998) (RT)

The Tribunal lacks the discretion under the Act to award an OAS pension to an applicant who had not yet resided 10 years in Canada on account of his or her financial situation.

D-32028 v. MHRD (August 6, 1998) (RT)

The applicant's ignorance of the fact that non-consecutive years could be used in determining the length of residency, resulting in a delay in applying, was not ground for awarding a benefit in excess of the partial pension to which she was entitled.

B-50542, B-50543 v. MHRD (February 1, 2000) (RT)

The intention to make Canada a permanent residence could not be equated with residing in Canada.

C-40317 v. MHRD (December 9, 1999) (RT)

The onus to prove residency is on the appellant. There is nothing in the *Old Age Security Act* which permits the Tribunal to reduce the number of years of residency. Therefore, the Tribunal has no jurisdiction to award remedies on compassionate grounds.

L-40431 v. MHRD (April 10, 2000) (RT)

While the Regulations permitted Canadians to travel abroad in missionary services without being penalized, it is implicit that the regulations assume that the Canadian will return to Canada to make their home, or intends to reside in Canada.

(b) Evidence

Canada (Minister of Human Resources Development) v. Ding, 2005 FC 76

Residency is a factual issue that requires an examination of the whole context of the individual under scrutiny. The "obvious intentions" of the resident to become a resident of Canada while present on a tourist visa should not be the sole basis of making a determination of residency. Several factors may be considered in determining whether the residence conditions have been observed: ties in the form of personal property; social ties in Canada; other fiscal ties in Canada (medical coverage, driver's licence, rental lease, tax records, etc.); ties in another country; regularity and length of visits to Canada, as well as the frequency and length of absences from Canada; and the lifestyle of the person or his establishment here.

Singer v. Canada (Attorney General), 2010 FC 607, affirmed 2011 FCA 178

The list of factors enumerated in *Ding* is not exhaustive. There may well be other factors which become relevant according to the particular circumstances of a case. The use of precedent for this purpose is dangerous as weight might be given to a factor in a particular set of circumstances that is inappropriate in a different context. The test is a fluid one. Sometime the fact that a person has obtained or applied for a permanent status will be relevant while in others it will not. This is true for most factors. However, presence in Canada at some point in time appears to be of particular importance if not crucial in all cases. While continuous presence is not required, it is difficult to imagine how one can be said to "ordinarily live" in Canada if this person has never actually been in Canada. Presence is, at some point in time, an essential element of this definition. The legislator made a clear policy decision when choosing to apply the threshold of July 1, 1977. The court cannot and should not interfere with such a decision. The liberal and purposive construction of the OAS Act is meant to enable the court to construe the statute in accordance with Parliament's intention. It is not meant as a tool to change the will of the legislator.

Tabry v. Canada (Attorney General), 2013 FC 286

When a law is adopted with a deadline, there will always be applicants who fail by a few days, and some who would qualify by a few days. While any applicant who narrowly misses the July 1, 1977 deadline is deserving of sympathy, given the language of the statute and the binding precedent of the *Singer* decision (above), the court cannot act on that sympathy. An internal Ministry memo describing a grace period relating to the July 1, 1977 rule does not trump the language of the OAS Act. The fact that the claimant had applied to immigrate to Canada in 1974 but had been delayed due to her spouse's error in her application was irrelevant.

De Carolis v. Canada (Attorney General), 2013 FC 366

The case law has laid down a non-exhaustive list of factors to consider when establishing residence. These factors are personal property, social and fiscal ties in Canada, ties in another country, regularity and length of visits to Canada, as well as the frequency and length of absences from Canada, the lifestyle of the person, and his or her establishment here. The burden of proof rests on the applicant.

De Bustamante v. Canada (Attorney General), 2008 FC 1111

Residence is a factual issue that requires an examination of the whole context of the individual under scrutiny.

Duncan v. Canada (Attorney General), 2013 FC 319

Settlement privilege attaches to settlement offers by the Minister expressly made "without prejudice", which offered a partial OAS pension, and such privilege is not waived by the decision of the Tribunal to include them in its hearing record. Had the Tribunal not found that the settlement offer was privileged, it would not be bound to adopt the position regarding the claimant's years of residence in Canada expressed Minister's letter, but it would at least have been required to assess and explain why it has come to a different conclusion.

L-79404 v. MSD (2004) (RT)

The burden of proof on an appellant may be formulated as follows:

1. A person wishing to assert a right shall prove the facts on which his claim is based.

2. Evidence is sufficient if it renders the existence of a fact more probable than its non-existence, unless the law requires more convincing proof.

3. Testimony is a statement whereby a person relates facts of which he or she has personal knowledge or whereby an expert gives his or her opinion.

4. The probative force of testimony is left to the appraisal of the Tribunal.

D-55075 v. MHRD (November 21, 2000); *D-55074 v. MHRD* (November 20, 2000) (RT)

The following factors should be taken into consideration in determining whether a person makes their home in and ordinarily live in Canada:

1. Ties in the form of personal property (e.g. house, business, furniture, automobile, bank account, credit card);

2. Social ties in Canada (e.g. membership with organizations or associations, or professional membership);

3. Other ties in Canada (e.g. hospital and medical insurance coverage, driver's licence, rental, lease, loan or mortgage agreement, property tax statements, electoral voters

list, life insurance policies, contracts, public records, immigration and passport records, provincial social services records, public and private pension plan records, federal and provincial income tax records);

4. Ties in another country;

5. Regularity and length of stay in Canada and the frequency and length of absences from Canada; and

6. The person's mode of living — i.e., whether his or her living in Canada is substantially deep rooted and settled.

S-42357 v. MHRD (December 15, 1999) (RT)

In determining whether the recipient actually resided in Canada during a given time period, objective and reliable documentary evidence such as passports, medical records and voter's lists represents the best evidence available, as opposed to oral testimony and information in investigation reports which are essentially hearsay.

W-32003 v. MHRD (July 31, 1998) (RT)

The applicant's statement that Canadian immigration authorities had promised her a visa before July 1977, should be given little weight in absence of documentary evidence. If applicant had been granted such a promise, her name would have appeared in a letter to her husband from the Canadian Embassy in February 1997, which it did not.

S-37376 v. MHRD (March 22, 2000) (RT)

The question of the applicant's marital status or spouse's whereabouts is not relevant to a determination of residency.

G-40287 and G-40288 v. MHRD (July 7, 1999), (RT)

The Tribunal refused to consider signed statement by the recipients admitting that they had been living mostly outside Canada for the past five years, on the ground that the statements were being challenged because the recipients claimed to have been pressured into signing the statement, and refused an opportunity to consult a lawyer before signing.

(c) Absences Longer Than One Year

Perera v. MNHW, 75 F.T.R. 310, [1994] F.C.J. No. 351 (T.D.) See also *Kuthiala v. MNHW,* [1995] F.C.J. No. 164 (T.D.).

Whether or not the individual makes his or her home and ordinarily lives in Canada is a question of fact to be determined in the particular circumstances. While an absence from Canada exceeding one year is obviously a factor to be considered, it is not determinative of the question. Section 21(4) of the Regulations does not state otherwise. The effect of s. 21(4) is simply that an absence of a temporary nature not exceeding one year shall be deemed not to have interrupted the person's residence. It does not necessarily follow that an absence in excess of one year interrupts the person's period of residence. Physical presence of the applicant is only determinative of eligibility if the applicant cannot establish that he or she has resided in Canada for the required 10-year period and is attempting to establish eligibility based on the second criteria in s. 3(1)(b), i.e., that the applicant has been present in Canada during the period specified therein.

K-57129 v. MHRD (November 1, 2002) (RT)

Section 21 of the OAS Regulations does not require an intent to return to Canada within 12 months. The question is simply whether there was an intent to return to Canada.

S-61596 v. MHRD (September 5, 2001) (RT)

Section 21(4) of the Regulations, which states that absence from Canada for the purpose of attending university shall be deemed not to have interrupted residence in Canada, assumes that student will return to Canada after they have completed their studies.

472

S-31486 v. MHRD (January 21, 1999) (RT)

Medical treatment is not an exception under the Act. However, whether an individual makes his home ordinarily in Canada is a question of fact to be determined in each case. Whether an absence exceeded one year is only a fact to be taken into account. (Note: *Perera* decision applied.)

S-40289 v. MHRD; S-40290 v. MHRD (June 4, 1999) (RT)

The fact that the applicant kept his returning resident permit while living abroad for longer than one year is indicative, but not determinative, of whether he made his home and ordinarily lived in Canada.

G-53918 v. MHRD (March 23, 2000) (RT)

Exceptions to the maximum one-year absence rule are few. Too broad of an interpretation would have the effect of nullifying the residence requirement.

J-32512 v. MHRD (June 16, 1998) (RT)

A CCRA determination that the applicant was a resident of Canada for particular years while physically out of the country could not be equated with the residency requirements of the *Old Age Security Act.*

(d) Canadian Charter of Rights and Freedoms

Pawar v. Canada, [1999] F.C.J. No. 1421 (C.A.)

The distinction in s. 3 based on the length and timing of residence in Canada does not discriminate against applicants on the basis of any of the enumerated grounds in s. 15 of the *Canadian Charter of Rights and Freedoms* or grounds analogous thereto. Nor do the distinctions based on whether the applicant has been born abroad, or whether they have accumulated credits in a country with whom Canada has negotiated a reciprocal social security agreement, discriminate on the ground of "national or ethnic origin", and are not analogous either.

Shergill v. Canada, 2003 FCA 468

The residence requirement for an OAS pension does not involve any form of discrimination analogous to the enumerated grounds in s. 15(1) of the *Charter of Rights.* This issue was settled by the Federal Courts' decisions in *Pawar,* for which the Supreme Court of Appeal has refused leave to appeal. The Supreme Court of Canada's later decision in *Lavoie v. Canada* did not require Parliament to discriminate in favour of citizens, regardless of length of residence, nor did it have anything to do with old age security.

Sell v. Canada (Attorney General), 2007 FC 1313

The Charter of Rights was not in effect when the *OAS Act* was amended in 1977 to introduce the residency requirement for the award of a full monthly pension, and the Charter has no retrospective application. The date of a claimant's entry into Canada is an event, that is, a specific, discrete occurrence, and not a matter of ongoing status, and did not give rise to a retrospective application of the Charter.

C-61948 v. MHRD (September 11, 2003) (RT)

Canadian citizenship is irrelevant as an appropriate criterion to either qualify for benefits or quantify a partial pension.

Canada v. Pattison, [1990] F.C.J. No. 1142 (T.D.)

The residence requirements under the Regulations do not violate the mobility rights guaranteed by s. 6 of the *Canadian Charter of Rights and Freedoms.* Neither do the provisions discriminate against applicants on the basis of any of the enumerated grounds in s. 15 of the Charter or grounds analogous thereto.

473

Old Age Security Act

S-71345 v. MHRD (November 5, 2002) (RT). See also *S-37685 v. MHRD* (June 26, 2002) (RT); *S-37686 v. MHRD* (June 26, 2002) (RT).

An applicant cannot bring a Charter challenge to the OAS residency requirements where the same person had previously been part of an unsuccessful class action suit on the same issue, which issue had been dealt with by the Federal Court of Appeal in *Pawar*.

(d.1) Standard of Review

Canada (Minister of Human Resources Development) v. Chhabu (2005), 280 F.T.R. 296

Residency is a question of fact to be determined in the particular circumstances. Where the proceedings are more factually than legally driven, the appropriate standard of review is reasonableness. The issue of residency in relation to OAS eligibility is one that the Review Tribunal is regularly called upon to determine. The factual circumstances of each case call for findings that fall within its expertise and thus militate in favour of deference. In interpreting the definition of residency, however, the Court is equally or better positioned. The *OAS Act* confers a benefit to certain individuals and establishes who is entitled to the receipt of benefits and to what extent. To that end, it involves the adjudication of an individual's rights. The conferment of benefits, however, is balanced with the interests of fairness and financial responsibility. The Minister is charged with the administration and integrity of the Act and the public interest in ensuring that applicants are not paid benefits to which they are not entitled. Thus, the Act provides for the adjudication of individual rights but is also polycentric in nature. This factor results in neither a high nor a low degree of deference. Where the nature of the question involves applying the correct legal test to various facts and is therefore one of mixed fact and law, this factor favours more deference.

Daoud v. HRSD, 2012 FCA 13

Although determining the place of residence for purposes of OAS eligibility involves questions of fact and credibility, which are subject to a very stringent standard of review, an extension of the period for seeking judicial review may be granted where the claimant was diligent in seeking review and the application raised errors of law regarding the interpretation and scope of the OAS Act and regarding the burden of proof that applies when establishing place of residence. It is up to the Tribunal, not the Federal Court on judicial review, to weigh the evidence presented to it. The reviewing court cannot assess the evidence in a manner that would be more favourable to the claimant.

Sell v. Canada (Attorney General), 2007 FC 1313

On a question of mixed fact and law, where the question in issue is legally driven the applicable standard of review is that of correctness.

(e) Example Cases — Residence not Established

- Claimant sent son to school in Canada in 1991, and five years later came to live with him; claimant returned to home country repeatedly, staying there for up to 11 months at a time; claimant maintained home country passport which continued to list his ancestral home as his address: *Singh v. Canada (Attorney General),* 2013 FC 437

- Clamaint had filed tax returns in Canada, owned real estate, carried out business activities, and contributed to the QPP. However, there were long and frequent absences, as demonstrated by passport stamps, that he had family ties and business interests in Italy, and his lifestyle was such that he travelled a lot and had no furniture, just some clothes, in his residence in Canada: *De Carolis v. Canada (Attorney General),* 2013 FC 366

- Claimant, born in the United States, quit her job in New York in 1976 as part of a relationship with Montreal man and shuttled back and forth between both cities over the next two years before finally marrying him in 1978; claimant kept furniture with her mother in New York; no proof of ties to Montreal before 1978, and claimant refused to authorize release of government records to prove her claim: *Saraffian v. Canada (Human Resources and Skills Development),* 2012 FC 1532, affirmed 2013 FCA 232

- Rest of family received medical approval for immigration on May 27, 1977, but applicant was required to obtain more tests; applicant eventually found to be in good health, but because of delay did not receive visa until July 21, 1977 and did not arrive in Canada until after July 24, 1977: *Singer v. Canada (Attorney General)*, 2010 FC 607

- Claimant's absence for period of about 27 months of a 35-month period justifies interruption of residence: *Valdivia De Bustamante v. Canada (Attorney General)*, 2008 FC 1111

- Previous short-term visits to Canada on visitor's permit not included in 10-year residence period: *L-79404 v. MSD* (2004) (RT)

- German-born spouse of Canadian-born missionary not having initial period of actual residence in Canada; periods of time participating in the German Social Benefit Plan excluded from operation of s. 21(5) of the OAS Regulations: *S-77319 v. MSD* (2004) (RT)

- Applicants returning to native country every year or two for stays of between 6 and 12 months at a time; major portion of applicant's income and liquid assets retained in native land: *D-55075 v. MHRD* (November 21, 2000); D-55074 v. MHRD (November 20, 2000) (RT)

- Investigation by Ministry triggered by applicant's son-in-law, who later recanted claiming he was angry at applicant; evidence of the applicant and her family members being contradictory, while the evidence of three independent third-party witnesses indicated that the applicant did not ordinarily reside in Canada: *S-43385 v. MHRD* (May 6, 1999) (RT)

- Recipient possessing only an Italian passport, had a spouse residing in Italy, and he lived in his brother's condominium in Montreal although he was able to travel regularly between Italy and Canada by virtue of a pass given by one of his children, an airline employee; recipient making contradictory statements over the years which affected his credibility: *D-35910 v. MHRD* (April 6, 1999) (RT)

- Applicant residing in Canada for only three years after moving from the Philippines, and had never participated in that country's social insurance plan: *V-38205 v. MHRD* (August 20, 1999) (RT)

- Applicant's son dying in India; applicant taking advantage of opportunity to come to Canada in following year, but returning four months later to help protect his daughter-in-law and grandchildren during civil war in India for following two years; applicant arriving in Canada on one-way airline ticket, but also returning to India on one-way ticket; during two-year period in India, applicant living off of income of land he owned while maintaining his returning resident permit; applicant ordinarily resident in India during two year period: *S-40289 v. MHRD*; *S-40290 v. MHRD* (June 4, 1999) (RT)

- Applicant remaining in U.K. while husband returning to Canada after separation; fact that applicant remained married to husband although separated not relevant to determining residence: *S-37376 v. MHRD* (March 22, 2000) (RT)

- Applicant couple owning house in Detroit and husband working in Michigan from 1950 to 1980; three children born in U.S., with last child's birth certificate showing usual residence as being Detroit; while couple bought property in Canada in 1949, this property was listed as a seasonal dwelling and property tax notices listed their Detroit address; couple not residing in Canada until selling Detroit house and living full time in Canadian property in 1981: *R-50065 v. MHRD*; *R-50075 v. MHRD* (February 24, 2000) (RT)

- Applicant falsely stating in original application that he had lived continuously in Canada from 1971 to February 1992, claim made to obtain the maximum possible benefit from the government; claim for years 1983–1986, based on six months' residence with son in 1983, six months in 1984 and three months in 1986, not accepted: *R-48244 v. MHRD* (April 14, 2000) (RT)

475

- Applicant coming to Canada from Iran as refugee following 1979 revolution; wife and children moving back to England; applicant travelling extensively around the world as a consultant, and staying at a "bed and breakfast" rather than alleged home in Guelph: *P-33693 v. MHRD* (November 30, 1999) (RT)

- Applicant giving U.S. address as return address in application to the U.S. immigration department for authorization to go to Crete; applicant having U.S. driver's licence and while giving Canadian address following automobile accident, that address belonging to another party; applicant destroying all documents that could have proven departures and entries into Canada, and unable to provide notices of assessment from CCRA for the years in question as requested: *P-38184 v. MHRD* (April 6, 1999) (RT)

- Nothing on file to prove that applicant resided in Canada anywhere from 1950 to 1992; numerous inconsistencies in evidence; applicant renting apartment in Canada and applying for SIN in 1991 after husband dying: *P-37058 v. MHRD* (April 6, 1999) (RT)

- Applicant importing her car and goods valued at $14,408 into Canada in November 1991, and treated for medical problems from March 1992 to March 1993, no evidence to confirm residence in Canada before and after these dates: *L-49149 v. MHRD* (May 2, 2000) (RT)

- Time spent by applicant, who was from Poland, in Soviet concentration camp during World War II not relevant in determining length of residency in Canada; no international agreements in effect with either Poland or Soviet Union: *M-28469 v. MHRD* (September 1, 1998) (RT)

- Applicant from Zambia working in Canada for 10 years before returning to Zambia in 1967, initially to teach, but subsequently engaged in missionary work; applicant never again residing in Canada and 1992 marriage licence indicating New York residence: *L-40431 v. MHRD* (April 10, 2000) (RT)

- Applicant absent from Canada for three years following denial of Return Residence Permit; applicant failing to appeal decision of Immigration Officer: *Kuthiala v. MNHW*, [1995] F.C.J. No. 164 (T.D.)

- Applicant returning to India to visit after six months in Canada, but becoming ill and physicians advising not to return to Canada; no evidence to support claim that applicant continued to pay half of rent on son's apartment in Canada during two-year period back in India: *C-40317 v. MHRD* (December 9, 1999) (RT)

- Parties having obtained landed immigrant status in Canada, purchasing a home and motor vehicle and opening a bank account, but residing in Canada for only four months before returning to South Africa for 21 months to attend to sale of their farm: *B-50542, B-50543 v. MHRD* (February 1, 2000) (RT)

- Applicant, a foreign national, working at embassy in Canada for 13 years prior to retirement, at which point he obtained permanent resident status; applicant applying for OAS pension 2 months before s. 21(2.1) of Regulations coming into force in 1983; right to pension not vesting until application approved: *Ata v. Canada*, [1985] F.C.J. No. 800 (C.A.)

- Applicant arriving in Canada and working here for 16 years before leaving to work for a Canadian company in U.K. for 15 years before retiring to South Africa; applicant failing to demonstrate intention to permanently return to Canada while working in U.K. and an physical return for 6 months: *F-31928 v. MHRD* (July 31, 1998) (RT)

- Visitor's visas over a four-year period not being sufficient documentary proof that the applicant actually resided in Canada during that time: *F-48994 v. MHRD* (March 23, 2000) (RT)

- A 17-month absence from Canada for personal and family reasons not fitting into any categories under Act regarding absences of more than a year; series of "returning resident permits" documentation received by applicant not relevant to OAS residency purposes: *G-43194 v. MHRD* (June 16, 1999) (RT)

● While in India, applicant contracted cellulitis in legs and underwent treatment; medical report from Indian physician stating that applicant unable to travel; medical information on file not establishing that condition being so severe that she could not return to Canada for treatment: *G-53918 v. MHRD* (March 23, 2000) (RT)

● Applicant moving to Canada in September 1984 and allegedly deciding to stay permanently in Canada in 1986; applicant returning to India "to finish business" in March 1986 until September 14, 1986, from September 15, 1986 to September 14, 1987, and from September 15, 1987 to November 1987; departures for such long periods of time were longer than necessary to tidy up business: *J-31234 v. MHRD* (October 13, 1998) (RT)

● Applicant going to the U.S. to live and work for 31 years, although returning to Canada each summer for her vacations and for winter holidays; such visits not re-starting the calculation of the prescribed six-month absence allowable under sec. 11(7)(c): *L-33570 v. MHRD* (July 6, 1998) (RT)

● Applicant giving only oral testimony asserting Canadian residence, without adducing such evidence as electricity/telephone bills or income tax receipts; testimony having many contradictions, and applicant had falsely represented his Canadian residence before when making his first application for OAS benefits: *R-40690 v. MHRD* (March 23, 2000) (RT)

(f) Example Cases — Residence Established

● 14-month absence to care for son who was ill; although claimant purchased one-way ticket to India, she continued to maintain a home, family and bank accounts in Canada: *K-57129 v. MHRD* (November 1, 2002) (RT)

● Applicant spending 18-month period in India obtaining medical treatment, period of absence should be included in calculating the ten-year residence requirement: *S-31486 v. MHRD* (January 21, 1999) (RT)

● Applicant obtaining permanent residence status in 1984, and maintaining house in Montreal and "vacation house" in New Jersey; testimonial evidence indicating applicant and spouse spending most of their time in Montreal and frequenting local establishments; no satisfying evidence led by Minister to contradict applicant's witnesses: *M-40316 v. MHRD* (March 1, 2000) (RT)

● Evidence in applicant's passport supported position that he returned to Canada for the purpose of completing one full year of residence: *T-48791 v. MHRD* (February 24, 2000) (RT)

● Applicant bringing family to Canada from Zambia in work/study program with United Church, for which he did not require a work permit; applicant living in Canada from August 1973 to October 1976, and from September 1978 to July 1981, although returning to Zambia on occasion to help his community with what he had learned; applicant maintaining bank account in Canada and his continued ties with Zambia related only to church activities: *L-39253 v. MHRD* (June 18, 1999) (RT)

● Applicant living 8 years with husband in U.S. before returning to Canada in 1967 to live with mother after alleged breakdown of marriage; 1985 Nova Scotia property deed listing applicant and ex-husband as New York residents merely indicative that applicant's mother wanted them to reconcile; applicant having taken all necessary steps to get rid of her U.S. green card, although she was not required to: *L-32017 v. MHRD* (October 14, 1998) (RT)

● Applicant not speaking or writing English, and living in a manner somewhat different from other Canadian residents; applicant dependent on daughter for many aspects of living; applicant not having bank account and daughter consistently signing her cheques: *I-28455 v. MHRD* (May 21, 1999) (RT); *I-28456 (Estate of) v. MHRD* (May 21, 1999) (RT)

- Applicant receiving CPP disability benefits while residing in Germany; art. 11(*a*) of social security treaty with Germany not requiring that applicant be a CPP contributor: *Canada (Attorney General) v. Simon*, [1998] 4 F.C. J. No. 670 (T.D.)

- Applicant qualifying as a missionary for purposes of s. 21(5)(*b*)(vi), having been invited by Roman Catholic Church in Mexico to do missionary work there; not necessary that applicant had not been sent by Church hierarchy in Canada: *Carota v. MNHW*, [1988] F.C.J. No. 439 (C.A.)

- Applicant attending university in U.S. in 1946–47 and from 1947 to 1951, then serving internationally as missionary from 1951 until retirement in 1984; applicant obtaining U.S. citizenship in 1952; U.S. citizenship not a bar to full OAS entitlement: *Canada v. Barnes*, [1994] F.C.J. No. 1864 (T.D.) (Note: In this judicial review proceeding, the judge found no grounds for overriding the Review Tribunal's exercise of its discretion.)

- Applicant returning to India numerous times to assist her widowed son; son dying while applicant in India, causing her to prolong stay for more than one year to care for grandchildren; applicant previously diligent in maintaining her immigrant status and keeping her trips within permissible lengths: *D-40739 v. MHRD* (June 4, 1999) (RT)

---

4. *Residence in Canada must be or have been legal* — **(1) A person who was not a pensioner on July 1, 1977 is eligible for a pension under this Part only if**

(*a*) on the day preceding the day on which that person's application is approved that person is a Canadian citizen or, if not, is legally resident in Canada; or

(*b*) on the day preceding the day that person ceased to reside in Canada that person was a Canadian citizen or, if not, was legally resident in Canada.

(2) *Regulations respecting legal residence* — **The Governor in Council may make regulations respecting the meaning of legal residence for the purposes of subsection (1).**

——————— **Notes** ———————

Related Regulations

- Section 22 — "Legal residence" defined
- Section 23 — Further information required

4.1. *Presumption* — **If the Minister intends to waive the requirement for an application in respect of a person under subsection 5(4) and the information available to the Minister under this Act with respect to that person includes the prescribed information, the person is presumed, in the absence of evidence to the contrary, to have met the requirements of**

(*a*) subparagraph 3(1)(*b*)(iii) or (*c*)(iii) or paragraph 3(2)(*b*); or

(*b*) paragraph 4(1)(*a*) or (*b*).

(S.C. 2012, c. 19, s. 449.)

5. *Limitations* — **(1) No pension may be paid to any person unless that person is qualified under subsection 3(1) or (2), an application therefor has been made by or on behalf of that person and the application has been approved, and, except as provided**

in this Act, no pension may be paid to any person in respect of any period prior to the day on which that person's application is approved.

(2) *Application deemed to have been made and approved* — Where an allowance ceases to be payable to a person by reason of that person having reached sixty-five years of age, the Minister may deem an application under subsection (1) to have been made by that person and approved, on the day on which the person reached that age. (S.C. 1995, c. 33, s. 2; 2000, c. 12, s. 209.)

(3) *Incarcerated persons* — No pension may be paid in respect of a period of incarceration — exclusive of the first month of that period — to a person who is subject to a sentence of imprisonment

    (*a*) that is to be served in a penitentiary by virtue of any Act of Parliament; or

    (*b*) that exceeds 90 days and is to be served in a prison, as defined in subsection 2(1) of the *Prisons and Reformatories Act*, if the government of the province in which the prison is located has entered into an agreement under section 41 of the *Department of Employment and Social Development Act*. (2012, c. 19, s. 296; 2013, c. 40, s. 236(1)(g)(i).)

(2010, c. 22, s. 3.)

(4) *Waiver of application* — The Minister may, on the day on which a person attains 65 years of age, waive the requirement referred to in subsection (1) for an application if the Minister is satisfied, based on information that is available to him or her under this Act, that the person is qualified under subsection 3(1) or (2) for the payment of a pension. (S.C. 2012, c. 19, s. 450.)

(5) *Notice of intent* — If the Minister intends to waive the requirement for an application in respect of a person, the Minister shall notify the person in writing of that intention and provide them with the information on which the Minister intends to rely to approve the payment of a pension. (S.C. 2012, c. 19, s. 450.)

(6) *Inaccuracies* — The person shall, before the day on which they attain 65 years of age, file with the Minister a statement in which the person corrects any inaccuracies in the information provided by the Minister under subsection (5). (S.C. 2012, c. 19, s. 450.)

(7) *Declining waiver* — The person may, before the day on which they attain 65 years of age, decline a waiver of the requirement for an application by notifying the Minister in writing of their decision to do so. (S.C. 2012, c. 19, s. 450.)

(8) *Cancellation of waiver* — Even if the requirement for an application is intended to be waived in respect of a person under subsection (4), the Minister may, before the day on which the person attains 65 years of age, require that the person make an application for payment of a pension and, in that case, the Minister shall notify the person in writing of that requirement. (S.C. 2012, c. 19, s. 450.)

(S.C. 1995, c. 33, s. 2; 2000, c. 12, s. 209; 2010, c. 22, s. 3; 2012, c. 19, ss. 296 and 450; 2013, c. 40, s. 236.)

———————— **Notes** ————————

Related Regulations

- Section 3 — Application form
- Section 4 — Application on other's behalf
- Section 5 — Effective date of approval

● Section 7 — Rounding off partial monthly pension

5.1. *Withdrawal of application* — **(1) An applicant may withdraw an application for a pension by giving a written notice of their withdrawal to the Minister at any time before payment of the pension commences. (S.C. 2007, c. 11, s. 15.)**

(2) *Effect of withdrawal* — **If an application for a pension is withdrawn under subsection (1), the withdrawn application shall not after that time be used for the purpose of determining the applicant's eligibility for a pension. (S.C. 2007, c. 11, s. 15.)**

(S.C. 2007, c. 11, s. 15.)

——————— Notes ———————

Larmet v. Canada (Human Resources and Skills Development), 2012 FC 1406

The rationale for the right to withdraw an application under s. 5.1 of the OAS Act is related to a desire to minimize the tax effects of OAS benefits arising from the receipt of unexpected income. Parliament was apparently concerned that individuals receiving OAS not be pushed into a higher taxation bracket by virtue of the receipt of those benefits. Section 5.1 of the OAS Act and s. 5 of the Regulations do not preclude a claimant from withdrawing his or her application and resubmitting after commencing to receive OAS benefits. If these provisions were intended to bar retroactive recovery in some situations to the prejudice of an otherwise entitled applicant some reference to that purpose would have been made.

Information from Statistics Canada

6. *Census statistics* — **Subject to the conditions specified in the regulations, the Minister is entitled, for the purpose of ascertaining the age of any pensioner or any applicant for a pension, to obtain from Statistics Canada, on request, any information respecting the age of a pensioner or applicant that is contained in the returns of any census taken more than thirty years before the date of the request.**

Amount of Pension

7. *Basic amount of full pension* — **(1) The amount of the full monthly pension that may be paid to any person for a month in the payment quarter commencing on January 1, 1985 is two hundred and seventy-three dollars and eighty cents.**

(2) *Quarterly adjustment of basic amount of full pension* — **Where a full monthly pension has been authorized to be paid to a person, the amount of the pension shall be adjusted quarterly, in such manner as may be prescribed by regulation, so that the amount that may be paid to that person for a month in any payment quarter commencing after March 31, 1985 is the amount obtained by multiplying**

  (a) the amount of the pension that might have been paid to that person for a month in the three-month period immediately before that payment quarter

by

  (b) the ratio that the Consumer Price Index for the first adjustment quarter that relates to that payment quarter bears to the Consumer Price Index for the second adjustment quarter that relates to that payment quarter.

(3) *No decrease in amount of full pension* — **Notwithstanding subsection (2), the amount of a full monthly pension that may be paid to a pensioner for any month in a**

payment quarter shall be not less than the amount of the full monthly pension that was or may be paid to a pensioner for any month in the three-month period immediately before that payment quarter.

(4) *Effect of reduction in Consumer Price Index* — Where, in relation to any payment quarter, the Consumer Price Index for the first adjustment quarter is lower than the Consumer Price Index for the second adjustment quarter,

> (*a*) no pension adjustment shall be made pursuant to subsection (2) in respect of that payment quarter; and
>
> (*b*) no pension adjustment shall be made pursuant to that subsection in respect of any subsequent payment quarter until, in relation to a subsequent payment quarter, the Consumer Price Index for the first adjustment quarter that relates to that subsequent payment quarter is higher than the Consumer Price Index for the second adjustment quarter that relates to the payment quarter referred to in paragraph (*a*), in which case the second adjustment quarter that relates to the payment quarter referred to in that paragraph shall be deemed to be the second adjustment quarter that relates to that subsequent payment quarter.

—————————— **Notes** ——————————

Related Regulations

- Section 8 — Manner of quarterly adjustment of benefit
- Section 9 — Determination of average CPI index for period of months

---

7.1. *Voluntary deferral — full monthly pension* — **(1)** If a person applies for their pension after they become qualified to receive a full monthly pension, the amount of that pension, as calculated in accordance with section 7, is increased by 0.6% for each month in the period that begins in the month after the month in which the person becomes qualified for that pension and that ends in the month in which the person's application is approved. (S.C. 2012, c. 19, s. 451.)

(2) *Voluntary deferral — partial monthly pension* — If a person applies for their pension after they become qualified to receive a partial monthly pension, the amount of that pension, as it is calculated in accordance with subsection 3(3) at the time that they become qualified for that pension, is increased by 0.6% for each month in the period that begins in the month after that time and that ends in the month in which the person's application is approved. (S.C. 2012, c. 19, s. 451.)

(3) *Greatest amount of pension* — A person who is qualified to receive a monthly pension shall, unless they decide otherwise, receive the greatest of the following amounts:

> (*a*) the amount of the full monthly pension as it is increased under subsection (1), if the person is qualified to receive a full monthly pension,
>
> (*b*) the amount of the partial monthly pension as it is increased under subsection (2), and
>
> (*c*) the amount of the partial monthly pension as it is calculated under subsection 3(3) at the time that the person's application is approved.

(S.C. 2012, c. 19, s. 451.)

(4) *Limitation* — Despite subsections (1) and (2), the amount of a pension is not increased for any month (*a*) before July 2013;

(*b*) after the month in which the person attains 70 years of age; or

(*c*) in which the person's pension would not be paid by virtue of subsection 5(3), or would be suspended under subsection 9(1) or (3), if the person were a pensioner.

(S.C. 2012, c. 19, s. 451.)

(S.C. 2012, c. 19, s. 451.)

Payment of Pension

8. *Commencement of pension* — **(1)** Payment of pension to any person shall commence in the first month after the application therefor has been approved, but where an application is approved after the last day of the month in which it was received, the approval may be effective as of such earlier date, not prior to the day on which the application was received, as may be prescribed by regulation.

(2) *Exception* — Notwithstanding subsection (1), where a person who has applied to receive a pension attained the age of sixty-five years before the day on which the application was received, the approval of the application may be effective as of such earlier day, not before the later of

(*a*) a day one year before the day on which the application was received, and (S.C. 1995, c. 33, s. 3(1).)

(*b*) the day on which the applicant attained the age of sixty-five years,

as may be prescribed by regulation.

(2.1) *Incarcerated persons* — Despite subsection (1), if the application by a person described in subsection 5(3) is approved while that person is incarcerated, payment of their pension shall commence in respect of the month in which they are released but only after they notify the Minister in writing before or after their release. (2010, c. 22, s. 4.)

(3) *Duration* — Subject to this Act, the pension shall continue to be paid during the lifetime of the pensioner and shall cease with the payment for the month in which the pensioner dies. (S.C. 2010, c. 22, s. 4.)

(S.C. 1995, c. 33, s. 3(1).)

——————— Notes ———————

Related Regulations

- Section 15 — Assignment of SIN's to applicants
- Section 24 — Payment to person other than beneficiary
- Section 25(2) — Notice of change of address
- Section 26 — Suspension of payments

Case Law

§1. Pre-1995 Eligibility

L-67880 v. MHRD (October 7, 2002) (RT)

Section 5(2) of the OAS Regulations was properly approved under the steps provided for in the *Statutory Instruments Act*. The 1995 amendments to s. 8 of the *OAS Act* reducing the 5-year period of retroactivity to 11 months therefore have the effect of law. The fact that the Minister may have known about the appellant's age when he applied for the CPP in 1997, that by itself did not impose a duty on the Minister to remind the appellant that he was also eligible for OAS benefits. The onus is on all Canadians to apply for an OAS pension, and this is particularly true where the applicant is an experienced practising lawyer.

M-35904 v. MHRD (April 21, 1999) (RT)

The Tribunal may consider the fact that the Minister usually keeps a 100-year shelf-life for applications invalidly filed, and keeps a record of notes sent out to that effect. In the absence of any documentary evidence that a premature application was sent before 1995, the applicant claim for retroactive benefits beyond the current 12-month maximum was dismissed despite testimony from witnesses testified that he had done so.

T-32177 v. MHRD (October 16, 1998) (RT). See also *B-46575 v. MHRD* (December 1, 1999) (RT).

Regardless of whether the Minister took adequate steps to inform the public of the reduced period of retroactivity under the Bill C-54 amendments, the general principle applies that ignorance of the law is no excuse. To ignore the legislative scope of Bill C-54 would be to exceed the law and ignore the plain words of the Act.

F-37734 v. MHRD (January 8, 1999) (RT)

In November 1995, s. 8 was amended by Bill C-54 to restrict retroactive payment to one year instead of five years. The restriction applied to all applications made after the amendment came into effect, even though the applicant became entitled to apply prior to that date. The Tribunal is bound to apply the legislation in force at the date of application.

F-41008 v. MHRD (June 16, 1999) (RT)

Where corroborating evidence of the applicant and his counsel indicated that the application had originally made in 1992, although it was not date stamped by a Ministry official at the time, the 5-year retroactive payment could be grandfathered to the applicant. The application had been refused at the time pending further documentation, as the applicant's birth certificate was insufficient.

K-32202 v. MHRD (October 16, 1998) (RT)

The applicant became eligible for OAS benefits in May 1994, but knowing that the law at that time allowed for retroactive benefits of up to five years she delayed applying until January 1996. The legislation in place at the time of the application applied notwithstanding the applicant's lack of knowledge of the change in the five-year retroactivity legislation.

L-43525 v. MHRD (July 23, 1999) (RT)

The right to apply for OAS at age 65, or put off the application to a later date, was not extinguished by Bill C-54. Bill C-54 did not apply to those pensioners who were 65 years old prior to Bill C-54 being put into law. An applicant, who in 1985 had opted for an early-retirement plan called the "Integration with the Old Age Security Option" (providing for an equivalent to their OAS pension to be added onto his regular benefits) and what the applicant was advised was an "automatic" adjustment at age 65 to deduct such amounts from subsequent OAS payments, was entitled to retroactive payments beyond the current one-year period.

D-60343 v. MHRD (October 18, 2000) (RT)

Not being aware of the reduction of the period of retroactivity from five years to one year was no excuse.

§2. Commencement of Pension

J-32511 v. MHRD (June 15, 1998) (RT)

An applicant cannot revoke her election to receive increased OAS pension as of a later date where no issue is taken with the applicant's execution of the election form or with any of its terms.

483

§3. Retroactive Benefits

Canada (Minister of Human Resources Development) v. Esler, 2004 FC 1567. See also *Canada (Procureur général) v. Vinet-Proulx*, 2007 FC 99.

The Review Tribunal is a pure creature of statute and as such, has no inherent equitable jurisdiction which would allow it to ignore the clear legislative provision contained in s. 8(2) and use the principle of fairness to grant retroactive benefits in excess of the statutory limit.

Larmet v. Canada (Human Resources and Skills Development), 2012 FC 1406

Where a claimant failed to seek retroactive benefits in her initial application, s. 5.1 of the OAS Act and s. 5 of the Regulations did not preclude a claimant from withdrawing his or her application and resubmitting after commencing to receive OAS benefits. If these provisions were intended to bar retroactive recovery in some situations, to the prejudice of an otherwise entitled applicant, some reference to that purpose would have been made.

---

9. *Suspension of pension where pensioner leaves Canada* — **(1) Where a pensioner, having left Canada either before or after becoming a pensioner, has remained outside Canada after becoming a pensioner for six consecutive months, exclusive of the month in which the pensioner left Canada, payment of the pension for any period the pensioner continues to be absent from Canada after those six months shall be suspended, but payment may be resumed with the month in which the pensioner returns to Canada.**

(2) *No suspension after 20 years' residence* — **In the circumstances described in subsection (1), payment of the pension may be continued without suspension for any period the pensioner remains outside Canada if the pensioner establishes that at the time the pensioner left Canada the pensioner had resided in Canada for at least twenty years after attaining the age of eighteen years.**

(3) *Suspension of pension where pensioner ceases to reside in Canada* — **Where a pensioner ceases to reside in Canada, whether before or after becoming a pensioner, payment of the pension shall be suspended six months after the end of the month in which the pensioner ceased to reside in Canada, but payment may be resumed with the month in which the pensioner resumes residence in Canada.**

(4) *No suspension where pensioner had 20 years' residence in Canada* — **In the circumstances described in subsection (3), payment of the pension may be continued without suspension if the pensioner establishes that at the time the pensioner ceased to reside in Canada the pensioner had resided in Canada for at least twenty years after attaining the age of eighteen years.**

(5) *Failure to comply with Act* — **Where a pensioner fails to comply with any of the provisions of this Act or the regulations, payment of the pension may be suspended, and where a pension is so suspended, payment may be resumed when the pensioner has complied with those provisions.**

--- **Notes** ---

Related Regulations

- Section 26 — Suspension of payments

- Section 25(1) — Notice of absence from Canada

Case Law

§1. Absence from Canada

G-62699 v. MHRD (August 23, 2001) (RT)

In calculating the years of residence in Canada of a pension recipient who moves to the U.S., the period before the Canada-U.S. convention came into effect in January 1952 must be included as well as the time after the appellant started receiving the OAS pension while still residing in Canada.

R-35014 v. MHRD; R-40776 v. MHRD (Aug 19, 1999) (RT)

Under s. 9(3), the only exception to suspending a person's pension after six months of being outside of Canada is where the total residence has been 20 years after age 18. Neither the Minister nor the Review Tribunal have the discretion to create variances even in cases of hardship, for example where the recipient became seriously ill while visiting abroad.

W-32004 v. MHRD; W-32006 v. MHRD (January 31, 2000) (RT)

After nearly 19 years of residence in Canada, the fact that the applicant had to stay longer than expected on a holiday expected to care for a sick relative, and was financially unable to return to complete the 20-year residence requirement to export the pension, was irrelevant. A person must have 20 years residence in Canada to receive pension benefits abroad.

A-42613 v. MHRD (July 8, 1999) (RT)

The fact that a recipient has American legal residence status should not prevail over her actual residence in Canada. In this case, the reason for getting a U.S. residence card was to facilitate the recipient's trips to visit her children in the U.S., and her longest period of absence from Canada was only three months.

P-53311 v. MHRD (April 25, 2000) (RT)

The applicant's various brief trips to Greece, totalling 11 months over a 24-year period, while she resided in South Africa were not sufficient to trigger the social security agreement between Canada and Greece and give her credit towards the 20-year residence requirement under s. 9(4). This was particularly so, as the applicant was receiving a grant for the aged in South Africa which would be cancelled if the applicant had left country for more than six months.

G-40287 and G-40288 v. MHRD (July 7, 1999), (RT)

The applicants continued to reside in Canada despite returning to Lebanon from December to April every year to visit their children.

M-32551 v. MHRD (April 6, 1999) (RT)

The applicant had been living with her son in Canada, but left to return to Chile for 10 months because her daughter was very ill. She then returned to Chile for two months when her daughter died, and then for two periods just shy of six months each to take care of her grandchildren. Since then, she has not returned to Chile. While the Minister was entitled to suspend pension benefits for the first period from six months after date of departure until the applicant's return, payments should resume the month of return to Canada despite the subsequent absences.

§2. Non-Compliance with Act

Whitton v. Canada (Attorney General), [2002] FCA 46

The Minister may not refuse to pay OAS benefits to a person who is otherwise eligible on the ground that the person is suspected of having fraudulently cashed benefit cheques issued to the person's deceased mother for 20 years.

9.1. *Request that pension cease to be payable* — **(1) Any pensioner may make a request to the Minister in writing that their pension cease to be payable.**

(2) *When pension ceases to be payable* — A pension shall cease to be payable on the last day of the month in which the Minister approves a request under subsection (1).

(3) *Request for reinstatement* — A pensioner whose pension has ceased to be payable under subsection (2) may make a request in writing to the Minister that their pension be reinstated.

(4) *When reinstatement effective* — A pension shall be reinstated and payment shall commence in the month following the month in which the Minister receives a request under subsection (3) or in the month chosen by the pensioner in the request, whichever is later.

(S.C. 1995, c. 33, s. 4.)

—————————— **Notes** ——————————

Larmet v. Canada (Human Resources and Skills Development), 2012 FC 1406

Obiter: The concern that individuals receiving OAS not be pushed into a higher taxation bracket by virtue of the receipt of such benefits was presumably the rationale behind s. 9.1 of the OAS Act which allows a person to suspend the payment of benefits.

————————————————

9.2. *Resumption of pension* — Payment of a pension that is suspended by virtue of subsection 5(3) shall resume in respect of the month in which a pensioner is released but only after they notify the Minister in writing before or after their release.

(2010, c. 22, s. 5.)

9.3. *Request to cancel pension* — **(1)** A pensioner may, in the prescribed manner and within the prescribed time after payment of a pension has commenced, request cancellation of that pension. (S.C. 2012, c. 19, s. 453.)

(2) *Effect of cancellation* — If the request is granted and the amount of any pension and related supplement and allowance is repaid within the prescribed time,

    (a) the application for that pension is deemed never to have been made; and

    (b) the pension is deemed for the purposes of this Act not to have been payable during the period in question.

(S.C. 2012, c. 19, s. 453.)

(S.C. 2012, c. 19, s. 453.)

Part II

Monthly Guaranteed Income Supplement

Interpretation

10. *Definitions* — The definitions in this section apply in this Part.

"base calendar year" **means the last calendar year ending before the current payment period.**

"current payment period" **means the payment period in respect of which an application for a supplement is made by an applicant.**

"previous payment period" **means the payment period immediately before the current payment period.**

(S.C. 1998, c. 21, s. 106.)

Supplement Payable

11. *Supplement payable* — **(1) Subject to this Part and the regulations, for each month in any payment period, a monthly guaranteed income supplement may be paid to a pensioner. (S.C. 1998, c. 21, s. 119(2)(b).)**

(2) *Requirement for application* — **Subject to subsection (4), no supplement may be paid to a pensioner for a month in any payment period unless an application for payment of a supplement has been made by the pensioner and payment of the supplement for months in that year has been approved under this Part. (S.C. 1998, c. 21, s. 119(2)(b).)**

S. 11(2) will be replaced by S.C. 2012, c. 19, s. 454(1) on proclamation, and will read as follows:

(2) *Requirement for application* — **Subject to subsections (3.1) and (4), no supplement may be paid to a pensioner for a month in any payment period unless an application for payment of a supplement has been made by the pensioner and payment of the supplement for months in that year has been approved under this Part.**

(3) *Application deemed to be made and approved* — **Where an allowance ceases to be payable to a person by reason of that person having reached sixty-five years of age, the Minister may deem an application under subsection (2) to have been made by that person and approved, on the day on which the person reached that age. (S.C. 1998, c. 21, s. 107; 2000, c. 12, s. 209.)**

S. 11(3.1) to (3.5) will be added by S.C. 2012, c. 19, s. 454(2) on proclamation, and will read as follows:

(3.1) *Waiver of application* — **The Minister may, in respect of a person, waive the requirement referred to in subsection (2) for an application for payment of a supplement for any month or months in a payment period if, on the day on which the person attains 65 years of age, the Minister is satisfied, based on information available to him or her under this Act, that the person is qualified under this section for the payment of a supplement.**

(3.2) *Notice of intent* — **If the Minister intends to waive the requirement for an application in respect of a person under subsection (3.1), the Minister shall notify the person in writing of that intention and provide them with the information on which the Minister intends to rely to approve the payment of a supplement.**

(3.3) *Inaccuracies* — **The person shall, before the day on which they attain 65 years of age, file with the Minister a statement in which the person corrects any inaccuracies in the information provided by the Minister under subsection (3.2).**

(3.4) *Declining waiver* — **The person may, before the day on which they attain 65 years of age, decline a waiver of the requirement for an application by notifying the Minister in writing of their decision to do so.**

(3.5) *Cancellation of waiver* — **Even if the requirement for an application is intended to be waived in respect of a person under subsection (3.1), the Minister may, before the day on which the person attains 65 years of age, require that the person make an application for payment of a supplement and, in that case, the Minister shall notify the person in writing of that requirement.**

Old Age Security Act

(4) *Waiver of application* — The Minister may waive the requirement referred to in subsection (2) for an application for payment of a supplement for any month or months in a payment period if an application for payment of a supplement has been made in respect of any payment period before that payment period. (S.C. 1998, c. 21, s. 119(1)(*a*); 2007, c. 11, s. 16(1).)

(5) *Notice where subsequent application required* — Where the requirement for an application for payment of a supplement for any month or months in a payment period has been waived under subsection (4) and an application is required for payment of a supplement for any subsequent month or months in that payment period, the Minister shall, not later than fifteen days before that subsequent month or the first of those subsequent months, notify the pensioner in writing that an application is required. (S.C. 1998, c. 21, s. 119(1)(*a*).)

(6) *Cancellation of waiver* — Notwithstanding that the requirement for an application for payment of a supplement for any month or months has been waived under subsection (4), the Minister may require that the pensioner make an application for payment of a supplement for that month or for any of those months, and in such a case, the Minister shall, not later than fifteen days before that month or the first of those months, notify the pensioner in writing that an application is required.

(7) *Limitations on payment of supplement* — No supplement may be paid to a pensioner for

(a) any month that is more than eleven months before the month in which the application is received or is deemed to have been made or in which the requirement for an application has been waived, as the case may be;

(b) any month for which no pension may be paid to the pensioner;

(c) any month throughout which the pensioner is absent from Canada having commenced to be absent from Canada either before or after becoming a pensioner and having remained outside Canada before that month for six consecutive months, exclusive of the month in which the pensioner left Canada; (S.C. 1996, c. 18, s. 51(1).)

(d) any month throughout which the pensioner is not resident in Canada, having ceased to reside in Canada, either before or after becoming a pensioner, six months before the beginning of that month; or (S.C. 1996, c. 18, s. 51(1).)

(e) any month during which the pensioner is

(i) a specially qualified individual, and

(ii) a person in respect of whom an undertaking by a sponsor is in effect as provided under the *Immigration and Refugee Protection Act*[4]. (S.C. 1996, c. 18, s. 51(1); 2001, c. 27, s. 264; 2007, c. 11, s. 16(2).)

S. 11(7)(e) will be replaced by S.C. 2014, c. 20, s. 371(1) on proclamation, and will read as follows:

(e) any month during which the pensioner is a person in respect of whom an undertaking by a sponsor is in effect as provided under the *Immigration and Refugee Protection Act*.

---

[4] Subparagraphs 11(7)(e)(ii), 19(6)(d)(ii) and 21(9)(c)(ii) of the *Old Age Security Act*, as they read immediately before the day on which this Act receives royal assent, continue to apply to any person who, before that day, is a beneficiary of a supplement or an allowance under that Act or has made an application for payment of a supplement or an allowance under that Act (S.C. 2007, c. 11, s. 37).

(8) *Application of para. (7)(e)* — **Paragraph (7)(e) does not apply to a pensioner where an event as provided by the regulations has occurred. (S.C. 1996, c. 18, s. 51(1).)**

S. 11(8) will be replaced by S.C. 2014, c. 20, s. 371(2) on proclamation, and will read as follows:

(8) *Application of para. (7)(e)* — **Paragraph (7)(e) does not apply**

(a) to a person who was qualified to receive a pension or an allowance immediately before the day on which this paragraph comes into force, whether or not they had applied for it; or

(b) to a pensioner if an event as provided by the regulations has occurred.

(S.C. 1995, c. 33, s. 5; 1996, c. 18, s. 51(1); 1998, c. 21, ss. 107, 119(1)(a), (2)(b); 2000, c. 12, s. 209; 2001, c. 27, s. 264; 2007, c. 11, s. 16.)

——————— **Notes** ———————

Synopsis

This section provides for a supplemental amount (the Guaranteed Income Supplement or "GIS") to be paid to OAS pension recipients who have little or no other income. GIS recipients are required to reapply every year. The GIS is not available to foreign residents, although it continues for six months after a recipient leaves Canada. Retroactive GIS payments are only available for up to 11 months prior to the date of the application. If the applicant is married and living with his or her spouse, or is a common-law partner, the combined income must be considered for determining eligibility (see s. 15).

Related Regulations

- Section 10 — Approval of application for supplement

- Section 22.1 — Sponsored immigrants' exceptions

- Section 23 — Further information required

Case Law

T-76276 v. MHRD (October 15, 2003) (RT)

Retroactive benefits beyond the 11-month limitation were justified where the Ministry had previously issued and suspended GIS payments to the recipient based on internal information, with no application filed or required. The recipient was entitled to expect that no application by him was required.

J-71328 and J-71330 v. MHRD (April 29, 2003) (RT)

The Review Tribunal has no authority or discretion to award GIS benefits to sponsored immigrants during the sponsorship term, despite any difficult financial circumstances they may be experiencing.

C-46120 v. MHRD (April 10, 2000) (RT)

In the absence of proof of a prior GIS application, a Review Tribunal's jurisdiction is confined to reviewing whether the decision of the Minister in awarding the benefits under the application before it has been done according to the legislative requirements. There was no argument that the eleven-month retroactivity payment was incorrect.

S-46930 v. MHRD (February 24, 2000) (RT)

Circumstances as to why a person had not made a GIS application earlier are not relevant to determining whether the Minister has fulfilled their obligations under the legislation.

Old Age Security Act

P-40873 v. MHRD (January 19, 1999) (RT)

Whether or not the applicant was fully informed that GIS benefits were available at the time she started to receive her OAS pension, the Tribunal was without jurisdiction to change the legislative provisions in the Act to increase the period of retroactivity beyond 11 months.

Y-28466 v. MHRD (February 25, 1999) (RT)

The applicant delayed in applying for GIS benefits for three years because he did not know that RRSP contributions were deductible in computing income for GIS purposes. He had been informed by a Human Resources officer at the time of the initial application that entitlement was based on "gross income". Nevertheless, the applicant had admittedly overlooked an instruction note regarding RRSP contributions sent with the first application, and such error on his part caused in late application.

L-33570 v. MHRD (July 6, 1998) (RT)

The applicant went to the U.S. to live and work for 31 years, although she returned to Canada each summer for her vacations and for winter holidays. It was held that, although she returned at least every six months, such visits did not re-start the calculation of the prescribed six-month absence allowable under sec. 11(7)(*c*) of the *Old Age Security Act*.

Amount of Supplement

12. *Amounts on April 1, 2005* — **(1) The amount of the supplement that may be paid to a pensioner for any month in the payment quarter commencing on April 1, 2005 is,**

　　(*a*) in the case of a person other than a person described in paragraph (*b*), five hundred and sixty-two dollars and ninety-three cents, and

　　(*b*) in the case of a person who, on the day immediately before that payment quarter, had a spouse or common-law partner to whom a pension may be paid for any month in that payment quarter, (S.C. 2000, c. 12, s. 207(1).)

　　　　(i) in respect of any month in that payment quarter before the first month for which a pension may be paid to the spouse or common-law partner, five hundred and sixty-two dollars and ninety-three cents, and

　　　　(ii) in respect of any month in that payment quarter commencing with the first month for which a pension may be paid to the spouse or common-law partner, three hundred and sixty-six dollars and sixtyseven cents,

　　minus one dollar for each full two dollars of the pensioner's monthly base income.

(S.C. 1998, c. 21, s. 108(1); 2000, c. 12, s. 207(1); 2005, c. 30, s. 136.)

　　(1.1) *Increase on January 1, 2006* — **The amount of the supplement that may be paid to a pensioner for any month in the payment quarter commencing on January 1, 2006 is the amount of the supplement that would otherwise be payable plus**

　　(*a*) eighteen dollars, in the case of a person described in paragraph (1)(*a*) or subparagraph (1)(*b*)(i); and

　　(*b*) fourteen dollars and fifty cents, in the case of a person described in subparagraph (1)(*b*)(ii).

(S.C. 2005, c. 30, s. 136.)

　　(1.2) *Increase on January 1, 2007* — **The amount of the supplement that may be paid to a pensioner for any month in the payment quarter commencing on January 1, 2007 is the amount of the supplement that would otherwise be payable plus**

(*a*) eighteen dollars, in the case of a person described in paragraph (1)(*a*) or subparagraph (1)(*b*)(i); and

(*a*) fourteen dollars and fifty cents, in the case of a person described subparagraph (1)(*b*)(ii).

(S.C. 2005, c. 30, s. 136.)

(2) *Indexation* — Subject to subsections (1.1) and (1.2), the amount of the supplement that may be paid to a pensioner for any month in any payment quarter commencing after June 30, 2005 is the amount obtained by multiplying

(*a*) the maximum amount of the supplement that might have been paid to the pensioner for any month in the three-month period immediately before that payment quarter

by

(*b*) the ratio that the Consumer Price Index for the first adjustment quarter that relates to that payment quarter bears to the Consumer Price Index for the second adjustment quarter that relates to that payment quarter,

minus one dollar for each full two dollars of the pensioner's monthly base income.

(S.C. 1998, c. 21, s. 108(1); 1999, c. 22, s. 88(1); 2005, c. 30, s. 136.)

(3) *No decrease in maximum amount of supplement* — Notwithstanding subsection (2), the maximum amount of the supplement that may be paid to a pensioner for any month in a payment quarter shall be not less than the maximum amount of the supplement that was or may be paid to a pensioner for any month in the three month period immediately before that payment quarter.

(4) *Effect of reduction in Consumer Price Index* — Where, in relation to any payment quarter, the Consumer Price Index for the first adjustment quarter is lower than the Consumer Price Index for the second adjustment quarter,

(*a*) no supplement adjustment shall be made pursuant to subsection (2) in respect of that payment quarter; and

(*b*) no supplement adjustment shall be made pursuant to that subsection in respect of any subsequent payment quarter until, in relation to a subsequent payment quarter, the Consumer Price Index for the first adjustment quarter that relates to that subsequent payment quarter is higher than the Consumer Price Index for the second adjustment quarter that relates to the payment quarter referred to in paragraph (*a*), in which case the second adjustment quarter that relates to the payment quarter referred to in that paragraph shall be deemed to be the second adjustment quarter that relates to that subsequent payment quarter.

(5) *Guaranteed minimum income for pensioners* — Despite subsection (2), the amount of the supplement that may be paid to a pensioner for any month after December 1997 is the amount determined by the formula (S.C. 1998, c. 21, s. 108(2).)

$$[(A - B) \times C] - D/2$$

where

A   is the aggregate of

(*a*) the maximum amount of the supplement that, but for this subsection, might have been paid to the pensioner for that month, and

(*b*) the amount of the full monthly pension;

B   is the pensioner's monthly pension;

491

C is the pensioner's special qualifying factor for the month; and

D is the pensioner's monthly base income rounded, where it is not a multiple of two dollars, to the next lower multiple of two dollars. (S.C. 1998, c. 21, s. 108(3); 1999, c. 22, s. 88(2).)

   (5.1) *Enhancement of supplement for certain married pensioners* — Where the aggregate of the pensions and supplements payable for a month to two pensioners, each of whom is the other's spouse or common-law partner, is less than the aggregate of the pension and supplement that would be payable for that month to one of them if the other were not a pensioner, the Minister may, notwithstanding subsection (2), pay to one of them for that month (S.C. 2000, c. 12, s. 207(1).)

   (*a*) the amount of supplement that would be payable for that month to that pensioner, if the other were not a pensioner,

minus

   (*b*) the aggregate of the pension and supplement payable for that month to the other. (S.C. 1996, c. 18, s. 52(2).)

(S.C. 2000, c. 12, s. 207(1).)

   (6) *Definition of "monthly base income"* — In this section, "monthly base income" means, in relation to the calculation of the supplement for a month in any given payment quarter,

   (*a*) in the case of a person other than an applicant described in paragraph (*b*) or (*c*), one-twelfth of the income of that person for the base calendar year;

   (*b*) in the case of an applicant who, on the day immediately before the current payment period, was the spouse or common-law partner of a person to whom no pension may be paid for any month in the current payment period, the amount determined by the formula (S.C. 1998, c. 21, s. 108(4); 2000, c. 12, s. 207(1).)

$$A/24 - B/2$$

where

A is the aggregate of the incomes of the applicant and the spouse or common-law partner for the base calendar year, and (S.C. 2000, c. 12, s. 207(1).)

B is the product
   (i) obtained by multiplying the amount of the full monthly pension that might have been paid to a pensioner for any month by the applicant's special qualifying factor for the month, and
   (ii) rounded, where that product is not a multiple of four dollars, to the next higher multiple of four dollars; and (S.C. 1998, c. 21, s. 108(5); 1999, c. 22, s. 88(3).)

   (*c*) in the case of an applicant who, on the day immediately before the current payment period, was the spouse or common-law partner of a person to whom a pension may be paid for any month in the current payment period, (S.C. 1998, c. 21, s. 119(1)(*b*); 2000, c. 12, s. 207(1).)

   (i) in respect of any month in the current payment period before the first month for which a pension may be paid to the spouse or common-law partner, the amount determined for the applicant for the month under paragraph (*b*), and (S.C. 1996, c. 18, s. 54(1); 1998, c. 21, s. 119(1)(*b*); 2000, c. 12, s. 207(1).)

(ii) **in respect of any month in that payment period commencing with the first month for which a pension may be paid to the spouse or common-law partner, one twenty-fourth of the aggregate of the incomes of the applicant and the spouse or common-law partner for the base calendar year. (S.C. 1998, c. 21, s. 119(1)(b); 2000, c. 12, s. 207(1).)**

(S.C. 1996, c. 18, s. 52; 1998, c. 21, s. 108; 1998, c. 21, s. 119(1)(b); 1999, c. 22, s. 88; 2000, c. 12, s. 207(1).)

—————— Notes ——————

Related Regulations

- Section 8 — Manner of quarterly adjustment of benefit
- Section 9 — Determination of average CPI index for period of months

Case Law

Gaisford v. Canada (Attorney General), 2011 FCA 28

The guaranteed income supplement is dependent upon a person's income as its purpose is to supplement the monthly OAS pension for those seniors with limited income. The guaranteed income supplement is thus adjusted to take into account the income of a beneficiary in accordance with adjustment formulas set out in the OAS. Compulsory RRIF withdrawals and the gross-up of dividend revenues are taxable amounts for the purposes of the ITA and therefore must be included in a recipient's income for the purposes of determining the guaranteed income supplement.

P-77645 v. MSD (2004) (RT)

To be granted a monthly GIS benefit under the *OAS Act*, the appellant must meet four criteria:

1. receive Old Age Security benefits (s. 11(1));
2. submit an application (s. 11(2) of Act; s. 10 of Regulations);
3. reside in Canada (s. 11(7) of Act); and
4. have an income not exceeding the set limit (s. 12 of Act).

The definition of "pension income" under s. 14 of the OAS Regulations does not include withdrawals from an RRSP. Therefore, the monies in that type of account, unless converted to a RRIF account, are considered like those in an ordinary savings account. RRSPs and RRIFs are two separate entities, and are not interchangeable.

S-75500 v. MSD (2004) (RT)

The illness of an applicant's immigration sponsor does not result in a sponsorship breakdown for the purposes of s. 22.1 of the Regulations. The Canada–Jamaica social security agreement did not bar Canada from unilaterally changing the rules in this regard.

B-74059 v. MSD; B-74060 v. MSD (2004) (RT)

Despite how spouses might describe their marital status — whether married or separated — they can remain married and not be legally separated if they exhibit behaviour which is more consistent with marriage than separation. Couples need not physically cohabitate or have conjugal relations for a marriage to survive.

12.1. *Additional amount —paragraph 12(1)(a) —* **(1) The amount that may be added to the amount of the supplement that may be paid under section 12 to a pensioner referred to in paragraph 12(1)(a) for any month in a payment quarter beginning after June 30, 2011 is the amount determined by the formula**

493

$$A \times B - C/4$$

where

A is \$50;

B is the pensioner's special qualifying factor for the month; and

C is

(*a*) in the case of a pensioner who has no spouse or common-law partner, $^1/_{12}$ of the pensioner's income for the base calendar year in excess of \$2,000 rounded, if it is not a multiple of four dollars, to the next lower multiple of four dollars, and

(*b*) in the case of a pensioner who, on the day immediately before the current payment period, had a spouse or common-law partner to whom no benefit may be paid for any month in the current payment period, $^1/_{24}$ of the aggregate of the income of the pensioner and his or her spouse or common-law partner for the base calendar year in excess of \$4,000 rounded, if it is not a multiple of four dollars, to the next lower multiple of four dollars.

(2011, c. 15, s. 13.)

(2) *Additional amount — paragraph 12(1)(b)* — The amount that may be added to the amount of the supplement that may be paid under section 12 to a pensioner referred to in paragraph 12(1)(*b*) for any month in a payment quarter beginning after June 30, 2011 is the amount determined by the formula

$$A \times B - C/4$$

where

A is

(*a*) in the case of a pensioner referred to in subparagraph 12(1)(*b*)(i), \$50, and

(*b*) in the case of a pensioner referred to in subparagraph 12(1)(*b*)(ii), \$35;

B is the pensioner's special qualifying factor for the month; and

C is $^1/_{24}$ of the aggregate of the income of the pensioner and his or her spouse or common-law partner for the base calendar year in excess of \$4,000 rounded, if it is not a multiple of four dollars, to the next lower multiple of four dollars.

(2011, c. 15, s. 13.)

(3) *Indexation* — For the purpose of calculating the amount payable under subsection (1) or (2) for any month in a payment quarter beginning after September 30, 2011, the amount to be determined for A in that subsection is the amount obtained by multiplying

(*a*) the amount determined for A for any month in the three-month period immediately before that payment quarter

by

(*b*) the ratio that the Consumer Price Index for the first adjustment quarter that relates to that payment quarter bears to the Consumer Price Index for the second adjustment quarter that relates to that payment quarter.

(2011, c. 15, s. 13.)

(4) *No decrease* — Despite subsection (3), the amount determined for A for any month in a payment quarter shall not be less than the amount determined for A for any

month in the three-month period immediately before that payment quarter. (2011, c. 15, s. 13.)

(5) *Effect of reduction in Consumer Price Index* — If, in relation to any payment quarter, the Consumer Price Index for the first adjustment quarter is lower than the Consumer Price Index for the second adjustment quarter,

(a) no adjustment to the amount determined for A shall be made under subsection (3) in respect of that payment quarter; and

(b) no adjustment to the amount determined for A shall be made under subsection (3) in respect of any subsequent payment quarter until, in relation to a subsequent payment quarter, the Consumer Price Index for the first adjustment quarter that relates to that subsequent payment quarter is higher than the Consumer Price Index for the second adjustment quarter that relates to the payment quarter referred to in paragraph (a), in which case the second adjustment quarter that relates to the payment quarter referred to in that paragraph is deemed to be the second adjustment quarter that relates to that subsequent payment quarter.

(2011, c. 15, s. 13.)

(2011, c. 15, s. 13.)

Calculation of Income

13. *Calculation of income* — For the purposes of determining the amount of supplement that may be paid to a pensioner for a month before July 1, 1999, the income for a calendar year of a person or an applicant is the income of that person or applicant for that year computed in accordance with the *Income Tax Act*, except that (S.C. 1998, c. 21, s. 109.)

(a) there shall be deducted from the person's or applicant's income from office or employment for that year

(i) a single amount in respect of all offices and employments of that person or applicant equal to the lesser of five hundred dollars and one fifth of the person's or applicant's income from office or employment for that year,

(ii) the amount of employee's premiums paid by the person or applicant during the year under the *Employment Insurance Act*, and

(iii) the amount of employee's contributions made by the person or applicant during the year under the *Canada Pension Plan* or a provincial pension plan as defined in section 3 of that Act;

(b) there shall be deducted from the person's or applicant's self-employed earnings for that year

(i) the amount of contributions made in respect of those self-employed earnings by the person or applicant during the year under the *Canada Pension Plan* or a provincial pension plan as defined in section 3 of that Act, and

(ii) the amount of premium paid by the person or applicant during the year under Part VII.1 of the *Employment Insurance Act*; and

(S.C. 2009, c. 33, s. 32.)

(c) there shall be deducted from the person's or applicant's income for that year, to the extent that those amounts have been included in computing that income,

(i) the amount of any benefit under this Act and the amount of any similar payment under a law of a provincial legislature,

Old Age Security Act

(ii) the amount of any allowance under the *Family Allowances Act* and the amount of any similar payment under a law of a provincial legislature,

(iii) the amount of any death benefit under the *Canada Pension Plan* or a provincial pension plan as defined in section 3 of that Act,

(iv) the amount of any grant under a program that is a prescribed program of the Government of Canada relating to home insulation or energy conversion for the purposes of paragraphs 12(1)(*u*) and 56(1)(*s*) of the *Income Tax Act*, and

(v) the amount of any social assistance payment made on the basis of a means, a needs or an income test by a registered charity as defined in subsection 248(1) of the *Income Tax Act* or under a program provided for by an Act of Parliament or a provincial legislature that is neither a program prescribed under the *Income Tax Act* nor a program under which the amounts referred to in subparagraph (i) are paid.

(S.C. 1990, c. 39, s. 57; 1998, c. 21, s. 109; 2009, c. 33, s. 32.)

———————— Notes ————————

Case Law

Canada (Minister of Human Resources Development) v. Gerstel, 2006 FCA 93 (CanLII)

While the computation of income under the OAS Act must be made in accordance with the rules provided under the federal *Income Tax Act* ("ITA"), subject to the stated exceptions, there was no requirement that this income be the same as that reported under the ITA. Since the capital cost allowance ("CCA") deduction is optional under the ITA, it was open to a GIS recipient and his spouse not to claim CCA for income tax purposes, but to do so for OAS Act purposes.

Canada v. Dechant, 2009 FCA 200

Despite the *Gerstel* decision (above), a GIS claimant is not entitled to adopt an accrual method for calculating income under the OAS Act, while maintaining a cash method for income tax purposes.

Naidoo v. Canada (Minister of Human Resources Development) 2003 TCC 394

"Income" under s. 13 of the *OAS Act* is computed in accordance with the federal *Income Tax Act*. Where a couple receiving GIS benefits borrowed against their life insurance policy, after being advised by the insurer that the net amount borrowed in a year must be included in income for income tax purposes, they were not entitled to relief when the increase in deemed income resulted in a reduction in their GIS entitlement. The court had no power to undo the transaction, even though it could have been fashioned in a way that avoided the harsh result to the couple.

———————————

Statement or Estimate of Income

14. *Statement of income to be made* — **(1) Every person by whom an application for a supplement in respect of a current payment period is made shall, in the application, make a statement of the person's income for the base calendar year. (S.C. 1998, c. 21, s. 110(1).)**

(1.01) *Waiver — statement of income* — **The Minister may waive the requirement to make a statement of income under subsection (1) if that information has been made available to the Minister under this Act and, in that case, the statement is deemed to have been made for the purposes of this Part. (S.C. 2007, c. 11, s. 17(1).)**

(1.1) *Minister may estimate income* — Where the requirement for an application for payment of a supplement for any month has been waived under subsection 11(4), the Minister may, on the basis of the information available to the Minister,

S. 14(1.1), the portion before paragraph (*a*), will be replaced by S.C. 2012, c. 19, s. 455 on proclamation, and will read as follows:

(1.1) *Minister may estimate income* — If the requirement for an application for payment of a supplement for any month has been waived under subsection 11(3.1) or (4), the Minister may, on the basis of the information available to him or her,

(*a*) estimate the applicant's income for the base calendar year; and

(*b*) in the case of an applicant who is a person described in subsection 15(2), estimate the income of the applicant's spouse or common-law partner for the base calendar year. (S.C. 2000, c. 12, s. 207(1).)

(1.2) *Statement of income where income estimated* — Where a person's income for a base calendar year has been estimated under subsection (1.1), the Minister may require that the person make a statement to the Minister of their income for any month in that year. (S.C. 1995, c. 33, s. 6.)

(2) *Additional statement if retirement in current payment period* — If in a current payment period a person who is an applicant, or is an applicant's spouse or common-law partner who has filed a statement as described in paragraph 15(2)(*a*), ceases to hold an office or employment or ceases to carry on a business, that person may, not later than the end of the second payment period after the current payment period, in addition to making the statement of income required by subsection (1) in the case of the applicant or in addition to filing a statement as described in paragraph 15(2)(*a*) in the case of the applicant's spouse or common-law partner, file a statement of the person's estimated income for the calendar year in which the person ceased to hold that office or employment or ceased to carry on that business, which income shall be calculated as the total of

(*a*) any pension income received by the person in that part of that calendar year that is after the month in which the person ceases to hold that office or employment or to carry on that business, divided by the number of months in that part of that calendar year and multiplied by 12,

(*b*) the income from any office or employment or any business for that calendar year other than income from the office, employment or business that has ceased, and

(*c*) the person's income for the base calendar year calculated as though, for that year, the person had no income from any office or employment or any business and no pension income.

(S.C. 1998, c. 21, s. 110(2); 2000, c. 12, s. 207(1); 2007, c. 11, s. 17(2).)

(3) *Additional statement if retirement in the last month of the calendar year that is in the current payment period* — Despite subsection (2), if in the last month of a calendar year that ends in the current payment period a person who is an applicant, or is an applicant's spouse or common-law partner who has filed a statement as described in paragraph 15(2)(*a*), ceases to hold an office or employment or ceases to carry on a business, the person may, not later than the end of the second payment period after the current payment period, in addition to making the statement of income required by subsection (1) in the case of the applicant or in addition to filing a statement as described in paragraph 15(2)(*a*) in the case of the applicant's spouse or common-law partner, file a statement of the person's estimated income for the calendar year that is immediately after the month in which the person ceased to hold that office or employment or ceased to carry on that business, which income shall be calculated as the total of

(a) any pension income received by the person in that calendar year,

(b) the income from any office or employment or any business for that calendar year other than income from the office, employment or business that has ceased, and

(c) the person's income for the base calendar year calculated as though, for that year, the person had no income from any office or employment or any business and no pension income.

(S.C. 1998, c. 21, s. 110(2); 2000, c. 12, s. 207(1); 2007, c. 11, s. 17(2).)

(4) *Additional statement if loss of pension income in current payment period* — **If in a current payment period a person who is an applicant, or is an applicant's spouse or common-law partner who has filed a statement as described in paragraph 15(2)(a), suffers a loss of income due to termination of or reduction in pension income, the person may, not later than the end of the second payment period after the current payment period, in addition to making the statement of income required by subsection (1) in the case of the applicant or in addition to filing a statement as described in paragraph 15(2)(a) in the case of the applicant's spouse or common-law partner, file a statement of the person's estimated income for the calendar year in which the loss is suffered, which income shall be calculated as the total of**

(a) any pension income received by the person in that part of that calendar year that is after the month immediately before the month in which the loss is suffered, divided by the number of months in that part of that calendar year and multiplied by 12,

(b) the income from any office or employment or any business for that calendar year, and

(c) the person's income for the base calendar year calculated as though, for that year, the person had no income from any office or employment or any business and no pension income.

(S.C. 1998, c. 21, s. 110(2); 2000, c. 12, s. 207(1); 2007, c. 11, s. 17(2).)

(5) *Additional statement if retirement before current payment period* — **If, in the circumstances described in paragraphs (a) and (b), a person who is an applicant, or is an applicant's spouse or common-law partner who has filed a statement as described in paragraph 15(2)(a), ceases to hold an office or employment or ceases to carry on a business, the person may, not later than the end of the payment period that is immediately after the current payment period, in addition to making the statement of income required by subsection (1) in the case of the applicant or in addition to filing a statement as described in paragraph 15(2)(a) in the case of the applicant's spouse or common-law partner,**

(a) if the person ceases to hold that office or employment or to carry on that business in the last calendar year ending before the payment period, file a statement of the person's estimated income for the calendar year ending in the current payment period, which income shall be calculated as the total of

(i) any pension income received by the person in that calendar year,

(ii) the income from any office or employment or any business for that calendar year, other than income from the office, employment or business that has ceased, and

(iii) the person's income for the base calendar year calculated as though, for that year, the person had no income from any office or employment or any business and no pension income; and

(*b*) if the person ceases to hold that office or employment or to carry on that business in a month that is before the payment period and after the last calendar year ending before the payment period, file a statement of the person's estimated income for the calendar year ending in the current payment period, which income shall be calculated as the total of

(i) any pension income received by the person in that part of that calendar year that is after the month in which the person ceases to hold that office or employment or to carry on that business, divided by the number of months in that part of that calendar year and multiplied by 12,

(ii) the income from any office or employment or any business for that calendar year, other than income from the office, employment or business that has ceased, and

(iii) the person's income for the base calendar year calculated as though, for that year, the person had no income from any office or employment or any business and no pension income.

(S.C. 1998, c. 21, s. 110(2); 2000, c. 12, s. 207(1); 2007, c. 11, s. 17(2).)

(6) *Additional statement if loss of pension income before current payment period —* If, in the circumstances described in paragraph (*a*) or (*b*), a person who is an applicant, or is an applicant's spouse or common-law partner who has filed a statement as described in paragraph 15(2)(*a*), suffers a loss of income due to a termination of or reduction in pension income, the person may, not later than the end of the payment period that is immediately after the current payment period, in addition to making the statement of income required by subsection (1) in the case of the applicant or in addition to filing a statement as described in paragraph 15(2)(*a*) in the case of the applicant's spouse or common-law partner,

(*a*) if the loss is suffered in the last calendar year ending before the payment period, file a statement of the person's estimated income for the calendar year ending in the current payment period, which income shall be calculated as the total of

(i) any pension income received by the person in that calendar year,

(ii) the income from any office or employment or any business for that calendar year, and

(iii) the person's income for the base calendar year calculated as though, for that year, the person had no income from any office or employment or any business and no pension income; and

(*b*) if the loss is suffered in a month that is before the payment period and after the last calendar year ending before the payment period, file a statement of the person's estimated income for the calendar year ending in the current payment period, which income shall be calculated as the total of

(i) any pension income received by the person in that part of that calendar year that is after the month immediately before the month in which the loss is suffered, divided by the number of months in that part of that calendar year and multiplied by 12,

(ii) the income from any office or employment or any business for that calendar year, and

(iii) the person's income for the base calendar year calculated as though, for that year, the person had no income from any office or employment or any business and no pension income.

(S.C. 1998, c. 21, s. 110(2); 2000, c. 12, s. 207(1); 2007, c. 11, s. 17(2).)

(7) *Where statement filed under subsection (2), (3) or (4)* — Where under subsection (2), (3) or (4) a statement of estimated income is filed by an applicant or an applicant's spouse or common-law partner, no supplement calculated on the basis of that statement may be paid to the applicant for any month in the current payment period before (S.C. 1998, c. 21, s. 119(1)(c); 2000, c. 12, s. 207(1).)

(a) the month immediately following the month shown in the statement as the month in which the applicant or the applicant's spouse or common-law partner, as the case may be, ceased to hold the office or employment or ceased to carry on the business, or (S.C. 2000, c. 12, s. 207(1).)

(b) the month shown in the statement as the month in which the applicant or the applicant's spouse or common-law partner, as the case may be, suffered the loss of income due to termination or reduction of pension income, (S.C. 2000, c. 12, s. 207(1).)

whichever is applicable.

(S.C. 1998, c. 21, ss. 110, 119(1)(c); 2000, c. 12, s. 207; 2007, c. 11, s. 17.)

——————— Notes ———————

Related Regulations

- Section 13 — Month in which loss of income occurs
- Section 14 — Definition of "pension income"
- Section 16 — Proof of spousal relationship

Case Law

P-77645 v. MSD (2004) (RT)

The Review Tribunal is competent to rule on the issue of whether the interpretation of "income" and "pension income", (as defined in s. 14(4) of the *OAS Act*, in relation to s. 14 of the Regulations) equates income from an RRSP to income from a RRIF. However, the Tribunal would not be competent to rule on the issue of whether a Minister's decision is unfounded because it addresses the computation of the appellant's income. The non-withdrawal of RRSP funds in a subsequent year does not constitute a reduction in pension income for that year.

L-81415 v. MSD (2004) (RT)

The estimate of previous year's income required by s. 14(4) of the *OAS Act* must actually be received by the Minister by June 30 of the following year, regardless of when it was mailed.

Canada (Attorney General) v. Comeau, 2004 FC 1034

The Review Tribunal is not authorized to direct how the Minister should treat a claimant's "income", including the inclusion or exclusion of RRSP redemptions, for the taxation year in question. Appeals on that ground are to be taken to the Tax Court of Canada.

Rysdyk v. Canada (Minister of Human Resources Development) 2003 TCC 123

By virtue of s. 56(1)(a)(i)(C.1) of the *Income Tax Act*, a pension paid to a Canadian resident under the "General Old Age Pensions" laws of the Netherlands, was to be included in the recipient's income. Therefore, the recipient's GIS entitlement was reduced to reflect the additional income.

W-74590 v. MHRD (December 19, 2003) (RT)

The receipt of an unusual distribution of a pension fund surplus in the previous year does not constitute a reduction in "pension income" in the current year, and therefore did not permit the recipient to use an estimate of his 2002 income for purposes of calculating his GIS entitlement. There had been no reduction of pension income in 2002 but merely a lack of further distributions of surplus.

F-76282 v. MHRD (December 18, 2003) (RT)

An RRSP is not a "pension income" for the purposes of s. 14 of the OAS Regulations, and cannot be viewed as a reason for a person to exercise an option to be paid on his or her estimated income for GIS purposes.

S-76079 v. MHRD (November 26, 2003) (RT)

The fact that a GIS recipient collapsed her RRSP in a given year did not mean that GIS for the following period could be adjusted to reflect her estimated income for the previous calendar year. Section 14 of the OAS Regulations did not include payments from an RRSP as part of the definition of "pension income".

A-72583 v. MHRD (May 20, 2003) (RT)

The Minister does not have the discretion to treat a GIS applicant's cashed-out RRSP funds as pension income, and does not have a duty to inform applicants that they may roll their RRSP into a RRIF instead of cashing it out. The Review Tribunal does not have the power to consider whether the cashing of an RRSP ought to be treated as "Other Income". To determine a pensioner's income for calculating the GIS, the Ministry relies on information supplied by the Canada Customs and Revenue Agency. The Tax Court of Canada is the proper forum for any dispute regarding the amount of income or about what is to be included as income.

B-71841 v. MHRD (January 22, 2003) (RT)

Under s. 14(6), the option to have a GIS entitlement based on estimated income rather than their actual income for the preceding calendar year was only available where a person suffered a loss of income due to a termination or reduction of pension income. A GIS benefits recipient was not eligible to exercise the option to have her GIS entitlement based on estimated income where he or she had withdrawn lump sum RRIF payments in the previous year, leaving a balance of funds in the RRIF. The RRIF must be fully depleted before the recipient was entitled to exercise the option.

F-70170 v. MHRD (October 28, 2002) (RT). See also *F-70171 v. MHRD* (October 28, 2002) (RT).

The Review Tribunal has no power to determine whether RRSP proceeds, withdrawn and applied to a first Homebuyer's Plan and not repaid, constitute income to Guaranteed Income Supplement recipients. The Minister must rely on income information provided by the CCRA, and a recipient was required to appeal to the Tax Court of Canada if he or she disagreed with the Agency's determination.

G-58977 v. MHRD (November 3, 2000) (RT)

RSP withdrawals do not constitute "pension income" for the purposes of s. 14. Payments from an RSP do not qualify as an "annuity" under s. 14(*a*) of the Regulations or as "superannuation or pension payments" under s. 14(*f*). The Review Tribunal has authority to hear the appeal of the Minister's exercise of discretion under s. 14 to use the estimated income in the enumerated circumstances.

W-55585 v. MHRD (October 27, 2000)

The option under s. 14(4) to base the widowed spouse's allowance entitlement on the estimated income for the current year rather than the actual income for the preceding year was only available where pension income had been reduced or terminated. The receipt of a retroactive payment in the preceding year did not mean that pension income had been reduced in the current year.

Old Age Security Act

D-34801 v. MHRD (September 3, 1998) (RT)

Whether or not the applicant is illiterate and unaware of the legislative requirement for annual applications, the legislation makes no provision for missed applications.

G-41508 v. MHRD (May 10, 1999) (RT)

The Minister is not obligated to forgive an overpayment of GIS when it was the fault of the applicant in declaring her income on the GIS renewal form.

Spouses and Common-Law Partners[5]

15. *Information required with application for supplement* — **(1) Every person by whom an application for a supplement in respect of a payment period is made shall, in the application, state whether the person has or had a spouse or common-law partner at any time during the payment period or in the month before the first month of the payment period, and, if so, the name and address of the spouse or common-law partner and whether, to the person's knowledge, the spouse or common-law partner is a pensioner. (S.C. 2000, c. 12, s. 207(1).)**

(1.1) *Statement if application waived* — **If the requirement for an application for payment of a supplement for any month has been waived under subsection 11(4) for a person who did not have a spouse or common-law partner immediately before the last payment period in respect of which a supplement was paid or, if no supplement was ever paid to the person, immediately before the last payment period in respect of which an application for payment of a supplement was received but who has a spouse or common-law partner immediately before the current payment period, the person shall notify the Minister without delay of the date of that change, the name and address of the spouse or common-law partner and whether, to the person's knowledge, the spouse or common-law partner is a pensioner. (S.C. 2000, c. 12, s. 207(1); 2007, c. 11, s. 18(1).)**

(2) *Statement by spouse or common-law partner* — **Subject to subsections (3), (4.1) and (4.2), where a person makes an application for a supplement in respect of a payment period and the person has or had a spouse or common-law partner at any time during the payment period or in the month before the first month of the payment period, the application shall not be considered or dealt with until such time as**

> **(a) the applicant's spouse or common-law partner files a statement in prescribed form of the spouse's or common-law partner's income for the base calendar year; (S.C. 2000, c. 12, s. 207(1).)**

> **(b) an application for a supplement in respect of the current payment period is received from the applicant's spouse or common-law partner; or (S.C. 2000, c. 12, s. 207(1).)**

> **(c) the income of the applicant's spouse or common-law partner for the base calendar year is estimated under subsection 14(1.1). (S.C. 2000, c. 12, s. 207(1).)**

(S.C. 2000, c. 12, s. 194(1).)

(2.1) *Waiver — subsection (1)* — **The Minister may waive the requirement to submit the information described in subsection (1) if that information has been submitted to the Minister in a joint application referred to in subsection 19(4). (S.C. 2007, c. 11, s. 18(2).)**

---

[5] Heading amended by 2000, c. 12, s. 193, effective July 31, 2000.

(2.2) *Waiver — paragraph 2(a)* — The Minister may waive the requirement to file a statement under paragraph 2(*a*) if the information has been made available to the Minister under this Act, and, if that is the case, the statement is deemed to have been filed for the purposes of this Part. (S.C. 2007, c. 11, s. 18(2).)

> S. 15(2.3) and (2.4) will be added by S.C. 2012, c. 19, s. 456 on proclamation, and will read as follows:
>
> **(2.3)** *Notice of intent* — If the Minister intends to waive the requirement for an application in respect of a person under subsection 11(3.1) and the person has a spouse or common-law partner, the Minister shall notify the spouse or common-law partner in writing of that intention and provide the spouse or common-law partner with the information regarding them on which the Minister intends to rely to approve the payment of a supplement.
>
> **(2.4)** *Inaccuracies* — The person's spouse or common-law partner shall, before the day on which the person attains 65 years of age, file with the Minister a statement in which the spouse or common-law partner corrects any inaccuracies in the information provided by the Minister under subsection (2.3).

(3) *Direction by Minister where no statement filed by spouse or common-law partner or where spouses or common-law partners living apart* — Where an application for a supplement in respect of any payment period has been made by a person, the Minister may, after any investigation of the circumstances that the Minister considers necessary, direct that the application be considered and dealt with as though the person did not have a spouse or common-law partner on the last day of the previous payment period, in any case where (S.C. 2000, c. 12, s. 207(1).)

    (*a*) no application or statement as described in subsection (2) has been filed by or received from the spouse or common-law partner of the person and no estimate of the income of the spouse or common-law partner of the person has been made under subsection 14(1.1); or (S.C. 2000, c. 12, s. 207(1).)

    (*b*) the Minister is satisfied that the person, as a result of circumstances not attributable to the person or the spouse or common-law partner, was not living with the spouse or common-law partner in a dwelling maintained by the person or the spouse or common-law partner at the time the application was made. (S.C. 2000, c. 12, s. 207(1).)

(3.1) *Continuing direction* — A direction made under subsection (3) in respect of a payment period is deemed to be a direction made in respect of every subsequent payment period, but the Minister may, after any investigation of the circumstances that the Minister considers necessary, cancel the direction.

(3.2) *Direction — spouse or common-law partner of incarcerated person* — The Minister may, after any investigation that the Minister considers necessary, direct, in respect of any month in a payment period, that an application for a supplement be considered and dealt with as though the applicant did not have a spouse or common-law partner on the last day of the previous payment period if the Minister is satisfied that, at any time during the preceding month, the applicant was the spouse or common-law partner of an incarcerated person described in subsection 5(3), except for the month in which the applicant's spouse or common-law partner is released. (2010, c. 22, s. 6.)

(3.3) *Continuing direction* — A direction made under subsection (3.2) continues to apply in respect of every subsequent month until the month before the month in which the spouse or common-law partner is released. However, the Minister may, after any investigation of the circumstances that the Minister considers necessary, cancel the direction. (2010, c. 22, s. 6.)

(4) *Notification of release* — Every applicant who is the subject of a direction under subsection (3.2) shall inform the Minister without delay of their spouse or common-law partner's release. (2010, c. 22, s. 6.)

(4.1) *Direction by Minister where spouses separated* — Where an application for a supplement in respect of a payment period that commences after June 30, 1999 has been made by a person, the Minister, if satisfied that the person is separated from the person's spouse, having been so separated for a continuous period of at least three months, exclusive of the month in which the spouses became separated, shall direct that the application be considered and dealt with as though the person had ceased to have a spouse at the end of the third such month.

(4.2) *Where applicant ceases to have a common-law partner otherwise than by death* — Where an application for a supplement in respect of a payment period that commences after June 30, 1999 is made by a person who at any time in the payment period ceases to have a common-law partner otherwise than by reason of the common-law partner's death, the supplement paid to the person, for any month in that payment period after the third month following the month in which the person ceased to have a common-law partner, shall be calculated as though the person did not have a common-law partner on the last day of the previous payment period. (S.C. 2000, c. 12, s. 194(3).)

(5) *Review of direction where statement subsequently filed by spouse or common-law partner* — Where, after the Minister has made a direction under subsection (3) with respect to an application for a supplement made in respect of a payment period that ends before July 1, 1999, a statement or application as described in subsection (2) is filed by or received from the applicant's spouse or common-law partner, the Minister may review the direction previously made and direct that any supplement paid to the applicant or the spouse or common-law partner for any month in that payment period after the month in which the review is made be calculated either on the basis that the applicant and the spouse or common-law partner were spouses or common-law partners of each other on the last day of the previous payment period or as though they had not been spouses or common-law partners on that day, according as the direction may specify. (S.C. 2000, c. 12, s. 207(1).)

(5.1) *Review of direction where statement subsequently filed by spouse or common-law partner* — Where, after the Minister has made a direction under subsection (3) based on paragraph (3)(*a*), with respect to an application for a supplement made in respect of a payment period that commences after June 30, 1999 and a statement or application as described in subsection (2) is filed by or received from the applicant's spouse or common-law partner, the Minister shall review the direction previously made and shall direct that any supplement paid to the applicant or the spouse or common-law partner for months in that payment period after the month in which the review is completed be calculated on the basis that the applicant and the spouse or common-law partner were spouses or common-law partners of each other on the last day of the previous payment period, unless there is some other reason for a direction to be made under subsection (3). (S.C. 2000, c. 12, s. 207(1).)

(6) *Direction by Minister where applicant becomes a spouse or separation ceases* — [Repealed by 2000, c. 12, s. 194(4).]

(6.1) *Application for supplement in certain cases* — Where an application for a supplement in respect of a payment period that commences after June 30, 1999 is made by

(a) a person who did not have a spouse or common-law partner immediately before a particular month in the payment period but has a spouse or common-law partner at the end of that month,

(b) a person in respect of whom a direction is made under subsection (3) based on paragraph (3)(b) who no longer meets the conditions set out in that paragraph, or

(c) a person described in subsection (4.1) who ceases to be separated from the person's spouse,

the calculation of the supplement shall be made, for any month after the month in which the person began to have a spouse or common-law partner, as though the person had a spouse or common-law partner on the last day of the previous payment period. (S.C. 2000, c. 12, s. 194(4).)

(7) *Direction by Minister where applicant ceases to have a spouse* — [Repealed by 2000, c. 12, s. 194(4).]

(7.1) *Where applicant ceases to have a spouse* — Where an application for a supplement in respect of a payment period that commences after June 30, 1999 is made by a person who at any time in the payment period ceases to have a spouse, the supplement paid to the person, for any month in that payment period after the month in which the person ceased to have a spouse, shall be calculated as though the person did not have a spouse on the last day of the previous payment period.

(7.2) *Where applicant ceases to have a common-law partner by reason of death* — Where an application for a supplement in respect of a payment period that commences after June 30, 1999 is made by a person who at any time in the payment period ceases to have a common-law partner by reason of the common-law partner's death, the supplement paid to the person, for any month in that payment period after the month in which the common-law partner died, shall be calculated as though the person did not have a common-law partner on the last day of the previous payment period. (S.C. 2000, c. 12, s. 194(5).)

(8) *Saving provision* — Nothing in subsections (6.1) to (7.2) shall be construed as limiting or restricting the authority of the Minister to make a direction under subsections (3) to (5.1). (S.C. 2000, c. 12, s. 194(5).)

(9) *Notification of change* — Every applicant shall inform the Minister without delay if they separate from, or cease to have, a spouse or common-law partner, or if they had a spouse or common-law partner at the beginning of a month, not having had a spouse or common-law partner at the beginning of the previous month. (S.C. 2000, c. 12, s. 207(1).)

(S.C. 1998, c. 21, s. 111; 2000, c. 12, ss. 194 and 207; 2007, c. 11, s. 18; 2010, c. 22, s. 6.)

Old Age Security Act

————————— **Notes** —————————

Case Law

§1. Generally

Canada (Minister of Human Resources Development) v. Leavitt, 2005 FC 664

Parliament chose to use objective criteria in s. 15(3)(*b*) — if a person is a spouse, living in the matrimonial home, that person does not meet the requirements to receive the higher level of GIS benefits. The objective of the legislation was to address the situation where one partner was in a hospital or nursing home or other care facility. The situation contemplated by Parliament was one where the partners were forced into living in separate residences and not one where the partners were no longer in a "conjugal relationship that is marriage".

Kombargi v. Canada (Minister of Social Development), 2006 FC 1511

While spouses living under the same roof may in fact be separated, such arrangements are probably not the norm and when they do occur, the task of proving a separation is made all the more difficult. However, it would be an error of law for the Review Tribunal to suggest that such arrangements can never occur.

L-76456 v. MSD (2004) (RT)

The requirement in s. 15(3)(*b*) that the separation of the parties must not be attributable to one of them in order to qualify as an involuntary separation establishes an objective test.

D-51012 v. MHRD (February 24, 2000) (RT)

The Act does not make a distinction between those who pay their ex-spouses support as opposed to those who do not. Section 15(4) (now s. 15(4.1)) gives the Minister the authority to consider a person as single commencing six months (now 3 months) after separation. Consequently, the amount of GIS to which an applicant who is paying spousal support is entitled must be calculated according to the rate of a single person. However, amounts paid in spousal support are deductible from the income that the GIS amount is based upon.

F-44416 v. MHRD (November 30, 1999) (RT)

A lack of ability by the applicant in making the decisions governing his or her circumstances is relevant in determining whether the applicant is maintaining a dwelling with a spouse.

S-62303 v. MHRD (April 5, 2001) (RT)

Sleeping in separate beds in the same room in a nursing home constituted involuntary separation, entitling each spouse to payment of GIS on the basis of the "single pensioner's rate."

§2. Parties Cohabitating or in a Spousal Relationship

- Wife returning home from nursing home so that husband could care for her, arranging to have paid help: *Canada (Minister of Human Resources Development) v. Leavitt,* 2005 FC 664

- GIS recipient alleging that his accountant had advised him to declare that he was living common-law with his secretary, for income tax purposes, so he applied the same to his GIS renewal; improbable that recipient did not understand the significance of "common-law"; Minister's decision finding relationship to be common-law upheld; couple co-habiting for 15 consecutive years, and publicly represented each other as common-law spouses: *R-40334 v. MHRD* (June 1, 1999) (RT)

- Couple sharing home expenses and taxes, cohabiting during 20 or 40 years, and publicly representing themselves as spouses: *P-29843 v. MHRD* (July 6, 1998) (RT)

- Applicant having excellent reasons for wanting legal separation, including husband's alcoholism and verbal abuse making her fear for her security and physical integrity and resulting in insomnia, not an involuntary separation in that she had good reasons for separating, formed the intention, consulted a lawyer and obtained the separation: *L-33607 v. MHRD* (June 22, 1998) (RT)

506

§3. No Spousal Relationship or Cohabitation

- Spouses becoming involuntarily separated when one spouse admitted to nursing home; status unchanged when spouse returned to family home because nursing home could not give her adequate care: *L-81159 v. MSD* (2004) (RT); *L-81160 v. MSD* (2004) (RT)

- Wife leaving husband because of his alcoholism and unacceptable behaviour: *L-76456 v. MSD* (2004) (RT)

- Applicant living with a man after her husband's death; applicant had previously informed Ministry that she had lived common-law since her deceased spouse's death; applicant had never introduced man as her husband, nor did he introduce her as his wife; couple never shared property together, and maintained separate beds; applicant considering the man to be her "companion"; (Note: A dissenting opinion found the applicant to lack credibility on this point): *Mc-32964 v. MHRD* (1998) (RT)

- Applicant nursing-home resident being granted GIS benefits before being placed into room with her husband, was unable to make decisions surrounding her own care and was subject to degree of control exercised under *Nursing Homes Act*; applicant and husband were not in fact living in dwelling "maintained by the person or a spouse" within meaning of s. 15(3): *F-44416 v. MHRD* (November 30, 1999) (RT)

- Applicant's husband making statutory declaration in divorce proceedings that couple had been living apart for one year; divorce and declaration rebutting applicant's claim that parties had never lived apart: *O-29844 v. MHRD* (June 3, 1999) (RT)

§4. Jurisdiction

Canada (Minister of Human Resources Development) v. Leavitt, 2005 FC 664

The Review Tribunal has the jurisdiction to hear an appeal with respect to the amount of a GIS benefit, even where the amount paid to the pensioner has been adjusted by Ministerial direction under s. 15(3.1) when the pensioner moved into and out of a nursing home. Such a determination cannot be equated with a purely discretionary exercise of the Minister's power, which would not be subject to appeal.

§5. Notification of change of marital status

Barry v. Canada (Attorney General), 2010 FC 1307

Under s. 15(9), the onus is on a claimant to report his or her marital status not only to the CRA but also to the Minister. This requirement existed even without the annual notice from the Minister, whom the applicant had to provide with the information, the notice simply being a reminder and not a precondition to the application of s. 15(9). It was irrelevant for this purpose that the claimant had informed the CRA of his change of status. Section 39(1) of the *Canada Revenue Agency Act* does not require the CRA to provide the Minister with the information he required.

Payment of Supplement

16. *Consideration of application or waiver* **— (1) The Minister shall, without delay after receiving an application for payment of a supplement under subsection 11(2) or after waiving the requirement for an application for payment of a supplement under subsection 11(4), as the case may be, consider whether the applicant is entitled to be paid a supplement, and may approve payment of a supplement and fix the amount of the supplement, or may determine that no supplement may be paid. (S.C. 1995, c. 33, s. 8.)**

S. 16(1) will be replaced by S.C. 2012, c. 19, s. 457 on proclamation, and will read as follows:

16. *Consideration of application or waiver* — **(1) The Minister shall, without delay after receiving an application for payment of a supplement under subsection 11(2) or after waiving the requirement for an application for payment of a supplement under subsection 11(3.1) or (4), as the case may be, consider whether the applicant is entitled to be paid a supplement, and may approve payment of a supplement and fix its amount, or may determine that no supplement may be paid.**

(2) *Notification of applicant* — Where particulars of the basis on which the amount of any supplement that may be paid to an applicant was fixed by the Minister are requested by the applicant or where the Minister determines that no supplement may be paid to the applicant, the Minister shall forthwith in writing notify the applicant of the basis on which that amount was fixed or of the decision that no supplement may be paid to the applicant and the Minister's reasons therefor, as the case may be.

(S.C. 1995, c. 33, s. 8.)

——————— **Notes** ———————

Related Regulations

- Section 23 — Further information required
- Section 24 — Payment to person other than beneficiary
- Section 25(2) — Notice of change of address
- Section 26 — Suspension of payments

---

17. *Payment of supplement to be made in arrears* — **Payment of a supplement for any month shall be made in arrears at the end of the month, except that where payment of a supplement in respect of months in any payment period is approved after the end of the month for which the first payment of the supplement may be made, payments of the supplement for the month in which payment of the supplement is approved and for months before that month may be made at the end of that month or at the end of the month immediately after that month.**

(S.C. 1998, c. 21, s. 112.)

Adjustment of Payments

18. *Adjustment of payments of supplements* — Where it is determined that the income for a base calendar year (in this section referred to as the "actual income") of an applicant for a supplement does not accord with the income of the applicant (in this section referred to as the "shown income") calculated on the basis of a statement or an estimate made under section 14, the following adjustments shall be made:

    (a) if the actual income exceeds the shown income, any amount by which the supplement paid to the applicant for months in the payment period exceeds the supplement that would have been paid to the applicant for those months if the shown income had been equal to the actual income shall be deducted and retained out of any subsequent payments of supplement or pension made to the applicant, in any manner that may be prescribed; and

    (b) if the shown income exceeds the actual income, there shall be paid to the applicant any amount by which the supplement that would have been paid to the applicant for months in the payment period if the actual income had been equal to the shown income exceeds the supplement paid to the applicant for those months.

(S.C. 1998, c. 21, s. 113.)

————————— **Notes** —————————

Case Law

Grenier v. Canada (Human Resources Development), 2008 FCA 130.

Where the "actual income" earned in the reference year chosen by the claimant under s. 14 of the Act exceeded the claimant's "shown income" (of $11,892) in his application, and adjustment had to be made under s. 18. The Minister was entitled to recover the resulting overpayment.

F-70170 v. MHRD (October 28, 2002) (RT). See also *F-70171 v. MHRD* (October 28, 2002) (RT).

The *OAS Act* did not prevent the Minister from applying its provisions regarding a GIS overpayment made over two consecutive payment periods, which had been calculated on the basis of the spouse's statement of estimated income. The wording of the GIS information sheet issued by the Ministry was not binding on the Tribunal. Where there was a delay by the Minister in processing an overpayment, the Tribunal was in no position to speculate why it took longer for the adjustment to be made once it was determined.

S-53653 v. MHRD (February 24, 2000) (RT)

The unpredictability of an amount received — e.g., a lump-sum amount from a previous employer — did not constitute an exception in the calculation of actual income. Under s. 18(1), when the actual income exceeds one's declared income, the overpayment is to be recovered.

———————————————

S. 18.1 and 18.2 will be added by S.C. 2012, c. 19, s. 458 on proclamation, and will read as follows:

Cessation of Payment

18.1. *Request that supplement cease to be payable* — If a pensioner makes a request to the Minister in writing that their supplement cease to be payable, it shall cease to be payable on the last day of the month in which the Minister approves the request and shall not resume until the later of the month after the month in which the Minister receives a new application for the supplement and the month chosen by the pensioner in the application.

Cancellation of Payment

18.2. *Request to cancel supplement* — (1) A pensioner may, in the prescribed manner and within the prescribed time after payment of a supplement has commenced, request cancellation of that supplement.

(2) *Effect of cancellation* — If the request is granted and the amount of any supplement and related allowance is repaid within the prescribed time,

    (a) the application for that supplement is deemed never to have been made; and

    (b) the supplement is deemed for the purposes of this Act not to have been payable during the period in question.

Old Age Security Act

509

Part III
Monthly Allowances[6]
Allowance Payable

19. *Payment of allowance* — **(1)** Subject to this Act and the regulations, an allowance may be paid to the spouse, common-law partner or former common-law partner of a pensioner for a month in a payment period if the spouse, common-law partner or former common-law partner, as the case may be,

(a) in the case of a spouse, is not separated from the pensioner, or has separated from the pensioner where the separation commenced after June 30, 1999 and not more than three months before the month in the payment period;

(a.1) in the case of a former common-law partner, has separated from the pensioner where the separation commenced after June 30, 1999 and not more than three months before the month in the payment period;

(b) in the case of a spouse, common-law partner or former common-law partner, has attained sixty years of age but has not attained sixty-five years of age; and

(c) in the case of a spouse, common-law partner or former common-law partner, has resided in Canada after attaining eighteen years of age and prior to the day on which their application is approved for an aggregate period of at least ten years and, where that aggregate period is less than twenty years, was resident in Canada on the day preceding the day on which their application is approved.

(S.C. 2000, c. 12, s. 196(1).)

(1.1) *Incarcerated common-law partner* — For the purposes of subsection (1), common-law partners do not become former common-law partners if the sole reason for their separation is that one of the partners is an incarcerated person described in subsection 5(3) or paragraph 19(6)(f). (2010, c. 22, s. 7(1).)

(1.2) *Incarcerated spouse* — For the purposes of paragraph (1)(a), a spouse is not considered to be separated from the pensioner if the sole reason for the separation is that the pensioner is an incarcerated person described in subsection 5(3). (2010, c. 22, s. 7(1).)

(2) *Residence in Canada must be or have been legal* — A person is eligible for an allowance under this section only if (R.S.C. 1985, c. 34 (1st Supp.), s. 2(1); S.C. 2000, c. 12, ss. 207(1) and 209.)

(a) on the day preceding the day on which that person's application for an allowance is approved that person is a Canadian citizen or, if not, is legally resident in Canada; or (S.C. 2000, c. 12, s. 209.)

(b) on the day preceding the day that person ceased to reside in Canada that person was a Canadian citizen or, if not, was legally resident in Canada.

(3) *Regulations respecting legal residence* — The Governor in Council may make regulations respecting the meaning of legal residence for the purposes of subsection (2).

(4) *Must apply annually* — Subject to subsection (4.1), no allowance may be paid under this section to the spouse or common-law partner of a pensioner in any payment period unless a joint application of the pensioner and the spouse or common-law partner, or an application described in section 30, has been made for payment of an allowance in respect of that payment period and payment of the allowance has been

---

[6] Heading amended by 2000, c. 12, s. 195, effective July 31, 2000.

approved under this Part. (R.S.C. 1985, c. 34 (1st Supp.), s. 2(2); 1995, c. 33, s. 10; 1998, c. 21, s. 119(1)(*d*); 2000, c. 12, ss. 207(1) and 209.)

S.C. 2012, c. 19, s. 459(1) will replace s. 19(4) with s. 19(3.1) and (4) on proclamtion, and will read as follows:

(3.1) *Presumption* — **If the Minister intends to waive the requirement for an application in respect of a person under subsection (4.02) and the information available to the Minister under this Act with respect to that person includes the prescribed information, the person is presumed, in the absence of evidence to the contrary, to have met the requirements of**

(*a*) **paragraph (1)(***c***); or**

(*b*) **paragraph (2)(***a***) or (***b***).**

(4) *Annual application* — **Subject to subsections (4.02) and (4.1), no allowance may be paid under this section to a pensioner's spouse or common-law partner in any payment period unless a joint application of the pensioner and the spouse or common-law partner, or an application described in section 30, has been made for payment of an allowance in respect of that payment period and payment of the allowance has been approved under this Part.**

(4.01) *Treated as joint application* — **If the pensioner is an incarcerated person described in subsection 5(3), their spouse or common-law partner may apply for an allowance individually and, for the purposes of subsection (4), that application shall be considered and dealt with as though it were a joint application of the pensioner and the spouse or common-law partner. (2010, c. 22, s. 7(2).)**

S. 19(4.02) to (4.07) will be added by S.C. 2012, c. 19, s. 459(2) on proclamation, and will read as follows:

(4.02) *Waiver of application* — **The Minister may, in respect of a person, waive the requirement referred to in subsection (4) for an application for an allowance for any month or months in a payment period if the Minister is satisfied, based on information available to him or her under this Act, that the person is qualified under this section for the payment of an allowance.**

(4.03) *Timing of waiver* — **The Minister may only waive the requirement referred to in subsection (4) in respect of a person**

(*a*) **on the day on which the pensioner's spouse or common-law partner attains 60 years of age; or**

(*b*) **on the day on which the pensioner attains 65 years of age if, on that day, the spouse or common-law partner is at least 60 years of age.**

(4.04) *Notice of intent* — **If the Minister intends to waive the requirement for an application in respect of a person under subsection (4.02), the Minister shall notify the person in writing of that intention and provide them with the information on which the Minister intends to rely to approve the payment of an allowance.**

(4.05) *Inaccuracies* — **The person shall, before the day referred to in paragraph (4.03)(***a***) or (***b***), file with the Minister a statement in which the person corrects any inaccuracies in the information provided by the Minister under subsection (4.04).**

(4.06) *Declining waiver* — **The person may, before the day referred to in paragraph (4.03)(***a***) or (***b***), decline the waiver of the requirement for an application by notifying the Minister in writing of their decision to do so.**

(4.07) *Cancellation of waiver* — Even if the requirement for an application has been waived in respect of a person under subsection (4.02), the Minister may, before the day referred to in paragraph (4.03)(*a*) or (*b*), require that the person make an application for payment of an allowance and, in that case, the Minister shall notify the person in writing of that requirement.

(4.1) *Waiver of application* — The Minister may waive the requirement referred to in subsection (4) for an application for payment of an allowance for any month or months in a payment period if an application for payment of an allowance has been made in respect of any payment period before that payment period. (S.C. 1995, c. 33, s. 10; 1998, c. 21, s. 119(1)(*d*); 2000, c. 12, ss. 207(1) and 209; 2007, c. 11, s. 19(1).)

(4.2) *Notice where subsequent application required* — Where the requirement for an application for any month or months in a payment period has been waived under subsection (4.1) and an application is required for payment of an allowance for any subsequent month or months in that payment period, the Minister shall, not later than fifteen days before that subsequent month or the first of those subsequent months, notify the spouse or common-law partner in writing that an application is required. (S.C. 1995, c. 33, s. 10; 1998, c. 21, s. 119(1)(*d*); 2000, c. 12, ss. 207(1) and 209.)

(4.3) *Cancellation of waiver* — Notwithstanding that the requirement for an application for any month or months has been waived under subsection (4.1), the Minister may require that an application referred to in subsection (4) be made for payment of an allowance for that month or for any of those months, and in such a case, the Minister shall, not later than fifteen days before that month or the first of those months, notify the spouse or common-law partner in writing that an application is required. (R.S.C. 1985, c. 34 (1st Supp.), s. 2; 1995, c. 33, s. 10; 2000, c. 12, ss. 207(1) and 209.)

(5) *Cessation of allowance* — An allowance under this section ceases to be payable on the expiration of the month in which the spouse, common-law partner or former common-law partner in respect of whom it is paid dies, becomes the spouse or common-law partner of another person, or no longer meets the conditions set out in subsection (1). (S.C. 1998, c. 21, s. 114(3); 2000, c. 12, s. 196(2).)

(6) *Limitations* — No allowance may be paid under this section to the spouse or common-law partner of a pensioner pursuant to an application therefor for (R.S.C. 1985, c. 34 (1st Supp.), s. 2(3); 2000, c. 12, ss. 207(1) and 209.)

   (*a*) any month that is more than 11 months before the month in which the application is received or is deemed to have been made or in which the requirement for an application has been waived, as the case may be; (S.C. 2007, c. 11, s. 19(2).)

   (*b*) any month for which no supplement may be paid to the pensioner; (S.C. 1996, c. 18, s. 53(1).)

   (*c*) any month throughout which the spouse or common-law partner is absent from Canada, having left Canada either before or after becoming entitled to an allowance under this Part and having remained outside Canada before that month for six consecutive months, exclusive of the month in which he left Canada; (S.C. 1996, c. 18, s. 53(1); 2000, c. 12, ss. 196(3), 207(1) and 209.)

   (*d*) any month during which the spouse or common-law partner is (S.C. 2000, c. 12, s. 207(1).)

      (i) a specially qualified individual, and

(ii) a person in respect of whom an undertaking by a sponsor is in effect as provided under the *Immigration and Refugee Protection Act*;[7] (S.C. 1996, c. 18, s. 53(1); 2000, c. 12, s. 196(3); 2001, c. 27, s. 265; 2007, c. 11, s. 19(3).)

S. 19(6)(*d*) will be replaced by S.C. 2014, c. 20, s. 372(1) on proclamation, and will read as follows:

(*d*) any month during which the spouse or common-law partner is a person in respect of whom an undertaking by a sponsor is in effect as provided under the *Immigration and Refugee Protection Act*;

(*e*) in the case of a common-law partner who was not a spouse immediately before the coming into force of this paragraph ("spouse" having in this paragraph the meaning that it had immediately before that coming into force), notwithstanding subsection 23(2), any month before the month in which this paragraph comes into force; or (S.C. 2000, c. 12, s. 196(3).)

(*f*) any period of incarceration — exclusive of the first month of that period — during which the spouse or common-law partner is subject to a sentence of imprisonment

(i) that is to be served in a penitentiary by virtue of any Act of Parliament, or

(ii) that exceeds 90 days and is to be served in a prison, as defined in subsection 2(1) of the *Prisons and Reformatories Act*, if the government of the province in which the prison is located has entered into an agreement under section 41 of the *Department of Employment and Social Development Act.* (2012, c. 19, s. 297; 2013, c. 40, s. 236(1)(g)(ii).)

(6.1) *Application of par. (6)(b)* — Paragraph (6)(*b*) does not apply to a spouse or common-law partner of a pensioner in respect of a month for which a supplement would be payable to the pensioner if

(*a*) the special qualifying factor of that pensioner for that month were equal to one; or

(*b*) the pensioner were not precluded from receiving a supplement by virtue of the application of subsection 5(3).

(S.C. 1996, c. 18, s. 53(2); 2000, c. 12, s. 207(1); 2010, c. 22, s. 7(4).)

(6.2) *Application of para. (6)(d)* — Paragraph (6)(*d*) does not apply to a spouse or common-law partner where an event as provided by the regulations has occurred. (S.C. 1996, c. 18, s. 53(2); 2000, c. 12, s. 207(1).)

S. 19(6.2) will be replaced by S.C. 2014, c. 20, s. 372(2) on proclamation, and will read as follows:

(6.2) *Application of para. (6)(d)* — Paragraph (6)(*d*) does not apply to a spouse or common-law partner

(*a*) who was qualified to receive an allowance immediately before the day on which this paragraph comes into force, whether or not they had applied for it; or

(*b*) if an event as provided by the regulations has occurred.

---

[7] Subparagraphs 11(7)(*e*)(ii), 19(6)(*d*)(ii) and 21(9)(*c*)(ii) of the *Old Age Security Act*, as they read immediately before the day on which this Act receives royal assent, continue to apply to any person who, before that day, is a beneficiary of a supplement or an allowance under that Act or has made an application for payment of a supplement or an allowance under that Act (S.C. 2007, c. 11, s. 37).

(6.3) *Resumption of allowance* — **Payment of an allowance that is suspended by virtue of paragraph (6)(*f*) shall resume in respect of the month in which the spouse or common-law partner is released but only if they**

(*a*) **have notified the Minister in writing before or after their release; and**

(*b*) **continue to be eligible for an allowance.**

(2010, c. 22, s. 7(5).)

(7) *Amount of allowance to spouse or common-law partner of pensioner* — **The amount of the allowance that may be paid under this section to the spouse or common-law partner of a pensioner shall be determined in accordance with subsection 22(3). (R.S.C. 1985, c. 34 (1st Supp.), s. 2(4); 2000, c. 12, ss. 207(1) and 209.)**

(R.S.C. 1985, c. 34 (1st Supp.), s. 2; 1995, c. 33, s. 10; 1996, c. 18, s. 53; 1998, c. 21, ss. 114, 119; 2000, c. 12, ss. 196, 207 and 209; 2001, c. 27, s. 265; 2007, c. 11, s. 19; 2010, c. 22, s. 7; 2012, c. 19, s. 297; 2013, c. 40, s. 236.)

———————— **Notes** ————————

Synopsis

This section provides for monthly amounts to be paid to the spouses of OAS recipients, where the spouses are between the ages of 60 and 64. Of course, when the spouse turns 65 she may be eligible to receive an OAS pension in her own right. The Allowance must be applied for every year. It is also available to spouses in that age range where the OAS recipient has died, unless the spouse remarries or is in a common-law relationship (see s. 21). Payments may be retroactive for up to one year prior to the application being made (see s. 23(2)). Up until 1995, the period of retroactivity was five years.

Related Regulations

- Sections 11–12 — Approval of application for spouse's (now monthly) allowance
- Section 16 — Proof of spousal relationship
- Section 17 — Where spouse deemed separated from pensioner
- Section 22 — "Legal residence" defined
- Section 22.1 — Sponsored immigrants' exceptions
- Section 23 — Further information required
- Section 25(3) — Notification of separation

Case Law

§1. Generally

Egan v. Canada, [1995] 2 S.C.R. 513

The objective of the spouse's allowance (now Monthly Allowance) is to benefit low income cohabiting spouses of whom only one has attained the age of sixty-five and the other has attained the age of sixty, by providing them with income equivalent to what they would receive if both spouses were pensioners. This is a pressing and substantial objective.

Canada (Attorney General) v. Comeau, 2004 FC 1034

The Review Tribunal is not authorized to direct how the Minister should treat a claimant's "income", including the inclusion or exclusion of RRSP redemptions, for the taxation year in question. Appeals on that ground are to be taken to the Tax Court of Canada.

Collins v. Canada, [2002] FCA 82

It is not an error to find that the granting of an income tested allowance to a cohabiting spouse, while denying it to a separated spouse in similar financial circumstances, is discriminatory within the meaning of s. 15 of the Charter of Rights by creating a distinction based on a personal characteristic intrinsic to human dignity. However, the exclusion of separated spouses from eligibility for a spouse's allowance under the OAS Act is as pressing and substantial as the spouse's allowance itself, and is justified under s. 1 of the Charter. While purely financial considerations are not sufficient to justify the infringement of Charter rights, they are relevant to determining the standard of deference for the test of minimal impairment when reviewing legislation that is enacted for a purpose which is not financial.

Collins v. Canada, [2000] 2 F.C. 3 (T.D.)

Denial of the spouse's allowance (now monthly allowance) to separated spouses does not violate the equality rights of separated spouses under s. 15 of the *Canadian Charter of Rights and Freedoms*. The pressing and substantial objectives of the spousal allowance provisions, including the survivor's allowance, are to provide benefits in limited and specific circumstances. The exclusion of separated individuals is not inconsistent with these pressing and substantial objectives and at least in part, is itself pressing and substantial. The object of the allowance is not so broad that it can be characterized as a comprehensive benefit program for all those in financial need between the ages of 60 and 64.

Canada (Minister of Human Resources and Development) v. Néron 2004 CF 101

Married spouses who are living apart are considered "separated" for the purposes of s. 17(c) of the OAS Regulations even if divorce proceedings have not been commenced by either spouse. No other federal or provincial legislation is referred to in the provision, and therefore the word "separated" in the section is to be taken in its ordinary sense. The date that divorce proceedings are commenced is not one of the circumstances enumerated in s. 17 for determining the date on which the couple separated.

S-36753 v. MHRD (October 19, 1998) (RT)

A spouse's intention not to return to the applicant is sufficient to find them legally and *de facto* separated.

§2. Example Cases — Separated Spouses

- Applicant's spouse having made arrangements in advance to move in with her daughter for the sole purpose of living separately and apart from the applicant; spouse making representation to various people that she was separated: *S-36753 v. MHRD* (October 19, 1998) (RT)

- Parties not separated until husband moving out of matrimonial home; fact that wife was sleeping overnight outside the home before that time was attributable to work demands; landlord corroborating wife's claim: *T-22599 v. MHRD* (December 10, 1997) (RT)

§3. Example Cases — 11-Month Maximum Applying

- Erroneous advice from accountant and financial advisor that applicant not eligible for widowed spouse's allowance benefits: *B-67374 v. MHRD* (January 15, 2003) (RT)

- Section 28.1 not relevant where applicant, who alleges that psychiatric difficulties prevented timely application, lacked medical evidence to support his claim: *M-26032 v. MHRD* (December 9, 1997), (RT)

- Client service officer allegedly failing to inform applicant of her right to Widowed Spouse Allowance when she went to office in 1989; applicant not formally applying until 1994: *M-34716 v. MHRD* (March 9, 1999) (RT)

- Applicant unaware of entitlement to the widowed spouse's benefits, and alleged that she had not been told of the benefits at the time when she applied for early retirement under CPP: *S-28465 v. MHRD* (July 31, 1998) (RT)

Old Age Security Act

20. *Failure to comply with Act* — **Payment of an allowance under section 19 or 21 may be suspended if the beneficiary fails to comply with any of the provisions of this Act or the regulations, but payment may be resumed when the beneficiary complies with those provisions.**

(R.S.C. 1985, c. 34 (1st Supp.), s. 3; 2000, c. 12, s. 209.)

————————— Notes —————————

Related Regulations

Section 26 — Suspension of payments

Case Law

B-33166 v. MHRD (December 11, 1997) (RT)

A separated spouse now residing full-time in the U.S. did not qualify for what is now called a monthly allowance.

———————————————

21. *Payment of allowance to survivors* — **(1) Subject to this Act and regulations, for each month in any payment period, an allowance may be paid to a survivor who (S.C. 1998, c. 21, s. 119(1)(e); 2000, c. 12, ss. 208(1) and 209.)**

    (a) **has attained sixty years of age but has not attained sixty-five years of age; and**

    (b) **has resided in Canada after attaining eighteen years of age and prior to the day on which their application is approved for an aggregate period of at least ten years and, where that aggregate period is less than twenty years, was resident in Canada on the day preceding the day on which their application is approved. (S.C. 2000, c. 12, s. 208(2).)**

(2) *Residence in Canada must be or have been legal* — **A survivor is eligible for an allowance under this section only if (S.C. 2000, c. 12, ss. 208(1) and 209.)**

    (a) **on the day preceding the day on which their application for an allowance is approved they are a Canadian citizen or, if not, are legally resident in Canada; or (S.C. 2000, c. 12, ss. 208(2) and 209.)**

    (b) **on the day preceding the day they ceased to reside in Canada they were a Canadian citizen or, if not, were legally resident in Canada. (S.C. 2000, c. 12, s. 208(2).)**

(3) *Meaning of "legal residence"* — **The Governor in Council may make regulations respecting the meaning of "legal residence" for the purposes of subsection (2).**

(4) *Must apply annually* — **Subject to subsections (5) and (5.1), no allowance may be paid to a survivor under this section in any payment period unless the survivor has made an application for an allowance in respect of that payment period and payment of the allowance has been approved under this Part. (R.S.C. 1985, c. 34 (1st Supp.), s. 4; 1995, c. 33, s. 11(1); 1998, c. 21, s. 119(1)(f); 2000, c. 12, ss. 208(1) and 209.)**

S.C. 2012, c. 19, s. 460 will replace s. 21(4) with s. 12(3.1) to (4.5) on proclamation, and will read as follows:

(3.1) *Presumption* — **If the Minister intends to waive the requirement for an application in respect of a survivor under subsection (4.1) and the information available to the Minister under this Act with respect to the survivor includes the prescribed information, the survivor is presumed, in the absence of evidence to the contrary, to have met the requirements of**

(*a*) paragraph (1)(*b*); or

(*b*) paragraph (2)(*a*) or (*b*).

(**4**) *Annual application* — Subject to subsections (4.1), (5) and (5.1), no allowance may be paid to a survivor under this section in any payment period unless the survivor has made an application for an allowance in respect of that payment period and payment of the allowance has been approved under this Part.

(**4.1**) *Waiver of application* — The Minister may, in respect of a survivor, waive the requirement referred to in subsection (4) for an application for payment of an allowance for any month or months in a payment period if, on the day on which the survivor attains 60 years of age, the Minister is satisfied, based on information available to him or her under this Act, that the survivor is qualified under this section for the payment of an allowance.

(**4.2**) *Notice of intent* — If the Minister intends to waive the requirement for an application in respect of a survivor under subsection (4.1), the Minister shall notify the survivor in writing of that intention and provide them with the information on which the Minister intends to rely to approve the payment of an allowance.

(**4.3**) *Inaccuracies* — The survivor shall, before the day on which they attain 60 years of age, file with the Minister a statement in which the survivor corrects any inaccuracies in the information provided by the Minister under subsection (4.2).

(**4.4**) *Declining waiver* — The survivor may, before the day on which they attain 60 years of age, decline a waiver of the requirement for an application by notifying the Minister in writing of their decision to do so.

(**4.5**) *Cancellation of waiver* — Even if the requirement for an application is intended to be waived in respect of a survivor under subsection (4.1), the Minister may, before the day on which the survivor attains 60 years of age, require that the survivor make an application for payment of an allowance and, in that case, the Minister shall notify the survivor in writing of that requirement.

(**5**) *Exception to application requirement* — Where the spouses or the common-law partners had, before the death of the pensioner, made a joint application for the allowance under section 19 for months in the payment period of the pensioner's death or the following payment period, no application is required to be made by the pensioner's survivor under subsection (4) in respect of the payment of an allowance under this section for months in the payment period in respect of which the joint application was made. (S.C. 2000, c. 12, s. 197(1).)

(**5.1**) *Waiver of requirement for application* — The Minister may waive the requirement referred to in subsection (4) for an application for payment of an allowance for any month or months in a payment period if an application for payment of an allowance has been made in respect of any payment period before that payment period. (S.C. 1995, c. 33, s. 11(2); 1998, c. 21, s. 119(1)(*g*); 2000, c. 12, ss. 208(1) and 209; 2007, c. 11, s. 20(1).)

(**5.2**) *Notice where subsequent application required* — Where the requirement for an application for payment of an allowance for any month or months in a payment period has been waived under subsection (5.1) and an application is required for payment of an allowance for any subsequent month or months in that payment period, the Minister shall, not later than fifteen days before that subsequent month or the first of those subsequent months, notify the survivor in writing that an application is required. (S.C. 1995, c. 33, s. 11(2); 1998, c. 21, s. 119(1)(*g*); 2000, c. 12, ss. 208(1) and 209.)

(**5.3**) *Cancellation of waiver* — Notwithstanding that the requirement for an application for payment of an allowance for any month or months has been waived under subsection (5.1), the Minister may require that the survivor make such an application for that month or for any of those months, and in such a case, the Minister shall, not later than fifteen days before that month or the first of those months, notify the survivor in writing that an application is required. (S.C. 1995, c. 33, s. 11(2); 2000, c. 12, ss. 208(1) and 209.)

(6) *Commencement of allowance* — An allowance may be paid under this section commencing with the month following the month in which the applicant becomes a survivor or attains sixty years of age, whichever is later. (S.C. 2000, c. 12, ss. 208(1) and 209.)

(7) *No allowance payable before September, 1985* — Notwithstanding subsections (6) and 23(2), no allowance may be paid under this section for any month prior to September, 1985. (S.C. 2000, c. 12, s. 209.)

(7.1) *Limitations* — In the case of a survivor who was not a widow immediately before the coming into force of this subsection ("widow" having in this subsection the meaning that it had immediately before that coming into force),

(a) no allowance may be paid under this section unless the survivor became a survivor on or after January 1, 1998; and

(b) no allowance may be paid under this section for any month before the month in which this subsection comes into force.

(S.C. 2000, c. 12, s. 197(2).)

(8) *Cessation of allowance* — An allowance under this section ceases to be payable on the expiration of the month in which the survivor in respect of whom it is paid dies, attains sixty-five years of age or ceases to be a survivor. (S.C. 2000, c. 12, ss. 208(1) and 209.)

(9) *Limitations* — [8]No allowance may be paid under this section to a survivor pursuant to an application therefor for (S.C. 2000, c. 12, ss. 208(1) and 209.)

(a) any month more than 11 months before the month in which the application is received or is deemed to have been made or in which the requirement for an application has been waived, as the case may be; (S.C. 1998, c. 21, s. 115(2); 2007, c. 11, s. 20(2).)

(b) any month throughout which the survivor is absent from Canada, having absented themselves from Canada either before or after becoming entitled to an allowance under this Part and having remained out of Canada before that month for six consecutive months, exclusive of the month in which they left Canada; or (S.C. 1998, c. 21, s. 115(2); 2000, c. 12, ss. 208(1), (2) and 209.)

(c) any month during which the survivor is (S.C. 2000, c. 12, s. 208(1).)

(i) a specially qualified individual, and

(ii) a person in respect of whom an undertaking by a sponsor is in effect as provided under the *Immigration and Refugee Protection Act*; or[9] (S.C. 2001, c. 27, s. 266; 2007, c. 11, s. 20(3).)

S. 21(9)(c) will be replaced by S.C. 2014, c. 20, s. 373(1) on proclamation, and will read as follows:

(c) any month during which the survivor is a person in respect of whom an undertaking by a sponsor is in effect as provided under the *Immigration and Refugee Protection Act*; or

---

[8] Subsection (9) as amended by 1998, c. 21, s. 115(2) is deemed to have come into force on April 1, 1996, pursuant to 1998, c. 21, s. 115(4).

[9] Subparagraphs 11(7)(e)(ii), 19(6)(d)(ii) and 21(9)(c)(ii) of the *Old Age Security Act*, as they read immediately before the day on which this Act receives royal assent, continue to apply to any person who, before that day, is a beneficiary of a supplement or an allowance under that Act or has made an application for payment of a supplement or an allowance under that Act (S.C. 2007, c. 11, s. 37).

(*d*) any period of incarceration — exclusive of the first month of that period — during which the survivor is subject to a sentence of imprisonment

(i) that is to be served in a penitentiary by virtue of any Act of Parliament, or

(ii) that exceeds 90 days and is to be served in a prison, as defined in subsection 2(1) of the *Prisons and Reformatories Act*, if the government of the province in which the prison is located has entered into an agreement under section 41 of the *Department of Employment and Social Development Act*. (2012, c. 19, s. 298; 2013, c. 40, s. 236(1)(g)(iii).)

(9.1) *Application of paragraph (9)(c)* — [10]**Paragraph (9)(c) does not apply to a survivor where an event as provided by the regulations has occurred.** (S.C. 1998, c. 21, s. 115(3); 2000, c. 12, s. 208(1).)

S. 21(9)(c) will be replaced by S.C. 2014, c. 20, s. 373(1) on proclamation, and will read as follows:

(9.1) *Application of paragraph (9)(c)* — **Paragraph (9)(c) does not apply to a survivor**

(*a*) **who was qualified to receive an allowance immediately before the day on which this paragraph comes into force, whether or not they had applied for it; or**

(*b*) **if an event as provided by the regulations has occurred.**

(9.2) *Resumption of allowance* — **Payment of an allowance suspended by virtue of paragraph (9)(d) shall resume in respect of the month in which the survivor is released but only if they**

(*a*) **have notified the Minister in writing before or after their release; and**

(*b*) **continue to be eligible for an allowance.**

(2010, c. 22, s. 8(2).)

(10) *Amount of allowance to survivor* — **The amount of the allowance that may be paid under this section to a survivor shall be determined in accordance with subsection 22(4).** (S.C. 2000, c. 12, ss. 208(1) and 209.)

(11) *Special case* — **Where subsection (5) applies, subsection (10) also applies in respect of months in the payment period in respect of which the joint application was made and that are after the pensioner's death.** (S.C. 1998, c. 21, s. 115(4).)

(12) *Eligibility of applicants* — **A person's eligibility for an allowance under this section in respect of a deceased spouse or common-law partner is not affected by the eligibility of another person for an allowance under this section in respect of that deceased spouse or common-law partner.** (S.C. 2000, c. 12, ss. 207(1) and 209.)

(R.S.C. 1985, c. 34 (1st Supp.), s. 4; 1995, c. 33, s. 11; 1998, c. 21, ss. 115, 119; 2000, c. 12, ss. 197, 207, 208 and 209; 2001, c. 27, s. 266; 2007, c. 11, s. 20; 2010, c. 22, s. 8; 2012, c. 19, s. 298; 2013, c. 40, s. 236.)

——————— **Notes** ———————

Related Regulations

- Sections 11-12 — Approval of application for spouse's [now monthly] allowance
- Section 16 — Proof of spousal relationship
- Section 22 — "Legal residence" defined

[10] Subsection (9.1) as added by 1998, c. 1998, c. 115(3) is deemed to have come into force on April 1, 1996, pursuant to 1998, c. 21, s. 115(4).

Old Age Security Act

Case Law

B-49043 v. MHRD (April 6, 2000) (RT)

The pensioner's ignorance of the existence of the widowed spouse's allowance at the time of the spouse's death does not confer authority on the Review Tribunal to award a longer period of retroactivity than the 11-month statutory maximum.

P-61416 v. MHRD (October 26, 2001) (RT)

In order to give notice under the Act, a recipient of survivor's benefits must take reasonable and adequate measures to specifically inform the Minister of any change in his or her marital status. Passive notice such as an income tax return does not constitute legal notice.

D-31990 v. MHRD (December 11, 1997) (RT)

The Tribunal could not grant longer retroactive payments of a survivor's allowance beyond the 11 months allowed by the legislation, despite the applicant's claim that at the age of sixty years, she was unaware of her entitlement to the allowance.

Amount of Allowance

22. *Definitions* — **(1) In this section,**

"base calendar year" **has the same meaning as in section 10; (S.C. 1998, c. 21, s. 116(2).)**

"current fiscal year" **Repealed. (S.C. 1998, c. 21, s. 116(1).)**

"current payment period" **means the payment period in respect of which an application for an allowance is made under this Part; (S.C. 1998, c. 21, s. 116(4); 2000, c. 12, s. 209.)**

"income", **for the purposes of determining the amount of benefits under this Part that may be paid for a month before July 1, 1999, means the income calculated as prescribed by section 13; (S.C. 1998, c. 21, s. 116(2).)**

"monthly income" **of a survivor in a current payment period is the amount that equals one-twelfth of their income for the base calendar year; (R.S.C. 1985, c. 34 (1st Supp.), s. 5(1); S.C. 1998, c. 21, s. 119(1)(h); 2000, c. 12, ss. 208(1) and (2).)**

"monthly joint income" **of a pensioner and the pensioner's spouse or common-law partner in a current payment period is the amount that equals one-twelfth of the total incomes of the pensioner and the spouse or common-law partner for the base calendar year; however, for the purpose of calculating the allowance that may be paid to the pensioner's spouse or common-law partner under subsection (3) for the months during which the pensioner is an incarcerated person described in subsection 5(3) — exclusive of the first month of incarceration and the month of release — it is the amount that equals one-twelfth of the income of the spouse or common-law partner for the base calendar year; (2010, c. 22, s. 9(1).)**

"pension equivalent" **means, in respect of any month in a payment quarter, the amount of the full monthly pension payable for that month under section 7;**

"residual income of the survivor" **for a month in a current payment period means the amount determined by the formula (S.C. 2000, c. 12, s. 208(1).)**

$$A - B$$

where

A   is the monthly income of the survivor in the current payment period, and (S.C. 2000, c. 12, s. 208(1).)

B is the product

    (*a*) obtained by multiplying four-thirds of the rounded pension equivalent by the survivor's special qualifying factor for the month, and (S.C. 2000, c. 12, s. 208(1).)

    (*b*) rounded, where that product is not a multiple of four dollars, to the next higher multiple of four dollars; (S.C. 1999, c. 22, s. 89(2).)

(R.S.C. 1985, c. 34 (1st Supp.), s. 5(1); 1996, c. 18, s. 54; S.C. 1998, c. 21, s. 116(2); 1999, c. 22, s. 89(2).)

"residual joint income" of a pensioner and the pensioner's spouse or common-law partner for a month in a current payment period means the amount determined by the formula (S.C. 2000, c. 12, ss. 206 and 207(1).)

$$A - B$$

where

A is the monthly joint income of the pensioner and the pensioner's spouse or common-law partner in the current payment period, and (S.C. 2000, c. 12, ss. 206 and 207(1).)

B is the product

    (*a*) obtained by multiplying four-thirds of the rounded pension equivalent by the spouse's or common-law partner's special qualifying factor for the month, and (S.C. 2000, c. 12, s. 207(1).)

    (*b*) rounded, where that product is not a multiple of four dollars, to the next higher multiple of four dollars; (S.C. 1999, c. 22, s. 89(1).)

(S.C. 1996, c. 18, s. 54; 1998, c. 21, s. 116(2).)

"rounded pension equivalent" means the pension equivalent rounded to the next higher multiple of three dollars when the pension equivalent is not a multiple of three dollars; (S.C. 1998, c. 21, s. 116(2); 1999, c. 22, s. 89(3).)

"rounded supplement equivalent" means the supplement equivalent rounded to the next higher multiple of one dollar when the supplement equivalent is not a multiple of one dollar; (S.C. 1998, c. 21, s. 116(2); 1999, c. 22, s. 89(3).)

"supplement equivalent" means, in respect of any month in a payment quarter, the amount of the supplement that would be payable for that month under subsection 12(1), (1.1), (1.2), (2), (3) or (4), as the case may be, to a pensioner whose spouse or common-law partner is also a pensioner when both the pensioner and the spouse or common-law partner have no income in the base calendar year and both are in receipt of a full pension; (S.C. 2000, c. 12, s. 198(1); 2005, c. 30, s. 137(1).)

"supplement equivalent for the survivor" means, in respect of any month in a payment quarter, the amount determined under subsection (4.1), (4.2), (4.3) or (4.4), as the case may be. (R.S.C. 1985, c. 34 (1st Supp.), s. 5(1); 2000, c. 12, s. 208(1); 2005, c. 30, s. 137(1).)

(2) *Effect on supplement under Part II* — Where, under this Part, an application has been made and approved or the requirement for an application has been waived in respect of the spouse or common-law partner of a pensioner for any month in a payment quarter, the amount of the supplement that may be paid for that month to the pensioner, in lieu of the amount of the supplement provided under Part II for that month, is the amount determined by the formula (S.C. 2000, c. 12, s. 207(2).)

$$[(A - B) \times C] - D/4$$

where

Old Age Security Act

A is the total of the supplement equivalent in respect of that month and the amount of the full monthly pension for that month;

B is the pensioner's monthly pension for that month;

C is the pensioner's special qualifying factor for that month; and

D is the residual joint income of the pensioner and the spouse or common-law partner for that month rounded, where that income is not a multiple of four dollars, to the next lower multiple of four dollars. (S.C. 1995, c. 33, s. 12; 1996, c. 18, s. 54(1); 1998, c. 21, s. 116(5); 1999, c. 22, s. 89(4); 2000, c. 12, ss. 206 and 207(2).)

(2.1) *Limitation* — No supplement under subsection (2) may be paid to an incarcerated person described in subsection 5(3) for any month for which no pension may be paid. (2010, c. 22, s. 9(2).)

(3) *Allowance to spouse or common-law partner of pensioner* — The amount of the allowance that may be paid under section 19 for any month in a payment quarter to the spouse or common-law partner of a pensioner is (S.C. 2000, c. 12, s. 207(1) and 209.)

(a) where there is no monthly joint income of the pensioner and spouse or common-law partner in the current payment period, the total of (S.C. 1998, c. 21, s. 116(6); 2000, c. 12, ss. 206 and 207(1).)

(i) the product obtained by multiplying the pension equivalent in respect of the month by the spouse's or common-law partner's special qualifying factor for the month, and (S.C. 2000, c. 12, s. 207(1).)

(ii) the product obtained by multiplying the supplement equivalent in respect of the month by the spouse's or common-law partner's special qualifying factor for the month; (S.C. 2000, c. 12, s. 207(1).)

(b) where the monthly joint income of the pensioner and spouse or common-law partner in the current payment period is equal to or less than the product (S.C. 2000, c. 12, ss. 206 and 207(1).)

(i) obtained by multiplying four-thirds of the rounded pension equivalent in respect of the month by the spouse's or common-law partner's special qualifying factor for the month, and (S.C. 2000, c. 12, s. 207(1).)

(ii) rounded, where that product is not a multiple of four dollars, to the next higher multiple of four dollars, (S.C. 1999, c. 22, s. 89(5).)

the amount determined by the formula (S.C. 1998, c. 21, s. 116(8).)

$$(A \times B) + C$$

where

A is the supplement equivalent in respect of the month,

B is the spouse's or common-law partner's special qualifying factor for the month, and (S.C. 2000, c. 12, s. 207(1).)

C is the greater of zero and the amount determined by the formula

$$(D \times B) - 3/4E$$

where

B is the spouse's or common-law partner's special qualifying factor for the month, (S.C. 2000, c. 12, s. 207(1).)

D is the pension equivalent in respect of the month, and

E is the monthly joint income of the pensioner and the spouse or common-law partner in the current payment period rounded, where that income is not a multiple of four dollars, to the next lower multiple of four dollars; and (S.C. 1998, c. 21, s. 116(8); 1999, c. 22, s. 89(6); 2000, c. 12, ss. 206 and 207(1).)

(c) where the monthly joint income of the pensioner and spouse or common-law partner in the current payment period is more than the product (S.C. 2000, c. 12, ss. 206 and 207(1).)

(i) obtained by multiplying four-thirds of the rounded pension equivalent in respect of the month by the spouse's or common-law partner's special qualifying factor for the month, and (S.C. 2000, c. 12, s. 207(1).)

(ii) rounded, where that product is not a multiple of four dollars, to the next higher multiple of four dollars, (S.C. 1999, c. 22, s. 89(7).)

the amount determined by the formula (S.C. 1998, c. 21, s. 116(9); 2000, c. 12, s. 206.)

$$(A \times B) - C/4$$

where

A   is the supplement equivalent in respect of the month,

B   is the spouse's or common-law partner's special qualifying factor for the month, and (S.C. 2000, c. 12, s. 207(1).)

C   is the residual joint income of the pensioner and spouse or common-law partner for that month rounded, where that income is not a multiple of four dollars, to the next lower multiple of four dollars. (R.S.C. 1985, c. 34 (1st Supp.), s. 5(2); 1996, c. 18, s. 54(2); 1998, c. 21, s. 116(10); 1999, c. 22, s. 89(8); 2000, c. 12, ss. 206 and 207(1).)

(4) *Allowance to survivor* — The amount of the allowance that may be paid under section 21 for any month in a payment quarter to a survivor is (S.C. 2000, c. 12, ss. 208(1) and 209.)

(a) where there is no monthly income of the survivor in the current payment period, the total of (S.C. 1998, c. 21, s. 116(11); 2000, c. 12, s. 208(1).)

(i) the product obtained by multiplying the pension equivalent of the survivor in respect of the month by the survivor's special qualifying factor for the month, and (S.C. 2000, c. 12, s. 208(1).)

(ii) the product obtained by multiplying the supplement equivalent for the survivor in respect of the month by the survivor's special qualifying factor for the month; (S.C. 2000, c. 12, s. 208(1).)

(b) where the monthly income of the survivor in the current payment period is equal to or less than the product (S.C. 2000, c. 12, s. 208(1).)

(i) obtained by multiplying four-thirds of the rounded pension equivalent in respect of the month by the survivor's special qualifying factor for the month, and (S.C. 2000, c. 12, s. 208(1).)

(ii) rounded, where that product is not a multiple of four dollars, to the next higher multiple of four dollars, (S.C. 1999, c. 22, s. 89(9).)

the amount determined by the formula (S.C. 1998, c. 21, s. 116(12).)

$$(A \times B) + C$$

where

A   is the supplement equivalent for the survivor in respect of the month, (S.C. 2000, c. 12, s. 208(1).)

B   is the survivor's special qualifying factor for the month, and (S.C. 2000, c. 12, s. 208(1).)

C   is the greater of zero and the amount determined by the formula

$$(D \times B) - 3/4E$$

where

B   is the survivor's special qualifying factor for the month, (S.C. 2000, c. 12, s. 208(1).)

D   is the pension equivalent in respect of the month, and

E   is the monthly income of the survivor in the current payment period rounded, where that income is not a multiple of four dollars, to the next lower multiple of four dollars; and (S.C. 1998, c. 21, s. 116(13); 1999, c. 22, s. 89(10); 2000, c. 12, s. 208(1).)

   (*c*) where the monthly income of the survivor in the current payment period is more than the product (S.C. 2000, c. 12, s. 208(1).)

      (i) obtained by multiplying four-thirds of the rounded pension equivalent in respect of the month by the survivor's special qualifying factor for the month, and (S.C. 2000, c. 12, s. 208(1).)

      (ii) rounded, where that product is not a multiple of four dollars, to the next higher multiple of four dollars, (S.C. 1999, c. 22, s. 89(11).)

the amount determined by the formula (S.C. 1998, c. 21, s. 116(14).)

$$(A \times B) - C/2$$

where

A   is the supplement equivalent for the survivor in respect of the month, (S.C. 2000, c. 12, s. 208(1).)

B   is the survivor's special qualifying factor for the month, and (S.C. 2000, c. 12, s. 208(1).)

C   is the residual income of the survivor in respect of the month rounded, where that residual income is not a multiple of two dollars, to the next lower multiple of two dollars. (R.S.C. 1985, c. 34 (1st Supp.), 5(3); 1996, c. 18, s. 54(1); 1998, c. 28, s. 116(15); 1999, c. 22, s. 89(12); 2000, c. 12, s. 208(1).)

   (4.1) *Supplement equivalent for the survivor* — The amount of the supplement equivalent for the survivor is

   (*a*) four hundred and fifty-four dollars and nine cents, for any month in the payment quarter commencing on April 1, 2005;

   (*b*) the amount of the supplement equivalent for the survivor that would otherwise be payable plus eighteen dollars, for any month in the payment quarter commencing on January 1, 2006; and

   (*c*) the amount of the supplement equivalent for the survivor that would otherwise be payable plus eighteen dollars, for any month in the payment quarter commencing on January 1, 2007.

(S.C. 2005, c. 30, s. 137(2).)

   (4.2) *Indexation of supplement equivalent for the survivor* — Subject to paragraphs (4.1)(*b*) and (*c*), the amount of the supplement equivalent for the survivor for any month in a payment quarter commencing after June 30, 2005 is the amount obtained by multiplying

   (*a*) the amount of the supplement equivalent for the survivor for any month in the three-month period immediately before that payment quarter

by

(*b*) the ratio that the Consumer Price Index for the first adjustment quarter that relates to that payment quarter bears to the Consumer Price Index for the second adjustment quarter that relates to that payment quarter.

(S.C. 2005, c. 30, s. 137(2).)

(4.3) *No decrease* — Despite subsection (4.2), the amount of the supplement equivalent for the survivor for any month in a payment quarter may not be less than the amount of the supplement equivalent for the survivor for any month in the three-month period immediately before that payment quarter. (S.C. 2005, c. 30, s. 137(2).)

(4.4) *Reduction in Consumer Price Index* — If, in relation to any payment quarter, the Consumer Price Index for the first adjustment quarter is lower than the Consumer Price Index for the second adjustment quarter,

(*a*) no adjustment of the supplement equivalent for the survivor is to be made under subsection (4.2) in respect of that payment quarter; and

(*b*) no adjustment of the supplement equivalent for the survivor is to be made under that subsection in respect of any subsequent payment quarter until, in relation to a subsequent payment quarter, the Consumer Price Index for the first adjustment quarter that relates to that subsequent payment quarter is higher than the Consumer Price Index for the second adjustment quarter that relates to the payment quarter referred to in paragraph (*a*), in which case the second adjustment quarter that relates to the payment quarter referred to in that paragraph is deemed to be the second adjustment quarter that relates to that subsequent payment quarter.

(S.C. 2005, c. 30, s. 137(2).)

(5) *Reinstatement of supplement* — Where the allowance payable to the spouse or common-law partner of a pensioner under this Part is suspended or terminated for any month, the pensioner may, notwithstanding subsection (2), be paid, for that month, the amount of supplement provided under Part II. (S.C. 2000, c. 12, ss. 207(1) and 209.)

(6) *Reinstatement of supplement* — Where, by reason of the amount of the monthly joint income, the aggregate of the amount of allowance payable to a pensioner's spouse or common-law partner for a month and the amount of supplement payable to the pensioner for that month under this Part is less than the amount of supplement that would be payable to the pensioner under Part II, the pensioner may, notwithstanding subsection (2), be paid, for that month, the amount of supplement provided under Part II minus the amount, if any, of allowance payable to that pensioner's spouse or common-law partner for that month. (S.C. 2000, c. 12, s. 198(2).)

(7) *Deemed Part II application* — For the purposes of subsections (5) and (6), an application made and approved under this Part shall be deemed to have been made and approved under Part II.

(R.S.C. 1985, c. 34 (1st Supp.), s. 5; 1995, c. 33, s. 12; 1996, c. 18, s. 54; 1998, c. 21, ss. 116, 119(1)(*h*); 1999, c. 22, s. 89; 2000, c. 12, ss. 198, 206, 207(1) and (2), 208(1) and 209; 2005, c. 30, s. 137; 2010, c. 22, s. 9.)

———————— Notes ————————

Case Law

F-44953 v. MHRD; F-44669 v. MHRD (January 11, 2000), (RT)

It was appropriate for the Minister to adjust the spouse's allowance benefits payable to take into account the income recorded in the name of the spouse for 1997 that exceeded the estimate. The Minister was entitled to recover any overpayment where the spouse's actual income exceeded the estimate.

22.1. *Additional amount — subsection 22(2)* — **(1) The amount that may be added to the amount of the supplement that may be paid to a pensioner referred to in subsection 22(2) for any month in a payment quarter beginning after June 30, 2011 is the amount determined by the formula**

$$A \times B - C/4$$

where

A   **is $35;**

B   **is the pensioner's special qualifying factor for the month; and**

C   **is $1/24$ of the aggregate of the income of the pensioner and his or her spouse or common-law partner for the base calendar year in excess of $4,000 rounded, if it is not a multiple of four dollars, to the next lower multiple of four dollars.**

(2011, c. 15, s. 14.)

(2) *Additional amount — subsection 22(3)* — **The amount that may be added to the amount of the allowance that may be paid to a spouse or common-law partner referred to in subsection 22(3) for any month in a payment quarter beginning after June 30, 2011 is the amount determined by the formula**

$$A \times B - C/4$$

where

A   **is $35;**

B   **is the special qualifying factor for the spouse or common-law partner for the month; and**

C   **is $1/24$ of the aggregate of the income of the pensioner and his or her spouse or common-law partner for the base calendar year in excess of $4,000 rounded, if it is not a multiple of four dollars, to the next lower multiple of four dollars.**

(2011, c. 15, s. 14.)

(3) *Additional amount — subsection 22(4)* — **The amount that may be added to the amount of the allowance that may be paid to a survivor referred to in subsection 22(4) for any month in a payment quarter beginning after June 30, 2011 is the amount determined by the formula**

$$A \times B - C/4$$

where

A   **is $50;**

B   **is the special qualifying factor for the spouse or common-law partner for the month; and**

C   **is $1/12$ of the survivor's income for the base calendar year in excess of $2,000 rounded, if it is not a multiple of four dollars, to the next lower multiple of four dollars.**

(2011, c. 15, s. 14.)

(4) *Indexation* — **For the purpose of calculating the amount payable under any of subsections (1) to (3) for any month in a payment quarter beginning after September 30, 2011, the amount to be determined for A in that subsection is the amount obtained by multiplying**

(a) **the amount determined for A for any month in the three-month period immediately before that payment quarter**

by

(*b*) the ratio that the Consumer Price Index for the first adjustment quarter that relates to that payment quarter bears to the Consumer Price Index for the second adjustment quarter that relates to that payment quarter.

(2011, c. 15, s. 14.)

(5) *No decrease* — Despite subsection (4), the amount determined for A for any month in a payment quarter shall not be less than the amount determined for A for any month in the three-month period immediately before that payment quarter. (2011, c. 15, s. 14.)

(6) *Effect of reduction in Consumer Price Index* — If, in relation to any payment quarter, the Consumer Price Index for the first adjustment quarter is lower than the Consumer Price Index for the second adjustment quarter,

(*a*) no adjustment to the amount determined for A shall be made under subsection (4) in respect of that payment quarter; and

(*b*) no adjustment to the amount determined for A shall be made under subsection (4) in respect of any subsequent payment quarter until, in relation to a subsequent payment quarter, the Consumer Price Index for the first adjustment quarter that relates to that subsequent payment quarter is higher than the Consumer Price Index for the second adjustment quarter that relates to the payment quarter referred to in paragraph (*a*), in which case the second adjustment quarter that relates to the payment quarter referred to in that paragraph is deemed to be the second adjustment quarter that relates to that subsequent payment quarter.

(2011, c. 15, s. 14.)

(2011, c. 15, s. 14.)

Commencement of Allowance

23. *Commencement of allowance* — **(1)** Payment of an allowance to any person under this Part shall commence in the first month after the application therefor has been approved, but where an application is approved after the last day of the month in which it was received, the approval may be effective as of such earlier date, not prior to the day on which the application was received, as may be prescribed by regulation. (S.C. 2000, c. 12, s. 209.)

(1.1) *Commencement where waiver of application* — Where the requirement for an application for payment of an allowance has been waived under this Part, the payment of the allowance shall not commence more than eleven months before the month in which the requirement for an application is waived. (S.C. 1995, c. 33, s. 13; 2000, c. 12, s. 209.)

(2) *Exception* — Notwithstanding subsection (1), where a person who has applied to receive an allowance attained the age of sixty years before the day on which the application was received, the approval of the application may be effective as of such earlier day, not before the later of (S.C. 2000, c. 12, s. 209.)

(*a*) a day one year before the day on which the application was received, and

(*b*) the day on which the person attained the age of sixty years, (S.C. 2000, c. 12, s. 199.)

as may be prescribed by regulation.

(3) *Incarcerated persons* — Despite subsections (1) and (1.1), if the application for an allowance by a person described in paragraph 19(6)(*f*) or 21(9)(*d*) is approved while that person is incarcerated, payment of their allowance shall commence in respect of the month in which they are released but only if they

(*a*) have notified the Minister in writing before or after their release; and

527

(*b*) continue to be eligible for an allowance.

(S.C. 2010, c. 22, s. 10.)

(S.C. 1995, c. 33, s. 13; 2000, c. 12, ss. 199 and 209; 2010, c. 22, s. 10.)

———————— Notes ————————

Related Regulations

- Section 25(2) — Notice of change of address
- Section 25(3) — Notice of death of beneficiary
- Section 26 — Suspension of payments

Case Law

C-49310 v. MHRD (January 20, 2000) (RT)

The Tribunal's powers are limited to what is permitted in the *Old Age Security Act*, and that limitation is a retroactive payment of the monthly allowance up to eleven months before the month the application was received. The applicant's claim that she did not receive the original notification from the Minister of her entitlement was not relevant.

————————————————

Payment of Allowance

24. *Consideration of application or waiver* — **(1) The Minister shall, without delay after receiving an application for an allowance under subsection 19(4) or 21(4) or after waiving the requirement for an application for an allowance under subsection 19(4.1) or 21(5.1), as the case may be, consider whether the applicant is entitled to be paid an allowance, and may approve payment of an allowance and fix the amount of benefits that may be paid, or may determine that no allowance may be paid. (S.C. 1995, c. 33, s. 14; 2000, c. 12, s. 209.)**

S. 24(1) will be replaced by S.C. 2012, c. 19, s. 462 on proclamation, and will read as follows:

24. *Consideration of application or waiver* — **(1) The Minister shall, without delay after receiving an application for an allowance under subsection 19(4) or 21(4) or after waiving the requirement for an application for an allowance under subsection 19(4.02) or (4.1) or 21(4.1) or (5.1), as the case may be, consider whether the applicant is entitled to be paid an allowance, and may approve payment of an allowance and fix the amount of benefits that may be paid, or may determine that no allowance may be paid.**

(2) *Notification to applicants or applicant* — **Where particulars of the basis on which the amount of any allowance that may be paid in respect of an application was fixed by the Minister are requested by an applicant or where the Minister determines that no allowance may be paid in respect of the application, the Minister shall forthwith in writing notify the applicants or applicant of the basis on which that amount was fixed or of the decision that no allowance may be paid in respect of the application and the Minister's reasons therefor, as the case may be. (S.C. 2000, c. 12, s. 209.)**

(S.C. 1995, c. 33, s. 14; 2000, c. 12, s. 209.)

———————— Notes ————————

Related Regulations

- Section 23 — Further information required

• Section 24 — Payment to person other than beneficiary

---

25. *Payment of an allowance to be made in arrears* — **Payment of an allowance for any month shall be made in arrears at the end of the month, except that where payment of an allowance in respect of any payment period is approved after the end of the month for which the first payment of the allowance may be made, payments thereof for the month in which payment of the allowance is approved and for months preceding that month may be made at the end of that month or at the end of the month next following that month.**

(S.C. 1998, c. 21, s. 119(2)(c); 2000, c. 12, s. 209.)

26. *Application of Part II* — **(1) Sections 6, 14, 15 and 18 apply, with such modifications as the circumstances require, in respect of an allowance under this Part and in respect of any application or any waiver of the requirement for an application for an allowance. (S.C. 1995, c. 33, s. 15; 2000, c. 12, s. 200.)**

(1.1) *Information previously submitted* — **For greater certainty, the Minister may waive the requirements of subsections 14(1) and 15(1) and (2) in respect of an application for an allowance under this Part if the information required under those subsections has already been submitted to or filed with the Minister in respect of an application for a supplement under Part II. (S.C. 2007, c. 11, s. 21.)**

(2) *Idem* — **The provisions of subsection 11(2) and sections 16 to 18 apply, with such modifications as the circumstances require, in respect of the supplement payable to the pensioner pursuant to subsection 22(2). (R.S.C. 1985, c. 34 (1st Supp.), s. 6.)**

(R.S.C. 1985, c. 34 (1st Supp.), s. 6; 1995, c. 33, s. 15; 2000, c. 12, s. 200; 2007, c. 11, s. 21.)

S. 26.01 and 26.02 will be added by S.C. 2012, c. 19, s. 463 on proclamation, and will read as follows:

Cesssation of Payment

26.01. *Request that allowance cease to be payable* — **If a person makes a request to the Minister in writing that their allowance cease to be payable, it shall cease to be payable on the last day of the month in which the Minister approves the request and shall not resume until the later of the month after the month in which the Minister receives a new application for the allowance and the month chosen by the person in the application.**

Cancellation of Payment

26.02. *Request to cancel allowance* — **(1) A person may, in the prescribed manner and within the prescribed time after payment of an allowance has commenced, request cancellation of that allowance.**

(2) *Effect of cancellation* — **If the request is granted and the amount of the allowance is repaid within the prescribed time,**

    (*a*) **the application for that allowance is deemed never to have been made; and**

    (*b*) **the allowance is deemed for the purposes of this Act not to have been payable during the period in question.**

Part IV
General
Effect of Waiver[11]

26.1. *Deeming provision* — When the requirement for an application for a benefit is waived by the Minister under this Act, the application is deemed to have been made by the applicant on the day on which the requirement is waived and, for greater certainty, the applicant shall not be paid that benefit for any month that is more than 11 months before the month in which the application is deemed to have been made.

(S.C. 2007, c. 11, s. 22.)

26.2. *Inviting persons to apply* — The Minister may invite persons to make an application for benefits under this Act and may, for that purpose, collect personal information and make available or use personal information available to him or her under this Act.

(S.C. 2012, c. 19, s. 464.)

Adjustment in Consumer Price Index

27. *Where basis of Consumer Price Index changed* — Where at any time the Consumer Price Index for Canada, as published by Statistics Canada under the authority of the *Statistics Act*, is adjusted to reflect a new time basis or a new content basis, a corresponding adjustment shall be made in the Consumer Price Index with respect to any adjustment quarter that is used for the purpose of calculating the amount of any benefit that may be paid under this Act.

Reconsiderations and Appeals

27.1. *Request for reconsideration by Minister* — **(1)** A person who is dissatisfied with a decision or determination made under this Act that no benefit may be paid to the person, or respecting the amount of a benefit that may be paid to the person, may, within ninety days after the day on which the person is notified in writing of the decision or determination, or within any longer period that the Minister may, either before or after the expiration of those ninety days, allow, make a request to the Minister in the prescribed form and manner for a reconsideration of that decision or determination. (S.C. 1997, c. 40, s. 100(1).)

(1.1) *Reconsideration — penalty* — A person against whom a penalty has been assessed under section 44.1 or, subject to the regulations, any person on their behalf, who is dissatisfied with the decision to impose a penalty or with the amount of the penalty may, within ninety days after the day on which the person is notified in writing of the decision or determination, or within any longer period that the Minister may, either before or after the expiration of those ninety days, allow, request the Minister in the prescribed form and manner to reconsider the decision or determination. (S.C. 1997, c. 40, s. 100(1).)

(2) *Decision of Minister* — The Minister shall, without delay after receiving a request referred to in subsection (1) or (1.1), reconsider the decision or determination, as the case may be, and may confirm or vary it and may approve payment of a benefit, determine the amount of a benefit or determine that no benefit is payable, and shall without delay notify, in writing, the person who made the request of the Minister's decision and of the reasons for it. (S.C. 1997, c. 40, s. 100(2).)

(S.C. 1997, c. 40, s. 100.)

---

[11] Heading added by S.C. 2007, c. 11, s. 22.

———————— **Notes** ————————

Related Regulations

- Section 29 — Request for reconsideration

Case Law

Canada (Minister of Human Resources Development) v. Tucker 2003 FCA 278

Decisions relating to the forgiveness of an overpayment or the repayment of an underpayment made as a result of erroneous advice are not decisions "respecting the amount of any benefit that may be paid to that person" within the meaning of s. 27.1(1). The OAS Act provides no other specific right of appeal of such a decision. The only remedy available to a recipient under the circumstances was to apply to the Federal Court for judicial review of the Minister's decision.

Canada (Attorney General) v. Bannerman, 2003 FCT 208

A request for reconsideration under s. 27.1(1) and the decision on the request for reconsideration are conditions precedent to a right of appeal to a Review Tribunal. Only a decision on a reconsideration request may be appealed to a Review Tribunal.

Canada (Minister of Human Resources Development) v. Dublin Estate, 2006 FC 152

Under s. 27.1(2), a Minister may confirm or vary the initial decision, and may approve payment of a benefit, determine the amount of a benefit, or determine that no benefit is payable. Under CPP s. 82(11), a Review Tribunal may confirm or vary a decision of the Minister made under s. 27.1(2), and may take any action in relation to that decision, that might have been taken by the Minister under that subsection. The Review Tribunal did not have jurisdiction to order the Minister to make an *ex gratia* payment.

Kiefer v. Canada (Attorney General), 2008 FC 786

Section 27.1(1) enables an individual, dissatisfied with a decision or determination made under the *OAS Act,* to request reconsideration by the Minister. Section 28(1) provides that a person who makes a request under s. 27.1(1) and who is dissatisfied with the decision of the Minister, may appeal the decision to a Review Tribunal under CPP s. 82(1). Section 82(1) of the CPP states that a party, dissatisfied with a decision of the Minister under s. 27.1(2) of the *OAS Act,* may appeal the decision to a Review Tribunal. However, CPP s. 83(1), which enables parties to seek leave to appeal decisions of the Review Tribunal (made under s. 82 of the CPP) to the PAB, specifically excludes decisions made under s. 28(1) of the *OAS Act* from the operation of CPP s. 83(1). Put another way, CPP s. 83(1) carves out an exception regarding the right to seek leave to appeal to the PAB with respect to appeals under s. 28(1) of the *OAS Act.* The only recourse available for unsuccessful appellants whose appeals to the Review Tribunal were lodged pursuant to s. 27.1(1) and 28(1) of the *OAS Act* is to seek judicial review of the Review Tribunal's decision in the Federal Court because no right to seek leave to appeal to the PAB exists. Rather, it is expressly excluded.

Buchan v. Canada (Attorney General), 2007 FC 1141

Section 84(2) of the CPP appears to be confined to a decision of the Minister made under "this Act", meaning the CPP. *Quaere* whether s. 84(2) permits the court to re-open or vary the Minister's decision under OAS Act s. 27.1(1).

Canada (Attorney General) v. Vinet-Proulx, 2007 FC 99

On a request for reconsideration of the Minister's initial decision, the Minister is not authorized under s. 27.1(2) to allow the retroactive payment of a pension for a period previous to one year prior to an application for benefits. Section 8(2) of the *OAS Act* and s. 5(2) of the OAS Regulations are clear and do not give the Minister any discretion: the approval of the application for benefits cannot take effect any earlier than one year before the date the application in question was received. Therefore, the Review Tribunal did not have jurisdiction to award pension benefits retroactively beginning on a date prior to one year prior to the application, as this is contrary to the legislative and regulatory provisions on which the Minister's initial decision and revised decision are based.

L-63827 v. MSD (2004) (RT)

A Ministry document sent to an appellant purporting to be explanatory in nature but taking a different position on various points from the Minister's initial position by way of offering the appellant a compromise constituted a new decision, giving the appellant the right to seek reconsideration by the Minister prior to the appeal to the Review Tribunal.

Canada (Minister of Human Resources Development) v. Leavitt, 2005 FC 664

The Review Tribunal has the jurisdiction to hear an appeal with respect to the amount of a GIS benefit, even where the amount paid to the pensioner has been adjusted by Ministerial direction under s. 15(3.1) when the pensioner moved into and out of a nursing home. Such a determination cannot be equated with a purely discretionary exercise of the Minister's power, which would not be subject to appeal.

P-41238 v. MHRD (May 7, 1999) (RT)

The Review Tribunal had authority to hear and dispose of claims concerning erroneous advice and administrative error in connection with the application of the Act. The Tribunal is not bound by the Department's internal policies, including policies on such matters as the standard of proof in determinations regarding erroneous advice and administrative error. The Review Tribunal had authority to review a Ministerial decision.

---

28. *Appeal — benefits* **— (1) A person who is dissatisfied with a decision of the Minister made under section 27.1, including a decision in relation to further time to make a request, or, subject to the regulations, any person on their behalf, may appeal the decision to the Social Security Tribunal established under section 44 of the *Department of Employment and Social Development Act.* (1997, c. 40, s. 101; 2012, c. 19, s. 236(1); 2013, c. 40, s. 236(1)(g)(iv).)**

(2) *Reference as to income* **— If, on an appeal to the Social Security Tribunal, it is a ground of the appeal that the decision made by the Minister as to the income or income from a particular source or sources of an applicant or beneficiary or of the spouse or common-law partner of the applicant or beneficiary was incorrectly made, the appeal on that ground must, in accordance with the regulations, be referred for decision to the Tax Court of Canada, whose decision, subject only to variation by that Court in accordance with any decision on an appeal under the *Tax Court of Canada Act* relevant to the appeal to the Social Security Tribunal, is final and binding for all purposes of the appeal to the Social Security Tribunal except in accordance with the *Federal Courts Act.* (S.C. 1995, c. 33, s. 16; 2000, c. 12, s. 207(1); 2002, c. 8, s. 182(1)(z.5); 2012, c. 19, s. 236(1).)**

(3) *Stay of benefits pending judicial review* **— If a decision is made by the Social Security Tribunal in respect of a benefit, the Minister may stay payment of the benefit until the later of (S.C. 2012, c. 19, s. 236(2).)**

(a) the expiration of the period allowed for making an application under the *Federal Courts Act* for judicial review of the decision, and (S.C. 2002, c. 8, s. 182(1)(z.5).)

(b) where Her Majesty has made an application under the *Federal Courts Act* for judicial review of the decision, the month in which all proceedings in relation to the judicial review have been completed. (S.C. 1995, c. 33, s. 16; (S.C. 2002, c. 8, s. 182(1)(z.5).)

(R.S.C. 1985, c. 34 (1st Supp.), s. 7; R.S.C. 1985, c. 51 (4th Supp.), s. 15; 1995, c. 33, s. 16; 1997, c. 40, s. 101; 2000, c. 12, s. 207; S.C. 2002, c. 8, s. 182; 2012, c. 19, s. 236; 2013, c. 40, s. 236.)

——————— **Notes** ———————

Related Regulations

● Sections 38–47 — Reference to Tax Court of Canada

Case Law

§1. General Principles

Kiefer v. Canada (Attorney General), 2008 FC 786

The only recourse available for unsuccessful appellants whose appeals to the Review Tribunal were lodged pursuant to s. 27.1(1) and 28(1) of the *OAS Act* is to seek judicial review of the Review Tribunal's decision in the Federal Court because no right to seek leave to appeal to the PAB exists. Rather, it is expressly excluded.

Canada (Minister of Human Resources Development) v. Chhabu, (2005), 280 F.T.R. 296, 35 Admin. L.R. (4th) 193 (Fed. Ct.). See also *Kiefer v. Canada (Attorney General),* 2008 FC 786

The applicable standard of review with respect to decisions of the Review Tribunal is reasonableness. A decision will be unreasonable only if there is no line of analysis within the given reasons that could reasonably lead the tribunal from the evidence before it to the conclusion at which it arrived. If any of the reasons that are sufficient to support the conclusion are tenable in the sense that they can stand up to a somewhat probing examination, then the decision will not be unreasonable and a reviewing court must not interfere. This means that a decision may satisfy the reasonableness standard if it is supported by a tenable explanation, even if this explanation is not one that the reviewing court finds compelling.

Canada (MHRD) v. Heaman, 2004 FC 1155

The jurisdiction of a statutory body such as the Review Tribunal is limited to that set out in its enabling statute. Where the Minister took the position that pay equity monies were a retroactive salary adjustment that should have been included for the purposes of calculating the claimant's GIS, the Review Tribunal was under a statutory duty, pursuant to s. 28(2) to refer the claimant's appeal to the Tax Court of Canada for adjudication.

Canada (Attorney General) v. Bannerman, 2003 FCT 208

There is no direct right of appeal from an original determination of the Minister without having first applied for redetermination and having received a decision flowing from that request. A request for reconsideration under s. 27.1(1) and the decision on the request for reconsideration are conditions precedent to a right of appeal to a Review Tribunal. Only a decision on a reconsideration request may be appealed to a Review Tribunal.

Canada (Attorney General) v. Pabla, [1994] F.C.J. No. 1698 (T.D.)

The Review Tribunal has a duty to interpret provisions of the Act and Regulations before applying them. It is wrong in law for the Tribunal to grant the applicant the benefit of the doubt because of an ambiguity in the provisions. The Tribunal must determine if the applicant has proven that he or she meets of the requirements of one of the provisions and indicate the facts on which it bases its decision. The Tribunal has no authority to entertain constitutional challenges.

Canada (Attorney General) v. Landry, [1997] F.C.J. No. 224 (T.D.)

It is not open to a Review Tribunal to take the law into its own hands and attempt to apply a scheme under the OAS in the same manner as under the CPP, which deals with the same broad subject matter, merely because it thinks the schemes should be the same. The Tribunal cannot expressly disregard the law.

Mian v. Canada (Attorney General), [2001] FCT 433 (C.A.)

To secure a reopening of a case, new evidence need only be such as to support a conclusion that there is a reasonable possibility as opposed to probability that it could lead the Tribunal to change its original decision. A finding that "these new facts are persuasive or determinative at all" was consistent with this threshold.

B-49043 v. MHRD (April 6, 2000) (RT)

The pensioner's ignorance of the existence of the widowed spouse's allowance at the time of the spouse's death does not confer authority on the Review Tribunal to award a longer period of retroactivity than the 11-month statutory maximum.

G-58977 v. MHRD (November 3, 2000) (RT)

The Review Tribunal has authority to hear the appeal of the Minister's exercise of discretion under s. 14 to use the estimated income in the enumerated circumstances.

C-42295 v. MHRD (October 5, 2000) (RT)

The Tribunal did not have the authority to forgive overpayments in whole or in part.

N-50900 v. MHRD (February 1, 2000) (RT)

The Tribunal is not bound by the terminology in an information booklet.

W-44040 v. MHRD (March 24, 1999) (RT)

Where the appellant already accepted a partial pension benefit, the Tribunal has no jurisdiction to re-open the issue.

F-41008 v. MHRD (June 16, 1999) (RT)

Appeal rights are not limited to certain sections in the Act. The Tribunal may review a Minister's decision whether to take remedial action for erroneous advice or administrative error under s. 32.

T-32177 v. MHRD (October 16, 1998) (RT)

The Tribunal is bound by the law, and can only interpret and enforce the governing legislative provisions. The Tribunal does not have "equitable" jurisdiction.

C-40317 v. MHRD (February 25, 2000) (RT)

The Tribunal does not have jurisdiction to reduce the number of years of required residency on compassionate grounds.

S-46930 v. MHRD (February 24, 1999) (RT)

The extent to which the Minister has or has not taken steps to ensure that people are aware of the provisions regarding benefits is not within the scope of the Tribunal's jurisdiction.

C-46120 v. MHRD (February 10, 2000) (RT)

Where it is argued that an administrative error had been made because the Minister did not respond to a request to determine why GIS benefits not had been paid pursuant to an alleged previous application, a Review Tribunal's jurisdiction is confined to reviewing whether the decision of the Minister in awarding the benefits under the current application has been done according to the legislative requirements.

C-49310 v. MHRD (November 3, 1999) (RT)

The Tribunal does not have equitable jurisdiction. Its powers are limited to what is permitted in the *Old Age Security Act*, despite an applicant's claim that she did not received a notification from the Minister of her entitlement to a benefit.

D-31990 v. MHRD (November 17, 1997) (RT)

The Tribunal is bound by the provisions of the *Old Age Security Act*, and cannot deviate from the legislation. Where the legislation clearly states a maximum retroactivity of eleven months; and this amount has been paid, the Tribunal is bound by the legislation.

T-32201 v. MHRD (June 22, 1999) (RT)

The Tribunal does not have the jurisdiction to exercise the Minister's discretion in granting overpayment remission.

§1.1. Jurisdiction of Commissioner of Review Tribunal

Stevens Estate v. Canada (Attorney General), 2011 FC 103. See also *Lambie v. Canada (Attorney General)*, 2011 FC 104

The Commissioner in the exercise of his or her case management function does not have the jurisdiction to close a claimant's OAS appeal file without convening a Review Tribunal to hear the appeal. An appellant has a *de novo* right of appeal from reconsideration decisions by the Minister before the Review Tribunal. Section 82 of the CPP provides that a Review Tribunal hearing must be scheduled. Any discretion conferred by s. 3(2) of the Review Tribunal Rules of Procedure, which provides that the Commissioner may take steps to obtain information an applicant failed to provide in order to rectify the failure to comply with s. 3(1) of the Rules, does not displace the mandatory requirements of the CPP s. 82 and the Rules. A Review Tribunal hearing on an OAS reconsideration appeal is a *de novo* hearing. Accordingly, an appellant may introduce new issues in the Review Tribunal appeal hearing. Therefore, the Commissioner is in no position to conclusively determine beforehand that an appeal is not within the Review Tribunal's purview. The Commissioner may not close an appeal file and deny an appellant's opportunity to a *de novo* hearing. The purpose of s. 3(2) of the Rules is to enable the Commissioner to facilitate the preparation of a proper appeal for the Review Tribunal's consideration. This may involve inquiry to identify proper grounds and factual evidence required for a Review Tribunal if an appellant does not articulate as such.

§2. Judicial Review of Review Tribunal OAS Decision

- See also commentary and cases under CPP s. 84

Alberta (Information and Privacy Commissioner) v. Alberta Teachers' Association, 2011 SCC 61, [2011] 3 SCR 654. See also *Canada (Canadian Human Rights Commission) v. Canada (Attorney General)*, 2011 SCC 53, [2011] 3 SCR 471.

Unless the situation is exceptional, the interpretation by the tribunal of its own statute or statutes closely connected to its function, with which it will have particular familiarity should be presumed to be a question of statutory interpretation subject to deference on judicial review. Inadequacy of reasons was not a stand-alone basis for quashing a decision in judicial review. The reviewing court may, if found necessary, look at the record for the purpose of assessing the reasonableness of the outcome.

Flitcroft v. Canada (Attorney General), 2012 FC 782

Obiter: While the existing jurisprudence indicates that the standard of review of Review Tribunal decisions on pure questions of law should be on a correctness standard, the Supreme Court of Canada's decision in *Alberta Teachers'* might well require a change in that approach.

Hussaini v. Canada (Attorney General), 2011 FC 26

Only persons who are directly affected by the order sought may be named as parties to an application for judicial review. The spouse of the claimant is not a proper party to judicial review proceedings. By virtue of s. 303(2) of the *Federal Court Rules*, the proper respondent is the Attorney General, not the Minister of Social Development. Federal Court Rule 81(2) grants discretion in the court to draw an adverse inference where an affidavit is based on belief. The Rule does not necessarily prescribe that the failure by an applicant to file her own affidavit necessarily leads to dismissal of the application. An application for judicial review can proceed without an affidavit being filed on behalf of the applicant or applicants. In any event, an application for judicial review proceeds on the basis on the record that was before the subordinate decision-maker. In the absence of evidence based on personal knowledge, any error must appear on the face of that record. The necessary facts are contained in that record, which is attached to an affidavit filed on behalf of the Minister. The necessary facts are accordingly before the Court. The claimant's affidavit should be struck where it was unsigned but not sworn, all of the attached exhibits were unidentified, and the affidavit was largely argumentative. This does not mean that it must be physically removed from the record, but only that it would not be considered by the reviewing court.

Canada (Attorney General) v. Comeau, 2004 FC 1034. See also *Canada (Minister of Human Resources Development) v. Leavitt*, 2005 FC 664.

On the issue of whether the RT had jurisdiction to hear the appeal in question, the appropriate standard of review is correctness.

Old Age Security Act

Canada (Minister of Human Resources Development) v. Leavitt, 2005 FC 664

Obiter: Where the Review Tribunal was required to apply the facts to the relevant provisions of the statute, the decision as a whole would likely attract a degree of deference of reasonableness *simpliciter.* [Author's note: The Court found that the Tribunal's decision was not supportable under any standard.]

Canada (MHRD) v. Heaman, 2004 FC 1155. See also *Canada (Attorney General) v. Comeau* 2004 FC 1034.

In the domain of statutory interpretation, the Review Tribunal possesses no superior expertise relative to the Federal Court. A Review Tribunal consists of three persons, only one of whom is required to be a member of the bar of a province (OAS Act s. 82(7)(a)). The purpose of the OAS Act is not stated anywhere in the statute and the *Canada Pension Plan* contains neither a right of appeal nor a privitive clause in respect of Review Tribunal decisions. Thus, the applicable standard of review is correctness.

Kuthiala v. MNHW, [1995] F.C.J. No. 164 (T.D.)

Although the terms of s. 28 of the *Federal Court Act* are quite broad in scope, courts in the presence of a privative clause will only interfere with the findings of a specialized tribunal where it is found that the decision of that tribunal cannot be sustained on any reasonable interpretation of the facts or of the law. This is the preferable formulation of the "patently unreasonable" test. (Note: This decision was made under the former s. 28(1). There is no longer a privative clause in the OAS. Section 84(1) of the *Canada Pension Plan* provides that the decision of a Review Tribunal, "except for judicial review under the *Federal Court Act*", is final and binding for all purposes of the CPP.)

Daoud v. HRSD, 2012 FCA 13

Although determining the place of residence for purposes of OAS eligibility involves questions of fact and credibility, which are subject to a very stringent standard of review, an extension of the period for seeking judicial review may be granted where the claimant was diligent in seeking review and the application raised errors of law regarding the interpretation and scope of the OAS Act and regarding the burden of proof that applies when establishing place of residence.

Dhaliwal v. Canada (Attorney General), 2003 FCT 162

The fact that a senior official with the Office of the Commissioner of the Review Tribunals felt compelled to apologize to the applicants for judicial review for the confusion and the delays in responding to them and to suggest that they might "wish to bring our delay to the attention of the Federal Court in support of a request to extend the time to apply for judicial review of the Review Tribunal's decision," was a relevant factor in justifying a late application for judicial review. However, the applicants still require an arguable case to take to the Federal Court for judicial review.

§3. Res Judicata and Issue Estoppel

● See also cases under CPP **s. 84 §5 Res Judicata / Finality Clause / New Facts**

S-71345 v. MHRD (November 5, 2002) (RT). See also *S-37686 v. MHRD* (June 26, 2002) (RT).

The principle of "issue estoppel" precludes a party from attempting to re-litigate some point, question or fact that has already been adjudicated. The principle applies where:

  1. the same question has been decided,

  2. the judicial decision which is said to create the estoppel was final, and

  3. the parties to the judicial decision were the same persons as the parties to the proceeding in which the estoppel is raised.

§4. Confidentiality orders

Singer v. Canada (Attorney General), 2011 FCA 3

Confidentiality orders extending to documentation tendered in appeals are the exception, and if required, should be made so as to minimize the impact of the order on the open court principle. A confidentiality order should only be granted when such an order is necessary to prevent a serious risk to an important interest because reasonably alternative measures will not prevent the risk, and the salutary effects of the confidentiality order outweigh its deleterious effects, including the effects on the right to free expression, which includes the public interest in open and accessible court proceedings. In appeal or judicial review proceedings under the OAS Act, it is appropriate to order that the claimant's SIN number be redacted from all affidavit evidence and exhibits. An order to seal the claimant's affidavit evidence and related exhibits would overreach the purpose of protecting the claimant's SIN number, particularly in light of the alternative measures easily available to achieve the same result.

Incapacity

28.1. *Incapacity when application actually made* — **(1) Where an application for a benefit is made on behalf of a person and the Minister is satisfied, on the basis of evidence provided by or on behalf of that person, that the person was incapable of forming or expressing an intention to make an application on the person's own behalf on the day on which the application was actually made, the Minister may deem the application to have been made in the month preceding the first month in which the relevant benefit could have commenced to be paid or in the month that the Minister considers the person's last relevant period of incapacity to have commenced, whichever is the later. (S.C. 1995, c. 33, s. 17.)**

(2) *Where previous incapacity* — **Where an application for a benefit is made by or on behalf of a person and the Minister is satisfied, on the basis of evidence provided by or on behalf of that person, that**

(a) **the person was incapable of forming or expressing an intention to make an application before the day on which the application was actually made,**

(b) **the person had ceased to be so incapable before that day, and**

(c) **the application was made**

(i) **within the period beginning on the day on which that person had ceased to be incapable and comprising the same number of days, not exceeding twelve months, as in the period of incapacity, or**

(ii) **where the period referred to in subparagraph (i) comprises fewer than thirty days, not more than one month after the month in which that person ceased to be so incapable,**

the Minister may deem the application to have been made in the month preceding the first month in which the relevant benefit could have commenced to be paid or in the month that the Minister considers the person's last relevant period of incapacity to have commenced, whichever is the later. (S.C. 1995, c. 33, s. 17.)

(3) *Period of incapacity* — **For the purposes of subsections (1) and (2), a period of incapacity must be a continuous period, except as otherwise prescribed. (S.C. 1995, c. 33, s. 17.)**

(4) *Application* — **This section applies only to persons who were incapacitated on or after January 1, 1995. (S.C. 1995, c. 33, s. 17.)**

(S.C. 1995, c. 33, s. 17; 2000, c. 12, s. 201.)

—————— **Notes** ——————

Related Regulations

● Section 24 — Payment to person other than beneficiary

Case Law

● See also digests under CPP s. 60 §2 Incapacity

Canada (Attorney General) v. Poon, 2009 FC 654.

When interpreting s. 28.1, the question is not whether a person is capable of dealing with the consequences of an application, but rather whether that person was capable of forming or expressing an intention to apply or not. The incapacity must be continuous. Mere personality and memory problems do not constitute incapacity, particularly where the claimant had admitted that she was a procrastinator at the time she finally made the application.

C-70042 v. MHRD (October 22, 2002) (RT)

The capacity threshold should be set at a low level. It is not a matter of general, as opposed to specific, intent. Ignorance of the law and lack of knowledge about available benefits or about the right to apply is not lack of capacity to form intention. Ability to perform the actions of day-to-day life is considered evidence of capacity to form and express an intention. The applicant's memory loss related to his long-term alcohol addiction did not mean that he lacked the capacity to form and express an intention to apply for Guaranteed Income Supplement benefits although he was eligible, where he still had the ability to perform the actions of day-to-day life.

M-86396 v. Minister of Social Development Canada (December 14, 2005)

Evidence that the alcoholic claimant had been very depressed, was not eating and was very confused about everything, was sufficient to establish incapacity to make an application for benefits at the time.

C-78795 v. MSD (2004) (RT)

Where a committee for a claimant's estate has been appointed, the incapacity of the claimant herself is no longer relevant.

M-26032 v. MHRD (December 9, 1997) (RT)

Section 28.1 cannot be considered where the applicant, who alleged that psychiatric difficulties prevented his timely application, did not have any medical evidence to support his claim.

V-35107 v. MHRD (July 30, 1998) (RT)

A person cannot be considered incapable of forming or expressing the intention to apply for the sole reason that they did not know the law. In spite of mental health problems, including poor judgment, limited intelligence, and weak education, the evidence must indicate a mental or physical problem so severe as to cause incapacity in the sense of the legislation.

D-60343 v. MHRD (October 18, 2000) (RT)

A diagnosis of narcolepsy did not constitute incapacity under the *OAS Act*.

Death[12]

29. *Application for pension by estate, etc.* — **(1) Despite anything in this Act, an application for a pension that would have been payable to a deceased person who, before their death, would have been entitled, on approval of an application, to payment of that pension under this Act may be made within one year after the person's death by the estate or succession, by the liquidator, executor or administrator of the estate or succession or heir of that person or by any person that may be prescribed by regulation.[13] (S.C. 2007, c. 11, s. 23.)**

(2) *Pension payable to estate or other persons* — **If an application is made under subsection (1), the pension that would have been payable to a deceased person referred to in that subsection shall be paid to the estate or succession or to any person that may be prescribed by regulation. (S.C. 2007, c. 11, s. 23.)**

(3) *Application deemed to have been received on date of death* — **Any application made under subsection (1) is deemed to have been received on the date of the death of the person who, before their death, would have been entitled to payment of the pension. (S.C. 2007, c. 11, s. 23.)**

---

[12] Heading amended by 2000, c. 12, s. 201, effective July 31, 2000.

[13] Section 29 of the *Old Age Security Act*, as it read immediately before the day on which this Act receives royal assent, continues to apply in respect of any application made under that section before that day (S.C. 2007, c. 11, s. 38).

(4) (Repealed by S.C. 2007, c. 11, s. 23.)

(S.C. 2007, c. 11, s. 23.)

———————— Notes ————————

Case Law

Canada (MHRD) v. Dublin (Estate), 2004 FC 1184

Section 29 is a general provision designed to allow the estate or heir of an individual who was eligible for benefits with the opportunity to make an application for those benefits within a limited period of time after his or her death. Although its purpose is ameliorative, the provision is clear that such benefits may only be paid if the application is made within one year of death. The terms "may" or "peuvent" in s. 29 clearly refer only to whether or not benefits will be paid. It authorizes when an application may be made, however it does not imply that the Minister has the discretion to consider applications made more than one year after a potential recipient's death.

Obiter: In unique circumstances where the delay was entirely outside the control of the claimant, the court may strongly recommend that the Minister make an *ex gratia* payment.

[Editor's note: In *Canada (Minister of Human Resources Development) v. Dublin Estate*, 2006 FC 152, the Federal Court stated that the Review Tribunal did not have jurisdiction to order the Minister to make an *ex gratia* payment of OAS benefits.]

R-73571 v. MHRD (June 13, 2003) (RT)

The Minister may waive strict compliance with the statutory time limits on applications for OAS benefits, when the Ministry's conduct amounts to administrative error. A letter written by the Ministry 14 months after the death of the deceased informing the deceased's estate that it had 60 days to reply constituted a waiver of the one requirement for applying.

Canada (Minister of Human Resources Development) v. Reisinger, 2004 FC 893

The Minister has no obligation to warn a claimant represented by counsel of a deadline clearly outlined in the *OAS Act.* Section 29 pertains to all benefits, and not simply to the OAS pension.

———————————————

30. *Retroactive application by survivor* — **(1) Despite paragraph 19(6)(*b*), if a person dies and the person's survivor would have been entitled to an allowance under section 19 had the survivor and the deceased person made a joint application for it before the death of the deceased person, the survivor may make application for an allowance under section 19 within one year after the death of the deceased person. (S.C. 1985, c. 34 (1st Supp.), s. 8(1); 2000, c. 12, s. 202; 2007, c. 11, s. 24(1).)**

(2) *Treated as joint application* — **An application referred to in subsection (1) shall be considered and dealt with as though it had been a joint application of the survivor and the deceased person and had been received on the date of the death of the deceased person. (S.C. 2000, c. 12, s. 202.)**

(3) *Limitation* — **(Repealed by S.C. 2007, c. 11, s. 24(2).) (R.S.C. 1985, c. 34 (1st Supp.), s. 8(2); 2000, c. 12, s. 209; 2007, c. 11, s. 24(2).)**

(R.S.C. 1985, c. 34 (1st Supp.), s. 8; 2000, c. 12, ss. 202 and 209; 2007, c. 11, s. 24.)

31. *Presumption as to death of applicant or beneficiary* — **(1) Where an applicant or beneficiary has disappeared under circumstances that, in the opinion of the Minister, raise beyond a reasonable doubt a presumption that the applicant or beneficiary is dead, the Minister may issue a certificate declaring that the applicant or beneficiary is presumed to be dead and stating the date on which the death is presumed to have occurred, and thereupon the applicant or beneficiary shall be deemed for all purposes of this Act to have died on the date so stated in the certificate.**

Old Age Security Act

539

(2) *Change of presumed date of death* — **If, after issuing a certificate under subsection (1), the Minister is satisfied from new information or evidence that the date of death is different from that stated in the certificate, the Minister may revoke the certificate and issue a new certificate stating a different date, in which case the applicant or beneficiary shall be deemed for all purposes of this Act to have died on the date so stated in the new certificate.**

(3) *Where person presumed dead reappears* — **If, after issuing a certificate under this section, the Minister is satisfied from new information or evidence that the applicant or beneficiary named in the certificate is alive, the Minister shall forthwith revoke the certificate and cause that person's benefits to be re-instated effective the month following the date of the person's presumed death stated in the certificate, subject to the provisions of this Act relating to the person's eligibility to receive those benefits.**

(4) *Death certificates issued by other authorities* — **For the purposes of this section, the Minister is not bound by the issuance or revocation of a death certificate by any other authority.**

——————— Notes ———————

Case Law

R-33563 v. MHRD (December 18, 1997) (RT)

The Minister was entitled to determine that OAS retirement pension recipient had died after his abandoned car was found, and an extensive ground and air search was unsuccessful in locating the recipient. The presumed date of death was when the RCMP concluded the survivor rate was zero, based on the searches having demonstrated that the chances of him surviving was remote. A subsequent court order obtained by the recipient's spouse indicating the date of death to be nearly two years later did not constitute new evidence where there was nothing by way of factual evidence or reasonable conjecture to show that the recipient did in fact survive beyond the presumed date of death.

Erroneous Advice or Administrative Error[14]

32. *Where person denied benefit due to departmental error, etc.* — **Where the Minister is satisfied that, as a result of erroneous advice or administrative error in the administration of this Act, any person has been denied a benefit, or a portion of a benefit, to which that person would have been entitled under this Act, the Minister shall take such remedial action as the Minister considers appropriate to place the person in the position that the person would be in under this Act had the erroneous advice not been given or the administrative error not been made. (S.C. 1995, c. 33, s. 18.)**

(S.C. 1995, c. 33, s. 18; 2000, c. 12, s. 203.)

——————— Notes ———————

Case Law

§1. Generally

Canada (Minister of Human Resources Development) v. Tucker, 2003 FCA 278. See also *Canada (MHRD) v. Mitchell,* 2004 FC 437; *Stevens Estate v. Canada (Attorney General),* 2012 FC 622.

The Review Tribunal did not have the power to entertain an appeal of the Minister's decision made under s. 32 to remit all or any portion of an overpayment to the recipient. Decisions relating to the forgiveness of an overpayment or the repayment of an underpayment made as a

---

[14] Heading amended by 2000, c. 12, s. 203, effective July 31, 2000.

result of erroneous advice are not decisions "respecting the amount of any benefit that may be paid to that person" within the meaning of s. 27.1(1). The only remedy available to a recipient under the circumstances was to apply to the Federal Court for judicial review of the Minister's decision.

Grosvenor v. Canada (Attorney General), 2011 FC 799

A finding as to whether erroneous advice has been provided is a purely factual determination. As a consequence, the Minister's delegate's decision is to be reviewed on the standard of reasonableness. In reviewing a decision against the reasonableness standard, the court must consider the justification, transparency, and intelligibility of the decision-making process, and whether the decision falls within a range of possible acceptable outcomes which are defensible in light of the facts and the law. Where an issue of procedural fairness arises, the task for the court is to determine whether the process followed by the decision-maker satisfied the level of fairness required in all of the circumstances. The onus is on the claimant to satisfy the Minister's delegate that he had received erroneous information regarding his entitlement to OAS benefits, and that he had relied upon this information to his detriment.

Canada (Attorney General) v. Vinet-Proulx, 2007 FC 99

A review tribunal does not have jurisdiction to set aside a decision of the Minister made under s. 32. In such a case, it is the Federal Court that has jurisdiction. Under s. 32, the Minister has authority to pay a retroactive pension in a case in which it is more likely that a previous application for benefits had been sent in by an applicant and received by the Minister on a certain date but subsequently lost because of an administrative error.

Canada (MHRD) v. Myrheim, 2004 FC 884

The Review Tribunal does not have power to entertain an appeal from the Minister's decision that having already applied for and then cancelled receipt of OAS benefits, the applicant was not entitled to reapply for OAS benefits. The procedure would be for the Minister to make a decision under s. 32 of the *Old Age Security Act,* and for the applicant to seek judicial review of that decision in the Federal Court.

Canada (Minister of Human Resources Development) v. Reisinger, 2004 FC 893

While the Minister may exercise discretion under s. 32 to deem an application to have been received within the deadline, that discretion should not be confused with authority to alter a deadline already imposed by statute. The Review Tribunal does not have the power to review a decision of the Minister not to extend the deadline. The Federal Court can review the decision, but only where the applicant applies for judicial review of that decision within 30 days of the decision or obtains an extension of time. The standard of review would be whether the Minister's discretionary decision was patently unreasonable, i.e., clearly wrong. The Minister has a wide discretion. However, the Minister's refusal to extend the statutory deadline despite letters sent by Department staff to the applicant giving respond by dates of after the statutory period expired could constitute a patently unreasonable decision.

Tomar v. Canada (Attorney General), 2008 FC 292

The statement on the Information Sheet given to applicants to the effect that the Information Sheet contained general information concerning OAS benefits reflecting the legislation, but that the *OAS Act* governed if there were any differences between the contents of the Information Sheet and the Act was effective to put applicants on notice regarding the residency requirements for the award of a full OAS pension, and clearly directed applicants to the Act if there were any doubts about the conditions to be met for the award of OAS benefits. In any case, the Information Sheet had given no information that was inconsistent with the statutory requirements.

L-81415 v. MSD (2004) (RT)

The Review Tribunal did not have jurisdiction to waive a statutory time limit, despite an ambiguous letter sent by the Minister instructing the claimant to "return" the completed form by the deadline.

K-67133 v. MHRD (July 15, 2002) (RT)

Ministry officials have a positive duty to inform CPP applicants of their eligibility for the OAS. Failure to do so constituted erroneous advice for the purposes of s. 32 and the Review Tribunal can therefore order retroactive payment of benefits beyond the 11-month statutory limit.

541

Old Age Security Act

P-41238 v. MHRD (May 7, 1999) (RT)

The Review Tribunal had authority to hear and dispose of claims concerning erroneous advice and administrative error in connection with the application of the Act. The Tribunal is not bound by the Department's internal policies, including policies on such matters as the standard of proof in determinations regarding erroneous advice and administrative error. The Review Tribunal had authority to review a Ministerial decision.

N-28458 v. MHRD (December 10, 1997) (RT)

In order to make a claim based on erroneous advice, the applicant must supply sufficient information to allow the Minister to conduct an investigation.

P-41288 v. MHRD (May 7, 1998) (RT)

The decision of the Federal Court of Appeal in *Pincombe* did not apply to bar appeals of the Minister's response to a claim alleging erroneous advice or administrative error under the *OAS Act*. Section 28 does not enumerate any particular sections under which appeals may be brought. Therefore, nothing is precluded from a right of appeal. The Tribunal is not bound by Ministerial internal policies, particularly regarding the burden of proof required for a determination of administrative error and erroneous advice. (Note: The Review Tribunal considers this to be the controlling case on this point, and cases issued subsequently (see below) have followed it. The issue has not yet been tested at the Federal Court level.)

O-42754 v. MHRD (June 4, 1999) (RT)

"Erroneous advice" can include the failure to give advice.

N-32007 v. MHRD (December 11, 1997) (RT)

With respect to erroneous advice, the law is clear that the Tribunal lacks the discretionary power the Act gives to the Minister. The Tribunal is therefore without jurisdiction to hear the appeal of the Minister's finding of no record to support the applicant's appeal.

D-35733 for the Estate of the Late Mrs. B. v. MHRD (September 30, 1999) (RT)

This provision cannot be used in instances where, at the most, the applicant was mistaken. The onus is on the applicant to provide evidence to satisfy the requirement that a government official provided wrong information.

Mc-30363 v. MHRD (December 10, 1997) (RT); *Mc-30789 v. MHRD* (December 18, 1997) (RT)

The erroneous advice must be provided by parties charged with the administration of the Act and not that of other parties such as the applicant's family physician.

F-41008 v. MHRD (June 16, 1999) (RT)

Appeal rights are not limited to certain sections in the Act. The Tribunal may review a Minister's decision whether to take remedial action for erroneous advice or administrative error under s. 32.

H-49921 v. MHRD (April 6, 2000) (RT)

Section 32 gives jurisdiction to the Minister to put the applicant in the position that they would have been in, had the erroneous advice not been given. While the Review Tribunal has jurisdiction to review the Minister's decision, it does not follow that the Tribunal also has the jurisdiction to rectify a case of erroneous advice. The Tribunal would be acting outside the scope of its powers if it were to assume the authority given to the Minister under s. 32.

M-34716 v. MHRD (March 9, 1999) (RT)

Where an administrative error is made by the Minister, the Review Tribunal has no authority to alter the Minister's decision. The Federal Court of Appeal's decision in *Pincombe v. Canada*, while under the CPP, was equally applicable to s. 32 of the OAS Act.

§2. Erroneous Advice or Administrative Error not Shown

- Claimant reported change of marital status to CRA, but not to Minister as required by s. 15(9); failure of Minister to make inquiries not an administrative error: *Barry v. Canada (Attorney General)*, 2010 FC 1307

- Section 32 does not impose an obligation on the Minister to ensure that everyone under the Act who is entitled to a benefit in fact knows about or applies for that benefit: *G-55761 v. MHRD* (October 18, 2000) (RT)

- Applicant unaware of entitlement to the widowed spouse's benefits, and alleged that she had not been told of the benefits at the time when she applied for early retirement under CPP: *S-28465 v. MHRD* (July 31, 1998) (RT)

- Applicant claiming to be widow, when in fact she was in a common-law relationship; applicant providing no evidence of administrative error in advice given to her: *D-35733 for the Estate of the Late Mrs. B. v. MHRD* (September 30, 1999) (RT)

- Applicant informed that application being returned to her because of incomplete information, but never receiving application; no record that application was, in fact, received by Minister: *H-41512 v. MHRD* (May 21, 1999) (RT)

- Applicant told by Ministry in 1995 that he could wait up to five years before applying for OAS pension and receive them retroactively; amendments later reducing period to 11 months; no onerous positive duty on Minister to inform Canadians of such changes in the law; advice being accurate at time: *G-46893 v. MHRD* (March 9, 2000) (RT)

- Client service officer allegedly failing to inform applicant of her right to Widowed Spouse Allowance when she went to office in 1989; applicant not formally applying until 1994; client not entitled to retroactive payments beyond 11 month maximum: *M-34716 v. MHRD* (March 9, 1999) (RT)

- Family doctor erroneously telling Canada Manpower and Immigration that applicant's family was previously examined for immigration purposes, thereby creating administrative delay in issuance of visa to applicant: *Mc-30363 v. MHRD* (December 10, 1997) (RT); *Mc-30789 v. MHRD* (December 18, 1997) (RT)

- Minister giving conflicting information booklets to the appellant with respect to period of retroactivity: *N-50900 v. MHRD* (February 1, 2000) (RT)

- No finding as to whether applicant was fully informed that the GIS benefits were available at the time she started to receive her OAS pension; Tribunal lacking jurisdiction to increase the period of retroactivity beyond 11 months in any event: *P-40873 v. MHRD* (January 19, 1999) (RT)

§3. Erroneous Advice or Administrative Error Shown

- Applicant applying in person for retirement pension five weeks after turning 65; applicant told by Ministry officials that he had to file last two income tax returns before qualifying for CPP, but not told of right to apply for OAS pension or GIS benefits: *K-67133 v. MHRD* (July 15, 2002) (RT)

- Corroborating evidence of applicant and counsel indicating that application originally made in 1992, although not date stamped by Ministry official; application had been refused at time pending further documentation: *F-41008 v. MHRD* (June 16, 1999) (RT)

- Ministry client services representative filing to inform 65-year-old CPP applicant of her OAS entitlements: *O-42754 v. MHRD* (June 4, 1999) (RT)

Availability of Information

33. *Definitions* — **(1) The following definitions apply in this section and sections 33.1 and 39.**

"administration" **includes the development, operation, evaluation and enforcement of policies and programs.**

"federal institution" **means a department or any other body referred to in Schedule I, I.1, II or III to the *Financial Administration Act.***

"public officer" **means an officer or employee of a federal institution, or a prescribed individual or a member of a prescribed class of individuals.**

(S.C. 2012, c. 19, s. 299.)

(2) *Interpretation* **— The definition of a word or expression in subsection (1) does not affect its interpretation in any other provision of this Act. (S.C. 2012, c. 19, s. 299.)**

(S.C. 1998, c. 19, s. 288; 1997, c. 40, s. 102; 2003, c. 22, s. 178; 2005, c. 35, s. 55; 2012, c. 19, s. 299.)

33.01. *Protection of information* **— (Repealed by S.C. 2012, c. 19, s. 299.)**

(S.C. 1997, c. 40, s. 102; 2005, c. 35, s. 56; 2007, c. 11, s. 25; 2012, c. 19, s. 299.)

───────────── **Notes** ─────────────

Related Regulations

● Section 28.1 — Information made available

Case Law

Singer v. Canada (Attorney General), 2011 FCA 3

Confidentiality orders extending to documentation tendered in appeals are the exception, and if required, should be made so as to minimize the impact of the order on the open court principle. A confidentiality order should only be granted when such an order is necessary to prevent a serious risk to an important interest because reasonably alternative measures will not prevent the risk, and the salutary effects of the confidentiality order outweigh its deleterious effects, including the effects on the right to free expression, which includes the public interest in open and accessible court proceedings. In appeal or judicial review proceedings under the OAS Act, it is appropriate to order that the claimant's SIN number be redacted from all affidavit evidence and exhibits. An order to seal the claimant's affidavit evidence and related exhibits would overreach the purpose of protecting the claimant's SIN number, particularly in light of the alternative measures easily available to achieve the same result.

─────────────────────

33.02. *Availability of information within certain departments* **— (Repealed by S.C. 2012, c. 19, s. 299.)**

(S.C. 1997, c. 40, s. 102; 2005, c. 35, s. 57; 2012, c. 19, s. 299.)

33.03. *Availability of information within federal institutions* **— (Repealed by S.C. 2012, c. 19, s. 299.)**

(S.C. 1997, c. 40, s. 102; 2005, c. 35, s. 58; 2005, c. 38, s. 138; 2005, c. 49, s. 7; 2012, c. 19, s. 299.)

33.04. *Exception re war crimes* **— (Repealed by S.C. 2012, c. 19, s. 299.)**

(S.C. 1997, c. 40, s. 102; 2012, c. 19, s. 299.)

33.05. *Availability of information to provincial authorities* **— (Repealed by S.C. 2012, c. 19, s. 299.)**

(S.C. 1997, c. 40, s. 102; 2012, c. 19, s. 299.)

33.06. *Availability of information to certain persons or bodies* **— (Repealed by S.C. 2012, c. 19, s. 299.)**

(S.C. 1997, c. 40, s. 102; 2005, c. 35, s. 60; 2012, c. 19, s. 299.)

33.07. *Where Minister may permit information to be made available* — **(Repealed by S.C. 2012, c. 19, s. 299.)**

(S.C. 1997, c. 40, s. 102; 2012, c. 19, s. 299.)

33.08. *Evidence and production of documents* — **(Repealed by S.C. 2012, c. 19, s. 299.)**

(S.C. 1997, c. 40, s. 102; 2005, c. 35, s. 61; 2012, c. 19, s. 299.)

33.09. *Offence* — **(Repealed by S.C. 2012, c. 19, s. 299.)**

(S.C. 1997, c. 40, s. 102; 2005, c. 35, s. 61; 2012, c. 19, s. 299.)

33.1. *Information obtained under other Acts* — **Despite any other Act or law,**

(*a*) **the Minister of National Revenue or any person that he or she designates may make available to the Minister, or to a public officer of the Department of Employment and Social Development that is designated by the Minister, a report providing information that is available to the Minister of National Revenue, if the information is necessary for the administration of this Act; (2013, c. 40, s. 237(1)(*l*).)**

(*b*) **the Minister of Citizenship and Immigration and officers and employees of the Department of Citizenship and Immigration may make available to the Minister, or to a public officer of the Department of Employment and Social Development, any information that was obtained in the administration of the** *Citizenship Act* **or the** *Immigration and Refugee Protection Act,* **if the information is necessary for the administration of this Act; and (2013, c. 40, s. 237(1)(*l*).)**

(*c*) **the Commissioner of Corrections or staff members of the Correctional Service of Canada may make available to the Minister or a public officer of the Department of Employment and Social Development any personal information that was obtained in the administration of the** *Corrections and Conditional Release Act,* **if the information is necessary for the administration of this Act. (2013, c. 40, s. 237(1)(*l*).)**

(S.C. 1997, c. 40, s. 102; 2012, c. 19, s. 299; 2013, c. 40, s. 237.)

33.11. *Information obtained under other Acts and relative to Social Insurance Numbers* — **(Repealed by S.C. 2012, c. 19, s. 299.)**

(S.C. 1997, c. 40, s. 102; 2000, c. 12, s. 207(1); 2001, c. 27, s. 267; 2005, c. 35, s. 66 2010, c. 22, s. 11; 2012, c. 19, s. 465; 2012, c. 19, s. 299.)

33.12. *Research or statistical purposes* — **(Repealed by S.C. 2012, c. 19, s. 299.)**

(S.C. 2005, c. 35, s. 62; 2012, c. 19, s. 299.)

33.13. *Use of information for research purposes* — **(Repealed by S.C. 2012, c. 19, s. 299.)**

(S.C. 2005, c. 35, s. 62; 2012, c. 19, s. 299.)

Regulations

34. *Regulations* — **The Governor in Council may make regulations for carrying the purposes and provisions of this Act into effect and, without restricting the generality of the foregoing, may make regulations**

(*a*) **prescribing the manner of making any application, statement or notification required or permitted by this Act, the information and evidence to be made available or allowed to be made available in connection therewith and the procedure to be followed in dealing with and approving applications; (S.C. 1995, c. 33, s. 21(1).)**

(b) prescribing the manner in which the average of the Consumer Price Index for any period of months shall be determined and the manner in which any such average that is determined to be a fraction of a whole number shall be expressed;

(c) defining the expression "pension income" for the purposes of section 14;

(d) for determining, for the purposes of any provision of section 14, the month in which or the month immediately before the month in which an applicant or an applicant's spouse or common-law partner ceased to hold an office or employment, ceased to carry on a business or suffered a loss of income due to termination or reduction of private pension income; (R.S.C. 1985, c. 1 (4th Supp.), s. 28; 2000, c. 12, s. 207(1).)

(e) prescribing the circumstances that shall be deemed to constitute, or prescribing what shall be or shall be deemed to be, an application by or on behalf of persons who are qualified for a pension under this Act and who, on or before December 31, 1951, applied for or were granted a pension as defined in the *Old Age Pensions Act*, chapter 156 of the Revised Statutes of Canada, 1927, and prescribing the time at which such applications shall be deemed to have been made or approved;

(f) prescribing the information and evidence to be made available or allowed to be made available by beneficiaries and the circumstances and form in which the information or evidence shall be submitted; (S.C. 1995, c. 33, s. 21(2).)

(g) providing for the assignment of Social Insurance Numbers by the Minister to applicants and beneficiaries, and to the spouses or common-law partners of applicants and beneficiaries, to whom such numbers have not earlier been assigned; (S.C. 2000, c. 12, s. 204(1).)

(h) defining residence and presence in Canada and defining intervals of absence from Canada that shall be deemed not to have interrupted residence or presence in Canada;

(i) providing, in the case of an allowance the amount of which is less than such amount not exceeding two dollars as may be prescribed in the regulations, for the payment of the allowance to the beneficiary at such intervals less frequently than monthly as may be prescribed in the regulations, or for the payment monthly of the prescribed amount to the beneficiary; (R.S.C. 1985, c. 34 (1st Supp.), s. 9(1); 2000, c. 12, s. 209.)

(j) providing for the suspension of payment of a benefit during an investigation into the eligibility of the beneficiary and the reinstatement or resumption of the payment thereof;

(k) prescribing the circumstances in which the spouse or common-law partner of a pensioner shall be deemed to be separated from the pensioner for the purposes of paragraph 19(1)(a) and subsection 19(5); (R.S.C. 1985, c. 34 (1st Supp.), s. 9(2); 2000, c. 12, s. 207(1).)

(l) prescribing the circumstances in which a pensioner shall be deemed to be separated from the pensioner's spouse for the purposes of subsections 15(4.1) and (6.1); (S.C. 2000, c. 12, s. 204(2).)

(m) prescribing the manner in which any amount required by this Act to be deducted and retained out of any benefit payment shall be so deducted and retained;

(m.1) setting out the circumstances in which the Minister may allow a longer period to make a request under subsection 27.1(1) or (1.1); (S.C. 2012, c. 19, s. 237(1).)

(n) prescribing the procedure to be followed on any reference under subsection 28(2); (S.C. 1995, c. 33, s. 21(3).)

(*o*) providing for the making of any application or statement, or the doing of any other act or thing required or permitted by this Act, by any person or agency, and for the payment of a benefit to any person or agency, on behalf of any other person or beneficiary if it is established in any manner and by any evidence that may be prescribed by the regulations that the other person or beneficiary is, by reason of infirmity, illness, insanity or other cause, incapable of managing their own affairs, and prescribing the manner in which any benefit authorized to be paid to the person or agency shall be administered and expended for the benefit of the other person or beneficiary and accounted for; (S.C. 1996, c. 18, s. 56; 1998, c. 21, s. 117; 2007, c. 11, s. 26(1).)

(*p*) providing events for the purposes of subsections 11(8), and 19(6.2) and 21(9.1); and (S.C. 1998, c. 21, s. 117.)

(*q*) prescribing anything that must or may be prescribed by regulations made under this Act; and (S.C. 1998, c. 21, s. 117.)

(*r*) (Repealed by S.C. 2012, c. 19, s. 237(2), in force June 29, 2012.)

(*s*) (Repealed by S.C. 2012, c. 19, s. 237(2), in force June 29, 2012.)

(R.S.C. 1985, c. 34 (1st Supp.), s. 9; R.S.C. 1985, c. 1 (4th Supp.), s. 28; 1995, c. 33, s. 21; 1996, c. 18, s. 56; 1998, c. 21, s. 117; 2000, c. 12, ss. 204, 207 and 209; 2007, c. 11, s. 26; 2012, c. 19, 237.)

34.1. *Personal Information Protection and Electronic Documents Act* — (**Repealed** by S.C. 2012, c. 19, s. 238, in force June 29, 2012.)

(2007, c. 11, s. 27; 2012, c. 19, s. 238.)

Form of Documents

35. *Form of applications, statements and notifications* — **Every application, statement or notification required or permitted by this Act shall be made or given in such form as the Minister may require.**

Benefits

35.1. *Making claim or providing information in person* — **The Minister may require an applicant or other person or a group or class of persons to be at a suitable place at a suitable time in order to make an application for benefits in person or to provide additional information about an application.**

(S.C. 1997, c. 40, s. 103.)

36. *Benefit not assignable* — **(1) A benefit shall not be assigned, charged, attached, anticipated or given as security, and any transaction purporting to assign, charge, attach, anticipate or give as security a benefit is void.**

(1.1) *Benefit not subject to seizure or execution* — **A benefit is exempt from seizure and execution, either at law or in equity.** (S.C. 1995, c. 33, s. 22.)

(2) *Exception* — **Despite subsections (1) and (1.1), if a provincial authority or a municipal authority in a province pays a person any advance or assistance or welfare payment for a month or a portion of a month that would not be paid if a benefit under this Act had been paid for that period and subsequently a benefit becomes payable or payment of a benefit may be made under this Act to that person for that period, the Minister may, in accordance with any terms and conditions that may be prescribed, deduct from the benefit and pay to the provincial authority or municipal authority, as the case may be, an amount not more than the amount of the advance or assistance or welfare payment paid.** (S.C. 1997, c. 40, s. 104.)

(3) *Reimbursement of Department of Veterans Affairs* — **Notwithstanding subsections (1) and (1.1), where any benefit is received for a month or any portion of a month after this subsection comes into force under any Act of Parliament that is administered**

by the Minister of Veterans Affairs, that would not have been received if a benefit under this Act had been paid for that period and subsequently a benefit becomes payable or payment of a benefit may be made under this Act to that person for that period, the Minister may deduct from the benefit and pay to the Department of Veterans Affairs an amount not exceeding the amount of the benefit if that person had, on or before receiving the benefit from the Department of Veterans Affairs, consented in writing to the deduction and payment by the Minister. (S.C. 1995, c. 33, s. 22.)

(S.C. 1995, c. 33, s. 22; 1997, c. 40, s. 104.)

———————— Notes ————————

Related Regulations

- Section 28.1 — Deductions from benefits

Case Law

Bouchard v. Canada (Attorney General), 2009 FCA 321. See also *Maheux v. Canada,* 2011 FC 901.

The Crown is not bound by the seizure exemption provisions set out in OAS Act s. 36, and can claim such monies by virtue of s. 224.1 of the *Income Tax Act.* Under s. 17 of the *Interpretation Act,* no enactment is binding on the Crown or affects the Crown or its rights or prerogatives in any manner, unless otherwise indicated. The provisions of the CPP and OAS Act appear to be aimed at ensuring that benefits payable under them be for the beneficiary's own use by preventing that person from alienating or encumbering them. Although OAS Act s. 36 applies to third parties, there is no indication of any intention to bind the Crown.

———————————————————

37. *Return of benefit where recipient not entitled* — **(1) A person who has received or obtained by cheque or otherwise a benefit payment to which the person is not entitled, or a benefit payment in excess of the amount of the benefit payment to which the person is entitled, shall forthwith return the cheque or the amount of the benefit payment, or the excess amount, as the case may be. (S.C. 1991, c. 44, s. 33(1).)**

(2) *Recovery of amount of payment* — **If a person has received or obtained a benefit payment to which the person is not entitled, or a benefit payment in excess of the amount of the benefit payment to which the person is entitled, the amount of the benefit payment or the excess amount, as the case may be, constitutes a debt due to Her Majesty and is recoverable at any time in the Federal Court or any other court of competent jurisdiction or in any other manner provided by this Act. (S.C. 1997, c. 40, s. 105; 2007, c. 11, s. 28(1).)**

(2.01) *Recovery of amount of interest* — **Interest payable under this Act constitutes a debt due to Her Majesty and is recoverable at any time in the Federal Court or any other court of competent jurisdiction or in any other manner provided by this Act. (S.C. 2007, c. 11, s. 28(1).)**

(2.02) *Recovery of amount of penalty* — **The amount of a penalty imposed on a person under section 44.1 constitutes a debt due to Her Majesty and is recoverable at any time in the Federal Court or any other court of competent jurisdiction or in any other manner provided by this Act. (S.C. 2007, c. 11, s. 28(2).)**

(2.1) *Set-off* — **If any amount is or becomes payable to the person or to the person's estate or succession under this Act or any other Act or program administered by the Minister, the amount of the debt may be deducted and retained out of the amount payable in the prescribed manner. (S.C. 1997, c. 40, s. 105.)**

(2.2) *Certificates* — **All or part of the debt that has not been recovered may be certified by the Minister**

(*a*) without delay, if in the Minister's opinion the person liable to pay the amount is attempting to avoid payment; and

(*b*) in any other case, on the expiration of 30 days after the default.

(S.C. 1997, c. 40, s. 105.)

(2.3) *Judgment* — On production to the Federal Court, the certificate shall be registered in the Court. When it is registered, it has the same force and effect, and all proceedings may be taken, as if the certificate were a judgment obtained in the Court for a debt of the amount specified in the certificate. (S.C. 1997, c. 40, s. 105.)

(2.4) *Judgment* — A certificate registered under subsection (2.3) may also be registered in the superior court of a province as if it were a document evidencing a judgment of that court. (S.C. 1997, c. 40, s. 105.)

(2.5) *Costs* — All reasonable costs and charges for the registration of the certificate are recoverable in the same way as if they had been certified and the certificate registered under this section. (S.C. 1997, c. 40, s. 105.)

(2.6) *Charge on land* — A document issued by the Federal Court or by a superior court of a province evidencing a certificate in respect of a debtor registered under subsection (2.3) or (2.4) may be recorded for the purpose of creating security, or a charge, lien or legal hypothec, on land in a province, or on an interest in land in a province, held or owned by the debtor, in the same manner as a document evidencing a judgment of the superior court of the province against a person for a debt owing by the person may be recorded in accordance with the law of the province to create security, or a charge, lien or legal hypothec, on land, or an interest in land, held or owned by the person. (S.C. 2001, c. 4, s. 111.)

(2.7) *Garnishment* — If the Minister knows or suspects that a person is or is about to become indebted or liable to make a payment to a person liable to make a payment to Her Majesty under this Act, the Minister may, by a notice served personally or by confirmed delivery service, require the first person to pay the money otherwise payable to the second person in whole or in part to the Receiver General on account of the second person's liability. (S.C. 1997, c. 40, s. 105; 2007, c. 11, s. 28(4).)

(2.8) *Debt due to the Crown* — An amount not paid as required by a notice under subsection (2.7) is a debt due to Her Majesty. (S.C. 1997, c. 40, s. 105.)

(2.9) *Proof of personal service* — If provision is made by this Act or the regulations for personal service of a request for information or a notice or demand, an affidavit of the person effecting service stating that

(*a*) the person has charge of the appropriate records and has knowledge of the facts in the particular case,

(*b*) such a request, notice or demand was served personally on a named day on the person to whom it was directed, and

(*c*) the person identifies as an exhibit attached to the affidavit a true copy of the request, notice or demand,

is evidence of the personal service and of the request, notice or demand.

(S.C. 1997, c. 40, s. 105.)

(3) *Amount deducted or retained* — [Repealed by 1997, c. 40, s. 105.]

(4) *Remission of amount owing* — Notwithstanding subsections (1), (2) and (3), where a person has received or obtained a benefit payment to which that person is not entitled or a benefit payment in excess of the amount of the benefit payment to which that person is entitled and the Minister is satisfied that

(a) the amount or excess of the benefit payment cannot be collected within the reasonably foreseeable future,

(b) the administrative costs of collecting the amount or excess of the benefit payment are likely to equal or exceed the amount to be collected,

(c) repayment of the amount or excess of the benefit payment would cause undue hardship to the debtor, or

(d) the amount or excess of the benefit payment is the result of erroneous advice or administrative error in the administration of this Act,

the Minister may, unless that person has been convicted of an offence under any provision of this Act or of the *Criminal Code* in connection with the obtaining of the benefit payment, remit all or any portion of the amount or excess of the benefit payment. (S.C. 1995, c. 33, s. 23(2).)

(5) *Exclusion of Financial Administration Act* — Section 155.1 of the *Financial Administration Act* does not apply in relation to amounts owing to Her Majesty under this Act. (S.C. 2007, c. 11, s. 28(5).)

(S.C. 1991, c. 44, s. 33; 1995, c. 33, s. 23(2); 1997, c. 40, s. 105; 2001, c. 4, s. 111; 2007, c. 11, s. 28.)

——————— Notes ———————

Related Regulations

● Section 27 — Recovery of overpayments

Case Law

Canada (Minister of Human Resources Development) v. Tucker, 2003 FCA 278

The Review Tribunal did not have power to entertain an appeal of the Minister's decision made under s. 37(4)(d) of the OAS Act to remit all or any portion of an overpayment to the recipient. The only remedy available to a recipient under the circumstances was to apply to the Federal Court for judicial review of the Minister's decision.

Whitton v. Canada (Attorney General), [2002] FCA 46

The Minister may not set off against OAS benefits payable to a person on the ground that the person is suspected of having fraudulently cashed benefit cheques issued to the person's deceased mother for 20 years. Such person was not the recipient of the amounts that he allegedly appropriated by fraud. The benefits that he was accused of cashing were not benefits that were paid to him.

Elguindy v. Canada, 2003 FCT 796

Where a monthly OAS payment was direct deposited in the recipient's bank account after her death, and this amount was withdrawn by the recipient's daughter to pay for the recipient's funeral expenses, the daughter was a person who "obtained", otherwise than by cheque, a benefit payment to which she was not entitled for the purposes of s. 37(1). The use to which the daughter claimed to have put the funds was irrelevant. It was open to the Ministry to then notify the daughter that such "debt" would be collected in full from any Government of Canada benefits which may become payable to her in the future.

M-79271 v. MSD (2004) (RT)

Where the applicant is already receiving OAS benefits, the burden of proving that the applicant is not eligible to receive such benefits is on the Ministry.

W-75880 v. MHRD (November 4, 2003) (RT)

The appellant was already in receipt of OAS and GIS benefits when he married. On his next three annual GIS applications, the appellant indicated his marital status as "married". The application form requires only persons who are applying for GIS benefits for the first time to furnish a copy of the marriage certificate if they are married. The appellant did not provide a copy of his marriage certificate. The appellant was paid GIS benefits for the three years at the single rate. It was held that the Minister's failure to take proper and timely notice of the appellant's change in marital status, as clearly stated on his GIS application form for three consecutive years, amounted to erroneous advice or administrative error. The appellant was entitled to a complete remission of the resulting overpayment.

T-34054 v. MHRD (August 15, 2000) (RT)

The Minister could not recover overpayments of Widowed Spouse's Allowance, because an official had advised the recipient that she did not have to disclose a survivorship pension as a source of income.

B-63980 v. MHRD (October 18, 2001) (RT)

A person who applies for GIS benefit jointly with his or her spouse is not to be penalized for the spouse's non-reporting of additional income where there is no evidence that the person was aware of the unreported income.

B-50411 v. MHRD; B-50412 v. MHRD (June 29, 2000) (RT)

The Review Tribunal does not have the power to intervene where the Minister uses its discretionary power to forgive part of an overpayment. The Tribunal could not order the Minister to return the amount collected to the recipient.

R-36780 v. MHRD; R-45514 v. MHRD (September 10, 1999) (RT)

Where the Minister's investigation revealed facts to presume that the pension recipient had never truly resided in Canada, or at least did not accumulate enough years of residence to be eligible for a pension, the conclusion that the recipient did not have the required residence or presence in Canada is maintained in absence of proof to the contrary.

D-35733 for the Estate of the Late Mrs. B. v. MHRD (September 30, 1999) (RT)

The repayment provision of section 37(2) does not apply to any overpayment made before July 13, 1995, therefore claims by the Minister for that period may be statute barred. A recipient whose benefit was calculated on the basis of her being a widow, although she was in fact living in a common-law union with another person, was held not to have "willfully misrepresented" her situation for the purposes of the provision, so as to obviate the limitation period.

R-41304 v. MHRD (April 7, 1999) (RT)

Where amounts are paid erroneously to a person, they are a debt due payable to the Crown which can only be waived by the Minister regardless of whether it was the person's error or the Minister's that resulted in the payments.

G-41508 v. MHRD (May 10, 1999) (RT)

The Minister is not obligated to forgive an overpayment of GIS when it was the fault of the applicant in declaring her income on the GIS renewal form.

Oaths and Affidavits

38. *Commissioners for oaths, etc.* — **(1) Any officer or employee of Her Majesty who is authorized by the Minister for the purpose may, in the course of their employment and subject to any other Act of Parliament or any Act of the legislature of a province, administer oaths and take and receive affidavits, declarations and solemn affirmations and every person so authorized has, with respect to any such oath, affidavit, declaration or affirmation, all the powers of a commissioner for taking affidavits. (S.C. 1995, c. 33, s. 24.)**

(2) *Acceptance of oaths, etc.* — **The Minister may accept, for the purposes of the administration of this Act or the regulations, any oath administered or affidavit, declaration or solemn affirmation given by any officer or employee of any department in, or other portion of, the federal public administration specified in Schedule I, IV or V to the *Financial Administration Act* or of any department of the government of a**

province who has all the powers of a commissioner for taking affidavits. (S.C. 1995, c. 33, s. 24; 2003, c. 22, 179.)

(S.C. 1995, c. 33, s. 24; 2003, c. 22, 179.)

Agreements

39. *Payment of provincial benefit* — **(1)** Where a province provides benefits similar to or as a supplement to benefits payable under this Act for a pensioner or a pensioner's spouse or common-law partner within that province, the Minister may, with the approval of the Governor in Council, enter into an agreement with the government of that province whereby the provincial benefit that is payable to a pensioner or a pensioner's spouse or common-law partner may be included with the amount of the benefit under this Act and paid on behalf of the government of that province in such manner as the agreement may provide. (S.C. 2000, c. 12, s. 205.)

(1.1) *Administration of provincial benefits* — The agreement may provide for the Minister to administer the provincial benefits on behalf of the government of that province in accordance with the terms and conditions set out in the agreement. (S.C. 2007, c. 11, s. 29.)

(2) *Province to reimburse expenses* — It shall be a term of the agreement that the government of the province that is a party to the agreement shall reimburse the Minister for the expenses incurred by the Minister under that agreement. (S.C. 2007, c. 11, s. 29.)

(S.C. 2000, c. 12, s. 205; 2007, c. 11, s. 29.)

40. *Reciprocal arrangements re administration, etc.* — **(1)** Where, under any law of a country other than Canada, provision is made for the payment of old age or other benefits including survivors' or disability benefits, the Minister may, on behalf of the Government of Canada, on such terms and conditions as may be approved by the Governor in Council, enter into an agreement with the government of that country for the making of reciprocal arrangements relating to the administration or operation of that law and of this Act, including, without restricting the generality of the foregoing, arrangements relating to

    (a) the exchange of such information obtained under that law or this Act as may be necessary to give effect to any such arrangements;

    (b) the administration of benefits payable under this Act to persons resident in that country, the extension of benefits under that law or this Act to persons employed in or resident in that country and the increase or decrease in the amount of the benefits payable under that law or this Act to persons employed in or resident in that country;

    (c) the administration of benefits payable under that law to persons resident in Canada, the extension of benefits under that law or this Act to persons employed in or resident in Canada and the increase or decrease in the amount of the benefits payable under that law or this Act to persons employed in or resident in Canada;

    (d) the totalization of periods of residence and periods of contribution in that country and periods of residence in Canada; and

    (e) the payment by that country and Canada respectively, where applicable as a result of totalization, of prorated benefits based on periods of residence and periods of contribution in that country and periods of residence in Canada.

(2) *Regulations for giving effect to agreements* — For the purpose of giving effect to any agreement entered into under subsection (1), the Governor in Council may make such regulations respecting the manner in which this Act shall apply to any case or class of cases affected by the agreement, and for adapting this Act thereto, as appear to the Governor in Council to be necessary for that purpose, and any regula-

tions so made may provide therein for the making of any financial adjustments required under the agreement and for the crediting or charging of the amount of any such adjustments to the Consolidated Revenue Fund.

———————— Notes ————————

Case Law

§1. United States

Gumboc v. Canada (Attorney General), 2014 FC 185

Read together, Article V of the Canada-U.S. Social Security Agreement and s. 21(5.3) of the OAS Regulations confirm that while while working in the U.S., an applicant cannot argue for the purposes of the OAS to be a Canadian resident, regardless of any ties maintained to Canada. With respect to periods during which a claimant worked in both the U.S. and Canada, Article VI(6) of the Canada/U.S. Agreement states that people living in the U.S. and performing services that are covered as employment or self-employment in both the U.S. and Canada shall not be treated as residents of Canada for OAS purposes. However, Article VIII of the Agreement allows applicants who have not accumulated the required years of residence to qualify for a partial pension by using their periods of coverage in the U.S. to establish a notional residence in Canada. When applying the OAS Act leads to denying any pension because the residency requirements of 10 years cannot be met, Article VIII comes to the rescue in that it allows for a pension to be paid. It entitles individuals to a pension. However, the Article is silent as to how the pension is to be calculated. The answer is given at Article IX(1). When Article VIII and IX are read together, it can be seen that Article VIII merely provides for the eligibility to a pension while Article IX indicates how that pension is to be calculated. Article VIII is informative as to who can get a pension; Article IX is informative as to how much that pension will be. The Article makes it clear that the pension is to be calculated exclusively on the basis of the periods of residence in Canada.

Canada (Minister of Human Resources Development) v. Stiel (F.C.), 2006 FC 466, [2006] 4 F.C.R. 489

Where the claimant had been a Canadian resident for 14 years, but a resident of the United States for the last 33 years, she was not entitled to a partial payment of OAS pension. Neither her U.S. residence nor her spousal benefit under U.S. law could be considered as "quarters of coverage" within the meaning of Article VIII (2)(*a*) of the Canada-U.S. Agreement. The Canada-U.S. Agreement contains many references to periods of residence in Canada, from which can be inferred that the intent of the Agreement is to treat a period of residence as different from a period of contribution. Therefore, only periods of contribution in the United States — and not periods of residence — are used in calculation of the entitlement to OAS pension in Canada. If Canada had wished to totalize periods of U.S. residence, it could have done so.

K-38682 v. MHRD (July 7, 1999) (RT)

In order for a U.S. resident to benefit from the social security agreement between Canada and the United States to qualify for a OAS pension, the applicant must have periods of residence in Canada on or after January 1952. Three years of Canadian residence between 1942 and 1945 after turning 18 were insufficient.

S-38795 v. MHRD (September 1, 1998) (RT)

Under the U.S. social security agreement, periods of residence in Canada can be combined with contributions to the social security scheme in the U.S. to reach the 20-year requirement for people living outside Canada to qualify for a pension.

§2. Greece

P-53311 v. MHRD (April 25, 2000) (RT)

The applicant's various brief trips to Greece, totaling 11 months over a 24-year period, while she resided in South Africa were not sufficient to trigger the social security agreement between Canada and Greece and give her credit towards the 20-year residence requirement under s. 9(4) of the Act. This was particularly so, as the applicant was receiving a grant for the aged in South Africa which would be cancelled if the applicant had left country for more than six months.

Old Age Security Act

553

§3. The Philippines

(Note: Canada has a Supplementary Agreement with the Philippines which covers that country's Government Social Security System. The agreement came into effect on July 1, 2001.)

V-38205 v. MHRD (August 20, 1999) (RT)

The applicant had not worked when she resided in the Philippines and did not participate in that country's social insurance plan. Therefore, it was not possible to receive any credits under the reciprocal agreement between the Philippines and Canada.

M-36696 v. MHRD (September 1, 1998) (RT)

While the applicant widow may benefit from widower's benefits under the Philippines' Social Security System ("SSS"), she herself was not a contributor to the plan. The legislation stipulates that only contributors to the SSS plan may benefit from the international agreement. As a result, the agreement was of no assistance to her in seeking an OAS pension.

A-42155 v. MHRD (March 24, 1999) (RT). See also *B-38217 v. MHRD* (September 1, 1998) (RT).

The Canada-Philippines agreement stipulates that only contributions made to the Philippines' Social Security System ("SSS") could be considered for the purpose of establishing the 10-year residency requirement in Canada. The Tribunal had no jurisdiction to determine that contributions to that country's Government Social Security System ("GSIS"), which was not provided for in the Agreement, could be taken into account, despite evidence that the GSIS and the SSS were to be considered as identical for pension eligibility purposes in the Philippines.

S-38163 v. MHRD (September 1, 1998) (RT)

The applicant's contributions to the Government Service Insurance System while an employee of the Philippines could not count towards his required residency period in Canada. The International Social Security Agreement with the Philippines came into force only with contributions to the Social Security System being included for the purposes of qualifying for Old Age Security pensions. The Tribunal has no jurisdiction to change the legislation.

§4. Germany

Canada (Attorney General) v. Simon, [1998] 4 F.C. J. No. 670 (T.D.)

It was not patently unreasonable for the Review Committee to interpret the phrase "subject to the Canada Pension Plan" in article 11(*a*) of the Canada-Germany treaty on social security as including the situation where the applicant resided in Germany while receiving CPP disability benefits. Evidence was not admissible that the Minister's previous practice was to interpret the phrase as requiring that the applicant have been a CPP contributor while living abroad. It could not be inferred from Germany's acquiescence in this practice that Germany implicitly agreed with this interpretation.

§5. Jamaica

Singer v. Canada (Attorney General), 2010 FC 607, affirmed 2011 FCA 178

Under the Jamaica–Canada agreement, the concept of totalization only enables the person entitled to a full pension under ss. 3(1)(*a*) and (*b*) without recourse to the provisions of the agreement, that does not meet the requirement for 20 years of residence in Canada, to the payment of a partial pension calculated in accordance with the Canadian legislation, outside of Canada. The agreement has nothing to do and does not deal at all with how one qualifies for a full old age pension pursuant to s. 3(1)(*b*)(i) of the OAS Act. A claimant must qualify under the Canadian legislation *per se* to be entitled to a full pension.

---

41. *Coming into force of agreements* **— (1) The Governor in Council may, by order, declare any agreement entered into under section 40 to be in force and, when any such order comes into force, the agreement to which it relates has the force of law in Canada during such period as by the terms of the agreement it remains in force.**

(2) *Publication* **— Notice of the day an agreement entered into under section 40 comes into force and of the day it ceases to be in force shall be given by proclamation**

of the Governor in Council published, with the text of the agreement, in the *Canada Gazette*.

42. *Tabling order* — **(1)** An order under section **41** shall be laid before each House of Parliament within the first **15** days on which that House is sitting after the order is made. (S.C. 2007, c. 11, s. 30.)

(2) *Coming into force of order* — An order referred to in subsection (1) shall come into force on the thirtieth sitting day after it has been laid before Parliament pursuant to that subsection unless before the twentieth sitting day after the order has been laid before Parliament a motion for the consideration of either House, to the effect that the order be revoked, signed by not less than fifty members of the House of Commons in the case of a motion for the consideration of that House and by not less than twenty members of the Senate in the case of a motion for the consideration of the Senate, is filed with the Speaker of the appropriate House.

(3) *Consideration of motion* — Where a motion for the consideration of the House of Commons or Senate is filed as provided in subsection (2) with respect to a particular order referred to in subsection (1), that House shall, not later than the sixth sitting day of that House following the filing of the motion, in accordance with the rules of that House, unless a motion to the like effect has earlier been taken up and considered in the other House, take up and consider the motion.

(4) *Time for disposition of motion* — A motion taken up and considered in accordance with subsection (3) shall be debated without interruption for not more than five hours and, on the conclusion of the debate or at the expiration of the fifth such hour, the Speaker of the House of Commons or the Senate, as the case may be, shall forthwith put, without further debate or amendment, every question necessary for the disposal of the motion.

(5) *Procedure on adoption of motion* — If a motion taken up and considered in accordance with subsection (3) is adopted, with or without amendments, a message shall be sent from the House adopting the motion informing the other House that the motion has been so adopted and requesting that the motion be concurred in by that other House.

(6) *Procedure in other House* — Within the first fifteen days next after receipt by it of a request pursuant to subsection (5) that the House receiving the request is sitting, that House shall, in accordance with the rules thereof, take up and consider the motion that is the subject of the request and all questions in connection therewith shall be debated without interruption for not more than five hours and, on the conclusion of the debate or at the expiration of the fifth such hour, the Speaker of the House of Commons or the Senate, as the case may be, shall forthwith put, without further debate or amendment, every question necessary to determine whether or not the motion in question is concurred in.

(7) *Where motion adopted and concurred in* — Where a motion taken up and considered in accordance with this section is adopted by the House in which it was introduced and is concurred in by the other House, the particular order to which the motion relates shall stand revoked but without prejudice to the making of a further order of a like nature to implement a subsequent agreement between the Government of Canada and the government of the country that was a party to the agreement to which the order related.

(8) *Where motion not adopted or concurred in* — Where a motion taken up and considered in accordance with this section is not adopted by the House in which it was introduced or is adopted, with or without amendments, by that House but is not concurred in by the other House, the particular order to which the motion relates comes into force immediately on the failure to adopt the motion or concur therein, as the case may be.

Old Age Security Act

(9) *Definition of expression "sitting day"* — For the purposes of subsection (2), a day on which either House of Parliament sits shall be deemed to be a sitting day.

(S.C. 2007, c. 11, s. 30.)

43. *Negative resolution of Parliament* — When each House of Parliament enacts rules whereby any regulation made subject to negative resolution of Parliament within the meaning of section 39 of the *Interpretation Act* may be made the subject of a resolution of both Houses of Parliament introduced and passed in accordance with the rules of those Houses, section 42 of this Act is thereupon repealed and an order made thereafter under section 41 is an order made subject to negative resolution of Parliament within the meaning of section 39 of the *Interpretation Act.*

Offences[15]

44. *Offences* — **(1)** Every person who

(a) knowingly makes a false or misleading statement in any application or statement required or permitted by this Act or makes any such application or statement that by reason of any non-disclosure of facts is false or misleading or obtains any benefit payment by false pretences, or (S.C. 1998, c. 21, s. 118.)

(b) being the payee thereof, negotiates or attempts to negotiate any cheque to which that person is not entitled, (S.C. 1998, c. 21, s. 118.)

(c) [Repealed by S.C. 1998, c. 21, s. 118.]

is guilty of an offence punishable on summary conviction.

(2) *Form of information or complaint* — No information or complaint for an offence under this Act is open to objection on the ground that the information or complaint is for more than one matter of complaint or that it relates to more than one offence.

(3) *Limitation period* — Any proceedings under this Act in respect of an offence may be commenced at any time within, but not later than, five years after the Minister becomes aware of the subject-matter of the proceedings. (S.C. 1997, c. 40, s. 106.)

(4) *Saving* — No proceeding shall be commenced under this section or the *Criminal Code* for an act or omission if a penalty for that act or omission has been imposed under section 44.1. (S.C. 1997, c. 40, s. 106.)

(S.C. 1997, c. 40, s. 106; 1998, c. 21, s. 118.)

———————— Notes ————————

Case Law

Whitton v. Canada (Attorney General), [2002] FCA 46

The fraudulent negotiation of an OAS pension cheque by a person other than the payee is not an offence under the Act.

———————————————

Administrative Monetary Penalties[16]

44.1. *Penalties* — **(1)** The Minister may impose on a person a penalty for each of the following acts or omissions if the Minister becomes aware of facts that in the Minister's opinion establish that the person has

(a) made a statement or declaration in an application or otherwise that the person knew was false or misleading;

---

[15] Heading replaced by S.C. 2007, c. 11, s. 31.

[16] Heading added by S.C. 2007, c. 11, s. 32.

(*a.1*) knowingly failed to correct any inaccuracies in the information provided by the Minister as required by subsection 5(6), 11(3.3), 15(2.4), 19(4.05) or 21(4.3); (2012, c. 19, s. 466.)

(*b*) made a statement or declaration in an application or otherwise that the person knew was false or misleading because of the non-disclosure of facts;

(*c*) knowingly failed to declare to the Minister all or some of the person's income;

(*d*) received or obtained by cheque or otherwise a benefit payment to which the person knew that they were not entitled, or a benefit payment that the person knew was in excess of the amount of the benefit payment to which they were entitled, and did not return the cheque or the amount of the benefit payment, or the excess amount, as the case may be, without delay; or (S.C. 2007, c. 11, s. 33(2).)

(*e*) participated in, assented to or acquiesced in an act or omission mentioned in any of paragraphs (*a*) to (*d*).

(1.1) *Purpose of penalty* — The purpose of the penalty is to promote compliance with this Act and not to punish. (S.C. 2007, c. 11, s. 33(4).)

(2) *Maximum penalty* — The Minister may set the amount of the penalty for each act or omission at not more than $10,000.

(3) *Limitation on imposition of penalties* — A penalty shall not be imposed on a person under subsection (1) if

(*a*) a prosecution for the act or omission has been initiated against the person; or

(*b*) five years have passed since the day on which the Minister became aware of the act or omission.

(4) *Rescission, etc., of penalty* — The Minister may rescind the imposition of a penalty under subsection (1), or reduce the penalty,

(*a*) on the presentation of new facts;

(*b*) on being satisfied that the penalty was imposed without knowledge of, or on the basis of a mistake as to, some material fact;

(*c*) on being satisfied that the penalty cannot be collected within the reasonably foreseeable future; or

(*d*) on being satisfied that payment of the penalty would cause undue hardship to the debtor.

(S.C. 2007, c. 11, s. 33(5).)

(S.C. 1997, c. 40, s. 107; 2007, c. 11, s. 33; 2012, c. 19, s. 466.)

Administration and Enforcement[17]

44.2. *Interpretation* — (1) The definitions in this subsection apply in this section.

"document" includes moneys, securities, books, records, letters, accounts, statements (financial or otherwise), correspondence, memoranda, film, microform, videotape, photographs, machine-readable records and other documentary material, regardless of form or characteristics, and any copy or printout of any of them.

"dwelling-house" means the whole or a part of a building or structure that is kept or occupied as a permanent or temporary residence and includes

(*a*) a building within the yard of a dwelling-house that is connected to it by a doorway or by a covered and enclosed passageway; and

(*b*) a unit that is designed to be mobile and to be used as a permanent or temporary residence and that is being used as such a residence.

---

[17] Heading added by S.C. 2007, c. 11, s. 34.

"judge" means a judge of a superior court having jurisdiction in the province where the matter arises or a judge of the Federal Court.

(2) *Inspections* — The Minister may, at any reasonable time, for any purpose relating to the administration or enforcement of this Act, examine any document that relates or may relate to the entitlement of a person to a benefit or the amount of a benefit and, for that purpose, the Minister may

(*a*) subject to subsection (3), enter any premises or place where the Minister believes a document relating to the entitlement of a person to a benefit or the amount of that a benefit is or should be kept; and

(*b*) require the owner, occupant or person in charge of the premises or place to give the Minister all reasonable assistance and to answer all proper questions relating to the administration or enforcement of this Act and, for that purpose, require the owner, occupant or person in charge of the premises or place to attend at those premises or that place with the Minister.

(3) *Warrant required to enter dwelling-house* — If the premises or place referred to in subsection (2) is a dwelling-house, the Minister may not enter that dwelling-house without the consent of the occupant except under the authority of a warrant issued under subsection (4).

(4) *Warrant* — On *ex parte* application by the Minister, a judge may issue a warrant authorizing the Minister to enter a dwelling-house subject to the conditions that may be specified in the warrant, if the judge is satisfied by information on oath that

(*a*) there are reasonable grounds to believe that the dwelling-house is a premises or place referred to in subsection (2);

(*b*) entry into the dwelling-house is necessary for a purpose relating to the administration or enforcement of this Act; and

(*c*) entry into the dwelling-house has been refused or that there are reasonable grounds to believe that entry will be refused.

(5) *Other access to document* — If the judge is not satisfied that entry into that dwelling-house is necessary for a purpose relating to the administration or enforcement of this Act but is satisfied that access to a document that is or should be kept in the dwelling-house has been or may be expected to be refused, the judge may

(*a*) order the occupant of the dwelling-house to provide the Minister with reasonable access to the document; and

(*b*) make any other order that is appropriate in the circumstances to carry out the purposes of this Act.

(6) *Requirement to provide documents or information* — Despite any other provision of this Act, the Minister may, subject to subsection (7), for any purpose relating to the administration or enforcement of this Act, by notice served personally or by confirmed delivery service, require that any person provide, within the reasonable time that is stipulated in the notice, any information or additional information or any document.

(7) *Unnamed persons* — The Minister shall not impose on a person, in this section referred to as a "third party", a requirement under subsection (6) to provide information or a document relating to one or more unnamed persons unless the Minister first obtains the authorization of a judge under subsection (8).

(8) *Judicial authorization* — On *ex parte* application by the Minister, a judge may, subject to the conditions that the judge considers appropriate, authorize the Minister to impose on a third party a requirement under subsection (6) relating to one or more unnamed persons, in this section referred to as the "group", where the judge is satisfied by information on oath that

(*a*) the person or group is ascertainable; and

(*b*) the requirement is made to verify compliance by the person or persons in the group with a duty or obligation under this Act.

(**9**) *Service of authorization* — If an authorization is granted under subsection (8), the authorization shall be served together with the notice referred to in subsection (6).

(**10**) *Review of authorization* — If an authorization is granted under subsection (8), a third party on whom a notice is served under subsection (6) may, not later than 15 days after the service of the notice, apply to the judge who granted the authorization or, if that judge is unable to act, to another judge of the same court, for a review of the authorization.

(**11**) *Powers on review* — On hearing an application under subsection (10), a judge may cancel the authorization previously ranted if the judge is not then satisfied that the conditions in paragraphs (8)(*a*) to (*d*) have been met, and the judge may confirm or vary the authorization if the judge is satisfied that those conditions have been met.

(**12**) *Copies as evidence* — When a document is inspected, examined or provided in accordance with this section, the person by whom it is inspected or examined or to whom it is provided may make, or cause to be made, one or more certified copies of it and any such copy is evidence of the nature and content of the original document and has the same probative force as the original document would have if it were proven in the ordinary way.

(**13**) *Compliance* — No person shall interfere with any person doing anything that the person is authorized under this section to do or prevent or attempt to prevent any person from doing any such thing.

(S.C. 1997, c. 40, s. 107.)

Consolidated Revenue Fund

45. *Payment out of C.R.F* — All benefits payable under this Act shall be paid out of the Consolidated Revenue Fund.

Administration and Annual Report

46. *Administration* — This Act shall be administered by the Minister of Employment and Social Development.

(1996, c. 11, s. 95(*k*); 2005, c. 35, s. 67(*e*)(ii); 2012, c. 19, s. 694(*f*)(ii); 2013, c. 40, s. 238(1)(*k*)(ii).)

46.1. *Electronic means* — (Repealed by S.C. 2012, c. 19, s. 239, in force June 29, 2012.)

47. *Annual report* — The Minister shall submit to Parliament annually, as soon as possible after the termination of each fiscal year, if Parliament is then in session or, if not, as soon as possible after the commencement of the next session of Parliament, a report covering the administration of this Act and including an account of receipts and disbursements during the previous fiscal year.

Old Age Security Act

Old Age Security Regulations

C.R.C. 1978, c. 1246, as amended by SOR/78-699, gazetted September 13, 1978 and effective August 31, 1978; SOR/81-285, gazetted April 22, 1981 and effective May 1, 1981; SOR/81-803, gazetted October 28, 1981 and effective October 9, 1981; SOR/83-84, gazetted January 26, 1983 and effective January 14, 1983, by SOR/84-49, gazetted January 11, 1984 and effective December 22, 1983; SOR/84-656, gazetted August 22, 1984 and effective August 9, 1984; SOR/86-956, gazetted October 1, 1986 and effective September 11, 1986; SOR/88-238, gazetted April 27, 1988 and effective April 14, 1988; SOR/89-269, gazetted June 7, 1989 and effective May 18, 1989; SOR/90-813, gazetted December 5, 1990 and effective November 22, 1990; SOR/93-40, gazetted February 10, 1993 and effective January 28, 1993; SOR/96-521, gazetted December 5, 1996 and effective January 1, 1997; SOR/97-530, gazetted December 12, 1997 and effective November 27, 1997; SOR/99-193, gazetted May 12, 1999 and effective April 22, 1999; SOR/2000-133, gazetted April 12, 2000 and effective March 30, 2000; SOR/2000-412, gazetted December 20, 2000 and effective November 30, 2000; SOR/2001-148, gazetted May 9, 2001 and effective April 26, 2001; SOR/2002-221, gazetted June 19, 2002 and effective June 6, 2002; 2004-249, gazetted December 1, 2004 and effective November 16, 2004; 2010-45, gazetted March 17, 2010 and effective February 23, 2010 except section 26, in force April 20, 2011; SOR/2013-20, effective March 1, 2013; SOR/2013-23, effective February 14, 2013, except sections 2 and 5–9 came into force March 1, 2013; sections 3 and 4 came into force on July 1, 2013; SOR/2013-62, effective April 1, 2013.

Regulations for Carrying into Effect the Purposes and Provisions of the Old Age Security Act

Short Title

1. These Regulations may be cited as the Old Age Security **Regulations.**

Interpretation

2. (1) In these Regulations,

"Act" **means the** *Old Age Security Act*;

"appeal" **means an appeal referred to in subsection 28(1) of the Act or made in respect of a reference; (SOR/96-521, s. 1(2).)**

"applicant" **(Repealed by SOR/96-521, s. 1(1).);**

"appellant" **means a person who makes an appeal referred to in subsection 28(1) or (2) of the Act or in respect of a reference; (SOR/90-813, s. 1(2); SOR/96-521, s. 1(2).)**

"application form" **means the form of application required by the Minister;**

"beneficiary" **includes a person on whose behalf a benefit has become payable; (SOR/96-521, s. 1(3).)**

"Board" **(Revoked by SOR/89-269, s. 1(1).)**

"Court" **means the Tax Court of Canada constituted by the** *Tax Court of Canada Act*; **(SOR/89-269, s. 1(2).)**

"Minister" **(Repealed by SOR/96-521, s. 1(1).)**

"reference" **means a reference to the Tax Court of Canada pursuant to subsection 28(2) of the Act; (SOR/90-813, s. 1(2); SOR/96-521, s. 1(2).)**

"Regional Director" **(Revoked by SOR/96-521, s. 1(1).)**

"request for reconsideration" **means a request made to the Minister for reconsideration under section 27.1 of the Act; (SOR/96-521, s. 1(3).)**

"Review Committee" **(Revoked by SOR/90-813, s. 1(1).)**

"Review Tribunal" **(Revoked by SOR/96-521, s. 1(1).)**

"secretary" **(Repealed by SOR/96-521, s. 1(1).).**

(1.1) In these Regulations,

    (a) **a reference to the age of "60 years" is to be read for the applicable period set out in column 1 of the table to subsection 2.2(1) of the Act as a reference to the corresponding age in column 2; and**

    (b) **a reference to the age of "65 years" is to be read for the applicable period set out in column 1 of the table to subsection 2.2(2) of the Act as a reference to the corresponding age in column 2.**

(SOR/2013-23, s. 1.)

(2) For the purposes of these Regulations, residence and presence in Newfoundland prior to the date of union of Newfoundland with Canada are deemed to be residence and presence in Canada respectively. (SOR/81-285, s. 1(2).)

(3) For the purpose of the definition "public officer" in subsection 33(1) of the Act, a prescribed individual is a person employed in a federal institution or whose services are required by a federal institution, on a casual or temporary basis or under a student employment program. (SOR/99-193, s. 1.)

(SOR/81-285, s. 1; SOR/89-269, s. 1; SOR/90-813, s. 1; SOR/96-521, s. 1; SOR/99-193, s. 1; SOR/2013-23, s. 1.)

Part I

Applications

Forms for Applications

3. (1) Where required by the Minister, an application for a benefit shall be made on an application form.

(2) Subject to subsections 5(2) and 11(3) of the Act, an application is deemed to have been made only when an application form completed by or on behalf of an applicant is received by the Minister.

(SOR/96-521, s. 2.)

4. (1) Where the Minister considers that a person is unable for a sufficient reason to make a request for a reconsideration or to make an appeal, an application, a statement or a notice, the request for reconsideration, appeal, application, statement or notice may be made on that person's behalf by a responsible person or agency. (SOR/96-521, s. 3.)

(2) Where a person is or has been in receipt of assistance pursuant to the *Unemployment Assistance Act* or the *Canada Assistance Plan*, an application for a pension may be made on behalf of that person by the appropriate provincial authority. (SOR/90-813, s. 2.)

(SOR/90-813, s. 2; SOR/96-521, s. 3.)

Approval of an Application for a Pension

5. (1) Subject to subsection (2), where the Minister

(a) is satisfied that an applicant is qualified for a pension in accordance with sections 3 to 5 of the Act, and (SOR/90-813, s. 4(1).)

(b) approves the application after the last day of the month in which it was received, (SOR/96-521, s. 4(1).)

the Minister's approval shall be effective on the latest of

(c) the day on which the application was received,

(d) the day on which the applicant became qualified for a pension in accordance with sections 3 to 5 of the Act, and (SOR/90-813, s. 3(2).)

(e) the date specified in writing by the applicant.

(SOR/83-84, s. 1.)

(2) Where the Minister is satisfied that an applicant mentioned in subsection (1) attained the age of 65 years before the day on which the application was received, the Minister's approval of the application shall be effective as of the latest of (SOR/96-521, s. 4(2).)

(a) the day that is one year before the day on which the application was received; (SOR/96-521, s. 4(2).)

(b) the day on which the applicant attained the age of 65 years;

(c) the day on which the applicant became qualified for a pension in accordance with sections 3 to 5 of the Act; and (SOR/90-813, s. 3(3).)

(d) the month immediately before the date specified in writing by the applicant. (SOR/96-521, s. 4(3).)

(3) Where the Minister, under subsection 5(2) or 11(3) of the Act, deems an application to have been made and approved, the Minister's approval shall be effective on the day on which the person attained the age of 65 years. (SOR/96-521, s. 4(4).)

(4) If the Minister waives the requirement for an application in respect of a person under subsection 5(4) of the Act, the Minister's approval is effective on the day on which the person attains the age of 65 years. (SOR/2013-23, s. 2.)

(SOR/84-656, s. 1; SOR/90-813, s. 3; SOR/96-521, s. 4; SOR/2013-23, s. 2.)

OAS REGULATIONS

563

Payment of an Allowance Under Two Dollars

6. Where a spouse, common-law partner or survivor is entitled under Part III of the Act to an allowance in an amount that does not exceed $2 monthly, an allowance of $2 is payable monthly to that spouse, common-law partner or survivor.

(SOR/89-269, s. 2; SOR/2000-412, s. 1.)

Manner of Rounding Off Amount of Partial Monthly Pension

7. Where the amount of a partial monthly pension referred to in subsection 3(3) of the Act, as increased under subsection 7.1(2) of the Act if applicable, contains a fraction of a dollar that is represented by three or more digits, (SOR/90-813, s. 4; SOR/2013-23, s. 3.)

    (*a*) if the third digit is less than 5, the third and subsequent digits shall be dropped; and

    (*b*) if the third digit is 5 or greater than 5, the second digit shall be increased by 1 and the third and subsequent digits shall be dropped.

(SOR/90-813, s. 4; SOR/2013-23, s. 3.)

Manner of Quarterly Adjustment of Benefit

8. (1) Where the amount of a full monthly pension or supplement is adjusted quarterly pursuant to subsection 7(2) or 12(2) of the Act,

    (*a*) there shall be an adjustment to the nearest cent, in accordance with subsection (2), of the product obtained

        (i) by multiplying the amount referred to in paragraph 7(2)(*a*) of the Act by the ratio referred to in paragraph 7(2)(*b*) of the Act, or

        (ii) by multiplying the amount referred to in paragraph 12(2)(*a*) of the Act by the ratio referred to in paragraph 12(2)(*b*) of the Act; and

(SOR/90-813, s. 5.)

    (*b*) the ratios referred to in paragraph (*a*) shall be expressed as decimal fractions in accordance with subsection (3).

(2) Where the product referred to in subparagraph (1)(*a*)(i), as increased under subsection 7.1(1) of the Act if applicable, or the product referred to in subparagraph (1)(*a*)(ii), contains a fraction of a dollar that is represented by three or more digits, (SOR/2013-23, s. 4.)

    (*a*) if the third digit is less than 5, the third and subsequent digits shall be dropped; and,

    (*b*) if the third digit is 5 or greater than 5, the second digit shall be increased by 1 and the third and subsequent digits shall be dropped.

(3) Where the ratios referred to in paragraph (1)(*a*) contain a fraction that is less than 1, that fraction shall be expressed as a decimal fraction of four digits after the decimal point, and

    (*a*) where the fourth digit after the decimal point is less than 5, the fourth digit after the decimal point shall be dropped; and

    (*b*) where the fourth digit after the decimal point is 5 or greater than 5, the third digit after the decimal point shall be increased by 1 and the fourth digit after the decimal point shall be dropped.

(SOR/90-813, s. 5; SOR/2013-23, s. 4.)

Determination of Average Consumer Price Index for Period of Months

9. (1) The average of the Consumer Price Index for Canada for a period of months shall be determined by dividing the aggregate of the Consumer Price Index for Canada, as published by Statistics Canada under the authority of the *Statistics Act*, for each month in that period by the number of months in that period.

(2) Where the quotient obtained pursuant to subsection (1) contains a fraction that is less than 1, such fraction shall be expressed as a decimal fraction of two digits after the decimal point and

    (*a*) the second digit after the decimal point shall be dropped if that digit is less than 5; or

    (*b*) the first digit after the decimal point shall be increased by one and the second digit shall be dropped if the second digit is five or greater than 5.

Approval of Application for a Supplement

10. Where the Minister is satisfied that a pensioner is eligible for a supplement under section 11 of the Act, the Minister shall approve an application for a supplement by that pensioner in accordance with that section.

(SOR/96-521, s. 5.)

Approval of Application for an Allowance

11. The Minister shall approve an application for an allowance for the spouse or common-law partner of a pensioner or for a survivor where the spouse, common-law partner or survivor is entitled to an allowance under section 19 or 21 of the Act.

(SOR/96-521, s. 5; SOR/2000-412, s. 2, 3.)

12. (1) Subject to subsections (2) and (3), where the Minister approves an application for an allowance after the last day of the month in which the application was received, the Minister's approval shall be effective as of the later of (SOR/2000-412, s. 4(1).)

    (*a*) the day on which the application was received, and

    (*b*) the day on which the spouse, common-law partner or survivor became entitled to an allowance under section 19 or 21 of the Act.

(SOR/2000-412, s. 4(2).)

(2) Where the spouse or common-law partner of a pensioner attains the age of 60 years before the day on which the application for an allowance in respect of the spouse or common-law partner is received, the approval of the application by the Minister shall be effective as of the latest of (SOR/2000-412, s. 4(3).)

    (*a*) the day that is one year before the day on which the application was received,

    (*b*) the day on which the spouse or common-law partner attained the age of 60 years, and

    (*c*) the day on which the spouse or common-law partner became entitled to an allowance under section 19 of the Act.

(SOR/2000-412, s. 4(4).)

(3) Where a survivor is entitled to an allowance under section 21 of the Act before the day on which an application in respect of the survivor is received, the approval of the application by the Minister shall be effective as of the later of (SOR/2000-412, s. 4(5).)

(*a*) the day that is one year before the day on which the application was received, and

(*b*) the day on which the survivor became entitled to an allowance under section 21 of the Act. (SOR/2000-412, s. 4(6).)

(SOR/96-521, s. 5; SOR/2000-412, s. 4.)

Month in which Loss of Income Occurs

13. For the purposes of section 14 of the Act, (SOR/90-813, s. 8.)

(*a*) the month in which an applicant or an applicant's spouse or common-law partner (SOR/2000-412, s. 5(1).)

   (i) ceases to hold an office or employment shall be the month in which the last day in respect of which he receives income from that office or employment falls, or

   (ii) ceases to carry on a business shall be the month in which the last day on which he actively carries on that business falls; and

(*b*) the month in which an applicant or an applicant's spouse or common-law partner suffers a loss of income due to termination or reduction of pension income shall be the month in which that termination or reduction actually occurs. (SOR/2000-412, s. 5(2).)

(SOR/90-813, s. 8; SOR/2000-412, s. 5.)

Definition of Pension Income

14. For the purposes of section 14 of the Act, "pension income" means the aggregate of amounts received as (SOR/90-813, s. 9.)

(*a*) annuity payments;

(*b*) alimony and maintenance payments;

(*c*) employment insurance benefits; (SOR/2001-148, s. 1(1).)

(*d*) disability benefits deriving from a private insurance plan;

(*e*) any benefit, other than a death benefit, under the *Canada Pension Plan* or a provincial pension plan as defined in the *Canada Pension Plan*;

(*f*) superannuation or pension payments, other than a benefit received pursuant to the Act or any similar payment received pursuant to a law of a provincial legislature; (SOR/86-956, s. 1; SOR/2001-148, s. 1(2).)

(*g*) compensation under a federal or provincial employee's or worker's compensation law in respect of an injury, disability or death; (SOR/2001-148, s. 1(2).)

(*h*) income assistance benefits under an agreement referred to in subsection 33(1) of the *Department of Human Resources Development Act* by reason of a permanent reduction in the work force as described in that subsection; and (SOR/2001-148, s. 1(2).)

(*i*) income assistance benefits under the Plant Workers' Adjustment Program, the Fisheries Early Retirement Program or the Northern Cod Adjustment and Recovery Program by reason of a permanent reduction in the workforce. (SOR/2001-148, s. 1(2).)

(SOR/84-656, s. 3; SOR/86-956, s. 1; SOR/90-813, s. 9; SOR/2001-148, s. 1.)

Assignment of Social Insurance Numbers to Applicants, Beneficiaries, Spouses or Common-law Partners

15. Where a Social Insurance Number has not been assigned to an applicant or beneficiary or to the spouse or common-law partner of an applicant or beneficiary, the Minister may assign or cause to be assigned a Social Insurance Number to the applicant or beneficiary or to the spouse or common-law partner of the applicant or beneficiary.

(SOR/2000-412, s. 6.)

Relationship Evidence[1]

16. If the Minister has not received sufficient evidence or information in support of an application to determine the relationship between the applicant and their spouse or common-law partner, the applicant or their representative shall allow the Minister access to the following documents:

(*a*) in the case of spouses,

   (i) an official copy or extract of the record of marriage issued by a competent authority or a certified copy of one, or

   (ii) if the Minister has sufficient reason to believe that an official copy or extract of the record of marriage or a certified copy is not available,

      (A) a statutory declaration setting out information as to the marriage, and

      (B) other evidence of the marriage; and

(*b*) in the case of common-law partners,

   (i) a statutory declaration setting out information as to the relationship of the common-law partners, and

   (ii) other evidence of the relationship.

(SOR/96-521, s. 27(*a*); SOR/2000-412, s. 7; SOR/2004-249, s. 5.)

17. (Repealed by SOR/2000-412, s. 8.)

Evidence of Age and Identity[2]

18. (1) Subject to section 19, the Minister shall determine the age and identity of an applicant for the purposes of the Act in accordance with whichever of subsections (2) to (2.2) is applicable. (SOR/96-521, s. 27(*b*); SOR/2004-249, s. 7(1).)

(2) The Minister shall determine the age and identity of an applicant on the basis of any information provided to the Minister by the Canada Employment Insurance Commission under subsection 28.2(5) of the *Department of Human Resources and Skills Development Act.* (SOR/96-521, s. 27(*b*); SOR/2004-249, s. 7(1); SOR/2013-20, s. 6.)

(2.1) The Minister shall determine the age and identity of an applicant on the basis of a birth certificate or a certified copy of one. (SOR/2004-249, s. 7(1).)

(2.2) If there is sufficient reason to believe that a birth certificate is not available, the Minister shall determine the age and identity of an applicant on the basis of any other evidence and information with respect to the age and identity of the applicant that is available from any source. (SOR/2004-249, s. 7(1).)

---

[1] Heading amended by SOR/2004-249, s. 5.

[2] Heading amended by SOR/2004-249, s. 6.

(3) If the Minister is unable to determine the age and identity of an applicant under any of subsections (2) to (2.2), the Minister shall, subject to the following conditions, request that Statistics Canada search the census records for information as to the age and identity of the applicant: (SOR/96-521, s. 27(*b*); SOR/2004-249, s. 7(2).)

    (*a*) any such request shall be made in the form prescribed by the Chief Statistician of Canada and shall bear the signed consent of the person concerning whom the information is sought and shall provide such specific information as may be necessary for the purpose of making a search of the census records; and

    (*b*) any information supplied by Statistics Canada shall be kept confidential and shall not be used for any purpose other than that of establishing the age of the applicant as required under the Act, the *Canada Assistance Plan* or the *Canada Pension Plan*, as the case may be. (SOR/96-521, s. 7(1).)

(4) (Repealed by SOR/96-521, s. 7(2).)

(SOR/96-521, s. 7, 27; SOR/2004-249, s. 7; SOR/2013-20, s. 6.)

19. Where the age of an applicant has been determined under the *Canada Pension Plan*, that determination may be accepted by the Minister for the purposes of the Act.

(SOR/96-521, s. 8.)

19.1. (Repealed by SOR/96-521, s. 8.)

Residence

20. (1) To enable the Minister to determine a person's eligibility in respect of residence in Canada, the person or someone acting on the person's behalf shall provide a statement giving full particulars of all periods of residence in Canada and of all absences from Canada that are relevant to that eligibility. (SOR/2013-23, s. 5.)

(2) Unless the Minister requires otherwise under the Act, a person is not required to provide a statement under subsection (1) in the circumstances set out in subsection 5(2) or (5), 11(3) or (4), 19(4.1) or 21(5) or (5.1) of the Act. (SOR/2013-23, s. 5.)

(SOR/96-521, s. 27(*c*); SOR/2013-23, s. 5.)

21. (1) For the purposes of the Act and these Regulations,

    (*a*) a person resides in Canada if he makes his home and ordinarily lives in any part of Canada; and

    (*b*) a person is present in Canada when he is physically present in any part of Canada.

(2) A person who lives on a ship outside the territorial waters of Canada shall, while so living, be deemed not to be living in any part of Canada.

(2.1) Notwithstanding subsection (1), a person who is not a Canadian citizen or a permanent resident of Canada does not reside in Canada for the purposes of the Act and these Regulations during any period in which he is present in Canada

    (*a*) for the purpose of carrying out his duties as a properly accredited diplomat, consular officer, representative or official of

        (i) a country other than Canada,

        (ii) the United Nations or any of its agencies, or

        (iii) any intergovernmental organization in which Canada participates;

(*b*) as a member of a military force present in Canada for training or for any other purpose in connection with the defence or security interests of Canada or under any treaty or agreement between Canada and another country;

(*c*) as the spouse, common-law partner or dependant of a person referred to in paragraph (*a*) or (*b*) or the dependant of that person's spouse or common-law partner; or (SOR/2000-412, s. 9(1).)

(*d*) as a member of the staff of or as a person otherwise accompanying a person referred to in paragraph (*a*), (*b*) or (*c*).

(SOR/83-84, s. 2.)

(3) For the purposes of the Act and these Regulations, where a person becomes the spouse or common-law partner of a person residing in Canada while the person residing in Canada is absent from Canada in any of the circumstances specified in paragraph (5)(*a*) or (*b*), the period outside Canada of the spouse after their marriage or of the common-law partner after becoming such a partner is considered a period of residence and presence in Canada, if

(*a*) the spouse or common-law partner returns to Canada either before or within six months after the return of the person residing in Canada or within six months after that person's death if that person dies while so absent from Canada; or

(*b*) the spouse or common-law partner attains, during that period outside Canada, an age at which the spouse or common-law partner is eligible to be paid a pension under the Act.

(SOR/2000-412, s. 9(2).)

(4) Any interval of absence from Canada of a person resident in Canada that is

(*a*) of a temporary nature and does not exceed one year;

(*b*) for the purpose of attending a school or university, or

(*c*) specified in subsection (5),

shall be deemed not to have interrupted that person's residence or presence in Canada.

(5) The absences from Canada referred to in paragraph (4)(*c*) of a person residing in Canada are absences under the following circumstances:

(*a*) while that person was employed out of Canada

(i) by the United Nations or one of its specialized agencies,

(ii) by the North Atlantic Treaty Organization,

(iii) by the Commonwealth Secretariat,

(iv) by the Organization of Economic Cooperation and Development,

(v) by l'Agence de coopération culturelle et technique, or

(vi) by a Canadian firm or corporation as a representative or member thereof,

if during his employment out of Canada he

(vii) had in Canada a permanent place of abode to which he intended to return, or

(viii) maintained in Canada a self-contained domestic establishment,

and he returned to Canada within six months after the end of his employment out of Canada or he attained, while employed out of Canada, an age at which he was eligible to be paid a pension under the Act;

(*b*) while that person was employed or engaged out of Canada

OAS REGULATIONS

(i) by the Government of Canada or by the government or a municipal corporation of any province,

(ii) in the performance of services in another country under a development or assistance program that is sponsored or operated in that country by the Government of Canada or of a province or by a non-profit Canadian agency,

(iii) as a member of the Canadian Forces, pursuant to and in connection with the requirements of his duties,

(iv) in work for Canada connected with the prosecution of any war,

(v) as a member of the armed forces of any ally of Canada during any war,

(vi) as a missionary with any religious group or organization,

(vii) as a worker in lumbering, harvesting, fishing or other seasonal employment,

(viii) as a transport worker on trains, aircraft, ships or buses running between Canada and points outside Canada or other similar employment, or

(ix) as an employee, a member or an officer of an international charitable organization,

if he returned to Canada within six months of the end of his employment or engagement out of Canada or he attained, while employed or engaged out of Canada, an age at which he was eligible to be paid a pension under the Act;

(c) while that person was accompanying their spouse or common-law partner who was absent from Canada in any of the circumstances specified in paragraph (a) or (b) or for the purpose of attending school or university, if that person

(i) returned to Canada either before or within six months after the return of their spouse or common-law partner or within six months after the death of their spouse or common-law partner, if their spouse or common-law partner died while so absent from Canada, or (SOR/2000-412, s. 9(3).)

(ii) while so absent from Canada, attained an age at which he was eligible to be paid a pension under the Act;

(d) while that person was awaiting transportation to Canada during or immediately after World War II, if he

(i) was unable to return to Canada owing to the dislocation of transportation facilities, and

(ii) returned to Canada when transportation became available;

(e) while that person was accompanying his spouse who was resident in Canada and awaiting transportation to Canada during or immediately after World War II, if that person

(i) was unable to return to Canada owing to the dislocation of transportation facilities, and

(ii) returned to Canada when transportation became available; or

(f) while that person was a dependent person and was accompanying and residing outside Canada with the person on whom he was dependent, if the person on whom he was dependent resided in Canada and was absent from Canada in any of the circumstances specified in paragraph (a) or (b) and if the dependent person

(i) returned to Canada before or within six months after the return of the person on whom he was dependent or within six months after that person's death, if that person died while so absent from Canada, or

(ii) while so absent from Canada, attained an age at which he was eligible to be paid a pension under the Act.

(5.1) Where, by virtue of an agreement entered into under subsection 40(1) of the Act, a person is subject to the Act while residing in a country other than Canada, the absence from Canada of that person, the person's spouse or common-law partner and dependants of the person or of the person's spouse or common-law partner, if the spouse, common-law partner or dependants, as the case may be, reside with the person in that country, shall, for the purposes of an allowance, not be considered to have interrupted the residence or presence in Canada of the person, spouse, common-law partner or dependants. (SOR/96-521, s. 13; SOR/2000-412, s. 9(4).)

(5.2) Where a person who is resident in Canada is subject to the legislation of a country other than Canada by virtue of an agreement entered into under subsection 40(1) of the Act, and the person's spouse or common-law partner or the dependant of the person or of the person's spouse or common-law partner engages in pensionable employment as defined in the *Canada Pension Plan* or in the plan of a province providing a comprehensive pension plan, any period in such pensionable employment shall, for the purposes of the Act and these Regulations, be considered to be a period of residence in Canada. (SOR/96-521, s. 9; SOR/2000-412, s. 9(4).)

(5.3) Where, by virtue of an agreement entered into under subsection 40(1) or the Act, a person is subject to the legislation of a country other than Canada, that person shall, for the purposes of the Act and these Regulations, be deemed not to be resident in Canada. (SOR/96-521, s. 9.)

(6) For the purposes of paragraph (5)(*f*), "dependent person" means, with respect to a person who was absent from Canada in any of the circumstances specified in paragraph 5(*a*) or (*b*), that person's father, mother, child or foster child of the person's spouse or common-law partner. (SOR/2000-412, s. 9(6).)

(7) "Dependant" means

(a) with respect to a person who does not reside in Canada within the meaning of subsection (2.1),

(b) with respect to a person who is deemed to be resident in Canada within the meaning of subsection (5.1), or

(c) with respect to a person referred to in subsection (5.2) who, while resident in Canada is subject to the legislation of a country other than Canada,

that person's father, mother, brother, sister, child or foster child or the father, mother, child or foster child or the person's spouse or common-law partner. (SOR/81-285, s. 5(3); SOR/83-84, s. 3; SOR/2000-412, s. 9(6).)

(8) For the purposes of section 4.1 of the Act as it relates to the requirement of subparagraph 3(1)(*c*)(iii) of the Act, the prescribed information is information indicating that the person, for at least 40 years, for all or part of each of those years,

(a) had unadjusted pensionable earnings under the *Canada Pension Plan* that were above the person's basic exemption for that year, or had unadjusted pensionable earnings under *An Act respecting the Québec Pension Plan*, R.S.Q., c. R-9 that were above the person's personal exemption for that year;

(b) received a retirement pension or disability pension under either the *Canada Pension Plan* or *An Act respecting the Québec Pension Plan*, R.S.Q., c. R-9; or

(c) had time excluded from a contributory period under the *Canada Pension Plan* because the person was a family allowance recipient, or had time not

OAS REGULATIONS

included in a contributory period under *An Act respecting the Québec Pension Plan*, R.S.Q., c. R-9 because the person was a recipient of family benefits.

(SOR/2013-23, s. 6.)

(9) For the purposes of subsection (8),

(a) in relation to the *Canada Pension Plan*, "basic exemption", "contributory period" and "unadjusted pensionable earnings" have the same meaning as in subsection 2(1) of that Act and "family allowance recipient" has the same meaning as in subsection 42(1) of that Act; and

(b) in relation to *An Act respecting the Québec Pension Plan*, R.S.Q., c. R-9, "recipient of family benefits", "personal exemption", "unadjusted pensionable earnings" and "contributory period" have the same meaning as in paragraph 1(v) and sections 43, 98 and 101 of that Act respectively.

(SOR/2013-23, s. 6.)

(SOR/81-285, s. 5; SOR/83-84, ss. 2, 3; SOR/89-269, s. 6; SOR/96-521, s. 9; SOR/2000-412, s. 9; SOR/2013-23, s. 6.)

Legal Residence

22. (1) For the purposes of subsections 4(1), 19(2) and 21(2) of the Act, "legal residence", with respect to a person described in any of those subsections, means that, on the applicable day specified in paragraph (a) or (b) of those subsections, that person (SOR/90-813, s. 11(1); SOR/2013-23, s. 8.)

(a) is or was lawfully in Canada pursuant to the immigration laws of Canada in force on that day;

(b) is or was a resident of Canada and is or was absent from Canada but

(i) is deemed, pursuant to subsection 21(4) or (5) or under the terms of an agreement entered into under subsection 40(1) of the Act, not to have interrupted the person's residence in Canada during that absence, and (SOR/96-521, s. 10(1).)

(ii) was lawfully in Canada pursuant to the immigration laws of Canada immediately prior to the commencement of the absence; or

(c) is not or was not a resident of Canada but is deemed, pursuant to subsection 21(3) or under the terms of an agreement entered into under subsection 40(1) or the Act, to be or to have been resident in Canada. (SOR/96-521, s. 10(2).)

(2) For the purposes of section 4.1 of the Act as it relates to the requirement of paragraph 4(1)(a) of the Act, the prescribed information is both

(a) a current residential address in Canada; and

(b) the prescribed information that is referred to in subsection 21(8).

(SOR/2013-23, s. 8.)

(SOR/78-699, s. 1; SOR/81-285, s. 6; SOR/89-269, s. 7; SOR/90-813, s. 11; SOR/96-521, s. 10; SOR/2013-23, s. 8.)

22.01. *Application of International Agreements* — The agreements referred to in the schedule, which were entered into under subsection 40(1) of the Act for the making of reciprocal arrangements relating to the administration or operation of the Act, shall, in order to give full effect to the Act, be applied in Canada in a manner that extends to common-law partners the treatment afforded to spouses.

(SOR/2000-412, s. 10.)

22.1. *[Sponsored immigrants' exceptions]* — (1) For the purposes of subsections 11(8), 19(6.2) and 21(9.1) of the Act, the following are events in relation to a sponsor referred to in those subsections: (SOR/2000-412, s. 11(1).)

(a) the death of a sponsor;

(b) the sponsor's conviction of an offence under the *Criminal Code* relating to the sponsored individual;

(c) a determination that the sponsor is a bankrupt as defined in section 2 of the *Bankruptcy and Insolvency Act*; and

(d) the sentencing of the sponsor to a term of imprisonment of more than six months. (SOR/97-530, s. 1.)

(2) *[Eligible sponsor]* — Subsection (1) applies to a sponsor

(a) whose undertaking in respect of a pensioner, the spouse or common-law partner of a pensioner, or a survivor, as the case may be, was in effect on or after March 7, 1996; and (SOR/2000-412, s. 11(2).)

(b) to whom an event referred to in any of paragraphs (1)(a) to (d) occurred on or after March 7, 1996. (SOR/97-530, s. 1.)

(SOR/97-530, s. 1; SOR/2000-412, s. 11.)

Further Information and Investigation before or after the Approval of an Application or before or after the Requirement of an Application is Waived

23. (1) The Minister, at any time before or after approval of an application or after the requirement for an application is waived, may require the applicant, the person who applied on the applicant's behalf, the beneficiary or the person who receives payment on the applicant's behalf, as the case may be, to make available or allow to be made available further information or evidence regarding the eligibility of the applicant or the beneficiary for a benefit. (SOR/96-521, s. 12.)

(2) The Minister may at any time make an investigation into the eligibility of a person to receive a benefit including the capacity of a beneficiary to manage his own affairs. (SOR/96-521, s. 27(d).)

(SOR/96-521, ss. 12, 27.)

Payment to Person other than Beneficiary

24. (1) Where a person or agency provides evidence satisfactory to the Minister that a beneficiary, by reason of infirmity, illness, insanity or other cause, is incapable of managing his own affairs, the Minister may direct the benefit to be paid on behalf of such beneficiary

(a) to any person or agency that the Minister is satisfied is authorized by or pursuant to any law of Canada or of a province to manage the affairs of that beneficiary; or

(b) where the Minister is not satisfied that any person or agency is so authorized, to any person or agency that the Minister may appoint for such purpose and that has entered into an agreement with the Minister to administer and expend the benefit on behalf of that beneficiary in accordance with the terms of the agreement.

(SOR/83-84, s. 4; SOR/96-521, s. 27(*e*).)

(2) The Minister shall furnish to a person or agency appointed under subsection (1) to receive a benefit such directions regarding the administration and expenditure of the benefit as the Minister considers in the best interests of the beneficiary. (SOR/96-521, s. 27(*e*).)

(3) Any person or agency appointed under subsection (1) shall account for the benefit payments received and the disbursements made, the account to be in such form and to be made at such times as the Minister may require. (SOR/96-521, s. 27(*e*).)

(4) Where a benefit is paid to any person or agency to be administered and expended for and on behalf of a beneficiary, the notices required by section 25 shall be given by such person or agency.

(5) A benefit payment may be made to the estate of a deceased beneficiary or, if there is no estate, to a person or agency designated by the Minister, where

(*a*) an amount is payable as a benefit to the deceased beneficiary; or

(*b*) a benefit payment made to the beneficiary or made on behalf of the beneficiary by cheque or otherwise is returned to the Minister after the beneficiary's death. (SOR/96-521, s. 13.)

(SOR/83-84, s. 4; SOR/96-521, ss. 13, 27.)

Notices by or on Behalf of an Applicant or Beneficiary

25. (1) Where an applicant or a beneficiary has absented himself from Canada for a period in excess of one month, he shall forthwith give notice thereof to the Minister and within one month of his return to Canada shall notify the Minister of his return.

(2) An applicant or a beneficiary shall notify the Minister of the address to which his benefit is to be sent and, in the event of any change of such address, shall forthwith notify the Minister of the change.

(3) Where joint applicants for an allowance become separated, the beneficiary and the pensioner shall immediately notify the Minister thereof. (SOR/2000-412, s. 12.)

(4) Where the beneficiary of an allowance dies, the pensioner shall immediately notify the Minister thereof. (SOR/2000-412, s. 12.)

(5) (Revoked by SOR/81-825, s. 7.)

(SOR/81-285, s. 7; SOR/96-521, s. 27(*f*); SOR/2000-412, ss. 11, 12.)

Suspension of Payments

26. (1) The Minister shall suspend the payment of a benefit in respect of any beneficiary where it appears to him that the beneficiary is ineligible for payment of the benefit and may suspend the payment where it appears to him that further inquiry into the eligibility of the beneficiary is necessary, and such suspension shall continue until evidence satisfactory to the Minister is given that the beneficiary is eligible for the benefit.

(2) When payment of any benefit that has been suspended under subsection (1) is resumed, the Minister shall cause payment of the benefit to be made for any portion of the period of suspension during which the beneficiary was eligible for benefit. (SOR/96-521, s. 27(*g*).)

(SOR/96-521, s. 27.)

Cancellation of Pension

26.1. (1) For the purposes of subsection 9.3(1) of the Act, a request for cancellation of a pension shall be made to the Minister in writing no later than six months after the day on which payment of the pension begins. (SOR/2013-23, s. 9.)

(2) For the purposes of subsection 9.3(2) of the Act, the amount of any pension and related supplement or allowance shall be repaid no later than six months after the day on which the request is granted. (SOR/2013-23, s. 9.)

(SOR/2013-23, s. 9.)

Recovery of Overpayments

27. For the purpose of subsection 37(2.1) of the Act, an amount of indebtedness that is owing may be deducted and retained out of the whole or any portion of a benefit that is payable to the person or the person's estate or succession, under this Act or any other Act or program administered by the Minister, that will recover the overpayment in a single payment or in instalments, in any amount that does not cause undue hardship to the person or the person's estate or succession.

(SOR/96-521, ss. 14, 27(*h*); SOR/99-193, s. 2.)

28. (Repealed by SOR/99-193, s. 2.)

Deductions from Benefits

28.1. (1) For the purposes of subsection 36(2) of the Act, the Minister may make a deduction from a benefit payable under the Act if

(*a*) the provincial authority or the municipal authority that paid the advance, assistance or welfare payments submits a record of the payment to the Minister, together with an irrevocable consent to the deduction signed by the person receiving the payment; (SOR/96-521, s. 16(1); SOR/99-193, s. 3.)

(*b*) the record and consent referred to in paragraph (*a*) are received by the Minister prior to the expiration of one year after the day on which the consent is signed;

(*c*) the Minister and the provincial authority or the municipal authority that paid the advance, assistance or welfare payment referred to in paragraph (*a*) have concluded an agreement in respect of the procedure to be followed in submitting records and consents; and (SOR/96-521, s. 16(2).)

(*d*) the amount deducted exceeds $50.

(2) For the purpose of subsection 36(2) of the Act, if, for any reason, no deduction has been made or a deduction and payment have been made by the Minister for an amount that is less than the amount that might have been paid under that subsection, the Minister shall not authorize any other deduction and payment. (SOR/99-193, s. 3; SOR/2002-221, s. 5.)

(SOR/89-269, s. 8; SOR/93-40, s. 1; SOR/96-521, s. 16; SOR/99-193, s. 3; SOR/2002-221, s. 5.)

Access to Privileged Information[3]

28.2. (Repealed by SOR/2013-20, s. 7.)

(SOR/99-193, s. 3; SOR/2013-20, s. 7.)

28.3. (Repealed by SOR/2013-20, s. 7.)

(SOR/2010-45, s. 24; SOR/2013-20, s. 7.)

Prescribed Federal Institutions and Federal Acts[4]

28.4. (Repealed by SOR/2013-20, s. 7.)

(SOR/2010-45, s. 24; SOR/2013-20, s. 7.)

Part II

Reconsiderations

Request for Reconsideration[5]

29. A request for a reconsideration under section 27.1 of the Act shall be made in writing and be conveyed to the Minister and shall set out

   (a) the name, address and Social Insurance Number or Account Number of the person; and

   (b) the grounds for the request for a reconsideration and a statement of the facts that form the basis of that request.

(SOR/96-521, s. 17; SOR/2000-133, s. 10.)

29.1. (1) For the purposes of subsection 27.1(1) and (1.1) of the Act and subject to subsection (2), the Minister may allow a longer period to make a request for reconsideration of a decision or determination if the Minister is satisfied that there is a reasonable explanation for requesting a longer period and the person has demonstrated a continuing intention to request a reconsideration. (SOR/2013-62, s. 1.)

(2) The Minister must also be satisfied that the request for reconsideration has a reasonable chance of success, and that no prejudice would be caused to the Minister or a party by allowing a longer period to make the request, if the request for reconsideration

   (a) is made after the 365-day period after the day on which the person is notified in writing of the decision or determination; or

   (b) is made by a person who has applied again for the same benefit.

(SOR/2013-62, s. 1.)

(3) The Minister may take any necessary steps to obtain information that the Minister may require to decide whether to allow a longer period to make a request for reconsideration. (SOR/2013-62, s. 1.)

(SOR/2013-62, s. 1.)

30. (Repealed by SOR/96-521, s. 18.)

---

[3] Heading added by SOR/2010-45, s. 23 and repealed by SOR/2013-20, s. 7.

[4] Heading added by SOR/2010-45, s. 24 and repealed by SOR/2013-20, s. 7.

[5] Heading added by SOR/2010-45, s. 25.

31. (Repealed by SOR/96-521, s. 18.)

32. (Repealed by SOR/96-521, s. 18.)

33. (Repealed by SOR/96-521, s. 18.)

34. (Repealed by SOR/96-521, s. 18.)

35. (Repealed by SOR/96-521, s. 18.)

36. (Repealed by SOR/96-521, s. 13.)

37. (Repealed by SOR/96-521, s. 18.)

Reference to Tax Court of Canada

38. If a ground of appeal referred to in subsection 28(2) of the Act is set out in an appeal brought under subsection 28(1) of the Act, the Social Security Tribunal must

(a) notify the appellant and the Minister that the appeal on that ground has been referred to the Court for decision under subsection 28(2) of the Act; and

(b) transmit to the Registrar of the Court a copy of the documents filed in the appeal that are relevant to the ground of appeal referred to in subsection 28(2) of the Act.

(SOR/96-521, s. 19; SOR/2013-62, s. 2.)

38.1. (1) Where an appeal is made in relation to a reference under subsection 28(2) of the Act and the Minister is of the opinion that a person other than the appellant may be directly affected by the decision of the Court, the Minister shall so notify the Social Security Tribunal. (SOR/2013-62, s. 5(a).)

(2) On notification, the Social Security Tribunal shall so notify the Registrar of the Court and the Registrar shall add that person as a party to the appeal. (SOR/2013-62, s. 5(a).)

(SOR/96-521, s. 19; SOR/2013-62, s. 5.)

39. (1) The Registrar of the Court, on receipt of the documents transmitted by the Social Security Tribunal pursuant to paragraph 38(b), shall immediately notify the Chief Judge of the Court, the Social Security Tribunal, the Minister and any person added as a party to the appeal of that receipt. (SOR/96-521, s. 20; SOR/2013-62, s. 5(b).)

(2) When the Chief Judge of the Court is notified pursuant to subsection (1), the Chief Judge shall appoint a judge of the Court to hear the reference.

(SOR/89-269, s. 11; SOR/96-521, s. 20; SOR/2013-62, s. 5.)

Date and Place of Reference

40. (1) The Registrar of the Court, in consultation with the judge of the Court appointed pursuant to subsection 39(2) to hear the reference, shall fix the date, time and place for the hearing of the reference. (SOR/89-269, s. 12(1).)

(2) The hearing of a reference shall be held in the city, town or village in which or nearest to which the appellant is ordinarily resident unless the appellant consents in writing to the hearing being held at some other place.

(3) The Registrar of the Court shall, by registered mail, notify the appellant, the Social Security Tribunal, the Minister and any person added as a party to the appeal

577

OAS REGULATIONS

of the date, place and time fixed for the hearing of the reference. (SOR/96-521, s. 21; SOR/2013-62, s. 5(*c*).)

(SOR/89-269, s. 12; SOR/96-521, s. 21; SOR/2013-62, s. 5.)

Procedure before Tax Court of Canada

41. **(1)** Proceedings before the Court shall be informal and shall be conducted in a summary manner.

(2) The judge appointed pursuant to subsection 39(2), subject to the right of all parties or their representatives to be heard, shall determine the procedure to be followed at the hearing of the reference.

(SOR/89-269, s. 13.)

42. The judge appointed pursuant to subsection 39(2) may, with the consent of the appellant, require that written submissions be filed by the appellant, the Minister and any person added as a party to the appeal in addition to or in lieu of an oral hearing.

(SOR/89-269, s. 22; SOR/96-521, s. 22.)

Decision of Tax Court of Canada

43. (Repealed by SOR/2000-133, s. 11.)

44. **(1)** The judge appointed pursuant to subsection 39(2) shall advise the Registrar of the Court of the judge's decision.

(2) The Registrar of the Court, after being advised of the decision in accordance with subsection (1), shall forward to the appellant, the Social Security Tribunal, the Minister and any person added as a party to the appeal a certified copy of the decision. (SOR/96-521, s. 24; SOR/2013-62, s. 5(*d*).)

(SOR/89-269, s. 13; SOR/96-521, s. 24; SOR/2013-62, s. 5.)

45. No costs shall be awarded on the disposition of a reference and no fees shall be charged to the appellant by the Court.

(SOR/89-269, s. 13.)

46. If an appeal sets out a ground of appeal that is not referred to the Court under subsection 28(2) of the Act and a ground of appeal that has been referred to the Court under that subsection, the Social Security Tribunal, on receipt of a certified copy of the decision of the Court, must proceed in accordance with the *Social Security Tribunal Regulations*.

(SOR/96-521, s. 25; SOR/2013-62, s. 3.)

47. All notices, requests and other documents shall be addressed to the person to whom they are required to be sent, forwarded or mailed at his last known address.

Interest on Amounts Owing to Her Majesty

48. **(1)** The following definitions apply in this section.

"average bank rate" means the simple arithmetic mean of the bank rates that are established during the month before the month in respect of which interest is being calculated.

578

"bank rate" means the rate of interest established weekly by the Bank of Canada as the minimum rate at which the Bank of Canada makes short-term advances to members of the Canadian Payments Association.

"debt" means

(a) a debt due under subsection 37(2) of the Act in respect of which a penalty has been imposed under section 44.1 of the Act; or

(b) a debt due under subsection 37(2.02) of the Act.

"demand for payment" means a demand for payment in writing and includes a notification of a decision to impose a penalty under section 44.1 of the Act or of the amount of a penalty imposed under that section.

"due date" means, in respect of a debt,

(a) where a payment schedule has been established, any day on which a scheduled payment is to be made; or

(b) where no payment schedule has been established, the day that is 120 days after the day on which a demand for payment was issued.

(SOR/2010-45, s. 26.)

(2) Interest is payable on all debts that are recoverable on or after the day on which this section comes into force. (SOR/2010-45, s. 26.)

(3) The accrual of interest on a debt, at the rate set out in subsection (4), begins on the due date. (SOR/2010-45, s. 26.)

(4) Interest accrues on a debt at a rate that is calculated daily and compounded monthly at the average bank rate plus three per cent. (SOR/2010-45, s. 26.)

(5) Interest does not accrue on a debt during the period in which a reconsideration under subsection 27.1(2) of the Act, an appeal under subsection 28(1) of the Act or section 55 of the *Department of Human Resources and Skills Development Act* or a judicial review under the *Federal Courts Act* is pending in respect of that debt. (SOR/2010-45, s. 26; SOR/2013-62, s. 4(1).)

(6) The accrual of interest on a debt or on a portion of the debt, as applicable, ceases on

(a) the day before the day on which a scheduled payment in respect of the debt or a payment of the debt in full is received by Her Majesty;

(b) the day on which the debt or the portion of the debt is remitted under subsection 37(4) of the Act;

(c) the day on which the penalty that constitutes the debt is reduced or the decision imposing that penalty is rescinded under

(i) subsection 44.1(4) of the Act, or

(ii) the latest of the following decisions in respect of a decision or determination of the Minister under section 44.1 of the Act:

(A) a decision of the Minister under subsection 27.1(2) of the Act, and

(B) a decision on an appeal under subsection 28(1) of the Act or section 55 of the *Department of Human Resources and Skills Development Act* or a judicial review under the *Federal Courts Act*; (SOR/2013-62, s. 4(2).)

(d) the day on which the accrued interest is remitted under subsection (7); or

(e) the day on which the debtor dies.

(SOR/2010-45, s. 26.)

OAS REGULATIONS

(7) The conditions under which the Minister may remit in whole or in part the interest payable under this section are that

(a) the interest has ceased to accrue in accordance with paragraph (6)(c);

(b) the interest cannot be collected within the reasonably foreseeable future;

(c) the administrative costs of collecting the interest would exceed the amount of that interest; and

(d) the payment of the interest would result in undue hardship to the debtor.

(SOR/2010-45, s. 26.)

(SOR/2010-45, s. 26; SOR/2013-62, s. 4.)

Schedule

(Sections 21 and 22)

(Repealed by SOR/96-521, s. 26.)

(Sections 22.01)

Country	Agreement
Antigua and Barbuda	Agreement on Social Security between Canada and Antigua and Barbuda, signed at Ottawa on September 2, 1992
Australia	Reciprocal Agreement on Social Security between the Government of Canada and the Government of Australia, signed at Canberra on July 4, 1988 Protocol amending the Reciprocal Agreement on Social Security between the Government of Canada and the Government of Australia, signed at Ottawa, on October 11, 1990
Austria (Republic of)	Agreement on Social Security between the Government of Canada and the Government of the Republic of Austria signed at Vienna on February 24, 1987 Supplementary Agreement to the Agreement on Social Security between Canada and the Republic of Austria, signed at Vienna on September 12, 1995
Barbados	Agreement on Social Security between the Government of Canada and the Government of Barbados, signed at Bridgetown on February 11, 1985
Belgium	Agreement on Social Security between the Government of Canada and the Government of Belgium, signed at Brussels on May 10, 1984
Chile (Republic of)	Agreement on Social Security between the Government of Canada and the Government of the Republic of Chile, signed on November 18, 1996
Croatia (Republic of)	Agreement on Social Security between the Government of Canada and the Government of the Republic of Croatia, signed on April 22, 1998
Cyprus (Republic of)	Agreement on Social Security between Canada and the Republic of Cyprus, signed at Ottawa on January 24, 1990
Denmark	Agreement on Social Security between the Government of Canada and the Government of Denmark, signed at Copenhagen on April 12, 1985
Dominica (Commonwealth of)	Agreement on Social Security between the Government of Canada and the Government of the Commonwealth of Dominica, signed at Roseau on January 14, 1988
Finland (Republic of)	Agreement on Social Security between the Government of Canada and the Government of the Republic of Finland, signed at Ottawa on October 28, 1986
France	Agreement on Social Security between the Government of Canada and the Government of France, signed at Ottawa on February 9, 1979
Germany (Federal Republic of)	Agreement on Social Security between the Government of Canada and the Government of the Federal Republic of Germany, signed at Bonn on November 14, 1985
Greece (Hellenic Republic)	Agreement on Social Security between Canada and the Hellenic Republic, signed at Toronto on November 10, 1995

Country	Agreement
Grenada	Agreement on Social Security between the Government of Canada and the Government of Grenada, signed on January 8, 1998
Guernsey	Agreement on Social Security between Jersey, Guernsey and Canada, in force in Canada as of January 1, 1994
Iceland	Agreement on Social Security between the Government of Canada and the Government of Iceland, signed at Gimli on June 25, 1988
Ireland	Agreement on Social Security between Canada and Ireland, signed at Ottawa on November 29, 1990
Israel	Interim Agreement on Social Security between the Government of Canada and the Government of Israel, signed at Jerusalem on April 9, 2000
Italy (Italian Republic)	Agreement on Social Security between Canada and Italy, signed at Toronto on November 17, 1977 Agreement on Social Security between Canada and the Italian Republic, signed at Rome on May 22, 1995
Jamaica	Agreement between the Government of Canada and the Government of Jamaica with respect to Social Security, signed at Kingston, Jamaica on January 10, 1983
Jersey	Agreement on Social Security between Jersey, Guernsey and Canada, in force in Canada as of January 1, 1994
Korea (Republic of)	Agreement on Social Security between Canada and the Republic of Korea, signed at Seoul on January 10, 1997
Luxembourg	Agreement on Social Security between the Government of Canada and the Government of Luxembourg, signed at Ottawa on May 22, 1986
Malta (Republic of)	Agreement on Social Security between Canada and the Republic of Malta, signed at Toronto on April 4, 1991
Mexico (United Mexican States)	Agreement on Social Security between Canada and the United Mexican States, signed at Ottawa on April 25, 1995
Morocco (Kingdom of)	Convention on Social Security between the Government of Canada and the Government of the Kingdom of Morocco, signed on July 1, 1998
Netherlands (Kingdom of the)	Agreement on Social Security between the Government of Canada and the Government of the Kingdom of the Netherlands, signed at The Hague on February 26, 1987
New Zealand	Agreement on Social Security between Canada and New Zealand, signed on April 9, 1996
Norway (Kingdom of)	Agreement on Social Security between the Government of Canada and the Government of the Kingdom of Norway, signed at Oslo on November 12, 1985
Philippines (Republic of the)	Agreement on Social Security between Canada and the Republic of the Philippines, signed at Winnipeg on September 9, 1994 Supplementary Agreement to the Agreement on Social Security between the Government of Canada and the Government of the Republic of the Philippines, signed at Winnipeg on November 13, 1999
Portugal	Agreement between Canada and Portugal with respect to Social Security, signed at Toronto on December 15, 1980

Country	Agreement
Saint Lucia	Agreement on Social Security between the Government of Canada and the Government of Saint Lucia, signed at Castries on January 5, 1987
Saint-Vincent and the Grenadines	Agreement on Social Security between the Government of Canada and the Government of Saint-Vincent and the Grenadines, signed on January 6, 1998
Slovenia (Republic of)	Agreement on Social Security between the Government of Canada and the Government of the Republic of Slovenia, signed on May 17, 1998
Spain	Protocol to the Convention on Social Security between Canada and Spain, signed at Ottawa on October 19, 1995
St. Kitts and Nevis (Federation of)	Agreement on Social Security between Canada and the Federation of St. Kitts and Nevis, signed at Ottawa on August 17, 1992
Sweden	Agreement on Social Security between the Government of Canada and the Government of Sweden, signed at Stockholm on April 10, 1985
Switzerland (Swiss Confederation)	Convention on Social Security between Canada and the Swiss Confederation, signed at Ottawa on February 24, 1994
Trinidad and Tobago (Republic of)	Agreement on Social Security between the Government of Canada and the Government of the Republic of Trinidad and Tobago, signed on April 9, 1997
Turkey (Republic of)	Agreement on Social Security between the Government of Canada and the Government of the Republic of Turkey, signed on June 19, 1998
United Kingdom of Great Britain and Northern Ireland	Memorandum of Understanding between the Government of Canada and the Government of the United Kingdom of Great Britain and Northern Ireland concerning Co-operation and Mutual Assistance in the Administration of Social Security Programmes, signed on January 16, 1997
United States of America	Agreement between the Government of Canada and the Government of the United States of America with respect to Social Security, signed at Ottawa on March 11, 1981
	Supplementary Agreement between the Government of Canada and the Government of the United States of America with respect to Social Security, signed at Ottawa on May 10, 1983 Second Supplementary Agreement amending the Agreement between the Government of Canada and the Government of the United States of America with respect to Social Security, signed on May 28, 1996
	Administrative Understanding on Mutual Assistance, concluded pursuant to the Agreement between the Government of Canada and the Government of the United States of America with respect to Social Security and signed on December 4, 1996
Uruguay (Eastern Republic of)	Agreement on Social Security between the Government of Canada and the Government of the Eastern Republic of Uruguay, signed at Ottawa on June 2, 1999

(SOR/2000-412, s. 13.)

Department of Employment and Social Development Act [1] (Parts 5 and 6)

S.C. 2005, c. 34, Parts 5 and 6 as replaced by 2012, c. 19, s. 224, effective June 29, 2012.

Part 5

Social Security Tribunal

Establishment and Administration

44. *Establishment of Tribunal* — **(1) There is established a tribunal to be known as the Social Security Tribunal, consisting of a General Division and an Appeal Division. (2012, c. 19, s. 224.)**

(2) *General Division* — **The General Division consists of the Income Security Section and the Employment Insurance Section. (2012, c. 19, s. 224.)**

(2012, c. 19, s. 224.)

——————————— Notes ———————————

Case Law

Atkinson v. Canada (Attorney General), 2014 FCA 187

The creation of the SST represents a major overhaul of the appeal processes regarding claims for Employment Insurance and income security benefits. It was intended to provide a more efficient, simplified, and streamlined appeal processes for CPP, OASA, and Employment Insurance decisions by offering a single point of contact for submitting an appeal. The changes made are not limited to the composition and structure of the SST, but also to the rules of practice.

45. *Composition* — **(1)** The Tribunal consists of not more than 74 full-time members to be appointed by the Governor in Council. **(2012, c. 19, s. 224.)**

(2) *Chairperson and Vice-chairpersons* — The Governor in Council designates one of the full-time members to hold office as the Chairperson and three full-time members to hold office as Vice-chairpersons, one of whom is responsible for the Appeal Division, one of whom is responsible for the Income Security Section and one of whom is responsible for the Employment Insurance Section. **(2012, c. 19, s. 224.)**

(3) *Part-time members* — In addition, the Tribunal consists of any number of part-time members, to be appointed by the Governor in Council if, in the Governor in Council's opinion, the workload of the Tribunal so requires, so long as the combined time devoted to their functions and

[1] Title changed from *Department of Human Resources and Skills Development Act* by S.C. 2013, c. 40, s. 205.

duties does not exceed the combined time that would be devoted by 11 full-time members. **(2012, c. 19, s. 224.)**

(4) *Mandate* — Each full-time member of the Tribunal is to be appointed for a term of not more than five years, and each part-time member is to be appointed for a term of not more than two years. A member may be reappointed for one or more additional terms. **(2012, c. 19, s. 224.)**

(5) *Tenure* — Each member of the Tribunal holds office during good behaviour and may be removed for cause by the Governor in Council at any time. **(2012, c. 19, s. 224.)**

(2012, c. 19, s. 224.)

46. *Vice-chairpersons* — **(1)** Each Vice-chairperson exercises any powers and performs any duties and functions that the Chairperson may assign. **(2012, c. 19, s. 224.)**

(2) *Members* — Each member exercises any powers and performs any duties and functions that the Vice-chairperson who is responsible for the Division or Section for which they hear matters may assign. **(2012, c. 19, s. 224.)**

(3) *Assignment* — Subject to section 47, the Chairperson may assign members to hear matters in the Appeal Division, the Income Security Section or the Employment Insurance Section. **(2012, c. 19, s. 224.)**

(2012, c. 19, s. 224.)

47. *Employment Insurance Section* — The Minister must consult a committee composed of the Chairperson of the Tribunal and the commissioners referred to in paragraphs 20(2)(c) and (d) before recommending to the Governor in Council any person to be appointed as a member of the Tribunal who may hear matters in the Employment Insurance Section.

(2012, c. 19, s. 224.)

48. *Full-time occupation* — **(1)** Each full-time member of the Tribunal must devote the whole of their time to the performance of their duties under this Act. **(2012, c. 19, s. 224.)**

(2) *Part-time members* — A part-time member of the Tribunal must not accept or hold any office or employment inconsistent with their duties under this Act. **(2012, c. 19, s. 224.)**

(2012, c. 19, s. 224.)

49. *Remuneration* — **(1)** Each member of the Tribunal is paid the remuneration fixed by the Governor in Council. **(2012, c. 19, s. 224.)**

(2) *Expenses — full-time members* — Each full-time member of the Tribunal is entitled to be paid reasonable travel and living expenses incurred by them while absent from their ordinary place of work in the course of performing their duties under this Act. **(2012, c. 19, s. 224.)**

(3) *Expenses — part-time members* — Each part-time member of the Tribunal is entitled to be paid reasonable travel and living expenses incurred by them while absent from their ordinary place of residence in the course of performing their duties under this Act. **(2012, c. 19, s. 224.)**

(4) *Federal public administration* — Members of the Tribunal are deemed to be employed in the federal public administration for the purposes of the *Government Employees Compensation Act* and any regulations made under section 9 of the *Aeronautics Act*. **(2012, c. 19, s. 224.)**

(5) *Not employed in public service* — Unless the Governor in Council otherwise orders in a class of cases, members of the Tribunal are deemed not to be employed in the public service for the purposes of the *Public Service Superannuation Act.* **(2012, c. 19, s. 224.)**

(2012, c. 19, s. 224.)

50. *Immunity* — No civil proceedings lie against any member of the Tribunal for anything done or said in good faith in the exercise or purported exercise of a power or in the performance or purported performance of a duty or function of the Tribunal.

(2012, c. 19, s. 224.)

51. *Absence — Chairperson* — **(1)** In the event of the absence or incapacity of the Chairperson or if the office of Chairperson is vacant, the Vice-chairperson of the Appeal Division acts as Chairperson and may exercise all the powers and perform all the duties and functions of the Chairperson. **(2012, c. 19, s. 224.)**

(2) *Absence — other* — If subsection (1) does not apply owing to the absence or incapacity of the Vice-chairperson of the Appeal Division, or if the office of Vice-chairperson of the Appeal Division is vacant, the Minister may authorize another Vice-chairperson to act as Chairperson and that Vice-chairperson may exercise all the powers and perform all the duties and functions of the Chairperson. **(2012, c. 19, s. 224.)**

(3) *Absence — Vice-chairperson* — In the event of the absence or incapacity of a Vice-chairperson or if the office of a Vicechairperson is vacant, the Chairperson may authorize a member to act, on any terms and conditions that the Chairperson may specify, as Vice-chairperson for the time being. **(2012, c. 19, s. 224.)**

(2012, c. 19, s. 224.)

Organization of Tribunal

Appeal to Tribunal — General Division

52. *Appeal — Time limit* — **(1)** An appeal of a decision must be brought to the General Division in the prescribed form and manner and within,

   (a) in the case of a decision made under the *Employment Insurance Act*, 30 days after the day on which it is communicated to the appellant; and

   (b) in any other case, 90 days after the day on which the decision is communicated to the appellant.

(2012, c. 19, s. 224.)

(2) *Extension* — The General Division may allow further time within which an appeal may be brought, but in no case may an appeal be brought more than one year after the day on which the decision is communicated to the appellant. **(2012, c. 19, s. 224.)**

(2012, c. 19, s. 224.)

———————— **Notes** ————————

The 90-day limit for CPP and OAS appeals from a Ministerial reconsideration is the same as under the previous scheme. However, the absolute limit of one year is new.

DESD ACT

Related Social Security Tribunal Regulations

- Section 4 (Requests to Tribunal)
- Sections 5–9 (Filing with Tribunal)
- Section 23 (Filing of appeal)
- Section 24 (Appeal form and contents)
- Section 25 (Extension of time for bringing appeal)
- Section 26 (Documents to be filed by Minister)
- Section 27 (Time to respond)
- Section 28 (Decision or further hearing)
- Section 29 (Decision made without delay)

Case Law

[Editor's note: The following cases were decided under the previous CPP ss. 82–84, now repealed.]

§1. Extension of Time to Appeal

Canada (Attorney General) v. Berhe, 2008 FC 967

The proper test on granting an extension of time to appeal the Minister's redetermination to the Review Tribunal is whether the applicant has demonstrated:

1. a continuing intention to pursue his or her application;
2. that the application has some merit;
3. that no prejudice to the respondent arises from the delay; and
4. that a reasonable explanation for the delay exists.

However, the underlying consideration which must be borne in mind in dealing with the application is whether, in the circumstances presented, to do justice between the parties calls for the grant of the extension. A strong case on the merits may counterbalance a less satisfactory justification for the delay. The standard of review as to whether a Commissioner has considered the proper factors in the exercise of his discretion to extend time for an appeal to the Review Tribunal is a question of law and should consequently be reviewed on a standard of correctness.

Canada (Attorney General) v. Pentney, 2008 FC 96

The Commissioner should give reasons to the Minister for extending the time to appeal, particularly in the case of a lengthy delay, or to the applicant explaining the reasons for refusing an extension of time. For high-volume decision-makers such as the Commissioner, the recommendations of investigatory officials can constitute adequate reasons, if the recommendations are accepted by the Commissioner. An extension after three years was not warranted where the claimant had not appealed in the interim because he was already receiving disability benefits from a private insurer.

Canada (Attorney General) v. Blondahl, 2009 FC 118

Motions for an extension are often dealt with in brief orders by the Federal Court, and there is generally no need for extensive reasons in such cases. What is important is that a decision that is subject to judicial review must contain enough to enable the parties to assess their possible grounds of review and for the court to exercise its jurisdiction. The Review Tribunal should, at minimum, adopt the practice of stating the test it applied by simply referring to a decision in which it is articulated, such as *Pentney.* In addition, it should state which of the four factors set out in this test the Tribunal found to be determinative in the exercise of its discretion as well as any other case-specific factors it found determinative. The existence of a continuing intention to pursue an appeal will often come to light when a prospective appellant explains why he or she did not in fact appeal earlier.

Canada (Attorney General) v. Schneider, 2008 FC 764

The decision of the Commissioner of the Review Tribunal to allow a longer period than 90 days to submit an appeal from the Minister respecting certain pension benefits is largely administrative in nature and, while requiring consideration of established legal criteria for granting an extension, the Commissioner must look at the factual circumstances of each case to make a determination which, as such, is a matter of mixed fact and law. The determination is one of an administrative nature such that it should be reviewed on a standard of reasonableness with substantial deference afforded to the Commissioner.

Halcro v. MNHW (April 26, 1988), CP 1057 (PAB)

The Minister is entitled to exercise discretion not to extend the time for appealing where the claimant was able to appeal the initial decision, but chose not to do so owing to a lack of medical evidence at the time to confirm his or her disability. New evidence which subsequently became available did not constitute new facts which would allow for the reopening of the original decision.

---

53. *Dismissal* — **(1) The General Division must summarily dismiss an appeal if it is satisfied that it has no reasonable chance of success. (2012, c. 19, s. 224.)**

(2) *Decision* — **The General Division must give written reasons for its decision and send copies to the appellant and the Minister or the Commission, as the case may be, and any other party. (2012, c. 19, s. 224.)**

(3) *Appeal* — **The appellant may appeal the decision to the Appeal Division. (2012, c. 19, s. 224.)**

(2012, c. 19, s. 224.)

Notes

This section has no counterpart under the previous scheme. It provocatively suggests that not every claimant will be entitled to "have his or her day in court." Such summary treatment might fairly be applied to the situation where the claimant is seeking relief which is legally beyond the jurisdiction of the SST to provide. Where the issues in dispute are factual in nature, or mixed fact and law, it is likely that a higher court would rule that a full hearing is mandatory under the Charter — see *Singh v. Minister of Employment and Immigration,* [1985] 1 SCR 177.

Related Social Security Tribunal Regulations

- Section 22 (Summary dismissal)
- Section 34 (Appeal of summary dismissal)
- Section 35 (Appeal form and contents)
- Section 36 (Time to respond)
- Section 37 (Decision or further hearing)
- Section 38 (Decision made without delay)

---

54. *Decision* — **(1) The General Division may dismiss the appeal or confirm, rescind or vary a decision of the Minister or the Commission in whole or in part or give the decision that the Minister or the Commission should have given. (2012, c. 19, s. 224.)**

(2) *Reasons* — **The General Division must give written reasons for its decision and send copies to the appellant and the Minister or the Commission, as the case may be, and any other party. (2012, c. 19, s. 224.)**

───────────── **Notes** ─────────────

Synopsis

This section is similar to the former CPP s. 84(11), and confers power on the SST General Division to affirm, overturn, or vary a Minister's decision. Subsection (2) codifies the requirement of written reasons.

Related Social Security Tribunal Regulations

- Section 3 (Informal conduct)
- Section 4 (Requests to Tribunal)
- Section 10 (Adding parties)
- Section 11 (Requests to adjourn or postpone)
- Section 12 (Failure to appear)
- Section 13 (Joining of appeals or applications)
- Section14 (Withdrawal)
- Section 15 (Pre-hearing conference)
- Section 16 (Dispute resolution)
- Section 17 (Settlement conference)
- Section 18 (Agreement between parties)
- Section 19 (When decisions deemed communicated)
- Section 20 (Notice of constitutional issues — filing and service)
- Section 21 (Form of hearing)

Case Law

§0.1. Proceedings in the SST

Y.Z. v. Minister of Human Resources and Skills Development, 2013 SSTAD 4 (CanLII)

Section 4 of the SST Regulations provides that a party may request the tribunal to provide for any matter concerning a proceeding. Section 68 of the CPP Regulations provides that where a claimant claims that she is disabled, she shall supply certain information to the Minister. This includes information regarding her occupation and earnings, and to undergo such special examinations and provide reports as the Minister deems necessary for the purpose of determining the disability of that person. It was appropriate to dismiss the claim where the claimant failed to respond to numerous requests by the Minister to provide a Consent for Service Canada to Obtain Personal Information, a Consent to Attend an Independent Medical Examination ("IME"), and a Request Sheet for Additional Information CPP Disability ("Questionnaire").

M.Z. v. Minister of Human Resources and Skills Development (August 29, 2014) AD-13-33 (SSTAD)

A claimant had been denied a full opportunity to present his case where he was given only 45 minutes to argue his case, despite the fact that no complaint of procedural fairness was made at the RT hearing.

[Editor's note: The following cases were decided under the previous CPP ss. 82–84, now repealed.]

§1. Powers and Jurisdiction of Review Tribunal

Canada (Minister of Human Resources Development) v. Dublin Estate, 2006 FC 152

Under s. 82(11), a Review Tribunal may confirm or vary a decision of the Minister made under OASA s. 27.1(2), and may take any action in relation to that decision that might have been taken by the Minister under that subsection. Under OASA s. 27.1(2), a Minister may confirm or vary the initial decision, and may approve payment of a benefit, determine the amount of a benefit, or determine that no benefit is payable.

The Review Tribunal did not have jurisdiction to order the Minister to make an *ex gratia* payment.

Canada (Attorney General) v. Vinet-Proulx, 2007 FC 99

The issues of determining on what date an application for benefits was sent by an applicant and of determining on what date the application in question was received by the Department are questions of fact that are within the jurisdiction of the Review Tribunal. It may decide the issue on the basis of the testimonies heard and the documents filed, or even on the basis of presumptions, on a balance of probabilities. The Review Tribunal does not have any jurisdiction in equity and may not, for example, order the Minister to make an *ex gratia* payment.

Upshall v. Canada (Attorney General), 2009 FCA 284

The Review Tribunal under CPP ss. 81 and 82 may, amongst other things, hear the appeal of a former spouse who is dissatisfied with any decision made under s. 55.1, where the essence of the former spouse's argument was that the Minister's interpretation of s. 55.1 was unfair, discriminatory, and wrong in law. Only if the argument was that the benefit had been denied due to departmental error did the Tribunal lack jurisdiction to consider the appeal.

Pincombe v. Canada (Attorney General) (October 21, 1994), CP 3291, CEB & PG (TB) ¶8555 (PAB)

The decision to remedy or not in CPP s. 66 is placed wholly within the Minister's department. Neither the Review Tribunal nor the PAB have jurisdiction to hear appeals from the Minister's decision or to interfere with the discretion exercised.

MSD v. Kendall (June 7, 2004), CP 21960 (PAB)

The Review Tribunal's power under s. 82(11) to confirm or vary a Minister's decision under s. 81 does not include the jurisdiction to conduct a roving appellate power over a prior application brought by the claimant which has ended in a refusal by the Minister. The term "decision" as used in s. 82(1) means a decision on the merits and cannot include a discretionary ruling of the Minister to refuse to entertain an application for a reconsideration because it was out of time.

Robsob-Belfrey v. MHRD (January 8, 2004), CP 15822 (PAB)

Where the Minister had never, on the record, considered and given a decision in writing on the issue of capacity, no appeal could be heard. Such a step was a necessary basis for the appeal procedure, and neither the Review Tribunal nor the PAB had jurisdiction to determine the matter without a formal decision of the Minister. Even though all parties were prepared to proceed on the issues, their consent could not confer jurisdiction on the PAB.

Graham v. MHRD (June 1997), CP 5230, CEB & PG ¶8692 (PAB)

The Review Tribunal is a statutory tribunal that must find its jurisdiction in the CPP. It does not possess any equitable jurisdiction, and therefore lacks the authority to forgive the repayment of disability benefits that have been paid in error to a claimant.

Doherty v. MEI (July 15, 1996), CP 4207, CEB & PG (TB) ¶8651 (PAB)

A decision of the Minister, under s. 81, includes a s. 55.3 decision, and therefore the Review Tribunal has jurisdiction to review a s. 55.3 Ministerial decision.

§2. Practice and Procedure

Duncan v. Canada (Attorney General), 2013 FC 319

Settlement privilege attaches to settlement offers by the Minister expressly made "without prejudice" which offered a partial OAS pension, and such privilege is not waived by the decision of the Tribunal to include them in its hearing record. Had the Tribunal not found that the settlement offer was privileged, it would not have been bound to adopt the position regarding the claimant's years of residence in Canada expressed in the Minister's letter, but it would at least have been required to assess and explain why it has come to a different conclusion.

Callihoo v. Canada (Attorney General) (2000), FC T-859-99 (Fed. T.D.)

Even if one member of the Review Tribunal demonstrated little or no knowledge of one of the conditions claimed to affect the applicant, that in itself raises no grounds for finding bias or a lack of impartiality on the part of that one member or of the three-person tribunal. There is no requirement that a member of the Tribunal have knowledge of each of the many conditions that underlie a claim for disability benefits. A member's decision is not based on his or her own understanding of medical conditions, but upon his or her assessment of the reports of medical examiners, which are provided in the main by the applicant for benefits. The Tribunal's ultimate decision is dependent upon the medical evidence in the record, and particular factual errors made by the Tribunal are not basic to this decision.

Sudnik v. MHRD (January 23, 2004), CP 19633 (PAB)

There is no statutory requirement that Review Tribunal hearings be recorded. As the appeal from the Review Tribunal to the Pension Appeals Board is by way of trial *de novo*, a transcript would not be necessary or required, except in exceptional cases. A claimant is not denied a fair hearing at the Review Tribunal level because there was no transcript. On an Application for Leave to Appeal or Judicial Review, the claimant could put forward all the facts by way of affidavit evidence. The deponents could be cross-examined on their affidavits.

St. Gelais v. MEI (September 13, 1994), CP 3046, CEB & PG (TB) ¶8558

All issues should be determined at each stage of the process to avoid unnecessarily prolonging what is already a lengthy process. This includes the making of a finding as to whether disability exists where the Review Tribunal dismissed the claim on the ground that the claimant had not made the minimum contributions within the qualifying period.

Headlam v. MEI (July 12, 1996), CP 3506, CEB & PG (TB) ¶8638

Res judicata applies to decisions of the Review Tribunal, which by virtue of s. 84(1) are as final and binding for all purposes of the CPP as a decision of the PAB. If there are new facts, then an application would have to made to the Review Tribunal that heard the matter in the first instance.

§3. Adjournments

Groke v. MHRD (October 29, 2001), CP 15563 (PAB)

Where the Review Tribunal failed to adjourn the hearing after stating that the evidence in the hearing was incomplete in that testing of the applicant had not been completed, the Tribunal's decision was not "final and binding" within the meaning of s. 84(1) and was not subject to *res judicata*.

Baptista v. MHRD (May 14, 1999), CP 07159 (PAB)

Due to the backlog of cases, the PAB must exercise discretion when granting adjournments.

Walters v. MHRD (November 4, 1996), CP 2639, CEB & PG (TB) ¶8655 (PAB)

The claimant's failure to comply with the requirements for raising a constitutional issue, after being granted two adjournments, was ground for dismissal of the appeal. The granting of a further adjournment in such circumstances would amount to an abuse of process.

§4. Language of Proceedings

Beaudoin v. Canada (MNHW), [1993] 3 FC 518 (C.A.)

Section 14 of the *Official Languages Act* entitles any person to use his or her official language of choice before a federal tribunal, and s. 15 obligates the tribunal to ensure that such evidence is heard as requested. An unrepresented party's *bona fide* request, on notice, for a hearing in the other official language must always be respected in full, and its denial amounts to a denial of natural justice, since it fetters the requesting party's ability to present a case in his or her own way. The PAB is required to take such a request at face value and not attempt to persuade the claimant to accept a hearing in English.

Garcia v. Canada (Attorney General), [2001] FCA 200

Courts are not required, as a matter of course, to inform a party of his or her right to an interpreter or to inquire as to whether a party is having trouble understanding the proceedings. Where a self-represented party has presented his or her case in previous proceedings with success, and never asked for an interpreter and it was not evident that assistance was required, the PAB did not lose jurisdiction by determining the case without providing an interpreter.

Gill v. Canada (Attorney General), 2011 FCA 195

Where a translator is used for the claimant's testimony, problems of interpretation at the hearing should have been raised at the first opportunity.

Casasanta v. Canada (Minister of Human Resources Development), 2002 FCA 495

On the date of the claimant's hearing before the PAB on a disability pension claim, he was affected by pain medications to the extent that he was unable to follow the proceedings. He also has difficulty with English, his first language being Italian, was self-represented and thus was unfamiliar with the procedures. The claim was denied by the PAB. Although there was no reason to believe that the PAB was aware of any the claimant's difficulties, and he did not advise the PAB of these problems or ask for an adjournment, the claimant cannot be said to have had a fair hearing in such highly unusual circumstances. No fault was to be ascribed to the PAB.

(2012, c. 19, s. 224.)

Appeal Division

55. *Appeal* — **Any decision of the General Division may be appealed to the Appeal Division by any person who is the subject of the decision and any other prescribed person.**

Notes

This section authorizes the bringing of appeals of decisions by the General Division, but is subject to the leave requirement imposed by section 56.

Related Social Security Tribunal Regulations

- Section 42 (Time to respond after leave granted)
- Section 43 (Decision or further hearing)
- Section 44 (Decision made without delay)

(2012, c. 19, s. 224.)

56. *Leave* — **(1) An appeal to the Appeal Division may only be brought if leave to appeal is granted. (2012, c. 19, s. 224.)**

(2) *Exception* — **Despite subsection (1), no leave is necessary in the case of an appeal brought under subsection 53(3) [summary dismissal by General Division]. (2012, c. 19, s. 224.)**

(2012, c. 19, s. 224.)

Notes

This section imposes a leave requirement on appeals from decisions of the General Division, except for summary dismissals. This carries forward the leave requirement on appeals to the Pension Appeals Board from the Review Tribunal.

Related Social Security Tribunal Regulations

- Section 39 (Leave to appeal)

- Section 41 (Written questions and submissions)

Case Law

§0.1. Leave to Appeal to SST Appeal Division

(a) General Principles

M.C.M. v. Minister of Human Resources and Skills Development, 2013 SSTAD 2

According to subsections 56(1) and 58(3) of the DHRSDA, "an appeal to the Appeal Division may only be brought if leave to appeal is granted" and "the Appeal Division must either grant or refuse leave to appeal". Subsection 58(2) provides that "leave to appeal is refused if the Appeal Division is satisfied that the appeal has no reasonable chance of success". In assessing the application, the Appeal Division is guided by previous decisions of the Federal Court (see below), which have decided that to be granted leave to appeal, the applicant must demonstrate that one ground of appeal has a reasonable chance of success. This can be done by adducing new evidence, or identifying an error of law or an error of significant fact made by the tribunal below. If new evidence is put forward, it must be such that it raises a genuine doubt as to whether the tribunal below would have reached the decision it did. The tribunal deciding whether to grant leave to appeal ought not to substitute its view of the persuasive value of the evidence for that of the tribunal who made the findings of fact. Such an argument does not raise a ground of appeal that has a reasonable chance of success.

(b) Example Situations

M.C.M. v. Minister of Human Resources and Skills Development, 2013 SSTAD 2

On an application for disability benefits, the recent diagnosis that the claimant has had Bipolar II, undiagnosed, for 35 years raised a genuine doubt as to whether the tribunal below would have reached the decision rejecting the claim it did had this information been before it.

[Editor's note: The following cases were decided under the previous CPP ss. 82–84, now repealed.]

§1. Test for Granting Leave

Martin v. Canada (MHRD), [1999] F.C.J. No. 1972 (Fed. C.A.)

On an application for leave to appeal the decision of the Review Tribunal, it is an error for the Vice-Chairman to consider whether the applicant for leave could succeed on the merits of the application. It is sufficient for the applicant to raise an arguable case or question of law or jurisdiction.

Canada (Attorney General) v. Kermenides, 2009 FC 429

The words set out in the reasons given for refusal to grant leave should not be reduced to a mantra. The member refusing leave should not be required to follow a strict formula or be tied strictly to words such as "some arguable ground" and should not use words such as "no reasonable chance on appeal". The reasons provided should make it clear to the reader that the member, in arriving at the decision whether to refuse leave, was not deciding the merits of the matter itself, but was determining whether a party could make some reasonable argument challenging the merits of the decision of the Review Tribunal.

Canada (Attorney General) v. Pelland, 2008 FC 1164

On a leave application, the PAB must determine whether there is some arguable ground on which the appeal might succeed. It should not decide whether the applicant could actually succeed.

Canada (Minister of Human Resources Development) v. Hogervorst, 2007 FCA 41

While Rule 7 of the *Pension Appeals Board Rules of Procedure (Benefits)* expressly states that an application for leave to appeal "shall be disposed of *ex parte* unless the Chairman or Vice-Chairman directs otherwise", the process should be guided by some common sense. Where more than seven years and a multitude of proceedings had elapsed since the rendering of the decision sought to be appealed, and the Minister was at all times a party to all the proceedings, the member of the PAB to whom the application for leave to appeal was brought should have sought a direction from either the Chairman or the Vice-Chairman as to the appropriateness of seeking submissions from the Minister in response to the application. This would ensure fairness to the Minister and increase the likelihood of a more enlightened decision as well as promote the credibility of the PAB itself.

Canada (Attorney General) v. Deschamp, 2007 FC 610

On a leave application, the PAB has jurisdiction to grant leave to appeal where it is alleged that the Review Tribunal erred in conducting a reconsideration hearing in the absence of a specific request by the claimant and that it erred in finding new facts.

Davies v. Canada (MHRD) (1999), FC T-1789-98

Subsections 83(1) and (2) clearly provide the statutory authority for the Chairman, Vice-Chairman, or member designate to make the decision of whether to grant or deny leave to appeal. The wording of these sections, combined with that of the final and binding clause in subsection 84(1), give the PAB a clear mandate to assess applications for leave to appeal.

Kerth v. Canada (MHRD), [1999] F.C.J. No. 1252 (T.D.). See also *Kurniewicz v. Canada (MMI)* (1974), 6 N.R. 225 (F.C.A.).

A leave to appeal proceeding is a preliminary step to a hearing on the merits, and is therefore is a first and lower hurdle for the applicant to meet than the one that must be met on the hearing of the appeal on the merits. Some arguable ground upon which the proposed appeal might succeed is needed in order for leave to be granted.

Callihoo v. Canada (Attorney General) (2000), FC T-859-99 (Fed. T.D.)

The proper test on an application for leave to appeal to the PAB from the Review Tribunal is whether the application raises an arguable case, without otherwise assessing the merits of the application. In the absence of significant new or additional evidence not considered by the Review Tribunal, an application for leave may raise an arguable case where the leave decision-maker finds the application raises a question of an error of law, measured by a standard of correctness, or an error of significant fact that is unreasonable or perverse in light of the evidence.

Mrak v. Canada (Minister of Human Resources Development), 2007 FC 672

The grant of leave is an interlocutory proceeding which does not decide the merits of an appeal which, itself, in the case of the Board is conducted *de novo.* The test in *Callihoo* is appropriate in the context of an application for judicial review challenging the grant of leave, with the additional requirement that the applicant must establish special circumstances to justify such a judicial review. The policy of the law is that unless there are special circumstances there should not be an appeal or immediate judicial review of an interlocutory judgment.

Kiefer v. Canada (Attorney General), 2008 FC 786

Section 83(1) carves out an exception regarding the right to seek leave to appeal to the PAB with respect to appeals under s. 28(1) of the *OAS Act.*

Canada (Attorney General) v. Farrell, 2006 FC 636

Under section 7 of the PAB's Rules of Procedure, it is either the Chairman or Vice-Chairman of the PAB that decides whether an application for leave for appeal to the PAB should be disposed of otherwise than *ex parte.* Where an application has been long-standing, the applicant's leave to appeal motion should not be *ex parte.*

Wihksne v. Canada (Attorney General) (2000), T-1451-99 (Fed. T.D.)

In refusing a leave application, the PAB is not restricted to using the exact words of the statute in citing the legal test of disability, as long it indicates that the Review Tribunal's decision was based on the weight of the evidence, that the laws were established, that the weight is a matter for the Tribunal hearing the case, and that the case before it was not an arguable case in which one can say that the weight should have been otherwise.

O'Leary v. MHRD, (February 24, 2003), CP 19041 (PAB)

The granting of leave by a lone judge of the PAB cured any defect in an appeal from a redetermination by the Review Tribunal under s. 84(2) based on new facts, because the judge must have realized, on reading the materials filed with the PAB, that leave should be granted from the original decision of the Review Tribunal and did so.

Canada (Minister of Human Resources Development) v. Ash, 2002 FCA 462

Where the decision granting leave noted one of the issues as being "If the Review Tribunal was wrong in its interpretation of the effect of division of the unadjusted pensionable earnings attributed to her, is she entitled to a disability pension by reason of her June 1989 stroke (as acknowledged by the Tribunal) by reason of the application of Section 44(1)(*b*)(iii) and what is the effective date of the payment of the first disability benefit?", the PAB was entitled to grant the claimant a disability pension automatically upon finding that the claimant had met the contributory requirements. While one could read the words "as acknowledged by the Tribunal" as referring only to the 1989 stroke and not to the fact that the disability itself had been acknowledged by the Tribunal, it could not be said that the PAB's reading and understanding of that paragraph was unreasonable, let alone improper.

§2. Practice and Procedure

Canada (Attorney General) v. Handa, 2006 FC 1148

In order for the doctrine of *functus officio* to apply, there must have been a final decision made by the PAB. The PAB's assumption that the applicant was no longer interested in pursuing the leave application did not constitute a final decision on the application for leave.

Canada v. Small, 2007 FC 678. See also *Canada (Minister of Human Resources Development) v. Roy,* 2005 FC 1456

An arguable issue cannot simply be assumed. Granting leave to appeal in the absence of proper reasons, especially where the designated PAB member questions whether a case is arguable, is an error of law, whatever standard of review is applied.

Canada (Minister of Human Resources Development) v. Penna, 2005 FC 469

It is an error of law to grant leave to appeal to the PAB where no application for an extension of time to seek leave, fully complying with the appropriate Rules, had been filed by the self-represented claimant, and no extension of time to file the application for leave had been granted.

§3. Standard of Review of Leave Decision (see also cases under s. 68§1(f))

Kaminski v. Canada (Attorney General), 2014 FC 238

The question of whether the tribunal member applied the correct test with respect to granting leave is reviewable on a standard or correctness, while the application of the test in granting or refusing leave to appeal is reviewable on a standard of reasonableness.

---

57. *Appeal — time limit —* **(1) An application for leave to appeal must be made to the Appeal Division in the prescribed form and manner and within,**

    (*a*) **in the case of a decision made by the Employment Insurance Section, 30 days after the day on which it is communicated to the appellant; and**

    (*b*) **in the case of a decision made by the Income Security Section, 90 days after the day on which the decision is communicated to the appellant.**

(2012, c. 19, s. 224.)

    (2) *Extension —* **The Appeal Division may allow further time within which an application for leave to appeal is to be made, but in no case may an**

application be made more than one year after the day on which the decision is communicated to the appellant. (2012, c. 19, s. 224.)

(2012, c. 19, s. 224.)

—————————— Notes ——————————

The 90-day limit for seeking leave to appeal CPP and OAS decisions of the General Division is the same as under the previous scheme. However, the absolute limit of one year is new.

Related Social Security Tribunal Regulations

• Section 40 (Application for leave form and contents)

Case Law

[Editor's note: The following cases were decided under the previous CPP s. 83(1), now repealed.]

Canada (Minister of Human Resources Development) v. Gattelaro, 2005 FC 833. See also *Canada (Minister of Human Resources Development) v. Hogervorst,* 2007 FCA 41.

The intent of Parliament as expressed in CPP s. 83(1) is to limit the time period for extending the appeal period to 90 days. While a designated member may extend the time period beyond 90 days, the authority to extend the statutory limitation should not be exercised arbitrarily or capriciously, and the following criteria must be considered and weighed:

1. A continuing intention to pursue the application or appeal;

2. The matter discloses an arguable case;

3. There is a reasonable explanation for the delay; and

4. There is no prejudice to the other party in allowing the extension.

Allowing appeals, absent compelling reasons, long after the expiry of time leads to a lack of certainty and finality for both the Minister and all parties to the process. Where the time for appealing expired over seven years prior to the appeal being brought, prejudice on the Minister's part could be presumed.

Obiter. It is difficult to see how the PAB can reach a fair, principled decision on applications for an extension of time to appeal on an *ex parte* basis; that is, without the submissions from the Minister.

Lavin v. Canada (Attorney General), 2011 FC 1387

Under s. 83(1) of the CPP, the PAB has broad discretion to permit a party to appeal a tribunal's decision outside the normal 90-day limitation period. However, this decision only confers a benefit — it is not a matter of right. The PAB must weigh and consider the four *Gattellaro* factors in making its decision. The record should clearly demonstrate that all of these factors have been addressed by the decision-maker. However, an extension may be granted even if one of the factors mentioned in this test is not satisfied.

Canada (Attorney General) v. McGee, 2007 FCA 208

An extension of time granted by a designated member of the PAB that is not challenged by way of judicial review thereby becomes final and binding. The full panel of the PAB does not have jurisdiction to hear an appeal from the extension granted.

Canada (Minister of Human Resources Development) v. Hogervorst, 2007 FCA 41. See also *Kabatoff v. Canada (Human Resources Development),* 2007 FC 820

It is not appropriate to grant an extension for leave to appeal a Review Tribunal decision seven years after it was made. Such an appeal constituted a collateral attack on a subsequent Tribunal decision refusing a second application by the same applicant on the ground of no new facts. The decision to grant leave to appeal could have given rise to inconsistent decisions, and did not recognize and give effect to the principle of finality. The granting, without any explanation or justification whatsoever, of an extension of time and leave to challenge a final decision more than seven years after it was rendered can only give rise to a reasonable inference that the discretion was, if not arbitrarily, at least improperly exercised, especially when two more binding and final decisions to the same effect on the same issue, between the same litigants, remain effective and unchallenged. Such circumstances imposed upon the judge sitting in judicial review the duty to scrupulously review the member's decision and provide adequate reasons. Whether the appellant has, at law, an arguable case may be otherwise expressed as whether the appellant, legally, has a reasonable chance of success. This is not purely a question of fact, but is at best a mixed question of fact and law.

Sheard v. Canada (Attorney General) 2010 FC 458

On a request for to the Chair or Vice-Chair of the PAB for an extension of time to appeal a Review Tribunal decision, the appellant must provide the following information:

     (a) the date of the Review Tribunal's decision;

     (b) the date that she received it, and the place where the decision was made;

     (c) her full name and mailing address;

     (d) the name of her representative, if she has one, and contact information for that person;

     (e) the grounds on which she is relying in seeking leave to appeal; and

     (f) a summary of the facts and the evidence on which she intends to rely.

In addition, the appellant must explain why she is seeking an extension of time. Normally, this involves showing that:

     (a) she had always intended to appeal the Tribunal's decision;

     (b) her appeal has some merit;

     (c) she has a reasonable explanation for her delay in seeking leave to appeal; and

     (d) granting the extension of time will not cause the Minister any particular difficulties.

There are no statutory limitations on the scope of discretion conferred on the Chair, Vice-Chair or designated member of the PAB to grant an extension of time.

Canada (Minister of Human Resources Development) v. Penna, 2005 FC 469

It is an error of law to grant leave to appeal to the PAB where no application for an extension of time to seek leave, fully complying with the appropriate Rules, had been filed by the self-represented claimant, and no extension of time to file the application for leave had been granted.

Canada (Minister of Human Resources Development) v. Dawdy, 2006 FC 429 (CanLII)

It is clear from the wording of s. 83(1) that a claimant who does not apply for leave to appeal a decision to the PAB within the 90-day period must first be granted a discretionary extension of time to seek leave. Rules 4 and 5 of the Pension Appeals Board Rules of Procedure (Benefits) outline the required information that must be present in an application for leave and require that the applicant state grounds on which an extension is sought. A delay of approximately 10 months could arguably be considered prejudice to the Minister.

Belo-Alves v. MHRSD, 2009 FC 413

Where, prior to the Federal Court of Appeal's decision in *Mazzotta*, the claimant had declined to seek judicial review to overturn the Tribunal's finding of no new facts, although she very much disagreed with it, the claimant could still be granted an extension two years later. An understanding of the claimant's life situation — including poverty, fear, continuing poor health, and serious life burdens — was important when attempting to understand her actions in failing to appeal. Factors which would be in play only on the leave to appeal application itself should not be considered on the application for an extension of time.

Canada (Minister of Human Resources Development) v. Roy, 2005 FC 1456 (CanLII)

An extension of time where there has been an 18-month delay would arguably result in prejudice to the Minister, given that hearings before the PAB are generally *de novo.*

Canada (Minister of Human Resources Development) v. Eason, 2005 FC 1698 (CanLII)

An application for an extension of time is not granted automatically or as of right. The decision is discretionary and such discretion should be exercised using a principled approach with a view to the four criteria listed in *Gattelaro.* In the absence of any reasons for decision, it is an error in law to fail to properly apply the correct criteria to the application for an extension of time. The granting of an extension of time cannot be inferred from the PAB's decision. Even if the party seeking leave makes a request for an extension of time, the PAB commits a reviewable error by granting leave without explicitly considering and granting the request for an extension of time.

Halcro v. MNHW (April 26, 1988), CP 1057 (PAB)

The PAB may, in a proper case, exercise the powers of the Minister to extend the time for appealing an initial decision.

---

58. *Grounds of appeal* **— (1) The only grounds of appeal are that**

(a) the General Division failed to observe a principle of natural justice or otherwise acted beyond or refused to exercise its jurisdiction;

(b) the General Division erred in law in making its decision, whether or not the error appears on the face of the record; or

(c) the General Division based its decision on an erroneous finding of fact that it made in a perverse or capricious manner or without regard for the material before it.

(2012, c. 19, s. 224.)

(2) *Criteria* **— Leave to appeal is refused if the Appeal Division is satisfied that the appeal has no reasonable chance of success. (2012, c. 19, s. 224.)**

(3) *Decision* **— The Appeal Division must either grant or refuse leave to appeal. (2012, c. 19, s. 224.)**

(4) *Reasons* **— The Appeal Division must give written reasons for its decision to grant or refuse leave and send copies to the appellant and any other party. (2012, c. 19, s. 224.)**

(5) *Leave granted* **— If leave to appeal is granted, the application for leave to appeal becomes the notice of appeal and is deemed to have been**

filed on the day on which the application for leave to appeal was filed. (2012, c. 19, s. 224.)

(2012, c. 19, s. 224.)

————————— **Notes** —————————

Case Law

§0.1. SST Decisions

M.Z. v. Minister of Human Resources and Skills Development (August 29, 2014) AD-13-33 (SSTAD)

Reasonableness is the appropriate standard of review on appeals with respect to errors of law, mixed fact and law, and errors of fact. However, no deference was owed to the tribunal below on questions of procedural fairness. The claimant could argue a breach of procedural fairness for the first time on appeal.

[Editor's note: The following cases were decided under the previous CPP ss. 82–84, now repealed.]

§1. Practice, Procedure, and Evidence

Canada (Minister of Human Resources Development) v. Milton, 2004 FCA 235

The PAB is master of its own procedure. Where, on an application to terminate benefits under s. 70, counsel for the Minister had had an opportunity to call the recipient as a witness, and to cross-examine him, in the course of presenting the evidence on behalf of the Minister, it cannot be said that the PAB's refusal to permit cross-examination, after the evidence of both parties was in, deprived the Minister of a reasonable opportunity of effectively participating at the hearing before the PAB. The PAB may well have concluded that, given the important part played by the medical reports in this case, and their content, any evidence that the recipient might have given was likely to be of relatively little significance to the PAB's determination.

Leduc v. Turner 2010 FCA 99

The absence of a transcript of a PAB hearing does not constitute a breach of the PAB's duty of procedural fairness where the court is able to deal effectively with the issues raised in the application for judicial review. The PAB's failure to refer in its reasons to oral evidence favouring the applicant's position indicated only that the evidence was given little weight, not that it was disregarded.

Kent v. Canada (Attorney General), 2006 FCA 375

An allegation of procedural unfairness by the PAB must be made in the notice of application for judicial review, or memorandum of fact and law. It is too late to raise the allegation that the applicant had been denied a fair hearing by the PAB for the first time at the judicial review hearing.

Evans v. Canada (Attorney General), 2011 FCA 281

Where the claimant does not attend the hearing personally or via a representative, the PAB was entitled to weigh the evidence and find that the claimant had not met his or her onus of proof to resolve conflicting documentary evidence submitted in support of the claim.

Gorgiev v. Canada (Minister of Human Resources Development), 2005 FCA 55

The rejection by the claimant of the Minister's settlement offer is not capable of being construed as an admission by the claimant.

Obiter: Where the claimant has disclosed the fact that the Minister made a settlement offer which was rejected by the claimant, the PAB could act on its own motion to have the disclosure struck from the record, simply on the basis that it was not relevant.

P.A. v. MHRSD (August 26, 2010), CP 26258 (PAB), judicial review denied 2011 FCA 75

A motion for discovery as part of a new fact application could not be used as a fishing expedition where in fact there were no "new facts". The claimant was hoping that if he could discover people within the Ministry, he could get an admission that he was disabled within the meaning of s. 42(2) before the date set by the Review Tribunal, and that this admission would constitute a new fact. Such an application was an abuse of process.

Weir (Estate of) v. HRSD (October 17, 2007), CP 24882 (PAB)

Where the deceased claimant's estate had no official estate trustee or administrator and the spouse of the deceased was separated from her husband at the time of death, the spouse was permitted to prosecute the appeal on behalf of her late husband's estate after filing a statutory declaration with the PAB confirming that she was the deceased's widow and with the written consent of his two children witnessed by a commissioner of oaths.

---

59. *Decision* — **(1) The Appeal Division may dismiss the appeal, give the decision that the General Division should have given, refer the matter back to the General Division for reconsideration in accordance with any directions that the Appeal Division considers appropriate or confirm, rescind or vary the decision of the General Division in whole or in part. (2012, c. 19, s. 224.)**

(2) *Reasons* — **The Appeal Division must give written reasons for its decision and send copies to the appellant and any other party. (2012, c. 19, s. 224.)**

(2012, c. 19, s. 224.)

--- **Notes** ---

This section is similar in effect to the former CPP s. 83(11).

Case Law

[Editor's note: The following cases were decided under the previous CPP ss. 82–84, now repealed.]

§1. Reasonable Apprehension of Bias

Gorgiev v. Canada (Minister of Human Resources Development), 2005 FCA 55

The disclosure to the PAB during the hearing of a previous settlement offer made by the Minister and its rejection by the claimant did not give rise to a reasonable apprehension of bias on the part of the PAB against the claimant in the circumstances. The members of the PAB, all of whom are judges or retired judges, must be taken to know that the reasonableness of a settlement cannot be assessed properly except by the parties themselves, because only the parties have all of the relevant information. The only information available to the PAB at the time of the disclosure of the rejected settlement offer was the material in the appeal record. The members of the PAB must also be taken to know that it was quite proper for the claimant to choose to have the matter heard and decided by the Board. In any case, the disclosure was more likely to reflect negatively on the position of the Minister than the position of the claimant.

§2. Reasons for Decision

(a) General Principles

R. v. Sheppard, [2002] 1 S.C.R. 869

The duty to give reasons, where it exists, arises out of the circumstances of a particular case. Where it is plain from the record why an accused has been convicted or acquitted, and the absence or inadequacy of reasons provides no significant impediment to the exercise of the right of appeal, the appeal court will not on that account intervene. On the other hand, where the path taken by the trial judge through confused or conflicting evidence is not at all apparent, or there are difficult issues of law that need to be confronted but which the trial judge has circumnavigated without explanation, or where there are conflicting theories for why the trial judge might have decided as he or she did, at least some of which would clearly constitute reversible error, the appeal court may in some cases consider itself unable to give effect to the statutory right of appeal. In such a case, one or other of the parties may question the correctness of the result, but will wrongly have been deprived by the absence or inadequacy of reasons of the opportunity to have the trial verdict *properly* scrutinized on appeal. In such a case, even if the record discloses evidence that on one view could support a reasonable verdict, the deficiencies in the reasons may amount to an error of law and justify appellate intervention. It will be for the appeal court to determine whether, in a particular case, the deficiency in the reasons precludes it from properly carrying out its appellate function.

R. v. Burns, [1994] 1 S.C.R. 656

Failure to indicate expressly that all relevant considerations have been taken into account in arriving at a verdict is not a basis for allowing an appeal under s. 686(1)(a) of the *Criminal Code.* This accords with the general rule that a trial judge does not err merely because he or she does not give reasons for deciding one way or the other on problematic points. The judge is not required to demonstrate that he or she knows the law and has considered all aspects of the evidence. Nor is the judge required to explain why he or she does not entertain a reasonable doubt as to the accused's guilt. Failure to do any of these things does not, in itself, permit a court of appeal to set aside the verdict.

Baker v. Canada (Minister of Citizenship and Immigration), [1999] 2 S.C.R. 817

In certain circumstances, the duty of procedural fairness will require the provision of a written explanation for a decision. The strong arguments demonstrating the advantages of written reasons suggest that, in cases where the decision has important significance for the individual, when there is a statutory right of appeal, or in other circumstances, some form of reasons should be required.

Newfoundland and Labrador Nurses Union v. Newfoundland and Labrador (Treasury Board), 2011 SCC 62, [2011] 3 SCR 708. See also *McLaughlin v. Canada (Attorney General),* 2012 FC 556.

The SCC's decision in *Baker* stands for the proposition that in certain circumstances, the duty of procedural fairness will require some form of reasons for a decision. It did not say that reasons were *always* required, and it did not say that the *quality* of those reasons is a question of procedural fairness. Not any alleged deficiencies or flaws in the reasons fall under the category of a breach of the duty of procedural fairness and are therefore subject to a correctness review. The breach of a duty of procedural fairness is an error in law. Where there are no reasons in circumstances where they are required, there is nothing to review. But where there *are* reasons, there is no such breach. Any challenge to the reasoning/result of the decision should therefore be made within the reasonableness analysis.

(b) CPP Decisions

Garcia v. Canada (Attorney General), [2001] FCA 200

Section 83(11) expressly imposes upon the PAB the obligation to notify in writing the parties to the appeal of its decision and of its reasons therefor. The PAB's failure to provide a full written explanation for its decision breaches the Board's duty of procedural fairness owed to the applicant and constitutes a reviewable error. It is not sufficient for the PAB to merely quote from or cite some of the medical reports and other evidence without accepting, rejecting, or analyzing it, and then simply conclude that in its opinion the applicant does not meet the strict requirements of the CPP with no explanation for the conclusion expressly stated.

Canada (Minister of Human Resources Development) v. Quesnelle, 2003 FCA 92

A double standard as to the adequacy of a tribunal's reasons depending on which way it decides a dispute should not be applied. The Minister represents the public interest in the financial integrity of the CPP and its due administration according to law, and there is a public interest in ensuring that claimants are not paid benefits to which they are not entitled. Both parties are entitled to a fair hearing before the PAB and, without reasons that adequately explain the basis of a decision, neither party can be assured that, when a decision goes against it, its submissions and evidence have been properly considered. Moreover, without adequate reasons, the losing party may be effectively deprived of the right to apply for judicial review. The fact that the PAB comprises serving and former federally appointed judges (s. 83(5)-(5.5)) is an indication that Parliament expected more by way of reasons than a finding that the claimant and a treating physician to be credible despite a great amount of evidence that the claimant's disability was not severe. Unlike many of those serving on administrative tribunals, the members and temporary members of the PAB are not unfamiliar with the writing of reasons for decision in matters where a careful analysis of the law and conflicting evidence is required. While members of the PAB may be called upon to hear a relatively large number of appeals, many of the cases that they hear are fairly straightforward and the workload can be shared among the three members who comprise a panel of the PAB.

Doucette v. MHRD, 2004 FCA 292

The Supreme Court of Canada's decision in *Sheppard* provides one basis upon which to assess the adequacy of the PAB's reasons in a particular case — i.e., do the reasons provide a sufficient basis for the Federal Court of Appeal to exercise its review function? The reasons under review should be fairly considered and in performing that exercise, the Court should examine the record on which the decision under review is based. The Court could exercise its review function where the PAB refers to "serious concerns" regarding the claimant's disability expressed in a medical report without identifying what those concerns are, as long as the report itself was clear about the nature of the concerns. While the PAB could have explained its reasoning more thoroughly, its reasoning could still be discerned from the language used.

Oliveira v. Canada (Minister of Human Resources Development), 2003 FCA 213

The PAB need not make express reference in its reasons to all the oral and documentary evidence presented. However, judicial review is available where it was apparent on the face of the reasons that the PAB in denying the claim actually ignored evidence of a specialist that the claimant's condition had progressed to a point that she could no longer be gainfully employed and that her condition was permanent.

Marrone v. Canada (Attorney General), 2008 FCA 216

The PAB's decision must contain meaningful analysis of the applicable law and of the evidence.

Atri v. Canada (Attorney General), 2007 FCA 178

Where the applicant is seeking to establish that his age is as set out in documents issued by his native country rather than his Canadian immigration documents, he is entitled as a matter of fairness to be told by the PAB why it did not accept his national documents as proof of his age, especially where the applicant alleged that his Identification Booklet is a birth certificate. The PAB failed to discharge its statutory duty to provide adequate reasons for its decision where it did not refer specifically to the national documents, nor explain why it preferred the immigration documents as proof of the applicant's age.

Giannaros v. Canada (Minister of Social Development), 2005 FCA 187

The Court should not intervene because it is of the opinion that the PAB failed to express themselves in a way acceptable to the Court. The reasons under review should be fairly considered and in performing that exercise, the Court should examine the record on which the decision under review is based. Judicial review should not be granted on this basis where the Court can discern the PAB's reasoning from the language it has used, although it is obvious that the PAB could have explained its reasoning more fully.

Giordano v. Canada (Attorney General), 2005 FCA 71

It is not necessary that the PAB's reasons contain an extensive analysis of the claimant's personal circumstances and the various medical reports that were before it, where the PAB's focus was on the claimant's failure to seek work otherwise than at her previous employer's factory and where no sedentary work was available. The PAB was entitled to focus on the relevant date for determining the claimant's disability and discount evidence of evaluations subsequent to that date.

Palumbo v. Canada 2005 FCA 117

The PAB is not required to refer to every one of what may be a considerable number of reports before it. Expert reports on which the claimant relies may be omitted from discussion in the PAB's reasons where they were not of sufficient probative significance to warrant treatment.

Dossa v. Canada (Pension Appeal Board), 2005 FCA 387

The PAB is not required or expected to refer to every report. Furthermore, it is entitled to prefer some evidence over other evidence, as long as that evidence is not of such probative significance that doing so would amount to a failure to discharge its elementary duty to engage in a meaningful analysis of the evidence. It is not the function of the Federal Court of Appeal to reweigh the evidence and retry the case. There is no bar to the PAB relying on hearsay evidence as long as it is not unfairly used.

Osborne v. Canada (Attorney General), 2005 FCA 412

Although the PAB did not expressly deal with the side effects caused by the claimant's medication, it could easily be inferred from the PAB's overall consideration of the medical and therapeutic reports before it, that it was fully aware of the treatment modalities being used by the claimant, including his use of medication.

Whiteley v. Canada (Minister of Social Development), 2006 FCA 72

In rendering a decision, the PAB is required to analyze the law and the evidence in a meaningful way. It is not enough to relate the evidence and then immediately conclude that the onus on the claimant had not been met.

Canada (Attorney General) v. Fink, 2006 FCA 354

In awarding a disability pension, it is not sufficient for the PAB to merely state that it took into account the totality of the evidence and then to conclude that applicant had met her burden of proof. Analysis is required.

Johnson v. Canada (Attorney General), 2007 FCA 66

Where none of the evidence directly addressed the applicant's condition during his MQP, but there was some evidence that could have been interpreted to favour the applicant's claim, it is incumbent upon the PAB to explain why they chose not to interpret the evidence that way, particularly where it is not clear from the record why they made that choice.

Thornton v. Canada (Social Development), 2007 FCA 65

The PAB was not obliged to refer to post-MQP reports which did not bear on the applicant's condition before the expiry of the MQP.

Minister of Human Resources Development v. Uzoni, 2005 FCA 313

The PAB is entitled to decline to draw an adverse inference from the claimant's absence from the hearing where the absence was adequately explained by a physician. In such circumstances, the PAB is not required to elaborate its reasons why it did not draw the adverse inference requested by the Minister.

Lalonde v. Canada (Minister of Human Resources Development), 2002 FCA 211

While to describe a person as having "a certain capacity to work" necessarily implies that that person suffers from a certain incapacity to work, the PAB could not leave it at that. Under CPP s. 83(11), the PAB must notify in writing the parties to the appeal "of its decision and of its reasons therefore". In the presence of such a provision, the reasons must be proper, adequate, and intelligible, and must enable the person concerned to assess whether he has grounds of appeal or, in this case, of judicial review. Thus, at the broadest level of accountability, the giving of reasoned judgments is central to the legitimacy of judicial institutions in the eyes of the public. The "real world" context requires that PAB consider the words "regularly", "substantially" and "gainful" found in the definition of "severe". The "real world" context presupposes that the PAB consider the particular circumstances of the claimant, her age, education level, language proficiency, and past work and life experience, as well as whether a claimant's refusal to undergo physiotherapy treatment is unreasonable and what impact that refusal might have on the claimant's disability status should the refusal be considered unreasonable.

Wirachowsky v. Canada (December 20, 2000), Doc. A-72-97 (Fed. C.A.)

The PAB's failure to consider all of the medical evidence before it meant that the decision denying the applicant's appeal could not stand, where the medical opinions corroborated the information supplied by the applicant in the questionnaire attached to his application for the disability pension. The phrase "semi-sedentary work" referred to in the medical evidence and the PAB's decision is incapable of conveying clear meaning for the purposes of assessing disability under the CPP.

Peters v. Canada (Minister of Human Resources Development), (May 11, 2000) Doc. A-865-97 (Fed. C.A.)

Judicial review was granted where the PAB erroneously stated (i) that none of the medical reports indicated the existence of an inability or of a functional deficiency, although one doctor had concluded that the claimant was incapable of even light office duties as a result of her neck and shoulder injuries sustained in a car accident, (ii) that it had not been established that she had undergone surgery to the shoulder, when in fact the evidence indicated that several procedures, including arthroscopic surgery, had been performed, and (iii) that the injuries were soft tissue, while the evidence showed multidirectional instability in the shoulder.

Lutzer v. Canada (Minister of Human Resources Development), [2002] FCA 190

After stating the correct test and such factors as the claimant's age and education, the PAB was not required to explain the reasoning leading to its conclusion that the claimant was not entitled to a disability pension.

Kellar v. Canada (Minister of Human Resources Development), [2002] FCA 204

The PAB is not required to refer to every piece of evidence before it, but only to those that have significant probative value. Where medical reports were written using false assumptions and various doctors who examined the claimant were unable to diagnose any specific cause of the symptoms of which she complained, the PAB was not obliged in law to set out its conclusions on the reports.

Canada (Attorney General) v. Dale, 2006 FC 1364

The CPP does not require that written reasons be provided where leave to appeal to the PAB is granted.

§3. Record of Proceedings

Burton v. Pension Appeals Board, 2008 FCA 140

There appears to be no statutory duty to record a PAB proceeding. But while the Pension Appeals Board Rules of Procedure (Benefits) are silent on the recording of hearings before the PAB, s. 10.1(1) of the Rules allows a party to submit, by motion in writing, to the Chairman or Vice-Chairman "any matter that arises, in the course of an appeal or seeking leave to appeal, that can be considered in advance of the hearing of the appeal without the personal appearance of the parties". In the absence of a transcript or sworn probative evidence as to what transpired at the PAB hearing with respect to an alleged instance of bias, it is impossible for the reviewing court to either verify the allegation or assess the credibility of that allegation.

Garcia v. Canada (Attorney General), [2001] FCA 200

In the absence of a statutory right to a recording of PAB proceedings under the CPP, a reviewing court must determine whether the record provided allows it to properly dispose of the application for appeal or review. Where affidavits are offered to establish facts underlying the issues on review, the opposing party must establish some basis on which such affidavits can be rejected or ignored. Uncontradicted affidavit evidence in conjunction with the application for judicial review provides an adequate record for the court to review factual findings made by the PAB in order to determine whether a ground of review was well-founded.

Bagri v. Canada (Attorney General), 2006 FCA 134

The fact that the PAB made no reference to the applicant's oral testimony did not mean that the reviewing court could not determine if the PAB thereby erred without a transcript of the hearing, where the principal substantive issues in the case concerned the adequacy of the medical evidence relevant to the claim that she qualified for long-term disability benefit as of a particular date.

Sudnik v. MHRD (January 23, 2004), CP 19633 (PAB)

There is no statutory requirement that Review Tribunal hearings be recorded. As the appeal from the Review Tribunal to the Pension Appeals Board is by way of trial *de novo*, a transcript would not be necessary or required, except in exceptional cases. A claimant is not denied a fair hearing at the Review Tribunal level because there was no transcript. On an Application for Leave to Appeal or Judicial Review, the claimant could put forward all the facts by way of affidavit evidence. The deponents could be cross-examined on their affidavits.

General

60. *Head office* — **(1) The head office of the Tribunal is in the National Capital Region described in the schedule to the *National Capital Act* or at any other place within Canada that may be designated by the Governor in Council. (2012, c. 19, s. 224.)**

(2) *Residence* — The Chairperson and the Vice-chairpersons must reside within the distance from the place referred to in subsection (1) that is determined by the Governor in Council. (2012, c. 19, s. 224.)

(2012, c. 19, s. 224.)

S. 60.1 will be added by S.C. 2014, c. 20, s. 466 on proclamation, and will read as follows:

60.1. *Services and facilities* — **(1)** The Minister may provide the Chief Administrator of the Administrative Tribunals Support Service of Canada with any administrative services and facilities that are necessary to enable him or her to provide support services and facilities to the Tribunal. **(2014, c. 20, s. 466.)**

(2) *Spending authority* — The Minister may spend revenues obtained from the provision of services and facilities to the Chief Administrator, in the fiscal year in which they are received or, unless an appropriation Act provides otherwise, in the next fiscal year. **(2014, c. 20, s. 466.)**

(2014, c. 20, s. 466.)

61. *Tribunal sittings* — Every application to the Tribunal is to be heard before a single member.

(2012, c. 19, s. 224.)

62. *Tribunal hearings* — All or part of a Tribunal hearing may be held in private if the Tribunal is of the opinion that the circumstances of the case so require.

(2012, c. 19, s. 224.)

─────────────── **Notes** ───────────────

SST policies regarding the conduct of hearings are reproduced after these provisions.

───────────────────────

63. *Expenses and allowances* — The Chairperson may in any particular case for special reasons reimburse any party required to attend a hearing for travel or living expenses or pay to them any other allowance, including compensation for lost remuneration, as are fixed by the Minister.

(2012, c. 19, s. 224.)

S. 63 will be replaced by S.C. 2014, c. 20, s. 467 on proclamation, and will read as follows:

63. *Expenses and allowances* — **(1)** Any party who is required to attend a hearing may, if the Chairperson in any particular case for special reasons considers it warranted, be reimbursed for their travel or living expenses up to the amounts determined by the Chief Administrator of the Administrative Tribunals Support Service of Canada, or be paid any allowance, including compensation for lost remuneration, in accordance with the rates fixed by that Chief Administrator. **(2014, c. 20, s. 467.)**

(2) *Payments* — Any amount to be paid under subsection (1) may be paid out of moneys appropriated by Parliament for the expenditures of the Administrative Tribunals Support Service of Canada. (2014, c. 20, s. 467.)

(2014, c. 20, s. 467.)

64. *Powers of tribunal* — (1) The Tribunal may decide any question of law or fact that is necessary for the disposition of any application made under this Act. (2012, c. 19, s. 224.)

(2) *Canada Pension Plan* — Despite subsection (1), in the case of an application relating to the *Canada Pension Plan*, the Tribunal may only decide questions of law or fact as to

(a) whether any benefit is payable to a person or its amount;

(b) whether any person is eligible for a division of unadjusted pensionable earnings or its amount;

(c) whether any person is eligible for an assignment of a contributor's retirement pension or its amount; and

(d) whether a penalty should be imposed under Part II of that Act or its amount. (2012, c. 31, s. 204.)

(2012, c. 19, s. 224.)

(3) *Employment Insurance Act* — If a question specified in section 90 of the *Employment Insurance Act* arises in the consideration of an application, it must be determined by an authorized officer of the Canada Revenue Agency, as provided by that section. (2012, c. 19, s. 224.)

(2012, c. 19, s. 224; 2012, c. 31, s. 204.)

—————————— Notes ——————————

Sections 64(1)–(2) are very similar to the former CPP s. 84(1) in effect. Section 64(3) is not likely to be relevant on CPP or OAS appeals. Section 90(1) of the *Employment Insurance Act* reads as follows:

90. — (1) *Request for ruling* — An employer, an employee, a person claiming to be an employer or an employee or the Commission may request an officer of the Canada Revenue Agency authorized by the Minister to make a ruling on any of the following questions:

(a) whether an employment is insurable;

(b) how long an insurable employment lasts, including the dates on which it begins and ends;

(c) what is the amount of any insurable earnings;

(d) how many hours an insured person has had in insurable employment;

(e) whether a premium is payable;

(f) what is the amount of a premium payable;

(g) who is the employer of an insured person;

(h) whether employers are associated employers; and

(i) what amount shall be refunded under subsections 96(4) to (10).

Case Law

§0.1. Powers of Social Security Tribunal

J.T. v. Minister of Human Resources and Skills Development, 2013 SSTAD 9

The SST has jurisdiction to deal with properly raised constitutional matters. Section 2(*d*) of the *Canadian Bill of Rights* does not guarantee a right to counsel. It states that a person cannot be compelled to give evidence if he is denied counsel. This does not impose an obligation on governments or the tribunal to provide counsel to a party in a legal matter, but if they choose to have counsel, they are entitled to have counsel represent them. There is no guarantee in the CPP nor any other legislation that counsel will be provided for a claimant in a disability hearing. Such a right to counsel is not a principle of fundamental justice.

F.S. v. Minister of Human Resources and Skills Development (March 3, 2014) CP 26328 (SSTAD)

Where neither the appellant nor his counsel attended the hearing of the appeal, the hearing may proceed. The Minister's oral request for dismissal for want of prosecution or abandonment should be dismissed where it had not been made with notice to the appellant.

J.Z. v. Minister of Human Resources and Skills Development (May 1, 2014) CP 29170 (SSTAD)

The Appeal Division could order the production of income information from a claimant either based on s. 68 of the CPP Regulations, or alternatively, under the common law right of access to relevant information when someone is claiming damages flowing from disability.

[Editor's note: The following cases were decided under the previous CPP ss. 82–84, now repealed.]

§1. Powers of Tribunals

Nova Scotia (Workers' Compensation Board) v. Martin; Nova Scotia (Workers' Compensation Board) v. Laseur, 2003 SCC 54

The current approach to the jurisdiction of administrative tribunals to subject legislative provisions to Charter scrutiny can be summarized as follows:

1. The first question is whether the administrative tribunal has jurisdiction, explicit *or* implied, to decide questions of law arising under the challenged provision.

2. (a) Explicit jurisdiction must be found in the terms of the statutory grant of authority.

   (b) Implied jurisdiction must be discerned by looking at the statute as a whole. Relevant factors will include the statutory mandate of the tribunal in issue and whether deciding questions of law is necessary to fulfilling this mandate effectively; the interaction of the tribunal in question with other elements of the administrative system; whether the tribunal is adjudicative in nature; and practical considerations, including the tribunal's capacity to consider questions of law. Practical considerations, however, cannot override a clear implication from the statute itself.

3. If the tribunal is found to have jurisdiction to decide questions of law arising under a legislative provision, this power will be presumed to include jurisdiction to determine the constitutional validity of that provision under the Charter.

4. The party alleging that the tribunal lacks jurisdiction to apply the Charter may rebut the presumption by (a) pointing to an explicit withdrawal of authority to consider the Charter; or (b) convincing the court that an

examination of the statutory scheme clearly leads to the conclusion that the legislature intended to exclude the Charter (or a category of questions that would include the Charter, such as constitutional questions generally) from the scope of the questions of law to be addressed by the tribunal. Such an implication should generally arise from the statute itself, rather than from external considerations.

Sudnik v. MHRD (January 23, 2004), CP 19633 (PAB)

The Supreme Court of Canada's decision in *Martin* clearly establishes that the PAB has the jurisdiction to hear a Charter application regarding the CPP. However, the PAB has no jurisdiction to conduct a judicial review of the Review Tribunal's decision.

Tranchemontagne v. Ontario Disability Support Program, 2006 SCC 14

Statutory tribunals empowered to decide questions of law are presumed to have the power to look beyond their enabling statutes in order to apply the whole law — including human rights legislation — to a matter properly before them.

Mazzotta v. Canada (Attorney General), 2007 FCA 297

Section 84(1) is designed to ensure that all questions of fact and law pertaining to the question of whether a benefit is payable to a person would be determined by the Review Tribunal and, on appeal, by the PAB. Parliament did not envisage a split of the process between the Federal Court, the Federal Court of Appeal, and the adjudicative mechanisms which it put in place and which it invested with broad powers to determine the merits of claims along with all the factual and legal questions that inevitably accompany these claims.

Canada (MHRD) v. Skoric, [2000] 3 FC 265 (C.A.)

The PAB has no broad regulatory responsibilities, but performs only the adjudicative function of hearing appeals from the Review Tribunal.

Garcia v. Canada (Attorney General) (2001), Doc. A-218-00 (Fed. C.A.)

The PAB's reasoning leading to its final disposition must be fully explained. It is not sufficient to simply recite the evidence without expressly accepting, rejecting, or analyzing it, and then conclude that in its opinion the applicant does not meet the strict requirements of the CPP.

Oliveira v. Canada (Minister of Human Resources Development), 2004 FCA 136

The fact that the PAB purported to grant leave did not confer on it any jurisdiction that the PAB did not otherwise have.

Canada (Attorney General) v. Matheson, 2007 FCA 383

Where the PAB approves a settlement between the parties by way of consent judgment, the PAB is *functus officio* and lacked jurisdiction to subsequently amend the settlement on a subsequent motion by one of the parties. The correct procedure is for the party seeking to set aside the settlement to apply to a court to annul the agreement. Before the parties can start afresh, the impugned agreement must be invalidated. There cannot be a valid agreement if the consent of one or both parties is vitiated.

Canada (Attorney General) v. McGee, 2007 FCA 208

The PAB's jurisdiction is over decisions of a Review Tribunal. Nowhere in the CPP can it be found that the PAB possesses the statutory power to sit on an appeal or to review a final and binding decision rendered by one of its members.

Spears v. Canada (Attorney General) 2004 FCA 193

Section 16(1) of the *Pension Appeals Board Rules of Procedure (Benefits)*, which expressly authorizes the panel to "summon before it by subpoena any person and require him to give evidence on oath and to produce such documents as it deems requisite", provides the PAB with ample authority to require the testimony of the Ministry's doctor at the hearing.

Canada (Minister of Human Resources Development) v. Dublin Estate, 2006 FC 152

The Review Tribunal did not have jurisdiction to order the Minister to make an *ex gratia* payment of OAS benefits.

Lazar v. Canada (Attorney General) (1999), Doc. T-459-98 (Fed. T.D.)

The statutory jurisdiction of the Review Tribunal and the PAB "to determine any question of law" relating to whether a benefit is payable under this section is broad enough to enable them to hear and decide Charter challenges to the validity of the enabling legislation, or any questions of common law relating to the procedural fairness of the decision-making process, that are relevant to an appellant's entitlement to a pension.

Obiter: On proceeding to determine whether the claimant had ceased to be eligible to receive a long-term disability pension, it may be that neither the Review Tribunal nor the PAB may have jurisdiction to set aside a claimant's indebtedness to the Crown. However, given that the Minister is unlikely to attempt to collect in this situation, such a limit on the jurisdiction of the statutory tribunals is not sufficient to render the rights of appeal inadequate alternative remedies to an application for judicial review.

Buchan v. Canada (Attorney General), 2007 FC 1141

Section 84(2) appears to be confined to a decision of the Minister made under "this Act", meaning the CPP. *Quaere* whether s. 84(2) permits the reopening or varying of the Minister's decision under OAS s. 27.1(1).

Canada (Attorney General) v. Dale, 2006 FC 1364

Neither the Review Tribunal nor the PAB has jurisdiction to entertain an appeal of a decision of the Minister under s. 66(4).

C.S. v. MHRSD (February 2, 2012), CP 28021 (PAB)

The doctrine of *functus officio* states that once an administrative tribunal or court has reached its decision, it cannot afterwards alter its award except to correct clerical mistakes or errors arising from an accidental slip or omission.

MSD v. Menard (July 14, 2006), CP 22041 (PAB)

The PAB has no authority to impute contributions. By virtue of s. 97, the PAB is without jurisdiction to alter or rectify the record of earnings filed. Only the Minister has such statutory jurisdiction.

McMaster v. MSD (March 31, 2006), CP 23010 (PAB)

Neither the Review Tribunal nor the PAB have the authority to decide on the incapacity of a person to form or express an intention to make an application for disability benefits until the Minister makes a decision under s. 81.

Sudnik v. MHRD (January 23, 2004), CP 19633 (PAB)

The PAB has no jurisdiction to conduct a judicial review of the Review Tribunal's decision.

Meseyton v. MHRD (June 4, 2004), CP 21108 (PAB)

The PAB is a statutory board and it therefore derived all of its powers, solely, from the statute that created it, namely, the CPP. While the members of the PAB were all judges or former judges of a superior court of a province and thus as members of those courts enjoyed a broad equitable jurisdiction, they had no such expanded jurisdiction when sittings as members of the PAB and were bound strictly by the express provisions and wording of the CPP.

B.P. v. MHRSD (June 18, 2010), CP 25325 (PAB)

The PAB cannot deem that the application for a death benefit also includes an application for a survivor's pension. Section 60(1) provides that no benefit is payable unless an application for the benefit is presented to the Minister by a claimant.

Robsob-Belfrey v. MHRD (January 8, 2004), CP 15822 (PAB)

Where the Minister had never, on the record, considered and given a decision in writing on the issue of capacity, no appeal could be heard. Such a step was a necessary basis for the appeal procedure, and the consent of all parties could not confer jurisdiction on the PAB to continue.

MSD v. Kovac (December 2, 2004), CP 21098 (PAB)

Where the Review Tribunal hears a new application after the initial application has been dismissed, it is required to address the proper procedure of a s. 84(2) reconsideration, and turn their minds to the issue of *res judicata*. For the PAB to ignore such failure by the Review Tribunal would set a dangerous precedent allowing unsuccessful applicants to circumvent the provisions. The CPP establishes specific procedures for each step of an appeal. Applicants are treated fairly by the appeal process and should be required to abide by it.

MSD v. Kendall (June 7, 2004), CP 21960 (PAB)

The CPP makes no mention of an equitable jurisdiction for either the Board or the Tribunal. Each of these adjudicative bodies must exercise its statutory powers resolutely but neither must overstep the bounds of the CPP and indulge in fairness considerations which are unsupported in the express language of the CPP.

Robsob-Belfrey v. MHRD (January 8, 2004), CP 15822 (PAB)

Where the Minister had never, on the record, considered and given a decision in writing on the issue of capacity, no appeal could be heard. Such a step was a necessary basis for the appeal procedure, and neither the Review Tribunal nor the PAB had jurisdiction to determine the matter without a formal decision of the Minister.

Spiece v. MHRD (April 7, 2003), CP 19047 (PAB)

Section 83(11) gave the PAB the power to conduct a full hearing of the claimant's case, including new evidence she was seeking to introduce before the Review Tribunal under s. 84(2).

Meron v. MHRD (November 5, 2001), CP 16783 (PAB)

The PAB has no authority to make an award of costs in favour of the applicant to reimburse her for her costs of preparing the appeal.

Larone v. MHRD (February 23, 2000), CP 09254 (PAB)

The PAB does not have jurisdiction to deal with the matter of recovery of any overpayment of disability benefits to a claimant, which are dealt with under s. 66.

Brandon v. MHRD

The PAB does not have jurisdiction to forgive the repayment of overpayments to a claimant on compassionate grounds.

Davies v. Canada (MHRD) (1999), Doc. FC T-1789-98

Section 84(1) is designed to provide the Review Tribunal with the mandate to determine if an applicant should be granted benefits and the amount of benefits, and to give the PAB discretion to determine whether leave to appeal is granted or denied to an applicant who has been refused disability benefits. The decisions of the PAB are not appealable other than by judicial review to the Federal Court.

MHRD v. Mansfield (August 10, 1999), CP 06175, CEB & PG (TB) ¶8806 (PAB). See also *Makeiv v. MNHW* (February 9, 1994), CP 2579, CEB & PG (TB) ¶8537 (PAB).

The PAB does not possess any equitable jurisdiction, and is bound solely by the provisions of the CPP and the evidence placed before it.

Graham v. MHRD (June 13, 1997), CP 5230, CEB & PG (TB) ¶8692 (PAB)

The PAB is a statutory tribunal which must find its jurisdiction in the CPP. It does not possess any equitable jurisdiction, and therefore lacks the authority to forgive the repayment of disability benefits that have been paid in error to a claimant.

Curto v. MHRD (October 9, 1996), CP 3841 (PAB)

The PAB is not a court of equity, and cannot base its decision on equity or equitable principles. It is a purely statutory Board created by legislation by the Government of Canada, approved by a majority of the provinces, and is bound by the provisions of that legislation and limited to the powers expressed therein. The PAB is mandated to base its decisions on the legal tenets and principles expressed in the CPP, and lacks equitable jurisdiction. That the applicant's former family physician had destroyed the medical records for the critical period, between 11 and 16 years previously, could not justify a finding of disability commencing at that time in the absence of other evidence.

Doherty v. MEI (July 15, 1996), CP 4207, CEB & PG (TB) ¶8651 (PAB)

A decision of the Minister, under s. 81 includes a s. 55.3 decision, and therefore the PAB has jurisdiction to review a s. 55.3 Ministerial decision.

Wiemer v. Ganim (1996), Doc. T-1121-95 (Fed. T.D.)

The PAB has no inherent power, and does not have the statutory authority to refer a matter back to the Minister for another consideration just after the PAB found the Minister's original consideration, which had been upheld by the Review Tribunal, to have been wrong.

Pincombe v. Canada (Attorney General) (October 21, 1994), CP 3291, CEB & PG (TB) ¶8555 (PAB)

The decision to remedy or not, in CPP s. 66, is placed wholly within the Minister's department. Neither the Review Tribunal nor the PAB have jurisdiction to hear appeals from the Minister's decision or to interfere with the discretion exercised.

§2. Effect of Departmental Guidelines

Atkinson v. Canada (Attorney General), 2014 FCA 187

While this definition of "benevolent employer" is not binding on the Federal Court, it is relevant on an application for judicial review as the SST's application of this definition nonetheless provides insight into the factors that contributed to the SST's decision, and enables the court to assess whether its application of paragraph 42(2)(*a*) was reasonable.

Boles v. MEI (June 30, 1994), CP 2794, CEB & PG (TB) ¶8553 (PAB)

The PAB cannot consider CPP guidelines generated and utilized as a practical matter within the Department in reaching a conclusion as to what Parliament intended to constitute a "substantially gainful occupation" under the CPP.

Lummiss v. MHRD (May 3, 1999), CP 8299 (PAB)

The criterion or benchmark in the guidelines as to the amount of money an applicant can earn without being considered "substantially gainfully employed" is not binding upon the Board, but it is a significant factor to be considered, with others, when deciding this issue.

§3. Practice and Procedure

K.B. v. MHRSD (May 11, 2012), CP 26646 (PAB)

After the close of the hearing, it is unacceptable for the applicant's counsel to send a "Summary of Argument" and an email from a witness for his client for the purpose of confirming, correcting, and adding to her testimony given at the hearing There must be a finality to hearings. If counsel feels compelled to continue a hearing after its conclusion, he or she must follow the appropriate procedure by bringing the appropriate motion.

§4. Onus of Proof and Credibility

MacNeil v. MHRD (January 16, 1998), Doc. A-806-96 (Fed. C.A.)

It is a function of the PAB to assess the credibility of witnesses appearing before it. Drawing inferences from the applicant's demeanour at the hearing as to the legitimacy of his back pain and hearing complaints did not constitute a denial of natural justice. The PAB was not required to bring to the applicant's attention its intent to draw adverse inferences from his demeanour in the hearing room and to give him the opportunity to rebut these inferences.

Jones v. Canada (Attorney General), 2010 FC 740

There is no statutory onus on the Ministry to obtain whatever evidence is available from the family doctor or any specialist listed in an application or prior application, whether or not it is filed by the claimant, to explain the CPP to the claimant, and to tell the claimant what information is missing from his or her file, including whether the claimant should file additional evidence. If there was such an onus, then the fact that the CPP Regulations put the burden of proof on the claimant would have no meaning.

Bird v. MHRD (August 23, 2000), CP 11632 (PAB). See also *MacNeil* (above).

It is an error for the Review Tribunal not only to make their own assessment of the applicant's physical ability based on his or her demeanour at the hearing, but also to rely on that assessment as an important, if not decisive, factor in their decision. It may be proper, in some rare cases, to make such observations and subsequently draw conclusions from them, but, in the normal run of cases, it should not be done.

Moore v. MHRD (September 10, 2001), CP 15717 (PAB)

The applicant need not do more than establish, on the whole of the evidence, that it is more likely than not that he or she meets the disability requirements of the Plan, as well as the contributory requirements. Convincing proof or proof of the claim beyond a reasonable doubt, as in a criminal prosecution, is inappropriate and is not required.

MHRD v. Zambito (June 29, 2001), CP 07681 (PAB)

Even on a Minister's appeal from a majority decision of the Review Tribunal, the onus of establishing a severe and prolonged disability remains on the applicant through the entire process, including the trial *de novo* before the PAB. Any onus on the Minister is addressed at the leave to appeal level.

Dasuki v. MHRD (August 31, 2001), CP 09419 (PAB)

The failure of the applicant to be present to answer questions about her condition and to have her credibility tested is a factor the PAB must consider.

Amicucci v. MHRD (April 12, 1998), CP 5071 (PAB)

In all proceedings before either the Review Tribunal or the PAB, the onus and responsibility to establish that the applicant or appellant, as the case may be, meets the qualifying criteria necessary to entitle him or her to pension benefits, lies upon the applicant or appellant. That party must bring him or herself within those criteria, and it is not incumbent upon the Minister to establish that the applicant is not so qualified. The standard of proof, which the applicant or appellant must meet, is one of reasonable probability. In a claim for disability pension, this is normally done through the production before the adjudicating body of objective and clinical medical reports from which it may be reasonably inferred that the party is, in fact, and in all probability, unable to engage in any form of substantially gainful employment, although the *viva voce* evidence given by or on behalf of the applicant or appellant is always to be given due weight.

MEI v. Bouliane (May 30, 1996), CP 4268 (PAB)

On an appeal by the Minister, the onus is on the Minister to prove a *prima facie* case only as the hearing is *de novo*. Once the *prima facie* case is made out, the onus then reverts back to the claimant.

MHRD v. Duhra (January 21, 1998), CP 5021 (PAB)

Given that the onus is on the claimant, the PAB needs to be able to assess his or her credibility and expect the claimant to give oral testimony. Credibility is difficult to assess on the basis of documentary evidence alone.

Dinas v. MHRD (April 25, 1997), CP 4024 (PAB)

Credibility is a major issue, and the claimant's evasiveness can be a significant factor. The PAB is entitled to draw an adverse inference from the fact that potential witnesses for the claimant, in this case the claimant's spouse or child, were not called to fill gaps in the evidence.

Di Caro v. MHRD (April 24, 1997), CP 4068 (PAB)

The claimant's failure to testify in person, unless adequately explained, will weigh heavily in the balance against the genuineness of the claim.

Abate v. MHRD (February 26, 1997), CP 4031 (PAB)

The onus is not on the Minister to disprove disability or to obtain further medical information.

MHRD v. Glimm (September 1, 1998), CP 5942 (PAB)

Throughout the entire process, from the initial application to the PAB hearing, the onus of proof rests on the claimant. There is no onus on the Minister to establish that the claimant does have a capacity for work. The onus shifts to the Minister only after the claimant has established a *prima facie* case of incapacity.

Burns v. MNHW (October 22, 1993), CP 2605, CEB & PG (TB) ¶8522 (PAB). See also *Lazzara v. MEI* (May 10, 1995), CP 3494 (PAB).

Chronic pain syndrome involves a very heavy onus on a disability pension claimant to establish entitlement.

---

65. *Canada Pension Plan* — **If, in the Minister's opinion, a person in addition to the appellant may be directly affected by the decision of the Tribunal relating to any of the following appeals, the Minister must notify the Tribunal of all such persons, and the Tribunal must add as a party to the appeal any such person who is not already a party to it:**

    (a) an appeal in respect of a survivor's pension payable to the survivor of a deceased contributor within the meaning of the *Canada Pension Plan*;

615

(*b*) an appeal in respect of a division of unadjusted pensionable earnings under section 55, 55.1 or 55.2 of the *Canada Pension Plan*; or

(*c*) an appeal in respect of an assignment of a contributor's retirement pension under section 65.1 of the *Canada Pension Plan.*

(2012, c. 19, s. 224.)

66. *Amendment of decision* — **(1) The Tribunal may rescind or amend a decision given by it in respect of any particular application if**

(*a*) **in the case of a decision relating to the *Employment Insurance Act*, new facts are presented to the Tribunal or the Tribunal is satisfied that the decision was made without knowledge of, or was based on a mistake as to, some material fact; or**

(*b*) **in any other case, a new material fact is presented that could not have been discovered at the time of the hearing with the exercise of reasonable diligence.**

(2012, c. 19, s. 224.)

(2) *Time limit* — **An application to rescind or amend a decision must be made within one year after the day on which a decision is communicated to the appellant. (2012, c. 19, s. 224.)**

(3) *Limit* — **Each person who is the subject of a decision may make only one application to rescind or amend that decision. (2012, c. 19, s. 224.)**

(4) *Division* — **A decision is rescinded or amended by the same Division that made it. (2012, c. 19, s. 224.)**

(2012, c. 19, s. 224.)

—————————— **Notes** ——————————

This provision replicates s. 84(2) of the CPP, which is repealed effective April 1, 2013. Three notable differences are that (1) the new section codifies the common law due diligence requirement, (2) the application must be brought within one year of the original decision, and (3) a claimant can only bring the application once with respect to a particular decision.

Case Law

[Editor's note: The following cases were decided under the previous CPP ss. 82–84, now repealed.]

§1. Practice and Procedure

Canada (Attorney General) v. Jagpal, 2008 FCA 38

This provision provides for an exceptional recourse. It makes an exception to the finality principle which characterizes judicial or quasi-judicial decisions. The provision ought to be interpreted in a manner which ensures procedural fairness to the parties who were either bound by, or entitled to rely upon, the final decision under a new attack. On a new facts application, the tribunal is required to determine two issues: whether there are new facts submitted by the person who brings the application, and whether these new facts are of sufficient force to justify rescinding or amending the earlier decision. These two issues are inextricably linked and decided on the basis of the same evidence. Usually, they are decided at the same time by the same tribunal member(s). This makes sense in terms of efficiency as well as fairness to the parties who do not have to attend two hearings. The hearing of a new facts application should not be split into two hearings: one at which the tribunal decides the issue of "new facts", and another at which the tribunal will decide whether the new facts justify rescinding the earlier decision. The determination of whether the submitted facts amount to new facts within the meaning of the provision is not a mere formality or a mere threshold. It is a key issue upon which the jurisdiction of the tribunal to rescind its earlier decision depends. If no new facts are found, the decision cannot be rescinded.

Canada (Attorney General) v. Richard, 2008 FCA 69

"New facts" within the meaning of the provision cannot include facts that are before the tribunal by way of an appeal. The tribunal must determine first if the two documents could be admitted as new facts because (1) they establish the existence of a condition which was in existence at the time of the original hearing but could not have been discovered with the exercise of reasonable diligence, and (2) this evidence may reasonably be expected to affect the outcome. Once it was determined that the additional evidence qualified as new facts, the tribunal had to determine if, combined with the documents that were before it at the original hearing, the claimant was disabled within the meaning of the CPP as of the MQP termination date. The tribunal is not entitled to collapse the two proceedings in to one and hear, at the same time, the new facts application and the appeal on the second application.

Mazzotta v. Canada (Attorney General), 2007 FCA 297

The proper legal test for establishing whether new facts are material so as to fall within the statutory provision is whether the proposed new facts may reasonably be expected to affect the outcome of the initial decision. Whether "there was a reasonable possibility as opposed to probability that the new evidence could lead the Tribunal to change its original decision" was an incorrect test.

Sherratt v. MHRSD (May 14, 2009), CP 25572 (PAB)

Mazzotta makes it clear that the determination of an application made under this provision is a two-step process:

1. The appellate tribunal must first decide on the admissibility of the new facts; those tendered at first instance and accepted by it or, if it be the case, different ones now being tendered to the appellate tribunal. If the appellate tribunal does not accept the tendered evidence as new facts, that ends the matter, and the appellate tribunal grants the appeal and rescinds the decision under appeal. In such event, the original decision remains final and binding for all purposes, by reason of s. 82.

2. If the appellate tribunal determines as admissible new facts, either those tendered and accepted at first instance or different ones tendered to the appellate tribunal, it then proceeds *de novo*, to determine, on all the evidence, whether to grant or deny benefits.

The appellate tribunal's ruling on new facts should form part of its final decision only once it has heard all of the evidence.

Jagpal v. Canada (Attorney General), 2006 FCA 26

New evidence obtained after the hearing before the tribunal should be dealt with by way of a reconsideration of the claim under this provision, not on judicial review.

Canada (Minister of Human Resources Development) v. Landry, 2005 FCA 167

The limits that the provision places on the appellate tribunal's jurisdiction means that it must consider the facts on which the first instance decision was originally based and the facts that it admitted as new facts when it revised the decision. The facts that are presented to the appellate tribunal at the hearing, and that it may itself characterize as new, whether or not those facts were submitted at first instance, should be added to those facts. Strictly speaking, the appellate tribunal should be limited to the new facts that were submitted at first instance. However, because it also has the power to review its own decision, based on new facts, the appellate tribunal could also be asked to do so once it has made its decision regarding the first instance

617

decision. It is therefore better for it, on the appeal of the original decision, to rule immediately on the new facts that were not submitted at first instance but that are now before the appellate tribunal. Moreover, with respect to the facts that were presented at first instance but rejected, in purely practical terms, the appellate tribunal must be able to review this refusal to consider those facts to be new facts. In order to rule on the merits of the application for disability benefits, the appellate tribunal could not have had regard to the facts rejected at first instance or to facts presented to the appellate tribunal that had not been presented at first instance without first satisfying itself, and deciding, that they were new facts. [Note: the PAB in *Sherratt v. MHRSD* (May 14, 2009), CP 25572 (PAB) held that the invitation in *Landry* for the PAB to "rule immediately" on the motion to adduce new facts was not binding.]

§2. Test for Admissibility of New Facts

Varrette v. Sainsbury, [1928] SCR 72. See also *Dove v. MSD* (September 7, 2004), CP 22419 (PAB), *Macri v. MSD* (January 6, 2005), CP 22830 (PAB).

A new hearing should be granted only where the new evidence proposed to be adduced could not have been obtained by reasonable diligence before the original hearing and is such that, if adduced it would be practically conclusive.

Canada (Attorney General) v. MacRae, 2008 FCA 82. See also *Higgins v. Canada (Attorney General),* 2009 FCA 322.

In order for evidence to be admissible as a "new fact", the evidence must meet a two-part test: (1) it must establish a fact (usually a medical condition in the context of the CPP) that existed at the time of the original hearing but was not discoverable before the original hearing by the exercise of due diligence (the "discoverability test"), and (2) the evidence must reasonably be expected to affect the result of the prior hearing (the "materiality test"). Courts have considered medical reports written after the original hearing of the application to be admissible pursuant to s. 84(2) of the CPP where, for example, the condition which they attest to exist at the time of the original hearing but could not have been diagnosed or known to the applicant through the exercise of due diligence by the applicant. However, in cases where the medical reports reiterate what is already known or has been diagnosed, the reports will not be considered as evidencing new facts. A mental disability may exist prior to a claimant's MQP date but may not have been diagnosed prior to that time.

Mazzotta v. Canada (Attorney General), 2007 FCA 297

The materiality test for the purpose of s. 84(2) is met if the proposed new facts may reasonably be expected to affect the outcome. This test is not a mere formality that can be ignored, overlooked, or bypassed. The test is there to strike a balance between, on the one hand, the need to have disability claims assessed fairly and the need, on the other hand, to secure, in the public interest, the finality and enforcement of previous decisions which are *res judicata*.

Kent v. Canada (Attorney General), 2004 FCA 420

The question of materiality is a question of mixed fact and law, in the sense that it requires a provisional assessment of the importance of the proposed new facts to the merits of the claim for the disability pension. In the context of an application to reconsider a decision relating to entitlement to benefits under the CPP, the test for the determination of new facts should be applied in a manner that is sufficiently flexible to balance, on the one hand, the Minister's legitimate interest in the finality of decisions and the need to encourage claimants to put all their cards on the table at the earliest reasonable opportunity, and on the other hand, the legitimate interest of claimants, who are usually self-represented, in having their claims assessed fairly, on the merits. These considerations generally require a broad and generous approach to the determination of due diligence and materiality. For most disabling conditions, it is reasonable to expect the claimant to present a complete picture of his or her disability at the time of the first application, or on a first appeal to the

Review Tribunal or the PAB. However, there are some disability claims, such as those based on physical and mental conditions that are not well understood by medical practitioners, that must be assessed against the background of an evolving understanding of a claimant's condition, treatment, and prognosis. It is especially important in such cases to ensure that the new facts rule is not applied in an unduly rigid manner, depriving a claimant of a fair assessment of the claim on the merits.

Ezerzer v. Canada (Minister of Human Resources Development), 2006 FC 812

The decision in *Kent* suggests that in certain situations, a disability can exist without being properly diagnosed. When this occurs, a less rigid assessment of whether someone qualifies for a disability pension should be applied.

Forfar v. Canada (Attorney General), 2007 FC 460

New facts are not necessarily new events. They are "new" if they could not have been discovered by the exercise of due diligence and presented at the original hearing. However, irrespective of the sense in which new is used, they must be relevant, or material.

§3. New Evidence — Example Cases

(a) Admitted / Determinative

- Where original doctor focused on physical symptoms only, evidence of pre-MQP mental health issues was admissible. The claimant could not be faulted for the failure of medical practitioners to have paid more attention to his mental health at the time: *Canada (Attorney General) v. MacRae*, 2008 FCA 82

- Facts relating to lack of improvement and inability to obtain work: *Arthurs v. Canada (Minister of Social Development)*, 2006 FC 1107

- New diagnosis of depression, which had not been asserted in original application; diagnosis based not on speculation but on patient history: *Ezerzer v. Canada (Minister of Human Resources Development)*, 2006 FC 812

- Psychologist's report obtained after MQP addressing for first time issue of whether or not there is "a severe and prolonged mental disability": *Van Every v. MHRD* (May 25, 2001), CP 12783 (PAB)

- Two reports prepared by neurosurgeon following four operations on claimant for rare condition; reports both dated after the date of the first Review Tribunal proceedings: *MHRD v. MacDonald*, [2002] FCA 48

(b) Not Admitted / Not Determinative

- Reinstatement of benefits after termination for non-compliance with Minister's request for information: *C.S. v. MHRSD* (February 2, 2012), CP 28021 (PAB)

- Diagnosis of secondary fibromyalgia syndrome three years after MQP, when she had been diagnosed with fibromyalgia; while primary and secondary fibromyalgia have different causes, their symptoms are identical: *Taker v. Canada (Attorney General)*, 2012 FCA 39

- Subsequent worker's compensation decision awarding the applicant a benefit for permanent disability did not automatically qualify as a new fact, where the provincial pension regime did not set out the same requirements as the CPP: *Harvey v. Canada (Attorney General)*, 2010 FC 74

- Documents presented relate to the diagnosis of degenerative disc disease, which was well known and investigated prior to original Review Tribunal hearing: *B.S.M. v. MHRSD* (September 17, 2010), CP 27031 (PAB)

- Claimant submitted new medical reports and an "updated" questionnaire on application for reconsideration; there were numerous similarities between first and second applications and questionnaires; documents presented relate to the diagnosis of degenerative disc disease, which was well known and investigated prior to the 2003 RT hearing: *R.A. v. MHRSD* (January 13, 2011), CP 26660 (PAB)

- Where medical information was produced seven years after the original hearing and MQP, the only reasonable conclusion was that such information did not exist at the time of the original hearing and could not reasonably be expected to have affected the original decision denying disability benefits. No evidence was adduced as to what, if any, steps had been taken, at the relevant time, to find the new evidence, nor was there any explanation as to why the new evidence could not have been provided at the original hearing: *W.D. v. MHRSD* (September 9, 2010), CP 25863 (PAB)

- Reports indicating a sharp deterioration in the claimant's condition after the MQP; existing condition just became more acute: *Gilroy v. Canada (Attorney General)*, 2010 FCA 302

- Physician put after the fact diagnosis of fibromyalgia at 1999, but moved it back to 1994 when informed of MQP date: *Gaudet v. Canada (Attorney General)* 2010 FCA 59

- Earlier diagnosis of sleep apnea would not have materially affected earlier decision, and in fact would have facilitated claimant's recovery: *Walker v. Canada (Attorney General)*, 2011 FCA 189

- Some evidence before first Review Tribunal hearing of applicant's psychiatric issues, so reports based on referrals for treatment of these issues made well after the first hearing did not constitute new facts; applicant had chosen not to proceed on the basis of his psychiatric issues as a ground of disability at the first hearing and did not exercise the reasonable diligence required to discover the additional medical reports subsequently relied upon as new facts: *R.M. v. MHRSD* (March 29, 2010), CP 26142 (PAB)

- "Newly discovered" medical reports merely confirmed that claimant had serious knee problems for which she sought medical attention; this was already known to Tribunal at original hearing: *Murphy v. Canada (Attorney General)*, 2008 FC 351

- Vocational Services Report dated a year after the RT hearing concluding that the claimant would not be able to function successfully in a competitive work environment, even on a part-time basis; report not discoverable because it did not exist at relevant time; functional ability assessment had been recommended prior to original hearing and MQP, but had not been done: *Sherratt v. MHRSD* (May 14, 2009), CP 25572 (PAB)

- New diagnosis with somatization disorder: *M.R. v. MHRSD (January 22, 2009)*, CP 24200 (PAB)

- A letter from an orthopaedic surgeon did not constitute new facts where the claimant had the letter at the time of the original Review Tribunal hearing but did not explain why she did not take it to the hearing. Claimant did not demonstrate the due diligence required nor could the proposed new facts reasonably be expected to affect the outcome of the original decision: *HRSD v. Sverkas* (January 17, 2008), CP 20822 (PAB)

- Claimant, whose MQP ended in December 1992, unsuccessfully applied for disability benefits in 1990 and 1996, appealing up to the PAB level both times. Claimant reapplied in 2000, using a report from Dr. B who was his physician from 1991 to 1993. Dr. B had not filed a report in the earlier proceedings, because the claimant thought his report from another physician would be sufficient. PAB dismissed the appeal because Dr. B's report could have been available in the earlier hearings and it was simply a rehash of all the evidence already considered previously: *Taylor v. MHRD* (April 20, 2004), CP 20684 (PAB). Note: judicial review being sought.

- Claimant applied three times for disability benefits, twice prior to MQP expiry and once after. First two were denied by Review Tribunal with leave to appeal to PAB denied both times. On his third application, the Review Tribunal ruled in favour of claimant, and stated (wrongly) that its decision was based partly on evidence not available on the first Tribunal hearing. On the Minister's appeal to PAB of the third Tribunal decision, the PAB dismissed claim on grounds of *res judicata*. If there were truly new facts, the proper procedure would have been for claimant to reapply to the Tribunal under s. 84(2). The Tribunal had no jurisdiction to hear new application after MQP: *Adamo v. MHRD* (January 16, 2004), CP 20427 (PAB)

- Independent assessment dating applicant's fibromyalgia to before the expiry of her MQP being issued shortly before PAB hearing; PAB acknowledging existence of fibromyalgia diagnosis while denying benefits: *Roper v. MHRD* (July 12, 2001), CP 17744 (PAB)

- Psychiatrist report detailing current problems based on examination four years after expiry of MQP: *MHRD v. Wade* (April 8, 2002), CP 14460 (PAB)

- New medical opinion based on clinical data already in existence; evidence not conclusive in any event: *Leonard v. MHRD* (March 19, 1998), CP 03893, CEB & PG (TB) ¶8706 (PAB)

- Claimant receiving medical report one hour before hearing, but not seeking adjournment: *Giampa v. MEI* (May 8, 1996), CP 3255, CEB & PG (TB) ¶8627 (PAB)

(c) Specific Types of Situations

Arthurs v. Canada (Minister of Social Development), 2006 FC 1107

The condition of fibromyalgia is difficult to prove by objective findings. Therefore, the test for new facts should be applied less rigidly in order to fairly assess such a disability claim.

L.D. v. MHRSD (January 26, 2012), CP 26351 (PAB)

Section 84(2) does not provide the PAB with authority to move back into earlier stages of this case and decide collateral issues, such as the alleged negligence raised against the agents who previously represented the appellant.

Macri v. MSD (January 6, 2005), CP 22830 (PAB)

The claimant did not establish that additional notes of a treating physician could not have been adduced at the first hearing, when other notes of the physician had been adduced.

Roper v. MHRD (July 12, 2001), CP 17744 (PAB)

The date of the emergence of fibromyalgia and its effect are not new facts within the meaning of the section.

§4. Res Judicata and Issue Estoppel

Kaminski v. Canada (Attorney General), 2014 FC 238

Issue estoppel is a branch of the *res judicata* doctrine, and engages the inherent power of the Court to prevent the misuse of its procedure by precluding the relitigation of issues, so as not to violate such principles as judicial economy, consistency, finality, and the integrity of the administration of justice. The doctrine applies where issues have been conclusively decided in prior proceedings, including the proceedings of administrative officers and tribunals. Determining whether issue estoppel applies involves a two-step process. First, it must be determined whether the moving party has established the three preconditions for its operation:

1. that the same question has been decided;

2. that the judicial decision which is said to create the estoppel was final; and

3. that the parties to the judicial decision or their privies were the same persons as the parties to the proceedings in which the estoppel is raised or their privies.

If the three preconditions are met, the court must still determine whether, as a matter of discretion, issue estoppel *ought* to be applied.

---

67. *Time limits* — **The Chairperson or a Vice-Chairperson may in any particular case for special reasons extend the time within which the Tribunal is required by regulation to make a decision under subsections 54(1), 58(3) and 59(1).**

(2012, c. 19, s. 224.)

68. *Decision final* — **The decision of the Tribunal on any application made under this Act is final and, except for judicial review under the *Federal Courts Act*, is not subject to appeal to or review by any court.**

(2012, c. 19, s. 224.)

———————— **Notes** ————————

This section is similar in effect to the CPP s. 84.

Note that judicial review of a CPP or OAS decision refusing leave to appeal is made to the Federal Court under ss. 18 and 18.1 of the *Federal Court Acts*, whereas judicial review of substantive CPP or OAS decisions are made directly to the Federal Court of Appeal under s. 28 of that Act.

Federal Courts Act

18. — **(1)** *Extraordinary remedies, federal tribunals.* — Subject to section 28, the Federal Court has exclusive original jurisdiction

(*a*) to issue an injunction, writ of *certiorari*, writ of prohibition, writ of *mandamus* or writ of *quo warranto*, or grant declaratory relief, against any federal board, commission or other tribunal; and

(*b*) to hear and determine any application or other proceeding for relief in the nature of relief contemplated by paragraph (*a*), including any proceeding brought against the Attorney General of Canada, to obtain relief against a federal board, commission or other tribunal.

. . .

18.1. — **(1)** *Application for judicial review* — An application for judicial review may be made by the Attorney General of Canada or by anyone directly affected by the matter in respect of which relief is sought.

(2) *Time limitation* — An application for judicial review in respect of a decision or an order of a federal board, commission or other tribunal shall be made within 30 days after the time the decision or order was first communicated by the federal board, commission or other tribunal to the office of the Deputy Attorney General of Canada or to the party directly affected by it, or within any further time that a judge of the Federal Court may fix or allow before or after the end of those 30 days.

(3) *Powers of Federal Court* — On an application for judicial review, the Federal Court may

(a) order a federal board, commission or other tribunal to do any act or thing it has unlawfully failed or refused to do or has unreasonably delayed in doing; or

(b) declare invalid or unlawful, or quash, set aside or set aside and refer back for determination in accordance with such directions as it considers to be appropriate, prohibit or restrain, a decision, order, act or proceeding of a federal board, commission or other tribunal.

(4) *Grounds of review* — The Federal Court may grant relief under subsection (3) if it is satisfied that the federal board, commission or other tribunal

(a) acted without jurisdiction, acted beyond its jurisdiction or refused to exercise its jurisdiction;

(b) failed to observe a principle of natural justice, procedural fairness or other procedure that it was required by law to observe;

(c) erred in law in making a decision or an order, whether or not the error appears on the face of the record;

(d) based its decision or order on an erroneous finding of fact that it made in a perverse or capricious manner or without regard for the material before it;

(e) acted, or failed to act, by reason of fraud or perjured evidence; or

(f) acted in any other way that was contrary to law.

(5) *Defect in form or technical irregularity* — If the sole ground for relief established on an application for judicial review is a defect in form or a technical irregularity, the Federal Court may

(a) refuse the relief if it finds that no substantial wrong or miscarriage of justice has occurred; and

(b) in the case of a defect in form or a technical irregularity in a decision or an order, make an order validating the decision or order, to have effect from any time and on any terms that it considers appropriate.

* * *

28. — **(1)** *Judicial review* — The Court of Appeal has jurisdiction to hear and determine applications for judicial review made in respect of any of the following federal boards, commissions or other tribunals:

...

(d) the Pension Appeals Board established by the *Canada Pension Plan.*

...

(2) *Section applies* — Sections 18 to 18.5, except subsection 18.4(2), apply, with any modifications that the circumstances require, in respect of any matter within the jurisdiction of the Federal Court of Appeal under subsection (1) and, when they apply, a reference to the Federal Court shall be read as a reference to the Federal Court of Appeal.

(3) *Federal Court deprived of jurisdiction* — If the Federal Court of Appeal has jurisdiction to hear and determine a matter, the Federal Court has no jurisdiction to entertain any proceeding in respect of that matter.

Note that procedures in the Federal Court of Appeal with respect to CPP appeals are governed by the *Tax Court of Canada Rules of Procedure* respecting the *Canada Pension Plan.*

Case Law

[Editor's note: The following cases were decided under the previous CPP ss. 82–84, now repealed.]

Contents

§1. Judicial Review

(a) General Principles of Administrative Law

Baker v. Canada (MCI), [1999] 2 S.C.R. 817

The fact that a decision is administrative and affects "the rights, privileges or interests of an individual" is sufficient to trigger the application of the duty of fairness. The existence of a duty of fairness, however, does not determine what requirements will be applicable in a given set of circumstances. The concept of procedural fairness is eminently variable and its content is to be decided in the specific context of each case. All of the circumstances must be considered in order to determine the content of the duty of procedural fairness. However, several factors are relevant to determining what is required by the common-law duty of procedural fairness in a given set of circumstances:

1. *The nature of the decision being made and the process followed in making it* — The closeness of the administrative process to the judicial process should indicate how much of those governing principles should be imported into the realm of administrative decision-making. The more the process provided for, the function of the tribunal,

the nature of the decision-making body, and the determinations that must be made to reach a decision resemble judicial decision-making, the more likely it is that procedural protections closer to the trial model will be required by the duty of fairness.

2. *The nature of the statutory scheme and the terms of the statute pursuant to which the body operates* — The role of the particular decision within the statutory scheme and other surrounding indications in the statute help determine the content of the duty of fairness owed when a particular administrative decision is made.

3. *The importance of the decision to the individual or individuals affected* — The more important the decision is to the lives of those affected, and the greater its impact on that person or those persons, the more stringent the procedural protections that will be mandated.

4. *The legitimate expectations of the person challenging the decision* — If a legitimate expectation is found to exist, this will affect the content of the duty of fairness owed to the individual or individuals affected by the decision. If the claimant has a legitimate expectation that a certain procedure will be followed, this procedure will be required by the duty of fairness. Similarly, if a claimant has a legitimate expectation that a certain result will be reached in his or her case, fairness may require more extensive procedural rights than would otherwise be accorded. Nevertheless, the doctrine of legitimate expectations cannot lead to substantive rights outside the procedural domain. This doctrine is based on the principle that the "circumstances" affecting procedural fairness take into account the promises or regular practices of administrative decision-makers, and that it will generally be unfair for them to act in contravention of representations as to procedure, or to backtrack on substantive promises without according significant procedural rights.

5. *The choices of procedure made by the agency itself* — This is particularly important when the statute leaves to the decision-maker the ability to choose its own procedures, or when the agency has an expertise in determining what procedures are appropriate in the circumstances.

This list of factors is not exhaustive. Other factors may also be important, particularly when considering aspects of the duty of fairness unrelated to participatory rights. Underlying all these factors is the notion that the purpose of the participatory rights contained within the duty of procedural fairness is to ensure that administrative decisions are made using a fair and open procedure, appropriate to the decision being made and its statutory, institutional, and social context, with an opportunity for those affected by the decision to put forward their views and evidence fully and have them considered by the decision-maker.

An oral hearing is not always necessary to ensure a fair hearing and consideration of the issues involved. The flexible nature of the duty of fairness recognizes that meaningful participation can occur in different ways in different situations.

In certain circumstances, the duty of procedural fairness will require the provision of a written explanation for a decision. The strong arguments demonstrating the advantages of written reasons suggest that, in cases such as this — where the decision has important significance for the individual, when there is a statutory right of appeal, or in other circumstances — some form of reasons should be required.

Procedural fairness also requires that decisions be made free from a reasonable apprehension of bias by an impartial decision-maker. The apprehension of bias must be a reasonable one, held by reasonable and right-minded persons, applying themselves to the question and obtaining thereon the required information. The test is "what would an informed person, viewing the matter realistically and practically — and having thought the matter through — conclude? Would he or she think that it is more likely than not that the decision-maker, whether consciously or unconsciously, would not decide fairly?"

625

(b) Judicial Review Generally

(i) Standard of review

Alberta (Information and Privacy Commissioner) v. Alberta Teachers' Association, 2011 SCC 61, [2011] 3 SCR 654. See also *Canada (Canadian Human Rights Commission) v. Canada (Attorney General)*, 2011 SCC 53, [2011] 3 SCR 471

Unless the situation is exceptional, the interpretation by the tribunal of its own statute or statutes closely connected to its function, with which it will have particular familiarity should be presumed to be a question of statutory interpretation subject to deference on judicial review. Inadequacy of reasons was not a stand-alone basis for quashing a decision in judicial review. The reviewing court may, if found necessary, look at the record for the purpose of assessing the reasonableness of the outcome.

The power to uphold an outcome is not a *carte blanche* to reformulate a tribunal's decision in a way that casts aside an unreasonable chain of analysis in favour of the court's own rationale for the result.

Dunsmuir v. New Brunswick, 2008 SCC 9. See also *Handa v. Canada (Attorney General)*, 2008 FCA 223

The previously extant two reasonableness standards of review are to be collapsed into one — "reasonableness". This is normally the standard to be applied on a judicial review of the exercise of statutory discretion by an administrative decision-maker. When applying this deferential standard, reviewing courts are to consider whether a decision is unreasonable by reference to the range of acceptable choices left to the decision-maker by the legislation, to the reasons for decision, and to the decision itself. In determining which of the remaining standards of review, correctness or reasonableness, is applicable within a given set of circumstances, a two-step process is to be followed. First, the court must ascertain whether the jurisprudence has already determined in a satisfactory manner the degree of deference to be accorded with regard to a particular category of question. Second, where the first inquiry proves unfruitful, the court must proceed to an analysis of the factors making it possible to identify the proper standard of review.

Law Society of New Brunswick v. Ryan, 2003 SCC 20

When undertaking a correctness review, the court may undertake its own reasoning process to arrive at the result it judges correct. In contrast, when deciding whether an administrative action was unreasonable, a court should not at any point ask itself what the correct decision would have been. Applying the standard of reasonableness gives effect to the legislative intention that a specialized body will have the primary responsibility of deciding the issue according to its own process and for its own reasons. The standard of reasonableness does not imply that a decision-maker is merely afforded a "margin of error" around what the court believes is the correct result.

There is a further reason that courts testing for unreasonableness must avoid asking the question of whether the decision is correct. Unlike a review for correctness, there will often be no single right answer to the questions that are under review against the standard of reasonableness. For example, when a decision must be taken according to a set of objectives that exist in tension with each other, there may be no particular trade-off that is superior to all others. Even if there could be, notionally, a single best answer, it is not the court's role to seek this out when deciding if the decision was unreasonable.

How will a reviewing court know whether a decision is reasonable given that it may not first inquire into its correctness? The answer is that a reviewing court must look to the reasons given by the tribunal. A decision will be unreasonable only if there is no line of analysis within the given reasons that could reasonably lead the tribunal from the evidence before it to the conclusion at which it arrived. If any of the reasons that are sufficient to support the conclusion are tenable in the sense that they can stand up to a somewhat probing examination, then the decision will not be unreasonable and a reviewing court must not interfere. This means that a decision may satisfy the reasonableness standard if it is supported by a tenable explanation even if this explanation is not one that the reviewing court finds compelling. This does not mean that every element of the reasoning given must independently pass a test for reasonableness. The question is rather whether the reasons, taken as a whole, are tenable as support for the decision. At all times, a court applying a standard of reasonableness must assess the basic adequacy of a reasoned decision remembering that the issue under review does not compel one specific result. Moreover, a reviewing court should not seize on one or more mistakes or elements of the decision which do not affect the decision as a whole.

Dr. Q. v. College of Physicians and Surgeons of British Columbia, 2003 SCC 19

The pragmatic and functional approach applies whenever a court reviews the decision of an administrative body. Under this approach, the standard of review is determined by considering four contextual factors:

1. *The presence or absence of a privative clause or statutory right of appeal* — A statute may afford a broad right of appeal to a superior court or provide for a certified question to be posed to the reviewing court, suggesting a more searching standard of review. A statute may be silent on the question of review; silence is neutral, and does not imply a high standard of scrutiny. Finally, a statute may contain a privative clause, militating in favour of a more deferential posture. The stronger a privative clause, the more deference is generally due.

2. *The expertise of the tribunal relative to that of the reviewing court on the issue in question* — This factor recognizes that legislatures will sometimes remit an issue to a decision-making body that has particular topical expertise or is adept in the determination of particular issues. Where this is so, courts will seek to respect this legislative choice when conducting judicial review. Yet expertise is a relative concept, not an absolute one. Greater deference will be called for only where the decision-making body is, in some way, more expert than the courts and the question under consideration is one that falls within the scope of this greater expertise. Thus, the analysis under this heading has three dimensions: the court must characterize the expertise of the tribunal in question; it must consider its own expertise relative to that of the tribunal; and it must identify the nature of the specific issue before the administrative decision-maker relative to this expertise. Relative expertise can arise from a number of sources and can relate to questions of pure law, mixed fact and law, or fact alone. The composition of an administrative body might endow it with knowledge uniquely suited to the questions put before it and deference might, therefore, be called for under this factor. For example, a statute may call for decision-makers to have expert qualifications, to have accumulated experience in a particular area, or to play a particular role in policy development. Similarly, an administrative body might be so habitually called upon to make findings of fact in a distinctive legislative context that it can be said to have gained a measure of relative institutional expertise. Simply put, "whether because of the specialized knowledge of its decision-makers, special procedure, or non-judicial means of implementing the Act", an administrative body called upon to answer a question that falls within its area of relative expertise will generally be entitled to greater curial deference

3. *The purposes of the legislation and the provision in particular* — If the question before the administrative body is one of law or engages a particular aspect of the legislation, the analysis under this factor must also consider the specific legislative purpose of the provision(s) implicated in the review. As a general principle, increased deference is called for where legislation is intended to resolve and balance competing policy objectives or the interests of various constituencies — i.e., the legislation is "polycentric". A statutory purpose that requires a tribunal to select from a range of remedial choices or administrative responses, is concerned with the protection of the public, engages policy issues, or involves the balancing of multiple sets of interests or considerations will demand greater deference from a reviewing court. The express language of a statute may help to identify such a purpose. For example, provisions that require the decision-maker to "have regard to all such circumstances as it considers relevant" or confer a broad discretionary power upon a decision-maker will generally suggest policy-laden purposes and, consequently, a less searching standard of review. Reviewing courts should also consider the breadth, specialization, and technical or

627

scientific nature of the issues that the legislation asks the administrative tribunal to consider. In this respect, the principles animating the factors of relative expertise and legislative purpose tend to overlap. A legislative purpose that deviates substantially from the normal role of the courts suggests that the legislature intended to leave the issue to the discretion of the administrative decision-maker and, therefore, militates in favour of greater deference. In contrast, a piece of legislation or a statutory provision that essentially seeks to resolve disputes or determine rights between two parties will demand less deference. The more the legislation approximates a conventional judicial paradigm involving a pure *lis inter partes* determined largely by the facts before the tribunal, the less deference the reviewing court will tend to show.

4. *The nature of the question — law, fact, or mixed law and fact —* When the finding being reviewed is one of pure fact, this factor will militate in favour of showing more deference towards the tribunal's decision. Conversely, an issue of pure law counsels in favour of a more searching review. This is particularly so where the decision will be one of general importance or great precedential value. Finally, with respect to questions of mixed fact and law, this factor will call for more deference if the question is fact-intensive, and less deference if it is law-intensive.

The above four factors may overlap. The overall aim is to discern legislative intent, keeping in mind the constitutional role of the courts in maintaining the rule of law. Consideration of the four factors should enable the reviewing judge to address the core issues in determining the degree of deference. It should not be viewed as an empty ritual, or applied mechanically. The virtue of the pragmatic and functional approach lies in its capacity to draw out the information that may be relevant to the issue of curial deference.

Starson v. Swayze, 2003 SCC 32. See also *R. v. Owen*, 2003 SCC 33

Where the standard of review is based on reasonableness *simpliciter*, there is no basis for judicial interference with findings of fact or the inferences drawn from the facts absent demonstrated unreasonableness. This means that the tribunal's conclusion must be upheld provided it was among the range of conclusions that could reasonably have been reached on the law and evidence. If the tribunal's decision is such that it could reasonably be the subject of disagreement among tribunal members properly informed of the facts and instructed on the applicable law, the Court should in general decline to intervene. The fact that the reviewing court would have come to a different conclusion does not suffice to set aside the tribunal's conclusion.

Baker v. Canada (MCI), [1999] 2 S.C.R. 817

Discretionary decisions, like all other administrative decisions, must be made within the bounds of the jurisdiction conferred by the statute, but with considerable deference given to decision-makers by courts in reviewing the exercise of that discretion and determining the scope of the decision-maker's jurisdiction. The degree of discretion in a grant of power can range from one where the decision-maker is constrained only by the purposes and objects of the legislation, to one where it is so specific that there is almost no discretion involved. In between, there may be any number of limitations placed on the decision-maker's freedom of choice, sometimes referred to as "structured" discretion.

The "pragmatic and functional" approach recognizes that standards of review for errors of law are appropriately seen as a spectrum, with certain decisions being entitled to more deference, and others entitled to less. Three standards of review have been defined: patent unreasonableness, reasonableness *simpliciter*, and correctness. The standard of review of the substantive aspects of discretionary decisions is best approached within this framework, especially given the difficulty in making rigid classifications between discretionary and non-discretionary decisions. The pragmatic and functional approach takes into account considerations such as the expertise of the tribunal, the nature of the decision being made, and the language of the provision and the surrounding legislation. It includes factors such as whether a decision is "polycentric" and the intention revealed by the statutory language. The amount of choice left by Parliament to the administrative decision-maker and the nature of the decision being made are also important considerations in the analysis. The spectrum of standards of review can incorporate the principle that, in certain cases, the legislature has demonstrated its intention to leave greater choices to decision-makers than in others, but that a court must intervene where such a decision is outside the scope of the power accorded by Parliament.

Incorporating judicial review of decisions that involve considerable discretion into the pragmatic and functional analysis for errors of law should not be seen as reducing the level of deference given to decisions of a highly discretionary nature. In fact, deferential standards of review may give substantial leeway to the discretionary decision-maker in determining the "proper purposes" or "relevant considerations" involved in making a given determination. The pragmatic and functional approach can take into account the fact that the more discretion that is left to a decision-maker, the more reluctant courts should be to interfere with the manner in which decision-makers have made choices among various options. However, though discretionary decisions will generally be given considerable respect, that discretion must be exercised in accordance with the boundaries imposed in the statute, the principles of the rule of law, the principles of administrative law, the fundamental values of Canadian society, and the principles of the Charter.

Newfoundland and Labrador Nurses Union v. Newfoundland and Labrador (Treasury Board) 2011 SCC 62, [2011] 3 SCR 708. See also *McLaughlin v. Canada (Attorney General)*, 2012 FC 556

The SCC's decision in *Baker* stands for the proposition that in certain circumstances, the duty of procedural fairness will require some form of reasons for a decision. It did not say that reasons were *always* required, and it did not say that the *quality* of those reasons is a question of procedural fairness. Not any alleged deficiencies or flaws in the reasons fall under the category of a breach of the duty of procedural fairness and are therefore subject to a correctness review. The breach of a duty of procedural fairness is an error in law. Where there are no reasons in circumstances where they are required, there is nothing to review. But where there *are* reasons, there is no such breach. Any challenge to the reasoning/result of the decision should therefore be made within the reasonableness analysis.

Suresh v. Canada (MCI), [2002] SCC 1. See also *Ahani v. Canada (MCI)*, [2002] SCC 2

The Supreme Court of Canada's decision in *Baker v. Canada* does not authorize courts reviewing decisions on the discretionary end of the spectrum to engage in a new weighing process. The Minister's task is to make a decision that conforms to the legislated criteria and procedures as well as the Constitution. The court's task, if called upon to review the Minister's decision, is to determine whether the Minister has exercised his or her decision-making power within the constraints imposed by the legislation and the Constitution. If the Minister has considered the appropriate factors in conformity with these constraints, the court must uphold his or her decision. It cannot set it aside even if it would have weighed the factors differently and arrived at a different conclusion.

Pushpanathan v. Canada (MCI), [1998] 1 S.C.R. 982

In determining the standard of review applicable in a judicial review proceeding, the overriding consideration is the intention of the legislature: did it intend that a reviewing court accord the decision under review deference, or was a full right of appeal intended, or does the relevant standard fall somewhere on the spectrum that lies between these two poles? The standard of review must also be determined by reference to the specific nature of the decision under review. The same standard will not necessarily apply to all decisions of the same decision-maker. The factors to be assessed are: (1) the legislative provisions governing the review process, including whether there is a privative clause; (2) the degree of expertise of the tribunal with respect to the question in issue, as compared to the degree of expertise the reviewing court has on that subject; (3) the purpose of the legislation and the nature of the decision-maker; that is, whether the decision-maker is balancing public policy considerations (sometimes vaguely worded) as opposed to adjudicating the rights of individuals; and (4) the nature of the decision under review, including whether it is a question of law or a question of fact.

Callihoo v. Canada (Attorney General) (2000), FC Doc. T-859-99 (Fed. T.D.). See also *Wihksne v. Canada (Attorney General)* (2000), Doc. T-1451-99 (Fed. T.D.)

At the correctness end of the spectrum, a reviewing court can reverse a decision if it is found to be simply incorrect. At the other end of the spectrum, the decision can only be set aside if the error made by the decision-maker is so unreasonable that it is without any foundation in evidence or law. Between the extremes of the spectrum, a standard of reasonableness may be appropriate where the decision under review does not concern only a question of law and it is sufficient if it can be supported by reasons that will stand up to a somewhat probing analysis.

Mulveney v. Canada (Human Resources Development), 2007 FC 869

Expertise, which may be derived from specialized knowledge about a subject or from experience and skill in the determination of particular issues, is the most important of the four factors set out in the *Dr. Q.* decision.

Ezerzer v. Canada (Minister of Human Resources Development), 2006 FC 812

On judicial review, a court can consider only evidence that was before the administrative decision-maker whose decision is being reviewed and not new evidence.

(ii) Other matters

Layden v. HRSD, 2009 FCA 14

On an application for judicial review, the reviewing court can only exceptionally decide a case on the merits. The Federal Court of Appeal cannot engage in an examination of the evidence as such, unless a particular result is so inevitable on the facts that any other conclusion would be perverse. Where an application is successful, the matter must then be referred back to the deciding authority with a direction.

(b.1) Judicial Review of SST Decisions

Atkinson v. Canada (Attorney General), 2014 FCA 187

Typically, a privative clause in a statute points towards a standard of reasonableness. However, the s. 68 privative clause explicitly enables the Federal Court to review the SST's decisions. Therefore, the existence of this privative clause does not support a deferential standard of review. However, the differences between the SST and the PAB's structure, membership, and mandate do not diminish the need to apply a deferential standard in reviewing the SST's decisions. One of the SST's mandates is to interpret and apply the CPP, and it will encounter this legislation regularly in the course of exercising its functions. Moreover, s. 64(2) of the DESDA also restricts the type of questions of law or fact that the SST may decide with respect to the CPP, presumably in order to better ensure that the SST is only addressing issues that fall within its expertise. These factors suggest that Parliament intended for the SST to be afforded deference by the Federal Court, as it has greater expertise in interpreting and applying the CPP. The SST's interpretation and application of CPP s. 42(2)(a) is therefore reviewable on a standard of reasonableness.

M.Z. v. Minister of Human Resources and Skills Development (August 29, 2014) AD-13-33 (SSTAD)

Reasonableness is the appropriate standard of review on appeals with respect to errors of law, mixed fact and law, and errors of fact. However, no deference was owed to the tribunal below on questions of procedural fairness. The claimant could argue a breach of procedural fairness for the first time on appeal.

(c) Judicial Review of Tribunal Decisions by Federal Court

Farrell v. Canada (Attorney General), 2010 FCA 181

On judicial review from the PAB regarding a disability claim, the power of the Federal Court of Appeal has definite limits. It is restricted in three very important ways:

1. Unless a constitutional objection is present, the court must follow the laws that Parliament has written, as they have been written. In s. 42(2)(a)(i) of the Plan,

Parliament provides that a disability is severe only if "by reason thereof the [applicant] is incapable regularly of pursuing any substantially gainful occupation" as of the end of the "minimum qualifying period". The court, and all of the administrative bodies and the PAB, below, for that matter, cannot change that language. All must apply it as written.

2. The Court of Appeal's earlier decisions are binding on the court and cannot be changed, unless they are "manifestly wrong".

3. Most importantly, the Court of Appeal is not allowed to act like the PAB, with all of the fact-finding and other powers that the PAB has. Rather, the court has the power only to review — not redo — the PAB's decision in light of the factual findings it made. In reviewing the decision, the court must ask itself this question: did the PAB's decision fall within a range of possible, acceptable outcomes which are defensible in respect of the facts and the law?

Kaminski v. Canada (Social Development), 2008 FCA 225

After *Dunsmuir*, the appropriate standard of review of this question of mixed fact and law is now reasonableness. Accordingly, the intervention of the Federal Court of Appeal will only be warranted where the impugned decision does not fall within a range of possible, acceptable outcomes which are defensible in respect of the facts and law. [Note: the pre-*Dunsmuir* cases below refer to the patent unreasonableness standard, especially for pure questions of fact, which the Supreme Court of Canada in *Dunsmuir* (see above) collapsed into a single reasonableness standard.] See also *Belo Alves v. Canada (Attorney General)*, 2011 FCA 169.

Gaudet v. Canada (Attorney General), 2013 FCA 254

In an application for judicial review, the Federal Court of Appeal's powers are limited. It is not allowed to retry the factual issues, reweigh the evidence, or redo what the tribunal did. Rather, it is to assess whether the tribunal reached an outcome that was acceptable and defensible on the facts and the law. This is a deferential standard. Where the decision is mainly factual, the range of defensible and acceptable outcomes available to the tribunal is relatively wide. Even if sworn, documents containing information about an applicant's recent condition and giving some background to a medical report in the record are not normally admissible on an application for judicial review.

D'Errico v. Canada (Attorney General), 2014 FCA 95

It is one thing for an administrative decision maker to issue sparse reasons to sophisticated parties who regularly engage in a specialized area — e.g., labour arbitration — and who are familiar with the legal and factual landscape. It is quite another to issue adverse reasons to a claimant for a CPP disability benefit on a record that calls for explanation. Normally where judicial review is granted, the Federal Court of Appeal grants *certiorari* and remits the matter to the tribunal for reconsideration. It is for the tribunal to decide the merits of cases, not the court. Normally, the court awards *mandamus* only where the outcome of the case on the merits is a foregone conclusion — in other words the evidence can lead only to one result. One recognized exception is where there has been substantial delay and the additional delay caused by remitting the matter to the administrative decision maker for redecision threatens to bring the administration of justice into disrepute. In such circumstances, the court exceptionally may direct that a certain result be reached. The word "exceptionally" recognizes that administrative tribunals should be allowed another chance to decide the merits of the matter and not have the reviewing court do it for them. But the circumstances may support resort to the latter option in certain cases where remitting the issue to the tribunal undermines the goal of expedient and cost-efficient decision making, which often motivates the creation of specialized administrative tribunals in the first place. Disability benefits are meant to address a very serious condition, one that prevents the earning of meaningful income to sustain oneself. Parliament could not have intended the final disposition of disability benefits in these circumstances to take eight years.

Simpson v. Canada (Attorney General), 2012 FCA 82

A tribunal need not refer in its reasons to each and every piece of evidence before it, but is presumed to have considered all the evidence. Assigning weight to evidence, whether oral or written, is the province of the trier of fact. Accordingly, a court hearing an appeal or an application for judicial review may not normally substitute its view of the probative value of evidence for that of the tribunal that made the impugned finding of fact. Even if the PAB misapprehended some of the evidence, the reviewing court will consider whether such mistakes would not have made good pervasive evidential weaknesses in the claimant's case.

Brennan v. Canada (Attorney General), 2011 FCA 318

Before reaching a conclusion, the PAB does not have to address every piece of evidence that is inconsistent with evidence it accepts. The fact that it does not mention expert reports to the contrary does not establish that the PAB was not alert to the evidence as a whole when it made its decision.

Michaud v. Canada (Attorney General), 2011 FCA 126

Although the PAB did not express any view on the claimant's credibility, it was open to the PAB to prefer the documentary and medical evidence before it to the claimant's oral evidence.

McMeekin v. Canada (Attorney General), 2011 FCA 165

Unlike the Federal Court, the Federal Court of Appeal does not schedule specific days for hearing motions. The usual practice is to deal with all motions on the basis of written submissions under Rule 369 of the *Federal Courts Rules*. The moving party or a respondent is entitled to request an oral hearing, but such a request is granted only in cases of urgency or other special circumstances.

Mazzotta v. Canada (Attorney General), 2007 FCA 297

The CPP contains adjudicative and review mechanisms and a process designed to provide an easy, flexible and affordable access to these mechanisms. An ultimate but limited access to the Federal Court of Appeal by way of judicial review ensures that the process will remain, to the benefits of the parties to a claim, within the boundaries of legality. In other words, the Federal Court of Appeal acts as a watchdog of the lawfulness of the process.

Cooke v. Canada (Minister of Human Resources Development), 2005 FCA 280

In an application for judicial review of a decision of the PAB, the Federal Court cannot undertake a completely new hearing of the matter that was before the PAB. Nor can the Court exercise any authority that Parliament has given to the PAB. The Court will only review the decision of the PAB (and reasons) against the evidence that was presented to the PAB, and consider whether the hearing itself was properly conducted. An application for judicial review will not succeed unless the applicant establishes one of the grounds stipulated in s. 18.1(4) of the *Federal Courts Act.* An applicant for judicial review must tell the Court why he or she believes the PAB's decision discloses one or more of those grounds of review. This is done first in the notice of application, and in more detail in the memorandum of fact and law. The Court considers the submissions of the parties relating to the alleged grounds of review in a manner that is consistent with the extensive jurisprudence relating to standards of review. Generally, for PAB decisions, the standard of review for questions of law is correctness. However, the Court generally will defer to the PAB with respect to findings of fact (that is, a finding of fact will be accepted absent palpable and overriding error). The Court's assessment of the PAB decision cannot take into account any evidence that was not before the PAB when it made its decision, except where there are allegations of procedural errors. The evidence that may properly be considered by the Court, to the extent it is relevant to the issues raised in the application for judicial review, must be presented to the Court in the form of properly sworn affidavits in either the applicant's application record, or the respondent's application record; it does not matter which because any party in an application for judicial review may refer to material in the application record of the other party. Documentary exhibits that were before the PAB are normally appended to an affidavit that is included in one or the other of the application records. If, after considering all of the permissible evidence and the submissions of the parties, the Court concludes that the PAB made an error that requires the intervention of the Court, the remedy normally is to set the decision aside and send the matter back to the PAB for reconsideration. The Court cannot award damages or the payment of money, and it cannot award a disability pension to the claimant. If the claimant's application is successful, the most he or she can expect from the Court is an order for a new hearing before a different panel of the PAB.

Dossa v. Canada (Pension Appeal Board), 2005 FCA 387

The standard of review to be applied by the Federal Court of Appeal on an application for judicial review of a PAB decision is correctness for questions of law. On matters of fact, the standard of review is patent unreasonableness. The standard of review for findings of disability by the PAB is patently unreasonable.

Canada (Attorney General) v. Burnham, 2008 FCA 380

A judgment disposing of an appeal or an application for judicial review may be made on consent without a hearing. The correct way to request a consent judgment is by filing a notice of motion in proper form, in a motion record, with one or more supporting affidavits containing the information that is required to demonstrate that the judgment should be made. The motion may be made jointly by the parties, or by one party with the consent of the other party, signified in writing. The information required to dispose of the judgment should be in a properly sworn affidavit, and not merely a draft order. The record should be a request for a judgment, which is the purpose of a notice of motion. It is generally advisable, when a request for a consent judgment is submitted, to include in the motion record a copy of all applicable statutory provisions — e.g., the relevant provisions of the CPP.

Canada (Minister of Human Resources Development) v. Hogervorst, 2006 FC 401. See also *Canada (Attorney General) v. Dale,* 2006 FC 1364

On an application for leave to appeal to the PAB, a decision of a designated member of the PAB to extend the time and to grant leave is discretionary. The appropriate standard of review to assess the decision of a designated member of the PAB is correctness on questions of law, patent unreasonableness on questions of fact, and reasonableness on questions of mixed fact and law.

Arthurs v. Canada (Minister of Social Development), 2006 FC 1106. See also *Taylor v. Canada (Minister of Human Resources Development),* 2005 FCA 293

A decision of the Review Tribunal under s. 84(2) on whether to reconsider an earlier decision, given new facts, is reviewable on a standard of patent unreasonableness.

Osborne v. Canada (Attorney General), 2005 FCA 412

Under the patently unreasonable test, the Federal Court of Appeal may only interfere if the PAB's decision is "clearly irrational" or "evidently not in accordance with reason".

Carter v. Canada (Minister of Social Development), 2006 FCA 172

On an application for judicial review, the court may decline to conduct the review on the basis of submissions that were not, but could have been, argued before the administrative tribunal whose decision is being challenged. However, where the issues raised by counsel for the applying party were questions of law, and the party was not represented by counsel until her case reached the Federal Court of Appeal, and the Minister is not prejudiced by having to respond, the court may exercise its discretion to decide the merits of counsel's arguments.

Hussaini v. Canada (Attorney General), 2011 FC 26

Federal Court Rule 81(2) merely grants discretion in the court to draw an adverse inference where an affidavit is based on belief. The Rule does not necessarily prescribe that the failure by an applicant to file her own affidavit necessarily leads to dismissal of the application. An application for judicial review can proceed without an affidavit being filed on behalf of the applicant or applicants. In any event, an application for judicial review proceeds on the basis on the record that was before the subordinate decision-maker. In the absence of evidence based on personal knowledge, any error must appear on the face of that record. The necessary facts are contained in that record, which is attached to an affidavit filed on behalf of the Minister. The necessary facts are accordingly before the Court. The claimant's affidavit should be struck where it was unsigned but not sworn, all of the attached exhibits were unidentified, and the affidavit was largely argumentative. This does not mean that it must be physically removed from the record, but only that it would not be considered by the reviewing court.

Jagpal v. Canada (Attorney General), 2006 FCA 26

New evidence obtained after the hearing before the PAB should be dealt with by way of a reconsideration of the claim under s. 84(2), not on judicial review.

McLaughlin v. Canada (Attorney General), 2012 FC 556

The general rule is that an applicant on judicial review can only rely on evidence that was before the decision-maker. There are limited exceptions to this general principle, namely, where the evidence is directed toward an alleged breach of natural justice or of the duty of fairness, where the evidence is necessary to understand the scope of the inferior tribunal's jurisdiction, or where the evidence merely provides uncontroversial background facts for the assistance of the court. Portions of an affidavit containing evidence not put before the PAB should be struck on judicial review. Where the applicant's affidavit on judicial review was prepared with the assistance of counsel and is expressed in clearer and more convincing terms than the applicant's written submissions to the PAB, the facts in these paragraphs were all before the PAB and, accordingly, may be restated by the applicant in her affidavit.

Spears v. Canada (Attorney General), 2004 FCA 193

The determination of the meaning of "severe" disability under s. 42(2)(a)(i) was a question of law to be reviewed on a standard of correctness. Whether the claimant's disability is "severe" for the purpose of s. 42(2)(a)(i) is a question of mixed law and fact. Since the determination of this latter question has a high factual component, it is reviewable on a standard of patent unreasonableness.

Canada (Attorney General) v. Hutchison, 2004 FCA 105

The statutory test under s. 18.1(4)(d) of the *Federal Courts Act* — i.e., whether the decision was made in a perverse or capricious manner or without regard to the material before it — may be applied in determining whether the decision is patently unreasonable.

Canada (Minister of Human Resources Development) v. Angheloni, 2003 FCA 140. See also *Lalonde v. Canada (Minister of Human Resources Development)*, 2002 FCA 211

The standard of review to be applied by the FCA on an application for judicial review of a decision of the PAB stands at the correctness end of the spectrum on matters of law. On matters of fact, the standard of review is that of patent reasonableness.

Carepa v. Canada (Minister of Social Development), 2006 FC 1319. See also *Sketchley v. Canada (Attorney General)*, [2005] F.C.J. No. 2056, 2005 FCA 404

Where procedural fairness is the issue, the pragmatic and functional analysis does not apply. Rather, the task for the court is to isolate any act or omission relevant to the question of procedural fairness, and to determine whether the process followed by the Tribunal satisfied the level of fairness required in all of the circumstances. That is, given that questions of procedural fairness are reviewed as questions of law, no deference is due: the decision-maker has either complied with the content of the duty of fairness appropriate for the particular circumstances, or has not.

Powell v. Canada (Minister of Human Resources Development), (June 23, 2000), Doc. A-472-98 (Fed. C.A.)

Where the applicant claims that the PAB, while embarked on a s. 42(2)(a) analysis, ignored "the material before it", the standard applicable for statutory review is that of patent unreasonableness.

Canada (Minister of Human Resources Development) v. Skoric, [2000] 3 FC 265 (C.A.)

The PAB has no broad regulatory responsibilities, but performs only the adjudicative function of hearing appeals from the Review Tribunal. The effect of the finality clause is to restrict the jurisdiction that the PAB would otherwise have had to reconsider its decisions, subject to its power to reconsider its decisions "on new facts" under s. 84(2). The standard of review of a decision of the PAB interpreting the CPP is towards the correctness end of the spectrum. Little deference should be shown to the PAB's interpretation of its constitutive legislation, especially in the absence of evidence indicating that PAB members acquire considerable expertise in the CPP as a result of the volume of appeals that they hear and decide.

Lutzer v. Canada (Minister of Human Resources Development), [2002] FCA 190

Judicial review would not be granted where the PAB's application of the relevant statutory provision to the facts before it was not unreasonable.

Villani v. Canada (Attorney General), [2001] FCA 248

The standard of review of a PAB decision involving the interpretation and application of the definition of a "severe" disability within the meaning of CPP s. 42(2)(*a*)(i) was correctness, at the least deferential end of the spectrum. However, as long as the PAB applies the correct legal test for severity, it will be in a position to judge on the facts whether, in practical terms, an applicant is incapable regularly of pursuing any substantially gainful occupation. The assessment of the applicant's circumstances is a question of judgment with which the Federal Court of Appeal will be reluctant to interfere.

MHRD v. Rafuse, [2002] FCA 31

On an application for judicial review, the role of the Federal Court with respect to the PAB's findings of fact is strictly circumscribed. In the absence of an error of law in a tribunal's fact-finding process, or a breach of the duty of fairness, the court may only quash a decision of the PAB for factual error if the finding was perverse or capricious or made without regard to the material before the PAB. If, as a result of an error of law, the PAB has omitted to make a relevant finding of fact, including a factual inference, the matter should normally be returned to the tribunal to enable it to complete its work.

Obiter: While the directions that the court may issue when setting aside a PAB decision include directions in the nature of a directed verdict, this is an exceptional power that should be exercised only in the clearest of circumstances. Such will rarely be the case when the issue in dispute is essentially factual in nature, particularly when the PAB has not made the relevant finding.

Vogt v. MHRD, [2002] FCA 52

The conclusion of the PAB after a review of the substantive evidence that there was no reliable objective evidence to support a finding that the claimant suffered from a disability such as to prevent him from regularly pursuing a substantially gainful employment will not be interfered with if the decision is not patently reasonable. It was not necessary for the PAB to have given reasons for not believing the claimant where its reasons were sufficiently comprehensive to demonstrate the reasoning on which its conclusions were based.

Lutzer v. MHRD, [2002] FCA 190

After stating the correct test and such factors as the applicant's age and education, the PAB was not required to explain the reasoning leading to its conclusion that the applicant was not entitled to a disability pension. Judicial review would not be granted where the PAB's application of the relevant statutory provision to the facts before it was not unreasonable.

Kellar v. MHRD, [2000] FCA 204

The PAB is not required to refer to every piece of evidence before it, but only to those that have significant probative value. Where medical reports were written using false assumptions and various doctors who examined the applicant were unable to diagnose any specific cause of the symptoms of which she complained, the PAB was not obliged in law to set out its conclusions on the reports.

Doyle v. MHRD, [2002] FCA 280

Where the PAB stated in its decision that there was no medical evidence, although there was in fact some medical evidence in the record, the Court could infer that this evidence was ignored and grant judicial review.

Canada (MHRD) v. Skoric, [2000] 3 FC 265 (C.A.)

The standard of review of a decision of the PAB interpreting the CPP is towards the correctness end of the spectrum. Little deference should be shown to the PAB's interpretation of its constitutive legislation, especially in the absence of evidence indicating that PAB members acquire considerable expertise in the CPP as a result of the volume of appeals that they hear and decide.

Wiemer v. Ganim (1996), Doc. T-1121-95 (Fed. T.D.)

In light of s. 28 of the *Federal Court Act*, the Trial Division must not, and must not purport to, perform judicial review in respect of a decision of the PAB. However, an order of the PAB purporting to refer a matter back to the Minister is plainly an excess of jurisdiction, which can be ignored without judicial review proceedings.

Sudnik v. Canada (Attorney General), 2004 FCA 271

During judicial review proceedings from the PAB sought by the unsuccessful claimant, abusive or irrelevant questions put to the Minister's medical advisor on written examination could be struck out, with costs against the claimant.

(d) Judicial Review of Ministerial Determination

Bartlett v. Canada (Attorney General), 2012 FCA 230

"Courtesy letters" of explanation from Ministry officials addressing why the original decision of the Ministry must stand but for the first time specifically denying the claimant's request for interest on retroactive payments were orders that could be the subject of judicial review. The last letter invited the claimant to seek judicial review if she wished to pursue the matter further.

(e) Examples of Successful Judicial Review Applications

- Tribunal gave inadequate reasons in dismissing application; already six years since application for disability benefits made; if remitted back to tribunal, entire proceeding could take eight years; *mandamus* issued to direct that claimant's application succeed: *D'Errico v. Canada* (Attorney General), 2014 FCA 95

- Failure to consider the combined effect of claimant's physical and neurological injuries was an error that rendered the tribunal's decision unreasonable; no physician ever provided an opinion which stated that claimant was capable of doing sedentary or limited work; report indicating such capability referenced by the tribunal was not from claimant's family doctor, but from a physiotherapist who was not treating the claimant for her psychological or neurological symptoms: *Dauti v. Canada (Attorney General)*, 2013 FCA 259

- Majority of PAB panel failed to consider the evolution and deterioration of claimant's medical condition over the years; reports intended to rebut family physician's report were not directed at claimant's MQP, and were at best equivocal about her condition: *Nahajowicw v. Canada (Attorney General)*, 2011 FCA 293

- PAB relying on evidence of claimant's family physician over that of two specialists, with no meaningful explanation as to why: *Canada (Attorney General) v. Ryall*, 2008 FCA 164

- In dismissing claim, PAB simply stating that "The Board has reviewed the testimony and evidence provided by the parties. The Board has some concerns about the quality and quantity of paper and reports that were submitted for the members' consideration. The Board finds that the Appellant has failed to substantiate her claim for a pension under the governing statute": *Marrone v. Canada (Attorney General)*, 2008 FCA 216

- PAB's brief reasons did not address important items of evidence that appeared to be inconsistent with conclusion that claimant's disability precluded her from employment, in particular, fact that claimant was working 11 months following end of MQP; PAB not mentioning two letters by same doctor, whose report was relied upon to support finding of disability, to the effect that claimant was capable of desk work, and denying having said that she was totally disabled; it was impossible to tell from PAB's reasons why it reached decision that it did: *Canada (Minister of Human Resources Development) v. Bartelds*, 2006 FCA 123

- PAB found that applicant had not worked since November 1997, yet ultimately based its decision on statement in 1999 medical report that applicant "uses all of his tools using his left hand and this becoming [*sic*] more and more difficult for him"; PAB inferring from hearsay and ambiguous statement that applicant still working and denying claim: *O'Liari v. The Attorney General of Canada*, 2003 FCA 375

- PAB using wrong test, asking whether "the employment in which the applicant is now engaged cannot be described as something at which the applicant is regularly engaged", instead of whether the applicant is "incapable regularly of pursuing any substantially gainful occupation": *Canada (Attorney General) v. Lemoine*, 2003 FCA 330

- MQP was six years before the hearing date; PAB putting too much emphasis on improvement in claimant's condition before hearing, and not giving enough weight to medical reports contemporaneous with MQP which indicated permanent disability: *Cochran v. Canada (Attorney General)*, 2003 FCA 343

(f) Judicial Review of Leave to Appeal Decision

(i) General principles

Layden v. HRSD, 2008 FC 619, affirmed on other grounds 2009 FCA 14

Decisions of the Chair or Vice-Chair of the PAB or their delegates in the exercise of the jurisdiction confined to them by statute, are not decisions of the PAB itself. Judicial review of such decisions is to the Federal Court. This principle is unaffected by the Federal Court of Appeal's decision in *Mazzotta v. Canada (Attorney General)*, [2007] F.C.J. No. 1209. The standard of review analysis does not apply where judicial review is sought based upon an alleged denial of procedural fairness. Rather, the task for the court is to determine whether the process followed in a given case satisfied the level of fairness required in all of the circumstances. A reviewing court has the final say in relation to questions of procedural fairness. The vast majority of decisions from the Federal Court dealing with decisions made with respect to applications for leave to appeal from decisions of the Review Tribunal involve cases where leave was denied. The leave provisions in section 7 of the *Pension Appeals Board Rules of Procedure* are unusual, in that applications for leave are presumptively dealt with, without notice to the opposing party. It may be that most applications for leave are brought by pension claimants, and that the Minister is content to simply address the matter before the PAB. Where the Minister brings the application for leave, the duty of full and frank disclosure on the Minister in an *ex parte* application for leave to appeal brought before a senior member of the PAB is no different than the duty imposed on parties in any other kind of *ex parte* proceeding. That is, counsel for the Minister must do more than simply present the Minister's own case in the best possible light, but must state the case fairly, and, in addition, must inform the member of any points of fact or law which favours the claimant. [Note: The Federal Court of Appeal essentially labelled the trial judge's statements regarding the obligation of the Crown to disclose as *obiter dicta*, and observed (at para. 7) that "this is an issue that is best left for determination in another case at some future time".]

Lavin v. Canada (Attorney General), 2011 FC 1387

There are two issues involved in the review of a PAB member's decision to grant leave to appeal: whether the right test was applied, and whether the member committed a reviewable error in applying that test. The first issue is a question of law and is therefore reviewable on the correctness standard. The second issue requires the PAB member to apply the test to the facts and is therefore a question of mixed fact and law that is reviewable on the reasonableness standard. In reviewing the member's decision on the standard of reasonableness, the Court should not intervene unless the member came to a conclusion that is not transparent, justifiable, and intelligible and within the range of acceptable outcomes based on the evidence before it.

Canada (Attorney General) v. Carroll, 2011 FC 1092. See also *Devlin v. Canada (Attorney General),* 2013 FC 746.

An arguable case required the applicant to put forward new or additional evidence, raise an issue not considered by the tribunal, or point to an error in the tribunal decision.

Zavarella v. Canada (Attorney General), 2010 FC 815

On a judicial review of a designated PAB member's decision, the Court can only consider the evidence that was before that member. It cannot speculate as to the nature of the additional evidence that the claimant may be able to adduce, let alone place any weight on that evidence, in making its decision.

Canada (Attorney General) v. St. Louis, 2011 FC 492

There is no obligation under the statutory scheme to give reasons for granting leave to appeal the Review Tribunal's decision. Where no reasons were given, it is for the reviewing court to determine whether there was an arguable case for which to grant leave.

Canada (Attorney General) v. Leer, 2012 FC 932

It was an error for the designated PAB member to suggest that the need for the Minister to provide clearer answers to questions could serve as a basis for granting leave, when the member also expressed the hope that the matter would not proceed to the stage of an appeal.

Canada (Attorney General) v. Skrzypek, 2011 FC 823. See also *Canada (Attorney General) v. Carroll,* 2011 FC 1092 and *Canada (Attorney General) v. Sarahan,* 2012 FC 52

Where the applicant for leave had failed to provide grounds for seeking leave in his or her application, the PAB member was required to set out reasons for granting leave.

Canada (Attorney General) v. Skryzpek, 2011 FC 823

Where the claimant's application for leave to appeal was simply accompanied by a letter restating the alleged ailments, and no reasons for granting leave were given, the Minister's application for judicial review was allowed. It cannot be expected that reviewing judges will embark on a search of the record to find pieces of evidence which could support or particularize broad allegations made by a party to the review.

Canada (Attorney General) v. Montesano, 2011 FC 398

Although the PAB Rules do not provide for an appeal in respect of a decision to grant leave to appeal, such a decision may be judicially reviewed by the Federal Court. Judicial review will be granted where the claimant failed to provide the information required by Rule 4, had not been expressly excused from doing so, the decision granting leave was not recorded, and the PAB member failed to give any reasons for granting leave.

Canada (Attorney General) v. Zakaria, 2011 FC 136

The question of whether the claimant has an arguable case at law is akin to determining whether he or she, legally, has a reasonable chance of success. An arguable case in the context of an application for disability benefits requires a decision-maker to consider the statutory criteria under the Plan that the disability in question be both severe and prolonged. Rule 4 of the Pension Appeals Board Rules of Procedure (Benefits) provides that an application for leave to appeal shall contain the grounds upon which the applicant relies to obtain leave to appeal, allegations of fact, reasons he intends to submit, and documentary evidence he intends to rely on in support of the appeal.

Canada (Attorney General) v. Graca, 2011 FC 615

Where leave to appeal is granted without reasons on an application brought five years after the Review Tribunal decision, judicial review should be granted. The decision to grant an extension of time is discretionary, and must be explicitly considered by the member. There is no automatic inference that just because a member granted leave, he or she must have also granted an extension of time. It is incumbent upon the member to support the exercise of discretion with reasons.

Fancy v. Canada (Social Development), 2008 FC 1414

Where, in considering whether to grant leave to appeal, the board was required to assess the factual evidence (mainly medical) against the legal test for disability under the CPP and to decide if there was an arguable case, the question was of mixed fact and law. On an application for judicial review, the standard of review was reasonableness.

Canada (Attorney General) v. Borai, 2008 FC 999

The PAB does not have jurisdiction to grant leave to appeal a decision of the Review Tribunal affirming the Minister's decision denying survivor benefits where the grounds upon which leave was sought was the failure of the RT to alter the date of disability of the claimant's deceased spouse. Neither the RT nor the PAB have jurisdiction over the issue of the disability date in respect of the claimant's spouse.

Vincent v. Canada (Attorney General), 2007 FC 724

Whether the PAB applied the proper test in granting leave to appeal the decision of the Review Tribunal is a question of law, reviewable on the standard of correctness. While the PAB must provide reasons for refusing an application for leave to appeal, no such duty exists when leave to appeal is granted. Where no reasons were given for the decision, it must be determined whether the PAB erred in law or in its appreciation of the facts in finding whether an arguable issue was raised, even if it is assumed that the PAB applied the correct test.

(ii) Appeal of dismissal by trial division

Gramaglia v. Canada (Attorney General), [1999] F.C.J. No. 1913 (Fed. C.A.)

The standard of review on an appeal from the dismissal by the Trial Division of an application for judicial review of the decision of the Vice-Chairman of the PAB refusing leave to appeal the decision of a Review Tribunal where no new evidence was adduced with the application for leave, was whether the Trial Division judge had erred in principle or in law or that he misapprehended the facts of the application. In the exercise of its discretion, the Trial Division was entitled to dismiss the appeal where it found that the evidence before the Vice-Chairman, and the evidence before the Review Tribunal, had been considered by each of them and their conclusions could not be said to be unreasonable.

(iii) Judicial review of PAB's decision to grant leave to appeal

Mrak v. HRSD, [2007] F.C.J. No. 909

The granting of leave is an interlocutory proceeding which does not decide the merits of an appeal. Therefore, on an application for judicial review of a decision granting leave, the applicant must establish the existence of "special circumstances" justifying judicial review from the decision. There is no statutory requirement that reasons be given when leave to appeal is granted.

Layden v. HRSD, 2008 FC 619, affirmed on other grounds 2009 FCA 14

There are a number of reasons why, in the absence of special circumstances, interlocutory rulings made by administrative tribunals should not be challenged until the tribunal has rendered its final decision. These include the fact that the application may be rendered moot by the ultimate outcome of the case, and the risk of the fragmentation of the process, with the accompanying costs and delays. In some cases, there may also be a possibility that the tribunal may end up modifying its original ruling as the hearing unfolds. However, special circumstances exist where the fairness of the leave process is not a matter that would be dealt with by the PAB, whose mandate, once leave is granted, is to conduct a *de novo* hearing into the merits of her claim for a disability pension, not to revisit the leave process. They also exist where the case raises concerns with respect to the integrity of the leave process that may not otherwise be addressed.

Canada (Attorney General) v. Zakaria, 2011 FC 136

The "arguable case" test set out in *Callihoo* has been held to apply to decisions of designated members granting leave to appeal. Where a claimant failed to provide new evidence with the leave application or identify an error of law or an error of significant fact by the Review Tribunal and obtained leave to appeal in any event, the reviewing court allowed the Minister's application for judicial review and remit the leave application to a different designated member of the board for redetermination.

(iv) Judicial review of PAB's refusal to grant leave

MHRD v. Rafuse, [2002] FCA 31

Where a member of the PAB had used an incorrect test in refusing leave to appeal a decision of the Review Tribunal, it was an error of law for the Federal Court to grant leave to appeal. The Court had no power to substitute its view for that of the PAB on the proper disposition of the leave application, or to set aside the refusal of leave and remit the matter with a direction that the PAB grant leave to appeal. Despite the delay, the appropriate approach was to remit the matter to another member of the PAB for determination of the application for leave using the correct test.

Martin v. Canada (MHRD), [1999] F.C.J. No. 1972 (Fed. C.A.)

The proper test in considering whether the Court can overrule the PAB's decision to refuse leave to appeal is the legality of the decision and not the correctness. Unless the Vice-Chairman considered irrelevant factors or acted contrary to law, the Court should show deference to its decision.

Wihksne v. Canada (Attorney General) (2000), Doc. T-1451-99 (Fed. T.D.)

On a review of the PAB's decision as to whether leave to appeal the decision of the Review Tribunal should be granted, the standard is reasonableness. In refusing a leave application, the board is not restricted to using the exact words of the statute in citing the legal test of disability, as long as it indicates that the Review Tribunal's decision was based on the weight of the evidence, that the laws were established, that the weight is a matter for the Tribunal hearing the case, and that the case before it was not an arguable case in which one can say that the weight should have been otherwise.

Callihoo v. Canada (Attorney General) (2000), FC T-859-99 (Fed. T.D.)

The review of a decision concerning an application for leave to appeal to the PAB from the Review Tribunal involves two issues:

1. Whether the decision-maker has applied the right test. That is, whether the application raises an arguable case without otherwise assessing the merits of the application.

2. Whether the decision-maker has erred in law or in appreciation of the facts in determining whether an arguable case is raised. If new evidence is adduced with the application or the application raises an issue of law or of relevant significant facts not appropriately considered by the Review Tribunal in its decision, an arguable issue is raised for consideration and it warrants the grant of leave.

In the absence of significant new or additional evidence not considered by the Review Tribunal, an application for leave may raise an arguable case where the leave decision-maker finds the application raises a question of an error of law, measured by a standard of correctness, or an error of significant fact that is unreasonable or perverse in light of the evidence.

Obiter: The Federal Court of Appeal in *Skoric* considered the decision of the PAB on its merits, circumstances distinguishable from where the issue arises in relation to the standard of review of a decision in regard to an application for leave to appeal. The issue in *Skoric* was clearly a legal one and the standard of review required little deference to the PAB decision.

Barcellona v. Canada (Attorney General), 2007 FC 324

Questions relating to breaches of procedural fairness are not subject to a pragmatic and functional analysis but are reviewable on a standard of correctness. The alleged failure of the PAB to grant the applicant time within which to appoint a representative relevant to his application was a matter of procedural fairness. The requirement that the applicant raise an arguable case means that an applicant bears the burden of setting forth grounds for an appeal. It is not necessary for the PAB to use the words "no arguable case" in disposing of an application for leave to appeal.

Kerth v. Canada (MHRD), [1999] F.C.J. No. 1252 (T.D.)

The standard applicable to reviewing the propriety of the test used by a member of the PAB when determining a request for leave to appeal a decision of the Review Tribunal is closer to the non-deferential end of the spectrum. There is not a great deal of difference between relative expertise of the PAB and the Federal Court in determining the principles applicable to leave to appeal applications. However, PAB members do have greater expertise in dealing with the underlying factual subject matter. Where the ground for leave is primarily the existence of additional evidence, the issue to be considered in relation to the leave application is whether the new evidence filed in support of the leave application raises a genuine doubt as to whether the Tribunal would have reached the decision it did, if the additional evidence had been before it.

Davies v. Canada (MHRD) (1999), FC T-1789-98

The exercise of discretion by a member designate of the PAB on an application for leave to appeal is a decision of the PAB. The provision applies to an application for judicial review of a decision by the Chairman or the Vice-Chairman of the PAB on a leave to appeal application. The PAB is specialized in the task of considering the evidence and assessing the relevant provisions of the Act before deciding if an individual qualifies as "disabled" under the Act.

In balancing the four factors in *Pushpanathan* to arrive at the appropriate standard of review for a decision of the PAB, a middle to lower level of deference should be accorded on leave applications. The principles expressed in *Kerth* are approved, except that the PAB does have a special expertise that ordinary judges do not have. Only evidence that was before the decision-maker can be considered on judicial review.

Enquist v. Canada (Attorney General), 2005 FC 587. See also *Lima v. Canada (Minister of Human Resources Development),* [2001] F.C.J. No. 220 (T.D.), affirmed 2006 FCA 47

The designated member of the PAB hearing the leave application is not required to use the words "arguable case" in reaching his decision, where the reasons demonstrate that the designated member concluded that the new evidence submitted by the claimant did not give rise to an arguable case.

(v) Example cases — leave application sent back to tribunal for reconsideration

- Successful application for leave merely reiterated claimant's position that he was unable to work due to several conditions which prevent him from working because the pain is severe and prolonged; no additional evidence furnished to PAB member; member must have applied wrong test for granting leave, or misapplied it: *Canada (Attorney General) v. Zakaria,* 2011 FC 136

- Statement in granting leave to appeal that appellant "may have" arguable case, in conjunction with lack of analysis of evidence; correct test was whether appellant "has" arguable case: *Canada (Attorney General) v. Schultz,* 2006 FC 1351

- Leave to appeal refused on basis that appellant had shown no "demonstrated error" on part of Review Tribunal; this was more onerous test than "arguable case" test: *Falbo v. Canada (Attorney General),* 2007 FC 578

- PAB applying Federal Court of Appeal's *Giannaros* decision in coming to refusing leave to appeal; *Giannaros* decision was judicial review of a decision on the merits of case, whereas test on leave application is whether arguable case has been raised: *Canada (Minister of Human Resources Development) v. Lewis,* 2006 FC 322 (CanLII)

641

- Claimant for retirement pension raising issue of his or her disability and its impact on calculation of contributory period; onus on Ministry and tribunals to determine whether the claimant was in fact disabled: *Van De Wetering v. Canada (Attorney General)*, 2003 FCT 588

- Review Tribunal stating that "neither the specialist nor the family doctor state that [applicant] is disabled from doing all work"; arguable issue existing as to whether Tribunal erred; Tribunal also ignoring testimony of family members: *Grenier v. MHRD*, [2001] FCT 1059

- PAB noting that claimant worked full time during period in question "for rehabilitative purposes": *Bagri v. Canada* (Attorney General), [2001] FCT 638

- PAB member citing lack of objective evidence as ground for refusing claim based on chronic pain syndrome: *Lima v. MHRD*, [2001] FCT 86

- New Functional Abilities Report alone constituting sufficient evidence of arguable case: *Burley v. MHRD*, [2001] FCT 127

- Incorrect test applied when PAB member finding Review Tribunal's decision to be "a reasonable interpretation of the evidence" and stated that he had "not been persuaded that another hearing would or could reach a different result": *Cameron v. Canada* (Attorney General), [2001] FCT 383

- Arguable case as to proper interpretation of requirement that claimant be "incapable regularly of pursuing any substantially gainful occupation" under s. 42(2)(a)(i): *Martin v. Canada (MHRD)*, [1999] F.C.J. No. 1972 (Fed. C.A.)

- Evidentiary dispute as to whether claimant had been offered modified work; questions raised requiring weighing of evidence, evaluation of claimant's credibility, and interpretation of documentary evidence: *Paproski v. MHRD* (2000), T-1959-99 (Fed. T.D.)

- Chairman committing error of law by refusing leave on grounds that Review Tribunal exercised its function properly and committed no error: *Salls v. MHRD* (2000), T-2204-98 (Fed. T.D.)

- Evidence before PAB in support of leave to appeal application being more substantial than that presented to the Tribunal: *Kerth v. Canada (Minister of Human Resources Development)*, [1999] F.C.J. No. 1252 (T.D.)

- Arguable point as to whether Tribunal ignored evidence of sole medical witness who testified before it; witness giving uncontroverted evidence as to the applicant's functional incapacity; no medical witnesses for Minister: *Korese v. MHRD* (2000), Doc. FC T-1686-99 (Fed. T.D.)

- Reference to lack of objective evidence in support of CPS-based application missing the point; CPS diagnosis not amenable to objective evidence: *Lima v. Canada (MHRD)* (2001), Doc. T-1794-99 (Fed. T.D.)

- Medical reports supporting applicant's claim to have been disabled during MQP: *MHRD v. Rafuse*, [2002] FCA 31

- Functional Abilities Evaluation report concluding that applicant's options for finding suitable gainful employment were limited raising arguable case; member designate not referring to report: *Burley v. Canada (MHRD)* (2001), Doc. T-1462-99 (Fed. T.D.)

(vi) Example cases — refusal of leave upheld

- Chiropractor suffered torn fibrocartilage and other injuries to his left wrist, but no medical or psychiatric evidence to indicate he could not pursue retraining opportunities or other types of employment related or unrelated to chiropractic medicine, which would not require physical manipulation of patients; no new evidence presented on judicial review, and did not pursue any other employment or retraining opportunities: *Williams v. Canada (Attorney General)*, 2010 FC 701

- PAB member not mentioning "arguable case" test but finding that Review Tribunal's decision was "not unreasonable" and "could be supported by the evidence"; additional evidence of physician not adding anything new to original report: *Duncan v. MHRD*, [2001] FCT 736

- PAB member satisfying test by stating unequivocally that "no panel of the PAB would disagree with the conclusion reached by the Review Tribunal"; not necessary to expressly state "there is no arguable case": *Lima v. MHRD*,]2001[FCT 86 [matter remitted back to PAB for other reasons]

- Although second letter from applicant's rheumatologist absent from Review Tribunal's and PAB's record, it contained virtually no new material and did not materially assist applicant's case: *Zimmerman v. MHRD*, [2001] FCT 1393

- Applicant not filing any new evidence before PAB to support application for leave to appeal; refusal to grant leave not unreasonable: *Davies v. Canada (MHRD)* (1999), T-1789-98 (Fed. T.D.)

(g) Time for Seeking Judicial Review

- See *Federal Courts Act* ss. 18.1(2), 28(2) reproduced above under CPP s. 84, which impose a 30-day deadline on applications for judicial review following a decision

Grewal v. Canada (Minister of Employment and Immigration), [1985] 2 FC 263 (C.A.)

As conferred by s. 18.1(2) of the *Federal Court Act*, the authority to extend the time for judicial review is unrestricted. "Special reasons" are not required. However, the authority must not be exercised arbitrarily or capriciously, and the period should only be extended when there are sound reasons for doing so. The underlying consideration is to ensure that justice is done between the parties. The decision must be one which is subject to judicial review, and the applicant must have an arguable case. In determining whether there is any satisfactory reason or proper justification for not bringing the application in time, the Court must take into account whether the applicant intended within the period to bring the application and had that intention continuously thereafter. Any abandonment of that intention, and laxity or failure of the applicant to pursue it as diligently as could reasonably be expected of him or her could but militate strongly against the case for an extension. The length of the period for which an extension is required and whether any and what prejudice to an opposing party will result from an extension being granted are also relevant. But in the end, whether or not the explanation justifies the necessary extension must depend on the facts of the particular case, and it would be wrong to lay down or fetter the discretionary power conferred by s. 18.1(2). [Note: s. 18.1(2) applies to the judicial review of PAB decisions by virtue of s. 28(2)]

Canada (Attorney General) v. Hennelly (June 2, 1999), Doc. A-617-95 (Fed. C.A.). See also *Marshall v. Canada*, 2002 FCA 172

On an application for an extension of time for seeking judicial review, the presence or absence of consent for an extension of time is not determinative. The proper test is whether the applicant has demonstrated:

1. a continuing intention to pursue his or her application;

2. that the application has some merit;

3. that no prejudice to the respondent arises from the delay; and

4. that a reasonable explanation for the delay exists.

Any determination of whether or not the applicant's explanation justifies the granting of the necessary extension of time will turn on the facts of each particular case.

Canada (Attorney General) v. Hryciw, 2008 FCA 70

An order extending the time for filing her affidavit and her record may be granted even where the above conditions under *Hennelly* are not met, but only to file a memorandum of fact and law. Prejudice to the other side could be inferred where the party in default sought to file an affidavit containing evidence that is not already on the record, although such prejudice could be remedied by permitting cross-examination on the affidavit or permitting the Crown to amend its memorandum of fact and law.

Thanos v. Canada (Attorney General), 2005 FCA 407

The presence of an arguable case as one of the factors which, according to the circumstances, could be taken into account when deciding whether to grant an extension of time to file an application for judicial review. In determining whether there is an arguable case, a relevant factor would be that the PAB had already granted leave to the claimant to appeal to the PAB.

Budget Steel Ltd. v. Seaspan 175 (The), 2003 FCT 390

The test in *Hennelly* is completely consistent with that of *Grewal.* Indeed, *Hennelly* perhaps provides a gloss on *Grewal,* where the elements bearing on a time extension were open-ended, but did include the requirements of a satisfactory explanation for the delay, that there be an arguable case and that there be no prejudice to the respondent resulting from the granting of an extension. The applicable factors set out as the test in *Hennelly* are to be balanced with the overall view of doing justice between the parties.

Canada (Attorney General) v. Vincent (Estate), 2004 FC 1016

The Federal Court may hear an application for judicial review of an interlocutory decision of the Review Tribunal with respect to standing.

Bartlett v. Canada (Attorney General), 2012 FCA 230

"Courtesy letters" of explanation from Ministry officials addressing why the original decision of the Ministry must stand but for the first time specifically denying the claimant's request for interest on retroactive payments were orders that could be the subject of judicial review. Therefore, they could extend the time for applying for judicial review although the original decision had been issued years before. The last letter invited the claimant to seek judicial review if she wished to pursue the matter further.

Canada (Minister of Human Resources Development) v. Baker, 2004 FC 1639

It is appropriate to seek judicial review of the granting of leave to appeal to the PAB a decision of the Review Tribunal dismissing a subsequent application on the grounds of *res judicata* in the absence of new facts. Although the granting of leave to appeal was not a final decision, the matter goes to the jurisdiction of the PAB to even hear the appeal.

Daoud v. HRSD, 2012 FCA 13

Although determining the place of residence for purposes of OAS eligibility involves questions of fact and credibility, which are subject to a very stringent standard of review, an extension of the period for seeking judicial review may be granted where the claimant was diligent in seeking review and the application raised errors of law regarding the interpretation and scope of the OAS Act and regarding the burden of proof that applies when establishing place of residence.

Mitcham v. Canada (Attorney General), 2003 FCA 70

Where the claimant had contacted his MP within 30 days of the PAB decision denying his claim for a CPP disability pension, who in turn contacted the Minister, neither one informing the claimant of his right to apply for judicial review, the claimant was entitled to proceed with a judicial review application six months after the time limit for doing so had expired. The claimant had not been well served either by the PAB, his Member of Parliament, or ministerial or departmental staff.

Regulations

69. *Governor in Council* — **The Governor in Council may make regulations respecting the manner in which the Tribunal may conduct its business, including regulations respecting**

(a) the procedure to be followed on appeals to the Tribunal;

(b) the circumstances under which information is deemed to have been communicated or received;

(c) the time within which the Tribunal must make a decision under subsections 54(1), 58(3) and 59(1);

(d) any special reasons for the purposes of section 63;

(e) the power to exclude any person from a hearing when oral evidence concerning a circumstance of sexual or other harassment is being given; and

(f) anything that, by this Part, is to be prescribed by regulation.

(2012, c. 19, s. 224.)

70. *Regulations — electronic documents and electronic information —* (1) The Governor in Council may, for the purposes of this Part, make regulations referred to in paragraphs 73(1)(c), (d) and (f). (2012, c. 19, s. 224.)

(2) *Regulations — definitions —* The Governor in Council may, for the purposes of regulations made under subsection (1), make regulations defining "electronic", "electronic document", "electronic information", "electronic signature" and "technology". (2012, c. 19, s. 224.)

(3) *Incorporation by reference —* Subsections 73(2) to (5) apply to regulations made under this section. (2012, c. 19, s. 224.)

(2012, c. 19, s. 224.)

Part 6

Electronic Administration or Enforcement

70.1. *Application —* This Part applies to the following Acts, programs and activities:

(a) the *Canada Pension Plan*;

(b) the *Old Age Security Act*;

(c) the *Employment Insurance Act*;

(d) the *Canada Student Financial Assistance Act*;

(e) the *Canada Student Loans Act*;

S. 70.1(e.1) will be added by S.C. 2014, c. 20, s. 485 on proclamation, and will read as follows:

(e.1) the *Apprentice Loans Act*; (2014, c. 20, s. 485.)

(f) the *Canada Labour Code*;

(g) any programs that are supported by grants or contributions under section 7; and

(h) any activities in respect of which the administration or enforcement is the responsibility of the Minister under the *Immigration and Refugee Protection Regulations*.

(2013, c. 40, s. 211.)

71. *Powers —* (1) Subject to the regulations, the Minister may administer or enforce electronically the Acts, programs and activities referred to in paragraphs 70.1(a) to (e), (g) and (h), the Minister of Labour may administer or enforce electronically the *Canada Labour Code* and the Commission may administer or enforce electronically the *Employment Insurance Act*, including for the purposes of (2013, c. 40, s. 212.)

(a) creating, communicating, making available, collecting, receiving, storing, or managing or otherwise dealing with documents or information;

(b) providing any services, benefits or other assistance;

(c) providing notifications;

(d) verifying the identity of a person or entity;

(e) entering into agreements or arrangements; and

(f) making, receiving or verifying an electronic signature.

(2012, c. 19, s. 224.)

(2) *Restriction* — The Minister and the Commission must not require persons or entities to apply electronically for, or receive electronically, services, benefits or other assistance except for classes of persons or entities and those services, benefits or other assistance that are prescribed by the regulations. (2012, c. 19, s. 224.)

(2012, c. 19, s. 224; 2013, c. 40, s. 212.)

——————— Notes ———————

Case Law

Canada (Attorney General) v. Jodhan, 2012 FCA 161

The method by which the federal government permits online access to potential claimants violates s. 15 of the Charter to the extent that it discriminates against visually impaired persons. The visually impaired have not been "reasonably accommodated" because they allegedly can obtain the same information available online by other channels, namely in person, by telephone, and by mail. These other channels are difficult to access, less reliable, and not complete. Moreover, they fail to provide the visually impaired with independent access or the same dignity and convenience as the services online. For the blind and visually impaired, accessing information and services online gives them independence, self-reliance, control, ease of access, dignity, and self-esteem. A person is not handicapped if she does not need help. Making the government online information and services accessible provides the visually impaired with "substantive equality."

72. *Electronic manner of filing documents* — (1) Unless another manner of filing a document or information is expressly required by a provision of an Act referred to in section 70.1 or any of its regulations, by a term or condition of a program referred to in paragraph 70.1(g) or by a provision of a regulation referred to in paragraph 70.1(h), the filing of an electronic version of the document or information is to be considered as the filing of a document or information in accordance with the provision or the term or condition. (2012, c. 19, s. 224; 2013, c. 40, s. 213(1).)

(2) *Power to prescribe form or manner of filing* — A provision of an Act referred to in section 70.1 or any of its regulations, or a term or condition of a program referred to in paragraph 70.1(g) or a provision of a regulation referred to in paragraph 70.1(h), that provides for a power to issue, prescribe or in any other manner establish a form or to establish the manner of filing a document or information includes the power to do so with respect to an electronic document or information. (2012, c. 19, s. 224; 2013, c. 40, s. 213(1).)

(3) *Written documents or information* — A requirement under a provision of an Act referred to in section 70.1 or any of its regulations, or a term or condition of a

program referred to in paragraph 70.1(*g*) or a provision of a regulation referred to in paragraph 70.1(*h*), that a document be in writing or information be provided in writing is satisfied by an electronic document or information if the electronic document or information (2013, c. 40, s. 213(2).)

(*a*) is readable or perceivable so as to be usable for subsequent reference;

(*b*) is in a format that does not prevent it from being retained by the recipient; and

(*c*) meets the prescribed requirements, if any.

(2012, c. 19, s. 224.)

(4) *Signatures* — A requirement under a provision of an Act referred to in section 70.1 or any of its regulations, or a term or condition of a program referred to in paragraph 70.1(*g*) or a provision of a regulation referred to in paragraph 70.1(*h*), for a signature is satisfied by an electronic signature if the electronic signature (2013, c. 40, s. 213(3).)

(*a*) is reliable for the purposes for which it is required;

(*b*) is reliably linked with the electronic document in respect of which the signature is required; and

(*c*) meets the prescribed requirements, if any.

(2012, c. 19, s. 224.)

(5) *Meaning of "filing"* — In this section, "filing" includes all manner of transmitting, regardless of how it is designated. (2012, c. 19, s. 224.)

(2012, c. 19, s. 224; 2013, c. 40, s. 213.)

73. *Regulations* — (1) The Governor in Council may make regulations

(*a*) providing for circumstances in which subsection 71(1) does not apply;

(*b*) defining, enlarging or restricting the meaning of any word or expression used but not defined in this Part;

(*c*) respecting the creation, communication, making available, collection, reception, storage or management of, or any other method of dealing with, electronic documents or electronic information, and their admissibility in any proceedings, including establishing

(i) criteria for the reliability of electronic documents, electronic information or electronic signatures,

(ii) the date and hour when an electronic document or electronic information is deemed to be sent or received and the place where it is deemed to be sent or received, (2013, c. 40, s. 214(1).)

(iii) the technology to be used and process to be followed for making, receiving or verifying an electronic signature, and

(vi) whether an electronic document must be signed with an electronic signature;

(*d*) establishing criteria for the validity of an agreement or arrangement entered into electronically;

(*e*) respecting terms and conditions for providing or receiving electronically services, benefits or other assistance, including the payment of amounts electronically;

(*f*) respecting the technology to be used and the process to be followed for verifying electronically the identity of any person or entity;

(g) respecting the establishment and operation of electronic systems or any other technology to be used in the administration or enforcement of an Act referred to in section 70.1, of a program referred to in paragraph 70.1(g) or of a provision of a regulation referred to in paragraph 70.1(h), and respecting the manner in which and the extent to which any provision of that Act or its regulations, any term or condition of that program or any provision of that regulation applies to the electronic systems; and (2013, c. 40, s. 214(2).)

(h) prescribing anything that by this Part is to be prescribed.

(2012, c. 19, s. 224.)

(2) *Incorporation by reference* — A regulation made under this section may incorporate by reference any document, regardless of its source, either as it exists on a particular date or as it is amended from time to time. (2012, c. 19, s. 224.)

(3) *Accessibility* — The Minister, the Minister of Labour or the Commission, as the case may be, shall ensure that any document that is incorporated by reference in a regulation in respect of which the administration or the enforcement is their responsibility is accessible. (2012, c. 19, s. 224; 2013, c. 40, s. 214(3).)

(4) *Defence* — A person is not liable to be found guilty of an offence for any contravention in respect of which a document that is incorporated by reference in the regulation is relevant unless, at the time of the alleged contravention, the document was accessible as required by subsection (3) or it was otherwise accessible to the person. (2012, c. 19, s. 224.)

(5) *No registration or publication* — For greater certainty, a document that is incorporated by reference in the regulation is not required to be transmitted for registration or published in the *Canada Gazette* by reason only that it is incorporated by reference. (2012, c. 19, s. 224.)

(2012, c. 19, s. 224; 2013, c. 40, s. 214.)

Social Security Tribunal Regulations

SOR/2013-60, effective April 1, 2013, as amended by S.C. 2013, c. 40, s. 236.

Interpretation

1. *Definitions* — **The following definitions apply in these Regulations.**

"Act" means the *Department of Employment and Social Development Act.* **(2013, c. 40, s. 236(3)(a).)**

"business day" means a day other than a Saturday or a Sunday or other holiday.

"party" means

> **(a) in a proceeding before the Income Security Section, the appellant, the Minister and any person added as a party under section 65 of the Act or section 10;**
>
> **(b) in a proceeding before the Employment Insurance Section, the appellant, the Commission and any person added as a party added under section 10;**
>
> **(c) in a proceeding before the Appeal Division, the appellant, all other parties to the proceeding in the General Division and any person added as a party under section 65 of the Act or section 10; and**
>
> **(d) in a proceeding to rescind or amend a decision, the applicant, the Minister or the Commission, any person added as a party under section 65 of the Act or section 10 and, if the proceeding is before the Appeal Division, all other parties to the proceeding in the General Division.**

2. *General principle* — **These Regulations must be interpreted so as to secure the just, most expeditious and least expensive determination of appeals and applications.**

(2013, c. 40, s. 236.)

General Provisions

Conduct of Proceedings

3. *Informal conduct* — **(1) The Tribunal**

> **(a) must conduct proceedings as informally and quickly as the circumstances and the considerations of fairness and natural justice permit; and**
>
> **(b) may, if there are special circumstances, vary a provision of these Regulations or dispense a party from compliance with a provision.**

(2) *Proceeding by way of analogy* — **If a question of procedure that is not dealt with by these Regulations arises in a proceeding, the Tribunal must proceed by way of analogy to these Regulations.**

4. *Requests to Tribunal* — **A party may request the Tribunal to provide for any matter concerning a proceeding, including the extension of a time limit imposed by these Regulations, by filing the request with the Tribunal.**

Filing with Tribunal

5. *Filing* — **(1) Any document required to be filed by these Regulations must be filed with the Tribunal at the address, facsimile number or email address — or in accordance with the electronic filing procedure — provided by the Tribunal on its website.**

(2) *Tribunal to provide copy to other parties* — **The Tribunal must provide a copy of any document filed by a party to the other parties to the proceeding without delay.**

(3) *Exception* — **The Tribunal is not required to provide a copy of a document if it has previously provided a copy of the document to the other parties to the proceeding.**

6. *Change in contact information* — **A party must file with the Tribunal a notice of any change in their contact information without delay.**

7. *Deemed filing dates* — **The date of filing of an appeal, application or other document is deemed to be**

   (a) **in the case of a document that is filed at the Tribunal's address or sent by mail or by facsimile, the date indicated by the date received stamp placed on the document by the Tribunal; and**

   (b) **in the case of a document that is filed by email or in accordance with the Tribunal's electronic filing procedure, the date of receipt indicated by the Tribunal's time stamp.**

8. *Deemed originals* — **An appeal, application or other document that is filed by email, facsimile or the Tribunal's electronic filing procedure is deemed to be the original of the document and the Tribunal may provide an electronic copy of it and certify the copy as a true copy.**

9. *Electronic version* — **If the Tribunal creates an electronic version of an appeal, application or other document that is filed at the Tribunal's address or sent by mail, the electronic version is deemed to be the original version of the document and the Tribunal may provide an electronic copy of it and certify the copy as a true copy.**

Participation of Parties

10. *Adding parties* — **(1) The Tribunal may, on its own initiative or if a request is filed, add any person as a party to a proceeding if the person has a direct interest in the decision.**

(2) *Request to be added as party* — **Any person may request that they be added as a party to a proceeding by filing a request that contains**

   (a) **the person's full name, address, telephone number and, if any, facsimile number and email address;**

   (b) **a statement that sets out why the person has a direct interest in the decision;**

(c) the name, address, telephone number and, if any, facsimile number and email address of any person authorized to represent the person; and

(d) a declaration that the information provided is true to the best of the person's knowledge.

11. *Requests to adjourn or postpone* — (1) A party may request that a hearing be adjourned or postponed by filing a request, with supporting reasons, with the Tribunal.

(2) *Subsequent requests by party* — If the Tribunal grants an adjournment or postponement at the request of a party, the Tribunal must not grant the party a subsequent adjournment or postponement unless the party establishes that it is justified by exceptional circumstances.

12. *Failure to appear* — (1) If a party fails to appear at a hearing, the Tribunal may proceed in the party's absence if the Tribunal is satisfied that the party received notice of the hearing.

(2) *Previous adjournment or postponement* — The Tribunal must proceed in a party's absence if the Tribunal previously granted an adjournment or postponement at the request of the party and the Tribunal is satisfied that the party received notice of the hearing.

13. *Joining of appeals or applications* — The Tribunal may, on its own initiative or if a request is filed by a party, deal with two or more appeals or applications jointly if

(a) a common question of law or fact arises in the appeals or applications; and

(b) no injustice is likely to be caused to any party to the appeals or applications.

14. *Withdrawal* — (1) Subject to subsection (2), a person may withdraw their appeal or application at any time before a decision is rendered by filing a notice with the Tribunal.

(2) *Exception* — In the case of a hearing held by teleconference, videoconference, other means of telecommunication or the personal appearance of the parties, a party may not withdraw their appeal or application after the conclusion of the hearing.

Conferences and Other Procedures

15. *Pre-hearing* — (1) The Tribunal may, on its own initiative or if a request is filed by a party, request the parties to participate in a pre-hearing conference on any matter concerning an appeal or an application to rescind or amend a decision.

(2) *Form of conference* — A pre-hearing conference may be held by teleconference, videoconference, other means of telecommunication or the personal appearance of the parties.

16. *Dispute resolution* — The Tribunal may, on its own initiative or if a request is filed by a party, request the parties to participate in a dispute resolution process in order to encourage the parties to resolve the appeal or application.

17. *Settlement conference* — **(1)** **The Tribunal may, on its own initiative or if a request is filed by a party, hold a settlement conference with the parties for the purpose of resolving the appeal or application in whole or in part.**

(2) *Member who holds conference* — **A member of the Tribunal who holds a settlement conference must not hear the appeal or application unless the parties consent to it.**

(3) *No disclosure* — **All matters discussed at a conference and all documents relating to a settlement conference are confidential and cannot be disclosed to any person by the Tribunal or the parties unless the parties consent.**

(4) *Form of conference* — **A settlement conference may be held by teleconference, videoconference, other means of telecommunication or the personal appearance of the parties.**

18. *Agreement between parties* — **The parties to an appeal or an application may request the Tribunal to make a decision based on an agreement between the parties by filing the request and the agreement, signed by all the parties, with the Tribunal.**

Deemed Communication of Decisions and Other Documents

19. *When decisions deemed communicated* — **(1)** **A decision made under subsection 53(1), 54(1), 58(3), 59(1) or 66(1) of the Act is deemed to have been communicated to a party**

(*a*) **if sent by ordinary mail, 10 days after the day on which it is mailed to the party;**

(*b*) **if sent by registered mail or courier, on**

  (i) **the date recorded on the acknowledgement of receipt, or**

  (ii) **the date it is delivered to the last known address of the party; and**

(*c*) **if sent by facsimile, email or other electronic means, the next business day after the day on which it is transmitted.**

(2) *Other documents sent by Tribunal* — **Subsection (1) also applies to any other document sent by the Tribunal to a party.**

Constitutional Issues

20. *Filing and service* — **(1)** **If the constitutional validity, applicability or operability of any provision of the** *Canada Pension Plan*, **the** *Old Age Security Act*, **the** *Employment Insurance Act*, **Part 5 of the** *Department of Employment and Social Development Act* **or the regulations made under any of those Acts is to be put at issue before the Tribunal, the party raising the issue must (2013, c. 40, s. 236(3)(*a*).)**

(*a*) **file a notice with the Tribunal that**

  (i) **sets out the provision that is at issue, and**

  (ii) **contains any submissions in support of the issue that is raised; and**

(*b*) **at least 10 days before the date set for the hearing of the appeal or application, serve notice of that issue on the persons referred to in subsection 57(1) of the** *Federal Courts Act* **and file a copy of the notice and proof of service with the Tribunal.**

(2) *Failure to prove service* — **If the proof of service required by paragraph (1)(***b***) has not been filed in accordance with that paragraph, the Tribunal may, on its own initiative or on the request of a party, adjourn or postpone the hearing.**

(3) *Time limits for documents and submissions* — **If a notice is filed under paragraph (1)(***a***), the time limits for filing documents or submissions set out in these Regulations do not apply and the Tribunal may direct the parties to file documents or submissions within the time limits it establishes.**

(2013, c. 40, s. 236.)

Form of Hearing

21. *Notice of hearing* — **If a notice of hearing is sent by the Tribunal under these Regulations, the Tribunal may hold the hearing by way of**

(*a*) **written questions and answers;**

(*b*) **teleconference, videoconference or other means of telecommunication; or**

(*c*) **the personal appearance of the parties.**

Summary Dismissal

22. *Notice to appellant* — **(1) Before summarily dismissing an appeal pursuant to subsection 53(1) of the Act, the General Division must give notice in writing to the appellant and allow the appellant a reasonable period of time to make submissions.**

(2) *Decision made without delay* — **After the appellant has been allowed a reasonable period of time to make submissions, the General Division must make its decision without delay.**

Appeals to General Division

Filing of Appeal

23. *Filing* — **An appeal of a decision to the General Division is brought by filing the appeal at the address, facsimile number or email address — or in accordance with the electronic filing procedure — provided by the Tribunal on its website.**

24. *Appeal form and contents* — **(1) An appeal must be in the form set out by the Tribunal on its website and contain**

. (*a*) **a copy of the decision that was made under subsection 81(2) or (3) of the *Canada Pension Plan*, subsection 27.1(2) of the *Old Age Security Act* or section 112 of the *Employment Insurance Act*;**

(*b*) **the date the decision was communicated to the appellant;**

(*c*) **if a person is authorized to represent the appellant, the person's name, address, telephone number and, if any, facsimile number and email address;**

(*d*) **the grounds for the appeal;**

(*e*) **any documents or submissions that the appellant relies on in their appeal;**

(*f*) **an identifying number of the type specified by the Tribunal on its website for the purpose of the appeal;**

(g) the appellant's full name, address, telephone number and, if any, facsimile number and email address; and

(h) a declaration that the information provided is true to the best of the appellant's knowledge.

(2) *Identifying number* — For the purposes of paragraph (1)(f), the Tribunal must specify on its website a type of identifying number which may include

(a) the appellant's social insurance number or the business number assigned to the appellant by the Minister of National Revenue;

(b) the number assigned to a decision made under subsection 81(2) or (3) of the *Canada Pension Plan*, subsection 27.1(2) of the *Old Age Security Act* or section 112 of the *Employment Insurance Act*; or

(c) any other type of identifying number.

25. *Extension of time for bringing appeal* — A person who does not file an appeal within the time limits set out in subsection 52(1) of the Act may request an extension of time by filing their appeal with a statement that sets out the reasons why the General Division should allow further time for the bringing of the appeal.

Appeals Before Income Security Section

26. *Documents to be filed by Minister* — The Minister must, within 20 days after the day on which the Minister receives a copy of an appeal, file the following with the Income Security Section:

(a) a copy of the application that gave rise to the decision being appealed;

(b) if applicable, the information relating to the marriage that is referred to in subsection 54(2) of the *Canada Pension Plan Regulations*;

(c) a copy of any notification given in accordance with section 46 or 46.1 of the *Canada Pension Plan Regulations*;

(d) a copy of any notification given in accordance with subsection 60(7) of the *Canada Pension Plan* or section 16 or 24 of the *Old Age Security Act*;

(e) a copy of the request made to the Minister for a reconsideration under subsection 81(1) of the *Canada Pension Plan* or subsection 27.1(1) of the *Old Age Security Act*; and

(f) a copy of the decision that was made under subsection 81(2) or (3) of the *Canada Pension Plan* or subsection 27.1(2) of the *Old Age Security Act* and any documents relevant to the decision.

27. *Time to respond* — (1) Within 365 days after the day on which the appeal is filed, the parties may

(a) file additional documents or submissions with the Income Security Section; or

(b) file a notice with the Income Security Section stating that they have no documents or submissions to file.

(2) *Additional time* — If a party files documents or submissions within 30 days before the end of the 365-day period, the other parties have an

additional 30 days after the end of that period to file documents or submissions in response.

28. *Decision or further hearing* — After every party has filed a notice that they have no documents or submissions to file — or at the end of the applicable period set out in section 27, whichever comes first — the Income Security Section must without delay

    (*a*) make a decision on the basis of the documents and submissions filed; or

    (*b*) if it determines that further hearing is required, send a notice of hearing to the parties.

29. *Decision made without delay* — If a notice of hearing is sent to the parties, the Income Security Section must make its decision without delay after the conclusion of the hearing.

Appeals Before Employment Insurance Section

30. *Documents to be filed by Commission* — The Commission must, within 7 business days after the day on which it receives a copy of an appeal, file the following with the Employment Insurance Section:

    (*a*) a copy of the request for a reconsideration made under section 112 of the *Employment Insurance Act*;

    (*b*) the documents in the Commission's possession that are relevant to the decision being appealed;

    (*c*) a copy of the decision being appealed; and

    (*d*) the submissions, if any, of the Commission.

31. *Notice of hearing or summary dismissal* — (1) The Employment Insurance Section must, at the time it sends copies of the documents filed by the Commission to the other parties, send all the parties

    (*a*) a notice of hearing; or

    (*b*) a notice of summary dismissal referred to in section 22.

(2) *Notice of summary dismissal* — If the Employment Insurance Section sends a notice of summary dismissal but does not summarily dismiss the appeal, it must send a notice of hearing to the parties without delay.

(3) *Section 53 of the Act* — For greater certainty, subsection (1) does not preclude the application of section 53 of the Act at any time during the proceedings.

32. *Reference of questions* — The Employment Insurance Section may, at any time prior to its decision, refer any question arising in relation to a claim for benefits to the Commission for investigation and report.

33. *Decision made without delay* — The Employment Insurance Section must make its decision without delay after the conclusion of the hearing.

Appeal of Summary Dismissal

34. *Appeal of summary dismissal* — An appeal of a decision of the Income Security Section or the Employment Insurance Section to summarily dismiss an appeal is brought by filing the appeal with the Appeal Division at the address, facsimile number or email address — or in accordance

655

with the electronic filing procedure — provided by the Tribunal on its website.

35. *Appeal form and contents* — **(1) An appeal must be in the form set out by the Tribunal on its website and contain**

(*a*) a copy of the decision to summarily dismiss;

(*b*) if a person is authorized to represent the appellant, the person's name, address, telephone number and, if any, facsimile number and email address;

(*c*) the grounds for the appeal;

(*d*) any statements of fact that were presented to the General Division and that the appellant relies on in the appeal;

(*e*) an identifying number of the type specified by the Tribunal on its website for the purpose of the appeal;

(*f*) the appellant's full name, address, telephone number and, if any, facsimile number and email address; and

(*g*) a declaration that the information provided is true to the best of the appellant's knowledge.

(2) *Identifying number* — **For the purposes of paragraph (1)(*e*), the Tribunal must specify on its website a type of identifying number which may include**

(*a*) the appellant's social insurance number or the business number assigned to the appellant by the Minister of National Revenue;

(*b*) the number assigned to a decision made under subsection 81(2) or (3) of the *Canada Pension Plan*, subsection 27.1(2) of the *Old Age Security Act* or section 112 of the *Employment Insurance Act*; or

(*c*) any other type of identifying number.

36. *Time to respond* — **Within 45 days after the day on which the appeal is filed, the parties may**

(*a*) file submissions with the Appeal Division; or

(*b*) file a notice with the Appeal Division that states that they have no submissions to file.

37. *Decision or further hearing* — **After every party has filed a notice that they have no submissions to file — or at the end of the period set out in section 36, whichever comes first — the Appeal Division must without delay**

(*a*) make a decision on the appeal; or

(*b*) if it determines that further hearing is required, send a notice of hearing to the parties.

38. *Decision made without delay* — **If a notice of hearing is sent to the parties, the Appeal Division must make its decision without delay after the conclusion of the hearing.**

Appeals to Appeal Division

39. *Leave to appeal* — **An application for leave to appeal a decision of the General Division is brought by filing the application with the Appeal Division at the address, facsimile number or email address — or in accordance with the electronic filing procedure — provided by the Tribunal on its website.**

40. *Application for leave form and contents* — **(1) An application for leave to appeal must be in the form set out by the Tribunal on its website and contain**

(*a*) **a copy of the decision in respect of which leave to appeal is being sought;**

(*b*) **if a person is authorized to represent the applicant, the person's name, address, telephone number and, if any, facsimile number and email address;**

(*c*) **the grounds for the application;**

(*d*) **any statements of fact that were presented to the General Division and that the applicant relies on in the application;**

(*e*) **if the application is brought by a person other than the Minister or the Commission, the applicant's full name, address, telephone number and, if any, facsimile number and email address;**

(*f*) **if the application is brought by the Minister or the Commission, the address, telephone number, facsimile number and email address of the Minister or the Commission, as the case may be;**

(*g*) **an identifying number of the type specified by the Tribunal on its website for the purpose of the application; and**

(*h*) **a declaration that the information provided is true to the best of the applicant's knowledge.**

(2) *Identifying number* — **For the purposes of paragraph (1)(*g*), the Tribunal must specify on its website a type of identifying number which may include**

(*a*) **in the case of an applicant other than the Minister or the Commission, the applicant's social insurance number or the business number assigned to the applicant by the Minister of National Revenue;**

(*b*) **the number assigned to a decision made under subsection 81(2) or (3) of the *Canada Pension Plan*, subsection 27.1(2) of the *Old Age Security Act* or section 112 of the *Employment Insurance Act*; or**

(*c*) **any other type of identifying number.**

41. *Written questions and submissions* — **Before granting or refusing an application for leave to appeal, the Appeal Division may**

(*a*) **request further information from the applicant by way of written questions and answers; and**

(*b*) **send a copy of the application for leave to the parties and request that they file submissions.**

42. *Time to respond* — **Within 45 days after the day on which leave to appeal is granted, the parties may**

(*a*) **file submissions with the Appeal Division; or**

(*b*) **file a notice with the Appeal Division stating that they have no submissions to file.**

43. *Decision or further hearing* — **After every party has filed a notice that they have no submissions to file — or at the end of the period set out in section 42, whichever comes first — the Appeal Division must without delay**

(*a*) **make a decision on the appeal; or**

(*b*) if it determines that further hearing is required, send a notice of hearing to the parties.

44. *Decision made without delay* — If a notice of hearing is sent to the parties, the Appeal Division must make its decision without delay after the conclusion of the hearing.

Rescinding of Amending Decisions

45. *Application to rescind or amend* — An application to rescind or amend a decision of the General Division or the Appeal Division is brought by filing the application at the address, facsimile number or email address — or in accordance with the electronic filing procedure — provided by the Tribunal on its website.

46. *Application form and contents* — (1) An application to rescind or amend a decision must be in the form set out by the Tribunal on its website and contain

(*a*) a copy of the decision that is the object of the application;

(*b*) if a person is authorized to represent the applicant, the person's name, address, telephone number and, if any, facsimile number and email address;

(*c*) a statement of the new facts or new material fact, as the case may be, that would allow the General Division or the Appeal Division to rescind or amend a decision under section 66 of the Act;

(*d*) any documents relied on by the applicant as evidence of the new facts or new material fact;

(*e*) if the application is brought by a person other than the Minister or the Commission, the applicant's full name, address, telephone number and, if any, facsimile number and email address;

(*f*) if the application is brought by the Minister or the Commission, the address, telephone number, facsimile number and email address of the Minister or the Commission, as the case may be;

(*g*) an identifying number of the type specified by the Tribunal on its website for the purpose of the application; and

(*h*) a declaration that the information provided is true to the best of the applicant's knowledge.

(2) *Identifying number* — For the purposes of subparagraph (1)(*g*), the Tribunal must specify on its website a type of identifying number which may include

(*a*) in the case of an applicant other than the Minister or the Commission, the applicant's social insurance number or the business number assigned to the applicant by the Minister of National Revenue;

(*b*) the number assigned to a decision made under subsection 81(2) or (3) of the *Canada Pension Plan*, subsection 27.1(2) of the *Old Age Security Act* or section 112 of the *Employment Insurance Act*; or

(*c*) any other type of identifying number.

47. *Time to respond* — A party may, within 30 days after the day on which the General Division or the Appeal Division sends a copy of the application, (*a*) file documents or submissions with the General Division or the Appeal Division, as the case may be; or

(*b*) file a notice with the General Division or the Appeal Division, as the case may be, that they have no documents or submissions to file.

48. *Decision or further hearing* — After every party has filed a notice that they have no documents or submissions to file — or at the end of the period set out in section 47, whichever comes first — the General Division or the Appeal Division, as the case may be, must without delay

(*a*) make a decision on the application; or

(*b*) if it determines that further hearing is required, send a notice of hearing to the parties.

49. *Decision made without delay* — If a notice of hearing is sent to the parties, the General Division or the Appeal Division, as the case may be, must make its decision without delay after the conclusion of the hearing.

Coming into Force

50. *April 1, 2013* — These Regulations come into force on April 1, 2013.

Policies of the Social Security Tribunal

The policies below, to be followed by parties appearing at the Social Security Tribunal, were published online at: http://www.canada.ca/en/sst/hearing information/index.html.

Form of hearing

1. **This section explains:**

- the different forms of hearings

- the responsibilities of the parties for oral hearings

- the expectations of witnesses at oral hearings; and

- who is responsible for expenses associated with oral hearings.

2. **Form of hearings**

- A Member of the Employment Insurance Section or a Member of the Income Security Section may decide to summarily dismiss an appeal, if the Member is satisfied that the appeal has no reasonable chance of success. In such cases, there is no hearing.

- A Member will decide how an appeal will proceed, including whether or not a hearing will be held.

- Under the *Social Security Tribunal Regulations*, a hearing may be in writing or oral.

- If the Member decides to hold a hearing, the Tribunal will inform the parties of the form of hearing.

- **Hearing in writing:** If the Member decides that clarifications are needed and can be obtained through written questions and answers, the hearing will be in writing.

- **Oral hearing:** If the Member decides that an oral hearing is required, the Member will decide whether the hearing will be held by way of teleconference, videoconference, or the personal appearance of the parties (i.e.: in-person hearing).

  — An oral hearing by teleconference means that the parties will take part in the hearing by telephone.

  — An oral hearing by videoconference means that the parties will appear by videoconference before the Member who is in another location. Videoconferencing allows the parties to interact with the Member via simultaneous video and audio transmissions.

  — An oral hearing by personal appearance is when the Member and the parties are physically in the same hearing room.

- At the Income Security Section and at the Appeal Division, the Member may decide that a hearing is not necessary and that a decision will be made on the basis of the documents and the submissions already on file. This is otherwise known as proceeding on the basis of the record.

Responsibilities of the parties regarding a written hearing

- The parties are responsible for responding to the written questions within the timeframe set by the Member. If a party fails to respond to all of the written questions within the established period of time, the Member may proceed without the additional information.

Responsibilities of the parties regarding an oral hearing

- When an oral hearing is scheduled, the form, location, date and time shall be communicated to the parties as part of a Notice of Hearing letter.

- Once the oral hearing has been scheduled, all of the parties are expected to attend at the location, date and time specified in the Notice of Hearing letter.

- If a party is not available on the date and time indicated in the Notice of Hearing letter, the party is required to contact the Tribunal within the timeframe specified in the letter. If a party fails to attend a scheduled hearing without prior notice, the Member may proceed in the party's absence.

- A party must notify the Tribunal of any change in their contact information without delay.

- If a party wishes to bring a witness to the oral hearing, the party is responsible for ensuring that the witness is available at the location, date and time of the oral hearing.

- Teleconference: If the oral hearing is held by way of teleconference, the parties are responsible for having access to a telephone on the date and time of the hearing. While the location to hold the teleconference is at each party's discretion, all parties are responsible for ensuring that the chosen location will facilitate discussion and participation during the hearing.

  — A party may use a cellular telephone to participate in a teleconference. The party is responsible for ensuring that the telephone will be functional for the duration of the hearing (i.e.: adequately charged and used within the established range of the local cellular network).

  — If a party does not have access to a telephone, the party is required to contact the Tribunal without delay and within the timeframe specified in the Notice of Hearing letter.

- Videoconference or personal appearance: If the oral hearing is held by way of videoconference or personal appearance by the parties, it will be scheduled at the hearing location nearest to the Appellant's address on file.

- It is possible for an oral hearing to proceed via a combination of methods, such as teleconference, videoconference and personal appearance.

Requirement for witnesses at oral hearings only

- Persons who are witnesses, including the parties, are required to provide testimony under oath or solemn affirmation.

- Witnesses are required to make a solemn affirmation unless they request to make an oath on a religious book.

- Witnesses who request to make an oath must bring their own religious book to the oral hearing; otherwise a solemn affirmation will be required.

- Persons who are witnesses should not normally act as a representative for a party.

Expenses and allowances related to an oral hearing only

- The parties are responsible for all expenses related to their participation in the oral hearing; that includes transportation, meals, hotel accommodation, etc.

- A party who wishes to bring a witness to the hearing is responsible for all expenses related to the participation of the witness in the oral hearing.

- According to the *Department of Employment and Social Development Act*, the Chairperson of the Social Security Tribunal, may, for special reasons reimburse a party required to attend a hearing for travel and living expenses or pay to them any other allowance.

Language of hearing, interpreters and language of documents

1. **This section explains:**

- the language in which the hearing is conducted;

- the role of the interpreter; and

- the requirements regarding the translation of documents in French or English

2. **Language of hearings**

- Tribunal hearings are conducted in French or English.

- The appellant has the right to decide in which of the official languages the hearing will be held. Unless the appellant indicates otherwise, the hearing will be conducted in the official language in which the appeal notice was written.

3. **Interpreter**

- If a party does not speak or sufficiently understand either French or English, the party must inform the Tribunal as soon as possible, so that appropriate arrangements can be made for an interpreter to be provided by the Tribunal at no cost.

- The role of the interpreter is to verbally translate what is said at the hearing. The interpreter establishes direct communication between the person requiring interpretation services and the other participants in the hearing. In other words, the role of the interpreter is to be a conduit for communication rather than an active participant.

4. Language of documents and translation

- All documents sent to the Tribunal must be in French or English. Any documents sent to the Tribunal in a language other than French or English will not be accepted. They will be returned to the party who submitted the documents.

- Documents in a language other than French or English must be translated into French or English and the translation is the responsibility of the party.

- The translated document must contain the name and coordinates of the translator in a printed format and an oath or a solemn affirmation written statement by the translator that the translation is accurate.

- The party must provide the Tribunal with both the document in its original language and the translated version.

- The party is responsible for all costs and expenses related to the translation of the document.

- The Tribunal can verify the translation to ensure that it is accurate.

Tribunal Hearing Recordings

1. This policy explains:

- who may record Tribunal hearings; and

- how to obtain a copy of the audio recording.

2. Recording Tribunal hearings

2.1 Under the *Department of Human Resources and Skills Development Ac*t, the *Canada Pension Plan* and the *Old Age Security Act*, there is no requirement for the Tribunal to record hearings conducted by telephone, videoconference or in person.

2.2 However, the Tribunal audio-records its hearings using a digital audio-recording device. There are several advantages to recording hearings; among them it ensures a complete record in case of an appeal.

2.3 Parties to the appeal are not permitted to record Tribunal hearings.

2.4 Audio recordings of hearings are kept by the Tribunal, along with all the documents and information related to a specific appeal file.

3. Copy of recording

3.1 There is no legal requirement for the Tribunal to provide transcripts of hearings. The Tribunal does not make or use transcripts of its hearings.

3.2 Parties to an appeal may request a copy of the audio recording of their hearing free of charge by completing the Audio Recording Request form (PDF format) and sending it to the Tribunal. This form is available on the Tribunal's website or by request.

3.3 The party requesting a copy of the recording must agree to use the audio recording for purposes related to his or her appeal only and to keep it confidential.

3.4 If a party to the appeal wants to use the audio recording for other purposes, the party must request the copy of the recording under the *Access to Information Act*.

3.5 The Tribunal usually approves audio recording requests from parties upon receipt of a completed Request form. In unusual circumstances, the Tribunal Member that heard the appeal may issue specific directions about the recording.

3.6 Requests of audio-recordings from anyone who is not a party to the appeal, must be made under the *Access to Information Act*.

3.7 The Tribunal cannot guarantee the audio quality of copies of audio recordings.

Index

Index

669

Index

671

Index

677